W9-AJL-494

# Fodor's 2023

# ESSENTIAL SPAIN

# Welcome to Spain

Spain conjures images of flamenco dancers, café-lined plazas, white hillside villages, and soaring cathedrals. Beyond these traditional associations, this modern country offers top-notch art museums, inventive cuisine, and exciting nightlife. From the Pyrenees to the coast, its landscapes and varied cultures are worth exploring. Especially enticing is the national insistence on enjoying everyday pleasures. This book was produced in the middle of the COVID-19 pandemic. As you plan your upcoming travels to Spain, please confirm that places are still open and let us know when we need to make updates by writing to us: editors@fodors.com.

## TOP REASONS TO GO

★ **Cool Cities:** Barcelona, Madrid, Seville, Granada, Valencia, Bilbao, San Sebastián, and Salamanca.

★ **Amazing Architecture:** From the Moorish Alhambra to Gaudí's eclectic Sagrada Família.

★ **History:** From Segovia's Roman aqueduct to Córdoba's Mezquita, history comes alive.

★ **Superlative Art:** Masterpieces by Goya, El Greco, Picasso, Dalí, and Miró thrill.

★ **Tapas and Wine:** Spain's justly famed small bites pair perfectly with its Riojas.

★ **Beautiful Beaches:** From Barcelona's city beaches to Ibiza's celebrated strands.

# Contents

**1 EXPERIENCE SPAIN** ...... 9
25 Ultimate Experiences ......10
What's Where ......20
Spain Today ......24
Spain's Best Museums ......28
Spain's Best Beaches ......30
Spain's Most Beautiful Villages ......32
What to Watch and Read Before You Go to Spain ......34
History You Can See ......36

**2 TRAVEL SMART** ...... 39
Know Before You Go ......40
Getting Here and Around ......42
Before You Go ......48
Essentials ......49
Contacts ......53
Great Itineraries ......54
Helpful Phrases in Spanish ......62
On the Calendar ......64

**3 MADRID** ...... 67
Welcome to Madrid ......68
Eating and Drinking Well in Madrid ......70
Planning ......72
Sol ......78
Palacio ......87
Moncloa ......92
Chueca ......96
Malasaña ......101
Barrio de las Letras ......103
Retiro ......111
Salamanca ......124
La Latina ......128
Lavapiés ......135
Arganzuela ......139
Chamberí ......140
Chamartín ......144
Tetuán ......146

**4 CENTRAL SPAIN** ...... 147
Welcome to Central Spain ......148
Eating and Drinking Well in Central Spain ......150
Planning ......153
Toledo ......158

Almagro ......168
Cuenca ......169
Sigüenza ......172
Segovia ......173
Sepúlveda ......180
San Lorenzo de El Escorial ......181
Ávila ......181
Salamanca ......184
Burgos ......192
León ......197
Astorga ......202
Villafranca del Bierzo ......203
Jerte and El Valle del Jerte (Jerte Valley) ......204
La Vera and Monasterio de Yuste ......207
Cáceres ......208
Trujillo ......213
Guadalupe ......215
Mérida ......218

**5 GALICIA, ASTURIAS, AND CANTABRIA** ...... 221
Welcome to Galicia, Asturias, and Cantabria ......222
Eating and Drinking Well in Galicia, Asturias, and Cantabria ......224
El Camino de Santiago ......226
Planning ......231
Santiago de Compostela ......233
Ourense and La Ribeira Sacra ......241
Lugo ......243
Muxía ......243
Fisterra ......245
Muros ......245
Cambados ......245
Pontevedra ......247
Vigo ......249
Baiona ......251
Tui ......252
A Coruña ......253
Betanzos ......257
Viveiro ......258
Luarca ......259
Oviedo ......260
Gijón ......263

Ribadesella .................................266
Llanes...................................267
Cangas de Onís ......................269
Potes ....................................270
Santander..............................271
Santillana del Mar .................277

**6 THE BASQUE COUNTRY,
NAVARRA, AND LA RIOJA ........ 279**
Welcome to The Basque Country,
Navarra, and La Rioja....................280
Eating and Drinking Well in the
Basque Country.............................282
Planning......................................285
Bilbao..........................................288
Bermeo........................................302
Mundaka .....................................302
Axpe Atxondo...............................305
Getaria and Zumaia ......................306
San Sebastián ..............................308
Vitoria-Gasteiz.............................317
Laguardia ....................................321
Pasaia .........................................323
Hondarribia .................................325
Pamplona ....................................326
Logroño........................................331
La Rioja Alta ................................333
Haro.............................................335

**7 THE PYRENEES ...........................337**
Welcome to The Pyrenees.............338
Eating and Drinking Well in the
Pyrenees .....................................340
Planning......................................344
Camprodon..................................347
Beget...........................................349
Sant Joan de les Abadesses ........351
Ripoll ..........................................351
Ribes de Freser and Vall de Núria.....352
Puigcerdà ....................................354
Llívia ...........................................356
Bellver de Cerdanya.....................356
La Seu d'Urgell ............................358
Sort.............................................359
Parc Nacional d'Aigüestortes i
Estany de Sant Maurici.................360

El Prado: Madrid's Brush
With Greatness .................... 116
Temple Expiatori de la
Sagrada Família.................... 459
Alhambra: Palace-Fortress.......... 661

Vielha .........................................361
Arties...........................................364
Salardú ........................................365
Zaragoza......................................367
Huesca.........................................371
Alquézar ......................................372
Aínsa ...........................................375
Parque Nacional de Ordesa y
Monte Perdido...............................377
Jaca .............................................378
Monasterio de San Juan de la Peña...380
Hecho and Ansó Valleys.................381
Roncal Valley................................383
Roncesvalles (Orreaga) .................384
Burguete (Auritz)...........................385
Baztan Valley................................385

**8 BARCELONA.................................387**
Welcome to Barcelona ...................388
Eating and Drinking Well
in Barcelona .................................390
Planning......................................393
La Rambla....................................398
Barri Gòtic...................................408
El Raval .......................................423
Sant Pere and Born/La Ribera .........431
La Ciutadella and Barceloneta .........443
The Eixample ...............................453
Gràcia .........................................473
Upper Barcelona: Sarrià and
Pedralbes ....................................477
Montjuïc and Poble Sec .................483

# Contents

**9 CATALONIA, VALENCIA, AND THE COSTA BLANCA** ............ 489

Welcome to Catalonia, Valencia, and the Costa Blanca .........................490

Eating and Drinking Well in Catalonia and Valencia ........................492

Planning ...........................................495

Girona ..............................................498

Figueres ...........................................505

Besalú ..............................................508

Tossa de Mar ...................................509

Sant Feliu de Guixols ......................512

S'Agaró .............................................513

Calella de Palafrugell and Around .....514

Begur and Around ...........................515

Cadaqués and Around .....................516

Montserrat .......................................518

Sitges ..............................................519

Santes Creus ...................................521

Santa Maria de Poblet .....................522

Tarragona ........................................522

Valencia ...........................................525

Albufera Nature Park .......................535

Dénia ...............................................535

Calpe (Calp) .....................................537

Altea ................................................538

Alicante (Alacant) ............................540

**10 IBIZA AND THE BALEARIC ISLANDS** ...................... 543

Welcome to Ibiza and the Balearic Islands .................................544

Eating and Drinking Well in the Balearic Islands .............................546

Best Beaches of the Balearics ..........548

Planning ...........................................551

Ibiza ................................................554

Formentera ......................................563

Mallorca ..........................................564

Menorca ...........................................584

**11 SEVILLE AND AROUND** ................. 595

Welcome to Seville and Around .........596

Flamenco .........................................598

Planning ...........................................601

Centro ..............................................604

Barrio de Santa Cruz ........................611

El Arenal and Parque María Luisa .....615

Barrio de la Macarena ......................619

Triana ..............................................620

Itálica ..............................................622

Córdoba ...........................................623

Ronda ..............................................635

Around Ronda: Caves, Romans, and Pueblos Blancos .......................638

Arcos de la Frontera .........................639

Jerez de la Frontera .........................640

Cádiz ................................................645

**12 GRANADA AND AROUND** ............. 649

Welcome to Granada and Around .....650

Eating and Drinking Well in Andalusia ......................................652

Planning ...........................................655

La Alhambra .....................................657

Realejo .............................................668

Sacromonte ......................................669

Albayzín ...........................................669

Centro ..............................................672

Outskirts of Granada ........................674

Priego de Córdoba ...........................676

Baeza ...............................................677

Úbeda ..............................................678

The Sierra Nevada ...........................680

The Alpujarras ..................................681

**13 COSTA DEL SOL AND COSTA DE ALMERÍA** ...................... 683

Welcome to Costa del Sol and Costa de Almería .......................684

Eating and Drinking Well Along Spain's Southern Coast ....................686

Best Beaches of the Southern Coast .............................688

Planning ...........................................691

The Cabo de Gata Nature Reserve ....695

Agua Amarga ...................................697

Almería ............................................697

Almuñécar ........................................700

Nerja ................................................702

The Axarquía ...................................704

Málaga .............................................705

Antequera ..............................713
The Guadalhorce Valley ..............715
Torremolinos ........................716
Fuengirola ..........................718
Mijas ...............................720
Marbella ............................722
Ojén ................................726
Estepona ............................727
Casares .............................729
Tarifa ..............................730
Gibraltar ...........................733

14 THE CANARY ISLANDS ............... 737
Welcome to The Canary Islands .......738
Planning ............................741
Tenerife ............................745
Gran Canaria ........................762
Lanzarote ...........................774
Fuerteventura .......................789
La Palma ............................795

INDEX ............................ 801

ABOUT OUR WRITERS ............... 816

MAPS

Travel Times by Train ..............26–27
Madrid Metro ........................80
Sol, Palacio, and Moncloa ..........82–83
Chueca and Malasaña .................98
Barrio de las Letras ................104
Retiro and Salamanca ............112–113
La Latina, Lavapiés, and Arganzuela.129
Chamberí, Chamartín, and Tetuán .....142
Castile–La Mancha ...................156
Toledo ..............................160
Castile and León ....................174
Segovia .............................176
Salamanca ...........................186
Burgos ..............................194
León ................................200
Extremadura .........................206
Santiago de Compostela and
Eastern Galicia .....................234

Santiago de Compostela ..............238
The Costa da Morte and Rías Baixas..244
A Coruña and Rías Altas .............254
Western Asturias ....................259
Picos de Europa .....................270
Cantabria ...........................273
Bilbao ..........................296–297
The Basque Coast ....................305
Navarra and La Rioja ................324
Eastern Catalan Pyrenees and
La Cerdanya .........................348
Western Catalan Pyrenees ............360
Aragón and the Central Pyrenees .....369
The Navarran and Basque Pyrenees..382
Barcelona Metro .....................400
La Rambla ...........................402
Barri Gòtic .....................410–411
El Raval ............................424
Sant Pere and La Ribera .........432–433
La Ciutadella and Barceloneta ...444–445
The Eixample ....................454–455
Gràcia ..............................474
Upper Barcelona: Sarrià and
Pedralbes ...........................478
Montjuïc and Poble Sec ..............484
Northern Catalonia and the
Costa Brava .........................500
Valencia and the Costa Blanca .......526
Valencia ............................530
Ibiza and Formentera ................556
Mallorca ............................566
Menorca .............................585
Seville .........................606–607
Córdoba .........................626–627
Granada .........................658–659
Granada Side Trips ..................675
Costa de Almería and Costa Tropical..698
Málaga and Inland ...................706
Málaga ..............................708
Gibraltar ...........................732
Tenerife ............................748
Gran Canaria ........................763
Lanzarote and Fuerteventura .........776
La Palma ............................796

# EXPERIENCE SPAIN

# 25 ULTIMATE EXPERIENCES

Spain offers terrific experiences that should be on every traveler's list. Here are Fodor's top picks for a memorable trip.

## 1 Park Güell

A sweeping view of Barcelona awaits you at this architectural park, Gaudí's pièce de résistance in urban planning. Peer out from the mosaic benches over gingerbread-like houses and fountains guarded by giant tiled lizards. *(Ch. 8)*

## 2 Picos de Europa

A national park where you can hike between lakes, meadows, and snowy peaks, this mountain range on Spain's northern coast is a top outdoor adventure. *(Ch. 5)*

## 3 Gorgeous Cathedrals

Towering temples in cities including León and Burgos have been presided over by bishops for centuries and are some of the greatest marvels in Spain. *(Ch. 4)*

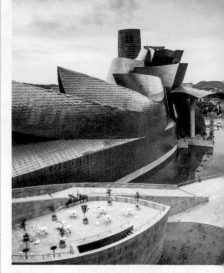

## 4 Food tours

Take a delicious dive into Spanish culture by trying dishes like tortilla española (Spanish potato omelet) and paella with a local guide who knows the best haunts.

## 5 Guggenheim Bilbao

Thought-provoking works by world-renowned international artists will entrance you at Bilbao's riverfront museum, a titanium work of art itself. *(Ch. 6)*

## 6 Beaches

You can't go wrong on the Iberian Peninsula, where you can choose between the sun-drenched beaches of the Mediterranean and the wild, brisk shores of the Atlantic.

## 7 Flamenco

A foot-stomping whirlwind of click-clacking castanets, guitar solos, and gut-wrenching vocals will have you shouting "¡Olé!" at the tablaos (flamenco venues) of Sevilla. *(Ch. 11)*

# 8 El Escorial

A leisurely day trip from the hustle and bustle of Madrid, this medieval town's main attraction is a gargantuan royal residence set high on a hill. *(Ch. 4)*

# 9 Córdoba Mosque

The ancient Mezquita's engraved columns and candy cane–striped double arches are an enchanting reminder of Andalusia's 10th-century Islamic grandeur. *(Ch. 11)*

## 10 Barri Gòtic

Barcelona's most ancient quarter is a maze of cobblestone streets and stone arcades that empty into medieval plaças. It also boasts some of the city's chicest boutiques. *(Ch. 8)*

## 11 Rioja wine caves

Don't miss the bodegas in Haro, in the heart of Rioja Alta, for their centuries of history and mysterious cellars, draped with penicillin mold and cobwebs. *(Ch. 6)*

## 12 Mérida

Tour the remnants of an ancient Roman city, home to one of the best-preserved stone amphitheaters in Europe. The UNESCO Site is the largest of its kind in Spain. *(Ch. 4)*

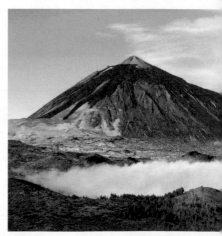

## 13 Canary Islands volcanoes

The tallest mountain in Spain is also an active volcano—and you can climb it. Make it to the peak of 12,000-foot El Teide, and you'll be rewarded with bird's-eye views. *(Ch. 14)*

# 14 Alhambra

Nothing epitomizes the Moors' power and ingenuity like this centuries-old fortress. Set aside a few hours to take in arched courtyards and intricate arabesques. *(Ch. 12)*

## 15 Sagrada Família

Gaudí's iconic church is a soaring fantasy world of vivid stained glass and zoomorphic motifs. It is slated for completion in 2026 after 150 years of construction. (Ch. 8)

## 16 Toledo

When Toledo was the ancient capital of Spain, Muslims, Jews, and Christians cohabitated in harmony—hence the city's nickname, "City of Three Cultures." (Ch. 4)

## 17 Skiing

Some of the best slopes in western Europe (and with reasonable ticket prices) can be found in the Pyrenees, the mountain range Spain shares with France and Andorra. (Ch. 7)

## 18 Retiro Park

The tree-shaded trails, artwork, and gardens here are an oasis right in Madrid's city center. Look for the Palacio de Cristal, an impressive iron-and-glass greenhouse. (Ch. 3)

# 19 ¡Feria!

Vibrant ferias, or fairs, are some of the country's wildest parties, with traditional dance performances, carnival rides, street food, and makeshift discotecas. *(Ch. 11)*

# 20 Paradores

Want to hole up in a property with personality and a true sense of place? Look to the paradores, a state-run network of accommodations in historic buildings.

## 21 Cuenca's hanging houses

It doesn't get much more picturesque than these buildings perched on a cliffside overlooking the Huécar River. They seem to defy gravity as they jut over the ravine. *(Ch. 4)*

## 22 Museums in Madrid

Madrid's Golden Triangle is home to three world-class museums within blocks of each other. Don't miss Picasso's Guernica at Museo Reina Sofia. *(Ch. 3)*

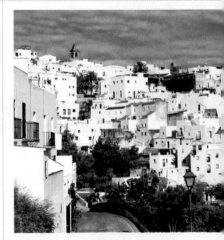

## 23 Segovia aqueduct

This work of Roman engineering has stood for more than 2,000 years—mind-boggling, considering that mortar is entirely absent from construction. *(Ch. 4)*

## 24 Pueblos blancos

Road trip through these stark white villages on Andalusian hilltops, one of southern Spain's most postcard-perfect attractions. *(Ch. 11)*

# 25 Santiago de Compostela

The best way to reach the Galician capital is hiking the Camino de Santiago, an old Christian pilgrimage route; you don't have to be religious to appreciate the hike. *(Ch. 5)*

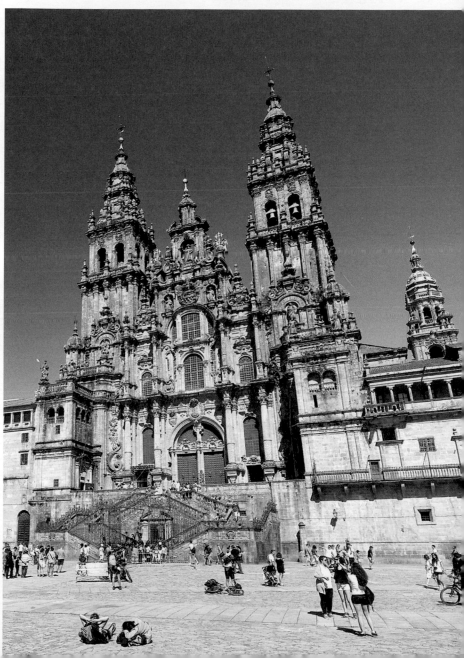

# WHAT'S WHERE

**1 Madrid.** Its boundless energy creates sights and sounds larger than life. The Prado, Reina Sofía, and Thyssen-Bornemisza museums make this one of the greatest repositories of Western art in the world.

**2 Central Spain.** From Madrid there are several important excursions, notably Toledo, as well as Segovia and Salamanca. Other cities in Castile–La Mancha and Castile-León worth visiting include León, Burgos, Soria, Sigüenza, Ávila, and Cuenca. Extremadura, Spain's remote borderland with Portugal, is often overlooked but has some intriguing places to discover.

**3 Galicia and Asturias.** On the way to Galicia to pay homage to St. James, pilgrims once crossed Europe to this corner of Spain so remote it was called *finis terrae* ("world's end"). Galicia's capital, Santiago de Compostela, still resonates with mystic importance. In nearby Asturias, villages nestle in green highlands, backed by the snowcapped Picos de Europa mountains, while sandy beaches stretch along the

Atlantic. East, in Cantabria, is the Belle Époque beach resort of Santander.

**4 The Basque Country, Navarra, and La Rioja.** The Basque region is a country within a country, proud of its own language and culture, and home to the wild, dramatic coast of the Bay of Biscay. Nearby Navarra and La Rioja are famous for the running of the bulls in Pamplona and for excellent wines, respectively.

**5 The Pyrenees.** Cut by some 23 steep north–south valleys on the Spanish side alone, with four independent geographical entities— the valleys of Camprodón, Cerdanya, Aran, and Baztán—the Pyrenees have a wealth of areas to explore, with different cultures and languages, as well as world-class ski resorts.

**6 Barcelona.** La Rambla, in the heart of the Ciutat Vella, is packed day and night with artists, street entertainers, vendors, and vamps, all preparing you for Barcelona's startling architectural landmarks. But treasures lie beyond the tourist path, including Antoni Gaudí's sinuous Casa Milà and his unique Sagrada Família church, masterpieces of Modernisme.

# WHAT'S WHERE

**7 Catalonia, Valencia, and the Costa Blanca.** The mountain-backed plain of the Levante is dotted with Christian and Moorish landmarks and Roman ruins. Valencia's signature paella fortifies visitors touring the city's medieval masterpieces and modern architecture, while the Costa Blanca has party-till-dawn resort towns. The rice paddies and orange groves of the Costa Blanca lead to the palm-fringed port city of Alicante.

**8 Ibiza and the Balearic Islands.** Ibiza still generates buzz as a summer playground for club-goers from all over, but even this isle has its quiet coves. Mallorca has some heavily tourist–populated pockets, along with pristine mountain vistas in the island's interior. On serene Menorca, the two cities of Ciutadella and Mahón have different histories, cultures, and points of view.

**9 Seville.** One of Andalusia's landlocked provinces, seductive Seville is a vibrant city known for its food, Moorish architecture, and flamenco. Don't miss the Mezquita in nearby Córdoba.

**10 Granada.** Christian and Moorish cultures are dramatically counterposed here. Especially notable is the romantic Alhambra.

**11 Costa del Sol and Costa de Almería.** A popular "sun-holiday" destination, the Costas have vast holiday resorts occupying much of the Mediterranean coast. Respites include Málaga, a vibrant city with world-class art museums; Marbella, a pristine Andalusian old quarter; and villages such as Casares that seem immune to the goings-on along the water.

**12 Canary Islands.** Fuerteventura, the least-visited and least-developed of the four largest volcanic islands, boasts endless white beaches, while Gran Canaria is an isle of contrasts from the desert dunes in the south to the verdant central peaks. Lanzarote's ocher-and-gold landscape is dotted with long beaches and white villages. Tenerife has the most attractions plus Spain's highest peak, the Pico de Teide.

# Spain Today

## POLITICS

Since the advent of democracy in 1978 and until 2014, Spanish politics was dominated by the two largest parties: the socialist Partido Socialista Obrero Español (PSOE) and the right-wing Partido Popular (PP). In 2014, however, as Spain continued to battle an economic crisis and as some high-profile corruption scandals came to light, the political scenario changed. "Renovation" became the watchword, and Spaniards clamored for more ethical behavior from public figures. On the back of this, two new parties entered the political arena: Unidas Podemos (Together We Can), a left-wing grassroots party; and Ciudadanos (Citizens), a pro-business, center-right party that strongly opposes Catalan nationalism. General elections in June 2016 resulted in a deadlock, with no party reaching the required 176-seat majority. The PP under Prime Minister Mariano Rajoy, however, formed a minority government with support from Ciudadanos.

In October 2017, a push for Catalan independence, led by separatist parties, created a major constitutional crisis. Separatist politicians presided over an independence referendum that had been outlawed by Spanish courts. The ruling PP government in Madrid took a hard-line stance against the independence movement, sending national police and civil guards into Catalonia to halt voting. To punish the renegade region, Madrid imposed emergency rule on Catalonia, suspending its autonomy and jailing top regional politicians—who remained in prison until 2021, when they were pardoned. This should ease tensions but it remains to be seen what will follow.

In 2018, Spain's national court found that the ruling PP had been profiting from illegal kickbacks in return for contracts since 1989 and confirmed that the party had been running an illegal, off-the-books accounting structure. The Socialist party under Pedro Sanchez won a parliamentary no-confidence motion and brought down Rajoy's government. Sanchez—who seeks a negotiated solution to the Catalan issue—became prime minister, supported in a coalition by Podemos and regional separatist parties.

Despite the coalition, the parties continued to clash over a number of policies. In May 2021, the leader of Podemos, Pablo Iglesias, stepped down as deputy prime minister, and Spain faced an uncertain future as the PP and Vox, Spain's populist radical right-wing party, gained ground.

## THE ECONOMY

After Spain went into recession in 2008, stringent financial measures were imposed by the European Union and the IMF. Unemployment soared to 26% and youth unemployment reached double that. Since 2014, the economy has bounced back: GDP growth for 2017 was 3.1%, one of the highest rates in Europe, and Spain surpassed the United States to become the world's second-most-visited country after France. When COVID-19 hit in March 2020, it had an unprecedented effect on the economy, and GDP shrank by 10.8% (the worst since 1970), the repercussions of which are yet to be fully seen. Despite this, thanks in part to high vaccination rates, restrictions are now all but lifted, and the economy is forecast to bounce back strongly.

## RELIGION

The state-funded Catholic Church, closely tied to the right-wing PP and with the national Cadena Cope radio station as its voice, continues to have considerable social and political influence in Spain, with members of secretive groups such as Opus Dei and the Legionarios de Cristo holding key government and industry positions.

Despite the church's influence, at street level Spain has become a secular country, as demonstrated by the fact that 70% of Spaniards supported the decidedly un-Catholic law allowing gay marriage—which has been legal since 2005. And although more than 75% of the population claims to be Catholic, less than 20% go to church on a regular basis.

More than 1 million Muslims reside in Spain, making Islam the country's second-largest religion.

## THE ARTS

Spain's devotion to the arts is clearly shown by the attention, both national and international, paid to its annual Princesa de Asturias prize, where Princess Leonor hands out accolades to international high achievers such as Frank Gehry, Francis Ford Coppola, Martin Scorsese, and Marina Abramovic, and to homegrown talent such as the writer Antonio Muñoz Molina and actress and director Núria Espert.

Film is at the forefront of the Spanish arts scene. Spain's most acclaimed director, Pedro Almodóvar, is still at it, releasing a short in 2020 starring Tilda Swinton (filmed during lockdown) and *Parallel Mothers* starring long-time muse, Penelope Cruz, in 2021. *The Bookshop*, an English-language film directed and produced by Spaniards, won Best Film and Best Director awards at the 2018 Goya Awards, Spain's version of the Oscars.

While authors such as Miguel Delibes, Rosa Montero, and Maruja Torres flourish in Spain, few break onto the international scene, with the exception of Arturo Pérez Reverte, whose books include *Captain Alatriste* and *The Fencing Master*, and Carlos Ruiz Zafón, author of the acclaimed *Shadow of the Wind*, *The Angel's Game*, and *Prisoner of Heaven*.

Spain's contribution to the fine arts is still dominated by three names: the Mallorca-born artist Miquel Barceló; the Basque sculptor Eduardo Chillida (who died in 2002); and the Catalan abstract painter Antoni Tàpies (who passed away in 2012).

## SPORTS

With Real Madrid and FC Barcelona firmly established as international brands, and with La Liga recognized as one of the world's most exciting leagues, soccer remains the nation's favorite sport. The national soccer team, known as La Roja (The Red One), won the World Cup in 2010 and has won the European Cup three times—a record tied only by Germany. In other sports, national heroes include Rafael Nadal, the first tennis player to hold Grand Slam titles on clay, grass, and hard court; Garbiñe Muguruza, the 2017 Wimbledon champion; six-time NBA All-Star Pau Gasol and his two-time All-Star brother, Marc; and WNBA star Anna Cruz, who plays for the Minnesota Lynx. Motorsports are hugely popular in Spain; Formula 1 champion Fernando Alonso has recently retired, but all-time-great Marc Marquez continues to dominate in Grand Prix motorcycle road racing.

## IMPACT OF COVID-19 ON SPAIN

Spain was hit hard by COVID-19. The government imposed a state of alarm, closed its borders, and enforced heavy restrictions. All of this had a huge effect on an economy that relies heavily on tourism and which was only just starting to recover from its long economic recession. The state of alarm was lifted in May 2021, and Spain looked optimistically toward a summer tourism revival. In April 2022, Spain lifted the compulsory use of face masks except on public transport and a small number of selected establishments.

**KEY**

○ AVE train stations

░ AVE train service

–○– Local train service

< time > Shortest travel time between stations

A Coruña
< 1hr 46min >
< 27min >
Santiago de Compostela
Lugo
< 4hrs 9min >
Oviedo
Gijón
< 2hrs 10min >
< 2hrs 39min >
Santander
< 2hr 56min >
Bilbao
< 37min >
< 50min >
Ourense
< 3hrs 46min >
León
< 35min >
< 2hrs 25min >
Miranda
< 1hr 30min >
Vigo
< 1hr 25min >
< 1hr 9min >
Burgos
< 47min >
< 51min >
Palencia
< 22min >
Zamora
< 24min >
Valladolid 24min
Medina del Campo
< 39min >
< 44min >
< 57min >
Salamanca
< 1hr 11min >
Ávila
< 1hr 30min >
MADRID
< 3hr 17min >
< 30min >
< 1hr 54min >
Toledo
< 1hr 27min >
PORTUGAL
Cáceres
< 38min >
< 1hr 45min >
< 50min >
Alcázar de San Juan
< 36min >
< 36min >
Mérida
< 3hr 44min >
Ciudad Real
Badajóz
< 30min >
< 50min >
Valdepeñas
Zafra
< 45min >
< 2hrs 29min >
< 3hrs 17min >
< 1hr 41min >
< 2hr 24min >
Córdoba
< 1hr 36min >
Jaén
< 41min >
< 1hr 22min >
Seville
< 2hr 27min >
< 55min >
Huelva
< 1hr 22min >
< 1hr 24min >
< 49min >
Granad
< 2hr
< 50min >
Antequera
< 1hr 12min >
< 32min >
Jerez
< 2hrs 34min >
Málaga
Cádiz
GIBRALTAR (UK)
Algeciras

0 — 100 miles
0 — 150 km

# Travel Times by Train

San Sebastián
< 1 hr 39min >
< 25min >
Irún-Hendaya
FRANCE

Vitoria-
Gasteiz
< 51min >
Pamplona/Iruña
PYRENEES
ANDORRA

< 59min >
Logroño

Huesca
Girona

Soria
< 1 hr 53min >
< 45min >
< 3 hr 47min >
< 38min >
COSTA BRAVA

< 3hrs 1min >
< 1 hr 17min >
< 39min >
< 1 hr 28min >
< 34min >
Barcelona
Zaragoza
Lleida
< 25min >

< 1hr 51min >
< 2hrs 23min >
Tarragona

Teruel
< 1 hr 20min >

< 54min >
Cuenca
< 2h 32min >
Castellón de la Plana

< 53min >
< 47min >
< 33min >
Valencia

< 57min >
< 1 hr 50min >

Albacete
< 46min >
Alicante

< 2hr 14min >
< 1 hr 47min >
Murcia

< 4hrs 50min >
< 1 hr 24min >
< 1 hr 14min >
< 2 hr 16min >

Lorca
< 54min >
Cartagena

< 32min >
Almería

## TRAVEL TIMES

| Destination | Fastest Times |
|---|---|
| Madrid to Barcelona | 2 hrs 30 min |
| Madrid to Bilbao | 4 hrs 32 min |
| Madrid to Seville | 2 hrs 23 min |
| Madrid to Granada | 3 hrs 17 min |
| Madrid to Santander | 4 hrs 4 min |
| Madrid to Valencia | 1 hr 40 min |
| Madrid to Santiago de Compostela | 3 hrs |
| Barcelona to Bilbao | 6 hrs 32 min |
| Barcelona to Valencia | 2 hrs 47 min |
| Seville to Granada | 2 hr 27 min |

# Spain's Best Museums

## CIUTAT DE LES ARTES I LAS CIÈNCIES (CITY OF ARTS AND SCIENCES), VALENCIA

This incredible collection of buildings in Valencia houses some of the world's most cutting-edge science and art exhibits in an enormous piece of modern architecture.

## MUSEU NACIONAL D'ART DE CATALUNYA (MNAC), BARCELONA

Catalonia's national art museum isn't just a literal palace, it's also a shrine to history, culture, and the spirit of the Catalonian people. MNAC has the finest collection of Romanesque frescoes and devotional sculpture in the world, most rescued from abandoned chapels in the Pyrenees in an astonishing feat of restoration.

## THEATRE-MUSEU DALÍ, FIGUERES

Dalí himself supervised the renovation work on this former municipal building, recognizable for its red and gold paint job and the iconic white eggs that crown it. The museum pays homage to the artist's creativity and imagination, and houses many memorable works. You won't find his greatest paintings here, but you will find his crypt!

## FUNDACIÓ JOAN MIRÓ, BARCELONA

High on the hill of Montjuïc, overlooking Barcelona, the Fundació Joan Miró houses the largest collection of works by the revolutionary artist, most of which are assembled from his own private collection, as well as temporary exhibitions by new artists. The building was designed by the artist's close friend, the avant-garde architect Josep Lluís Sert.

## THE GUGGENHEIM MUSEUM, BILBAO

Frank Gehry's groundbreaking Guggenheim Museum Bilbao is a complex work of art in its own right and one of the great pieces of architecture of the 21st century. It's also one of the world's best contemporary art museums. Highlights include works by Andy Warhol, Anish Kapoor, Jeff Koons, Louise Bourgeois, and Eduardo Chillida.

## MUSEO THYSSEN-BORNEMISZA, MADRID

Set in a palace on the Paseo del Prado, the Thyssen offers the opportunity to check a lot of important art off your bucket list as you explore European painting from the Middle Ages through the late 20th century.

## MUSEO DEL PRADO, MADRID

The Prado is one of Spain's largest and most visited museums and a highlight of a visit to Madrid. Wander through rooms filled with dazzling works by the great European masters, all housed in a magnificent neoclassical building that first opened more than 200 years ago.

## MUSEU PICASSO, BARCELONA

Five elegant medieval and early Renaissance palaces in Barcelona's La Ribera house a collection of more than 4,000 works by Pablo Picasso, who studied at La Llotja art school. The collection focuses primarily on these formative years and includes pre-adolescent portraits and sketched landscapes.

## CENTRO DE ARTE REINA SOFÍA, MADRID

The Reina Sofía is specifically dedicated to Spanish modern and contemporary art, with works by practically all the major Spanish artists of the 20th century—Picasso, Dalí, Miró, Julio González, Antoni Tàpies, Alfonso Ponce de León, and Antonio Saura. Picasso's *Guernica* is the top attraction.

## MUSEO ARQUEOLÓGICO NACIONAL (NATIONAL ARCHEOLOGICAL MUSEUM), MADRID

A modern showcase of ancient treasures, MAN went from hidden gem to one of Madrid's top museums, home to one of the most outstanding archaeological collections in Europe.

# Spain's Best Beaches

### CALA MACARELLA AND CALA MACARELLETA, MENORCA

These picture-perfect coves, situated alongside each other on the southwest coast of the island, offer impeccably clear waters, white beaches, and shallow, glimmering rock pools.

### PLAYA LOS LANCES, TARIFA

Located where the Mediterranean and the Atlantic meet, Tarifa is ideal for kitesurfing and for spotting dolphins and whales. The main attraction is the 6-mile-long paradise of powdery white sand and the protected nature reserve.

### PLAYA DE CORRALEJO, FUERTEVENTURA, CANARY ISLANDS

Incredibly popular with kitesurfers, all the Grandes Playas (or big beaches) of the Corralejo Natural Park offer pristine white powder sand and crystal-clear turquoise water.

### BOGATELL, BARCELONA

Barceloneta may be the best known of Barcelona's city beaches, but Bogatell is the beach of choice among locals in the know. Why? Not only is it less crowded than tourist-heavy Barceloneta, it is also cleaner and less popular with local pickpockets. The downside, meanwhile, is that it requires a slightly longer trek from the city center. It's also home to one of Catalonia's best-loved seafood restaurants, Xiringuito Escribà.

### PLAYA LAS ARENAS, VALENCIA

Given that Las Arenas literally translates as "the sands," it goes without saying that Valencia's most famous beach has been blessed with some pristine golden powder. The water is calm and shallow, making it suitable for swimmers of all ages and abilities, as well as for windsurfing and other water sports. The wide, busy promenade that runs alongside the grand beach is packed with bars and restaurants.

### LA CONCHA, SAN SEBASTIÁN

San Sebastián's emblematic seashell-shaped La Concha ranks as one of the most famous urban beaches in the world. Sheltered from the elements by Monte Urgull on one side and Monte Igueldo on the other, and facing Isla de Santa Clara island across a short stretch of water, La Concha's water is nearly always calm, making it an ideal spot for swimming, paddling, and sunbathing.

### PLAYA DE LA RIBERA, SITGES
The dreamy seaside town of Sitges is located some 40 km (25 miles) down the coast from Barcelona and offers pristine, white powder sand and a lively scene.

### PLAYA DE LA VICTORIA, CÁDIZ
The most famous urban beach in the Andalusian city of Cádiz, Playa de la Victoria has a spacious, golden sand beach; a generous boardwalk with a seemingly infinite number of beach bars; and several popular beachfront hotels.

### EL PLAYAZO, COSTA DE ALMERIA
Few places in Europe remain as wild and unspoiled as Cabo de Gata, the UNESCO Biosphere Reserve in the southeastern corner of the Iberian Peninsula. Its wild, arid landscape is a mix of secluded rocky coves, jagged cliffs, and idyllic white sandy beaches.

### PLAYA DE SES ILLETES, FORMENTERA
While every corner of Formentera screams exclusivity, the chicest spot of all is Platja de Ses Illetes, part of the Ses Salines National Park. The residents are pretty, too.

### ISLAS CIES, VIGO
One of the last unspoiled refuges of the Spanish coastline, these islands off the coast of Galicia in northernmost Spain are designated a nature conservation and wildlife site and home to seven beautiful beaches.

### ES TRENC, MALLORCA
Popular with nudists and day-trippers, Es Trenc has excellent facilities and a variety of restaurants and beach bars and is an ideal spot to let it all hang out—if that's what you're into.

# Spain's Most Beautiful Villages

## FORNELLS, MENORCA

For a guaranteed quiet escape, head to the northern fishing village of Fornells, whose whitewashed houses wrap around a picturesque marina. Dive by day, then make your way to one of the seafood restaurants for the daily catch.

## CADAQUÉS, GIRONA

Dalí, Lorca, Duchamp, Buñuel, Picasso—Spain's visionaries flocked to this whitewashed town on the Costa Brava for much the same reasons travelers continue to visit today: its laid-back, bohemian attitude; blindingly white houses; tiny harborside restaurants; and stupefyingly gorgeous sunsets.

## CASARES, MÁLAGA

This quintessential Andalusian village—whitewashed houses and terra-cotta roofs—produced one of the region's greatest thinkers and patriots, Blas Infante. Visit the museum in his childhood home, then wander up to the ruins of a Moorish castle.

## SAN CRISTÓBAL DE LA LAGUNA

The UNESCO-protected center of San Cristóbal de La Laguna (simply "La Laguna" to locals) takes on a tropical feel with wide plazas, Baroque churches, and pastel-painted houses with carved-wood balconies. What La Laguna may lack in beaches (it's 15 minutes from the coast) it makes up for with a student-driven nightlife scene, fascinating history (don't miss the Museo de Historia de Tenerife), and immaculately preserved colonial architecture.

## ALQUÉZAR, HUESCA

One of the best-preserved villages of the region of Aragón, sandwiched between Catalonia and Navarra, Alquézar spirals out like a nautilus from its central *castillo*. Start there and wind your way down to the base of the village through one-car-wide streets and arcaded plazas, pausing at the designated viewpoints to snap pics of the foothills of the Pyrenees.

## FORNALUTX, MALLORCA

Overlooking a spectacular backdrop of the Tramuntana mountain range, this is one of Mallorca's highest and most charming villages. The steep cobbled streets are lined with honey-hued stone buildings embellished with bright green shutters and colorful flowers.

## CUDILLERO, ASTURIAS

Gravity-defying cliff-top houses? Check. Sleepy port surrounded by cafés and seafood restaurants? Check. Centuries-old churches and palaces? Also yes.

## ALMAGRO, CIUDAD REAL

Drama geeks and literature buffs fawn over Almagro, whose Corral de Comedias is the only preserved medieval theater in Europe, founded in 1628. This quaint Manchegan town is known for its *berenjenas de Almagro* (pickled baby eggplant) best sampled at the tapas bars that line the green-and-white Plaza Mayor, a relic of the 1500s; near the plaza are granite mansions bearing the heraldic shields of their former owners and a splendid parador housed in a 17th-century convent.

## BEGET, CATALONIA

Beget is nestled against a backdrop of forested mountains, all but hidden amid the lush green valleys of the Pyrenees. Medieval bridges span the river, which flows past the village's historic stone houses and a Romanesque church. There's all manner of hiking trails that start and finish here, best capped off with a *vermut* in the village plaza.

## HONDARRIBIA, GIPUZKOA

Hondarribia is one of the Basque Country's most charming towns, thanks to its white, green, and red fishermen's homes and tree-shaded promenades. Wind your way down to the harbor on foot, and ferry over to the town of Hendaye. Then stay at the parador, housed in a medieval bastion.

# What to Watch and Read Before You Go to Spain

### HOMAGE TO CATALONIA
### BY GEORGE ORWELL

Orwell's journals directly document his time at war in Catalonia, and his first-person narrative provides a view of war-torn Barcelona that today may seem wholly foreign.

### THE SHADOW OF THE WIND
### BY CARLOS RUIZ ZAFÓN

Daniel Sempere is 10 years old when his father, a bookseller in post–civil war Barcelona, takes him to a mysterious labyrinth filled with treasured but forgotten tomes, and tells him to pick one that he will then dedicate his life to preserving. What follows is a tale of a young man who discovers a mysterious person—or perhaps creature—is destroying all remaining works of Julián Carax, the author whose book he now protects. The Shadow of the Wind story of life, death, and history may be fictional, but its setting in a war-torn Spain is forceful, and the fact that it's sold more than 15 million copies hints at its compelling universe.

### THE BEST THING THAT CAN
### HAPPEN TO A CROISSANT
### BY PABLO TUSSET

Pablo "Baloo" Miralles is the lazy, debaucherous scion of a well-to-do Spanish family. When his elder (and more accomplished) brother inexplicably disappears, Baloo suddenly finds himself pulled into the dealings of the family's powerful financial firm, a turn of events that inspires him to try to locate his missing sibling. Within this satirical quasi-detective story is a modern-day tale about the city of Barcelona.

### FOR WHOM THE BELL TOLLS
### BY ERNEST HEMINGWAY

All the typical Hemingway elements are present in this fictional account of the Spanish Civil War: romance, bravado, glory, death, and tragedy. It's an incredibly evocative slice of historical fiction that is almost impossible to put down once started.

### MARKS OF IDENTITY BY
### JUAN GOYTISOLO

A searing masterpiece from one of Spain's greatest novelists and poets describes the return of an exile to Barcelona. Goytisolo comes to the conclusion that every man carries his own exile with him, wherever he lives. The narrator (Goytisolo) rejects Spain itself and searches instead for poetry. This is a shocking and influential work, and an affirmation of the ability of the individual to survive the political tyrannies of the last century and the current one. Marks of Identity was banned in Spain until after Franco's death.

### MONSIGNOR QUIXOTE
### BY GRAHAM GREENE

This novel provides a wonderful journey through Spain in the company of Monsignor Quixote, an aging village priest, and his friend Sancho Panza, the communist ex-mayor. It's a contemporary reimagining of Miguel Cervantes's classic Don Quixote but set in Spain in the 1980s rather than the 1600s.

### THE NEW SPANIARDS
### BY JOHN HOOPER

How was the transition from dictatorship to democracy accomplished so smoothly? How did a country noted for sexual repression find itself in the European vanguard in legalizing gay marriage? What's the deal with the Spanish royal family? Read Hooper's fascinating study, considered one of the clearest insights into the sociology and culture of modern Spain.

## ¡AY CARMELA! DIRECTED BY CARLOS SAURA

This 1990 film portrays the ethical and personal dilemmas a group of nomadic comedians faces during the Spanish Civil War. The film features a scene where Carmela, played by Carmen Maura, tries to teach a Polish prisoner, an International Brigadist, how to pronounce the /ñ/ sound in the word "España."

## BIUTIFUL DIRECTED BY ALEJANDRO GONZÁLEZ IÑÁRRITU

Alejandro González Iñárritu's first feature since *Babel,* and his fourth emotionally moving film is the story of a single father of two (Javier Bardem) in Barcelona who finds out he has terminal cancer and tries to find someone to care for his children before his death. While melancholy, this is also a story of redemption as a father seeks a better life for his children.

## ALL ABOUT MY MOTHER DIRECTED BY PEDRO ALMODÓVAR

After Manuela's 17-year-old son Esteban is killed before her eyes she decides to move to Barcelona in order to find his father, a transvestite named Lola who doesn't know that Esteban exists. It's a brilliantly directed tale which sensitively examines a variety of complex topics such as bereavement, addiction, gender identity, and the impacts of HIV. It also earned director Pedro Almodóvar the Best Director award at the 1999 Cannes Film Festival and the Academy Award for Best Foreign Language Film in 2000.

## WOMEN ON THE VERGE OF A NERVOUS BREAKDOWN DIRECTED BY PEDRO ALMODÓVAR

This Academy Award–nominated black comedy was Pedro Almodóvar's international breakthrough and secured his place at the forefront of modern Spanish cinema. Madrid-based Pepa resolves to kill herself with a batch of sleeping-pill-laced gazpacho after her lover leaves her. Fortunately, she is interrupted by a deliciously chaotic series of events.

## BELLE EPOQUE DIRECTED BY FERNANDO TRUEBA

It is 1931 in Spain and the country's monarchy is facing its final days. During this time of confusion and conflicting loyalties, Fernando, whose allegiance is to the republic, deserts from the army and goes on the run into the beautiful Spanish countryside. There he meets Manolo, a painter with the same political beliefs and four young, beautiful daughters.

## A GUN IN EACH HAND DIRECTED BY CESC GAY

Catalan director Cesc Gay recruited some top-notch Spanish actors and actresses for this comedy. Told through a series of vignettes, *A Gun In Each Hand* explores how changing gender roles in Spain affect modern relationships and speaks to how Spanish ideas about masculinity and relationships are evolving, and how the evolution can benefit women in Spain.

## PAN'S LABYRINTH DIRECTED BY GUILLERMO DEL TORO

Set in the early years of Franco's dictatorship, this film follows an imaginative kid, Ofelia, who moves with her pregnant mother to her future stepfather's house. In her new home, she meets the faun, Pan, who tells her she might be the lost princess of an underground world. While she faces mythological creatures and terrifying beasts, a rebellion is taking place in her stepfather's military post.

## FAMILY UNITED BY DANIEL SANCHEZ AREVALO

Combining two of Spain's greatest passions—football and family—this Spanish comedy takes place at a family wedding in a mountain-village near Madrid during the 2010 World Cup soccer final.

# History You Can See

## ANCIENT SPAIN

The story of Spain, a romance-tinged tale of counts, caliphs, crusaders, and kings, begins long before written history. The Basques were among the first here, fiercely defending the green mountain valleys of the Pyrenees. Then came the Iberians, believed to have crossed the Mediterranean from North Africa around 3000 BC. The Celts arrived from the north about a thousand years later. The seafaring Phoenicians founded Gadir (now Cádiz) and several coastal cities in the south three millennia ago. The parade continued with the Greeks, who settled parts of the east coast, and then the Carthaginians, who founded Cartagena around 225 BC and dubbed the then-wild, forested, and game-rich country "Ispania," after their word for rabbit: *span*.

**What to See:** Near Barcelona, on the Costa Brava, rocket yourself back almost 3,000 years at **Ullastret,** a settlement occupied by an Iberian people known as the Indiketas. On a tour, actors guide groups through the homes and fortifications of some of the peninsula's earliest inhabitants, the defensive walls attesting to the constant threat of attack and the bits of pottery evidence of the settlement's early ceramic industry. Not far away in **Empúries** are ruins of the Greek colony established in the 6th century BC. At the **Museo de Cádiz** in Andalusia, you can view sarcophagi dating back to the 1100 BC founding of the city.

In Madrid, the outstanding **National Archaeological Museum** displays more than 1 million years of artifacts unearthed in what is now Spain, from Paleolithic tools found in Madrid's Manzanares River basin to 19th-century textiles and musical instruments.

## THE ROMAN EPOCH

Modern civilization in Iberia began with the Romans, who expelled the Carthaginians and turned the peninsula into three imperial provinces. It took the Romans 200 years to subdue the fiercely resisting Iberians, but their influence is seen today in the fortifications, amphitheaters, aqueducts, and other ruins in cities across Spain, as well as in the country's legal system and in the Latin base of Spain's Romance languages and dialects.

**What to See:** Segovia's nearly 3,000-foot-long **Acueducto Romano** is a marvel of Roman engineering. Mérida's Roman ruins are some of Spain's finest, including its **bridge, theater,** and **outdoor amphitheater.** Tarragona was Rome's most important city in Catalonia, as the **walls, circus,** and **amphitheater** bear witness, while Zaragoza boasts a **Roman amphitheater** and a **Roman fluvial port** that dispatched flat-bottom riverboats loaded with wine and olive oil down the Ebro.

## THE VISIGOTHS AND MOORS

In the early 5th century, invading tribes crossed the Pyrenees to attack the weakening Roman Empire. The Visigoths became the dominant force in central and northern Spain by AD 419, establishing their kingdom at Toledo and eventually adopting Christianity. But the Visigoths, too, were to fall before a wave of invaders. The Moors, an Arab-led Berber force, crossed the Strait of Gibraltar in AD 711 and swept through Spain in an astonishingly short time, launching almost eight centuries of Muslim rule. The Moorish architecture and Mudejar Moorish-inspired Gothic decorative details found throughout most of Spain tell much about the splendor of the Islamic culture that flourished here.

**What to See:** Moorish culture is most spectacularly evident in Andalusia, derived from the Arabic name for the Moorish reign on the Iberian Peninsula, al-Andalus, which meant "western lands." The fairy-tale **Alhambra** palace overlooking Granada captures the refinement of the Moorish aesthetic, while the earlier 9th-century **Mezquita** at Córdoba bears witness to the power of Islam in al-Andalus.

## SPAIN'S GOLDEN AGE

By 1085, Alfonso VI of Castile had captured Toledo, giving the Christians a firm grip on the north. In the 13th century, Valencia, Seville, and finally Córdoba—the capital of the Muslim caliphate in Spain—fell to Christian forces, leaving only Granada in Moorish hands. Nearly 200 years later, the so-called Catholic Monarchs—Ferdinand of Aragón and Isabella of Castile—were joined in a marriage that would change the world. Finally, on January 2, 1492—244 years after the fall of Córdoba—Granada surrendered and the Moorish reign was over.

The year 1492 was the beginning of the nation's political golden age: Christian forces conquered Granada and unified all of present-day Spain as a single kingdom; in what was, at the time, viewed as a measure promoting national unity, Jews and Muslims who did not convert to Christianity were expelled from the country. The departure of educated Muslims and Jews was a blow to the nation's agriculture, science, and economy from which it would take nearly 500 years to recover. The Catholic Monarchs and their centralizing successors maintained Spain's unity, but they sacrificed the spirit of international free trade that was bringing prosperity to other parts of Europe. Carlos V weakened Spain with his penchant for waging war, and his son, Felipe II, followed in the same expensive path, defeating the Turks in 1571 but losing the "Invincible Spanish Armada" in the English Channel in 1588.

**What to See:** Commemorate Columbus's voyage to America in Seville, Huelva, Granada, Cádiz, and Barcelona, all of which display venues where "the Discoverer" was commissioned, was confirmed, set out from, returned to, or was buried. Wander through the somber **Escorial,** a monastery northwest of Madrid commissioned by Felipe II in 1557 and finished in 1584, the final resting place of most of the Habsburg and Bourbon kings of Spain ever since.

## WAR OF THE SPANISH SUCCESSION

The War of the Spanish Succession (1700–14) ended with the fall of Barcelona, which sided with the Habsburg Archduke Carlos against the Bourbon Prince Felipe V. El Born market, completed in 1876, covered the buried remains of the Ribera neighborhood, where the decisive battle took place. Ribera citizens were required to tear down a thousand houses to clear space for the Ciutadella fortress, from which fields of fire were directed, quite naturally, toward the city the Spanish and French forces had taken a year to subdue. The leveled neighborhood, then about a third of Barcelona, was plowed under and forgotten by the victors, though never by Barcelonians.

**What to See:** In Barcelona, the **Fossar de les Moreres cemetery,** next to the Santa María del Mar basilica, remains a powerful symbol for Catalan nationalists who gather there every September 11, Catalonia's National Day, to commemorate the fall of the city in 1714.

## SPANISH CIVIL WAR

Spain's early-19th-century War of Independence required five years of bitter guerrilla fighting to rid the peninsula of Napoleonic troops. Later, the Carlist wars set the stage for the Spanish Civil War (1936–39), which claimed more than half a million lives. Intellectuals and leftists sympathized with the elected government; the International Brigades, with many American, British, and Canadian volunteers, took part in some of the worst fighting, including the storied defense of Madrid. But General Francisco Franco, backed by the Catholic Church, got far more help from Nazi Germany, whose Condor legions destroyed the Basque town of Gernika (in a horror made infamous by Picasso's monumental painting *Guernica*), and from Fascist Italy. For three years, European governments stood by as Franco's armies ground their way to victory. After the fall of Barcelona in January 1939, the Republican cause became hopeless. Franco's Nationalist forces entered Madrid on March 27, 1939, and thus began nearly 40 years of dictatorship under Franco. This dark period in recent Spanish history ended on November 20, 1975, when Franco died.

**What to See:** Snap a shot of **Madrid's Plaza Dos de Mayo,** in the Malasaña neighborhood, where officers Daoiz and Velarde held their ground against the superior French forces at the start of the popular uprising against Napoléon. The archway in the square is all that remains of the armory Daoiz and Velarde defended to the death. Trace the shrapnel marks on the wall of the **Sant Felip Neri church** in Barcelona, evidence of the 1938 bombing of the city by Italian warplanes under Franco's orders. East of Zaragoza, **Belchite** was the scene of bloody fighting during the decisive Battle of the Ebro. The town has been left exactly as it appeared on September 7, 1937, the day the battle ended.

### RETURN TO DEMOCRACY

After Franco's death, Spain began the complex process of national reconciliation and a return to democracy. Despite opposition from radical right-wing factions and an attempted coup d'état in February 1981, Spain celebrated the first general elections for 40 years in 1977 and approved a democratic constitution in 1978.

# Chapter 2

# TRAVEL SMART

Updated by
Elizabeth Prosser

★ **CAPITAL:**
Madrid

**POPULATION:**
47.35 million

**LANGUAGE:**
Spanish

$ **CURRENCY:**
Euro

**COUNTRY CODE:**
34

△ **EMERGENCIES:**
112

**DRIVING:**
On the right

⚡ **ELECTRICITY:**
220v/50 cycles; electrical
plugs have two round prongs

**TIME:**
Six hours ahead of New York

**WEB RESOURCES:**
www.spain.info/en
www.parador.es
www.spainisculture.com

Bay of
Biscay

Madrid
★
SPAIN

Mediterranean Sea

# Know Before You Go

Should you tip? When can you eat? Do you need to plan ahead for the major attractions or can you just show up? We've got answers and a few tips to help you make the most of your visit to this beautiful country.

## CATALAN CULTURE IS STRONG

Before the rise of modern-day Spain there was Aragon, a kingdom on the Iberian Peninsula whose territories included the regions we know as Catalonia and Aragon, as well as Roussillon, a part of southern France. The Catalan people and their culture are tenacious, and Barcelona—the capital of Catalonia—remains strongly Catalan. This means that you'll see signage printed in both Spanish and Catalan and will also hear Catalan being spoken. The wealthy Catalan region has about 7.5 million people, with their own language, parliament, flag, and anthem. While you won't be expected to learn the language, it's a sign of respect to learn at least a few Catalan words. (Speaking of regional differences, in the Spanish south, the culture and architecture was strongly influenced by the Moors, the name given to Spain's Muslim population who came across the Straight of Gibraltar from northern Africa.)

## A SLOWER WAY OF LIFE

Spanish life has a slower rhythm than you may be accustomed to. Meals are later (lunch starts at around 2 and dinner at around 10 or 11) and are languorous experiences that last for hours. Sundays are especially slow, especially in smaller towns (and in the off season) where many stores and some restaurants are closed for the day. Stores and restaurants keep familiar hours in tourist-centric areas, and while it's unlikely that you'll be refused service if you want to eat lunch at noon, you'll definitely stand out as a tourist. As for the fabled afternoon siesta, while it does still exist in some more rural communities, in cities like Barcelona and Madrid, it really just takes the form of a long, leisurely lunch.

## SPAIN IS GAY FRIENDLY

While it's true that Spain is Catholic-majority and generally takes religion quite seriously, this country also legalized gay marriage in 2005, a full decade before the United States. While Spain as a whole is generally tolerant, specific areas have also built international reputations for being welcoming to gay travelers and have gay-friendly beaches, restaurants, and nightclubs, and hold yearly Pride parades. Some particularly welcoming destinations are the capital city Madrid, which is said to be one of the most LGBT-friendly cities in all of Europe, the seaside resort town of Sitges, Barcelona, the island of Maspalomas in the Canary Islands, and parts of the bass-thumping club island Ibiza.

## BOOK AHEAD

There are a few major attractions in Spain that rank high on most traveler bucket lists, and if you are hoping to check some of the world's top attractions off your list, too, you'll need to plan ahead. For big-ticket sights like the Alhambra, the Sagrada Família, Park Güell, and the Picasso Museum, book tickets before you arrive. Otherwise, lines can be long, and there is no guarantee that tickets will be available when you visit, especially at peak times. Booking in advance gives you an allocated time (there is zero flexibility with this at most attractions, so be sure to arrive on time).

## THE RAIN IN SPAIN...

Everyone knows the saying "the rain in Spain stays mainly in the plain," thanks to Eliza Doolittle's elocution exercise in *My Fair Lady*. While you may have sung along as Professor Higgins asked excitedly, "Where does it rain?" It turns out the rain in Spain doesn't really fall or stay upon the plain at all. On the contrary, it favors the country's rocky, steep northwestern corner, Galicia.

## PACK FOR A VARIED CLIMATE AND TERRAIN

If you're planning to travel across different regions of Spain, keep in mind that the landscape and climate can change rather dramatically. While Catalonia and Aragon are rolling, arid, and quite dry, Basque Country has generally mild temperatures but significant rainfall, even during the drier months, and southern cities like Seville have a dry Mediterranean climate that can get quite hot during the day. Spain also has placid beaches, coastal plains, tropical islands, and the dramatic Pyrenees mountain range. You'll need to pack accordingly if you will be in more than one climate zone.

## SKIP THE PLANE AND TAKE A TRAIN

Flights from one region of Spain to another are cheap and easy, but don't discount the country's high-speed rail network. It's fast, comfortable, and a great way to get from city to city. You can get from Madrid to Seville in 2 hours and 20 minutes without any of the hassles or stresses of air travel. Also, did we mention that you can bring food and alcohol on board with you?

## WINE IS INEXPENSIVE

Spain is the third largest producer of wine in the world, after France and Italy, and almost half the wine (in a normal vintage) production is sold at low prices—like 5 to 10 euros a bottle. It's key to a fun and frugal vacation to know that just because this wine is inexpensive, it doesn't mean it's cheap.

## DON'T JUST EAT PAELLA

Delicious as it is, there's a lot more to Spanish cuisine than paella. As with any country, Spanish recipes are strongly influenced by culture, tradition, and environment. In northwestern Basque Country, the name of the game is *pintxos* (pronounced pinchos), which is that region's version of tapas—numerous little bites, often on a toothpick, eaten alongside beer or wine. Vegetables are the main attraction in the Navarra region: look for Lodosa piquillo peppers, Tudela artichokes, and white asparagus. On the western border where Spain meets Portugal, the greatest treasure is *jamón ibérico*, thinly sliced cured ham made from pigs fattened up on foraged acorns. In the Andalusian south—where they were invented—tapas reign supreme. Think about the region you're in before you order. If you're on the coast, fish is the way to go. If you're inland, consider a dish made with meat.

## GO TO THE BEACH

While most of Europe visits Spain for their beach holidays, the rest of the world is more interested in Spain's vibrant cities, culture, and history. But if you find yourself on one of Spain's gorgeous beaches, you'll wonder why people don't visit for the beaches alone. Spain has a great many seaside towns that offer a range of popular and less-traveled stretches of sand. Even major coastal cities like Barcelona have beaches. If you're looking for something truly special though, head to the Canary Islands, which are famous for their soft sands and clear, azure waters.

## TIPPING ISN'T MANDATORY (MOST OF THE TIME)

Thanks to decent worker protections, Spanish servers earn a living wage and don't depend on tips to survive. That said, it is customary in a casual restaurant to round up your bill and leave the change, but it isn't expected or required. If you eat in a formal restaurant, there is an expectation that you'll tip, but the maximum is still only 10%.

# Getting Here and Around

##  Air

Flying time from New York to Madrid is about seven hours; from London, it's just over two hours.

Regular nonstop flights serve Spain from many major cities in the eastern United States; flying from other North American cities usually involves a stop. If you're coming from North America and want to land in a city other than Madrid or Barcelona, consider flying a European carrier.

The Visit Europe from oneworld (which includes American Airlines, Iberia, and British Airways among others) is the most useful aviation pass for Spain. It is available only to residents of countries outside Europe and must be booked before departure with a Oneworld member airline. The pass gives you access to 200 destinations in 50 countries in Europe and North Africa. It's available as an add-on to an international flight to Europe booked with any of the airlines in the Oneworld alliance, and is accepted for as long as the international ticket is valid. You must buy a minimum of two coupons for flights within Europe, but there's no maximum.

A number of low-cost carriers operate from the United Kingdom to Spain such as Vueling (⊕ www.vueling.com) and Jet2 (⊕ www.jet2.com). They provide competition to the market's main players, easyJet (⊕ www.easyjet.com) and Ryanair (⊕ www.ryanair.com). All these carriers offer frequent flights, cover small cities as well as large ones, and have very competitive fares.

### AIRPORTS
Most flights from North America land in, or pass through, Madrid's Barajas Airport (MAD). The other major gateway is Barcelona's Prat de Llobregat (BCN).

From the United Kingdom and elsewhere in Europe, regular flights also touch down in Málaga (AGP), Alicante (ALC), Palma de Mallorca (PMI), and many other smaller cities.

### FLIGHTS
From North America, Air Europa flies to Madrid and Barcelona; American Airlines, part of the Oneworld Alliance, and Iberia fly to Madrid and Barcelona; Delta flies direct to Madrid only. Note that some of these airlines use shared facilities and do not operate their own flights. Within Spain, Iberia is the main domestic airline and also operates low-cost flights through its budget airlines Iberia Express and Vueling. Air Europa and Ryanair both offer inexpensive flights on most domestic routes. The earlier before your travel date you purchase the ticket, the more bargains you're likely to find. Air Europa, Iberia Express, Vueling, and Ryanair also have flights from Spain to other destinations in Europe.

Iberia runs a shuttle, the Puente Áereo, offering flights just over an hour long between Madrid and Barcelona, every 30 minutes (more often during peak travel times) 6:45 am–9:45 pm. You don't need to reserve; you can buy your tickets at the airport ticket counter upon arriving or book online at ⊕ www.iberia.com/es/air-shuttle. Passengers can also use the self-service check-in counters to avoid the line. Puente Áereo departs from Terminal T1 in Barcelona; in Madrid, the shuttle departs from Terminal 4.

## ○ Boat

Regular car ferries connect the United Kingdom with northern Spain. Brittany Ferries sails from Plymouth to Santander, and from Portsmouth to Santander and

Bilbao. Trasmediterránea and Baleària connect mainland Spain to the Balearic and Canary islands.

Direct ferries from Spain to Tangier leave daily from Tarifa and Algeciras on FRS, Inter Shipping, and Trasmediterránea. Otherwise, you can take your car either to Ceuta (via Algeciras, on Baleària) or Melilla (via Málaga, on Trasmediterránea)—two Spanish enclaves on the North African coast—and then move on to Morocco.

# 🚌 Bus

You can travel to Spain on modern buses (Eurolines/National Express, for example) from major European cities, including London, Paris, Rome, Frankfurt, and Prague. Although it may once have been the case that international bus travel was significantly cheaper than air travel, budget airlines have changed the equation. For perhaps a little more money and a large saving of travel hours, flying is increasingly the better option.

Within Spain, a number of private companies provides bus service, ranging from knee-crunchingly basic to luxurious. Fares are almost always lower than the corresponding train fares, and service covers more towns, though buses are less frequent on weekends. Smaller towns don't usually have a central bus depot, so ask the tourist office where to wait for the bus. Spain's major national long-haul bus line is ALSA.

Most of Spain's larger companies have buses with comfortable seats and adequate legroom; on longer journeys (two hours or longer), a movie is shown on board, and earphones are provided. Except on smaller regional lines, all buses have bathrooms on board; most long-haul buses also usually stop at least once every two to three hours for a snack and bathroom break. Smoking is prohibited on board.

ALSA has four luxury classes in addition to its regular seating. Premium, available on limited routes from Madrid, includes a number of services such as à la carte meals and a private waiting room, while Supra+ and Supra Economy include roomy leather seats and onboard meals. You also have the option of *asientos individuales*, individual seats (with no other seat on either side) that line one side of the bus. The last class is Eurobus, with a private waiting room, comfortable seats, and plenty of legroom. The Supra+ and Eurobus usually cost, respectively, up to one-third and one-fourth more than the regular seats.

If you plan to return to your initial destination, you can save by buying a round-trip ticket. Also, some of Spain's smaller regional bus lines offer multitrip passes, which are worthwhile if you plan to move back and forth between two fixed destinations within the region. Generally, these tickets offer savings of 20% per journey; you can buy them at the station. The general rule for children over 3 is that if they occupy a seat, they pay full fare. Check the bus websites for *ofertas* (special offers).

At bus station ticket counters, most major credit cards (except American Express) are accepted. If you buy your ticket on the bus, it's cash only.

During peak travel times (Easter, August, and Christmas), it's a good idea to make a reservation at least a week in advance.

# Getting Here and Around

## 🚗 Car

Your own driver's license is valid in Spain, but U.S. citizens are highly encouraged to obtain an International Driving Permit (IDP). The IDP may facilitate car rental and help you avoid traffic fines—it translates your state-issued driver's license into 10 languages so officials can easily interpret the information on it. Permits are available from the American Automobile Association.

Driving is the best way to see Spain's rural areas. The main cities are connected by a network of excellent four-lane divided highways (*autovías* and *autopistas*), which are designated by the letter *A* and have speed limits—depending on the area—of 80 kph (50 mph)–120 kph (75 mph). If the artery is a toll highway (*peaje*), it is designated *AP.* The letter *N* indicates a *carretera nacional*: a national or intercity route, with local traffic, which may have four or two lanes. Smaller towns and villages are connected by a network of secondary roads maintained by regional, provincial, and local governments, with an alphabet soup of different letter designations.

### RENTAL CARS

Alamo, Avis, Budget, Enterprise, Europcar, and Hertz have branches at major Spanish airports and in large cities. Smaller regional companies and wholesalers offer lower rates. The online outfit Pepe Car has been a big hit with travelers; in general, the earlier you book, the less you pay. Rates run as low as €15 per day, taxes included. All agencies have a range of models, but virtually all cars in Spain have manual transmission. Rates in Madrid begin at the equivalents of $60 per day and $190 per week for an economy car with air-conditioning, manual transmission, and unlimited mileage, including 21% tax. A small car is cheaper and prudent for the tiny roads and parking spaces in many parts of Spain.

Anyone age 18 or older with a valid license can drive in Spain, but rental agencies require a minimum driver age of 21 and most rental agencies will not rent cars to drivers under 23.

### ROAD CONDITIONS

Spain's highway system includes some 6,000 km (3,600 miles) of well-maintained superhighways. Still, you'll find some stretches of major national highways that are only two lanes wide, where traffic often backs up behind trucks. Autopista tolls are steep, but as a result these highways are often less crowded than the free ones. If you're driving down through Catalonia, be aware that there are more tolls here than anywhere else in Spain. This can result in a quicker journey, but at a sizable cost. If you spring for the autopistas, you'll find that many of the rest stops are nicely landscaped and have cafeterias with decent but overpriced food.

Most Spanish cities have notoriously long morning and evening rush hours. Traffic jams are especially bad in and around Barcelona, Madrid, and Seville. If possible, avoid the morning rush, which can last until noon, and the evening rush, which lasts 7–9. Also be aware that at the beginning, middle, and end of July and August, the country suffers its worst traffic jams (delays of six to eight hours are common) as millions of Spaniards embark on, or return from, their annual vacations.

### ROADSIDE EMERGENCIES

Rental agencies Hertz and Avis have (optional) 24-hour breakdown service. If you belong to AAA, you can get emergency assistance from the Spanish counterpart, RACE.

## RULES OF THE ROAD

Spaniards drive on the right and pass on the left, so stay in the right-hand lane when not passing. Children under 12 may not ride in the front seat, and seat belts are compulsory for both front- and backseat riders. Speed limits are 30 kph (19 mph) or 50 kph (31 mph) in cities, depending on the type of street, 90 kph (59 mph) or 100 kph (62 mph) on national highways, 120 kph (75 mph) on the autopista or autovía. The use of cell phones by drivers, even on the side of the road, is illegal, except with completely hands-free devices.

Severe fines are enforced throughout Spain for driving under the influence of alcohol. Spot Breathalyzer checks are often carried out, and you will be cited if the level of alcohol in your bloodstream is found to be 0.05% or above.

Spanish highway police are increasingly vigilant about speeding and illegal passing. Police are empowered to demand payment on the spot from non-Spanish drivers. Police disproportionately target rental-car drivers for speeding and illegal passing, so play it safe.

## 🚃 Train

*The chart here has information about popular train routes. Prices are for one-way fares (depending on seating and where purchased) and subject to change.*

International trains run from Madrid to Lisbon (10 hours 30 minutes, overnight) and Barcelona to Paris (6 hours 40 minutes).

Spain's wonderful high-speed train, the 290-kph (180-mph) AVE, travels between Madrid and Seville (with a stop

### Train Travel Times

| Route | Time |
| --- | --- |
| Madrid to Barcelona: €45–€91 | High-speed AVE trains make the trip in 2 hours 30 minutes |
| Madrid to Bilbao: €22–€40 | Semi-express Alvia train time is 4 hours 32 minutes |
| Madrid to Málaga: €35–€70 | Fastest AVE trains take 2 hours 25 minutes |
| Madrid to Seville: €35–€66 | Fastest AVE trains take 2 hours 23 minutes |
| Madrid to Granada: €35–€70 | Fastest AVE trains take 3 hours and 17 minutes |
| Madrid to Santander: €27–€55 | Semi-express Alvia is 4 hours 4 minutes |
| Madrid to Valencia: €23–€80 | Fastest AVE trains take 1 hour 40 minutes |
| Madrid to Santiago de Compostela: €30–€60 | Fastest Alvia trains take 3 hours |
| Barcelona to Bilbao: €30–€50 | Running time about 6 hours 32 minutes |
| Barcelona to Granada: €40–€115 | High-speed AVE trains take 6h and 25 min |
| Barcelona to Valencia: €27–€50 | Fastest time 2 hours 47 minutes |
| Seville to Granada: €24–€50 | Running time about 2 hours 22 minutes |

in Córdoba) in 2½ hours; prices start at about €50 each way. It also serves the Madrid–Barcelona route, cutting travel time to just under three hours. From Madrid you can also reach Lleida, Huesca (one AVE train daily), Valencia, Málaga, Toledo, and Valladolid.

# Getting Here and Around

From summer 2021, the state-run rail system (RENFE) introduced tariffs based on demand on AVE train services. Tickets at less popular times (e.g. midday or mid-week) are up to 75% cheaper in all three classes: *Básico*, *Elige,*and *Premium*. The low-cost AVE service, known as Avlo (⊕ *avlorenfe.com*), offers routes between Madrid, Barcelona, and Zarragoza with one-way tickets from as little as €7. The company plans to add other Avlo routes in 2022.

The fast Talgo service is also efficient, but other elements of the rail system are still a bit subpar by European standards, and some long-distance trips with multiple stops can be tediously slow. Although some overnight trains have comfortable sleeper cars, first-class fares that include a sleeping compartment are comparable to, or more expensive than, airfares.

Most Spaniards buy train tickets in advance online or at the train station's *taquilla* (ticket office). The lines can be long, so give yourself plenty of time. For popular train routes, you will need to reserve tickets more than a few days in advance and pick them up at least a day before traveling. The ticket clerks at the stations rarely speak English, so if you need help or advice in planning a more complex train journey, you may be better off going to a travel agency that displays the blue-and-yellow RENFE sign. A small commission (e.g., €2.50) should be expected. For shorter, regional train trips, you can often buy your tickets from machines in the train station. Note that you must provide your full name and identity details (e.g. passport number) for all AVE tickets.

You can use a credit card for train tickets at most city train stations, but in smaller towns and villages it may be cash only. Seat reservations are required on most long-distance and some other trains, particularly high-speed trains, and are wise on any train that might be crowded. You need a reservation if you want a sleeping berth.

The easiest way to make reservations is to go to the English version of the REN-FE website (click "Welcome" on the top line) or use the RenfeTicket smartphone app (to buy tickets using the app, you need to register and to have bought a RENFE ticket with your credit card). Book early if you're traveling during Holy Week, on long holiday weekends, or in July and August. (The site allows you to make reservations up to 62 days in advance, which is important in qualifying for online purchase discounts.)

Caveats: You cannot buy tickets online for certain regional lines or for commuter lines (*cercanías*). Station agents cannot alter your reservations; you must do this yourself online. Some ticket types, e.g. Básico for the AVE, allow no changes. The RENFE website may not work with all browsers, but it does accept all major credit cards, including American Express.

## DISCOUNTS

If you purchase a ticket on the REN-FE website for the AVE or any of the Grandes Líneas (the faster, long-distance trains, including the Talgo), you can get a discount of 20%–60%, depending on how far ahead you book and how you travel: discounts on one-way tickets tend to be higher than on round-trips. Discount availabilities disappear fast: the earliest opportunity is 62 days in advance of travel. If you have a domestic or an international airline ticket and want to take the AVE within 48 hours of your arrival but haven't booked online, you can still get a 10% discount on the AVE one-way ticket and 25% for a round-trip ticket with a dated return. On regional trains, you get a 10% discount on round-trip tickets (15% on AVE medium-distance trains).

■TIP➜ If there are more than two of you traveling on the AVE, look for the word "mesa" in the fare column, quoting the price per person for four people travelling together and sitting at the same table. If you select the price, it tells you how much the deal is for one, two, and three people. You have to buy all the tickets at the same time, but they're between 20% and 60% cheaper than regular tickets.

## RAIL PASSES

If you're coming from the United States and are planning extensive train travel in Europe, check Rail Europe for Eurail passes. Whichever pass you choose, you must buy it before you leave for Europe.

Spain is one of 33 European countries in which you can use the Eurail Global Pass, which buys you unlimited rail travel in all participating countries for the duration of the pass. Choose from passes that allow a set number of days to travel during a one-, two-, or three-month period, or passes offering continuous travel within the chosen period. There are discounts for children (ages 4–11) and youths (ages 12–27).

If Spain is your only destination, a Eurail Spain Pass allows between three and eight days of unlimited train travel in Spain within a one-month period for $272–$499 (first class) and $204–$337 (second class). There are also combination passes for those visiting Spain and Portugal, Spain and France, and Spain and Italy.

Many travelers assume that rail passes guarantee them seats on the trains they wish to ride: not so. Reserve seats even if you're using a rail pass.

# Before You Go

## ✏ Immunizations

COVID-19 has disrupted travel since March 2020, and travelers should expect sporadic ongoing issues. Always travel with a mask in case it's required, and keep up to date on the most recent testing and vaccination guidelines for Spain.

## 🌐 Passports and Visas

Visitors from the United States, Australia, Canada, New Zealand, and the United Kingdom need a valid passport to enter Spain.

### VISAS

Visas are not necessary for those with U.S. passports valid for a minimum of six months and who plan to stay in Spain for tourist or business purposes for up to 90 days. Should you need a visa to stay longer than this, contact the Spanish consulate office nearest to you in the United States to apply for the appropriate documents.

## 🇺🇸 U.S. Embassy/Consulate

Embassies are located in Madrid while some countries also maintain consulates in Barcelona. The United States also maintains consular agencies in Fuengirola, Las Palmas, Palma de Mallorca, Seville, and Valencia.

## 🧳 What to Pack

Pack light. Although baggage carts are free and plentiful in most Spanish airports, they're rare in smaller train stations and most bus stations. Madrid,

north and northeastern Spain, and Granada and the Sierra Nevada can be bitterly cold from late fall through early spring, while the Mediterranean and southern regions are generally much milder. It makes sense to wear casual, comfortable clothing and shoes for sightseeing, but you'll want to dress up a bit in large cities, especially for fine restaurants and nightclubs. On the beach, anything goes; it's common to see women of all ages wearing only bikini bottoms, and many of the more remote beaches allow nude sunbathing.

## 📅 When to Go

**High season:** June through mid-September is the most expensive and popular time to visit the coast and islands. Inland cities are quieter but hot, and many businesses close for August. Sunshine is guaranteed almost everywhere, except in the north where weather is changeable.

**Low season:** Winter offers the least appealing weather, though it's the best time for airfares and hotel deals. The Mediterranean coast can be balmy during the daytime, even in December—and there are no crowds—but nighttime temperatures drop.

**Value season:** May, June, and September are lovely with warm weather, saner airfares, and good hotel offers. You can hang with the locals without the tourist crowds. October still has great weather, though temperatures start to fall by November. Bring an umbrella in March and April.

# Essentials

## 🧭 Communications

### PHONES

The good news is that you can now make a direct-dial telephone call from virtually any point on earth. The bad news? You can't always do so cheaply. Calling from a hotel is almost always the most expensive option; hotels usually add huge surcharges to all calls, particularly international ones. In some countries you can phone from call centers or even the post office. Calling cards usually keep costs to a minimum, but only if you purchase them locally. And then there are cell phones, which are sometimes more prevalent—particularly in the developing world—than landlines; as expensive as mobile phone calls can be, they are still usually a much cheaper option than calling from your hotel.

The country code for Spain is 34. The country code is 1 for the United States and Canada.

If you're going to be traveling in Spain for an extended period, buy a local SIM card (ensure your phone is unlocked), use Skype or FaceTime, or install a free messenger app on your smartphone, such as Viber or WhatsApp.

## 🍴 Dining

Sitting around a table eating and talking is a huge part of Spanish culture, defining much of people's daily routines. Sitting in the middle of a typical bustling restaurant here goes a long way toward building understanding of how fundamental food can be to Spanish lives.

Although Spain has always had an extraordinary range of regional cuisines, in the past decade or so its restaurants

have won it international recognition at the highest levels. A new generation of Spanish chefs—led by the revolutionary Ferran Adrià—has transformed classic dishes to suit contemporary tastes, drawing on some of the freshest ingredients in Europe and bringing an astonishing range of new technologies into the kitchen.

Smoking is banned in all eating and drinking establishments in Spain.

### MEALS AND MEALTIMES

Outside major hotels, which serve morning buffets, breakfast (*desayuno*) is usually limited to coffee and toast or a roll. Lunch (*comida* or *almuerzo*) traditionally consists of an appetizer, a main course, and dessert, followed by coffee and perhaps a liqueur. Between lunch and dinner the best way to snack is to sample some tapas at a bar; normally you can choose from quite a variety. Dinner (*cena*) is somewhat lighter, with perhaps only one course. In addition to à la carte selections, most restaurants offer a *menú del día* (daily fixed-price menu) consisting of a starter, main plate, beverage, and dessert. The menú del día is traditionally offered only at lunch, but increasingly it's also offered at dinner in popular tourist destinations. If your waiter does not suggest it when you're seated, ask for it: "*¿Hay menú del día, por favor?*"

Mealtimes in Spain are later than elsewhere in Europe, and later still in Madrid and the southern region of Andalusia. Lunch starts around 2 or 2:30 (closer to 3 in Madrid) and dinner after 9 (as late as 11 or midnight in Madrid). Weekend eating times, especially dinner, can begin upward of an hour later. In areas with heavy tourist traffic, some restaurants open a bit earlier.

# Essentials

Most prices listed in menus are inclusive of 10% value-added tax (I.V.A.), but not all. If I.V.A. isn't included, it should read, "10% I.V.A. no incluido en los precios" at the bottom of the menu. Unless otherwise noted, the restaurants listed in this guide are open daily for lunch and dinner.

Prices in the reviews are the average cost of a main course or equivalent combination of smaller dishes at dinner or, if dinner is not served, at lunch.

## PAYING

Credit cards are widely accepted in Spanish restaurants, but some smaller establishments do not take them. If you pay by credit card and you want to leave a small tip above and beyond the service charge, leave the tip in cash. ■TIP→ See Tipping for guidelines.

## WINES, BEER, AND SPIRITS

Apart from its famous wines, Spain produces many brands of lager, the most popular of which are San Miguel, Cruzcampo, Aguila, Voll Damm, Mahou, and Estrella. There's also a thriving craft-beer industry, and most large towns and cities have bars specializing in local brews. Jerez de la Frontera is Europe's largest producer of brandy and is a major source of sherry. Catalonia is a major producer of cava (sparkling wine). Spanish law prohibits the sale of alcohol to people age 18 or younger.

## 🛏 Lodging

By law, hotel prices in Spain must be posted at the reception desk and should indicate whether the value-added tax (I.V.A. 10%) is included. Note that high-season rates prevail not only in summer but also during Holy Week and local fiestas. In much of Spain, breakfast is normally *not* included.

## HOTELS AND BED-AND-BREAKFASTS

The Spanish government classifies hotels with one to five stars, with an additional rating of five-star GL (Gran Lujo) indicating the highest quality. Although quality is a factor, the rating is technically only an indication of how many facilities the hotel offers. For example, a three-star hotel may be just as comfortable as a four-star hotel but lack a swimming pool.

All hotel entrances are marked with a blue plaque bearing the letter *H* and the number of stars. The letter *R* (for *residencia*) after the letter *H* indicates an establishment with no meal service, with the possible exception of breakfast. The designations *fonda* (*F*), *pensión* (*P*), *casa de huéspedes* (*CH*), and *hostal* (*Hs*) indicate budget accommodations: these are no longer official categories, but you'll still find them across the country. In most cases, especially in smaller villages, rooms in such buildings will be basic but clean; in large cities, these rooms can be downright dreary.

When inquiring in Spanish about whether a hotel has a private bath, ask if it's an *habitación con baño*. Although a single room (*habitación sencilla*) is usually available, singles are often on the small side. Solo travelers might prefer to pay a bit extra for single occupancy of a double room (*habitación doble uso individual*). Make sure you request a double bed (*cama de matrimonio*) if you want one—if you don't ask, you will usually end up with two singles.

The Spanish love small country hotels and agritourism. Rusticae (⊕ www.rusticae.es) is an association of more than 120 independently owned hotels in restored palaces, monasteries, mills, and estates, generally in rural Spain. Similar associations serve individual regions, and tourist offices also provide lists of establishments. In Galicia, *pazos* are beautiful, old, often stately homes converted into small luxury hotels; Pazos de Galicia (⊕ www.pazosdegalicia.com) is the main organization for them. In Cantabria, *casonas* are small-to-large country houses, but they may not have individual websites, so check the regional tourist office websites for booking and contact information.

A number of *casas rurales* (country houses similar to B&Bs) offer pastoral lodging either in guest rooms or in self-catering cottages. You may also come across the term *finca,* for country estate house. Many *agroturismo* accommodations are fincas converted to upscale B&Bs.

## PARADORES

The Spanish government operates nearly 100 paradores—upscale hotels often in historic buildings or near significant sites. Rates are reasonable, considering that most paradores have four or five-star amenities, and the premises are invariably immaculate and tastefully furnished, often with antiques or reproductions. Each parador has a restaurant serving regional specialties, and you can stop in for a meal without spending the night. Paradores are popular with foreigners and Spaniards alike, so make reservations well in advance.

---

## 💲 Taxes

Value-added tax, similar to sales tax, is called I.V.A. in Spain (pronounced "*ee*-vah," for *impuesto sobre el valor añadido*). It's levied on both products and services, such as hotel rooms and restaurant meals. When in doubt about whether tax is included, ask, "*¿Está incluido el I.V.A.?*" The I.V.A. rate for hotels and restaurants is currently 10%, regardless

of their number of stars. A special tax law for the Canary Islands allows hotels and restaurants there to charge 7% I.V.A. Menus will generally note at the bottom whether tax is included ("*I.V.A. incluido*") or not ("*más 10% I.V.A.*").

Although food, pharmaceuticals, and household items are taxed at the lowest rate (4%), most consumer goods are now taxed at 21%. A number of shops participate in Global Refund (formerly Europe Tax-Free Shopping), a VAT refund service that makes getting your money back relatively hassle-free. You cannot get a refund on the VAT for such items as meals, or services such as hotel accommodations or taxi fares.

When making a purchase that qualifies for Global Refund, find out whether the merchant gives refunds—not all stores do, nor are they required to—and ask for a V.A.T. refund form. Have the form stamped like any customs form by customs officials when you leave the country or, if you're visiting several European Union countries, when you leave the EU. After you're through passport control, take the form to a refund-service counter for an on-the-spot refund (which is usually the quickest and easiest option), or mail it to the address on the form (or the envelope with it) after you arrive home. You receive the total refund stated on the form, but the processing time can be long, especially if you request a credit-card adjustment.

Global Blue is a Europewide service with 300,000 affiliated stores and more than 700 refund counters at major airports and border crossings. The refund form, called a Tax Free Check or Refund Cheque, is the most common across the European continent. The service issues refunds in the form of cash, check, or credit-card adjustment.

# Essentials

## 💲 Tipping

Aside from tipping waiters and taxi drivers, Spaniards tend not to leave extra in addition to the bill. Restaurant checks do not list a service charge on the bill but consider the tip included. If you want to leave a small tip in addition to the bill, tip 5%–10% of the bill (and only if you think the service was worth it), and leave less if you eat tapas or sandwiches at a bar—just enough to round out the bill to the nearest €1.

## 🧭 Tours

### SPECIAL-INTEREST TOURS

**Madrid and Beyond**

SPECIAL-INTEREST TOURS | An array of customized private luxury tours (no two are the same) is offered by this company, focusing on culinary, cultural, and sports-related themes. ☎ 9117/758-0063 in Spain ⊕ www.madridandbeyond.com ✉ Prices available on application.

**Toma Tours**

SPECIAL-INTEREST TOURS | This company provides personalized and small-group tours with the focus on discovering Andalusia's culture, landscape, and gastronomy beyond the guidebook. ☎ 650/733116 ⊕ tomaandcoe.com ✉ From €1,690.

### ART

**Escorted Spain Tours**

SPECIAL-INTEREST TOURS | Based in the United States, this company offers a range of tours with accents on art, cultural history, and the outdoors. ☎ 800/942–3301 ⊕ www.escortedspaintours.com ✉ From €1,135.

### BIRD-WATCHING

**Discovering Doñana**

SPECIAL-INTEREST TOURS | In the Coto Doñana National Park in Andalusia, this company offers some of the best guided bird-watching tours and expeditions in Spain. ☎ 620/964369 ⊕ www.discoveringdonana.com ✉ From €165.

### CULINARY AND WINE

**Artisans of Leisure**

SPECIAL-INTEREST TOURS | This company offers personalized food-and-wine and cultural tours to Spain. ☎ 800/214–8144, 212/243–3239 ⊕ www.artisansofleisure.com ✉ From €7,685.

**Cellar Tours**

SPECIAL-INTEREST TOURS | Based in Madrid, Cellar Tours offers a wide array of wine and culinary tours to Spain's main wine regions. ☎ 911/436553 in Spain, 310/496–8061 in U.S. ⊕ www.cellartours.com ✉ From €700.

### HIKING

**Spain Adventures**

SPECIAL-INTEREST TOURS | This company offers hiking and biking around Spain, as well as unusual tours such as yoga and cooking. ☎ 772/564–0330 ⊕ www.spainadventures.com ✉ From €3,090.

### LANGUAGE PROGRAMS

**Go Abroad**

SPECIAL-INTEREST TOURS | This is one of the best resources for language schools and international programs in Spain. ⊕ www.goabroad.com.

### VOLUNTEER PROGRAMS

**Spain Savvy**

SPECIAL-INTEREST TOURS | Owned and operated by an American expat in Seville, this company designs custom itineraries including culturally immersive experiences and top-notch properties. ☎ 717/702559 ⊕ www.spainsavvy.com ✉ From €300.

# Contacts

## ✈ Air

**CONTACTS Air Europa.** ☎ 911/401501 ⊕ www. aireuropa.com. **Iberia.** ☎ 901/111500 ⊕ www. iberia.com. **Transportation Security Administration.** ⊕ www.tsa.gov.

**AIRLINES Air Europa.** ☎ 911/401501 ⊕ www. aireuropa.com. **Iberia Express.** ☎ 919/046342 ⊕ www.iberiaex-press.com. **Vueling.** ☎ 900/645000 ⊕ www.vueling.com.

**AIRPORTS AENA.** ☎ 913/211000 ⊕ www. aena.es. **Madrid–Barajas (MAD).** ✉ ☎ 902/404704 ⊕ www.aeropuertoma-drid-barajas.com.

## 🚌 Bus

**CONTACTS ALSA.** ✉ Carrer de Virat s/n, ☎ 902/242–2242 ⊕ www.alsa.es. **Flixbus.** ⊕ www.flixbus.es.

## 🚗 Car

**CAR RENTAL COMPANIES**
**Budget.** ☎ 902/112569 Customer Service, 902/112585 Bookings ⊕ www.budget.com.

**Enterprise.** ☎ 902/100101 ⊕ www.enterprise.es. **Europcar.** ☎ 911/505000 ⊕ www.europcar.es. **Hertz.** ☎ 917/497765 Bookings ⊕ www.hertz.com. **Pepe Car.** ☎ 916/350317 ⊕ www.pepecar.com.

**EMERGENCY SERVICE RACE.** ☎ 900/100992 for info, 900/112222 for assistance ⊕ www.race.es.

## 🚆 Train

**TRAIN CONTACTS Eurail.** ⊕ www.eurail.com. **Rail Europe.** ⊕ www.raileurope. com. **RENFE.** ☎ 912/320320 for tickets and info ⊕ www.renfe.es.

## ⚠ Emergencies

**FOREIGN EMBASSIES AND CONSULATES**
**U.S. Embassy.** ✉ Calle Serrano 75, ☎ 91/587–2200 U.S.-citizen emergencies ⊕ es.usembassy.gov.

**GENERAL EMERGENCY CONTACTS Emergency telephone number.** ☎ 112. **Fire department.** ☎ 080. **Local police.** ☎ 092. **Medical service.** ☎ 061. **National police.** ☎ 091.

## 🛏 Lodging

**APARTMENT RENTALS**
**HolidayLettings.** ⊕ www. holidaylettings.co.uk. **Vrbo.** ⊕ www.vrbo.com. **Interhome.** ☎ 800/268–2615 ⊕ www.inter-homeusa.com. **Villas and Apartments Abroad.** ☎ 212/213–6435 ⊕ www.vaanyc.com.

**PARADORS Paradores de España.** ☎ 913/742500 in Spain ⊕ www.parador.es.

## ⛴ Boat

**CONTACTS Brittany Ferries.** ☎ 0330/159–7000 in U.K., 902/108147 in Spain ⊕ www.brittany-ferries. com. **FRS.** ☎ 950/081830 ⊕ www.frs.es. **Inter Shipping.** ☎ 956/684729. **Trasmediterránea.** ☎ 902/454645 ⊕ www. trasmediterranea.es.

# Great Itineraries

## Madrid to the Alhambra, 10-day Itinerary

This trip takes in the best of vibrant Madrid and its world-class art museums and showcases some of Castile's historic gems before whisking you to the Moorish south where Córdoba's majestic mosque, Seville's fragrant orange blossoms, and Granada's "heaven on earth" await.

### DAYS 1–3: MADRID

Start the day with a visit to either the **Prado,** the **Museo Thyssen-Bornemisza,** or the **Centro de Arte Reina Sofía.** Then head to the elegant **Plaza Mayor**—a perfect jumping-off point for a tour of the Spanish capital. To the west, see the **Plaza de la Villa, Palacio Real** (the Royal Palace), **Teatro Real** (Royal Theater), and the royal convents; to the south, wander around the maze of streets of **La Latina** and **El Rastro** and try some local tapas.

On Day 2, visit the sprawling **Barrio de las Letras,** centered on the Plaza de Santa Ana. This was the favorite neighborhood of writers during the Spanish golden literary age in the 17th century (Cervantes lies buried under a convent nearby), and it's still crammed with theaters, cafés, and good tapas bars. It borders the Paseo del Prado on the east, allowing you to comfortably walk to any of the art museums in the area. If the weather is pleasant, take an afternoon stroll in the **Parque del Buen Retiro.**

For your third day in the capital, wander in **Chueca** and **Malasaña,** the two funky hipster neighborhoods most favored by young madrileños. Fuencarral, a landmark pedestrianized street that serves as the border between the two, is one of the city's trendiest shopping enclaves. From there you can walk to the **Parque del Oeste** and the **Templo de Debod**—the best spot from which to see the city's sunset. Among the lesser-known museums, consider visiting the captivating **Museo Sorolla,** Goya's frescoes and tomb at the **Ermita de San Antonio de la Florida,** or the **Real Academia de Bellas Artes de San Fernando** for classic painting. People-watch at any of the terrace bars in either Plaza de Chueca or Plaza del Dos de Mayo in Malasaña.

**Logistics:** If you're traveling light, the subway (Metro Línea 8) or the bus (No. 203 during the day and N27 at night) will take you from the airport to the city for €5. The train costs €2.60 and a taxi is a fixed price of €30. Once in the center consider walking or taking the subway rather than cabbing it in gridlock traffic.

### DAYS 4 AND 5: CASTILIAN CITIES

There are several excellent options for half- or full-day side trips from Madrid to occupy Days 4 and 5. **Toledo** and **Segovia** are two of the oldest Castilian cities—both have delightful old quarters dating back to the Romans. There's also **El Escorial,** which houses the massive monastery built by Felipe II. Two other nearby towns also worth visiting are **Aranjuez** and **Alcalá de Henares.**

**Logistics:** Toledo and Segovia are stops on the high-speed train line (AVE), so you can get to either of them in a half hour from Madrid. To reach the old quarters of both cities, take a bus or cab from the train station or take the bus from Madrid. Buses and trains both go to El Escorial. Reach Aranjuez and Alcalá de Henares via the intercity train system.

### DAY 6: CÓRDOBA OR EXTREMADURA

**Córdoba,** the capital of both Roman and Moorish Spain, was the center of Western art and culture between the 8th and 11th centuries. The city's breathtaking

**Mezquita** (mosque), which is now a cathedral, and the medieval **Jewish Quarter** bear witness to the city's brilliant past. From Madrid, you could also rent a car and visit the lesser-known cities in the north of **Extremadura,** such as **Guadalupe** and **Trujillo,** and overnight in **Cáceres,** a UNESCO World Heritage Site, then return to Madrid the next day.

**Logistics:** The AVE will take you to Córdoba from Madrid in less than two hours. One alternative is to stay in Toledo, also on the route heading south, and then head to Córdoba the next day, although you need to return to Madrid by train first. Once in Córdoba, take a taxi for a visit out to the summer palace at Medina Azahara.

### DAYS 7 AND 8: SEVILLE

Seville's **cathedral,** with its tower La Giralda, **Plaza de Toros Real Maestranza,** and **Barrio de Santa Cruz** are visual feasts. Forty minutes south by train, you can sip the world-famous sherries of **Jerez de la Frontera,** then munch jumbo shrimp on the beach at **Sanlúcar de Barrameda.**

**Logistics:** From Seville's AVE station, take a taxi to your hotel. After that, walking and hailing the occasional taxi are the best ways to explore the city. A rental car is the best option to reach towns beyond

**Tip**

Spain's modern freeways and toll highways are as good as any in the world—with the exception of the signs, which are often tiny and hard to decipher as you sweep past them at the routine speed of 120 kph (74 mph).

Seville, except for Jerez de la Frontera, where the train station is an architectural gem in its own right.

### DAYS 9 AND 10: GRANADA

The hilltop **Alhambra** palace, Spain's most visited attraction, was conceived by the Moorish caliphs as heaven on earth. Try any of the city's famous tapas bars and tea shops, and make sure to roam the magical, steep streets of the **Albayzín,** the ancient Moorish quarter.

**Logistics:** The Seville–Granada leg of this trip is best accomplished by renting a car; Antequera makes a good quick stop on the way. However, the Seville–Granada trains (three daily, about 2½ hours, €40) are one alternative. Another idea is to head first from Madrid to Granada, and then from Granada to Seville via Córdoba.

# Great Itineraries

## Barcelona and the North Coast, 16-day Itinerary

Dive into happening Barcelona, with its unique blend of Gothic and Gaudí architecture, colorful markets, and long city beaches. Then head to the verdant north for culinary sophistication in San Sebastián and to check out the Guggenheim in chic Bilbao. Next, wind your way along the wild, rugged coastline, taking in the mountains, fishing ports, bagpipes, and Europe's best seafood along the way.

### DAYS 1–3: BARCELONA
To get a feel for Barcelona, begin with **La Rambla** and the **Boquería** market. Then set off for the **Gothic Quarter** to see the **Catedral de la Seu, Plaça del Rei,** and the Catalan and Barcelona government palaces in **Plaça Sant Jaume.** Next, cross Via Laietana to the **Born-Ribera** (waterfront neighborhood) for the Gothic **Santa Maria del Mar** and nearby **Museu Picasso.**

Make Day 2 a Gaudí day: Visit the **Temple Expiatori de la Sagrada Família,** then **Park Güell.** In the afternoon see the **Casa Milà** and **Casa Batlló,** part of the Manzana de la Discòrdia on Passeig de Gràcia. **Palau Güell,** off the lower Rambla, is probably too much Gaudí for one day, but don't miss it.

On Day 3, climb **Montjuïc** for the **Museu Nacional d'Art de Catalunya,** in the hulking **Palau Nacional.** Investigate the **Fundació Miró, Estadi Olímpic,** the **Mies van der Rohe Pavilion,** and **CaixaForum** exhibition center. At lunchtime, take the cable car across the port for seafood in **Barceloneta** and then stroll along the beach.

**Logistics:** In Barcelona, walking or taking the subway is better than cabbing it.

### DAY 4: SAN SEBASTIÁN
San Sebastián is one of Spain's most beautiful—and delicious—cities. Belle Époque buildings nearly encircle the tiny bay, and tapas bars flourish in the old quarter. Not far from San Sebastián is historic **Pasajes (Pasaia) de San Juan.**

**Logistics:** Take the train from Barcelona to San Sebastián (5 hours 30 minutes) in the afternoon. You don't need a car in San Sebastián proper, but visits to cider houses in Astigarraga, Chillida Leku on the outskirts of town, and many of the finest restaurants around San Sebastián are possible only with your own transportation or a taxi (the latter with the advantage that you won't get lost). The freeway west to Bilbao is beautiful and fast, but the coastal road is recommended at least as far as Zumaia.

### DAYS 5 AND 6: THE BASQUE COAST
The Basque coast between San Sebastián and Bilbao has a succession of fine beaches, rocky cliffs, and picture-perfect fishing ports. The wide beach at **Zarautz,** the fishermen's village of **Getaria,** the **Zuloaga Museum in Zumaia,** and **Bermeo**'s port and fishing museum should all be near the top of your list.

### DAYS 7 AND 8: BILBAO
Bilbao's **Guggenheim Museum** is worth a trip for the building itself, and the **Museo de Bellas Artes** has an impressive collection of Basque and Spanish paintings. Restaurants and tapas bars are famously good in Bilbao.

**Logistics:** In Bilbao, use the subway or the Euskotram, which runs up and down the Nervión estuary.

## DAYS 9 AND 10: SANTANDER AND CANTABRIA

The elegant beach town of **Santander** has an excellent summer music festival every August. Nearby, **Santillana del Mar** is one of Spain's best Renaissance towns, and the museum of the **Altamira Caves** displays reproductions of the famous underground Neolithic rock paintings discovered here. Exploring the **Picos de Europa** will take you through some of the peninsula's wildest reaches, and the port towns along the coast provide some of Spain's most pristine beaches.

## DAYS 11–13: OVIEDO AND ASTURIAS

The coast road through **Ribadesella** and the cider capital **Villaviciosa** to **Oviedo** is scenic and punctuated with tempting beaches. Oviedo, its **cathedral,** and the simplicity of its pre-Romanesque churches are worlds away from the richness of Córdoba's Mezquita and Granada's Alhambra.

**Logistics:** The A8 coastal freeway gets you quickly and comfortably to Gijón, then hop on the A66 to Oviedo. From there, head back to the A8 and go west through Avilés and into Galicia via the coastal N634—a slow but scenic route to Santiago.

## DAYS 14–16: SANTIAGO DE COMPOSTELA AND GALICIA

Spain's northwest corner, with **Santiago de Compostela** at its spiritual and geographic center, is a green land of bagpipes and apple orchards. The Albariño wine country, along the Río Miño border with Portugal, and the *rías* (estuaries), full of delicious seafood, will keep you steeped in *enxebre*—Gallego for "local specialties and atmosphere."

**Logistics:** The four-lane freeways AP9 and A6 whisk you from Lugo and Castro to Santiago de Compostela and to the Rías Baixas. By car is the only way to tour Galicia. The AC862 route around the upper northwest corner and the Rías Altas turns into the AP9 coming back into Santiago.

# Great Itineraries

## Andalusia with Madrid and Barcelona

### ANDALUSIA 7-DAY ITINERARY

Head south to a land of fiery flamenco passion, unique Moorish treasures, impossibly white villages, and delicious sherry and tapas. As you make your way from Córdoba to Granada via Seville, Jerez de la Frontera, and Málaga, prepare yourself to see some of Europe's finest monuments, prettiest villages, and loveliest—albeit most sweltering—landscapes.

### DAY 1: CÓRDOBA

Córdoba's breathtaking **Mezquita** (mosque), now a cathedral, is an Andalusian highlight, and the medieval **Jewish Quarter** is lovely to explore. If you're here during May, visit the **Festival de los Patios** (Patio Festival).

### DAYS 2–3: SEVILLE

The city that launched Christopher Columbus to the New World, **Seville** is a treasure trove of sights. Start with the **cathedral** and climb La Giralda for great views of the city. Move on to the richly decorated *alcázar* (fortress), still an official royal residence, with its many beautiful patios, and where, more recently, much of the *Game of Thrones* epic was filmed. The **Jewish Quarter** in Santa Cruz is a charming labyrinth of alleyways and squares. In the afternoon, cross to **Triana** over the Guadalquivir River and lose yourself in the quiet streets, which are the birthplace of many a flamenco artist.

**Logistics:** Take the high-speed train (AVE) to Seville from Córdoba (45 minutes). Seville is a compact city and easy to navigate so it's best to explore on foot—or pick up a municipal bicycle at one of the hundreds of Sevici bike stations spread out across the city.

### DAY 4: JEREZ DE LA FRONTERA AND RONDA VIA ARCOS DE LA FRONTERA

**Jerez de la Frontera** is the world's sherry headquarters and home to some of the greatest *bodegas* (wineries). Visit Domecq, Harvey, or Sandeman, and, if you have time, watch the world's finest dancing horses at the prestigious Royal Andalusian School of Equestrian Art. The lovely cliff-top village of **Arcos de la Frontera,** one of Andalusia's prettiest *pueblos blancos* (white villages), makes a great stop on the way to **Ronda.** One of the oldest towns in Spain, Ronda is famed for its spectacular position and views; get the best photo from the Juan Peña El Lebrijano Bridge.

**Logistics:** Rent a car in Seville and take the highway to Jerez de la Frontera before making your way to Ronda via Arcos de la Frontera. If you have time, stop off in the lovely village of Grazalema.

### DAY 5: MÁLAGA

Start your exploration of the capital of the **Costa del Sol, Málaga,** with the **Roman theater,** Moorish **alcazaba** (citadel), and Gothic **cathedral.** Stroll down to the Muelle Uno on the port for views of the city skyline and **Gibralfaro** castle before returning to the center to visit the **Museo Picasso** and browse the shops in Larios and surrounding streets.

**Logistics:** Leave Ronda early and enjoy the scenic drive to Málaga via the A367 and A357. In Málaga, explore on foot, leaving your car in a central lot or at your hotel.

### DAYS 6–7: GRANADA

Allow a good half day to visit the hilltop **Alhambra** palace and Generalife gardens. From there, walk down to the city center to the **cathedral** and **Capilla Real,** the shrine of Isabella of Castile and Ferdinand of Aragón. Finish your day with

PORTUGAL

Córdoba
ANDALUSIA
Seville
Arcos de la
Frontera
Granada
Jerez de
la Frontera
Ronda
Málaga
Grazalema
COSTA DEL SOL
*Mediterranean Sea*

some tapas at one of the many famous tapas bars. On Day 7, walk up to the Albayzín, the ancient Moorish quarter, for a leisurely wander around the narrow streets. Take your time in the Plaza de San Nicolás and admire the magnificent views of the Alhambra and Sierra Nevada before you leave.

**Logistics:** The drive to Granada from Málaga takes about 1 hour 30 minutes. Granada is best explored on foot, so leave your car at the hotel.

## MADRID AND BARCELONA, 6-DAY ITINERARY

Combining Spain's two largest and greatest cities on a six-day itinerary gives you the chance to take in the contrasts of imperial Madrid and Moderniste Barcelona. Both cities are vibrant, energetic cultural centers showcasing some of Europe's greatest art and architecture as well as Spanish gastronomy at its best. You can also get a taste for Spain's late-night fun, sample its colorful markets, and stay at some of the country's best lodgings. However, Madrid and Barcelona feel very different, and you'll find huge contrasts in their landscapes, culture, and ambience. By visiting them both

### Tip

Rent a car with a GPS navigation system to help you find your way from one Andalusian city to the next. Help with navigating is also useful in the cities themselves.

you'll get a good idea of the many facets that make up Spain.

*For what to do on your days in Madrid, see the "Madrid to the Alhambra" itinerary. For Barcelona, see the "Barcelona, the North Coast, and Galicia" itinerary.*

**Logistics:** Take the high-speed train (AVE) from Madrid to Barcelona (2 hours 30 minutes). For the return journey, fly from Barcelona to Madrid Barajas Airport in time to catch your flight home.

# Great Itineraries

## 5 Days: Madrid Plus Granada or Seville and Side Trips

### DAYS 1 AND 2: MADRID

Start the day with a visit to either the Prado, the Museo Thyssen-Bornemisza, or the Centro de Arte Reina Sofía. Then head to the elegant Plaza Mayor—a perfect jumping-off point for a tour of the Spanish capital. To the west, see the Plaza de la Villa, Palacio Real (the Royal Palace), Teatro Real (Royal Theater), and the royal convents; to the south, wander around the maze of streets of La Latina and El Rastro and try some local tapas.

On Day 2, visit the sprawling Barrio de las Letras, centered on the Plaza de Santa Ana. This was the favorite neighborhood of writers during the Spanish golden literary age in the 17th century (Cervantes lies buried under a convent nearby), and it's still crammed with theaters, cafés, and good tapas bars. From here, you can pop to the Paseo del Prado on the east and visit any of the art museums in the area. After lunch, take an afternoon stroll in the Parque del Buen Retiro or wander in Chueca or Malasaña, the two funky hipster neighborhoods favored by young locals. From here, walk to the Parque del Oeste and the Templo de Debod to marvel at the city's sunset.

### GRANADA

**Getting Here:** Four daily flights connect Granada with Madrid, and it's easy to get to the city from the airport by taxi, airport bus, or rental car. There are a couple of daily high-speed AVE trains from Madrid to Granada daily.

**Day 3:** After arriving in Granada, visit the Catholic Monarchs' tomb at the Capilla Real before exploring more Moorish monuments such as the Palacio Madraza (seminary) or El Bañuelo (bathhouse). Stroll around the Moorish Albayzín neighborhood for extraordinary views of Granada's highlight, the Alhambra, and the Sierra Nevada backdrop, extra special at sunset. Dine on the city's excellent tapas or take in a flamenco show.

**Day 4:** Granada's star of the show is, of course, La Alhambra, the most visited attraction in Spain. Its palace, fortress, patios, gardens, and museums alone merit the trip to Granada and need at least half a day to do them justice. Try to get an early-morning ticket to experience this wonder with fewer crowds. Note: reserve your ticket as far in advance as possible and show up at your ticketed time (preferably, before) or you will not be allowed entry. Get lunch early before you pick up your hired car for a side trip excursion.

## EVENING 4, DAY 5: SIDE TRIP OPTIONS

**Option 1:** Drive north to Priego de Córdoba (1¼ hours) to see one of the region's prettiest towns with a plethora of baroque churches, white facades decked with geraniums and stunning views. From here, drive to Córdoba and your hotel. Spend the next day exploring the Mezquita (mosque) and the Jewish Quarter and dine on the city's famous oxtail stew or *flamenquín* (pork fritter) washed down with local Montilla wine.

**Option 2:** Drive northeast to Baeza (1½ hours) and then to Úbeda, two jewels in Spain's Renaissance crown. Both are home to stunning architecture, seen in intricate facades on the many monuments; allow more time for Úbeda where you can visit the historic potter's quarter.

**Option 3:** Head south for the Sierra Nevada (1 hour drive) for a paradise of skiing in winter and trekking and climbing in summer. Or explore the Alpujarras, a unique mountain region dotted with picturesque Moorish villages set in stunning landscapes where time appears to have stopped still.

## SEVILLE

**Getting Here:** Andalusia's second-largest airport, after Málaga, is in Seville and there are flights from Madrid every four hours or so. From Madrid, the best approach to Andalusia is via the high-speed AVE. In just 2½ hours, the spectacular ride winds through olive groves and rolling fields of Castile to Córdoba and on to Seville. From Seville's Santa Justa train station, get a cab (or rental car) to your hotel.

**Day 3:** Must-sees in the Andalusian capital include the cathedral with its La Giralda tower and the Reales Alcazares Moorish palace. Between visits, explore the nearby Barrio de Santa Cruz neighborhood with its typical architecture, orange blossom trees, and tiny squares. Dine early on delicious tapas at one of the traditional *tavernas* before an evening stroll along the banks of the Guadalquivir River.

**Day 4:** Start with a visit to one of the city's great private houses—Palacio de las Dueñas, Casa de Pilatos, or Palacio de la Condesa de Lebrija—to see how the other half lived in the city. After lunch on tapas, admire the Plaza de Toros Real Maestranza (bullring) and stroll around the Parque de María Luisa before an aperitif in the bar at the Hotel Alfonso XIII. Then take in a flamenco show.

## DAY 5: DAY TRIP OPTIONS

Seville is perfectly placed for several excellent side trips: taste the world-famous sherries of Jerez de la Frontera and admire the dancing horses before dining on Spain's freshest seafood at Puerto de Santa María or Sanlúcar de Barrameda; visit Spain's largest and one of its greatest Roman sites at Itálica, just outside Seville; drive to Ronda, one of Andalusia's most beautiful white towns, perched on a river gorge and the cradle of bullfighting; head for Europe's oldest city, the maritime Cádiz and soak up the history in its narrow streets and along the fortress walls; or go to Córdoba where the city's breathtaking Mezquita (mosque) and medieval Jewish Quarter await you. Don't miss the vibrant flower-packed patios while you're there.

# Helpful Phrases in Spanish

## BASICS

| | | |
|---|---|---|
| Hello | Hola | oh-lah |
| Yes/no | Sí/no | see/no |
| Please | Por favor | pore fah-**vore** |
| May I? | ¿Me permite? | may pair-**mee**-tay |
| Thank you | Gracias | **Grah**-see-as |
| You're welcome | De nada | day **nah**-dah |
| I'm sorry | Lo siento | lo see-**en**-toh |
| Good morning! | ¡Buenos días! | **bway**-nohs **dee**-ahs |
| Good evening! | ¡Buenas tardes! (after 2pm) | **bway**-nahs-**tar**-dess |
| | ¡Buenas noches! (after 8pm) | **bway**-nahs **no**-chess |
| Good-bye! | ¡Adiós!/¡Hasta luego! | ah-dee-**ohss/ah**-stah **lwe**-go |
| Mr./Mrs. | Señor/Señora | sen-**yor**/ sen-**yohr**-ah |
| Miss | Señorita | sen-yo-**ree**-tah |
| Pleased to meet you | Mucho gusto | **moo**-cho **goose**-toh |
| How are you? | ¿Que tal? | keh-tal |

## NUMBERS

| | | |
|---|---|---|
| one | un, uno | oon, **oo**-no |
| two | dos | dos |
| three | tres | tress |
| four | cuatro | **kwah**-tro |
| five | cinco | **sink**-oh |
| six | seis | saice |
| seven | siete | see-**et**-eh |
| eight | ocho | o-cho |
| nine | nueve | new-**eh**-vey |
| ten | diez | dee-**es** |
| eleven | once | **ohn**-seh |
| twelve | doce | **doh**-seh |
| thirteen | trece | **treh**-seh |
| fourteen | catorce | ka-**tohr**-seh |
| fifteen | quince | **keen**-seh |
| sixteen | dieciséis | dee-**es**-ee-**saice** |
| seventeen | diecisiete | dee-**es**-ee-see-**et**-eh |
| eighteen | dieciocho | dee-**es**-ee-o-cho |
| nineteen | diecinueve | dee-**es**-ee-new-**ev**-eh |
| twenty | veinte | **vain**-teh |
| twenty-one | veintiuno | **vain**-te-**oo**-noh |
| thirty | treinta | **train**-tah |
| forty | cuarenta | kwah-**ren**-tah |
| fifty | cincuenta | seen-**kwen**-tah |
| sixty | sesenta | sess-**en**-tah |
| seventy | setenta | set-**en**-tah |
| eighty | ochenta | oh-**chen**-tah |
| ninety | noventa | no-**ven**-tah |
| one hundred | cien | see-**en** |
| one thousand | mil | meel |
| one million | un millón | oon meel-**yohn** |

## COLORS

| | | |
|---|---|---|
| black | negro | **neh**-groh |
| blue | azul | ah-**sool** |
| brown | marrón | mah-**ron** |
| green | verde | **ver**-deh |
| orange | naranja | na-**rahn**-hah |
| red | rojo | **roh**-hoh |
| white | blanco | **blahn**-koh |
| yellow | amarillo | ah-mah-**ree**-yoh |

## DAYS OF THE WEEK

| | | |
|---|---|---|
| Sunday | domingo | doe-**meen**-goh |
| Monday | lunes | **loo**-ness |
| Tuesday | martes | **mahr**-tess |
| Wednesday | miércoles | me-**air**-koh-less |
| Thursday | jueves | hoo-**ev**-ess |
| Friday | viernes | vee-**air**-ness |
| Saturday | sábado | **sah**-bah-doh |

## MONTHS

| | | |
|---|---|---|
| January | enero | eh-**neh**-roh |
| February | febrero | feh-**breh**-roh |
| March | marzo | **mahr**-soh |
| April | abril | ah-**breel** |
| May | mayo | **my**-oh |
| June | junio | **hoo**-nee-oh |
| July | julio | **hoo**-lee-yoh |
| August | agosto | ah-**ghost**-toh |
| September | septiembre | sep-tee-**em**-breh |
| October | octubre | oak-**too**-breh |
| November | noviembre | no-vee-**em**-breh |
| December | diciembre | dee-see-**em**-breh |

## USEFUL WORDS AND PHRASES

| | | |
|---|---|---|
| Do you speak English? | ¿Habla usted inglés? | ah-**blah** oos-**ted** in-**glehs** |
| I don't speak Spanish. | No hablo español | no **ah**-bloh es-pahn-**yol** |
| I don't understand. | No entiendo | no en-tee-**en**-doh |
| I understand. | Entiendo | en-tee-**en**-doh |
| I don't know. | No sé | no seh |
| I'm American. | Soy americano (americana) | soy ah-meh-ree-**kah**-no (ah-meh-ree-**kah**-nah) |
| What's your name? | ¿Cómo se llama? | koh-mo seh **yah**-mah |
| My name is . . . | Me llamo . . . | may **yah**-moh |
| What time is it? | ¿Qué hora es? | keh o-rah es |
| How? | ¿Cómo? | **koh**-mo |
| When? | ¿Cuándo? | **kwahn**-doh |
| Yesterday | Ayer | ah-**yehr** |
| Today | hoy | oy |
| Tomorrow | mañana | mahn-**yah**-nah |
| Tonight | Esta noche | es-tah **no**-cheh |
| What? | ¿Qué? | keh |
| What is it? | ¿Qué es esto? | keh es **es**-toh |

| | | |
|---|---|---|
| Why? | ¿Por qué? | pore **keh** |
| Who? | ¿Quién? | kee-**yen** |
| Where is . . . | ¿Dónde está . . . | dohn-deh es-**tah** |
| . . . the train station? | la estación del tren? | la es-tah-see-**on** del trehn |
| . . . the subway station? | estación de metro | la es-ta-see-**on** del **meh**-sah . . . |
| . . . the bus stop? | la parada del autobus? | la pah-**rah**-dah del ow-toh-**boos** |
| . . . the terminal? (airport) | el aeropuerto | el air-oh-**pwar**-toh |
| . . . the post office? | la oficina de correos? | la oh-fee-**see**- nah deh koh-**rreh**-os |
| . . . the bank? | el banco? | el **bahn**-koh |
| . . . the hotel? | el hotel? | el oh-**tel** |
| . . . the museum? | el museo? | el moo-**seh**-oh |
| . . . the hospital? | el hospital? | el ohss-pee-**tal** |
| . . . the elevator? | el ascensor? | el ah-sen-**sohr** |
| Where are the restrooms? | el baño? | el **bahn**-yoh |
| Here/there | Aquí/allí | ah-**key**/ah-**yee** |
| Open/closed | Abierto/cerrado | ah-bee-**er**-toh/ ser-**ah**-doh |
| Left/right | Izquierda/derecha | iss-key-**eh**-dah/ dare-**eh**-chah |
| Is it near? | ¿Está cerca? | es-**tah sehr**-kah |
| Is it far? | ¿Está lejos? | es-**tah leh**-hoss |
| I'd like . . . | Quisiera . . . | kee-see-**ehr**-ah |
| . . . a room | un cuarto/una habitación | oon **kwahr**-toh/**oo**-nah ah-bee-tah-see-**on** |
| . . . the key | la llave | lah **yah**-veh |
| . . . a newspaper | un periódico | oon pehr-ee-**oh**-dee-koh |
| . . . a stamp | un sello de correo | oon **seh**-yo deh korr-**eh**-oh |
| I'd like to buy . . . | Quisiera comprar . . . | kee-see-**ehr**-ah kohm-**prahr** |
| . . . soap | jabón | hah-**bohn** |
| . . . suntan lotion | crema solar | **kreh**-mah soh-**lar** |
| . . . envelopes | sobres | **so**-brehs |
| . . . writing paper | papel | pah-**pel** |
| . . . a postcard | una tarjeta postal | oon-ah tar-**het**-ah post-**ahl** |
| . . . a ticket | un billete (travel) | oon bee-**yee**-teh |
| | una entrada (concert etc.) | oona en-**trah**-dah |
| How much is it? | ¿Cuánto cuesta? | **kwahn**-toh **kwes**-tah |
| It's expensive/cheap | Es caro/barato | es **kah**-roh/ bah-**rah**-toh |
| A little/a lot | Un poquito/mucho | oon poh-**kee**-toh/ **moo**-choh |
| More/less | Más/menos | mahss/**men**-ohss |
| Enough/too (much) | Suficiente/ | soo-fee-see-**en**-teh/ |
| I am ill/sick | Estoy enfermo(a) | es-**toy** en-**fehr**-moh(mah) |
| Call a doctor | Llame a un medico | **ya**-meh ah oon **med**-ee-koh |

**DINING OUT**

| | | |
|---|---|---|
| I'd like to reserve a table . . . | Quisiera reservar una mesa . . . | kee-**syeh**-rah rreh-sehr-**bahr oo**-nah meh-sah . . . |
| . . . for two people. | para dos personas. | **pah**-rah dohs pehr-**soh**-nahs |
| . . . for this evening. | para esta noche. | **pah**-rah **ehs**-tah noh-cheh |
| . . . for 8 PM | para las ocho de la noche. | **pah**-rah lahs **oh**-choh deh lah noh-cheh |
| A bottle of . . . | Una botella de . . . | **oo**-nah bo-**teh**-yah deh |
| A cup of . . . | Una taza de . . . | **oo**-nah **tah**-sah deh |
| A glass of . . . | Un vaso (water, soda, etc.) de... | oon **vah**-so deh |
| | Una copa (wine, spirits, etc.) de... | oona **coh**-pah deh |
| Bill/check | La cuenta | lah **kwen**-tah |
| Bread | El pan | el pahn |
| Breakfast | El desayuno | el deh-sah-**yoon**-oh |
| Butter | La mantequilla | lah man-teh-**kee**-yah |
| Coffee | Café | kah-**feh** |
| Dinner | La cena | lah **seh**-nah |
| Fork | El tenedor | el ten-eh-**dor** |
| I don't eat meat | No como carne | noh koh-moh **kahr**-neh |
| I cannot eat . . . | No puedo comer . . . | noh **pweh** doh koh-**mehr** |
| I'd like to order . . . | Quiero pedir . . . | kee-**yehr**-oh peh-**deer** |
| I'd like . . . | Me gustaría . . . | Meh goo-stah-**ee**-ah |
| I'm hungry/thirsty | Tengo hambre/sed | **Tehn**-goh **hahm**-breh/seth |
| Is service/the tip included? | ¿Está incluida la propina? | es-**tah** in-cloo-**ee**-dah lah pro-**pee**-nah |
| Knife | El cuchillo | el koo-**chee**-yo |
| Lunch | La comida | lah koh-**mee**-dah |
| Menu | La carta, el menú | lah **cart**-ah, el meh-**noo** |
| Napkin | La servilleta | lah sehr-vee-**yet**-ah |
| Pepper | La pimienta | lah pee-mee-**en**-tah |
| Plate | plato | |
| Please give me . . . | Por favor déme . . . | pore fah-**vor deh**-meh |
| Salt | La sal | lah sahl |
| Spoon | Una cuchara | **oo**-nah koo-**chah**-rah |
| Sugar | El ázucar | el ah-**su**-kar |
| Tea | té | teh |
| Water | agua | **ah**-gwah |
| Wine | vino | **vee**-noh |

Help! Socorro soh-**koh**-roh
Stop! Pare pah-reh

# On the Calendar

## January

**La Tamborrada.** Every January 19 and 20, more than 100 platoons of Donostiarras (San Sebastián natives) dress up as chefs and Napoleonic soldiers and bang drums as they parade through the streets. The tradition was born out of a mockery of Napoleon's troops, who would march around the city in a similar fashion. Today it's San Sebastián's biggest street party. ⊠ *San Sebastián* 🖃 *Free.*

**Processo dels Tres Tocs** *(Procession of the Three Knocks).* This festival, held in Ciutadella on January 17, celebrates the 1287 victory of King Alfonso III of Aragón over the Moors. ⊠ *Ciutadella.*

## February

**Carnival.** In February and March, on this first major fiesta of the year after Three Kings' Day (January 6), cities, towns, and villages across the region erupt with festive fun, including parades, parties, and wild costumes.

**Festes de Santa Eularia.** Ibiza's boisterous winter carnival, held on February 12, includes folk dancing and music. ⊠ *Eivissa.*

## March

**Cherry Blossom Festival** *(Fiesta del Cerezo en Flor).* For approximately two weeks between March and early May, depending on the year, Spain's prized cherry-growing region, the Jerte Valley, turns pink and white as more than a million cherry trees bloom in unison. Throughout the area, a series of live concerts, street markets, and gastronomic presentations accompany nature's show. ⊠ *Jaraíz de la Vera* 🕾 *92/747–2558* ⊕ *www.turismovalledeljerte.com.*

## April

**Feria de Abril** *(April Fair).* Held two weeks after Easter, this secular celebration focuses on horses, pageantry, and bullfights. ⊠ *Seville.*

## May

**Antxua Eguna** *(Getaria Anchovy Festival).* Join Getaria locals the first weekend of May as they celebrate the moment anchovies reach their plump seasonal prime with gallons of Txakolí and mountains of grilled fresh fish. ⊠ *Getaria.*

**Cruces de Mayo** *(Festival of Crosses).* Celebrated throughout the Spanish-speaking world, this ancient festival is a highlight of Córdoba's calendar of events, with lots of flower-decked crosses and other floral displays, processions, and music in early May. ⊠ *Córdoba.*

**Festival de los Patios** *(Patio Festival).* This celebration, awarded UNESCO World Heritage status in 2012, is held during the second week of May, a fun time to be in the city, when owners throw open their flower-decked patios to visitors (and to judges, who nominate the best), and the city celebrates with food, drink, and flamenco. ⊠ *Córdoba* ⊕ *turismodecordoba.org.*

**WOMAD Cáceres.** The World of Music, Arts, and Dance draws crowds of around 75,000 in early May. Main stages are set up in the magical surroundings of this ancient city's plazas for free concerts, and other events include shows staged in the Gran Teatro, children's events, and a grand procession. ⊠ *Calle San Antón 0, Cáceres* ⊕ *www.womadespana.com.*

# June

**Festes de Sant Joan.** At this event June 23–24, riders in costume parade through the streets of Ciutadella on horseback, urging the horses up to dance on their hind legs while spectators pass dangerously under their hooves. ⊠ *Ciutadella.*

# July

**Bilbao BBK Live.** One of Spain's hottest pop and rock music festivals, BBK Live draws more than 100,000 fans each year with its lineup of big-name artists. In 2022, headliners included LCD Soundsystem, Stromae, and the Killers. Those who have outgrown noisy, muddy campgrounds will appreciate the "glamping" accommodation option. ⊠ *Bilbao* ⊕ *www. bilbaobbklive.com* ✆ *From €145.*

**Festival de Teatro Clásico.** In Mérida, the highlight of the cultural calendar is this annual festival held in the restored Roman amphitheater from early July through mid-August. It features opera as well as classical drama and celebrated its 67th year in 2021. ⊠ *Pl. Margarita Xirgu, Mérida* ☎ *92/400–9480* ⊕ *www.festivald-emerida.es.*

**Jazzaldia.** Drawing many of the world's top performers, this late-July festival in San Sebastián attracts an international crowd of jazz devotees. The 2022 lineup included Diana Krall, Herbie Hancock, and Iggy Pop. ⊠ *San Sebastián* ⊕ *www. jazzaldia.eus* ✆ *From €25.*

**Ortigueira Festival.** This major Celtic music festival, which takes place in early or mid-July over four days in the coastal city of Ortigueira, attracts folk musicians from around the world. ⊠ *A Coruña* ☎ *981/923093 for tourist office* ⊕ *www. festivaldeortigueira.com.*

**San Fermín.** Pamplona's main event, immortalized by Ernest Hemingway in his 1926 novel, *The Sun Also Rises,* is best known for its running of the bulls, a tradition that's dangerous for humans and ultimately lethal for the animals involved. Ethics aside, a huge part of the festival is consumed by nontaurine activities such as processions, live music acts, and fireworks. Held each year July 6–14, the festival begins daily at 8 am with a herd of fighting bulls let loose to run through the narrow streets to the bullring alongside daredevils testing their speed and agility in the face of possible injury or death. The atmosphere is electric, and hotel rooms overlooking the course come at a price. ⚠ **Recent years have seen a disturbing increase in sex crimes; it's advisable for travelers, especially women, to take commonsense precautions, including being aware of your surroundings and not walking alone at night.** ⊠ *Pamplona* ⊕ *www.sanfermin.com.*

**Virgen del Carmen.** The patron saint of sailors (Our Lady of Mount Carmel) is honored July 15–16 in Formentera with a blessing of the boats in the harbor. The holiday is also celebrated on Ibiza. ⊠ *Sant Antoni.*

# August

**Aste Nagusia.** The "Big Week," a nine-day event celebrating Basque culture, is held in Bilbao in mid-August with a fine series of street concerts, bullfights, and fireworks displays. ⊠ *Bilbao.*

**Festa do Viño Albariño** *(Albariño Wine Festival).* On the first Sunday of August, the town of Cambados, capital of Albariño country, draws thousands to witness its processions, concerts, cultural events, fireworks, and other revelry honoring local vineyards and wineries—including

# On the Calendar

wine tastings from around 40 different Rías Baixas wineries. The festival has been held since the early 1950s. ⊠ *Cambados* ⊕ *www.fiestadelalbariño.com.*

**Fiesta de la Virgen Blanca** *(Festival of the White Virgin).* This weeklong festival (August 4–9) celebrates Vitoria's patron saint with bullfights and street parties. The festivities begin with the arrival of Celedón, a well-dressed dummy that "flies" over the main square holding an umbrella. ⊠ *Vitoria.*

**Sant Ciriac.** Capped with a spectacular fireworks display over the walls of Eivissa's old city, this festival (on August 8) celebrates the Reconquest of Ibiza from the Moors. ⊠ *Eivissa.*

**Sant Lluís.** Celebrations of this saint's day, which are held during the last weekend of August in the town of Sant Lluís, on Menorca, center on an equestrian cavalcade called La Qualcada. ⊠ *Sant Lluís.*

## September

**Barcelona Acció Musical (BAM).** This quarter-century old festival held in Barcelona showcases emerging talents from the Catalan region. ☎ *010 Barcelona information: daily 24 hrs (in Catalan and Spanish))* ⊕ *www.barcelona.cat/bam.*

**Fiestas de la Mare de Déu de Gràcia.** Held September 6–9 in Mahón, this celebration is Menorca's final blowout of the season. ⊠ *Mahón.*

**Fiesta de Otoño** *(Autumn Festival).* In September, this festival in Jerez celebrates the grape harvest and includes a procession, the blessing of the harvest on the steps of the cathedral, and traditional-style grape treading. ⊠ *Jerez de la Frontera.*

**International Jazz Festival.** Famous jazz artists from around the world come together in the fall in Barcelona for this annual jazz festival. ☎ *93/481–7040* ⊕ *www.jazz.barcelona.*

**San Sebastián International Film Festival.** Glitterati descend on the city for its international film fest in the second half of September. Exact dates vary, so check the website for details. ⊠ *San Sebastián* ⊕ *www.sansebastianfestival.com.*

## October

**Festa do Marisco** *(Seafood Festival).* Galicia's famous culinary event, held in O Grove in October, draws crowds to feast on a stunning number of seafood delicacies. ⊠ *O Grove* ⊕ *www.turismogrove.es.*

**Fiesta de la Rosa del Azafrán** *(Consuegra Saffron Festival).* This festival, held in the last weekend of October since 1963, celebrates the annual saffron harvest, one of La Mancha's longest-standing traditions. Watch a saffron-plucking contest, savor locally made Manchego cheeses, and marvel at folk dance spectacles—all with a backdrop of Don Quixote–style windmills. ☎ *92/547–5731 Consuegra tourist office* ⊕ *www.consuegra.es.*

## December

**Encuentros Flamencos.** Some of the country's best performers are featured in this early-December event in Granada. ⊠ *Granada.*

**Los Escobazos.** On December 7, the city is filled with bonfires celebrating the Virgen de la Concepción. Watch out for the locals play-fighting with torches made out of brooms—or if you're feeling daredevilish, join in. ⊠ *Jarandilla de la Vera* ☎ *92/756–0460 tourist office.*

# Chapter 3

# MADRID

Updated by
Benjamin Kemper

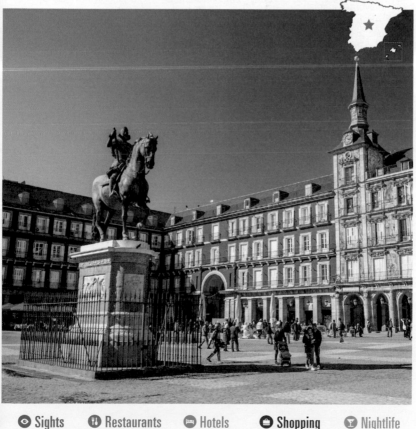

| ◉ Sights | 🍴 Restaurants | 🛏 Hotels | 🛍 Shopping | 🍸 Nightlife |
|---|---|---|---|---|
| ★★★★★ | ★★★★☆ | ★★★★☆ | ★★★★★ | ★★★★★ |

# WELCOME TO MADRID

## TOP REASONS TO GO

★ **Hit the Centro Histórico:** The Plaza Mayor, on any late night when it's almost empty, evokes the stately, somber glory of Golden Age Spain.

★ **Stroll down museum row:** Feast your eyes on works by your favorite Spanish artists—from Goya to Velázquez to Picasso—in the Prado, Reina Sofía, and Thyssen-Bornemisza.

★ **Nibble tapas into the night:** Indulge in a madrileño style of dining and sample local wines while grazing on small plates (both traditional and modern) on Cava Baja, Calle Ponzano, and beyond.

★ **Relax in the Retiro gardens:** Unwind at a *chiringuito* (refreshment stand) and enjoy some primo people-watching.

★ **Burn the midnight oil:** As other European cities tuck themselves in, madrileños swarm the bars and clubs in lively neighborhoods such as Malasaña, Chueca, Lavapiés, and Letras—and stretch the party until dawn.

**1 Sol.** The bustling heart of Madrid with clothes, souvenirs, and tapas bars.

**2 Palacio.** Madrid's noblest corner and home to the Royal Palace, Royal Theater, and newly pedestrianized Plaza de España and Sabatini Gardens.

**3 Moncloa.** A posh residential quarter with down-home restaurants and a tranquil off-the-radar park.

**4 Chueca.** The "gayborhood," as famous for its come-one-come-all nightclubs as for its trendy boutiques and restaurants.

**5 Malasaña.** Once a haven for rockers and rebels, now it's mostly fashion boutiques, third-wave coffee shops, and chic cocktail bars.

**6 Barrio de las Letras.** The historical stomping grounds of Spain's literary legends is where locals go for high-end tapas bars and where well-heeled travelers post up in style.

**7 Retiro.** The surprisingly nontouristy district fringing the city's most iconic park.

**8 Salamanca.** High-society types flock here for upscale tapas, special-occasion dinners, and exclusive shopping.

**9 La Latina.** El Rastro flea market lures the crowds to Madrid's most castizo (rootsy) neighborhood that hasn't lost its rakish edge.

**10 Lavapiés.** Ever countercultural and independently minded, Lavapiés is a multicultural mecca packed with eye-catching modern art.

**11 Arganzuela.** A vibrant contemporary art center and new riverside park put this sleepy residential neighborhood on the map.

**12 Chamberí.** Welcome to Madrid's newest culinary frontier lined with restaurants helmed by up-and-coming chefs.

**13 Chamartín.** Fans cheer till they're hoarse at Real Madrid soccer matches in this northern district.

**14 Tetuán.** You won't bump into any tour buses in this working-class neighborhood with international restaurants and old-timey tapas bars.

# EATING AND DRINKING WELL IN MADRID

A selection of tapas, including smoked ham and peppers.

As Spain's largest city situated in the center of the peninsula, Madrid continues to be the "breakwater of the many Spains" that poet Antonio Machado famously wrote about. It is home to countless regional Spanish restaurants serving everything from Valencian paella to Basque *pintxos* (skewered snacks), but traditional Madrid fare closely resembles that of Castile.

With a climate sometimes described as *nueve meses de invierno y tres de infierno* (nine months of winter and three of hell), it's no surprise that local grub is often comfort food. Garlic soup, stewed chickpeas, and roast suckling pig and lamb are standard components of Madrid feasts, as are baby goat and deeply flavored beef from Ávila and the Sierra de Guadarrama. *Cocido madrileño* (a meat-packed winter stew) and *callos a la madrileña* (stewed tripe) are favored local specialties, while *jamón ibérico* (Iberian ham)—a specialty of the *dehesas,* or rolling oak forests of Extremadura and Andalusia—is a special-occasion treat.

## TAPAS

Itinerant grazing from tavern to tavern is especially popular in Madrid, beneficiary of tapas traditions from every corner of Spain. The areas around Plaza de Santa Ana, Plaza Mayor, Calle Ponzano, and Cava Baja buzz with excitement as crowds drink beer and wine while devouring platefuls of *boquerones en vinagre* (vinegar-cured anchovies), *calamares a la romana* (fried squid), *albóndigas* (meatballs), and the like.

## SOUPS

Sopa de ajo (garlic soup), also known as sopa castellana, is a homey soup that starts with an unapologetically garlicky ham-bone stock. Stale bread is then torn in to thicken it up, followed by a cracked egg—a final enriching flourish. Caldo—hot, meaty broth flavored with ham ends and served in coffee mugs—is a Madrid favorite on wet winter days. It is often marketed in restaurant windows (look for " ¡Hay caldo!" signs).

## STEWS

Cocido madrileño is Madrid's ultimate comfort food and one of its oldest dishes: a boiled dinner of chickpeas, vegetables, potatoes, sausages, pork, and hen simmered for hours and presented in multiple courses. Estofado de judiones de La Granja (broad-bean stew) is another soul-satisfying favorite: pork, quail, ham, or whatever meat is available simmers with onions, tomatoes, carrots, and luxuriously creamy broad beans from the Segovian town of La Granja de San Ildefonso.

## ROASTS

Asadores (restaurants specializing in roasts) are an institution in and around Madrid, where cochinillo asado, or roast suckling pig, is the crown jewel. Wherever you taste it, the preparation is largely the same: milk-fed piglets are

Ingredients for a classic cocido madrileño.

roasted in oak-burning wood ovens and emerge shatteringly crisp yet tender enough to carve using the blunt edge of a plate. Lechazo, or milk-fed lamb, is another asador stalwart that emerges from wood ovens accompanied by the aromas of Castile's wide meseta: woodsmoke, rosemary, and thyme.

## WINES

The traditional Madrid house wine, a coarse Valdepeñas from La Mancha, south of the capital, has fallen out of favor as better-quality cuvées from Rioja and Ribera del Duero (for reds) and Rueda and Rías Baixas (for whites) have become more readily available. Deep-pink rosados, the best of which hail from Rioja, Catalonia, and Navarra, are increasingly popular, as is cava, Spanish bubbly from Catalonia. Natural wines—made without additives or pesticides in family-run bodegas (wineries)—are becoming trendier by the minute and can be enjoyed at a number of specialty bars and restaurants.

A hearty clam-and-bean stew

3

Madrid EATING AND DRINKING WELL IN MADRID

Madrid, the Spanish capital since 1561, is Europe's city that never sleeps—a vibrant and increasingly international metropolis with an infectious appetite for art, music, and epicurean pleasures.

Madrid has many modern barrios such as Salamanca, Chamberí, and Chamartín, but the historic center—between the Royal Palace and Parque del Buen Retiro—is the main attraction for international visitors. A conglomeration of Belle Époque buildings with intricate facades, terra-cotta-roofed residences, and redbrick Mudejar Revival churches, Madrid is a stately stunner. Madrileños love being outdoors as much as possible. Restaurant patios (*terrazas*), flea markets, and parks and plazas are always abuzz when the sun's out.

Then there's the art—the legacy of one of the most important global empires ever assembled. King Carlos I (1500–58), who later became Emperor Carlos V (or Charles V), set out to collect the best specimens from all European schools of art, many of which found their way to Spain's palaces and, later, to the Prado Museum. Between the classical Prado, the contemporary Reina Sofía, the wide-ranging Thyssen-Bornemisza, and Madrid's smaller artistic repositories—the Real Academia de Bellas Artes de San Fernando, the Convento de las Descalzas Reales, the Sorolla Museum, and the Lázaro Galdiano Museum, to name a few—there are more paintings here than you could admire in a lifetime.

Not all of the city's most memorable attractions are centuries old. The CaixaForum arts center is an architectural triumph by Jacques Herzog and Pierre de Meuron. Futuristic towers by Norman Foster and César Pelli have changed the city's northern landscape. Other recent developments include Madrid Río, which added nearly 300 acres of green space and six miles of footpaths along the banks of the Manzanares River, and the renovated Plaza de España, which was completed in 2021 and now spills over into the surrounding parks and pedestrian areas.

# Planning

## When to Go

Madrid is hot and dry in summer—with temperatures reaching 40°C (105°F) in July and August—and chilly and damp in winter, with minimum temperatures around 1°C (low 30s). Snow in the city is rare; in January 2021, Madrid was clobbered by the biggest winter storm in over a half-century. Perhaps the most pleasant time to visit is spring, especially May, when the city honors its patron saint with street fairs and celebrations. June and September to December are also pleasant, generally temperate times to visit.

Avoid Madrid in July and August—especially August, as locals flee the punishing heat for the coasts and mountains, and many restaurants, bars, and shops shutter.

# Planning Your Time

Madrid's most valuable art treasures are on display within a few blocks of Paseo del Prado. This area is home to the Museo del Prado, whose collection amasses masterworks by Velázquez, Goya, El Greco, and others; the Centro de Arte Reina Sofía, whose eclectic contemporary art pieces include Picasso's *Guernica*; and the Museo Thyssen-Bornemisza, whose collection stretches from the Renaissance to the 21st century. Each can take hours to explore, so it's best to alternate museum visits with less intellectually rigorous activities. If you're short on time and want to pack everything in, recharge at tapas bars and cafés in the neighboring Barrio de las Letras.

Any visit to Madrid should include a walk among the historical sights and churches between Puerta del Sol and the Palacio Real. Be sure to stop in the Plaza Mayor, Plaza de la Villa, and Plaza de Oriente. Those with time to go beyond the standard sights should spend time strolling and people-watching in the trendy barrios of Lavapiés, Chamberí, Malasaña, and Chueca.

# Getting Here and Around

## AIR

Madrid's Adolfo Suárez Madrid–Barajas Airport is Europe's seventh-busiest aviation hub. Terminal 4 (T4) handles flights from 25 carriers including Oneworld partners that handle the bulk of flights to and from the U.S. such as American Airlines, British Airways, and Iberia. All other U.S. airlines use Terminal 1 (T1).

Airport terminals are connected by bus service and also to Línea 8 of the metro, which reaches the city center in 30–45 minutes for around €5 (€1.50–€2 plus a €3 airport supplement). For €5 there are also convenient buses (Nos. 203 and 203 Exprés) to the Atocha train station (with stops on Calle de O'Donnell and Plaza de Cibeles) and to Avenida de América (note that bus drivers don't take bills greater than €20), where you can catch the metro or a taxi to your hotel. Taxis charge a flat fee of €30 from the airport to anywhere in the city center.

## BIKE

**BiciMAD** (*www.bicimad.com*) is Madrid's bike-share service with docks scattered around the city center. The bikes are electric, meaning you hardly have to pedal, and are an excellent alternative to the metro and buses, provided the weather is good and you're comfortable riding in traffic (separate bike lanes are virtually nonexistent). Avid urban cyclists staying for a month or more may wish to purchase a €25 yearly membership, which drastically lowers the cost of individual rides to €1.10 for up to one hour, but occasional users can pay €2 for up to one hour, buying a ticket at each service station. The bikes can be borrowed from, and returned to, any station in the system. In 2021 the BiciMAD GO service was added allowing users to retrieve and leave certain bikes directly on the sidewalk; download the BiciMAD app for details. ⚠ **After docking your bike, be sure to click closed the circular lock above the back wheel, lest you be charged 50 cents extra.**

## BUS

Buses are generally less convenient than trains, though they're sometimes faster and cheaper. Madrid has no central bus station: Most destinations south and east are serviced by Estación del Sur, while Intercambiador de Moncloa and Estación de Avenida de América service northern destinations. All have eponymous metro stops (except for Estación del Sur, serviced by Méndez Álvaro). Tickets can be purchased with a card inside the station or with exact change on the bus.

Blue city buses (€1.50 one-way) run about 6 am–11:30 pm. Less-frequent night buses run through the night on heavily trafficked routes. Línea Cero (look for buses marked 001 and 002) is a fare-free bus line launched in 2020. Contactless credit cards are accepted as payment on all blue buses in addition to cash (exact change is recommended).

**BUS STATIONS Estación de Avenida de América.** ⊠ *Av. de América 9, Salamanca* ☏ *90/242–2242 for ALSA Bus Company* ⊕ *www.crtm.es/tu-transporte-publico/intercambiadores.aspx* Ⓜ *Av. de América.* **Estación del Sur.** ⊠ *Calle Méndez Álvaro s/n, Atocha* ☏ *91/468–4200* ⊕ *www.estaciondeautobuses.com* Ⓜ *Méndez Álvaro.* **Intercambiador de Moncloa.** ⊠ *Calle Princesa 89, Moncloa* ☏ *012 for Madrid's public hotline* ⊕ *www.crtm.es* Ⓜ *Moncloa.*

## CAR

It's best to ditch your rental car when in Madrid as traffic and expensive parking cause headaches, though a car is handy for trips to smaller locales with limited public transportation options; many national highways radiate from Madrid including the A6 (Segovia, Salamanca, Galicia); the A1 (Burgos and the Basque Country); the A2 (Guadalajara, Barcelona, France); the A3 (Cuenca, Valencia, the Mediterranean coast); the A4 (Aranjuez, La Mancha, Granada, Seville); the A42 (Toledo); and the A5 (Talavera de la Reina, Portugal). The city is surrounded by ring roads (M30, M40, and M50), from which most of these highways are easily picked up. There are also toll highways (marked R2, R3, R4, and R5) that bypass major highways, and the A41, a toll highway connecting Madrid and Toledo.

**Madrid 360** is a sweeping new environmental scheme that prohibits most nonresident vehicles—rentals included—from entering the city center. This zone is delineated by double red lines, large roadside signs, and wavy logos painted clearly on the asphalt; entering without the proper permissions will result in fines. Be sure to ask your rental car agency about the specific restrictions on your vehicle as they relate to Madrid 360. Zero-emissions vehicles are not affected, so if you plan on driving in the city center, it may be worth spending the extra euros on an eco-friendly car.

## SUBWAY

To ride the metro, you must buy a refillable Tarjeta de Transporte Público (Public Transportation Card), which costs a nonrefundable €4 and can be obtained at ticketing machines inside any metro station. Each journey costs €1.50–€2, depending on how far you're traveling within the city. There are no free transfers between the metro and bus systems. The **Abono Turístico** (Tourist Pass) allows unlimited use of public buses and the metro for one day (€9 for Zone A, €17 for Zone T) to seven days (€36 for Zone A, €71 for Zone T); buy it at tourist offices, metro stations, and select newsstands. The metro runs 6 am–1:30 am, though a few entrances close earlier.

After nearly four years of renovations, the Gran Vía metro station is finally back in business as of late 2021. Architecture buffs will appreciate the new neoclassical entryway on Calle Montera, a meticulous recreation of Antonio Palacios's 1920 structure that was subsequently demolished.

**SUBWAY INFORMATION Metro Madrid.** ☏ *90/244–4403* ⊕ *www.metromadrid.es.*

## TAXI

Taxis are well-regulated and work under several tariff schemes. Meters start at €2.50 (€3.15 nights, weekends, and holidays). There is a fixed taxi fare of €30 to or from the airport from the city center. Book a taxi by phone or via the Free Now app, which interfaces with official city taxis. Ride-hailing apps Uber, Cabify, and

Bolt are generally more economical than official taxis. In 2021, it became possible to rent a Lime electric scooter via the Uber app. ■TIP➔ **Uber recently entered into an agreement with city taxis, so if you order an Uber and a white taxi pulls up, don't be alarmed.**

The rise of Uber and similar ride-hailing apps has led to a standoff between traditional taxis and vehicles for hire. Taxi strikes are increasingly frequent, so if you plan on using a taxi service, be sure to inquire locally to ensure they're running.

**Blablacar** is Spain's leading rideshare app in intercity travel. Its free platform allows you to book ahead using a credit card and message your driver to set meeting and drop-off points. Blablacar is the most affordable way to travel to Madrid's outlying cities and beyond as drivers aren't allowed to make a profit (you essentially help the driver offset the price of gas and tolls).

### TAXI SERVICES **Radio Taxi Gremial.**
☎ 91/447–3232, 91/447–5180 ⊕ www.radiotaxigremial.com. **Radioteléfono Taxi.** ☎ 91/547–8200 ⊕ www.radiotelefono-taxi.com. **Tele-Taxi.** ☎ 91/371–2131 ⊕ www.tele-taxi.es.

# Tours

### Plaza Mayor Tourist Office
CULTURAL TOURS | Madrid's main tourist office, open 365 days a year, is a treasure trove of maps and resources. Staff happily recommend bus, Segway, cycling, and walking tours to meet your needs. ✉ Casa de la Panadería, Pl. Mayor 27, Sol ☎ 91/578–7810 ⊕ www.esmadrid.com.

### BIKE TOURS
Biking in Madrid can be a white-knuckle experience for those unaccustomed to biking in traffic, but for leisurely sightseeing through parks and along the river, bike tours can be a pleasant activity.

### BravoBike
BICYCLE TOURS | FAMILY | BravoBike offers guided bike tours in English (from €15 for two hours). It also offers multiday guided and self-guided tours in destinations including Toledo, Segovia, Andalusia, and the Camino de Santiago pilgrimage route. ✉ Calle Juan Álvarez Mendizábal 19, Moncloa ☎ 91/758–2945, 60/744–8440 for WhatsApp ⊕ www.bravobike.com 🎫 From €15.

## BUS TOURS
### Madrid City Tours
BUS TOURS | FAMILY | The ubiquitous red double-decker tourist buses make 1½-hour circuits of the city, allowing you to get on and off at various attractions. Beyond the one- and two-day passes, consider: the "Historic Madrid" tour, the "Modern Madrid" tour, or the "Night Tour" (June 16–September 15 only), all with recorded English commentary. ☎ 91/369–2732 ⊕ www.madrid.city-tour.com 🎫 From €21.

## WALKING TOURS
### Association of Official Tourist Guides of the Region of Madrid (APIT)
CULTURAL TOURS | FAMILY | This operator offers custom history and art walks by government-certified travel guides in 15 languages. ✉ Sol ☎ 91/542–1214 ⊕ www.apit.es.

### Carpetania Madrid
WALKING TOURS | This 20-year-old company offers niche, brainy Spanish-only tours and literary walks on topics like "Women of Malasaña" and "Almodóvar's Madrid." ✉ Calle Jesús del Valle 11, Malasaña ☎ 91/531–4018 ⊕ www.carpetaniamadrid.com 🎫 From €10.

### Devour Tours
FOOD AND DRINK TOURS | FAMILY | Devour is a dependable food tour company catering to hungry travelers of all interests. In Madrid, walks run the gamut from a "Tapas, Taverns & History" neighborhood

tapas crawl to a "Prado Museum Tour & VIP Botín Lunch" that culminates in a meal at the world's oldest restaurant. ✉ Cortes ☎ 91/902–4660, 415/969–9277 U.S. phone number ⊕ www.devourtours.com ✉ From €99.

★ **Walk and Eat Spain**

FOOD AND DRINK TOURS | FAMILY | It doesn't get more ear-to-the-ground than these small-group food tours in Malasaña. On the €89 2½-hour mercado tour, one of a handful of itineraries, you'll meet local characters ranging from olive vendors to ham slicers to beloved local chefs—and feast on the greatest hits of Spanish food while amassing a shopping bag of edible souvenirs. Kid-friendly tours are also available. ✉ Calle de Fuencarral 78, Malasaña ☎ 67/171–7874 ⊕ www.walkandeat-spain.com ✉ From €89 Ⓜ Tribunal.

# Restaurants

Spain is an essential foodie pilgrimage, and no Spanish city holds a candle to Madrid when it comes to variety of national and international cuisines. The pandemic hit the restaurant industry hard, though not as hard as it did hotels. Restaurants were largely allowed to remain open throughout, albeit with expanded outdoor dining and strict curfews in place. But lamentably, a number of beloved restaurants were forced to shutter.

Younger madrileños gravitate toward trendy neighborhoods like taberna-lined Malasaña, LGBT+-friendly Chueca, rootsy La Latina, and multicultural Lavapiés for their boisterous and affordable restaurants and bars. Dressier travelers and those visiting with family, on the other hand, will feel more at home in the quieter, more sedate restaurants of Salamanca, Chamberí, Ibiza, and Retiro. Of course, these are broad-brush generalizations, and there are plenty of exceptions.

## What It Costs in Euros

|  | $ | $$ | $$$ | $$$$ |
|---|---|---|---|---|
| **RESTAURANTS** | | | | |
|  | under €17 | €17–€23 | €24–€30 | over €30 |

# Hotels

There's a dizzying array of hotels to choose from in Madrid, from grande-dame icons that once hosted Lorca and Hemingway to quirky boutique hotels with art-lined walls and plant-based breakfast buffets.

## What It Costs in Euros

|  | $ | $$ | $$$ | $$$$ |
|---|---|---|---|---|
| **HOTELS** | | | | |
|  | under €125 | €125–€174 | €175–€225 | over €225 |

# Nightlife

Unlike in other European cities, where partying is a pastime geared mostly toward the young, there are plenty of bars and discotecas with mixed-age crowds in Madrid. It's not uncommon for children to play on the sidewalks past midnight while multigenerational families and friends convene over coffee or cocktails at an outdoor café. There's a lot of overlap between dining, bar-hopping, and nightlife in Madrid—some bars serve tapas and cocktails and blast DJ sets till the wee hours—but this section is geared toward establishments that revolve around drinking, dancing, and entertainment.

Madrid is a sundown-to-sunup party city, but those with earlier bedtimes will feel at home at the sleek cafés, cervecerías (pubs), and cocktail bars on Calle Jorge

## Where Should I Stay?

| | Neighborhood Vibe | Pros | Cons |
|---|---|---|---|
| Palacio, Moncloa, La Latina, and Sol | Anchored by the Plaza Mayor, this historic area is full of taverns and narrow streets | Old-world feel; central location; lodging and dining for every budget and style | Labyrinthine streets make it tough to navigate; noisy; tourist traps galore |
| Barrio de las Letras | A magnet for upscale tourists, this classic literary nest has several pedestrian-only streets | Picturesque plazas; fashionable hotels and restaurants; steps from big museums | Congested around Plaza de Santa Ana; some bars and restaurants are overpriced; lots of tourists and expats |
| Chueca and Malasaña | Vibrant and bustling, this is where you want to be if you don't plan on being in bed before midnight | Electric with busy nightlife, alternative shops, and charming cafés | Loud, especially on weekends; 20-minute walk from most attractions; older buildings mean smaller digs |
| Salamanca, Retiro, Moncloa, and Chamberí | Swanky yet sedate, these are the neighborhoods many high-end hotels and restaurants call home | Quiet at day's end; good restaurants and upscale shopping; not touristy | Bland and conservative; restaurant staff and locals can be snooty; expensive |
| Chamartín | Corporate, buttoned-up, and quiet, this is business central | Near the financial district, Berbabéu Stadium, and Chamartín Railway Station; hidden-gem dining spots. | A taxi or metro ride from sights; architecturally unattractive |

Juan (Barrio Salamanca), Calle Ponzano (Chamberí), and Plaza de Santa Ana (Letras).

More rambunctious party scenes can be found in Malasaña, with its underground discotecas and rocker bars around Plaza de Dos de Mayo; Chueca, with its legendary LGBT+ (yet totally hetero-friendly) venues off the eponymous plaza; and Sol, home to a number of popular mega-clubs with flashy visuals and multiple floors.

## Shopping

Madrid is a leader in contemporary art and design, but you'll have no trouble finding traditional crafts, such as ceramics, woven baskets, guitars, and leather goods. Note that family-run shops and

boutiques generally close during lunch hours, on Saturday afternoons, and all day Sunday.

Madrid has three main shopping areas. The most commercial stretches from Callao to Puerta del Sol (taking in Calle Preciados, Gran Vía, and the streets north of Puerta del Sol) and includes major department stores and international clothing chains such as El Corte Inglés, Zara, Nike, Bershka, and Primark.

The place to shop for timeless, classic fashion is Salamanca, bounded roughly by Calles Serrano, Juan Bravo, Jorge Juan (and its mews), and Velázquez; the shops on Goya extend as far as Alcalá. The streets just off the Plaza de Colón, particularly Calle Serrano and Calle Ortega y Gasset, have the widest selection of designer goods—think Prada, Loewe, Armani, and Louis Vuitton—as well as big-name Spanish designers including Purificación García, Bimba y Lola, and Roberto Verino. More high-end boutiques can be found on and around Calle Lagasca and Calle Claudio Coello.

For eclectic finds and trendier threads, Chueca, Malasaña, Lavapiés, and the streets around the Conde Duque cultural center are your best bets. Calle Fuencarral, between Gran Vía and Tribunal metro station, has the most shops in this area with outposts from Diesel, Adidas, and Footlocker—but don't miss out on less corporate, and often more exciting, boutiques on nearby Calles Hortaleza, Almirante, Piamonte, Velarde, and Corredera Alta de San Pablo. The latter two have several terrific vintage fashion shops.

# Sol

Built in the 16th century around the Puerta del Sol, this neighborhood used to mark the city's geographic center, which today sits a tad to its east. Sol encompasses, among other sights, the monumental Plaza Mayor and the popular pedestrian shopping area around Callao.

There's never a dull moment in Puerta del Sol, the bustling semicircular plaza where friends gather, buskers perform, and bar crawls begin. The Puerta (gate) designation is a holdover from when this spot bore entry into the medieval city walls; Sol (sun), on the other hand, is a reference to a sun carving that adorned the gate. Let your gaze wander to the clocktower atop the Casa de Correos, the oldest building on the square, where political dissidents were jailed and tortured under Franco's regime. Today, it ushers Madrid into the New Year each December as onlookers partake in the Spanish tradition of eating 12 grapes in the last 12 seconds of the year.

⚠ Beware of closures, delays, and construction noise around Sol in 2023 as the square is being renovated through the middle of the year.

## ◉ Sights

### Mercado de San Miguel
MARKET | Adjacent to the Plaza Mayor, this mercado gastronómico is a feast for the senses. Its bustling interior—a mixture of tapas spots and grab-and-go counters—sits beneath a fin-de-siècle glass dome reinforced by elaborate wrought iron. Enjoy a glass of wine and maybe a snack here, but save your appetite: the market, as gorgeous as it may be, has become overpriced and underwhelming in recent years. There are two diamonds in the rough: Rocambolesc, with its futuristic ice creams by the Roca brothers, and Daniel Sorlut, a posh oyster bar. ⊠ *Pl. de San Miguel, Sol* ⊕ *www.mercadodesanmiguel.es* Ⓜ *Ópera.*

### ★ Plaza Mayor
PLAZA/SQUARE | A symbol of imperial Spain's might and grandeur, this public square is often surprisingly quiet, perhaps since most locals wrote it off long ago as too touristy. The plaza was finished in 1619 under Felipe III, whose equestrian statue stands in the center, and is one of the largest in Europe, measuring 360 feet by 300 feet. It's seen it all: *autos-da-fé* (public burnings of heretics), the canonization of saints, criminal executions, royal marriages, bullfights (until 1847), and all manner of other events. The plot was once occupied by a city market, and many of the surrounding streets retain names of the trades and foods once headquartered there (e.g., Cutlers' Street, Lettuce Street). The plaza's oldest building, Casa de la Panadería (Bakery House), has brightly painted murals and gray spires; it is now the tourist office. Opposite sits Casa de la Carnicería (Butcher Shop), now a boutique hotel. The plaza is closed

## Did You Know?

The Casa de la Panadería (Bakery House), on the left side of this photo of the Plaza Mayor, is the oldest building in the plaza and was originally a bread shop. It's recognizable by the colorfully painted facade.

# Madrid Metro

to motorized traffic, making it a pleasant if touristy spot to enjoy a cup of coffee. ⊠ *Sol* Ⓜ *Sol.*

## Puerta del Sol

**PLAZA/SQUARE** | Crowded with locals, tourists, hawkers, and street performers, the Puerta del Sol is the nerve center of Madrid. It is in the throes of a massive renovation through at least mid-2023, so beware of possible closures. A brass plaque in the sidewalk on the south side of the plaza marks Kilometer Zero, the point from which all distances in Spain are measured. The restored 1756 French-Neoclassical building near the marker now houses the offices of the regional government, but during Franco's reign, it was the headquarters of his secret police and is still known colloquially as the Casa de los Gritos (House of Screams). Across the square are a bronze statue of Madrid's official symbol, a bear with a *madroño* (strawberry tree), and a statue of King and Mayor Carlos III on horseback. Puerta del Sol has been the nucleus of countless protests and political movements through the centuries. It was here, in 2011, that the 15-M movement started as a sleep-in against government austerity measures and blossomed into an organized revolution. The grassroots political party Podemos was created as a result. The 15-M demonstrations would go on to inspire Occupy Wall Street and other pro-democracy and anti-capitalist protests around the world. ⊠ *Sol* Ⓜ *Sol.*

## Real Academia de Bellas Artes de San Fernando (*St. Ferdinand Royal Academy of Fine Arts*)

**ART MUSEUM** | Designed by José Benito de Churriguera in the waning baroque years of the early 18th century, this museum showcases 500 years of Spanish painting, from José Ribera and Bartolomé Esteban Murillo to Joaquín Sorolla and Ignacio Zuloaga. The tapestries along the stairways are stunning. The gallery displays paintings up to the 18th century, including some by Goya. Guided tours are usually available (check the website for times). The same building houses the Instituto de Calcografía (Prints Institute), which sells limited-edition prints from original plates engraved by Spanish artists. There are often classical concerts and literary events in the small upstairs hall: tickets can be purchased on the website. ⊠ *Calle de Alcalá 13, Sol* ☎ *91/524–0864* ⊕ *www.realacademia-bellasartessanfernando.com* ⊠ *€8 (free Wed.)* ⊘ *Closed Mon. and Aug.* Ⓜ *Sol.*

# 🍴 Restaurants

## La Casa del Abuelo

**$$ | TAPAS** | This rustic tapas hall is the oldest of three branches of a beloved local chain, and it has barely changed since it was founded in 1906. The tapa to try here is *gambas al ajillo*, shrimp sautéed with garlic. **Known for:** traditional atmosphere; bold proprietary Toro wines; killer gambas al ajillo. ⑤ *Average main: €19* ⊠ *Calle de la Victoria 12, Sol* ☎ *91/521–2319* ⊕ *www.lacasadelabuelo.es* Ⓜ *Sol.*

## La Pulpería de Victoria

**$$ | SPANISH | FAMILY** | A modern, urban interpretation of a traditional Galician *pulpería* (octopus restaurant), this casual spot specializes in *polbo á feira*, boiled octopus cut into coins, drizzled with olive oil, and dusted with smoked paprika. Pair it with an icy glass of Albariño and a heap of blistered *padrón* peppers. **Known for:** variety of Galician wines; ocean-fresh shellfish; Galician-style octopus. ⑤ *Average main: €20* ⊠ *Calle de La Victoria 2, Sol* ☎ *91/080–4929* ⊕ *www.pulperiade-victoria.com* Ⓜ *Sol.*

## ★ Lambuzo

**$$ | SPANISH | FAMILY** | This laid-back Andalusian barroom, one of three locations (the others are in Retiro and Chamberí), embodies the joyful spirit of that sunny region. Let the cheerful waitstaff guide

Sol, Palacio,
and Moncloa

## Sights ▼

1 Casa de Campo .......... A1
2 Catedral de la
   Almudena ............... B6
3 Ermita de San Antonio
   de la Florida ............. A3
4 Jardines de Sabatini ... B4
5 Madrid Río ............... A8
6 Mercado de
   San Miguel ............. D6
7 Monasterio de la
   Encarnación ............ C4
8 Monasterio de las
   Descalzas Reales ....... D5
9 Museo Cerralbo ......... B2
10 Museo del Traje ......... A1
11 Palacio Real ............. B5
12 Parque del Oeste ....... A1
13 Plaza de la Villa ......... C6
14 Plaza de Oriente ........ C5
15 Plaza Mayor ............. D6
16 Puerta del Sol ........... E5
17 Real Academia
   de Bellas Artes
   de San Fernando ....... G5
18 San Nicolás
   de los Servitas .......... C6
19 Teleférico ............... A4

## Restaurants ▼

1 Casa Lafu ................ C3
2 Casa Mingo ............. A4
3 Cuenllas ................. A1
4 La Casa del Abuelo ..... G6
5 La Copita Asturiana ..... C8
6 La Pulpería de
   Victoria .................. F5
7 Lambuzo ................ D5
8 Le Bistroman Atelier .... C5
9 Paco Roncero
   Restaurante ............. G5

## Quick Bites ▼

1 Chocolatería
   San Ginés ............... E5
2 Chocolatería
   Valor ..................... E4
3 Four ...................... C6

## Hotels ▼

1 Ateneo Hotel ............ F5
2 Dear Hotel ............... C2
3 Four Seasons Hotel
   Madrid .................. G5
4 Generator Madrid ...... D3
5 Gran Meliá Palacio
   de Los Duques .......... C4
6 Hotel Indigo Madrid –
   Gran Vía ................. D4
7 Hotel Indigo Madrid –
   Princesa ................. B1
8 Hotel Intur Palacio
   San Martín .............. D4
9 Iberostar Las Letras
   Gran Vía ................. G4
10 The Madrid Edition ...... E5
11 Mayerling Hotel .......... E7
12 Room Mate
   Macarena ............... E4

you through the extensive menu, which includes fried seafood, unconventional croquetas (flecked with garlicky shrimp, for instance), and heftier shareables like creamy oxtail rice and seared Barbate tuna loin. **Known for:** free marinated carrots with every drink; a shoal's worth of seafood dishes; carefree Andalusian vibe. $ *Average main: €22* ⊠ *Calle de las Conchas 9, Sol* ☎ *91/143–4862* ⊕ *www. barlambuzo.com* ⊘ *Closed Mon. No dinner Sun.* Ⓜ *Ópera.*

### Paco Roncero Restaurante

$$$$ | ECLECTIC | Occupying an aerie above one of Madrid's oldest, most exclusive gentlemen's clubs, the dining room and rooftop terrace of this tasting-menu-only restaurant (formerly known as La Terraza del Casino) are decorated with playful, almost circuslike elements such as bright blue pushcarts, checkered floors, and yellow velvet chairs. The cuisine is as thrilling and whimsical as the decor with dishes ranging from crunchy sardines with *ají romesco* sauce to roast squab with foie and locally foraged mushrooms. **Known for:** foams, jellies, and flamboyant flourishes; two Michelin stars; Instagrammable interiors. $ *Average main: €95* ⊠ *Calle Alcalá 15, Sol* ☎ *91/532–1275* ⊕ *www.pacoroncerorestaurante.com* ⊘ *Closed Sun. and Mon.* 🎩 *Jacket required* Ⓜ *Sol.*

## ☕ Coffee and Quick Bites

### Chocolatería San Ginés

$ | CAFÉ | FAMILY | San Ginés is to Madrid what Café du Monde is to New Orleans: a historical fried-dough mecca. For generations this 19th-century café has been frying spirals of piping-hot churros and *porras* (the churro's fatter, chewier cousin—try them) day and night. **Known for:** a local institution; central location; chocolate con churros. $ *Average main: €4* ⊠ *Pasadizo de San Ginés, Sol* ⊹ *Enter by Arenal 11* ☎ *91/365–6546* ⊕ *www. chocolateriasangines.com* Ⓜ *Sol.*

## 🛏 Hotels

### Ateneo Hotel

$ | HOTEL | This economical and somewhat dated property is set in an 18th-century building that once housed the Ateneo, a club founded in 1835 to promote freedom of thought. **Pros:** sizable rooms; some rooms have skylights and balconies; triples and quadruples available. **Cons:** uninspired decor; noisy area; major pedestrian artery. $ *Rooms from: €100* ⊠ *Calle de Montera 22, Sol* ☎ *91/521–2012* ⊕ *www.hotel-ateneo.com* ⇌ *44 rooms* ⦿ *No Meals* Ⓜ *Gran Vía, Sol.*

### Four Seasons Hotel Madrid

$$$$ | HOTEL | You'll feel like a VIP as you step into the grand lobby—with its gilt-topped columns, enormous central skylight, and sleek spiral staircase—of what was Madrid's most hotly anticipated hotel when it opened in 2020. **Pros:** above-and-beyond service touches; celebrity-chef restaurant; original artwork by emerging Spanish artists. **Cons:** situated above chain restaurants and boutiques; wildly expensive; little sense of place. $ *Rooms from: €995* ⊠ *Calle de Sevilla 3, Sol* ☎ *91/088–3333* ⊕ *www. fourseasons.com* ⇌ *200 rooms* ⦿ *Free Breakfast* Ⓜ *Sol.*

### Iberostar Las Letras Gran Vía

$$$ | HOTEL | A modern, clubby hotel on the stately avenue of Gran Vía, Iberostar Las Letras is a welcoming oasis from the area's constant hubbub of tourists and shoppers. **Pros:** state-of-the-art gym; happening rooftop bar; many rooms have balconies. **Cons:** awkward bathroom design; no spa; lackluster service and food in Gran Clavel. $ *Rooms from: €220* ⊠ *Gran Vía 11, Sol* ☎ *91/523–7980* ⊕ *www.iberostar.com* ⇌ *110 rooms* ⦿ *No Meals* Ⓜ *Banco de España.*

### Mayerling Hotel

$$ | HOTEL | Minimalism at just the right value is the key at this former textile wholesaler's premises, now a 22-room

The Puerta del Sol, Madrid's central transportation hub, is sure to be passed through by every visitor to the city.

boutique hotel a few blocks off Plaza Mayor and Plaza de Santa Ana. Serene (if slightly clinical) white rooms come in three sizes—standard, superior, and triple—and are decorated with colorful headboards, charcoal valances, and small open closets. **Pros:** triples available; prime location; 24-hour complimentary coffee, snacks, and juices. **Cons:** no restaurant or gym; white walls show smudges; rooms are smallish by U.S. standards. ⑤ *Rooms from: €150* ✉ *Calle del Conde de Romanones 6, Sol* ☎ *91/420–1580* ⊕ *www.mayerlinghotel.com* ⇥ *22 rooms* ⑩ *No Meals* Ⓜ *Tirso de Molina.*

 Nightlife

### DANCE CLUBS
### ★ Cocó Madrid

**DANCE CLUBS** | This club, with its wild color palette, huge dance floor, and better-than-average cocktails, is best known for its branded DJ nights: La Discoteca (formerly Chá Chá; tickets via ⊕ dice.fm) on Fridays and Mondo Disko (Thursdays

and Saturdays) that rage until dawn with house and electronic music often by international DJs. ✉ *Calle Alcalá 20, Sol* ☎ *91/445–7938* ⊕ *www.mondodisko.es* ✷ *Closed Mon.–Wed.* Ⓜ *Sevilla.*

### Sala El Sol

**DANCE CLUBS** | Madrid's oldest discoteca continues to win over patrons with all-night dancing to live music (starting around midnight Thursday–Saturday) and DJ sets. Check the website to see what's on the docket, and prepurchase tickets for parties like Trueno, popular among techno-heads. ✉ *Calle Jardines 3, Sol* ☎ *91/532–6490* ⊕ *www.salaelsol. com* ✷ *Closed Mon.* Ⓜ *Gran Vía.*

### ❶ Performing Arts

### Círculo de Bellas Artes

**CONCERTS** | Concerts, theater, dance performances, art exhibitions, and other events are all part of the calendar at this performance and entertainment venue. There is also an extremely popular (and overpriced) café and rooftop restaurant-bar with breathtaking views of the city. ⊠ *Calle del Marqués de Casa Riera 2, Top floor, Sol* ☎ *90/242–2442* ⊕ *www.circulobellasartes.com* ⊡ *€5* Ⓜ *Banco de España.*

## 🍽 Shopping

### CLOTHING
**Capas Seseña**

OTHER ACCESSORIES | Seseña is the oldest cape tailor in the world and one of Madrid's most emblematic shops. Since 1901, this family-run business has outfitted the likes of Picasso, Hemingway, and Michael Jackson in traditional merino wool and velvet capes, some lined with red satin. ⊠ *Calle de la Cruz 23, Sol* ☎ *91/531–6840* ⊕ *www.sesena.com* ⊙ *Closed Sun.* Ⓜ *Sol.*

### CRAFTS AND DESIGN
**El Arco Artesanía**

CRAFTS | El Arco sells contemporary, whimsical handicrafts from all over Spain, including modern ceramics, handblown glassware, jewelry, and leather items. ⊠ *Pl. Mayor 9, Sol* ☎ *60/663–4935* ⊕ *www.artesaniaelarco.com* Ⓜ *Sol.*

**Taller Puntera**

CRAFTS | You can watch the artisans at work at this inviting atelier-boutique hybrid situated steps from the Plaza Mayor. Regardless of what catches your eye—a leather card holder, handbag, or perhaps a hand-bound notebook—you'll be pleasantly surprised by the affordable prices. ⊠ *Pl. del Conde de Barajas 4, Sol* ☎ *91/364–2926* ⊕ *www.puntera.com* ⊙ *Closed Sun.* Ⓜ *Ópera, Tirso de Molina.*

### FANS
★ **Casa de Diego**

OTHER SPECIALTY STORE | Established in 1823, Casa de Diego manufactures fans, umbrellas, and classic Spanish walking sticks with ornamented silver handles and also sells traditional Spanish ornamental combs, mantillas, and castanets.

## Gourmet Experience Gran Vía 🍴

On the rooftop of El Corte Inglés, Spain's largest department store, there's a gourmet food court with some of the best views in the city. Grab a couple of tapas and a glass of wine after perusing the shops around Callao (though don't fill up here as the food is nothing raveworthy). Take the second entrance to El Corte Inglés as you're walking down Callao on Calle Carmen and across from Fnac.

The British royal family buys autograph fans here for signing on special occasions. ⊠ *Puerta del Sol 12, Sol* ☎ *91/522–6643* ⊕ *www.casadediego.info* ⊙ *Closed Sun.* Ⓜ *Sol.*

## 🏃 Activities

### SPAS
**Hammam Al Ándalus**

SPAS | Walk through a nondescript door off the noisy Plaza de Jacinto Benavente and suddenly you're in a serene Moorish-style bathhouse decorated with carved arches and Andalusian tile. Flickering candles light the way to a steam room, a relaxation area, shallow pools of varying temperatures, and a massage parlor where professional masseurs offer treatments ranging from 15 minutes to one hour. It's not an authentic hammam by any stretch, but it's the best-priced spa experience in town and a good rainy-day activity for adult travelers. ⊠ *Calle de Atocha 14, Sol* ⊕ *www.madrid.hammamalandalus.com* ⊡ *€55–€120* Ⓜ *Sol.*

# Palacio

Madrid's oldest neighborhood, Palacio is the home of the imposing Palacio Real (Royal Palace). This is where Muhammad I established the city's first military post in the 9th century, essentially founding the city. The quarter, bounded by the Plaza Mayor to the east, is a maze of cobblestone streets lined with homey restaurants and old-school cafés and shops.

## ◉ Sights

### Catedral de la Almudena

CHURCH | The first stone of the cathedral, which faces the Royal Palace, was laid in 1883 by King Alfonso XII, and the resulting edifice was consecrated by Pope John Paul II in 1993. La Almudena is controversial due to its hodgepodge of architectural styles; it is playfully mocked by madrileños, who sometimes call it *la fea* (the ugly one). Built on the site of the old church of Santa María de la Almudena (the city's main mosque during Arab rule), the cathedral has a wooden statue of Madrid's female patron saint, the Virgin of Almudena, allegedly discovered after being hidden by Christian devotees during the so-called Reconquest. The cathedral's name is derived from the place where the relic was found, within the wall of the old citadel (in Arabic, *al-mudayna*). ⊠ *Calle Bailén 10, Palacio* ☎ *91/542–2200* ⊕ *www.catedraldelaalmudena.es* ☞ *Free; museum and cupola €7* Ⓜ *Ópera.*

### Jardines de Sabatini (*Sabatini Gardens*)

GARDEN | The manicured gardens to the north of the Palacio Real, located where the royal stables once were, are a pleasant place to rest or watch the sun set. Renovated in 2022 as part of the Plaza de España overhaul, they are named for the prolific 18th-century architect who designed the Puerta de Alcalá, Royal Botanical Garden, and San Francisco el Grande convent, among other key sights. ⊠ *Calle Bailén, Palacio* Ⓜ *Ópera.*

### Madrid Río

CITY PARK | FAMILY | Madrid Río takes in some 32 km (20 miles) of green space and bike-friendly paths along the lazy, shallow Manzanares River, beginning at the Puente de los Franceses in the northwest and terminating at the Pasarela Legazpi in the southeast. A popular place to enter is Segovia Bridge, downhill from the Royal Palace; a Christmas market is held here with craft kiosks and food stalls. Outdoor concerts (check out the Veranos de la Villa series; lineups are posted online) and informal riverside dining round out the park's offerings. Note to nature lovers: Madrid Río connects to Casa de Campo, Parque del Oeste, and Madrid's 64-km (40-mile) Anillo Verde ("Green Ring") bike path. ⊠ *Palacio* ⊕ *www.esmadrid.com/en/whats-on/veranos-de-la-villa* Ⓜ *Príncipe Pío, Pirámides, Legazpi.*

### Monasterio de la Encarnación (*Monastery of the Incarnation*)

RELIGIOUS BUILDING | Once connected to the Palacio Real by an underground passageway, this cloistered Augustinian convent now houses fewer than a dozen nuns. It was founded in 1611 by Queen Margarita de Austria, the wife of Felipe III, and has several artistic treasures including a reliquary where a vial with the dried blood of St. Pantaleón is said to liquefy every July 27. The ornate church has superb acoustics for medieval and Renaissance choral concerts. ⊠ *Pl. de la Encarnación 1, Palacio* ☎ *91/454–8803 for tourist office* ⊕ *www.patrimonionacional.es/en/visita/royal-monastery-la-encarnacion* ☞ *€6 (free Wed. and Thurs. 4–6:30)* ☺ *Closed Mon.* Ⓜ *Ópera.*

★ **Monasterio de las Descalzas Reales**
(*Monastery of the Royal Discalced/Bare-foot Nuns*)
RELIGIOUS BUILDING | After a 20-month closure for renovations, this important 16th-century monastery reopened to the public in December 2021 with 200 new works from its art collection on display. The plain brick-and-stone facade belies an opulent interior strewn with paintings by Francisco de Zurbarán, Titian, and Pieter Brueghel the Elder—all part of the dowry of new monastery inductees—as well as a hall of sumptuous tapestries crafted from drawings by Peter Paul Rubens. Fifty works from the collection were meticulously restored as part of the recent renovations. The convent was founded in 1559 by Juana of Austria, one of Felipe II's sisters, who ruled Spain while he was in England and the Netherlands. It houses 33 different chapels—the age of Christ when he died and the maximum number of nuns allowed to live at the monastery—with more than 120 immaculately preserved crucifixes among them. Eighteen nuns still live here and grow vegetables in the garden. No photos allowed. ■TIP➜ **You must take a tour in order to visit the convent, and tickets must be bought online ahead of time (they sell out fast); those who don't speak Spanish can access an English guide through the app.** ⊠ *Pl. de las Descalzas Reales 3, Palacio* ☎ *91/454–8800* ⊕ *www.patri-monionacional.es/en/real-sitio/monaster-io-de-las-descalzas-reales* ⌑ *€6* ☾ *Closed Mon.* ⚲ *Reservations and pre-purchased tickets required* Ⓜ *Sol.*

★ **Palacio Real** (*Royal Palace*)
CASTLE/PALACE | Emblematic of the oldest part of the city, the Royal Palace awes visitors with its sheer size and monumental presence. The palace was commissioned in the early 18th century by the first of Spain's Bourbon rulers, Felipe V. Outside, you can see the classical French architecture on the graceful Patio de Armas; inside, 2,800 rooms compete with each other for over-the-top opulence.

A two-hour guided tour in English points out highlights including the Salón de Gasparini, King Carlos III's private apartments; the Salón del Trono, a grand throne room; and the banquet hall, set with gleaming china. Also within are the Museo de Música (Music Museum), with the world's largest collection of five-stringed instruments by Antonio Stradivari; the Painting Gallery, with works by Spanish, Flemish, and Italian artists; the Armería Real (Royal Armory), with suits of armor and medieval torture implements; and the Real Oficina de Farmacia (Royal Pharmacy). The palace also takes in the Biblioteca Real (Royal Library), with a first edition of Miguel de Cervantes's *Don Quixote*, and the Real Cocina (Royal Kitchen; tickets sold separately), which occupies 800 square meters (8,600 square feet) and has remained largely unchanged since the late 18th century. Opened to the public in 2017, its framed handwritten menus, antediluvian wood-burning ovens, enormous copper cauldrons, wooden iceboxes, and nearly 3,000 antique kitchen utensils make it a must-stop for foodies. In 2021 the seven-room Bailén Wing, containing mirrors, tapestries, armaments, and more, reopened after a 25-year hiatus. The same year, the palace's most iconic viewpoint overlooking the Campo del Moro gardens also reopened after 15 years of sluggish renovations. ⊠ *Calle Bailén, Palacio* ☎ *91/454–8800* ⊕ *www.patrimoniona-cional.es/visita/palacio-real-de-madrid* ⌑ *From €12* Ⓜ *Ópera.*

**Plaza de la Villa**
PLAZA/SQUARE | Madrid's town council met in this medieval-looking complex from the Middle Ages until 2009, when it moved to the Palacio de Cibeles. It now houses municipal offices. The oldest building on the plaza is the Casa de los Lujanes, the one with the Mudejar tower.

Built as a private home in the late 15th century, the house carries the Lujanes crest over the main doorway. Also on the plaza's east end is the brick-and-stone Casa de la Villa, built in 1629, a classic example of Dutch-influenced Madrid design, with clean lines and spire-topped corner towers. Connected by an overhead walkway, the Casa de Cisneros was commissioned in 1537 by the nephew of Cardinal Cisneros. It's one of Madrid's rare examples of the flamboyant plateresque style, which has been likened to splashed water. Sadly, none of these landmarks are open to the public on a regular basis. ⊠ *Palacio* Ⓜ *Sol, Ópera.*

### Plaza de Oriente

PLAZA/SQUARE | This stately semicircular plaza, sandwiched between the Palacio Real and the Teatro Real, is flanked by massive statues of Spanish monarchs that were meant to be mounted atop the palace. Queen Isabel of Farnesio, one of the first royals to live in the palace, had them removed because she was afraid their enormous weight would bring the roof down. (That's the official reason; according to local lore, the queen wanted the statues removed because her own likeness wouldn't have been placed front and center.) A Velázquez drawing of King Felipe IV is the inspiration for the statue in the plaza's center. It's the first equestrian bronze ever cast with a rearing horse. The sculptor, Italian artist Pietro de Tacca, enlisted Galileo Galilei's help in configuring the statue's weight so it wouldn't tip over. The 2021 overhaul of Plaza de España eliminated all car traffic between Plaza de Oriente and Plaza de España and added pleasant footpaths and fountains. ⊠ *Palacio* Ⓜ *Ópera.*

### San Nicolás de los Servitas (*Church of St. Nicholas of the Servites*)

RELIGIOUS BUILDING | There's some debate over whether this church, the oldest in central Madrid, once formed part of an Arab mosque. It was more likely built

after the so-called Reconquest of Madrid in 1083, but the brickwork and horseshoe arches are evidence that it was crafted by either Mudejars (workers of Islamic origin) or Christian Spaniards well versed in the style. Inside, exhibits detail the Islamic history of early Madrid. ⊠ *Pl. de San Nicolás, Palacio* ☎ *91/559–4064* 🖃 *Suggested donation* Ⓜ *Ópera.*

## 🍴 Restaurants

### Casa Lafu

$$ | CHINESE | FAMILY | If you haven't tried Chinese food in Madrid, then you're missing out—the city has some of the best Chinese restaurants in Europe thanks to a vibrant immigrant community. Casa Lafu, with its serene white-tablecloth dining room, stands out for its expertly prepared repertoire of regional dishes, from Sichuan-style *má là* (spicy) plates to Shanghainese wine-cooked meats and Cantonese dim sum. **Known for:** rare regional specialties; upscale Chinese cuisine at affordable prices; hot pot. ⑤ *Average main: €19* ⊠ *Calle Flor Baja 1, Palacio* ☎ *91/548–7096* ⊕ *www.casalafu.com* Ⓜ *Santo Domingo.*

### ★ La Copita Asturiana

$$ | SPANISH | FAMILY | In the heart of the tourist fray but blissfully under the radar, this teensy lunch-only restaurant (est. 1959) with an old tin bar serves all the Asturian favorites, from *fabada* (bean stew) to *cachopo* (ham-and-cheese-stuffed cutlets) to creamy rice pudding. Asturian cider is the requisite beverage. **Known for:** kitsch decor; easy-on-the-wallet prices; northern Spanish comfort food. ⑤ *Average main: €18* ⊠ *Calle de Tabernillas 13, Palacio* ☎ *91/365–1063* ⊕ *www.lacopitaasturiana.com* ☉ *Closed Sat. No dinner* Ⓜ *Tirso de Molina.*

### Le Bistroman Atelier

$$$ | FRENCH | For a country that borders France, Spain has a surprising dearth of good French restaurants, which makes

Le Bistroman all the more remarkable—not only is the food good by Spanish standards, it would be a hit in Paris with its homemade *everything*, from terrines to breads to pastries. Wild game (venison, squab) features prominently on the menu, and other highlights include an old-school cheese cart and throwback desserts like babas au rhum and vanilla bean soufflé. **Known for:** varied French wine list; elevated bistro cooking; exquisite bouillabaisse (call to order in advance). ⑤ *Average main: €29* ⊠ *Calle de la Amnistia 10, Palacio* ☎ *91/447–2713* ⊕ *www.lebistroman.es* ⊘ *Closed Mon.* Ⓜ *Ópera.*

## ☕ Coffee and Quick Bites

### Chocolatería Valor

$ | **CAFÉ** | **FAMILY** | Trace the western side of the Monasterio de las Descalzas Reales until you reach Chocolatería Valor, an ideal spot to indulge in piping-hot churros dipped in thick hot chocolate. Valor's churros are chewy, puffy, and snipped into batons, more akin to *porras* (churros' baking-soda-leavened sibling) than to standard crispy churros. **Known for:** outdoor seating; family-friendly atmosphere; one of the best chocolaterías in town. ⑤ *Average main: €6* ⊠ *Calle Postigo de San Martín 7, Palacio* ☎ *91/899–4062* ⊕ *www.valor.es* Ⓜ *Callao.*

### Four

$ | **CAFÉ** | Expertly pulled espressos, natural wines, and unexpectedly outstanding food—think velvety truffled scrambles, flavorful quiches, and cinnamon-scented pear cake—have made this café on Plaza del Biombo an instant hit with locals and expats, many of whom treat the roomy communal table like a coworking space (just be considerate and order more than a coffee if you plan on staying awhile). **Known for:** €15 weekday prix fixe; industrial-chic decor plus sunny patio seating; genial bilingual staff. ⑤ *Average main: €10* ⊠ *Calle Calderón de la Barca 8,*

*Palacio* ☎ *62/257–1608* ⊕ *www.fourmadrid.com* ⊘ *Closed Tues.* Ⓜ *Ópera.*

##  Hotels

### Generator Madrid

$ | **HOTEL** | Generator Madrid might be a budget hotel with shared (up to eight-person) rooms, but it runs circles around most of the city's big-name hotels in the design department, and guests can't get enough of the rooftop bar, plush towels, and Instagram-ready interiors. **Pros:** bubbly staff and fellow guests; USB sockets in rooms; PlayStation in the lobby. **Cons:** no laundry facilities or kitchen; storing luggage in lockers is exorbitant at €2 per hour; towels (€5 rental) not included in the rate. ⑤ *Rooms from: €45* ⊠ *Calle de San Bernardo 2, Palacio* ☎ *91/047–9801* ⊕ *www.staygenerator.com* ⟲ *129 rooms* ¹⊙¹ *No Meals* Ⓜ *Callao.*

### ★ Gran Meliá Palacio de Los Duques

$$$$ | **HOTEL** | Spanish-art lovers will geek out at this luxurious oasis with an expansive courtyard tucked behind Gran Vía, where reproductions of famous Diego Velázquez paintings feature in every room. **Pros:** Dos Cielos, one of the city's best hotel restaurants; rooftop bar and splash pool; underfloor heating and deep-soak tubs. **Cons:** no great views from rooms; rooftop often off-limits because of private events; rooms are less attractive than public areas. ⑤ *Rooms from: €384* ⊠ *Cuesta Santo Domingo 5, Palacio* ☎ *91/276–4747* ⊕ *www.melia.com* ⟲ *180 rooms* ¹⊙¹ *No Meals* Ⓜ *Santo Domingo.*

### Hotel Indigo Madrid – Gran Vía

$$$ | **HOTEL** | A hip, vibrant hotel off the bustling Gran Vía thoroughfare, Indigo is best known for its stunning rooftop lounge and outdoor infinity pool, rare features in Madrid. **Pros:** sceney rooftop infinity pool; well-equipped gym; restaurant that punches above its weight. **Cons:** dated decor; loses vitality in cold-weather months; interior rooms get little natural

light. ⑥ *Rooms from: C105* ✉ *Calle de Silva 6, Palacio* 🏠 *91/200-8585* ⊕ *www.indigomadrid.com* ⇆ *85 rooms* ⦿ *No Meals* Ⓜ *Santo Domingo.*

### Hotel Intur Palacio San Martín
**$$ | HOTEL |** In an unbeatable location across from Monasterio de las Descalzas Reales, this hotel—once the U.S. embassy and later a luxurious residential building crowded with noblemen—has the architectural bones of a turn-of-the-century mansion with its hand-carved ceilings, marble foyers, and intricate iron balconies. **Pros:** good variety at breakfast; lobby with glass-domed atrium; spacious rooms. **Cons:** church bells in the morning; bare-bones gym; bland interiors. ⑤ *Rooms from: €128* ✉ *Pl. de San Martín 5, Palacio* 🏠 *91/701-5000* ⊕ *www.intur.com* ⇆ *103 rooms* ⦿ *No Meals* Ⓜ *Ópera, Callao.*

### ★ The Madrid Edition
**$$$$ | HOTEL |** The visionary hotelier best known for creating Studio 54, Ian Schrager, is the brains behind Madrid's most buzzed-about hotel opening of 2022, one of Marriott's übertrendy Edition properties. **Pros:** exquisite Mexican breakfasts; serene Natura Bissé spa and spacious gym with the latest Technogym equipment; central location across from Las Descalzas Reales convent. **Cons:** overlooks a scruffy, unkempt square; photo-snapping influencers left and right; minor service foibles. ⑤ *Rooms from: €650* ✉ *Pl. de Celenque 2, Palacio* 🏠 *91/954-5420* ⊕ *www.editionhotels.com/madrid* ⇆ *200 rooms* ⦿ *No Meals* Ⓜ *Sol, Ópera.*

### Room Mate Macarena
**$$$ | HOTEL |** A newer addition to the Room Mate chain, Macarena opened in 2020 smack on the Gran Vía thoroughfare. **Pros:** photogenic and flamboyant design; gleaming new property; rooftop open till 2 am on weekends. **Cons:** interiors could be too loud for some; breakfasts more befitting of a youth hostel; pool looks bigger in photos than in person. ⑤ *Rooms from: €220* ✉ *Gran Vía 43, Palacio* 🏠 *91/116-1191* ⊕ *www.room-matehotels.com* ⇆ *130 rooms* ⦿ *No Meals* Ⓜ *Santo Domingo, Callao.*

## 🍸 Nightlife

### DANCE CLUBS
#### Cool
**DANCE CLUBS |** This gritty, Berlin-style underground club hosts techno-driven dance parties on weekend nights. The most popular parties are the mixed-crowd Stardust (Fridays), with mostly techno music, and the LGBT+-focused Yass Club (Saturdays), with a mix of pop, house, and hip-hop. ✉ *Calle Isabel la Católica 6, Palacio* 🏠 *63/459-6212* ⊕ *www.salacoolmadrid.com* Ⓜ *Santo Domingo.*

#### Velvet
**DANCE CLUBS |** Trippy and chameleonlike, thanks to colorful LED lights and the undulating shapes of the columns and walls, this is the place to go if you want a late-night drink without the thunder of a full-blown DJ. ✉ *Calle Jacometrezo 6, Palacio* 🏠 *63/341-4887* ⊕ *www.velvetdisco.es* ⊘ *Closed Mon.–Wed.* Ⓜ *Callao.*

### MUSIC CLUBS
#### ★ Café Berlín
**LIVE MUSIC |** For a space so small, Café Berlín packs a huge acoustic punch and draws an international, eclectic crowd. Before midnight, catch nightly live music acts in a panoply of styles (flamenco, swing, soul, and more); from around 1 am on, drop in for the disco-inflected DJ sets that ooze good vibes until 6 am. ✉ *Costanilla de los Ángeles 20, Palacio* 🏠 *91/559-7429* ⊕ *www.berlincafe.es* Ⓜ *Santo Domingo.*

#### El Amante
**DANCE CLUBS |** With two winding floors filled with nooks hosting the city's best-heeled crowds, this might be the closest thing you'll find in Madrid to a posh

private New York club. Music is usually bass-heavy electronic or house. The door is tough, so be sure to dress to impress (no sneakers allowed). Get here before 1:30 am or be ready to wait in line. ⊠ *Calle Santiago 3, Palacio* ☎ *91/755–4460* Ⓜ *Ópera.*

## 🏀 Performing Arts

### ★ Teatro Real

OPERA | This resplendent Neoclassical theater is the city's premier venue for opera and dance performances. Built in 1850, it fell into disuse from 1925 to 1966 because of political upheaval. A major restoration project endowed it with golden balconies, plush seats, and state-of-the-art stage equipment. Opera buffs rave about the choir, said to be one of the best in the world. The theater sometimes hosts flamenco on Friday evenings in the smaller auditorium. ⊠ *Pl. de Isabel II, Palacio* ☎ *91/516–0660* ⊕ *www.teatroreal.es* Ⓜ *Ópera.*

### FLAMENCO

#### Corral de la Morería

FOLK/TRADITIONAL DANCE | A Michelin-starred dinner followed by a world-class flamenco performance in the same building sounds too good to be true, but at Corral de la Morería, the food (Basque with an Andalusian twist) is as invigorating as the twirling and stomping bailaoras. Opt for an elegant, market-driven prix-fixe menu to be enjoyed during the show, or splurge on an exclusive tasting experience at the four-table Gastronómico restaurant that earned the venue its coveted star. Wine pairings, which hinge on rare back-vintage sherries and other *vinos generosos* (fortified wines), are well worth the extra euros. ⊠ *Calle de la Morería 17, Palacio* ☎ *91/365–8446* ⊕ *www.corraldelamoreria.com* Ⓜ *La Latina.*

## 🛍 Shopping

### CERAMICS

#### ★ Antigua Casa Talavera

CRAFTS | Opened in 1904, this is the best of Madrid's many ceramics vendors. Despite the name, the finest wares sold here are from Manises, near Valencia, but the blue-and-yellow Talavera ceramics are also excellent. All pieces are hand-painted and bear traditional Spanish motifs that have been used for centuries. ⊠ *Calle de Isabel la Católica 2, Palacio* ☎ *91/547–3417* ⊕ *www.antiguacasatalavera.com* ⊙ *Closed Sat.* Ⓜ *Santo Domingo.*

### SPECIALTY STORES

#### Alambique

OTHER SPECIALTY STORE | Amateur and professional cooks will love this terrific little shop (est. 1978) that sells everything from paella pans to earthenware cazuelas to olive-wood cheese boards. Cooking classes in Spanish are also available. ⊠ *Pl. de la Encarnación 2, Palacio* ☎ *91/547–4220* ⊕ *www.alambique.com* ⊙ *Closed Sun.*

# Moncloa

Moncloa is sprawling, diverse, unurbanized in certain pockets, and less touristy than other city-center neighborhoods. It takes in high-society residential communities like Aravaca and Puerta de Hierro, livelier urban areas like Argüelles (where college kids commandeer entire sidewalk cafés), and parks like the manicured Parque del Oeste, sections of the Madrid Río esplanade, and the more rugged Casa de Campo.

## 👁 Sights

### ★ Casa de Campo

CITY PARK | FAMILY | Over five times the size of New York's Central Park, Casa de Campo is Madrid's largest park and a

## Did You Know?

In 1997 the Teatro Real
returned to its intended
use as a dedicated opera
house—it was a major
European opera venue
when it first opened in
1850, but in the interim
years it was also used as
a parliamentary debate
chamber, a dance hall, a
temporary war barracks,
and even a gunpowder
storage facility.

nature-lover's paradise, complete with bike trails, picnic tables, pine forests, lakeside restaurants (seek out Villa Verbena, run by the folks behind Triciclo in Barrio de las Letras), and a public outdoor pool (€5 entry). See if you can spot wildlife like hawks, foxes, hares, and red squirrels—and, from November to May, a flock of sheep cared for by a real-deal shepherd. The park's name ("country house") is a holdover from when the grounds were the royal family's hunting estate. It became public property in May 1931 with the arrival of the Spanish Second Republic, which dissolved royal landholdings. ✉ *Moncloa* Ⓜ *Casa de Campo, Lago, Batán.*

### Ermita de San Antonio de la Florida (*Goya's Tomb*)

CHURCH | Built between 1792 and 1798 by Italian architect Francisco Fontana, this Neoclassical chapel was financed by King Carlos IV, who also commissioned Goya to paint the vaults and the main dome. Goya depicted events of the 13th century (such as St. Anthony of Padua resurrecting a dead man) as if they had happened in his own time five centuries later, with naturalistic images never used before to paint religious scenes. Opposite the image of the frightening dead man on the main dome, Goya painted himself as a man covered with a black cloak. Goya, who died in Bordeaux in 1828, is buried here (without his head, which was stolen in France) under an unadorned gravestone. ✉ *Glorieta de San Antonio de la Florida 5, Moncloa* ☎ *91/542–0722* ⊕ *www.sanantoniodelaflorida.es* 🎟 *Free* ☉ *Closed Mon.* Ⓜ *Príncipe Pío.*

### Museo Cerralbo

ART MUSEUM | One of Madrid's most captivatingly opulent museums is also one of its least known. This former palace, built in 1893 by the marquis of the same name, preserves the nobleman's art collection including works by El Greco,

Tintoretto, Van Dyck, and Zurbarán. These hang in gilded and frescoed halls appointed with ornate period furniture. ✉ *Calle de Ventura Rodríguez 17, Moncloa* ☎ *91/547–3646* ⊕ *www.culturaydeporte. gob.es/mcerralbo/en/home.html* 🎟 *€3. Free Thurs. 5–8 pm, Sun.* ☉ *Closed Mon.* Ⓜ *Ventura Rodríguez.*

### Museo del Traje (*Costume Museum*)

OTHER MUSEUM | Trace the evolution of dress in Spain here, from rare old royal burial garments to French fashion pieces of Felipe V's reign and the haute couture creations of Balenciaga and Pertegaz. Explanatory notes are in English, and the museum has a superb modern Spanish restaurant, Café de Oriente, overlooking the gardens. ✉ *Av. Juan de Herrera 2, Moncloa* ☎ *91/550–4700* ⊕ *www. culturaydeporte.gob.es/mtraje/inicio. html* 🎟 *€3. Free Sat. after 2:30 and Sun.* ☉ *Closed Mon.* Ⓜ *Ciudad Universitaria.*

### ★ Parque del Oeste

CITY PARK | FAMILY | This is many madrileños' favorite park for its pristine yet unmobbed paths and well-pruned lawns and flower beds. From dawn to dusk, expect to see dogs cavorting off leash, couples sprawled out beneath the trees, and groups of friends playing frisbee and fútbol. From Paseo del Pintor Rosales, meander downhill toward Avenida de Valladolid, crossing the train tracks, and you'll hit Madrid Río; walk southwest and you'll find Templo de Debod and, beyond, the newly pedestrianized Plaza de España. This park also contains the city's only cable car (see "Teleférico") and, 100 yards beneath it, a rose garden (Rosaleda; free entry) containing some 20,000 specimens of more than 650 rose varieties that reach their peak in May. In the quieter northern section of the park (along Avenida Séneca), you'll happen upon Civil War–era bunkers interspersed among plane-tree-lined promenades, a sobering reminder that Parque del Oeste

░░░ ░░░ ░░░░░░░ ░░░░░ ░░ ░░░░░░░ ░░░░░ ance against Franco's armies. ✉ *Paseo del Pintor Rosales, Moncloa* Ⓜ *Argüelles, Moncloa, Ventura Rodríguez, Pl. de España.*

### Teleférico

**AMUSEMENT RIDE | FAMILY** | Kids and adults alike appreciate the sweeping views from this retro cable car, which swoops you 2.5 km (1.6 miles) from the Rosaleda gardens (in the Parque del Oeste) to the center of Casa de Campo in about 10 minutes. If you're feeling active, take a (very) long hike to the top and ride back into the city, or pause in Casa de Campo for primo picnicking.

■ **TIP→** This is not the best way to get to the zoo and theme park, located approximately 2 km (1 mile) from the drop-off point in Casa de Campo. You're better off riding the Teléferico out and back, then taking the bus to the zoo. ✉ *Estación Terminal Teleférico, Paseo de Pintor Rosales, at Calle Marqués de Urquijo, Moncloa* ☎ *91/541-1118* ⊕ *teleferico.emtmadrid.es* 🎫 *€6* Ⓜ *Argüelles.*

## 🍴 Restaurants

### Casa Mingo

**$ | SPANISH | FAMILY** | Madrid's oldest *sidrería* (cider house) is a grand, cathedral-like hall with barrel-lined walls, double-height ceilings, and creaky wooden chairs. The star menu item is roast chicken, hacked up unceremoniously and served in a puddle of cider jus—old-school bar food at its finest. **Known for:** a Madrid institution; roast chicken; Asturian cider. ⑤ *Average main: €16* ✉ *Paseo de la Florida 34, Moncloa* ☎ *91/547-7918* ⊕ *www.casamingo.es* Ⓜ *Príncipe Pío.*

### ⭐ Cuenllas

**$$$ | SPANISH** | Epitomizing old-world luxury, Cuenllas (KWEN-yas) is Moncloa's most venerable dining establishment, in business since 1939. After sitting down

at the bar or in the dining room for a meal of Spanish bistro fare (think warm saltcod brandade, Santoña anchovy canapés, and marinated partridge) accompanied by reserva wines, peruse the adjoining "Ultramarinos" gourmet shop for edible souvenirs including caviar, cheeses, wines, and homemade charcuterie. **Known for:** charmingly old-fashioned waiters; French-inflected Spanish dining; standout traditional wine list. ⑤ *Average main: €25* ✉ *Calle Ferraz 5, Moncloa* ☎ *91/559-1705* ⊕ *www.cuenllas.es* ⊘ *Closed Sun.* Ⓜ *Ventura Rodríguez.*

##  Hotels

### ⭐ Dear Hotel

**$$$ | HOTEL** | Catty-corner to Plaza de España, Dear Hotel is a sleek urban property designed by Tarruella Trenchs Studio, the firm behind such lauded projects as H10 La Mimosa hotel in Barcelona and La Bien Aparecida restaurant in Madrid. **Pros:** all rooms face out; Scandi-chic furnishings; swanky rooftop bar with 360-degree views. **Cons:** cramped lobby; no gym or spa; tiny pool. ⑤ *Rooms from: €186* ✉ *Gran Vía 80, Moncloa* ☎ *91/412-3200* ⊕ *www.dearhotelmadrid. com* 🛏 *162 rooms* ⑩ *No Meals* Ⓜ *Pl. de España.*

### Hotel Indigo Madrid – Princesa

**$$ | HOTEL** | This bright budget option opened in 2019 in the heart of residential Argüelles, steps from the bustling shopping street Calle Princesa. **Pros:** five-minute walk from Parque del Oeste; rain showers; cheery decor. **Cons:** bathrooms are basic; so-so breakfast; poor soundproofing. ⑤ *Rooms from: €135* ✉ *Calle del Marqués de Urquijo 4, Moncloa* ☎ *91/548-1900* ⊕ *www.ihg.com* 🛏 *101 rooms* ⑩ *No Meals* Ⓜ *Argüelles.*

# Chueca

Chueca, a subsection of Justicia district, is named after the Plaza de Chueca, which is in turn named after Federico Chueca, author and composer of *zarzuelas* (short musical plays). Today the neighborhood is Spain's most iconic LGBT+ quarter, its unofficial title since the 1980s, when the first gay bars arrived on the scene. Nowadays most young LGBT+ madrileños live and party elsewhere because of the barrio's soaring rents, tourist crowds, and increasingly older clientele, but for a fun, carefree, and rowdy night out, Chueca never disappoints regardless of your age or orientation. That said, the "gayborhood" has plenty of attractions beyond nightlife ranging from museums to pretty plazas to fantastic galleries and restaurants.

## ⊙ Sights

### Museo del Romanticismo (*Museum of Romanticism*)

HISTORY MUSEUM | To catch a glimpse of how the Spanish bourgeoisie lived in the early 19th century, step into this former palace of a marquis. Each room sparkles with ornate period furniture, evocative portraits, and other historical artifacts culled from the height of Spanish Romanticism. It's worth spending a few minutes admiring the flamboyantly decorated fans and backlit lithophanes. The museum can be seen in an hour or two, but don't rush out: the plant-filled interior patio is a lovely, tranquil place to enjoy tea and pastries. ⊠ *Calle de San Mateo 13, Chueca* ☏ *91/448–1045* ⊕ *www.culturaydeporte. gob.es/mromanticismo/en/inicio.html* ⛢ *€3. Free Sat. after 2 pm.* ⊙ *Closed Mon.* Ⓜ *Tribunal.*

### Mercado San Antón

MARKET | Chueca's neighborhood mercado has been reborn. In 2022, the three-floor complex underwent a massive renovation that gutted and revamped the second floor entirely and added 16 new stalls, the buzziest of which are Chuka Sando (katsu sandos made with real-deal shokupan bread) and an offshoot of the centennial Café Comercial. After browsing the more traditional grocery stalls on the ground floor, take the escalator up to the second for a rollicking *tapeo* (tapas crawl), or go up one additional floor to dine at Nudos, a sceney rooftop restaurant and bar owned by the folks behind the Spanish craft gin Nordés. ⊠ *Calle de Augusto Figueroa 24, Chueca* ☏ *91/330– 0730* ⊕ *www.mercadosananton.com.*

## 🍴 Restaurants

### Casa Hortensia Restaurante y Sidrería

$$ | SPANISH | FAMILY | Approximate a vacation to northern Spain by dining at this true-blue Asturian restaurant (or at the more casual sidrería in the bar area), where that region's unsung comfort-food dishes—such as *fabada* (pork-and-bean stew), Cabrales cheese, and *cachopo* (cheese-stuffed beef cutlets)—take center stage. The obligatory tipple is *sidra,* bone-dry Asturian cider that's aerated using a battery-powered gadget designed for this task. **Known for:** local crowd; cider bottles with fun DIY aerators; authentic fabada. ⓢ *Average main: €20* ⊠ *Calle Farmacia 2, 2nd and 3rd fl., Chueca* ✛ *Situated in what appears to be an apartment building* ☏ *91/539–0090* ⊕ *www.casahortensia.com* ⊙ *Closed Mon. No dinner Sun.* Ⓜ *Chueca.*

### ★ Casa Salvador

$$ | SPANISH | Whether you approve of bullfighting or not, the culinary excellence of Casa Salvador—a checkered-table-cloth, taurine-themed restaurant that opened in 1941—isn't up for debate. Sit down to generous servings of feather-light fried hake, hearty oxtail stew, and other stodgy (in the best way) Spanish classics, all served by hale old-school waiters clad in white jackets. **Known for:**

cloud-light fried hake and stewed oxtail; walls packed with bullfighting paraphernalia; time-warpy decor. $ *Average main: €20* ⊠ *Calle de Barbieri 12, Chueca* 🕾 *91/521–4524* ⊕ *www.casasalvadormadrid.com* ☽ *Closed Sun. No dinner Mon.* Ⓜ *Chueca.*

### Celso y Manolo

$$ | TAPAS | This hip neighborhood favorite has around a dozen tables and an extensive, eclectic menu geared toward sharing that features game meats, seafood, and cheeses from the mountainous northern region of Cantabria. Organic wines sourced from around the country make for spot-on pairings. **Known for:** varied menu; Cantabrian specialties; market-driven cuisine. $ *Average main: €19* ⊠ *Calle Libertad 1, Chueca* 🕾 *91/531–8079* ⊕ *www.celsoymanolo.es* Ⓜ *Chueca.*

### NaDo Madrid

$$$$ | SPANISH | In a converted brick-walled coal cellar that stretches like a subway tunnel behind an unmarked door is one of Madrid's buzziest restaurants. Galician chef Iván Domínguez coaxes exquisite ingredients from his home region—ocean-fresh cockles, horse mackerel, baby lágrima peas, crackly cornbread baked in cabbage leaves—into minimalist fine-dining fare that both surprises and satisfies. **Known for:** open kitchen puts you in the center of the action; creative riffs on traditional Galician cuisine; ultratrendy hotspot. $ *Average main: €50* ⊠ *Calle de Prim 5, Chueca* 🕾 *91/445–1208* ⊕ *www.nado.es* ☽ *Closed Mon. and Tues. No dinner Sun.* Ⓜ *Chueca.*

### ★ Roostiq

$$$ | EUROPEAN | Fire is the secret ingredient at Roostiq, where pizzas sizzle and puff in a wood-burning oven and meat, fish, and vegetables char until tender over white-hot embers. Even the cheesecake is of the Basque "burnt" variety, all brown and caramel-y on the outside and

gooey within. **Known for:** trendy industrial digs; 150 Champagnes to choose from; open-hearth roasts and pizzas. $ *Average main: €26* ⊠ *Calle de Augusto Figueroa 47, Chueca* 🕾 *91/853–2434* ⊕ *www.roostiqmadrid.com* ☽ *No dinner Sun.* Ⓜ *Chueca.*

## ☕ Coffee and Quick Bites

### ★ Faraday

$ | CAFÉ | Faraday is a chic little café known for its meticulously roasted beans, mathematically precise baristas, and gorgeous midcentury modern furniture. Laptops are allowed. **Known for:** excellent coffee; closed 2–4 pm; great music. $ *Average main: €5* ⊠ *Calle de San Lucas 9, Chueca* ⊕ *www.faraday-cafeteria.negocio.site* Ⓜ *Alonso Martínez, Chueca.*

## 🛏 Hotels

### ★ Only YOU Boutique Hotel

$$$$ | HOTEL | The Ibizan owners of this hotel bring that island's mix of glamour, energy, and cutting edge music and design to one of Madrid's most happening neighborhoods. **Pros:** outstanding tapas at Padrino bar; all-day breakfast; double-paned glass blocks out street noise. **Cons:** no bathtubs in some upgraded rooms; rooms above Calle Barquillo can be pricey; breakfast lacks quality and variety. $ *Rooms from: €255* ⊠ *Calle Barquillo 21, Chueca* 🕾 *91/005–2222* ⊕ *www.onlyyouhotels.com* ⇥ *125 rooms* ˮⓄˮ *No Meals* Ⓜ *Chueca.*

### The Principal Madrid

$$$$ | HOTEL | Dozens of hotels flank Gran Vía, Madrid's main artery, but the five-star Principal rises above the fray—and not just on account of its swanky rooftop cocktail bar. **Pros:** outdoor breakfasts and rooftop with 360-degree views; luxurious feel with personal touches; Ramón Freixa–helmed restaurant. **Cons:** middling breakfast; rooftop pool is tiny; rooms

## Chueca and Malasaña

### KEY
- **1** Sights
- **1** Restaurants
- **1** Quick Bites
- **1** Hotels

### Sights ▼
1 Mercado San Antón.... **D3**
2 Museo del Romanticismo ......... **D1**
3 Palacio de Liria ......... **A3**

### Restaurants ▼
1 Bar La Gloria ............. **A1**
2 Bodega de la Ardosa....**C2**
3 Casa Hortensia Restaurante y Sidrería ................... **D2**
4 Casa Macareno......... **B1**
5 Casa Salvador........... **D3**
6 Celso y Manolo ......... **D4**
7 La Colmada.............. **B1**
8 NaDo Madrid............. **E3**
9 Roostiq................... **E3**

### Quick Bites ▼
1 Faraday ................... **E2**
2 Misión Café.............. **C3**
3 Toma Café 1 .............. **C2**

### Hotels ▼
1 Only YOU Boutique Hotel ......... **E3**
2 The Principal Madrid... **D4**
3 URSO Hotel and Spa ... **D1**

not fully soundproofed. $ Rooms from: €433 ⊠ Calle Marqués de Valdeiglesias 1, Chueca ☎ 91/521–8743 ⊕ www.theprincipalmadridhotel.com ☞ /6 rooms ⏵⃝ No Meals Ⓜ Chueca.

### URSO Hotel and Spa

$$$$ | HOTEL | In a Neoclassical building so stunning that it was featured in Almodóvar's film *Parallel Mothers*, URSO boasts old-world comfort and avant-garde design to satisfy alternative types and jet-setters alike. **Pros:** stunning facade; calming rooms; Natura Bissé spa with 7-meter hydromassage pool. **Cons:** smallish gym and chilly pool; entry-level rooms are dark and cramped; bar closes at midnight. $ *Rooms from: €320* ⊠ Calle de Mejía Lequerica 8, Chueca ☎ 91/444–4458 ⊕ www.hotelurso.com ☞ 78 rooms ⏵⃝ No Meals Ⓜ Alonso Martínez, Tribunal.

## 🎧 Nightlife

Most of Chueca's LGBT+-oriented venues—including all of those listed below—are welcoming to customers of all genders and sexual orientations.

### BARS

#### Café Belén

CAFÉS | The handful of tables at this rootsy bar are rarely empty on weekends, thanks to the candlelit, cozy atmosphere and picture windows that open in summer. Expect a young, mixed crowd. Weeknights are more mellow. ⊠ Calle Belén 5, Chueca ☎ 91/308–2747 ⊕ www.elcafebelen.com ⊘ Closed Mon. Ⓜ Chueca.

#### Del Diego

COCKTAIL LOUNGES | There are no fripperies of modern mixology to be found at Del Diego, and that's just how the dyed-in-the-wool regulars like it. This legendary bar has been pouring flawless classic cocktails like dirty martinis and white Russians since the late 1990s, and amigos, you'd better believe they're all that

and a bag of chips. ⊠ Calle de la Reina 12, Chueca ☎ 91/523–3106 ⊕ www.deldiego.com ⊘ Closed Sun. and Mon. Ⓜ Gran Vía.

### ★ Macera Taller Bar

COCKTAIL LOUNGES | The age-old technique of maceration rules at Macera, where bartenders treat spirits like blank canvases, imbuing them with surprising flavor combinations. Gin is steeped with fresh cilantro, lime, and jalapeño until it achieves a zippy grassy piquancy. Whiskey might be infused with almonds, fresh cherries, mint, or vanilla bean. ■TIP→ There's a second, clubbier outpost on Calle Ventura de la Vega 7 in Barrio de Las Letras. ⊠ Calle San Mateo 21, Chueca ☎ 91/011–5810 ⊕ www.maceradrinks.com Ⓜ Alonso Martínez, Tribunal.

### Vinoteca Vides

WINE BARS | This dressed-down wine bar is a great spot to sample classically styled Spanish wines at a terrific price. There's a particularly deep selection of grippy *monastrells*, a dark, high-alcohol grape ubiquitous in southern Spain. ⊠ Calle Libertad 12, Chueca ☎ 91/531–8444 ⊕ www.vinotecavides.es Ⓜ Chueca.

## DANCE CLUBS

### Fulanita de Tal

DANCE CLUBS | Chueca's favorite lesbian bar hosts popular concerts and dusk-to-3:30 am dance parties in an intimate, unpretentious space. The music varies night to night and mixes pop, oldies, reggaeton, and electro. ⊠ Calle de Regueros 9, Chueca ☎ 91/319–5069 ⊕ www.fulanitadetal.es ⊘ Closed Mon.–Wed. Ⓜ Alonso Martínez, Chueca.

### ★ Pavoneo

BARS | One of Chueca's buzziest new gay bars, Pavoneo caters to well-dressed creatives, selfie-snapping influencers, and models on their nights off. The bartenders may not know what a Negroni is—even if they have all the requisite ingredients—but mira, you came for the scene, not for the mixology. ⊠ *Calle de Belén 9, Chueca* ☎ *64/679–6485* ⊙ *Closed Sun.–Wed.* Ⓜ *Chueca.*

## MUSIC CLUBS

### Café Libertad 8

**LIVE MUSIC** | Almost every classic madrileño songwriter, musician, and poet has passed through this timeworn hangout, which opens at 3:30 pm (entertainment starts at 9). Acoustic guitar concerts priced at less than €10 a head are fantastic—and virtually tourist-free. ⊠ *Calle de la Libertad 8, Chueca* ☎ *91/532–1150* ⊕ *www.libertad8cafe.com* Ⓜ *Chueca.*

### Intruso Bar

**LIVE MUSIC** | Easy to miss (it's tucked inside a building just a block off Fuencarral), this is one of Chueca's best lounge-bars, and it's open until past 5 am nightly. There are live DJs and funk and jazz bands starting around 9; expect a mixed-age crowd. ⊠ *Calle Augusto Figueroa 3, Chueca* ⊕ *www.intrusobar.com* Ⓜ *Chueca.*

### Museo Chicote

**LIVE MUSIC** | This landmark cocktail bar–lounge is said to have been one of Hemingway's haunts, and much of the interior can be traced to the 1930s, but modern elements (like the in-house DJ and hordes of international visitors) keep this spot firmly in the present. ⊠ *Gran Vía 12, Chueca* ☎ *91/532–6737* ⊕ *www.museochicote.com* Ⓜ *Gran Vía.*

## 🛍 Shopping

### BOUTIQUES AND FASHION

#### Mans Concept

**MEN'S CLOTHING** | Owned by Andalusian fashion wunderkind Jaime Álvarez, this is Madrid's most cutting-edge made-to-measure menswear boutique. Ready-made clothes are also available in the shop and online. ⊠ *Calle San Bernardino 15, Chueca* ⊕ *www.mansconceptmenswear.com* ⊙ *Closed weekends* Ⓜ *Alonso Martínez, Chueca.*

#### Oteyza

**MIXED CLOTHING** | Every garment sold at master tailor Oteyza takes at least two months to make, and the classic craftsmanship shows in the immaculate suits, jackets, and shirts. Get fitted while you're in Madrid and pony up the euros for shipping—you won't regret it. ⊠ *Calle Conde de Xiquena 11, Chueca* ☎ *91/448–8623* ⊕ *www.deoteyza.com* ⊙ *Closed Sun.* Ⓜ *Chueca.*

#### ★ Pez

**HOUSEWARES** | A favorite among local fashionistas, this store has two branches—one dedicated to high-end women's wear and another to furniture and decor—on the same street. ⊠ *Calle de Regueros 2 and 15, Chueca* ☎ *91/308–6677* ⊕ *www.pez-pez.es* ⊙ *Closed Sun.* Ⓜ *Chueca.*

#### Próxima Parada

**WOMEN'S CLOTHING** | The bubbly owner of this womenswear store culls daring, colorful garments from Spanish designers for her devoted (mostly 40-and-above) clientele. ⊠ *Calle Conde de Xiquena 9, Chueca* ☎ *91/523–1929* ⊕ *www.facebook.com/tiendaproximaparada* ⊙ *Closed Sun.* Ⓜ *Chueca.*

### CERAMICS

#### Guille García-Hoz

**CERAMICS** | This renowned ceramicist is known for painted plates and gleaming white urns decorated with animal motifs. ⊠ *Calle de Génova 4, 5th fl., ext. derecha, Chueca* ☎ *91/308–3149* ⊕ *www.guillegarciahoz.com* ⊙ *Closed weekends* Ⓜ *Chueca.*

### FOOD AND WINE

#### La Productería

**FOOD** | You'll find organic local cheeses, gourmet tinned food, charcuterie, and natural wine at this pocket-size shop. ⊠ *Calle de Barbieri 21, Chueca* ☎ *60/835–7175* ⊕ *www.laproducteria. com* ⊘ *Closed Sun. and Mon.* Ⓜ *Chueca.*

### Poncelet Cheese Bar

**FOOD** | At this gourmet cheese bar and shop, you can find more than 120 different cheeses from all over Spain as well as some 300 others. Marmalades, wines, and other assorted cheese accompaniments are available. ⊠ *Calle de Argensola 27, Chueca* ☎ *91/308–0221* ⊕ *www. poncelet.es* ⊘ *Closed Mon. and Tues.* Ⓜ *Alonso Martínez.*

# Malasaña

Malasaña has a youthful, off-beat pulse rivaled only, perhaps, by Lavapiés, its more multicultural counterpart. Formerly called Barrio de las Maravillas, the neighborhood is centered on Plaza de Dos de Mayo, which commemorates the May 2 uprising against French occupation in 1808. Manuela Malasaña, for whom the barrio is named, was a martyr in the conflict. In the 19th century, the neighborhood was a hotbed of early Spanish feminism with such legendary residents as Carmen de Burgos, Rosalía de Castro, and Emelia Pardo Bazán. At the end of the 20th century, Malasaña emerged once again as a countercultural mecca amidst the cathartic post-Franco social movement called the Movida Madrileña; its rough-and-ready streets featured prominently in pop culture thanks to music and film icons like Alaska, Mecano, Hombres G, and Pedro Almodóvar. These days the neighborhood is cleaner and less rambunctious than it was in its rakish heyday, thanks to massive waves of gentrification in the 2000s and 2010s, but its rebellious spirit lives on—just drop in on Plaza de Dos de Mayo any weekend night, and you'll find crowds of locals partying gleefully while flouting open container laws.

## ◉ Sights

### Palacio de Liria (*Liria Palace*)

**HISTORIC HOME** | In 2019, this working palace belonging to the House of Alba, one of Spain's most powerful noble families, formally opened to the public. Its sumptuous halls and creaky passages are hung with works selected from what many consider to be Spain's finest private art collection—you'll spot Titians, Rubens, Velázquezes, and other instantly recognizable paintings. In the library, Columbus's diaries from his voyage to the New World are on display as well as the first Spanish-language Bible and other priceless official documents. The Neoclassical palace was built in the 18th century but was bombed during the Spanish Civil War (only the facade survived), its works thankfully safeguarded during the conflict. The Duchess of Alba oversaw the reconstruction of the palace to its precise original specifications. ■**TIP**→ **Visits are by tour only, but if online tickets are sold out, try your luck as a walk-in.** ⊠ *Calle de la Princesa 20, Malasaña* ☎ *91/230–2200* ⊕ *www.palaciodeliria. com* ⊠ *€15 (includes tour)* Ⓜ *Ventura Rodríguez.*

## ◉ Restaurants

### Bar La Gloria

**$ | SPANISH | FAMILY** | Your reward for overlooking the soulless IKEA furnishings of this family-run dinette is honest home-cooked food served at exceptionally reasonable prices for the neighborhood. Try Cordoban-style *flamenquines* (ham-and-cheese-stuffed pork), salmon tartare, or (on Sunday) a crave-worthy paella Valenciana. **Known for:** local crowd; Sunday paella; budget weekday prix fixes. ⑤ *Average main: €15* ⊠ *Calle del Noviciado 2, Malasaña* ☎ *91/083–1401* ⊕ *www.barlagloria.es* ⊘ *Closed Mon. No dinner Sun.* Ⓜ *Noviciado.*

### ★ Bodega de la Ardosa

$$ | SPANISH | A 19th-century *bodega* (wine vendor), with barrel tables and dusty gewgaws hanging from the walls, Bodega de la Ardosa is a welcome anachronism in modern Malasaña and a tourist magnet for good reason. The bar's claim to fame—and the dish madrileños make special trips for—is its award-winning *tortilla española,* or Spanish omelet, always warm with a runny center. **Known for:** draft vermú and unfiltered sherry "en rama"; tortilla española; 100-plus years of history. $ *Average main: €17* ⊠ *Calle Colón 13, Malasaña* ☎ *91/521–4979* ⊕ *www.laardosa.es* Ⓜ *Tribunal.*

### ★ Casa Macareno

$$ | TAPAS | FAMILY | Whether you pull up a stool at at the marble bar or sit down for a soup-to-nuts feast in the azulejo-lined dining room, you're in for some of Madrid's finest traditional tapas with a twist here. Madrileños come from far and wide to share heaped plates of *ensaladilla rusa* (tuna-flecked potato salad), a house specialty, as well as textbook-perfect croquetas and hefty steaks served with sherry gravy and house-cut fries. **Known for:** over-and-above service; dependably exceptional old-school tapas; hidden gem in Malasaña. $ *Average main: €18* ⊠ *Calle de San Vicente Ferrer 44, Malasaña* ☎ *91/166–0921* ⊕ *www.casamacareno.com* Ⓜ *Tribunal, Noviciado.*

### La Colmada

$ | TAPAS | The first thing you'll notice about this teeny seafood-centric tapas bar is its bright blue walls, a nod to the sea. Sure, you could cobble together a full meal from the menu of delectable cheeses, cured sausages, hams, and *conservas* (canned seafood; seek out La Pureza and Ana María brands), but La Colmada is better suited to casual, booze-fueled snacking. **Known for:** affordable Spanish wines; jovial atmosphere; top-quality canned delicacies. $ *Average main: €11* ⊠ *Calle del Espíritu Santo 19,* *Malasaña* ☎ *91/017–6579* ⊕ *www.lacolmada.com* ◔ *Closed Sun.* Ⓜ *Tribunal.*

## ☕ Coffee and Quick Bites

### ★ Misión Café

$ | CAFÉ | From the owners of Hola Coffee, Madrid's preeminent third-wave coffee shop, comes this über-trendy, roomier outpost two blocks from Gran Vía. Beyond the single-origin espressos and other classics made from roasted-in-house beans, there are warming chai lattes, shrubs, and (seasonal) cold brew. **Known for:** cool-kid hangout; killer pastries; complex brews made with roasted-in-Madrid beans. $ *Average main: €11* ⊠ *Calle de los Reyes 5, Malasaña* ☎ *91/064–0059* ⊕ *www.mision.cafe* Ⓜ *Noviciado, Plaza de España.*

### Toma Café 1

$ | CAFÉ | The originator of Madrid's third-wave coffee revolution, Toma—with two other locations in Chamberí (Toma Café Olavide and Proper Sound)—is a favorite among expats and local coffee geeks. After satisfying your cold brew, flat white, or pour-over cravings in the newly renovated digs, indulge in any of the delicious open-face tostas. **Known for:** major expat hangout; always busy; excellent coffee selection. $ *Average main: €10* ⊠ *Calle de la Palma 49, Malasaña* ☎ *91/704–9344* ⊕ *www.tomacafe.es* Ⓜ *Noviciado.*

## 🌙 Nightlife

### BARS

### V Manneken

BARS | V Manneken is downright debonair. Cut-glass decanters filled with scotch sit on the marble bar top; gold-framed oil paintings accent the walls; and yellowed, out-of-print books sit on tables for you to thumb through while sipping staunchly classic cocktails like Cream Fizzes, Last Words, and Tom Collinses. ⊠ *Calle Marqués de Sta. Ana 30, Malasaña* ☎ *61/564–2480* ◔ *Closed Sun. and Mon.* Ⓜ *Tribunal.*

## DANCE CLUBS
### Café La Palma
DANCE CLUBS | This feel-good nightclub with a bar, chill-out area, and medium-size dance floor draws a mixed-age, LGBT+-friendly crowd with live performances and DJ sets that rage until 6 am. ⊠ *Calle de la Palma 62, Malasaña* ☎ *91/522–5031* ⊕ *www.cafelapalma.com* ⊘ *Closed Mon. and Tues.* Ⓜ *Noviciado.*

### Tupper Ware
DANCE CLUBS | Throw on a graphic tee and a pair of ripped jeans and fist-pump the night away at this alternative rock and indie bar that blasts throwback cult classics till 3 am daily. ⊠ *Corredera Alta de San Pablo 26, Malasaña* ☎ *91/446–4204* Ⓜ *Tribunal.*

## 🛍 Shopping

### BOUTIQUES AND FASHION
### Sportivo
MEN'S CLOTHING | Time to bust out the big bucks—Sportivo is one of the best menswear boutiques in the city, with two floors of hand-picked garments by the buzziest designers out of Spain, France, Japan, and beyond. ⊠ *Calle Conde Duque 20, Malasaña* ☎ *91/542–5661* ⊕ *www.sportivostore.com.*

# Barrio de las Letras

Barrio de las Letras (just "Letras" to locals) is known for its charming balconied buildings and electric restaurant and bar scene. It's named for the writers and playwrights of the Spanish Golden Age who lived here. Once a *castizo* (Madrid jargon for "old-school") part of town, Letras is now packed with well-to-do tourists and Madrid's nouveau riche. In short, it's a *scene.*

Letras is a historical (read: unofficial) neighborhood that technically belongs to the district of Cortes, but madrileños use its colloquial, more descriptive name. At the heart of the barrio is Plaza de Santa Ana with its noble buildings, iconic theater, and crowded tapas bars, though you'll see more locals wining and dining on and around the pedestrianized Calle de Huertas. As you explore, remember to look down—sidewalks here bear quotes in bronze from the neighborhood's one-time denizens—Quevedo, Góngora, Lope de Vega, and Cervantes, to name a few.

## 👁 Sights

### CaixaForum
ART MUSEUM | Swiss architects Jacques Herzog and Pierre de Meuron (who designed London's Tate Modern) converted an early-20th-century power station into a stunning arts complex that arguably turns Madrid's "Golden Triangle" of art museums into a quadrilateral. Belonging to one of the country's wealthiest foundations (La Caixa bank), the structure seems to float above the sloped public plaza, with a tall vertical garden designed by French botanist Patrick Blanc on its northern side contrasting with a geometric rust-color roof. Inside, the soaring exhibition halls display ancient as well as contemporary art including pieces from La Caixa's proprietary collection. ⊠ *Paseo del Prado 36, Barrio de las Letras* ☎ *91/330–7300* ⊕ *www.caixaforum.es* 💷 *€6* Ⓜ *Estación del Arte.*

### ★ Museo Thyssen-Bornemisza
ART MUSEUM | The far-reaching collection of the Thyssen's almost 1,000 paintings traces the history of Western art with examples from every important movement, from 13th-century Italian Gothic through 20th-century American pop art. The works were gathered from the 1920s to the 1980s by Swiss industrialist Baron Hans Heinrich Thyssen-Bornemisza and his father. The museum, opened in 1992, occupies the spacious late-18th-century Villahermosa Palace. The baron donated the entire collection

## Barrio de las Letras

### Sights ▼

1 CaixaForum............... **E5**
2 Museo
Thyssen-Bornemisza... **D2**
3 Plaza de Santa Ana..... **B3**

### Restaurants ▼

1 Amano ................... **B3**
2 Casa González ........... **C3**
3 El Barril de las Letras.... **C3**
4 Gofio..................... **C3**
5 La Dolores ............... **D3**
6 La Sanabresa ............ **C4**
7 Taberna La Elisa ........ **D4**
8 Triciclo .................. **D4**
9 Vinoteca Moratín ....... **D4**

### Quick Bites ▼

1 Chocolat Madrid........ **D4**

### Hotels ▼

1 Catalonia
Puerta del Sol .......... **A3**
2 DoubleTree by Hilton
Madrid-Prado............ **C2**
3 Gran Hotel Inglés ....... **B2**
4 Hotel Catalonia
Las Cortes .............. **B3**
5 Hotel Urban.............. **C2**
6 ME Madrid
Reina Victoria .......... **B3**
7 NH Collection Madrid
Suecia.................... **D1**
8 NH Collection
Paseo del Prado ........ **D3**
9 Urban Sea
Atocha 113.............. **D5**
10 Westin Palace .......... **D2**

to Spain in 1993, and a subsequent renovation added the baroness's personal collection (considered of lesser quality). One could argue that the Thyssen boasts mostly minor works from major artists and major works from minor artists—even still, the collection traces the development of Western humanism as no other in the world. It includes works by Hans Holbein, Gilbert Stuart, and many Impressionists and Postimpressionists, plus a number of German Expressionist paintings. In summer, the rooftop terrace (closed Mondays; accessible via a separate entrance on Calle Zorrilla) is an appealing place to unwind with a coffee or cocktail. ■TIP➔ **To enter the museum for free (Mondays only), you must reserve online ahead of time.** ⊠ *Paseo del Prado 8, Barrio de las Letras* ☎ *91/369-0151* ⊕ *www.museothyssen.org* ✉ *€13 (free Mon.)* Ⓜ *Banco de España.*

**Plaza de Santa Ana**

PLAZA/SQUARE | This plaza was the heart of the theater district in the 17th century—the Golden Age of Spanish literature—and is now one of Madrid's most happening nightlife centers. A statue of 17th-century playwright Pedro Calderón de la Barca faces the Teatro Español, where other literary legends such as Lope de Vega, Tirso de Molina, and Ramón del Valle-Inclán released some of their world-renowned plays. Opposite the theater, beside the ME by Meliá hotel, is the diminutive Plaza del Ángel, with one of Madrid's best jazz clubs, Café Central. Cervecería Alemana, a favorite haunt of Hemingway, is on the southeast corner and makes phenomenally tender fried calamari. ⊠ *Barrio de las Letras* Ⓜ *Sol, Sevilla.*

 **Restaurants**

**Amano**

$$ | TAPAS | "A mano" means "by hand" in Spanish, and lest this experimental white-walled tapas and wine bar come

across as pretentious, there's an entire section of the menu devoted to finger food. Whet your appetite with one-bite wonders like fried eggplant drizzled with honey and garlicky *salmorejo* (a cold tomato soup), then settle in for heftier plates like stewed oxtail, which basically melts on fork impact. **Known for:** stylish minimalist interiors; varied wine list with French selections; innovative vegetable-driven tapas. ⑤ *Average main: €22* ⊠ *Pl. de Matute 4, Barrio de las Letras* ☎ *91/527-7970* ⊕ *www.amanorest.com* ⊘ *Closed Mon. and Tue.* Ⓜ *Antón Martín.*

★ **Casa González**

$ | SPANISH | This gourmet shop (est. 1931) doubles as a cozy bar where you can sample most of the stuff on the shelves including canned asparagus, charcuterie, anchovies, and a varied, well-priced selection of Spanish cheeses and wines. It also serves good, inexpensive breakfasts. **Known for:** quaint setting; delectable sobrassada-honey toast; regional wines and cheeses. ⑤ *Average main: €9* ⊠ *Calle León 12, Barrio de las Letras* ☎ *91/429 5618* ⊕ *www.casagonzalez.es* Ⓜ *Antón Martín.*

**El Barril de las Letras**

$$$ | SEAFOOD | Seafood lovers shouldn't miss this modern, Ibiza-chic marisquería with original wrought-iron columns, white tablecloths, and ample alfresco seating. The griddled prawns from Dénia are always a treat, as is the cloudlike roasted sole and any number of rice dishes. **Known for:** outdoor dining; impeccable seafood; romantic ambience. ⑤ *Average main: €25* ⊠ *Calle de Cervantes 28, Barrio de las Letras* ☎ *91/186-3632* ⊕ *www.barrildelasletras.com* Ⓜ *Antón Martín.*

**Gofio**

$$$$ | FUSION | Savor a rare taste of Canary Island cuisine—with quite a few twists—at this envelope pushing restaurant helmed by Tenerife-born chef Safe Cruz that was awarded a Michelin star in 2019. Expect foaming, smoking concoctions

The vertical outdoor garden is a stunning element of the CaixaForum cultural center. The sculpture in front of the building is changed periodically.

that incorporate traditional Canarian specialties like green *mojo* (cilantro-parsley sauce), Gomero goat cheese, and—of course—gofio (stoneground cornflour). **Known for:** gorgeous, uncontrived plating; smoky volcanic wines; Canarian "fusion". ⑤ *Average main: €65* ⊠ *Calle Lope de Vega 9, Barrio de las Letras* ☎ *91/599–4404* ⊕ *www.gofiorestaurant. com* ⊘ *Closed Mon. and Tues.* Ⓜ *Antón Martín.*

### La Dolores
$ | TAPAS | A lively corner bar (established in 1908) with a colorful trencadís-tiled facade, this is a solid spot for a cold beer and a nosh after visiting the nearby museums. Try the *matrimonio* ("marriage") tapa, which weds one pickled and one cured anchovy on a slice of crusty baguette. **Known for:** mixed crowd of foreigners and locals; refreshing cañas; affordable no-nonsense tapas. ⑤ *Average main: €12* ⊠ *Pl. de Jesús 4, Barrio de las Letras* ☎ *91/429–2243* Ⓜ *Antón Martín.*

### La Sanabresa
$ | SPANISH | FAMILY | Most budget prix fixes in Madrid are limited to lunch, but La Sanabresa offers a budget three-course dinner as well. Choose from a menu of over 20 appetizers and over 40 entrées that reads like a highlight reel of grandmotherly Spanish cuisine: gazpacho, ensaladilla rusa, fried anchovies, chicken cutlets, and on and on. **Known for:** satisfying soups and stews; trusty traditional holdout in a gentrified area; prix fixes are a steal. ⑤ *Average main: €12* ⊠ *Calle del Amor de Dios 12, Barrio de las Letras* ☎ *91/429–0338* ⊘ *Closed Sun.* Ⓜ *Antón Martín.*

### ★ Taberna La Elisa
$$ | TAPAS | The old-fashioned azulejo walls, painted red facade, and squat wooden barstools might fool you into thinking this newcomer is any old tavern, but behind the swinging door, cooks are busy plating novel takes on tapas that you didn't know needed improving. Take the crispy pig ear, doused in the usual

spicy brava sauce—It gets an unorthodox hit of freshness from tarragon-packed mojo verde. **Known for:** trendy crowd; Andalusian-style decor; flavor-bomb tapas. $ *Average main: €23* ✉ *Calle de Santa María 42, Barrio de las Letras* ☎ *91/421-6409* ⊕ *www.eltriciclo.es/la-elisa* Ⓜ *Antón Martín.*

### Triciclo

$$$ | TAPAS | Triciclo serves inventive Spanish-style bistronomie—think baby Asturian favas with mushrooms and seaweed and spot prawn ravioli with saffron and borage. This may be the only restaurant in town that serves raciones in one-third portions as well as half and full ones—ideal for creating your own tasting menu whether at the bar or in the dining room. **Known for:** excellent service; top-quality ingredients; tapas with a modern twist. $ *Average main: €27* ✉ *Calle Santa María 28, Barrio de las Letras* ☎ *91/024-4798* ⊕ *www.eltriciclo.co* ☾ *Closed Sun.* Ⓜ *Antón Martín.*

### ★ Vinoteca Moratín

$$ | SPANISH | You'd be hard-pressed to find a more romantic restaurant than this snug wine bar with a rotating menu of a dozen or so dishes and eclectic Spanish wines. Antique wooden tables are tucked among bookshelves and wine cabinets, and fresh flowers grace the entryway and wait stations. **Known for:** intimate ambience; seasonal bistro fare; Spanish wine list with quirky small-production bottles. $ *Average main: €18* ✉ *Calle de Moratín 36, Barrio de las Letras* ☎ *91/127-6085* ⊕ *www.vinotecamoratin.com* ☾ *Closed Sun.* Ⓜ *Antón Martín.*

## ☕ Coffee and Quick Bites

### ★ Chocolat Madrid

$ | CAFÉ | FAMILY | Always crisp and never greasy—that's the mark of a well-made churro, and Madrid Chocolat's piping-hot baskets of fried dough always hit the spot. **Known for:** bright and comfortable dining area; city's best churros; terrific grilled ham-and-cheese sandwiches to boot. $ *Average main: €6* ✉ *Calle de Santa María 30, Barrio de las Letras* ⊕ *www.chocolatmadrid.com* Ⓜ *Antón Martín.*

## 🛏 Hotels

### Catalonia Puerta del Sol

$$ | HOTEL | The regal cobblestone corridor leading to the reception desk, the atrium with granite ashlar walls, and the magnificent wooden staircase (presided over by a lion statue) reveal this building's 18th-century origins. **Pros:** grand, quiet building; generous breakfast bar; spacious rooms. **Cons:** smoking permitted in the courtyard; rooms are slightly dated; rather uncharming street. $ *Rooms from: €145* ✉ *Calle de Atocha 23, Barrio de las Letras* ☎ *91/369-7171* ⊕ *www.hoteles-catalonia.es* ⛌ *63 rooms* ⦿ *No Meals* Ⓜ *Tirso de Molina.*

### DoubleTree by Hilton Madrid-Prado

$$$$ | HOTEL | This DoubleTree may appear corporate, but any stuffiness is mitigated by a warm staff eager to help with every need. **Pros:** relaxing earth-tone accents; one of the city's best Japanese restaurants; excellent in-room amenities. **Cons:** no sense of place; dull bar; no valet parking. $ *Rooms from: €264* ✉ *Calle de San Agustín 3, Barrio de las Letras* ☎ *91/360-0820* ⊕ *www.hilton.com* ⛌ *61 rooms* ⦿ *No Meals* Ⓜ *Antón Martín.*

### Gran Hotel Inglés

$$$$ | HOTEL | This legendary hotel, inaugurated in 1853, is the oldest in Madrid—and after a long, painstaking renovation by Rockwell Group, it reopened in 2018 to great fanfare. **Pros:** one of the city's most iconic hotels; made-to-order breakfasts featuring artisanal Spanish products; magazine-cover-worthy design. **Cons:** occasional street noise; phenomenally expensive; disappointing Casa Lobo restaurant. $ *Rooms from: €765* ✉ *Calle Echegaray 8, Barrio de las Letras*

🕾 *91/360–0001* ⊕ *www.granhotelingles.
com* ⤻ *48 rooms* ¶◎¶ *No Meals* Ⓜ *Sevilla.*

## Hotel Catalonia Las Cortes

**$$$** | **HOTEL** | In a late-18th-century palace
formerly owned by the Duke of Noblejas,
this hotel, a few yards from Plaza de
Santa Ana, still bears traces of opulence
and grandeur. **Pros:** blissfully underpriced;
gorgeous architectural details; big walk-in
showers. **Cons:** no bar; no gym, pool,
or spa; common areas are rather dull.
⑤ *Rooms from: €180* ⊠ *Calle del Prado
6, Barrio de las Letras* 🕾 *91/389–6051*
⊕ *www.cataloniahotels.com/en/hotel/
catalonia-las-cortes* ⤻ *74 rooms* ¶◎¶ *No
Meals* Ⓜ *Sevilla, Antón Martín.*

## Hotel Urban

**$$$$** | **HOTEL** | A five-minute walk from
Puerta del Sol and the Retiro, Hotel
Urban blends buttoned-up business
aesthetics with tropical accents in the
form of Papua New Guinean artifacts and
other rare museum-grade works. **Pros:**
stellar à la carte breakfasts; celebrity chef
restaurant; roof deck that's a destination
in itself. **Cons:** early-aughts interiors in
desperate need of renovation; tiny gym
with no treadmill; smallish rooms with
so-so soundproofing. ⑤ *Rooms from:
€275* ⊠ *Carrera de San Jerónimo 34, Barrio de las Letras* 🕾 *91/787–7770* ⊕ *www.
derbyhotels.com* ⤻ *103 rooms* ¶◎¶ *No
Meals* Ⓜ *Sevilla.*

## ★ ME Madrid Reina Victoria

**$$$** | **HOTEL** | In an unbeatable location,
this historic hotel used to play host to
visiting bullfighters (hence the bulls'
heads hanging in the lounge), but it's
decidedly more hip these days under the
management of Meliá's youthful subdivi-
sion, ME. **Pros:** cool, clubby vibe; rooftop
bar with great views of city; unbeatable
location. **Cons:** key cards demagnetize
easily; plaza-facing rooms can be noisy;
some rooms are cramped. ⑤ *Rooms
from: €195* ⊠ *Pl. Santa Ana 14, Barrio de
las Letras* 🕾 *91/531–4500* ⊕ *www.melia.
com* ⤻ *192 rooms* ¶◎¶ *No Meals* Ⓜ *Sol.*

## NH Collection Madrid Suecia

**$$$** | **HOTEL** | The building housing the NH
Collection Madrid Suecia was once home
to Ernest Hemingway and Che Guevara;
today's guests are decidedly tamer,
but the retro aesthetic lives on in the
hotel's brown velvet couches, towering
tropical plants, and suave concierges.
**Pros:** renovated rooms; nine-minute walk
from Prado Museum; rooftop bar with
great views. **Cons:** overpriced restaurant;
windowless gym; robes and slippers not
provided in entry-level rooms. ⑤ *Rooms
from: €220* ⊠ *Calle del Marqués de Casa
Riera 4, Barrio de las Letras* 🕾 *91/200–
0570* ⊕ *www.nh-hotels.com* ⤻ *123
rooms* ¶◎¶ *No Meals* Ⓜ *Banco de España.*

## NH Collection Paseo del Prado

**$$$** | **HOTEL** | In a turn-of-the-20th-century
palace overlooking Plaza de Neptuno, this
hotel preserves the building's erstwhile
grandeur with wooden headboards, gold-
tramed mirrors, tutted sofas, and wing
chairs. **Pros:** within the Golden Triangle
of museums; "lazy Sunday checkout" at
3 pm; gym with panoramic views. **Cons:**
uninspiring interiors; inconsistent food
at Estado Puro; need to upgrade to get
good views. ⑤ *Rooms from: €216* ⊠ *Pl.
Cánovas del Castillo 4, Barrio de las Letras* 🕾 *91/330–2400* ⊕ *www.nh-hoteles.
com* ⤻ *115 rooms* ¶◎¶ *No Meals* Ⓜ *Banco
de España.*

## Urban Sea Atocha 113

**$** | **HOTEL** | A metropolitan outpost of the
Blue Sea resort chain, Urban Sea Atocha
113 is a basic 36-room hotel just north
of the eponymous railway station. **Pros:**
equidistant between Barrio de las Letras
and Lavapiés; single rooms ideal for solo
travelers; complimentary 24-hour coffee
in lobby. **Cons:** exterior rooms facing Calle
Atocha are noisy and pricey; in-room
sinks and bathrooms with no doors
in some rooms; bare-bones services.
⑤ *Rooms from: €124* ⊠ *Calle Atocha
113, Barrio de las Letras* 🕾 *91/369–2895*
⊕ *www.blueseahotels.com* ⤻ *36 rooms*
¶◎¶ *No Meals* Ⓜ *Estación del Arte.*

## Westin Palace

$$$$ | **HOTEL** | Situated inside the "Golden Triangle," the Westin Palace is known for its unbeatable location, stately facade, and classical decor. **Pros:** historic grand hotel; rooms have USB ports and antifog mirrors; 24-hour gym with adjoining roof deck. **Cons:** last renovation won't meet design lovers' expectations; overpriced; standard rooms face a backstreet. ⑤ *Rooms from: €312* ⊠ *Pl. de las Cortés 7, Barrio de las Letras* ☎ *91/360–8000* ⊕ *www.palacemadrid.com* ↩ *467 rooms* ⏽⏽ *No Meals* Ⓜ *Banco de España, Sevilla.*

# ▼ Nightlife

## BARS

### La Venencia

**WINE BARS** | This dusty sherry-only bar hasn't changed a lick since the Spanish Civil War, from its no-tipping policy to its salty waiters to its chalked bar tabs. The establishment is named for the tool used to extract sherry through the bunghole of a barrel.

⚠ **No photography allowed.** ⊠ *Calle de Echegaray 7, Barrio de las Letras* ☎ *91/429–7313* Ⓜ *Sol.*

### ★ Salmon Guru

**COCKTAIL LOUNGES** | Regularly featured on best-of lists, Salmon Guru is Madrid's— and perhaps Spain's—most innovative coctelería. Come here to impress and to geek out over eye-popping concoctions like the Chipotle Chillón, made with mezcal, absinthe, and chipotle syrup. The *nueva cocina* tapas are almost as impressive as the drinks. ⊠ *Calle de Echegaray 21, Barrio de las Letras* ☎ *91/000–6185* ⊕ *www.salmonguru.es* ☉ *Closed Mon.* Ⓜ *Antón Martín.*

### Viva Madrid

**COCKTAIL LOUNGES** | The Argentine celebrity mixologist behind the bar Salmon Guru has converted one of Madrid's oldest tabernas, built in 1856, into a see-and-be-seen cocktail hot spot. The building's architectural bones remain, from the carved-wood bar to the arched doorways to the tiled walls, but the rest, particularly the flamboyantly garnished drinks and well-dressed crowd they attract, feels distinctly current. ⊠ *Calle Manuel Fernández y González 7, Barrio de las Letras* ☎ *91/605–9774* ⊕ *www.restaurantevivamadrid.com* Ⓜ *Sevilla, Antón Martín.*

## DANCE CLUBS

### Discoteca Azúcar

**DANCE CLUBS** | Salsa dancing is a fixture of Madrid nightlife. Even if you don't have the guts to twirl and shake with the pros on the dance floor, you'll be almost as entertained sipping a mojito on the sidelines. Entry with two cocktail vouchers costs €12. ⊠ *Calle de Atocha 107, Barrio de las Letras* ☎ *91/429–6208* ⊕ *www.azucarsalsadisco.com* ☉ *Closed Sun.–Wed.* Ⓜ *Estación del Arte.*

### Independance Club

**DANCE CLUBS** | Your favorite underground European artist has likely played at this perennially packed venue with a large subterranean dance floor and good sound and lights. Check the website for upcoming bands and DJs. ⊠ *Calle de Atocha 127, Barrio de las Letras* ☎ *68/351–6474* ⊕ *independanceclub.com* ☉ *Closed Sun.–Weds.* Ⓜ *Estación del Arte.*

### ★ Teatro Kapital

**DANCE CLUBS** | Madrid's most famous nightclub, Kapital has seven floors—each of which plays a different type of music (spun by top local and international DJs, of course)—and room for 2,000 partiers, plus a small movie theater and rooftop terrace. Dress to impress for this one: no sneakers, shorts, or tanks allowed. VIP tables overlooking the dance floor (approximately €170 for four people) are a worthwhile splurge if you can swing it. ⊠ *Calle Atocha 125, Barrio de las Letras* ☎ *91/420–2906* ⊕ *www.grupo-kapital. com* ☉ *Closed Mon. and Tue.* Ⓜ *Estación del Arte.*

## MUSIC CLUBS

### ★ Café Central

LIVE MUSIC | Madrid's best-known jazz venue is swanky, and the musicians are often internationally known. Performances are usually 9–11 nightly, and tickets can be bought at the door or online. ⊠ *Pl. de Ángel 10, Barrio de las Letras* ☏ *91/369–4143* ⊕ *www.cafecentralmadrid.com* ☾ *Closed Mon.* Ⓜ *Antón Martín.*

## 🛍 Shopping

### BOUTIQUES AND FASHION

### ★ Andrés Gallardo

JEWELRY & WATCHES | Madrid's porcelain whisperer, Gallardo fashions second-hand shards and custom-made porcelain elements into runway-ready jewelry and accessories. ⊠ *Calle de San Pedro 8, Barrio de las Letras* ☏ *91/053–5352* ⊕ *www.andresgallardo.com* ☾ *Closed Sun.* Ⓜ *Antón Martín.*

### Elisa & Eduardo Rivera

MIXED CLOTHING | A block off Plaza de Santa Ana, this is the flagship store of two young Spanish designers with clothes and accessories for both men and women. All garments are handmade in an atelier 40 minutes north of Madrid. Other stores can be found on Calle Sagasta 4 and Calle Clavel 4. ⊠ *Pl. del Ángel 4, Barrio de las Letras* ☏ *91/843–5852* ⊕ *www.eduardorivera.es* Ⓜ *Sol.*

### Santacana

OTHER SPECIALTY STORE | Keep your hands warm—and stylish—during Madrid's chilly winters with a pair of custom handmade gloves by Santacana, a family-run glover that's been open since 1896. ⊠ *Calle Huertas 1, Barrio de las Letras* ☏ *91/704–9670* ⊕ *www.santacana.es* Ⓜ *Antón Martín.*

# Retiro

Straighten your tie and zhuzh your hair— you've arrived in Madrid's equivalent of New York's Upper East Side or London's Kensington: a charming, tree-lined playground for the rich complete with luxury apartments, Michelin-starred restaurants, and one of Europe's most scenic parks, Parque del Buen Retiro.

But get off the main shopping streets and you'll see that these districts are not all glitz and glam. East and south of the park, you'll find upper-middle-class neighborhoods like Ibiza and Pacífico with their fair share of modest apartments and mom-and-pop bars and restaurants. And in addition to the eponymously named park, the Retiro district holds the prestigious Museo del Prado, an essential stop on any Madrid itinerary. The sliver of Retiro real estate called Paseo del Arte, sandwiched between the western side of the park and the Paseo del Prado, is where you'll find some of the city's most exclusive and expensive homes.

## 👁 Sights

### Cuesta de Moyano

PEDESTRIAN MALL | Home to Europe's most expansive permanent book fair since 1925, this pedestrian avenue has around 30 wooden stalls filled with new and second-hand books. In addition to being a pleasant street to stroll—it connects Paseo del Prado with Retiro park—this is also a good place to find collectible and first-edition books. The tourist information kiosk hands out free English-language maps and brochures. ⊠ *Cuesta de Moyano, Retiro* ⊕ *www.cuestamoyano.es.*

### Estación de Atocha

TRAIN/TRAIN STATION | Madrid's main train station is a steel-and-glass hangar built in the late 19th century by Alberto Palacio Elissague, who became famous for his

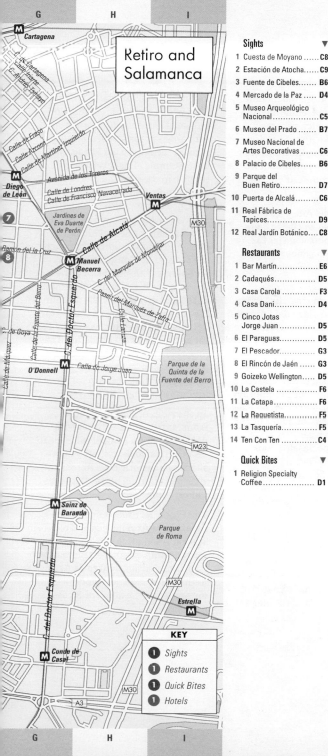

## Retiro and Salamanca

### Sights ▼

1 Cuesta de Moyano ...... **C8**
2 Estación de Atocha...... **C9**
3 Fuente de Cibeles....... **B6**
4 Mercado de la Paz ..... **D4**
5 Museo Arqueológico Nacional.................. **C5**
6 Museo del Prado ....... **B7**
7 Museo Nacional de Artes Decorativas ....... **C6**
8 Palacio de Cibeles...... **B6**
9 Parque del Buen Retiro............. **D7**
10 Puerta de Alcalá ...... **C6**
11 Real Fábrica de Tapices.................. **D9**
12 Real Jardín Botánico.... **C8**

### Restaurants ▼

1 Bar Martín................. **E6**
2 Cadaqués................ **D5**
3 Casa Carola ............. **F3**
4 Casa Dani................ **D4**
5 Cinco Jotas Jorge Juan ............. **D5**
6 El Paraguas............. **D5**
7 El Pescador............. **G3**
8 El Rincón de Jaén ...... **G3**
9 Goizeko Wellington..... **D5**
10 La Castela ............... **F6**
11 La Catapa................. **F6**
12 La Raquetista............. **F5**
13 La Tasquería............. **F5**
14 Ten Con Ten ............. **C4**

### Quick Bites ▼

1 Religion Specialty Coffee.................. **D1**

### Hotels ▼

1 Barceló Emperatriz...... **C1**
2 Gran Meliá Fénix......... **C4**
3 Heritage Madrid Hotel...................... **E2**
4 Hotel Palacio Del Retiro, Autograph Collection.... **C6**
5 ICON Wipton ............ **D5**
6 Mandarin Oriental Ritz, Madrid.............. **B7**
7 Only YOU Atocha ........ **C9**
8 Rosewood Villa Magna ................... **C3**
9 Tótem Madrid ........... **D4**
10 VP Jardín de Recoletos................. **C5**

### KEY

1 Sights
1 Restaurants
1 Quick Bites
1 Hotels

# The Art Walk (Paseo del Prado)  ⊙

Any visit to Madrid should include a stroll along the museum-lined Paseo del Prado, which became a UNESCO World Heritage Site along with Parque del Buen Retiro in 2021. You can tour the area in about two hours (longer, of course, if you visit the Prado).

■ TIP→ The Paseo del Arte pass allows you to visit the Prado, the Reina Sofía, and the Thyssen-Bornemisza for €32. You can buy it at any of the three museums and don't have to visit all on the same day.

The Paseo del Prado stretches from Plaza de Cibeles to Plaza del Emperador Carlos V (also known as Plaza de Atocha) and is home to Madrid's three main art museums—the Prado, Reina Sofía, and Thyssen-Bornemisza—as well as the CaixaForum, an art institution with fabulous temporary exhibitions. In earlier times the Paseo marked the eastern boundary of the city, and in the 17th century it was given a cleaner neoclassical look. A century later, King Carlos III designed a leafy nature walk with glorious fountains and a botanical garden to provide respite to madrileños during the scorching summers.

Start your walk on Plaza Cánovas del Castillo, with its Fuente de Neptuno (Fountain of Neptune); on the northwestern corner is the **Museo Thyssen-Bornemisza**. To your left, across from the plaza, is the elegant, just-renovated Mandarin Oriental Ritz, which abuts the colonnaded Palace of the Bolsa (historical stock exchange); across from it on the right is the **Museo del Prado**, the best example of neoclassical architecture in the city and one of the world's best-known museums. It was enlarged in 2007 with the addition of what's widely known as "Moneo's cube," architect Rafael Moneo's steel-and-glass building that encloses the cloister of Monasterio de los Jerónimos. This monastery, the oldest building in this part of town (built in 1503), is dwarfed by the museum. It once sat at the core of the **Parque del Buen Retiro**, which stretched as far as the Paseo del Prado until the 19th century, when Queen Isabel II sold a third of its terrain to the state. Always bustling, it is a great place to unwind after sightseeing.

To the right of the Prado, across from Murillo Gate, is the **Jardín Botánico**, also a wonderful place to relax with a book or sketch in the shade of an exotic tree. Across the street is a sloping plaza that leads to **CaixaForum**.

The Paseo del Prado ends at the **Estación de Atocha**, a grand old train station resembling the overturned hull of a ship. To its west, across from Calle Atocha, lies **Centro de Arte Reina Sofía**, Madrid's modern art museum and the home of Picasso's *Guernica*.

work with Ricardo Velázquez on the Palacio de Cristal (Glass Palace) in the Parque del Buen Retiro. It is the site of one of the 2004 Al-Qaeda train bombings that collectively killed 193 and injured over 2,000, the topic of the 2022 Netflix documentary *11M: Terror in Madrid.* Today, following renovations by architect Rafael Moneo, the station's main hall resembles a greenhouse; it's filled with tropical trees and contains a busy turtle pool, a magnet for kids. ⚠ **Beware of detours and delays through 2024. In 2022, the city greenlit a €69 million renovation that will reroute the station's main entrance through the iconic wrought-iron façade facing Calle de Atocha.** ✉ *Paseo de Atocha, Retiro* ☎ *91/243–2323* Ⓜ *Estación del Arte, Atocha RENFE.*

**Fuente de Cibeles** (*Cybele Fountain*)
**FOUNTAIN** | The Plaza de Cibeles, where three of Madrid's most affluent districts (Centro, Retiro, and Salamanca) intersect, is both an epicenter of municipal grandeur and a crash course in Spanish architecture. Two palaces, Buenavista and Linares (baroque and baroque revival, respectively), sit on the northern corners of the plaza and are dwarfed by the ornate Palacio de Cibeles. In the center of the plaza stands one of Madrid's most defining symbols, Cybele Fountain, a depiction of the Roman goddess of the Earth driving a lion-drawn chariot. During the civil war, patriotic madrileños risked life and limb to sandbag it as Franco's Nationalist aircraft bombed the city. ✉ *Retiro* Ⓜ *Banco de España.*

★ **Museo del Prado** (*Prado Museum*)
**ART MUSEUM** | The Prado was first commissioned by King/Mayor Carlos III in 1785 as a natural science museum, but by the time the building was completed in 1819, its purpose had changed to exhibiting the art gathered by Spanish royalty since the time of Ferdinand and Isabella. The Prado's jewels are its works

by the nation's three great masters, Goya, Velázquez, and El Greco—though the museum also holds masterpieces by Flemish, Dutch, German, French, and Italian artists, collected when their lands were part of the Spanish Empire. The most famous canvas of all, Velázquez's *Las Meninas* (*The Maids of Honor*), combines a self-portrait of the artist with a mirror reflection of the king and queen. Among Goya's early masterpieces are portraits of the family of King Carlos IV; later works include his famous "black paintings." Other highlights include the *Garden of Earthly Delights* by Hieronymus Bosch and two of El Greco's greatest works, *The Resurrection* and *The Adoration of the Shepherds.* ✉ *Paseo del Prado, Retiro* ☎ *91/330–2800* ⊕ *www.museodelprado.es* ✎ *€15 (permanent collection free Mon.–Sat. 6–8 pm, Sun. 5–7 pm)* Ⓜ *Banco de España, Estación del Arte.*

**Museo Nacional de Artes Decorativas**
**ART MUSEUM** | This palatial building showcases 70,000 items including textiles, furniture, jewelry, ceramics, glass, crystal, and metalwork. The collection starts with medieval and Renaissance items on the first floor and ends with 18th- and 19th-century pieces on the top floor. The ground floor rotates temporary exhibitions and avant-garde works. This museum can be seen as part of the Abono Cinco Palacios, a €12 pass that grants access to five mansion-museums over a 10-day period. ✉ *Montalbán 12, Retiro* ☎ *91/532–6499* ⊕ *mnartesdecorativas.mcu.es* ✎ *€3 (free Thurs. after 5 and Sun.)* ⊘ *Closed Mon.* Ⓜ *Retiro.*

**Palacio de Cibeles** (*Cybele Palace*)
**VIEWPOINT** | This ornate building on the southeast side of Plaza de la Cibeles, built at the start of the 20th century and formerly called Palacio de Comunicaciones, is a massive stone compound bearing French, Viennese, and traditional

*Continued on page 121*

# EL PRADO:
## MADRID'S BRUSH WITH GREATNESS

One of the world's top museums, the Prado is to Madrid what the Louvre is to Paris, or the Uffizi to Florence: a majestic city landmark and premier art institution that merits the attention of every traveler who visits the city.

The Prado celebrated its 200th anniversary in 2019, and its unparalleled collection of Spanish paintings (from the Romanesque period to the 19th century—don't expect to find Picassos here) makes it one of the most visited museums in the world. Foreign artists are also well represented—the collection includes masterpieces of European painting such as Hieronymus Bosch's *Garden of Earthly Delights*, *The Annunciation by Fra Angelico*, *Christ Washing the Disciples' Feet* by Tintoretto, and *The Three Graces* by Rubens—but the Prado is best known as home to more paintings by Diego Velázquez and Francisco de Goya than anywhere else.

Originally meant by King Charles III to become a museum of natural history, the Prado nevertheless opened, in 1819, as a sculpture and painting museum under the patronage of his grandchild, King Philip VII. For the first bewildered *madrileños* who crossed the museum's entrance back then, there were only about 300 paintings on display. Today there are more than 3 million visitors a year and 2,000-plus paintings are on display (the whole collection is estimated at about 8,000 canvases, plus 1,000 sculptures).

**WHEN TO GO**
The best time to visit the Prado is during lunch time, from 1-3, to beat the rush.

**HUNGRY?**
If your stomach rumbles during your visit, check out the café/restaurant in the foyer of the new building.

**CONTACT INFORMATION**
✉ Paseo del Prado s/n, 28014 Madrid
☎ (+34) 91 330 2800.
⊕ www.museodelprado.es
Ⓜ Banco de España, Estación del Arte

**HOURS OF OPERATION**
🕓 Mon.–Sat. 10 AM–8 PM, Sun. 10 AM–7 PM, Closed New Year's Day, Fiesta del Trabajo (May 1), and Christmas.

**ADMISSION**
€15. Free Mon. to Sat. 6 PM–8 PM, Sun. 5 PM-7 PM. To avoid lines, buy tickets in advance online.

The Trinity by El Greco, 1577. Oil on canvas.

# THREE GREAT MASTERS

### FRANCISCO DE GOYA 1746–1828

Goya's work spans a staggering range of tone, from bucolic to horrific, his idyllic paintings of Spaniards at play and portraits of the family of King Carlos IV contrasting with his dark, disturbing "black paintings." Goya's attraction to the macabre assured him a place in posterity, an ironic statement at the end of a long career in which he served as the official court painter to a succession of Spanish kings, bringing the art of royal portraiture to unknown heights.

Goya found fame in his day as a portraitist, but he is admired by modern audiences for his depictions of the bizarre and the morbid. Beginning as a painter of decorative Rococo figures, he evolved into an artist of great depth in the employ of King Charles IV. The push-pull between Goya's love for his country and his disdain for the enemies of Spain yielded such masterpieces as *Third of May 1808*, painted after the French occupation ended. In the early 19th century, Goya's scandalous *The Naked Maja* brought him before the Spanish Inquisition, whose judgment was to end his tenure as a court painter.

Francisco de Goya

### DIEGO VELÁZQUEZ 1599–1660

A native of Seville, Velázquez gained fame at age 24 as court painter to King Philip IV. He developed a lifelike approach to religious art in which both saints and sinners were specific people rather than generic types. The supple brushwork of his ambitious history paintings and portraits was unsurpassed. Several visits to Rome, and his friendship with Rubens, made him the quintessential baroque painter with an international purview.

Diego Velázquez

### DOMENIKOS THEOTOKOPOULOS (AKA "EL GRECO") 1541–1614

El Greco's art was one of rapture and devotion, but beyond that his style is almost impossible to categorize. "The Greek" found his way from his native Crete to Spain through Venice; he spent most of his life in Toledo. His twisted, elongated figures imbue both his religious subjects and portraits with a sense of otherworldliness. While his palette and brushstrokes were inspired by Italian Mannerism, his approach to painting was uniquely his own. His inimitable style left few followers.

Domenikos Theotokopoulos

# SIX PAINTINGS TO SEE

### SATURN DEVOURING ONE OF HIS SONS (1819)
FRANCISCO DE GOYA Y LUCIENTES

In one of fourteen nightmarish "black paintings" executed by Goya to decorate the walls of his home in the later years of his life, the mythological God Kronos, or Saturn, cannibalizes one of his children in order to derail a prophecy that one of them would take over his throne. *Mural transferred to canvas.*

Saturn Devouring One of His Sons

### THE GARDEN OF DELIGHTS OR LA PINTURA DEL MADROÑO (1500)
HIËRONYMUS BOSCH

Very little about the small-town environment of the Low Countries where the Roman Catholic Bosch lived in the late Middle Ages can explain his thought-provoking, and downright bizarre, paintings. His depictions of mankind's sins and virtues, and the heavenly rewards or demonic punishments that await us all, have fascinated many generations of viewers. The devout painter has been called a "heretic," and compared to Salvador Dalí for his disturbingly twisted renderings. In this three-panel painting, Adam and Eve are created, mankind celebrates its humanity, and hell awaits the wicked, all within a journey of 152 inches! *Wooden Triptych.*

The Garden of Delights

### LAS MENINAS (THE MAIDS OF HONOR) (1656-57)
DIEGO VELÁZQUEZ DE SILVA

Velázquez's masterpiece of spatial perspective occupies pride-of-place in the center of the Spanish baroque galleries. In this complex visual game, *you* are the king and queen of Spain, reflected in a distant hazy mirror as the court painter (Velázquez) pauses in front of his easel to observe your features. The actual subject is the Princess Margarita, heir to the throne in 1656. *Oil on canvas.*

Las Meninas

### STILL LIFE (17th Century; no date)
FRANCISCO DE ZURBARÁN

Best known as a painter of contemplative saints, Zurbarán, a native of Extremadura who found success working with Velázquez in Seville, was a peerless observer of beauty in the everyday. His rendering of the surfaces of these homely objects elevates them to the stature of holy relics, urging the viewer to touch them. But the overriding mood is one of serenity and order. *Oil on canvas.*

Still Life

### DAVID VICTORIOUS OVER GOLIATH (1599)
MICHELANGELO MERISI (CARAVAGGIO)

Caravaggio used intense contrasts between his dark and light passages (called *chiaroscuro* in Italian) to create drama in his bold baroque paintings. Here, a surprisingly childlike David calmly ties up the severed head of the giant Philistine Goliath, gruesomely featured in the foreground plane of the picture. The astonishing realism of the Italian painter, who was as well known for his tempestuous personal life as for his deftness with a paint brush, had a profound influence on 17th century Spanish art. *Oil on canvas.*

David Victorious over Goliath

### THE TRINITY (1577)
DOMENIKOS THEOTOKOPOULOS (EL GRECO)

Soon after arriving in Spain, Domenikos Theotokopoulos created this view of Christ ascending into heaven supported by angels, God the Father, and the Holy Spirit. It was commissioned for the altar of a convent in Toledo. The acid colors recall the Mannerist paintings of Venice, where El Greco was trained, and the distortions of the upward-floating bodies show more gracefulness than the anatomical contortions that characterize his later works. *Oil on canvas.*

The Trinity

## PICASSO AND THE PRADO

The Prado contains no modern art, but one of the greatest artists of the 20th century had an important history with the museum. **Pablo Picasso** (1891–1973) served as the director of the Prado during the Spanish civil war, from 1936 to 1939. The Prado was a "phantom museum" in that period, Picasso once noted, since it was closed for most of the war and its collections hidden elsewhere for safety.

Picasso with his wife
Jacqueline Roque

Later that century, the abstract artist's enormous *Guernica* hung briefly on the Prado's walls, returning to Spain from the Museum of Modern Art in 1981. Picasso had stipulated that MoMA give up his anti-war masterpiece after the death of fascist dictator Francisco Franco, and it was displayed at the Prado and the Casón del Buen Retiro until the nearby Reina Sofia was built to house it in 1992.

Picasso in his atelier

Spanish influence. It first served as the city's main post office and, after renovations, is now an administrative building housing the mayor's office, a cultural center called CentroCentro (a pleasant place to study or work), several exhibition halls, dining options (on the second and sixth floors), and a rooftop lookout. ⊠ Pl. de Cibeles, Retiro ☎ 91/480–0008 ⊕ www.centrocentro.org ⧉ Free, Mirador Madrid €3 ⊗ Closed Mon. Ⓜ Banco de España.

★ **Parque del Buen Retiro** (El Retiro)
**CITY PARK** | **FAMILY** | Once the private playground of royalty and a UNESCO World Heritage site since 2021, Madrid's crowning park is a vast expanse of green encompassing formal gardens, fountains, lakes, exhibition halls, children's play areas, outdoor cafés, and a puppet theater (shows on Saturday and Sunday at 12:30). The park, especially lively on weekends, also holds a book fair in May and occasional flamenco concerts in summer. From the entrance at the Puerta de Alcalá, head straight toward the center to find the Estanque (pond), presided over by a grandiose equestrian statue of King Alfonso XII. The 19th-century Palacio de Cristal (Glass Palace) was built to house exotic plants—and, horrifically, actual tribesmen displayed as a "human zoo"—from the Philippines. The Rosaleda (Rose Garden) is bursting with color and heady with floral scents for most of the summer. Madrileños claim that a statue called the Ángel Caído (Fallen Angel) is the only one in the world depicting the Prince of Darkness before his fall from grace. ⊠ Puerta de Alcalá, Retiro Ⓜ Retiro.

**Puerta de Alcalá**
**NOTABLE BUILDING** | This triumphal arch, today a popular backdrop for photos, was built by Carlos III in 1778 to mark the site of one of the ancient city gates. You can still see numerous bullet and cannonball holes on its exterior, left intentionally as a reminder of Madrid's tumultuous past. ⊠ Calle de Alcalá, Retiro Ⓜ Retiro.

**Real Fábrica de Tapices**
**FACTORY** | Tired of previous monarchs' dependency on Belgian and Flemish thread mills and craftsmen, King Felipe V decided to establish the Royal Tapestry Factory in Madrid in 1721. It was originally housed near Alonso Martínez and moved to its current location in 1889. Some of Europe's best artists collaborated on the factory's tapestry designs, the most famous of whom was Goya, who produced a number of works on display at the Prado. The factory, the most renowned of its kind in Europe, is still in operation—you can tour the workshop floor and watch weavers at work. They apply traditional weaving techniques from the 18th and 19th centuries to modern and classic designs—including Goya's. Prebooking online is required, and all visitors get a tour (English tours usually begin at 12:30 pm weekdays; check website for updates). ⊠ Calle de Fuenterrabía 2, Retiro ☎ 91/434–0550 ⊕ www.realfabricadetapices.com ⧉ €5 ⊗ Closed weekends and Aug. ⧉ Reservation required Ⓜ Menéndez Pelayo, Estación del Arte.

**Real Jardín Botánico** (Royal Botanical Garden)
**GARDEN** | **FAMILY** | You don't have to be a horticulturalist to appreciate the breadth of the exotic plant collection here. Opened in 1781 and emblematic of the Age of Enlightenment, this lush Eden of bonsais, orchids, cacti, and more houses more than 5,000 species of living plants and trees in just 20 acres. Its dried specimens number over a million, and many were brought back from exploratory voyages to the Americas. ⊠ Pl. de Murillo 2, Retiro ☎ 91/420–3017 ⊕ www.rjb.csic.es ⧉ €6 Ⓜ Estación del Arte.

# 🍴 Restaurants

## Bar Martín

$ | **SPANISH** | This hole-in-the-wall opened in 1940 serves no-frills Castilian classics like *patatas revolconas* (mashed potatoes with paprika and pork rinds), ham croquettes, and meatballs so good they're often gone before the dinner rush. Don't expect to find a seat unless you go at off hours. **Known for:** outdoor parkside dining; crowds on weekends; affordable Spanish bar food. ⑤ *Average main: €11* ⊠ *Av. de Menéndez Pelayo 17, Retiro* ☎ *91/573–1167* Ⓜ *Ibiza.*

## La Castela

$$ | **TAPAS** | **FAMILY** | Traditional taverns with tin-top bars, vermouth on tap, and no-nonsense waiters are a dying breed in Madrid, but this one, just a couple of blocks from the Parque del Buen Retiro, has stood the test of time. It's always busy with locals clamoring over plates of sautéed wild mushrooms, tuna ventresca and roasted pepper salad, and stewed chickpeas with langoustines. **Known for:** neighborhood crowd; friendly staff; colorfully plated tapas. ⑤ *Average main: €19* ⊠ *Calle Doctor Castelo 22, Retiro* ☎ *91/574–0015* ⊕ *www.restaurantelacastela.com* ⊘ *No dinner Sun.* Ⓜ *Ibiza.*

## ★ La Catapa

$$$ | **SPANISH** | La Catapa's tapas are classic but never old hat, inventive but never pretentious. The burst-in-your-mouth croquetas and garlicky razor clams may lure the crowds, but the hidden gems are in the vegetable section: it's hard to decide between the artichoke *menestra* with crisped jamón, ultra-creamy *salmorejo* (gazpacho's richer, more garlicky sibling), and umami-packed seared mushrooms. **Known for:** a Retiro institution; decadent cream-filled pastry "cigars"; elevated tapas. ⑤ *Average main: €23* ⊠ *Calle Menorca 14, Retiro* ☎ *68/614–3823* ⊘ *Closed Sun. and Mon.* Ⓜ *Ibiza.*

## La Raquetista

$$ | **FUSION** | A relative newcomer on Retiro's traditional tapas scene, La Raquetista has quickly become known for nueva cocina dishes that vary from night to night including tuna "pastrami," uni with potato cream, and Segovian suckling pig tacos, all served bar-side or in a snug five-table dining room. **Known for:** unusual Spanish wines; to-die-for torreznos (fried pork rinds); eye-popping fusion tapas. ⑤ *Average main: €21* ⊠ *Calle del Dr. Castelo 19, Retiro* ☎ *91/831–1842* ⊕ *www.laraquetista.com* ⊘ *No dinner Sun.* Ⓜ *Ibiza.*

# 🛏 Hotels

## Hotel Palacio Del Retiro, Autograph Collection

$$$$ | **HOTEL** | An early-20th-century palace built for a noble family with extravagant habits (the elevator carried their horses up and down from the rooftop exercise ring), this hotel mixes old-world elegance with modern bells and whistles. **Pros:** spacious, elegant rooms; bathrooms stocked with all sorts of complimentary products; within walking distance of the Prado. **Cons:** cumbersome room keys; lower rooms facing the park can get noisy; pricey breakfast. ⑤ *Rooms from: €337* ⊠ *Calle de Alfonso XII 14, Retiro* ☎ *91/523–7460* ⊕ *www.ac-hotels.com* ➟ *50 rooms* ⍾ *No Meals* Ⓜ *Retiro.*

## ★ Mandarin Oriental Ritz, Madrid

$$$$ | **HOTEL** | A €99-million renovation by Mandarin Oriental completed in 2021 breathed new life to this grande dame overlooking the Prado Museum, replacing mustard-colored drapes, dim sconces, and faded carpets with bright whites, gold accents, and stunning contemporary art. **Pros:** celebrity chef restaurant; the epitome of modern luxury; new fitness center and chandelier-lighted pool. **Cons:** priced too high for the vast majority of travelers; inconsistent El Jardín restaurant; many museum-grade antiques were

You can rent rowboats at the lake in the Parque del Buen Retiro; it's a great way to cool off in the summer.

auctioned off in the revamp. $ Rooms from: €865 ⊠ Pl. de la Lealtad 5, Retiro ☎ 91/701–6767 ⊕ www.mandarinoriental.com ⇨ 153 rooms ⊙ No Meals Ⓜ Banco de España.

### Only YOU Atocha
$$$ | HOTEL | One of the trendiest, most youthful hotels in town, Only YOU Atocha has a swanky high-design lobby, rooftop restaurant, spacious gym, and industrial-chic accommodations. **Pros:** gorgeous designer furniture; cloud-soft beds; intriguing pop-ups and events. **Cons:** looks out over major intersection; food quality falls short across the board; exterior-facing rooms are very noisy. $ Rooms from: €200 ⊠ Paseo de la Infanta Isabel 13, Retiro ☎ 91/409–7876 ⊕ www.onlyyouhotels.com ⇨ 205 rooms ⊙ No Meals Ⓜ Estación del Arte.

## 🍸 Nightlife

### Florida Park
GATHERING PLACES | Retiro Park is now a nightlife destination, thanks to Florida, the see-and-be-seen leisure complex with six venues: El Pabellón, a white-tablecloth restaurant; La Galería, an informal tapas bar; La Terraza, a chic rooftop terrace; Los Kioscos, an indoor-outdoor bar with live music; La Cúpula, a cocktail bar open late; and La Sala, a tony nightclub that heats up on weekends. ⊠ Parque del Buen Retiro, Paseo de la República Dominicana 1, Retiro ☎ 91/827–5275 ⊕ www.floridapark.es Ⓜ Ibiza.

## 🛍 Shopping

### Qava
FOOD | Featuring exclusively Spanish cheeses from small producers, Qava doesn't just source and sell killer cheeses that make great gifts—it also ages each wheel to perfection in on-site "caves." Sample them in an eight-table tasting

area alongside carefully selected wines. The 11 pm closing time means you can work Qava into a tapas crawl or—if you're feeling European—make it a final dessert stop. ⌧ *Calle del Dr. Castelo 34, Retiro* ☎ *91/853–2853* ⊕ *www.qavadequesos. com* Ⓜ *Ibiza, O'Donnell.*

# Salamanca

Salamanca was part of the 19th-century urban expansion called the Ensanche, which bulldozed the city walls to make way for new gridded neighborhoods. The area was originally intended to provide shelter for the working class, but because of its desirable parkside location, it swiftly became a hot spot for the well-to-do, a legacy that remains as the district contains the most expensive homes per square foot in the country.

## ◉ Sights

### ★ Mercado de la Paz

**MARKET** | Salamanca's gleaming main market is a hangarlike food emporium selling everything from wild game to softball-size Calanda peaches to sashimi-grade tuna to the country's finest jamón and canned seafood. Standout restaurants here include Casa Dani (arguably the city's best Spanish omelet; see separate entry) and Matteo Cucina Italiana (osteria-style pastas and risotto). ⌧ *Calle Ayala 28, Salamanca* ☎ *91/435–0743* ⊕ *www.mercadodelapaz.com* ⊗ *Closed Sun., Sat. after 2 pm* Ⓜ *Serrano.*

### Museo Arqueológico Nacional (*National Archaeological Museum*)

**HISTORY MUSEUM** | **FAMILY** | This museum boasts three large floors filled with Spanish relics, artifacts, and treasures ranging from ancient history to the 19th century. Among the highlights are *La Dama de Elche*, the bust of a wealthy 5th-century-BC Iberian woman (notice that her headgear vaguely resembles the

mantillas and hair combs still associated with traditional Spanish dress); the ancient Visigothic votive crowns discovered in 1859 near Toledo, believed to date back to the 7th century; and the medieval ivory crucifix of Ferdinand and Sancha. There is also a replica of the early cave paintings in Altamira (access to the real thing, in Cantabria Province, is highly restricted).

■ **TIP→ Consider getting the multimedia guide offering select itineraries to make your visit more manageable.** ⌧ *Calle de Serrano 13, Salamanca* ☎ *91/577–7912* ⊕ *www.man.es* ⌦ *€3 (free Sat. after 2 and Sun. before 2)* ⊗ *Closed Mon.* Ⓜ *Colón, Serrano.*

## 🍴 Restaurants

### ★ Cadaqués

**$$$$** | **CATALAN** | Never has an open kitchen in Madrid been so mesmerizing: at Cadaqués, black-clad cooks tend to rows of paella pans sizzling over pluming orange wood embers and flip Flintstones-worthy steaks and whole fish licked by open flame. It feels like the type of rustic experience you'd encounter at the Mediterranean seaside, but Cadaqués sits squarely on Jorge Juan, Madrid's poshest street. **Known for:** refined Mediterranean decor with well-heeled clientele to match; a slice of the Levant in Madrid; best rice dishes in town. ⑤ *Average main: €55* ⌧ *Calle de Jorge Juan 35, Salamanca* ☎ *91/360–9053* ⊕ *restaurantecadaques. com* Ⓜ *Velázquez.*

### Casa Carola

**$$$$** | **SPANISH** | **FAMILY** | Locals flock to Casa Carola for one dish, *cocido madrileño*, Madrid's famous boiled dinner whose roots can be traced to a medieval Sephardic stew called *adafina*. Served ritualistically in three courses, or *vuelcos*— broth, then chickpeas and vegetables, then meats—it's an essential Madrid experience, especially in the cold-weather months. **Known for:** warm service; old-timey interiors; cocido madrileño served in three courses. [$] *Average main: €30* ✉ *Calle de Padilla 54, Salamanca* ☎ *91/401–9408* ⊕ *www.casacarola.com* ✪ *No dinner. Closed mid-June–mid-Sept.* Ⓜ *Lista.*

### ★ Casa Dani

$ | SPANISH | Casa Dani is a legendary bar in Mercado de la Paz whose *tortilla de patata* is easily the best in town, and perhaps the country (if first place in the National Spanish Omelet Championship of 2019 is any indication). Each hefty wedge is packed with caramelized onions and served hot and slightly runny. **Known for:** long lines that are worth the wait; value prix-fixe lunch; possibly world's best tortilla española. [$] *Average main: €12* ✉ *Mercado de la Paz, Calle de Ayala 28, Salamanca* ✛ *Back right corner* ☎ *91/576 6026* ⊕ *www.casadani.es* ✪ *Closed Sun. No dinner* Ⓜ *Serrano.*

### Cinco Jotas Jorge Juan

$$$ | TAPAS | Cinco Jotas Ibérico ham is a sight to behold, translucent and shimmering like shards of red stained glass, a shade darker than prosciutto and twice as fragrant. That's because this famous producer uses only 100% purebred, acorn-fed Iberian hogs. **Known for:** Ibérico pork dishes beyond just ham; tranquil and elegant patio; the Rolls Royce of jamón. [$] *Average main: €28* ✉ *Calle Puigcerdà, Local 2, Salamanca* ☎ *91/575–4125* ⊕ *www.cincojotas.es* Ⓜ *Serrano.*

### ★ El Paraguas

$$$$ | SPANISH | This low-ceiling dining room filled with plush armchairs, starched white tablecloths, and colorful bouquets is a welcoming spot to feast on refined Asturian dishes like sea urchin gratin, morels stuffed with truffled foie gras, pheasant with braised green beans, and suckling lamb confit. Weather permitting, you can request a patio table to watch Madrid's one percent parade down Calle Jorge Juan. **Known for:** romantic dining room and terrace; fantastic seafood; haute Asturian cuisine. [$] *Average main: €34* ✉ *Calle Jorge Juan 16, Salamanca* ☎ *91/431–5950* ⊕ *www.elparaguas.com* ✪ *No dinner Sun.* Ⓜ *Serrano.*

### El Pescador

$$$ | SEAFOOD | Owned by the proprietors of one of the best fish markets in town, Pescaderías Coruñesas, this seafood restaurant with a warm, modern interior welcomes guests with an impressive window display of fresh seafood—red and white prawns, Kumamoto oysters, goose barnacles, and the renowned Galician Carril clams are just some of what you might see. Fish (including turbot, sole, grouper, and sea bass) is cooked to your liking in the oven, on the grill, in a pan with garlic, or battered and fried. **Known for:** crisp Galician wines; dayboat fish; extravagant seafood displays. [$] *Average main: €27* ✉ *Calle de Jose Urtega y Gasset 75, Salamanca* ☎ *91/402–1290* ⊕ *www.marisqueriaelpescador.net* ✪ *Closed Sun.* Ⓜ *Lista, Núñez de Balboa.*

### El Rincón de Jaén

$$ | SPANISH | FAMILY | An Andalusian taberna, El Rincón de Jaén evokes the raucous energy and down-home cuisine of that sunny region. Start with *pescaíto frito,* a mix of seafood that's lightly fried and served with lemon halves, before moving on to more substantial dishes like the peeled tomato salad topped with oil-cured tuna belly (easily one of the best salads in town) and whole roasted fish and braised meats. **Known for:** complimentary tapas with drinks; tomato and tuna salad; Andalusian joie de vivre. [$] *Average main: €23* ✉ *Calle Don Ramón de la Cruz 88, Salamanca* ☎ *91/401–6334* ⊕ *elrincondejaen.com* Ⓜ *Lista.*

### Goizeko Wellington

$$$ | SPANISH | The seasoned Basque chef of this quiet white-tablecloth standby serves dependably delectable fine-dining versions of Spanish classics like steamed

hake with seaweed-garlic refrito, cured tuna salad with crab vinaigrette, and a phenomenal roast suckling pig doused in syrupy jus. Save room for house-made desserts, which number over 15 and play nicely with sweet Muscatel wine or sherry. **Known for:** elegant yet comfortable atmosphere; excellent acoustics; elevated Basque cuisine. $ *Average main: €27* ⊠ *Hotel Wellington, Calle de Villanueva 34, Salamanca* ☎ *91/577–6026* ⊕ *www. goizekowellington.es* ☾ *Closed Sun.* Ⓜ *Retiro, Príncipe de Vergara.*

### La Tasquería

$ | TAPAS | La Tasquería draws restaurant industry pros and food writers with its bold menu revolving around off-cuts like liver, kidneys, tripe, and tongue—onetime staples of the Spanish diet that fell out of favor but are now getting a modern makeover. Even the squeamish should consider ordering delectable dishes like lamb necks with corn and huitlacoche, and brain-and-potato omelet. **Known for:** good-value €55 tasting menu; craft beers and sherries; offal everything. $ *Average main: €16* ⊠ *Calle Duque de Sesto 48, Salamanca* ☎ *91/451–1000* ⊕ *www. latasqueria.com* Ⓜ *Príncipe de Vergara.*

### Ten Con Ten

$$$ | SPANISH | This "gin bar" helped start the Spanish *gin-tónic* craze of the late 1980s, and though perhaps not as avant-garde as it once was, the quality of food and drinks at Ten Con Ten is consistently fantastic. Grab a cocktail at one of the wooden high-tops in the bar area, or sit down for a soup-to-nuts dinner in the classy dining room at the back—just remember to book a table weeks, if not months, in advance. **Known for:** hand-cut jamón ibérico; memorable gastro-bar fare; expertly made gin-tónics. $ *Average main: €25* ⊠ *Calle de Ayala 6, Salamanca* ☎ *91/575–9254* ⊕ *www.restaurantetenconten.com* Ⓜ *Serrano.*

## ☕ Coffee and Quick Bites

### Religion Specialty Coffee

$ | CAFÉ | After browsing the art collection at Museo Lázaro Galdiano, walk north a block to reach this charming café suited to both working and schmoozing. There are sandwiches, chia bowls, smoothies, and pastries on the menu, in addition to teas and the usual coffee drinks. **Known for:** well-made coffees and teas; laptop-friendly; affordable brunch. $ *Average main: €9* ⊠ *Calle de María de Molina 24, Salamanca* ☎ *91/069–8221* ⊕ *www. religioncoffee.es* Ⓜ *Gregorio Marañón.*

## 🛏 Hotels

### Barceló Emperatriz

$$ | HOTEL | Worthy of an empress as its name implies, this sumptuous property on a tree-shaded block offers knowledgeable concierge services, healthy breakfast options (tahini toast! spirulina omelets!), an updated gym, and an extensive pillow menu. **Pros:** luxury on a budget; solid little gym; king-size beds and in-room hot tubs. **Cons:** small pool and gym; 10-minute taxi from center of town; cramped lobby. $ *Rooms from: €155* ⊠ *Calle de López de Hoyos 4, Salamanca* ☎ *91/342–2490* ⊕ *www.barcelo. com* ⇄ *146 rooms* ⦿| *No Meals* Ⓜ *Núñez de Balboa.*

### Gran Meliá Fénix

$$$$ | HOTEL | A Madrid institution that has played host to the likes of the Beatles, Cary Grant, and Rita Hayworth, this hotel has an impressive lobby with marble floors, antique furniture, and a stained-glass dome ceiling. **Pros:** celebrity hangout Hortensio restaurant; above-and-beyond service; great breakfast buffet. **Cons:** VIP policy excludes standard-room guests from certain areas; guest rooms showing some wear; small bathrooms could use update. $ *Rooms from: €281* ⊠ *Calle de Hermosilla 2, Salamanca*

🏨 91/431–6700 🌐 www.melia.com ⤲ 225 rooms ○l No Meals Ⓜ Colón.

## Heritage Madrid Hotel

$$$$ | **HOTEL** | Hotel Orfila's newer stylish sibling, the Relais & Château–approved Heritage lies north of Salamanca's commercial hubbub in a stately residential area. **Pros:** standout old-meets-new furnishings; plush towels and robes; "secret" rooftop bar and terrace. **Cons:** unprofessional front desk staff; no gym, pool, or sauna; far from most sights. ⑤ Rooms from: €422 ✉ Calle de Diego de León 43, Salamanca ☎ 91/088–7070 🌐 www.heritagemadridhotel.com ⤲ 46 rooms ○l No Meals Ⓜ Avenida de América.

## ICON Wipton

$$$ | **HOTEL** | Whites, grays, and dark woods define this boutique hotel on Salamanca's most opulent street, Jorge Juan. **Pros:** calming atmosphere; standout breakfasts; location on main dining and nightlife street. **Cons:** small desks in guest rooms; noise travels from ground-floor bar; entry-level rooms are a tight fit. ⑤ Rooms from: €180 ✉ Calle de Jorge Juan 17, Salamanca ☎ 91/435–5411 🌐 www.iconwipton.com ⤲ 61 rooms ○l No Meals Ⓜ Serrano, Velázquez.

## ★ Rosewood Villa Magna

$$$$ | **HOTEL** | Barrio Salamanca's most distinctive hotel, which reopened in late 2021 under the Rosewood umbrella after a yearlong eight-figure renovation, is now one of the swankiest properties in Spain. **Pros:** Madrid's best hotel breakfast and high tea; inviting spa and public areas with fireplaces and cushy sofas; impeccable service. **Cons:** unrenovated bathrooms feel comparatively old-fashioned; big-city surroundings lack charm; Amós restaurant still getting its footing. ⑤ Rooms from: €850 ✉ Paseo de la Castellana 22, Salamanca ☎ 91/587–1234 🌐 www.rosewoodhotels.com/en/villa-magna ⤲ 154 rooms ○l No Meals Ⓜ Rubén Darío, Colón.

## Tótem Madrid

$$$ | **HOTEL** | Tótem checks all the boxes for a solid boutique hotel: genial service, streamlined design, sought-after location, terrific food and cocktails. **Pros:** charming tree-lined block; bubbly service; excellent cocktail bar and restaurant. **Cons:** interior rooms not as pleasant; disappointing breakfast; many attractions not within walking distance. ⑤ Rooms from: €206 ✉ Calle Hermosilla 23, Salamanca ☎ 91/426–0035 🌐 www.totem-madrid.com ⤲ 64 rooms ○l No Meals Ⓜ Serrano.

## VP Jardín de Recoletos

$$ | **HOTEL** | **FAMILY** | This high-end apartment-hotel offers great value on a quiet street just a couple of blocks from Retiro Park, the Prado, and shopping areas. **Pros:** spacious rooms with kitchens; good value with periodic deals via website; good restaurant. **Cons:** breakfast not served in the garden; could use a redesign; the garden closes at midnight and can be noisy. ⑤ Rooms from: €161 ✉ Calle Gil de Santivañes 6, Salamanca ☎ 91/781–1640 🌐 www.recoletos-hotel.com ⤲ 43 rooms ○l No Meals Ⓜ Colón.

# ⊻ Nightlife

## DANCE CLUBS

### Bling Bling

**DANCE CLUBS** | This glitzy, ever-crowded nightclub attracts a well-heeled local crowd with house, reggaeton, and remixed pop tracks. Dress to impress: this isn't an easy door. ✉ Calle Génova 28, Salamanca ☎ 91/064–4479 Ⓜ Colón.

# 🎭 Performing Arts

## Auditorio Nacional de Música

**CONCERTS** | This is Madrid's main concert hall, with spaces for both symphonic and chamber music. ✉ Calle del Príncipe de Vergara 146, Salamanca ☎ 91/337–0140 🌐 www.auditorionacional.mcu.es Ⓜ Cruz del Rayo, Prosperidad.

# 🛍 Shopping

## BOUTIQUES AND FASHION

Salamanca is Madrid's quintessential shopping district with a high concentration of large and small shops and boutiques on Calles Claudio Coello, Lagasca, and the first few blocks of Serrano.

### Adolfo Domínguez

**MIXED CLOTHING** | This popular Galician designer creates simple, sober, elegant lines for both men and women. Of the numerous locations around the city, the flagship at Calle Serrano 5 is the most varied. There are also two large stores at Madrid–Barajas Airport. ⊠ *Calle de Serrano 5, Salamanca* ☎ *91/436–2600* ⊕ *www. adolfodominguez.com* Ⓜ *Serrano.*

### Loewe

**LEATHER GOODS** | Luxury Spanish fashion house Loewe (Lo-EH-veh), which is having a moment among trendy young Spaniards, carries designer purses, accessories, and clothing made of butter-soft leather in gorgeous jewel tones. The store at Serrano 26 displays the women's collection; men's items are a block away at Serrano 34. ⊠ *Calle de Serrano 26 and 34, Salamanca* ☎ *91/577–6056* ⊕ *www. loewe.com* Ⓜ *Serrano.*

### Purificación García

**HANDBAGS** | For women and men searching for elegant all-day wear, this store offers some standout pieces, particularly handbags. There's another branch at Claudio Coello 95. ⊠ *Calle de Serrano 28, Salamanca* ☎ *91/435–8013* ⊕ *www. purificaciongarcia.com* Ⓜ *Serrano.*

## FOOD AND WINE

### Lavinia

**WINE/SPIRITS** | Every attendant is a sommelier at this sprawling wine store. Beyond the 4,000-plus bottles from nearly every viticultural region imaginable, there are books, glasses, and bar accessories on sale. A Spanish restaurant on-site pours some 50 wines by the glass and has outdoor seating (skip the food; it's overpriced and underwhelming). ⊠ *Calle de José Ortega y Gasset 16, Salamanca* ☎ *91/426–0604* ⊕ *www.lavinia.es* ⊘ *Closed Sun.* Ⓜ *Núñez de Balboa.*

### Mantequerías Bravo

**WINE/SPIRITS** | Stock up on Spanish wines, olive oils, cheeses, and hams at this old-timer that's been around since 1931 and is situated in the heart of Salamanca's shopping area. ⊠ *Calle de Ayala 24, Salamanca* ☎ *91/576–7641* ⊕ *www. mantequeriasbravo.com* ⊘ *Closed Sun.* Ⓜ *Serrano.*

## JEWELRY

### Coolook

**JEWELRY & WATCHES** | Spanish jeweler Mar Aldeguer sells nature-inspired jewelry made from precious and semiprecious metals and stones at this welcoming boutique. There's another branch at Calle Barquillo 34. ⊠ *Calle Serrano 84, Salamanca* ☎ *91/626–3920* ⊕ *www.coolook. es* ⊘ *Closed Tues. and Sun.*

## TEXTILES

### ★ Ábbatte

**FABRICS** | Every blanket, tablecloth, throw, and rug sold at this deservedly pricey textile shop is woven by hand using the finest natural fibers in the Cistercian abbey of Santa María de la Sierra in Segovia. ⊠ *Calle Villanueva 27, Salamanca* ☎ *91/622–5530* ⊕ *www.abbatte.com* ⊘ *Closed Sun.*

# La Latina

This is perhaps Madrid's most *castizo* (loosely, "authentic") neighborhood, with its deep-rooted history and hardscrabble spirit. Its layout has changed little since medieval times, with sinuous cobblestone streets emptying onto wide plazas, but its demographic makeup has in the last decade or so due to soaring rents and ever more Airbnbs. Though its mom-and-pop businesses preserve

# La Latina, Lavapiés, and Arganzuela

**KEY**
- Sights
- Restaurants
- Quick Bites
- Hotels

## Sights ▶

| | |
|---|---|
| 1 Basílica de San Francisco el Grande | A2 |
| 2 Cava Baja | C1 |
| 3 Centro de Arte Reina Sofía | H3 |
| 4 Matadero Madrid | E3 |
| 5 Mercado de Antón Martín | G2 |
| 6 Mercado de la Cebada | C2 |
| 7 Plaza de la Paja | B1 |
| 8 Tabacalera | E3 |

## Restaurants ▶

| | |
|---|---|
| 1 Bar Santurce | C2 |
| 2 Bar Toboggan | E3 |
| 3 Casa Botín | C1 |
| 4 Casa Gerardo | B3 |
| 5 Casa Revuelta | C1 |
| 6 El Rincón de Marco | E3 |
| 7 Juana la Loca | B2 |
| 8 La Buríona | G2 |
| 9 La Oveja Negra | F3 |
| 10 La Teranga | E3 |
| 11 Los Huevos de Lucio | C1 |
| 12 Melo's | F2 |
| 13 Pantao | E3 |
| 14 Restaurante Badila | E2 |
| 15 Taberna de Antonio Sánchez | E2 |

## Quick Bites ▶

| | |
|---|---|
| 1 Hola Coffee | G3 |
| 2 Plántate Café | E2 |

## Hotels ▶

| | |
|---|---|
| 1 Artrip | F3 |
| 2 CoolRooms Palacio de Atocha | F1 |
| 3 The Hat | D1 |
| 4 Hotel Freedom | F1 |
| 5 Posada del León de Oro | C1 |

0 100 m
0 500 ft

the old-world aesthetic of La Latina of yore, the neighborhood has all but lost its original inhabitants and, with them, its pleasingly gritty edge. But that doesn't keep madrileños from flocking here every chance they get, especially around August 15, when the neighborhood's famous Verbena de la Paloma street fair unfolds to the oompah of the *chotis* (a type of folk dance). When exploring, architecture buffs should keep an eye out for La Latina's *casas a la malicia*, illegally constructed apartments from the 16th to 18th century recognizable for their asymmetrical, randomly placed windows. Their confusing floor plan was intended to dupe the municipal authorities into believing they contained fewer dwellings (allowing landlords to evade property taxes), one of many examples of this neighborhood's unruly character.

Officially part of the Palacio neighborhood, this bustling area—bordered by Calle de Segovia to the north; Calle Toledo to the east; Puerta de Toledo to the south; and Calle Bailén, with its imposing Basílica de San Francisco, to the west—houses some of the city's oldest buildings, plenty of sloping streets, and an array of unmissable tapas spots—especially on Cava Baja and Cava Alta and in the area around Plaza de la Paja.

## ◉ Sights

### Basílica de San Francisco el Grande
**CHURCH** | In 1760 Carlos III built this basilica on the site of a Franciscan convent, allegedly founded by St. Francis of Assisi in 1217. The dome, 108 feet in diameter, is the largest in Spain, even larger than that of St. Paul's in London. The seven main doors, of American walnut, were carved by Casa Juan Guas. Three chapels adjoin the circular church, the most famous being that of **San Bernardino de Siena** containing a Goya masterpiece depicting a preaching San Bernardino. The figure standing on the right, not looking up, is a self-portrait of Goya. The 16th-century Gothic choir stalls came from La Cartuja del Paular, in rural Segovia Province. ⊠ *Pl. de San Francisco, La Latina* ☎ *91/365–3800* ⊠ *€5 guided tour (in Spanish); free self-guided Sat.* ⊘ *Closed Sun. and Mon.* Ⓜ *Puerta de Toledo, La Latina.*

### Cava Baja
**STREET** | Madrid's most popular tapas street is crowded with excellent (if arguably overpriced) tapas bars and traditional tabernas. Its lively, and rather touristy, atmosphere spills over onto nearby streets and squares including Almendro, Cava Alta, Plaza del Humilladero, and Plaza de la Paja. Expect full houses and long wait times on weekend nights. ⊠ *La Latina* Ⓜ *La Latina.*

### Mercado de la Cebada
**MARKET** | **FAMILY** | An unrenovated building and budget-friendly tapas and groceries make this market a local favorite for both shopping and snacking. The hangarlike space is at its busiest on Saturday from noon to 3 pm, when seafood stalls transform into makeshift fish and shellfish restaurants, frying, steaming, and boiling their freshest wares and serving them on plastic plates alongside jugs of unlabeled table wine—quite the party. Once buzzed and sated, pop into La Pecera, a chic stall dedicated to prints, paintings, and photography by local artists. ⊠ *Pl. de la Cebada, La Latina* ☎ *91/366–6966* ⊕ *www. mercadodelacebada.com* ⊘ *Closed Sun.* Ⓜ *La Latina.*

### ★ Plaza de la Paja
**PLAZA/SQUARE** | At the top of a hill, on Costanilla San Andrés, sits the most important square of medieval Madrid. It predates the Plaza Mayor by at least two centuries. The sloped plaza's jewel is the Capilla del Obispo (Bishop's Chapel), built between 1520 and 1530, where peasants deposited their tithes, called *diezmas*—one-tenth of their crop. Architecturally the chapel traces the transition

# A Good Walk: Old Madrid

*Wander around Puerta del Sol for a look at Madrid's oldest buildings, bustling taverns, and cobblestone alleys. Allow about two hours, or more if you visit the Palacio Real or Monasterio de la Encarnación.*

Begin at **Puerta del Sol**, the center of Madrid and a major social and transportation hub, then take Calle Mayor to **Plaza Mayor.** Inaugurated in 1620 on the site of a thriving street market, this is Madrid's historical main square, where you'll find the Casa de la Panadería (Bakery House)—an imposing building with mythological figures painted on its facade, home of the main tourist office.

Exit Plaza Mayor through the "Cutler's Arch" (Arco de Cuchilleros) and go down the stairs: to the right is Calle Cava de San Miguel—an ancient-looking stretch of colorful taverns that inches uphill to the posh Mercado de San Miguel and Calle Mayor; to the left is Calle de Cuchilleros ("Cutlers' Street"), which leads to the Plaza de Puerta Cerrada, or "Closed Gate," named for the city gate that once stood here. The mural up to your right reads *Fui sobre agua edificada; mis muros de fuego son* ("I was built on water; my walls are made of fire"), a reference to the city's origins as a fortress with abundant springs and flint ramparts. Cross the street to **Calle Cava Baja**, packed with taverns and restaurants. At Plaza del Humilladero, walk past Plaza de San Andrés and take Costanilla de San Andrés from Plaza Puerta de Moros, down to **Plaza de la Paja**, which was renovated in 2022. The **Capilla del Obispo** (Bishop's Chapel), on the south edge of the plaza, completed in 1535, houses one of Spain's most magnificent Renaissance altarpieces. Look right on narrow Calle Príncipe Anglona—at its end you'll see a tall redbrick Mudejar tower, the only original element belonging to San Pedro el Real (St. Peter the Royal), one of Madrid's oldest churches.

Cross Calle Segovia to Plaza de la Cruz Verde, take the stairs (Calle del Rollo) to your right, go straight to Calle Cordón, then turn left. Walk up the stairs and cross the Plaza del Cordón and Calle Sacramento to get to **Plaza de la Villa**; noteworthy buildings here are (west) the former city hall main office, finished in 1692; (east) the Casa and Torre de los Lujanes, the oldest civil building in Madrid, dating to the mid-15th century; and (south) the Casa Cisneros, from the 16th century. Turn left on Calle Mayor and walk to Calle San Nicolás; on the corner is the Palacio del Duque de Uceda, a residential building from the 17th century now used as military headquarters. Turn right onto Calle San Nicolás (San Nicolás de los Servitas is Madrid's oldest standing church, with a Mudejar tower dating to the 17th century) and walk to Plaza de Ramales, where you'll find a display of a ruined section of the foundation of the medieval Iglesia de San Juan, demolished in the 19th century. Take Calle San Nicolas until it becomes Calle de Lepanto, which leads to the **Plaza de Oriente.** The equestrian statue of Felipe IV was sculpted from a drawing by Velázquez, who worked and died in what is now a residential building on the east side of the plaza. Take a breather in the plaza, then visit the **Palacio Real**, the adjacent **Jardines de Sabatini**, or nearby **Monasterio de la Encarnación.**

from the blocky Gothic period, which gave the structure its basic shape, to the Renaissance, the source of its decorations. It houses a polychrome altarpiece with scenes from the New Testament and a carved alabaster cenotaph by Francisco Giralte that art historians fawn over. Seven cloistered nuns live in the building and hold Mass in the chapel on Sundays at 6:30 pm and at several other times during the week (check the schedule on the door or call for details). To visit the chapel it is imperative to reserve in advance; tours are in Spanish only. The chapel is part of the complex of the domed church of San Andrés, one of Madrid's oldest. At the northern tip of the plaza there's a pretty little 18th-century park, Jardín del Príncipe de Anglona, that locals call Madrid's secret garden. ⊠ *La Latina* ☎ *91/559–2874* ✎ *reservascapilladelobispo@archimadrid.es* 🎫 *€4 (Capilla del Obispo)* ⊙ *Chapel tours only Tues. 9:30-12:30 and Thurs. 4-5:30* ⬧ *Reservation required to visit chapel* Ⓜ *La Latina.*

# 🍴 Restaurants

## Casa Botín

$$$ | SPANISH | According to *Guinness World Records*, Madrid is home to the world's oldest restaurant, Botín, established in 1725 and a favorite of Ernest Hemingway. The final scene of *The Sun Also Rises* is set in this very place. **Known for:** roving music ensembles called "tunas"; roast lamb and suckling pig; world's oldest restaurant. ⑤ *Average main: €27* ⊠ *Calle Cuchilleros 17, La Latina* ☎ *91/366–4217* ⊕ *www.botin.es* Ⓜ *Tirso de Molina.*

## ★ Casa Gerardo

$ | TAPAS | Huge *tinajas*, clay vessels once filled to the brim with bulk wine (now defunct), sit behind the bar at this raucous no-frills bodega specializing in Spanish cheese and charcuterie. Ask the waiters what they've been drinking and eating lately, and order precisely that. **Known for:** frazzled yet friendly staff; wide selection of wines and charcuterie; unforgettable old-world atmosphere. ⑤ *Average main: €10* ⊠ *Calle Calatrava 21, La Latina* ☎ *91/221–9660* ⊙ *Closed Mon.* Ⓜ *La Latina, Puerta de Toledo.*

## ★ Casa Revuelta

$ | SPANISH | Many tapas bars serve *pincho de bacalao* (battered cod; an old-school standby) but none hold a candle to Revuelta's rendition, which is crisp, featherlight, and not too salty. Elbow your way to the 1930s-era bar and ask for a pincho de bacalao and a glass of Valdepeñas, a Manchegan red that comes chilled in tiny stemless glasses—just like the olden days. **Known for:** time-warp decor; midmorning vermú (vermouth) rush; battered salt cod canapés. ⑤ *Average main: €8* ⊠ *Calle Latoneros 3, La Latina* ☎ *91/366–3332* ⊙ *Closed Mon. No dinner Sun.* Ⓜ *La Latina.*

## ★ Juana la Loca

$$$ | TAPAS | This tony gastro-bar serves newfangled tapas that are well worth their higher-than-usual price tag. Spring for the tempura soft-shell crab bao with chive mayonnaise, garlicky artichoke flatbread, or any other tapa del día, but whatever you do, order the famous tortilla de patata, irresistible with its molten core and handfuls of caramelized onions. **Known for:** cheek-by-jowl crowds; earth-shatteringly good tortilla de patata; nueva cocina tapas done right. ⑤ *Average main: €24* ⊠ *Pl. Puerta de Moros 4, La Latina* ☎ *91/366–5500* ⊕ *www.juanalaloca.es* ⊙ *No lunch Mon.* Ⓜ *La Latina.*

## Los Huevos de Lucio

$$ | SPANISH | Don't let the crowds dissuade you from entering this Cava Baja stalwart—tables and barstools open up fast. The nonnegotiable dish to try here is *huevos estrellados*, "bashed" fried eggs tucked between olive-oil-fried potatoes and topped with optional

add ons like jamón, txistorra sausage, and *pisto* (Spanish ratatouille). **Known for:** uproarious atmosphere; great salads and vegetable dishes; fried egg nirvana. ⑤ *Average main: €18* ✉ *Calle Cava Baja 30, La Latina* ☎ *91/366–2984* ⊕ *www. loshuevosdelucio.com* ⊗ *Closed Tues.* Ⓜ *La Latina.*

 ## Hotels

### ★ The Hat

$ | **HOTEL** | The Hat epitomizes the fast-growing category of "designer hostels," affordable properties geared toward the younger set with sleek multiperson (and some private) rooms, bumping weekend events, and generous breakfasts. **Pros:** rooftop bar; bountiful breakfasts; steps from Plaza Mayor. **Cons:** location means tourists are everywhere; some rooms are dark; hotel guests not prioritized on rooftop, which fills up fast. ⑤ *Rooms from: €64* ✉ *Calle Imperial 9, La Latina* ☎ *91/772–8572* ⊕ *www. thehatmadrid.com* ⇱ *42 rooms* ◯⃓ *Free Breakfast* Ⓜ *Tirso de Molina.*

### Posada del León de Oro

$$ | **HOTEL** | More like a luxurious village inn than a metropolitan hotel, this refurbished late-19th-century property was built atop the remains of a stone wall that encircled the city in the 12th century, which you can see through glass floor panels at the hotel entrance and in the casual restaurant. **Pros:** bargain prices in an unbeatable location; high ceilings with exposed wood beams; restaurant with more than 300 Spanish wines. **Cons:** cramped entry-level rooms; late-night noise; interior-facing rooms are small. ⑤ *Rooms from: €169* ✉ *Calle Cava Baja 12, La Latina* ☎ *91/119–1494* ⊕ *www. posadadelleondeoro.com* ⇱ *27 rooms* ◯⃓ *No Meals* Ⓜ *La Latina.*

## ▽ Nightlife

### BARS
#### Delic

**CAFÉS** | This warm, inviting café-bar is an all-hours hangout. Homesick travelers will find comfort in Delic's carrot cake, brownies, and pumpkin pie (seasonal), while low-key revelers will appreciate the bar's coziness and late hours (open until 2:30 am on weekends). ✉ *Pl. de la Paja, Costanilla de San Andrés 14, La Latina* ☎ *91/364–5450* ⊕ *www.delic.es* ⊗ *Closed Mon.* Ⓜ *La Latina.*

### El Viajero

**BARS** | You can find fine modern raciones here (the ultracreamy burrata stands out), but this place is better known for its middle-floor bar, which fills up with a cocktail-drinking after-work crowd, and rooftop terrace decorated with potted plants. Beware of the 10% surcharge that comes with outdoor dining, and expect so-so service. ✉ *Pl. de la Cebada 11, La Latina* ☎ *91/366–9064* ⊕ *www. elviajeromadrid.com* ⊗ *Closed Mon.* Ⓜ *La Latina.*

### ★ Sala Equis

**CABARET** | This übertrendy cinema-bar hybrid occupies a former adult film theater. The first floor is a high-ceilinged bar with bleacher seating, deck chairs, cushy sofas, and an ivy-covered wall. Upstairs, there's a quieter lounge with velvet walls and warm neon lights; continue to the top floor and you've reached the main attraction, a 55-seat cinema with cocktail service that plays art-house films (buy tickets online in advance). The Spanish movies don't have subtitles, but there are frequent screenings of undubbed English films. ✉ *Calle del Duque de Alba 4, La Latina* ☎ *91/429–6686* ⊕ *www.salaequis. es* Ⓜ *Tirso de Molina.*

The bustling Rastro flea market takes place every Sunday 10–2; you never know what kind of treasures you might find.

# 🛍 Shopping

## CRAFTS AND DESIGN

### ★ Cocol

CRAFTS | There's no better shop in Madrid for top-quality Spanish artisan wares. The shelves in this tiny independently owned boutique off Plaza de la Paja are lined with everything from exquisite Andalusian pottery to hand-sewn blankets, antique esparto baskets, and leather soccer balls. ⊠ Costanilla de San Andrés 18, La Latina ☎ 91/919–6770 ⊕ www. cocolmadrid.es Ⓜ La Latina.

## FLEA MARKETS

### ★ El Rastro

MARKET | FAMILY | On Sunday morning, Calle de Ribera de Curtidores is closed to traffic and jammed with outdoor booths selling everything under the sun—this is its weekly transformation into the Rastro flea market. Find everything from antique furniture to rare vinyls of flamenco music and keychains emblazoned with "CNT," Spain's old anarchist trade union. Practice your Spanish by bargaining with vendors over paintings, heraldic iron gates, new and used clothes, and even hashish pipes. Plaza General Vara del Rey has some of El Rastro's best antiques, and the streets beyond—Calles Mira el Río Alta and Mira el Río Baja—boast all sorts of miscellany. The market shuts down shortly after 2 pm, in time for a street party to start in the area known as La Latina at and around the bar El Viajero in Plaza Humilladero.

■ TIP→ Off the Ribera are two galerías, courtyards with higher-quality, higher-priced antiques shops. ⊠ Calle de Ribera de Curtidores, La Latina ⏱ Closed Mon.–Sat. Ⓜ La Latina.

## FOOD AND WINE

### Madrid & Darracott

WINE/SPIRITS | More than just a neighborhood wine shop with a well-curated cellar, Madrid & Darracott, opened in 2019, hosts themed wine tastings Thursday to Sunday evenings in English. Wondering about the difference between Rioja and Ribera del Duero or what makes cava sparkle? Reserve your spot online and show up sober—the pours are generous. ⊠ *Calle del Duque de Rivas 8, La Latina* ☎ *91/219–1975* ⊕ *www.madriddarracott. com* Ⓜ *Tirso de Molina.*

## 🎭 Performing Arts

### ★ Flamenco La Quimera

**FOLK/TRADITIONAL DANCE** | **FAMILY** | Prepare for a soulful, invigorating show at this old-school, not-too-kitschy flamenco tablao adjacent to the Plaza Mayor. The start times are 8 and 10 pm nightly, and the festivities spill over into a flamenco-fueled foot-stomping party that starts at midnight (€12). ⊠ *Calle de Cuchilleros 7, La Latina* ☎ *91/356–9361* ⊕ *www.tablaolaquimera.com* 🍽 *€65 dinner package or €35 drink-only ticket* Ⓜ *Sol, Ópera.*

# Lavapiés

Lavapiés, which has overtaken Malasaña and La Latina as Madrid's trendiest neighborhood, has the city's highest concentration of immigrants—mostly Chinese, Indian, and North and West African—and as a result the area has plenty of international markets and inexpensive restaurants. It also has the highest concentration of extant *corralas*—a type of shared working-class building (now protected by the city after many years of abandonment) that became popular in Madrid in the 17th century. Within, apartments revolve around a central patio, which serves as the community's social hub.

## 👁 Sights

### ★ Centro de Arte Reina Sofía

**ART MUSEUM** | Madrid's premier museum of modern art, housed in a historic hospital building, features more than 1,000 works on four floors (the tip of the iceberg from a collection of over 23,000). Painting is the focus here, but photography and cinema are also represented. The new collection contextualizes the works of the great modern masters—Picasso, Miró, and Salvador Dalí—and of other famed artists, such as Juan Gris, Jorge Oteiza, Pablo Gargallo, Julio Gonzalez, Eduardo Chillida, and Antoni Tàpies, into broad historical narratives to explain the evolution of modern art. This means, for instance, that the Dalís are not all displayed together in a single area, but scattered around the 38 rooms. The museum's showpiece is Picasso's *Guernica*: the huge black-and-white canvas depicts the horror of the Nazi Condor Legion's ruthless bombing of innocent civilians in the Basque town of Gernika in 1937 during the Spanish Civil War. Check out the rooftop area for scenic city views. ⊠ *Calle de Santa Isabel 52, Lavapiés* ☎ *91/467–5062* ⊕ *www.museoreinasofia. es* 🍽 *From €12 (free Mon. and Wed.–Sat. after 7 pm, Sun. 12:30–2:30)* 🕐 *Closed Tues.* Ⓜ *Atocha.*

### ★ Mercado de Antón Martín

**MARKET** | Go on an international tapas crawl here—nibbling on tacos (at Cutzamala), sushi (at Yokaloka), homemade croissants (at Cafés Tornasol), and more—without so much as stepping outside. Doppelgänger, an eclectic tasting-menu-only cubbyhole headed by a young Somali-Spanish chef, is currently all the rage; the same goes for newly opened Garage Bar, dedicated to natural wines. ⊠ *Calle de Santa Isabel 5, Lavapiés* ☎ *91/369–0620* ⊕ *www. mercadoantonmartin.com* 🕐 *Closed Sun.* Ⓜ *Antón Martín.*

**Tabacalera** (*Tabacalera Art Promotion*) **ART MUSEUM** | This cultural center, which occupies a dilapidated 18th-century cigarette factory, is divided into two parts. On the building's northwest corner, there's the city-funded exhibition and event space (called Espacio Promoción del Arte), a free-entry hub of contemporary art that's always worth peeking into, while at the southwest corner is the city's most famous art squat. The latter (with no official opening schedule) feels like a slice of Copenhagen's Christiania in Madrid with its political, in-your-face graffiti and sculptural art. ⊠ *Calle de Embajadores 51, Lavapiés* ☎ *91/701–7045* ⊕ *www.promociondelarte.com/tabacalera* 🎫 *Free* ⊙ *Closed Mon.* Ⓜ *Lavapiés.*

##  Restaurants

### Bar Santurce

$ | **TAPAS** | This take-no-prisoners abuelo bar near the top of the Rastro is famous for griddled sardines, served hot and greasy in an odiferous heap with nothing but a flick of crunchy salt. Beware, supersmellers: eau de sardine is potent perfume. **Known for:** busy on Sunday; inexpensive and unfussy; sardine mecca. ⑤ *Average main: €10* ⊠ *Pl. General Vara del Rey 14, Lavapiés* ☎ *64/623–8303* ⊕ *www.sites.google.com/barsanturce.com/barsanturce-en* ⊙ *Closed Mon.* Ⓜ *La Latina.*

### El Rincón de Marco

$ | **CUBAN** | **FAMILY** | Step straight into Havana at this hidden Cuban bar and restaurant where rumbas and sones flow from the speakers and regulars burst into impromptu dance parties. Whatever you end up eating—a €7 *ropa vieja* (cumin-scented beef stew), or perhaps the heftier €10 *picapollo* (fried chicken)—be sure to nab an order or two of fried plantains for the table. **Known for:** music that makes you want to dance; kitschy decor; home-cooked Cuban food. ⑤ *Average main: €10* ⊠ *Calle Cabestreros 8, Lavapiés* ☎ *91/210–7500* ⊙ *Closed Mon.* Ⓜ *Lavapiés.*

### La Burlona

$$ | **TAPAS** | Indulge in some self-pampering, or impress a special someone at this sunlight-flooded gastro-tavern with minimalist decor that serves creatively plated dishes that taste as good as they look. Squash blossoms come stuffed with garlicky revolcona potatoes, oysters on the half-shell arrive swimming in blood orange escabeche, and gazpacho is gussied up with shiso tempura and sushi-grade tuna. **Known for:** secret bar below; more than 30 small-production wines by the bottle; eye-popping modern tapas. ⑤ *Average main: €21* ⊠ *Calle de Santa Isabel 40, Lavapiés* ☎ *91/018–0018* ⊙ *Closed Mon.* Ⓜ *Lavapiés.*

### La Oveja Negra

$ | **VEGETARIAN** | Traveling as a vegan in Madrid is becoming easier and easier, thanks to affordable, inviting restaurants with palate-popping food like Oveja Negra. Try vegan takes on Spanish classics: sidra-braised soy chorizo, leek-and-squash croquetas, and meatless pâtés, to name a few dishes. **Known for:** punk atmosphere; laid-back vibe; tasty vegan cuisine. ⑤ *Average main: €13* ⊠ *Calle Buenavista 42, Lavapiés* ☎ *65/533–6474* ⊕ *ovejavegana.com* ⊙ *Closed Mon. and Tues.* Ⓜ *Lavapiés.*

### La Teranga

$ | **AFRICAN** | **FAMILY** | To get a literal taste of Lavapiés's vibrant West African community, step into this family-run Senegalese hole-in-the-wall that serves the neighborhood's best *mafé* (meat-and-peanut stew), *samousas* (spicy meat-filled turnovers), and *thieboudienne* (Senegal's national dish, made with fish and vegetables)—at exceptionally affordable prices. **Known for:** Senegalese home cooking; almost exclusively West African clientele; warm and welcoming staff. ⑤ *Average main: €9* ⊠ *Calle de Caravaca 12, Lavapiés* ☎ *60/214–1016* Ⓜ *Lavapiés.*

## ★ Melo's

$ | SPANISH | This beloved old Galician bar changed hands in 2021—it's now run by three twentysomething Madrid natives who couldn't bear to see their favorite neighborhood hangout disappear—but the menu of eight infallible dishes has miraculously stayed the same (save for the addition of battered cod, a secret family recipe of one of the new business partners). Come for the jamón-flecked croquetas, blistered Padrón peppers, and griddled football-size zapatilla sandwiches; stay for the dressed-down conviviality and the *cuncos* (ceramic bowls) overflowing with slatey Albariño. **Known for:** battered cod grandfathered in from Casa Revuelta; oversize ham croquetas; old-school Galician bar food. $ *Average main: €11* ⊠ *Calle del Ave María 44, Lavapiés* 🕾 *91/527–5054* Ⓜ *Lavapiés.*

### Restaurante Badila

$ | SPANISH | FAMILY | This mom-and-pop lunch-only staple has paper tablecloths, walls hung with ceramic plates, and a chalked menu. The ever-rotating prix fixe menu is the move here—for €15 (or €18 on weekends), choose from, say, rustic bean stew, a huge T-bone steak, or a wild-mushroom scramble followed by homemade chocolate cake. **Known for:** bubbly staff; lovingly made modern Spanish food; great-value prix fixe. $ *Average main: €16* ⊠ *Calle de San Pedro Martir 6, Lavapiés* 🕾 *91/429–7651* ⊙ *No dinner* Ⓜ *Tirso de Molina.*

### Taberna de Antonio Sánchez

$$ | SPANISH | A Lavapiés landmark opened in 1786, this taberna's regulars have included realist painter Ignacio Zuloaga, countless champion bullfighters, and King Alfonso XIII. Sip on a sudsy *caña*, or half pint, in the creaky, characterful bar area along with a free tapa or two, and then scram—there's much better food to be had in this barrio. **Known for:** cold cañas poured from an ancient pewter tap; museum-grade bullfighting paraphernalia; centuries-old decor. $ *Average*

main: €16 ⊠ *Calle del Mesón de Paredes, Lavapiés* 🕾 *91/539–7826* ⊕ *www.tabernaantoniosanchez.com* ⊙ *No dinner Sun.* Ⓜ *Lavapiés.*

## ☕ Coffee and Quick Bites

### ★ Hola Coffee

$ | CAFÉ | Spaniards love their morning cafés con leche and afternoon *cortados* (espresso with steamed milk), but it was hard to find a truly great cup of joe in Madrid until Hola Coffee came along with its multilayered third-wave espressos and cold brews made with beans the company roasts itself. From-scratch baked goods and open-faced sandwiches will make you want to stay awhile. **Known for:** alternative music and atmosphere; multilingual expat staff and clientele; third-wave coffees made with house-roasted beans. $ *Average main: €9* ⊠ *Calle del Dr. Fourquet 33, Lavapiés* 🕾 *91/056–8263* ⊕ *www.hola.coffee* Ⓜ *Lavapiés.*

### Plántate Café

$ | CAFÉ | This coffee shop with exposed-brick walls is an adorable breakfast nook worth seeking out for its single-origin brews and well-priced plant-based brunches. **Known for:** popular with expats; expertly pulled espressos; plenty of vegan options. $ *Average main: €13* ⊠ *Calle del Mesón de Paredes 28, Lavapiés* 🕾 *91/023–0291* ⊕ *www.facebook.com/plantatecafe* Ⓜ *Lavapiés.*

## 🛏 Hotels

### Artrip

$$$ | HOTEL | A stone's throw from Madrid's "Golden Triangle" of museums, Artrip is a little-known gem of a hotel ideally suited to art-loving travelers. **Pros:** free portable Wi-Fi; youthful design touches; independently owned. **Cons:** no parking; small showers; street noise. $ *Rooms from: €212* ⊠ *Calle de Valencia 11, Lavapiés* 🕾 *91/539–3282* ⊕ *www.artriphotel.com* ⊅ *17 rooms* ⊙ *No Meals* Ⓜ *Embajadores.*

### CoolRooms Palacio de Atocha

$$$$ | HOTEL | The splashiest new (2018) hotel in this part of town is situated at the northern edge of Lavapiés, five minutes on foot from both Sol and Antón Martín market. **Pros:** exceptionally spacious rooms even at the entry level; neon signs and clubby, young atmosphere; fresh flowers and plants galore. **Cons:** overeager and occasionally harried staff; unheated shallow pool; no gym. ⑤ *Rooms from: €300* ✉ *Calle de Atocha 34, Lavapiés* ☎ *91/088–7780* ⊕ *www.coolrooms.com* ⤳ *35 rooms* ❍| *No Meals* Ⓜ *Antón Martín, Sol.*

### Hotel Freedom

$ | HOTEL | FAMILY | Rooms in this inexpensive and cheerful hotel overlooking Plaza de Antón Martín have turquoise walls, crimson sofas, and multicolor headboards. **Pros:** independently owned; trendy location; immaculately clean. **Cons:** no restaurant, bar, gym, or room service; no breakfast; lobby-adjacent room is noisy. ⑤ *Rooms from: €120* ✉ *Calle de Santa Isabel 4, Lavapiés* ☎ *91/073–6271* ⊕ *www.hotelfreedom.com* ⤳ *21 rooms* ❍| *No Meals* Ⓜ *Antón Martín.*

## ⓨ Nightlife

### BARS AND CAFÉS

★ **Bendito Vinos y Vinilos**

WINE BARS | This unassuming stall inside Mercado de San Fernando is a wine-industry hangout—one of the city's top spots for sampling hard-to-find natural and biodynamic wines from Spain and beyond. Pair whatever wine the bartenders are drinking lately with Bendito's well-priced cheeses and charcuterie such as *mojama* (cured tuna) from Andalusia and ribbons of smoky *cecina* (beef "ham") from León. ✉ *Mercado de San Fernando, Calle de Embajadores 41, Lavapiés* ☎ *66/175–0061* ⊕ *www.benditovino.com* ⊙ *Closed Mon.* Ⓜ *Lavapiés.*

### La Caníbal

WINE BARS | At this hot spot for wine geeks with communal tables ideally suited to large groups, you can pull up a stool and choose from dozens of boutique bottles or some 15 small-production Spanish wines on tap. ✉ *Calle de Argumosa 28, Lavapiés* ☎ *91/539–6057* ⊕ *www.lacanibal.com* Ⓜ *Estación del Arte.*

### Savas

BARS | Lavapiés upped its cocktail game with Savas, a pocket-size bar that has quickly become a cult hangout for mixology geeks and neighborhood scenesters. The classic cocktails are expertly made—think White Russians and Tom Collinses at about €9 apiece—and local craft beers by La Virgen are on offer. ✉ *Calle de la Sombrerería 3, Lavapiés* ⊙ *Closed Tues.* Ⓜ *Lavapiés.*

## MUSIC AND DANCE CLUBS

### Club 33

DANCE CLUBS | This intimate nightclub caters to a local, alternative crowd and is a favorite stop on the lesbian party circuit, though revelers of all orientations are welcome. ✉ *Calle de la Cabeza 33, Lavapiés* ☎ *91/369–3302* ⊕ *www.club33madrid.es* ⊙ *Closed Sun.–Wed.* Ⓜ *Lavapiés.*

## ⚫ Performing Arts

### La Casa Encendida

CONCERTS | Film festivals, alternative art shows, dance performances, and weekend events for children are held here. In summer, check the website for outdoor concerts on the rooftop, which is open to the public and a pleasant place to unwind with a book when nothing is on. A coffee and pastry at the laptop-friendly Pum Pum Café outpost on the ground floor is always a treat. ✉ *Ronda de Valencia 2, Lavapiés* ☎ *91/506–3875* ⊕ *www.lacasaencendida.es* ▱ *Free* Ⓜ *Embajadores, Lavapiés.*

A typical evening scene: beer and tapas on the terrace of one of Madrid's many tapas bars

# Shopping

## CRAFTS

### ★ Yolanda Andrés

CRAFTS | These are not your grandma's embroideries: in Yolanda Andrés's thought-provoking pieces, which she describes as "paintings with thread," she interprets the centuries-old technique through a modern-day lens—with stunning results. Beyond the framed artwork (don't miss the technicolor "Artichoke" line), there are embroidered pillowcases, totes, and more. ⊠ Calle Encomienda 15, Lavapiés ☏ 91/026–0742 ⊕ www. yolandaandres.com ⊙ Closed Tues. and Sun. Ⓜ Tirso de Molina.

# Arganzuela

Arganzuela is such a huge district that a born-and-bred madrileño would never say, "let's meet in Arganzuela." Locals instead speak in terms of the neighborhood's many subdistricts: Imperial,

Legazpi, Las Delicias, Palos de Moguer, La Chopera, Las Acacias, and Atocha. The lack of historical sights—with the notable exception of Matadero Madrid—keeps this blue-collar area largely off tourists' radar.

# Sights

### ★ Matadero Madrid

ARTS CENTER | What was once Madrid's largest slaughterhouse is now one of its most vibrant arts and cultural centers. Built in the early 1900s on a then-undeveloped swath of land on the outskirts of town, the Matadero Municipal de Legazpi was in operation from 1925 to 1996. At its peak, it comprised 64 buildings and processed over 500 cattle and 5,000 sheep per day. The complex is a stunning example of Spanish fin-de-siècle civil architecture, all stone-and-redbrick facades punctuated by wide doorways and arched windows. Today its bays are thronged with families, tourists, and plenty of pierced-and-tattooed artists.

Check the website for events ranging from film screenings to poetry slams to art exhibits and design fairs. After moseying from building to building, rest your legs at La Cantina del Matadero, a casual restaurant inside the complex where artists and spectators break bread in the form of tapas and fresh-out-of-the-oven pizzas. ✉ *Pl. de Legazpi 8, Arganzuela* ☎ *91/318–4670* ⊕ *www.mataderomadrid. org* ✆ *Free* Ⓜ *Legazpi.*

## 🍴 Restaurants

### Bar Toboggan
$ | **INTERNATIONAL** | Thanks to independently owned gems like Toboggan, La Chopera neighborhood is beginning to attract a younger, cooler crowd. This corner bar with outdoor seating serves mouthwatering international tapas ranging from tacos to tortilla to homemade hummus in a sunlit space decorated with plants and metal barstools. **Known for:** good-vibes-only atmosphere; open till 2 am daily; local La Virgen beer. Ⓢ *Average main: €11* ✉ *Pl. de Rutilio Gacis 2, Local 1, Arganzuela* ☎ *91/245–6432* ⊕ *www. bartoboggan.com* Ⓜ *Legazpi.*

### Piantao
$$$ | **ARGENTINE** | Across the street from Matadero Madrid, this upmarket Argentine *asador* (steak house) hits all the high notes with its daintily crimped empanadas, regional breads, gutsy South American wines, and flame-licked vegetables and steaks airlifted in from La Pampa with just the right amount of char. **Known for:** gooey dulce de leche cheesecake; attentive and knowledgeable service; industrial yet refined digs. Ⓢ *Average main: €25* ✉ *Paseo de la Chopera 69, Arganzuela* ☎ *91/467–5402* ⊕ *www.piantao.es* ◎ *No dinner Sun.* Ⓜ *Legazpi.*

## 🍸 Nightlife

### La Riviera
**LIVE MUSIC** | One of Madrid's largest nightlife venues, with nine bars and an outdoor terrace, La Riviera hosts big-name DJs, local and international bands, and sundown-to-sunup raves. It's a key party spot on the Madrid Pride week (early July) circuit. ✉ *Paseo Bajo de la Virgen del Puerto, Arganzuela* ☎ *91/365–2415* ⊕ *www.salariviera.com* Ⓜ *Puerta del Ángel.*

### Sala Caracol
**LIVE MUSIC** | Live techno, jazz, funk, and rock shows with reasonably priced tickets keep music-loving madrileños returning to this underground nightclub just south of Lavapiés. ✉ *Calle de Bernardino Obregón 18, Arganzuela* ☎ *91/527–3594* ⊕ *www.salacaracol.com* Ⓜ *Embajadores.*

# Chamberí

Until recently, Chamberí was largely overlooked by tourists due to its reputation as a staid and sleepy residential neighborhood, but in the last several years, it has established itself as the city's gastronomic nerve center with innovative tapas bars and fusion fine-dining restaurants springing up left and right.

## ◉ Sights

### Andén Cero (*Platform Zero*)
**OTHER MUSEUM** | **FAMILY** | The so-called ghost station of Chamberí is now a locomotive museum managed by Metro Madrid. It occupies the grand old Chamberí station, built in 1919 and defunct since 1966. There are vintage advertisements, old maps, and other memorabilia. Tours (free) and placards are in Spanish only. ■TIP→ **Don't wait for staff to come fetch you after watching the introductory film—just head down to the platform.** ✉ *Pl.*

de Chamberí, Chamberí ☎ 90/044–4404 ⊕ www.metromadrid.es/en/who-we-are/anden-cero ☜ Free ⊙ Closed Mon.–Thu. Ⓜ Iglesia, Bilbao.

### Calle Ponzano

STREET | Locals will tell you that this street boasts more bars per square foot (nearly 100 in total) than anywhere else on earth. Alternative facts aside, there's a bar for every taste here, from tile-walled tabernas to louche cocktail lounges to newfangled fusion spots. Start with a caña or glass of vermú at a time-worn standby like El Doble (No. 58) or Fide (No. 8) before sampling traditional tapas at Taberna Alipio Ramos (No. 30) or La Máquina (No. 39). More eclectic, refined bites can be found at the tuna-centric DeAtún (No. 59), cheffy Sala de Despiece (No. 11), and modern Basque Arima (No. 51). ⊠ Calle Ponzano, Chamberí ⊕ www.ponzaning.es Ⓜ Iglesia, Alonso Cano.

### ★ Mercado de Vallehermoso

MARKET | Choose from made-to-order pinsas (ancient Roman pizzas with a cloud-like crust) at Di Buono, flaky Argentine ompanadas at Graciana, refined market cuisine at El 2, updated Spanish street food at Miga Cana, and high-octane Thai curries at Kitchen 154, among other flavor-packed options at this city-block-size market in the heart of Chamberí. ⊠ Calle de Vallehermoso 36, Chamberí ☎ 91/138–9995 ⊕ www.mercadovallehermoso.es ⊙ No dinner Sun. Ⓜ Quevedo.

### ★ Museo Sorolla

ART MUSEUM | See the world through the once-in-a-generation eye of Spain's most famous impressionist painter, Joaquín Sorolla (1863–1923), who lived and worked most of his life at this home and garden that he designed and decorated. Every corner is filled with exquisite artwork—including plenty of original Sorollas—and impeccably selected furnishings, which pop against brightly colored walls that evoke the Mediterranean

coast, where the painter was born. The museum can be seen as part of the Abono Cinco Palacios, a €12 pass that grants access to five mansion-museums. ⊠ Paseo del General Martínez Campos 37, Chamberí ☎ 91/310–1584 ⊕ museosorolla.mcu.es ☜ €3 (free Sat. after 2 and all day Sun.) ⊙ Closed Mon. Ⓜ Rubén Darío, Gregorio Marañón.

## 🍴 Restaurants

### Las Tortillas de Gabino

$$$ | TAPAS | At this lively restaurant you'll find crowds of Spaniards gobbling up one of the city's finest, most upscale renditions of tortilla española with unconventional add-ins like octopus, potato chips, and truffles. The menu also includes plenty of equally succulent non-egg choices (the rice dishes in particular stand out). **Known for:** carefully selected wines; date-night ambience; fancy tortillas. ⑤ Average main: €24 ⊠ Calle Rafael Calvo 20, Chamberí ☎ 91/319–7505 ⊕ www.lastortillasdegabino.com ⊙ Closed Sun. Ⓜ Rubén Darío.

### Perretxico Chamberí

$$ | BASQUE | The new Madrid outpost of a legendary Vitoria-Gasteiz (Basque Country) pintxo bar, Perretxico is known for its "cocido donut"—cocido being Spain's famous boiled dinner of chickpeas, various meats, and sausages. These are blended into a paste, stuffed inside a doughnut, and served alongside a demitasse of umami-packed bone broth for dunking, a wink to the classic doughnut-coffee combo. **Known for:** Chamberí hot spot; inventive Basque pintxos; cocido doughnut. ⑤ Average main: €17 ⊠ Calle Rafael Calvo 29, Chamberí ☎ 91/192–0069 ⊕ www.perretxico.es ⊙ No dinner Sun. Ⓜ Rubén Darío.

### Restaurante Barrera

$$$ | SPANISH | Duck into this cozy hole-in-the-wall and be treated like family—Ana, the owner, recites the nightly menu to

## Sights ▼

1 Andén
   Cero ......... **B7**

2 Calle
   Ponzano ..... **B5**

3 Mercado de
   Valle-
   hermoso .... **A6**

4 Museo
   Sorolla ...... **C6**

## Restaurants ▼

1 Casa
   Sotero ....... **C2**

2 DiverXO ..... **C2**

3 Las Tortillas
   de Gabino ... **B6**

4 Perretxico
   Chamberí ... **C6**

5 Restaurante
   Barrera ...... **B6**

6 Sacha ....... **C2**

7 Sala de
   Despiece.... **B6**

8 Sylkar ....... **B5**

9 Taberna
   San
   Mamés ...... **A5**

10 Tripea ....... **A6**

## Quick Bites ▼

1 Ciento Trenta
   Grados ...... **A6**

## Hotels ▼

1 Hotel NH
   Collection
   Madrid
   Euro-
   building .... **C2**

2 Hotel
   Orfila ........ **B8**

3 Hotel
   Sardinero ... **B7**

4 Hyatt Regency
   Hesperia
   Madrid ..... **C6**

5 Intercontinental
   Madrid ...... **C6**

6 The Pavilions
   Madrid ...... **C8**

**KEY**

1 *Sights*

1 *Restaurants*

1 *Quick Bites*

1 *Hotels*

Chamberí, Chamartín
and Tetuán

each table and flits around with a smile
until the last guest saunters out. Barrera's famous patatas revolconas (papri-
ka-spiced mashed potatoes topped with
crispy pork belly), are always on offer;
they might be followed by roast suckling
lamb, wine-braised meatballs, or seared
dayboat fish depending on the night.
Inquire about prices when ordering to
avoid sticker shock. **Known for:** unhurried
all-night dining; terrific patatas revolconas
and ensaladilla rusa; homey, romantic
atmosphere. ⑤ *Average main: €25*
✉ *Calle de Alonso Cano 25, Chamberí*
☎ *91/594–1757* ⊘ *Closed Mon. No dinner
Sun.* Ⓜ *Alonso Cano.*

### Sala de Despiece

**$$ | SPANISH |** The opening of this
ultratrendy butcher-shop-themed
restaurant spurred the revival of Calle
Ponzano as Madrid's most exciting tapas
street. Feast on eye-catching, impeccably
prepared dishes like carpaccio-truffle
roll-ups and grilled octopus slathered in
chimichurri.✉ **Known for:** see-and-be-
seen crowd; playful industrial decor;
local celebrity chef. ⑤ *Average main:
€22* ✉ *Calle de Ponzano 11, Chamberí*
☎ *91/752–6106* ⊕ *www.saladedespiece.
com* Ⓜ *Iglesia, Alonso Cano.*

### ★ Sylkar

**$$ | SPANISH | FAMILY |** Budget time for
a siesta after dining at this phenomenal down-home restaurant that hasn't
changed a lick since opening a half-century ago. Whether you're in the boisterous
downstairs bar or cozy upstairs dining
room with cloth napkins and popcorn
walls, you'll be blown away by Sylkar's
lovingly prepared specialties including
creamy ham croquetas, braised squid in
ink sauce, battered hake, and the best
tortilla española in Madrid for those in
the runnier-the-better camp. **Known for:**
free tapa with every drink; irreverent
banter with the waitstaff; legendary
tortilla española. ⑤ *Average main: €21*
✉ *Calle de Espronceda 17, Chamberí*

☎ *91/554–5703* ⊘ *Closed Sun. No dinner
Sat.* Ⓜ *Alonso Cano.*

### Taberna San Mamés

**$$$ | SPANISH |** What's that firetruck-red
stew on every table in this tiny neighborhood tavern? *Callos a la madrileña*,
Madrid-style tripe flavored with industrial
quantities of garlic and smoky Extremaduran paprika. ■TIP→ **Known for:** cozy,
traditional digs; neighborhood crowd;
abuela-approved tripe stew. ⑤ *Average
main: €27* ✉ *Calle de Bravo Murillo
88, Chamberí* ☎ *91/534–5065* ⊕ *www.
tabernasanmames.es* ⊘ *Closed Sun. No
dinner Mon.* Ⓜ *Cuatro Caminos.*

### Tripea

**$$$$ | FUSION |** Young-gun chef Roberto
Martínez Foronda continues to turn food
critics' heads with his Spanish-fusion
restaurant hidden inside the Mercado de
Vallehermoso, Chamberí's traditional market. The ever-changing tasting menu—a
steal at €40—takes cues from *chifa* (Peru-
vian-Chinese) and *nikkei* (Peruvian-Japa-
nese) culinary canons and incorporates
fresh ingredients from the market. **Known
for:** foodie buzz; Spanish-fusion cuisine;
experimental tasting menus. ⑤ *Average
main: €40* ✉ *Mercado de Vallehermoso,
Calle de Vallehermoso 36, Chamberí*
☎ *91/828–6947* ⊕ *www.tripea.es*
⊘ *Closed Sun. and Mon.* Ⓜ *Quevedo.*

## ☕ Coffee and Quick Bites

### Ciento Treinta Grados

**$ | CAFÉ |** These carb geeks cut no
corners—breads here are leavened with
sourdough and made with organic stoneground flours, and the beans for their
complex coffees are roasted in house.
Drop into the postage-stamp dinette
for breakfast or an afternoon pick-me-
up, and savor airy all-butter croissants
and any range of sweet and savory
pastries and breads. **Known for:** location
across from Mercado de Vallehermoso;
house-roasted coffee beans; sourdough

breads and pastries. $ *Average main:*
*€7 ✉ Calle de Fernando el Católico 17,*
*Chamberí ☎ 91/006–7076 ⊕ cientotrein-*
*tagrados.com* Ⓜ *Quevedo.*

##  Hotels

### Hotel Orfila

**$$$$ | HOTEL |** On a leafy residential street,
this 1886 town house bearing the Relais
& Château fleur-de-lis feels more like a
country estate than a city-center hotel.
**Pros:** tranquil year-round dining terrace;
historical art and furniture; old-world
comfort. **Cons:** expensive room service via poorly designed app; no gym;
dining is not up to standard. $ *Rooms*
*from: €577 ✉ Calle Orfila 6, Chamberí*
*☎ 91/702–7770 ⊕ www.hotelorfila.com*
*➳ 32 rooms* ¡Ⓞ¡ *No Meals* Ⓜ *Alonso*
*Martínez.*

### Hotel Sardinero

**$ | HOTEL |** Steps from the trendy Mala-
saña and gay-friendly Chueca districts,
and slightly off the tourist track, Hotel
Sardinero occupies a turn-of-the-century palace directly above the Alonso
Martínez metro stop. **Pros:** good deals on
rates; gorgeous neoclassical facade; two
rooftop terraces. **Cons:** kettles and cof-
feemakers only available on request; no
restaurant; some guests report plumbing
issues. $ *Rooms from: €120 ✉ Pl. Alon-*
*so Martínez 3, Chamberí ☎ 91/206–2160*
*⊕ www.hotelsardineromadrid.com ➳ 63*
*rooms* ¡Ⓞ¡ *No Meals* Ⓜ *Alonso Martínez.*

### Intercontinental Madrid

**$$$$ | HOTEL |** Chauffeur-driven town cars
snake around the block day and night at
the Intercontinental Madrid, a classically
decorated hotel frequented by dignitar-
ies, diplomats, and other international
bigwigs. **Pros:** dependable if starchy
elegance; excellent business facilities;
24-hour gym. **Cons:** street-facing rooms
can be noisy; removed from the center;
cookie-cutter business hotel decor.

$ *Rooms from: €278 ✉ Paseo de la*
*Castellana 49, Chamberí ☎ 91/700–7300*
*⊕ www.ihg.com ➳ 302 rooms* ¡Ⓞ¡ *No*
*Meals* Ⓜ *Gregorio Marañón.*

### The Pavilions Madrid

**$$$ | HOTEL |** Hitting the sweet spot
between high-end luxury and state-of-
the-art design, the Pavilions is a boutique
hotel that stands out for its original art
and sculpture by top Spanish artists,
much of it available for purchase. **Pros:**
design on a budget; indoor-outdoor pool
and wellness area; breakfast in solarium.
**Cons:** drab facade; unexciting block; small
gym. $ *Rooms from: €220 ✉ Calle Ama-*
*dor de los Ríos 3, Chamberí ☎ 91/310–*
*7500 ⊕ www.pavilionshotels.com/madrid*
*➳ 29 rooms* ¡Ⓞ¡ *No Meals* Ⓜ *Colón.*

## ⊙ Nightlife

### MUSIC CLUBS
#### ★ Clamores

**LIVE MUSIC |** Jive to live jazz concerts and
DJ sets until 5:30 am on weekdays and 6
am on weekends. Check the website for
performance listings and to buy tickets,
which rarely creep above €15. ✉ *Calle de*
*Albuquerque 14, Chamberí ☎ 91/445–*
*5480 ⊕ www.salaclamores.es* Ⓜ *Bilbao.*

# Chamartín

This sprawling neighborhood, which
extends to the north of the city from
Avenida de América, wasn't annexed to
Madrid until 1948. During the following
decades, and due to the construction of
new sights such as the Chamartín Train
Station and the National Auditorium of
Music, it has been gaining popularity
among madrileños as a good and lively
place to live. The area has many office
buildings, convention centers, and business hotels.

# ¡GOOOOOOAALL!

Fútbol (or soccer) is Spain's number one sport, and Madrid has four teams: Real Madrid, Atlético Madrid, Rayo Vallecano, and Getafe. For tickets, book online or call a week in advance to reserve and pick them up at the stadium—or, if the match isn't sold out, stand in line at the stadium of your choice. Ticket prices vary according to several factors: the importance of the rival, the seat location, the day of the week the match takes place, whether the match is aired on free TV or not, and the competition (Liga, Copa del Rey, Champions League or Europa League). Final dates and match times are often confirmed only a few days before, so it can be hard to reserve in advance. That said, Real Madrid and Atlético Madrid never play at home the same week, so there is a football match every single week in the city.

### Stadiums

**Campo de Fútbol de Vallecas** To enjoy a spirited match without the long lines and inflated price tag, step up to Rayo Vallecano's box office. The team's second-tier status doesn't make the games any less thrilling (think college ball vs. NBA), especially when you catch them on their home turf in Vallecas, which seats 14,708. You can feel good about your ticket purchase, too, since Rayo is known for its community activism. When the pandemic hit, the team's charitable foundation sewed and distributed 12,000 masks for undersupplied hospitals. ✉ *Calle del Payaso Fofó 0, Puente de Vallecas, Madrid* ☎ *91/478–4329* ⊕ *www.rayovallecano.es* Ⓜ *Portazgo.*

**Santiago Bernabéu Stadium** Home to Real Madrid, this stadium seats 85,400 and offers daytime tours of the facilities. A €590 million gut renovation is on track to be completed by mid-2023, turning the stadium into a sleek, UFO-like coliseum from the future; tour and game schedules may be affected, so check the website for updates. ✉ *Paseo de la Castellana 140, Chamartín* ☎ *91/398–4300* ⊕ *www.realmadrid.es* Ⓜ *Santiago Bernabéu.*

**Wanda Metrpolitano** Since 2017, Atlético Madrid (Real Madrid's rival team) has called this stadium in the San Blas–Canillejas district home.

✉ *Av. de Luis Aragones 4, San Blas–Canilejas, Madrid* ⊕ *www.atleticodemadrid.com/wandametropolitano* Ⓜ *Estadio Metropolitano.*

## 🍴 Restaurants

### ★ DiverXO

**$$$$ | ECLECTIC |** When you ask a madrileño about a remarkable food experience—something that stirs the senses beyond feeding one's appetite—DiverXO is often the first name you'll hear. There's just one take-no-prisoners tasting menu (called a "canvas") that runs €365 and incorporates a dizzying array of international ingredients and chemical processes.

**Known for:** Madrid's only Michelin three-star; courses that use the whole table as a canvas; punk-rock fine dining. 💲 *Average main: €365* ✉ *NH Hotel Eurobuilding, Calle Padre Damian 23, Chamartín* ☎ *91/570–0766* ⊕ *www.diverxo.com* ⊘ *Closed Sun.–Tues.* Ⓜ *Cuzco.*

### ★ Sacha

**$$$$ | SPANISH |** Settle into an unhurried feast at Sacha, a cozy bistro with soul-satisfying food and hand-selected wines, and you might never want to leave—especially if you strike up a conversation with chef Sacha himself, who's quite the storyteller. The cuisine is regional Spanish—think butifarra sausages with sautéed mushrooms or razor clams with black garlic emulsion—with just enough imagination to make you wonder why the restaurant isn't better known. **Known for:** hard-to-find wines; impeccable steak tartare; Spanish bistro fare. $ *Average main: €30* ⊠ *Calle Juan Hurtado de Mendoza 11, Chamartín* ☎ *91/345–5952* ⊕ *www.restaurantesacha.com* ☻ *Closed Sun.* Ⓜ *Cuzco.*

## 🛏 Hotels

### ★ Hotel NH Collection Madrid Eurobuilding

$$ | HOTEL | The towering NH Collection Madrid Eurobuilding, located blocks from Real Madrid's home stadium, is a state-of-the-art luxury property with large, airy rooms and an enormous pool and gym complex. **Pros:** 180-degree views from some rooms; bargain rates; excellent gym and spa. **Cons:** very quiet area at night; hotel can't secure bookings at DiverXO; inconsistent service. $ *Rooms from: €130* ⊠ *Calle de Padre Damián 23, Chamartín* ☎ *91/353–7300* ⊕ *www.nh-hotels.com* ⇌ *440 rooms* ⦿ *No Meals* Ⓜ *Cuzco.*

### Hyatt Regency Hesperia Madrid

$$$$ | HOTEL | The legendary Hesperia hotel was bought and renovated by Hyatt Regency and is all about comfortable business stays. **Pros:** corporate-chic decor; 24-hour room service; spacious rooms. **Cons:** miles from the city center; stuffy, business feel; interior rooms can be dark. $ *Rooms from: €359* ⊠ *Paseo de la Castellana 57, Chamartín* ☎ *91/210–8800* ⊕ *www.hesperia.com* ⇌ *169 rooms* ⦿ *No Meals* Ⓜ *Gregorio Marañón.*

# Tetuán

As Madrid grew dramatically in the second half of the 19th century, rough-and-tumble barrios like Tetuán got a face-lift. Today, its main artery, Bravo Murillo, divides the more developed, business-oriented eastern section from the more residential and multicultural western area of the neighborhood.

## 🍴 Restaurants

### ★ Casa Sotero

$ | TAPAS | Crackly fried pig ear, fat wedges of tortilla de patata, and garlicky rabbit *al ajillo* are a few of the many old-school standbys that have kept this tile-lined cubbyhole bar in business since 1934. **Known for:** off-the-radar gem that's worth the hike; phenomenally affordable; classic Madrid tapas and breakfasts. $ *Average main: €9* ⊠ *Calle José Castán Tobeñas 1, Tetuán* ☎ *91/570–6481* ⊕ *www.casasotero.org* ☻ *Closed Mon.* Ⓜ *Pl. de Castilla, Valdeacederas.*

## 🎭 Nightlife

### DANCE CLUBS

**Oh My Club**

DANCE CLUBS | At this hopping venue, popular among young Latinx locals, you'll find plenty of space to dance (under the gaze of go-go girls) to rap, hip-hop, and reggaeton, and also quieter nooks where you can chat and sip a drink. ⊠ *Calle Rosario Pino 14, Tetuán* ☎ *91/340–7537* ⊕ *www.ohmyclub.es* ☻ *Closed Mon.* Ⓜ *Cuzco.*

# CENTRAL SPAIN

**4**

Updated by
Benjamin Kemper

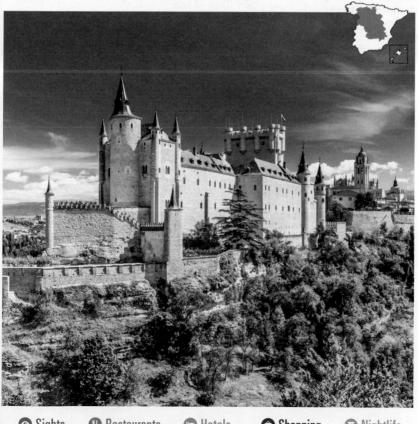

| ● Sights | ⑪ Restaurants | 🛏 Hotels | 🛍 Shopping | ☝ Nightlife |
|----------|---------------|----------|-------------|-------------|
| ★★★★★ | ★★★★☆ | ★★★☆☆ | ★★★★☆ | ★★★☆☆ |

# WELCOME TO CENTRAL SPAIN

## TOP REASONS TO GO

★ **Discover the Toledo of El Greco:** Tour the Renaissance painter's home and studio on an El Greco–themed tourist trail in the stunning city that the Greek-born painter called home.

★ **Be mesmerized by Cuenca's Hanging Houses:** The Casas Colgadas seem to defy gravity, clinging to a cliffside with views over Castile–La Mancha's parched plains.

★ **Wander Salamanca's old and new cathedrals:** Compare the intricate Late Gothic detail of the new with the Romanesque simplicity of the old.

★ **Visit Segovia's aqueduct:** Miraculously this soaring 2,000-year-old Roman aqueduct, constructed without mortar, still functions today.

★ **Time-travel to the Middle Ages:** The skyline of medieval Cáceres—with its ancient spires, towers, and cupolas—belies myriad up-to-the-minute cultural attractions.

**1 Toledo.** Uncover a treasure trove of medieval art and restored synagogues, mosques, and churches.

**2 Almagro.** Relish in small-town charm and an evening tapeo (tapas crawl) on the plaza.

**3 Cuenca.** Explore the Ciudad Encantada ("Enchanted City") with its alien rock formations.

**4 Sigüenza.** Marvel at one of Spain's most stunning Gothic cathedrals.

**5 Segovia.** Climb the watchtower of the Alcázar, said to have inspired Walt Disney.

**6 Sepúlveda.** Explore a medieval dungeon and 11th-century church in a town some call the most beautiful in Spain.

**7 San Lorenzo de El Escorial.** Bask in the grandeur of Habsburg Spain in the eponymous palace complex.

**8 Ávila.** Trace some of the best-preserved city walls in Europe and duck into ancient convents.

**9 Salamanca.** See if you can spot the "lucky frog" on the plateresque facade of Spain's oldest university.

**10 Burgos.** Taste the famous "morcilla de Burgos" (local blood sausage) after visiting the imposing cathedral.

**11 León.** Snap photos of vivid stained-glass panels in this city's Gothic cathedral.

**12 Astorga.** Feast your eyes on one of Gaudí's least-known masterpieces, the Episcopal Palace.

**13 Villafranca del Bierzo.** Vineyard-hop through the cult-favorite Bierzo wine region.

**14 El Valle del Jerte.** Get a front-row seat to one of Spain's most breathtaking natural displays.

**15 La Vera and Monasterio de Yuste.** Detour here for natural springs and the retirement estate of King Carlos V.

**16 Cáceres.** Time-travel back a few centuries in the UNESCO-protected old town, a filming site for *Game of Thrones*.

**17 Trujillo.** Contemplate Spain's fraught colonial past in the cradle of the conquistadores.

**18 Guadalupe.** Admire this jewel of a monastery in the foothills of the Sierra de Villuercas.

**19 Mérida.** Tour the immaculately restored Roman amphitheater.

ASTURIAS
CANTABRIA
NAVARRA

Villafranca del Bierzo
13
León
11
LA RIOJA
12
Astorga
Burgos
10
PORTUGAL
Soria
Toro
Zamora
Valladolid
Sepúlveda 6
*Duero R.*
CASTILE AND LEÓN
Medinaceli
ARAGON
Salamanca
Segovia 5
Sigüenza
9
Ávila 8
4
San Lorenzo de El Escorial 7
MADRID
*SIERRA DE GREDOS*
La Vera
MADRID
Alcalá de Henares
Plasencia
15
14
Jerte and El Valle del Jerte
Aranjuez
Tarancón
Cuenca
3
Toledo 1
CASTILE-LA MANCHA
Cáceres 16
Guadalupe 18
Mota del Cuervo
17
Trujillo
Consuegra
Alcázar
La Roda
Malagon
Tomelloso
adajoz
Ciudad Real 2
Manzanares
Albacete
19
Mérida
Almagro
Valdepenas
Hellín
EXTREMADURA
Zafra
Puertollano
ANDALUSIA
MURCIA

0          30 mi
0          30 km

# EATING AND DRINKING WELL IN CENTRAL SPAIN

Roast lamb with potatoes

In Spain's central *meseta*, or arid, high plateau, rustic cooking provides comfort and energy. Roast lamb, pork, and goat are staples, as are soups, stews, and *migas*—breadcrumbs fried with meats and sausages.

Classic Castilian dishes include *cordero* (lamb) and *cochinillo* (suckling pig), roasted in wood-burning ovens, and *perdiz* (partridge), either marinated in *escabeche* (spiced vinaigrette), or served Toledo-style (braised in white wine). Broad-bean dishes are common around Ávila and La Granja (Segovia), while *trucha* (trout) and *cangrejos de río* (crayfish that are usually imported these days) are Guadalajara specialties. Some of Castile's most surprising cuisine is found in Cuenca, where Sephardic and Moorish influences appear in dishes like gazpacho *pastor,* a stew made with several meats and a matzolike flatbread. Across Spain's rural interior, wild mushrooms are a constant, most often cooked with little more than salt and olive oil in earthenware dishes; more elaborate preparations include *níscalos estofados* (stewed saffron milk cap mushrooms) and *setas a la segoviana*, a fragrant braise of king trumpet mushrooms.

## WHAT DON QUIXOTE ATE

"Somewhere in La Mancha, in a place whose name I do not care to remember..." begins the epic *Don Quixote*, yet the wines and hearty dishes of this region are some of Spain's most memorable. Cervantine menus based on dishes mentioned in the book are favorites at taverns throughout Quixote country southeast of Madrid. They usually feature *gachas manchegas* (a thick porridge of fried grass-pea flour and pork) and *duelos y quebrantos* (scrambled eggs and bacon).

## LAMB

*Cordero asado,* roast lamb, is a favorite throughout Castile, while the subcategory of *lechazo,* or milk-fed lamb, is even more prized for its mild, ultratender meat, one of Spain's great delicacies.

## PARTRIDGE

*Perdiz a la toledana* is one of Castile–La Mancha's most classic dishes and a masterpiece of *cocina de caza,* Spanish game-meat cooking. The partridges are braised in wine with vinegar, olive oil, onions, garlic, and bay leaves until the sauce is thick and rich. October to February is hunting season for partridge and the best time to try it—just watch out for steel shot in the meat.

## VEGETABLE STEW

*Pisto manchego,* a ratatouille-like vegetable stew with peppers, onions, tomatoes, and zucchini flavored with garlic and (sometimes) cumin, is a classic. Served in earthenware *cazuelas,* often with a fried egg on top, it makes a wonderful light lunch with a bit of crusty bread and a glass of raspy local wine.

## MIGAS DEL PASTOR

Translated as "shepherd's bread crumbs," this ancient dish is made with stale bread that's softened with water and fried in olive oil with lots of garlic

Migas were created as a way to use up leftover bread.

and (optionally) eggs, bacon, chorizo, peppers, or potato. Fresh grapes are a traditional accompaniment.

## GAZPACHO PASTOR (SHEPHERD'S STEW)

Andalusian gazpacho is a cold soup, but in La Mancha, especially around Cuenca, gazpacho is a thick, hot braise made with virtually everything in the barnyard. Partridge, hare, rabbit, hen, peppers, paprika, and *tortas de cenceña* (a flatbread with Jewish roots made especially for this dish) all find their way into the pot.

## WINES OF CENTRAL SPAIN

Central Spain's finest wines are red, and most are bold, oaky, and high in alcohol. Wines made in the traditional style include Dominio de Valdepusa's Petit Verdot and Syrah blends (Toledo); Ribera del Duero's famed Tempranillos by Pingus, Protos, and Pago de Carraovejas; Extremadura's concentrated reds from Bodegas Habla and Ruiz Torres; and Bierzo's berry-forward Mencías from the likes of Descendientes de J. Palacios. Notable natural and biodynamic wineries in this area include Esencia Rural (Toledo), Envínate (Extremadura), Uva de Vida (Toledo), and Vinos Ambiz (Ávila). Winery visits are generally by appointment only.

Pisto manchego incorporates a variety of stewed vegetables.

Madrid, in the center of Spain, is an excellent jumping-off point for exploring, and the high-speed train puts many destinations within easy reach. The "Castiles," which bracket Madrid to the north and south, and Extremadura, bordering Portugal, are steeped in tradition and feel a world away from the ultramodern Spanish capital.

There's something of an underlying unity in Castile, the high, wide steppe of central Spain planted with olive trees and grapevines and punctuated with tiny medieval towns and the occasional scrubby sierra.

Over the centuries, poets and authors have characterized Castile as austere and melancholy. Gaunt mountain ranges frame the horizons; gorges and rocky outcrops break up flat expanses; and the fields around Ávila and Segovia are littered with giant boulders. Castilian villages are built predominantly of granite, and their severe, formidable look contrasts markedly with the whitewashed walls of most of southern Spain.

The very name Extremadura, literally "the far end of the Duero" (as in the Douro River), expresses the wild, isolated, and end-of-the-line character of the region bordering Portugal. With its poor soil and minimal industry, Extremadura hardly experienced the economic booms felt in other parts of Spain, and it's still the country's poorest province—but for the tourist, this otherworldly, lost-in-time feel is unforgettable. No other place in Spain has as many Roman monuments as

Mérida, capital of the vast Roman province of Lusitania, which included most of the western half of the Iberian Peninsula. Mérida guarded the Vía de la Plata, the major Roman highway that crossed Extremadura from north to south, connecting Gijón with Seville. The economy and the arts declined after the Romans left, but the region revived in the 16th century when explorers and conquerors of the so-called New World—from Francisco Pizarro and Hernán Cortés to Francisco de Orellana, first navigator of the Amazon—returned to their birthplace. These men built the magnificent palaces that now glorify towns such as Cáceres and Trujillo, and they turned the remote monastery of Guadalupe into one of the great artistic repositories of Spain.

## MAJOR REGIONS

**Castile–La Mancha** is the land of Don Quixote, Miguel de Cervantes's chivalrous hero. Some of Spain's oldest and noblest cities are found here, steeped in culture and legend, though many have fallen into neglect due to rural flight and lack of investment. Traditional towns here are treeless warrens of whitewashed one-floor houses with indigo-painted plinths—squint and you could be in North

Africa. Toledo, the pre-Madrid capital of Castile, is the main destination, though travelers willing to venture farther afield can explore Cuenca with its Hanging Houses; Almagro with its green-and-white plaza and splendid parador; or Consuegra or Campo de Criptana, both of which sit under the gaze of Don Quixote–esque windmills.

**Castile–León** is Spain's windswept interior, stretching from the dry plains of Castile–La Mancha to the hilly vineyards of Ribera del Duero, and up to the foot of several mountain ranges: the Sierra de Gredos, Sierra de Francia, and northward toward the towering Picos de Europa. The area combines two of Spain's old kingdoms, Léon and Old Castile, each with their many treasures of palaces, castles, and cathedrals. The region's crown jewel is Segovia with its Roman aqueduct and 12th-century Alcázar, though medieval Ávila is a close second. Farther north lie Salamanca, dominated by dusky sandstone buildings, and the ancient capitals of Burgos and León. Burgos, an early outpost of Christianity, has what most consider the most beautiful Gothic cathedral in Spain. León is a vibrant college town with a budget-friendly tapas scene and a nationally famous modern art museum.

Rugged **Extremadura** is a nature lover's paradise, so bring your mountain bike (or plan on renting one), hiking boots, and binoculars. The lush Jerte Valley and the craggy peaks of the Sierra de Gredos mark upper Extremadura's fertile landscape. South of the Jerte Valley is the 15th-century Yuste Monastery in the village of Cuacos de Yuste. Don't miss medieval Cáceres—boasting one of the best-kept old towns in Europe—and Mérida, with its immaculately preserved Roman amphitheater. Extremadura's other main towns—Badajoz, Trujillo, Olivenza, and Zafra—are charming (if a tad sleepy) and virtually tourist-free.

# Planning

## When to Go

July and August can be brutally hot, and November through February can get bitterly cold, especially in the mountains. May and October, when the weather is sunny but relatively cool, are the two best months to visit.

Spring is the ideal season in Extremadura, especially in the countryside, when the valleys and hills bloom with wildflowers. The stunning spectacle of cherry blossom season in the Jerte Valley and La Vera takes place around mid-March (for more information, visit ⊕ www.turismovalledeljerte.com). Fall is also a good time for Extremadura, though there may be rain starting in late October.

## Planning Your Time

Madrid is an excellent hub for venturing farther into Spain, but with so many choices, we've divided destinations into must-see, stand-alone excursions and worthy pit stops en route to other parts of the country. Some are day trips; others are best overnight.

The top stand-alone destinations from Madrid are **Toledo, Segovia** (add **Sepúlveda** if time allows), **Salamanca,** and **Sigüenza,** in order of importance. Salamanca should be an overnight trip as it's farther and has buzzy nightlife, while the others can be long day-trips.

If you're traveling to other areas in Spain and beyond, we suggest seeing the following destinations along the way:

Visiting Salamanca? Stop in **Ávila** (buses go direct to Salamanca without stopping, but most trains stop in Ávila).

Visiting Santander, San Sebastián, or Bilbao? Stop in **Burgos.**

Visiting Asturias? Stop in **León.**

Visiting Galicia? Stop in **Villafranca del Bierzo** or **Astorga.**

Visiting Córdoba or Granada? Stop in **Almagro.**

Visiting Valencia? Stop in **Cuenca.** Most trains, including the high-speed AVE to Valencia, call there.

Visiting Portugal? Stop in **Extremadura.**

Extremadura is a neglected destination, even for Spanish tourists, but it's a beautiful part of the country with fascinating cities like Cáceres (a UNESCO World Heritage Site) and Trujillo, both of which have been used as filming locations for *Game of Thrones.* You can get a lightning impression of Extremadura in a day's drive from Madrid (or on a pit stop on the way to Lisbon), though overnighting is preferable. It's about 2½ hours from Madrid to **Jerte**; from there, take the A66 south to **Cáceres** before heading east to **Trujillo** on the N521. Split your time evenly between Cáceres and Trujillo. If you have more time, spend a day exploring the Roman monuments in **Mérida** and do some world-famous bird-watching in the **Parque Natural de Monfragüe,** near **Plasencia.** A deeper dive into the region must include a visit to the stunning **Monasterio de Yuste,** where Spain's founding emperor, Carlos V, died in 1558.

# Getting Here and Around

## AIR

The only international airport in central Spain is Madrid's Barajas; Salamanca, León, and Valladolid have domestic airports but receive very few flights. Extremadura's only airport is Badajoz, which services Madrid and Barcelona only.

**AIRPORT Madrid–Barajas Adolfo Suárez Airport.** ☎ *91/321–1000* ⊕ *www.aena.es.*

## BUS

Bus connections between Madrid and the "Castiles" are frequent and cheap; there are several stations and stops in Madrid. Because of unpredictable travel patterns due to COVID-19, some of the below routes may not be fully operational. Double-check all timetables on carriers' websites for up-to-date information.

Buses to Toledo (1 hour) leave every half hour from the southern Plaza Elíptica, and buses to Segovia (1¼ hours) leave every hour from La Sepulvedana's headquarters, near Príncipe Pío. Jiménez Dorado sends buses to Ávila (1¾ hours) from the Estación del Sur. ALSA has service to León (4½ hours), Valladolid (2¼ hours), and Soria (3 hours). Avanza serves Cuenca (2¾ hours), Salamanca (3 hours), and Burgos (2½ hours).

From Burgos, buses head north to the Basque Country; from León, you can press on to Asturias. Service between towns is not as frequent as it is to and from Madrid, so in some cases, you may find it quicker to return to Madrid and make your way from there. Online reservations are rarely necessary but might save you a few bucks and the minutes you'd otherwise spend waiting in line.

Buses to Extremadura's main cities from Madrid typically leave on time. Some examples of destinations from Madrid are: Cáceres (seven daily), Guadalupe (two daily), Trujillo (12 daily), and Mérida (seven daily). For schedules and prices, check the tourist offices or consult the individual bus lines. Note that it's best to avoid rush hour as journeys can be delayed.

A headache-free way to plan bus travel is www.omio.com, a scheduling and purchasing site that allows you to view different prices and bus companies on one platform.

**CONTACTS ALSA.** ☎ *90/242-2242*
⊕ *www.alsa.es*. **Avanza.** (*Auto-Res*)
☎ *91/272-2832* ⊕ *www.avanzabus.com*.
**La Sepulvedana.** ☎ *90/211-9699* ⊕ *lasepul-vedana.es*. **Movelia.** ☎ *90/264-6428*
⊕ *www.movelia.es*.

## CAR

Major highways—the A1 through A6—spoke out from Madrid, making Spain's farthest corners no more than five- to six-hour drives. If possible, avoid returning to Madrid on major highways at the end of a weekend or a holiday. The beginning and end of August are also notorious for traffic jams, as is Semana Santa (Holy Week), which starts on Palm Sunday and ends on Easter Sunday. National (toll-free) highways and back roads are slower but provide one of the great pleasures of driving around the Castilian countryside: surprise encounters with castles, quaint villages, and spectacular vistas.

If you're driving from Madrid to Extremadura, the six-lane A5 moves quickly. The A66, or Vía de la Plata, which crosses Extremadura from north to south, is also effective. The fastest way from Portugal is the (Portuguese) A6 from Lisbon to Badajoz (not to be confused with the Spanish A6, which runs northwest from Madrid to Galicia). Side roads—particularly those that cross the wilder mountainous districts, such as the Sierra de Guadalupe—differ in terms of upkeep but are wonderfully scenic.

### MILEAGE FROM MADRID:

- Madrid to Burgos is 243 km (151 miles).
- Madrid to Cáceres is 299 km (186 miles).
- Madrid to Cuenca is 168 km (104 miles).
- Madrid to Granada is 428 km (266 miles).
- Madrid to Léon is 334 km (208 miles).
- Madrid to Salamanca is 212 km (132 miles).
- Madrid to Segovia is 91 km (57 miles).
- Madrid to Toledo is 88 km (55 miles).
- Madrid to Ávila is 114 km (71 miles).

## RIDESHARE

As slow, right-lane-cruising buses and clunky old trains make intercity travel in Castile a nuisance, travelers of all ages are increasingly taking rideshares, the most popular of which is Blablacar. Its free platform allows you to book ahead via debit or credit card and message with the driver to set pickup and drop-off points. It's not only the quickest way from A to B without a rental car but also often the cheapest, since drivers aren't allowed to make a profit on trips (the amount you pay only offsets costs for tolls and gas). Check⊕ www.blablacar.com for details.

## TRAIN

The main towns in Castile and León and Castile–La Mancha are accessible by multiple daily trains from Madrid, with tickets running about €10–€30, depending on train speed (the high-speed AVE service costs more), the time of day, and the day of the week. Several towns make feasible day trips: there are commuter trains from Madrid to Segovia (30 minutes), Guadalajara (30 minutes), and Toledo (30 minutes). Trains to Toledo depart from Madrid's Atocha station; trains to Salamanca, Burgos, and León depart from Chamartín; and both stations serve Ávila, Segovia, and Sigüenza, though Chamartín has more frequent service. Trains from Segovia go only to Madrid, but you can change at Villalba for Ávila and Salamanca.

For Extremadura, notoriously rickety and sluggish trains from Madrid stop at Monfragüe, Plasencia, Cáceres, Mérida, Zafra, and Badajoz and run roughly six times daily. At the time of writing, an Alvia (fast train) service between Plasencia and Badajoz was scheduled to be completed by August 2022, shaving 45 minutes off that itinerary and, therefore, from journeys to Madrid as well. Currently the journey from Madrid to Cáceres takes about four hours; within the province there are services between

Badajoz and Cáceres (three daily, 1 hour 55 minutes), Mérida (five daily, 40 minutes), Plasencia (two daily, 2 hours 40 minutes), and beyond. Several cities have separate train stations for normal versus AVE high-speed rail service; the newer AVE stations are often farther from town centers.

⚠ **Expect delays and schedule changes due to the €20 million project to update the Extremaduran train network.**

**CONTACTS RENFE.** ☎ *90/232–0320* ⊕ *www.renfe.com.*

## Restaurants

This is Spain's rugged heartland, bereft of touristy hamburger joints and filled instead with traditional tabernas, which attract Spanish foodies from across the country. Some of the most renowned restaurants in this region are small and family-run, while a few new avant-garde spots in urban areas serve up modern architecture as well as experimental fusion dishes.

*Restaurant reviews have been shortened. For full information, visit Fodors.com.*

## Hotels

Small, independently owned hotels abound in Castile and León, and many of the country's best-reviewed paradores (⊕ *www.paradores.es*) are in quiet towns such as Almagro, Ávila, Cuenca, and Sigüenza. Paradores in Toledo, Segovia, and Salamanca are modern buildings with magnificent views and, in the case of Segovia, have wonderful indoor and outdoor swimming pools. Reacting to a spate of bad press and unsatisfactory customer reviews, the parador brand invested €21 million in its Castile and León properties in 2019, but it came under fire again in 2020 when—despite raking in €14 million in profits the year prior—it cut most workers' salaries by a quarter in the midst of the COVID-19 outbreak. Corporate politics aside, there are plenty of pleasant alternatives to paradores such as Segovia's Hotel Infanta Isabel; Salamanca's Hotel Rector; and Cuenca's Posada de San José, housed in a 16th-century convent.

In Extremadura, paradores occupy buildings of great historical and architectural interest; the Extremaduran government also runs a few *hospederías,* regional offshoots of the parador chain. Most "highend" hotels, with a few exceptions (such as the space-age Miluna bubble hotel in Toledo), are modern boxes with little character. You're almost always better off staying in a charming, underrated *hotel rural* or *casa rural* (guesthouse).

*Hotel reviews have been shortened; for full information, visit Fodors.com.*

## What It Costs in Euros

| | $ | $$ | $$$ | $$$$ |
|---|---|---|---|---|
| **RESTAURANTS** | | | | |
| | under €12 | €12–€17 | €18–€22 | over €22 |
| **HOTELS** | | | | |
| | under €100 | €101–€150 | €151–€200 | over €200 |

# Tours

In summer, the tourist offices of Segovia, Toledo, and Sigüenza organize Trenes Turísticos (miniature tourist trains) that glide past all the major sights; contact local tourist offices for schedules.

A great way to get to know Extremadura is by bike (in any season but scorching summer). You can essentially forgo maps by following the ancient Roman road, the Vía de la Plata, which runs north to south along the A66 and passes by Plasencia, Cáceres, Mérida, and Zafra. Note that areas north of Cáceres province, including the Jerte Valley, La Vera, and Guadalupe, are mountainous and uneven: be prepared for an invigoratingly bumpy ride. The regional government has also opened four Vías Verdes, or "green way" paths geared toward hiking and biking, along disused railroads; a notable (if rugged) one goes from Logrosán (a couple of miles southwest of Guadalupe) to Villanueva de la Serena (east of Mérida and near Don Benito). Check tourist offices for maps of these and other trails.

### ★ Equiberia
**GUIDED TOURS | FAMILY |** Horseback tours ranging 5–10 days offer a unique way to experience the gorges, fields, and forests of the Sierra de Gredos, Segovia, Ávila, and beyond; ask about their Menorca tours if you're headed to that island. ⊠ *Camino Cepedamingo, Ávila* ✛ *in Navarredonda de Gredos* ☎ *68/934–3974* ⊕ *www.equiberia.com* ✉ *From €1,200.*

### Valle Aventura
**GUIDED TOURS | FAMILY |** Hiking, horseback riding, cycling, and kayaking trips in the Jerte Valley can be organized with this company. ⊠ *Garganta de los Infiernos Actividades en la Naturaleza* ☎ *63/663–1182* ⊕ *www.valleaventura.com* ✉ *From €180.*

# Toledo

*88 km (55 miles) southwest of Madrid.*

The spiritual capital of Castile, Toledo sits atop a rocky mount surrounded on three sides by the Río Tajo (Tagus River). When the Romans arrived here in 192 BC, they built their fortress (the Alcázar) on the highest point of the rock. Later, the Visigoths remodeled the stronghold.

In the 8th century, the Moors arrived and strengthened Toledo's reputation as a center of religion and learning. Today, the Moorish legacy is evident in Toledo's strong crafts tradition, the mazelike streets, and the predominance of brick construction (rather than the stone of many of Spain's historical cities). For the Moors—an imprecise catch-all term for Islam-practicing North African settlers of the Iberian Peninsula—beauty was to be savored from within rather than displayed on the surface. Even Toledo's cathedral—one of the most richly endowed in Spain—is hard to see from the outside, largely obscured by the warren of houses around it.

Alfonso VI, aided by El Cid ("Lord Conqueror"), captured the city in 1085 and dubbed himself emperor of Toledo. Under the Christians, the town's strong intellectual life was maintained, and Toledo became famous for its school of translators, who taught Arab medicine, law, culture, and philosophy. Religious tolerance continued, and during the rule of Pedro the Cruel (so named because he allegedly had members of his own family murdered to advance his position), a Jewish banker, Samuel Levi, became the royal treasurer and one of the wealthiest men in the booming city. By the late 1400s, however, hostility toward Jews and Arabs had grown as the ruthlessly intolerant Catholic monarchs established Toledo as a bastion of the Catholic church.

Under Toledo's long line of cardinals—most notably Mendoza, Tavera, and Cisneros—Renaissance Toledo was a center of the humanities. Economically and politically, however, the city began to decline at the end of the 15th century. The expulsion of the Jews from Spain in 1492, as part of the Spanish Inquisition, eroded Toledo's economic and intellectual prowess. Then, when Madrid became the permanent center of the Spanish court in 1561, Toledo lost its political importance too, and the expulsion from Spain of the converted Arabs (Moriscos) in 1601 meant the departure of most of the city's artisans. The years the painter El Greco spent in Toledo—from 1572 to his death in 1614—were those of the city's decline, which is greatly reflected in his works.

In the late 19th century, after hundreds of years of neglect, the works of El Greco came to be widely appreciated, and Toledo was transformed into a major tourist destination—even if the cosmopolitan luxury one might expect from such a hot spot never quite arrived. The winding streets and steep hills can be tough to navigate, especially when you're searching for a specific sight, so take a full day (or three) to absorb the town's medieval trappings—and relish in getting lost from time to time.

**A note on COVID-19:** Travel restrictions devastated Toledo as the city lost its economic engine: 2 million annual tourists. When shopping and making bookings, seek out family-run establishments to help them recover.

## GETTING HERE AND AROUND

The best way to get to Toledo from Madrid is the high-speed AVE train, which leaves from Madrid some nine times daily from Atocha station and gets you there in 30 minutes. From the ornate Neo-Mudejar train station, take a taxi or bus (L61 or L62), or walk the 1½ km (1 mile) to the city center.

# El Greco: the Titan of Toledo

"Crete gave him his life, and brushes; Toledo, a better land, where he begins with Death to attain Eternity." With these words, the Toledan poet Fray Hortensio Paravicino paid homage to his friend El Greco—and to the symbiotic connection between El Greco and his adopted city of Toledo. El Greco's intensely individual and expressionist style—elongated and often distorted figures, electric colors, and haunting mysticism—was seen as strange and disturbing, and his work remained largely underappreciated until the late 19th century, when he found wide acclaim and joined the ranks of Velázquez and Goya as a master of Spanish painting.

Born Doménikos Theotokópoulos on the Island of Crete, El Greco ("the Greek") received his artistic education

and training in Italy and then moved to Spain around 1577, lured in part by the prospect of painting frescoes for the royal monastery of El Escorial. King Felipe II, however, rejected El Greco's work for being too unusual. In Toledo, El Greco finally came into his own, creating many of his greatest works and honing his singular style and vision until his death in 1614. His masterpiece *The Burial of Count Orgaz*, which hangs in Toledo's Chapel of Santo Tomé, pays tribute to Toledan society. Perhaps the most famous rendering of Toledo is El Greco's dramatic *View of Toledo*, in which the cityscape crackles with a sinister energy underneath a stormy sky. El Greco's other famous landscape, *View and Plan of Toledo*, can be seen at Toledo's Museo de El Greco.

ALSA buses leave Madrid every half hour from Plaza Elíptica and take 1¼ hours.

## TOURS

### ★ Toledo de la Mano

**GUIDED TOURS** | Toledophile Adolfo Ferrero, author of a 200-page guidebook about the town, delves far deeper on his private tours than those run by competitors, touching on the city's multicultural history and its significance in medieval Europe. Groups of up to 55 people can be accommodated. ⊠ *Calle Nuncio Viejo 10, Toledo* ☎ *62/917–7810* ⊕ *www.toledodelamano. com* 🎫 *From €150.*

### Toledo Train Vision

**TRAIN TOURS** | **FAMILY** | This unabashedly touristy "train" chugs past many of Toledo's main sights, departing from the Plaza de Zocodover every hour on the hour during the week, and every 30 minutes on weekends. The tour takes 45–50

minutes and has recorded information in 16 languages (including English, Spanish, and French) plus children's versions in those three languages, too. Buy tickets at the kiosk in Plaza de Zocodover. ⊠ *Pl. de Zocodover, Toledo* ☎ *62/530–1890* ⊕ *www.toledotrainvision.com* 🎫 *€7.*

## VISITOR INFORMATION

**CONTACTS Toledo Tourist Office.** ⊠ *Pl. de Zocodover 8, Toledo* ☎ *92/526–7666, 68/785–4965, 92/523–9121* ⊕ *www. turismo.toledo.es.*

 **Sights**

### Alcázar

**MILITARY SIGHT** | Originally a Moorish citadel (*al-qasr* is Classical Arabic for "fortress"), Toledo's Alcázar is on a hill just outside the walled city, dominating the horizon. The south facade—the building's most severe—is the work of Juan

Toledo

KEY
- ● Sights
- ● Restaurants
- ● Hotels
- 🛈 Tourist Information

TO N400/401 →

**Sights** ▼

1 Alcázar ................... **D4**
2 Calle del Comercio ...... **C3**
3 Cathedral ................. **C4**
4 Convento de
San Clemente .......... **B3**
5 Convento de Santo
Domingo el Antiguo .... **B3**
6 Hospital de Tavera ....... **C1**
7 Iglesia de
San Ildefonso ........... **C3**
8 Iglesia de San Román ... **C3**
9 Iglesia de
Santo Tomé ............. **B4**
10 Mezquita del
Cristo de al Luz .......... **C3**

11 Monasterio de San Juan
de los Reyes ............. **A4**
12 Museo de
Santa Cruz .............. **D3**
13 Museo del Greco ....... **B4**
14 Museo Ruiz de Luna ..... **A3**
15 Plaza de Zocodover .... **D3**
16 Puente de Alcántara .... **E3**
17 Puente de
San Martín ............... **A4**
18 Sinagoga de Santa María
La Blanca ................ **B4**
19 Sinagoga del
Tránsito ................. **B4**

**Restaurants** ▼

1 Bar Ludeña .............. **D3**
2 Cervecería
Entrecalles .............. **D3**
3 Churrería
Santo Tomé ............. **B4**
4 El Trébol ................. **D3**
5 Restaurante Iván
Cerdeño ................. **A3**

**Hotels** ▼

1 Antídoto Rooms ......... **D3**
2 Hacienda del
Cardenal ................. **C2**
3 Hotel Sercotel
Pintor El Greco .......... **B4**
4 Miluna ................... **A1**

de Herrera, of Escorial fame, while the east facade incorporates a large section of battlements. The finest facade is the northern, one of many Toledan works by Miguel Covarrubias, who did more than any other architect to introduce the Renaissance style here. The building's architectural highlight is his Italianate courtyard, which, like most other parts of the building, was largely rebuilt after the Spanish Civil War, when the Alcázar was besieged by the Republicans. Though the Nationalists' ranks were depleted, they held on to the building. Dictator Francisco Franco later turned the Alcázar into a monument to Nationalist bravery. It now houses the Museo del Ejército (Military Museum), which was formerly in Madrid.

■**TIP→** Hang onto your ticket—it's needed when you exit the museum. ⊠ *Cuesta de los Capuchinos, Toledo* ☎ *92/523–8800* ⊕ *www.museo.ejercito.es* ⊠ *From €5 (free Sun.).*

## Calle del Comercio

**STREET** | Near Plaza de Zocodover, this is the town's narrow and busy pedestrian thoroughfare. It's lined with bars and shops and shaded in summer by awnings. It was repaved in 2021. ⊠ *Calle del Comercio, Toledo.*

## ★ Cathedral

**CHURCH** | One of the most impressive structures in all of Spain, this is a must-see on any visit to the city. The elaborate structure sits on the site of what was once Toledo's great mosque (of which only a column and the cistern remain). It owes its impressive Mozarabic chapel, with an elongated dome crowning the west facade, to El Greco's only son. The rest of the facade is mainly early 15th century. Immediately to your right is a beautifully carved plateresque doorway by Covarrubias, marking the entrance to the Treasury, which houses a small crucifixion scene by the Italian painter Cimabue and an extraordinarily intricate

late-15th-century monstrance by Juan del Arfe. The ceiling is an excellent example of Mudejar (11th- to 16th-century Moorish-influenced) workmanship. From here, walk around to the ambulatory. In addition to Italianate frescoes by Juan de Borgoña and an exemplary baroque illusionism by Narciso Tomé known as the Transparente, you'll find several El Grecos, including one version of *El Espolio* (*Christ Being Stripped of His Raiment*), the first recorded instance of the painter in Spain. ⊠ *Calle Cardenal Cisneros 1, Toledo* ☎ *92/522–2241* ⊕ *www.catedral-primada.es* ⊠ *From €10.*

## Convento de San Clemente

**CHURCH** | Founded in 1131, this is Toledo's oldest and largest convent—and it's still in use. The handful of nuns who live here produce sweet wine and marzipan. The impressive complex, a bit outside the city center, includes ruins of a mosque on which a chapel was built in the Middle Ages, those of an Islamic house and courtyard (with an ancient well and Arab baths), and those of a Jewish house from the same period. Tours, offered twice daily (though not dependably—be forewarned), might include a visit to the kitchen where the Mother Superior will let you sample some sweets if she's in a good mood. Skip the touristy marzipan shops and buy the real stuff here. There's also an adjacent cultural center with rotating history exhibits. ⊠ *Calle San Clemente, Toledo* ☎ *92/525–3080* ⊠ *€6* ⊙ *Closed sporadically (call before visiting).*

## Convento de Santo Domingo el Antiguo

(*Convento de Santo Domingo de Silos; Santo Domingo Convent*)
**CHURCH** | This 16th-century Cistercian convent houses the earliest of El Greco's Toledo paintings as well as the crypt where the artist is believed to be buried. The friendly nuns at the convent—of whom eight remain—will show you around its odd little museum,

## Did You Know?

The alcázar of Toledo has dominated the city since at least the 3rd century. It is the setting for an important scene of Franquist lore: During the Spanish Civil War, the Nationalist colonel Moscardó was defending the building against overwhelming Republican forces. The Republicans held his son hostage, demanding the alcázar be surrendered. To his son's entreaties to "surrender or they will shoot me," the father replied, "Then commend your soul to God and die like a hero."

which includes decaying bone relics of little-known saints and a life-size model of John the Baptist's decapitated head. ⊠ *Pl. Santo Domingo el Antiguo, Toledo* ☎ *92/522–2930* 🎟 *€2.*

### Hospital de Tavera (*Hospital de San Juan Bautista*)

**HOSPITAL** | Architect Alonso de Covarrubias's last work, this hospital lies outside the city walls, beyond Toledo's main northern gate. A fine example of Spanish Renaissance architecture, the building also houses the Museo de Duque de Lema in its southern wing. The most important work in the museum's miscellaneous collection is a painting by 17th-century artist José Ribera. The hospital's monumental chapel holds El Greco's *Baptism of Christ* and the exquisitely carved marble tomb of Cardinal Tavera, the last work of Alonso de Berruguete. Descend into the crypt to experience some bizarre acoustical effects. A full ticket includes the hospital, museum, old pharmacy, and Renaissance patios; a partial ticket includes everything except the museum. Guided tours are available at 45-minute intervals. ⊠ *Calle Duque de Lerma 2 (aka Calle Cardenal Tavera), Toledo* ☎ *92/522–0451* ⊕ *www. fundacionmedinaceli.org/monumentos/ hospital* 🎟 *€6.*

### ★ Iglesia de San Ildefonso (*San Ildefonso Church, The Jesuits*)

**CHURCH** | Sometimes called "Los Jesuitas," for the religious order that founded it, the Iglesia de San Ildefonso is named for Toledo's patron saint, a 7th-century bishop. It was consecrated in 1718 after the baroque stone facade with twin Corinthian columns took 150 years to build. Its semispherical dome is one of the icons of Toledo's skyline. This impressive building's tower affords some of the best views over Toledo. ⊠ *Pl. Juan de Mariana 1, Toledo* ☎ *92/525–1507* 🎟 *€3.*

### Iglesia de San Román

**CHURCH** | Hidden in a virtually unspoiled part of Toledo, this early-13th-century Mudejar church (built on the site of an earlier Visigoth one) is now the **Museo de los Concilios y de la Cultura Visigoda** (Visigoth Museum) with exhibits of statuary, manuscript illustrations, jewelry, and an extensive collection of frescoes. The church tower is adjacent to the ruins of Roman baths. ⊠ *Calle San Román, Toledo* ☎ *92/522–7872* 🎟 *€2 (free Fri. and Sat. 4:30–6:30 and Sun. 10–2:30).*

### ★ Iglesia de Santo Tomé (*Santo Tomé Church*)

**CHURCH** | Not to be confused with the marzipan shop bearing the same name, this chapel topped with a Mudejar tower was built specially to house El Greco's most masterful painting, *The Burial of Count Orgaz.* Using vivid colors and splashes of light, it portrays the benefactor of the church being buried with the posthumous assistance of St. Augustine and St. Stephen, who have appeared at the funeral to thank the count for his donations to religious institutions named after the two saints. Though the count's burial took place in the 14th century, El Greco painted the onlookers in contemporary 16th-century costumes and included people he knew; the boy in the foreground is one of El Greco's sons, and the sixth figure on the left is said to be the artist himself. Santo Tomé is Toledo's most visited church besides the cathedral, so to avoid crowds, plan to visit as soon as the building opens. ⊠ *Pl. del Conde 4, Calle Santo Tomé, Toledo* ☎ *92/525–6098* ⊕ *www.santotome.org* 🎟 *€3.*

### Mezquita del Cristo de la Luz (*Mosque of Christ of the Light*)

**MOSQUE** | Originally a tiny Visigothic church, the mosque-chapel was transformed into a mosque during the Moorish occupation. The Islamic arches and vaulting survived, making this the most important relic of Moorish Toledo, even if a glaringly out-of-place sculpture of Jesus on the cross is the centerpiece of the building today. Legend has it that the chapel got its name when Alfonso VI's horse, striding triumphantly into Toledo in 1085, fell to its knees out front (a white stone marks the spot). It was then "discovered" that a candle had burned continuously behind the masonry the whole time the Muslims had been in power. Allegedly, the first Mass of the Reconquest was held here, and later a Mudejar apse was added. There are remnants of a Roman house in the yard nearby. ⊠ *Cuesta de Carmelitas Descalzos 10, Toledo* ☎ *92/525-4191* ⌖ *€3.*

### ★ Monasterio de San Juan de los Reyes

CHURCH | This convent church in western Toledo was erected by Ferdinand and Isabella to commemorate their victory at the Battle of Toro in 1476. (It was also intended to be their burial place, but their wish changed after Granada was recaptured from the Moors in 1492, and their actual tomb is in that city's Capilla Real.) The breathtakingly intricate building is largely the work of architect Juan Guas, who considered it his masterpiece and asked to be buried there himself. In true plateresque fashion, the white interior is covered with inscriptions and heraldic motifs. ⊠ *Calle San Juan de los Reyes 2, Toledo* ☎ *92/522-3802* ⊕ *www.sanjuandelosreyes.org* ⌖ *€3.*

### Museo de Santa Cruz

ART MUSEUM | In a 16th-century Renaissance hospital with a stunning Classical-Plateresque facade, this museum is open all day without a break (unlike many of Toledo's other sights). Works of art have replaced the hospital beds, and among the displays is El Greco's *Assumption* of 1613, the artist's last known work. A small archaeology museum is set in the hospital's delightful cloister. ⊠ *Calle Cervantes 3, Toledo*

☎ *92/522-1402* ⌖ *€4, free Wed. after 4 and Sun.* ⊙ *Closed Sun. after 2:30.*

### Museo del Greco (*El Greco Museum*)

ART MUSEUM | This house that once belonged to Peter the Cruel's treasurer, Samuel Levi, is said to have later been El Greco's home, though historians now believe he actually lived across the street. Nevertheless, the interior of the El Greco Museum is decorated to resemble a typical house of the artist's time. The house is now incorporated into a revamped El Greco museum with several of the artist's paintings, including a panorama of Toledo with the Hospital of Tavera in the foreground, and works by several of El Greco's students (including his son) and other 16th- and 17th-century artists. Medieval caves have been excavated at the site, and there's a beautiful garden in which to take refuge from Toledo's often-scorching summer heat. The impressive museum complex has been the centerpiece for Toledo tourism since the "El Greco 2014" festival, marking the 400th anniversary of the artist's death. ⊠ *Paseo del Tránsito, Toledo* ☎ *92/522-3665* ⌖ *€3 (free Sat. after 2 and Sun.).*

### Museo Ruiz de Luna

ART MUSEUM | Most of the region's pottery is made in Talavera de la Reina, 76 km (47 miles) west of Toledo. At this museum you can watch artisans throw local clay, then trace the development of Talavera's world-famous ceramics, chronicled through some 1,500 tiles, bowls, vases, and plates back to the 14th century. ⊠ *Pl. de San Augustín, Calle San Agustín el Viejo 13, Talavera de la Reina* ☎ *92/580-0149* ⊕ *cultura.castillalamancha.es* ⌖ *€3* ⊙ *Closed Mon.*

### Plaza de Zocodover

PLAZA/SQUARE | Toledo's main square was built in the early 17th century as part of an unsuccessful attempt to impose a rigid geometry on the chaotic Moorish streets. Over the centuries, this tiny plaza has hosted bullfights, executions

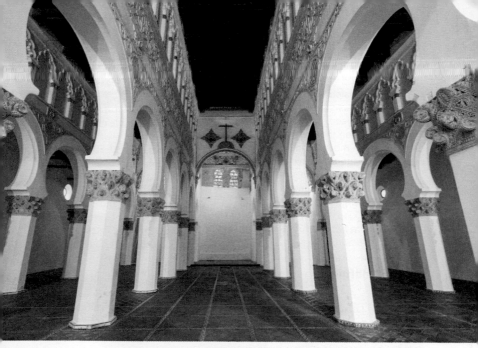

Toledo's Santa María la Blanca synagogue is a fascinating symbol of cultural cooperation: built by Islamic architects, in a Christian land, for Jewish use.

(autos-da-fé) of heretics during the Spanish Inquisition, and countless street fairs. Today it's home to the largest and oldest marzipan store in town, Santo Tomé. You can catch intracity buses here, and the tourist office is on the south side of the plaza. ✉ *Pl. Zocodover, Toledo.*

### Puente de Alcántara

**BRIDGE** | Roman in origin, this is the city's oldest bridge. Next to it is a heavily restored castle built after the Christian capture of 1085 and, above this, a vast and severe military academy, an eyesore of Francoist architecture. From the other side of the Río Tajo, the bridge offers fine views of Toledo's historic center and the Alcázar. ✉ *Calle Gerardo Lobo, Toledo.*

### Puente de San Martín

**BRIDGE** | This pedestrian bridge on the western edge of Toledo dates to 1203 and has splendid horseshoe arches. At 40 meters (131 feet) long, it was one of the longest bridges in the world at the time of construction. ✉ *Puente de San Martín, Toledo.*

### ★ Sinagoga de Santa María La Blanca

**SYNAGOGUE** | Founded in 1203, Toledo's second synagogue—situated in the heart of the Jewish Quarter—is nearly two centuries older than the more elaborate Tránsito, just down the street. Santa María's white interior has a forest of columns supporting capitals with fine filigree work, a wonder of Mudejar architecture. It was a center of study and prayer until the 1355 assault on the Jewish Quarter and subsequent pogroms in 1391. ✉ *Calle de los Reyes Católicos 4, Toledo* ☎ *92/522–7257* ⛭ *€3.*

### ★ Sinagoga del Tránsito (*Museo Sefardí, Sephardic Museum*)

**SYNAGOGUE** | This 14th-century synagogue's plain exterior belies sumptuous interior walls embellished with colorful Mudejar decoration. There are inscriptions in Hebrew and Arabic glorifying God, Peter the Cruel, and Samuel Levi (the original patron). It's a rare example of architecture reflecting Arabic as the lingua franca of medieval Spanish Jews. It's said that Levi imported cedars from

Lebanon for the building's construction, echoing Solomon when he built the First Temple in Jerusalem. This is one of only three synagogues still fully standing in Spain (two in Toledo, one in Córdoba), from an era when there were hundreds—though more are in the process of being excavated. Adjoining the main hall is the **Museo Sefardí,** a small but informative museum of Jewish culture in Spain. ⊠ *Calle Samuel Levi 2, Toledo* ☏ *92/522–3665* ⊕ *www.mecd.gob.es/ msefardi/home.html* 🖾 *€3 (free Sat. afternoon and Sun.).*

##  Restaurants

### Bar Ludeña

$ | SPANISH | Locals and visitors come together at this old-timey tapas bar for steaming cauldrons of *carcamusas toledanas,* a local meat stew studded with peas and chorizo. (Give the rest of the menu a pass.) **Known for:** rustic ambience; free tapa with every drink; hearty carcamusa stew. ⑤ *Average main: €12* ⊠ *Pl. de la Magdalena 10, Toledo* ☏ *92/522–3384* ◷ *Closed Wed.*

### Cervecería Entrecalles

$ | SPANISH | With 10 artisanal beers on tap and 150 available by the bottle— many of them locally brewed—Entrecalles is Toledo's premier craft beer bar. A basic but well-executed bar-food menu (burgers, *patatas bravas, croquetas*) provides ballast for all the suds; the prix-fixes are a steal. **Known for:** budget-friendly food; welcoming staff; heaven for beer geeks. ⑤ *Average main: €11* ⊠ *Calle de la Paz, Toledo* ☏ *92/504–1678* ⊕ *www. cerveceriaartesana.es* ◷ *Closed Mon.*

### ★ Churrería Santo Tomé

$ | SPANISH | FAMILY | Recharge at this adorable four-table churro shop , established over a century ago, with hot homemade churros dipped in melted chocolate so thick it's almost spreadable. The 6 am opening time means you can indulge in

churros for breakfast like a local. **Known for:** local institution; coffee and hot chocolate; fresh and featherlight churros. ⑤ *Average main: €5* ⊠ *Calle Santo Tomé 27, Toledo* ☏ *92/521–6324* ◷ *Closed Mon.*

### ★ El Trébol

$$ | SPANISH | You can't leave Toledo without indulging in one of El Trébol's famous *bombas,* fried fist-size spheres of mashed potato stuffed with spiced meat and anointed with aioli. They're best enjoyed on the twinkly outdoor patio with a locally brewed beer in hand. **Known for:** local craft beers; most pleasant patio in town; to-die-for bombas. ⑤ *Average main: €15* ⊠ *Calle de Santa Fe 1, Toledo* ☏ *92/528–1297* ⊕ *www.cerveceriatrebol. com.*

### ★ Restaurante Iván Cerdeño

$$$$ | SPANISH | The buzziest opening in Toledo in recent memory, chef Iván Cerdeño's namesake restaurant, inaugurated in 2019, is a beacon of Castilian *alta gastronomía*—think architectural dishes composed of foams, spherified sauces, and edible flowers served in a minimal white-tablecloth dining room. The ever-rotating tasting menus (5, 7, or 10 courses) almost always feature local game such as partridge or roe deer. **Known for:** secluded location across the Tagus; culinary hot spot; two-Michelin-star dining. ⑤ *Average*

main: €80 ⊠ *Cigarral del Ángel, Ctra. de la Puebla, Toledo* ☎ *92/522–3674* ⊕ *www. ivancerdeno.com* ⏱ *Closed Mon.–Wed.*

# 🛏 Hotels

### ★ Antídoto Rooms

**$ | HOTEL |** Antídoto is a breath of fresh air in Toledo's mostly staid hotel scene: expect turquoise beamed ceilings, poured-concrete floors, and designer light fixtures. **Pros:** chic modern hotel in the heart of the old town; friendly staff; exceptional value. **Cons:** sheets could be softer; in-room bathrooms with no curtains and transparent doors; awkward room layout. ⑤ *Rooms from: €86* ⊠ *Calle Recoletos 2, Toledo* ☎ *68/976–6605* ⊕ *www.antidotorooms.com* ⤴ *10 rooms* ⋔ *No Meals.*

### Hacienda del Cardenal

**$$ | HOTEL |** Once a summer palace for Cardinal Lorenzana, who lived in the 1700s, this serene three-star hotel with a pool on the outskirts of the old town hits the sweet spot between rustic and refined. **Pros:** lovely courtyard; spacious rooms; convenient dining. **Cons:** stairs inconvenient for those with heavy luggage; parking is pricey; restaurant often full. ⑤ *Rooms from: €108* ⊠ *Paseo de Recaredo 24, Toledo* ☎ *92/522–4900* ⊕ *www.elhostaldelcardenal.com* ⤴ *27 rooms* ⋔ *Free Breakfast.*

### Hotel Sercotel Pintor El Greco

**$$$ | HOTEL |** Next to the painter's house, this former 17th-century bakery is a chic, contemporary hotel managed by the Sercotel chain. **Pros:** parking garage adjacent; complimentary wine and olives; cozy decor. **Cons:** bar area sometimes closed for private events; elevator goes to the second floor only; street noise in most rooms. ⑤ *Rooms from: €184* ⊠ *Alamillos del Tránsito 13, Toledo* ☎ *92/528–5191* ⊕ *www.hotelpintorelgreco.com* ⤴ *60 rooms* ⋔ *No Meals.*

### ★ Miluna

**$$$$ | HOTEL |** Taking a page from the playbook of Aire de Bardenas, Navarra's avant-garde bubble hotel, Miluna opened in 2018 on the outskirts of Toledo. **Pros:** a bubble hotel that won't break the budget; the ideal place to unplug; telescopes in every room. **Cons:** no alternate dining options in vicinity; uncomfortable in winter and summer when temperatures are extreme; expensive and limited reservations. ⑤ *Rooms from: €269* ⊠ *C. Valdecarretas, Parcela 364, Toledo* ☎ *92/567–9229* ⊕ *www.miluna.es* ⤴ *4 rooms.*

# 👜 Shopping

The Moors established silver, damascene (metalwork inlaid with gold or silver), pottery, embroidery, and marzipan traditions here. A turn-of-the-20th-century art school next to the Monasterio de San Juan de los Reyes keeps some of these crafts alive. For inexpensive pottery, stop at the large stores on the outskirts of town, on the main road to Madrid. Many shops are closed on Sunday.

### Confitería Santo Tomé

**CANDY |** Since 1856, Santo Tomé has been Spain's most famous maker of marzipan, a Spanish confection made from sugar, honey, and almond paste. Visit the main shop on the Plaza de Zocodover, or take a tour of the old convent-turned-factory where it's actually made at Calle Santo Tomé 3 (advance booking required). ⊠ *Pl. de Zocodover 7, Toledo* ☎ *92/522–1168, 92/522–3763* ⊕ *www.mazapan.com.*

### El Baúl de la Piker

**MIXED CLOTHING |** There's no shortage of throwback treasures at this independently owned vintage shop specializing in women's wear. Keep an eye out for retro leather pieces—Toledo has long been known for its fine leather artisanship. ⊠ *Calle Trastámara 17, Toledo* ☎ *92/567–2083* ⊕ *www.elbauldelapiker. com* ⏱ *Closed Sun.*

## ★ La Encina de Ortega

**FOOD** | This is a one-stop-shop for local wines, olive oil, Manchego cheese, and—most notably—ibérico pork products (ham, chorizo, dry-cured sausages) made from pigs raised on the family farm. Stick around for charcuterie boards and generously poured glasses of wine. ⊠ *Calle La Plata 22, Toledo* ☎ *92/510–2072* ⊕ *www.laencinadeortega.com* ⊘ *Closed Sat. afternoon, Sun.*

# Almagro

*215 km (134 miles) south of Madrid.*

The center of this noble town contains the only preserved medieval theater in Europe. It stands beside the ancient Plaza Mayor, where 85 Roman columns form two colonnades supporting green-frame 16th-century buildings. Enjoy casual tapas—such as pickled baby eggplant (*berenjenas de Almagro*), a hyperlocal specialty known the country over—and rustic Manchegan wines in the bars lining the square. Near the plaza are granite mansions emblazoned with the heraldic shields of their former owners and a splendid parador in a restored 17th-century convent.

## GETTING HERE AND AROUND

Almagro can be reached by train from Madrid, with one scheduled departure per day departing from Atocha or Chamartín stations for the 2½-hour journey, but it's probably best to rent a car or book a Blablacar rideshare. The drive south from the capital takes you across the plains of La Mancha, where Don Quixote's adventures unfolded.

## VISITOR INFORMATION

**CONTACTS Almagro Tourist Office.** ⊠ *Pl. Mayor 1, Almagro* ☎ *92/686–0717* ⊕ *www.ciudad-almagro.com.*

# ◉ Sights

## Corral de Comedias

**PERFORMANCE VENUE** | Appearing almost as it did in 1628 when it was built, this theater has wooden balconies on four sides and the stage at one end of the open patio. During the golden age of Spanish theater—the time of playwrights Pedro Calderón de la Barca, Cervantes, and Lope de Vega—touring actors came from all over Europe to Almagro, once a burgeoning urban center for its mercury mines and lace industry. Few such theaters stand today. Forgo the tourist-oriented spectacles unless you're thoroughly bilingual or a Spanish theater buff: poor acoustics and archaic Spanish scripts make it difficult to understand what's going on. An international classical theater festival takes place here in July. ⊠ *Pl. Mayor 18, Almagro* ☎ *92/686–1539* ⊕ *www.corraldecomedias.com* ▤ *From €4.*

## ★ Museo Etnográfico Campo de Calatrava

**HISTORY MUSEUM** | For a window into what agrarian life was like in this area in centuries past, pop into this tiny museum presided over by the passionate historian who amassed the antique curiosities on display. The influence of the Central European "Fúcares" families on the area is especially fascinating. A guided tour, in Spanish, takes a little less than an hour and is well worth it. ⊠ *Calle Chile 6, Almagro* ☎ *65/701–0077* ⊕ *www.museodealmagro.com* ▤ *€5.*

## Museo Nacional del Teatro

**HISTORY MUSEUM** | **FAMILY** | This museum, housed in the ancestral seat of the Calatrava Order of knights, displays models of the Roman amphitheaters in Mérida (Extremadura) and Sagunto (near Valencia), both still in use, as well as costumes, pictures, and documents relating to the history of Spanish theater. Kids love handling the antique instruments previously used for sound effects during productions. ⊠ *Calle del Gran Maestre 1, Almagro* 🕾 *02/828–1014, 02/620–1018* 🌐 *museoteatro.mcu.es* 🎫 *€3 (free Sat. afternoon and Sun. morning)* 🕐 *Closed Mon.*

## 🛏 Hotels

### ★ Parador de Almagro

**$$ | HOTEL |** Five minutes from the Plaza Mayor of Almagro, this parador is a finely restored 16th-century Franciscan convent with cells, cloisters, and patios. **Pros:** pretty indoor courtyards; ample free parking; outdoor pool. **Cons:** inconsistent restaurant; double-bed rooms smaller than normal rooms; occasionally untidy public areas. ⑤ *Rooms from: €129* ⊠ *Ronda de San Francisco 31, Almagro* 🕾 *92/686–0100* 🌐 *www.parador.es* 🛏 *54 rooms* 🍽 *No Meals.*

# Cuenca

*168 km (105 miles) southeast of Madrid, 150 km (93 miles) northwest of Valencia.*

Cuenca is one of the most surreal-looking towns in Spain, built on a sloping escarpment with precipitous sides plunging down to the Huécar and Júcar rivers. When real estate grew scarce a few centuries back, local builders constructed gravity-defying homes that dangle over the abyss. These Casas Colgadas ("Hanging Houses") are a unique architectural attraction. The old town's dramatic setting grants spectacular views of the surrounding countryside, and its cobblestone streets, cathedral, churches, and taverns contrast starkly with the modern town, which sprawls beyond the river gorges. Though somewhat isolated, Cuenca makes a good overnight stop if you're traveling between Madrid and Valencia, or even a worthwhile detour between Madrid and Barcelona.

## GETTING HERE AND AROUND

From Madrid, buses leave for Cuenca about every two hours from Conde de Casal. From Valencia, four buses leave every four to six hours, starting at 8:30 am. A high-speed AVE train leaves Madrid approximately every hour and stops in Cuenca (after about 55 minutes) on its way to Valencia. Slower, cheaper trains also run several times daily between Cuenca and Valencia, Madrid, Albacete, and Alicante, on the coast. Rideshares (such as Blablacar) to and from the city are plentiful.

## VISITOR INFORMATION

**CONTACTS Cuenca Tourist Office.** ⊠ *Calle Alfonso VIII 2, Cuenca* 🕾 *96/924–1051* 🌐 *www.visitacuenca.es.*

## 👁 Sights

Cuenca has a cathedral and more than a dozen churches, but visitors are allowed inside only about half of them. The best views of the city are from the square in front of a small palace at the very top of town, where the town tapers out to the narrowest of ledges. Here, gorges flank the precipice, and old houses sweep down toward a distant plateau. The lower half of the old town is a maze of tiny streets, any of which will take you up to the Plaza del Carmen. From here the town narrows and a single street, Calle Alfonso VIII, continues the ascent to the Plaza Mayor, which passes under the arch of the town hall.

### ★ Casas Colgadas (*Hanging Houses*)

**NOTABLE BUILDING |** As if Cuenca's famous Casas Colgadas, suspended impossibly over the cliffs below, were not eye-popping enough, they also house one of Spain's finest museums, the Museo de Arte Abstracto Español (Museum of Spanish Abstract Art)—not to be confused with the adjacent Museo Municipal de Arte Moderno. Projecting over the town's eastern precipice, these houses

Cuenca's precarious Casas Colgadas (Hanging Houses) are also home to the well-regarded Museum of Abstract Art.

originally formed a 15th-century palace, which later served as a town hall before falling into disrepair in the 19th century. In 1927 the cantilevered balconies were rebuilt, and in 1966 the painter Fernando Zóbel created the world's first museum devoted exclusively to abstract art. The works he gathered—by such renowned names as Carlos Saura, Eduardo Chillida, Lucio Muñoz, and Antoni Tàpies—are primarily by exiled Spanish artists who grew up under Franco's regime. The museum has free smartphone audio guides that can be downloaded from the website. ⊠ *Calle de los Canónigos, Cuenca* ☎ *96/921–2983* ⊕ *www.march. es/arte/cuenca* 🎫 *Free.*

### Catedral de Cuenca

**CHURCH** | Built in the 12th century atop ruins of a conquered mosque, the cathedral, which looms over the Plaza Mayor, lost its Gothic character in the Renaissance. Inside are the tombs of the cathedral's founding bishops, an impressive portico of the Apostles, and a Byzantine reliquary. There's also a museum in the once-cellar of the Bishop's Palace containing a jewel-encrusted Byzantine diptych of the 13th century, a Crucifixion by the 15th-century Flemish artist Gerard David, a variety of carpets from the 16th through 18th centuries, and two small El Grecos. An excellent audio guide is included in the price of admission. ⊠ *Pl. Mayor, Cuenca* ☎ *96/922–4626* ⊕ *www. catedralcuenca.es* 🎫 *€6.*

### Ciudad Encantada (*Enchanted City*)

**NATURE SIGHT** | **FAMILY** | Not an "Enchanted City" as its name implies, Ciudad Encantada—situated 35 km (22 miles) north of Cuenca—is a series of large, fantastic mushroomlike rock formations erupting in a landscape of pines. It was formed over thousands of years by the forces of water and wind on limestone rocks, and you can see it in under two hours. See if you can spot formations named *Cara* (Face), *Puente* (Bridge), *Amantes* (Lovers), and *Olas en el Mar* (Waves in the Sea). Rent a car to get here, or arrange a visit with Ecotourism Cuenca (⊕ *www. ecoturismocuenca.com* ☎ *61/650–7695*).

✉ *Ciudad Encantada, Cuenca* 📞 *63/490.9952* ⊕ *www.ciudadencantada.es* 💲 *€5.*

## ★ Puente de San Pablo

**BRIDGE** | If you don't have a fear of heights, cross this narrow 16th-century footbridge to take in the vertiginous view of the river and equally thrilling panorama of the Casas Colgadas. It's by far the best view of the city. If you've read the popular English novel *Winter in Madrid* by C. J. Sansom, you'll recognize this bridge from the final scene. ✉ *Cuenca.*

## 🍴 Restaurants

Much of Cuenca's cuisine is based on wild game, but farm-raised lamb, rabbit, and poultry are ubiquitous on menus. Trout from the adjacent river (and, increasingly, from farms) is the fish of choice, and it turns up in entrées and soups. In almost every restaurant you'll find *morteruelo*—Cuenca's pâté of *jabalí* (wild boar), rabbit, partridge, hen, liver, pork loin, and spices—as well as gazpacho Manchego (aka *galiano*), a meat stew thickened with dry flatbread, a remnant of the Sephardic culinary canon. For dessert, try *alajú*, a hard sugar candy containing honey, almonds, and lemon that's great with cheese; or the more ubiquitous *torrijas*, bread slices dipped in milk or wine, fried until custardy, and sprinkled with cinnamon-sugar.

### Figón del Huécar

**$$$** | **SPANISH** | This family-run white-table-cloth restaurant serves updated Castilian classics in an airy dining room set in a medieval stone house overlooking the old city (ask for an outdoor table when booking). Specialty dishes include Manchegan *migas* (fried pork and bread crumbs), *ajoarriero* (pounded potatoes, garlic, bacalao, and olive oil), and veal with potatoes *al montón* (fried with garlic). **Known for:** elegant dining room; scrumptious desserts; breathtaking views. 💲 *Average main: €20* ✉ *Ronda de Julián Romero 6, Cuenca* 📞 *96/924–0062, 62/906–3366*

⊕ *www.figondelhuecar.es* ⊗ *Closed Mon. No dinner Sun.*

## ★ La Ponderosa

**$$** | **TAPAS** | La Ponderosa is a quintessential yet elevated Castilian bar where locals mingle at high volume while tossing back local wine and munching on well-priced seasonal delicacies like griddled wild asparagus, suckling lamb chops, and seared wild mushrooms. It's a standing-room-only joint, so if you want to sit, you'll have to come early and find a place on the terrace. **Known for:** buzzy atmosphere; simple and delicious vegetable dishes; hidden-gem local wines. 💲 *Average main: €15* ✉ *Calle de San Francisco 20, Cuenca* 📞 *96/921–3214* ⊗ *Closed Sun. and July.*

### Trivio

**$$$$** | **SPANISH** | The punchy, artfully presented dishes at Trivio—think wild game tartare and house-pickled vegetables—are an anomaly in a region known for its stodgy country fare. Choose between 9- and 15-course tasting menus in the dining room, or opt for a casual à la carte experience in the Bistró-Bar. **Known for:** pretty plating; award-winning croquettes; bold tasting menus. 💲 *Average main: €50* ✉ *Calle Colón 25, Cuenca* 📞 *96/903–0593* ⊕ *www.restaurantetrivio.com* ⊗ *Closed Mon. No dinner Sun.*

## 🏨 Hotels

### Cueva del Fraile

**$** | **HOTEL** | **FAMILY** | Surrounded by dramatic landscapes, this family-friendly three-star lodging occupies a 16th-century building on the outskirts of town. **Pros:** beautiful interior garden terrace; good value; outdoor swimming pool and tennis courts. **Cons:** interiors show their age; no a/c in some rooms; location 7 km (4½ miles) from town. 💲 *Rooms from: €87* ✉ *Ctra. Cuenca–Buenache, Km 7, Cuenca* 📞 *96/921–1571* ⊕ *www.hotelcuevadelfraile.com* ⊗ *Closed Jan.* 🛏 *75 rooms* 🍽 *No Meals.*

★ **Parador de Cuenca**

$$$ | HOTEL | The rooms are luxurious and serene at the exquisitely restored 16th-century convent of San Pablo, pitched on a precipice across a dramatic gorge from Cuenca's city center. **Pros:** great views of the hanging houses and gorge; consistently good restaurant; spacious rooms. **Cons:** calls to reception sometimes go unanswered; secure garage parking sometimes unavailable; expensive breakfast not always included in room rate. ⑤ *Rooms from: €180* ✉ *Subida a San Pablo, Cuenca* ☎ *96/923–2320* ⊕ *www.parador.es* ⌁ *63 rooms* ❢⃝❢ *No Meals.*

★ **Posada de San José**

$ | B&B/INN | FAMILY | This family-friendly inn, housed in a centuries-old convent, clings to the top of the Huécar gorge in Cuenca's old town. **Pros:** cozy historical rooms; well-prepared local food; stunning views of the gorge. **Cons:** sloping floors can be vertiginous when lying in bed; certain rooms are cramped; built to 17th-century proportions, some doorways are low. ⑤ *Rooms from: €97* ✉ *Calle Julián Romero 4, Cuenca* ☎ *96/921–1300, 63/981–6825* ⊕ *www.posadasanjose.com* ⌁ *31 rooms* ❢⃝❢ *No Meals.*

# Sigüenza

*132 km (82 miles) northeast of Madrid.*

The ancient university town of Sigüenza dates back to Roman, Visigothic, and Moorish times and still has splendid architecture and an awe-inspiring Gothic cathedral. It's one of the rare Spanish towns that has not surrendered to modern development and sprawl. If you're coming from Madrid via the A2, the approach, through craggy hills and ravines, is dramatic. Sigüenza is an ideal base for exploring the countryside on foot or by bike, thanks to the Ruta de Don Quixote, a network of paths named for Cervantes's literary hero that passes through the town center and nearby villages.

## GETTING HERE AND AROUND

There are several train departures daily to Sigüenza from Madrid's Chamartín station, and the journey takes about 1½ hours. Sigüenza's train station is a 10-minute walk from the historic walled center. Buses depart from Madrid's Avenida de América station once a day and take 2 hours. If you arrive by car, park near the train station to avoid the narrow cobblestone streets of the city center. Rideshares, such as Blablacar, are another option, provided there are trips that align with your schedule.

## TOURS

### Tren Medieval

TRAIN TOURS | FAMILY | Leaving from Madrid's Chamartín station, this delightful medieval-themed train service runs to Sigüenza mid-April through mid-November. The (otherwise thoroughly modern) train comes populated with minstrels, jugglers, and other entertainers, and it's a great activity for Spanish-speaking children. The ticket price includes round-trip fare, a guided visit to Sigüenza, entry to the main monuments and museums, and discounts at area restaurants. ✉ *Estación de Sigüenza, Sigüenza* ☎ *90/232–0320* ⊕ *www.renfe.com/es/es/experiencias* ▨ *€35* ⊗ *Closed winter.*

# ⊙ Sights

### Castillo de Sigüenza

CASTLE/PALACE | FAMILY | This enchanting castle overlooking wild, hilly countryside from above Sigüenza is now a parador. Non-guests can visit the dining room and common areas. The structure was founded by the Romans and rebuilt at various later periods. Most of the current building was erected in the 14th century, when it became a residence for the queen of Castile, Doña Blanca de Borbón, who was banished here by her husband, Pedro the Cruel. During the Spanish Civil War the castle was the scene of fierce battles, and much of the structure was destroyed. The lobby has an exhibit on the subsequent restoration with photographs of the bomb damage. If you have a half-hour to spare, there's a lovely walking path around the hilltop castle with a 360-degree view of the city and countryside below. ⊠ *Pl. de Castillo, Sigüenza* ☎ *94/939–0100* ⌨ *Free.*

### Catedral de Sigüenza

**CHURCH | FAMILY |** Begun around 1150 and completed in the 16th century, Sigüenza's cathedral combines Romanesque, Gothic, and Renaissance architecture. Wander from the late-Gothic cloister to a room lined with 17th-century Flemish tapestries, then onto the north transept, housing the 15th-century plateresque tomb of Dom Fadrique of Portugal. The Chapel of the Doncel (to the right of the sanctuary) contains Don Martín Vázquez de Arca's tomb, commissioned by Queen Isabella, to whom Don Martín served as *doncel* (page) before an untimely death at the gates of Granada in 1486. In a refurbished early-19th-century house next to the cathedral's west facade, the small Diocesan Museum has a prehistoric section and religious art from the 12th to 18th century. It also runs the weekend tours of the burial chambers (catacombs) under the cathedral—a spooky favorite for kids. ⊠ *Calle Serrano Sanz 2, Sigüenza* ☎ *94/939–1023* ⊕ *www.catedralsiguenza.es* ⌨ *€6 including museum.*

### Plaza Mayor

**PLAZA/SQUARE |** The south side of the cathedral overlooks this harmonious arcaded Renaissance square that hosts a medieval market on weekends. ⊠ *Plaza Mayor, Sigüenza.*

## 🍽 Restaurants

### Bar Alameda

**$$ | TAPAS | FAMILY |** This family-run bar and restaurant punches above its weight with market-driven tapas that reflect a sense of place. Spring for the stuffed foraged mushrooms or seared Sigüenza-style blood sausage. **Known for:** family-friendly atmosphere; local wines by the glass; thoughtfully prepared tapas. Ⓢ *Average main: €15* ⊠ *Calle de la Alameda 2, Sigüenza* ☎ *67/727–7773* ⊘ *Closed Wed.*

## 🛏 Hotels

### ★ Parador de Sigüenza

**$$$ | HOTEL | FAMILY |** This fairy-tale 12th-century castle has hosted royalty for centuries, from Ferdinand and Isabella right up to Spain's present king, Felipe VI. **Pros:** excellent food; plenty of parking; sense of history and place. **Cons:** occasionally surly service; bland, modern furniture that doesn't jibe with the space; much of castle is a neo-medieval replica. Ⓢ *Rooms from: €200* ⊠ *Pl. del Castillo, Sigüenza* ☎ *94/939–0100* ⊕ *www.parador.es* ⇥ *81 rooms* ⧖ *Free Breakfast.*

# Segovia

*91 km (57 miles) north of Madrid.*

Medieval Segovia rises on a steep ridge that juts above a stark, undulating plain. It's defined by its ancient monuments, excellent cuisine, embroideries and textiles, and old-fashioned charm. An important military town in Roman times, Segovia was later established by the Moors as a major textile center. Captured by the Christians in 1085, it was enriched by a royal residence, and in 1474, Henry IV's half sister Isabella the Catholic (married to Ferdinand of Aragón) was crowned queen of Castile here. By that time Segovia was a bustling city of about 60,000 (its population hovers

around 52,000 today), but its importance soon diminished as a result of its taking the losing side of the Comuneros in the popular revolt against Emperor Carlos V. Though the construction of a royal palace in nearby La Granja in the 18th century somewhat revived Segovia's fortunes, it never recovered its former vitality. In the early 20th century, Segovia's sleepy charm won over artists and writers, among them painter Ignacio Zuloaga and poet Antonio Machado. Today the streets swarm with day-trippers from Madrid—if you can, visit sometime other than sweltering summer, and spend the night to have much of the city to yourself.

You'll want to hit the triumvirate of basic sights: the aqueduct, Alcázar, and cathedral. Come evening, don't miss the bustling food and nightlife scene around the Plaza Mayor.

### GETTING HERE AND AROUND

High-speed AVE trains from Madrid's Chamartín station—the fastest and costliest option—take 30 minutes and drop you at Guiomar station, about 7 km (4 miles) outside Segovia's center. City buses 11 and 12 are timed to coincide with arriving trains. Bus 11 will take you to the foot of the aqueduct after about a 15-minute ride, and Bus 12 drops you near the bus station.

Avanza buses depart Madrid (Moncloa station) for Segovia roughly every 45 minutes. Direct routes take 55 minutes and cost around €5 each way. There are also plentiful Blablacar options. (Check ⊕ www.blablacar.com or the app for details.)

Urbanos de Segovia operates the 13 inner-city bus lines and one tourist line, which are better options for getting around than struggling through the narrow streets (and problematic parking) with a car. Segovia's central bus station is a five-minute walk from the aqueduct along the car-free Paseo de Ezequiel González.

### ESSENTIALS

**BUS CONTACTS Bus Station.** ⊠ Paseo de Ezequiel González, Segovia ☎ 92/142–7705. **Avanza.** ⊠ Pl. la Estación de Autobuses, Segovia ⊕ www.avanzabus.com. **Urbanos de Segovia.** ⊠ Segovia ☎ 90/233–0080 ⊕ segovia.avanzagrupo.com.

**VISITOR INFORMATION Segovia Tourist Office.** ⊠ Pl. Azoguejo 1, Segovia ☎ 92/146–6720, 92/146–6721 ⊕ www.turismodesegovia.com.

## ● Sights

### ★ Alcázar

**CASTLE/PALACE | FAMILY |** It's believed that the Walt Disney logo is modeled after the silhouette of this turreted castle. Possibly dating to Roman times, the Alcázar was expanded in the 14th century, remodeled in the 15th, altered again toward the end of the 16th, and completely reconstructed after being gutted by a fire in 1862, when it was used as an artillery school. The exterior, especially when seen below from the Ruta Panorámica, is awe-inspiring, as are the superb views from the ramparts. Inside, you can enter the throne room, chapel, and bedroom used by Ferdinand and Isabella as well as a claustrophobia-inducing winding tower. The intricate woodwork on the ceiling is marvelous, and the first room you enter, lined with knights in shining armor, is a crowd pleaser, particularly for kids. There's also a small armory museum, included in the ticket price. ⊠ Pl. de la Reina Victoria, Segovia ☎ 92/146–0759, 92/146–0452 ⊕ www.alcazardesegovia.com ☑ €9 for castle, tower, and museum.

### ★ Aqueduct of Segovia

**RUINS |** Segovia's Roman aqueduct is one of the greatest surviving examples of Roman engineering and the city's main sight. Stretching from the walls of the old town to the lower slopes of the Sierra de Guadarrama, it's about 2,952 feet long

# Segovia

**KEY**

- ● Sights
- ● Restaurants
- ● Hotels
- 🛈 Tourist Information

0   200 yards

0   200 meters

**Sights** ▶

1 Alcázar..............................B2
2 Aqueduct of Segovia............H2
3 Catedral de Segovia.............E2
4 Iglesia de la Vera Cruz.........D1
5 Iglesia de San Millán..........G3
6 Palacio Real de La Granja......H3
7 Plaza Mayor......................E2

**Restaurants** ▶

1 Casa Duque.......................G3
2 El Fogón Sefardí.................E2
3 Mesón de Cándido................G2
4 Mesón de José María.............F2

**Hotels** ▶

1 Áurea Convento Capuchinos......E1
2 Hotel Infanta Isabel............E2
3 Hotel Spa La Casa Mudéjar.......E2

and rises in two tiers to a height of 115 feet. The raised section of stonework in the center originally carried an inscription, of which only the holes for the bronze letters remain. Neither mortar nor clamps hold the massive granite blocks together, but miraculously, the aqueduct has stood since the end of the 1st century AD. ⚠ Climbing onto the aqueduct for photos or otherwise is strictly prohibited. ✉ Pl. del Azoguejo, Segovia.

★ **Catedral de Segovia**

CHURCH | Segovia's 16th-century cathedral was built to replace an earlier one destroyed during the revolt of the Comuneros against Carlos V. It's one of the country's last great examples of the Gothic style. The designs were drawn up by the leading late-Gothicist Juan Gil de Hontañón and executed by his son Rodrigo, in whose work you can see a transition from the Gothic to the Renaissance style. The interior, illuminated by 16th-century Flemish windows, is light and uncluttered (save for the wooden neoclassical choir). Across from the entrance, on the southern transept, is a door opening into the late-Gothic cloister, the work of architect Juan Guas. Off the cloister, a small museum of religious art, installed partly in the first-floor chapter house, has a white-and-gold 17th-century ceiling, a late example of *artesonado* (a Mudejar technique using intricately joined wooden slats). ✉ Pl. Mayor, Segovia ☎ 92/146–2205 ⊕ www.catedralsegovia.es 🔁 From €3 (free Sun. Mass).

**Iglesia de la Vera Cruz**

CHURCH | This isolated Romanesque church on the outskirts of town was built in 1208 for the Knights Templar. Like other buildings associated with the order, it has 12 sides, inspired by the Church of the Holy Sepulchre in Jerusalem. It's about a 45-minute walk from town (you can see this church on a cliffside from the castle windows), but the trek pays off in full when you climb the bell tower and see the Segovia skyline silhouetted against the Sierra de Guadarrama. ⚠ **Change is not given for bills larger than €20.** ✉ Ctra. de Zamarramia, Segovia ☎ 92/143–1475 🔁 €3 (free Tues. 4–6 pm).

**Iglesia de San Millán**

CHURCH | Built in the 12th century and a model example of the Segovian Romanesque style, this church, a five-minute walk outside the town walls, is an architectural marvel. The exterior is notable for its arcaded porch, where church meetings were once held. The virtually untouched interior is dominated by massive columns, whose capitals carry such carved scenes as the Flight into Egypt and the Adoration of the Magi. The vaulting on the crossing shows the Moorish influence on Spanish medieval architecture. It opens for Mass only. ✉ Av. Fernández Ladreda 26, Segovia ☎ 92/146–3876 ⊕ www.parroquiasanmillansegovia.com 🔁 Free.

★ **Palacio Real de La Granja** (*Royal Palace of La Granja*)

CASTLE/PALACE | If you have a car, don't miss the Palacio Real de La Granja in the town of La Granja de San Ildefonso, on the northern slopes of the Sierra de Guadarrama. The palace site was once occupied by a hunting lodge and a shrine to San Ildefonso, administered by Hieronymite monks from the Segovian monastery of El Parral. Commissioned by the Bourbon king Felipe V in 1719, the palace has been described as the first great building of the Spanish Bourbon dynasty. The Italian architects Juvarra and Sachetti, who finished it in 1739, were responsible for the imposing garden facade, a late-baroque masterpiece anchored by a giant order of columns. The interior was gutted by fire, but the collection of 15th- to 18th-century tapestries warrants a visit.

Outside, walk through the magnificent gardens: terraces, ornamental ponds,

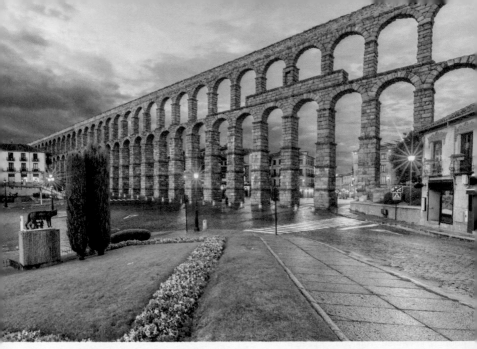

Segovia's Roman aqueduct, built more than 2,000 years ago, is remarkably well preserved.

lakes, classical statuary, woods, and baroque fountains dot the mountainside. Provided there is enough rainfall, on Wednesday, Saturday, and Sunday evenings in the summer (April–August, 5:30–7 pm), the illuminated fountains are turned on, one by one, creating an effect to rival that of Versailles. Dates and start times sometimes change on a whim, so call ahead. ⊠ *Pl. de España 15, San Ildefonso* ⊕ *About 11 km (7 miles) southeast of Segovia on N601* ☎ *92/147–0019, 92/147–0020* ⊕ *www.patrimonionacional. es* ⊠ *€9.*

### Plaza Mayor

**PLAZA/SQUARE** | In front of the cathedral, this historic square comes alive every night and especially on weekends, when visiting Madrileños and locals gather at casual cafés that line the perimeter. There's a gazebo in the middle that occasionally hosts live music. (Otherwise it's occupied by children playing while their parents dine nearby.) ⊠ *Pl. Mayor, Segovia.*

## 🍴 Restaurants

### Casa Duque

$$$$ | SPANISH | FAMILY | Segovia's oldest restaurant, founded in 1895 and still run by the same family, has a rustic interior with wood beams and bric-a-brac hanging on the walls. The decor suits the unfussy (if perhaps overpriced) cuisine, which features roast meats and stewed local *judiones* (broad *beans*). **Known for:** back-in-time setting; genial English-language menus and service; no-knife-needed cochinillo asado (roast suckling pig). ⑤ *Average main: €30* ⊠ *Calle Cervantes 12, Segovia* ☎ *92/146–2487, 92/146–2486* ⊕ *www.restauranteduque.es.*

### ★ El Fogón Sefardí

$$$ | SPANISH | This tavern in Segovia's historic Jewish quarter is owned by La Casa Mudéjar Hospedería hotel and has won awards for the region's best tapas. The extensive menu highlights Segovian specialties like cochinillo as well as traditional Sephardic Jewish cuisine (though it's not a kosher kitchen), plus a

variety of well-executed *raciones* (shared plates). **Known for:** generous salads; great cochinillo; Sephardic-influenced cuisine. $ *Average main: €21* ⊠ *Calle Judería Vieja 17, Segovia* ☎ *92/146–6250* ⊕ *www. lacasamudejar.com.*

### Mesón de Cándido

$$$$ | SPANISH | Beginning life as an inn in the 18th century, Cándido was declared a national monument in 1941, and today displays photos of famous patrons including Ernest Hemingway, Salvador Dalí, and Princess Grace. The suckling pig (cochinillo) is the star; partridge stew and roast lamb are also memorable, especially on cold afternoons. ■TIP→ **Ask for a table overlooking the aqueduct, just a few feet away, and be sure to book ahead. Known for:** famous former patrons like Ernest Hemingway; historical building; wood-fired-oven-roasted cochinillo. $ *Average main: €25* ⊠ *Pl. de Azoguejo 5, Segovia* ☎ *92/142–5911* ⊕ *www.mesondecandido.es.*

### ★ Mesón de José María

$$$$ | SPANISH | According to foodies, this old-timey *mesón* (traditional tavern-restaurant) serves the most delectable cochinillo in town, but there are plenty of lighter, fresher dishes to choose from as well. Expect a boisterous mix of locals and tourists. **Known for:** local crowd (a rarity in this touristy town); beamed dining room; best cochinillo in town. $ *Average main: €28* ⊠ *Calle Cronista Lecea 11, Segovia* ✛ *off Pl. Mayor* ☎ *92/146–1111, 92/146–6017* ⊕ *www.restaurantejosemaria.com.*

## 🛏 Hotels

### Áurea Convento Capuchinos

$$$$ | HOTEL | Áurea is a clean-cut Eurostars property whose guest rooms have tufted black leather headboards, beamed ceilings, and walls hung with photographs of local sights. **Pros:** standout buffet breakfasts; steps from the cathedral; over-and-beyond service. **Cons:** little in the way of local flavor; fee to use the swimming pool; no in-room temperature controls. $ *Rooms from: €275* ⊠ *Pl. Capuchinos 2, Segovia* ☎ *92/141–5250* ⊕ *www.eurostarshotels.co.uk/aurea-convento-capuchinos.html* ⬖ *62 rooms* ¶⚫ *No Meals.*

### Hotel Infanta Isabel

$$ | HOTEL | On the corner of the Plaza Mayor, this classically appointed hotel boasts cathedral views in a bustling shopping area. **Pros:** lived-in, cozy ambience; some rooms have balconies overlooking the plaza; central location. **Cons:** decidedly unhip decor; rooms facing the plaza can be noisy on weekends; some rooms are cramped and oddly shaped. $ *Rooms from: €128* ⊠ *Pl. Mayor 12, Segovia* ☎ *92/146–1300* ⊕ *www. hotelinfantaisabel.com* ⬖ *37 rooms* ¶⚫ *No Meals.*

### Hotel Spa La Casa Mudéjar

$$ | HOTEL | Built in the 15th century as a Mudejar palace, this historical property has spacious rooms and a well-priced spa (€35 per person; adults only) that's popular even with nonguests. **Pros:** terrific restaurant serving rare Sephardic dishes; affordable spa; historic building with Roman ruins. **Cons:** beds are nothing special; no nearby parking; forgettable interiors. $ *Rooms from: €148* ⊠ *Calle Isabel la Católica 8, Segovia* ☎ *92/146–6250* ⊕ *www.lacasamudejar.com* ⬖ *40 rooms* ¶⚫ *No Meals.*

## 👜 Shopping

After Toledo, the province of Segovia is Castile's most important area for traditional artisanry. Glass and crystal are specialties of La Granja, and ironwork, lace, basketry, and embroidery are famous in Segovia. The area around Plaza San Martín is a good place to buy crafts.

# Castillo de Coca

Perhaps the most famous medieval site near Segovia—worth the 52 km (32-mile) detour northwest of the city en route to Ávila or Valladolid—is the Castillo de Coca. Built in the 15th century for Archbishop Alonso de Fonseca I, the salmon-hued castle is a turreted Mudejar structure of plaster and red brick surrounded by a deep moat. It looks like a stage set for a fairy tale, and, indeed, it was intended not as a fortress but as a place for the notoriously pleasure-loving archbishop to hold riotous parties. The interior, now occupied by a forestry school, has been modernized, with only fragments of the original decoration preserved. ⊕ *www.castillodecoca.com*

### Calle Daoíz
NEIGHBORHOODS | Leading to the Alcázar, this street overflows with locally made (if tourist-oriented) ceramics, textiles, and gift shops. ⊠ *C. Daoiz, Segovia.*

# Sepúlveda

*58 km (36 miles) northeast of Segovia.*

A walled village with a commanding position, Sepúlveda has a charming main square, but the main reasons to visit are its 11th-century Romanesque church and striking gorge with a scenic hiking trail.

### GETTING HERE AND AROUND
Sepúlveda is about 1 hour north of Madrid on the A1. There are several buses (and Blablacar rideshares) a day from both Segovia and Madrid. The city is perched atop a hill overlooking a ravine, so you'll likely want transportation to the top. Don't park or get off the bus too soon.

### VISITOR INFORMATION
CONTACTS **Sepúlveda Tourist Office.** ⊠ *Pl. del Trigo 6, Sepúlveda* ☎ *92/154–0425* ⊕ *sepulveda.es.*

# Sights

### El Salvador
CHURCH | This 11th-century wonder is the oldest Romanesque church in the province. The carvings on its capitals, probably by a Moorish convert, are quite outlandish. ⊠ *Calle Subida a El Salvador 31, Sepúlveda* ☜ *Free.*

### ★ Ermita de San Frutos
CHURCH | This 11th-century hermitage is in ruins, but its location, on a peninsula jutting out into a bend 100 meters above the Duratón River, is extraordinary. You'll need a car to get there, about 15 minutes' drive west of Sepúlveda. After parking, walk along the marked path— the surrounding area is a natural park and a protected nesting ground for rare vultures—and try to go at sunset, when the sun sets the monastery and river aglow. Inside the monastery, there's a small chapel and plaque describing the life of San Frutos, the patron saint of Segovia. An ancient pilgrimage route stretches 77 km (48 miles) from the monastery to Segovia's cathedral, and pilgrims still walk it each year. As an add-on to the trip, you can rent kayaks from NaturalTur to paddle the river (⊕ www.naturaltur. com; ☎92/152–1727). ⊠ *Carrascal del Río, Burgomillodo, Sepúlveda* ☜ *Free.*

# 🍴 Restaurants

### ★ Fogón del Azogue

**$$$$** | **SPANISH** | **FAMILY** | The menu at this white-tablecloth aerie, which overlooks rolling farmland, hinges on local delicacies like fried blood sausage, creamy ham croquettes, and—naturally, since we're in Segovia province—crackly roast milk-fed lamb and suckling pig. The spacious venue is well suited to hosting large groups. **Known for:** brick-oven-roasted pork and lamb; wraparound windows with gorgeous views; refined Castilian cuisine. ⓢ *Average main: €23* ✉ *Calle de San Millán 6, Sepúlveda* ☎ *69/020–2772* ⊗ *Closed Tues.–Wed. No dinner Sun.–Fri.*

# San Lorenzo de El Escorial

*50 km (31 miles) northwest of Madrid.*

An hour from Madrid, and within Madrid province, San Lorenzo de El Escorial makes for a leisurely day trip away from the hustle and bustle of the Spanish capital. The medieval town's main attraction is the Real Sitio de San Lorenzo de El Escorial, the Royal Site of San Lorenzo of El Escorial. A dozen or so trains leave daily from the Madrid Sol train station, or you can take the C3 regional line from Atocha, Chamartín, Nuevos Ministerios, or Recoletos. The journey takes about an hour, and the entrance to El Escorial is about a 15-minute walk from the train station.

# 👁 Sights

### ★ Real Monasterio de San Lorenzo de El Escorial

**CASTLE/PALACE** | A UNESCO World Heritage Site and one of Spain's most visited landmarks, the imposing El Escorial palace complex was commissioned by Felipe II after the death of his father in the 1500s and remains the most complete and impressive monument of the later Renaissance in Spain. The monastery was built as an eternal memorial for his relatives, and the crypt here is the resting place of the majority of Spain's kings, from Charles V to Alfonso XIII. A fantasy land of gilded halls, hand-painted chambers, and manicured French gardens, the gargantuan royal residence also houses an important collection of paintings by Renaissance and baroque artists donated by the crown. The library alone is worth the entry fee—its vibrant frescoes and leather-bound tomes spur the imagination. ✉ *Pl. de España 1, San Lorenzo de El Escorial* ☎ *91/890–5903* ⊕ *www.patrimonionacional.es/en/visita/royal-site-san-lorenzo-de-el-escorial* ⓢ *€12 (free 3–7 on Wed. and Sun.)* ⊗ *Closed Mon.* Ⓜ *El Escorial.*

# 🍴 Restaurants

### ★ Charolés Restaurante

**$$$** | **SPANISH** | **FAMILY** | According to Spain's top food critics, this restaurant ladles out the best *cocido madrileño* in all the land. Each component of the multicourse boiled dinner, from the chickpeas to the chorizo to the pickled peppers, is sourced from top-notch producers from around the peninsula. **Known for:** within walking distance of the palace; cozy historical decor; probably the world's best cocido madrileño. ⓢ *Average main: €22* ✉ *Calle Floridablanca 24, San Lorenzo de El Escorial* ☎ *91/890–5975* ⊕ *www.charolesrestaurante.com.*

# Ávila

*114 km (71 miles) northwest of Madrid.*

On a windy plateau littered with giant boulders, with the Sierra de Gredos in the background, Ávila is a walled fairy-tale

Ávila's city walls, which still encircle the old city, have a perimeter of about 2½ km (1½ miles).

town. After it was wrested from the Moors in 1090, soaring crenelated walls were erected around its perimeter—by some 1,900 builders, who allegedly finished the task in just nine years. The walls have nine gates and 88 cylindrical towers bunched together, making them unique to Spain in form—they're quite unlike the Moorish defense architecture that the Christians adapted elsewhere. They're most striking when seen from afar; for the best views (and photos), cross the Adaja River, turn right on Carretera de Salamanca, and walk uphill about 250 yards to a monument of pilasters surrounding a cross known as the Four Posts.

Ávila's fame is largely due to St. Teresa. Born here in 1515 to a noble family of Jewish origin, Teresa spent much of her life in Ávila, leaving a legacy of convents and the ubiquitous *yemas* (candied egg yolks), originally distributed free to the poor and now sold at high prices to tourists. The town comes to life during the Fiestas de la Santa Teresa in October, a weeklong celebration that includes lighted decorations, parades, singing in the streets, and religious observances.

## GETTING HERE AND AROUND

Jiménez Dorado (⊕ www.jimenezdorado. com) and Avanza (⊕ avila.avanzagrupo. com) serve Ávila and its surrounding villages. Some two dozen trains depart for Ávila each day from Chamartín station, and there are usually plentiful Blablacar rideshares available. The city itself is easily managed on foot.

## VISITOR INFORMATION

**CONTACTS Ávila Tourist Office.** ⊠ *Av. de Madrid 39* ☎ *92/020–6200* ⊕ *www. turismoavila.com.*

## ⊙ Sights

**Basílica de San Vicente** (*Basilica of St. Vincent*)
**CHURCH** | Where this massive Romanesque basilica stands, it's said that St. Vincent was martyred in 303 AD with his sisters, Sts. Sabina and Cristeta.

Construction began in 1130, though the complex was restored in the late 19th and early 20th centuries. The west front, shielded by a vestibule, displays damaged but expressive carvings depicting the death of Lazarus and the parable of the rich man's table. The sarcophagus of St. Vincent forms the centerpiece of the interior. The extraordinary, Eastern-influenced canopy above the sarcophagus is a 15th-century addition. Combined, these elements form one of Spain's most prized examples of Romanesque architecture. ⊠ *Pl. de San Vicente 1, Ávila* ☎ *92/022–5969* ⊕ *www.basilicasanvicente.es* ✉ *€3 (free Sun.).*

**Casa de los Deanes** (*Deans' Mansion*)
HISTORIC HOME | This 15th-century building houses the cheerful **Museo Provincial de Ávila,** full of local archaeology and folklore. Part of the museum's collection is housed in the adjacent Romanesque temple of San Tomé el Viejo, a few minutes' walk east of the cathedral apse. ⊠ *Pl. de Nalvillos 3, Ávila* ☎ *92/021–1003* ✉ *€2 (free Sat. and Sun.)* ☾ *Closed Mon.*

★ **Catedral de Ávila**
CHURCH | The battlement apse of Ávila's cathedral forms the most impressive part of the city's walls. Entering the town gate to the right of the apse, you can reach the sculpted north portal by turning left and walking a few steps. The west portal, flanked by 18th-century towers, is notable for the crude carvings of hairy male figures on each side. Known as "wild men," these figures appear in many Castilian palaces of this period. The Transitional Gothic structure, with its granite nave, is considered to be the first Gothic cathedral in Spain. Look for the early-16th-century marble sepulchre of Bishop Alonso de Madrigal. Known as El Tostado (the Toasted One) for his swarthy complexion, the bishop was a tiny man of enormous intellect. When on one occasion Pope Eugenius IV ordered him to stand—mistakenly thinking him to be on his knees—the bishop pointed to the space between his eyebrows and hairline, and retorted, "A man's stature is to be measured from here to here!" ⊠ *Pl. de la Catedral, Ávila* ☎ *92/021–1641* ⊕ *catedralavila.es* ✉ *€7.*

**Convento de Santa Teresa**
CHURCH | This Carmelite convent was founded in the 17th century on the site of the St. Teresa's birthplace. Teresa's account of an ecstatic vision, in which an angel pierced her heart, inspired many baroque artists, most famously the Italian sculptor Giovanni Bernini. There's a small museum with creepy relics, including one of Teresa's fingers. You can also see the small and rather gloomy garden where she played as a child. ⊠ *Pl. de la Santa 2, Ávila* ☎ *92/021–1030* ⊕ *www.santateresadejesus.com* ✉ *Church and reliquary free, museum €2.*

**Real Monasterio de Santo Tomás**
CHURCH | In an unlikely location—among apartment blocks a good 10-minute walk from the walls—is one of the most important religious institutions in Castile. The monastery was founded by Ferdinand and Isabella with the backing of Inquisitor-General Tomás de Torquemada, largely responsible for the expulsion of the Jews per the Alhambra Decree, who is buried in the sacristy. Further funds were provided by the confiscated property of converted Jews who were dispossessed during the Inquisition. Three decorated cloisters lead to the church; inside, a masterful high altar (circa 1506) by Pedro Berruguete overlooks a serene marble tomb by the Italian artist Domenico Fancelli. One of the earliest examples of the Italian Renaissance style in Spain, this work was built for Prince Juan, the only son of Ferdinand and Isabella, who died at 19. After Juan's burial here, his heartbroken parents found themselves unable to return. ⊠ *Pl. de Granada 1, Ávila* ☎ *92/022–0400* ⊕ *www.monasteriosantotomas.com* ✉ *€4.*

# 🍴 Restaurants

## Las Cancelas

$$$ | SPANISH | Locals flock to this little tavern for tapas and fat, juicy steaks served in the boisterous barroom or white-tablecloth dining area, set in a covered arcaded courtyard. There are 14 hotel rooms available, too—simple, endearingly well-worn arrangements at moderate prices. **Known for:** good value; quaint, romantic dining room; chuletón de Ávila (gargantuan local steak). $ *Average main: €21* ✉ *Calle de la Cruz Vieja 6, Ávila* ☎ *92/021–2249* ⊕ *www.lascancelas.com* ⊗ *Closed Jan.–early Feb. No dinner Sun.*

## ★ Restaurante El Molino de la Losa

$$$$ | SPANISH | FAMILY | At the edge of the serene Adaja River, El Molino, housed in a 15th-century mill, is one of the most idyllic restaurants in the region. Lamb, the chef's specialty, is roasted in a medieval wood oven; it's best preceded by smoky, bacon-y *revolcona* (mashed) potatoes or a bowl of stewed white beans from nearby El Barco de Ávila. **Known for:** refined old-school cuisine; stunning location with views of the river and city walls; succulent roast lamb. $ *Average main: €30* ✉ *Calle Bajada de la Losa 12, Ávila* ☎ *92/021–1101, 92/021–1102* ⊕ *www.elmolinodelalosa.com* ⊗ *Closed Tues. No dinner Sun.–Wed.*

# 🛏 Hotels

## ★ Best Western Premier Sofraga Palacio

$$ | HOTEL | A breath of fresh air on Ávila's aging hotel scene, this 2021 property strikes a delicate balance between old and new. **Pros:** pleasingly mellow decor; exquisite local ham, preserves, and cheeses at breakfast; historical building with character. **Cons:** restaurant is a bit overpriced for the area; popular wedding venue; design a bit cookie-cutter in spots. $ *Rooms from: €129* ✉ *Calle López Núñez 1, Ávila* ☎ *92/025–4080* ⊕ *www.bestwestern.com* ➥ *27 rooms* ⦿ *Free Breakfast.*

## Palacio de los Velada

$$ | HOTEL | This four-star hotel occupies a beautifully restored 16th-century palace in the heart of the city next to the cathedral, an ideal spot if you like to relax between sightseeing. **Pros:** gorgeous glass-covered patio; bountiful breakfast buffet; amiable service. **Cons:** lack of power outlets; expensive off-site parking; some rooms don't have views because the windows are so high. $ *Rooms from: €105* ✉ *Pl. de la Catedral 10, Ávila* ☎ *92/025–5100* ⊕ *www.hotelpalaciodelosvelada.com* ➥ *145 rooms* ⦿ *Free Breakfast.*

## Parador de Ávila

$$$ | HOTEL | FAMILY | Post up in a 16th-century medieval castle attached to the massive town walls at this parador whose standout feature is its lush garden containing archaeological ruins. **Pros:** gorgeous garden and views; family-friendly rooms and services; good restaurant. **Cons:** underwhelming breakfast; interiors need a refresh; 10-minute walk to the action. $ *Rooms from: €155* ✉ *Marqués de Canales de Chozas 2, Ávila* ☎ *92/021–1340* ⊕ *www.parador.es* ➥ *61 rooms* ⦿ *No Meals.*

# Salamanca

*212 km (132 miles) northwest of Madrid.*

Salamanca's radiant sandstone buildings, mathematically proportioned Plaza Mayor, and meandering river make it one of the most majestic and beloved cities in Spain. For centuries, its eponymous university has imbued the city with an intellectual verve, a stimulating arts scene, and—in recent decades—raging nightlife to match. You'll see more foreign

Salamanca's Plaza Mayor once hosted bullfights.

students here per capita than anywhere else in Spain.

If you approach from Madrid or Ávila, your first glimpse of Salamanca will be the city rising from the wide and winding Tormes River. In the foreground is a 15-arch Roman bridge; soaring above it is the combined bulk of the old and new cathedrals. Piercing the skyline to their right is the Renaissance monastery and church of San Esteban. Behind these, and largely out of sight from the river, is a medieval warren of palaces, convents, and university buildings that culminates in the Plaza Mayor. Despite enduring considerable damage over the centuries, Salamanca remains one of Spain's greatest cities architecturally, a veritable showpiece of the Spanish Renaissance.

## GETTING HERE AND AROUND

You'll feel rushed if you try to visit Salamanca from Madrid in an out-and-back day trip. To fully enjoy its splendor, plan on an overnight. Approximately 13 trains depart Madrid for Salamanca daily, several of which are high-speed ALVIA itineraries that take just over an hour and a half. Avanza buses leave from the Estación Sur de Autobuses; Blablacar rideshares (about 2 hours and 15 minutes) are faster and more affordable.

Once in town, Salamanca de Transportes runs 64 municipal buses equipped with lifts for passengers with limited mobility on routes throughout the city. You may opt to take a bus in order to reach the train and bus stations on the outskirts of the city.

**CONTACTS Salamanca de Transportes.**
✉ *Calle Gran Vía 4, Salamanca* ☎ *92/321–2829* ⊕ *www.salamancadetransportes. com.*

## VISITOR INFORMATION
**CONTACTS Salamanca City Tourist Office.**
✉ *Pl. Mayor 32, Salamanca* ☎ *92/321–8342* ⊕ *www.salamanca.es.*

# Salamanca

**KEY**
- ● Sights
- ● Restaurants
- ● Hotels

0     200 yards
0     200 meters

**Sights** ▼

1 Casa de Las Conchas ... **C4**
2 Convento de Las Dueñas .............. **D5**
3 Convento de San Estéban ............. **D6**
4 La Catedral Vieja and La Catedral Nueva ...... **B5**
5 Museo de Art Nouveau y Art Déco – Casa Lis .... **B6**
6 Palacio de Monterrey ... **C3**
7 Plaza Mayor ............. **D3**
8 Puente Romano ......... **A6**
9 Universidad de Salamanca ........... **B5**

**Restaurants** ▼

1 Bambú Tapas y Brasas ................... **C3**
2 Consentido ............. **D3**
3 La Hoja 21 ................. **C5**
4 Patio de la Abuela ...... **D1**
5 Tapas 2.0 ................. **C4**
6 Valencia ................. **C2**

**Hotels** ▼

1 Grand Hotel Don Gregorio ............. **C5**
2 Hotel Rector ............. **C6**
3 Microtel Placentinos ... **B4**
4 Revolutum Hostel ........ **C4**

# ◉ Sights

**Casa de Las Conchas** (*House of Shells*)

HISTORIC HOME | This house, whose facade is covered in scallop shell carvings, was built around 1500 for Dr. Rodrigo Maldonado de Talavera, a chancellor of the Order of St. James, whose symbol is the shell. Among the playful plateresque details are the lions over the main entrance, engaged in a fearful tug-of-war with the Talavera crest. The interior has been converted into a public library. Duck into the charming courtyard, which has an intricately carved upper balustrade that imitates basketwork. ⊠ *Calle Compañía 2, Salamanca* ☎ *92/326–9317* ☜ *Free*.

★ **Convento de Las Dueñas** (*Convent of the Dames*)

CHURCH | Founded in 1419, this convent hides a 16th-century cloister that is the most fantastically decorated in Salamanca, if not all of Spain. The capitals of its two superimposed Salmantine arcades are crowded with a baffling profusion of grotesques that can absorb you for hours. Don't forget to look down: the interlocking diamond pattern on the ground floor of the cloister is decorated with the knobby vertebrae of goats and sheep. It's an eerie yet perfect accompaniment to all the grinning, disfigured heads sprouting from the capitals looming above you. The museum has a fascinating exhibit on Spain's little-known slavery industry. ■TIP➜ **Seek out the traditional sweets made by the nuns.** ⊠ *Pl. del Concilio de Trento, Salamanca* ☎ *92/321–5442* ☜ *€2*.

★ **Convento de San Estéban** (*Convent of St. Stephen*)

CHURCH | The convent's monks, among the most enlightened teachers at the university in medieval times, introduced Christopher Columbus to Isabella (hence his statue in the nearby Plaza de Colón, back toward Calle de San Pablo). The complex was designed by one of the

monks who lived here, Juan de Álava. The west facade, a thrilling plateresque masterwork in which sculpted figures and ornamentation are piled up to a height of more than 98 feet, is a gathering spot for tired tourists and picnicking locals, but the crown jewel of the structure is a glowing golden sandstone cloister with Gothic arcading punctuated by tall, spindly columns adorned with classical motifs. The church, unified and uncluttered but also dark and severe, allows the one note of color provided by the ornate and gilded high altar of 1692. An awe-inspiring baroque masterpiece by José Churriguera, it deserves five minutes of just sitting and staring. ⊠ *Pl. Concilio de Trento 1, Salamanca* ☎ *92/321–5000* ⊕ *www.conventosanesteban.es* ☜ *€4* ⊗ *Museum closed Mon.*

★ **La Catedral Vieja and La Catedral Nueva**

CHURCH | Nearest the river stands the Catedral Vieja (Old Cathedral), built in the late 12th century and one of the most riveting examples of the Spanish Romanesque. Because the dome of the crossing tower has strange, plumelike ribbing, it's known as the Torre del Gallo (Rooster's Tower). The much larger Catedral Nueva (New Cathedral) went up between 1513 and 1526 under the late-Gothic architect Juan Gil de Hontañón. Controversially, a 1992 restoration added an astronaut carving to the facade

---

## Fonseca's Mark ◉

Nearly all of Salamanca's outstanding Renaissance buildings bear the five-star crest of the powerful and ostentatious Fonseca family. The most famous of them, Alonso de Fonseca I, was the archbishop of Santiago and later of Seville; he was also a notorious womanizer and a patron of the Spanish Renaissance.

---

**4**

**Central Spain** SALAMANCA

as a wink to the modern era—see if you can spot it. Both cathedrals are part of the same complex, though they have different visiting hours, and you need to enter the New to get to the Old. ⊠ *Pl. de Anaya and Calle Cardenal Pla y Deniel, Salamanca* ☎ *92/321–7476, 92/328–1123* ⊕ *www.catedralsalamanca.org* ⊠ *€6 (includes Catedral Nueva and Catedral Vieja).*

### Museo de Art Nouveau y Art Déco – Casa Lis

ART MUSEUM | Sure, the best thing about this museum is probably the stunning Moderniste building it's housed in, but the collections—comprising 19th-century paintings and glass, French and German china dolls, Viennese bronze statues, and more—are a welcome reprieve from all the churrigueresque convents and churches. ⊠ *Calle Gibraltar 14, Salamanca* ☎ *92/312–1425* ⊕ *www.museocasalis. org* ⊠ *€5 (free Thurs. 11–2).*

### Palacio de Monterrey

CASTLE/PALACE | Built in the mid-16th century by Rodrigo Gil de Hontañón and one of the most stunning Renaissance palaces in Spain, this lavish abode was meant for an illegitimate son of Alonso de Fonseca I. The building, which opened to the public in 2018, is flanked by towers and has an open arcaded gallery running the length of the upper level. Such galleries—often seen on the ground floor of palaces in Italy—were intended to provide privacy for the women of the house and to cool the floor below during the summer. Walking the halls on either the day- or nighttime tour, feast your eyes on seldom-before-seen Titians, Coellos, and other masterpieces presided over by the Alba family. ⊠ *Pl. de las Agustinas, Salamanca* ☎ *92/321–3020* ⊕ *www. palaciodemonterrey.com* ⊠ *From €7 (free Tues. at 10:30 am with prior booking).*

### ★ Plaza Mayor

PLAZA/SQUARE | In the 1730s Alberto and Nicolás Churriguera built Salamanca's Plaza Mayor, one of the largest and most beautiful squares in Spain. The lavishly elegant, pinkish *ayuntamiento* (town hall) dominates its northern side. The square and its arcades are popular gathering spots for Salmantinos of all ages, and its terrazas are the perfect spot for a coffee break. At night, the plaza swarms with students meeting "under the clock" on the plaza's north side. *Tunas* (roving musicians in traditional garb) often meander among the cafés and crowds, playing for smiles, applause, and tips. ⊠ *Plaza Mayor, Salamanca.*

### Puente Romano (*Roman Bridge*)

BRIDGE | Next to this bridge is an Iberian stone bull, and opposite the bull is a statue commemorating the young hero of the 16th-century picaresque novel *The Life of Lazarillo de Tormes and of His Fortunes and Adversities,* a masterpiece of Spanish literature. There's also a 300-meter track and a network of paths on the south side of the bridge ideal for jogging. ⊠ *Salamanca.*

### Universidad de Salamanca

COLLEGE | The university's walls, like those of the cathedral and other structures in Salamanca, often bear large ocher lettering recording the names of famous university graduates. The earliest names are said to have been written in the blood of the bulls killed to celebrate the successful completion of a doctorate (call it medieval graffiti!). The elaborate facade of the Escuelas Mayores (Upper Schools) dates to the early 16th century; see if you can spy the eroded "lucky" frog that's become the symbol of the city—legend has it that students who do on their first try will pass all their exams. The interior of the Escuelas Mayores, drastically restored in parts, is disappointing after the splendor of the facade and not worth entering unless you're a diehard

## Did You Know?

Salamanca's "new" cathedral was built in the 16th century to help reinforce the deteriorating "old" cathedral, which dates to the 12th. Today you can see both, entering the new to get to the old.

Spanish literature buff. But if you are, the lecture hall of Fray Luis de León, where Cervantes, Pedro Calderón de la Barca, and numerous other luminaries of Spain's golden age once sat, is of interest, as is the grand library. Don't miss the serene courtyard (free entry) of the Escuelas Menores (Lower Schools) that wraps around the patio in front of the Escuelas Mayores. ✉ *Calle Libreros, Salamanca* ☎ *92/329–4400, 95/222–2998* ⊕ *www. usal.es* 🖾 *Free to view facade, €10 to enter (free Mon. morning).*

## 🍴 Restaurants

### Bambú Tapas y Brasas

$$$ | TAPAS | Bambú is two restaurants in one: there's a jovial basement tapas bar serving gargantuan tapas and beers, and then there's the far more sedate white-tablecloth dining room, whose alta cocina menu is as experimental as it is expensive. Both are worthwhile options; go with the vibe that suits you best. **Known for:** terrific grilled meats; upscale dining room; free tapas with every drink at the bar. ⑤ *Average main: €20* ✉ *Calle Prior 4, Salamanca* ☎ *92/326–0092* ⊕ *www.bambubrasas.com* 🕙 *No dinner Mon.*

### ★ Consentido

$$$$ | MODERN EUROPEAN | In his 30s, Salamanca-born chef Carlos Hernández del Río cut his teeth in such star-studded kitchens as Elkano, Zuberoa, and DiverXO before returning to his roots in 2020 to open this restaurant showcasing the best ingredients, techniques, and wines from his native region—with a few geeky French touches. Expect immaculately prepared appetizers like griddled fresh artichokes with Béarnaise followed by mains including stewed chickpeas with sherry and pork and marinated Tormes river trout, all served in a bright dining room with checkerboard tile floors and designer furniture. **Known for:** rising-star chef; homemade breads and pâtés; hottest restaurant in town. ⑤ *Average main: €24* ✉ *Pl. del Mercado 8, Salamanca* ☎ *92/370–8261* ⊕ *www. restaurante-consentido.es* 🕙 *Closed Mon. and Tues.*

### ★ La Hoja 21

$$$ | SPANISH | Just off the Plaza Mayor, this upscale restaurant has a glass facade, high ceilings, butter-yellow walls, and minimalist art—a welcome relief from the dime-a-dozen Castilian mesones. Savor traditional fare with a twist, such as ibérico pork ravioli and langoustine-stuffed trotters at dinner, or spring for the €19 lunch prix fixe, an absolute steal, served Tuesday through Thursday. **Known for:** romantic, low-key atmosphere; phenomenally affordable menú del día (prix fixe); nuanced yet unpretentious modern fare. ⑤ *Average main: €22* ✉ *Calle San Pablo 21, Salamanca* ☎ *92/326–4028* ⊕ *www.lahoja21. com* 🕙 *Closed Mon. No dinner Sun.*

### Patio de la Abuela

$ | TAPAS | *Jeta*—crackly, juicy fried pig snout sliced into bite-size pieces—is the raison d'être of this locals-oriented gem 1½ km (1 mile) north of the city center. Pair it with an ice-cold beer, and you've got the perfect aperitivo or late-night snack—for under €5. **Known for:** pilgrimage-worthy porky bits; pleasant patio; best budget eats in town. ⑤ *Average main: €4* ✉ *Calle Salesas 2, Salamanca* ☎ *92/362–1370* 🕙 *Closed Mon. and Tues.*

### ★ Tapas 2.0

$$ | TAPAS | Decidedly modern, dependably delicious, and shockingly cheap, Tapas 2.0 might pull you back for a second meal. The cool *ensaladilla rusa* (tuna-and-potato salad), a specialty, is perhaps one of the best in Spain; then there are more substantial dishes, like stewed broad beans with octopus and shrimp, and saucy chicken cannelloni, all complemented by a wine list featuring unexpected pours like German Riesling. **Known for:** best tapas in town;

uncommon wines; award-winning ensaladilla rusa. $ *Average main: €14* ✉ *Calle Felipe Espino 10, Salamanca* ☎ *92/321–6448* ⊕ *www.tapastrespuntocero.es.*

### Valencia

$$$ | SPANISH | Despite its Mediterranean name, this traditional, family-run restaurant serves up Castilian specialties like garlic soup, partridge salad, local river trout, white asparagus, and suckling lamb. The tiny front bar is decorated with black-and-white photos of local bullfighters, and is usually packed with locals (as is the back room). **Known for:** outdoor seating; soul-warming Castilian fare; hidden-gem local hangout. $ *Average main: €20* ✉ *Calle Concejo 15, Salamanca* ☎ *92/321-7868* ⊕ *www.restaurantovalencia.com* ⊙ *Closed Mon. and Tues. Sept.–May, Sun. and Mon. June–Aug.*

## 🛏 Hotels

### Grand Hotel Don Gregorio

$$$$ | HOTEL | This upscale boutique hotel has spacious, contemporary rooms in a building with roots in the 15th century. **Pros:** quiet and comfortable; spa and in-room massages; complimentary cava upon arrival. **Cons:** hodgepodge, passé decor; no outdoor space for lounging; overpriced restaurant. $ *Rooms from: €245* ✉ *Calle San Pablo 80–82, Salamanca* ☎ *92/321–7015* ⊕ *www.hoteldongregorio.com* ⤴ *17 rooms* ❢⊘ *Free Breakfast.*

### ★ Hotel Rector

$$$$ | HOTEL | From the stately entrance to the high-ceiling guest rooms, this charming 13-room hotel offers a fairy-tale European experience. **Pros:** good value for a luxury hotel; good location; personal service. **Cons:** breakfast could be more ample; no balconies; parking costs extra. $ *Rooms from: €259* ✉ *Paseo Rector Esperabé 10, Salamanca* ☎ *92/321–8482* ⊕ *www.hotelrector.com* ⤴ *13 rooms* ❢⊘ *No Meals.*

### ★ Microtel Placentinos

$ | B&B/INN | This is a cheap-and-cheerful B&B tucked down a quiet pedestrian street in Salamanca's historic center, near the Palacio de Congresos convention center and a short walk from the Plaza Mayor. **Pros:** some rooms have whirlpool baths; short walk to bus station; quirky decor. **Cons:** boring breakfast buffet; some accommodations are cramped; rooms by interior staircase can be noisy. $ *Rooms from: €90* ✉ *Calle Placentinos 9, Salamanca* ☎ *92/328–1531* ⊕ *www.microtelplacentinos.com* ⤴ *9 rooms* ❢⊘ *Free Breakfast.*

### Revolutum Hostel

$ | HOTEL | What some might call a "designer hostel," this is the best modern budget hotel in Salamanca. **Pros:** breakfast included; special rates for families and longer stays; all rooms have private bathrooms. **Cons:** small bathrooms in some rooms; you have to make your own bed in some rooms; deposit required for towels. $ *Rooms from: €55* ✉ *Calle Sánchez Barbero 7, Salamanca* ☎ *92/321-7656* ⊕ *www.revolutumhostel.com* ⤴ *20 rooms* ❢⊘ *Free Breakfast.*

## 🍸 Nightlife

Particularly in summer, Salamanca sees the greatest influx of foreign students of any city in Spain. By day they study Spanish, and by night they fill Salamanca's bars and clubs.

### BARS AND CAFÉS
### ★ The Doctor Cocktail

COCKTAIL LOUNGES | This petite, unpretentious coctelería off the Plaza Mayor serves an enormous breadth of drinks, from colorful tiki numbers (some with pyrotechnics) to Prohibition-era classics, until 1:30 am daily. ✉ *Calle Doctor Pinuela 5, Salamanca* ☎ *92/326–3151.*

## Mist Cocktail Bar

COCKTAIL LOUNGES | Sip fabulously gaudy cocktails both classic and experimental at this bar that also pulls excellent single-origin espressos. Weather permitting, try to snag a spot on the large outdoor patio. ⊠ *Calle Bordadores 14, Salamanca* ☎ *92/321–4530* ⊕ *www.cafenieblabar. com.*

## 🎭 Performing Arts

### Teatro Liceo

MUSIC | This 732-seat theater, 40 yards from Plaza Mayor, is a renovated 19th-century building erected over an 18th-century convent. It hosts classic and modern performances of opera, dance, and flamenco as well as film festivals. ⊠ *Calle del Toro 23, Salamanca* ☎ *92/328–1716* ⊕ *www.ciudaddecultura. org.*

## 🛍 Shopping

### El Rastro

MARKET | This Sunday flea market—named after the larger one in Madrid—is held just outside Salamanca's historic center. It has some 400 stalls. ⊠ *Av. de Aldehuela, Salamanca.*

### ★ Luis Méndez

JEWELRY & WATCHES | Luis and his two brothers are independent third-generation jewelers whose work is distinguished by intricate filigree. The most stunning specimens—costing more than €1,000—are fashioned out of gold and pearls, but there are more affordable options made from silver and semiprecious stones. Visit their boutique, or purchase from the online Etsy catalog. ⊠ *Calle Meléndez 8, Bajo 2, Salamanca* ☎ *92/326–0725, 92/344–9111* ⊕ *www. luismendez.net.*

### ★ Mercado Central

FOOD | FAMILY | At Salamanca's most historic market with more than 50 stalls you can stock up on local gourmet specialties—such as farinato sausages, jamón ibérico, and sheep's cheeses—and round out your shopping spree with a glass of wine at any of the traditional tapas counters. ⊠ *Pl. del Mercado, Salamanca* ☎ *92/321–3000* ⊕ *www.mercadocentralsalamanca.com* ⊗ *Closed Sun.*

# Burgos

*243 km (151 miles) north of Madrid on A1.*

On the banks of the Arlanzón River, this small city boasts some of Spain's most outstanding Gothic architecture. If you approach on the A1 from Madrid, the spiky twin spires of Burgos's cathedral, rising above the main bridge, welcome you to the city. Burgos's second pride is its heritage as the city of El Cid, the part-historical, part-mythical hero of the so-called Reconquest of Spain. For better and for worse, the city has long been synonymous with both militarism and religion, and even today more nuns fill the streets than almost anywhere else in Spain.

Burgos was born as a military camp—a fortress built in 884 under Christian king Alfonso III, who was struggling to defend the upper reaches of Old Castile from the constant forays of the Arabs. It was vital in the defense of so-called Christian Spain, and its reputation as an early outpost of Christianity was cemented with the founding of the Royal Convent of Las Huelgas in 1187, and as it became a stop for pilgrims on the Camino de Santiago.

In 1938, as the Spanish Civil War raged, soon-to-be dictator Francisco Franco made Burgos his first seat of government, a testament to the city's conservative leanings. Today Burgos is a modern Spanish city like any other, and happily, its name is more likely to recall its famous *queso fresco* (quark) and *morcilla* (blood sausage) than its fraught political past.

The small city of Burgos is famous for its magnificent Gothic cathedral.

## GETTING HERE AND AROUND

From Madrid, Burgos can be reached by train, with about a dozen daily departures from Chamartín (2½ hours on the fast ALVIA and 4½ on the regional line). Note that the Rosa Manzano train station is 5 km (3.1 miles) from the city center. By bus, there's hourly service from various Madrid stations. Blablacar rideshares are generally available as well. Once in town, explore on foot or with the help of municipal bus routes, which form a tight web.

## VISITOR INFORMATION

**CONTACTS Burgos Tourist Office.** ⊠ Pl. de Alonso-Martínez 7 ☎ 94/720–3125 ⊕ turismo.aytoburgos.es.

## ◉ Sights

### Arco de Santa María

**NOTABLE BUILDING** | Across the Plaza del Rey San Fernando from the cathedral, this is the city's main gate, rebuilt in the 16th century by King Charles V. Walk through toward the river and look above the arch at the 16th-century statues of the first Castilian judges, El Cid, King Carlos I, and Spain's patron saint, James. ⊠ Burgos.

### Cartuja de Miraflores (Miraflores Charterhouse)

**CHURCH** | The plain facade of this 15th-century Carthusian monastery, some 3 km (2 miles) outside the historic center, belies a richly decorated interior. There's an altarpiece by Gil de Siloe that is said to be gilded with the first gold plundered in the Americas. ⊠ Ctra. Fuentes Blancas, Burgos ☎ 94/725–2586 ⊕ www.cartuja.org ⊠ Free.

### ★ Catedral de Burgos

**CHURCH** | The cathedral contains such a wealth of art and other treasures that the local burghers lynched their civil governor in 1869 for trying to take an inventory of it, fearing that he was plotting to steal their riches. Just as opulent is the sculpted flamboyant Gothic facade. The cornerstone was laid in 1221, and the two 275-foot towers were completed in the 14th century, though the final chapel was not finished until 1731. There are 13

# Burgos

**KEY**

- ① Sights
- ① Restaurants
- ① Hotels

## Sights ▶

1. Arco de Santa María...... **E2**
2. Cartuja de Miraflores..... **E2**
3. Catedral de Burgos........ **E2**
4. Monasterio de las Huelgas........... **A3**
5. Museo de la Evolución Humana................ **G2**
6. Paseo del Espolón........ **F2**

## Restaurants ▶

1. Casa Ojeda.................. **G1**

## Hotels ▶

1. Crisol Mesón del Cid..... **E2**
2. Landa............................ **F3**

0 ___ 200 yards

0 ___ 200 meters

chapels, the most elaborate of which is the hexagonal Condestable Chapel. You'll find the tomb of El Cid (1026–99) and his wife, Ximena, under the transept. El Cid (Rodrigo Díaz de Vivar) was a feudal warlord revered for his victories over the Moors, though he fought for them as well; the medieval *Song of My Cid* transformed him into a Spanish national hero.

At the other end of the cathedral, high above the West Door, is the Reloj de Papamoscas (Flycatcher Clock), named for the sculptured bird that opens its mouth as the hands mark each hour. The grilles around the choir have some of the finest wrought-iron work in central Spain, and the choir itself has 103 delicately carved walnut stalls, no two alike. The 13th-century stained-glass windows were destroyed in 1813, one of many cultural casualties of Napoléon's retreating troops. The excellent free audio guide has a kid friendly option. ☒ *Pl. de Santa María, Burgos* ☎ *94/720–4712* ⊕ *www. catedraldeburgos.es* ▧ *€9.*

**Monasterio de las Huelgas** (*Monasterio de las Huelgas*)

CHURCH | This convent on the outskirts of town, founded in 1187 by King Alfonso VIII, is still run by Cistercian nuns. There's a small on-site textile museum, but the building's main attraction is its stained-glass panels, some of the oldest in Spain. Admission includes a guided tour (Spanish only), which is the only way to view the monastery. ⚠ **The monastery closes from 2 to 4 pm.** ☒ *Calle de Los Compases, Burgos* ☎ *94/720–6045* ⊕ *www.patrimonionacional.es* ▧ *€6* ⊗ *Closed Mon.*

★ **Museo de la Evolución Humana**

SCIENCE MUSEUM | FAMILY | This airy, modern natural history museum traces human evolution from primate to the present day. There are life-size replicas of our ancient ancestors, plus hands-on exhibits and in-depth scientific explanations (in English) that will fascinate visitors of all ages. Pair with a museum-led

visit to the Atapuerca archaeological site (inquire at reception or online to arrange). ☒ *Paseo Sierra de Atapuerca, Burgos* ☎ *94/725–7103* ⊕ *www.museoevolucionhumana.com* ▧ *€6 (free Tues. and Thurs. at 7 pm and Wed. afternoon)* ⊗ *Closed Mon.*

**Paseo del Espolón**

PROMENADE | The Arco de Santa María frames the city's loveliest promenade, the Espolón. Shaded with black poplars, it follows the riverbank. ☒ *Burgos.*

## 🍽 Restaurants

**Casa Ojeda**

$$$$ | SPANISH | This restaurant—a Castilian classic—is known for refined Burgos standbys, especially *cochinillo* (suckling pig) and lamb served straight from the 200-year-old wood oven. Wines by the glass are local and reasonably priced. **Known for:** tried-and-true Castilian cuisine; old-school waitstaff; fall-off-the-bone lamb. ⑤ *Average main: €26* ☒ *Calle Vitoria 5, Burgos* ☎ *94/720–9052* ⊕ *www. restauranteojeda.com* ⊗ *No dinner Sun.*

## 🛏 Hotels

**Crisol Mesón del Cid**

$$ | HOTEL | Previously a 15th-century printing press and newly under the Eurostars umbrella, this hotel has bright, airy guest rooms (ask for one facing the cathedral) with tile floors and exposed brick and stone walls. **Pros:** cathedral views from upgraded rooms; central location; comfy, clean digs. **Cons:** some rooms are noisy; could use a face-lift; parking is a tight squeeze. ⑤ *Rooms from: €139* ☒ *Pl. Santa María 8, Burgos* ☎ *94/720–8715* ⊕ *www.mesondelcid.es* ⇆ *55 rooms* ⦿ *Free Breakfast.*

★ **Landa**

$$$$ | HOTEL | FAMILY | If you've ever dreamed of holing up in a luxurious castle, consider booking a room at

# Side Trips from Burgos

## Monastery of Santo Domingo de Silos

For a sojourn with masters of the Gregorian chant, head to the monastery where 1994's triple-platinum album *Chant* was recorded. Located 58 km (36 miles) southeast of Burgos, the monastery has an impressive two-story cloister that's lined with intricate Romanesque carvings. Try to drop in for an evening vespers service. It's a unique experience that's well off the tourist path. Single men can stay here for up to eight days (€50 per night with full board). Guests are expected to be present for breakfast, lunch, and dinner but are otherwise left to their own devices. ⊕ www.abadiadesilos.es

## Ojo Guareña

If you have a day to spare or are traveling on to Cantabria, stop at this breathtaking hermitage hewn into a karst cliffside surrounded by leafy woodlands situated a mile south of Cueva. A national monument, the cave complex housing the religious structure stretches 90 km (56 miles), and there's rock art throughout the many chambers that depicts the cave as a dwelling for early humans. Archaeologists date the site's use from the Middle Paleolithic to the Middle Ages. A worthwhile guided tour of the hermitage lasts 45 minutes; even more scintillating is the tour of nearby Palomera Cave (by appointment only). ⊕ www.merindad-desotoscueva.es

Landa, a converted 14th-century palace some 5 km (3 miles) from the city center surrounded by lush gardens. **Pros:** stunning indoor-outdoor swimming pool; beautiful lobby; surprisingly affordable for level of luxury. **Cons:** inconsistent food quality and unprofessional restaurant staff; car required; roads to and from town are busy. ⑤ *Rooms from: €237* ✉ *Ctra. de Madrid–Irún, Km 235, Burgos* ☎ *94/725–7777* ⊕ *www.landa.as* ↩ *37 rooms* ⑩ *No Meals.*

## 🅨 Nightlife

Due to its student population, Burgos has an energetic *vida nocturna* (nightlife), especially in Las Llanas, near the cathedral. House wines and *cañas* (half-pints) flow freely through the crowded tapas bars along Calles Laín Calvo and San Juan, near the Plaza Mayor. Calle Puebla, a small, dark street off Calle San Juan, also gets constant revelers. Order a drink at any Burgos bar, and the bartender will plunk down a free *pinchito* (small tapa)—a longstanding tradition.

### Bardeblás

**CAFÉS** | This intimate bar stays open until 4:30 am on the weekends, inviting you to stay awhile—and you just might, thanks to its strong and affordable drinks and catchy throwback jams. ✉ *Calle de la Puebla 29, Burgos* ☎ *94/720–1162.*

### Cervecería Flandes

**PUBS** | With 12 beers on tap that run the gamut from Belgian ales to rare Castilian microbrews, this Burgos stalwart attracts a diverse crowd of students, travelers, and beer geeks. Just don't expect any fancy food here—potato chips, nachos, and other sundry snacks are the only grub available. ✉ *Pl. Huerto del Rey 21, Burgos* ☎ *65/993–4813* ⊕ *www.cerveceriaflandes.es.*

# 🛍 Shopping

Ribera del Duero reds, bottled south of the city along the eponymous river, aren't as well known as Rioja, but they can be equally (if not more) sublime with their leathery, spicy depth. Snap up a bottle or two as well as some Burgos-style *morcilla* (blood sausage) and fresh local cheese. Beyond culinary finds, keep your eye out for small artisan shops specializing in ceramics and textiles.

### ★ Delicatessen Ojeda

**FOOD** | A food lover's paradise, this pristine, well-lit store carries all the Castilian delicacies you can imagine, from Burgos-style morcilla and cheese to roasted oil-packed peppers and top-quality dried beans and pulses. ✉ *Calle de Vitoria 5, Burgos* 🕿 *94/720–4832* ⊕ *www.delicatessenojeda.com* 🕙 *Closed Mon.*

# León

*334 km (208 miles) northwest of Madrid, 184 km (114 miles) west of Burgos.*

León, the ancient capital of Castile and León, straddles the banks of the Bernesga River in the high plains of Old Castile; today it's a wealthy and conservative provincial capital and prestigious university town. The wide avenues of western León are lined with boutiques, and the twisting alleys of the half-timber old town hide the bars, bookstores, and chocolaterías popular with students.

Historians say that the city was not named for the proud lion that has been its emblem for centuries but rather for the Roman word *legio* (legion), a reference to the fact that the city was a camp for the Roman legions in AD 70. The capital of Christian Spain was moved here from Oviedo in 914 as the Reconquest spread south, ushering in the city's most prosperous era.

---

## El Camino de Santiago ◉

West of Burgos, the León-bound N120 crosses the ancient Camino de Santiago, or Way of St. James, revealing lovely old churches, tiny hermitages, ruined monasteries, and medieval villages across rolling fields. West of León, you can follow the well-worn Camino pilgrimage route as it approaches the giant cathedral in Santiago de Compostela.

---

As you wander the old town, you can see fragments of the 6-foot-thick ramparts that were once part of the Roman walls. Look down and you might notice small brass scallop shells set into the street. The scallop is the symbol of St. James; the town government installed them to mark the path for modern-day pilgrims heading north to Santiago de Compostela.

### GETTING HERE AND AROUND

León can be reached by train from Madrid with a dozen or so departures daily from Chamartín station; the journey takes 2¼ hours on the high-speed ALVIA or AVE and between three and four hours on trains making local stops. ALSA has several bus departures daily from Madrid, and there are generally plentiful Blablacar rideshares available.

### VISITOR INFORMATION

**CONTACTS León Tourist Office.** ✉ *Pl. Regla 2, León* 🕿 *90/220–3030, 98/723–7082* ⊕ *www.turismocastillayleon.com.*

# ◉ Sights

### Antiguo Convento de San Marcos

**CHURCH** | Originally a home for knights of the Order of St. James, who patrolled the Camino de Santiago, this monastery was

The colorful panels on León's MUSAC, the Museum of Modern Art, were inspired by the rose window of the city's Gothic cathedral.

begun in 1513 by the head of the order, King Ferdinand. It is now a parador. The plateresque facade is a majestic swath of small, intricate sculptures (many depicting knights and lords) and ornamentation—one of the most impressive Renaissance works in Spain. Inside, a cloister full of medieval statues leads you to the bar, which still has the original defensive arrow slits as windows. As the Anexo Monumental del Museo de León, the convent also displays historic paintings and artifacts. ⊠ *Pl. de San Marcos 7, León* ☎ *98/724–5061, 98/723–7300* ⊕ *www. parador.es* 🖼 *Free* ⊙ *Closed Mon.*

### Basílica de San Isidoro

CHURCH | This sandstone basilica was built into the side of the city wall in 1063 and rebuilt in the 12th century on the site of an ancient Roman temple. Adjoining the basilica, the **Panteón de los Reyes** (Royal Pantheon), which has been called "the Sistine Chapel of Romanesque art," has vibrant 12th-century frescoes on its pillars and ceiling. Look for the agricultural calendar painted on one archway,

showing which farming task should be performed each month. Twenty-three kings and queens were buried here, but their tombs were destroyed by French troops during the Napoleonic Wars. Treasures in the adjacent **Museo de San Isidoro** include a jewel-encrusted agate chalice, a richly illustrated handwritten Bible, and polychrome wood statues of the Virgin Mary. Admission includes a guided tour of the Royal Pantheon and museum. ⊠ *Pl. de San Isidoro 4, León* ☎ *98/787–6161* ⊕ *www.museosanisidor- odeleon.com* 🖼 *€5* ⊙ *Closed Mon.*

### Casa Botines

ART MUSEUM | This Gaudí masterpiece, which housed a bank until 2017, is now an excellent museum dedicated to the Moderniste architect. Under the conical spires and behind the squamous facade are more than 5,000 works of art spanning eight centuries by such renowned masters as Sorolla, Madrazo, Gutiérrez, and Solana. Given that this is the largest of Gaudí's buildings to be opened as a museum, it's worth the extra few euros for a guided tour in English. ✉ *Calle Legión VII 3, León* ☎ *987/735–3247* ⊕ *www.casabotines.es* ✉ *From €5* 🕑 *Closed Tues.*

★ **Catedral de León**

CHURCH | The pride of León is its soaring cathedral, begun in 1205. It is an outstanding example of Gothic architecture complete with gargoyles, flying buttresses, and pointed arches. Its 2,000 square yards of vivid stained-glass panels—second only, perhaps, to those in Chartres, France—depict biblical stories and Castilian landscapes. A glass door to the choir gives an unobstructed view of nave windows and the painted altarpiece, framed with gold leaf. The cathedral also contains the sculpted tomb of King Ordoño II, who moved the capital of Christian Spain to León. The museum's collection boasts giant medieval hymnals, textiles, sculptures, wood carvings, and paintings. Look for the carved wood Mudejar archive, with a letter of the alphabet above each door—it's one of the world's oldest filing cabinets. Guided tours can be scheduled by phone. ✉ *Pl. de Regla, León* ☎ *987/787–5770* ⊕ *www.catedraldeleon.org* ✉ *From €7.*

**Fundación Vela Zanetti**

ART MUSEUM | This contemporary art museum, constructed using minimalist wood beams and glass panels inside a 15th-century mansion, pays homage to Zanetti, a 20th-century Castilian artist known for his thought-provoking murals portraying agrarian life. Some may remind you of works by El Greco for their shimmering luminosity. It's worth the stop, and you can view the exhibit in under an hour. ✉ *Casona de Villapérez, Calle Pablo Flórez, León* ☎ *987/724–4121* ✉ *Free* 🕑 *Closed Sun. and Mon.*

**MUSAC (Museo de Arte Contemporáneo de Castilla y León)** (*Museum of Modern Art of Castilla y León*)

ART MUSEUM | It's worth detouring to this museum for its facade alone, a modern technicolor masterpiece by famed

Spanish architects Mansilla + Tuñón. The endless rainbow of rectangles that encloses the building is an homage to the colorful stained glass of the cathedral. Inside, wander through rooms bearing the latest art and multimedia projects by locally and nationally acclaimed artists. Films and concerts are also shown throughout the year. ✉ *Av. de los Reyes Leoneses 24, León* ☎ *987/09–0000* ⊕ *www.musac.es* ✉ *€3 (free Sun. 5–9)* 🕑 *Closed Mon.*

**Museo de León**

HISTORY MUSEUM | This museum displays artifacts from the region from prehistoric to contemporary times, including sculptures, engravings, paintings, and furniture, but the crown jewel of the collection is the Cristo Carrizo (Carrizo Crucifix), a small 11th-century Romanesque ivory carving distinguished by its lifelike expression and powerful presence. Notice the figure's carefully coiffed hair and beard and the loincloth arranged in sumptuous Byzantine detail. ✉ *Pl. de Santo Domingo 8, León* ☎ *987/723–6405* ⊕ *www.museodeleon.com* ✉ *€1* 🕑 *Closed Mon.*

**Plaza de San Martín**

PLAZA/SQUARE | León's busiest tapas bars are in and around this 12th-century square. The area is called the Barrio Húmedo, or "Wet Neighborhood," allegedly because of the deluge of wine spilled here late at night. ✉ *León.*

**Plaza de Santa María del Camino**

PLAZA/SQUARE | This square was once called Plaza del Grano (Grain Square) because it was the site of the city's corn and bread market. Also here is the church of **Santa María del Camino,** where pilgrims stop on their way west to Santiago de Compostela. The fountain in the middle of the plaza depicts two cherubim clutching a pillar, symbolizing León's two rivers and the capital. ✉ *León.*

León

**Sights** ▼

1 Antiguo Convento de San Marcos...... **A2**

2 Basílica de San Isidoro....... **B3**

3 Casa Botines...... **A5**

4 Catedral de León ..... **D5**

5 Fundación Vela Zanetti....... **C3**

6 MUSAC (Museo de Arte Contemporáneo de Castilla y León) ...... **A2**

7 Museo de León ..... **A4**

8 Plaza de Santa María del Camino.. **B8**

9 Plaza de San Martín....... **C7**

10 Plaza Mayor....... **C6**

**Restaurants** ▼

1 Adonías del Pozo..... **A8**

2 El Rebote.... **B7**

3 Restaurante Sorrento .... **A9**

**Hotels** ▼

1 Hotel Real Colegiata de San Isidoro....... **B2**

2 NH Collection León Plaza Mayor ....... **D6**

**KEY**

1 *Sights*

1 *Restaurants*

1 *Hotels*

0        400 feet

0        100 meters

### Plaza Mayor

**MARKET** | This is the heart of the old town, and on Wednesday and Saturday mornings the arcaded plaza bustles with farmers selling produce and cheeses. ⊠ *León.*

## 🍴 Restaurants

### Adonías del Pozo

**$$$$** | **SPANISH** | In this softly lit dining room furnished with rustic tables and colorful ceramics, feast on top-of-the-line cured *cecina* (Leonese air-dried beef "ham"), roasted peppers, and chorizo. Grilled sea bream is a treat for seafood lovers; banana pudding with chocolate sauce is a treat for just about everyone. **Known for:** homey dining room; excellent sausages and roast meats; well-priced €22 menú del día. $ *Average main: €30* ⊠ *Calle Santa Nonia 16, León* 🕿 *98/720–6768, 98/725–2665* 🕙 *Closed Sun.*

### El Rebote

**$** | **TAPAS** | Though every drink comes with a complimentary croqueta at this pocket-size bar frequented by locals, the crisp, gooey orbs are so succulent that you'll want to order a few extra. Be sure to sample the smoky cured beef cecina rendition. **Known for:** sardine-can digs; quirky local wines by the glass; to-die-for croquetas. $ *Average main: €10* ⊠ *Pl. San Martín 9, León* 🕿 *98/721–3510* 🕙 *Closed Mon. and Tues.*

### ★ Restaurante Sorrento

**$$$** | **SPANISH** | **FAMILY** | León is a cold, windy town for much of the year, so it's no surprise that the local version of *cocido* (boiled dinner) is heartier than usual with mounds of green cabbage, spoonable blood sausage, and some 10 types of meat (chorizo, beef shanks, pork belly, and chicken, to name a few). Sample the city's best rendition at this spartan yet inviting downstairs restaurant outside the historic center—and be sure to bring an appetite. **Known for:** local crowd; warm service; soul-satisfying cocido leonés.

$ *Average main. €20* ⊠ *Calle Bernardo del Carpio 1, León* 🕿 *98/707–3270* 🕙 *Closed Mon.*

## 🛏 Hotels

### Hotel Real Colegiata de San Isidoro

**$** | **HOTEL** | Other hotels around town bill themselves as being steps from the main tourist attractions, but the Hotel Real Colegiata, which houses a Romanesque collegiate library and museum, is located within one. **Pros:** gorgeous historic building; great value; modern Spanish restaurant. **Cons:** no in-room coffee-making facilities; unrenovated rooms lack style; no gym, pool, or spa. $ *Rooms from: €99* ⊠ *Pl. Santo Martino 5, León* 🕿 *98/787–5088* ⊕ *www.hotelrealcolegiata.com* 🍴 *32 rooms* ❙⊙❙ *Free Breakfast.*

### ★ NH Collection León Plaza Mayor

**$$$** | **HOTEL** | This handsome hotel, housed in a palace overlooking the 17th-century Plaza Mayor, is awash with whites, dark woods, and neutral tones. **Pros:** subdued, elegant interiors; varied breakfasts; parking below building. **Cons:** parking is a tight squeeze; maintenance a little inconsistent; some furniture could use replacing. $ *Rooms from: €185* ⊠ *Pl. Mayor 15–17, León* 🕿 *98/734–4357* ⊕ *www.nh-collection.com* 🍴 *51 rooms* ❙⊙❙ *No Meals.*

## 🍸 Nightlife

León's most popular hangouts are clustered around the Plaza Mayor, frequented mainly by couples and families, and Plaza San Martín, where the college kids hang. The surrounding streets (Calles Escalerilla, Plegarias, Ramiro II, Matasiete, and Mulhacén) are packed with tapas bars. In the Plaza Mayor, you might want to start at La Pañería, The Harley, or Mama Tere. In Plaza de San Martín, begin your evening with tapas and *cortitos* (local slang for two-gulp glasses of beer) at Taberna Los Cazurros, El Rebote, or Mesón Jabugo. Then go clubbing at Studio 54, a discoteca housed in an old theater whose crowd gets progressively younger (and more LGBT+ friendly) as the night goes on.

# 🛍 Shopping

Tasty regional treats include roasted red peppers, potent brandy-soaked cherries, and candied chestnuts—but León's most prized artisanal product is *cecina*, air-dried beef that packs an umami punch similar to that of good jerky or a dry-aged steak. You can buy all of these items in food shops around the city. Note: Many stores in León are closed on Sunday.

### Prada a Tope

**FOOD** | Prada a Tope has a restaurant, winery, and gourmet store, plus a huge estate in the countryside outside León. It operates this small café and shop in the city whose delicacies include chestnuts in syrup, bittersweet figs and pears in wine, jams, and liqueurs. Not enough room in your suitcase? Order by mail from its website. ✉ *Calle Alfonso IX 9, León* ☎ *98/725–7221, 98/756–3366* ⊕ *www.pradaatope.es* ⊗ *Closed Mon.*

# Astorga

*46 km (29 miles) southwest of León.*

Astorga, where the pilgrimage roads from France and Portugal merge, once had 22 hospitals to lodge and care for ailing travelers. Though the city is no longer the bustling crossroads it once was, plenty of travelers visit this charming town for its eye-popping Gaudí masterpiece, *El Palacio Episcopal,* and its famed *cocido maragato,* a stick-to-your-ribs stew. It gets its name from the historical area Astorga is situated in, La Maragatería, which at one time stood apart from its neighbors for its special dialect, elaborate dress, and distinctive folk music.

## GETTING HERE AND AROUND

More than a dozen buses depart daily from León, and the trip takes about 45 minutes. If you're driving, there's ample parking. The city is navigable on foot once you've arrived.

## VISITOR INFORMATION

**CONTACTS Astorga Tourist Office.** ✉ *Pl. Eduardo de Castro 5, Astorga* ☎ *98/761–8222* ⊕ *www.aytoastorga.es.*

# 👁 Sights

★ **Centro de Interpretación del León Romano** (*Roman Museum*)
**RUINS | FAMILY** | This hidden-gem museum uses the archaeological record to show what life was like in Astorga during Roman times, when the city was called Asturica Augusta. The most memorable part of the experience is the Ruta Romana, a walking tour of Roman archaeological remains (combined tickets can be bought at the museum). Descriptions are in Spanish only. ✉ *Pl. San Bartolomé 2, Astorga* ☎ *98/761–6937* ⊕ *www.aytoleon.es* 🎟 *Free* ⊗ *Closed Mon.*

### La Catedral de Santa María de Astorga

**CHURCH** | The museum within this Gothic cathedral displays 10th- and 12th-century chests, religious silverware, and paintings and sculptures by Astorgans through the ages, but the real treasure is the cathedral itself. You'll be especially wowed by the chancel, which contains Spain's most elaborate Romanist (Late Renaissance) retable, and by the choir, sculpted from walnut wood in an exuberant Flemish style. ✉ *Pl. de la Catedral, Astorga* ☎ *98/761–5820* ⊕ *www.catedralastorga.com* 🎟 *From €6.*

★ **Palacio de Gaudí** (*Palacio Episcopal*)
**CASTLE/PALACE** | Opposite Astorga's cathedral is this fairy-tale neo-Gothic palace designed for a Catalan cleric by Gaudí in 1889. Though the humdrum interiors pale in comparison to the eye-popping exteriors, those interested in local ecclesiastical history shouldn't miss visiting the

Museo de Los Caminos (Museum of the Way). Guided tours are worthwhile and cost an extra €3; be sure to call ahead to book an English-language tour. ⊠ *Pl. de la Catedral, Glorieta Eduardo de Castro, Astorga* 🕾 *98/761–6882* ⊕ *www.palaciodegaudi.es* ⊠ *From €6* ⊗ *Closed Mon.*

##  Restaurants

### Restaurante Serrano

**$$$ | SPANISH |** This local hangout serves Astorgan dishes that incorporate wild game, foraged mushrooms, and regional meats. For a break from carnivorous Castilian cuisine, tuck into house-made pasta dishes or chickpeas stewed with fresh octopus, a house specialty. **Known for:** wild game; attentive old-school service; dishes using crème-de-la-crème "pico pardal" garbanzos. Ⓢ *Average main: €21* ⊠ *Calle Portería 2, Astorga* 🕾 *98/761–7866, 64/607–1736* ⊕ *www. restauranteserrano.es* ⊗ *Closed Mon.*

##  Hotels

### Hotel Vía de la Plata

**$$ | HOTEL | FAMILY |** A giant slate terrace with views of the countryside is the main draw of this airy, streamlined hotel with a vibe that feels more city than country. **Pros:** great views and service; gorgeous terrace; free parking. **Cons:** bookable only via online form or third party; small breakfast area; spa not included in rate. Ⓢ *Rooms from: €112* ⊠ *Calle Padres Redentoristas 5, Astorga* 🕾 *98/761–9000* ⊕ *www.hotelviadelaplata.es* ⇗ *38 rooms* ⊠ *Free Breakfast.*

# Villafranca del Bierzo

*135 km (84 miles) west of León.*

After crossing León's grape-growing region, where the funky, floral Bierzo wines are produced, you'll arrive in this medieval village, dominated by a massive (and still-inhabited) feudal fortress. Visit the Romanesque church of Santiago to see the *Puerta del Perdón* (Door of Pardon), a sort of spiritual consolation prize for exhausted Camino pilgrims who couldn't make it over the mountains. Stroll the streets and seek out the onetime home of the infamous Grand Inquisitor Tomás de Torquemada. If you've made it all the way here, don't leave Bierzo without visiting the area's most famous archaeological site, Las Médulas, whose bizarre stone formations are the remnants of Roman gold mines.

### GETTING HERE AND AROUND

A car is the best way to explore this rural region, though buses from León also service the area. You'll likely want your own transportation once you arrive anyway to visit Las Médulas, several kilometers away; it's also possible to hike or get there by bicycle.

### VISITOR INFORMATION

**CONTACTS Villafranca del Bierzo Tourist Office.** ⊠ *Av. Díaz Ovelar 10, Villafranca del Bierzo* 🕾 *98/754–0028* ⊕ *www.villafrancadelbierzo.org.*

## ◉ Sights

### ★ Las Médulas

**RUINS | FAMILY |** One of northern Spain's most impressive archaeological sites, this mountainous area of former Roman gold mines—located 24 km (15 miles) south of town—is a UNESCO World Heritage Site. The landscape is the result of an ancient mining technique in which myriad water tunnels were burrowed into a mountain, causing it to collapse. Miners would then sift through the rubble for gold. What's left at Las Médulas are half-collapsed mountains of golden clay with exposed tunnels peeking through lush green forest. Take in the best panorama from the Orellán viewpoint. There are hiking paths, a small archaeology exhibit, and a visitor center; the latter organizes 3-km (2-mile) walking tours—check schedules online, and call or email

ahead to book ( medulas@ccbierzo.com).
■ TIP➜ **A parking lot was added in 2021; the price is €3 per vehicle.** ☒ *Carucedo* ☎ *98/742–0708* ⊕ *www.patrimoniocastillayleon.com/en/las-medulas* ☒ *Free, archaeology center €2, Orellán tunnel €3, guided walking tour €5.*

### 🛏 Hotels

#### ★ Casa Rural do Louteiro
$ | **B&B/INN** | **FAMILY** | This charming, rustic inn in a tiny village near Las Médulas was lovingly converted from a series of medieval ruins. **Pros:** rustic details; fire pit on winter evenings; friendly staff. **Cons:** no housekeeping service; disorganized front-desk management; plenty of hiking and biking nearby, but you'll need a car to get here. ⑤ *Rooms from: €73* ☒ *Calle Louteiro 6, Orellán* ☎ *65/293–3419, 65/293–3971* ⊕ *www.casadolouteiro.com* ⌙ *3 cottages* ⦿ *No Meals.*

#### Parador de Villafranca del Bierzo
$$ | **HOTEL** | **FAMILY** | This modern two-story hotel built with local stone looks out over the Bierzo valley. **Pros:** indoor and outdoor swimming pools; free parking; quiet surroundings. **Cons:** noisy a/c in some rooms; rooms are plain and some overlook parking lot; lacks history of other paradores. ⑤ *Rooms from: €110* ☒ *Av. de Calvo Sotelo 28, Villafranca del Bierzo* ☎ *98/754–0175* ⊕ *www.parador.es* ⌙ *51 rooms* ⦿ *No Meals.*

# Jerte and El Valle del Jerte (Jerte Valley)

*220 km (137 miles) west of Madrid.*

Every spring, the Jerte Valley in northern Extremadura becomes one of Spain's top attractions for its riot of cherry blossoms. Unsurprisingly, this is where Spain's biggest cherry harvest originates, backed by the snowcapped Gredos mountains. Book ahead for March and April—peak cherry blossom season—and monitor the bloom date estimates on the tourist board's website (⊕ ⊕ www.turismovalledeljerte.com) or local Spanish-language news outlets like El Periódico Extremadura (⊕ ⊕ www.elperiodicoextremadura.com).

## GETTING HERE AND AROUND
You will need a car to get here and explore the valley. For a scenic route, follow N110 southwest from Ávila to Plasencia.

## VISITOR INFORMATION
**CONTACTS Valle del Jerte Tourist Office.** ☒ *Paraje Virgen de Peñas Albas (N110), Cabezuela del Valle* ☎ *92/747–2558* ⊕ *www.turismovalledeljerte.com.*

### 👁 Sights

#### Cabezuela del Valle
**TOWN** | Full of half-timber stone houses, this is one of the valley's best-preserved villages. Follow N110 to Plasencia, or, if you enjoy mountain scenery, detour from the village of Jerte to Hervás, traveling a narrow road that winds 35 km (22 miles) through forests of low-growing oak trees and over the Honduras Pass. ☒ *Cabezuela del Valle.*

#### Puerto de Tornavacas (*Tornavacas Pass*)
**VIEWPOINT** | There's no more striking introduction to Extremadura than the Puerto de Tornavacas—literally, the point "where the cows turn back." Part of the N110 road northeast of Plasencia, the pass marks the border between Extremadura and the stark plateau of Castile. Its elevation of 4,183 feet affords a breathtaking view of the valley formed by the fast-flowing Jerte River. The lower slopes are covered with a dense mantle of ash, chestnut, and cherry trees, whose richness contrasts with the granite cliffs of Castile's Sierra de Gredos, blanketed in garnacha grapevines. But cherries, of course, are the principal crop. Camping is popular in this area (contact the tourist office for more details), and even the

Cherry trees bloom in the Jerte Valley.

most experienced hikers can find some challenging trails. ✉ *Plasencia*.

##  Restaurants

### ★ La Cabaña

**$$ | SPANISH |** This homey, sun-drenched restaurant serves honest Extremaduran fare at an excellent price. Unlike at other dining options in the area, cooks here pay special attention to presentation and ingredient quality—attributes on display in the not-too-greasy migas, wonderfully juicy Iberian pork dishes, and refreshing tomato salads. **Known for:** bright, casual dining room; ibérico pork dishes; home-cooked food. ⑤ *Average main: €15* ✉ *Av. Ramón y Cajal 17, Jerte* ☎ *64/523–3953* ⊕ *www.restaurantelacabañajerte.es* ⊗ *No dinner Wed*.

## 🛏 Hotels

### Finca El Carpintero

**$ | B&B/INN | FAMILY |** This restored 150-year-old stone mill and farmhouse makes an ideal base for enjoying

the area's great outdoors. **Pros:** cozy atmosphere with a warm fireplace in winter; ideal country escape, especially in spring and fall; picturesque grounds and swimming pool. **Cons:** spent towels and small TVs; need a car; disparity in quality between rooms and suites. ⑤ *Rooms from: €75* ✉ *N110, Km 360.5, Tornavacas* ✛ *9 km (5½ miles) northeast of Jerte* ☎ *92/717–7089, 65/932–8110* ⊕ *www.fincaelcarpintero.com* ⇥ *8 rooms* ⑩ *Free Breakfast*.

### La Casería

**$$ | B&B/INN | FAMILY |** One of Extremadura's first rural guesthouses, this rambling home 10 km (6 miles) southeast of Jerte is on a spectacular 120-acre working farm, once a 16th-century Franciscan convent. **Pros:** privacy in the cottages; views of Jerte Valley; outdoor activities. **Cons:** far from all main sights and national parks; need a car to get here; main lodge often rented out to groups. ⑤ *Rooms from: €120* ✉ *N110, Km 378.5, Navaconcejo* ☎ *92/717–3141* ⊕ *www.lacaseria.es* ⇥ *9 rooms* ⑩ *Free Breakfast*.

# Extremaduran Food

Extremaduran food is simple and hearty. In addition to fresh produce, Extremadurans rely on pigs, and they use every part, including the *criadillas* (testicles—just don't confuse them with *criadillas de la tierra*, which are truffles). Meats are outstanding, most notably the complex and nutty *jamones ibérico de bellota* (hams from acorn-fed Iberian black pigs) such as those hailing from the Sierra de Montánchez, north of Cáceres, and the Dehesa de Extremadura, from the southern oak forests around Zafra. Equally irresistible are regional variations of chorizo made with potatoes (*patatera*) or squash (*calabacera*). *Caldereta de cordero* (lamb stew), redolent of garlic and wine, is particularly tasty, as is beef from longhorn retinto cows, a local breed. Game is common, and *perdiz al modo de Alcántara* (partridge cooked with truffles) is a specialty. Extremadurans make a tomato-less *gazpacho* using cucumbers, green peppers, and broth. The region's most famous dish is *migas*, bread crumbs fried in olive oil with garlic, and sometimes peppers, and sausage.

Local sheep, goat, and cow cheeses are known for their strong flavors. Seek out tortas, the round, semisoft washed-rind cheeses of Cáceres: Torta del Casar and Queso de La Serena are frequent prize-winners in international cheese competitions. Pimentón de la Vera, smoked paprika from the Vera Valley packaged in colorful, old-timey tins, makes a terrific souvenir. Round out your meals with *técula mécula*, an almond-flavored marzipan tart that combines the flavors of Spain and Portugal.

Marketed under the generic appellation Ribera del Guadiana, Extremadura's little-known grippy red wines are up-and-coming on the Spanish wine scene and a good value. Natural wine lovers should seek out bottles by Envínate, especially the monovarietal Tinta Amarela Parcela Valdemedel, made from the bold yet obscure tinta amarela (aka trincadeira preta) grape. Typical digestifs include liqueurs made from cherries or acorns.

# La Vera and Monasterio de Yuste

*45 km (28 miles) east of Plasencia.*

In northern Extremadura, the fertile La Vera region sits at the foot of the Gredos mountains, which are usually snowcapped through June. With its wildflowers, mountain vistas, and world-famous Yuste Monastery, the area welcomes hordes of tourists, especially in spring, its most beautiful season. One of the favorite souvenirs to take home is La Vera's famous smoky paprika, or "pimentón," available in three types: *dulce* (mild), *agridulce* (medium), and *picante* (hot). You're likely to see strings of red peppers hanging out to dry on the windowsills of area homes.

## GETTING HERE AND AROUND
You'll need a car to get here. Turn left off the C501 at Cuacos and follow signs to the monastery for 1 km (½ mile) until you arrive.

## VISITOR INFORMATION
**CONTACTS Jaraíz de la Vera Tourist Office.**
⊠ *Calle Mérida 17, Jaraíz de la Vera*
☎ *92/717–0587.*

# Parque Natural de Monfragüe 👁

At the junction of the Tiétar and Tajo rivers, 20 km (12 miles) south of Plasencia on the EX208 and 60 km (37 miles) southwest of La Vera via the EX203, lies Extremadura's only national park. This rocky, mountainous wilderness is known for its diverse plant and animal life including lynxes, boars, deer, foxes, black storks, imperial eagles, and the world's largest colony of black vultures, attracting bird-watchers from around the world. Bring binoculars and head for the lookout point called Salto del Gitano (Gypsy's Leap), on the C524 just south of the Tajo River—vultures can often be spotted wheeling in the dozens at close range. The park's visitor center and main entrance is in the hamlet of Villarreal de San Carlos. ⊕ *www.parquedemonfrague.com*

## 👁 Sights

★ **Monasterio de Yuste** (*Yuste Monastery*)
CHURCH | In the heart of La Vera—a region of steep ravines (*gargantas*), rushing rivers, and sleepy villages—lies the Monasterio de San Jerónimo de Yuste, founded by Hieronymite monks in the early 15th century. Badly damaged in the Peninsular War, it was left to decay after the suppression of Spain's monasteries in 1835, but has since been restored by the Hieronymites. Today it's one of the most impressive monasteries in all of Spain. Carlos V (1500–58), founder of Spain's vast 16th-century empire, spent his last two years in the Royal Chambers, enabling the emperor to attend mass within a short stumble of his bed. The guided tour also covers the church, the crypt where Carlos V was buried before being moved to El Escorial (near Madrid), and a glimpse of the monastery's cloisters. ⊠ *Ctra. de Yuste, Cuacos* ☎ *92/717–2197* ⊕ *www.patrimonionacional.es* 🎟 *From €7* ⏱ *Closed Mon.*

**Museo del Pimentón** (*Paprika Museum*)
OTHER MUSEUM | Tucked away in a 17th-century row house, this quirky museum tells the history of the locally made paprika, dubbed "red gold," for which Jaraíz de la Vera is best known. The three floors feature audiovisual presentations and examples of grinding tools and recipes. The museum is the centerpiece of the village's annual pepper festival, held in August. ⊠ *Pl. Mayor 7, Jaraíz de la Vera* ☎ *92/746–0810* ⊕ *museodelpimenton.business.site* 🎟 *Free* ⏱ *Closed Sun. afternoon and Mon.*

## 🛏 Hotels

★ **La Posada de los Sentidos**
$ | B&B/INN | FAMILY | There are five charming, rustic rooms in this rural hotel housed in a 16th-century convent house. **Pros:** views of the Gredos mountains; staff can arrange a variety of experiences; private garden with play area. **Cons:** rooms can get chilly on cold nights; soundproofing not ideal; shared kitchen with other guests. 💲 *Rooms from: €100* ⊠ *Calle Machín 19, Jarandilla de la Vera* ☎ *63/542–9779* ⊕ *www.laposadadelossentidos.es* ⇆ *5 rooms* 🍽 *No Meals.*

# Cáceres

*299 km (186 miles) west of Madrid, 125 km (78 miles) southwest of Monasterio de Yuste.*

The provincial capital and one of Spain's oldest cities, Cáceres is known for its UNESCO-protected old town, lively

The San Mateo church, with the Torre de las Cigüeñas (Tower of the Storks) in the background

tapeo, and avant-garde Helga Alvear art museum. The Roman colony called Norba Caesarina was founded in 35 BC, but when the Moors took over in the 8th century, they named the city Quazris, which eventually morphed into the Spanish Cáceres. Amazingly, some 22 Moorish towers survive in the historic center today. Ever since noble families helped Alfonso IX expel the Moors in 1229, the city has prospered; the pristine condition of the medieval and Renaissance quarter is the result of the families' continued occupancy of the palaces erected in the 15th century.

### GETTING HERE AND AROUND

Trains from Madrid take about 2½ hours and are the cheapest and easiest way to get to Cáceres. Once there, catch a city bus outside the train station, which takes you to Plaza Mayor in the historic quarter, or walk 15 minutes into town. From Madrid, Blablacar rideshares are an excellent option as well. The city center is walkable. If you drive, park on the outskirts as the winding, narrow medieval streets are difficult to navigate.

**TRAIN STATION Cáceres Train Station.**
✉ Av. Juan Pablo II 6, Cáceres 🕾 92/723–5061, 90/224–0202 ⊕ www.renfe.com.

### TOURS

**Cuenta Trovas de Cordel**
✉ Pl. Mayor, Cáceres 🕾 66/728–3187, 66/777–6205 ⊕ www.cuentatrovas.com.

### VISITOR INFORMATION

**CONTACTS Cáceres.** ✉ Pl. Mayor 1, Cáceres 🕾 92/701–0834, 92/721–7237 tours ⊕ turismo.caceres.es.

## 👁 Sights

### ★ Cáceres Museum

HISTORY MUSEUM | The Casa de las Veletas (House of the Weather Vanes) is a 12th-century Moorish mansion that is now used as the city's museum. Filled with archaeological finds from the Paleolithic through Visigothic periods, the museum also includes an art section with works by El Greco, Picasso, and

Miró. The highlight is the superbly preserved Moorish cistern—the aljibe—with horseshoe arches supported by mildewy stone pillars. ⊠ *Pl. de las Veletas 1, Cáceres* ☏ *92/701–0877* ⊕ *museodecaceres.juntaex.es* ⊡ *€2 (free Sun. and for EU residents)* ⊘ *Closed Mon.*

### ★ Ciudad Monumental

NEIGHBORHOOD | Travel back a few centuries in Cáceres's Ciudad Monumental (aka "casco antiguo" or "ciudad vieja"), one of the best-preserved medieval quarters in Europe. It's so convincingly ancient that *Game of Thrones* used it as a filming location. There isn't a single modern building to detract from its aura, a testament to the fact that Cáceres became a backwater plagued by war after Spain's Golden Age. It's virtually deserted in winter and occasionally dusted with a light coating of snow—a fairy-tale sight. Most of the city's main monuments are located here, but of Cáceres's approximately 100,000 residents, fewer than 400 reside within this tiny enclave. ⊠ *Cáceres.*

### Concatedral de Santa María

CHURCH | This Gothic church, built mainly in the 16th century, is now the cathedral and the city's most important religious site. The elegantly carved wooden reredos (dating to 1551), left unpainted according to Extremaduran custom, is barely visible in the gloom. Follow the lines of pilgrims to the statue of San Pedro de Alcántara in the corner; legend says that touching the stone figure's shoes brings luck. A small museum in the back displays religious artifacts. ⊠ *Pl. de Santa María, Cáceres* ☏ *92/721–5313* ⊕ *www.concatedralcaceres.com* ⊡ *€5.*

### Iglesia de San Mateo

CHURCH | Construction on this church began in the 14th century, purportedly over the ruins of a mosque, and took nearly 300 years to finish. The interior is austere, with a 16th-century choir and walls lined with the tombs of prominent Cáceres citizens. The church opens at 10 most mornings, but check with the tourist office in case of changes. ⊠ *Pl. de San Mateo, Cáceres* ☏ *92/724–6329* ⊡ *Free.*

### ★ Museo Helga de Alvear (*Visual Arts Center Foundation Helga de Alvear*)

ART MUSEUM | After a day spent meandering through medieval passageways and marveling at ancient churches, this contemporary art museum, presided over by one of Europe's great modern art collectors, is a breath of fresh air. Highlights include sculptures by Ai Weiwei and Dan Graham and paintings by Josef Albers and John Baldessari. A much-anticipated renovation by Tuñón Arquitectos (of Atrio fame), finished in 2021, added soaring galleries and multimedia spaces to house the gallerist's entire collection. If visiting on a weekend, be sure to reserve entry in advance online. ⊠ *Calle Pizarro 8, Cáceres* ☏ *92/762–6414* ⊕ *www.fundacionhelgadealvear.es* ⊡ *Free* ⊘ *Closed Mon.*

### ★ Museo Vostell Malpartida

ART MUSEUM | The first thing that grabs your attention at this museum—located 14 km (9 miles) outside town—is the landscape that surrounds it: the Los Barruecos nature reserve. Spanning 800 acres, the park's otherworldly landscape comprises rolling grasslands, lakes, and enormous, peculiarly shaped boulders, which you can explore on foot. These curious natural forms inspired Wolf Vostell, a German artist of the Fluxus and Happening movements, to turn a defunct yarn factory within the park into a museum. Today you can still take in his bizarre, thought-provoking work—including a Cadillac surrounded by dinner plates and a wall of rusty Guardia Civil motorcycles. ⊠ *Calle Los Barruecos, Cáceres* ☏ *92/701–0812* ⊕ *www.museovostell.org* ⊡ *€3* ⊘ *Closed Mon.*

### Palacio de los Golfines de Abajo

CASTLE/PALACE | Wander the halls of one of Cáceres's great noble homes on a memorable guided tour (English available). Begun in the late 15th century and finished in the late 16th—hence the sumptuous plateresque facade—the palace bears the insignia of the Catholic Monarchs, who greatly enriched the Golfín family. See if you can also spot the coat of arms of the Golfines, situated beneath a gothic double window on the top floor. ⊠ *Pl. de los Golfines 1, Cáceres* ⊕ *www.palaciogolfinesdeabajo.com* ⊠ *€3* ⊙ *Closed Mon.*

**Palacio del Capitán Diego de Cáceres**

CASTLE/PALACE | The battlement tower of this palace is also known as the Torre de las Cigüeñas (Tower of the Storks) for obvious reasons. It's now a military residence, but rooms are occasionally open for exhibitions. ⊠ *Pl. San Mateo, Cáceres.*

**Plaza Mayor**

PLAZA/SQUARE | This long, inclined, arcaded plaza contains several cafés, the tourist office, and—on breezy summer nights—nearly everyone in town. In the middle of the arcade opposite the old quarter is the entrance to the lively Calle General Ezponda, lined with tapas bars, student hangouts, and discotecas that keep the neighborhood electric with activity until dawn. The city's main Christmas market, selling candles, figurines, and sweets, is held here. ⊠ *Cáceres.*

**Santuario de la Virgen de la Montaña**

(*Sanctuary of the Virgin of the Mountain*) VIEWPOINT | Overlooking Cáceres's Ciudad Monumental is this 18th-century shrine dedicated to the city's patron saint. It's built on a mountain with stunning views of the old town, especially at sunset. The panorama is worth the 15-minute drive— or even the grueling two-hour climb past chalets and farms—even if the interior of the church is rather mundane (barring the gilded baroque altar). ⊠ *Ctra. Santuario Virgin de la Montaña, Cáceres* ⊠ *Free.*

# 🍽 Restaurants

★ **Atrio Restaurante Hotel**

$$$$ | SPANISH | This jaw-droppingly elegant award-winning restaurant and hotel, housed in a medieval building redesigned by star architect Mansilla + Tuñón, is the crown jewel of Extremaduran hospitality. The ground-floor restaurant specializes in refined contemporary cooking, and the menu changes according to what's in season in chef Toño Pérez's private garden. **Known for:** phenomenal luxury hotel on-site; interiors with bespoke furniture and original works by Warhol et al; zero-kilometer Extremaduran cuisine. ⑤ *Average main: €195* ⊠ *Pl. de San Mateo 1, Cáceres* ☎ *92/724–2928* ⊕ *www.restauranteatrio.com.*

**El Figón de Eustaquio**

$$$ | SPANISH | A fixture on the quiet and pleasant Plaza San Juan, this restaurant has been run by the same family for 70 years and counting. In its jumble of old-fashioned dining rooms with wood-beam ceilings, feast on regional delicacies including *venado de montería* (wild venison) and *perdiz estofada* (partridge stew) complemented by full-bodied local wines. **Known for:** pleasant outdoor patio; good selection of local wines; old-school Extremaduran cooking. ⑤ *Average main: €21* ⊠ *Pl. San Juan 12–14, Cáceres* ☎ *92/724–4362, 92/724–8194* ⊕ *www. elfigondeeustaquio.com.*

★ **La Marina**

$$ | SPANISH | FAMILY | The third-generation owner of this beloved bar keeps endangered Cacereño dishes alive such as eggs scrambled with lamb brains (a delicacy!); spicy stewed pig ear; and *zarangollo*, a garlicky, vinegary salad of blistered roasted peppers and parsley topped with flaked Spanish tuna. There is outdoor seating available. **Known for:** above-and-beyond service; griddled seafood and meats; sensational offal dishes. ⑤ *Average main: €14* ⊠ *Av. Virgen de la Montaña 18, Cáceres* ☎ *62/938–6238*

⊕ *www.lamarinacaceres.es* ⊘ *Closed Sun. No dinner Mon.*

**La Tapería**

$$ | TAPAS | This tiny taberna, which serves some of the best tapas in town, is always packed with locals. Order a few tostas (open-faced sandwiches on crusty peasant bread) and raciones (shared plates), and pair them with Extremaduran wines. **Known for:** free tapa with every drink; local hangout; fresh, filling tostas. ⑤ *Average main: €12* ⊠ *Calle Sánchez Garrido 1, bajo, Cáceres* ☎ *92/722-5147* ⊘ *Closed Mon.*

 **Hotels**

**Hotel Iberia Plaza Mayor**

$ | HOTEL | FAMILY | The halls of this budget hotel—confusingly not on the Plaza Mayor but rather 100 yards down a quiet side street—are painted deep red and adorned with old etchings of Cáceres scenes. **Pros:** great value; prime location; generous breakfast buffet. **Cons:** reservations by online form or third party only; no on-site parking; dated furniture and so-so soundproofing. ⑤ *Rooms from: €71* ⊠ *Calle Pintores 2, Cáceres* ☎ *92/724-7634* ⊕ *www.iberiahotel.com* ⇨ *38 rooms* ⦿⦿ *Free Breakfast.*

★ **NH Collection Cáceres Palacio de Oquendo**

$$$ | HOTEL | This 16th-century palace, which spans the length of Plaza San Juan on the edge of the old quarter, is now an NH Collection hotel that rivals the city's parador—at much lower rates. **Pros:** excellent value; quiet area close to Plaza Mayor; recent redesign. **Cons:** some rooms have only skylights (no windows); pricey breakfast and mediocre restaurant; no parking. ⑤ *Rooms from: €160* ⊠ *Pl. San Juan 11, Cáceres* ☎ *92/721-5800* ⊕ *www.nh-hotels.com* ⇨ *86 rooms* ⦿⦿ *No Meals.*

**Parador de Cáceres**

$$$ | HOTEL | This 14th-century palace in the old town boasts elegant

public spaces filled with antiques. **Pros:** stunning old building; spacious rooms; peaceful outdoor dining area. **Cons:** some bathrooms need updating; unattractive indoor dining room; spartan decor. ⑤ *Rooms from: €195* ⊠ *Calle Ancha 6, Cáceres* ☎ *92/721-1759* ⊕ *www.parador.es* ⇨ *39 rooms* ⦿⦿ *Free Breakfast.*

⑦ **Nightlife**

**El Corral de las Cigüeñas**

LIVE MUSIC | There's a hopping nighttime music scene at this charming old-town café with an outdoor patio. In winter months, the club is open evenings Thursday through Sunday. Hours vary depending on events; call ahead or check concert schedules online. Students with a valid ID get a discount. ⊠ *Cuesta de Aldana 6, Cáceres* ☎ *92/721-6425, 64/775-8245* ⊕ *www.elcorralcc.com* ⊘ *Closed Mon.–Wed.*

⬤ **Shopping**

Some of the best shopping in Cáceres is culinary: the city and surrounding countryside are renowned for producing unparalleled Iberian ham and chorizo, complex cheeses, grippy wines, and mouthwatering pastries. But there are also distinctive artisan crafts worth seeking out.

**Centro de Artesanía Casa Palacio de los Moraga**

CRAFTS | Eschew the usual souvenir shops and instead drop by this art collective that sells wallets, purses, pins, toys, clothes, and other decorative elements in leather and ceramics made by local artisans. ⊠ *Calle Cuesta de Aldana 1, Cáceres* ☎ *92/722-7453* ⊕ *www.artesanex.com* ⊘ *Closed Mon.*

**Pastelería Isa**

FOOD | The city's premier pastry shop since opening in 1952, "La Isa" is best known for its *mojicón*, an oversized orange-scented muffin native to

Extremadura that's the perfect café con leche sidekick. ⊠ *Pl. Mayor 25, Cáceres* 🕾 *92/724–8185.*

★ **Sierra de Montánchez**

**FOOD** | Satisfy your jamón cravings at this gourmet shop specializing in acorn-fed pork products. There are usually baskets of terrific La Dalia pimentón on sale as well; grab one or two tins here as they're hard to find outside Extremadura. ⊠ *Pl. de la Concepción 5, Cáceres* 🕾 *92/721– 2025* ⊕ *www.sierrademontanchez.es* ⊘ *Closed Sun.*

# Trujillo

*45 km (28 miles) east of Cáceres, 256 km (159 miles) southwest of Madrid.*

Trujillo rises up from the boulder-strewn fields like a great granite schooner under full sail. From above, the rooftops and towers are worn and medieval-looking. At street level, Renaissance architecture abounds in squares such as the Plaza Mayor, with its elegant San Martín church. As in Cáceres, storks' nests top many towers—the birds have become an emblem of Trujillo. With roots in Roman times, the city was captured from the Moors in 1232 and colonized by a number of leading military families. Today it's known for hosting Spain's most popular cheese festival, Feria del Queso, an odorous bacchanal that takes place every spring (inquire about dates and tickets at the local tourist office).

## GETTING HERE AND AROUND

There is no train service to Trujillo, but Avanza bus offers five departures daily from Madrid's Estacion de Sur (3½ hours). There are usually several Blablacar rideshares available each day as well. Take in Trujillo on foot, as the streets are mostly cobbled or crudely paved with stone (suitable footwear needed; prepare for hills, too). The two main roads into Trujillo leave you at the unattractive bottom end of town. Things get progressively older the farther you climb, but even on the lower slopes—where most of the shops are concentrated—you need walk only a few yards to step into what seems like the Middle Ages.

**BUS CONTACTS Avanza Bus.** 🕾 *91/272– 2832* ⊕ *www.avanzabus.com.*

## ESSENTIALS

**VISITOR INFORMATION Trujillo Tourist Office.** ⊠ *Pl. Mayor 6, Trujillo* 🕾 *92/732– 2677* ⊕ *www.trujilloturismo.org.*

# ◉ Sights

## Iglesia de Santa María La Mayor

**CHURCH** | Attached to a Romanesque bell tower, this Gothic church is the most beautiful in Trujillo. It's only occasionally used for Mass, and its interior has been virtually untouched since the 16th century. The upper choir has an exquisitely carved balustrade, and the coats of arms at each end indicate the seats Ferdinand and Isabella occupied when they came here to worship. Note the high altar, circa 1480, adorned with great 15th-century Spanish paintings. To see it properly illuminated, place a coin in the box next to the church entrance. Climb the tower for stunning views of the town and vast plains stretching toward Cáceres and the Sierra de Gredos.

■**TIP**➔ **The optional audio guide is worth the €1 fee.** ⊠ *Pl. de Santa María, Trujillo* 🖼 *From €2.*

★ **La Villa**

**HISTORIC DISTRICT** | This is Trujillo's old town, enclosed by restored stone walls. Follow them along Calle Almenas, which runs west from the Palacio de Orella- na-Pizarro, beneath the Alcázar de Los Chaves, a castle-fortress that was converted into a lodge in the 15th century and hosted dignitaries including Ferdinand and Isabella. Now a college, the building has seen better days. Continue west along the wall to the Puerta de San Andrés, one of La Villa's four surviving gates (there were originally seven). Views from the hilltop are particularly memorable at sunset, when spotlights illuminate the old quarter. ⊠ *Trujillo.*

### Palacio de Orellana-Pizarro

**CASTLE/PALACE** | The Palacio de Orellana-Pizarro, renovated by the conquistador Juan Pizarro himself in the 16th century, is now a school and has one of the most elegant Renaissance courtyards in town. The ground floor, open to visitors, has a deep, arched front doorway; on the second story is an elaborate Renaissance balcony bearing the crest of the Pizarro family. Miguel de Cervantes, on his way to thank the Virgin of Guadalupe for his release from prison, spent time writing in the palace. ⊠ *Trujillo* ⊕ *Behind Pl. Mayor* 🖾 *Free.*

### Pizarro House Museum

**HISTORY MUSEUM** | The Pizarro family residence is now a modest museum dedicated to the connection between Spain and Latin America. The first floor emulates a typical home from 15th-century Trujillo, and the second floor is divided into exhibits on Peru and Pizarro's life there. The museum explains the "Curse of the Pizarro," recounting how the conquistador and his brothers were killed in brutal battles with rivals; those who survived never again enjoyed the wealth they had achieved in Peru. Glaringly absent from the museum is any mention of what Pizarro's conquests wrought: mass murder of Incas, feudalism and enslavement, forced conversions to Catholicism, and so on. ■**TIP**➔ **The museum closes from 2 to 4.** ⊠ *Calleja del Castillo 1, Trujillo* 🖾 *€2.*

### ★ Plaza Mayor

**PLAZA/SQUARE** | One of the finest plazas in Spain, this Renaissance gem is dominated by a bronze equestrian statue of Francisco Pizarro—the work of American sculptor Charles Rumsey. Notice the Palacio del Marqués de la Conquista, the most dramatic building on the square with plateresque ornamentation and imaginative busts of the Pizarro family

flanking its corner balcony. It was built by Francisco Pizarro's half-brother Hernando. ⊠ *Pl. Mayor, Trujillo.*

### Trujillo Castle (*Alcazaba de Trujillo*)

**CASTLE/PALACE** | For spectacular views, climb this large fortress—a *Game of Thrones* filming location—built by the Moors in the 9th century over older Roman foundations. To the south are silos, warehouses, and residential neighborhoods. To the north are green fields and brilliant flowers, partitioned by a maze of nearly leveled Roman stone walls, and an ancient cistern. The castle's size underscores the historical importance of now-tiny Trujillo. ⊠ *Cerro Cabeza de Zorro, Trujillo* 🕾 *92/732–2677* 🖾 *€2.*

## 🍴 Restaurants

### ★ El 7 de Sillerías

**$$$** | **SPANISH** | Locals will point you here for fresh, reasonably priced tapas and mains including croquetas (try the wild mushroom rendition) and *secreto ibérico* (seared Iberian pork shoulder steak). The weekday lunch menú del día—three courses plus wine—is a steal. **Known for:** elevated Extremaduran classics; juicy ibérico pork steaks; pleasant patio out back. 🖲 *Average main: €20* ⊠ *Calle Sillerías 7, Trujillo* 🕾 *92/732–1856* ⊕ *www. el7desillerias.com* ⊗ *Closed Tues. No dinner Mon.*

### Restaurante Bizcocho Plaza

**$$$** | **SPANISH** | A Trujillo institution conveniently located on the Plaza Mayor, Bizcocho specializes in Extramaduran cuisine—think local jamón, cheese, and migas—and the stone-and-tile dining room is cozy and cool even in the summer. Reservations are essential on holiday weekends. **Known for:** well-presented plates; excellent Iberian pork dishes; central location. 🖲 *Average main: €20* ⊠ *Pl. Mayor 11, Trujillo* 🕾 *92/732–2017* ⊕ *www. restaurantebizcochoplaza.com.*

# 🛏 Hotels

### ★ Hotel Boutique Posada Dos Orillas

**$ | HOTEL |** This hotel occupies a 16th-century stagecoach inn on a quiet pedestrian street uphill from the Plaza Mayor. **Pros:** pleasant interiors; good weekend rates; beautiful terrace. **Cons:** small TVs; beds a little basic; no reserved parking. **⑤** *Rooms from: €72* ⊠ *Calle de los Cambrones 6, Trujillo* ☎ *92/765–9079* ⊕ *www.dosorillas.com* ↝ *13 rooms* ⏐❍⏐ *Free Breakfast.*

### Izán Trujillo

**$ | HOTEL | FAMILY |** Once a 16th-century convent, this dependable four-star hotel is a five-minute walk from the Plaza Mayor. **Pros:** air of calm throughout the property; central location yet quiet; friendly and efficient staff. **Cons:** one-note breakfasts with little variety; rooms vary in size; small swimming pool. **⑤** *Rooms from: €95* ⊠ *Pl. del Campillo 1, Trujillo* ☎ *92/745–8900* ⊕ *www.izanhoteles.es* ↝ *78 rooms* ⏐❍⏐ *No Meals.*

### ★ Parador de Trujillo

**$$$ | HOTEL | FAMILY |** In another of the region's 16th-century convents, this parador offers tranquility and comfort in cheery restored rooms awash with wall art and patterned textiles. **Pros:** peace and quiet in the heart of town; homey colorful decor; swimming pool. **Cons:** poor-quality bath products; rooms are a bit like monastery quarters—on the small side; pricey for the area. **⑤** *Rooms from: €160* ⊠ *Calle Santa Beatriz de Silva 1, Trujillo* ☎ *92/732–1350* ⊕ *www.parador.es* ↝ *50 rooms* ⏐❍⏐ *Free Breakfast.*

# 👜 Shopping

### Eduardo Pablos Mateos

**CRAFTS |** This workshop specializes in wood carvings, basketwork, and furniture made from esparto grass. Call ahead to confirm opening hours and to schedule a personal tour. ⊠ *Calle de San Judas 3, Trujillo* ☎ *92/732–1066, 60/617–4382 mobile.*

### La Despensa

**FOOD |** This gourmet shop on the corner of Plaza Mayor was once the wine cellar of a 16th-century palace. Now it sells local products including jamón, cheese, wine, and locally made beer at excellent prices. ⊠ *Cuesta de la Sangre 0, Trujillo* ☎ *65/450–3419.*

# Guadalupe

*200 km (125 miles) southwest of Madrid, 96 km (60 miles) east of Trujillo.*

Guadalupe's monastery is one of the most inspiring sights in Extremadura. Its story begins around 1300, when, as the story goes, a local shepherd uncovered a statue of the Virgin, supposedly carved by St. Luke. King Alfonso XI, who often hunted here, had a church built to house the statue and vowed to found a monastery should he defeat the Moors at the battle of Salado in 1340. After his victory, he kept his promise. The monastery's heyday came between the 15th and 18th centuries, when, under the rule of the Hieronymites, it was turned into a pilgrimage center rivaling Santiago de Compostela in importance. Pilgrims have sought out the monastery since the 14th century and, in recent decades, are joined by just as many tourists. Yet Guadalupe's isolation—a good two-hour drive from the nearest town—has protected it from the tour bus crowds. The surrounding area is known for its copperware, crafted here since the 16th century.

## GETTING HERE AND AROUND

A car is best as there's no train and bus service is sporadic. Park on the outskirts of town, then meander the hilly cobblestone streets on foot.

## ESSENTIALS

**VISITOR INFORMATION Guadalupe Tourist Office.** ⊠ *Pl. Santa María de Guadalupe, Guadalupe* ☎ *92/715–4128.*

## 👁 Sights

**Plaza Mayor** (*Plaza de Santa María de Guadalupe*)

PLAZA/SQUARE | In the middle of this tiny, irregularly shaped plaza—which is transformed during festivals into a bullring—is the 15th-century fountain where Columbus's two Native American servants were baptized in 1496. Here, as is the case across Extremadura, there's a conspicuous lack of reckoning or awareness regarding the region's role in the horrors of colonizing the Americas. ⊠ *Guadalupe.*

★ **Real Monasterio de Santa María de Guadalupe** (*Royal Monastery of Our Lady of Guadalupe*)

CHURCH | Looming in the background of the Plaza Mayor is the late-Gothic facade of Guadalupe's colossal monastery church, flanked by battlement towers. The (required, Spanish-only) guided tour begins in the Mudejar cloister and continues on to the chapter house, with hymnals, vestments, and paintings including a series of small panels by Zurbarán. The ornate 17th-century sacristy has a series of eight Zurbarán paintings, from 1638 to 1647. These austere representations of monks of the Hieronymite order and scenes from the life of St. Jerome are the artist's only significant paintings housed in the setting for which they were intended. The tour concludes in the garish late-baroque Camarín, the chapel where the famous *Virgen Morena* (*Black Virgin*) is housed. Each September 8, the virgin is brought down from the altarpiece and walked around the cloister in a procession with pilgrims following on their knees. Outside, the monastery's gardens have been restored to their original, geometric Moorish style. ⊠ *Pl. Santa María de Guadalupe, Guadalupe*

⤷ *Entrance on Pl. Mayor* ☎ *92/736–7000* ⊕ *www.monasterioguadalupe.com* ⊠ *€5.*

## 🛏 Hotels

**Casa Rural Abacería de Guadalupe**

$$ | B&B/INN | FAMILY | For a simple, inexpensive overnight stay, try this small, tidy guesthouse on a quiet side street near the center of the village, around the corner from the parador. **Pros:** private location; plenty of peace and quiet; good for families. **Cons:** no Wi-Fi; cold hallways in the winter; individual rooms are a bit small. ⑤ *Rooms from: €105* ⊠ *Calle Marqués de la Romana, Guadalupe* ☎ *92/715–4282, 65/020–8405* ⊕ *www.air-bnb.com* ⇆ *3 rooms* ⚬| *Free Breakfast.*

★ **Hospedería del Real Monasterio**

$ | HOTEL | An excellent and considerably cheaper alternative to the town parador, this inn was built around the 16th-century Gothic cloister of the monastery itself. **Pros:** guests get free monastery admission; helpful staff; magical surroundings for a pittance. **Cons:** uncomfortable beds; subpar food in the restaurant; church bells chime around the clock. ⑤ *Rooms from: €95* ⊠ *Pl. Juan Carlos I, Guadalupe* ☎ *92/736–7000* ⊕ *www.hospederiagua-dalupe.es* ⊗ *Closed mid-Jan.–mid-Feb.* ⇆ *47 rooms* ⚬| *No Meals.*

**Parador de Guadalupe**

$$ | HOTEL | This exquisite estate, once the 15th-century palace of the Marquis de la Romana, now houses one of Spain's finest paradores. **Pros:** stunning architecture; idyllic balconies; down-home Extremaduran cooking. **Cons:** old-world property with old-world amenities; long hike from reception to the farthest rooms; tight parking. ⑤ *Rooms from: €140* ⊠ *Calle Marqués de la Romana 12, Guadalupe* ☎ *92/736–7075* ⊕ *www.para-dor.es* ⇆ *41 rooms* ⚬| *Free Breakfast.*

Mérida's excellently preserved Roman amphitheater is the site of a drama festival every July.

# Mérida

*76 km (47 miles) south of Cáceres, 191 km (119 miles) north of Seville, 347 km (216 miles) southwest of Madrid.*

Mérida has some of the most impressive Roman ruins in Iberia. Founded by the Romans in 25 BC on the banks of the Río Guadiana, the city is strategically located at the junction of major Roman roads from León to Seville and Toledo to Lisbon. The glass-and-steel bus station, on the other side of the river from the town center, commands a good view of the strikingly long Roman bridge. On the bank opposite the ruins is the *alcazaba* (fortress).

Other Roman sites nearby require a drive. Across the train tracks in a modern neighborhood is the *circo* (circus), where chariot races were held. Little remains of the grandstands, which seated 30,000, but the outline of the circus is clearly visible and impressive for its size. Of the existing aqueduct remains, the most impressive is the Acueducto de los Milagros (Aqueduct of Miracles), north of the train station.

## GETTING HERE AND AROUND

There are several buses daily to Mérida from Badajoz (1 hour), Seville (2½ hours), Cáceres (45 minutes), Trujillo (1½ hours), and Madrid (4½ hours). There are also several daily trains, which take about the same travel time but cost more. Check the RENFE website (*www.renfe.com*) or tourist office for schedules. Alternatively, there are usually several Blablacar rideshare departures from Madrid and Mérida's neighboring cities each day. Once in Mérida, the city center is navigable on foot or by tourist train.

■TIP➔ At the tourist office or via the website , you can purchase a €16 combo ticket including entry to six sights: the Roman Theater and Amphitheater, Roman Circus, Alcazaba (Arab Citadel), Morería Archaeological Site, Crypt of the Basilica of Santa Eulalia, and House of Mithraeum and Columbarium.

## ESSENTIALS

**VISITOR INFORMATION Mérida Tourist Office.** ⊠ *Calle Santa Eulalia 66, Mérida* ☎ *92/438–0191* ⊕ *www.turismomerida. org.*

## ◉ Sights

### Alcazaba (Fortress)

RUINS | To get to this sturdy square fortress, built by the Romans and strengthened by the Visigoths and Moors, continue west from the Museo Nacional de Arte Romano, down Suárez Somonte toward the river and city center. Turn right at Calle Baños and you can see the towering columns of Templo de Diana, the oldest of the Roman buildings. To enter the Alcazaba, follow the fortress walls around to the side farthest from the river. Climb up to the battlements for sweeping river views, or go underground to see the *aljibe*, or cistern. ⊠ *Calle de Graciano, Mérida* ☎ *92/400–4908* ⊕ *www.turismomerida.org/what-to-see/ arab-citadel* ⊠ *€6.*

### Basílica de Santa Eulalia

CHURCH | Originally Visigothic, this basilica marks the site of a Roman temple as well as the alleged place where the child martyr Eulalia was burned alive in AD 304 for spitting in the face of a Roman magistrate. The site was a focal point for pilgrimages during the Middle Ages. In 1990, excavations revealed layer upon layer of Paleolithic, Visigothic, Byzantine, and Roman settlements. The popular €16 sightseeing combination ticket sold at the tourist office includes entry only into the underground crypt of the basilica; it's €2 to visit the main structure. ⊠ *Rambla Mártir Santa Eulalia, Av. de Extremadura 3, Mérida* ☎ *92/430–3407* ⊠ *€2.*

### Colección Visigoda

HISTORY MUSEUM | An abandoned 18th-century church contains this easily digestible museum compiling some of the most important Visigothic artworks on the Iberian Peninsula. It's a branch of the Museo Nacional de Arte Romano, in a separate location north of the Plaza de España, in Mérida's old town. ■TIP→ If you enjoy this museum and are traveling to Málaga, check out the recently opened Hergan Collection, which, according to some scholars, contains the most valuable ensemble of Visigothic art in the world including figurines recovered from an ancient shipwreck. ⊠ *Calle Santa Eulalia 1, Mérida* ☎ *92/430–0106* ⊕ *www.turismomerida.org/que-ver/coleccion-visigoda* ⊠ *Free.*

### ★ Morería Archaeological Site

RUINS | FAMILY | Mérida's Roman *teatro* (theater) and *anfiteatro* (amphitheater) are set in a verdant park, and the theater—the best preserved in Spain—seats 6,000 and is used for a classical drama festival each July. The amphitheater, which holds 15,000 spectators, opened in 8 BC for gladiatorial contests. Next to the entrance to the ruins is the main tourist office, where you can pick up maps and brochures. You can buy a ticket to see only the Roman ruins or, for a bit more, an *entrada conjunta* (joint admission), which also grants access to the crypt of the Basílica de Santa Eulalia and to the Alcazaba. To reach the monuments by car, follow signs for Museo de Arte Romano. Parking is usually easy to find. ⊠ *Av. de los Estudiantes, Mérida* ☎ *92/431–2530* ⊕ *www.turismomerida. org/what-to-see/moreria-archaeological-area* ⊠ *From €6.*

### ★ Museo Nacional de Arte Romano (National Museum of Roman Art)

HISTORY MUSEUM | Across the street from the entrance to the Roman sites and connected by an underground passage is Mérida's superb Roman art museum, in a building designed by the Spanish architect Rafael Moneo. Walk through a series of passageways to the luminous, cathedral-like main exhibition hall, which is supported by arches the same proportion and size (50 feet) as the Roman arch in the center of Mérida, the Arco de

Trajano (Trajan's Arch). Exhibits include mosaics, frescoes, jewelry, statues, pottery, household utensils, and other Roman works. The crypt beneath the museum contains the remains of several homes and a necropolis that were uncovered while the museum was being built in 1981. ⊠ *Calle José Ramón Mélida, Mérida* ☎ *92/431–1690, 92/431–1912* ⊕ *www.mecd.gob.es/mnromano/home.html* ☑ *€3. Free weekends after 2.* ⊙ *Closed Mon.*

### Plaza de España
**PLAZA/SQUARE** | Mérida's main square is lively day and night. The oldest building is a 16th-century palace, now the Hotel Ilunion Mérida Palace. Behind it stretches Mérida's most charming area, with Andalusian-esque white houses shaded by palms, in the midst of which stands the Arco de Trajano, part of a Roman city gate. It's a great place to people-watch over tapas at sunset. ⊠ *Mérida.*

## 🍴 Restaurants

### ★ El Puchero de la Nieta
**$$** | **SPANISH** | The drab, nothingburger interiors of this Mérida standby belie a well-executed menu of must-try dishes including *migas* (fried bread crumbs with bacon), jamón-wrapped melon, gazpacho, and whatever *puchero del día* (stew of the day) happens to be burbling out back. **Known for:** crowd-pleasing local comfort food; small digs (so call ahead!); €14 prix-fixe lunch. ⑤ *Average main: €12* ⊠ *Calle José Ramón Mélida 14, Mérida* ☎ *63/563–6434* ⊙ *Closed Tues. No dinner Mon.*

## 🛏 Hotels

### ★ Ilunion Mérida Palace
**$$$** | **HOTEL** | **FAMILY** | Dominating the Plaza de España, this five-star luxury hotel has a rooftop pool deck, Roman- and Moorish-theme design elements, and a twinkly central courtyard. **Pros:** outdoor pool, terrace, and solarium; standout breakfast; gym facilities. **Cons:** a bit far from the Roman ruins; middling hotel restaurant; plaza-facing rooms can be noisy in summer. ⑤ *Rooms from: €190* ⊠ *Pl. de España 19, Mérida* ☎ *92/438–3800* ⊕ *www.ilunionmeridapalace.com* ⇨ *76 rooms* ⦿ *No Meals.*

### Parador de Mérida (*Parador Vía de la Plata*)
**$$$$** | **HOTEL** | **FAMILY** | This spacious hotel exudes Andalusian cheerfulness with hints at its Roman and Moorish past—it was built over the remains of a Roman temple, later became a baroque convent, and then served as a prison. **Pros:** central location; dazzling-white interior; serene interior courtyard. **Cons:** could use a revamp; erratic Wi-Fi; restaurant not up to snuff. ⑤ *Rooms from: €220* ⊠ *Calle Almendralejo 56, Mérida* ☎ *92/431–3800* ⊕ *www.parador.es* ⇨ *81 rooms* ⦿ *No Meals.*

# GALICIA, ASTURIAS, AND CANTABRIA

Updated by
Megan Lloyd

| ⊙ Sights | 🍴 Restaurants | 🏨 Hotels | 🛍 Shopping | 🍸 Nightlife |
|---|---|---|---|---|
| ★★★★☆ | ★★★☆☆ | ★★★★☆ | ★★★☆☆ | ★★★☆☆ |

# WELCOME TO GALICIA, ASTURIAS, AND CANTABRIA

## TOP REASONS TO GO

★ **Ascend to food heaven:** Ancient Santiago de Compostela has more restaurants and bars per square mile than any other city around.

★ **Embark on remote mountain hikes:** Explore the spectacular Picos de Europa range on foot, and hole up in far-flung mountain villages.

★ **Clink glasses of local Albariño:** The Rías Baixas vineyards yield some of Spain's finest white wines.

★ **Live your idyllic seaside fantasy:** Watch the fishing boats come and go in busy ports like Vigo.

★ **Discover Santander:** There's enough music, architecture, opera, and theater in the Cantabrian capital to keep you busy for days (and nights).

The misty and mysterious regions of Galicia, Asturias, and Cantabria stretch east above Portugal, along Spain's windswept northern coast. Explorers once called this far-flung corner of the peninsula *finis terrae* (the end of the earth).

**1 Santiago de Compostela.** The exuberant final destination for Christian and (increasingly) secular pilgrims on the Walk of St. James.

**2 Ourense and La Ribeira Sacra.** Stunning medieval architecture, dramatic valleys, and natural hot springs.

**3 Lugo.** Beautifully preserved Roman ramparts.

**4 Muxía.** A quaint fishing village on a peninsula jutting into the Atlantic.

**5 Fisterra.** Once the "end of the earth," now an optional add-on finale to the Camino.

**6 Muros.** Famous for its late-afternoon fish auction.

**7 Cambados.** Consistently listed as one of Spain's prettiest towns.

**8 Pontevedra.** Home base for wine-soaked adventures in the Rías Baixas.

**9 Vigo.** A formidable port, red-roofed fishermen's houses, and a lively old town.

**10 Baiona.** The site of one of Spain's most popular paradores.

**11 Tui.** A fortified old border town.

**12 A Coruña.** The aristocratic epicenter of Galicia with bountiful shops and chic restaurants.

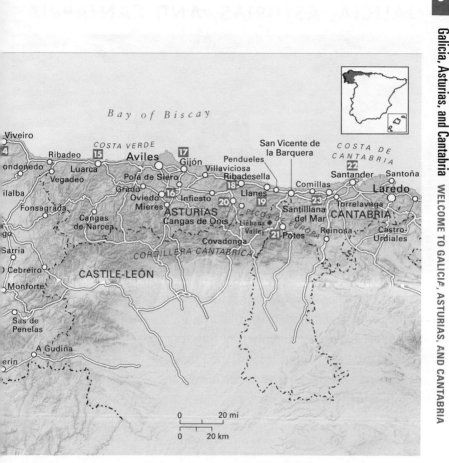

Bay of Biscay

COSTA VERDE

COSTA DE CANTABRIA

**13 Betanzos.** A charming medieval town at the confluence of two rivers.

**14 Viveiro.** Scenic unspoiled beaches make this a popular summer resort.

**15 Luarca.** The beloved white town on Asturias's Green Coast.

**16 Oviedo.** A timeless, stately city with palpable youthful energy.

**17 Gijón.** An ancient Roman port with uproarious and unpretentious nightlife.

**18 Ribadesella.** Synonymous with seafood, natural wonders, and canoe racing.

**19 Llanes.** The beach town Spaniards love for its colorful houses and mountain backdrop.

**20 Cangas de Onís.** Unofficial capital of Picos de Europa National Park.

**21 Potes.** Sigh-worthy cheeses and 9th-century bridges.

**22 Santander.** Cantabria's tranquil yet culture-packed capital.

**23 Santillana del Mar.** An architectural treasure trove of 15th- to 17th-century stone houses.

# EATING AND DRINKING WELL IN GALICIA, ASTURIAS, AND CANTABRIA

A plethora of seafood delicacies

Galicia, Asturias, and Cantabria are famous for seafood and fish so fresh that chefs frown on drowning the inherent flavors in sauces and seasonings. Inland, the Picos de Europa and the mountain meadows are rich in game, lamb, and beef.

The northern coast of Spain is justly famous for fish and seafood, and specialties include *merluza a la gallega* (steamed hake with paprika sauce) in Galicia and *merluza a la sidra* (hake in a cider sauce) in Asturias. Look also for Galician seafood treasures such as *vieiras* (scallops) and *pulpo a la gallega* (boiled octopus that's drizzled with olive oil and dusted with salt and paprika). The rainy weather means that bracing stews are a favorite form of sustenance, especially *fabada asturiana* (Asturian bean-and-sausage stew) and Galicia's *caldo gallego* (a thick soup of white beans, turnip greens, ham, and potatoes). Cantabria's cooking is part mountain fare, such as roast kid and lamb or *cocidos* (pork-and-bean stews) in the highlands, and part seafood dishes, such as *sorropotún* (a bonito, potato, and vegetable stew) along the coast.

### CABRALES CHEESE

Asturias is known for Spain's most pungent cheese, Cabrales, a blue made from raw cow milk (with goat curd added for a softer consistency). Produced in the Picos de Europa mountains of eastern Asturias, the cheese is prized both for the quality of the milk and the dry highland air used to cure it. It's often melted over roast meats or eaten as an appetizer or dessert with a nip of sherry.

## BEANS AND LEGUMES

Fabada asturiana is as famous in Spain as Valencia's paella or Andalusia's gazpacho. Not unlike French cassoulet, the hearty white bean stew is ladled out in copious quantities and—don't say we didn't warn you—often necessarily followed by a siesta. The secret to great fabada is the ultracreamy "de la Granja" bean grown in the region, which you can buy in vacuum-sealed bags as culinary souvenirs at gourmet shops. Fatback, *morcilla* (blood sausage), chorizo, and other regional pork products give fabada its signature smoky flavor. Other bean dishes to try include *verdinas con almejas* (beans with clams) and *pote* (boiled dinner with white beans and cabbage).

## VEGETABLES

Bitter and tart turnip greens (*grelos*) are a staple in Galicia, so celebrated that they have their own festival, La Festa do Grelo, held in February and March. As a side, they're often eaten with boiled pork shoulder (*lacón*), boiled potatoes, and chorizo. They make it into soups such as *caldo gallego*, which calls for the stalks and greens, *alubias* (white beans), and potatoes—plus pork for ballast and flavor.

The hearty and fortifying caldo gallego.

The classic octopus-and-potato combination.

## PULPO A LA GALLEGA

This Galician delicacy, also known as *polbo á feira*, consists of octopus that's been boiled (traditionally in a copper cauldron), cut into tentacled coins, drizzled with olive oil, sprinkled with salt and smoky paprika, and served on a wooden plate. A common variation adds an understory of boiled potato to soak up the heady brackish juices.

## TO DRINK

Wine lovers across the world know Galicia through its Albariño, the citrusy, slate-y white produced in the Rías Baixas that's become a fixture on restaurant menus. But there are plenty of other intriguing wines to try in northern Spain such as Ribeiro, a floral white blend traditionally sipped from shallow white ceramic cups called *cuncas*, and godello, Spain's current golden-boy grape that has somms swooning over its honeyed complexity. By contrast, Asturias makes little wine but over 10 million gallons of *sidra* (hard cider) annually. At Asturian restaurants, waiters dramatically decant ("escanciar") it from overhead to aerate it slightly. Those with a penchant for the hard stuff shouldn't miss Galicia's *queimada*, a potent "witches' brew" of grappalike *orujo* steeped with lemon peel, coffee beans, and sugar that's set aflame in an earthenware bowl.

# EL CAMINO DE SANTIAGO

Crossing meadows, mountains, and villages across Spain, about 350,000 travelers embark each year on a pilgrimage to Galicia's Santiago de Compostela, the sacred city of St. James. They're not all pious religious types these days, though a spiritual quest is generally the motivation. While some complete the hike alone, many more do it with friends or family.

### HISTORY OF THE CAMINO

The surge of spiritual seekers heading to Spain's northwest coast began as early as the 9th century, when news spread that the apostle James's remains were being kept there. By the middle of the 12th century, about 1 million pilgrims were arriving in Santiago de Compostela each year. An entire industry of food hawkers, hoteliers, and trinket sellers awaited their arrival. The pilgrims even had the world's first travel guide, the *Codex Calixtinus* (published in the 12th century), to help them on their way. Some made the journey in response to their conscience, to do penance for their sins against God, while others were sentenced by law to make the trek as payment for crimes against the state. Legend claims that St. James's body was transported secretly to the area by boat after his martyrdom in Jerusalem in AD 44. The idea had stuck by 814, when a hermit claimed to see miraculous lights in the sky, accompanied by the sound of angels singing, on a wooded hillside near Padrón. Human bones were quickly discovered at the site, and immediately—and perhaps somewhat conveniently—declared to be those of the apostle (the bones may actually have belonged to Priscillian, the leader of a 4th-century Christian sect). Word of this important find quickly spread across a relic-hungry Europe. Within a couple of centuries, the road to Santiago had become as popular as the other two major medieval pilgrimages, to Rome and to Jerusalem. After the 12th century, pilgrim numbers declined due to the dangers of robbery along the route, a growing skepticism about the genuineness of St. James's remains, and the rise of science in place of religion.

The Camino de Santiago passes through the medieval town of Logroño, capital of Spain's Rioja region.

### THE PILGRIMAGE TODAY

The pilgrims follow one of seven main routes, walking about 19 miles per day in a nearly 500-mile journey. Along the way, they encounter incredible local hospitality and trade stories with fellow adventurers. By the late 1980s, there were only about 3,000 pilgrims trickling into Santiago a year, but in 1993 the Galician government launched an initiative to increase the number of visitors to the region, and the popularity of the pilgrimage soared. In holy years, when St. James's Day (July 25) falls on a Sunday, the number of pilgrims usually doubles.

### WHO WAS ST. JAMES?

St. James the Great, brother of St. John the Evangelist (author of the Gospel of

Scallop shell symbols mark the routes of the Camino de Santiago.

John and the Book of Revelation), was one of Jesus's first apostles. Sent by Jesus to preach that the kingdom of heaven had come, he crossed Europe and ended up in Spain. Along the way, he saved a knight from drowning in the sea. As legend goes, the knight resurfaced covered in scallop shells: this is why Camino pilgrims carry this seashell on their journey. St. James is said to have been beheaded by King Herod Agrippa on his return to Judea in AD 44 but rescued by angels. He was subsequently transported in a rudderless stone boat back to Spain, where his lifeless body was encased in a rock. James is said to have resurfaced to aid the Christians in the Reconquest Battle of Clavijo, gaining him the (rather problematic) title of Matamoros, or Moor Killer. When the body of St. James was "found," people came in droves to see his remains—the Spanish and Portuguese name for St. James is Santiago. The belief arose that sins would be cleansed through the penance of this long walk, an idea encouraged by the Church.

### THE PILGRIMAGE EXPERIENCE

Not everyone does the route in one go. Some split it into manageable chunks and take years to complete the whole course. Most, however, walk

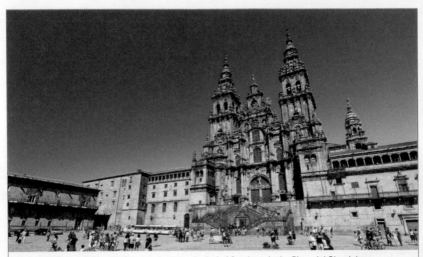

At the end of the Camino de Santiago is the cathedral of Santiago, in the Plaza del Obradoiro.

an average of 30 km (19 miles) per day to arrive in Santiago after a monthlong trek. The route sometimes follows a mountain trail and other times passes through villages and fields. It is generally so well marked that most travelers claim not to need a map (bringing one is highly recommended, however): simply follow the route markers—scallop shells on blue backgrounds with an arrow beneath, posted on buildings or painted on rocks and trail posts. Walking is not the only option: bicycles are common and will cut the time needed to complete the pilgrimage in half; horseback riding can also be arranged. Every town along the route has an official Camino *albergue* (hostel), often in an ancient monastery or original pilgrim's hospice. They are basic and generally accommodate 40–150 people. You can bunk for free—though a donation is expected—in the company of fellow walkers but may stay only one night, unless severe Camino injuries prevent you from moving on. Be aware that these places fill up fast. Walkers get first priority, followed by cyclists and those on horseback, with organized

walking groups at the bottom of the pecking order. If there is no room at the official albergues, there are plenty of paid hostels along the route. Wherever you stay, get your Pilgrims' Passport, or *credencial*, stamped, as proof of how far you've walked.

## A TYPICAL DAY

A typical day on the Camino involves walking hard through the morning to the next village in time to get a free bed. The afternoon is for catching up with fellow pilgrims, having a look around town, and doing a bit of washing. The people you meet along the way and the camaraderie with fellow pilgrims are highlights of the trip for many, regardless of age. Some albergues serve a communal evening meal, but there is always a bar in town that offers a lively atmosphere and a cheap (€8–€12) pilgrim's set menu (quality and fare vary; it consists of three courses plus bread and beverage). Over dinner, walkers compare sore feet, guzzle local wine, and make new walking partners for the following day. Make sure you're back to the albergue by curfew, usually 10 or 11, lest you find a locked door.

## THE FINISH LINE

Arriving at the end of the Camino de Santiago is an emotional experience. It is common to see small groups of pilgrims, hands clasped tightly together, tearfully approaching the moss- and lichen-covered cathedral in Santiago's Plaza del Obradoiro. After entering the building through the Pilgrim's Door and hugging the statue of St. James, a special Mass awaits at midday, the highlight of which (if you time your arrival correctly) is seeing the *botafumeiro*, a giant incense-filled censer, swinging from the ceiling. Those that have covered more than 100 km (62 miles) on foot, or twice that distance on a bicycle—as shown by the stamped passport—can then collect their Compostela certificate from the pilgrim's office (near the cathedral, at Rúa do Vilar 1).

### USEFUL WEBSITES

The official Camino website (⊕ *www. caminodesantiago.gal*) has detailed route maps, packing lists, and a tab for booking albergues, though perhaps handier is the (unaffiliated yet well-reviewed) Way of St James app, which is free to download. The following are also treasure troves of information: ⊕ *www. caminodesantiago.me*, ⊕ *www.csj.org. uk*, and ⊕ *www.caminoadventures. com*.

### CAMINO TIPS

The most popular of the seven main routes of the Camino de Santiago is the 791-km (480-mile) **Camino francés** (French Way), which starts in France (in Saint-Jean-Pied-de-Port) and crosses the high *meseta* plains into Galicia. The **Camino norte** (Northern Way), which runs through the woodlands of Spain's rugged north coast, is also gaining in popularity.

The busiest time on the Camino is June–September; busy can mean crowded paths and booked-up albergues, particularly if you start the Camino on the first few days of the month. April, May, and late September are more tranquil. Making the journey in winter is not advised due to soggy and unpredictable weather.

As any seasoned hiker will tell you, the most important piece of equipment is your hiking boots, which should be as professional as your budget allows and broken in before you hit the trail. Other essentials include a good-quality—and waterproof (it rains year round in Galicia)—backpack, sleeping bag, sunscreen, and medical kit including Vaseline and blister remedies for sore feet. Don't forget a set of earplugs as well.

To get your Camino "passport"/credential ahead of time, contact a Camino confraternity group. Or just sort it out upon arrival—you can always snap one up last minute at common starting points, local churches, and popular albergues for about €2. For a complete list of confraternity groups in cities throughout Spain, visit ⊕ *www. oficinadelperegrino.com/en/preparation/confraternities-in-spain*.

You can also now digitize your passport by using the new credentials app on your phone. For information on the app, visit ⊕ *www.oficinadelperegrino.com/en/pilgrimage/the-credencial/*.

It's common today for families to walk the Camino de Santiago together.

Spain's green, mountainous north is en route to nowhere, an end in itself. Spaniards who have spent time in the region wax poetically about it and describe it with a palpable sense of nostalgia. Its ruggedness and open-armed hospitality evoke a humbler, simpler Spain of generations past. Galicians have a term for this wistful longing for people and places left behind: *morriña.*

Creeping north and northwest from the lonesome Castilian plains to the rocky seacoast, Galicia, Asturias, and Cantabria take in lush hills and scraggly vineyards, gorgeous *rías* (estuaries), and perhaps the country's wildest mountains, the Picos de Europa. Santander and the entire Cantabrian region are cool summer refuges with sandy beaches, high sierras (including part of the Picos), and tiny highland towns. Santander, once the main seaport for Old Castile, on the Bay of Biscay, is in a mountainous zone wedged between the Basque Country and Asturias.

Northwestern Spain has a Celtic feel with its shamrock-covered hills and oft-overcast skies. Ancient granite buildings wear a blanket of moss, and even the stone *hórreos* (granaries) are built on stilts above the damp ground. Swirling fog and heavy mist help keep local folktales of the supernatural alive. Rather than the usual flamenco guitar, a *gaita* (bagpipe) is the more common choice for buskers here, a legacy of the Celts who settled here in the 5th and 6th centuries BC.

Santiago de Compostela, where the cathedral holds the remains of the apostle James, has drawn pilgrims for 900 years, leaving churches, shrines, and former hospitals in their path. Asturias, north of the main pilgrim trail, has always maintained a separate identity, isolated by the rocky Picos de Europa. This and the Basque Country are the only parts of Spain never conquered by the Moors, so Asturian architecture shows little Moorish influence. According to lore (yet increasingly disputed), it was from a mountain base at Covadonga that the Christians won their first decisive battle against the Moors and launched the so-called Reconquest of Spain. Despite being very much its own region, Cantabria is in spirit much closer to Asturias—with which it shares the Picos de Europa, Castilian Spanish, and similar architecture—than its passionately independent neighbor, the Basque Country.

## MAJOR REGIONS

**Santiago de Compostela and Eastern Galicia.** Santiago isn't only for pilgrims—it's also a vibrant university town with terrific food and a charming old town whose crown jewel is its towering 13th-century cathedral.

**The Costa da Morte and Rías Baixas.** From the small fishing village of Malpica to Muros, from Fisterra (World's End) down to Vigo and the Portuguese border, this area also takes in the peaceful seaside towns of Cambados and Baiona, the gorgeous beaches of Las Islas Cíes, and the medieval streets of Pontevedra.

**A Coruña and Rías Altas.** Galicia has more coastline and unspoiled, nontouristy beaches than anywhere else in Spain. There are vast sandy expanses and tiny, tucked-away coves, but take note: the water is colder than the Mediterranean and the weather more temperamental

**Asturias.** The Senda Costera (Coastal Way) nature route between Pendueles and Llanes takes in some of Asturias's most spectacular coastal scenery, including noisy *bufones* (large waterspouts created naturally by erosion) and U-shaped Playa de Ballota. Asturias is bordered to the southeast by the imposing Picos de Europa, which are best accessed via the scenic coastal towns of Llanes or Ribadesella.

**Picos de Europa.** One of Spain's best-kept secrets, the "Peaks of Europe" straddle Asturias, Cantabria, and Castile and León. In addition to 8,910-foot peaks, there are deep caves, well-kept mountain refuges, and interesting wildlife. The region is also known for its fine cheeses.

**Cantabria.** Wide beaches, delectable sweets, and summer music-and-dance festivals are highlights in this rural region. The Liébana Valley, the Renaissance town at Santillana del Mar, and ports and beaches like San Vicente de la Barquera rank among northern Spain's finest treasures.

# Planning

## When to Go

Galicia sizzles (think highs of 95°F [35°C]) June–September, even if it's one of Spain's coolest regions. Summer is the best time for swimming, hiking, water sports, and live music. Asturias and Cantabria, in the mountains, are cooler than Galicia, though Galicia is rainier—not for nothing is this region called Green Spain. Avoid these three regions in winter (unless you like moody weather and solitude): the rain, wind, and freezing temperatures make most activities a pain. Spring and fall are safer bets as the weather is calmer and crowds are few.

## Planning Your Time

You can take a train, bus, or rideshare to Santiago de Compostela, but flying is most convenient. Budget one week, give or take, to cover Santiago and southern Galicia. From Santiago, you can drive down the PO550 to Cambados, stopping on the way at fishing villages along the Ría de Arousa. If you continue along the coastal road to Pontevedra, pause there to explore the medieval streets lined with tapas bars, then drive down to Vigo for a lunch of oysters on Rúa Pescadería. Continue south and arrive before dark at the Baiona Parador.

Alternatively, travel to A Coruña, and from there head north to some of Spain's loveliest beaches and Viveiro. From here cross into Asturias and post up in Luarca or Gijón. Another attractive option is zipping up the mountain passes into Picos de Europa and staying in a remote village.

Farther east, Santillana del Mar's Renaissance architecture, the Altamira Caves, and the Sardinero Beach at Santander are top spots, while the fishing villages and beaches around Llanes in eastern Asturias and San Vicente de la Barquera in Cantabria have beguiling ports and inlets. If you want to truly delve into the Picos de Europa and the region's rugged coastline, Asturias and Cantabria merit more than a week's exploration.

# Getting Here and Around

## AIR

There are airports in Santiago de Compostela, Santander, A Coruña, and Vigo, plus one near San Esteban de Pravia, 47 km (29 miles) north of Oviedo, Asturias's only airport. Santiago is the busiest of the bunch. Airport shuttles run by ALSA generally leave from the city bus station.

## BIKE

Cycling the Camino de Santiago de Compostela is becoming more popular every year, particularly with international visitors. The official *French Way by Bicycle* PDF is downloadable on ⊕ *www. caminodesantiago.gal* and available in print at the Santiago tourist office. It advises that the approximately 800-km (500-mile) route from the French border to Santiago is no cake walk—bridle paths, dirt tracks, rough stones, and mountain passes await. The best time of year to tackle it is late spring or early autumn. The Asturias tourist office outlines routes in that region on ⊕ *www.turismoasturias. es/en/turismo-activo/bici*. For something a little less arduous, try the final leg of the Camino Francés, from Sarria to Santiago, which takes 2–4 days.

## BIKE ROUTES

**Camino Ways**

This tour operator can help you bike the Camino with tailor-made packages for individuals and families, child-friendly accommodations if necessary, meals, luggage transfer, and bike rental. ⊠ *Calle Gomez Ulla 6, Santiago de Compostela* ☎ *923/990672* ⊕ *www.caminoways.com*.

**Camino de Santiago**
☎ *902/112000, 981/900643* ⊕ *www. caminodesantiago.gal*.

## BUS

ALSA runs buses every few hours from Madrid to Galicia and Asturias. On arrival, there is good bus service between cities such as Santiago, Vigo, Pontevedra, Lugo, A Coruña, Gijón, Oviedo, and Santander. However, train travel between the aforementioned is generally faster and more comfortable (and more expensive). Reaching smaller towns and villages by bus is usually possible but time-consuming and inconvenient. Galicia-based Monbus offers quick, inexpensive transportation between major cities like Santiago, A Coruña, Vigo, and Pontevedra, as well as smaller towns that may not be easily accessible by train.

**CONTACTS ALSA.** ☎ *902/422242* ⊕ *www. alsa.com*. **Monbus.** ☎ *900/929192* ⊕ *www.monbus.es*.

## CAR

Driving is the best way to get around. The four-lane A6 expressway links the area with central Spain; it takes about 6½ hours to cover the 650 km (403 miles) from Madrid to Santiago, and from Madrid, it's 240 km (149 miles) on the N1 or the A1 toll road to Burgos, after which you can take the N623 to complete the 162 km (100 miles) to Santander.

The expressway north from León to Oviedo and Gijón is the fastest way to cross the Cantabrian Mountains. The AP9 north–south Galician ("Atlantic") expressway links A Coruña, Santiago, Pontevedra, and Vigo, and the A8 in Asturias links Santander to Luarca and beyond. Local roads along the coast or through the hills are more scenic but slower.

## TRAIN

RENFE (⊕ *www.renfe.es*) runs several trains a day from Madrid to Santander (4½ hours), Oviedo (5 hours), and Gijón (5½ hours), and a separate line serves Santiago (4½ hours). The long-awaited high-speed AVE line connecting Ourense and Madrid (2½ hours) was also completed in December 2021. Local RENFE trains connect the region's major cities with most of the surrounding small towns, but there are often dozens of stops on the way. Narrow-gauge REN-FE–FEVE trains clatter slowly across northern Spain, connecting Galicia and Asturias with Santander, Bilbao, and Irún (on the French border).

RENFE's Transcantábrico Gran Lujo train tour (⊕ www.renfe.com) is an eight-day, 1,000-km (600-mile) journey through the Basque Country, Cantabria, Asturias, and Galicia. English-speaking guides narrate, and a private bus takes the group from train stations to natural attractions. Passengers sleep on the train in suites and dine on local specialties. Itineraries run April–October; the all-inclusive cost is around €6,000 for seven nights per person in a deluxe suite.

# Restaurants

From the humblest taverns to the haughtiest dining rooms, chefs in Galicia, Asturias, and Cantabria emphasize the use of fresh, local ingredients. Excellent, cheap meals can be found at smaller, family-run eateries, which usually stick to traditional foods and draw mostly local crowds. Restaurants that stray from the culinary norm—those with top-notch service, experimental cuisine, and elegant surroundings—tend to command a higher price tag.

*Restaurant reviews have been shortened. For full information, visit Fodors. com.*

# Hotels

Expect to feel at home in the region's traditional inns: they're usually small, centuries-old, family-owned properties, with pleasing gardens, exposed stone

walls, and genuine service. City hotels don't have the same country charm, but they make up for it with modern-day conveniences and (generally) spacious rooms. Chain hotels in the region may resemble their American counterparts, but they don't always come with ample parking, big breakfasts, fitness rooms, and other amenities that we've come to accept as standard. Book ahead for stays in May–September, high season.

*Hotel reviews have been shortened. For full information, visit Fodors.com.*

| What It Costs in Euros | | | |
|---|---|---|---|
| $ | $$ | $$$ | $$$$ |
| **RESTAURANTS** | | | |
| under €12 | €12–€17 | €18–€22 | over €22 |
| **HOTELS** | | | |
| under €90 | €90–€125 | €126–€180 | over €180 |

# Santiago de Compostela

*650 km (403 miles) northwest of Madrid.*

Welcome to one of the most beloved and beautiful cities not just in Galicia but in all of Spain. Wander down the cobblestone streets of the old town, and you'll gasp at the gorgeous mix of Romanesque, Gothic, and baroque buildings. Or pop into an art gallery or one of the city's many chic literary cafés to catch some poetry or local music. A large, lively university makes Santiago one of the most electric cities in Spain, and its cathedral makes it one of the most impressive. The building is opulent and awesome, yet its towers create a sense of harmony as a benign St. James, dressed in pilgrim's costume, looks down from his perch. Santiago de Compostela welcomes around 4 million visitors a year, with an extra million during Holy Years, which occur when St. James's Day (July 25) falls on a Sunday.

Santiago de Compostela and Eastern Galicia

■TIP➔ The next jubilee will be celebrated in 2027.

## GETTING HERE AND AROUND

Santiago is connected to Pontevedra (61 km [38 miles]) and A Coruña (57 km [35 miles]) via the AP9 tollway. The N550 is free but slower. Parking anywhere in the city center can be difficult unless you use one of the numerous car parks around the outside edge of the historical quarter.

Bus service out of Santiago's station is plentiful, with eight daily buses to Madrid (7–9 hours) and hourly buses to A Coruña and to the Santiago Airport.

High-speed Talgo trains to Madrid take just over six hours; there is daily service to Irún, on the French border, via León and Santander. Trains depart every hour for Galicia's other major towns.

Santiago's center is very pedestrian friendly, and the distances between attractions are relatively short, so walking is the best and often the only way around town.

**BUS STATION Santiago de Compostela Bus Station.** ⊠ Rúa de Clara Campoamor, Santiago de Compostela ☎ 981/542416.

**TRAIN STATION Santiago de Compostela Train Station.** ⊠ Rúa do Hórreo 75A, Santiago de Compostela ☎ 912/320320 RENFE.

## VISITOR INFORMATION
**CONTACTS Santiago de Compostela Tourist Office.** ⊠ Rúa do Vilar 63, Santiago de Compostela ☎ 981/555129 ⊕ www.santiagoturismo.com.

## TOURS
### Cathedral Roof Tours

VIEWPOINT | For a bird's-eye view of the city, join one of the tours arranged by the cathedral museum that takes you across the *cubiertas,* the granite steps of the cathedral roofs. Pilgrims made the same 100-foot climb in medieval times to burn their travel-worn clothes below the Cruz dos Farrapos (Cross of Rags). There is a limited number of English-language tours. ⊠ *Catedral de Santiago de Compostela, Praza do Obradoiro, Santiago de Compostela* ☎ *902/557812* ⊕ *www. catedraldesantiago.es* ⊠ *From €12.*

### Asociación Profesional de Guías Turísticos de Galicia

WALKING TOURS | Santiago's association of well-informed guides, an offshoot of the tourist office, can arrange walking tours of the city or tours to any place in Galicia. Spanish-language city tours depart Praza de Praterías at 12 and 6 and cost €12; private English tours can be arranged for around €80–€100. Look out for the yellow umbrella at the meeting point. Advance booking is mandatory either by phone or email (*info@guiasdegalicia.org*). ⊠ *Praza de Praterías, Santiago de Compostela* ☎ *606/985185* ⊕ *www.guiasdegalicia.org* ⊠ *From €12.*

## ⊙ Sights

### ★ Casco Antiguo (*Old Town*)

HISTORIC DISTRICT | The best way to spend your time in Santiago de Compostela is to simply wander the old town, losing yourself in its maze of narrow stone-paved streets and postage-stamp plazas. In the process you'll stumble on old *pazos* (manor houses), convents, and churches. The most beautiful pedestrian thoroughfares are Rúa do Vilar, Rúa do Franco, and Rúa Nova—portions of which are covered by arcaded walkways called *soportales,* designed to keep walkers out of the rain. Don't miss Praza da Quintana, bounded by the majestic walls of the cathedral and the 9th-century Monastery of San Paio de Antealtares, a favorite summer hangout for buskers and young travelers. ⊠ *Santiago de Compostela.*

### ★ Catedral de Santiago de Compostela
(*Cathedral of Santiago de Compostela*)
CHURCH | It's a new era for the Catedral: In 2020, the unsightly—and seemingly permanent—scaffolding came down to reveal one of Spain's most impressive (and painstakingly laborious) restorations. What was once a discolored, greenish, and weather-worn facade is now radiant, golden, and spotless—a befittingly grand finale to arduous pilgrimages. Although the facade is baroque, the interior holds one of the finest Romanesque sculptures in the world: the Pórtico de la Gloria, completed in 1188 by Maestro Mateo. It is the cathedral's original entrance, its three arches carved with figures from the Apocalypse, the Last Judgment, and purgatory. Below Jesus is a serene St. James, poised on a carved column. Look carefully and you can see five smooth grooves, formed by the millions of pilgrims who have placed their hands here over the centuries. On the back of the pillar, devotees lean forward to touch foreheads in the hope that his genius be shared.

St. James presides over the high altar in a bejeweled cloak, which pilgrims embrace upon arriving at the cathedral. The stairs behind the sculpture are the cathedral's focal point, surrounded by dazzling baroque decoration, sculpture, and drapery. The crypt beneath the altar, which houses the purported remains of James and his disciples St. Theodore and St. Athenasius, is generally closed to the public. A pilgrims' Mass is held daily at noon. ⊠ *Praza do Obradoiro, Santiago de Compostela* ☎ *902/044077 museum information and booking* ⊕ *www. catedraldesantiago.es/en* ⊠ *Cathedral free; €12 for museum, portico, and art exhibits.*

Santiago de Compostela's Praza do Obradoiro

## Centro Galego de Arte Contemporánea
(*Galician Center for Contemporary Art*)
ART MUSEUM | Santiago's premier contemporary art museum is housed in a stark yet elegant modern building that contrasts with Santiago's ancient feel. Inside, a lobby of gleaming Italian marble gives way to white-walled, high-ceilinged exhibition halls filled with mind-bending conceptual art—some of which might be a bit "out there" for the uninitiated. The temporary exhibits are excellent. Portuguese designer Álvaro Siza built this museum from smooth, angled granite to mirror the medieval convent of San Domingos de Bonaval next door. ⊠ *Rúa Valle Inclán 2, Santiago de Compostela* ☎ *981/546619* ⊕ *cgac.xunta.gal* ☒ *Free.*

## Cidade da Cultura
NOTABLE BUILDING | More than a decade in the making, Santiago's City of Culture is a controversial striated-stone-and-glass edifice on Monte Gaiás. It was meant to whisk Galician culture into the future but fell short: construction was stopped in 2013 due to delays and mismanagement. A pared-down version has since opened with a museum, an archive library, temporary art exhibits, and cultural attractions including concerts and talks. The design of the complex, by the American architect Peter Eisenman, takes inspiration from the shape of a scallop shell, the emblem of St. James. ⊠ *Monte Gaiás, Santiago de Compostela* ☎ *881/997565 museum information* ⊕ *www.cidadedacultura.gal* ☒ *Museum free, exhibits priced separately* ☉ *Museum closed Mon.*

## Hostal de los Reyes Católicos (*Hostel of the Catholic Monarchs*)
NOTABLE BUILDING | This hostel was built in 1499 by Ferdinand and Isabella to house the pilgrims who previously slept on Santiago's streets. It's the oldest refuge in the world and was converted from a hospital into a parador in 1954. The facade bears two Castilian coats of arms along with Adam, Eve, and various saints; inside, the four arcaded patios have gargoyle rainspouts said to be caricatures of 16th-century townsfolk.

Behind the lobby is the building's focal point, a Renaissance chapel in the shape of a cross. Thanks to the Parador Museo initiative, even non-overnight guests can behold these architectural treasures on a guided tour. ⊠ Praza do Obradoiro 1, Santiago de Compostela ⊕ www.civitatis. com/en/santiago-de-compostela/hostal-reyes-catolicas-tour ⊒ €12.

★ **Mercado de Abastos de Santiago** (Santiago City Market)

MARKET | Designed by architect Joaquín Vaquero Palacios, this charming stone building, built in 1941, houses a bustling traditional food market. It fills up around 11, when locals come to shop, but the operating hours are roughly 8 am to 3 pm. Whether you snap up local cheeses and tinned fish to take home or merely ogle Galicia's wondrous bounty of shellfish and produce, don't miss this market, one of Spain's most underrated foodie destinations. ⊠ Rua Ameas, Santiago de Compostela ☎ 981/583438 ⊕ www. mercadodeabastosdesantiago.com ⊘ Closed Sun.

**Museo do Pobo Galego** (Galician Folk Museum)

HISTORY MUSEUM | Next to the Centro Galego de Arte Contemporánea stands the medieval convent of San Domingos de Bonaval. The museum within holds photos, farm implements, traditional costumes, and other items illustrating aspects of traditional Galician life. The star attraction is the 13th-century self-supporting spiral granite staircase that still connects three floors. ⊠ San Domingos de Bonaval, Santiago de Compostela ☎ 981/583620 ⊕ www.museodopobo.gal ⊒ €4 (free Sun.) ⊘ Closed Mon.

**Museum of Pilgrimage and Santiago** (Pilgrimage Museum)

HISTORY MUSEUM | North of Acibechería (follow Ruela de Xerusalén) is the Museo das Peregrinacións containing Camino de Santiago iconography: sculptures, carvings, azabache (compact black coal,

or jet) items, and more. For an overview of the history of St. James, the cathedral, and the pilgrimage, as well as the Camino's role in the development of the city itself, this is a key visit. ⊠ Praza das Praterías 2, Santiago de Compostela ☎ 981/566110 ⊕ museoperegrinacions. xunta.gal ⊒ Free admission since the pandemic and at the time of writing. ⊘ Closed Mon. and some holidays.

**Pazo de Xelmírez** (Palace of Archbishop Xelmírez)

CASTLE/PALACE | Step into this rich 12th-century building to view an unusual example of Romanesque civic architecture, with a cool, clean, vaulted dining hall. The little figures carved on the corbels in this graceful, 100-foot-long space are drinking, eating, and listening to music with great medieval gusto. Each is different, so stroll around for a tableau of mealtime merriment.

■TIP→ The palace is attached to the cathedral. However, the entrance varies—it's best to ask at the cathedral museum where to enter the Pazo de Xelmírez. ⊠ Praza do Obradoiro, Santiago de Compostela ☎ 981/552985 ⊕ www.catedraldesantiago.es ⊒ €12, included in cathedral museum ticket.

**Praza do Obradoiro**

PLAZA/SQUARE | The imposing baroque facade of the cathedral dominates this sprawling square. Look for the stone slab in the center, which indicates "kilometer zero" on the pilgrimage trail. It is also the setting for the spectacular fireworks display on July 24 (the eve of St. James's Day). Traffic-free and flanked on all sides by historical buildings—including the 16th-century Hostal de los Reyes Católicos—it is the quintessential place to soak up the city's rich history. ⊠ Praza do Obradoiro, Santiago de Compostela.

# Santiago de Compostela

**KEY**

- **1** Sights
- **1** Restaurants
- **1** Hotels
- **i** Tourist Information

## Sights ▼

1. Casco Antiguo .......... **B4**
2. Catedral de Santiago de Compostela .......... **B3**
3. Centro Galego de Arte Contemporánea .......... **E1**
4. Cidade da Cultura ........ **E7**
5. Hostal de los Reyes Católicos ................ **A3**
6. Mercado de Abastos de Santiago ... **D4**
7. Museo do Pobo Galego .............. **E1**
8. Museum of Pilgrimage and Santiago ............ **D4**
9. Pazo de Xelmírez ....... **B3**
10. Praza do Obradoiro ..... **A3**

## Restaurants ▼

1. A Barrola ................. **A5**
2. A Tafona by Lucía Freitas ............. **E3**
3. Abastos 2.0 ............. **D4**
4. Carretas ................. **A2**
5. Casa Marcelo ........... **A3**
6. O Curro da Parra ........ **D3**
7. Restaurante Filigrana ... **A7**

## Hotels ▼

1. Hotel Costa Vella ......... **C1**
2. Hotel Monumento San Francisco ............ **B1**
3. Hotel Spa Relais & Châteaux A Quinta da Auga ................. **A7**
4. Parador Hostal dos Reis Católicos .......... **A3**
5. Pazo Cibrán ............... **E7**

# 🍴 Restaurants

## A Barrola

$$$ | SEAFOOD | A solid bet on a street packed with middling tourist eateries, this seafood restaurant has polished wood floors and a bustling terrace. The *caldo gallego, santiaguiños* (slipper lobsters), *arroz con bogavante* (rice with lobster), and seafood empanadas are superb—as any of the university-faculty regulars will tell you. **Known for:** raucous atmosphere; local delicacies; seafood feasts. $ *Average main: €20* ✉ *Rúa do Franco 29, Santiago de Compostela* 🕾 *981/577999* ⊕ *www.restaurantebarrola.com* ☽ *Closed Mon.*

## A Tafona by Lucía Freitas

$$$$ | SPANISH | This upscale restaurant by one of the region's most promising chefs serves elevated Galician cuisine in a bright, modern dining room with exposed stone walls. Menus feature a plethora of hyperlocal ingredients that have "first and last names," as the chef likes to say: Cambados oysters, Fisterra razor clams, Cachena beef, etc. **Known for:** finest Galician ingredients; experimental tasting menus; Michelin-starred dining. $ *Average main: €98* ✉ *Virxe da Cerca 7, Santiago de Compostela* 🕾 *981/562314* ⊕ *www.restauranteatafona.com* ☽ *Closed Mon. and Tues. No dinner Sun.*

## ★ Abastos 2.0

$$$$ | TAPAS | "From market to plate" is this *nueva cocina* restaurant's philosophy: chefs start and finish the day with an empty larder and a blank menu. The freshest fish and produce are handpicked at the neighboring Mercado de Abastos and coaxed into exciting dishes that defy tradition. **Known for:** contemporary design; market-fresh ingredients; inventive tapas. $ *Average main: €25* ✉ *Casetas 13–18, Pl. de Abastos, Santiago de Compostela* 🕾 *654/015937* ⊕ *www.abastosdouspuntocero.com* ☽ *Closed Sun.*

## Carretas

$$$$ | SEAFOOD | This casual seafood spot around the corner from the Hostal de los Reyes Católicos specializes in shellfish ranging from melt-in-your-mouth battered mini-scallops to a take-no-prisoners *variado de mariscos* platter with langoustines, king prawns, crab, and *percebes* (barnacles, a local delicacy). **Known for:** complimentary liqueurs with dessert; lively atmosphere; fresh seafood. $ *Average main: €25* ✉ *Rúa das Carretas 21, Santiago de Compostela* 🕾 *981/563111* ⊕ *www.restaurantecarretas.com* ☽ *No dinner Sun. Closed Mon.*

## ★ Casa Marcelo

$$$$ | FUSION | Fusing traditional Galician cuisine with Japanese, Mexican, and Peruvian, among others, Casa Marcelo whips up creatively plated dishes in an open-plan kitchen. The jovial dining area—always full and always loud—seats guests at long communal tables, a nod to the fact that the dishes are meant to be shared. **Known for:** extremely popular; impress-your-date cuisine; fusion tapas. $ *Average main: €30* ✉ *Rúa das Hortas 1, Santiago de Compostela* 🕾 *981/558580* ☽ *Closed Mon. and Tues. No dinner Sun.*

## O Curro da Parra

$$$ | SPANISH | Across from the market, this lively two-floor restaurant has exposed brick walls, wooden tables, and a menu of modern, seasonally driven dishes ranging from oyster *croquetas* to saucy local beef meatballs, plus an ever-changing variety of seafood preparations. **Known for:** fantastic wines; market-to-table cuisine; attractive plating. $ *Average main: €21* ✉ *Rúa Travesa 20, Santiago de Compostela* 🕾 *981/556059* ⊕ *www.ocurrodaparra.com.*

## ★ Restaurante Filigrana

$$$$ | SPANISH | Although the eggplant-colored walls, crystal chandeliers, and carefully chosen antique furniture evoke a traditional French dining room,

the food at this restaurant—attached to the A Quinta da Auga hotel—is unmistakably Galician. Try delicacies such as chestnut cream soup, fresh-caught hake, and bay scallops roasted in their shells with garlic-parsley oil. **Known for:** weekday lunch prix fixe; bucolic environs; old-school Galician fine dining. ⑤ *Average main: €25* ⊠ *Hotel Spa Relais & Châteaux A Quinta da Auga, Paseo da Amaia 23B, Santiago de Compostela* ☎ *981/534636* ⊕ *www.aquintadaauga.com.*

## 🛏 Hotels

### Hotel Costa Vella

$ | **B&B/INN** | **FAMILY** | At this classically Galician inn, there's an idyllic little garden and views of red-tile rooftops, the baroque convent of San Francisco, and the green hills beyond (ask for a garden view). **Pros:** charming views; warm, accommodating staff; ideal location. **Cons:** no elevator; thin walls and noise from other rooms carries; creaky floors. ⑤ *Rooms from: €87* ⊠ *Rúa Porta da Pena 17, Santiago de Compostela* ☎ *981/569530* ⊕ *www.costavella.com* ↻ *14 rooms* ⦿ *Free Breakfast.*

### Hotel Monumento San Francisco

$$$$ | **HOTEL** | Contemporary stained-glass windows add pizzazz to the solemn interior of this converted 13th-century convent that adjoins the church of the same name. **Pros:** indoor pool area with vaulted ceilings; independently owned; easily accessible by car. **Cons:** can get chilly at night; decor a bit corporate and dated; might be too quiet for some. ⑤ *Rooms from: €200* ⊠ *Campillo San Francisco 3, Santiago de Compostela* ☎ *981/581634* ⊕ *www.sanfranciscohm.com* ↻ *81 rooms* ⦿ *Free Breakfast.*

### ★ Hotel Spa Relais & Châteaux A Quinta da Auga

$$$$ | **HOTEL** | Tastefully converted from a 14th-century printing factory, this restored stone building is set among manicured gardens and beside the burbling Río Sar. Rooms drip with French crystal chandeliers and opulent antique furniture—handpicked by the owner—a level of attention to detail that's mirrored by the above-and-beyond service. **Pros:** destination restaurant; tranquil spa with pool; attentive service. **Cons:** small beds; Wi-Fi spotty in some rooms; 10-minute drive from town. ⑤ *Rooms from: €285* ⊠ *Paseo da Amaia 23B, Santiago de Compostela* ☎ *981/534636* ⊕ *www. aquintadaauga.com* ↻ *61 rooms* ⦿ *Free Breakfast.*

### ★ Parador Hostal dos Reis Católicos

$$$$ | **HOTEL** | One of the finest paradores in the country, this 15th-century building was once a royal hostel and hospital for sick pilgrims. **Pros:** views of Praza do Obradoiro; collectible antiques and paintings; excellent cuisine. **Cons:** pricey; popular with the tour-bus set; confusing corridors. ⑤ *Rooms from: €235* ⊠ *Praza do Obradoiro 1, Santiago de Compostela* ☎ *981/582200* ⊕ *www.parador.es* ↻ *137 rooms* ⦿ *Free Breakfast.*

### Pazo Cibrán

$ | **B&B/INN** | This comfortable 18th-century Galician manor house, 7 km (4 miles) from Santiago de Compostela, has an antiques-packed living room that overlooks gardens with magnolias, palms, and a bamboo walk. **Pros:** country hospitality; delightful gardens; picturesque old estate. **Cons:** only open for groups November–March; limited dining nearby; inaccessible without a car. ⑤ *Rooms from: €65* ⊠ *San Xulián de Sales 6, Vedra* ⟷ *Take N525 toward Ourense from Santiago and turn right at Km 11, after gas station* ☎ *981/511515* ⊕ *www.pazocibran. es* ↻ *11 rooms* ⦿ *Free Breakfast.*

## 🅨 Nightlife

Though weekends are always popping, Thursday is just as big a night in Santiago, since many students spend weekends at home with their families. For up-to-date info on concerts, films, and clubs, visit ⊕ *www.compostelacultura.gal.* Bars and seafood-centric tapas joints line the old streets south of the cathedral, particularly **Rúa do Franco, Rúa da Raiña,** and **Rúa do Vilar.** A great first stop, especially if you haven't eaten dinner, is **Rúa de San Clemente,** off Praza do Obradoiro, where several bars offer hefty free tapas with each drink.

## BARS

### Casa das Crechas

BARS | Drink to Galicia's Celtic roots here, with live music and Celtic wood carvings hanging from thick stone walls, while dolls of playful Galician witches ride their brooms above the bar. ⊠ *Vía Sacra 3, Santiago de Compostela* ☎ *981/560751* ⊕ *www.facebook.com/casadascrechas.*

### ★ O Filandón

BARS | Venture forth through the narrow cheese shop and you'll discover a cozy bar in the back, where an inviting log fire burns on chilly evenings and pilgrims gather and swap stories and pin handwritten notes to the walls (there are literally thousands). The *pinchos* (snacks) that como with drinks aro moro than gonerous: hunks of freshly baked bread with assorted charcuterie and cheeses. ⊠ *Rúa da Acibechería 6, Santiago de Compostela* ☎ *981/572738* ☙ *Closed Sun.*

### Pub Modus Vivendi

PUBS | Galicia's oldest pub is also one of its most unusual: Modus Vivendi is in a former stable. The old stone feeding trough is now a low table, and instead of stairs you walk on ridged stone inclines designed for the former occupants—horses and cattle. On weekends, the bar hosts live music (jazz, Spanish, Celtic) and sometimes storytelling. ⊠ *Praza Feixóo 1, Santiago de Compostela* ☎ *607/804140.*

## CAFÉS

With its melancholic and often chilly weather, Santiago is a great city for cozy coffee-drinking and people-watching. There are many cafés clustered around

the cathedral—particularly on Rúa Caldería and Rúa do Vilar.

### Café Casino

CAFÉS | Upholstered armchairs, mirrors, and wood paneling make this Art Nouveau café in a former casino especially atmospheric. ⊠ *Rúa do Vilar 35, Santiago de Compostela* ☎ *981/577503* ⊕ *www.cafecasino.gal.*

### Café Iacobus

CAFÉS | FAMILY | Dunk hot churros into melted chocolate at this cheery, snug café with stone walls and white tile floors. Another branch is at Rúa Caldería 42. ⊠ *Rúa da Senra 24, Santiago de Compostela* ☎ *981/585967.*

### Cafe Literarios

CAFÉS | Tranquil by day and lively at night, Cafe Literarios has colorful paintings, large windows, and plenty of outdoor tables. It overlooks the plaza. Stick to booze and coffee here as the food is distinctly underwhelming. ⊠ *Praza da Quintana 1, Santiago de Compostela* ☎ *981/882912.*

# Ourense and La Ribeira Sacra

*105 km (65 miles) southeast of Santiago de Compostela, 95 km (59 miles) east of Vigo.*

Despite the uninspiring backdrop of Ourense's new town, Galicia's third-largest city has bubbling thermal springs and an attractive medieval quarter whose animated streets, tapas bars, and plazas come alive on weekends. A smattering of notable historical monuments includes the colossal arches of the **Ponte Vella** (Roman bridge) spanning the Río Miño and the 13th-century Cathedral of San Martino. Between the cathedral and the Praza do Ferro is the **Os Vinos** area, ideal for tapas-hopping.

Ourense is a good starting point for exploring the dramatic landscapes of the Ribeira Sacra and Canón do Sil (Sil River Canyon), plus charming villages such as Allariz and Ribadavia. Ourense's surroundings brim with vineyards, trails, Romanesque churches, and monasteries.

**GETTING HERE AND AROUND**
RENFE and Monbus service Ourense from Santiago and Vigo in less than two hours. The A52 links Ourense to Vigo and Pontevedra, and the AG53 to Santiago.

**VISITOR INFORMATION**
**CONTACTS Lugo Tourist Office.** ✉ *Praza do Campo 11, Lugo* ☎ *982/251658.*

##  Sights

### Thermal Baths
**HOT SPRING** | Several hot springs along the Minho River at varying temperatures draw visitors from far and wide and are ideal for soaking weary muscles on the pilgrim trail. Some are free and others charge a small entrance fee. There is a tourist train that stops at the main baths, but the only ones guests can currently visit are in Outariz. At the time of writing, the other baths were closed due to new laws. ✉ *A Chavasqueira Thermal Baths, Campo da Feira, Ourense* ☎ *988/366064* ⊕ *www.turismodeourense.gal.*

## 🍴 Restaurants

### Fuentefría
$ | **SPANISH** | The *tostas* (open-faced sandwiches) are the tapa to try here. Whether your chosen toast-topper is smoked salmon, blue cheese, baked ham, or otherwise, you can't go wrong at this down-home bar. **Known for:** genial service; house-made empanada gallega; terrific tostas with local toppers. ⑤ *Average main: €8* ✉ *Rúa Viriato 6, Ourense* ☎ *697/487868.*

## 🛏 Hotels

### Casa Rural Torre Lombarda
$ | **B&B/INN** | Though this rustic, well-kept inn is a mere 20-minute drive from the city center, its natural surroundings and open-armed hospitality make you feel like you're much farther afield. **Pros:** old mill on-site; idyllic country escape not far from the city; free parking. **Cons:** no breakfast or 24-hour service; ill-suited for travelers with limited mobility; creaky floorboards. ⑤ *Rooms from: €59* ✉ *Praza Torre Lombarda* ☎ *988/554005* ⊕ *www.torrelombarda.com* ⇄ *9 rooms* ⦿l *No Meals.*

### Hotel Carrís Cardenal Quevedo
$$ | **HOTEL** | Steps from restaurants, shops, and lively tapas bars is this city-center hotel with smartly decorated rooms that exude an urban sensibility—think crisp white bedding and polished wooden floors. **Pros:** prime location; modern bells and whistles; good restaurant. **Cons:** uninspiring views; tight parking space; no in-room coffee. ⑤ *Rooms from: €105* ✉ *Rúa Cardenal Quevedo 28–30, Ourense* ☎ *988/375523* ⊕ *www.carrishoteles.com* ⇄ *39 rooms* ⦿l *Free Breakfast.*

### ★ Parador de Santo Estevo
$$$ | **HOTEL** | Clinging to the edge of the Canón do Sil, this parador, carefully built into the colossal 12th-century Benedictine Monasterio de Santo Estevo, stands out for its atmospheric setting and spectacular vistas. **Pros:** magnificent views; spa on site; historical sanctuary surrounded by nature. **Cons:** remote; popular wedding venue; mediocre food. ⑤ *Rooms from: €150* ✉ *Monasterio de Santo Estevo, Ourense* ⊹ *Off CV323 beyond Luintra, 26 km (16 miles) northeast of Ourense* ☎ *988/010110* ⊕ *www.parador.es* ⊙ *Closed Dec.–Feb.* ⇄ *77 rooms.*

# Lugo

*102 km (63 miles) east of Santiago de Compostela.*

Off the A6 freeway, Galicia's oldest provincial capital is notable for its 2-km (1½-mile) **Roman wall.** The beautifully preserved ramparts surround the old town. A walkway on top has good views. The baroque *ayuntamiento* (town hall) has a magnificent rococo facade overlooking the tree-lined **Praza Maior.** There's a good view of the Río Miño valley from the **Parque Rosalía de Castro,** outside the Roman walls near the cathedral, which mixes Romanesque, Gothic, baroque, and neoclassical styles.

## GETTING HERE AND AROUND
**CONTACTS Estación de Autobuses Lugo.** ⊠ *Prazo da Constitución, Lugo.* **Estación de Tren Lugo.** ⊠ *Pl. Conde de Fontao, Lugo* ☎ 912/320320 *RENFE* ⊕ *www. renfe.com.*

## VISITOR INFORMATION
**CONTACTS Lugo Tourist Office.** ⊠ *Praza do Campo 11, Lugo* ☎ *982/251658.*

## ◉ Sights

### City Walls
**PROMENADE** | A UNESCO World Heritage Site, the 3rd-century Roman walls encircling Lugo provide a picturesque 2-km (1-mile) walk and the best bird's-eye views of the town. There are 85 towers and 10 gates, and the walls have four staircases and two ramps providing access to the top. ⊠ *Lugo.*

## ⦿ Restaurants

### Paprica
$$$$ | SPANISH | With a focus on top-notch sourcing and modern takes on traditional Galician fare, this eatery offers creative, seasonal dishes in a contemporary setting. À la carte options are available, but the superb (€62) tasting menu is definitely worthwhile. **Known for:** local sourcing; affordable tasting menu; Galician fusion. $ *Average main: €25* ⊠ *Nóreas 10, Lugo* ☎ *982/255824* ⊕ *www.paprica.es* ⦿ *Closed Sun. and Mon.*

## 🛏 Hotels

### Fervenza Casa Grande
$ | B&B/INN | This centuries-old manor house situated 14 km (8 miles) south of Lugo is tucked away in a forest by the Río Miño. **Pros:** intimate feel; ideal hideaway for outdoorsy types; restaurant that's a destination in itself. **Cons:** inadequate soundproofing; rooms could use a refurb; removed from town. $ *Rooms from: €76* ⊠ *Ctra. Lugo–Paramo, Km 11, Lugo* ☎ *982/151610* ⊕ *www.fervenza. com* ⇄ *9 rooms.*

# Muxía

*75 km (47 miles) northwest of Santiago de Compostela, 30 km (18 miles) north of Fisterra.*

Muxía is a tiny (population: 4,700), far-flung fishing village surrounded by the soaring rocky cliffs and virgin beaches of the Costa da Morte. It's also close to many hiking trails that meander through lush green forests, making it a perfect rural getaway.

## ◉ Sights

### O Camiño dos Faros (*Way of the Lighthouses*)
**SCENIC DRIVE** | Three lighthouses can be visited by car within an hour and a half on this route. Expect extraordinary views of the vertiginous rocky cliffs and churning waters that earned this part of Galicia its nickname, Costa da Morte. Start at the Faro de Cabo Touriñán, which guards a narrow peninsula marking what was once believed to be the westernmost

point of continental Europe. A 20-minute drive away is the Faro da Punta da Barca, a stone lighthouse built in 1926 alongside the 16th-century Virxe da Barca sanctuary. Finish with Faro de Cabo Vilán, which juts dramatically above a red-rock promontory; it was the first in Spain to run by electricity. Alternatively the 200-km (124-mile) route can be hiked on a well-marked trail that runs from Malpica to Finisterre. ⊠ *Muxia* ⊕ *www.camino-dosfaros.com/en.*

##  Beaches

### Praia de Nemiña

**BEACH** | A favorite with surfers and sport fisherman, this somewhat undiscovered beach is buffered from the wind by green forested hills on either side. It's a fine place for a midday picnic or romantic stroll at sunset on fine white sand. **Amenities:** showers. **Best for:** sunset; surfing; walking. ⊠ *Muxia.*

## 🛏 Hotels

### Casa Fontequeiroso

**$$** | **B&B/INN** | Surrounded by green hills and pine forests and a five-minute drive from the beaches of Costa da Morte, this bed-and-breakfast has simple yet tasteful rooms with wooden furniture and red-tile floors. **Pros:** bucolic surroundings; bicycles available for guests; owner is a fantastic cook. **Cons:** no amenities nearby; lunch and dinner must be prebooked; remote. ⑤ *Rooms from: €95* ⊠ *Lugar de Queiroso, Nemiña* ☎ *981/748946* ⊕ *www.casafontequeiroso.com* ⏎ *6 rooms* ⦿| *Free Breakfast.*

# Fisterra

*50 km (31 miles) west of Santiago de Compostela, 75 km (48 miles) southwest of A Coruña.*

There was a time when this windswept outcrop over raging waters was thought to be the end of the earth—*finis terrae*—and many Spaniards continue to believe, incorrectly, that Fisterra is the westernmost point of Europe (that point is actually in Portugal). Despite this, many Camino pilgrims opt to hike to the "end of the earth" from Santiago de Compostela; indeed, arriving at Fisterra's picturesque lighthouse, beyond which there is nothing but the open Atlantic, is thrilling. The town all but shuts down in winter, but in summer it's a pleasant seaside resort with an attractive harbor.

**VISITOR INFORMATION**
**CONTACTS Fisterra Turismo.** ⊠ *Plaza da Constitución Nº31, Fisterra* 🕾 *627/239731* ⊕ *www.concellofisterra. gal/turismo/oficina_turismo/en.*

##  Sights

**Santa María das Areas**
CHURCH | Aside from legends, another draw in this tiny seaside town is its main plaza and the 12th-century church of Santa María das Areas. Romanesque, Gothic, and baroque elements combine in an impressive (if gloomy) facade. ⊠ *Rúa Alcalde Fernández 14, Fisterra.*

##  Hotels

**Hotel Naturaleza Mar da Ardora**
$$ | HOTEL | A two-minute walk from Mar de Fora Beach, this boutique hotel is surrounded by gardens and boasts stunning beach views. **Pros:** sweeping sea views; dinner on the terrace; on-site spa. **Cons:** dated interiors; noise carries between rooms; relatively pricey. ⑤ *Rooms from: €125* ⊠ *Playa de la Potiña 15, Fisterra*

🕾 *66 //64 1304* ⊕ *www.hotelmardaardora. com* 🖙 *6 rooms* ⦿| *Free Breakfast.*

# Muros

*65 km (40 miles) southwest of Santiago de Compostela, 55 km (34 miles) southeast of Fisterra.*

Muros is a popular summer resort with arcaded streets framed by Gothic arches. The quiet alleys of the old town reveal well-preserved Galician granite houses, but the real action takes place when fishing boats return from the mussel-breeding platforms to hawk their wares at the evening fish auction (usually 4 pm), announced by siren. Anyone is welcome, but only wholesalers can buy. Trays overflowing with octopus tendrils and cod carcasses line the floor, which is splattered with squid ink and fish blood (stand far away or wear rubber boots). Good beaches nearby include Praia de San Francisco and Praia da Area.

**GETTING HERE AND AROUND**
Monbus runs frequent buses between Muros and Santiago de Compostela and A Coruña. By car, take the AP9 north from Vigo and Pontevedra (just under 2 hours away) or the AC550 west from Santiago de Compostela and A Coruña (1½ hours).

**VISITOR INFORMATION**
**CONTACTS Muros Tourist Office.** ⊠ *Curro da Praza 1, Muros* 🕾 *981/826050* ⊕ *www.murosturismo.gal.*

# Cambados

*34 km (21 miles) north of Pontevedra, 61 km (37 miles) southwest of Santiago de Compostela.*

This breezy seaside town has a charming, almost entirely residential old quarter and is ground zero for Albariño

# Wine Tasting in Rías Baixas

## Albariño Wine

Rías Baixas, in southern Galicia, is the most important Denomination of Origin (D.O.) in the province and the largest global producer of Albariño, a crisp, young, and aromatic varietal that has international prestige. Albariño has been compared to riesling for its vibrant acidity, to Petit Manseng and Viognier for its peach and apricot notes, and to Pinot Gris for its floral bouquet. Its dry, slate-y qualities sing alongside local seafood.

Vineyards and bodegas are spread throughout Pontevedra province and beyond, with a particularly high density in Cambados, a major Albariño-producing area. With more than 7,000 growers and 20,000 individual vineyard plots in Rías Baixas, planning a wine trip to the region can feel overwhelming. Happily, free resources like **Ruta do Viño Rías Baixas** (⊕ www.rutadelvinoriasbaixas. com/en) and **Rías Baixas Wines** (⊕ www.riasbaixaswines.com) are available to help if you wish to self-guide. Set tours are a safer bet if you have limited time or want to learn as much as possible.

## Wine Tours

**Boots & Grapes Tours** Private custom tours of two bodegas in the Salnes region, including an English-speaking guide, run at approximately €340 (per couple) for four to five hours. ⊠ Pontevedra ☎ 637/158786 ⊕ www.bootsandgrapestours.com.

**North West Iberia Wine Tours** One-, three-, and six-day wine tours include transport, admissions, lunch, and wine tasting at two different locations as well as a visit to a local pazo (estate) and camellia garden. ⊠ Rúa Enrique Marinas Romero 30–5H, A Coruña ☎ 881/879910 ⊕ www.northwestiberiawinetours.com ⊡ From €180.

winemaking. The impressive main square, **Praza de Fefiñáns,** is bordered by an imposing bodega. Cambados's **cemetery** is one of the most picturesque in Spain: its tombs surround a mossy medieval church ruin.

### GETTING HERE AND AROUND

Cambados is less than an hour from either Santiago de Compostela (to the north), or Vigo and Pontevedra (to the south) all via the AP9.

## ● Sights

### Bodegas del Palacio de Fefiñanes

WINERY | Set in a 16th-century stone palace, this illustrious winery has been making wine since the 17th century and crafts textbook Albariños. The 1583 Albariño de Fefiñanes sees five years in Bordeaux barrels. Guided tours including tastings range from €12 to €24. Reservations recommended. ⊠ Pl. de Fefiñanes, Cambados ☎ 986/542204 ⊕ www. fefinanes.com ⊡ From €12.

### Don Olegario

WINERY | This award-winning, family-run winery offers an intimate tour followed by a tasting on the terrace overlooking the vineyards. ⊠ Refoxos, Corbillón, Cambados ☎ 986/520886 ⊕ www.donolegario.com ⊡ From €8 ⌂ Reservations essential.

### Pazo de Rubianes

GARDEN | The jewel of this property is the camellia garden, one of the largest and most impressive collections of flowers in the world. The camellias bloom

November, May, and peak February–April. The 15th-century manor house is decadently furnished and also worth a visit, as are the attached bodega and chapel. Gourmet picnic baskets with local products can be assembled for a leisurely lunch amid the vines and flowers. There are also guided tours, which last about two hours and include the gardens, winery, *pazo*, chapel, and a tasting. ⊠ *Rúa do Pazo 7, Cambados* ☎ 986/510534 ⊕ *www.pazoderubianes. com* ✉ *Self-guided tour (by appointment) free, guided tour €18.*

## 🍴 Restaurants

### María José

**$$ | SEAFOOD |** Across from the parador, this long-established restaurant produces inventive dishes like scallop salad, mango soup with mascarpone ice cream, and salmon with anchovy mayonnaise. Specialties include *arroz de marisco caldoso* (shellfish, stock, and rice). **Known for:** terrace tables with sea views; abundant portions at economical prices; unironic throwback 90s dining room. ⑤ *Average main: €14* ⊠ *C. San Gregorio 2–1, Cambados* ☎ 986/542281 ⊗ *No dinner Sun.–Tues.*

## 🛏 Hotels

### Parador de Cambados

**$$$ | HOTEL |** This airy mansion's rooms are warmly furnished with wrought-iron lamps, area rugs, and full-length wood shutters over small-pane windows. **Pros:** easily accessible; excellent dining; outdoor pool. **Cons:** limited parking; rooms showing wear; occasionally surly staff. ⑤ *Rooms from: €130* ⊠ *Paseo Calzada, Cambados* ☎ 986/542250 ⊕ *www.para-dor.es* ✉ *58 rooms* ⦿ *No Meals.*

### ★ Quinta de San Amaro

**$$$ | HOTEL |** This quirky rural hotel is a great base for wine tourism, thanks to the gorgeous vineyard views and

complimentary visit to a local winery. **Pros:** outstanding service and memorable restaurant; beautiful views; in the heart of wine country. **Cons:** small swimming pool; somewhat remote at a 15-minute drive from Cambados; need a car to get here. ⑤ *Rooms from: €140* ⊠ *Rúa San Amaro 6, Cambados* ☎ 630/877590 ⊕ *www.quintadesanamaro.com* ✉ *14 rooms* ⦿ *Free Breakfast.*

## 🛍 Shopping

### Cucadas

**CRAFTS |** Head to this crafts shop for its large selection of baskets, shells, copper items, and lace. ⊠ *Praza de Fefiñáns 8, Cambados* ☎ 986/542511 ⊕ *www. facebook.com/CUCADAS.1985.*

# Pontevedra

*135 km (84 miles) southeast of Fisterra, 59 km (37 miles) south of Santiago de Compostela.*

At the mouth of a *ría* (estuary), Pontevedra is a delightful home base for exploring Rías Baixas. Its well-preserved old quarter is a dense warren of pedestrian-only streets and handsome plazas flanked with elegant stone buildings, many of which are festooned with cascading flowers. The city got its start as a Roman settlement (its name comes from an old Roman bridge over the Río Lérez). In the 16th century it became an influential hub of fishing and international trade. Today, its streets and plazas are awash with charming bars and restaurants. Weekends are particularly busy.

### GETTING HERE AND AROUND

RENFE and Monbus offer quick, frequent service between Vigo and Pontevedra, a half-hour journey; the same bus and train routes also link Pontevedra to Santiago de Compostela and A Coruña to the north along the AP9.

**CONTACTS Estación de Autobuses Ponte-vedra.** ⊠ *Calle de la Estación, Pontevedra* ☎ *986/852408.*

## VISITOR INFORMATION

**CONTACTS Pontevedra Tourist Office.** ⊠ *Pl. de España 1, Pontevedra* ☎ *986/090890* ⊕ *www.visit-pontevedra.com.*

# ◉ Sights

### Adega Eidos

**WINERY** | This sleek winery overlooks Sanxenxo harbor and produces a modern, fruit-forward style of Albariño harvested from old, ungrafted vines grown on granite slopes. Only natural yeasts are used in the fermentation. Tours including nibbles, and a wine tasting cost approximately €5. ⊠ *Padriñán 65, Sanxenxo, Pontevedra* ☎ *986/690009* ⊕ *www. adegaeidos.com* 🎫 *From €7.*

### Museo de Pontevedra

**HISTORY MUSEUM** | Housed in two 18th-century mansions connected by a stone bridge, this museum includes exquisite Celtic jewelry, silver from all over the world, and several large model ships. The original kitchen, with a stone fireplace, is intact; below, descend steep wooden stairs to the reconstructed captain's chamber on the battleship *Numancia,* which limped back to Spain after the Dos de Mayo battle with Peru in 1866. Complete the loop by going upstairs in the first building, where there are Spanish, Italian, and Flemish paintings. ⊠ *Rúa Padre Amoedo Carballo 3, Pontevedra* ☎ *986/804100* ⊕ *www.museo.depo.gal* 🎫 *Free* ☉ *Closed Mon.*

### Pazo Baión

**WINERY** | Surrounded by Albariño vineyards, this 15th-century stone manor house stands in pleasant contrast to its 100-year-old boutique wine cellar, built in an Art Deco style. Winemaker José Hidalgo produces a silky Albariño with notes of citrus and floral aromas here. Reservations are required. ⊠ *Abelleira 6, Vilanova de Arousa, Pontevedra* ☎ *636/800234* ⊕ *www.pazobaion.com* 🎫 *From €15.*

### Real Basilica de Santa María la Mayor

**CHURCH** | The 16th-century seafarers' basilica has lovely, sinuous vaulting and, at the back of the nave, a Romanesque portal. There's also an 18th-century Christ by the Galician sculptor Ferreiro. ⊠ *Av. de Santa María 24, Pontevedra* ☎ *986/866185* 🎫 *Free.*

# 🍽 Restaurants

### Casa Solla

**$$$$** | **SPANISH** | Book a table at this terrace garden restaurant 2 km (1 mile) outside of town toward O Grove for a fine-dining culinary tour of the region. Local mackerel, chorizo, hake, and beef are mainstays here, as are traditional Galician cheeses and wines. **Known for:** ideal for special occasions; eye-popping plating; tasting menu only. ⑤ *Average main: €108* ⊠ *Av. Sineiro 7, San Salvador de Poio* ☎ *986/872884* ☉ *Closed Mon. No dinner Thurs. and Sun.*

### La Navarra

**$** | **TAPAS** | Join the locals leaning on wine-barrel tables to watch soccer and snack on Galician cheeses and spicy chorizo, which hangs from ceiling racks above the bar. **Known for:** good charcuterie and tostas; raucous sports bar; local hangout. ⑤ *Average main: €10* ⊠ *Rúa Princesa 13, Pontevedra* ☎ *986/851254* ☉ *Closed Sun.*

# 🛏 Hotels

### Parador de Pontevedra

**$$$** | **HOTEL** | A 16th-century manor house in the heart of the old quarter, this parador has guest rooms with recessed windows embellished with lace curtains and large wooden shutters; some face a small rose garden. **Pros:** interesting collection of bric-a-brac; free parking; tranquil yet central location. **Cons:** dungeon-y rooms; limited parking; confusing corridors. $ *Rooms from: €140* ⊠ *Rúa Barón 19, Pontevedra* ☎ *986/855800* ⊕ *www. parador.es* ⤴ *47 rooms* ⦿ *No Meals.*

# Vigo

*31 km (19 miles) south of Pontevedra, 90 km (56 miles) south of Santiago de Compostela.*

Vigo's formidable port is choked with trawlers and fishing boats and lined with clanging shipbuilding yards. The city's gritty exterior gives way to a compact and lively center that clings to a tiered hill rising over an ancient Roman settlement. A jumble of modernist buildings and red-roofed fisherman's houses hide the narrow streets of Vigo's appealing *casco vello* (old town). Vigo's highlights can be explored in a few hours.

Fishing is central to the livelihood of thousands who live and work in Vigo, and its fish market handles some of the largest quantities of fresh fish in Europe, which is consumed across the continent. From 10 to 3:30 daily, on **Rúa Pescadería** in the barrio of **La Piedra,** Vigo's famed *ostreras*—a group of rubber-gloved fisherwomen who have been peddling fresh oysters to passersby for more than decades—shuck the bushels of oysters hauled into port that morning. Competition has made them expert hawkers who cheerfully badger all who walk by their pavement stalls. When you buy half a dozen (for around €10), the women plate them and plunk a lemon on top; you can then take your catch into any nearby restaurant and turn it into a meal. A short stroll southwest of the old town brings you to the fishermen's barrio of **El Berbés.** Facing the port, it has several seafood restaurants, most with outdoor tables in summer.

## GETTING HERE AND AROUND

A small airport connects Vigo to a handful of destinations, like Madrid and Barcelona, but trains and buses are your best bet for transportation within Galicia. Northbound RENFE trains leave on the hour for Pontevedra, Santiago de Compostela, and A Coruña, making stops at smaller towns in between. Monbus and ALSA also connect Vigo to the same destinations via the AP9, while AUTNA runs a daily shuttle south to Porto and its international airport, a 2½-hour trip.

**CONTACTS Vigo Bus Station.** ⊠ *Av. de Madrid 57, Vigo* ☎ *986/373411.* **Vigo Train Station–Urzáiz.** ⊠ *Rúa Via Nte., Vigo* ☎ *912/320320 RENFE* ⊕ *www.renfe. com.*

## VISITOR INFORMATION

**CONTACTS Vigo Tourist Office.** ⊠ *Rúa López de Neira 8, Vigo* ☎ *986/224757* ⊕ *www.turismodevigo.org.*

## ◉ Sights

### ★ Islas Cíes

**ISLAND** | The Cíes Islands, 35 km (21 miles) west of Vigo, are among Spain's best-kept secrets. They form a pristine nature preserve that's one of the last unspoiled refuges on the Spanish coast. Starting on weekends in May and then daily June–late September, Naviera Mar de Ons (☎ *986/225272,* ⊕ *www. mardeons.com*) runs about eight boats from Vigo's harbor (subject to weather conditions), returning later in the day, for the €21 round-trip fare (tickets must be booked in advance on the website). The 45-minute ride brings you to white-sand beaches surrounded by turquoise waters brimming with marine life; there's also great birding. The only way to get around is your own two feet: it takes about an hour to cross the main island. If you want to stay overnight, there's a designated camping area. The tourist office has up-to-date information on timetables and crossings.

■ TIP➔ It is mandatory for travelers to the Cíes Islands to first obtain authorization from the Xunta de Galicia online portal (autorizacionillasatlanticas.xunta.gal/illasr). ⊠ Estación Marítima, Vigo ⊕ www.campingislascies.com ⊠ €20.

## Museo de Arte Contemporánea de Vigo (MARCO) (Museum of Contemporary Art)

ART MUSEUM | Housed in a refurbished prison on Vigo's main shopping drag, this museum doesn't have a permanent collection but hosts intriguing temporary exhibitions and solo shows of featured artists. ⊠ Rúa do Príncipe 54, Vigo ☎ 986/113900 ⊕ www.marcovigo.com ⊠ Free ⊙ Closed Mon.

## Parque Monte del Castro

CITY PARK | South of Vigo's old town, this is a quiet, stately park with sandy paths, palm trees, mossy embankments, and stone benches. Atop a series of steps are the remains of an old fort and a mirador (lookout) with fetching views of Vigo's coastline and the Islas Cíes. Along its shady western side lies the Castro de Vigo, the remains of Vigo's first Celtic settlement, dating to the 3rd century BC. ⊠ Av. Marqués de Alcedo, between Praza de España and Praza do Rei, Vigo ⊠ Free ⊙ Castro de Vigo closed Sun. and Mon. ⌨ Reservations required for Castro de Vigo.

## 🍴 Restaurants

### Cocedero Bar La Piedra

$ | SPANISH | Fancy it ain't, but this jovial tapas bar is where you can devour the freshest catch from the Rúa Pescadería fisherwomen, and it does a roaring lunch trade with Vigo locals. Expect heaping plates of marisco (shellfish) and scallops with roe at market prices, plus fresh and fruity Albariño, its trusty sidekick. Known for: simple, down-to-earth atmosphere; front-row seats for oyster hawkers; fresh seafood. ⑤ Average main: €10 ⊠ Rúa Pescadería 3, Vigo ☎ 986/431204.

### El Mosquito

$$$$ | SPANISH | Signed photos from the likes of King Juan Carlos and Julio Iglesias cover the walls of this elegant stone-wall restaurant opened in 1928. Specialties include lenguado a la plancha (grilled sole) and navajas (razor clams). Known for: extensive wine cellar; caramel flan; dependably good seafood. ⑤ Average main: €25 ⊠ Praza da Pedra 4, Vigo ☎ 616/504544 ⊕ www.elmosquitorestaurante.com ⊙ No dinner Sun.

### Tapas Areal

$$$ | TAPAS | This ample and lively bar flanked by ancient stone and exposed redbrick walls is a good spot for tapas and beer as well as Albariños and Ribeiros. Known for: fresh and modern tapas; good Albariño selection; buzzing atmosphere. ⑤ Average main: €18 ⊠ Rúa México 36, Vigo ☎ 986/418643 ⊕ www.tapasareal.com ⊙ Closed Sun.

## 🛏 Hotels

### Gran Hotel Nagari Boutique and Spa

$$$ | HOTEL | A short walk from the harbor, this boutique hotel has a glitzy early-aughts aesthetic in public spaces—think colorful plastic swivel chairs and gold brocade curtains—though guest rooms are more neutral, with white linens and sparse wall art; upgrades add in-room jacuzzis. Pros: a short stroll from the old town; excellent spa; rooftop pool with city and Atlantic views. Cons: confusing panel controls in rooms; spa and pool not complimentary; parking not complimentary. ⑤ Rooms from: €140 ⊠ Pl. de Compostela 21, Vigo ☎ 986/211111 ⊕ www.granhotelnagari.com ⇨ 63 rooms.

## 🍸 Nightlife

The streets around Praza de Compostela and the pedestrian-only Rúa Montero Ríos, down toward the waterfront, come alive in the early evening for drinks and tapas. Night owls should check out the snazzier cocktail bars in the Areal district (along Rúa Areal and Rúa de Rosalía de Castro) or the rock and indie scene in the Churruca neighborhood (Rúa Rogelio Abalde, Rúa Churruca) from midnight onward, where you can often stumble across live music.

### La Trastienda del Cuatro

**WINE BARS** | Around the corner from Praza de Compostela, this trendy wine bar (with a good upscale restaurant in the back) has a wide-reaching wine list complemented by modern tapas with winks to Asian and Latin cuisines. ⊠ *Rúa de Pablo Morillo 4, Vigo* ☎ *986/115881* ⊕ *www.latrastiendadelcuatro.com.*

## 🛍 Shopping

There's a large shopping center next to where the cruise ships dock. Close by you'll find Mercado da Pedra, the city's main market, where clothing, food, and a variety of goods are sold. For souvenirs, head to the old town, where there is an abundance of artisanal shops selling locally crafted leather, wood, and ceramics. On the aptly named Rúa Cesteiros (literally "street of basketmakers"), you can check out Vigo's famous handwoven baskets. Vigo's commercial shopping area is centered on Rúa Principe.

## 🏃 Activities

There are several horseback riding clubs in the hills around Vigo. The Galician Equestrian Federation is an excellent source of information.

### HORSEBACK RIDING
#### Granja O Castelo

**HORSEBACK RIDING** | The rural hotel Granja O Castelo conducts horseback rides along the main pilgrimage routes to Santiago, including those departing O Cebreiro and Braga (Portugal). ⊠ *Castelo 41, Ponte Caldelas* ☎ *986/425937, 608/381334* ⊕ *www.caminoacaballo.com* ➹ *from €1,395 for 4 days.*

# Baiona

*12 km (8 miles) southwest of Vigo.*

At the southern end of the AP9 freeway and the Ría de Vigo, Baiona (Bayona in Castilian) is a summer hideaway for affluent Galicians. When Columbus's *Pinta* landed here in 1492, Baiona became the first town to receive the news of the discovery of the so-called New World. Once a castle, **Monte Real** is one of Spain's most popular paradores; walk around the battlements for superb views. Inland from Baiona's waterfront is the jumble of streets that make up Paseo Marítimo; head west for seafood restaurants and lively cafés and bars. Calle Ventura Misa is one of the main drags. On your way into or out of town, check out Baiona's **Roman bridge.** The best nearby beach is Praia de América, north of town toward Vigo.

### GETTING HERE AND AROUND

ATSA buses leave every 30 minutes from Vigo, bound for Baiona and Nigrán. By car, take the AG57 from Vigo to the north or the PO340 from Tui to the southeast.

## 🛏 Hotels

### ★ Parador de Baiona

**$$$$** | **HOTEL** | This baronial parador, positioned on a hill within the perimeter walls of a medieval castle, has plush rooms, some with balconies and ocean views toward the Islas Cíes. **Pros:** stupendous medieval architecture; luxurious bathrooms; views of the ría. **Cons:** dark rooms; dinner can be disappointing; especially pricey for rooms with sea views. ⑤ *Rooms from: €250* ⊠ *Av. Arquitecto Jesús Valverde, Baiona* ☎ *986/355000* ⊕ *www.parador.es* ➹ *122 rooms* ❙⊘❙ *Free Breakfast.*

### Pazo da Touza

**$$** | **HOTEL** | This 16th-century stone manor house is surrounded by manicured gardens and has a terrace that looks out

The coastline of Baiona is one of the first things the crew of Columbus's ship the saw when they returned from their discovery of America.

onto a labyrinth of hedges. **Pros:** historical manor house; tranquil setting; immaculate gardens. **Cons:** popular wedding venue; some traffic noise from nearby road; 15-minute drive from Baiona. ⑤ *Rooms from: €110* ✉ *Rúa dos Pazos 119* ☎ *986/383047* ⊕ *www.pazodatouza. info* ⇨ *8 rooms* ⦿ *No Meals.*

# Tui

*14 km (9 miles) southeast of Baiona, 26 km (16 miles) south of Vigo.*

The steep, narrow streets of Tui, noble with their emblazoned mansions, are a reminder that this was one of the seven capitals of the Galician kingdom. Today it's an important border town; the mountains of Portugal are visible from the cathedral. Across the river in Portugal, the old fortress town of Valença contains reasonably priced shops, bars, restaurants, and a hotel with splendid views.

## GETTING HERE AND AROUND
From Vigo, take the scenic coastal route PO552, which goes up the banks of the Río Miño along the Portuguese border or, if time is short, jump on the inland A55; both routes lead to Tui.

## ◉ Sights

### Tui Cathedral
**CHURCH** | A crucial building during the medieval wars between Castile and Portugal, Tui's 12th-century Romanesque cathedral looks like a fortress. Its majestic cloisters surround a lush formal garden. Rooftop ("Cubiertas") tours take place every day but Sunday at 1:30 pm from July to September. ✉ *Pl. de San Fernando, Tui* ☎ *986/600511* ⊕ *www. catedraldetui.com* ⊠ *Free, €9 for rooftop tour.*

## 📖 Hotels

**Parador de Tui**

$$$ | HOTEL | This stately gran-ite-and-chestnut hotel on the bluffs overlooking the Miño is filled with local art, and the rooms are furnished with antiques including four-poster beds. **Pros:** enticing gardens; swimming pool (seasonal); restaurant with excellent seafood. **Cons:** dark rooms; somewhat pricey; a bit of a walk from Tui proper. ⑤ *Rooms from:* €150 ⊠ *Av. Portugal, Tui* ☎ *986/600300* ⊕ *www.parador.es* ⊘ *Closed Jan.–mid-Feb.* ⇨ *32 rooms* ◎ *No Meals.*

# A Coruña

*57 km (35 miles) north of Santiago de Compostela.*

One of Spain's busiest ports, A Coruña is often (mistakenly) overlooked by travelers. While the weather can be fierce, wet, and windy, there are frequent bouts of sunshine. The dramatic weather, along with a thriving commercial center and intriguing historic quarter, gives the city and its people a distinctive personality. It is also the wealthiest city in Galicia.

A Coruña takes pride in its gastronomy, and there is a buzzing nightlife scene as well as a host of interesting sights such as the world's oldest still-functioning lighthouse. The city's shining jewel is its emblematic row of glass-enclosed, white-paned galleries on the houses that line the harbor—a remarkable sight when the light catches them on a sunny day.

## GETTING HERE AND AROUND

The A9 motorway provides excellent access to and from Santiago de Compostela, Pontevedra, Vigo, and Portugal, while Spain's north coast and France are accessible along the N634.

Buses run every hour from A Coruña to Santiago. Trains also operate on an hourly basis to Santiago and Pontevedra from the city's San Cristóbal train station; Madrid can be reached in five hours on the high-speed AVE.

Outside the old town, the city's local buses shuttle between the Dársena de la Marina seafront and more far-flung attractions such as the Torre de Hércules lighthouse.

**CONTACTS A Coruña Bus Station.** ⊠ *Rúa Caballeros 21, A Coruña* ☎ *981/184335.* **A Coruña Train Station.** ⊠ *Av. Ferrocaril 2, A Coruña* ☎ *912/320320* ⊕ *www.renfe. com.*

### VISITOR INFORMATION

**CONTACTS A Coruña Tourist Office.** ⊠ *Pl. de María Pita 6, A Coruña* ☎ *981/923093* ⊕ *www.turismocoruna.com.*

## 👁 Sights

**Aquarium Finisterrae**

AQUARIUM | FAMILY | Situated next to the Torre de Hércules, this aquarium features interactive exhibits, an underwater hall, and a seal colony. A fitting tribute to Galicia's relationship with the sea, it focuses on the ecosystems of the Atlantic and Galician coast. ⊠ *Paseo Alcalde Francisco Vázquez 34, A Coruña* ☎ *981/189842* 🎫 €10.

**Castillo de San Antón (Museo Arqueológico e Histórico)**

HISTORY MUSEUM | At the northeastern tip of the old town is St. Anthony's Castle, a 16th-century fort that houses A Coruña's Museum of Archaeology. The collection includes remnants of the prehistoric Celtic culture that once thrived in these parts, including silver artifacts as well as ruins from *castros*, the Celts' stone forts. ⊠ *Paseo Alcalde Francisco Vázquez 2, A Coruña* ☎ *981/189850* 🎫 €2 ⊘ *Closed Mon.*

## A Coruña and Rías Altas

0 — 10 mi
0 — 10 km

### Colexiata de Santa María do Campo

CHURCH | Called St. Mary of the Field because the building was once beyond the city's walls, this Romanesque beauty dates to the mid-13th century. The facade depicts the Adoration of the Magi; the celestial figures include St. Peter, holding the keys to heaven. Because of an architectural miscalculation the roof is too heavy for its supports, so the columns inside lean outward and the buttresses outside have been thickened. The interior is often closed but the exterior alone is worth seeing. ⊠ *Rúa Damas 24, A Coruña.*

### Iglesia de Santiago

CHURCH | This 12th-century church, the oldest in A Coruña, was the first stop on the Camino Inglés (English route) toward Santiago de Compostela. Originally Romanesque, it's now a hodgepodge that includes Gothic arches, a baroque altarpiece, and two 18th-century rose windows. ⊠ *Rúa do Parrote 1, A Coruña.*

### Paseo Marítimo

PROMENADE | To see why sailors once nicknamed A Coruña "la ciudad de cristal" (the glass city), stroll the Paseo Marítimo, said to be the longest seaside promenade in Europe. Although the congregation of boats is charming, the real sight is across the street: a long, gracefully curved row of houses. Built by fishermen in the 18th century, they face away from the sea—it's said that at the end of a long day, these seafarers were tired of looking at the water. Nets were hung from the porches to dry, and fish was sold on the street below. When Galicia's first glass factory opened nearby, someone thought to enclose these porches in glass, like the latticed stern galleries of oceangoing galleons, to keep wind and rain at bay. The resulting emblematic glass galleries spread across the harbor and eventually throughout Galicia. The 13 km (8 miles) of flat surface with ocean views make it a wonderful jogging spot. ⊠ *Paseo Marítimo, A Coruña.*

## Praza de María Pita

**PLAZA/SQUARE** | The focal point of the old town, this bustling large plaza has a north side that's given over to the neoclassical Palacio Municipal, or city hall, built 1908–12 with three Italianate domes. The monument in the center, built in 1998, depicts the heroine Maior (María) Pita. When England's Sir Francis Drake arrived to sack A Coruña in 1589, the locals were only half-finished building the defensive Castillo de San Antón. A 13-day battle ensued. When María Pita's husband died, she took up his lance, slew the Briton who tried to plant the Union Jack, and revived the exhausted Coruñeses, inspiring other women to join the battle. The surrounding streets of the old town are a hive of activity, lined with tapas bars and shops. ⊠ *Pr. de María Pita, A Coruña.*

## ★ Torre de Hércules

**LIGHTHOUSE** | Much of A Coruña sits on a peninsula, on the tip of which sits this city landmark and UNESCO World Heritage Site—the oldest still-functioning lighthouse in the world. First installed during the reign of Trajan, the Roman emperor born in Spain in AD 98, the lighthouse was rebuilt in the 18th century and looks strikingly modern; all that remains from Roman times are inscribed foundation stones. Scale the 245 steps for superb views of the city and coastline—if you're here on a summer weekend, the tower opens for views of city lights along the Atlantic. Lining the approach to the lighthouse are sculptures depicting figures from Galician and Celtic legends. ⊠ *Av. de Navarra, A Coruña* ☎ *981/223730* ⊕ *www.torredeherculesa-coruna.com* ☜ *€3 (free Mon.).*

## ⊕ Beaches

### Orzán and Riazor Beaches

**BEACH** | A Coruña's Paseo Marítimo winds along two pleasant, well-maintained urban beaches, Playa del Orzán and Playa de Riazor. These long curves of fine golden sand tend to be busy in summer with chattering groups of local families and friends enjoying the milder climate. The area of Playa del Orzán in front of the hotel Meliá María Pita is popular with surfers. Cross the Paseo Marítimo for a choice of cafés and restaurants with animated terraces. Seafront kiosks sell ice cream and snacks. There is no natural shade, but you can rent sun loungers and parasols in summer. **Amenities:** food and drink; lifeguards; showers; toilets. **Best for:** surfing; swimming; walking. ⊠ *Paseo Marítimo, A Coruña.*

## ⊕ Restaurants

### El De Alberto

**$$$** | **SPANISH** | El De Alberto marries traditional Galician flavors with eye-catching modern presentation. Alberto, the passionate and friendly chef-owner, has no qualms about, say, dolloping kimchi sauce on local octopus or painting truffle butter on baked scallops (instead of the usual squirt of lemon). **Known for:** great value; cheerily decorated dining room; playful nueva cocina dishes. ⑤ *Average main: €18* ⊠ *Comandante Fontanes 1, A Coruña* ☎ *981/907411* ⊙ *Closed Mon. No dinner Sun.*

### La Penela

**$$$** | **SEAFOOD** | This sophisticated sea-foam-green dining room is the perfect place to feast on fresh fish while sipping Albariño. Don't miss the crabs or mussels with béchamel, a dish that La Penela is locally famous for. **Known for:** French-inflected seafood dishes; terrace dining; views of the harbor and Plaza de María Pita. ⑤ *Average main: €18* ⊠ *Pl. de María Pita 12, A Coruña*

🖮 *981/209200* ⊕ *www.lapenela.com* ⊘ *Closed Tues., No dinner Sun., Closed last 2 wks of Jan.*

## Hotels

**Hotel Lois**

$ | **B&B/INN** | Steps from the tapas bars of Calle Estrella, Hotel Lois is an excellent choice for its location alone, and its clean, contemporary style and excellent value for money make it all the more appealing. **Pros:** central location; discount at nearby car park; surrounded by restaurants. **Cons:** no access to street with car; no parking on-site; patchy Wi-Fi in some rooms. $ *Rooms from: €83* ✉ *Estrella 40, A Coruña* 🕾 *981/212269* ⊕ *hotel-lois. mydirectstay.com/es/index.html* ↘ *10 rooms* ⦿| *No Meals.*

**NH Collection A Coruña Finisterre**

$$$ | **HOTEL** | A favorite with businesspeople and families, the oldest and busiest of A Coruña's top hotels is a few minutes' walk from the port. **Pros:** port and city views; big-brand efficiency; heated pool. **Cons:** some rooms showing wear; unimpressive breakfast; inconvenient €20/day outdoor parking. $ *Rooms from: €130* ✉ *Paseo del Parrote 2–4, A Coruña* 🕾 *981/205400* ⊕ *www.nh-hotels.com/ hotel/nh-collection-a-coruna-finisterre* ↘ *92 rooms* ⦿| *No Meals.*

## Nightlife

Begin your evening in the **Praza de María Pita**: cafés and tapas bars proliferate off its western corners and inland. **Rúas Estrella, Franja, Riego de Agua, Barrera, and Galera** and the **Praza do Humor** have many tapas bars that get progressively busier as the night develops, some of which serve Ribeiro wine in bowls and free tapas with every drink. Start at the top of Calle Estrella (at the farthest end from Pr. María Pita) beginning with A Taberna de Cunqueiro (Rúa Estrella 22) and work your way back. Night owls head for the posh and pricey clubs around **Playa del Orzán** (Orzán Beach), particularly along Rúa Juan Canalejo. For lower-key entertainment, the old town has cozy taverns and plenty of bars that stay open into the early hours.

**Taberna da Galera**

**WINE BARS** | This trendy wine bar in the heart of the old town serves Galician *raciones* to a lively crowd. Feast on *tigres* (stuffed mussels), octopus tempura, or delightfully runny tortilla española, and accompany it all with a glass of fresh Ribeiro wine. ✉ *Rúa Galera 32, A Coruña* 🕾 *881/923996* ⊕ *www.tabernadagalera. com.*

## Shopping

**Rúa Real** and **Praza de Lugo** have boutiques with contemporary threads. A stroll down **Rúa San Andrés,** two blocks inland from Calle Real, or **Rúa Juan Flórez,** leading into the newer town, can yield some sartorial treasures. The Mercado Municipal de San Agustín, close to Praza de María Pita, is the place to go to stock up on local produce, tinned fish, and all kinds of charcuterie.

★ **Alfarería Aparicio**

**CRAFTS** | The glazed terra-cotta ceramics from Buño, a town 40 km (25 miles) west of A Coruña on the C552, are prized by aficionados. To see where they're made, drive there, then stop in this store to snap up some souvenirs. ✉ *Rúa Nova 4, A Coruña* 🕾 *981/711136* ⊕ *www.alfareriaaparicio.es.*

**Mundo Galego**

**FOOD** | Stop here for local cheese, wine, liqueur, and other Galician specialties. The shop also organizes tastings. ✉ *Rúa Galera 40, A Coruña* 🕾 *981/912038* ⊕ *www.facebook.com/mundogalego* ⊘ *Closed Sun.*

A Coruña is a major port town, but fashionistas might know it as where the first Zara clothing shop opened, back in 1975.

## 🏃 Activities

In A Coruña and the surrounding area, enjoy year-round outdoor activities including sailing, golf, and hiking. Swimmers and surfers can take advantage of the 2 km (1 mile) of beach and coastline in the heart of the city. *See Beaches section.*

# Betanzos

*25 km (15 miles) east of A Coruña, 65 km (40 miles) northeast of Santiago de Compostela.*

The charmingly frayed-at-the-edges medieval town of Betanzos is surrounded by parts of its old city wall. An important Galician port in the 13th century, the old town straddles the confluence of the Mendo and Mandeo Rivers and is known today for its white galleried houses, stately Gothic monuments, and lively taverns serving tortilla de Betanzos—an ultra-runny rendition of the classic Spanish omelet.

**GETTING HERE AND AROUND**
From Vigo and other destinations south, head north on the AP9; from A Coruña, head east for half an hour along the same freeway. The medieval center, with its narrow lanes rising up from the Pont Nova, is best explored on foot.

**VISITOR INFORMATION**
**CONTACTS Betanzos Tourist Office.** ✉ *Praza de Galicia 1, Betanzos* ☎ *981/776666* ⊕ *turismo.betanzos.es.*

## 👁 Sights

**Igrexa de San Francisco de Betanzos**
**CHURCH** | The 1292 monastery of San Francisco was converted into a church in 1387 by nobleman Fernán Pérez de Andrade. His magnificent tomb, to the left of the west door, has him lying on the backs of a stone bear and boar, with hunting dogs at his feet and an angel receiving his soul by his head. ✉ *Pl. de Fernán Pérez Andrade, Betanzos* ☎ *€2.*

# Two Great Detours

## A Beach Detour

**As Catedrais Beach** (*Las Catedrais Beach*) One of Spain's best-kept secrets, this spectacular stretch of sand, also known as Praia de Augas Santas (Beach of the Holy Waters) features vast rock formations, domes, arches, and caves that were naturally formed by wind and sea. In high season (July–September) it is mandatory to reserve a ticket to access the actual beach via ⊕ *ascatedrais.xunta.gal*. The arches are accessible for walks when the tide goes out; otherwise, the beach can be completely covered. **Amenities:** parking. **Best for:** beach walks; rock formations; spectacular natural scenery. ⊠ *A8, 516 exit, Ribadeo* 🖭 *Free*.

## Shopping Side Trip

**Cerámica de Sargadelos** Distinctive blue-and-white-glazed contemporary ceramics are made at Cerámica de Sargadelos, 21 km (13 miles) east of Viveiro. It's usually possible to watch artisans work (weekdays 9–1:15), but call ahead to check. ⊠ *Ctra. Paraño, Cervo* 🕾 *982/557841* ⊕ *www.sargadelos.com*.

### Igrexa de Santa María do Azogue de Betanzos

CHURCH | This 15th-century church, a few steps uphill from the church of San Francisco, is a national monument. It has Renaissance statues that were stolen in 1981 but subsequently recovered. ⊠ *Pl. de Fernán Pérez Andrade, Betanzos* 🖭 *Free*.

### Igrexa de Santiago de Betanzos

CHURCH | The tailors' guild put up the Gothic-style church of Santiago, which includes a Pórtico de la Gloria inspired by that of Santiago's cathedral. Above the door is a carving of St. James as the Slayer of the Moors—a title that hasn't aged particularly well. ⊠ *Rúa. de Lanzós 16, Betanzos* 🖭 *Free*.

# Viveiro

*121 km (75 miles) northeast of Betanzos.*

The once-turreted city walls of this popular summer resort are still partially intact. The **Semana Santa** processions, when penitents follow religious processions on their knees, are particularly noteworthy. The beaches in Viveiro Bay are some of the north's finest.

## GETTING HERE AND AROUND

Narrow-gauge FEVE trains connect Viveiro to Oviedo, Gijón, and other points east. By car, head east on the AP9 from A Coruña, then take the LU540 to Viveiro.

## VISITOR INFORMATION

**CONTACTS Viveiro Tourist Office.** ⊠ *Av. Ramón Canosa 3, Viveiro* 🕾 *982/560879* ⊕ *www.viveiroturismo.com*.

 Hotels

### Hotel Ego

$$ | HOTEL | The view of the ría from this hilltop hotel outside Viveiro is unbeatable, and every room has one. **Pros:** hilltop views; excellent restaurant; relaxing public areas. **Cons:** small spa; the facade resembles an airport terminal; a little generic. ⑤ *Rooms from: €100* ⊠ *Pl. de Area 1, off N642, Viveiro* 🕾 *982/560987* ⊕ *www.hotelego.es* ⤵ *45 rooms* ⑪ *No Meals*.

# Luarca

*92 km (57 miles) northeast of Oviedo.*

The village of Luarca (Ḷḷuarca in Asturian) is in a cove at the end of the Río Negro. It has a fishing port and, to the west, a sparkling bay. The town is a maze of cobblestone streets, stone stairways, and whitewashed houses hemmed in by a harborside decorated with painted flowerpots.

## GETTING HERE AND AROUND

To get to Oviedo, Gijón, and other destinations east, take a FEVE train or ALSA bus; it's about a two-hour trip. By car, take the A8 west along the coast from Oviedo and Gijón or east from A Coruña.

## VISITOR INFORMATION

**CONTACTS Luarca Tourist Office.** ⊠ *Calle Ramón Asenjo 25, Luarca* ☏ *985/640083* ⊕ *www.turismoluarca.com.*

##  Restaurants

### Barómetro

**$$$** | **SEAFOOD** | **FAMILY** | Decorated with an ornate barometer to gauge the famously unpredictable local weather, this family-run seafood spot is in a 19th-century building on the harbor. In addition to an inexpensive *menú del día* (prix fixe), there's outstanding seafood à la carte including fried *calamares* (squid) and uni-stuffed asparagus. **Known for:** excellent-value prix-fixe lunch; seafood noodle soup; popular with locals. $ *Average main: €18* ⊠ *Paseo del Muelle 5, Luarca* ☏ *985/470662* ⊘ *Closed Tues. No dinner Sun.*

## Sport

$$$ | SPANISH | This family-run restaurant has been going strong since the 1950s. Its large windows overlook the river, and its kitchen makes a mean *fabada asturiana* (bean-and-sausage stew). **Known for:** rollo de bonito (tuna meatballs in tomato sauce); day-boat seafood; riverside dining. ⑤ *Average main: €22* ⊠ *Calle Rivero 9, Luarca* ☎ *985/641078.*

## 🛏 Hotels

### ★ Hotel Rural 3 Cabos

$$ | B&B/INN | FAMILY | On a grassy hill with spectacular bay views, this cozy yet modern B&B makes for a charming stay. **Pros:** house-made cake at breakfast; free bike rental; stunning views of land and sea. **Cons:** restaurant open only to guests; car needed; out of the way (15-minute drive to Luarca). ⑤ *Rooms from: €110* ⊠ *Ctra. de El Vallín, Km 4, Luarca* ☎ *985/924252* ⊕ *www.hotelrural3cabos.com* ⊗ *Closed Jan. (can vary)* ⇩ *9 rooms* ⦿ *Free Breakfast.*

### Villa La Argentina

$$$ | B&B/INN | Built in 1899 by a wealthy *indiano* (a Spaniard who made his fortune in the Americas and returned), this charming Asturian mansion on the hill above Luarca offers modern apartments in the garden or Belle Époque suites in the main building. **Pros:** swimming pool; peace and quiet; lovely gardens. **Cons:** simple breakfast; not central; uphill walk from town. ⑤ *Rooms from: €135* ⊠ *Villar, Luarca* ☎ *985/640102* ⊕ *www.villalaargentina.com* ⊗ *Closed Jan. and Feb.* ⇩ *12 rooms* ⦿ *Free Breakfast.*

# Oviedo

*92 km (57 miles) southeast of Luarca, 50 km (31 miles) southeast of Cudillero, 30 km (19 miles) south of Gijón.*

Inland, the Asturian countryside morphs into rolling green hills punctuated with

## Cudillero 👁

The coastal road leads 35 km (22 miles) east of Luarca to this crayon-box fishing village clustered around a tiny port. The peridot hills, the shimmering water, and the pops of color among the white houses—a canny use of leftover boat paint—make this village one of the prettiest and most touristic in Asturias. Seafood and cider restaurants line the central street, which turns into a boat ramp at the bottom of town.

wooden tile-roof *hórreos* (granaries) strung with dried corn. A drive through the mountains and valleys brings you to Asturias's stately capital, Oviedo. Although its periphery is primarily industrial, the city has three of the most famous pre-Romanesque churches in Spain and a large university, giving it both ancient charm and youthful zest. Start your explorations with the two exquisite 9th-century chapels outside the city, on the slopes of Monte Naranco.

## GETTING HERE AND AROUND

Oviedo is served by the A66 tollway that links to Gijón and Avilés, where you can get on the A8 west to A Coruña or east toward Santander. Madrid is reached on the N630 south.

There are several buses per day to Gijón (30 minutes) and to Santiago and A Coruña (5 hours). Madrid is 4½ hours away by rail from Oviedo's RENFE station on Calle Uría. The FEVE service operates across the north coast, with Gijón easily reached in half an hour and Bilbao 7½ hours away.

Local buses operate along the main arteries of Oviedo, between the train station and shopping areas, but most of the action is in the historical center, where Oviedo's oldest buildings are clustered in the labyrinth of streets around the Plaza

Alfonso. Considering the short distances, walking is the best option, though taxis are inexpensive.

**CONTACTS Oviedo Bus Station.** ☒ *Calle Pepe Cosmen, Oviedo* ⊕ *www.estaciondeautobusesdeoviedo.com.* **Oviedo Train Station.** ☒ *Calle Uria, Oviedo* ☎ *912/320320 Renfe.*

### VISITOR INFORMATION
**CONTACTS Tourist Information Center of Asturias.** ☒ *Pl. de la Constitución 4, Oviedo* ☎ *984/493563* ⊕ *www.visitovido.info.*

##  Sights

### Catedral Metropolitana de San Salvador de Oviedo
**CHURCH |** Oviedo's Gothic cathedral was built between the 14th and 16th centuries around the city's most cherished monument, the *Cámara Santa* (Holy Chamber). King Ramiro's predecessor, Alfonso the Chaste (792–842), built it to hide the treasures of Christian Spain during the struggle with the Moors. Damaged during the Spanish Civil War, it has since been rebuilt. Inside is the gold-leaf Cross of the Angels, commissioned by Alfonso in 808 and encrusted with pearls and jewels. On the left is the more elegant Victory Cross, actually a jeweled sheath crafted in 908 to cover the oak cross used by Pelayo in the battle of Covadonga. ☒ *Pl. Alfonso II El Casto, Oviedo* ☎ *985/219642* ⊕ *www.catedraldeoviedo.com* ☒ *€7 (incudes audio guide).*

### San Julián de los Prados *(Santullano)*
**CHURCH |** Older than its more famous pre-Romanesque counterparts on Monte Naranco, the 9th-century church of Santullano has surprisingly well-preserved frescoes inside. Geometric patterns, rather than representations of humans or animals, cover almost every surface, along with a cross containing Greek letters. ☒ *C. Selgas 1, Oviedo* ☎ *687/052826* ⊕ *www.sanjuliandelosprados.com* ☒ *€2 (free 1st Mon. of each month)* ☉ *Closed Sun.*

### ★ Santa María del Naranco and San Miguel de Lillo
**CHURCH |** These two churches—the first with superb views and its plainer sister 300 yards uphill—are the jewels of an early architectural style called Asturian pre-Romanesque, a more primitive, hulking, defensive line that preceded Romanesque architecture by nearly three centuries. Commissioned as part of a summer palace by King Ramiro I when Oviedo was the capital of Christian Spain, these masterpieces have survived for more than 1,000 years. Tickets for both sites are available in the church of Santa María del Naranco. ☒ *Monte Naranco, Oviedo* ✛ *2 km (1 mile) north of Oviedo* ☎ *638/260163* ⊕ *www.santamariadelnaranco.es* ☒ *€4, includes guided tour (free Mon., without guide).*

## 🍴 Restaurants

### Casa Fermín
**$$$$ | SPANISH |** Skylights, plants, and an air of modernity belie the age of this sophisticated restaurant, which opened in 1924 and is now in its fourth generation. The nueva cocina menu changes seasonally, and there is also a tasting menu. **Known for:** special-occasion dining; exceptional seafood; inventive Asturian cuisine. ⑤ *Average main: €29* ☒ *C. San Francisco 8, Oviedo* ☎ *985/216452* ⊕ *www.casafermin.com* ☉ *Closed Sun., No dinner Mon.*

### La Corte de Pelayo
**$$$ | SPANISH |** Head to this renowned white-tablecloth restaurant and meeting spot on one of Oviedo's main thoroughfares for *cachopo*, a heart-stopping fried veal cutlet stuffed with ham and cheese—an Asturian speciality. If you prefer something a bit lighter, there are salads, fresh fish, and meat dishes. **Known for:** central location; lively atmosphere; wonderful cachopo. ⑤ *Average main: €20* ☒ *Calle San Francisco 21, Oviedo* ☎ *985/213145* ⊕ *www.lacortedepelayo.com* ☉ *No dinner Sun.*

## Tierra Astur

$$ | SPANISH | FAMILY | This *sidrería* (cider restaurant) is popular among locals and tourists alike, who come to enjoy the lively barroom atmosphere. Cider is poured from a great height, and traditional, family-style Asturian fare like *fabada* and *tablas* (cheese and charcuterie boards) are ideal for sharing. **Known for:** succulent chuletón (rib-eye steak); platters with over 40 types of meats and cheese; abundant Asturian cider. $ *Average main: €15* ⊠ *Calle Gascona 1, Oviedo* ☎ *985/202502* ⊕ *www.tierra-astur.com.*

## 🛏 Hotels

### Barceló Oviedo Cervantes

$$ | HOTEL | A playful revamp of this townhouse in the city center added a neo-Moorish portico to the original latticed facade and indulgent amenities like entertainment systems in some of the bathrooms. **Pros:** fun '70s design; on-site bar and restaurant; central location close to train station. **Cons:** subpar lighting in rooms; erratic service; uninteresting views. $ *Rooms from: €114* ⊠ *Calle Cervantes 13, Oviedo* ☎ *985/255000* ⊕ *www.barcelo.com* ↪ *72 rooms* ⦿ *No Meals.*

### ★ Eurostars Hotel de la Reconquista

$$$ | HOTEL | Occupying an 18th-century hospice emblazoned with a huge stone coat of arms, the luxurious Reconquista is by far the most distinguished hotel in Oviedo. **Pros:** great location; good breakfast buffet; spacious rooms. **Cons:** decor may be fusty for some; some street noise; some rooms have uninteresting views. $ *Rooms from: €135* ⊠ *Calle Gil de Jaz 16, Oviedo* ☎ *985/241100* ⊕ *www. eurostarshotels.co.uk* ↪ *142 rooms* ⦿ *Free Breakfast.*

## 🍸 Nightlife

Oviedo gets a little rowdy after dark on weekends, and there's plenty in the way of loud live music. Most of the bars are concentrated on Calle Mon and its continuation, Calle Oscura. Calle Canóniga, off Calle Mon, also has a number of bars. Calle Gascona is cider row, lined with *sidrerías* that spill out onto the street and serve tapas till late. Bartenders here pour the cider from a great height, which aerates the naturally still cider.

## 🛍 Shopping

Shops throughout the city carry azabache jewelry made of jet.

### Joyería Santirso

JEWELRY & WATCHES | This family-run shop has been selling silver jewelry, including Asturias's world-famous azabache, for five generations. ⊠ *Calle Rúa 7, Oviedo* ☎ *985/225304* ⊕ *www.joyeriasantirso. com* ⊗ *Closed Sun.*

### Mercado El Fontán

MARKET | Oviedo's main traditional market, built in 1885 in a structural rationalist style, brims with produce, cheeses, meats, and a jaw-dropping variety of fresh seafood. On Sunday morning there's an open-air *rastro* (flea market) on the adjoining square. ⊠ *Pl. 19 de Octubre, Oviedo* ☎ *985/204394* ⊕ *www. mercadofontan.es* ⊗ *Closed Sun.*

## 🏃 Activities

### SKIING

#### Fuentes de Invierno

SKIING & SNOWBOARDING | An hour's drive from Oviedo in the heart of the Cantabrian Mountains, Fuentes de Invierno has five chairlifts and 15 trails of varying difficulty. ⊠ *Ctra. del Puerto de San Isidro, Oviedo* ☎ *985/959106* ⊕ *www. fuentesdeinvierno.com* 🎫 *€27.*

### Valgrande Pajares

SKIING & SNOWBOARDING | This resort has two chairlifts, eight slopes, and cross-country trails. ⊠ *Estación Invernal y de Montaña Valgrande-Pajares, Brañillín, Pajares* ✛ *60 km (37 miles) south of Oviedo* ☎ *985/957097* ⊕ *www.valgrande-pajares.com* ✉ *€29.*

# Gijón

*30 km (19 miles) north of Oviedo.*

The Campo Valdés baths, dating to the 1st century AD, and other reminders of Gijón's time as an ancient Roman port remain visible downtown. Gijón (Xixón in Asturian) was almost destroyed in a 14th-century struggle over the Castilian throne, but by the 19th century it was a thriving port and industrial city. Today it is part fishing port, part summer resort, and part university town, packed with cafés, restaurants, and sidrerías. It's a bit scruffier than Oviedo but also more down-to-earth.

## GETTING HERE AND AROUND

Gijón is 30 minutes away from Oviedo by ALSA bus or FEVE train, both of which run every half hour throughout the day. The A8 coastal highway stretches east from Gijón to Santander, and west to Luarca and eventually A Coruña.

**CONTACTS Gijón Bus Station.** ⊠ *Calle Magnus Blikstad 2, Gijón* ⊕ *www.alsa.com/en/web/bus/bus-stations/gijon-station.* **Gijón Train Station.** ⊠ *Calle Sanz Crespo, Gijón* ☎ *912/432343* ⊕ *www.renfe.com.*

## VISITOR INFORMATION

**CONTACTS Gijón Tourist Office.** ⊠ *Calle Fermín García Bernardo, Gijón* ☎ *985/341771* ⊕ *www.gijon.es/es/turismo/informacion-turistica.*

## ◉ Sights

### Cimadevilla

VIEWPOINT | This steep peninsula—the old fishermen's quarter—is now the main nightlife hub. At sunset, the sidewalk in front of bar El Planeta (Tránsito de las Ballenas 4), overlooking the harbor, is a prime spot to join locals drinking Asturian cider. From the park at the highest point on the headland, beside Basque artist Eduardo Chillida's massive sculpture *Elogio del Horizonte* (*In Praise of the Horizon*), there's a panoramic view of the coast and city. ⊠ *Gijón.*

### ★ Muséu del Pueblu d'Asturies (*Museum of the Asturian People*)

HISTORY MUSEUM | Across the river, on the eastern edge of town, this rustic museum contains traditional Asturian houses, cider presses, a mill, and an exquisitely painted granary. Also here is the Museo de la Gaita (Bagpipe Museum) celebrating the area's centuries-old bagpiping tradition. There are bagpipes from other parts of the world on display as well. ⊠ *Paseo del Doctor Fleming 877, La Güelga, Gijón* ☎ *985/182960* ⊕ *www.gijon.es/es/directorio/museu-del-pueblu-dasturies* ✉ *Free* ☉ *Closed Mon.*

### Termas Romanas de Campo Valdés (*Roman Baths*)

RUINS | Dating to the time of Augustus, the ruins of Gijón's baths are under the plaza at the end of the beach. Visits take approximately 20 minutes, and there are no English descriptions. ⊠ *Campo Valdés, Gijón* ☎ *985/185151* ✉ *Free* ☉ *Closed Mon.*

## ⊕ Beaches

As capital of the Costa Verde, Gijón overlooks two attractive sandy beaches that are large enough to avoid overcrowding in summer.

**Playa de Poniente** (Sunset Beach)

BEACH | Tucked into the city's harbor, this horseshoe-shape curve of fine artificial sand and calm waters is wonderful for an evening stroll. **Amenities:** lifeguards; showers; toilets. **Best for:** sunset; swimming; walking. ✉ Calle Rodriguez San Pedro, Gijón.

**Playa de San Lorenzo**

BEACH | Gijón's other popular beach, beyond the headland from Playa de Poniente, has golden sand backed by a promenade that extends from one end of town to the other. Across the narrow peninsula and the Plaza Mayor is the harbor, where the fishing fleet comes in with the day's catch. As long as the tide is out, you can sunbathe. The waves are generally moderate, but weather and currents can be unpredictable. **Amenities:** food and drink; lifeguards; showers; toilets; water sports. **Best for:** sunset; swimming; walking. ✉ Av. Rufo García Rendueles, Gijón.

## 🍴 Restaurants

★ **La Galana**

$$$ | SPANISH | La Galana is a typical Asturian sidrería, colossal barrels lining the walls, thick wooden tables, and plenty of standing room at the bar, where locals munch on Cabrales cheese. The kitchen serves refined cider-house fare: Expect cheeses with quince jam, *pulpo a la brasa* (grilled octopus), and a range of creative tapas. **Known for:** lovingly prepared cider-house fare; great-value prix fixe; local cider. $ Average main: €20 ✉ Pl. Mayor 10, Gijón ☎ 985/172429 ⊕ www.restauranteasturianolagalana.es.

**Restaurante Auga**

$$$$ | SPANISH | This upscale, glass-enclosed dining room, housed in what was once Gijón's fish market, overlooks the harbor and serves imaginative seafood and meat dishes. Expect a variety of raw, grilled, smoked, foamed, and roasted

options, all plated with panache. **Known for:** alfresco dining; award-winning kitchen; harbor and sea views. $ Average main: €34 ✉ Calle Claudio Alvargonzález, Gijón ☎ 985/168186 ⊕ www.restauranteauga.com ⊙ Closed Mon., No dinner Sun.

## 🛏 Hotels

**Hostel Gijón Centro**

$ | B&B/INN | Steps from the harbor and Plaza Mayor, this tiny guesthouse offers rooms with large windows affording plenty of natural light, plus simple, modern decor and comfortable beds. **Pros:** excellent value; quiet; central location. **Cons:** simple lodging; no on-site facilities; tiny bathrooms. $ Rooms from: €80 ✉ Calle San Antonio 12, Gijón ☎ 657/029242 ⊕ www.hostelgijoncentro.es ⤴ 6 rooms ⦿ No Meals.

★ **Hotel El Mirador de Ordiales**

$ | B&B/INN | This cozy hilltop B&B offers exquisite views of the valley below and the snowcapped Picos de Europa in the distance. **Pros:** stunning views; spacious rooms; good base for hiking. **Cons:** breakfast is extra; few dining options in the area; far afield. $ Rooms from: €85 ✉ Camín de Ordiales 545, Siero ☎ 653/938156, 985/721020 ⊕ www.elmiradordeordiales.com ⤴ 3 rooms ⦿ No Meals.

**Parador de Gijón**

$$ | HOTEL | This is one of the most dressed-down and inviting paradores in Spain, and most rooms have wonderful views over the lake or park. **Pros:** park views; terrific restaurant; welcoming, down-to-earth staff. **Cons:** some distance from the old town; expensive for the area; austere guest rooms. $ Rooms from: €125 ✉ Av. Torcuato Fernández Miranda 15, Gijón ☎ 985/370511 ⊕ www.parador.es ⤴ 40 rooms.

# Ribadesella

*67 km (40 miles) east of Gijón, 84 km (50 miles) northeast of Oviedo.*

The N632 twists around green hills dappled with eucalyptus groves and affords glimpses of the sea, beaches, and snowcapped Picos de Europa. This fishing village and beach resort is famous for its seafood, cave formations, and canoe races (held on the Río Sella the first Saturday in August).

**GETTING HERE AND AROUND**
FEVE and ALSA connect Ribadesella to Gijón and Oviedo by train and bus, a journey of 1½–2 hours. By car, you can take the A8 from Gijón and Oviedo past Villaviciosa to Ribadesella.

**VISITOR INFORMATION**
**CONTACTS Ribadesella Tourist Office.**
✉ *Paseo Princesa Letizia, Ribadesella* ☎ *985/860038* ⊕ *www.ribadesella.es.*

##  Sights

**Rock Art Center of Tito Bustillo**
**CAVE** | Discovered in 1968, the cave here has 20,000-year-old paintings on a par with those in Lascaux, France, and Altamira. Giant horses and deer prance about the walls. To protect the paintings, no more than 375 visitors are allowed inside each day, so reservations are essential. The guided tour is in Spanish. Audioguides are available in English. There's also a museum of Asturian cave finds, open year-round. ✉ *Av. de Tito Bustillo, Ribadesella* ☎ *985/18560* ⊕ *www.centrotitobustillo.com* ◈ *€5, free Wed.* ۞ *Closed Mon. and Tues., Closed Nov.–Feb.*

##  Beaches

**Playa de Santa Marina**
**BEACH** | To the west of the Río Sella estuary, which divides the town, this gentle curve of golden sand is one of the prettiest beaches in Asturias. It's tucked beneath the town's seafront promenade, lined with 20th-century mansions. Moderate waves provide safe swimming conditions, although, as with all of Spain's Atlantic-facing beaches, currents and weather can be unpredictable. In high season (particularly in August) the beach can get very busy. This part of the coast is not called the "dinosaur coast" for nothing; over by the Punta'l Pozu Viewpoint, you can see footprints embedded in the rocks and cliff faces where they left their mark millions of years ago. Amenities listed are only available June–September. **Amenities:** food and drink; lifeguards; showers; toilets. **Best for:** surfing; swimming. ✉ *Paseo Agustin de Argüelles Marina, Ribadesella.*

##  Restaurants

**Arbidel**
**$$$$** | **SPANISH** | This award-winning, modern Asturian restaurant in the old town is adorned with rustic stone walls and a hand-painted mural. There are also inventive tapas and tasting menus (starting at €65). **Known for:** apple gazpacho with sardines; good-value tasting menus; experimental Asturian cuisine. ⑤ *Average main: €32* ✉ *Calle Oscuro 1, Ribadesella* ☎ *985/861440* ⊕ *www.arbidelrestaurante.com* ۞ *Closed Mon. and Tues., No dinner Sun.*

## 🛏 Hotels

**Hotel Ribadesella Playa**
**$$** | **B&B/INN** | Spending a night in this restored turn-of-the-20th-century mansion on the beach is pleasant and peaceful: it's family run and has a timeless, stately charm that may remind you of black-and-white European art films. **Pros:** proximity to the Tito Bustillo cave and the beach; good breakfast; lovely views of the Cantabrian sea. **Cons:** some rooms are small; noise from outside; limited availability in high season. ⑤ *Rooms*

*from:* €125 ⊠ *Calle Ricardo Cangus 3,
Ribadesella* ☎ 985/860715 ⊕ *www.hotel-ribadesellaplaya.com* ⊘ *Closed Nov.–Mar.*
🛏 *17 rooms* ⧖ *Free Breakfast.*

# Llanes

*40 km (25 miles) east of Ribadesella.*

This beach town is on a pristine stretch
of the Costa Verde. The shores in both
directions outside town have vistas of
cliffs looming over white-sand beaches and isolated caves. A long canal
connected to a small harbor cuts through
the heart of Llanes, and along its banks
rise colorful houses with glass galleries against a backdrop of the Picos de
Europa. At the daily portside fish market,
usually held around 1 pm, vendors display heaps of freshly caught seafood.

## GETTING HERE AND AROUND

The scenic A8 coastal route from Gijón
continues past Villaviciosa and Ribadesella and then winds through Llanes before
heading east toward Santander. FEVE
trains and ALSA buses make the trip in
2–3½ hours.

## VISITOR INFORMATION

**CONTACTS Llanes Tourist Office.** ⊠ *Calle
Marqués de Canillejas 1, Llanes*
☎ *985/400164* ⊕ *www.llanes.es.*

## ◉ Sights

### Basílica de Santa María del Conceyu

CHURCH | This 13th-century church rising
over the main square is an excellent
example of Romantic Gothic architecture.
⊠ *Pl. Christo Rey, Llanes* ⧖ *Free.*

### Mirador Panorámico La Boriza

VIEWPOINT | Dotting the Asturian coast
east and west of Llanes are *bufones*,
cavelike cavities that expel water when
waves are sucked in. These active blow-
holes shoot streams of water as high
as 100 feet at unpredictable intervals.
They are clearly marked so you can find

them, and there are barriers to protect
you when they expel water. There is one
east of Playa Ballota; try to watch it in
action from this mirador east of Llanes,
between the villages of Cué and Andrin.
If you miss the spurt, the view is still
worth a stop—on a clear day you can see
the coastline all the way east to Santander. ⊠ *Llanes* ⧖ *Free.*

### Plaza Cristo Rey

PLAZA/SQUARE | Peaceful and well con-
served, this plaza marks the center of the
old town, which is partially surrounded
by the remains of its medieval walls.
⊠ *Llanes.*

##  Beaches

### Playa Ballota

BEACH | One km (½ mile) east of Llanes is
the pristine and secluded Playa Ballota,
with private coves and one of the few
stretches of nudist sand in Asturias.
**Amenities:** food and drink (seasonal). **Best
for:** nudists; swimming; walking. ⊠ *Calle
Ballota, Llanes.*

### Playa de Torimbia

BEACH | Farther west of Llanes is the
partially nudist Playa de Torimbia, a
wild, virgin beach as yet untouched by
development. It is reached only via a
footpath—roughly a 15-minute walk. This
secluded crescent of fine, white sand
and crystal-clear waters is backed by
Asturias's green hills, making it one of
the region's most picturesque beaches.
Winds can be strong, and there is no real
infrastructure. **Amenities:** none. **Best for:**
nudists; solitude; swimming; walking.
⊠ *Llanes* ⊹ *Off C. Niembru, 8 km (5
miles) west of Llanes.*

### Playa de Toró

BEACH | On the eastern edge of town is
Playa de Toró, where fine white sands are
peppered with unique rock formations.
This pristine beach is ideal for sunbathing
and families. **Amenities:** lifeguards; showers; toilets. **Best for:** swimming. ⊠ *Av.
Ctra. de Toró, Llanes.*

Hiking in the Picos de Europa

## Playa del Sablón

**BEACH | FAMILY |** Steps from the old town is the protected Playa del Sablón (whose name derives from the Asturian word for "sand"), a little swath of beach that gets crowded on weekends. **Amenities:** food and drink; lifeguards; showers; toilets. **Best for:** swimming. ⊠ *Calle Sablón, Llanes.*

##  Restaurants

### El Bálamu

**$$$$ | SPANISH |** A restaurant housed inside the Llanes fish market and right on the water means you'll get the freshest catch in town. Watch your next meal come into the port on small fishing boats and enjoy simple preparations that highlight the natural quality of each fish, mollusk, and crustacean on the menu. **Known for:** exceptionally fresh seafood; tranquil seaside views; hospitable waitstaff. ⑤ *Average main: €25* ⊠ *Puerto Pesquero, Llanes* ☎ *985/413606.*

## 🛏 Hotels

### Hotel Caeaclaveles

**$$$ | HOTEL |** This ultramodern eco-hotel in the woods is an architectural marvel with its grass-topped roof, sinuous walls, full-length windows, and polished-cement ceiling. **Pros:** award-winning architecture; quiet and scenic; plenty of natural light. **Cons:** no children under nine; somewhat remote, car needed; decor pales in comparison to the exterior. ⑤ *Rooms from: €145* ⊠ *La Pereda, Carretera LLN-6, Km 2, Llanes* ☎ *985/925981* ⊕ *www.caeaclaveles.com* ⊙ *Closed mid-Dec.–Easter* 🗜 *5 rooms.*

### La Posada de Babel

**$$ | B&B/INN |** Outside Llanes, among oak, chestnut, and birch trees, you'll find this charming family-run inn with personalized attention and roaring fires in the public rooms. **Pros:** amiable staff; beautiful grounds; comfy base for hiking. **Cons:** room styles vary; closed in winter; tech could use a revamp. ⑤ *Rooms from: €117* ⊠ *La Pereda, Llanes* ⊹ *4 km (2½ miles)* southwest of Llanes ☎ 019/457804 ⊕ www.laposadadebabel.com ۞ Closed Dec.–Easter ⌷ 12 rooms ⏁ Free Breakfast.

# Cangas de Onís

25 km (16 miles) south of Ribadesella, 70 km (43 miles) east of Oviedo.

The first capital of so-called Christian Spain, Cangas de Onís is also the nerve center of the Picos de Europa National Park. It's tucked into a narrow valley carved by the Sella River and has the feel of a mountain village.

## VISITOR INFORMATION
**CONTACTS Cangas de Onís Tourist Office.**
✉ Av. Covadonga 1, Cangas de Onís ☎ 985/848005 ⊕ www.turismocangasdeonis.com.

##  Sights

**Picos de Europa Visitor Center**
VISITOR CENTER | To help plan your rambles, consult the scale model of the park outside the visitor center; staff inside can advise you on suitable routes. Stores on the same street sell English maps and guidebooks. ✉ Pedro Pidal Visitor Center, Av. Covadonga 1, Cangas de Onís ☎ 985/848614 ⊕ www.parquenacionalpicoseuropa.es/english/visitor-centres.

**Puente Romano de Cangas de Onís**
BRIDGE | A high, humpback medieval bridge (also known as the Puente Romano, or Roman Bridge, because of its style) spans the Río Sella gorge with a reproduction of Pelayo's Victory Cross, or La Cruz de la Victoria, dangling underneath. ✉ Cangas de Onís.

##  Restaurants

**Restaurante Los Arcos**
$$ | SPANISH | On one of the town's main squares, this busy smart-casual restaurant decorated in whites and grays

serves local cider, fine Spanish wines, and honest regional dishes. The well-priced lunch menu features mouthwatering revueltos (scrambled eggs with add-ins), seafood, and stews. **Known for:** scrambled eggs with blood sausage; over 40 local cheeses; great value. ⑤ Average main: €15 ✉ Hotel Los Lagos Nature, Pl. Camila Beceña 3, Cangas de Onís ☎ 985/849277 ⊕ www.loslagosnature.com/restauranteLosArcos.

##  Hotels

**Hotel Posada del Valle**
$$ | B&B/INN | A British couple converted this 19th-century stone farmhouse into an idyllic hillside inn with stunning views of the Picos. **Pros:** surrounded by nature; wealth of local knowledge at your fingertips; views of the Picos. **Cons:** restaurant does not serve lunch; limited breakfast; remote and difficult to find. ⑤ Rooms from: €95 ✉ Collía, Cangas de Onís ☎ 985/841157 ⊕ www.posadadelvalle.com ۞ Closed Nov.–Mar. ⌷ 12 rooms ⏁ No Meals.

★ **Parador de Cangas de Onís**
$$$ | HOTEL | On the banks of the Río Sella just west of Cangas, this friendly parador is made up of an 18th-century Benedictine monastery and a modern wing. **Pros:** gorgeous riverside location and mountain views; grounds steeped in history; notable restaurant. **Cons:** rooms on lower floor can be noisy; chilly corridors; limited menu not suited to vegetarians. ⑤ Rooms from: €145 ✉ Monasterio de San Pedro de Villanueva, Villanueva, Ctra. N625, Cangas de Onís ✛ From N634 take right turn for Villanueva ☎ 985/849402 ⊕ www.parador.es ⌷ 64 rooms ⏁ Free Breakfast.

##  Activities

The tourist office in Cangas de Onís can help you organize a Picos de Europa trek. The Picos visitor center in Cangas has general information, audiovisual components, route maps, and a useful scale model of the range.

### Astursella Aventura

**RAFTING** | This outdoor adventure company specializes in canoeing, rafting, and canyon rappelling in and around the Río Güeña. ⊠ *Ramón Prada Vicente 3, Cangas de Onís* ☎ *985/848370* ⊕ *www. astursellaaventura.com.*

### Cangas Aventura Turismo Activo

**MOUNTAIN CLIMBING** | Rafting, canoeing, jet-skiing, climbing, trekking, horseback riding, paintballing, and snowshoeing packages are all available here. ⊠ *Av. Covadonga 17 Bajo, Cangas de Onís* ☎ *985/849261* ⊕ *www.cangasaventura. com.*

## Potes

*115 km (69 miles) southwest of Santander, 81 km (50 miles) southeast of Cangas de Onís.*

Famed for its cheeses, the region of La Liébana is a highland domain whose main city is Potes. Potes is named for its ancient bridges and is known for the stunning 9th-century **monasteries** of Santo Toribio de Liébana, Lebeña, and Piasca that dot its perimeter. The gorges of the Desfiladero de la Hermida pass are 13 km (8 miles) north, and the rustic town of Mogrovejo is on the way to the vertiginous cable car at Fuente Dé, 10 km (6 miles) west of Potes.

## GETTING HERE AND AROUND

Potes is just over two hours from Gijón and Oviedo via the A8, and 1½ hours from Santander via the A8 and N621.

### VISITOR INFORMATION

**CONTACTS Potes Tourist Office.** ⊠ Pl. la Serna, Potes ☎ 942/730787 ⊕ www. ayuntamientodepotes.es.

##  Sights

### Teleférico Fuente Dé

**VIEWPOINT** | As you approach the parador of Fuente Dé, at the head of the valley northwest of the hamlet of Espinama, you'll see a wall of gray rock jutting 6,560 feet into the air. At the top is a tiny hut: El Mirador del Cable (the cable-car lookout point). Get there via a 2,625-foot funicular (€17 round-trip). After you exit the funicular, you can hike along the Ávila Mountain pasturelands, rich in wildlife, between the central and eastern massifs of the Picos. There's an official entrance to Picos de Europa National Park here. ⊠ Potes ☎ 942/736610 ⊕ entradas. telefericofuentede.com.

## Restaurants

### ★ El Bodegón

**$$ | SPANISH** | An invitingly cozy space awaits behind the ancient stone facade of this restaurant, 200 meters (656 feet) from the main plaza. Part of the house is original, but much has been renovated, providing an attractive combination of traditional mountain design and modern construction. **Known for:** affordable mountain cooking; popular spot; standout wines. ⑤ Average main: €15 ⊠ Calle San Roque 4, Potes ☎ 942/730247 ⊙ Closed Wed.

## Hotels

### Hotel del Oso

**$$ | HOTEL | FAMILY** | This homey and economical lodge is the perfect base for exploring the Picos de Europa. **Pros:** convenient base for hiking; swimming pool and tennis court; dependably good restaurant. **Cons:** some rooms are on the small side; lower floor rooms can be noisy; decor is outdated. ⑤ Rooms from: €94 ⊠ Cosgaya, Potes ☎ 942/733018 ⊕ www.hoteldeloso.es ⊙ Closed Dec. 15–Feb. 15 ☞ 49 rooms ᠁ No Meals.

### Hotel Valdecoro

**$ | B&B/INN** | In this family-run mountain house, which faces the main road through town, efficient staff tend to guest rooms with modern appointments, making for a pleasant stay. **Pros:** cozy mountain feel; lounge with a fireplace; fine rustic restaurant. **Cons:** no air-conditioning; rooms are tidy but unremarkable; on the main road. ⑤ Rooms from: €80 ⊠ Rte. Paco Wences, Calle Roscabao 5, Potes ☎ 942/730025 ⊕ www.hotelvaldecoro.es ⊙ Closed Jan. and Feb. ☞ 41 rooms ᠁ Free Breakfast.

# Santander

390 km (242 miles) north of Madrid, 154 km (96 miles) north of Burgos, 116 km (72 miles) west of Bilbao, 194 km (120 miles) northeast of Oviedo.

One of the great ports on the Bay of Biscay, Santander is surrounded by busy beaches, yet it manages to avoid the package-tour feel of many Spanish seaside resorts. A fire destroyed most of the old town in 1941, so the rebuilt city looks relatively modern. It comes to life in summer, when its music-and-dance festival draws students, tourists, and performers.

From the 1st to the 4th century, Roman Santander—then called Portus Victoriae—was a major port. Commercial life accelerated between the 13th and 16th centuries, but the waning of Spain's naval power and a series of plagues during the reign of Felipe II caused its fortunes to plummet. The economy was restarted after 1778, when Seville's monopoly on trade with the Americas was revoked and Santander entered fully into commerce with the so-called New World. In 1910 the Palacio de la Magdalena was built by popular subscription as a gift to Alfonso XIII and his queen, Victoria Eugenia, lending Santander prestige as one of Spain's royal watering holes.

The modern city benefits from several promenades and gardens, most of which face the bay. Walk east along the Paseo de Pereda, the main boulevard, to Puerto Chico, a small yacht harbor. Then follow Avenida Reina Victoria to find the tree-lined park paths above the first of the city's beaches, Playa de la Magdalena. Walk onto the Península de la Magdalena to the Palacio de la Magdalena, today the summer seat of the University of Menéndez y Pelayo. Beyond the Magdalena Peninsula, wealthy locals occupy mansions facing the long stretch of shoreline known as El Sardinero, Santander's best beach.

## CRUISE SHIP TRAVEL TO SANTANDER, SPAIN

Ferries dock at the passenger terminal, Estación Marítima, which is downtown. Facilities inside the terminal include a supermarket, café, and tourist information desk. The main tourist office is on Jardines de Pereda. The old town and commercial shopping area are both a short, easy walk away.

There are plenty of hotels close to the port, but consider overnighting in the more scenic Playa del Sardinero beach area; it's 5–10 minutes away from the center via taxi. Metered taxis can be hailed at the entrance of the terminal, and a one-way trip to Playa del Sardinero costs less than €12 (luggage usually costs extra). In Spain it is not customary to tip taxi drivers, but if you want to leave something, rounding up by €1 or €2 is acceptable. The train station (Plaza de las Estaciones) is about a 10-minute walk, and from here you can reach any of Spain's major cities. Local and national buses departing from the Estación de Autobuses (Calle Naveas de Tolosa) run to nearby destinations including Santillana del Mar, a 30-minute drive away.

## GETTING HERE AND AROUND

Santander is easily navigated on foot, but if you're looking to get to El Sardinero beach, hail a taxi or take the bus from the central urban transport hub at Jardines de Pereda.

**CONTACTS Santander Bus Station.**
✉ *Calle Navas de Tolosa, Santander* 🕾 *942/211995.* **Santander Train Station.**
✉ *Pl. de las Estaciones, Santander* 🕾 *912/320320 Renfe* ⊕ *www.renfe.com.*

## VISITOR INFORMATION
**CONTACTS Santander Tourist Office.**
✉ *Jardines de Pereda, Santander* 🕾 *942/203000* ⊕ *turismo.santander.es.*

# ⊙ Sights

### Catedral de Santander
CHURCH | The blocky cathedral marks the transition between Romanesque and Gothic. Though largely rebuilt in the neo-Gothic style after serious damage in the town's 1941 fire, the cathedral retained its 12th-century crypt. The chief attraction here is the tomb of Marcelino Menéndez y Pelayo (1856–1912), Santander's most famous literary figure. The cathedral is across Avenida de Calvo Sotelo from the Plaza Porticada. ✉ *Calle de Somorrostro, Santander* 🎟 *€1.*

### ★ Centro Botín

ARTS CENTER | Inaugurated in 2017, this futuristic museum and performance center designed by architect Renzo Piano was the biggest cultural opening in northern Spain in recent memory. It houses contemporary artwork by international artists. Worth a visit for the eye-popping architecture and views alone, the building overlooks the harbor and is surrounded by the Jardines de Pereda. There is a café on-site, as well as two viewing decks accessible free of charge. ⊠ *Jardines de Pereda, Muelle de Albareda, Santander* ☎ *942/047147* ⊕ *www.centrobotin.org/en* ⊠ *€8, viewpoint free* ⊙ *Closed Mon. (except mid-July–Aug.).*

### Gran Casino del Sardinero

CASINO | This elegant Belle Époque casino and restaurant—worth a quick visit even if gambling isn't your thing—is the heart of El Sardinero, the vacationer's quarter west of the old city. You can't miss it with its regal white facade, red awnings, and pleasant tree-shaded park. Around it you'll find expensive hotels and several fine restaurants. ⊠ *Pl. de Italia, Santander* ☎ *942/276054* ⊕ *www.grancasinosardinero.es* ⊠ *€3.*

### Palacio de la Magdalena

CASTLE/PALACE | Built on the highest point of the Peninsula de Magdalena and surrounded by 62 acres of manicured gardens and rocky beaches, this early-20th-century palace is the most distinctive building in Santander. It was originally a summer home for King Alfonso XIII and Queen Victoria Eugenia, and it has architectural influences from France and England. Today it is a venue for meetings, weddings, and classes. There are also daily guided visits—call in advance to schedule a tour in English. ⊠ *Av. Magdalena, Santander* ☎ *942/203084* ⊕ *www.palaciomagdalena.com* ⊠ *€5.*

# Puente Viesgo 👁

In 1903, four caves were discovered in this 16th-century hamlet in the Pas Valley under the 1,150-foot peak of Monte del Castillo. Two of these—Cueva del Castillo and Cueva de las Monedas—are open to the public. Bison, deer, bulls, and humanoid stick figures are depicted within the caves; the oldest designs are thought to be 35,000 years old. Most arresting are the paintings of 44 hands (35 of them remain). The painters are thought to have blown red pigment around their hands through a hollow bone, leaving the negative image. Reservations are essential via ⊕ *cuevas.culturadecantabria.com.*

## 🏖 Beaches

### Playa El Sardinero

BEACH | Santander's longest and most popular beach has a full range of amenities and fine, golden sand. Although this northeast-facing stretch is exposed, moderate waves in summer make it fine for bathing—despite the chilly water temperatures. In winter, it is a favorite among surfers, particularly the part of the beach in front of Hotel Chiqui. Enter the beach via the sun-dappled Piquío Gardens, where terraces filled with flowers and trees lead the way down to the beach. **Amenities:** food and drink; lifeguards; showers; toilets; water sports. **Best for:** surfing; swimming; walking. ⊠ *Santander.*

## 🍽 Restaurants

### Bodega del Riojano

$$$ | SPANISH | The paintings on wine-barrel ends that decorate this classic restaurant have given it the nickname "Museo

The Altamira Museum's replica of a Paleolithic cave displays paintings of bison.

Redondo" (Round Museum). The building dates back to the 16th century when it was a wine cellar, apparent in the heavy wooden beams overhead and the rough, rustic tables. **Known for:** elevated traditional Cantabrian and Riojan fare; historic setting; friendly service. $ *Average main: €19* ✉ *Calle Río de la Pila 5, Santander* ☎ *942/216750* ⊕ *www.bodegadelriojano. com* ☾ *No dinner Sun.*

### El Serbal

$$$$ | **SPANISH** | Five blocks from the marina, this white-tablecloth dining room with blue walls and hardwood floors pulls out all the stops: Order the tasting menu, for instance, and you'll sample no fewer than five varieties of olive oil. Mains hinge on Cantabrian seafood and run the gamut from cod *al pil pil* (with an emulsified garlic-oil sauce) to flambéed suckling pig to scallop tartare. **Known for:** elegant dining room; well-executed tasting menu; pristine seafood. $ *Average main: €25* ✉ *Calle de Andrés del Río 7, Santander* ☎ *942/222515* ⊕ *www.elserbal.com* ☾ *Closed Mon. No dinner Sun.*

### ★ La Casona del Judío

$$$$ | **SPANISH** | The two exquisite tasting menus at this tranquil Michelin-star establishment offer a whirlwind tour of modern Cantabrian cooking at a good value. Request a table in the romantically lit brick wine cellar, and savor such delicacies as roast partridge with celery-root puree, griddled tiger prawns, and ultracreamy rice pudding. **Known for:** modern Cantabrian cuisine; chatty chef; tasting menus. $ *Average main: €75* ✉ *Calle de Repuente 20, Santander* ☎ *942/342726* ⊕ *www.casonadeljudio.com* ☾ *Closed Mon., No dinner Sun.*

## 🛏 Hotels

### Abba Santander Hotel

$$$ | **HOTEL** | Abba Santander is a chain hotel with welcoming staff and modern conveniences. **Pros:** cheerful service; intriguing architectural details; central location. **Cons:** additional cost for parking; busy part of town; beds may be too firm for some. $ *Rooms from: €130* ✉ *Calle*

Calderón de la Barca 3, Santander
☎ 942/212450, 942/091516 bookings
⊕ www.abbahoteles.com/en/destina-
tions/abba-santander-hotel/hotel.html
⇗ 37 rooms ⊚ No Meals.

### Hotel Bahía

$$ | HOTEL | One of Santander's best-rated hotels is this plush, traditional standby overlooking the water and the cathedral. **Pros:** central location; friendly service; great for watching maritime traffic. **Cons:** no gym; outdated interiors; bells can be noisy on the cathedral side. Ⓢ Rooms from: €120 ⊠ Calle Cádiz 22, Santander ☎ 942/205000 ⊕ www.hotelbahias-antander.com ⇗ 188 rooms ⊚ No Meals.

### Las Brisas

$$$ | B&B/INN | This aparthotel used to be an aristocratic family's mansion by the sea. **Pros:** close to the shore; defiantly uncorporate; charming old-world feel. **Cons:** 30-minute walk from the city center; some rooms are a bit cramped; mildly disorganized. Ⓢ Rooms from: €143 ⊠ Calle la Braña 14, El Sardinero ☎ 942/270111 ⊕ www.hotellasbrisas. net ⊘ Closed Jan–Feb. 15 ⇗ 13 rooms ⊚ Free Breakfast.

## ☮ Nightlife

Most people start their evening in the tapas bars and taverns in and around Plaza de Cañadío, and Calle Hernán Cortés. Night owls continue on to Calle del Sol and Calle de Santa Lucía, which have pleasant spots for late-night drinking, some with live music.

### Cañadío

BARS | An after-work favorite, Cañadio draws a lively evening crowd for tempting tapas and chilled beer on tap. ⊠ Calle de Gómez Oreña 15, Santander ☎ 942/314149 ⊕ www.restaurantecanadio.com ⊘ Closed Sun. except in summer.

## ☺ Shopping

For most items, head to the center: The streets around the ayuntamiento (town hall) are good for clothing, shoes, and sportswear. At the bustling Mercado de la Esperanza, just behind the ayuntamiento, you can find fish and shellfish that have been freshly plucked from the Cantabrian Sea, as well as locally produced cheeses, cured sausages, and tinned fish. Open-air fruit and vegetable stalls mark the entrance.

### Mantequerías Cántabras

FOOD | Local delicacies—including Santander's most famed dessert, sobaos pasiegos (fluffy buttery cakes)—are sold here. ⊠ Mercado del Este, Calle Hernán Cortés 4, Santander ☎ 942/074787 ⊘ Closed Sun.

# Santillana del Mar

29 km (18 miles) west of Santander.

Santillana del Mar has a thriving tourism industry, thanks to cave art discovered 2 km (1 mile) north of town. The town itself is worth a visit of at least a day. Just as the Altamira Caves have captured the essence of prehistoric life, the streets, plazas, taverns, and manor houses of Santillana del Mar paint a vivid portrait of medieval and Renaissance village life in northern Spain. Its stunning ensemble of 15th- to 17th-century stone houses is one of Spain's greatest architectural collections.

### VISITOR INFORMATION

**CONTACTS Santillana del Mar Tourist Office.** ⊠ Calle Jesús Otero 20, Santillana del Mar ☎ 942/818812 ⊕ www.santillanadelmarturismo.com.

# ⊙ Sights

## Altamira Caves

CAVE | These world-famous caves, 3 km (2 miles) southwest of Santillana del Mar, have been called the Sistine Chapel of prehistoric art for the beauty of their drawings, believed to be some 18,000 years old. First uncovered in 1875, the caves are a testament to early mankind's admiration of beauty and surprising technical skill in representing it, especially in the use of rock forms to accentuate perspective.  *All visitors are entered into a lottery for tickets to enter the actual caves, yet only five are allowed in each week. The reproduction in the museum, however, is open to all.* ☒ *Museo de Altamira, Marcelino Sanz de Sautuola, Santillana del Mar* ☏ *942/818005* ⊕ *museodealtamira.mcu.es* ☒ *€3 (free Sat. afternoon and Sun.)* ⊙ *Closed Mon.*

## Colegiata de Santa Juliana

CHURCH | Santillana del Mar is built around the Colegiata, Cantabria's finest Romanesque structure. Highlights include the 12th-century cloister, famed for its sculpted capitals, a 16th-century altarpiece, and the tomb of Santa Juliana, who is the town's patron saint and namesake. ☒ *Pl. las Arenas 1A, Santillana del Mar* ☏ *639/830520* ☒ *€3.*

## Museo Diocesano

OTHER MUSEUM | Inside the 16th-century Regina Coeli convent is a museum devoted to liturgical art including wooden figures of saints, oil paintings of biblical scenes, altarpieces, and a collection of plundered treasures from the so-called New World. ☒ *Calle El Cruce, Santillana del Mar* ☏ *942/840317* ☒ *€3* ⊙ *Closed Mon.*

# ⊟ Hotels

## ★ Parador de Santillana Gil Blas

$$$ | HOTEL | Built in the 16th century, this imposing stone palace has baronial rooms with heavy wooden beams and splendid antique furnishings. **Pros:** storybook surroundings; attentive service; opulent decor. **Cons:** noise carries from the square into the rooms; drafty in winter; expensive. ⑤ *Rooms from: €145* ☒ *Pl. Ramón Pelayo 11, Santillana del Mar* ☏ *942/028028* ⊕ *www.parador.es* ⇌ *28 rooms* ⦿⧉ *No Meals.*

## Posada La Casa del Organista

$ | B&B/INN | A typical *casona montañesa* (mountain manor) with painstakingly crafted stone and wood details, this intimate, gentlemanly hideaway makes a comfortable base for exploring the town and surrounding countryside. **Pros:** good base; lovely views of tiled roofs and rolling hills; immaculately clean. **Cons:** no elevator; some rooms are small; difficult to book in high season. ⑤ *Rooms from: €84* ☒ *Calle Los Hornos 4, Santillana del Mar* ☏ *942/840352* ⊕ *www.casadelorganista.com* ⊙ *Closed Dec. 21–Jan. 20* ⇌ *14 rooms* ⦿⧉ *No Meals.*

# Chapter 6

# THE BASQUE COUNTRY, NAVARRA, AND LA RIOJA

Updated by
Benjamin Kemper

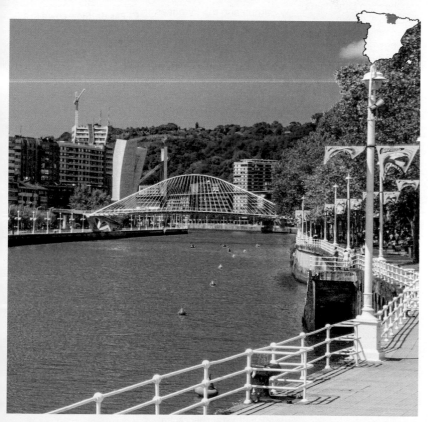

| ⦿ Sights | 🍴 Restaurants | 🛏 Hotels | 🛍 Shopping | 🍸 Nightlife |
|:---:|:---:|:---:|:---:|:---:|
| ★★★★★ | ★★★★★ | ★★★★☆ | ★★★★☆ | ★★★☆☆ |

# WELCOME TO THE BASQUE COUNTRY, NAVARRA, AND LA RIOJA

## TOP REASONS TO GO

★ **Explore the Basque coast:** From colorful fishing villages to tawny beaches, the dramatic Basque coast always delights the eye.

★ **Eat** *pintxos* **(bar snacks) in San Sebastián:** Nothing matches San Sebastián's Parte Vieja, where tavern-hoppers graze at counters heaped with eye-catching morsels.

★ **Appreciate Bilbao's art and architecture:** The gleaming titanium Guggenheim and the Museo de Bellas Artes (Fine Arts Museum) shimmer where steel mills and shipyards once stood, while verdant pastures can be seen in the distance.

★ **Swirl and sip your way through La Rioja:** Spain's most prestigious wine region takes in ancient cobwebbed *bodegas* and architectural wonders.

★ **Splurge on an avant-garde tasting menu:** Few areas on earth boast such a high concentration of renowned chefs making delicious, innovative food.

Inland from the Bay of Biscay, on the border with France, the Basque Country, Navarra, and La Rioja are a Spain apart, a land of dewy green hills, sprawling vineyards, and rocky meadowlands. These regions occupy a fertile slot situated between the Picos de Europa and the Pyrenees mountain ranges and are a cool, rainy reprieve from the sun-scorched Spanish *meseta* (high plain) to the south.

**1 Bilbao.** Go for the Guggenheim; stay for the pintxos and the quaint old town.

**2 Bermeo.** Take a peek at the most important fishing port in the Basque Country.

**3 Mundaka.** Surf the famous *ola izquierda* (left-breaking wave) with the pros.

**4 Axpe Atxondo.** Live your Basque rural fantasy in a tiny mountain town.

**5 Getaria and Zumaia.** Explore Balenciaga's old stomping grounds and taste the grilled turbot that Anthony Bourdain made famous.

**6 San Sebastián.** Make a pilgrimage to Spain's culinary mecca with more Michelin stars per capita than (almost) any other city on earth.

**7 Vitoria-Gasteiz.** Experience true-blue Basque culture without a tour bus in sight in the region's tranquil, eco-friendly capital.

**8 Laguardia.** Savor world-class wine in ultra-modern tasting rooms.

**9 Pasaia.** Slow down in a postcard-worthy fishing village just a few minutes' drive from San Sebastián.

**10 Hondarribia.** Stroll among colorful captains' houses before hopping on a ferry to France.

**11 Pamplona.** Visit the stately Navarran capital, synonymous with Hemingway and the running of the bulls.

**12 Logroño.** Make this scrappy, food-focused city your home base for enological adventures in La Rioja.

**13 La Rioja Alta.** Winery-hop through La Rioja's most coveted wine area.

**14 Haro.** Hole up in La Rioja's most wine-centric town, and feast on local roast lamb.

**15 Sierra Rioja Alta.** Hike, ski, and discover untamed nature in the Riojan highlands.

# EATING AND DRINKING WELL IN THE BASQUE COUNTRY

A restaurant rendition of the classic bacalao al pil pil.

Basque cuisine, Spain's most prestigious regional gastronomy, incorporates the refined culinary sensibilities of the French and the no-nonsense country cooking of inland Iberia—but it's no hybrid cuisine.

The distinctive seafood, meat, and vegetable dishes served here are often impossible to find elsewhere in Spain, thanks to hyperlocal ingredients and culinary secrets passed down from generation to generation.

The so-called Nueva Cocina Vasca (New Basque Cuisine) movement began nearly half a century ago as an echo of the nouvelle cuisine of France. Young chefs like Pedro Subijana and Juan Mari Arzak began deconstructing versions of classic Basque dishes like *marmitako* (tuna and potato stew) and *bacalao al pil pil* (salt cod bathed in emulsified garlic sauce) with the aim to redefine and promote Basque cooking globally. Today the region has the world's highest concentration of Michelin stars per capita—a flare for fancy cooking that has trickled down into a vibrant (and more affordable) pintxo culture.

## CIDER

Don't miss a chance to go to a *sagardotegi*, a boisterous cider house where homemade cider spurts into your glass straight from a *kupela* (an enormous barrel) to be quaffed in a single gulp. *Txuletas de buey* (juicy rib eyes grilled over coals) and *tortilla de bacalao* (cod omelet) provide ballast for the zingy, kombucha-tart cider. The cider-cod combination is linked to the Basque fishermen and whalers who carried cider, rather than wine, in their galleys.

## BABY EELS

*Angulas,* or elvers in English, are a Basque delicacy that has become an expensive treat, with prices reaching €1,200 a kilogram. The 3- to 4-inch-long eels look like spaghetti with eyes and are typically served in a small earthenware dish sizzling with olive oil, garlic, and a single slice of chili. A special wooden fork is used to eat them, to avoid any metallic taste and because the wood grips the slippery eels better than metal. Don't be misled by the "gulas" sold in lower-end *tapas* bars and groceries: they look just like angulas, but are made from processed whitefish.

## BACALAO

Cod—a staple of the Basque diet since the Stone Age—comes in various guises today. *Bacalao al pil pil* is a Bilbao favorite made by pan-cooking the desalted fillets with garlic and olive oil until a thick sauce forms; *pil pil* refers to the sound of the cod-oil emulsion bubbling in the pan.

## BESUGO A LA DONOSTIARRA

*Besugo* (sea bream) cooked San Sebastián style is baked in the oven, covered with flakes of garlic that look like scales, and enlivened at the last minute with vinegar and parsley. Locally available *aligote* (white bream) is similar and much less expensive.

A plate of phenomenally expensive angulas.

A hearty bowl of marmitako.

## OX

Traditionally the ox was a beast of burden in the Basque Country, fed and maintained with reverence and care, but today the term *buey* (ox) is synonymous with good eating. When slaughtered at the age of 12 or 13, oxen's flesh is tender and marbled with streaks of fat rich with grassy aromas. Nowadays, most steaks marketed as *txuletas de buey* (ox steaks) are in fact cut from beef—inaccurately labeled, but delicious nonetheless.

## TUNA AND POTATO STEW

*Marmitako,* the Basque answer to bouillabaisse, is a stick-to-your-ribs potato, yellowfin tuna, and red pepper stew. Beware: it sometimes has a strong fishy taste. One bite and you'll understand why the dish, named after the French for cooking pot (*marmite*), has long been the preferred restorative for weather-beaten seafarers.

## WINE

Basque Txakolí, a simple, zippy white (and, increasingly, rosé and even red) wine made from tart indigenous grapes, is refreshing with seafood and pintxos. Those who prefer a Basque red should spring for a Tempranillo from Rioja Alavesa, the part of Rioja wine country north of the Ebro.

Northern Spain is a misty land of green hills, low russet rooflines, and colorful fishing villages; it's also home to the formerly industrial cities of Bilbao and Vitoria-Gasteiz, now centers of art and architecture. The semiautonomous Basque Country—which spills over the French border—has a verdant landscape and a rugged coastline, and a distinct national and cultural entity.

The Navarra region is considered Basque in the Pyrenees—indeed, Euskera is spoken in much of the region's north (Spanish is spoken in the south). La Rioja, tucked between the Sierra de la Demanda mountain range separating La Rioja from the central Castilian steppe and the Ebro, is Spain's premier wine country.

Called País Vasco in Castilian Spanish and Euskal Herria in the linguistically mysterious, non-Indo-European Basque language, Euskera, the Basque region is essentially a country within a country, or a nation within a state (the semantics are much debated). Though a significant portion of Basques favor independence from Spain, the separatist terrorist organization ETA (Euskadi Ta Askatasuna, meaning "Basque Homeland and Liberty"), which used to cause some travelers pause, disbanded in 2018. There have been no significant politically motivated acts of violence in the region in years.

Basque culture, with its pre-Roman roots, is unlike that of any other region in Spain. In local festivals, locals play such rural sports as chopping mammoth tree trunks and lifting boulders. The Basques' competitive streak carries over into poetry and gastronomy; *bertsolariak* (amateur poets) improvise duels of sharp-witted verse, and gastronomic societies compete in cooking contests to see who can make the best *sopa de ajo* (garlic soup) or *marmitako*.

It's worth noting that the French Basque Country, though part of the same cultural unit, is not covered in for geographical reasons. In addition, although most locales and subjects in this chapter have both Basque and Castilian (Spanish) spellings, we've given preference to the most widely used name (e.g., pintxos, not pinchos, and San Sebastián, not "Donosti").

## MAJOR REGIONS

**Bilbao and inland Basque Country.** Starring the futuristic Museo Guggenheim Bilbao, Frank Gehry's titanium brainchild, Bilbao is one of Spain's artistic hot spots. The Basque capital of Vitoria is smaller and less flashy, but those who visit are rewarded with a remarkably well-preserved medieval quarter and affordable frills-free dining.

**San Sebastián and the coast.** Along the Bay of Biscay in Gipuzkoa province, colorful fishing villages and beach towns appear one after the other on the snaking BI-3438 coastal highway. Weaving through dense forests punctuated with jaw-dropping ocean views, this is one of the most scenic drives in Spain. After passing the sleepy port of Getaria and a handful of well-to-do resorts, you'll arrive in San Sebastián, Bilbao's aristocratic cousin, a city that invites you to slow down with its elegant boardwalks and leisurely pintxo crawls. East of San Sebastián is Pasaia (in Spanish: Pasajes), from which the Marquis de Lafayette set off to help the rebel forces in the American Revolution and where Victor Hugo spent a winter writing. Just shy of the French border is Hondarribia (Spanish: Fuenterrabía), a brightly painted, flower-festooned port town.

**Navarra and Pamplona.** Bordering the French and Aragonese Pyrenees and populated largely by Basques, Navarra grows progressively less Basque toward its southern and eastern edges. Pamplona, the ancient Navarrese capital, draws crowds with its annual festivities of San Fermín and the running of the bulls. Olite, south of Pamplona, has a storybook castle, while the towns of Puente la Reina and Estella are visually indelible stops on the Camino de Santiago.

**La Rioja** (named for the Río Oja), a rugged compendium of highlands, plains, and vineyards nourished by the Río Ebro, is synonymous with fine wine. Most inhabitants live along the Ebro, in the cities of Logroño and Haro, though the mountains and upper river valleys are arguably more scenic. A mix of Atlantic and Mediterranean climates, and cultures with Basque overtones, La Rioja comprises La Rioja Alta (Upper Rioja), the wetter and more mountainous western end (where most of the region's great wines come from), and La Rioja Baja (Lower Rioja), the dryer eastern extremity with a more Mediterranean climate and less prestigious wines. Logroño, the scruffy regional capital, straddles the two.

# Planning

## When to Go

Relatively clear skies and warm temperatures last from mid-April to mid-October, making the warm-weather months the best time of year to visit. Some shops and restaurants close in August.

Pamplona in July is bedlam, though for hard-core party animals it's heaven.

The Basque Country is rainy in the winter, but the bracing Atlantic weather can be invigorating if you're in the right mindset. Basque cuisine's heartiest, richest dishes taste their best when it's cold and damp outside—case in point: the menus at traditional cider houses, which (for the most part) are only available January to mid-May.

The September film festival in San Sebastián coincides with the spectacular whaleboat regattas, while the beaches are still ideal and mostly uncrowded.

When looking for a place to stay, remember that the north is an expensive, well-to-do part of Spain, which is reflected in room rates—though some steals can be found in the off-season (and on Airbnb). San Sebastián is particularly pricey, and Pamplona rates triple during San Fermín in July. Be sure to book far ahead for summer travel.

# Planning Your Time

A road trip through the Basque Country, Navarra, and La Rioja requires at least a week, but you can get a good sense of Bilbao and San Sebastián, the region's most essential cities, in two days each. The Baztan Valley (see The Pyrenees chapter); Pamplona; Laguardia; and La Rioja's capital, Logroño, are other top stops.

If you have a spare day or two, visit Mundaka and the coast of Bizkaia west of Bilbao; Getaria, Pasaia, and Hondarribia near San Sebastián; and the wineries of Haro in La Rioja, stopping in Vitoria on the way.

La Rioja also has some of the finest mountain landscapes in Spain in Sierra de la Demanda, and worthwhile culinary pilgrimages in the "gastronomical hotel" Echaurren in Ezcaray and in the legendary asador Terete in Haro.

There's also more to the area's festival scene than the world-famous San Fermín and its running of the bulls in Pamplona. From music and dance festivals to colorful religious processions to quirky food fairs like the Getaria Anchovy Festival, there are lots of events that can be worth planning a trip around (see "On the Calendar" in Travel Smart).

# Getting Here and Around

## AIR
Bilbao's airport serves much of this area, and there are smaller, often more expensive airports at Hondarribia (serving San Sebastián), Vitoria, Logroño, and Pamplona, which run mostly domestic flights.

**AIRPORTS Aeropuerto de Bilbao.** ⊠ 48180 Loiu, ⊕ www.aena.es.

## BICYCLE
Bicycle travel in the Basque Country and across the north of Spain is hilly and often wet, but for the iron-hearted, -lunged, -legged, and -bottomed, this is a scenic way to travel and terrific exercise, albeit somewhat perilous on the region's narrow roads.

## BUS
Frequent coach service connects the major cities to Madrid, Zaragoza, and Barcelona (with a layover or transfer to Spain's other destinations). The trip between Barcelona and Bilbao takes seven to eight hours.

Public bus service between cities and smaller towns is surprisingly comprehensive—and cheap. Consult Google Maps or visit a local tourist office for route information.

## CAR
Even the remotest points are an easy one-day drive from Madrid, and northern Spain is well-connected by freeways.

The drive from Madrid to Bilbao is 397 km (247 miles), about five hours; follow the A1 past Burgos to Miranda del Ebro, where you pick up the AP68. Car rentals are available in the major cities: Bilbao, Pamplona, San Sebastián, Hondarribia, and Vitoria. Note: The Basque word for calle is "kalea." We have standardized our addresses using "Calle" for ease of Google Mapping, but you will see Kalea on road signs in most Basque locales.

## TAXI
In cities, taxis can usually be hailed on the street, and drivers are generally amenable to longer trips (say, from San Sebastián to Astigarraga's cider houses). When booking a taxi outside the main cities, be sure to agree on a rate prior to traveling, or ensure there is a meter.

## TRAIN

Currently only snail-speed old RENFE trains connect Madrid and Barcelona to Bilbao, San Sebastián, and Logroño. The much-anticipated "Y Vasca" AVE route—over 30 years in the making and expected to be completed by 2028—will make the trip much quicker. Once you've arrived, a car is the most convenient way to get around, though if you aren't venturing too far into the countryside, you can rely on buses, rideshares, and—in Bilbao—the metro and tramway. The regional company FEVE runs a delightful if notoriously unreliable narrow-gauge train that winds through stunning landscapes. From San Sebastián, lines west to Bilbao (via Euskotren, which locals call *El Topo*, "The Mole") and east to Hendaye, France, depart from Estación de Amara; most long-distance trains use RENFE's Estación del Norte.

*See the Travel Smart chapter for more information about train travel.*

### RIDESHARE

If you don't have a car, the fastest, cheapest, and most eco-friendly way to get from Madrid or Barcelona to major destinations in the Basque Country, Navarra, and La Rioja is via the Blablacar rideshare app. Simply type your origin and destination into the app, select the itinerary that best suits your schedule, and confirm your booking via credit card. You can then text with the driver to arrange pickup and drop-off locations. Prices are low because drivers aren't allowed to make a profit (the fee you pay only helps offset the cost of gas and tolls). Download the app in your mobile provider's app store or browse trips on ⊕ *www.blablacar.com*.

# Restaurants

Foodies may never want to leave this corner of Spain, where avant-garde and down-home cooking styles merge seamlessly. Everywhere you look in the region's cities and towns, there are mom-and-pop taverns, pintxo bars, wine-and-cheese nooks, and *asadores*—restaurants specializing in grilled meats and fish. The Basque Country is well known for its Michelin-starred destination restaurants, venues sequestered in off-the-beaten-path villages that have become dining meccas such as Asador Etxebarri (in Atxondo), Martín Berasategui (in Lasarte), and Mugaritz (in Errenteria).

*Restaurant reviews have been shortened. For full information, visit Fodors. com.*

# Hotels

From glitz-and-glam grande dames in San Sebastián to architectural hideaways and rustic *agroturismos* in La Rioja, this part of Spain has a hotel for every type of traveler.

*Hotel reviews have been shortened. For full information, visit Fodors.com.*

| What It Costs in Euros | | | |
|---|---|---|---|
| $ | $$ | $$$ | $$$$ |
| **RESTAURANTS** | | | |
| under €15 | €15–€21 | €22–€27 | over €27 |
| **HOTELS** | | | |
| under €100 | €100–€139 | €140–€195 | over €195 |

# Bilbao

*102 km (63 miles) west of San Sebastián, 116 km (72 miles) east of Santander, 397 km (247 miles) north of Madrid.*

Time in Bilbao (Bilbo in Euskera) may be recorded as BG or AG—Before Guggenheim or After Guggenheim. Never has a single monument of art and architecture so radically changed a city, at least not in Spain. Frank Gehry's stunning museum, plus Norman Foster's sleek subway system, the Santiago Calatrava glass footbridge and airport, the leafy César Pelli Abandoibarra park and commercial complex next to the Guggenheim, and the Philippe Starck Azkuna Zentroa cultural center have breathed unprecedented creative energy and verve into what was once a sooty industrial hub.

Greater Bilbao contains almost 1 million inhabitants, nearly half the total population of the Basque Country. Founded in 1300 by Vizcayan noble Diego López de Haro, the city became an industrial center in the mid-19th century because of the abundance of minerals in the surrounding hills. An affluent industrial class grew up here, as did the working class in suburbs that line the *Margen Izquierda* (Left Bank) of the Nervión estuary.

Bilbao's newer attractions get more press, but the city's old treasures still quietly line the banks of the silty Nervión. The *Casco Viejo* (Old Quarter)—also known as *Siete Calles* (Seven Streets)—is a charming jumble of shops, bars, and restaurants on the river's right bank, near the Puente del Arenal bridge. This elegant proto-Bilbao nucleus was carefully restored after devastating floods in 1983. Throughout the Casco Viejo are ancient mansions emblazoned with family coats of arms, wooden doors, and fine ironwork balconies. The most interesting square is the 64-arch Plaza Nueva, where an outdoor market is pitched every Sunday morning.

Walking the banks of the Nervión is a satisfying jaunt. After all, this was how—while out on a morning jog—Guggenheim director Thomas Krens first discovered the perfect spot for his project, nearly opposite the right bank's Deusto University. From the Palacio de Euskalduna upstream to the colossal Mercado de la Ribera, parks and green zones line the river. César Pelli's Abandoibarra project fills in the half mile between the Guggenheim and the Euskalduna bridge with a series of parks, the Deusto University library, and a major shopping center.

On the left bank, the wide, late-19th-century boulevards of the Ensanche neighborhood, such as Gran Vía (the main shopping artery) and Alameda de Mazarredo, are the city's more aristocratic face. Bilbao's cultural institutions include, along with the Guggenheim, the Museo de Bellas Artes, and an opera society (Asociación Bilbaína de Amigos de la Ópera, or ABAO) with dozens of performances per year and tens of thousands of spectators. In addition, epicureans have long ranked Bilbao's culinary offerings among the best in Spain. Don't miss a chance to ride the Euskotren trolley line along the river from Atxuri Station to Basurto's San Mamés soccer stadium, reverently dubbed the "Catedral del Fútbol" (the Cathedral of Football).

## GETTING HERE AND AROUND

Euskotren's Tranvía Bilbao, running up and down the Ría de Bilbao (aka Nervión Estuary) past the Guggenheim to the Mercado de la Ribera, is an attraction in its own right: silent, swift, and panoramic as it glides up and down its grassy runway. The Euskotren that leaves from Atxuri Station north of the Mercado de la Ribera runs along a spectacular route through Gernika and the Urdaibai Biosphere Preserve to Mundaka and Bermeo, probably the best way short of a boat to see this lovely wetlands preserve.

Bilbobus provides local bus service 6:15 am 10:55 pm. Plaza Circular and Plaza Moyua are the principal hubs for all lines. Once the metro and normal bus routes stop service, take a night bus, known as a Gautxori ("night bird"). Six lines run every 30 minutes between Plaza Circular and Plaza Moyúa and the city limits on Friday 11:30 pm–2 am and on Saturday overnight until 7 am.

Metro Bilbao is linear, running down the Nervión estuary from Basauri, above, or east of, the Casco Viejo, all the way to the mouth of the Nervión at Getxo, before continuing to the beach town of Plentzia. The Moyúa station is the most central stop, and lies in the middle of Bilbao's Ensanche, or modern part. The second subway line runs down the left bank of the Nervión to Santurtzi. The fare is approximately €2 for a one-way ticket and around €1 with the Barik travel card (see below).

The reusable Barik card is good for metro and bus travel and for the Artxanda Furnicular, RENFE, and Euskotren trains and trams, and costs €3, plus a minimum additional value of €5. Cards can be purchased at Barik vending machines in all metro stations. One card can be used by up to 10 people. Transfers cost extra.

For up to 24, 48, or 72 hours, the Bilbao Bizkaia Card (⊕ www.bilbaobizkaiacard. com) allows for unlimited use of the metro, buses, train, tram, and Artxanda funicular railway all around the Bizkaia region; discounts on certain restaurants, bars, and shops; and free entry to a variety of cultural activities including more than 25 sights such as the Guggenheim, Museo de Bellas Artes de Bilbao, and Museo de Reproducciones Artísticas de Bilbao. The card costs €10 for 24 hours, €15 for 48 hours, and €20 for 72 hours.

**BUS AND SUBWAY INFORMATION Bilbobus.** ☎ 94/445–3471 ⊕ www.bilbobus. com. **Metro Bilbao.** ☎ 94/425–4025 ⊕ www.metrobilbao.eus.

**STATIONS Bilbao-Abando Railway Station.** ⊠ Pl. Circular 2, El Ensanche ☎ 94/479–5760 ⊕ www.adif.es. **Termibus Bilbao.** ⊠ Gurtubay 1, San Mamés ☎ 94/439–5077.

## VISITOR INFORMATION
**CONTACTS Bilbao Tourism Office.** ⊠ Pl. Circular 1, El Ensanche ☎ 94/479–5760 ⊕ www.bilbaoturismo.net Ⓜ Abando.

## TOURS
### Bilbao Paso a Paso
**GUIDED TOURS** | Bilbao Paso a Paso organizes walking tours, guided visits to the Guggenheim, hot-air-balloon rides, gastronomical tours around the city, LGBT+ itineraries, and excursions to nearby sights. ⊠ San Nicolás de Olabeaga 62B, Casco Viejo ☎ 94/415–3892 ⊕ www. bilbaopasoapaso.com 🖅 From €175 Ⓜ Olabeaga.

### Bilbao Turismo
**GUIDED TOURS** | Weekend guided tours, in English and Spanish, are conducted by the tourist office (reservations required). ⊠ Pl. Circular 1, El Ensanche ☎ 94/479 5760 ⊕ www.bilbaoturismo. net Ⓜ Abando.

### Bilboats
**BOATING | FAMILY** | One- and two-hour boat tours take you downstream from Plaza Pío Baroja, the city center, passing some of Bilbao's iconic buildings and bridges. Customized day trips can also be arranged. ⊠ Pl. Pío Baroja, Bilbao ☎ 94/642–4157 ⊕ www.bilboats.com 🖅 From €13 Ⓜ Moyúa.

## ◉ Sights
### Azkuna Zentroa
**NOTABLE BUILDING** | In the early 20th century, this was a municipal wine-storage facility used by Bilbao's Rioja wine barons. Now, the city-block-size, Philippe Starck–designed civic center has shops, cafés, restaurants, movie theaters, and nightlife venues. The complex regularly hosts film festivals and art exhibitions,

and it's a cozy place to take refuge on a rainy afternoon. ✉ *Pl. Arriquibar 4, El Ensanche* ☎ *94/401–4014* ⊕ *www. azkunazentroa.eus* Ⓜ *Moyúa.*

## Begoñako Basilika

**CHURCH** | Bilbao's most cherished religious sanctuary, dedicated to Bizkaia's patron saint, can be reached via 313 stairs from Plaza de Unamuno or by the gigantic elevator (Ascensor de Begoña) looming over Calle Esperanza 6. The Gothic nave was begun in 1519 and was completed in 1620 with the economic support of dozens of shipbuilders and merchants, whose businesses are commemorated on the inner walls. The high ground the basilica occupies was strategically important during the Carlist Wars of 1836 and 1873, and as a result La Begoña suffered significant damage that was not restored until the beginning of the 20th century. ✉ *Calle Virgen de Begoña 38, Begoñalde* ☎ *94/412–7091* 🔲 *Free* Ⓜ *Casco Viejo.*

## Biblioteca de Bidebarrieta

**LIBRARY** | This historic library and intellectual club was originally called *El Sitio* (The Siege) in memory of Bilbao's successful resistance to the Carlist siege of 1876. (Carlists were supporters of Fernando VII's brother, Don Carlos, over his daughter Isabella II as rightful heir to the Spanish throne.) Now a municipal library, the Bidebarrieta has a music auditorium that is one of Bilbao's most beautiful venues and a spot to check for the infrequent performances held there. The reading rooms are open to the public and are a good place to read newspapers, make notes, or just enjoy the historical echoes of the place. ✉ *Calle Bidebarrieta 4, Casco Viejo* ☎ *94/415–0915* 🔲 *Free* ⊙ *Closed Sun.* Ⓜ *Casco Viejo.*

## Catedral de Santiago de Bilbao (*St. James's Cathedral*)

**CHURCH** | Bilbao's oldest church was a pilgrimage stop on the coastal route to Santiago de Compostela. Work began in 1379, but fire delayed completion until the early 16th century. The florid Gothic style with Isabelline elements features a nave in the form of a Greek cross, with ribbed vaulting resting on cylindrical columns. The notable outdoor arcade was used for public meetings of early governing bodies. ✉ *Pl. de Santiago 1, Casco Viejo* ☎ *94/415–3627* ⊕ *www.catedralbilbao.com* 🔲 *€6* Ⓜ *Casco Viejo.*

## Convento de la Encarnación

**CHURCH** | The Basque Gothic architecture of this early-16th-century convent, church, and museum gives way to Renaissance and baroque ornamentation high on the main facade. The Museo Diocesano de Arte Sacro (Diocesan Museum of Sacred Art) occupies a carefully restored 16th-century cloister. The inner patio, ancient and intimate, is alone worth the visit. On display are religious silverwork, liturgical garments, sculptures, and paintings dating back to the 12th century. The convent is across from the Atxuri station just upstream from the Puente de San Antón. ✉ *Pl. de la Encarnación, Casco Viejo* ☎ *94/432–0125* ⊕ *www.eleizmuseoa.com* 🔲 *€3* ⊙ *Closed Mon.* Ⓜ *Casco Viejo.*

## Doña Casilda Iturrizar Park

**CITY PARK** | **FAMILY** | Bilbao's main park, stretching east toward the river from the Museo de Bellas Artes, is a lush collection of tree-shaded paths, duck ponds, fountains, and wide lawns. It's a sanctuary from the hard-edged Ensanche, Bilbao's modern, post-1876 expansion. Doña Casilda de Iturrizar was a well-to-do 19th-century Bilbao matron who married a powerful banker and used his wealth to support various cultural and beneficent institutions in the city, including this grassy refuge. ✉ *El Ensanche* Ⓜ *San Mamés.*

## Euskal Museoa Bilbao Museo Vasco (*Basque Museum of Bilbao*)

**HISTORY MUSEUM** | The world's best museum on Basque ethnography (and Bilbao's

cultural history) occupies a 16th-century convent. Highlights include El Mikeldi, a pre-Christian, Iron Age stone animal representation that may be 4,000 years old; the room dedicated to Basque shepherds and the pastoral way of life; and the exhibit "Mar de los Vascos" ("Sea of the Basques") about whaling, fishing, and maritime activities. Placards are in Spanish and Basque only. ✉ *Pl. Unamuno 4, Casco Viejo* ☎ *94/415–5423* ⊕ *www. euskalmuseoa.eus* ⌕ *€3 (free Thurs.)* ⊘ *Closed Tues.* Ⓜ *Casco Viejo.*

### Funicular de Artxanda

**VIEWPOINT** | Take a five-minute spin on the Artxanda Funicular, the railway up to the top of Artxanda Mountain, for some of the best views over Bilbao. At the summit, there's a park, hotel, sports complex, and a couple of good *asadores.* ✉ *Pl. de Funicular, Matiko* ☎ *94/445–4966* ⊕ *funicularartxanda.bilbao.eus* ⌕ *€5 round-trip* Ⓜ *Casco Viejo.*

### Iglesia de San Nicolás

**CHURCH** | Honoring the patron saint of mariners, San Nicolás de Bari, the city's early waterfront church was built over an earlier hermitage and consecrated in 1756. With a striking baroque facade over the Arenal, originally a sandy beach, the church weathered significant damage at the hands of French and Carlist troops in the 19th century. Sculptures by Juan Pascual de Mena adorn the interior. Look for the oval plaque to the left of the door marking the high-water mark of the flood of 1983. ✉ *Pl. de San Nicolás 1, Casco Viejo* ☎ *94/416–3424* ⌕ *Free* Ⓜ *Casco Viejo.*

### Itsasmuseum (*Maritime Museum of Bilbao*)

**OTHER MUSEUM** | **FAMILY** | This carefully researched nautical museum on the left bank of the Ría de Bilbao reconstructs the history of the Bilbao waterfront and shipbuilding industry beginning from medieval times. Temporary exhibits range from visits by extraordinary seacraft such as tall ships or traditional fishing vessels to thematic displays on 17th- and 18th-century clipper ships or the sinking of the *Titanic.* ✉ *Muelle Ramón de la Sota 1, San Mamés* ☎ *94/608–5500* ⊕ *www.itsasmuseum.eus* ⌕ *€6 (free Tues. Sept.–June)* ⊘ *Closed Mon.* Ⓜ *San Mamés.*

### Kaitxo

**FACTORY** | A 20-minute drive southwest to the village of Balmaseda is in fact a one-way ticket to chocolate-and-coffee heaven. On an hourlong factory tour, learn firsthand what goes into making some of Spain's finest "bean-to-bar" chocolate and award-winning single-origin coffees—and how both delicacies tie into Spain's rich food history—during a tour that culminates in a heady tasting. ✉ *Fábrica Kaitxo, Avda. Encartaciones 72, Bilbao* ☎ *94/680–0679* ⊕ *www.kaitxo. com* ⌕ *€12.*

### La Casa de la Villa (City Hall) (*Casa Consistorial*)

**GOVERNMENT BUILDING** | Architect Joaquín de Rucoba built this city hall in 1892, on the site of the San Agustín convent destroyed during the 1836 Carlist War. It shares the Belle Époque style of de Rucoba's Teatro Arriaga. The Salón Árabe, the highlight of the interior, was designed by the same architect who built Bilbao's Café Iruña, as their neo-Mudejar motifs suggest. ✉ *Pl. de Ernesto Erkoreka 1, El Arenal* ☎ *94/420–4200, 94/420–5298* ⌕ *Free* Ⓜ *Abando.*

### Los Jardines de Albia

**GARDEN** | Bilbaínos wax poetic about this welcoming town green surrounded by concrete jungle. Overlooking the square is the Basque Gothic **Iglesia de San Vicente Mártir,** whose amply robed sculpture of the Virgin—located on the main facade—had to be sculpted a second time after the original version was deemed too scantily clad, according to local legend. The Jardines de Albia are centered on the bronze effigy of writer Antonio de Trueba, by the famous Spanish sculptor Mariano Benlliure (1866–1947). ⊠ *Calle Colón de Larreátegui, El Ensanche* Ⓜ *Abando.*

## ★ Mercado de la Ribera

**MARKET** | This renovated triple-decker ocean liner, with its prow facing down the estuary toward the open sea, houses one of the best markets of its kind in Europe—and one of the biggest, with some 400 retail stands that run the gamut from fish markets to pintxo bars to wine shops. This is a good place to stock upon culinary souvenirs while indulging in a pintxo or three. ⊠ *Calle de la Ribera 22, Casco Viejo* ☎ *94/602–3791* ⊕ *mercadodelaribera.biz* ⊗ *Closed Sat. from 3 pm and Sun.* Ⓜ *Casco Viejo.*

## Museo de Bellas Artes (*Museum of Fine Arts*)

**ART MUSEUM** | Spain's number-three fine arts museum, bested only by Madrid's Prado and Seville's Museo de Bellas Artes, features works from every Spanish school and movement from the 12th through the 20th centuries. The collection of Flemish, French, Italian, and Spanish paintings includes works by El Greco, Francisco de Goya y Lucientes, Diego Velázquez, José Ribera, Paul Gauguin, and Antoni Tàpies. One large and excellent section traces developments in 20th-century Spanish and Basque art alongside works by better-known European contemporaries, such as Fernand Léger and Francis Bacon. Look for Zuloaga's famous portrait of La Condesa Mathieu de Moailles and Joaquín Sorolla's portrait of Basque philosopher Miguel de Unamuno. Expect to spend at least three hours here. ⊠ *Parque de Doña Casilda de Iturrizar, Pl. Museo 2, El Ensanche* ☎ *94/439–6060* ⊕ *www. museobilbao.com* ⊠ *Free* ⊗ *Closed Tues.* Ⓜ *Moyúa.*

## ★ Museo Guggenheim Bilbao

**ART MUSEUM** | It's hard to overstate the importance of the Guggenheim museum, Frank Gehry's architectural masterpiece of undulating titanium and chaotic, nature-inspired forms built on the riverfront. It all began when Guggenheim director Thomas Krens set out to find a venue for a major European museum and came up dry in Paris, Madrid, and other major cities. Having glumly accepted an invitation to Bilbao, Krens was out for a morning jog when he found what he was looking for—an empty riverside lot once occupied by shipyards and warehouses. He had a vision of a building that would symbolize Bilbao's macro-reconversion from steel to titanium, from heavy industry to art—and one that would be a nexus between the early-14th-century Casco Viejo and the 19th-century Ensanche, between the wealthy right bank and working-class left bank of the Nervión.

Frank Gehry's gleaming brainchild opened in 1997 and was hailed as "the greatest building of our time" by architect Philip Johnson and "a miracle" by Herbert Muschamp of the *New York Times*. At once suggestive of a silver-scaled fish and a mechanical heart, Gehry's sculpture in titanium, limestone, and glass echoes the Contemporary and Postmodern artworks it contains. The smoothly rounded jumble of surfaces and cylindrical shapes recalls Bilbao's shipbuilding and steel-manufacturing past, while transparent and reflective materials create a shimmering, futuristic luminosity. With the final section of La Salve Bridge over the Nervión folded into the structure, the Guggenheim is both a doorway to Bilbao and an urban forum: the atrium looks up into the center of town and across the river to the old quarter and the tranquil green hillsides of Artxanda, where livestock graze. Gehry achieved his goal of building a structure in which "you [could] feel your soul rise up."

The free audio guide offers an excellent synopsis of modern art, contemporary art, and the Guggenheim.

The collection, described by Krens as "a daring history of the art of the 20th century," consists of more than 250 works, most from the New York Guggenheim and the rest acquired by the Basque government. The second and third floors reprise the original Guggenheim collection of abstract expressionist, cubist, surrealist, and geometrical works. Legendary artists of the 20th century (including Kandinsky, Picasso, Ernst, Tàpies, Pollock, and Calder) are joined by more contemporary figures (Bruce Nauman, Txomin Badiola, Miquel Barceló, Jean-Michel Basquiat, and others). The ground floor is dedicated to large-format and installation work, some of which—like Richard Serra's *Serpent*—was created specifically for the space. Claes Oldenburg's *Knife Ship*, Robert Morris's walk-in *Labyrinth*, and pieces by Joseph Beuys, Christian Boltanski, Richard Long, Jenny Holzer, and others round out the heavyweight division in one of the largest galleries in the world.

Expect lines on holidays and weekends, especially late morning through early afternoon. Cut the wait time by buying tickets ahead of time online or around closing time for the following day. ✉ *Abandoibarra Etorbidea 2, El Ensanche* ☎ *94/435–9080* ⊕ *www.guggenheim-bilbao.eus* 🎫 *€16* 🕐 *Closed Mon. Sept.– June* Ⓜ *Moyúa.*

## Plaza Miguel de Unamuno (*Plaza Unamuno*)

PLAZA/SQUARE | This roomy square at the upper edge of the Casco Viejo honors Bilbao's greatest intellectual, Miguel de Unamuno (1864–1936), the philosopher, novelist, professor, and public figure. Unamuno wrote some of Spain's most seminal works including *Del sentimiento trágico de la vida en los hombres y los pueblos* (*The Tragic Sense of Life in Men and Nations*). His *Niebla* (*Mist*) is generally accepted as the first existentialist novel, published in 1914 when Jean-Paul Sartre was but nine years old. ✉ *Casco Viejo* Ⓜ *Casco Viejo.*

## Plaza Nueva (*Plaza Barria*)

PLAZA/SQUARE | This 64-arch neoclassical plaza, built in 1851, is known for its Sunday-morning flea market, December 21 Santo Tomás festivities, and tapas bars and restaurants. Note the size of the houses' balconies (the bigger the balcony, the richer the original proprietor) and the tiny windows near the top of the facades, where servants' quarters would've been. The building behind the coat of arms at the head of the square was once a government office but is now the Euskaltzaindia (Academy of the Basque Language). The coat of arms shows the tree of Gernika, a symbol of Basque autonomy. The bars and shops around the arcades include two Victor Montes establishments, one for pintxos at Plaza Nueva 8 and the other for sit-down dining at No. 2. Café Bar Bilbao (No. 6), aka Casa Pedro, has Belle Époque interiors accented by photos of early Bilbao, while Argoitia (No. 15), across the square, has a nice angle on the midday sun. ✉ *Casco Viejo* Ⓜ *Casco Viejo.*

## ★ Vizcaya Bridge (*Hanging Bridge*)

BRIDGE | This extraordinary 19th-century transporter bridge suspended by cables ferries cars and passengers across the Nervión, uniting the bourgeois Arenas and working-class Portugalete districts. Portugalete is a 15-minute walk from Santurce, where the quayside Hogar del Pescador Mandanga serves simple fish specialties like*besugo* and grilled sardines. ✉ *Barria 3, Las Arenas* ✛ *To reach bridge, take subway to Areeta, or drive across Puente de Deusto, turn left on Av. Lehendakari Aguirre, and follow signs for Las Arenas; it's a 10- or 15-min drive from downtown.* ☎ *94/480–1012* ⊕ *www.puente-colgante.com* 🎫 *From €1* Ⓜ *Areeta.*

### Zubizuri Bridge

**BRIDGE** | Santiago Calatrava's seagull-shaped bridge (the name means "white bridge" in Euskera) is a few minutes from the Guggenheim. Other creations by the cult architect include Bilbao Airport and Ondarroa's Puerto Bridge. ⊠ *El Ensanche* Ⓜ *Moyúa.*

##  Restaurants

### Asador Guetaria

**$$$$ | BASQUE** | With a wood-paneled dining room awash with antiques, this family operation is a longtime local favorite for top-quality fish and meats cooked over coals. In the open kitchen, wild *lubina* (sea bass), *rodaballo* (turbot), and other regional delicacies from land and sea cook to crackly perfection. **Known for:** homey, old-timey dining room; familial atmosphere; masterful grilled dishes. Ⓢ *Average main: €50* ⊠ *Colón de Larreátegui 12, El Ensanche* ☎ *94/424–3923, 94/423–2527* ⊕ *www.guetaria.com* Ⓜ *Moyúa.*

### ★ Azurmendi

**$$$$ | BASQUE** | The immersive gastro-experience at this envelope-pushing eco-restaurant by renowned Basque chef Eneko Atxa starts with nibbles in the indoor garden, continues on to the kitchen with a quick tour, and culminates in the dining room with a conceptual tasting menu featuring dishes like "dew water" and curd made with "a thousand flowers." **Known for:** a 10-minute drive out of town; most innovative restaurant experience in Bilbao; three-Michelin-star dining. Ⓢ *Average main: €260* ⊠ *Legina Auzoa, Bilbao* ☎ *94/455–8866* ⊕ *www. azurmendi.restaurant* ☾ *Closed Sun. and Mon.*

### Berton

**$$ | BASQUE** | The kitchen is open until midnight in this unfussy Casco Viejo pintxo spot. The industrial design—think tables with a green polyethylene finish and exposed pipes—belies a comfort-food-heavy menu with star dishes like octopus brochettes and juicy grilled steaks. **Known for:** night-owl hot spot; terrific value; top-quality steaks. Ⓢ *Average main: €16* ⊠ *Calle Jardines 8, Casco Viejo* ☎ *94/416–7035* ⊕ *www. berton.eus* Ⓜ *Casco Viejo.*

### ★ Bihotz

**$ | CAFÉ** | Rest your legs at this third-wave coffeehouse that uses a sleek La Marzocco machine and is furnished with cushy armchairs and floor lamps. There are also small-production vermouths and local craft beers to try alongside soups, sandwiches, and other snacks. **Known for:** homey, inviting ambience; excellent craft beer selection; best café con leche in town. Ⓢ *Average main: €8* ⊠ *Calle Arechaga 6, Casco Viejo* ☎ *94/471–9674* ⊕ *www.facebook.com/bihotzsanfrancisco* ☾ *Closed Mon.* Ⓜ *Casco Viejo.*

### ★ Bistró Guggenheim Bilbao

**$$$ | BASQUE** | Museum restaurants tend to be underwhelming, overpriced tourist traps, but Bistró—with its exuberantly colorful dining room and meticulously prepared modern Basque cuisine served by a knowledgeable waitstaff—is a blissful exception to the rule. Tartares, roast meats, local seasonal vegetables, and top-grade seafood are the building blocks of the three set menus, the most expensive of which is a five-course *degustación* for a paltry €38. **Known for:** river- and museum-side dining on a budget; homemade everything, including the bread; iconic interior design. Ⓢ *Average main: €22* ⊠ *Avda. Abandoibarra 2, El Ensanche* ☎ *94/423–9333* ⊕ *www.bistroguggenheimbilbao.com* ☾ *No dinner Sun.–Wed.* Ⓜ *Moyúa.*

### ★ Café Iruña

**$$ | CAFÉ** | This historical Bilbao haunt (est. 1903) in the Ensanche's most popular garden and square has azulejo-lined walls, dreamy murals of rural scenes, and a painted artesonado ceiling. Stick to tried-and-true classics like Basque

# Bilbao

## Sights ▼

1 Azkuna Zentroa ......... **E6**
2 Begoñako Basilika ...... **J1**
3 Biblioteca de
Bidebarrieta .............. **I4**
4 Catedral de Santiago
de Bilbao ................ **J4**
5 Convento de
la Encarnación .......... **J5**
6 Doña Casilda
Iturrizar Park ............ **C5**
7 Euskal Museoa Bilbao
Museo Vasco ........... **J4**
8 Funicular de
Artxanda ................ **F1**
9 Iglesia de
San Nicolás ............. **I3**
10 Itsasmuseum ............ **A6**
11 Kaitxo ................... **A7**

12 La Casa de la Villa
(City Hall) ................ **G2**
13 Los Jardines de
Albia ..................... **G3**
14 Mercado de la
Ribera ................... **J5**
15 Museo
de Bellas Artes .......... **C4**
16 Museo Guggenheim
Bilbao ................... **C2**

17 Plaza Miguel de
Unamuno ................ **J4**
18 Plaza Nueva ............. **I3**
19 Vizcaya Bridge .......... **A6**
20 Zubizuri Bridge ......... **F1**

## Restaurants ▼

1 Asador Guetaria ........ **E3**
2 Azurmendi .............. **J3**

**KEY**
- **1** Sights
- **1** Restaurants
- **1** Quick Bites
- **1** Hotels

| | | | |
|---|---|---|---|
| 3 | Berton | H4 | |
| 4 | Bihotz | I6 | |
| 5 | Bistró Guggenheim Bilbao | C2 | |
| 6 | Café Iruña | F4 | |
| 7 | Casa Rufo | G5 | |
| 8 | Etxanobe | E3 | |
| 9 | Gure Kabi | C5 | |
| 10 | Gure Toki | I3 | |

| | | |
|---|---|---|
| 11 | La Ribera | J5 |
| 12 | La Viña del Ensanche | E5 |
| 13 | Nido Bilbao | G2 |
| 14 | Pentxo | J5 |
| 15 | Txiriboga | I4 |

**Quick Bites** ▼

| | | |
|---|---|---|
| 1 | Salón de Juegos Concha | F5 |

**Hotels** ▼

| | | |
|---|---|---|
| 1 | Barceló Bilbao Nervión | G1 |
| 2 | Caravan Cinema | I4 |
| 3 | Castillo de Arteaga | H1 |
| 4 | Ercilla Hotel | D6 |
| 5 | Gran Hotel Domine Bilbao | C3 |

| | | |
|---|---|---|
| 6 | Hotel Artexte | B1 |
| 7 | Hotel Miró | A5 |
| 8 | Hotel Palacio Urgoiti | H1 |
| 9 | Hotel Sirimiri | J5 |
| 10 | Iturrienea Ostatua | H4 |
| 11 | NH Collection Villa de Bilbao | A6 |

steak frites or bacalao al pil pil. **Known for:** intricate neo-Mudejar dining room; packed with locals; no-nonsense Basque comfort food. $ *Average main: €16* ✉ *Los Jardines de Albia, Calle Berástegui 4, El Ensanche* ☎ *94/423–7021* ⊕ *www.cafeirunabilbao.net* Ⓜ *Moyúa.*

### ★ Casa Rufo
**$$ | BASQUE |** Charming and cozy, this centenarian Bilbao institution is essentially a series of nooks and crannies tucked into a fine food, wine, olive oil, cheese, and ham emporium. Leave it to the affable owners to recommend specialties such as *txuleton* (gigantic T-bone steak), which pairs wonderfully with the house Rioja or any number of pours from the 1,000-bottle-strong wine list. **Known for:** homey dining room; delectable txuleton de buey; deep wine list with hard-to-find selections. $ *Average main: €20* ✉ *Calle Hurtado de Amézaga 5, El Ensanche* ☎ *94/443–2172* ⊕ *www.casarufo.com* ⊙ *Closed Sun.* Ⓜ *Abando.*

### Etxanobe
**$$$$ | BASQUE |** This Nueva Cocina Vasca (New Basque Cuisine) favorite houses two concepts: La Despensa, with vibrant, internationally inflected *raciones* served beneath neon lights and Edison bulbs, and El Atelier, the sedate, white-tablecloth restaurant serving ultra-high-end seafood-centric tasting menus. Both are terrific in their own right; spring for whichever your budget will allow. **Known for:** standout seafood; look-at-me designer decor; casual and refined dining under one roof. $ *Average main: €35* ✉ *Calle de Juan de Ajuriaguerra 8, El Ensanche* ☎ *94/442–1071* ⊕ *www.atelieretxanobe.com* ⊙ *Closed Sun.* Ⓜ *Uribitarte.*

### Gure Kabi
**$$ | SPANISH | FAMILY |** This family-friendly restaurant off the tourist track serves a wide range of classic, lovingly prepared dishes ranging from creamy squid *croquetas* to griddled European lobster. The best value is the €15 weekday *menú del día* (prix fixe), which can be made

vegetarian upon request. **Known for:** killer prix-fixe lunch; locals-only vibe; Basque home cooking. $ *Average main: €17* ✉ *Calle Particular de Estraunza 4–6, El Ensanche* ☎ *94/600–4843* ⊕ *www.gurekabi.com* ⊙ *Closed Sun.* Ⓜ *Indautxu.*

### ★ Gure Toki
**$$ | BASQUE |** You'd be hard-pressed to find a more pleasant outdoor lunch in Bilbao than at this chic little pintxo bar with sunlit tables smack on the charming Plaza Nueva. Fried *rabas* (squid strips), *croquetas*, and locally made *txistorra* (smoky chorizo sausage) never come off the menu for good reason. **Known for:** efficient service; knockout pintxos; unbeatable location for people-watching. $ *Average main: €16* ✉ *Plaza Nueva 12, Casco Viejo* ☎ *94/415–8037* ⊕ *www.guretoki.com* ⊙ *Closed Wed.* Ⓜ *Zazpi Kaleak.*

### La Ribera
**$$$ | BASQUE | FAMILY |** Make a beeline to this gastro bar on the ground floor of the eponymous *mercado* to satisfy your Basque food cravings after you've ogled all the shimmering fresh fish, plump *jamones ibéricos* (Iberian hams), and sweet-smelling fruit. The *menú del día* (price varies) is usually a good deal, and the highbrow pintxos are consistently tasty. **Known for:** wide selection of sweet and savory snacks; good prix-fixe lunch; hip, young vibe. $ *Average main: €21* ✉ *Mercado de la Ribera, Calle de la Ribera 20, Casco Viejo* ☎ *94/657–5474* ⊕ *www.lariberabilbao.com* ⊙ *Closed Mon.–Wed.* Ⓜ *Casco Viejo.*

### ★ La Viña del Ensanche
**$$ | BASQUE |** Littered with used napkins and furnished with simple wood tables beneath hams hanging from the rafters, this lively, deceptively simple bar attracts locals and tourists alike for its exceptional pintxos. Don't pass up the deconstructed Galician-style octopus on a bed of mashed potatoes laced with *pimentón* (paprika) or the appetizer of house-made foie gras with three preserves. **Known for:** house-made foie gras; loud, convivial

atmosphere; croquetas flooded with top-shelf Joselito jamón. $ *Average main: €20* ⊠ *Diputazio 10, El Ensanche* ☎ *94/415–5615* ⊕ *www.lavinadelensanche.com* ☻ *Closed Sun.* Ⓜ *Moyúa.*

### Nido Bilbao

$$$ | BASQUE | Even the bread is homemade at this wildly popular Basque restaurant on the Left Bank that's renowned for throwback dishes like goose foie gras with raspberry coulis, dry-aged T-bone steaks, and house-made *morcilla* (blood sausage). A list of small-production and organic wines rounds out the hyperlocal dining experience. **Known for:** market cuisine; natural wine; house-made everything. $ *Average main: €24* ⊠ *Calle Barroeta Aldamar 3, El Ensanche* ☎ *94/436–0643* ⊕ *www.nidobilbao.com* ☻ *Closed Sun.* Ⓜ *Abando.*

### ★ Pentxo

$$ | BASQUE | FAMILY | Consistently delicious, shockingly affordable, and unapologetically old-school, Pentxo is the sort of restaurant Bilbaínos like to keep to themselves. Whether you pop in for a pintxo at the bar (the flash-fried *antxoas rellenas*, or stuffed anchovies, are a must) or come for a €16 prix-fixe lunch (opt for whatever seafood main is listed), you'll leave wishing you could be a regular. **Known for:** unbeatable lunch deal; outstanding pintxos and coffee drinks; local crowd. $ *Average main: €16* ⊠ *Calle Belostikale 20, Casco Viejo* ☎ *94/416–9472* ⊕ *www.restaurantepentxo.com* ☻ *Closed Sun.* Ⓜ *Casco Viejo.*

### Txiriboga

$ | TAPAS | Locals flock to this hole-in-the-wall for what might be the city's best *croquetas*—choose from *jamón* (ham), chicken, bacalao, or wild mushroom. The *rabas* (fried calamari) also stand out for their non-reasy, ultracrisp exterior. **Known for:** terrific calamari; quintessential Basque taberna; burst-in-your-mouth croquetas. $ *Average main: €10* ⊠ *Calle Santa Maria 13, Casco Viejo* ☎ *94/415–7874* ☻ *Closed Mon.* Ⓜ *Casco Viejo.*

## ☕ Coffee and Quick Bites

### Salón de Juegos Concha

$ | SPANISH | Locals know that this nondescript *salón de juegos* (literally "gambling hall") slings some of the city's best potato omelets, flipped nonstop from 8 am to midnight. The basic potato-and-onion rendition, gloriously gooey in the center, will set you back €2; more deluxe versions (with crab, *jamón ibérico*, etc.) are a tad pricier. **Known for:** hot Spanish omelet served around the clock; secret local haunt; shockingly affordable. $ *Average main: €4* ⊠ *Calle General Concha 1, Bilbao* ☎ *94/410–1971* Ⓜ *Moyúa.*

## 🛏 Hotels

### Barceló Bilbao Nervión

$$$ | HOTEL | Sandwiched between the Casco Viejo and the industrial area surrounding the Guggenheim, this corporate hotel soars seven stories over the Nervión, and its best rooms boast semicircular windows that make you feel like you're hovering over it. **Pros:** big-brand comforts; clean lines; great location. **Cons:** lacks local flavor; not terribly homey; no river views from interior rooms. $ *Rooms from: €175* ⊠ *Paseo Campo de Volantín 11, Casco Viejo* ☎ *94/445–4700* ⊕ *www.barcelo.com* ⇥ *350 rooms* ⓞ *No Meals* Ⓜ *Uribitarte.*

### Caravan Cinema

$$ | B&B/INN | This cozy, cinema-themed pension with in-room Nespresso machines and huge TVs is a great value. **Pros:** independently owned; cheerful staff; convenient to main sights. **Cons:** contact proprietor to schedule check-in time; inadequate soundproofing; some rooms overlook a gritty little courtyard. $ *Rooms from: €105* ⊠ *Calle Correo 11, Casco Viejo* ☎ *68/886–0907* ⊕ *www.caravan-cinema.com* ⇥ *11 rooms* ⓞ *No Meals* Ⓜ *Arriaga.*

## ★ Castillo de Arteaga

$$$$ | HOTEL | Built in the mid-19th century for Empress Eugenia de Montijo, wife of Napoléon III, this neo-Gothic limestone castle-cum-hotel with rooms in the watchtowers and defensive walls is one of the most extraordinary lodgings in the area (and Relais & Châteaux agrees). **Pros:** market-driven restaurant worth a trip in itself; palatial interiors; views over the wetlands. **Cons:** few restaurants in the area; spotty Wi-Fi in some rooms; isolated from the village and 30 minutes from Bilbao. $ *Rooms from: €200* ⊠ *Calle Gaztelubide 7, Gautegiz de Arteaga* ✛ *40 km (25 miles) northwest of Bilbao* ☎ *94/627–0440* ⊕ *www.castillodearteaga.com* ☾ *Closed late Dec.–early Mar.* ☞ *13 rooms* ⦿ *Free Breakfast.*

## Ercilla Hotel

$$$ | HOTEL | A prim business crowd fills this modern hotel under the Marriott Autograph Collection umbrella that's known for streamlined digs and professional service. **Pros:** favorite among journalists, politicians, and business-people; views from rooftop bar; steps from pintxo hot spots. **Cons:** lots of stairs; room keys deactivate easily; not the place for a quiet getaway. $ *Rooms from: €148* ⊠ *Calle Ercilla 37, Endantxu* ☎ *94/470–5700* ⊕ *www.ercilladebilbao.com* ☞ *325 rooms* ⦿ *Free Breakfast* Ⓜ *Moyúa.*

## Gran Hotel Domine Bilbao

$$$$ | HOTEL | This sleek art hotel across from the Guggenheim showcases the conceptual wit of Javier Mariscal, creator of Barcelona's 1992 Olympic mascot Cobi, and the structural know-how of Bilbao architect Iñaki Aurrekoetxea. **Pros:** poster child of Bilbao's renaissance; spacious, updated rooms; breakfast on the rooftop terrace. **Cons:** soundproofing could be better; unremarkable food; hard on the wallet. $ *Rooms from: €280* ⊠ *Alameda de Mazarredo 61, El Ensanche* ☎ *94/425–3300* ⊕ *www.granhoteldominebilbao.com* ☞ *145 rooms* ⦿ *No Meals* Ⓜ *Moyúa.*

## Hotel Artetxe

$ | B&B/INN | FAMILY | With rooms overlooking Bilbao from the heights of Artxanda, this Basque farmhouse with cheery interiors and eager young owners offers excellent value. **Pros:** peace and quiet on the outskirts of town; plenty of space for children to play; great service. **Cons:** no evening restaurant service; BYOB; far from the center. $ *Rooms from: €95* ⊠ *Calle de Berriz 112, Bilbao* ✛ *Off Ctra. Enékuri–Artxanda, Km 7* ☎ *94/474–7780* ⊕ *www.hotelartetxe.com* ☞ *12 rooms* ⦿ *Free Breakfast.*

## Hotel Miró

$$$ | HOTEL | Between the Guggenheim and the Museo de Bellas Artes, this quiet boutique hotel with floor-to-ceiling windows and impeccable service is the sister property of the Domine just up the street. **Pros:** pleasingly muted decor; views of the Guggenheim; on-site gym and free coffee and tea in the lobby. **Cons:** so-so soundproofing; interiors will strike many as passé; showing wear in places. $ *Rooms from: €190* ⊠ *Alameda de Mazarredo 77, El Ensanche* ☎ *94/661–1880* ⊕ *www.mirohotelbilbao.com* ☞ *50 rooms* ⦿ *No Meals* Ⓜ *Moyúa.*

## Hotel Palacio Urgoiti

$$ | HOTEL | FAMILY | This majestic hotel, occupying a reconstructed 17th-century country palace by the airport, is a peaceful country retreat with a 9-hole pitch-and-putt and nearby activities including sand, surf, and sailing 15 km (9 miles) away in Plentzia and equestrian activities in Mungia. **Pros:** handy train service into Bilbao; good home base for outdoor enthusiasts; convenient to the airport. **Cons:** freezing indoor pool; flights overhead; 15-minute drive to Bilbao. $ *Rooms from: €127* ⊠ *Calle Arritugane, Mungia* ✛ *13 km (8 miles) west of Bilbao,*

*2 km (1 mile) from airport* 🖼 *94/074 6868*
⊕ *www.palaciourgoiti.com* ⤳ *43 rooms*
🍽 *Free Breakfast.*

### Hotel Sirimiri
**$** | **HOTEL** | A small, attentively run hotel near the Atxuri station, this modest pensión has modern rooms with views of some of Bilbao's oldest architecture. **Pros:** handy to the Mercado de la Ribera, Casco Viejo, and the Atxuri train station; steps from tram; excellent buffet-style breakfast. **Cons:** thin walls; lacks character of surrounding buildings; tight quarters. $ *Rooms from: €99* ⊠ *Pl. de la Encarnación 3, Casco Viejo* ☎ *94/433–0759* ⊕ *www.hotelsirimiri.es* ⤳ *28 rooms* 🍽 *Free Breakfast* Ⓜ *Casco Viejo.*

### ★ Iturrienea Ostatua
**$$** | **B&B/INN** | This quirky, cozy hotel occupies a traditional town house in the Casco Viejo. **Pros:** budget-friendly; comfy interiors; attentive personnel. **Cons:** slow Wi-Fi; no on-site parking and the closest lot is expensive; exterior-facing rooms can be noisy. $ *Rooms from: €106* ⊠ *Calle Santa María 14, Casco Viejo* ☎ *94/416–1500* ⊕ *www.iturrieneaostatua.com* ⤳ *19 rooms* 🍽 *No Meals* Ⓜ *Casco Viejo.*

### NH Collection Villa de Bilbao
**$$** | **HOTEL** | The Bilbao outpost of this trusted chain is a great value and offers choice extras—morning newspapers at your door, good breakfast, comfortable rooms, and professional service—all in a central location within walking distance of all the main attractions. **Pros:** spacious rooms; scenic walk to the Bellas Artes and Guggenheim museums; near San Mamés stadium. **Cons:** poor bathroom maintenance; a bit cold and corporate; disorganized reception staff. $ *Rooms from: €115* ⊠ *Gran Vía 87, El Ensanche* ☎ *94/441–6000* ⊕ *www.nh-hoteles.com* ⤳ *139 rooms* 🍽 *No Meals* Ⓜ *San Mamés.*

## 🛍 Shopping

The main stores for clothing are found around Plaza Moyúa in El Ensanche, along streets such as Iparraguirre and Rodríguez Arias. The Casco Viejo has dozens of smaller shops, many of them in handsomely restored early houses with gorgeous wooden beams and ancient stones, specializing in an endless variety of products from crafts to antiques. Wool items, gourmet products, and wood carvings from around the Basque Country can be found throughout Bilbao. Basque *txapelak* (berets, or *boinas* in Spanish) are famous worldwide and make fine gifts.

### Ganboa Jewellery
**JEWELRY & WATCHES** | Try on handmade, one-of-a-kind jewelry at this tranquil boutique, whose Basque owner finds inspiration for her organic designs in nature. Prices range from approximately €10 to €300 per piece. ⊠ *Arechaga Kalea 5, Casco Viejo* ☎ *94/652–7989* ⊕ *www.ganboajewellery.com* ⊗ *Closed Sun.* Ⓜ *Casco Viejo.*

### ★ Proyecto Hemen
**CRAFTS** | Embodying Bilbao's electric urban pulse, this Casco Viejo concept store sells ceramics, textiles, accessories, and other up-to-the-minute statement pieces designed by its three young owners. ⊠ *Erronda Kalea 12, Casco Viejo* ☎ *94/657–8494* ⊕ *www.proyectohemen.com* ⊗ *Closed Sat. at 2 pm and Sun.* Ⓜ *Atxuri.*

## 🏃 Activities

### MULTISPORT
#### Bilbobentura
**KAYAKING** | There's perhaps no better way to take in Bilbao's intriguing urban landscape than on a kayak ride down the estuary. Bilbobentura offers ski packages, hiking tours, and bicycle, kayak, and SUP rentals. Rental rates begin at €8 for bicycles, €11 for single-person kayaks,

and €14 for stand-up paddle boards. ⊠ *Ramón de la Sota 1, San Mamés* 🕾 *66/073–4953* ⊕ *www.bilbobentura. com.*

## SOCCER

Soccer is religion in Bilbao, even if the scrappy Athletic Club has been on a decades-long losing streak. "The Lions" are often in the top half of the league standings and take special pleasure in tormenting powerhouses Madrid and Barcelona. The local rivalry with San Sebastián's Real Sociedad is as bitter as baseball's Yankees–Red Sox feud.

### San Mamés Stadium

SOCCER | Athletic Bilbao calls this decade-old arena on the Nervión its home turf. The largest stadium in the Basque Country, it seats over 53,000 and has a retractable roof that keeps spectators dry, rain or shine. ⊠ *Rafael Moreno Pitxitxi, San Mamés* 🕾 *94/441–3954* ⊕ *www. bilbaostadium.com* Ⓜ *San Mamés.*

# Bermeo

*34 km (21 miles) northeast of Bilbao, 9 km (5 miles) east of San Juan de Gaztelugatxe.*

Walk from the old town down to the port to get a sense of Bermeo's charm. Before the town became synonymous with commercial fishing (it once boasted the largest fishing fleet in Spain), it was a booming whaling center. In the 16th century, Bermeo whalers reportedly donated the tongue of every whale to raise money for the Church. Bermeo has one of only two wooden-boat shipyards on the northern coast, and the boats docked in its busy harbor make a colorful picture. Drive to the top of the windswept hill above town, where a cemetery overlooks the crashing waves below, then head west on the coastal road to explore the breathtaking island hermitage of San Juan de Gaztelugatxe, a must-see sight.

# Mundaka

*37 km (23 miles) northeast of Bilbao.*

Tiny Mundaka, famous among surfers all over the world for its left-breaking roller at the mouth of the Ría de Gernika, has much to offer nonsurfers as well. The town's elegant summer homes and stately houses bearing family coats of arms compete for pride of place with the hermitage on the Santa Catalina peninsula and the parish church's Renaissance doorway.

## VISITOR INFORMATION

CONTACTS Mundaka. ⊠ *Calle Josepa Deuna,* 🕾 *94/617–7201* ⊕ *www.mundakaturismo.com.*

## 🏖 Beaches

### Mundaka Beach

BEACH | This beach is said to have the longest surf break in Europe and among the best in the world, making it a magnet for surfers. In summer and fall this beach is off-limits to families who just want to splash around. Inland from the beach is the Urdaibai Natural Preserve, a UNESCO-designated biosphere. **Amenities:** lifeguards; water sports. **Best for:** surfing. ⊠ *Calle Matadero, Mundaka.*

## 🍴 Restaurants

### Baserri Maitea

$$$ | BASQUE | Eleven km (7 miles) south of Mundaka and 1 km (½ mile) northwest of Gernika, you'll find this restaurant in an idyllic 18th-century *caserío*, or traditional Basque farmhouse. Garlands of red peppers and garlic hang from wooden beams in the cathedral-like dining area, where loyal guests tuck into hearty yet refined fish and meats cooked over a wood-fire grill. **Known for:** personable waitstaff; bacalao dishes; spectacular ambience in a Basque farmhouse. Ⓢ *Average main: €27* ⊠ *Calle Atxondoa, Mundaka*

# Basque Culture

Nobody knows where the Basques came from or when they arrived in this windswept corner of the Iberian Peninsula. Though the first written records of the Basques are from Roman times, studies indicate that this "tribe" of proto-Europeans has inhabited the area for at least 7,000 years and perhaps reached North America before Columbus. A combination of impenetrable geography and a fierce warrior class kept the Basques somewhat isolated from the rest of the continent for hundreds, if not thousands, of years—enough time to establish and preserve their distinctive mythology, sports, food, and language.

## Basque Language

Although all Basques speak French north of the border and Spanish south of the border, many (approximately one-quarter of the population on the Spanish side) consider **Euskera** their first language. The mother tongue is so vital to the Basque identity that the cultural signifier "Basque" in Euskera is "Euskalduna," literally "Speaker of Basque." As Europe's only non-Indo-European language, Euskera is one of the great enigmas of linguistic scholarship. To the nonspeaker, it sounds like rough, consonant-heavy Spanish, though its highly complex grammar has no relation to the Romance languages.

## Basque Cuisine

Traditional Basque cuisine combines vegetables, Atlantic fish, beef, and lamb with a love of sauces that is rare south of the Pyrenees. The myriad award-winning chefs in the region have made Basque food seem innovative and fancy to foreigners, but most everyday Basques still eat as they always have—simply, from the land and sea. With the seemingly eternal trendiness of pintxos (the Basque equivalent of tapas), Basque cuisine solidified itself as part of the international culinary zeitgeist.

## Basque Sports

A Basque village without a *frontón* (pelota court) is as unimaginable as an American town without a baseball diamond. *Pelota*, or **jai alai** in Euskera, is the fastest-moving ball sport, according to Guinness World Records, with ball speeds reaching 150 mph. The game is played on a three-walled court 175 feet long and 56 feet wide with 40-foot side walls, and the object is to angle the ball along or off of the side wall so that it cannot be returned. Betting is popular.

*Herrikirolak* (rural sports) are based on farming and seafaring. Stone lifters (*harrijasotzaileak* in Euskera) heft weights up to 700 pounds. *Aizkolari* (axe men) chop wood in various contests, and the *gizon proba* (man trial) pits three-man teams moving weighted sleds. Then there are the *estropadak*, whaleboat rowers who compete in spectacular regattas (culminating in the September competition off La Concha beach in San Sebastián).

When it comes to **soccer**, Basque goaltenders have developed special fame in Spain, where Bilbao's Athletic Club and San Sebastián's Real Sociedad have won national championships with budgets far inferior to those of Real Madrid or FC Barcelona.

# Embattled Gernika

On April 26, 1937—market day—Gernika, 33 km (20 miles) east of Bilbao, was attacked by German and Italian air brigades at the behest of the Nationalist forces in what would be history's second terror bombing against a civilian population. (The first, much less famous, was against neighboring Durango, about a month earlier.) Gernika, a rural town, had been one of the symbols of Basque identity since the 14th century. As early as the Middle Ages, Spanish sovereigns had sworn under the ancient oak tree of Gernika to respect Basque *fueros*, local courts with the sort of autonomy that was anathema to Generalísimo Francisco Franco's Madrid-centered "National Movement," which promoted Spanish unity over local identity.

The planes of the Nazi Luftwaffe were sent with the blessings of Franco to experiment with saturation bombing of civilian targets and to decimate the traditional seat of Basque autonomy.

When the raid ended, between 153 and 1,654 civilians—the exact number of casualties is unclear—lay dead or dying in the ruins after weathering 30 tons of explosives; today Gernika remains a symbol of the atrocities of war, largely thanks to Picasso's famous canvas *Guernica*. The city was destroyed (although the oak tree miraculously emerged unscathed) and has been rebuilt as a modern if architecturally uninteresting town. Not until the 60th anniversary of the event did Germany officially apologize for the bombing.

When Spain's Second Republic commissioned Picasso to create a work for the Paris 1937 International Exposition, little did he imagine that his grim canvas protesting the bombing of a Basque village would become one of the most famous paintings in history.

Picasso's painting had its own struggle. The Spanish Pavilion in the International Exposition nearly substituted a more upbeat work, using *Guernica* as a backdrop. In 1939, Picasso ceded *Guernica* to New York's Museum of Modern Art, stipulating that the painting should return only to a democratic Spain. Over the next 30 years, as Picasso's fame grew, so did *Guernica*'s—as a work of art and a symbol of Spain's captivity. Its reinterpretation by Basque artist Agustín Ibarrola continues to draw thousands to Bilbao's Museo de Bellas Artes each year.

When Franco died in 1975, two years after Picasso, negotiations with Picasso's heirs for the painting's return to Spain were already underway. Now on display at Centro de Arte Reina Sofía (*See Madrid*), *Guernica* is home for good.

☎ 94/625–3408 ⊕ www.baserrimaitea.com ⊙ No dinner Sun.–Thurs.

## Portuondo

$$$$ | **BASQUE** | Sweeping beach views through picture windows, aromas of fresh fish cooking over hot coals, a sophisticated country dining room—these are a few reasons Portuondo, a 15-minute walk outside town, is a Mundaka stalwart. Those in the mood for something more informal can post up at the downstairs pintxo bar. **Known for:** buzzy pintxo bar; meats and fish grilled to perfection; scenic setting. $ *Average main: €30* ⊠ *Portuondo Auzoa*

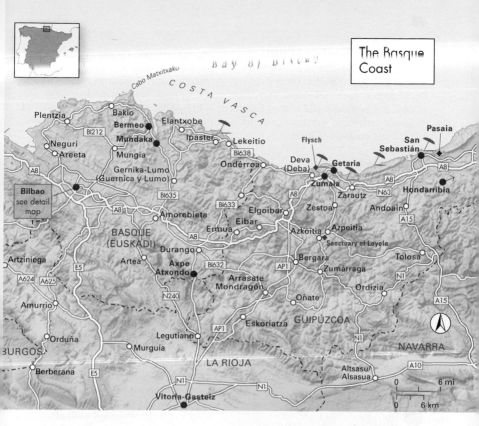

*1, Mundaka ⟐ Ctra. Gernika–Bermeo BI2235, Km 47 ☎ 94/687–6050 ⊕ www. restauranteportuondo.com ⊗ No dinner Mon.–Thurs.*

##  Hotels

### Atalaya

**$$ | HOTEL |** Tastefully converted from a private mansion, this 1911 landmark on the shore is a favorite for quick overnight rail getaways from Bilbao, and scenery along the 37-km (23-mile) train ride is spectacular. **Pros:** intimate retreat from Bilbao's sprawl and bustle; free parking; well-maintained sauna. **Cons:** outdated tech; limited menu in the restaurant; tight quarters in some rooms. **⑤** *Rooms from: €125 ⊠ Calle Itxaropen 1, Mundaka ☎ 94/687–6899 ⊕ www.atalayahotel.es ⇄ 13 rooms* ⊚*l No Meals.*

# Axpe Atxondo

*47 km (29 miles) east of Bilbao, 45 km (28 miles) south of Mundaka, 44 km (28 miles) south of Elantxobe.*

The village of Axpe, in the valley of Atxondo, sits in the shadow of 1,456-meter (4,777-foot) Mt. Anboto—one of the highest peaks in the Basque Country outside the Pyrenees. Anboto, with its spectral gray rock face, is a sharp contrast to the soft green meadows running up to the foot of the mountain. According to local lore, the Basque nature goddess Mari inhabits a cave close to the summit; in his *Mitología Vasca (Basque Mythology)*, ethnologist José María de Barandiarán describes Mari as "a beautiful woman, well constructed in all ways except for one foot, which was like that of a goat."

## GETTING HERE AND AROUND

From Bilbao, drive east on the A8/E70 toward San Sebastián. Get off at the Durango exit, 40 km (24 miles) from Bilbao, and take the BI632 toward Elorrio. At Apatamonasterio, turn right onto the BI3313 and continue to Axpe.

## 🍴 Restaurants

### ★ Asador Etxebarri

$$$$ | BASQUE | Of all the three-Michelin-star Basque temples, Bittor Arginzoniz's Etxebarri is the most exclusive, since it serves only lunch and reservations are limited. Here, grilling is elevated to an art form, with various types of woods, coals, and handmade tools carefully selected for the preparation of each dish. **Known for:** surprisingly unpretentious, laid-back atmosphere; temple of open-hearth cuisine; no. 3 spot on "World's 50 Best" restaurants list. $ *Average main: €60* ✉ *Pl. San Juan 1, Axpe* ☎ *94/658–3042* ⊕ *www.asadoretxebarri.com* ◷ *Closed Mon. No dinner. Closed Aug.*

## 🛏 Hotels

### ★ Mendi Goikoa Bekoa

$$$ | HOTEL | This handsome hillside estate is among the province's most exquisite hideaways. **Pros:** gorgeous setting; sweet, sweet silence; smart and attentive service. **Cons:** reservations via online form; not open year round; need a car to get here. $ *Rooms from: €140* ✉ *Barrio San Juan 33, Axpe* ☎ *94/682–0833* ⊕ *www.mendigoikoabekoa.com* ◷ *Closed Nov.–Easter* ⇌ *12 rooms* ⭐️ *Free Breakfast.*

# Getaria and Zumaia

*80 km (50 miles) east of Bilbao, 22 km (14 miles) west of San Sebastián.*

Getaria (Guetaria in Castilian) is known as the kitchen of Gipuzkoa province for its sought-after restaurants and taverns.

It is the birthplace of modiste Cristóbal Balenciaga (1895–1972), who is commemorated in a relatively new museum, and explorer Juan Sebastián Elcano (1487–1526), the first circumnavigator of the globe and Spain's most emblematic naval hero. Elcano took over and completed Magellan's voyage after Magellan was killed in the Philippines in 1521.

Getaria's galleonlike church, one of the Basque Country's crown jewels of Gothic architecture, has sloping wooden floors resembling a ship's deck. From Getaria you can walk an hour to Zarautz, the next town east, which has a wide family-friendly beach and plenty of taverns and cafés, plus a 12-km (7-mile) trail called the Anillo Verde Azul (EBU) that encircles the town.

Zumaia, the town west of Getaria, is a snug little port and summer resort with the Urola River flowing—back and forth, according to the tide—through town. It is best known for a dramatic sedimentary rock formation called the Flysch. Zumaia and Getaria are connected via the coast road and by several good footpaths.

## VISITOR INFORMATION

**CONTACTS Getaria Tourist Office.** ✉ *Parque Aldamar 2,* ☎ *94/314–0957* ⊕ *www.getariaturismo.eus.* **Zumaia Tourist Office.** ✉ *Pl. de Kantauri 13,* ☎ *94/314–3396* ⊕ *www.zumaia.eus.*

## ◉ Sights

### Cristóbal Balenciaga Museum

OTHER MUSEUM | The haute-couture maestro Cristóbal Balenciaga (1895–1972) was born in Getaria, and the impressive museum created in his honor is a must-see, regardless of your fashion sensibilities. The collection and interactive exhibits are distributed between two buildings, the mansion where Balenciaga was born and a starkly geometric monolith inaugurated in 2011. Feast your eyes on ever-rotating couture relics from the foundation's 1,200-item collection, from suits to gowns and accessories that represent his life's work. "Balenciaga is a couturier in the truest sense of the word," said Coco Chanel of her rival. "The others are simply fashion designers." ⊠ *Aldamar Parkea 6, Getaria* ☎ *94/300–8840* ⊕ *www.cristobalbalenciagamuseoa.com* ☜ *€10* ⊘ *Closed Mon. in Sept.–June.*

### ★ Flysch

**NATURE SIGHT | FAMILY** | The Flysch is the crown jewel of the Basque Coast Geopark, a 13-km (8-mile) stretch of coastline distinguished by spectacular cliffs and rock formations. Taking its name from the German for "slippery"—a reference to the slipping of tectonic plates that thrust the horizontal rock layers into vertical panels—the Flysch contains innumerable layers of sedimentary rock displaying some 20 million years of geological history. One such layer is black and devoid of fossils; it was identified by scientists as marking the Cretaceous–Paleogene extinction event, which caused the extinction of the dinosaurs. ⊠ *Playa de Itzurun, Zumaia* ☜ *Free.*

### Sanctuary of Loyola

**RELIGIOUS BUILDING** | This sanctuary, about 20 km (12 miles) south of Zumaia in Cestona, is an exuberant Churrigueresque-baroque structure erected in honor of Íñigo Lopez de Oñaz y Loyola (1491–1556) after he was canonized in 1622 for his defense of the Catholic Church against the tides of Martin Luther's Reformation. Almost two centuries later, Roman architect Carlos Fontana designed the basilica that memorializes the saint. The ornate construction contrasts with the austere lifestyle of St. Ignatius, who took vows of poverty and chastity after his conversion. Polychrome marble, flamboyant altar work, and a huge but delicate dome decorate the interior. The fortresslike tower house has the room where Ignatius (Eneko in Euskera) experienced conversion while recovering from a wound received in an intra-Basque battle. ⊠ *Loiola Auzoa 16,*

Cestona ✛ *From Bilbao, take Exit 48 toward Zestoa-Azpeitia* ⊕ *loyola.global* ☜ *€5.*

## 🍴 Restaurants

### ★ Asador Bedua

**$$$$ | BASQUE** | This idyllic fourth-generation asador in a centuries-old house draws the crowds with its flawless tortilla de bacalao, txuleta de buey, and local game and fish of all kinds such as *besugo a la donostiarra* (roast sea bream with garlic-vinegar sauce) and, when in season, *becada* (Eurasian woodcock) cloaked in meaty wine sauce. Fizzy Txakolí is the standard tipple, but there's also a surprisingly deep list of Champagnes and international bottles to choose from. **Known for:** warm service in both the stone-wall dining room and glassed-in terrace; ancient building overlooking a tidal river; pristine seafood and home-grown vegetables. ⑤ *Average main: €30* ⊠ *Cestona, Barrio Bedua, Cestona* ✛ *Up Urola, 3 km (2 miles) from Zumaia* ☎ *94/386–0551* ⊕ *www.bedua.eus.*

### ★ Elkano

**$$$$ | SEAFOOD** | Ever since Anthony Bourdain waxed poetic about award-winning Elkano's grilled turbot on *Parts Unknown,* the dish has become something of a holy grail among in-the-know foodies. Order the famous flatfish (at its fatty prime in May and June), and you'll receive what Bourdain called an "anatomy lesson" as the maître d' extols the virtues of each separate cut, culminating with the gelatinous fins—which you're encouraged to suck between your fingers, caveman style. **Known for:** impressive Champagne selection; reputation as an Anthony Bourdain favorite; grilled turbot. ⑤ *Average main: €60* ⊠ *Calle Herrieta 2, Getaria* ☎ *94/314–0024* ⊕ *www.restauranteelkano.com* ⊘ *Closed Tues. No dinner Sun.–Thurs.*

### ★ Segore Etxe-Berri

$$ | BASQUE | FAMILY | Hidden in the lush, hilly countryside southwest of Tolosa— and many miles off the tourist track—is this idyllic agroturismo comprised of a restaurant and five-room bed-and-breakfast housed in a traditional *caserío* (Basque farmhouse) perched on a hilltop. After snapping a few pics of the jaw-dropping views, tuck into a soul-satisfying Basque feast of roast chicken (raised on the property), stewed game meats, or fresh fish. **Known for:** meats and vegetables from the estate; outdoor playground for kids; culinary gem in the middle of nowhere. $ *Average main: €20* ✉ *Calle Valle Santa Marina, Albiztur* ☎ *94/358-0976* ⊕ *www.segore.com* ⊙ *Closed Tues. No dinner Mon.–Thurs.*

### 🛏 Hotels

#### Saiaz Getaria

$$ | HOTEL | An idyllic beach escape with panoramic views over the Bay of Biscay, this renovated 15th-century house on Getaria's uppermost street has cozily decorated rooms. **Pros:** historic property; discounts at nearby spa and gym; waves lull you to sleep. **Cons:** only two (first-come, first-served) parking spaces; spotty Wi-Fi; soundproofing could be better. $ *Rooms from: €118* ✉ *Roke Deuna 25, Getaria* ☎ *94/314-0143* ⊕ *www.saiazgetaria.com* ⊙ *Closed Dec. 20–Jan. 6* ⇆ *17 rooms.*

#### San Prudentzio

$ | HOTEL | FAMILY | Surrender to the slow pace of country life at this family-run hotel perched on a hilltop amid rolling vineyards. **Pros:** ground-floor terrace and lounge with a fireplace; well-stocked help-yourself bar and homemade tortilla de patata every morning; on the Camino de Santiago. **Cons:** steep 20-minute walk to Getaria; cleanliness could be improved; lacks the rustic charm of other rural lodgings. $ *Rooms from: €90* ✉ *San Prudentzio, Getaria* ⊕ *Follow signs for Barrio Askizu – San Prudentzio on the*
coastal road west of Getaria ☎ *94/314-0411* ⊕ *www.hotelsanprudentzio.com* ⇆ *10 rooms* ⊙ *No Meals.*

### 🛍 Shopping

Getaria, Zumaia, and the surrounding villages are great places to pick up locally canned anchovies, tuna, and sardines as well as bottles of Txakolí, pickled *piparra* peppers, and *sagardoa* (Basque cider). Of note is the *ventresca de bonito del norte* (oil-cured albacore tuna belly), so veined with delicious omega-3-rich fat that it's almost spreadable—the best canned tuna money can buy.

#### Salanort

FOOD | This highly regarded *conservas* company might be most famous for its anchovies, which are always plump and expertly packed, but you can also stock up on oil-packed bacalao and Idiazabal cheeses plus local wines and *patxaran*, a local digestif made with sloe berries. ✉ *Nagusia 22, Getaria* ☎ *94/314-0036* ⊕ *www.salanort.com.*

# San Sebastián

*100 km (62 miles) northeast of Bilbao.*

San Sebastián (Donostia in Euskera) is a majestic city arched around one of the finest urban beaches in the world, **La Concha**, so named for its shell-like shape, with Ondarreta and Zurriola beaches at the southwestern and northeastern ends. The Urgull and Igeldo promontories serve as bookends for La Concha, while Zurriola has Mount Ulia rising over its far end. The best way to take in San Sebastián is on foot: Promenades and pathways twist up the hills that surround the city and afford postcard-perfect views.

The first records of San Sebastián date to the 11th century. A backwater for most of Spain's history, the city had the good fortune in 1845 to woo Queen Isabella II, who was seeking relief from a skin ailment in the icy Atlantic waters. Doubt{.....} vacations were all the rage in late-19th-century Europe, and Isabella was followed by much of the aristocracy of the time. San Sebastián became—and remains—a favored summer retreat for Madrid's well-to-do.

The city is bisected by the **Urumea River,** which is crossed by three ornate bridges inspired by late-19th-century French architecture. At the mouth, the incoming surf smashes the rocks with such force that white foam erupts, and the sound is wild and Wagnerian. The city is laid out with wide streets on a grid pattern, thanks mainly to the dozen times it has been all but destroyed by fire. The last conflagration came after the French were expelled in 1813; English and Portuguese forces occupied the city, abused the population, and torched the place. Today, San Sebastián is an expensive seaside resort on par with Nice and Monte Carlo; in summer, French vacationers descend in droves. It is also, like Bilbao, a center of Basque nationalism.

Neighborhoods include the charming and increasingly over-touristed Parte Vieja, tucked under Mount Urgull; hip-and-happening Gros (so named for a corpulent Napoleonic general), across the Urumea to the north; commercial Centro, the main city nucleus around the cathedral; residential Amara, farther east toward the Anoeta sports complex; glitzy La Concha, at center stage around the beach; and stately El Antiguo, at the western end of La Concha. Alto de Miracruz is the high ground to the northeast toward France; Errenteria is inland east of Pasaia; Oiartzun is a village farther north; Astigarraga and Hernani are in apple-cider country to the east of Anoeta.

## GETTING HERE AND AROUND

San Sebastián is a very walkable city, though local buses (€1.85) are also convenient. Buses for Pasaia (Pasajes), Errenteria, Astigarraga, and Oiartzun originate in Calle Okendo, one block west of the Urumea River behind the Hotel María Cristina. Bus A-1 goes to Astigarraga; A-2 is the bus to Pasaia.

The regional train, Euskotren, is popularly known as El Topo (The Mole) for the amount of time it spends underground (€2–€7 per journey). It originates in Bilbao and tunnels its way to Hendaye, France, every 30 minutes or so. Euskotren also serves Bilbao by way of Lasarte–Oria, but buses and Blablacar rideshares will get you there in about half the time. It services neighboring towns including Lasarte-Oria (12 minutes), Pasaia (12 minutes), and Irun (30 minutes).

For the funicular up Mount Igeldo (943/213525; €4), the station is behind Ondarreta beach at the western end of La Concha.

**BUS CONTACTS Estación de Autobuses.** ⊠ Paseo de Federico García Lorca 1, ☎ 94/317–5150 ⊕ www.estaciondonostia.com.

**CAR RENTAL Europcar.** ⊠ Calle Gabarrari 22, ☎ 94/366–8530 ⊕ www.europcar.com.

**TRAIN CONTACTS Estación de Amara.** (Estación de Easo) ⊠ Pl. Easo 9, ☎ 90/254–3210 ⊕ www.renfe.com. **Estación de San Sebastián–Donostia.** (Estación del Norte) ⊠ Paseo de Francia 22, ☎ 90/224–3402 ⊕ www.renfe.com.

## VISITOR INFORMATION

**CONTACTS San Sebastián–Donostia Tourist Office.** ⊠ Alameda del Blvd. 8, ☎ 94/348–1166 ⊕ www.sansebastianturismoa.eus.

## ◉ Sights

Every corner of Spain champions its culinary identity, but San Sebastián is especially proud of its varied food scene. Many of the city's restaurants and pintxo bars are in the **Parte Vieja** (Old Quarter), on the east end of the bay beyond the elegant **Casa Consistorial** (City Hall) and formal **Alderdi Eder** gardens. The building

San Sebastián's famed, curving beach La Concha

that now houses city hall opened as a casino in 1887; after gambling was outlawed early in the 20th century, the town council moved here from the Plaza de la Constitución, the Parte Vieja's main square.

### Aquarium Donostia-San Sebastián

AQUARIUM | FAMILY | For a stroll through and under some 6,000 marine animals—ranging from tiger sharks to sea turtles, with one participative pool where kids are encouraged to touch and try to pick up fish—the aquarium is a great rainy-day activity. The illustrated history of Basque whaling and boatbuilding is also fascinating. ⊠ *Pl. Carlos Blasco de Imaz 1, Parte Vieja* 🕾 *94/344–0099* ⊕ *www. aquariumss.com* 🕾 *€13.*

### Catedral del Buen Pastor (*Cathedral of the Good Shepherd*)

CHURCH | You can see the facade of this 19th-century cathedral from the river, across town. With the tallest church spire in the province, the Catedral del Buen Pastor was constructed in the neo-Gothic style. It's worth a glimpse inside for its beautiful stained-glass windows. ⊠ *Pl. del Buen Pastor, Calle Urdaneta 12, Centro* 🕾 *94/346–4516* 🕾 *Free* 🕙 *Closed weekends.*

### ★ Chillida Leku Museum

ART MUSEUM | In Hernani, a 10-minute drive south of San Sebastián (close to both Martín Berasategui's restaurant in nearby Lasarte *and* the cider houses of the Astigarraga neighborhood, like Sidrería Petritegi), the Eduardo Chillida Sculpture Garden and Museum, in a 16th-century farmhouse, got a face-lift after years of neglect and finally reopened in 2019. It is a treat for anyone interested in contemporary art. ⊠ *Caserío Zabalaga, Barrio Jáuregui 66, Lasarte* 🕾 *94/333–6006* ⊕ *www.museochillidale-ku.com* 🕾 *€12* 🕙 *Closed Tues.–Thurs.*

### Iglesia de Santa María del Coro

CHURCH | Just in from the harbor, in the shadow of Monte Urgull, is this baroque church with a stunning carved facade of an arrow-riddled St. Sebastián flanked by two towers. The interior is strikingly restful considering the bustling area.

Note the sculptures *The Harmony of Sound,* by Maximilian Poizmann, to the right of the entrance, and *By the Cross to the Light,* by Eduardo Chillida, in the baptistery. ⊠ *Calle Mayor 12, Parte Vieja* ☎ *94/342–3124* ☞ *€3.*

### Isla de Santa Clara

**ISLAND | FAMILY |** You can visit the uninhabited Isla de Santa Clara, which rises from the center of the bay and shields La Concha from high swells. Ferries (around €7 round trip) run from the mainland every 30 minutes and are packed on summer weekends, and reaching the island from the beach is a fun challenge for experienced swimmers. There's a small bar at the ferry dock and lifeguard service at a beach that reveals itself only at low tide. Bring sturdy sandals as the coastline is rocky. In 2021, a 15-ton bronze fountain called *Hondalea* ("Sea Floor"), by Basque sculptor Cristina Iglesias, was unveiled within the lighthouse; its whooshing flows are meant to mimic the tides. ⊠ *San Sebastián* ⊕ *www.motorasdelaisla.com.*

### Kursaal

**PERFORMANCE VENUE |** Designed by the world-renowned Spanish architect Rafael Moneo and located at the mouth of the Urumea River, the Kursaal is San Sebastián's postmodern concert hall, film society, and convention center. The gleaming cubes of glass that make up this bright complex were conceived as a perpetuation of the site's natural geography, an attempt to underline the harmony between the natural and the artificial and to create a visual stepping-stone between the heights of Monte Urgull and Monte Ulia. Home of the Basque Country's symphony orchestra, the venue is also a favorite for ballet, opera, theater, and jazz performances. It has two auditoriums, a gargantuan banquet hall, meeting rooms, exhibition space, and a set of terraces overlooking the estuary. ⊠ *Av. de Zurriola 1, Gros* ☎ *94/300–3000* ⊕ *www.kursaal.eus.*

### ★ Monte Igeldo

**VIEWPOINT |** On the western side of the bay, this promontory is a must-visit. You can walk, drive up, or take the funicular (around €4 round trip), with departures every 15 minutes. From the top, you get a bird's-eye view of San Sebastián's gardens, beaches, parks, wide tree-lined boulevards, and Belle Époque buildings. There's also a small amusement park. ⊠ *Igueldo* ☎ *94/321–3525 for funicular* ⊕ *www.monteigueldo.es* ☯ *Closed most of Jan. and Wed. Nov.–Feb.*

### Tabakalera

**ARTS CENTER |** Occupying a century-old tobacco factory, this vibrant cultural center, inaugurated in 2015, epitomizes the creative, forward-thinking verve of San Sebastián. Check the website to see what performances, exhibitions, and screenings are planned ahead of your visit, and drop by to steep yourself in the city's here and now. The roof deck (free) affords pleasing views of the river directly below. ⊠ *Pl. Andre Zigarrogileak 1, Amara* ☎ *94/311–8855* ⊕ *www.tabakalera.eus* ☞ *Free.*

## 🅑 Beaches

### ★ La Concha

**BEACH | FAMILY |** San Sebastián's shell-shaped main beach is one of the most famous urban beaches in the world. Night and day, rain or shine, it's filled with locals and tourists alike, strolling and taking in the city's skyline and the uninhabited Isla de Santa Clara just offshore. Several hotels line its curved expanse including the grande dame Hotel de Londres y de Inglaterra. The beach has clean, pale sand and few rocks or seaweed, but only a bit of shade, near the promenade wall. Lounge chairs are available for rent. The calm surf makes it a favorite pick for families. **Amenities:** lifeguards; showers; toilets. **Best for:** sunrise; sunset; walking. ⊠ *Calle de la Concha Ibilbidea, La Concha.*

**Zurriola**

BEACH | Across the Urumea River from La Concha lies this sprawling, less touristy beach. Exposed to the open Atlantic, the beach boasts waves that are sometimes big enough to surf—and occasionally too dangerous for kids. **Amenities:** lifeguards; water sports. **Best for:** surfing. ⊠ *Zurriola Ibilbidea, Gros.*

##  Restaurants

### ★ Antonio Bar

$$ | TAPAS | Tuna carpaccio with pickled Basque peppers, battered hake cheeks, tripe and pork jowl stew—these are some of the classics you'll find on the menu at Antonio, a neighborhood stand-by that serves unpretentious pintxos at fair prices. Ask about nightly specials, which vary depending on what's in season. **Known for:** regional beers and wines; packed with locals; no-nonsense pintxo bar. Ⓢ *Average main: €17* ⊠ *Calle Bergara 3, Centro* ⊕ *www.antoniobar. com* ⊘ *Closed Sun.*

### ★ Arzak

$$$$ | BASQUE | One of the world's great culinary meccas, award-winning Arzak embodies the prestige, novelty, and science-driven creativity of the Basque culinary zeitgeist. The restaurant and its high-tech food lab—both helmed by founder Juan Mari Arzak's daughter Elena these days—are situated in the family's 19th-century home on the outskirts of San Sebastián. **Known for:** fresh flavors and striking plating; old-school hospitality; scintillating yet unpretentious culinary experience. Ⓢ *Average main: €255* ⊠ *Av. Alcalde Jose Elosegui 273, Alto de Miracruz* ☎ *94/327–8465, 94/328–5593* ⊕ *www.arzak.es* ⊘ *Closed Sun. and Mon., June 15–July 2, and 3 wks in early Nov.*

### Astelena 1997

$$$ | BASQUE | The narrow stone rooms of a defunct banana warehouse are now one of the finest spots for modern Basque dining. The €55 weekend tasting menu hinges on what's in season, though dishes like seared txuleton and hake in white wine sauce with clams never come off the menu for a reason. **Known for:** surprisingly good value for this part of town; fantastic seafood dishes; unpretentious yet elegant Basque cuisine. Ⓢ *Average main: €24* ⊠ *Euskal Herria 3, Parte Vieja* ☎ *94/342–5867* ⊕ *www. restauranteastelena.com* ⊘ *Closed Mon. and Tues. No dinner.*

### Bergara

$$ | TAPAS | Winner of many a miniature cuisine award (don't miss the prawn-filled *txalupa* tartlet), this Gros neighborhood standby offers outside-the-box takes on traditional tapas and pintxos. It also serves more substantial dishes for sit-down meals. **Known for:** lively atmosphere; heavenly foie gras; variety of newfangled and traditional pintxos. Ⓢ *Average main: €20* ⊠ *Calle General Arteche 8, Gros* ☎ *94/327–5026* ⊕ *www. pinchosbergara.es.*

### Bodegón Alejandro

$$$ | BASQUE | Hiding in the basement of a timber building in the heart of the Parte Vieja, this restaurant—where world-renowned chef Martín Berasategui cut his teeth—toes the line between traditional and contemporary Basque cuisine. A recent menu included Navarran white asparagus with hollandaise, poached hake with clam-and-pea sauce, and *brûléed torrijas* (Spanish "French" toast). **Known for:** seasonal vegetable delicacies like de lágrima peas and white asparagus; kilometer-zero dining; affordable and delectable tasting menus. Ⓢ *Average main: €24* ⊠ *Calle de Fermín Calbetón 4, Parte Vieja* ☎ *94/342–7158* ⊕ *www. bodegonalejandro.com* ⊘ *Closed Mon. and Tue.*

### ★ Casa Urola

$$$$ | BASQUE | FAMILY | Don't be put off by the slightly outdated decor of this Parte Vieja stalwart—the kitchen at Casa Urola is easily one of the city's most adroit.

Savor appetizers made with hard-to-find regional vegetables like cardoon, borage, and tiny *de lágrima* peas before moving onto entrées like seared squab, presented with a pâté of its own liver, and roasted hake loin, served with white wine and clams. **Known for:** city's best torrija; reputation as restaurant industry favorite; flawless Basque cuisine. $ *Average main: €28* ⊠ *Calle de Fermín Calbetón 20, Parte Vieja* ☎ *94/344–1371* ⊕ *www.casaurolajatetxea.es* ⊗ *Closed Tues. No dinner Sun.*

### ★ Ganbara

**$$$ | BASQUE |** This busy bar and sedate downstairs restaurant near Plaza de la Constitución is run by the third generation of the same family. Exquisite minimalist morsels range from white Huelva prawns to homemade foie gras to roast squab and—the house specialty—wild mushrooms topped with an egg yolk. **Known for:** lively and loud atmosphere in the bar area; traditional Basque pintxos; to-die-for wild mushrooms. $ *Average main: €26* ⊠ *Calle San Jerónimo 21, Parte Vieja* ☎ *94/342–2575* ⊕ *www.ganbarajatetxea.com* ⊗ *Closed Mon. and Tue. No dinner Sun.*

### Goiz Argi

**$ | TAPAS |** The specialty of this tiny bar—and the reason locals flock here in droves—is the garlicky seared-shrimp brochette. **Known for:** cheerful bartenders; good value; juicy shrimp skewers. $ *Average main: €9* ⊠ *Calle de Fermín Calbetón 4, Parte Vieja* ☎ *94/342–5204.*

### Gorriti Taberna

**$ | TAPAS |** Next to the open-air Brecha Market, this traditional little pintxo bar is a well-priced neighborhood standby with a genial old-school staff. **Known for:** simple, well-prepared Basque bites; casual local crowd; fabulous tortilla de bacalao. $ *Average main: €11* ⊠ *Calle San Juan 3, Parte Vieja* ☎ *94/342–8353* ⊕ *www.bargorriti.com* ⊗ *Closed Sun.*

### La Cepa de Bernardo

**$$$ | TAPAS |** This boisterous tavern established in 1948 has ceilings dangling with *jamones*, walls covered with old photos of San Sebastián, and a dining room packed with locals and tourists in equal measure. Everything from the Iberian ham to the little olive-pepper-and-anchovy combos called *"penaltis"* will whet your appetite, but those who opt for a full meal shouldn't overlook the dry-aged *txuleton*. **Known for:** €18 prix-fixe lunch; melt-in-your-mouth steak; hand-cut Iberian ham. $ *Average main: €23* ⊠ *Calle 31 de Agosto 7, Parte Vieja* ☎ *94/342–6394* ⊕ *www.barlacepa.com.*

### ★ La Viña

**$$ | TAPAS | FAMILY |** This centrally located, no-frills bar is almost always crowded, drawing busloads of tour groups as well as locals, who come to try the worth-the-hype "burnt" cheesecake with an oozy core. This silky, creamy dessert pairs perfectly with a cup of coffee, while, on the savory side, the underrated pintxos—red peppers stuffed with bacalao, croquetas, veal meatballs, what have you—sing alongside a glass of Rioja. **Known for:** wide variety of classic pintxos; old-timey ambience; world-famous cheesecake with a cult following. $ *Average main: €16* ⊠ *Calle 31 de Agosto 3, Parte Vieja* ☎ *94/342–7495* ⊕ *www.lavinarestaurante.com* ⊗ *Closed Mon.*

### ★ Martín Berasategui

**$$$$ | CONTEMPORARY |** Basque chef Martín Berasategui has more Michelin stars than any other chef in Spain, and at his flagship in the dewy village of Lasarte-Oria, it's easy to see why. Dishes are Basque at heart but prepared with exacting, French-inflected technique that comes through in dishes like artfully composed salads, elegant caviar preparations, and eel-and-foie-gras mille-feuilles—a Berasategui signature. **Known for:** artful mix of classic and avant-garde; idyllic, white-tablecloth outdoor terrace; once-in-a-lifetime dining experience.

⑤ *Average main: €88* ✉ *Calle Loidi 4, Lasarte* ✧ *8 km (5 miles) south of San Sebastián* ☎ *94/336–6471, 94/336–1599* ⊕ *www.martinberasategui.com* ⏱ *Closed Sun.–Tues. and mid-Dec.–mid-Jan.*

**Maun Grill Bar**

$$ | BASQUE | Opened in 2019 in Mercado de San Martín, Maun is not your typical no-frills "bar de mercado," but rather a gastronomical food counter whose mouthwatering dishes—such as fish stew, squid in ink sauce, and heirloom tomato salad—are made with ultrafresh ingredients sourced right there at the market. **Known for:** market-fresh cuisine; terrific value; promising young chef. ⑤ *Average main: €18* ✉ *Mercado San Martín, Urbieta Kalea 9, Centro* ☎ *60/323–4761* ⊕ *www.maungrillbar.com* ⏱ *Closed Mon.*

**Mugaritz**

$$$$ | ECLECTIC | This bucolic farmhouse in the hills above Errenteria, 8 km (5 miles) northeast of San Sebastián, is a veritable laboratory of modern cooking techniques helmed by (arguably) the most experimental chef in Spain today, Andoni Aduriz. The obligatory three-hour, 23-course experience is unabashedly abstract with dishes like "don't search, find" and "tradition: onion and squid," all complemented by zany wild-card wines. **Known for:** long, immersive dining experience; abstract dishes; most "out there" of the Basque three-stars. ⑤ *Average main: €242* ✉ *Otzazulueta Baserria, Aldura Aldea 20, Errenteria, San Sebastián* ☎ *94/352–2455, 94/351–8343* ⊕ *www.mugaritz.com* ⏱ *Closed Mon.–Wed. and mid-Jan.–mid-Apr.*

**Restaurante Kokotxa**

$$$$ | INTERNATIONAL | The menu at this award-winning restaurant in the heart of the Parte Vieja hinges on chef Daniel López's clean, innovative cuisine, which plays on traditional Basque and Spanish flavors and often adds an Asian twist. Opt for a market-driven *degustación* or López's signature tasting menu, which includes dishes like whole langoustine with Navarrese white beans and Sichuan-spiced squab in liver ragout. **Known for:** surprisingly casual atmosphere; Asian-inflected Basque cuisine; only Michelin-starred dining in the city center. ⑤ *Average main: €90* ✉ *Calle del Campanario 11, Parte Vieja* ☎ *94/342–1904* ⊕ *www.restaurantekokotxa.com* ⏱ *Closed Sun.–Tues.*

**Topa Sukalderia**

$$ | LATIN AMERICAN | FAMILY | This buzzy Latin-Spanish fusion restaurant in Gros is the brainchild of Andoni Luis Aduriz of two-Michelin-star Mugaritz. A breath of fresh air on the local dining scene serving colorful cocktails and saucy dishes to the backdrop of Cuban jazz, Topa prides itself on making everything from scratch, from its nixtamalized tortillas to its "thousand-day" mole (originally a gift of Enrique Olvera of Pujol). **Known for:** best margs and guac in town; casual concept by Mugaritz chef; Basque-Latin fusion cuisine. ⑤ *Average main: €20* ✉ *Calle Agirre Miramon 7, Gros* ☎ *94/356–9143* ⊕ *www.topasukalderia.com* ⏱ *Closed Tue.*

**★ Zelaia Sagardotegia**

$$$ | BASQUE | This traditional *sagardotegi* 7 km (4 miles) south of San Sebastián is where the region's top chefs—Juan Mari Arzak, Martín Berasategui, and Pedro Subijana, to name a few—ring in every cider season with a resounding ¡txotx! ("cheers" in Basque). Removed from the tourist track and open from mid-January to late April, Zelaia invites guests into its barrel-lined warehouses to chow down on an à la carte menu of bacalao-centric dishes, thick-cut steaks, and—for dessert—local cheeses with quince preserves and walnuts (vegetarian options are also available). **Known for:** unlimited cider drinking; food that's an echelon above other sagardotegis; authentic cider house. ⑤ *Average main: €27* ✉ *B0 Martindegi 29* ☎ *94/355–5851* ⊕ *www.zelaia.eus* ⏱ *Closed late Apr.–mid-Jan. and Sun.*

## Zuberoa

**$$$$ | BASQUE |** This is the kind of restaurant where the chef greets every table and meals start with an amuse-bouche of foie gras—in other words, a slice of old-school heaven. Market-driven meals (think roasted wild game, tiny de lágrima peas, and strawberry gazpacho) unfold to the backdrop of a 15th-century farmhouse with an ivy-lined patio (the latter is open in summer only). **Known for:** dining room in a 15th-century caserío; wonderfully hospitable chef; Michelin-starred old-world Basque cuisine. ⑤ *Average main: €43* ⊠ *Araneder Bidea, Barrio Iturriotz, San Sebastián* ☎ *94/349–1228* ⊕ *www.zuberoa.com* ⌚ *Closed Wed. year-round, and Sun. June–Oct. No dinner Sun. year-round, and Tues. Nov.–May.*

## 🛏 Hotels

### Arrizul Congress Hotel

**$$$$ | HOTEL |** This clean-cut urban hotel, located steps from the river and Zurriola Beach, opened in early 2017 and is a dependable option for families and business travelers alike. **Pros:** feels fresh and modern; within walking distance of all the main sights; triples are available. **Cons:** occasionally unprofessional front-desk staff; architectural foibles make some rooms awkward; so-so soundproofing means noisy mornings. ⑤ *Rooms from: €251* ⊠ *Calle Ronda 3, Gros* ☎ *94/332–7026* ⊕ *www.hotelarrizulcongress.com* ⌂ *46 rooms* ⟍◯⟍ *Free Breakfast.*

### ★ Hotel Arbaso

**$$$$ | HOTEL |** Arbaso means "ancestor" in Euskera, and though this three-year-old hotel is awash with modern comforts (e.g., Marshall speakers, gym and sauna, smart bidet toilets, Apivita cosmetics), it exudes Basqueness in its staff uniforms, inspired by traditional jai alai uniforms; cuisine at Narru restaurant, hinging on local meats and seafood; and design elements, drawing on the Basque Country's raw materials like wood and natural stone. **Pros:** variety of amenities, bespoke tours, and cultural experiences; designer-y newcomer with a strong sense of place; Narru restaurant helmed by renowned local chef. **Cons:** cramped reception area; street noise in some rooms; pricey breakfast. ⑤ *Rooms from: €283* ⊠ *Calle Hondarribia 24, Centro* ☎ *84/393–1400* ⊕ *www.hotelarbaso.com* ⌂ *50 rooms* ⟍◯⟍ *No Meals.*

### ★ Hotel María Cristina

**$$$$ | HOTEL |** Belle Époque grace and opulence are embodied here, in San Sebastián's most legendary hotel looming over the Urumea. **Pros:** elaborate white-tablecloth breakfasts; grand historic building; old-world elegance with new-world amenities. **Cons:** wildly expensive; views aren't as dramatic as from other top hotels; staff can be a bit stiff. ⑤ *Rooms from: €624* ⊠ *Paseo República Argentina 4, Centro* ☎ *94/343–7600* ⊕ *www.hotel-mariacristina.com* ⌂ *136 rooms* ⟍◯⟍ *No Meals.*

### Hotel de Londres y de Inglaterra

**$$$$ | HOTEL |** On the main beachfront promenade overlooking La Concha, this stately hotel has a regal, old-world feel and Belle Époque aesthetic that starts in the marble lobby, with its shimmering chandeliers, and continues throughout the hotel. **Pros:** best hotel views in town; professional service; cozy and comfortable rooms. **Cons:** middling breakfasts and noticeable wear and tear; you're paying for the location, location, location; street side can be noisy on weekends. ⑤ *Rooms from: €354* ⊠ *Zubieta 2, La Concha* ☎ *94/344–0770* ⊕ *www.hlondres.com* ⌂ *148 rooms* ⟍◯⟍ *Free Breakfast.*

### Hotel Parma

**$$$ | HOTEL |** Overlooking the Kursaal concert hall and the Zurriola beach at the mouth of the Urumea, this small but inviting two-star is also steps from the bar-lined Parte Vieja. **Pros:** Parte Vieja location; you can hear the crashing of the waves; river views. **Cons:** some rooms look out onto a scuzzy courtyard; interiors could use a face-lift; digs are a bit cramped and cluttered. ⑤ *Rooms from: €180* ✉ *Paseo de Salamanca 10, Parte Vieja* ☎ *94/342–8893* ⊕ *www.hotelparma.com* ☞ *27 rooms* ⊚ *Free Breakfast.*

### ★ One Shot Tabakalera House

$$$ | HOTEL | Locals call this four-star newcomer a "hotel within a museum" because of its location inside the Tabakalera cultural center, a hotbed of art and innovation inaugurated in 2015. **Pros:** avant-garde design; close to the RENFE train station; located within the city's cultural center. **Cons:** no coffeemakers in most rooms; no room service; 10-minute walk into town. ⑤ *Rooms from: €190* ✉ *Paseo Duque de Mandas 52, Amara* ☎ *94/393–0028* ⊕ *www.hoteloneshottabakalerahouse.com* ☞ *33 rooms* ⊚ *No Meals.*

### Pensión Nuevas Artes

$$ | B&B/INN | This tidy 10-room hotel four blocks east of the cathedral stands out for its rock-bottom (at least by local standards) prices. **Pros:** terrific value; steps from the cathedral and other top sights; cozy atmosphere. **Cons:** no a/c; bad soundproofing; no check-in between 2 and 5 pm. ⑤ *Rooms from: €109* ✉ *Urbieta 64, Centro* ☎ *94/347–4905* ⊕ *www.pension-nuevasartes.com* ☞ *10 rooms* ⊚ *No Meals.*

### Sansebay

$$$$ | HOTEL | FAMILY | At the foot of Mount Urgull sits this airy new (finished in 2020) boutique hotel with streamlined modern furnishings and stunning views out over La Concha and the old harbor. **Pros:** both standard and apartment-style digs are available; views of Isla Santa Clara from upgraded rooms; exquisite breakfasts and freshly baked cakes. **Cons:** reception closes at 11 pm; no gym; decor lacks sense of place. ⑤ *Rooms from: €247* ✉ *Mari Kalea 21, Parte Vieja* ☎ *94/343–5724* ⊕ *www.sansebayhotel.com* ☞ *29 rooms* ⊚ *No Meals.*

### Villa Soro

$$$$ | HOTEL | There's no better time to book a fairytale getaway at this iconic mansion-cum-hotel, which debuted under new ownership with a fresh face in spring 2022. **Pros:** new wellness area with treatment rooms and 24-hour gym; complimentary bikes and beach towels; tranquil country estate within arm's reach of the center. **Cons:** expensive considering the location; traditional, conservative aesthetics might not be for everyone; 10-minute taxi, bus, or bike ride from most sights. ⑤ *Rooms from: €323* ✉ *Av. de Ategorrieta 61, Gros* ☎ *94/329–7970* ⊕ *www.hotelvillasoro.com* ☞ *25 rooms* ⊚ *No Meals.*

### Zinema7 Hotel

$$$ | HOTEL | Set in the renovated Astoria Cinema, this film-themed hotel has a spacious lobby adorned with autographed photos of the many movie stars who have attended the famous San Sebastián Film Festival over the years. **Pros:** spacious rooms; varied, good-quality breakfast; fun and campy cinematographic decor. **Cons:** ugly high-rise building; not for non-cinephiles; 20-minute walk (or short bus ride) to beach and the Parte Vieja. ⑤ *Rooms from: €180* ✉ *Calle de la Sagrada Família 1, Centro* ☎ *94/344–5000* ⊕ *www.zinema7hotel.com* ☞ *102 rooms* ⊚ *No Meals.*

## ⓨ Nightlife

### BARS AND PUBS

#### Gu

COCKTAIL LOUNGES | The renovated Gu, with its floor-to-ceiling windows overlooking La Concha, is a glitzy indoor-outdoor cocktail bar and nightclub housed in a futuristic building resembling a cruise ship. ✉ *Ijentea 9, Centro* ☎ *84/398–0775* ⊕ *www.gusansebastian.com.*

### ★ Arenales

WINE BARS | Having the the most intriguing natural wine list in town is this newcomer postage-stamp bar's claim to

fame. Go for the spontaneously ferment-
ed oddball varietals; stay for the Argen-
tine-inflected pintxos and ever-rotating
vegetable-heavy menu. Reservations are
a must. ⊠ *Boulevard Zumardia 11, Centro*
☎ *94/343–5953* ⊕ *www.instagram.com/
arenales.bar.*

## DANCE CLUBS
### Bataplán
DANCE CLUBS | San Sebastián's top dance
club, in business for four decades, is near
the western end of La Concha. Guest
DJs and events determine the vibe,
although you can count on high-energy
dance music, a young clientele, and
enthusiastic imbibing. ⊠ *Paseo de la Concha 10, Centro* ☎ *94/346–0439* ⊕ *www.
bataplandisco.com* ۞ *Closed Mon.–Wed.*

## MUSIC CLUBS
### Akerbeltz
LIVE MUSIC | This feel-good dive bar is
a perfect late-night refuge for music
and drinks. ⊠ *Calle Mari 19, Parte Vieja*
☎ *94/346–0934, 94/345–1452* ۞ *Closed
Tue.*

### ★ ¡BE! Club
LIVE MUSIC | Formerly known as Bebop,
this San Sebastián classic—which
eschews the usual Top 40 in favor of
Latin, jazz, and unconventional dance
tunes—recently got a major face-lift
and is all the better for it. ⊠ *Paseo de
Salamanca 3, Parte Vieja* ☎ *94/347–8505*
⊕ *www.beclubss.com.*

# ⬤ Shopping

San Sebastián is a busy shopping center.
Wander Calle San Martín and the surrounding pedestrian-only streets to see
what's in the windows.

### Alboka Artesanía
CRAFTS | This is the best city-center shop
for Basque-made artisan items such as
patterned tablecloths and linens, goat-
skin jai alai balls, ceramics, and traditional
dress. ⊠ *Pl. Constitución 8, Parte Vieja*

☎ *94/342–6300* ⊕ *albokaartesania.com*
۞ *Closed Sun.*

### Casa Ponsol
HATS & GLOVES | Visit this milliner to buy a
*boina*, or traditional felt hat. The Leclerq
family has been hatting (and clothing) the
local male population since 1838. ⊠ *Calle
Narrica 4, at Calle Sarriegui 3, Parte Vieja*
☎ *94/342–0876* ⊕ *www.casaponsol.com*
۞ *Closed Sun.*

### Mimo Bite the Experience
FOOD | This posh gourmet food and wine
shop also hosts Basque cooking classes
and popular food tours. ⊠ *Calle Okendo
1, Centro* ☎ *94/342–1143* ⊕ *www.mimo.
eus.*

# Vitoria-Gasteiz

*62 km (39 miles) south of Bilbao, 100 km
(62 miles) west of Pamplona.*

The capital of the Basque Country, and
the region's second-largest city after
Bilbao, Vitoria-Gasteiz might be Euskadi's least "Basque" city, at least from a
foreigner's perspective, since it's neither
a seafaring port nor a mountain enclave.
It sprawls, instead, over the undulating
meseta de Álava (Álava plain) and functions as a modern industrial center with
plentiful cultural events, fine restaurants,
and museums—in other words, it's a
Basque city for Basques.

It takes in a strikingly well-preserved
Casco Medieval (Medieval Quarter).
Founded by Sancho el Sabio (the Wise) in
1181, the urban center was built largely
of granite, so Vitoria's oldest streets and
squares look weathered and ancient.
**Calle Cuchillería** ("La Kutxi" to locals)
is the old town's main tapas drag with
over 40 establishments packed into a
500-meter (1/3-mile) stretch.

### GETTING AROUND
Take the A1 and the PA34 from Pamplona, which takes one hour by car; buses
also run regularly between the two cities.

From Bilbao, hop on the AP68 and N622, which takes 44 minutes. Vitoria is a spread-out city, but the area you'll spend your time in is small, only about 1 km (½ mile) square, and easily covered on foot. An efficient tram service connects the city center to the train and bus stations.

**BUS STATION Estación de Autobuses de Vitoria–Gasteiz.** ⊠ *Pl. de Euskaltzaindia,* ☎ *94/516–1666.*

**CAR RENTALS Europcar.** ⊠ *Calle Adriano VI 29,* ☎ *94/520–0433* ⊕ *www.europcar. com.*

**VISITOR INFORMATION**
**CONTACTS Vitoria–Gasteiz.** ⊠ *Pl. España 1,* ☎ *94/516–1598* ⊕ *www.vitoria-gasteiz. org.*

# 👁 Sights

## ★ Artium Museum

**ART MUSEUM** | Officially named the Centro-Museo Vasco de Arte Contemporáneo, this former bus station is regarded as the third corner of the Basque modern art triangle, along with the Bilbao Guggenheim and San Sebastián's Chillida–Leku. The museum's permanent collection—including 20th- and 21st-century paintings and sculptures by Jorge Oteiza, Chillida, Agustín Ibarrola, and Nestor Basterretxea, among others—makes it one of Spain's finest treasuries of contemporary art. ⊠ *Calle Francia 24, Vitoria* ☎ *94/520–9020* ⊕ *www.artium. eus* 💲 *Free (donation recommended)* 🕑 *Closed Mon.*

## Bibat Museum

**HISTORY MUSEUM** | **FAMILY** | The 1525 Palacio de Bendaña and adjoining bronze-plated building are home to one of Vitoria's main attractions, the Bibat, which combines the Museo Fournier de Naipes (Playing-Card Museum) with the Museo de Arqueología. The *palacio* houses the 15,000 playing-card sets of Don Heraclio Fournier, who founded a famous playing-card factory in 1868. One of the largest and finest such collections in the world, it features hand-painted cards from Japan, round cards from India, and other ancient specimens dating to the 12th century. The Museo de la Arqueología, in the newest building, has Paleolithic dolmens, Roman art and artifacts, medieval objects, and the famous Stele del Jinete (Stele of the Horseback Rider), an early Basque tombstone. ⊠ *Calle Cuchillería 54, Vitoria* ☎ *94/520–3700* ⊕ *www.fourniermuseoabibat.eus* 💲 *Free* 🕑 *Closed Mon.*

## ★ Catedral de Santa María

**CHURCH** | Dating to the 14th century, this once-crumbling cathedral has been undergoing renovations for more than two decades—but it's open to visitors, which is its unique selling point. Guided tours begin in the bowels of the building, where the transition from Romanesque to Gothic styles is evident in the square pillars topped with cylindrical ones. The tour culminates in a visit to the bell tower followed by a hyperrealistic light show that gives visitors a sense of the cathedral's formerly colorful painted exterior through the ages. A prominent and active supporter of the project is British novelist Ken Follett, whose novel *World Without End* is about the construction of the cathedral. The renovation is slated to be completed once and for all within the next three years. ■**TIP→ Call ahead to book an English-language group tour, or use the free audio guide on the standard tours, which depart every 30 minutes or so.** ⊠ *Pl. Santa Maria, Vitoria* ☎ *94/525–5135* ⊕ *www.catedralvitoria.eus* 💲 *€11.*

## Museo de Armería de Álava

**OTHER MUSEUM** | Just south of the park, this weaponry museum has prehistoric hatchets, 20th-century pistols, and a sand-table reproduction of the 1813 battle between the Duke of Wellington's troops and the French. ⊠ *Paseo Fray Francisco 3, Vitoria* ☎ *94/518–1925* ⊕ *www.armamuseoa.eus* 💲 *Free* 🕑 *Closed Mon.*

**Museo de Bellas Artes de Álava** (*Museum of Fine Arts*)

ART MUSEUM | Paintings by Ribera, Picasso, and the Basque painter Zuloaga adorn the walls of this exuberant baroque building, whose collection spans from the 18th to the 20th century. ⊠ *Paseo Fray Francisco 8, Vitoria* ☎ *94/518–1918* ⊕ *www.arteederrenmuseoa.eus* 🎫 *Free* ☉ *Closed Mon.*

**Plaza de España**

PLAZA/SQUARE | Across Virgen Blanca, past the monument and the handsome Victoria Café stands this arcaded neoclassical square with the austere elegance typical of 19th-century municipal architecture. ⊠ *Pl. de España, Vitoria.*

**Plaza de la Virgen Blanca**

PLAZA/SQUARE | In the southwest corner of old Vitoria, this plaza—the nerve center of the Casco Viejo—is ringed by noble houses with covered arches and white-trim glass galleries. The monument in the center commemorates the Duke of Wellington's victory over Napoleon's army here in 1813. ⊠ *Pl. de la Virgen Blanca, Vitoria.*

**Street Art**

PUBLIC ART | In a city as noble and staid as Vitoria, you don't expect to find world-class street art, but that's precisely what's been drawing more and more tourists and artsy types to the parallel streets of Anorbin and Carnicerías in the old town. Feast your eyes on multistory, thought-provoking murals depicting family scenes, landscapes, and political issues. Of note is an enormous mural covering the entire side of a house opposite El Portalón restaurant. ⊠ *Cantón Anorbin, Vitoria.*

**Torre de Doña Ochanda**

CASTLE/PALACE | FAMILY | This 15th-century tower houses Vitoria's Museo de Ciencias Naturales, which contains botanical, zoological, and geological collections along with the museum's most prized items: pieces of amber from the nearby

archaeological site at Peñacerrada-Urizaharra. ⊠ *Calle Siervas de Jesús 24, Vitoria* ☎ *94/518–1924* 🎫 *Free* ☉ *Closed Mon.*

**Torre de los Anda**

HISTORIC HOME | This is the oldest house and defensive tower in Vitoria, constructed in the 15th century beside the cathedral. Though it's closed to the public, the courtyards and winding streets that surround it are worth exploring. ⊠ *Pl. de la Burullería, Vitoria.*

## 🍴 Restaurants

**Bar El Toloño**

$$ | TAPAS | The unassuming interiors of this Casco Viejo standby belie a sophisticated kitchen that has won numerous awards for its knockout pintxos including *txangurro gratinado* (crab gratin), *gildas* (olive-anchovy-pepper brochettes), and rabbit ravioli. Order and pay at the bar, then carry your nibbles outside to the first-come-first-served patio. **Known for:** aperitivo hour rush; devoted local crowd; worth-the-wait creative bites. ⑤ *Average main: €17* ⊠ *Cuesta San Francisco 3, Vitoria* ☎ *94/523–3336* ⊕ *www.tolonobar.com.*

**Bar La Torre de Anda**

$ | BASQUE | A little-known culinary gem on the ground floor of the 15th-century Torre de Anda, this down-home wine and cheese bar with three high-top tables is always stocked with smoky Idiazabal, limited-production Rioja Alavesa wines, and tart gildas. **Known for:** passionate and knowledgeable owner; in the heart of the old town; perfect spot for an aperitivo or midday snack. ⑤ *Average main: €10* ⊠ *Hedegile Kalea 110, Vitoria* ☎ *68/889–8988.*

**★ El Mesón**

$$ | BASQUE | Textbook-perfect Basque classics draw a local crowd at this Ensanche restaurant run by a seasoned husband-and-wife team on the cusp of retirement—so visit while you still can! Seasonal Basque delicacies, like earthy

*perretxico* mushrooms, meaty fresh anchovies, and tender white asparagus, round out a perennial menu whose star dishes include squid braised in its own ink and hake in *salsa verde*. **Known for:** over-and-beyond service; Basque restaurant classics done right; varied wine list. ⓢ *Average main: €18* ✉ *Ramon Ortiz de Zarate Kalea 5, Vitoria* ☎ *94/514–6191.*

### El Portalón

**$$$** | **SPANISH** | With creaky wood floors, bare brick walls, and ancient beams and coats of arms, this 15th-century inn turns out classical Castilian and Basque specialties reflective of the region. Try the *cochinillo lechal* (roast suckling pig) or any of the monkfish preparations. **Known for:** deep wine list; Basque comfort food; fairytale medieval building. ⓢ *Average main: €23* ✉ *Calle Correría 147, Vitoria* ☎ *94/514–2755* ⊕ *www.restauranteelportalon.com* ◔ *No dinner Sun.*

### ★ La Bodeguilla Lanciego

**$$$** | **BASQUE** | This inviting white-tablecloth taberna established in 1959 serves soul-satisfying cuisine in a cabinlike dining room decorated with taupe curtains, blond-wood chairs, and original artwork. Steak frites is the go-to here with roast turbot coming in a close second. **Known for:** books up weeks in advance; excellent txuletas; subtle, tasteful decor. ⓢ *Average main: €24* ✉ *Calle Olagibel 60, Vitoria* ☎ *94/525–0073* ⊕ *www.labodeguillalanciego.com* ◔ *Closed Sun.*

### Zaldiaran

**$$$** | **BASQUE** | Don't be put off by the outdated plating (think sorbet served in martini glasses); book a meal here for contemporary interpretations of Basque classics, such as tempura-battered artichokes and razor clams with yuzu vinaigrette. The tasting menu (€72) changes seasonally. **Known for:** impress-your-date ambience; good-value tasting menus; heavenly steak tartare. ⓢ *Average main: €25* ✉ *Av. Gasteiz 21, Vitoria*

☎ *94/513–4822* ⊕ *www.restaurantezaldiaran.com* ◔ *Closed Mon.–Wed. No dinner Thurs. and Fri.*

 ## Hotels

### Etxegana Hotel and Spa

**$$$** | **HOTEL** | **FAMILY** | On top of a mountain in the heart of Basque country's "little Switzerland," 20 minutes north of Vitoria-Gasteiz and 40 minutes south of Bilbao, this relaxing retreat features breathtaking views of the surrounding mountains and an excellent restaurant and spa. **Pros:** stunning views; family-run and welcoming; surrounded by nature. **Cons:** Wi-Fi could be better in some rooms; popular wedding venue; half-hour drive to town. ⓢ *Rooms from: €145* ✉ *Ipiñaburu 38, Zeanuri* ☎ *94/633–8448* ⊕ *www.etxegana.com* ⤢ *18 rooms* ❙⓿❙ *Free Breakfast.*

### ★ La Casa de los Arquillos

**$** | **B&B/INN** | Brightly lit, with clean Scandi-minimal design, this adorable B&B is steps from Plaza de España. **Pros:** unbeatable location; independently owned; good breakfast. **Cons:** some rooms don't have blackout drapes; no parking or 24-hour reception; rooms are up two flights of stairs. ⓢ *Rooms from: €90* ✉ *Paseo los Arquillos 1, Vitoria* ☎ *94/515–1259* ⊕ *www.lacasadelosarquillos.com* ⤢ *8 rooms* ❙⓿❙ *Free Breakfast.*

### Parador de Argómaniz

**$$** | **HOTEL** | This 17th-century palace has panoramic views over the Álava plains and feels like a time warp with its long stone hallways decorated with bulky, opulent antiques. **Pros:** contemporary rooms and comforts; excellent restaurant; gorgeous details and surroundings. **Cons:** noisy radiators might wake you up; no patio furniture on guest-room balconies; isolated at a 15-minute drive from Vitoria. ⓢ *Rooms from: €110* ✉ *Calle del Parador 14, Argómaniz* ✛ *East of Vitoria* off N104 toward Pamplona ☎ 94/529-3200 ⊕ www.parador.es ↘ 53 rooms ✺ No Meals.

### Silken Ciudad de Vitoria

$$ | HOTEL | FAMILY | The soaring atrium, expansive lobby, and turreted corner rooms lend this dependable seven-floor hotel a grand, conservative air. **Pros:** helpful veteran staff; local baked goods and homemade tortilla de patata at breakfast; comfortable, spacious rooms. **Cons:** not in a pretty part of town; no bedside outlets or lotion in the bathroom; feels a bit dark and dated. $ *Rooms from: €115* ⊠ *Gaztelako Atea 8, Vitoria* ☎ 94/514–1100 ⊕ *www.hoteles-silken.com* ↘ 149 rooms ✺ No Meals.

## 🌙 Nightlife

★ **Dazz**

LIVE MUSIC | Drop by this kitschy bar for live music and Basque comfort food in the evenings; there's usually an impressively smooth band playing rock, blues, or jazz. Lunch on the outdoor picnic tables is wonderful when the weather is nice. ⊠ *Calle Cuchillería 60, Vitoria* ☎ 94/556–1642 ⊕ *www.facebook.com/benat.lasa.3.*

## 🛍 Shopping

★ **Victofer Conservas Artesanas**

FOOD | This century-old purveyor that supplies top restaurants in the area is a great place to stock up on premium *conservas* (preserved and canned foods) and sacks of mottled *alubias de Álava* (Álava pinto beans). Tinned vegetables are Victofer's forte with piquillo peppers and white asparagus tips being particularly exceptional. ⊠ *Calle Cuchillería 14, Vitoria* ☎ 94/525–5305 ⊕ *www.victofer.com* ⊙ *Closed Sun.*

# Laguardia

*45 km (28 miles) south of Vitoria.*

Founded in 908 AD to stand guard—as its name suggests—over Navarra's southwestern flank, Laguardia is situated on a promontory overlooking the Río Ebro and the vineyards of La Rioja Alavesa wine country. The peaceful medieval town is an ideal outpost for vineyard-hoppers.

## VISITOR INFORMATION

CONTACTS **Laguardia Tourist Office.** ⊠ *Calle Mayor 52,* ☎ 94/560–0845 ⊕ *www.laguardia-alava.com.*

## 👁 Sights

Starting from the 15th-century Puerta de Carnicerías, or Puerta Nueva, the central portal off the parking area on the east side of town, the first landmark is the 16th-century **Ayuntamiento,** with its imperial shield of Carlos V. Farther into the square is the current town hall, built in the 19th century. A right turn down Calle Santa Engracia takes you past impressive façades—the floor inside the portal at No. 25 is a lovely stone mosaic, and a walk behind the triple-emblazoned 17th-century facade of No. 19 reveals a stagecoach, floor mosaics, wood beams, and an inner porch. The Puerta de Santa Engracia, with an image of the saint in an overhead niche, opens out to the right, and on the left, at the entrance to Calle Víctor Tapia, No. 17 bears a coat of arms with the Latin phrase *Laus Tibi* (Praise Be to Thee).

### Bodega El Fabulista

WINERY | This family-run bodega is famed for its down-to-earth, approachable tours, which explore the 16th-century caves below Laguardia and are followed by a tasting of three fruity carbonic-maceration wines for €15. ⊠ *Pl. San Juan, Laguardia* ☎ 94/562–1192 ⊕ *www.*

*bodegaelfabulista.com* 🖻 *From €8*
⊘ *Closed Sun.*

### Bodegas Baigorri

**WINERY** | This sleek, modern winery is
an architectural wonder of glass and
steel with floor-to-ceiling windows that
overlook the vineyards and a state-of-the-
art multilevel wine cellar. The two-hour
morning tour ends around 2 pm—the
perfect time to settle in for lunch at the
upstairs restaurant. The tasting menu
pairs the three-course menu with four
signature wines for around €50 and is
highly recommended. ⊠ *Ctra. Vitoria–
Logroño, Km 53, Logroño* ☎ *94/560–9420*
⊕ *www.bodegasbaigorri.com* 🖻 *From
€18* ⊘ *Closed Sun. and Mon.*

### Casa de la Primicia

**NOTABLE BUILDING** | Laguardia's oldest
civil structure, the 15th-century Casa
de la Primicia is where tithes of fresh
fruit were collected in medieval times.
Visit the restored underground bodega,
where tours culminate in a range of wine
tastings, one of which samples four local
varietals (Tempranillo, Graciano, Mazuelo,
and Garnacha). ⊠ *Calle Páganos 78,
Laguardia* ☎ *94/562–1266, 94/560–0296*
⊕ *www.bodegascasaprimicia.com*
🖻 *From €13.*

### Eguren Ugarte

**WINERY** | The family behind this majestic
winery has been in the business for five
generations. Surrounded by vineyards on
all sides, Eguren Ugarte offers a variety
of pre-bookable tours and tastings on
foot, horseback, and Segway. ⊠ *Ctra.
A124, Km 61, Páganos, Laguardia*
☎ *94/560–0766* ⊕ *www.egurenugarte.
com* 🖻 *From €15.*

### Galería Juanjo San Pedro

**ART GALLERY** | This gallery is filled with
colorful abstract paintings of landscapes
and rural life by a local artist. ⊠ *Calle
Mayor 11, Laguardia* ☎ *65/892–8580*
⊕ *www.juanjosanpedro.es* ⊘ *Closed Sun.*

### Herederos de Marqués de Riscal

**WINERY** | The village of Elciego, 6 km (4
miles) southeast of Laguardia, is the site
of the historic Marqués de Riscal winery.
Tours of the vineyards and cellars—
among the most legendary in La Rioja—
are conducted in English. Reservations
are required. The estate also includes the
stunning Frank Gehry–designed Hotel
Marqués de Riscal, crafted out of waves
of metal reminiscent of his Guggenheim Bilbao. ⊠ *Calle Torrea 1, Elciego*
☎ *94/560–6000* ⊕ *www.marquesderiscal.
com* 🖻 *From €21.*

### Hontza

**WINERY** | Small-production, minimal-in-
tervention wines produced according to
the biodynamic method are the specialty of this independent winery that's a
25-minute drive east of Laguardia. Tours
and tastings are by online appointment
only. ⊠ *2 Barriobusto Bidea, Laguardia*
⊕ *www.vinedoshontza.com.*

### ★ Santa María de los Reyes

**CHURCH** | Laguardia's architectural
masterpiece is this church's Gothic
polychrome portal—the only one of its
kind in Spain. Protected by a posterior
Renaissance facade, the door centers on
a lovely, lifelike effigy of La Virgen de los
Reyes (Virgin of the Kings), sculpted in
the 14th century and painted in the 17th
by Ribera. Guided tours are available by
pre-booking only; email the Laguardia
tourist office, and be sure to specify your
language (*turismo@laguardia-alava.com*).
⊠ *Calle Mayor 52, Laguardia* ☎ *94/560–
0845* 🖻 *Tours €4* ⚬ *Reservations via the
tourist office only.*

## 🛏 Hotels

### Hospedería de los Parajes

$$$ | **HOTEL** | Amenities at this traditional
hotel in a restored stone building include
a complimentary glass of wine at check-
in, to be taken in a 16th-century wine
cave. **Pros:** charming wine cellar; cozy,
grandmotherly digs; centrally located.

Cons: expensive and remote parking; Wi-Fi spotty in some rooms; poor natural light. $ Rooms from: €190 ⊠ Calle Mayor 46–48, Laguardia ☎ 94/562–1130 ⊕ www.hospederiadelosparajes.com ⤢ 18 rooms ⦿ Free Breakfast.

### Hotel Castillo El Collado

$$ | HOTEL | Guests are treated like royalty in this castlelike 18th-century manor house. Pros: old-world European feel; website features every room (so ask for the one you want); close to the heart of town. Cons: maintenance could be improved; underwhelming breakfast; spotty Wi-Fi in some rooms. $ Rooms from: €135 ⊠ Paseo El Collado 1, Laguardia ☎ 94/562–1200 ⊕ www. castillocollado.com ⤢ 10 rooms ⦿ Free Breakfast.

### ★ Hotel Marqués de Riscal, A Luxury Collection Hotel

$$$$ | HOTEL | Frank Gehry's post-Guggenheim hotel looks like an extraterrestrial colony in the middle of one of La Rioja's oldest vineyards. Pros: dazzling architecture; superb dining; dependable big-brand (Marriott) luxury. Cons: service isn't always five-star; interiors pale in comparison to the exterior; phenomenally expensive. $ Rooms from: €560 ⊠ Calle Torrea 1, Elciego ⊹ 6 km (4 miles) southwest of Laguardia ☎ 94/518–0880 ⊕ www.hotel-marquesderiscal.com ⤢ 43 rooms ⦿ Free Breakfast.

### Hotel Viura

$$$$ | HOTEL | The sharp angles and bright colors of this architecturally avant-garde luxury hotel cut a striking contrast to the vernacular architecture surrounding it, and the location—12 km (7 miles) west of Laguardia in the sleepy village of Villabuena de Álava—makes it a good base for exploring La Rioja Alavesa and neighboring Rioja Alta. Pros: quirky, Instagrammable architecture; king-size beds; rooftop gym and bar. Cons: soundproofing could be improved; no spa; not much to do in the village. $ Rooms from: €202 ⊠ Calle Mayor, Villabuena de Álava

☎ 94/560–9000 ⊕ www.hotelviura.com ⤢ 33 rooms ⦿ Free Breakfast.

### ★ Mayor de Migueloa

$$ | HOTEL | With its stone floors and rough-hewn ceiling beams, this 17th-century palace hotel transports you back in time, but it features thoroughly modern comforts: a terrific on-site tavern and winery (try the smoky, garlicky Riojana potatoes), cushy beds, framed prints, and flower-fringed wrought-iron balconies. Pros: quaint, countrified rooms; restaurant that's a destination in itself; off-season specials. Cons: no Wi-Fi in some rooms; exterior-facing rooms are noisy on weekends; parking is far. $ Rooms from: €110 ⊠ Calle Mayor de Migueloa 20, Laguardia ☎ 94/560–0187 ⊕ www.mayordemigueloa.com ⊙ Closed Jan. 8–Feb. 8 ⤢ 8 rooms ⦿ No Meals.

# Pasaia

*7 km (4 miles) east of San Sebastián.*

Three towns make up the busy little port of Pasaia (Rentería in Spanish): **Pasai Antxo** (Pasajes Ancho), an industrial area; **Pasai de San Pedro** (Pasajes de San Pedro), a large fishing harbor; and historic **Pasai Donibane** (Pasajes de San Juan), a colorful cluster of 16th- and 17th-century buildings. The most scenic way in is via Pasai de San Pedro, on the San Sebastián side of the strait: Catch a five-minute launch across the mouth of the harbor (approximately €2 round trip).

Pasaia has lots of history. In 1777, a 20-year-old General Lafayette set out from Pasai Donibane to aid the American Revolution. Victor Hugo spent the summer of 1843 here writing his *Voyage aux Pyrénées*; in fact, the **Victor Hugo House** is now the tourist office, its walls hung with the writer's drawings and memorabilia. The **Albaola boatbuilding factory,** a visitable center of maritime culture, is directed by Xabier Agote, who taught boatbuilding in Rockland, Maine.

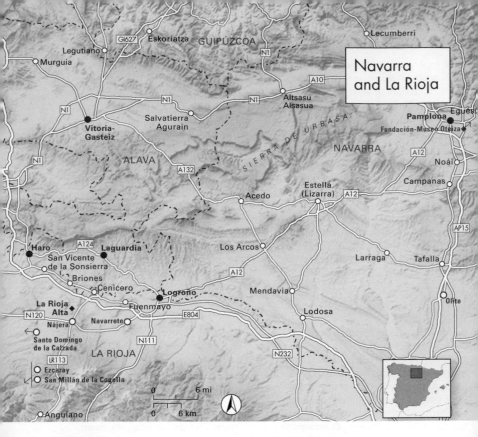

## ⊙ Sights

**Mater Boat Museum** (*Mater Ontzi Museo Ekoaktiboa*)

**NAUTICAL SIGHT** | **FAMILY** | A museum on the move, this traditional wooden Basque fishing boat called a *mater*—the last of its kind—was built in 1900 and today gives roving "eco-tours" of the coastline. Visitors can choose from experiences ranging from an out-to-sea itinerary exploring ancestral fishing methods to an in-depth tour through the bowels of the vessel centered on the art of shipbuilding and maintenance. ⊠ *Calle Arraunlari, Pasai Donibane* ☎ *61/981–4225* ⊕ *www.mater.eus* ⊠ *€7* ⊘ *Closed Jan. and Feb.*

## 🍴 Restaurants

**★ Casa Cámara**

**$$$$** | **SEAFOOD** | Four generations ago, Pablo Cámara turned this 19th-century fishing wharf on the Pasaia narrows into a first-class seafood restaurant with lovely views over the shipping lane. A steaming *sopa de pescado* (fish soup) is just the ticket on a wet Atlantic day, or try *cangrejo del mar* (spider crab with vegetable sauce) or the superb hake with salsa verde. **Known for:** quaint, old-timey ambience; pristine shellfish; pier-side dining. $ *Average main: €46* ⊠ *Calle San Juan 79, Pasai Donibane* ☎ *94/352–3699* ⊕ *www.casacamara.com* ⊘ *Closed Mon. No dinner Sun.–Thu.*

# Hondarribia

*20 km (13 miles) east of Pasaia.*

Hondarribia is the last fishing port before the French border and a wonderful day trip from San Sebastián. Lined with fishermen's homes and small fishing boats, the harbor is a scenic if slightly touristy spot. If you have a taste for history, follow signs up the hill to the medieval bastion and onetime castle of Carlos V, now a parador, and keep your eye out for coats of arms emblazoned on the corners of old buildings (as opposed to above entryways)—an Hondarribia peculiarity.

### VISITOR INFORMATION

**CONTACTS Hondarribia Tourist Office.** ⊠ *Pl. de Armas 9,* ☎ *94/364–3677* ⊕ *www. hondarribia.eus.*

##  Restaurants

### Alameda

$$$$ | **BASQUE** | The Txapartegi brothers—Mikel, Kepa, and Gorka—are the decorated chefs behind this restaurant in elegantly restored house with a sunny terrace. Count on seasonally rotated combinations of carefully chosen ingredients, from fish and duck to vegetables. **Known for:** scenic seaside environs; freshest seafood and meats; understated Michelin-starred dining. ⑤ *Average main: €36* ⊠ *Calle Minasoroeta 1, Hondarribia* ☎ *94/364–2789* ⊕ *www.restaurantealameda.net* ⊗ *Closed Mon.–Wed. No dinner.*

### ★ Hermandad de Pescadores

$$$ | **SEAFOOD** | Presided over by a legendary Basque fishermen's guild, this central restaurant serves the freshest fish money can buy at fair prices. At simple wooden tables and a handsome mahogany bar, locals dig into local comfort food—think sopa de pescado, steamed mussels, and clams *a la marinera* (in a thick, garlicky sauce). **Known for:** homey, unfussy dining room; booking up weeks in advance; affordable dayboat fish.

⑤ *Average main: €23* ⊠ *Calle Zuloaga 12, Hondarribia* ☎ *94/364–2738* ⊕ *www. hermandaddepescadores.com* ⊗ *Closed Mon. No dinner weekdays.*

## Hotels

### Basalore

$$$$ | **HOUSE** | San Sebastián's buzzy new Hotel Arbaso likes to call this luxurious hilltop villa with five rooms its finest "suite," but that's selling this sister property short; after all, most suites don't span 67 acres teeming with goats, sheep, and pampered Basque "Wagyu" cows (a passion project of the owner). **Pros:** unparalleled privacy and exclusivity; in the middle of nowhere yet accessible to nearby cities; endless room to spread out. **Cons:** books up quickly; off-the-charts expensive; a bit of a hike from San Sebastián. ⑤ *Rooms from: €4,500* ⊠ *Jaitzubia Auzoa 200, Hondarribia* ☎ *84/393–1420* ⊕ *hotelarbaso.com/ noticia/basalore-casa-lujo-hondarribia-nueva-web* ⊅ *5 rooms* ⑩ *No Meals.*

### Casa Artzu

$ | **B&B/INN** | **FAMILY** | Welcoming hosts run this budget-friendly inn in a 13th-century family farmhouse overlooking the Bidasoa estuary. **Pros:** great value; free parking; family-friendly. **Cons:** need a car; breakfast €3 extra; credit cards not accepted. ⑤ *Rooms from: €52* ⊠ *Barrio Montaña, Hondarribia* ☎ *94/364–0530* ⊕ *www.casaartzu.com* ⊅ *6 rooms* ⑩ *No Meals.*

### ★ Parador de Hondarribia

$$$$ | **HOTEL** | **FAMILY** | You can live like a medieval lord in this 10th-century bastion, home in the 16th century to Spain's founding emperor, Carlos V—hence its alternative name: Parador El Emperador. **Pros:** sweeping sea views; white-tablecloth breakfasts in the mossy courtyard; building that oozes medieval mystique. **Cons:** overpriced room rates and parking in high season; insipid furniture in guest rooms; no restaurant. ⑤ *Rooms from: €300* ⊠ *Pl. de Armas 14, Hondarribia*

☎ 94/364–5500 ⊕ www.parador.es ⤶ 36 rooms �‖ No Meals.

# Pamplona

*79 km (47 miles) southeast of San Sebastián.*

Founded by the Roman emperor Pompey as Pompaelo, or Pampeiopolis, Pamplona was successively taken by the Franks, Goths, and Moors. In 750, Pamplonians put themselves under the protection of Charlemagne and expelled their Arab rulers temporarily. But the foreign commander took advantage of this trust to destroy the city walls; when he was driven out once more by the Moors, the Navarrese took their revenge, ambushing and slaughtering the retreating Frankish army as it fled over the Pyrenees through the mountain pass of Roncesvalles in 778. This is the episode depicted in the 11th-century *Song of Roland,* although its anonymous French poet cast the Moors as the aggressors. In the ensuing centuries, Pamplona was a collection of three rival towns that would be forcibly incorporated into one city by Carlos III (the Noble, 1387–1425) of Navarra.

Of course, Pamplona (Iruña or Iruñea in Euskera) is best known for its running of the bulls, made famous by Ernest Hemingway in his 1926 novel, *The Sun Also Rises.* The occasion is the festival of San Fermín, July 6–14, when Pamplona's population triples (along with its hotel rates). Every morning of the festival, a rocket is shot off at 8 sharp, and the bulls kept overnight in the corrals at the edge of town are run through a series of closed-off streets leading to the bullring, an 850-meter (1/2-mile) dash. Running among them are Spaniards and foreigners feeling audacious (or perhaps foolhardy) enough to risk getting gored.

The degree of peril for the runners is difficult to gauge. Serious injuries are reported daily during the festival; deaths are rare but do occur. Some say the human cost is beside the point: After the bulls' desperate gallop through town, every one of them is killed slowly to cheers in the bullring, a reality that draws ire from many anti-bullfighting Spaniards and animal rights groups—and, in many cases, from uninitiated Americans who aren't as prepared as they think for the gory spectacle. Indeed, the festival comes under more scrutiny with each passing year, even if most attendees are not there to run but rather to party. Running is free, but tickets to *corridas* (bullfights) are pricey and can be difficult to finagle.

## GETTING HERE AND AROUND

**BUS STATION Estación de Autobuses de Pamplona.** ✉ Av. de Yanguas y Miranda 2, ☎ 90/202–3651 ⊕ www.estaciondeauto-busesdepamplona.com.

**CAR RENTALS Europcar.** ✉ Av. Pio XII 43, ☎ 94/817–2523 ⊕ www.europcar.com.

**TRAIN INFORMATION Estación de Pamplona.** ✉ Pl. de la Estación 1, Pamplona ☎ 90/232–0320, 90/243–2343 ⊕ www. renfe.com.

## VISITOR INFORMATION

**CONTACTS Pamplona Tourist Office.** ✉ Calle San Saturnino 2, ☎ 94/842–0700 ⊕ www.pamplona.es.

## ◉ Sights

### Archivo Real y General de Navarra

**HISTORIC SIGHT** | This Rafael Moneo–designed monolith of glass and stone, ingeniously contained within a Romanesque palace, is Pamplona's architectural pièce de résistance. With papers and parchments dating to the 9th century, the archive holds more than 75,000 linear feet of documents and has room for more than 55,500 feet more. The library and reading rooms are lined with cherrywood and crowned with a gilded ceiling. ✉ Calle Dos de Mayo, Pamplona

☎ 04/842–4667, 84/842–4623 ⊕ www.
navarra.es 🏛 Free ⊙ Closed weekends.

## Catedral de Pamplona

**CHURCH** | The fragile gabled Gothic arches
of this 14th-century cloister make it one
of the finest of its type in the country.
Inside are the tombs of Carlos III and his
wife, marked by an alabaster sculpture.
The well-preserved kitchen is one of just
three surviving Gothic kitchens of Spain.
The Museo Catedralicio Diocesano (Dioc-
esan Museum) houses religious art from
the Middle Ages and the Renaissance.
Call in advance for guided tours in English. ⊠ Calle Curia, Pamplona ☎ 94/821–
2594 ⊕ www.catedraldepamplona.com
🏛 €5 ⊙ Museum closed Sun.

## Ciudadela

**CITY PARK** | Take an evening paseo along-
side locals through this central park with
promenades and pools on the site of an
ancient fortress. ⊠ Pamplona.

## Fundación-Museo Oteiza

**ART MUSEUM** | This museum 12 km (7½
miles) east of Pamplona commemorates
Jorge Oteiza (1908–2003), the father
of modern Basque art. In his seminal
treatise, Quosque tandem, Oteiza called
for Basque artists to find their own aesthetic and not acquiesce to the Spanish
canon. Rejecting ornamentation in favor
of essential form, he created the school
of artists from which Eduardo Chillida
(1924–2002) emerged. The earth-tone
concrete slab of a building housing the
museum was Oteiza's home for more
than two decades. ⊠ Calle de la Cuesta
7, Pamplona ⊕ From town, take Ctra.
N150 east for 8 km (5 miles) to Alzuza
☎ 94/833–2074 ⊕ www.museooteiza.org
🏛 €4 (free Fri.) ⊙ Closed Mon.

## Javier (Xabier, Xavier)

**CASTLE/PALACE** | This gorgeous Navarran
hamlet 54 km (33½ miles) southeast of
Pamplona, perched atop a lush riverbed and gorge, is the birthplace of the
16th-century Roman Catholic missionary
Francis Xavier, cofounder of the Jesuit

order. There's a fine castle, cathedral, and
monastery, comfortable hotels, a couple
of restaurants, and an impressive visitor
center with rotating exhibits. Whatever
your religious persuasion, it's a beautiful
stop on your travels in the Pamplona
area. ⊠ Javier ☎ 94/888–4024 ⊕ www.
javier.es 🏛 Castle €3.

## Museo de Navarra

**HISTORY MUSEUM** | **FAMILY** | In a 16th-cen-
tury building once used as a hospital
for pilgrims on their way to Santiago de
Compostela, this museum has a collection of regional archaeological artifacts
and historical costumes. Placards are
Spanish-only. ⊠ Cuesta de Santo Domingo 47, Pamplona ☎ 84/842–6493 ⊕ www.
museodenavarra.navarra.es 🏛 €2 (free
Sat. afternoon and Sun.) ⊙ Closed Mon.

## Museo Universidad de Navarra

**ART MUSEUM** | Designed by celebrity archi-
tect Rafael Moneo, this contemporary
art museum and event space opened in
2014 on the University of Navarra campus. It has an exceptional photograph
collection dating to the birth of photography as an art form, and the permanent
art collection features classic works by
Rothko, Picasso, Kandinsky, and Tàpies.
⊠ Campus Universitario, Calle Universidad, Pamplona ☎ 94/842–5700 ⊕ www.
museo.unav.edu 🏛 €5.

## Olite

**TOWN** | **FAMILY** | An unforgettable glimpse
into the Kingdom of Navarra of the
Middle Ages is the reward for journeying
to this town. The 11th-century church of
San Pedro is revered for its finely worked
Romanesque cloisters and portal, but it's
the town's storybook castle—restored
by Carlos III in the French style and
brimming with ramparts, crenellated
battlements, and watchtowers—that
dazzles the imagination. You can walk
the ramparts, and should you get tired or
hungry, part of the castle has been converted into a parador, making a fine place
to grab a snack or catch a few z's. ⊠ 41

km (25 miles) south of Pamplona, Olite
🖥 94/874-0000 ⊕ www.olite.es.

### Plaza del Castillo
**PLAZA/SQUARE** | One of Pamplona's greatest charms is the warren of narrow streets near the Plaza del Castillo (especially Calle San Nicolás) filled with restaurants and bars. ✉ Pamplona.

## 🍴 Restaurants

### Café Iruña
**$$** | **CAFÉ** | Pamplona's gentry have been flocking to this ornate, French-style café since 1888, but in 1926 Ernest Hemingway made it part of world literary lore in *The Sun Also Rises*. You can have a drink with a bronze version of the author in his favorite perch at the far end of the bar, or enjoy views of the plaza from a table on the terrace. **Known for:** grand, ornate dining area; chocolate con churros; major tourist attraction. ⑤ *Average main:* €17 ✉ Pl. del Castillo 44, Pamplona 🖥 94/822-2064 ⊕ www.cafeiruna.com.

### Errejota
**$$$** | **SPANISH** | This warm, family-run restaurant in a stately mansion with a classically elegant interior is one of Pamplona's foremost addresses for refined cuisine. There's something for everyone on the diverse, internationally inflected menu, whose highlights include baby artichokes with langoustine tails and monkfish with black-olive vinaigrette and soy-anchovy mayonnaise. **Known for:** standout artichokes; white-tablecloth dining room; modern Navarrese cuisine. ⑤ *Average main:* €26 ✉ Pl. Príncipe de Viana 1, Pamplona 🖥 94/822-2097 ⊕ www.errejota. es ۞ Closed Mon. (except during San Fermín). No dinner Sun.-Wed.

### Europa Restaurante
**$$$$** | **SPANISH** | Pamplona's finest restaurant, in the hotel of the same name, the Europa offers refined, Michelin-starred Navarrese cooking with reasonably priced à la carte dishes as well as excellent tasting menus. The small and bright first-floor dining room is the perfect backdrop to dishes like slow-cooked lamb and pork and what might be the best bacalao al pil pil you'll ever taste. **Known for:** affordable tasting menus; nicest restaurant in town; seasonal vegetable dishes. ⑤ *Average main:* €33 ✉ Calle Espoz y Mina 11, Pamplona 🖥 94/822-1800 ⊕ www.hreuropa. com ۞ Closed Sun.

### ★ Gaucho
**$** | **TAPAS** | This legendary tavern (est. 1968), which remains surprisingly calm even during San Fermín, serves some of the city's best tapas. Choose between classics like garlicky mushroom brochettes and jamón-filled croquetas, or spring for more modern creations such as seared goose liver toasts or almond-encrusted morcilla. **Known for:** old-timey atmosphere; delicious tapas for all budgets; delectable foie gras. ⑤ *Average main:* €13 ✉ Calle Espoz y Mina 7, Pamplona 🖥 94/822-5073 ⊕ www. cafebargaucho.com.

### ★ La Mañueta
**$** | **SPANISH** | **FAMILY** | In 2022, Spain's oldest churrería—perhaps Pamplona's top culinary attraction—rang in 150 years. In this hole-in-the-wall resembling a medieval foundry, hypnotic whorls of dough fry to crackly perfection in vats of Navarran extra-virgin olive oil set over beechwood flame. **Known for:** churros with over a century of history; San Fermín rite of passage; limited hours. ⑤ *Average main:* €8 ✉ Calle Mañueta 8, Pamplona 🖥 94/822-7627 ▭ No credit cards ۞ Closed Aug.–Sept., Nov.–June.

## 🛏 Hotels

### ★ Gran Hotel La Perla
**$$$$** | **HOTEL** | The oldest hotel in Pamplona, where Ernest Hemingway conceived of his first novel, *The Sun Also Rises,* is a comfortable and conservative hotel with some early-20th-century accents such as velvet bergères and ornate headboards. **Pros:** staff are well-versed in history of

the property; good soundproofing; even entry-level rooms are spacious. **Cons:** no pool, gym, or spa; prices triple during San Fermín; rooms vary widely in aesthetic and quality. $ *Rooms from: €245* ⊠ *Pl. del Castillo 1, Pamplona* ☎ *94/822–3000* ⊕ *www.granhotellaperla.com* ⇆ *44 rooms* ¶Ol *Free Breakfast.*

### Hotel Maisonnave

$$ | **HOTEL** | **FAMILY** | This modern four-star is tucked away on a relatively quiet pedestrian street yet steps from the action on Plaza del Castillo and Calle Estafeta. **Pros:** friendly multilingual staff; lively bar and restaurant; great location. **Cons:** corporate vibes; decor feels dated; lacks sense of place. $ *Rooms from: €101* ⊠ *Calle Nueva 20, Pamplona* ☎ *94/822–2600* ⊕ *www.hotelmaisonnave.es* ⇆ *138 rooms* ¶Ol *Free Breakfast.*

### Pamplona Catedral Hotel

$$$ | **HOTEL** | In a renovated convent, this contemporary hotel steps from the cathedral offers a great value. **Pros:** above-and-beyond service; convenient location; exceptional breakfasts. **Cons:** somewhat seedy area; heating and a/c are not central; bleak interiors. $ *Rooms from: €167* ⊠ *Calle Dos de Mayo 4, Pamplona* ☎ *94/822–6688* ⊕ *www.pamplonacatedralhotel.com* ⇆ *49 rooms* ¶Ol *Free Breakfast.*

### Sercotel Hotel Europa Pamplona

$ | **HOTEL** | More famous for its world-class Michelin-starred restaurant on the ground floor, this modestly priced hotel is one of Pamplona's best-kept secrets, a block and half from the bullring and within shouting distance of party central, Plaza del Castillo. **Pros:** central location; special restaurant offers for hotel guests; good value. **Cons:** prices can double during San Fermín; rooms on the small side; noisy during the fiesta unless you score an interior room. $ *Rooms from: €95* ⊠ *Calle Espoz y Mina 11, Pamplona* ☎ *94/822–1800* ⊕ *www.hoteleuropa-pamplona.com* ⇆ *25 rooms* ¶Ol *Free Breakfast.*

## ⊻ Nightlife

### Canalla

**DANCE CLUBS** | Dress up, or you might flunk the bouncer's inspection at this lounge-y nightclub, filled until dawn with young singles and couples. Cover charge depends on visiting DJs and events, and Fridays are popular student nights. ⊠ *Av. Bayona 2, Pamplona* ☎ *67/921–9871* ⊕ *www.canalla.es* ⊙ *Closed Sun.–Wed.*

### Ozone

**DANCE CLUBS** | This techno haven is one of the most popular dance clubs in town. Cover charge depends on visiting DJs and events; check the website for lineups and prices. ⊠ *Calle Monasterio de Velate 5, Pamplona* ☎ *94/826–1593* ⊕ *www.ozonepamplona.com* ⊙ *Closed Sun.–Wed.*

## ⊕ Performing Arts

### Edificio Baluarte

**MUSIC** | The Congress Center and Auditorium, built in 2003 by local architectural star Patxi Mangado, is a sleek assemblage of black Zimbabwean granite. It contains a concert hall of exquisite acoustical perfection utilizing beechwood from upper Navarra's famed Irati *haya* (beech) forest. Performances and concerts, from opera to ballet, are held in this modern venue, built on the remains of one of the five bastions of Pamplona's 16th-century Ciudadela. ⊠ *Pl. del Baluarte, Pamplona* ☎ *94/806–6066* ⊕ *www.baluarte.com.*

### ★ Zentral

**CONCERTS** | A self-proclaimed "gastro club," with food and live music offerings, this venue hosts events ranging from Lindy Hop dance parties to lectures on food science. It morphs into a DJ-driven *discoteca* most nights after 1 am. ⊠ *Mercado de Santo Domingo, Calle de Santo Domingo, 1st fl., Pamplona* ☎ *94/822–0764* ⊕ *www.zentralpamplona.com.*

# 📛 Shopping

Botas are the leather wineskins from which Basques typically drink at bullfights or during fiestas, and the most iconic bota manufacturer, ZZZ, is from Pamplona. The art lies in drinking a stream of wine from a bota held at arm's length without spilling a drop.

### Caminoteca Pamplona

SPORTING GOODS | Owned by a former Camino pilgrim, this small store stocks everything and anything a hiker embarking on the Camino de Santiago could need, from backpacks, boots, hiking socks, and walking sticks to smaller but equally necessary items like blister ointment, rain ponchos, and sporks. ⊠ Calle de Curia 15, Pamplona ☎ 94/821–0316 ⊕ www.caminoteca.com.

### ★ Fragment

HOUSEWARES | This well-curated boutique run by young designers is the city's top spot to buy handmade jewelry and accessories, kitchenware, couture garments, and eye-catching stationery. ⊠ Calle Nueva 1, Pamplona ☎ 94/841 0430 ⊕ karlotalaspalas.com/fragment ۝ Closed Sun.

### Manterola

FOOD | Here you can buy La Cafetera toffee, a local café con leche–flavored sweet. The shop also sells Navarran wine and other delicacies. ⊠ Calle Tudela 5, Pamplona ☎ 94/822–3174 ⊕ www.manterola.es ۝ Closed Sun.

### Olentzero

SOUVENIRS | You can buy botas in most Navarrese towns, but Pamplona's Olentzero gift shop sells the best brand, Las Tres Cetas, written "ZZZ." ⊠ Calle de la Estafeta 42, Pamplona ☎ 94/882–0245 ⊕ www.olentzeroa.com.

# Logroño

85 km (53 miles) southwest of Pamplona.

A busy industrial city of about 150,000, Logroño has a lovely old quarter bordered by the Ebro and medieval walls, with **Bretón de los Herreros** and **Muro Francisco de la Mata** being its principal streets. Wine-loving travelers who prefer the bustle of a city to the quiet of the country should hole up here and take day trips to the outlying vineyards.

Near Logroño, the Roman bridge and the mirador (lookout) at **Viguera** are the main sights in the lower Iregua Valley. According to legend, Santiago (St. James) helped the Christians defeat the Moors at the **Castillo de Clavijo,** another panoramic spot. **Río Leza** is La Rioja's most dramatic canyon.

## GETTING HERE AND AROUND

**BUS STATION Estación de Autobuses de Logroño.** ⊠ Av. España 1, ☎ 94/123–5983 ⊕ www.logroño.es.

**TRAIN STATION Estación de Logroño.** ⊠ Av. de Colón 83, ☎ 90/243–2343 ⊕ www.adif.es.

## VISITOR INFORMATION

**CONTACTS Logroño Tourist Office.** ⊠ Calle Portales 50, ☎ 94/127–7000 ⊕ www.logroño.es.

# ◉ Sights

### Church of San Bartolomé

CHURCH | The oldest still-standing church in Logroño, San Bartolomé was built between the 13th and 14th centuries in a French Gothic style. Highlights include the 11th-century Mudejar tower and an elaborate 14th-century Gothic doorway. Some carvings on the stone facade depict scenes from the Bible. This is also a landmark on the Camino de Santiago pilgrimage path. ⊠ Pl. San Bartolomé 2, Logroño ☎ 94/125–2254 ⊴ Free.

**Concatedral de Santa María de la Redonda**

CHURCH | Noted for its twin baroque towers, the present-day cathedral was rebuilt in the 16th century in a Gothic style atop ruins of a 12th-century Romanesque church. ⊠ *Calle Portales 14, Logroño* ☎ *94/125–7611* ⊕ *www.laredonda.org* ⊞ *Free.*

**Puente de Piedra** (*Stone Bridge*)

BRIDGE | Many of Logroño's monuments, such as this elegant bridge, were built as part of the Camino de Santiago pilgrimage route. ⊠ *Av. de Navarra 1, Logroño.*

**Santa María de Palacio**

CHURCH | This 11th-century church is known as La Aguja (The Needle) for its pyramid-shaped 135-foot Romanesque-Gothic tower. ⊠ *Calle del Marqués de San Nicolás 30, Logroño* ⊞ *Free.*

**Santiago el Real** (*Royal St. James's Church*)

CHURCH | Note the equestrian statue of the saint Santiago Matamoros (aka St. James the Moorslayer) presiding over the main door of this church, which was reconstructed in the 16th century. ⊠ *Calle Barriocepo 6, Logroño* ☎ *94/120–9501* ⊕ *www.santiagoelreal.org* ⊞ *Free.*

## 🍴 Restaurants

For tapas, you'll find bars with signature specialties on the connecting streets **Calle del Laurel** and **Travesía de Laurel,** the latter also known as El Sendero de los Elefantes (Path of the Elephants)—an allusion to *trompas* (trunks), Spanish for a snootful. Try Bar Soriano for "champis" (*champiñones*, or mushrooms), Blanco y Negro for *matrimonio* ("wedded" white and salt-cured anchovies on a mini-baguette), and Bar Travesía for tortilla de patata. If you're ordering wine, a young "cosecha" or "clarete" comes in squat *chato* glasses, a crianza brings out the crystal, and a reserva or gran reserva (selected grapes aged over three years in oak and bottle) usually elicits goblets for proper swirling, nosing, and tasting.

**★ La Taberna de Baco**

$ | SPANISH | This bright, modern bar is a great spot to try seasonal, market-fresh tapas like heirloom tomato salad with chilies and raw onion or cheesy mushroom "carpaccio," but locals flock here for one dish in particular: *oreja a la plancha*, griddled pig's ear swimming in punchy *brava* (spicy) sauce. Shatteringly crisp and unapologetically rich, it's one of the best versions you'll have in Spain. **Known for:** amiable bartenders; wide selection of small-production wines; offal even the squeamish can learn to love. ⑤ *Average main: €14* ⊠ *Calle de San Agustín 10, Logroño* ☎ *94/121–3544* ⊕ *tabernadebaco.com.*

**★ Tondeluna**

$$ | SPANISH | Tondeluna has six communal tables (with 10 seats each), and all have views into the kitchen, where cooks plate dishes novel and familiar like glazed beef cheeks with apple puree and Getaria-style hake with melty *panadera* (thinly sliced roasted) potatoes. **Known for:** excellent value; lively dining room; balance of experimental and classic dishes. ⑤ *Average main: €17* ⊠ *Calle Muro de la Mata 9, Logroño* ☎ *94/123–6425* ⊕ *www.tondeluna.com* ⊗ *No dinner Sun.*

**Txebiko Cachetero**

$$ | SPANISH | A Calle del Laurel standby, this refined taberna with wood-paneled walls serves Riojan specialties like *cochinillo asado* (roast suckling pig) and pimentón-laced potatoes *a la riojana* (potato and chorizo stew). The neighboring La Brasa de Laurel (at No.16) is run by the same team and centers on high-end grilled meats and fish. **Known for:** crackly cochinillo and fresh seafood; upscale Riojan cuisine; personable waitstaff. ⑤ *Average main: €18* ⊠ *Calle del Laurel 3, Logroño* ☎ *94/122–8463* ⊕ *www.txebiko.com* ⊗ *Closed Sun. No dinner Mon.–Thu.*

The fertile soil and fields of the Ebro River Valley make some of Spain's most colorful landscapes.

## 🛏 Hotels

### Eurostars Marqués de Vallejo

$$ | **HOTEL** | Close to—but not within earshot of—the raucous food fight that is Calle del Laurel, this hotel by the cathedral is within walking distance of all the major sights. **Pros:** central location; pleasant public areas with art; clean, homey rooms. **Cons:** breakfast spread could use some love; no longer independently owned; street-side rooms can be noisy in summer. *⑤ Rooms from: €135 ⊠ Calle Marqués de Vallejo 8, Logroño ☎ 94/124–8333 ⊕ www.eurostarshotels.com ⇆ 50 rooms ⦿ Free Breakfast.*

### NH Logroño Herencia Rioja

$$ | **HOTEL** | This modern four-star hotel near the old quarter has contemporary, comfortable rooms, good facilities, a well-trained staff, and a businesslike buzz about it. **Pros:** clean, corporate comfort; excellent breakfast; steps from Calle del Laurel's tapas bonanza. **Cons:** tight, white-knuckle parking; cheerless interiors; undistinguished modern building.

*⑤ Rooms from: €131 ⊠ Calle Marqués de Murrieta 14, Logroño ☎ 94/121–0222 ⊕ www.nh-hoteles.com ⇆ 83 rooms ⦿ No Meals.*

# La Rioja Alta

The Upper Rioja, the most prized subregion of La Rioja's wine country, extends from the Río Ebro to the Sierra de la Demanda. La Rioja Alta has the most fertile soil, the best vineyards and agriculture, the most impressive castles and monasteries, a ski resort at Ezcaray, and the historic economic advantage of being on the Camino de Santiago.

## 👁 Sights

### Ezcaray

**TOWN** | Enter the Sierra de la Demanda by heading south from Santo Domingo de la Calzada on LR111. Your first stop is the town of Ezcaray, with its aristocratic houses emblazoned with family crests, of which the palace of Conde de

Torremúzquiz is the most distinguished. The town is famous for its mohair (angora goat wool) textiles, of which Mantas Ezcaray is the only remaining producer in Spain; the shop (⊠ *Calle Cristobal de Zamudio 12; www.mantasezcaray. com*) services fashion houses like Loewe and Armani. Good excursions from Ezcaray are the Valdezcaray ski station; the source of the Río Oja at Llano de la Casa; La Rioja's highest point, the 7,494-foot Pico de San Lorenzo; and the Romanesque church of Tres Fuentes, at Valgañón. The hamlet is also known for its wild mushrooms—and the resulting tapas served in its barrooms. ⊠ *Ezcaray* ☎ *94/135–4679 tourist office* ⊕ *www. ezcaray.org.*

### Nájera

**TOWN** | This town was the capital of Navarra and La Rioja until 1076, when the latter became part of Castile and the residence of the Castilian royal family. The monastery of Santa María la Real (⊕ *www.santamarialareal.net*), the "pantheon of kings," is distinguished by its 16th-century Claustro de los Caballeros (Cavaliers' Cloister), a flamboyant Gothic structure with 24 lacy plateresque Renaissance arches overlooking a grassy patio. The sculpted 12th-century tomb of Doña Blanca de Navarra is the monastery's best-known sarcophagus, while the 67 Gothic choir stalls dating from 1495 are among Spain's best. ⊠ *Nájera* ☎ *94/136–1083 tourist office* ⊕ *www. najera.es.*

### Navarrete

**TOWN** | This town, 14 km (9 miles) west of Logroño via the A12, has noble houses and the 16th-century Santa María de la Asunción church. The village is also famous for its painted ceramics; shop at any of the artisan shops in the town center. ☎ *94/144–1062 tourist office* ⊕ *www.navarrete.es/turismo.*

### ★ San Millán de la Cogolla

**TOWN** | This town, southeast of Santo Domingo de la Calzada, has two jaw-dropping monasteries on the UNESCO World Heritage Sites list. There's **Monasterio de Yuso**, where a 10th-century manuscript on St. Augustine's *Glosas Emilianenses* contains handwritten notes in what is considered the earliest example of the Spanish language, the vernacular Latin dialect known as Roman Paladino. And then there's the Visigothic **Monasterio de Suso** (⊕ *www.monasteriodesanmillan.com*), where Gonzalo de Berceo, recognized as the first Castilian poet, wrote and recited his 13th-century verse in the Castilian tongue, now the language of nearly 600 million people around the world. ⊠ *San Millán de la Cogolla* ☎ *94/137–3259 tourist office* ⊕ *www.sanmillandelacogolla.es/ oficina-de-turismo-san-millan* 🎫 *€4 for Suso Monastery, €7 for Yuso Monastery* ⊗ *Monasteries closed Mon.*

### Santo Domingo de la Calzada

**TOWN** | A stop on the Camino de Santiago, this town is named after an 11th-century saint who built roads and bridges for pilgrims and founded the hospital that is now a parador. The cathedral (⊠ *Calle Cristo 94/134–0033*) is a Romanesque-Gothic pile containing the saint's tomb, choir murals, and a walnut altarpiece carved by Damià Forment in 1541. The live hen and rooster in a plateresque stone chicken coop commemorate a legendary local miracle in which a pair of roasted fowl came back to life to protest the innocence of a pilgrim hanged for theft. Be sure to stroll through the beautifully preserved medieval quarter. ⊠ *Nájera* ✛ *On N120 20 km (12 miles) west of Nájera* ⊕ *www.santodomingodelacalzada.org.*

## 🛏 Hotels

### ★ Echaurren

**$$$$** | **HOTEL** | Rioja's renowned "gastro hotel," Echaurren is a food lover's paradise with two envelope-pushing restaurants and Relais & Châteaux–certified digs. **Pros:** Rioja's gastronomical mecca; highly personal service; comfortable beds. **Cons:** no bathtubs in most rooms; entry-level rooms are cramped; loud church bells. $ *Rooms from: €230* ✉ *Calle Padre José García 19, Ezcaray* ☎ *94/135-4047* ⊕ *www.echaurren.com* ⇆ *25 rooms* ❍❙ *Free Breakfast.*

### Hostal Nuestra Señora de Valvanera

$ | **HOTEL** | **FAMILY** | Housed in a monastery atop a 9th-century hermitage, this rural hotel run by a Benedictine community is an ideal base for hiking. **Pros:** cool for the summer; rooms of varying sizes for families; simplicity and silence. **Cons:** decidedly unhip; limited and inconsistent food; spartan accommodations. $ *Rooms from: €65* ✉ *Monasterio de Valvanera, Ctra. LR435, Ezcaray* ☎ *94/137-7044* ⊕ *www.monasteriodevalvanera.es/hospederia* ⇆ *28 rooms* ❍❙ *No Meals.*

### Hostería San Millan

$$ | **HOTEL** | This magnificent inn occupies a wing of the historic Monasterio de Yuso. **Pros:** historic site; good breakfasts; graceful building with spacious rooms. **Cons:** popular among the tour-bus set; monastic interiors; somewhat isolated. $ *Rooms from: €125* ✉ *Monasterio de Yuso, San Millán de la Cogolla* ☎ *94/137-3277* ⊕ *www.hosteriasanmillan.com* ⇆ *25 rooms* ❍❙ *Free Breakfast.*

### Hotel La Venta de Goyo

$ | **B&B/INN** | A favorite with anglers and hunters, this cheery inn across from the confluence of the Urbión and Najeril la Rivers has spartan wood-trimmed bedrooms with red-checked bedspreads and an excellent restaurant specializing in *caparrones* (kidney bean stew) and game dishes made from venison, wild boar, partridge, woodcock, and the like. **Pros:** excellent game and mountain cooking; unforgettable house-made jams; charming rustic bar. **Cons:** a bit isolated; hot in the summer; next to the road. $ *Rooms from: €40* ✉ *Puente Río Neila 2, Viniegra de Abajo* ☎ *94/137-8007* ⊕ *www.ventadegoyo.es* ⇆ *22 rooms* ❍❙ *No Meals.*

# Haro

*49 km (30 miles) west of Logroño.*

Haro is the wine capital of La Rioja. Its Casco Viejo (Old Quarter) and best taverns are concentrated along the loop known as La Herradura (the Horseshoe), with the Santo Tomás church at the apex of its curve and Calle San Martín and Calle Santo Tomás leading down to the upper left-hand (northeast) corner of Plaza de la Paz. Up the left side of the horseshoe, Bar La Esquina is the first of many tapas bars. Bar Los Caños, behind a stone archway at San Martín 5, is built into the vaults and arches of the former church of San Martín and serves excellent local crianzas and reservas and a memorable pintxo of quail egg, anchovy, hot pepper, and olive.

## VISITOR INFORMATION

**CONTACTS Haro Tourist Office.** ✉ *Pl. de la Paz 1,* ☎ *94/130-3580* ⊕ *www.haroturismo.org.*

## ◉ Sights

### Bodegas (*Wineries*)

**NEIGHBORHOOD** | Haro's century-old bodegas have been headquartered in the Barrio de la Estación (Train Station District) since the railroad opened in 1863 and are a fantastic place to go winery-hopping, since they're within walking distance of one another. They were built around the train station for streamlined export to France, whose wine industry at the time had been devastated by the phylloxera plague. Guided tours and tastings, some in English, can be arranged at the facilities themselves or through the tourist office. ✉ *Barrio de la Estación, Haro.*

### Bodegas Muga

**WINERY** | This sprawling, prestigious bodega offers visits, tours, and tastings (pre-book online) as well as a wine bar and restaurant. The standard fee includes a tasting of three wines. Segway and hot-air-balloon tours with partner companies can also be arranged ahead of time. ✉ *Barrio de la Estación, Haro* ☎ *94/130–6060* ⊕ *www.bodegasmuga.com* 🖃 *€25.*

**Santo Tomás**

CHURCH | The architectural highlight of Haro, this single-nave Renaissance and late-Gothic church was completed in 1564. It has an intricately sculpted plateresque portal on the south side and a gilded baroque organ facade towering over the choir loft. ✉ *Calle Santo Tomás 5, Haro* ☎ *94/131–1690* 🖃 *Free.*

#  Restaurants

### ★ Terete

$$$$ | SPANISH | A perennial local favorite, this rustic spot has been roasting lamb in wood ovens since 1877 and serves a hearty *menestra de verduras* (vegetables stewed with bits of ham) that is justly revered as a mandatory sidekick. With rough hand-hewn wooden tables distributed around dark stone and wood-beam dining rooms, the medieval stage-coach-inn environment matches the traditional roasts. **Known for:** stock of some of La Rioja's best reservas and crianzas; succulent roast lamb and suckling pig; 19th-century wood-burning oven. ⑤ *Average main: €30* ✉ *Calle Lucrecia Arana 17, Haro* ☎ *94/131–0023* ⊕ *www.terete. es* ⊘ *Closed Mon., 1st 2 wks in July, and last 2 wks in Nov. No dinner Sun.*

# THE PYRENEES

7

Updated by
Benjamin Kemper

| ⊙ Sights | 🍴 Restaurants | 🛏 Hotels | 🛍 Shopping | 🍸 Nightlife |
|---|---|---|---|---|
| ★★★★☆ | ★★★☆☆ | ★★★☆☆ | ★☆☆☆☆ | ★☆☆☆☆ |

# WELCOME TO THE PYRENEES

## TOP REASONS TO GO

★ **Revel in the Romanesque:** Feast your eyes on 900-year-old religious architecture in Taüll and marvel at the mural paintings of the Noguera de Tor Valley.

★ **Explore Spain's Grand Canyon:** The Parque Nacional de Ordesa y Monte Perdido has stunning scenery, along with marmots and mountain goats.

★ **Hike the highlands:** Trek the verdant highlands of the Basque Country's Baztan Valley, then hug the Bidasoa River down to colorful Hondarribia and the Bay of Biscay.

★ **Venture deep into rural Aragón:** The enchanting medieval town of Alquézar winds up to a 9th-century citadel that keeps watch over the Parque Natural de la Sierra y los Cañones de Guara, famous for prehistoric cave paintings.

★ **Ride the cogwheel train at Ribes de Freser, near Ripoll:** Ascend the gorge to the sanctuary and ski station at Vall de Núria, then hike to the remote highland valley and refuge of Coma de Vaca.

**1 Camprodon.** A stylish little mountain hub.

**2 Beget.** One of Catalonia's best-preserved stone villages.

**3 Sant Joan de les Abadesses.** Known for the 12th-century Romanesque church of Sant Joan.

**4 Ripoll.** Home of 9th-century Benedictine Monastery of Santa Maria.

**5 Ribes de Freser and Vall de Núria.** The starting point of the famous cogwheel train.

**6 Puigcerdà.** A base for skiers and hikers from both sides of the border.

**7 Llívia.** A small Spanish exclave surrounded on all sides by France.

**8 Bellver de Cerdanya.** The dictionary definition of a perfect Pyrenean mountain village.

**9 La Seu d'Urgell.** Ancient town facing the snowy rock wall of the Sierra del Cadí.

**10 Sort.** Home base for skiers and anglers.

**11 Parc Nacional d'Aigüestortes i Estany de Sant Maurici.** Among Spain's finest and wildest national parks.

**12 Taüll.** A Romanesque treasure box.

**13 Vielha.** A small Pyrenean city near the French border.

**14 Arties.** Lively mountain town with hiking, nature, and Romanesque art.

**15 Salardú.** A convenient base with Aranese speakers and fairy-tale bell towers.

**16 Zaragoza.** Home to the famous La Pilarica.

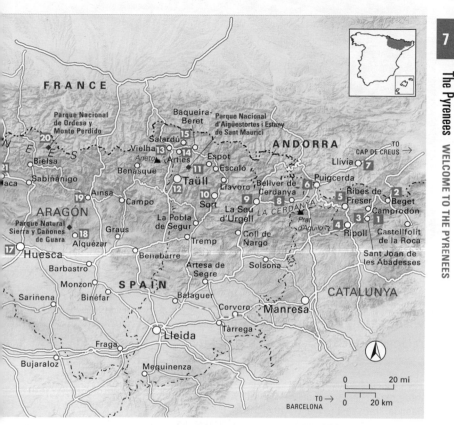

TO →
BARCELONA

**17 Huesca.** There's plenty of charm in the hilly medieval quarter.

**18 Alquézar.** A town that tops lists of Spain's most picturesque villages.

**19 Aínsa.** Walled hilltop village with cobblestone streets and sweeping views.

**20 Parque Nacional de Ordesa y Monte Perdido.** A stunning national park with swooping lammergeiers.

**21 Jaca.** Known for an 11th-century cathedral and fortress.

**22 Monasterio de San Juan de la Peña.** Popular with Holy Grail seekers.

**23 Hecho and Ansó Valleys.** Idyllic mountain villages dot dramatic gorges.

**24 Roncal Valley.** Known for farmland and sheep's cheese.

**25 Roncesvalles (Orreaga).** The first stop for pilgrims on the Camino de Santiago.

**26 Burguete (Auritz).** Made famous in Hemingway's *The Sun Also Rises*.

**27 Baztan Valley.** Scenic point between the central Pyrenees and the Atlantic.

# EATING AND DRINKING WELL IN THE PYRENEES

Grilled steak, chorizo and longaniza sausages with grilled peppers.

Pyrenean cuisine is hearty mountain fare characterized by thick soups, stews, roasts, and local game. Ingredients are prepared with slightly different techniques and recipes in each valley, village, and kitchen.

The culinary traditions of the Pyrenees match the area's three main cultural identities—Catalan, Aragonese, and Basque, from east to west. Within these, there are more niche local specialties, particularly in La Garrotxa, La Cerdanya, Ribagorça, Val d'Aran, Benasque, Alto Aragón, Roncal, and Baztan. Game is common throughout. Trout, mountain goat, deer, boar, partridge, rabbit, duck, and quail are roasted over coals or cooked in wine-y stews called *civets* in Catalonia and *estofados* in Aragón and the Basque Pyrenees. Fish and meat are sometimes seared on white-hot slate (*a la llosa* in Catalan, *a la piedra* in Spanish). Sheep, goat, and cow cheeses vary from valley to valley, along with types of sausages and charcuterie.

## WILD MUSHROOMS

Wonderfully aromatic wild mushrooms plucked from the mountainsides are available year-round but are especially abundant and varied in autumn. They're a constant in Pyrenean meat and egg dishes—particularly in non-breakfast scrambled egg dishes called *remenats* (*revueltos* in Spanish, *nahasiak* in Basque)—though they're equally divine on their own simply sautéed with garlic, parsley, and olive oil. Seek out varieties like *rovellons* (saffron milk caps), and *camagrocs* (a type of chanterelle).

## HEARTY STEWS

Cool climes and grueling farm work made filling meat-and-vegetable stews a mainstay of the Pyrenean table. The Pyrenees has its own rendition of French *garbure* with legumes, vegetables, potatoes, pork, chicken, and sometimes lamb or wild boar, all floating in a rich beef stock. *Olha aranesa* (Aranese soup)—a cousin to Catalan *escudella* and central Spain's *cocido madrileño*—is another Pyrenean power soup with pasta, chickpeas, white beans, and several cuts of pork that's served in multiple courses.

Wild black trumpet mushrooms

### PYRENEAN STEWS

Wild boar stew is known by different names in the various languages of the Pyrenees, but it's a gloriously gamy treat no matter where you try it. Wild boar is prepared in many different ways between Catalonia, Aragón, and the Basque Country, but most recipes include onions, carrots, mushrooms, peppers, sherry, and sweet paprika. *Civet d'isard* (mountain-goat stew), known as *estofado de ixarso* in the Pyrenees of Aragón, is another favorite, prepared in much the same way but with a more delicate taste. Civets are a rather distinctive family of stews; marinated in red wine, thickened with pig's blood, and flavored subtly with

chocolate, they are essentially medieval comfort food.

### TRINXAT

The Catalan verb *trinxar* means to chop or shred, and *trinxat* is winter cabbage, previously softened by frost, chopped fine and mixed with mashed potato and fatback or bacon. A quintessential high-altitude comfort food, trinxat plays the acidity of the cabbage against the saltiness of the pork and the butteriness of boiled potatoes.

### DUCK WITH TURNIPS

The Pyrenean dish *tiró amb naps* (duck with turnips) has its roots in pre-Columbian Europe, as do nearly all European recipes that use turnips instead of potatoes, an import from the Americas. The frequent use of duck (*pato* in Spanish, *anec* in Catalan, *tiró* in La Cerdanya) in the Cerdanya Valley two hours north of Barcelona is a taste acquired from French Catalunya, just over the Pyrenees.

Spring duckling with potatoes

The soaring mountain range that stretches from the Mediterranean to the Atlantic is striated by some three dozen gorgeous valleys, which were all but completely isolated from one another until around the 10th century. The region has retained much of its distinctive cultural identities as well as a palpably unbridled highland spirit. Local languages abound across the range, with Spanish and Euskera (Basque) spoken in upper Navarra; Aragonese (and its local varieties) in Aragón; and Catalan at the eastern end of the chain from Ribagorça to the Mediterranean. Spanish is spoken fluently by all, though often as a second language.

As the gateway between the Iberian Peninsula and the rest of Europe, the Pyrenees were always a strategic barrier—and a stronghold to be reckoned with: The Romans never subdued the "Vascones" (as Greek historian Strabo [63–21 BC] called the Basques) in the western Pyrenean highlands; Charlemagne lost Roland and his rear guard at Roncesvalles in 778, and his Frankish heirs lost all of Catalonia in 988; and Napoléon Bonaparte never completed his conquest of the peninsula, largely because of communications and supply problems posed by the Pyrenees. Hitler, whether for geographical or political reasons, decided not to use post–Civil War Spain to launch his African campaign in 1941. In fact, following the Spanish Civil War and World War II, the Pyrenees were a corridor to freedom for downed pilots, Jewish refugees, and POWs fleeing the Nazis and Franco's dictatorship.

## MAJOR REGIONS

**Eastern Catalan Pyrenees.** Catalonia's easternmost Pyrenean valley, the Vall de Camprodon, is still hard enough to reach that, despite pockets of Barcelona summer colonies, it has retained much of its farm culture and mountain wildness. It has several exquisite towns and churches and—more stunning still—dramatic mountains in the Sierra de Catllar. Start from Cap de Creus in the Empordà to get the full experience of the Pyrenean cordillera's rise from the sea; then move west through Beget, Camprodon, the Ter Valley, Sant Joan de les Abadesses, and Ripoll before heading north through Ribes de Freser and Vall de Nuria. Vallter 2000, La Molina, and Núria are ski resorts at either end of the Pyrenean heights on the north side of the valley.

**La Cerdanya.** Said to be in the shape of the handprint of God, this high pastureland is bordered north and south by snow-covered peaks. La Cerdanya starts in France, at Col de la Perche (near Mont Louis) and ends in the Spanish province of Lleida, at Martinet. Being split between two countries, and subdivided into two more provinces on each side, gives the valley an identity all its own. Puigcerdà is the largest town and is a lively base for skiers and hikers, while the Spanish enclave of Llívia is easily reached across the border. Bellver de Cerdanya showcases examples of traditional Pyrenean architecture, surrounded by refreshing mountain views, while the ancient town of La Seu d'Urgell houses the 11th-century chapel of Sant Miquel and the 14th-century convent of Sant Domenec—now a converted parador. Residents on both sides of the border speak Catalan, a Romance language derived from early Provençal French, and regard the valley's political border with undisguised hilarity. Unlike any other valley in the upper Pyrenees, this one runs east–west and is thus blessed with record sunlight hours.

**Western Catalan Pyrenees.** "The farther from Barcelona, the wilder" is the rule of thumb, and this is true of the rugged countryside and fauna in the western part of Catalonia. Sort, the capital of the Pallars Sobirà (Upper Pallars Valley), is the area's epicenter for skiing, fishing, and white-water kayaking. Three of the greatest destinations in the Pyrenees are in this region: the harmonious, Atlantic-influenced Val d'Aran with its capital, Vielha; the Noguera de Tor Valley (aka Vall de Boí), with its matching set of gemlike Romanesque churches in Taüll; and Parc Nacional d'Aigüestortes i Estany de Sant Maurici, which has a network of pristine lakes and streams. The main geographical units in this section are the valley of the Noguera Pallaresa River, the Val d'Aran headwaters of the Atlantic-bound Garonne, and the Noguera Ribagorçana River Valley (Catalonia's western limit).

**Aragón and Central Pyrenees.** The highest, remotest, and most spectacular range of the Pyrenees is the middle section, farthest from sea level. From Benasque on Aragón's eastern side to Jaca at the western edge are the great heights and most dramatic landscapes of Alto Aragón (Upper Aragón), including the Maladeta (11,165 feet), Posets (11,070 feet), and Monte Perdido (11,004 feet) peaks, the three highest points in the chain. The oft-bypassed cities of Zaragoza and Huesca are useful Pyrenean gateways and historic destinations in themselves. Both are charmingly provincial. Drive east out of Huesca into the Sierra de Guara, a UNESCO World Heritage Site, whose crown jewel is the historic village of Alquézar; hiking and other outdoor activities abound here. Farther north, stop at Aínsa for its 11th-century citadel and castle. The Parque Nacional de Ordesa y Monte Perdido (also a World Heritage site) boasts some of the region's best trails. Deep in Alto Aragón, Jaca has a fine 11th-century cathedral and fortress, and a lively personality all its own. The

**7**

**The Pyrenees**

Hecho and Ansó Valleys are the western-most valleys in Aragón and rank among the wildest and most unspoiled reaches of the Pyrenees. With only cross-country skiing available, it doesn't see hordes of winter tourists (unlike its neighbors).

**The Navarran and Basque Pyrenees.** Beginning in the Roncal Valley, the language you hear may be Euskera, the pre-Indo-European tongue of the Basques. The highlands of Navarra, from Roncesvalles and Burguete down through the Baztan Valley to Hondarribia, are a magical realm of rolling hillsides, folklore, and emerald pastures.

# Planning

## When to Go

If you're a hiker, stick to the summer (June–September, especially July), when the weather is better and there's less chance of a serious snowfall—not to mention blizzards or lightning storms at high altitudes.

October, with comfortable daytime temperatures and chillier evenings, is ideal for enjoying the still-green Pyrenean meadows and valleys and hillside hunts for wild mushrooms. November brings colorful leaves, the last mushrooms, and the first frosts.

For skiing, visit December–March. The green springtime thaw, mid-March–mid-April, is spectacular for skiing on the snowcaps as well as trout-fishing or golfing on the verdant valley floors.

August is the only crowded month, when all of Europe is on summer vacation and the cooler highland air is at its best.

# Planning Your Time

You could hike all the way from the Atlantic to the Mediterranean in some 43 days, but few have that kind of vacation time. Instead, consider a road trip—you can feasibly wind your way from one end of the mountain range to the other in about one week, though allotting 5–7 days in each of the following areas makes for a richer experience: La Cerdanya and the Eastern Catalan Pyrenees, easily accessed from Barcelona; the Western Catalan Pyrenees and Val d'Aran in the Lleida province of Catalonia; Jaca and the central Pyrenees, north of Zaragoza; or the Basque Pyrenees north of Pamplona.

A day's drive up through Figueres (in Catalonia) and Olot will bring you to the town of **Camprodon.** The picturesque villages dotted around this area—in particular **Beget, Sant Joan de les Abadesses,** and **Ripoll**—are worthy stops, especially for the famous monastery of Santa Maria de Ripoll with its 13th-century Romanesque portal. La Cerdanya's sunny plains are popular with walkers and mountain bikers year-round and skiers in La Molina and Masella in winter. **Puigcerdà, Llívia,** and **Bellver de Cerdanya** are must-visits, too.

To the west, the historic town of **La Seu d'Urgell** is a historical touchstone on the way to the **Parc Nacional d'Aigüestortes i Estany de Sant Maurici,** the **Val d'Aran,** and the winter-sports center Baqueira-Beret. Stop at **Taüll** and the **Noguera de Tor Valley** for Romanesque churches.

The central Aragonese Pyrenees reveal the most dramatic scenery with Aneto being the highest peak in the entire range. The **Parque Nacional de Ordesa y Monte Perdido** is Spain's most majestic canyon—reminiscent of North America's Grand Canyon. **Alquézar** and **Aínsa** are upper Aragón's best-preserved medieval towns, while **Zaragoza, Huesca,** and **Jaca** are the most populated cities.

Farther west, the lower Navarran Pyrenees give way to rolling pasturelands. **Roncesvalles** is the first stop for pilgrims on the life-affirming **Camino de Santiago,** and the peaceful **Baztan Valley** guards a land of ancient traditions.

# Getting Here and Around

## AIR
Barcelona's international airport, El Prat, is the main gateway to the Catalan Pyrenees from the east. From the north, the area can be reached via Toulouse Blagnac; from the west, your best bet for international flights is Biarritz Airport in France. Smaller airports at Zaragoza, Pamplona, and San Sebastián's Hondarribia are useful for domestic flights.

## BUS
Buses are the only mode of transportation that will get you around the Pyrenees without hiking or driving, but be forewarned that there's lots of zigzagging up and down valleys. In most cases, four daily buses, run by ALSA (⊕ www.alsa.com) or Avanza (⊕ www.avanzabus.com), connect the main pre-Pyrenean cities (Barcelona, Zaragoza, Huesca, and Pamplona) and key highland destinations (Puigcerdà, La Seu d'Urgell, Vielha, Benasque, and Jaca). ■ TIP→ **The time lost waiting for buses makes this option inefficient if you're on a tight schedule.**

## CAR
The easiest way (and in many cases, the *only* way) to tour the Pyrenees is by car—and it comes with the best scenery. The Eje Pirenaico (Pyrenean Axis, or N260) is a safe and carefully engineered cross-Pyrenean route that connects Cap de Creus—the Iberian Peninsula's easternmost point on the Mediterranean Costa Brava (east of Girona and Cadaqués)—with Cabo de Higuer, the lighthouse west of Hondarribia at the edge of the Atlantic Bay of Biscay.

The Collada de Toses (Tosses Pass) to Puigcerdà is the most difficult route into the Cerdanya Valley, but it's toll-free, has spectacular scenery, and you get to include Camprodón, Olot, and Ripoll in your itinerary. Safer and faster but more expensive (tolls total more than €22 from Barcelona to Bellver de Cerdanya) is the E9 through the Cadí tunnel. Once you're there, most of the Cerdanya Valley's two-lane roads are wide and well paved. As you go west, roads may become more difficult to navigate, winding dramatically through mountain passes.

## TRAIN
There are three small train stations deep in the Pyrenees: Ribes de Freser in the eastern Catalan Pyrenees, Puigcerdà in the Cerdanya Valley, and La Pobla de Segur in the Noguera Pallaresa Valley. The larger gateways are Zaragoza, Huesca, and Lleida. From Madrid, connect through Barcelona for the eastern Pyrenees, Zaragoza and Huesca for the central Pyrenees, and Pamplona or San Sebastián for the Navarran and Basque Pyrenees. For information on timetables and routes, consult ⊕ www.renfe.com. There are two new low-cost train companies servicing Barcelona: Ouigo (⊕ www.ouigo.com) and Avlo (⊕ www.avlorenfe.com).

# Hiking the Pyrenees

There are many reasons to visit the Pyrenees—skiing, food, art, and architecture, to name a few—but hiking is the region's biggest draw. No matter how spectacular the mountains seem from the road, they are exponentially more dazzling from upper hiking trails that are accessible only on foot. The natural splendor is best enjoyed on day hikes or overnight two-day treks to mountain huts (*refugios,* or *refugis* in Catalan) in the Ordesa or Aigüestortes national parks, in the Alberes range, or on the hike from Col de Núria to Ulldeter.

Local tourist offices provide maps and can recommend day hikes.

■TIP➜ Download the Wikiloc app (www. wikiloc.com) to track your hike, access offline topographic base maps, and share photos of your trek. It's a popular app locally, so you can download other users' hikes. A live-tracking feature allows you to share your location with family as a safety precaution.

Hiking in the Pyrenees should always be undertaken carefully: proper footwear, headwear, water supply, and weather-forecast awareness are essential. High-altitude climbs are not recommended for first-timers unless you hire a guide. There can be unexpected snowstorms even in summer.

## Restaurants

In the high Pyrenees, cozy stone inns, with their hearty cuisine and comfortable interiors, are a welcome sight after a day of hiking or sightseeing. Often family-run and relaxed, they rarely have a dress code, and nourishing meals frequently close with a complimentary *chupito* (shot) of local cassis and patxaran (sloe berry liqueur). Down in the main cities, restaurants tend to be more contemporary and slightly more expensive yet equally hospitable.

*Restaurant reviews have been shortened. For full information, visit Fodors. com.*

## Hotels

Most hotels in the Pyrenees are informal and outdoorsy, with a large fireplace in one of the public rooms. They are usually built of wood, glass, and stone and have steep slate roofs that blend in with the surrounding mountains. There's a high concentration of family operations passed down from generation to generation, though chain options also abound.

*Hotel reviews have been shortened. For full information, visit Fodors.com.*

### What It Costs in Euros

|  | $ | $$ | $$$ | $$$$ |
|---|---|---|---|---|
| **RESTAURANTS** | | | | |
| | under €16 | €16–€22 | €23–€28 | over €28 |
| **HOTELS** | | | | |
| | under €100 | €100–€139 | €140–€195 | over €195 |

## Tours

Trekking, horseback riding, adventure sports such as canyoning and ballooning, and more contemplative outings like bird-watching and botanical tours, are a few of the activities available at the main Pyrenean resorts.

Populated with trout, the Pyrenees' cold streams provide excellent angling from mid-March to the end of August. Notable places to cast a line are the Segre, Aragón, Gállego, Noguera Pallaresa, Arga, Esera, and Esca Rivers. Pyrenean ponds and lakes also tend to be rich in trout.

### Pyrenean Experience

**GUIDED TOURS** | British expat Georgina Howard specializes in showcasing Basque-Navarran culture, walking, and gastronomy. Tours include accommodations and meals. ✉ *Iaulin Borda, Ameztia, Ituren* ☎ *650/713759* ⊕ *www.pyrenean-experience.com* ✈ *From €1,100.*

# Skiing

Skiing is the main winter attraction in the Pyrenees, and the range holds over half of Spain's ski resorts. Baqueira-Beret, in Val d'Aran, is the most renowned ski resort. According to the Pyrenean Observatory of Climate Change (OPCC), the climate crisis is heating up the Pyrenees alarmingly fast, but thanks to snow machines, there is usually fine skiing December–March here and at more than 20 resorts including Vallter 2000 at Setcases in the Camprodon Valley and La Molina (with accessible facilities for those with limited mobility) and Masella in La Cerdanya. Although weekend skiing can be crowded in the eastern valleys, Catalonia's western Pyrenees have more breathing room; same goes for Aragón, whose main resorts are Cerler-Benasque, Panticosa, Formigal, Astún, and Candanchú. Numerous resorts offer heliskiing and cross-country skiing. Leading areas for the latter include Lles, in the Cerdanya; Salardú and Beret, in Val d'Aran; and Panticosa, Benasque, and Candanchú, in Aragón. Jaca, Puigcerdà, and Vielha also offer winter activities such as public skating sessions, figure-skating classes, and ice-hockey programs.

A good resource for up-to-date ski conditions and information is On the Snow (⊕ www.onthesnow.co.uk/spain/skireport). Tourist offices also provide insight.

# Camprodon

*127 km (79 miles) northwest of Barcelona, 80 km (50 miles) west of Girona.*

Camprodon, the capital of its *comarca* (county), is at the junction of the Ter and Ritort Rivers—both excellent trout streams. The rivers flow by, through, and under much of the town, giving it a highland waterfront character (as well as a long history of flooding). Its best-known symbol is the elegant 12th-century stone bridge that broadly spans the Ter River in the center of town. Camprodon owes much of its opulence to the summer residents from Barcelona who built mansions along **Passeig Maristany,** the leafy promenade at its northern edge.

## GETTING HERE AND AROUND
The C38 runs into the center of town from both north (France) and south (Barcelona, Vic, or Ripoll) directions. If coming from France, the southbound D115 changes into the C38 once over the Spanish border. The best way to explore is on foot, as the streets are narrow and can be tricky to navigate by car.

## VISITOR INFORMATION
**CONTACTS Camprodon Tourist Office.**
⊠ *Carrer Sant Roc 22, Camprodón* ☎ *972/740010* ⊕ *www.valldecamprodon. org.*

## 🛏 Hotels

★ **Fonda Rigà**
$ | **B&B/INN** | **FAMILY** | A highland inn with comfortable modern rooms and spectacular mountain views, this perch is an excellent base for hiking, horseback riding, and viewing Pyrenean flora and fauna. **Pros:** stunning views and quiet surroundings at a terrific value; outstanding restaurant; complimentary house wine and bottled water. **Cons:** bookings only by email or phone; remote from Camprodon; a serious 5-km (3-mile) drive above the valley floor. ⑤ *Rooms from: €57* ⊠ *Ctra. de Tregurà de Dalt, Km 4.8* ⊕ *At end of Tregurà route, 10 km (6 miles) up Ter Valley from Camprodón* ☎ *972/136000* ⊕ *www.fondariga.com* ⊗ *Closed Nov. 1–15 and 2 wks in late June/early July (dates vary)* ⇥ *16 rooms* ⊗| *Free Breakfast.*

### Hotel de Camprodon

**$ | HOTEL |** This elegant Moderniste building has rooms over the bustling Plaça Dr. Robert on one side and over the river on the other. **Pros:** central location; wonderful views over the river; charming Art Nouveau style and preserved features throughout. **Cons:** five-night minimum stay in summer; rooms on the square can be noisy in summer; no parking. ⑤ *Rooms from: €94* ⊠ *Pl. Dr. Robert 3, Camprodón* ☎ *972/740013* ⊕ *www. hotelcamprodon.com* ⤴ *50 rooms* ⋈ *No Meals.*

### Hotel Maristany

**$$$ | HOTEL |** A stately old chalet on Camprodon's grandest promenade, this lovely family-owned hotel offers a chance to live like the 19th- and 20th-century Barcelona aristocracy who spent their summers here. **Pros:** tranquil location outside the center; private parking; excellent restaurant. **Cons:** not in the heart of the action; so-so soundproofing; rooms and baths are somewhat cramped. ⑤ *Rooms from: €170* ⊠ *Av. Maristany 20, Camprodón* ☎ *972/130078* ⊕ *www.hotelmaristany. com* ⊘ *Closed Dec. 11–Easter* ⤴ *10 rooms* ⋈ *Free Breakfast* ☞ *Adults only.*

## 🎭 Performing Arts

### Festival de Música de Isaac Albéniz

**MUSIC |** Camprodon's most famous son is composer Isaac Albéniz (1860–1909), who spent more than 20 years in exile in France, where he became friends with musical luminaries such as Pablo Casals, Claude Debussy, and Gabriel Fauré. His celebrated classical guitar piece,

Asturias, is one of Spain's best-known works. In July and August, during the Isaac Albéniz Music Festival, a series of concerts by renowned artists and young talent from the European classical music scene is held in the monastery of Sant Pere. For an up-to-date concert schedule, contact the tourist office or visit the website. ⊠ *Sant Pere de Camprodón, Carrer Monestir 2, Camprodón* ⊕ *www. albeniz.cat.*

##  Shopping

### Cal Xec

**FOOD** | This legendary sausage and cheese store also sells vanilla-flavored Birbas cookies, a local favorite. ⊠ *Carrer Isaac Albéniz 1, Camprodón* ☎ *972/740084* ⊕ *www.calxec.com.*

### Mercat Setmanal

**CRAFTS** | Held every Sunday 9–2, this market sells all manner of artisanal food, crafts, clothing, antiques, and bric-a-brac. ⊠ *Pl. Dr. Robert, Camprodón.*

### Rocabruna

**TOWN** | From Camprodon, take the C38 north toward Molló and the French border. After 3 km (2 miles), turn east toward Rocabruna, a village of well-preserved stone houses at the source of the clear Beget River. Rocabruna is famous for two attractions: its 11th-century castle (now in ruins), built on a hilltop with superb views of the Beget Valley, La Garrotxa, and the Pyrenees, and the idyllic Can Po restaurant, a worthwhile stop on the way to Beget.

# Beget

*17 km (10 miles) east of Camprodon.*

The village of Beget, considered Catalonia's *més bufó* (cutest), was inaccessible by car until the mid-1960s, when a *pista forestal* (jeep track) was laid down. In 1980, Beget was finally fully connected to the rest of the world by an asphalt roadway, which can be hazardous when mist descends, as it often does. The GIV5223 road to Castellfollit de la Roca, 12 km (7 miles) away, winds scenically among the formerly volcanic peaks of the Alta Garrotxa. Beget's 30-some houses are eccentric stone structures with heavy wooden doors and a golden color particular to the Vall de Camprodón. Archaic stone bridges span the stream where protected trout swim in clear mountain water.

### GETTING HERE AND AROUND

Drive northeast out of Camprodon on Carrer Molló (C38) for 2 km (1 mile) before turning right onto the Carretera Camprodon–Beget (GIV5223) for 14 km (9 miles) to Beget. Cars are not allowed to enter the village, but there is parking just outside. When leaving, head toward Oix, which leads to Castellfollit de la Roca and the N260, to avoid having to retrace your steps back up the mountain.

## ◎ Sights

### Sant Cristòfol

**CHURCH** | The 12th-century Romanesque church of Sant Cristòfol (St. Christopher) has a diminutive bell tower and a rare six-foot Majestat—a polychrome wood carving of the risen Christ in head-to-foot robes that dates to the 12th century. If the church is closed (there are no regular hours, though visitors report having luck on weekday mornings and weekend afternoons), ask in the bar-restaurant behind the church, or in El Forn de Beget, and someone may direct you to the keeper of the key. ⊠ *Pl. Major, Beget* ☎ *No phone* 🎫 *€2.*

## Did You Know?

Trekking in the Pyrenees can be a very serious endeavor—it's possible to walk the entire way from the Atlantic Coast to the Mediterranean in about six weeks, but shorter one- or two-day hikes can be just as stunning.

# 🍴 Restaurants

### ★ Can Po

$ | **CATALAN** | In this ivy-covered stone-and-mortar farmhouse perched over a deep gully in nearby Rocabruna, feast on carefully prepared local dishes like *vedella amb crema de ceps* (veal in wild mushroom sauce) and the Catalan classic *oca amb peres* (goose stewed with pears). In winter, spring for the *civet de porc senglar* (stewed wild boar) or any of the wild mushroom dishes. **Known for:** soul-satisfying stews; cozy ambience; hearty mountain cuisine. 💲 *Average main: €15* ⌧ *Ctra. de Beget, Rocabruna* ☎ *972/741045* ⊙ *Closed Mon.–Wed.*

# 🛏 Hotels

### El Forn de Beget

$$ | **B&B/INN** | Overlooking the Trull River in the upper part of the village, this little stone hotel and restaurant has panoramic views over Alta Garrotxa. **Pros:** a true hideaway in the Pyrenees; classic mountain food; wonderful river views from the dining room. **Cons:** need a car to get here; remote location; rooms are small and close together. 💲 *Rooms from: €105* ⌧ *Carrer Josep Duñach "En Feliça" 9, Beget* ☎ *972/741230* ⊕ *www.elforndebeget.com* ⤳ *4 rooms* ❂ *Free Breakfast.*

# Sant Joan de les Abadesses

*14 km (9 miles) southwest of Camprodon.*

The site of an important church, Sant Joan de les Abadesses is named for the 9th-century abbess Emma and her successors. Emma was the daughter of Guifré el Pilós (Wilfred the Hairy), a hero of the Christian Reconquest of Ripoll whom some regard as the founder of Catalonia.

The town's arcaded Plaça Major offers a glimpse of its medieval past, as does the broad, elegant 12th-century bridge over the Ter.

## GETTING HERE AND AROUND

Exit southwest of Camprodon on Carrer Molló (C38) for 9 km (6 miles), passing through Sant Pau de Segúries. At the rotary, take the first exit onto the N260 for 4 km (2½ miles) to Sant Joan de les Abadesses. If you're coming from Ripoll, take the northbound N260 for 10 km (6 miles). Once here, it's an easy stroll.

## VISITOR INFORMATION

**CONTACTS Sant Joan de les Abadesses Tourist Office.** ⌧ *Pl. de la Abadía 9, Sant Joan de les Abadesses* ☎ *972/720599* ⊕ *www.santjoandelesabadesses.cat.*

# 👁 Sights

### Monastery of Sant Joan de les Abadesses

**CHURCH** | In the 12th-century Romanesque church of Sant Joan, the altarpiece—a 13th-century polychrome wood sculpture of the Descent from the Cross—is one of the most expressive and human of that epoch. Wilfred the Hairy gifted this church to his daughter, Emma, and did the same for his son Radulfo with the Monastery of Santa Maria de Ripoll. *See Ripoll sights.* ⌧ *Pl. de la Abadía, Sant Joan de les Abadesses* ☎ *972/722353* ⊕ *www.monestirsantjoanabadesses.cat* ⌦ *€5* ⌲ *No credit cards.*

# Ripoll

*10 km (6 miles) southwest of Sant Joan de les Abadesses, 105 km (65 miles) north of Barcelona.*

One of Catalonia's first Christian strongholds of the so-called Reconquest and a center of religious erudition during the Middle Ages, Ripoll is known as the bressol (cradle) of Catalonia's liberation from Moorish domination and the spiritual home of Guifré el Pilós (Wilfred the Hairy), the count of Barcelona who some historians claim founded the Catalan nation in the late 9th century. A dark, mysterious country town built around a 9th-century **Benedictine monastery**, Ripoll was a cultural focal point throughout French Catalonia and the Pyrenees, from the monastery's 879 founding until the mid-1800s, when Barcelona began to eclipse it.

### GETTING HERE AND AROUND

The C17 northbound from Vic heads into the center of Ripoll. From Camprodon and Sant Joan de les Abadesses, head southwest on the C38, which turns into the N260 to the town center. There are direct trains from Barcelona (2 hours; line R3 on the Cercanías commuter rail) and approximately two daily bus connections (1½ hours ⊕ www.teisa-bus.com). It's a 10-minute walk from the station to the center, and the small town is easy to explore on foot.

### VISITOR INFORMATION

**CONTACTS Ripoll Tourist Office.** ⊠ Pl. de l'Abat Oliva, Ripoll ☎ 972/702351 ⊕ www. visit.ripoll.cat.

## ⊙ Sights

### Monastery of Santa Maria de Ripoll

CHURCH | Decorated with a pageant of biblical figures, the 12th-century doorway to the church is one of Catalonia's great works of Romanesque art. It was crafted as a triumphal arch by stonemasons and sculptors of the Roussillon school, which was centered on French Catalonia and the Pyrenees. You can pick up a guide to the figures surrounding the portal in the nearby Centro de Interpretación del Monasterio, in Plaça de l'Abat Oliva. The center has an exhibition space (Catalan only) that explains the historical, cultural,

and religious relevance of this so-called cradle of Catalonia. It also provides information about guided tours. ⊠ Pl. Monasterio, Ripoll ☎ 972/704203 ⊕ www. monestirderipoll.cat ☑ €8.

# Ribes de Freser and Vall de Núria

14 km (9 miles) north of Ripoll.

The small town of Ribes de Freser is the starting point of the famous cremallera (cogwheel) train, which connects passengers with Núria, a small mountaintop ski resort and pilgrimage site, via a spectacular ascent through the Gorges of Núria.

### GETTING HERE AND AROUND

The N260 north of Ripoll goes straight to Ribes de Freser. Continue farther north on the GIV5217 to reach Queralbs by car. Queralbs and Ribes de Freser are easily explored on foot.

### VISITOR INFORMATION

**CONTACTS Vall de Ribes Tourist Office.** ⊠ Ctra. de Bruguera 2, Ribes de Freser ☎ 972/727728 ⊕ www.vallderibes.cat.

## ⊙ Sights

### Camí dels Enginyers

TRAIL | With a trailhead at the ski area of Núria, at an altitude of 6,562 feet, the dramatic—and occasionally heart-stopping—"engineers' path" is best done in summer. The three-hour trek, aided at one point by a cable handrail, leads to the remote highland valley of Coma de Vaca, where a cozy refuge and hearty replenishment await. Call ahead to make sure there's space, and check weather conditions. In the morning you can descend along the riverside Gorges de Freser trail, another three-hour walk, to Queralbs, where there are connecting trains to Ribes de Freser. ⊠ Refugi de

Coma de Vaca, Termino Municipal de Queralbs dentro del Espacio protegido Ter Freser, Queralbs ☎ 649/229012 ⊕ www.comadevaca.cat/index.php/en ☾ Closed Sept.–May.

## Queralbs

**TOWN** | The three-hour walk down the mountain from Vall de Núria to the sleepy village of Queralbs follows the course of the cogwheel train on a rather precipitous but fairly easy route (provided there's no snow). The path overlooks gorges and waterfalls overshadowed by sheer peaks before exiting into the quaint village of Queralbs, where houses made of stone and wood cling to the side of the mountain. There is a well-preserved Romanesque church, notable for its six-arch portico, marble columns, single nave, and pointed vault. ⊠ Queralbs ⊕ www.vallderibes.cat/en/pobles/queralbs.

## Santuari de la Mare de Déu de Núria

**CHURCH** | The legend of this Marian religious retreat is based on the story of Sant Gil of Nîmes, who did penance in the Núria Valley during the 7th century. The saint left behind a wooden statue of the Virgin Mary, a bell he used to summon shepherds to prayer, and a cooking pot; 300 years later, a pilgrim found these treasures in this sanctuary. The bell and the pot came to have special importance to infertile women, who, according to local lore, would be blessed with as many children as they wished after placing their heads in the pot and ringing the bell. ⊠ Vall de Núria ✛ 26 km (16 miles) north of Ripoll ☜ Free.

## ★ Vall de Núria Rack Railway (Cremallera)

**TRAIN/TRAIN STATION | FAMILY** | The 45-minute train ride from the town of Ribes de Freser up to Núria provides one of Catalonia's most eclectic excursions—in few other places in Spain does a train make such a precipitous ascent. The cogwheel train, nicknamed La Cremallera ("The Zipper" in English), was completed in 1931 to connect Ribes with the Santuari de la Mare de Déu de Núria (Mother of God of Núria) and with hiking trails and ski runs. ⊠ Estación de Ribes-Enllaç, Ribes de Freser ☎ 972/732020 ⊕ www.valldenuria.cat/en/summer/rack-railway/presentation ☜ €30 round-trip ☾ Closed weekdays in Nov.

## 🛏 Hotels

### Hostal Les Roquetes

**$ | B&B/INN** | A short walk from the cogwheel train and in the center of the village, this *hostal* has simple, cheerful rooms with red-tile floors; those with (small) terraces afford spectacular valley views. **Pros:** fantastic views; good base for walks in the area; fireplace in the common area. **Cons:** simple lodging; only accessible by local road or cogwheel train, and those times are limited; limited food options outside of weekends. ⑤ *Rooms from: €78* ⊠ Ctra. de Ribes 5, Queralbs ☎ 972/727369 ⊕ www.hostalroquetes.com ☾ Closed Nov. ⇆ 8 rooms ⑪ No Meals.

### Hotel Vall de Núria

**$$$ | HOTEL | FAMILY** | A mountain refuge and state-run hotel, this family-oriented base camp has double, triple, and quadruple rooms. **Pros:** in the heart of the Pyrenees; clean and simple; pristine mountain air. **Cons:** high rates for basic lodging; minimum two-night stay in high season; feels institutional and austere. ⑤ *Rooms from: €142* ⊠ Estación de Montaña Vall de Núria, Queralbs ☎ 972/732020 ⊕ www.valldenuria.cat/en ☾ Closed Nov. ⇆ 65 rooms, 12 apartments ⑪ Free Breakfast.

# Puigcerdà

*65 km (40 miles) northwest of Ripoll, 170 km (106 miles) northwest of Barcelona.*

Puigcerdà ("poo-cher-DA") is the largest town in the valley; in Catalan, *puig* means "hill," and *cerdà* derives from "Cerdanya." From the promontory upon which it stands, the views down across the meadows of the valley floor and up into the craggy peaks of the surrounding Pyrenees are dramatic. The 12th-century **Romanesque bell tower**—all that remains of the town church of Santa Maria, destroyed in 1936 at the outset of the Spanish Civil War—and the sunny sidewalk cafés facing it are among Puigcerdà's prettiest spots, as are the manmade lake dotted with rowboats in summer and the Gothic church of **Sant Domènec.**

A prime base for skiers and hikers from both sides of the border, Puigcerdà has lively restaurants, a bustling shopping promenade, and a popular new music festival called Summerfest Cerdanya. On Sunday, markets sell clothes, cheeses, fruits, vegetables, and wild mushrooms.

## GETTING HERE AND AROUND

From Ripoll take the northwest-bound N260 for 63 km (39 miles) toward Ribes de Freser. There are several commuter trains a day (they are less frequent on weekends) connecting Barcelona Sants to Puigcerdà (line R3). Buses go from Barcelona Estación del Nord (⊕ *www. alsa.com*). Once you reach the center, there is ample parking, and the easiest way to get around town is on foot.

## VISITOR INFORMATION

**CONTACTS Puigcerdà Tourist Office.** ⊠ *Pl. Santa Maria, Puigcerdà* ☎ *972/880542* ⊕ *www.puigcerda.cat.*

# ⊙ Sights

## Ligne de Cerdagne

**TRAIN/TRAIN STATION | FAMILY |** Affectionately called *le petit train jaune* ("the little yellow train"), this line runs from Bourg-Madame and La Tour de Querol, both easy hikes over the border into France from Puigcerdà (Bourg-Madame is the closest). The border at La Tour, a pretty hour-long hike from Puigcerdà, is marked by a stone painted with the Spanish and French flags. The *carrilet* (narrow-gauge railway) is the last in the Pyrenees and is used for tours as well as transportation; it winds slowly through La Cerdanya to the medieval walled town of Villefranche-de-Conflent, where it can also be picked up. The 63-km (39-mile) tour can take most of the day, especially if you stop to browse in Mont-Louis or Villefranche. The last section, between La Cabanasse and Villefranche, is the most picturesque. In low season the trains have infrequent and unpredictable timetables. ⊠ *Oficina de Turisme de la Cerdanya, Ctra. Cruïlla N152 N260, Puigcerdà* ☎ *972/140665 Cerdanya tourist office (Spain), 046/804–1547 Pyrénées Cerdagne tourist office (France)* ⊕ *www. pyrenees-cerdagne.com/en/le-train-jaune-english/the-schedules* 🎫 *€11 round trip.*

## Plaça Cabrinetty

**PLAZA/SQUARE |** With its porticoes and covered walks, this square named for a hero of the Carlist Wars is protected from the gusty mountain wind. It is ringed by pastel-painted Renaissance houses, some with decorative sgraffito designs and all with balconies. ⊠ *Puigcerdà.*

## Santa Maria Bell Tower

**VIEWPOINT |** The 12th-century Santa Maria church in the center of town was largely destroyed in 1936 during the Spanish Civil War, but the bell tower remains and is open to visitors. At the top, take in a 360-degree panorama of La Cerdanya's towns, bucolic farmlands, and snowy peaks. ⊠ *Pl. Santa Maria, Puigcerdà* ☎ *972/880542* ⊠ €2.

## 🍽 Restaurants

### Tap de Suro

$ | **CATALAN** | Named for the classic bottle stopper (*tap*) made of cork (*suro*), this wine store-cum-gastrobar is the perfect place to unwind over local cheeses, duck and goose liver, and other delicacies. Expect a varied and affordable tapas menu and an ever-rotating wine selection with labels from Spain and France. **Known for:** cozy; top-notch cheeses and charcuterie; intriguing wines from near and far. ⑤ *Average main: €14* ⊠ *Carrer Querol 21, Puigcerdà* ☎ *678/655928* ♥ *Closed Mon.*

## Hotels

### Hotel del Lago

$$ | **HOTEL** | A comfortable old favorite near Puigcerdà's emblematic lake, this spa hotel with old-fashioned decor consists of several salmon-pink spire-topped mansions arranged around a grassy central garden. **Pros:** lakeside real estate; short walk to the center; spa with hot tub and pool. **Cons:** no restaurant (only breakfast); pricey for its services; showing wear in spots. ⑤ *Rooms from: €130* ⊠ *Av. Dr. Piguillem 7, Puigcerdà* ☎ *972/881000* ⊕ *www.hotellago.com* ↝ *24 rooms* ⦿ *Free Breakfast.*

### Villa Paulita

$$$ | **HOTEL** | This stately town-house complex at the edge of the lake has some of the most sought-after rooms and food in the Cerdanya Valley. **Pros:** renowned restaurant with good breakfast; right on the lake; close to activity. **Cons:** overpriced for what it offers; underwhelming pool and spa; cramped entry-level rooms with outdated technology. ⑤ *Rooms from:*

## Tip 👁

The tourist office on the outskirts of Puigcerdà (⊠ *Oficina de Turisme del Consell Comarcal de la Cerdanya, corner of Ctra. N260 and N152* ☎ *972/880542*) has up-to-date information on the best hiking trails in La Cerdanya. If you're planning a long-distance hiking trip, local bus connections will get you to your starting point and retrieve you at the finish line.

*€161* ⊠ *Av. Pons i Gasch 15, Puigcerdà* ☎ *972/884622* ⊕ *www.villapaulitahotel.com* ↝ *38 rooms* ⦿ *Free Breakfast.*

## 🛍 Shopping

### Carrer Major

**NEIGHBORHOODS** | This is an uninterrupted pedestrian-only row of stores selling books, jewelry, fashion, sports equipment, and more. ⊠ *Puigcerdà.*

### Mercat Setmanal

**MARKET** | On Sunday morning (9–2), walk over to this lively weekly market that, like those in most Cerdanya towns, features local crafts and specialties such as herbs, goat cheese, wild mushrooms, honey, and baskets. ⊠ *Passeig 10 d'Abril, Puigcerdà.*

### ★ Pastisseria Confiteria Cosp

**FOOD** | For the best *margaritas* in town (no, not those—these are crunchy-edged madeleines made with almonds), head to what is allegedly the oldest commercial establishment in Catalonia, founded in 1806. ⊠ *Carrer Major 20, Puigcerdà* ☎ *972/880103.*

# Llívia

*6 km (4 miles) northeast of Puigcerdà.*

A Spanish exclave in French territory, Llívia was marooned by the 1659 Peace of the Pyrenees treaty, which ceded 33 villages to France. Incorporated as a *vila* (town) by royal decree of Carlos V—who spent a night here in 1528 and was impressed by the town's beauty and hospitality—Llívia managed to remain Spanish. In the town center, look for the mosaic commemorating Lampègia, *princesa de la paul i de l'amor* (princess of peace and of love), erected in memory of the red-haired daughter of the Duke of Aquitania and lover of Munuza, a Berber governor who ruled La Cerdanya in the 8th century in Islamic Spain.

## GETTING HERE AND AROUND
From Puigcerdà you could basically walk to Llívia, 6 km (4 miles) north just across the French border, but there are also buses from the Puigcerdà train station. By car, follow the Camí Vell de Llívia to the N154, which goes directly to Llívia.

## VISITOR INFORMATION
**CONTACTS Llívia Tourist Office.** ✉ *Carrer dels Forns 10, Llívia* ☎ *972/896313* ⊕ *www.llivia.org.*

## ⊙ Sights

### Mare de Déu dels Àngels
CHURCH | At the upper edge of town, this fortified church has wonderful acoustics. ✉ *Carrer dels Forns 13, Llívia* 🎫 *Free.*

### Museu de la Farmacia
NOTABLE BUILDING | Across from the Mare de Déu dels Àngels church, this ancient pharmacy, housed within the Museo Municipal, was founded in 1415 and is certifiably the oldest working pharmacy in Europe. ✉ *Carrer dels Forns 10, Llívia* ☎ *972/896313* ⊕ *www.patrimoni.gencat. cat/en/collection/esteve-pharmacy-llivia* 🎫 *€4* ⊗ *Closed Mon.*

## 🍴 Restaurants

### ★ Can Ventura
$$$ | CATALAN | In a flower-festooned 17th-century stone house is one of La Cerdanya's finest restaurants, which serves elevated Catalan fare with French touches. Beef a la llosa and duck with orange and spices are house specialties, and the wide selection of *entretenimientos* (hors d'oeuvres or tapas) is the perfect way to begin. **Known for:** additional bar area for drinks and tapas; cozy mountain lodge setting; beef seared on hot slate. ⑤ *Average main: €25* ✉ *Pl. Major 1, Llívia* 🎫 *972/896178* ⊕ *www. canventura.com* ⊗ *Closed Mon. and Thurs. No dinner Sun.*

### La Formatgeria de Llívia
$$$ | CATALAN | This restaurant on the eastern edge of town is inside a former cheese factory, and the proprietors continue the tradition by producing fresh cheese on the premises while you watch. In the restaurant, fine local cuisine and fondues come with panoramic views looking south toward Puigmal and across the valley. **Known for:** open fire in winter; homemade cheese; fondues and raclettes. ⑤ *Average main: €25* ✉ *Pl. de Ro, Gorguja, Llívia* 🎫 *972/146279* ⊕ *www.laformatgeria.com* ⊗ *Closed Tues. and Wed. (except Aug.).*

# Bellver de Cerdanya

*18 km (11 miles) southwest of Puigcerdà, 31 km (19 miles) southwest of Llívia.*

Bellver de Cerdanya has preserved its slate-roof-and-fieldstone Pyrenean architecture more successfully than many of La Cerdanya's larger towns. Perched on a promontory over the **Riu Segre,** which winds around much of the town, Bellver is essentially a fishing village plopped in the mountains, with trout as the protagonist. The town's Gothic church of

**Sant Jaume** and the arcaded **Plaça Major,** in the upper part of town, are exquisite examples of traditional Pyrenean mountain-village design.

### GETTING HERE AND AROUND
Take the southwest-bound N260 from Puigcerdà; once here, explore on foot.

### VISITOR INFORMATION
**CONTACTS Bellver de Cerdanya Tourist Office.** ⊠ *Pl. Major 12, Bellver de Cerdanya* ☎ *973/510016* ⊕ *www.bellver.org/ turisme.*

##  Hotels

**Aparthotel Bellver**
**$$** | **B&B/INN** | Rustic terra-cotta tiles, arresting mountain views, and stone rooms warmed by fireplaces lure tranquility-loving travelers to this unfussy inn in the town center. **Pros:** snug common area with fireplace; on-site parking; open year-round. **Cons:** books up quickly; no a/c; two-night minimum stay in July and August. ⑤ *Rooms from: €100* ⊠ *Carrer de la Batllia 61–63, Bellver de Cerdanya* ☎ *973/510627* ⊕ *www.aparthotelbellver.com* ⊘ *Erratic blackout dates (check ahead)* ↪ *12 apartments* ⊘¶ *Free Breakfast.*

# La Seu d'Urgell

*20 km (12 miles) south of Andorra la Vella (in Andorra), 45 km (28 miles) west of Puigcerdà, 200 km (120 miles) northwest of Barcelona.*

La Seu d'Urgell is an ancient town facing the snowy rock wall of the Sierra del Cadí. As the seat (*seu*) of the regional archbishopric since the 6th century, it has a rich legacy of art and architecture. The Pyrenean feel of the streets, with their dark balconies and porticoes, overhanging galleries, and colonnaded porches— particularly **Carrer dels Canonges**—makes Seu mysterious and memorable. Look for the medieval **grain measures** at the corner of Carrer Major and Carrer Capdevila. The tiny food shops on the arcaded Carrer Major are good places to assemble lunch for a hike.

### GETTING HERE AND AROUND
Take the N260 southwest from Puigcerdà via Bellver de Cerdanya. From the direction of Lleida, head north on the C13 for 63 km (39 miles), then take the C26 after Balaguer, before joining the C14 for 32 km (20 miles) and then the N260 into the center. There are buses daily from Barcelona. The town is compact and can be explored on foot.

**CONTACTS ALSA.** ⊠ *Calle Bisbe de Bell-Loch 1, La Seu d'Urgell* ☎ *902/422242* ⊕ *www.alsa.com.*

### VISITOR INFORMATION
**CONTACTS La Seu d'Urgell Tourist Office.** ⊠ *Carrer Major 8, La Seu d'Urgell* ☎ *973/351511* ⊕ *www.turismeseu.com.*

## ◉ Sights

### ★ Catedral de Santa Maria
**CHURCH** | This 12th-century cathedral is the finest in the Pyrenees, and the sunlight casting the rich reds and blues of Santa Maria's southeastern rose window into the deep gloom of the transept is a moving sight. The 13th-century cloister is famous for the individually hewn, often whimsical capitals on its 50 columns, crafted by the same Roussillon school of masons who carved the doorway on the church of Santa Maria in Ripoll. Don't miss the haunting 11th-century chapel of Sant Miquel or the Diocesan Museum, which has a collection of striking medieval murals from various Pyrenean churches and a colorfully illuminated 10th-century Mozarabic manuscript of the monk Beatus de Liébana's commentary on the apocalypse. ■ TIP→ **Be aware of the limited visiting hours: Monday through Friday from 10–1:30 and 4–6, and Saturdays from 10–1 only.** ⊠ *Pl. del Deganat, La Seu*

d'l Irgell ☎ 973/353242 ⊕ www.museud-
iocesaurgell.org 🎫 €4, includes museum
⊘ Closed Sun.

##  Hotels

### ★ Cal Serni

**$$$ | B&B/INN |** Ten minutes north in
the Pyrenean village of Calbinyà, this
enchanting 15th-century farmhouse and
inn exudes rustic charm with its stone-
walled rooms and traditional wooden furnishings. **Pros:** mountain solitude minutes
from La Seu; incredible views; window
into local country cooking. **Cons:** simple
lodgings; tight public spaces; small guest
rooms. ⑤ *Rooms from: €155* ⊠ *Ctra.
de Calbinyà, Valls de Valira, Calbinyà*
☎ *973/352809* ⊕ *www.calserni.com* 🛏 *6
rooms* ❑ *Free Breakfast.*

### El Castell de Ciutat

**$$$$ | HOTEL |** Outside town, the idyllic
mountain setting of this wood-and-slate
Relais & Château–approved property beneath La Seu's castle makes it
one of the finest places to stay in the
Pyrenees. **Pros:** best restaurant for
many miles; on-site spa; magnificent
Pyrenean panoramas. **Cons:** misses out
on the feel of the town; next to a busy
highway; standard upper-floor rooms
feel slightly cramped. ⑤ *Rooms from:
€210* ⊠ *Ctra. de Lleida (N260), Km 229,
La Seu d'Urgell* ☎ *973/350000* ⊕ *www.
hotelelcastell.com* 🛏 *33 rooms, 5 suites*
❑ *Free Breakfast.*

### Parador de la Seu d'Urgell

**$$ | HOTEL |** These comfortable quarters
in the center of town are built into the
14th-century convent of Sant Domènec.
**Pros:** next to the Santa Maria cathedral;
historic building; generous breakfasts
with local meats and cheeses. **Cons:**
no on-site parking; dated décor; feels
a bit institutional. ⑤ *Rooms from: €138*
⊠ *Calle Sant Domènec 6, La Seu d'Urgell*
☎ *973/352000* ⊕ *www.parador.es* 🛏 *79
rooms* ❑ *No Meals.*

# Sort

*59 km (37 miles) west of La Seu d'Urgell,
136 km (84 miles) north of Lleida, 259
km (161 miles) northwest of Barcelona.*

The capital of the Pallars Sobirà (Upper
Pallars Valley) is the area's epicenter for
skiing, fishing, and white-water kayaking.
The word *sort* is Catalan for "luck," and
its local lottery shop, La Bruixa d'Or (The
Gold Witch), became a tourist attraction
by living up to the town's name and
selling more than an average number of
winning tickets. Don't be fooled by the
modern town you see from the main
road. One block back, Sort is honey-
combed with tiny streets and protected
corners built to stave off harsh winter
weather.

## GETTING HERE AND AROUND

Heading west from La Seu d'Urgell, take
the N260 toward Lleida, then head west
again at Adrall, staying on the N260, and
drive 53 km (33 miles) over the Cantó
Pass to Sort.

## VISITOR INFORMATION

**CONTACTS Pallars Sobirà Tourist
Office.** ⊠ *Camí de la Cabanera 1, Sort*
☎ *973/621002* ⊕ *turisme.pallarssobira.
cat.*

## 🍴 Restaurants

### ★ Fogony

**$$$$ | SPANISH |** Come here for seasonal
and contemporary creations from an
acclaimed chef and supporter of the
slow-food movement, with a prix fixe
menu that may include dishes such as
*pollo a la cocotte con trufa* (organic blue-
foot chicken with truffle) and *solomillo
de ternera de los Pirineos con ligero
escabeche de verduras y setas* (filet of
Pyrenean veal with marinated vegetables
and mushrooms). This restaurant is one
of the best of its kind in the Pyrenees
and, if you hit Sort at lunchtime, it makes

an excellent reason to stop. **Known for:** award-winning menu; family run; part of the slow food movement. $ *Average main: €45* ✉ *Av. Generalitat 45, Sort* ☎ *973/621225* ⊕ *www.fogony.com* ⊗ *Closed Mon. and Tues. No dinner Sun.*

# Parc Nacional d'Aigüestortes i Estany de Sant Maurici

*33 km (20 miles) north of Sort, 168 km (104 miles) north of Lleida, 292 km (181 miles) northwest of Barcelona.*

Catalonia's only national park, which translates to "twisted waters" in Catalan, is the undisputed jewel of the Catalan Pyrenees. Its dramatic unspoiled landscape, reminiscent of the Alps, was shaped over 2 million years of glacial activity. Hikers can reach the park from the Noguera Pallaresa and Ribagorçana valleys, from the villages of Espot to the east, and from Taüll and Boí to the west. There are several visitor centers with maps and information on hiking routes and accommodation in the villages that border the park such as Espot and Boí.

## GETTING HERE AND AROUND

The C13 north up the Noguera Pallaresa Valley covers 34 km (21 miles) from Sort to Espot. One of the main entrances to the park is 4 km (2 miles) west of Espot, where there is also a parking lot. No cars are allowed inside the park (except official taxis/transport). Be sure to arrive early—preferably before 9 am—as parking lots have limited capacity and fill up quickly in high season.

## VISITOR INFORMATION

**CONTACTS Casa del Parc Nacional dc Boí (Park Information Center - Boí).** ⊠ *Carrer de les Graieres 2, Boí* ☎ *973/696189* ⊕ *www.vallboi.cat/en.* **Casa del Parc Nacional d'Espot (Park Information Center).** ⊠ *Carrer de Sant Maurici 5, Espot* ☎ *973/624036.*

## ◉ Sights

### ★ Parc Nacional d'Aigüestortes i Estany de Sant Maurici

**NATIONAL PARK** | Get ready to marvel at some of the most arresting mountain scenery in Europe. The terrain of this national park is formed by jagged peaks, steep rock walls, and deep glacial depressions filled with crystalline water, all of which lie in the shadow of the twin peaks of Els Encantats. Until the turn of the last century, this area was one of the remotest in Europe, known only to shepherds and hunters. Its 200-some streams, lakes, and lagoons intersperse with fir and birch forests and empty into the Noguera River watercourses: the Pallaresa to the east and the Ribagorçana to the west. Rain and snow are notably frequent in all areas. The land range sweeps from wildflower-blanketed meadows below 5,000 feet to rocky crests at nearly double that height; it's inhabited by Pyrenean chamois, golden eagles, capercaillies, and other fauna in great abundance. The twin Encantats measure more than 9,000 feet, and the surrounding peaks of Beciberri, Peguera, Montarto, and Amitges hover between 8,700 feet and a little less than 10,000 feet. The park offers an abundance of walking trails; the most popular is a day-hike from east to west, starting at the village of Espot and finishing in Boí. Less time is needed to see the glacial lakes at Circ de Colomèrs, a 40-minute drive south from Baqueira.

■ **TIP→** Driving inside the park is not permitted, so most visitors leave their cars at the closest entrance and then take a taxi or shuttle, stationed at the main parking areas, to the trailhead.

⊠ *Espot* ☎ *973/696189* ⊕ *parcsnaturals. gencat.cat/en/xarxa-de-parcs/aiguestortes/inici/index.html* ☑ *Free.*

# Vielha

*79 km (49 miles) northwest of Sort, 297 km (185 miles) northwest of Barcelona, 160 km (99 miles) north of Lleida.*

Vielha (Viella in Spanish), capital of the Val d'Aran, is a lively crossroads at the center of a movement to defend and reconstruct the valley's architectural, institutional, and linguistic heritage. At first glance, the town looks like a typical ski-resort base, but the compact and bustling old quarter has a Romanesque church and narrow streets filled with a good selection of restaurants, shops, and a couple of late-night bars. Hiking and climbing are popular around Vielha; guides are available year-round and can be arranged through the tourist office. The Festa Major (town fair), with traditional dances and local dishes, takes place every September 6 to 8.

## GETTING HERE AND AROUND

From the direction of Taüll, head south on the L500 for 15 km (9 miles) toward El Pont de Suerte. At Campament de Tor, turn right onto the northbound Carretera Lleida–Vielha (N230). Vielha's center is fairly compact, and everything can be reached on foot, but you'll need a car to get to Salardú, Arties, and the ski station of Baqueira-Beret.

## VISITOR INFORMATION

**CONTACTS Vielha Tourist Office.** ⊠ *Carrer Sarriulera 10, Vielha* ☎ *973/640688* ⊕ *www.visitvaldaran.com.*

# Hiking in the Pyrenees

Walking the Pyrenees, with one foot in France and the other in Spain, is exhilarating. Though the Alps are taller, the Pyrenees are less known and more remote, which has kept them comparatively pristine and untouristed.

In fall and winter, the Alberes Mountains between Cap de Creus, the Iberian Peninsula's easternmost point, and the border with France at Le Perthus are a grassy runway between the Côte Vermeille's curving beaches to the north and the green patchwork of the Empordà to the south. The well-marked GR (Gran Recorrido) 11 is a favorite two-day spring or autumn hike, with an overnight at the Refugi de la Tanyareda, just below Puig Neulós, the highest point in the Alberes.

The eight-hour walk from Coll de Núria to Ulldeter over the Sierra Catllar, above Setcases, is another grassy corridor in good weather, April–October. The luminous Cerdanya Valley is a hiker's paradise year-round, while the summertime Andorra hike is a scenic 360-degree tour of the tiny country.

The Parc Nacional d'Aigüestortes i Estany de Sant Maurici is superb for trekking from spring through fall. The ascent of the highest peak in the Pyrenees, the 11,168-foot Aneto peak above Benasque, is a long day's round-trip best approached in summer and only by fit and experienced hikers. Much of the hike is over the Maladeta Glacier, from the base camp at the Refugio de La Renclusa. There are also plenty of day hikes suitable for beginners here such as the *Ruta dels set llacs* (Route of the Seven Lakes), which winds among crystalline lakes in the Colomers Cirque.

In Parque Nacional de Ordesa y Monte Perdido, you can take day trips up to the Cola de Caballo waterfall and back around the southern rim of the canyon or, for true mountain goats, longer hikes via the Refugio de Góriz to La Brèche de Roland and Gavarnie or to Monte Perdido, the parador at La Pineta, and the village of Bielsa. Another prized walk involves bed and dinner in the base-camp town of Torla or a night up at the Refugio de Góriz at the head of the valley.

The section of the Camino de Santiago walk from Saint-Jean-Pied-de-Port to Roncesvalles is a marvelous 8- to 10-hour trek any time of year, though check weather reports October–June.

Local *excursionista* (outing) clubs can help you get started; local tourist offices may also have brochures and rudimentary trail maps. The higher reaches are navigable only in summer.

Some useful contacts for hiking are **Cercle d'Aventura** (☎972/881017), **Giroguies Senderisme** (☎972/303886), and **Guies de Meranges** (☎616/855535).

## 👁 Sights

### ★ Sant Miquèu

CHURCH | The octagonal 14th-century bell tower makes this 12th-century church unmistakable. Walk through the 13th-century portico, adorned with 59 figurines, then meander toward the 15th-century Gothic altar. Beside it is one of the most important examples of Romanesque Catalan art, the 12th-century wood carving *Crist de Mijaran*. Uniquely expressive for its time, this bust of Christ is believed to be the sole remnant of a monumental ensemble depicting the Descent from the Cross that was likely destroyed (or stolen) by the French in the 15th century. The bust, which spent the civil war years stashed away in Switzerland, today sits under glass in a temperature-controlled case. ⊠ *Pl. de la Iglesia, Vielha* 🕾 *973/640021* 🎫 *Free.*

## 🍴 Restaurants

### El Molí

$$$ | SPANISH | A picturesque riverside location, knotty pine walls, wood beams, and a rustic prix fixe that highlights regional specialties make this a lovely spot for a meal. There is a ground-floor dining room with large windows that frame a broad sweep of the river and a second, smaller dining room tucked up in the attic. **Known for:** flame-licked calçots (Catalan green onions) in season; river views; aged Pyrenean beef cooked over coals. ⑤ *Average main: €25* ⊠ *Carrèr Sarriulèra 26, Vielha* 🕾 *973/641718* ⊕ *www.hotelelmoli.es/en* ⊗ *Closed Wed.*

### ★ Era Coquèla

$$ | CATALAN | FAMILY | On a bank overlooking the Garonne, the white-tablecloth, tile-floor Era Coquèla is a Vielha institution, beloved by local families, repeat vacationers, and even truck drivers passing through town. Roast meats, civets (wine-and-game stews), and seasonal vegetable dishes are native-son chef Marc Nus's strongest suits—all are served by an enthusiastic and knowledgeable staff. **Known for:** well-priced set menus at lunch and dinner; removed from the tourist bustle; local favorite. ⑤ *Average main: €22* ⊠ *Avenguda Garona 29, Vielha* 🕾 *97/3642915* ⊕ *www.eracoquela.com* ⊗ *Closed Mon. No dinner Sun.*

## 🛏 Hotels

### Hotel El Ciervo

$ | HOTEL | In the old quarter, this family-run inn is unabashedly kitsch with tinsel, twinkly lights, and tchotchkes everywhere you look. **Pros:** cozy and inviting; amiable and knowledgeable owner; free daily guided hikes. **Cons:** "famous" multicourse breakfasts are underwhelming; books up months in advance; schlocky, gaudy budget furnishings. ⑤ *Rooms from: €99* ⊠ *Pl. de San Orencio 3, Vielha* 🕾 *973/640165* ⊕ *www.hotelelciervo.net* ⊗ *Closed Apr.–mid-June and last 2 wks Oct. and Nov.* ➪ *20 rooms* ⦿| *No Meals.*

## 🍸 Nightlife

### DeVins

WINE BARS | This popular wine bar (open evenings only) has a prime location overlooking the river and is known for its tapas, cheese boards, and wine. As the night wears on, locals pile in for well-made gin and tonics. ⊠ *Carrèr Major 23, Vielha* 🕾 *647/511146.*

### Saxo Blu

PUBS | Open until past 2 nightly, this good-vibes-only pub is the closest thing you'll find to a nightclub in this part of the Pyrenees. ⊠ *Carrèr Marrec 6, Vielha* 🕾 *97/3640972.*

# Santa Maria de Montgarri

Partly in ruins, this 11th-century chapel was once an important way station on the route into the Val d'Aran from France. The beveled hexagonal bell tower and the rounded stones, which look as if they came from a brook bottom, give the structure a curious stippled appearance. The Romería de Nuestra Señora de Montgarri (Feast of Our Lady of Montgarri), on July 2, is a country fair with food, games, music, and dance. The sanctuary can be reached by following the C142 road until Beret and then walking or off-roading 6 km (4 miles) along a dirt track. It is difficult to get there during the winter snow season.

## 🛍 Shopping

### ★ Eth Galin Reiau

**FOOD** | On the same square as the church, this shop has its own line of gourmet products ranging from locally produced pâté de foie gras and cheese to small-batch Val d'Aran cassis, marmalades, and honey. ⊠ Pl. de la Gleisa 2, Vielha ☎ 973/641941 ⊕ www.tiendagalinreiau.com ⊗ Closed Sun.

## 🏃 Activities

Skiing, white-water rafting, hiking, climbing, horseback riding, and fly-fishing are a few of the sports available in the Val d'Aran. There are terrific walks through the wooded valleys of the Río Garona, and mountain climbers can relish steep, well-marked hikes up the surrounding peaks: Maubermé (9,450 feet), Besiberri Nord (9,885 feet), and Tuc de Molières (9,873 feet).

### SKIING

### ★ Baqueira-Beret (Baqueira-Beret Ski Station)

**SKIING & SNOWBOARDING** | **FAMILY** | This ski center offers Catalonia's most varied and reliable skiing. Its 87 km (54 miles) of *pistes* (slopes), spread over 53 runs, range from the gentle Beret slopes to the vertical chutes of Baqueira. The Bonaigua area is a mixture of steep and gently undulating trails, with some of the longest, most varied runs in the Pyrenees. A dozen or so restaurants and four children's areas are scattered about the facilities, and the thermal baths at Tredós are 4 km (2½ miles) away. ☎ 973/639025 ⊕ www.baqueira.es 🎟 From €55.

# Arties

*7 km (4 miles) east of Vielha, 3½ km (2 miles) west of Salardú.*

Arties is a lively village with Romanesque, Gothic, and Renaissance architecture that straddles a clear river presided over by Montarto Peak.

### GETTING HERE AND AROUND

The C28 east out of Vielha reaches Arties in 7 km (4 miles). The village is small and best explored on foot. Cross the bridge over the river to hit the main square.

## 🍴 Restaurants

### Tauèrna Urtau Arties

**$$** | **TAPAS** | **FAMILY** | The area's beloved tapas chain is friendly, fun, and always busy with customers helping themselves to some 40 mouthwatering types of *pinchos* (dainty bar-side tapas ranging from mini hamburgers to fried king prawns to sautéed mushrooms). You can also have larger portions in the sit-down dining area. **Known for:** rollicking atmosphere; cider and local products; crowd-pleasing Basque dishes. ⑤ *Average main: €16* ✉ *Pl. Urtau 12, Arties* ☎ *973/640926* ⊕ *www.urtau.com* ⊘ *Closed Wed.*

## 🛏 Hotels

### ★ Casa Irene
**$$$ | B&B/INN |** Casa Irene exudes old-fashioned coziness with wood-beamed ceilings and plush armchairs, plus modern amenities. **Pros:** individualized attention; free shuttle to the slopes; understated yet tasteful decor. **Cons:** often booked up; dated decor; street-facing rooms can be noisy on summer nights. ⑤ *Rooms from: €180* ✉ *Carrer Major 22, Arties* ☎ *973/644364* ⊕ *www.hotelcasairene.com* ⊘ *Closed May, June, Oct., and Nov.* 🛏 *22 rooms* ⦿ *Free Breakfast.*

### Parador de Arties
**$$ | HOTEL |** Once the house of Gaspar de Portolà, the military officer who colonized California, this modern parador with friendly staff and an outdoor pool (seasonal) has views of the Pyrenees and is handy for exploring the Romanesque sights in nearby villages. **Pros:** panoramas from cozy public areas; free parking; quiet and personal for a parador. **Cons:** in need of renovation; requires driving; cold pool. ⑤ *Rooms from: €103* ✉ *Calle San Juan 1, Artiés* ☎ *973/640801* ⊕ *www.parador.es* ⊘ *Closed 40 days after Easter wk (dates vary)* 🛏 *54 rooms, 3 suites* ⦿ *No Meals.*

# Salardú

*9 km (6 miles) east of Vielha.*

Salardú is not only one of the most charming villages in the Pyrenees—it's also a key crossroads in the Val d'Aran,

convenient to Baqueira-Beret; Montarto Peak, Parc Nacional d'Aigüestortes (specifically the lakes and Tredòs baths at Circ de Colomèrs), and the wonderfully scenic hamlets of Unha, Bagergue, and Montgarri. The town itself, with some 700 inhabitants, is known for its steep streets and octagonal fortified bell tower.

**GETTING HERE AND AROUND**
The C28 east out of Vielha goes straight to Salardú and Tredós in 9 km (6 miles) and on to Baqueira-Beret in 13 km (8 miles). Most visitors ditch their car at the public parking lot in the center of town; the area is easily explored on foot.

## 🍴 Restaurants

### ★ Casa Rufus
**$$$ | SPANISH |** Pine walls and floors, red-and-white-check curtains, and flowy white tablecloths furnish this stuck-in-time restaurant in the gray-stone village of Gessa, between Vielha and Salardú. Try the rabbit stuffed with veal and pork, or call ahead to order an off-menu civet of mountain goat or venison. **Known for:** good stop-off on way to or from the Baqueira ski slopes; wide selection of local meat dishes; one of the best restaurants in the area. ⑤ *Average main: €23* ✉ *Carrer Sant Jaume 8, Gessa* ☎ *973/645246* ⊘ *Closed Tues.*

## 🛏 Hotels

### Hotel Val de Ruda
**$$$ | HOTEL |** For rustic surroundings—light on luxury but long on comfort—only a two-minute walk from the ski lift, this modern-traditional construction of glass, wood, and stone is a good choice. **Pros:** pleasant and outdoorsy; friendly-family service; terrific breakfasts. **Cons:** so-so soundproofing; open only during ski season; some upstairs rooms are cozy but tiny. ⑤ *Rooms from: €155* ✉ *Ctra. Baqueira-Beret Cota 1500, Salardú*

🛏 *073/045258* 🌐 *www.hotelvalderudab-aqueira.com* ☺ *Closed after Easter wk–Nov.* �']'" *35 rooms* 🍴 *Free Breakfast.*

# Zaragoza

*138 km (86 miles) west of Lleida, 307 km (191 miles) northwest of Barcelona, 164 km (102 miles) southeast of Pamplona, 322 km (200 miles) northeast of Madrid.*

Despite its sizable population of around 650,000, this sprawling provincial capital midway between Barcelona, Madrid, Bilbao, and Valencia retains a laid-back feel. It is a worthwhile detour from the tourist track yet still accessible via the AVE, Spain's high-speed railroad, with both Madrid and Barcelona only 90 minutes away.

The first decade of this century were major boom years here, and it's been rated one of Spain's most desirable places to live because of its air quality, affordability, and low population density. There are also a number of well-kept museums; most are free.

Straddling the Ebro, Zaragoza (pronounced tha-ra-GO-tha) was originally named Caesaraugusta after Roman emperor Augustus. It was a thriving river port by 25 BC, and its rich history is exemplified in its Roman ruins, Jewish baths, and umpteen architectural styles: Moorish, Romanesque, Gothic-Mudejar, Renaissance, baroque, neoclassical, Art Nouveau, and more. Parts of the **Roman walls** are visible near the city's landmark **Basílica de Nuestra Señora del Pilar.** Nearby, the medieval **Puente de Piedra** (Stone Bridge) spans the Ebro. Key sights include the **Lonja** (Stock Exchange), **La Seo cathedral,** the Moorish **Aljafería** (Fortified Palace and Jewel Treasury), **Mercado de Lanuza** (Produce Market), and many **Mudejar churches** in the old town.

Worthwhile excursions from Zaragoza include Goya's birthplace in **Fuendetodos,** 44 km (27 miles) to the southeast, and **Monasterio de Piedra,** an hour's drive southwest. Founded in 1195 by Alfonso II of Aragón, this lush oasis of caves, waterfalls, and suspended walkways surrounds a 12th-century Cistercian monastery and a 16th-century Renaissance section that is now a hotel (🌐 *www.monasteriopiedra.com*).

## GETTING HERE AND AROUND

Several trains per day link Zaragoza and Barcelona, Lleida, and Huesca (🌐 *www.renfe.com*). Buses link Zaragoza, Huesca, and Jaca (🌐 *aragon.avanzagrupo.com*). By car, travel west from Barcelona on the E90 motorway. Zaragoza's sights are accessible on foot.

**BUS STATION Estación Central de Autobuses.** ✉ *Calle Miguel Roca i Junyent 7, Zaragoza* ☎ *976/700599* 🌐 *www.estacion-zaragoza.es.*

## VISITOR INFORMATION

**CONTACTS Zaragoza Tourist Office.** ✉ *Pl. Nuestra Señora del Pilar, Zaragoza* ☎ *902/142008* 🌐 *www.zaragoza.es/turismo.*

## ◉ Sights

★ **Catedral–Basílica de Nuestra Señora del Pilar** (*Basilica of Our Lady of the Pillar*)
**CHURCH** | This basilica on the banks of the Ebro, often shortened to La Pilarica or El Pilar, is Zaragoza's symbol and pride. An immense baroque structure with 11 vivid tile-topped cupolas, La Pilarica is home to the Virgen del Pilar, patron saint of peninsular Spain and the entire Hispanic world. The fiestas honoring this most Spanish of saints, held in mid-October, are ushered in with processions, street concerts, bullfights, and traditional *jota* dancing. Among the basilica's treasures are two frescoes by Goya—one of them,

*El Coreto de la Vírgen,* painted when he was young, and the other, *Regina Martium,* after his studies in Italy. The bombs displayed to the right of the altar of La Pilarica chapel fell through the roof of the church in 1936 and miraculously failed to explode. Behind La Pilarica's altar is the tiny opening where the devout line up to kiss the rough marble pillar where La Pilarica is said to have been discovered. ✉ *Pl. del Pilar, Zaragoza* ⊕ *www.catedraldezaragoza.es/basilica* 🎫 *€9 (includes both cathedrals, museums, and bell tower)* ⊙ *Museum closed Sun. Tower closed Mon. in winter.*

### Catedral del Salvador de Zaragoza (La Seo)
*(Catedral de San Salvador)*
CHURCH | Zaragoza's main cathedral, at the eastern end of Plaza del Pilar, is the city's bishopric, or diocesan *seo* (seat). It was built in many architectural styles: Mudejar (brick-and-tile exterior), Gothic (altarpiece), churrigueresque (doorways), and baroque (facade). The Museo de Tapices within contains medieval tapestries. The nearby medieval Casa y Arco del Deán form one of the city's favorite corners. ✉ *Pl. de la Seo 4, Zaragoza* ☎ *976/291231* ⊕ *www.catedraldezarago-za.es/la-seo-catedral-del-salvador* 🎫 *€9 (includes both cathedrals, museums, and bell tower).*

### EMOZ (Escuela Museo Origami Zaragoza)
ART MUSEUM | FAMILY | Within Zaragoza's Centro de Historias, EMOZ houses one of the finest collections of origami in the world. These eye-popping exhibitions change themes seasonally and reveal the surprising story of Zaragoza's historical connection to the art of paper-folding. ✉ *Centro de Historias, Pl. San Agustín 2, Zaragoza* ☎ *876/034569* ⊕ *www.emoz.es* 🎫 *€3* ⊙ *Closed Mon.*

### IAACC Pablo Serrano
ART MUSEUM | A collection of works by 20th-century sculptor Pablo Serrano (1908–85) and his wife, Juana

Francés, are on display in this museum. ✉ *Paseo María Agustín 20, Zaragoza* ☎ *976/280659* ⊕ *www.iaacc.es* 🎫 *Free* ⊙ *Closed Mon.*

### Iglesia de San Pablo
CHURCH | After the basilica and La Seo, this church, with intricate Mudejar brickwork, is considered by Zaragozanos to be the "third cathedral." ✉ *Carrer San Pablo 42, Zaragoza* ☎ *976/446296* ⊕ *www.san-pablozaragoza.org* 🎫 *Free* ⊙ *Closed Sun.*

### Museo de Zaragoza
ART MUSEUM | This museum contains a treasure trove of works by Zaragoza's emblematic painter, Goya, including his portraits of Fernando VII and his best graphic works: *Desastres de la Guerra, Caprichos,* and *La Tauromaquia.* ✉ *Pl. de los Sitios 6, Zaragoza* ☎ *976/222181* ⊕ *www.museodezaragoza.es* 🎫 *Free* ⊙ *Closed Mon.*

### Museo del Foro de Caesaraugusta
RUINS | FAMILY | Remains of the Roman forum and elaborate sewage system can be seen here. Two more Roman sites, the thermal baths at Calle de San Juan y San Pedro and the river port at Plaza San Bruno, are also open to the public. You can organize in advance to see the presentation videos in English through the Museo del Teatro Romano (☎976/726075). English-language audio guides are also available. ✉ *Pl. de la Seo 2, Zaragoza* ☎ *976/721221* ⊕ *www. zaragoza.es/ciudad/museos/es/foro* 🎫 *€4* ⊙ *Closed Mon.*

### Museo del Teatro de Caesaraugusta
RUINS | In addition to the restored Roman amphitheater, built in the 1st century AD, you can see objects recovered in the excavation including theatrical masks, platters, and even hairpins. ✉ *Calle San Jorge 12, Zaragoza* ☎ *976/726075* ⊕ *www.zaragoza.es/ciudad/museos/es/teatro* 🎫 *€7* ⊙ *Closed Mon.*

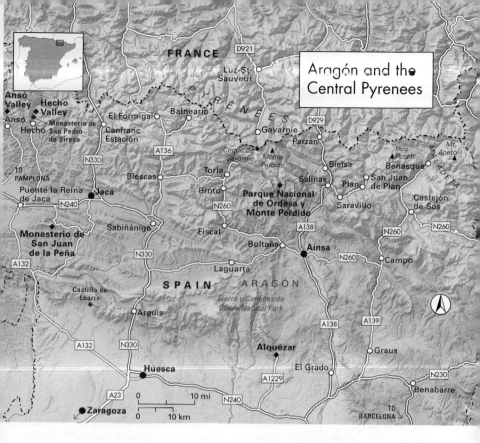

Map showing France, the Pyrenees, Spain, and Aragón with towns including Ansó, Hecho, Jaca, Huesca, Zaragoza, Aínsa, Benasque, and various roads and natural parks.

## Museo Goya Colección Ibercaja

**ART MUSEUM** | A small but mighty collection of Goya's works, particularly engravings, are on view here. QR codes are convenient stand-ins for English-language placards. ⊠ *Carrer Espoz y Mina 23, Zaragoza* ☎ *976/397387* ⊕ *museogoya. ibercaja.es* 🎟 *€6.*

## ★ Museo Pablo Gargallo

**ART MUSEUM** | This is one of Zaragoza's sightseeing treasures, both for the palace in which it is housed and for its collection: Gargallo, born near Zaragoza in 1881, was one of Spain's greatest modern sculptors. ⊠ *Pl. de San Felipe 3, Zaragoza* ☎ *976/724922* ⊕ *www.zaragoza.es/ciudad/museos/es/gargallo* 🎟 *€4* ⊘ *Closed Mon.*

## Palacio de La Aljafería

**CASTLE/PALACE** | This is one of Spain's three best-preserved Moorish palaces. If Córdoba's Mezquita shows the energy of the 10th-century Caliphate and Granada's Alhambra is the crowning 14th-century glory of al-Andalus (the 789-year Moorish empire on the Iberian Peninsula), then the late-11th-century Aljafería is the middle child. Originally a fortress and royal residence, and later a seat of the Spanish Inquisition, the Aljafería is now the home of the Cortes (Parliament) de Aragón. The 9th-century Torre del Trovador (Tower of the Troubadour) appears in Giuseppe Verdi's opera Il Trovatore. Visits by online reservation only. ⊠ *Diputados, Zaragoza* ☎ *976/289528* ⊕ *reservasonline.aljaferia. com* 🎟 *€5* ⊘ *Closed Thurs., and Fri. if parliament is in session.*

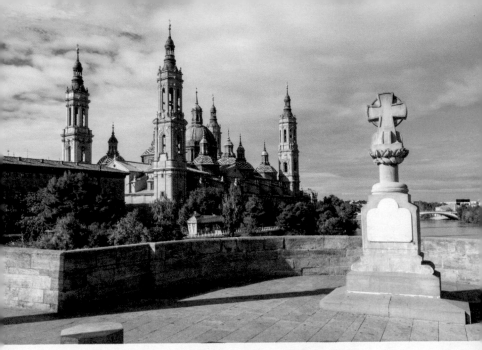

Overlooking the Río Ebro and Zaragoza's Basílica de Nuestra Señora del Pilar

# 🍴 Restaurants

### ★ El Tubo Neighborhood

$$ | SPANISH | El Tubo, the area surrounding the intersection of Calle Estébanes and Calle Libertad, is tapas central. Try to stick to one tapa per bar so you can sample as many spots as possible. **Known for:** packed pedestrianized streets; lively atmosphere; variety of tapas bars. ⑤ *Average main: €15* ⊠ *Calle Estébanes, Zaragoza.*

### Los Victorinos

$$ | TAPAS | Named after a much-feared and respected breed of fighting bull, this rustic tavern, located behind La Seo, is dripping with taurine paraphernalia. It offers an elaborate and inventive selection of pinchos and tapas. **Known for:** lively old-school atmosphere; zippy one-bite gildas (pickled brochettes); melt-on-your-tongue Iberian ham. ⑤ *Average main: €17* ⊠ *Calle José de la Hera 6, Zaragoza* ☎ *976/394213* ⊙ *Closed Mon.–Wed., No dinner Sun.*

### ★ Palomeque

$$$ | TAPAS | For upscale tapas, sharable *raciones*, and a more sedate atmosphere, step into Palomeque. Dishes hinge on market produce and fuse traditional recipes with playful modern plating. **Known for:** hidden gem; charmingly dated decor; dishes with local produce and meats. ⑤ *Average main: €26* ⊠ *Calle Agustín Palomeque 11, Zaragoza* ☎ *976/214082* ⊕ *www.restaurantepalomeque.es* ⊙ *Closed Sun. No dinner Sat.*

### Tragantúa

$$ | SPANISH | This rollicking wood-paneled dining room serves surprisingly sublime seafood, cooked *a la plancha* (on the griddle), *al horno* (in the oven), or folded into a variety of rice dishes. The beer is fresh and cold, and the house wines, largely from Upper Aragón's envelope-pushing Somontano D.O., are big and bold—and dangerously economical. **Known for:** comfy dining room; seafood so fresh you might as well be on the coast; excellent house wines. ⑤ *Average main: €21* ⊠ *Pl.*

Santa Marta, Zaragoza ☎ 976/299174
⊕ www.grupoloscabezudos.es ⊙ Closed
last 2 wks in June and 2nd wk in Jan.

## 🛏 Hotels

### ★ Hotel Sauce
$ | HOTEL | Hotel Sauce might be the
perfect budget hotel—it has quirky wall
art, midcentury modern furniture, bright
and uncluttered rooms, and a location
that can't be beat. **Pros:** central location;
excellent value; modern facilities and
café on-site. **Cons:** not many rooms;
rooms are too small for long stays; reception service can be erratic. $ Rooms
from: €74 ⊠ Espoz y Mina 33, Zaragoza
☎ 976/205050 ⊕ www.hotelsauce.com
⤳ 40 rooms ⊙ No Meals.

### Hotel Palafox Zaragoza
$$ | HOTEL | One of Zaragoza's top
hotels, Palafox combines contemporary
design with traditional urban service
and elegance. **Pros:** top comfort and
service; good restaurant; private parking
for guests. **Cons:** decor could use a
revamp; rooms not as impressive as
the public spaces; modern and some-
what antiseptic. $ Rooms from: €132
⊠ Calle Marqués Casa Jiménez, Zaragoza
☎ 976/237700 ⊕ www.palafoxhoteles.
com ⤳ 179 rooms ⊙ Free Breakfast.

# Huesca

68 km (42 miles) northeast of Zaragoza,
123 km (76 miles) northwest of Lleida.

Huesca has been a Roman colony, Moor-
ish stronghold, and capital of Aragón
(until the royal court moved to Zaragoza
in 1118). A quiet little urban center today,
it was so constantly embattled over the
centuries that the Spanish expression
"It's ringing like Huesca's bell" means
that something bad is about to happen.

The town's university was founded in
1354 and has a rigorous Aragonese stud-
ies department.

## GETTING HERE AND AROUND
From Zaragoza there are several trains
each day (⊕ www.renfe.com). Avanza
(⊕ www.avanzabus.com) runs buses
between Huesca and Zaragoza, Lleida,
and Jaca. By car from Zaragoza, head
northwest toward Huesca on the A23.
The center is small and walkable.

**CONTACTS Bus Station.** ⊠ Calle José Gil
Cávez 10, Huesca.

## VISITOR INFORMATION
**CONTACTS Huesca Tourist Office.** ⊠ Pl.
Luis López Allué, Huesca ☎ 974/292170
⊕ www.huescaturismo.com.

## ◉ Sights

### Huesca Cathedral
CHURCH | An intricately carved gallery tops
the eroded facade of Huesca's 13th-cen-
tury Gothic cathedral. Damián Forment, a
protégé of the 15th-century Italian master
sculptor Donatello, created the alabaster
altarpiece, which dates to 1533 and has
scenes from the Crucifixion. ⊠ Pl. de la
Catedral, Huesca ☎ 974/231099 ⊠ €4
⊙ Museum closed Sun.

### Museo de Huesca
HISTORY MUSEUM | This museum occu-
pies parts of the former royal palace of
the kings of Aragón and holds paintings
by Aragonese primitives, including La
Virgen del Rosario by Miguel Jiménez,
and several works by the 16th-century
Maestro de Sigena. The eight chambers,
set around an octagonal patio, include
the Sala de la Campana (Hall of the Bell),
where beheadings of errant nobles took
place. In 2022, the gallery dedicated to
Visigothic artifacts reopened with new
displays after lengthy renovations. ⊠ Pl.
de la Universidad, Huesca ☎ 974/220586
⊕ www.museodehuesca.es ⊠ Free
⊙ Closed Mon.

### San Pedro el Viejo

CHURCH | This Benedictine abbey has an 11th-century cloister. Ramiro II and his father, Alfonso I, the only Aragonese kings not entombed at San Juan de la Peña, rest in a side chapel. ⊠ *Pl. de San Pedro, Huesca* ⊕ *www.sanpedroelviejo. com* 🎫 *€4.*

 Restaurants

#### ★ Las Torres

$$$ | SPANISH | Huesca's top restaurant makes inventive use of local ingredients like wild mushrooms, wild boar, venison, and lamb. The glass-walled kitchen is as inviting as the food that emerges from it, and the wine list is strong on Somontano, Huesca's own D.O. **Known for:** excellent value; terrific tasting menus; Aragonese with a modern twist. Ⓢ *Average main: €25* ⊠ *Calle María Auxiliadora 3, Huesca* ☎ *974/228213* ⊕ *www. lastorres-restaurante.com* ☾ *No dinner Sun.–Tues. Closed 2 wks over Easter and last 2 wks of Aug.*

 Hotels

#### Abba Huesca

$$ | HOTEL | This modern hotel has quiet, minimalist rooms and a busy downstairs bar where guests and locals mingle. **Pros:** excellent value; on-site bar, restaurant, and outdoor pool; understated elegance. **Cons:** decor lacks pizzazz; unattractive neighborhood; not in the center. Ⓢ *Rooms from: €110* ⊠ *Calle de Tarbes 14, Huesca* ☎ *974/292900* ⊕ *www. abbahuescahotel.com* ⇝ *84 rooms* ⊙❘ *No Meals.*

#### Hostal San Marcos

$ | B&B/INN | FAMILY | In this 19th-century building that's now a budget hotel, guest rooms are snug and simple, with pine furniture, tile floors, and spotless bathrooms. **Pros:** central location; a steal; historic and elegant building. **Cons:** street noise; hodgepodge of patterns

everywhere; rooms feel cramped. Ⓢ *Rooms from: €60* ⊠ *Calle San Orencio 10, Huesca* ☎ *974/222931* ⊕ *www. hostalsanmarcos.es* ⇝ *29 rooms* ⊙❘ *Free Breakfast.*

## Castillo de Loarre 👁

This walled 11th-century monastery, 36 km (22 miles) west of Huesca off Route A132 on A1206, is nearly indistinguishable from the rock outcroppings that surround it. Inside the walls are a church, a tower, a dungeon, and even a medieval toilet. The complex—which many call the best-preserved Romanesque castle in Europe—affords views of almond and olive groves in the Ebro basin. ⊕ *www. castillodeloarre.es*

## 🛍 Shopping

#### Ultramarinos La Confianza

FOOD | Founded in 1871, La Confianza may be the oldest grocery store in Spain. It's in the porticoed Plaza Mayor in the old town and worth popping into to see the tiled floors and hand-painted ceiling, and to browse the shelves stacked high with local products, from dried fruit and nuts to specialty chocolates and salt cod. ⊠ *Pl. Mayor (Pl. López Allué), Huesca* ☎ *974/222632* ⊕ *www.ultramarinoslaconfianza.com* ☾ *Closed Sun.*

## Alquézar

*51 km (32 miles) northeast of Huesca, 123 km (76 miles) northeast of Zaragoza.*

As though carved from the ocher rock itself, Alquézar looms over the Parque Natural Sierra y Cañones de Guara and is

Mountain trekking in the Huesca province

one of Spain's prettiest towns. Its maze of winding cobbled streets and low archways coil around a central square, which stands out for its oblong shape and porched area that was built to provide shelter from the sun and rain. Look up as you walk—many facades bear coats of arms that date to the 16th century.

## GETTING HERE AND AROUND

From Huesca, take the A22 or N240 east for 29 km (18 miles) before merging onto the A1229 toward Alquézar. Cars cannot enter the old quarter, so the only way to see the town is on foot.

## VISITOR INFORMATION

**CONTACTS Alquézar Tourist Office.** ✉ Calle Arrabal 14, Alquézar ☎ 974/318940 ⊕ www.alquezar.es.

 **Sights**

### Bodegas Lalanne

**WINERY** | A 20-minute drive south of Alquézar drops you at this family-run wine estate that's been in business for over a century. Plan to spend about two hours here between the winery tour and tasting, in which you'll sample bold New World–style wines—Gewürztraminer, Cabernet Sauvignon, etc.—that are a hallmark of the Somontano D.O. Be sure to call ahead or book online. ✉ Ctra. A1232, Km 3.8, Alquézar ☎ 974/310689 ⊕ www. bodegaslalanne.eu ☞ From €36.

### Colegiata de Santa María la Mayor

**CHURCH** | The Colegiata, originally a 9th-century Moorish alcázar (citadel) for which the town is named, was conquered by the Christians in 1067. An interesting mix of Gothic, Mudejar, and Renaissance details are found in the shaded cloister, and there are biblical murals that date to the Romanesque era. The church, built in the 16th century, contains an almost life-size Romanesque figure of Christ, but restoration has taken away some of the building's charm—its interior brickwork is now only a painted representation. Visits are conducted via guided tour (Spanish only) and usually depart every 30 minutes. ⊠ *Diseminado Afueras, off Calle la Iglesia, Alquézar* ☎ *974/318940* ⊕ *www.patrimoniocul-turaldearagon.es/bienes-culturales/colegiata-de-santa-maria-alquezar* ⊠ *€3* ⊗ *Closed Jan. 6–Feb. 7.*

### Parque Cultural del Río Vero

**RUINS** | **FAMILY** | A UNESCO World Heritage Site, this park within the Sierra de Guara contains more than 60 limestone caves with prehistoric paintings. Some date to around 22,000 BC, though most are from between 12,000 and 4,000 BC. Information, guided tours, and kid-friendly activities are available through the interpretation center in Colungo; check the monthly schedule on the home page. Hours vary, so call ahead. ⊠ *Calle Las Braules 2, Colunga* ⊕ *9½ km (6 miles) east of Alquézar* ☎ *974/306006* ⊕ *www.parqueculturalriovero.com/en* ⊠ *Free, €4 for some exhibits.*

### ★ Pasarelas de Alquézar

**TRAIL** | **FAMILY** | Take a breathtaking riverside hike (1½ hours) on the Ruta de las Pasarelas loop, which hugs near-sheer cliffs that plunge into rushing turquoise waters. There's a waterfall, a cave, and plenty of placards with information on the surrounding nature and historical buildings. Be sure to bring plenty of water and to arrive early, since parking (follow the signs) is limited. Certain stretches are on metal pathways with steep drops, so those with limited mobility or a fear of heights should skip this one. The trail starts at Plaza de Rafael Ayerbe beside the ayuntamiento (town hall). No bikes or pets are allowed. ⊠ *Pl. Rafael Ayerbe, Alquézar* ☎ *682/932809* ⊕ *www.pasarelasdealquezar.com* ⊠ *€4.*

##  Restaurants

### Casa Pardina

$$$$ | **SPANISH** | Romantic dining at a reasonable price is the main draw at this restaurant with two fixed-price menus

offering dozens of dishes to choose from. The cuisine is distinctly Aragonese with a few modern twists (think local venison stewed with dates, plums, and honey), and the wine hails from nearby Somontano. **Known for:** locally sourced ingredients and local olive oil; set menu only; outdoor dining with sweeping views. ⑤ *Average main: €39* ⊠ *Calle Medio, Alquézar* ☎ *974/318425* ⊕ *www.casapardina.com* ⊗ *Closed Mon.–Wed. No dinner Sun.*

## 🛏 Hotels

### Hotel Santa María de Alquézar

$ | **B&B/INN** | **FAMILY** | Just outside the old town walls, this hotel has the best views around—overlooking the Río Vero canyon and the Colegiata de Santa María. **Pros:** phenomenal views; relaxed ambience; bright rooms. **Cons:** parking is tricky in high season; not inside the old town; some street noise. ⑤ *Rooms from: €95* ⊠ *Calle Arrabal, Alquézar* ☎ *974/318436* ⊕ *www.hotel-santamaria.com* ⊗ *Closed Jan.–mid-Feb.* ⇆ *21 rooms* ⦿⧓ *Free Breakfast.*

## 🏃 Activities

The Sierra de Guara is the largest nature reserve in Aragón and one of Europe's best places for canyoning (descending mountain gorges, usually in or near streams and other water sources).

### Avalancha

**ADVENTURE TOURS** | **FAMILY** | Avalancha is the leading local provider for canyoning and other adventure activities and provides equipment such as wet suits and helmets. All ages and levels are welcome. ⊠ *Paseo San Hipolito, Alquézar* ☎ *974/318299* ⊕ *www.avalancha.org.*

# Aínsa

*66 km (41 miles) southwest of Benasque, 113 km (70 miles) northeast of Huesca, 214 km (133 miles) northeast of Zaragoza.*

Don't be spooked by the uninspiring new town—Aínsa is one of the most picturesque towns in the Pyrenees. In its walled medieval quarter, stone houses festooned with flowers are jammed together along narrow cobbled streets. A stroll to the top of the promontory affords sweeping views of the surrounding mountains and Parque Nacional de Odesa.

## GETTING HERE AND AROUND

Head north out of Huesca on the E7, then take the N260 for a total of 98 km (61 miles) before hopping on the A2205 for 15 km (9 miles). Aínsa can only be explored on foot once you're through the old city walls.

## VISITOR INFORMATION

**CONTACTS Aínsa Tourist Office.** ⊠ *Av. Ordesa 5, Aínsa* ☎ *974/500767* ⊕ *www. villadeainsa.com.*

##  Sights

### Castillo de Aínsa

**CASTLE/PALACE** | The citadel and castle, originally built by the Moors in the 11th century, was conquered by the Christians and reconstructed in the 16th century. Take a walk along the ramparts for the best views of the town and surrounding landscape. ⊠ *Pl. Mayor 1, Aínsa* ☎ *974/318940* ⊕ *www.patrimoniocultur-aldearagon.es/bienes-culturales/castil-lo-de-ainsa* ☜ *Free.*

### Iglesia de Santa María

**CHURCH** | This 12th-century Romanesque church, with its quadruple-vaulted door and 13th-century cloister, is in the corner of the attractive, porticoed Plaza Mayor. ⊠ *Calle Santa Cruz, Aínsa* ☜ *Free.*

## 🛏 Hotels

### ★ Hotel Casa de San Martín

**$$$ | HOTEL** | Situated on a remote and wonderfully scenic stretch of the Eje Pirenaico (Pyrenean Axis Highway), midway between medieval Aínsa and the Parque Nacional de Ordesa y Monte Perdido, is this tasteful mountaintop B&B with verdant valley views, stone-wall rooms, and standout down-home cuisine. The British owner knows the surrounding trails through pine and oak forests like the back of his hand, and you can explore many of them without leaving the property, which spans over 200 acres. **Pros:** secluded eden in the mountains; in a converted monastery; noteworthy food and local wine. **Cons:** entry via 5-km (3-mile) gravel driveway; no pool; few nearby restaurants. ⓢ *Rooms from: €170* ⊠ *Calle Única 1, Aínsa* ☎ *974/338349* ⊕ *casadesanmartin.com* ➽ *9 rooms* ⏐◯⏐ *Free Breakfast.*

### Hotel Los Arcos

**$$$ | B&B/INN** | This six-bedroom hotel on the Plaza Mayor has exposed stone walls and simple (if dated) modern furnishings; some add whirlpools and wrought-iron balconies. **Pros:** excellent service; prime location; comfortable furnishings. **Cons:** expensive for the area; no elevator or parking; street noise. ⓢ *Rooms from: €140* ⊠ *Pl. Mayor 23, Aínsa* ☎ *974/500016* ⊕ *www.hotellosarcosainsa.com* ➽ *6 rooms* ⏐◯⏐ *Free Breakfast.*

### Hotel Los Siete Reyes

**$$ | B&B/INN** | One of two boutique hotels in Aínsa's Plaza Mayor, Los Siete Reyes occupies a handsome restored mansion with ample stone-walled bedrooms overlooking the square. **Pros:** charming and atmospheric; good views of the mountain or village; central location. **Cons:** patchy Wi-Fi; dark painted walls make rooms gloomy; noise from the square. ⓢ *Rooms from: €126* ⊠ *Pl. Mayor, Aínsa* ☎ *974/500681* ⊕ *www.lossietereyes.com* ➽ *6 rooms* ⏐◯⏐ *Free Breakfast.*

## Activities

**Tirolina Ordesa Pirineo**

ZIP LINING | FAMILY | Clocking in at 2 km (1¼ miles) in length and reaching speeds of up to 160 km (100 miles) per hour, this exhilarating zip-line that opened in 2021 whooshes above the Ara river amid rugged mountain peaks. The starting point is between Aínsa and Jaca, and the experience takes under one hour from start to finish. ✉ *Ctra. de Bergua, Pardina de Asue, Aínsa ⊕ in the village of Fiscal* ☎ *72/2592362* ⊕ *www.tirolinapirineos. com* ✉ *€43.*

# Parque Nacional de Ordesa y Monte Perdido

*79 km (49 miles) west of Bielsa, 45 km (30 miles) west of Aínsa, 92 km (57 miles) north of Huesca.*

This splendid but often overlooked park in the central Pyrenees was founded by royal decree in 1918. It expanded from 4,940 to 56,810 acres when provincial and national authorities added the Monte Perdido massif, head of the Pineta Valley, and Escuain and Añisclo Canyons.

### VISITOR INFORMATION

**CONTACTS Centro de Visitantes de Torla.** ✉ *Av. Ordesa, Torla* ☎ *974/486472* ⊕ *www.turismodearagon.com/en/ficha/ ordesa-y-monte-perdido.*

## Sights

★ **Ordesa and Monte Perdido National Park**
NATIONAL PARK | FAMILY | Welcome to the wildest, most unspoiled corner of the Pyrenees. The three main valleys of this national park—Ordesa, Pineta, and Añisclo—are carved out by the Ara River and its tributaries, the Arazas. They culminate in the majestic massif of Monte Perdido, which stands at 11,000 feet on the

### En Route: Broto

**Broto** is a typical Aragonese mountain town with a notable 16th-century Gothic church. Nearby villages, such as **Oto,** have stately manor houses with classic local features: baronial entryways, conical chimneys, and wooden galleries. **Torla** is Parque Nacional de Ordesa y Monte Perdido's main entry point, with regular buses (€5 round trip) that go up to the park entrance during summer; it is a popular base for hikers.

Franco-Spanish border; it's the highest of the park's three main mountains. The remote yet worthwhile valley of Las Gargantas de Escuaín is famous for its dolmen and soaring rock walls. Throughout the park, you'll find lakes, waterfalls, high mountain meadows, and forests of pine, fir, larch, beech, and poplar. Protected wildlife includes trout, boar, chamois, lammergeier, and the *sarrio* mountain goat (*Rupicapra pyrenaica*).

Well-marked mountain trails lead to waterfalls, caves, and spectacular observation points. The standard tour, a full-day's hike (eight hours), runs from the parking area in the Pradera de Ordesa, 8 km (5 miles) northeast of Torla, up the Arazas River, past the Gradas de Soaso (Soaso Risers, a natural stairway of waterfalls) to the Cola de Caballo (Horse's Tail), a fan of falling water at the head of the Cirque de Cotatuero, a dramatic natural amphitheater. There is one refuge, Refugio Góriz, north of the Cola de Caballo. A return walk on the south side of the valley, past the Cabaña de los Cazadores (Hunters' Hut), offers a breathtaking view followed by a two-hour descent back to the parking area. ✉ *Torla*

🖃 974/486472 ⊕ www.turismodearagon.
com/en/ficha/ordesa-y-monte-perdido
🖾 Free.

## 🍴 Restaurants

### A'Borda Samper
$ | SPANISH | FAMILY | At this wood-
beamed barroom, dine on comfort-food
tapas and mains like battered zucchini,
meatballs bobbing in tomato sauce, fried
eggs with sausage, and juicy steaks.
**Known for:** genial service; house-made
desserts; affordable country cooking.
⑤ Average main: €12 ⊠ Calle Travecinal,
Torla 🕾 619/321757.

## 🛏 Hotels

### Villa de Torla
$ | B&B/INN | FAMILY | This classic mountain
refuge, with sundecks, flower-fringed
terraces, and a private dining room, rents
a variety of rooms with typical Pyrenean
details—stone floors and wood paneling and trim. **Pros:** in a postcard-perfect
Pyrenean village; terrific value; great
amenities and restaurant on-site. **Cons:**
some rooms on the small side; not all
rooms have a private bathroom; street
noise in summer. ⑤ Rooms from: €95
⊠ Pl. Aragón 1, Torla 🕾 974/486156
⊕ www.hotelvilladetorla.com ⟿ 38
rooms ⦿ Free Breakfast.

# Jaca

24 km (15 miles) southwest of Biescas,
164 km (102 miles) north of Zaragoza.

Jaca, the municipal center of upper
Aragón, is anything but sleepy with plenty of standing-room tapas bars and cafés.
Founded in 1035 as the kingdom of
Jacetania, it was an important stronghold
during the so-called Reconquest of the
Iberian Peninsula and was never overtaken by the Moors. On the first Friday
of May, the town still commemorates

the decisive battle in which a battalion of
women, their hair and jewelry flashing in
the sun, allegedly intimidated the Moorish cavalry into retreat. Avoid the industri-
al-looking outskirts and head straight to
the atmospheric old town, where there's
a splendid 11th-century cathedral and fortress and bustling restaurants and bars.

## ⊙ Sights

### Canfranc International Railway Station
TRAIN/TRAIN STATION | FAMILY | In July and
August a guided train tour departs from
the Jaca RENFE station, heading to the
valley and Canfranc's magnificent Belle
Époque train station, abandoned since
1970 and slowly falling to pieces. The
station has a bewitching history and was
used as a location in the 1965 film Doctor
Zhivago. At the time of writing, a high-
end hotel slated to open in early 2023
was being constructed on-site by the
Barceló hotel group; additionally, Spain
was in serious talks with France about
reopening the route to Pau. A nontourist
train runs year-round between Jaca and
Canfranc. Reservations are essential;
call ahead or reserve your spot online.
⊠ Estación Internacional de Canfranc,
Jaca 🕾 974/373141 ⊕ www.canfranc.es/
venta-online.php 🖾 From €4.

### Ciudadela de Jaca
MILITARY SIGHT | The massive pentagonal
Ciudadela is an impressive example of
17th-century military architecture. It has
a display of more than 35,000 military
miniatures, arranged to represent different periods of history. Check the website
to confirm hours, which vary by month.
⊠ Av. del Primer Viernes de Mayo, Jaca
🕾 974/357157 ⊕ www.ciudadeladejaca.
es 🖾 €8.

### Jaca Cathedral
CHURCH | An important stop on the
pilgrimage to Santiago de Compostela,
Jaca's 11th-century Catedral de San
Pedro has lovely carved capitals and was

The Monasterio de San Juan de la Peña near Jaca

the first French-Romanesque cathedral in Spain, paving the way for later Spanish Romanesque architecture. Inside the cathedral and near the cloisters, the Museo Diocesano has excellent Romanesque and Gothic frescoes and artifacts collected from nearby churches. ⊠ *Pl. de San Pedro 1, Jaca* ⌑ *Cathedral free, museum €6.*

##  Restaurants

### La Tasca de Ana

$ | TAPAS | One of the best tapas bars in town, La Tasca de Ana is boisterous and filled with locals. With only a handful of tables and standing room by the bar, it's not the setting for a quiet romantic dinner, but it's a fine place to kick-start the evening with local wine and tapas like *rodolfitos* (battered langoustines) and stuffed piquillo peppers. **Known for:** lively atmosphere; delectable langoustines; quick and efficient service. ⑤ *Average main: €11* ⊠ *Calle Ramiro I 3, Jaca* ☎ *974/363621* ⊕ *www.latascadeana.com*

⊘ *Closed Mon., 2 wks in May, and 2 wks in Sept. No lunch weekdays.*

## 🛏 Hotels

### Gran Hotel

$ | HOTEL | This rambling hotel—Jaca's old grande dame—has seen better days, but its central location and budget rates makes it a good base. **Pros:** quiet location; within walking distance of sights; good value. **Cons:** no frills; needs renovation; charmless for the Pyrenees. ⑤ *Rooms from: €75* ⊠ *Paseo de la Constitución 1, Jaca* ☎ *974/360900* ⊕ *www. granhoteljaca.com* ⇱ *165 rooms* ⦿ *Free Breakfast.*

### ★ Hotel Barosse

$$$ | B&B/INN | In a village on the outskirts of Jaca, this adults-only bed-and-breakfast is worth sacrificing city-center conveniences. **Pros:** peaceful rural setting; friendly service; boutique-style accommodations. **Cons:** not suited to families with kids; not in the center

of Jaca; a car is necessary. $ *Rooms from: €148 ⊠ Calle de Estirás 4, Jaca ☎ 974/360582, 638/845992 ⊕ www. barosse.com ⊘ Closed Nov. ⇆ 5 rooms ¡○¡ Free Breakfast.*

### Hotel Rural El Mirador de los Pirineos
$$ | **B&B/INN** | On the way to the Monasterio de San Juan de la Peña, 10 km (6 miles) from Jaca, this tranquil, homey hotel has a spa and pool, making it a pleasant retreat. **Pros:** a peaceful and charming alternative to urban Jaca; perfect for R&R; idyllic setting. **Cons:** not luxurious; staff not always on hand; only two restaurants nearby. $ *Rooms from: €113 ⊠ Calle Ordana 8, Santa Cruz de la Serós ☎ 974/355593, 609/470 231 reservations ⊕ www.elmiradordelospirineos. com ⊘ Closed around Easter and 2 wks in Nov. ⇆ 7 rooms ¡○¡ Free Breakfast.*

### ★ Posada Naturista
$ | | **FAMILY** | Hit the reset button at this secluded, rustic retreat in an abandoned village deep in the mountains above Jaca that's the passion project of an Argentine back-to-the-land couple. **Pros:** stunning surroundings with scant light pollution; nourishing and flavorful food; sense of camaraderie among guests. **Cons:** noise from other rooms; shared bathrooms; miles from the nearest restaurant. $ *Rooms from: €55 ⊠ Calle Única, Jaca ✢ in Lastiesas Altas ☎ 97/4348087 ⊕ www.posadalastiesasaltas.es ⊘ Closed Nov.–Easter wk ¡○¡ All-Inclusive.*

## ▼ Nightlife

Jaca's music bars are concentrated in the *casco antiguo* (old town), on Calle Ramiro I, and along Calle Gil Bergés and Calle Bellido. In the porticoed Plaza de la Catedral, there are a number of bars with terraces, in the shade of the cathedral, to be enjoyed day or evening.

### Bar Casa Fau
**CAFÉS** | This busy bar with front-row seats to the cathedral serves coffee and soft drinks, a good selection of wine by the glass, and beer on tap—all of which can be accompanied by tapas and light snacks starting at 11 am. ⊠ *Pl. de la Catedral 3, Jaca ☎ 974/361594.*

## ⬤ Shopping

### Bodegas Langa
**WINE/SPIRITS** | This fifth-generation bar-meets-*bodega* (wine shop) stocks traditional wines and local products, but the tapas are internationally inflected and artfully plated, a testament to the young owner's training at the Basque Culinary Institute. ⊠ *Pl. San Pedro 5, Jaca ☎ 974/360494 ⊕ www.bodegaslanga.es.*

## 🏃 Activities

### Ski areas
**SKIING & SNOWBOARDING** | On the road to Somport and the French border, the ski areas of Candanchú and Astún are 32 km (20 miles) north of Jaca. ⊠ *Jaca ⊕ www. astun.com.*

# Monasterio de San Juan de la Peña

*23 km (14 miles) southwest of Jaca, 185 km (115 miles) north of Zaragoza, 90 km (56 miles) east of Pamplona.*

South of the Aragonese valleys of Hecho and Ansó is the Monastery of San Juan de la Peña, a site connected to the legend of the Holy Grail and one of the centers of Christian resistance during the 700-year Islamic reign of the Iberian Peninsula.

## GETTING HERE AND AROUND

From Jaca, drive 11 km (7 miles) west on the N240 toward Pamplona to a left turn clearly signposted for San Juan de la Peña. From there it's another 11 km (7 miles) on the A1603 to the monastery. Be prepared for switchbacks and tight turns. Parking is near the "new" redbrick monastery; buy tickets inside that building and catch a shuttle bus to the original, more important, monastery beneath the boulder.

## ◉ Sights

### ★ Monasterio de San Juan de la Peña

CHURCH | The origins of this cliffside sanctuary can be traced to the 9th century, when a hermit monk named Juan settled here on the *peña* (cliff). A monastery was founded on the spot in 920, and in 1071, Sancho Ramírez, son of King Ramiro I, made use of the structure, which was built into the mountain's rock wall, to found this Benedictine monastery. The highlight is the cloister, which is tucked under the cliff and dates to the 12th century. Partially in ruin, it contains intricately carved capitals depicting zoomorphic and biblical scenes of Paradise. The church of the new monastery contains the Kingdom of Aragon Interpretation Centre, where audio guides in English are available. ⊠ *Jaca ⊹ Off N240 on A1603* ☎ *974/355119* ⊕ *www.monasteriosan-juan.com* ⌨ *€12.*

# Hecho and Ansó Valleys

*The Hecho Valley is 49 km (30 miles) northwest of Jaca. The Ansó Valley is 25 km (15 miles) west of Hecho, 118 km (73 miles) east of Pamplona.*

The Ansó Valley is Aragón's western limit. Rich in fauna (mountain goats, wild boar, and even a bear or two), it follows the Veral River up to Zuriza. Towering over the head of the valley is Navarra's

## En Route ◉

From Ansó, head west to Roncal on the sinuous but panoramic 17-km (11-mile) road through the San Miguel highlands. To enjoy this route fully, count on taking a good 45 minutes to reach the Esca River and the Roncal Valley.

highest point, the 7,989-foot **Mesa de los Tres Reyes** (Plateau of the Three Kings), named not for the Magi but for the kings of Aragón, Navarra, and Castile, whose 11th-century kingdoms bordered one another here, allowing them to meet without leaving their respective realms. The **Selva de Oza** (Oza Forest), at the head of the Hecho Valley, is above the **Boca del Infierno** (Mouth of Hell), a tight draw that road and river barely squeeze through.

It's worth stopping at the pretty villages of **Ansó** and **Hecho,** where well-preserved stone houses bunch together along narrow cobbled streets overlooking the valley. In Ansó, on the last Sunday in August, residents don traditional medieval costumes and perform ancestral dances.

## GETTING HERE AND AROUND

You can reach the Hecho Valley from Jaca by heading west on the N240 and then north on the A176.

## VISITOR INFORMATION

CONTACTS **Hecho Tourist Office.** ⊠ *Paseo Ctra. de Oza 38, Hecho* ☎ *974/375505* ⊕ *www.valledehecho.es.*

## ◉ Sights

### Monasterio de San Pedro de Siresa (*Abbey of San Pedro de Siresa*)

CHURCH | The area's most important monument, the 9th-century retreat of Monasterio de San Pedro de Siresa presides

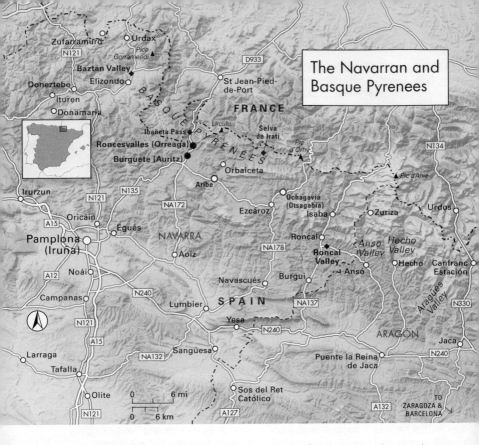

over the village of Siresa, 2 km (1 mile) north of Hecho. Only the 11th-century church remains, but it is a marvelous example of Romanesque architecture. Cheso, a medieval Aragonese dialect descended from the Latin spoken by the Siresa monks, is thought to be the closest to Latin of all Romance languages and dialects. It has been kept alive in the Hecho Valley, especially in the works of local poet Veremundo Méndez Coarasa. ✉ Calle San Pedro, Siresa ☎ 62/907–8513 🎫 €3 ⊙ Closed Mon.

## 🛏 Hotels

### Casa Blasquico

$ | **B&B/INN** | **FAMILY** | This pleasantly kitsch inn with bright painted walls is a typical mountain chalet with flower-draped balconies and a plethora of memorabilia on display. **Pros:** two cute dormered rooms; friendly service; fine mountain cuisine. **Cons:** no elevator; public rooms cluttered; rooms lack space. ⑤ Rooms from: €60 ✉ Pl. la Fuente 1, Hecho ☎ 974/375007, 657/892128 ⊕ www.casablasquico. es ⊙ Closed weekdays Nov.–Mar. 🛏 6 rooms ⑩ Free Breakfast.

### Hotel de Montaña Usón

$ | **B&B/INN** | For an eco-friendly (solar-powered) base for exploring the upper Hecho Valley or the Oza Forest, look no further than this adorable Pyrenean inn situated 7 km (4 miles) north of Hecho. **Pros:** friendly service; stunning views into the mountains; great value for the area. **Cons:** reception closes at 10 pm; remote setting; no elevator. ⑤ Rooms from: €65 ✉ Ctra. Selva de Oza (HU2131), Km 7, Usón ✛ From Hecho *follow signs for Siresa. From there it's about 5 km (3 miles) north* ☎ *608/729369* ⊕ *www.hoteluson.com* ☾ *Closed Nov.– Mar.* ⇨ *8 rooms, 4 apartments* ⏹️ *No Meals.*

★ **Posada Magoria**

$ | **B&B/INN** | Guest rooms in this carefully restored Art Nouveau house, now an eco-friendly B&B, have splendid views, crisp bedding, and knickknacks galore. **Pros:** homey, relaxed atmosphere; healthy retreat with knowledgeable owner; cozy ambience in beautiful surroundings. **Cons:** small rooms and bathrooms; scant restaurants in the area; thin walls—choose a room on a higher floor. ⑤ *Rooms from: €60* ⊠ *Calle Milagro 32A, Ansó* ☎ *974/370049* ⊕ *www.posadamagoria. com* ⇨ *7 rooms* ⏹️ *Free Breakfast.*

# Roncal Valley

*17 km (11 miles) west of Ansó Valley, 72 km (45 miles) west of Jaca, 86 km (53 miles) northeast of Pamplona.*

The Roncal Valley, the eastern edge of the Basque Pyrenees, is known across Spain for its eponymous sheep's cheese. Roncal is also the birthplace of Julián Gayarre (1844–90), the leading tenor of his time. The 34-km (21-mile) drive through the towns of **Burgui** and **Roncal** to **Isaba** winds through green hillsides past *caseríos,* traditional Basque farmhouses covered by long, sloping roofs that were designed to house animals on the ground floor and the family up above to take advantage of the body heat of the livestock. Burgui's red-tile roofs backed by rolling pastures contrast with the vertical rock and steep slate roofs of the Aragonese and Catalan Pyrenees. Isaba's wide-arch bridge across the Esca is a graceful reminder of Roman aesthetics and engineering.

## GETTING HERE AND AROUND

To get to the valley from Jaca, take the N240 west along the Aragón River; a right turn north on the A137 follows the Esca River from the head of the Yesa Reservoir up the Roncal Valley.

## VISITOR INFORMATION

**CONTACTS Roncal Tourist Office.** ⊠ *Ctra. del Roncal, Roncal* ☎ *948/475256* ⊕ *www.vallederoncal.es.*

## ◉ Sights

### Aribe

**TOWN** | Two kilometers (1 mile) south of Ochagavía, at Escároz, a small secondary roadway winds 22 km (14 miles) over the Abaurrea heights to Aribe, a tiny town—population 36—known for its triple-arch medieval bridge, ancient *hórreo* (granary), Zamariain viewpoint, and Zubi Esekia suspension bridge.

### El Tributo de las Tres Vacas (*Tribute of the Three Cows*)

**FAIRGROUND** | Nearly every July 13 since 1375, the "Tribute of the Three Cows" unfolds in the heart of the Roncal Valley on the French border. Local mayors, dressed in traditional gowns, gather near the summit of San Martín to receive the symbolic payment of three cows from their French counterparts, in memory of a settlement of ancient border disputes that's believed to be the oldest surviving "pact" of its kind in Europe. Feasting and joyous imbibing follow. ⊠ *Roncal.*

### Ochagavía (Otsagabia)

**TOWN** | The road west (NA140) to Ochagavía (Otsagabia in Basque) through the Portillo de Lazar (Lazar Pass) has views of the Anie and Orhi peaks, which tower over the French border. The village itself, with original cobblestone streets and riverside promenade, is a pleasant spot to stretch the legs. ⊠ *Roncal.*

**Selva de Irati** (*Irati Forest*)

FOREST | FAMILY | A 15-km (9-mile) detour north through the town of Orbaizeta up to the headwaters of the Irati River, at the Irabia Reservoir, gets you a good look at the Selva de Irati, one of Europe's major beech forests and the source of much of the lumber for the Spanish Armada. Today it's a popular nature reserve that's veined with trails from which you might glimpse wildlife like deer, woodpeckers, wild boar, and even wolverines. Notably it also contains megalithic cromlechs and dolmens around the villages of Azpegi and Orbaizeta. ⊠ *Roncal* ⊕ *www.visitnavarra.es/en/irati-forest.*

# Roncesvalles (Orreaga)

*64 km (40 miles) northwest of Isaba in the Roncal Valley, 48 km (30 miles) north of Pamplona.*

Roncesvalles (Orreaga in Basque) is a small village and the site of the Battle of Roncesvalles (or Battle of Roncevaux Pass), when Charlemagne's army, under the command of Roland, was attacked and overcome by Basque soldiers in AD 778. The battle became the inspiration for one of France's most revered literary poems, *Le Chanson de Roland* (*The Song of Roland*), written in the 11th century.

The village's strategic position, 23 km (14 miles) from the original starting line of Saint-Jean-Pied-de-Port in France, has made it the first stop-off point for pilgrims on the Camino de Santiago since the 10th century. Its Gothic Colegiata (built in the style of the Notre-Dame Cathedral in Paris), hospital, and 12th-century chapel have provided shelter since then. Mountains in this area rarely reach higher than 4,900 feet. This part of the Camino offers some of the trail's best scenery.

## GETTING HERE AND AROUND

The northbound N135 out of Pamplona goes straight to Roncesvalles.

## VISITOR INFORMATION

**CONTACTS Orreaga-Roncesvalles Tourist Office.** ⊠ *Calle de Nuestra Señora de Roncesvalles, Orreaga* ☎ *948/760301* ⊕ *www.roncesvalles.es.*

# ◉ Sights

### Ibañeta Pass

SCENIC DRIVE | This 3,468-foot pass, above Roncesvalles, is a gorgeous route into France. A menhir (monolith) marks the traditional site of the legendary battle in *The Song of Roland,* during which Roland fell after calling for help on his ivory battle horn. The well-marked eight-hour walk to or from Saint-Jean-Pied-de-Port (which does *not* follow the road) is the first and one of the most beautiful and dramatic sections of the Santiago pilgrimage. ⊠ *Orreaga.*

### Real Colegiata de Santa María de Roncesvalles

CHURCH | Built on the orders of King Sancho VII el Fuerte (the Strong), the Collegiate Church houses the king's tomb, which measures more than 7 feet long. ⊠ *Calle de Nuestra Señora de Roncesvalles, Orreaga* ☎ *948/760000* 🎟 *€5* ⊙ *Closed Wed. in Dec.–Feb.*

# 🛏 Hotels

### Casa de Beneficiados

$ | HOTEL | A favorite among Camino pilgrims, this hotel in a restored 18th-century building adjoining the Colegiata provides warm, low-lit, stone-walled common areas and modern, comfortable rooms. **Pros:** historic building with lots of character; oozes pilgrim-trail ambience; friendly service. **Cons:** take caution arriving by car in bad weather; simple food; apartments lack the charm of the common areas. ⑤ *Rooms from: €95*

Calle Nuestra Señora de Roncesvalles, Orreaga ☎ 948/760105 ⊕ www.hotelroncesvalles.com ⊘ Closed mid-Nov.–mid-Mar. ⌐ 16 rooms ⦿ No Meals.

# Burguete (Auritz)

*2 km (1 mile) south of Roncesvalles.*

Burguete (Auritz in Basque) lies between two mountain streams forming the headwaters of the Urobi River and is surrounded by meadows and forests. The town was immortalized in Ernest Hemingway's *The Sun Also Rises* with an evocative description of trout fishing here in an ice-cold stream. Upon returning to the village, he wrote, "The girl brought in a big bowl of hot vegetable soup and the wine. We had fried trout afterward and some sort of a stew and a big bowl full of wild strawberries [...] After supper we went up-stairs and smoked and read in bed to keep warm. Once in the night I woke and heard the wind blowing. It felt good to be warm and in bed."

**GETTING HERE AND AROUND**
The N135 northbound out of Pamplona goes to Burguete in 44 km (27 miles). From Roncesvalles, it's 2 km (1 mile) south on the N135.

## 🛏 Hotels

**Hotel Loizu**
$ | B&B/INN | FAMILY | An inn for pilgrims since the 18th century, the Loizu is now a country-style hotel that makes an excellent base for exploring the Selva de Irati. **Pros:** family-run; comfortable and ample rooms; friendly service. **Cons:** noise from other rooms; basic breakfast; bathrooms are a bit cramped. ⑤ *Rooms from: €93* ⊠ *Calle San Nicolás 13, Auritz* ☎ 948/760008 ⊕ www.loizu.com ⊘ *Closed mid-Dec.–Mar.* ⌐ *27 rooms* ⦿ *Free Breakfast.*

# Baztan Valley

*62 km (38 miles) northwest of Roncesvalles, 80 km (50 miles) north of Pamplona.*

Tucked between the Bidasoa River headwaters and the 3,545-foot peak of Gorramendi Mountain on the border with France lies the Baztan Valley. These rounded green hills are a scenic halfway stop-off point between the central Pyrenees and the Atlantic. Roads here meander through picture-perfect villages of geranium-covered white stone houses with red-tile roofs grouped around a central *frontón* (handball court).

This once-isolated pocket of the Basque-Navarran Pyrenees is peppered with smugglers' trails and is the site of the Camino de Baztanas, the oldest stretch of the Camino de Santiago. You can follow the ancient footsteps of pilgrims starting from the historic village of **Urdax.** Nearby, close to the village of **Zugarramurdi,** you can visit a collection of limestone caves, otherwise knowns as Las Cuevas de las Brujas (Witches' Caves), which bore witness to so-called witches' covens and their pagan rituals before their eventual and brutal persecution in the 1600s. In the valley's main town, **Elizondo,** stately homes and ancestral mansions, built by nobles returning with their fortunes from the Americas, straddle the banks of the Baztan River.

Try to be in the village of Ituren in late September for its carnival, the Day of the Joaldunak, which has been recognized as one of the oldest celebrations in Europe. Here you can see striking costumes hung with clanging cowbells as participants parade from farm to farm and house to house paying homage to their ancestors; some anthropologists argue that the rituals go back to pagan times. Check the exact dates of the event with the tourist office as each year's schedule depends on the phases of the moon.

## VISITOR INFORMATION
**CONTACTS Baztan Valley Tourist Office.**
✉ *Pl. de los Fueros, Elizondo* ☎ *94/858–1517* ⊕ *www.valledebaztan.com.*

#  Restaurants

### Casa Galarza
$$ | **BASQUE** | Stop here for Basque and Navarran comfort food served in an old stone house on the river. Start with any of the local vegetable specialties, such as tender asparagus spears swimming in tangy vinaigrette, before digging into heftier mains like monkfish-stuffed piquillo peppers and (seasonally) roast squab and milk-fed lamb. **Known for:** wood-beam dining room; house-made desserts; old-school Basque cooking. ⑤ *Average main: €17* ✉ *Calle Santiago 1, Elizondo* ☎ *948/580101* ⊘ *Closed Tues., 2 wks in Feb., last wk of Sept., and 1st wk of Oct. No dinner Mon.–Thurs. in Nov.–June.*

### ★ Donamaria'ko Benta
$$ | **BASQUE** | **FAMILY** | This family-run restaurant and B&B in a former 19th-century residence has a crackling fire in winter and a willow-shaded patio in summer. Prix fixes change seasonally and center on well-executed classics like *secreto ibérico con crema de hongos* (Iberian pork steak with wild mushroom cream) and *txangurro a la Donostiarra* (baked crab). **Known for:** friendly service; traditional Navarran recipes; riverside dining in summer. ⑤ *Average main: €17* ✉ *Barrio de las Ventas 4, Donamaria* ☎ *948/450708* ⊕ *www.donamariako.com* ⊘ *Closed Mon. and Dec. 10–Jan. 5. No dinner Sun.*

# BARCELONA

8

Updated by
Isabelle Kliger

| 👁 Sights | 🍴 Restaurants | 🛏 Hotels | 🛍 Shopping | 🍸 Nightlife |
|-----------|----------------|-----------|-------------|--------------|
| ★★★★★ | ★★★★★ | ★★★★★ | ★★★★★ | ★★★★★ |

# WELCOME TO BARCELONA

## TOP REASONS TO GO

★ **Explore La Boqueria:** Barcelona's produce market may be the most exciting cornucopia in the world.

★ **Visit Santa Maria del Mar:** The early Mediterranean Gothic elegance, rhythmic columns, and unbroken spaces make this church peerless.

★ **See La Sagrada Família:** Gaudí's unfinished masterpiece is the city's most iconic treasure.

★ **Experience El Palau de la Música Catalana:** This Art Nouveau tour de force is alive with music.

★ **Shop for fashion and design:** How could a city famous for its architecture not offer an abundance of innovative clothing, furniture, and design shops as well?

★ **Watch *castellers* and *sardanas:*** Human castles and Catalonia's national dance are two fun ways to appreciate Catalan culture.

**1** La Rambla. A stroll here passes the Boqueria market and other key sights.

**2** Barri Gòtic. The city's medieval Gothic Quarter surrounds the Catedral de la Seu.

**3** El Raval. A funky multicultural sprawl.

**4** Sant Pere and La Ribera. The the narrow cobblestone streets of La Ribera are filled with interesting shops and restaurants and the Picasso Museum.

**5** La Ciutadella and Barceloneta. Waterfront neighborhoods with great seafood restaurants.

**6** The Eixample. A post-1860 grid of city blocks, with the Sagrada Família church and several Gaudí buildings.

**7** Gràcia. This trendy bohemian neighborhood includes Gaudí's Park Güell.

**8** Upper Barcelona. Sarrià is an old-school neighborhood with gourmet shops and restaurants.

**9** Montjuïc and Poble Sec. Montjuïc features parks, open-air theaters, and museums. Poble Sec is known for its multiethnic vibe and up-and-coming food scene.

TO
TIBIDABO

Pl. de Francesc
Macià

Travessera de Gràcia

Avda. Diagonal

Park Güell

**7**

**GRÀCIA**

Carrer de Sant Antoni Maria Claret

C. de Indústria

Paris

C. del Comte d'Urgell

C. de Villaroel

C. de Casanova

C. de Muntaner

C. d'Aribau

Plaça de Joan
Carles I

C. del Rosselló

C. de Provença

C. de Mallorca

Avda. Diagonal

C. de Corsega

Passeig de S. Joan

C. de Bailèn

C. de Roger de Flor

C. de Nàpoles

C. de Sicília

C. de Sardenya

C. de Marina

La Sagrada
Família

C. del Comte Borrell

**6** **EIXAMPLE**

C. de València

C. d'Aragó

C. de la Diputació

Rambla de Catalunya

Passeig de Gràcia

C. de Balmes

C. de Pau Claris

C. de Roger d'Lluria

C. del Bruc

C. de Girona

C. de Bailèn

C. de València

C. d'Aragó

Carrer del Consell de Cent

Plaça
Tetuán

C. de la Diputació

Corts Catalanes

C. de Sepulveda

C. de Floridablanca

C. de Tamarit

de Manso

Plaça
Universitat

Ronda S. Pere

Rda. de
Sant Antoni

C. de Joaquim
Costa

**MACBA**

**3**

**RAVAL**

Hospital de
la Santa Creu

C. del Carme

C. de Hospital

**LA RAMBLA**

La Boqueria
Market

C. de Sant Pau

C. la Unió

C. Ferran

C. Nou de la Rambla

Pl. St.
Jaume
Plaça

C. Ample

Gran Via de les

Plaça de
Catalunya

Pl. Urquinaona

Fontanella

La Rambla

Jonqueres

Plaça de
Casp

C. d'Ausias Marc

**SANT PERE**

El Palau de la
Música Catalana

S. Pere Més Alt

S. Pere Més Baix

Avda. Catedral

**2**

**BARRI
GÒTIC**

Santa Maria
del Mar

C. Princesa

Via Laietana

C. Ciutat

Ferat

Corts Catalanes

Arc del Triomf

C. dels Almogàvers

C. de Ribes

P. de Carles I

**4**

**LA
RIBERA**

Passeig de
Lluís Companys

Passeig Pujades

Parc de la
Ciutadella

Passeig
del Born

C. del Comerç

Pg. Picasso

Avda. de la
Meridiana

Passeig de Carles I

Plaça Portal
de la Pau

Pg. de Colom

Pl. d'Antoni
López

Avda. d'Icària

**CIUTADELLA**

Estació de
França

**5**

C. de Wellington

Vila
Olímpica

Avda. d'Icària

**PORT
OLÍMPIC**

Rambla
de Mar

Moll de Sant Bertrán

Moll
d'Espanya

Passeig Joan
de Borbó

**BARCELONETA**

Rda. de Sant Pau

Pl. Prat

Pg. de Montjuïc

# EATING AND DRINKING WELL IN BARCELONA

A stew of broad beans and black and white botifarra sausage.

Barcelona cuisine draws from Catalonia's rustic country cooking and uses ingredients from the Mediterranean, the Pyrenees, and inland farmlands. Cosmopolitan influences and experimental contemporary innovation have combined to make Barcelona, historically linked to France and Italy, an important food destination.

The Mediterranean diet of seafood, vegetables, olive oil, and red wine comes naturally to Barcelona. Fish of all kinds, shrimp, shellfish, and rice dishes combining them are common, as are salads of seafood and Mediterranean vegetables. Vegetable and legume combinations are standard. Seafood and upland combinations, the classic *mar i muntanya* (surf and turf) recipes, join rabbit and prawns or cuttlefish and meatballs, while salty and sweet tastes—a Moorish legacy—are found in recipes such as duck with pears or goose with figs.

## CAVA

Order Champagne in Barcelona and you'll get anything from French bubbly to dirty looks. Ask, instead, for *cava*, sparkling wine from the Penedès region just southwest of the city. The first cava was produced in 1872 after the phylloxera plague wiped out most of Europe's vineyards. Cava (from the "cave" or wine cellar where it ferments) has a drier, earthier taste than Champagne, and slightly larger bubbles.

## SALADS

*Esqueixada* is a cold salad consisting of strips of raw, shredded, salt-cured cod marinated in oil and vinegar with onions, tomatoes, olives, and red and green bell peppers. Chunks of dried tuna can also be included, as well as chickpeas, roasted onions, and potatoes, too. *Escalibada* is another classic Catalan salad of red and green bell peppers and eggplant that have been roasted over coals, cut into strips, and served with onions, garlic, and olive oil.

Esqueixada, or raw codfish salad

## LEGUMES

*Botifarra amb mongetes* (sausage with white beans) is the classic Catalan sausage made of pork and seasoned with salt and pepper, grilled and served with stewed white beans and *allioli* (an olive oil and garlic emulsion); botifarra can also be made with truffles, apples, eggs, wild mushrooms, and even chocolate. *Mongetes de Sant Pau amb calamarsets* (tiny white beans from Santa Pau with baby squid) is a favorite *mar i muntanya*.

## VEGETABLES

*Espinaques a la catalana* (spinach with pine nuts, raisins, and garlic) owes a debt to the Moorish sweet-salt counterpoint and to the rich vegetable-growing littoral along the Mediterranean coast north and south of Barcelona. Bits of

bacon, fatback, or *jamón ibérico* may be added; some recipes use fine almond flakes as well. *Albergínies* (eggplant or aubergine) are a favorite throughout Catalonia, whether roasted, stuffed, or stewed, while *carxofes* (artichokes) fried to a crisp or stewed with rabbit is another staple.

## FISH

*Llobarro a la sal* (sea bass cooked in salt) is baked in a shell of rock salt that hardens and requires a tap from a hammer or heavy knife to break and serve. The salt shell keeps the juices inside the fish and the flesh flakes off in firm chunks, while the skin of the fish prevents excessive saltiness from permeating the meat. *Suquet* is a favorite fish stew, with scorpion fish, monkfish, sea bass, or any combination thereof, cooked with potatoes, onions, and tomatoes.

## DESSERTS

*Crema catalana* (Catalan cream) is the most popular dessert in Catalonia, a version of the French crème brûlée, custard dusted with cinnamon and confectioner's sugar and burned with a blowtorch (traditionally, a branding iron was used) before serving. The less sweet and palate-cleansing *mel i mató* (honey and fresh cheese) runs a close second in popularity.

A dessert of mel i mató (honey with fresh cheese)

# The infinite variety and throb of street life, the nooks and crannies of the medieval Barri Gòtic, the ceramic tile and stained glass of Moderniste facades, the art and music, the food (ah, the food!)— one way or another, Barcelona will find a way to get your full attention.

The Catalonian capital greeted the new millennium with a cultural and industrial rebirth comparable only to the late-19th-century Renaixença (Renaissance) that filled the city with its flamboyant Moderniste (Art Nouveau) buildings. An exuberant sense of style—from hip new fashions to cutting-edge interior design, to the extravagant visions of star-status postmodern architects—gives Barcelona a vibe like no other place in the world. Barcelona is Spain's most visited city, and it's no wonder: it's a 2,000-year-old master of the art of perpetual novelty.

Barcelona's present boom began on October 17, 1987, when Juan Antonio Samaranch, president of the International Olympic Committee, announced that his native city had been chosen to host the 1992 Olympics. This single masterstroke allowed Spain's so-called second city to throw off the shadow of Madrid and its 40-year "internal exile" under Franco, and resume its rightful place as one of Europe's most dynamic destinations. The Catalan administration lavished millions in subsidies from the Spanish government for the Olympics, then used the Games as a platform to broadcast the news about Catalonia's cultural and national identity from one end of the planet to the other. More Mediterranean than Spanish, historically closer and more akin to Marseille or Milan than to Madrid, Barcelona

has always been ambitious, decidedly modern (even in the 2nd century), and quick to accept the latest innovations. (The city's electric light system, public gas system, and telephone exchange were among the first in the world.) Its democratic form of government is rooted in the so-called Usatges Laws instituted by Ramon Berenguer I in the 11th century, which amounted to a constitution. This code of privileges represented one of the earliest known examples of democratic rule; Barcelona's Consell de Cent (Council of 100), constituted in 1274, was Europe's first parliament and one of the cradles of Western democracy. The center of an important seafaring commercial empire with colonies spread around the Mediterranean as far away as Athens, when Madrid was still a Moorish outpost on the arid Castilian steppe—it was Barcelona that absorbed new ideas and styles first. It borrowed navigation techniques from the Moors. It embraced the ideals of the French Revolution. It nurtured artists like Picasso and Miró, who blossomed in the city's air of freedom and individualism. Barcelona, in short, has always been ahead of the curve.

# Planning

## Planning Your Time

The best way to get around Barcelona is on foot; the occasional resort to subway, taxi, or tram will help you make the most of your visit. The comfortable FGC (Ferrocarrils de la Generalitat de Catalunya) trains that run up the center of the city from Plaça de Catalunya to Sarrià put you within 20- to 30-minute walks of nearly everything. The metro and the FGC close just short of midnight Monday–Thursday and Sunday, and at 2 am on Friday; on Saturday, the metro runs all night. The main attractions you need a taxi or the metro to reach are Montjuïc (Miró Foundation, MNAC, Mies van der Rohe Pavilion, CaixaFòrum, and Poble Espanyol), most easily accessed from Plaça Espanya; Park Güell above Plaça Lesseps; and the Auditori at Plaça de les Glòries. You can reach Gaudí's Sagrada Família by two metro lines (Nos. 2 and 5), but you may prefer the walk from the FGC's Provença stop, as it's an enjoyable half-hour jaunt that passes by three major Moderniste buildings: Palau Baró de Quadras, Casa Terrades (Casa de les Punxes), and Casa Macaia.

Sarrià and Pedralbes are easily explored on foot. The Torre Bellesguard and the Col.legi de les Teresianes are uphill treks; you might want to take a cab. It's a pleasant stroll from Sarrià down through the Jardins de la Vil.la Cecilia and Vil.la Amèlia to the Cátedra Gaudí (the pavilions of the Finca Güell, with Gaudí's amazing wrought-iron dragon gate); from there, you can get to the Futbol Club Barcelona through the Jardins del Palau Reial de Pedralbes and the university campus, or catch a two-minute taxi.

All of the Ciutat Vella (Barri Gòtic, Born-Ribera, La Rambla, El Raval, and Barceloneta) is best explored on foot. If you stay in Barceloneta for dinner, have the restaurant call you a taxi to get back to your hotel.

The city bus system is also a viable option—you get a better look at the city as you go—but the metro is faster and more comfortable. The tramway offers a quiet ride from Plaça Francesc Macià out Diagonal to the Futbol Club Barcelona, or from behind the Parc de la Ciutadella out to Glòries and the Fòrum at the east end of Diagonal.

## When to Go

For optimal weather and marginally fewer tourists, the best times to visit Barcelona and the rest of Catalonia are April–June and mid-September–mid-December. Catalans and Basques vacation in August, causing epic traffic jams at both ends of the month.

## Discounts and Deals

The very worthwhile **Barcelona Card** (⊕ www.barcelona-card.com) comes in three-, four-, and five-day versions (€46, €56, and €61). You get unlimited travel on public transport, free admission at numerous museums, and discounts on restaurants, leisure sights, and stores. Meanwhile, the two-day "Express" gives you free public transport and a discount on admissions. You can get the cards in Turisme de Barcelona offices in Plaça de Catalunya and Plaça Sant Jaume and at the Casa Batlló, the Aquarium, and the Poble Espanyol, among other sights; buy in advance online for a 10% discount.

## Getting Here and Around

### AIR

Most flights arriving in Spain from the United States and Canada pass through Madrid's Barajas (MAD), but the major gateway to Catalonia and other nearby regions is Spain's second-largest airport,

Barcelona's spectacular glass, steel, and marble Prat del Llobregat (BCN). The T1 terminal is a sleek, ultramodern facility that uses solar panels for sustainable energy and offers a spa, a fitness center, restaurants and cafés, and VIP lounges. This airport is served by numerous international carriers, but Catalonia also has two other airports that handle passenger traffic, including charter flights. One is just south of Girona, 90 km (56 miles) north of Barcelona and convenient to the resort towns of the Costa Brava. Bus and train connections from Girona to Barcelona work well and cheaply, provided you have the time. The other Catalonia airport is at Reus, 110 km (68 miles) south of Barcelona, a gateway to Tarragona and the beaches of the Costa Daurada. Flights to and from the major cities in Europe and Spain also fly into and out of Bilbao's Loiu (BIL) airport.

**AIRPORT INFORMATION Aeroport de Girona–Costa Brava.** (*GRO*) ✉ *17185 Vilobi de Onyar, Girona* ☎ *9102/321–1000 general info on Spanish airports* ⊕ *www. aena.es.* **Aeropuerto de Madrid (Adolfo Suárez Madrid-Barajas).** (*MAD*) ✉ *Av. de la Hispanidad s/n, Madrid* ☎ *91/321–1000 general info on Spanish airports* ⊕ *www. aeropuertomadrid-barajas.com/eng.* **Aeropuerto de Reus.** (*REU*) ✉ *Autovía Tarragona–Reus, Reus* ☎ *9/321–1000 general info on Spanish airports* ⊕ *www. aena.es/en/reus-airport/reus.html.* **Aeropuerto Internacional de Bilbao.** (*BIO*) ✉ *Loiu 48180, Bilbao* ☎ *902/404704 general info on Spanish airports* ⊕ *www. aeropuertodebilbao.net/en.* **Barcelona El Prat de Llobregat.** (*BCN*) ✉ *C–32B s/n, Barcelona* ☎ *902/404704 general info on Spanish airports* ⊕ *www.aena.es/en/barcelona-airport/index.html.*

## GROUND TRANSPORTATION

Check first to see if your hotel in Barcelona is one of the very few that provides airport-shuttle service. If not, visitors typically get into town by train, bus, taxi, or rental car.

Cab fare from the airport into town is €30–€35, depending on traffic, the part of town you're heading to, and the amount of baggage you have (there's a €3.10 surcharge for airport pickups/drop-offs, and a €1 surcharge for each suitcase that goes in the trunk). If you're driving your own car, follow signs to the Centre Ciutat, from which you can enter the city along Gran Vía. For the port area, follow signs for the Ronda Litoral. The journey to the center of town can take 25–45 minutes, depending on traffic.

The Aerobus leaves Terminal 1 at the airport for Plaça de Catalunya every 10 minutes 5:35 am–7:20 am and 10:25 pm–1:05 am, and every 5 minutes 7:30 am–10:20 pm. From Plaça de Catalunya the bus leaves for the airport every 5 or 10 minutes between 5 am and 12:10 am. The fare is €5.90 one way and €10.20 round trip. Aerobuses for Terminals 1 and 2 pick up and drop off passengers at the same stops en route, so if you're outward bound make sure that you board the right one. The A1 Aerobus for Terminal 1 is two-tone light and dark blue; the A2 Aerobus for Terminal 2 is dark blue and yellow.

The train's only drawback is that it's a 10- to 15-minute walk from your gate through Terminal 2 over the bridge. From Terminal 1 a shuttle bus drops you at the train. Trains leave the airport every 30 minutes between 5:42 am and 11:38 pm, stopping at Estació de Sants, for transfer to the Arc de Triomf, then at Passeig de Gràcia and finally at El Clot–Aragó. Trains going to the airport begin at 5:21 am from El Clot, stopping at Passeig de Gràcia at 5:27 am, and Sants at 5:32 am. The trip to Sants takes about 20 minutes, and the fare is €4.10. For getting around the city, the best bargain is the T10 (aka T-Casual) metro card; with it, you have ten rides on any of the subways, buses or FGC trains (Ferrocarils de la Generalitat to Catalunya, a separate system), with free transfers between them, all for €11.35. Take note: you can't share the card.

If you plan to make extensive use of public transportation, consider buying a "Hola Barcelona" card at the Tourist Information Center in Plaça Catalunya; the card gives you unlimited rides for anywhere from two to five days, at €14.76 to €34.38.

## CITY BUS, SUBWAY, AND TRAM

In Barcelona the underground metro, or subway, is the fastest, cheapest, and easiest way to get around. Metro lines run Monday through Thursday and Sunday 5 am–midnight, Friday to 2 am, Saturday and holiday evenings all night. The FGC trains run 5 am to just after midnight on weekdays and to 1:52 am on weekends and the eves of holidays. Sunday trains run on weekday schedules.

Transfers from a metro line to the FGC (or vice versa), or to a local bus, are free within an hour and 15 minutes. Note that in many stations, you need to validate your ticket at both ends of your journey. Maps showing bus and metro routes are available free from the tourist information office in Plaça de Catalunya.

**CONTACTS Transports Metropolitans de Barcelona.** (*TMB*) ⊠ *Carrer 60, 21–23, Barcelona* ☎ *93/298–7000* ⊕ *www.tmb. cat/en/home.*

## TAXI

In Barcelona taxis are black and yellow and show a green rooftop sign on the front right corner when available for hire. The meter currently starts at €2.10 and rises in increments of €1.07 every kilometer. These rates apply 6 am–10 pm weekdays. At hours outside of these, the rates rise 20%. There are official supplements of €1 per bag for luggage.

Trips to or from a train station entail a supplemental charge of €2.10; a cab to or from the airport, or the Barcelona Cruise Terminal, adds a supplemental charge of €4.20, as do trips to or from a football match. The minimum price for taxi service to or from the Barcelona airport is €20 for terminals T1, T2, and T3, and €39

from T4. There are cabstands (*parades,* in Catalan) all over town, and you can also hail cabs on the street, though if you are too close to an official stand they may not stop. You can call for a cab by phone 24 hours a day. Drivers do not expect a tip, but rounding up the fare is standard.

**CONTACTS Barna Taxi.** ⊠ *Calle Marina 82, Barcelona* ☎ *93/357–7755, 93/322–2222* ⊕ *www.barnataxi.com.* **Radio Taxi.** ⊠ *Carrer del Cánem 71, Barcelona* ☎ *93/303–3033* ⊕ *radiotaxi033.com.* **Taxi Class Rent.** ⊠ *Calle Espronceda 43, bajos, Barcelona* ☎ *93/307–0707* ⊕ *www.taxiclassrent. com/en.*

## TRAIN

International overnight trains to Barcelona arrive from many European cities, including Paris, Grenoble, Geneva, Zurich, and Milan; high-speed trains to and from Paris take about 5½ hours, and advance-purchase tickets online are competitive with flight prices. Almost all long-distance trains arrive at and depart from Estació de Sants, though many make a stop at Passeig de Gràcia that comes in handy for hotels in the Eixample or in the Ciutat Vella. Estació de França, near the port, handles primarily regional trains within Catalonia. Train service connects Barcelona with most other major cities in Spain; in addition a high-speed Euromed route connects Barcelona to Tarragona and Valencia.

Spain's intercity services (along with some of Barcelona's local train routes) are the province of the government-run railroad system—RENFE (Red Nacional de Ferrocarriles Españoles). The high-speed AVE train now connects Barcelona and Madrid (via Lleida and Zaragoza) in less than three hours. (Spain has more high-speed tracks in service than any other country in Europe.) The fast TALGO and ALTARIA trains are efficient, though local trains remain slow and tedious. The Catalan government's FGC (Ferrocarril de la Generalitat de Catalunya) also provide train service, notably to Barcelona's commuter suburbs of Sant Cugat, Terrassa, and Sabadell.

Information on the local/commuter lines (*rodalies* in Catalan, *cercanías* in Castilian) can be found on the RENFE website,⊕ ⊠ *www.renfe.com*. Rodalies go, for example, to Sitges from Barcelona, whereas you would take a regular RENFE train to, say, Tarragona. It's important to know whether you are traveling on RENFE or on rodalies (the latter distinguished by a stylized C), so you don't end up in the wrong line.

Both Catalonia and the Basque Country offer scenic railroad excursions. The day train from Barcelona to Madrid runs through bougainvillea-choked towns before leaping out across Spain's central *meseta* (plateau) via Zaragoza, most trains arriving at Atocha Station in Madrid in about 2½ hours. The train from Barcelona's Plaça de Catalunya north to Sant Pol de Mar and Blanes runs along the edge of the beach.

First-class train service in Spain, with the exception of the *coche-cama* (Pullman) overnight service, barely differs from second class or *turista*. The TALGO or the AVE trains, however, are much faster than second-class carriers like the slowpoke Estrella overnight from Barcelona to Madrid, both with limited legroom and general comforts. The AVE is the exception: these sleek, comfortable bullet trains travel between Barcelona and Madrid or between Madrid and Seville. Some 30 AVE trains a day connect Barcelona and Madrid, with departures from 5:50 am to 9:15 pm. Trips take from 2 hours 30 minutes to 3 hours 10 minutes.

During peak travel times (Easter, August, and Christmas), it's important to make a reservation weeks or even months in advance; on routes between major cities (Barcelona to Bilbao or Madrid, for example), it's a good idea to reserve well in advance, especially for overnight trips.

**STATIONS Estació de França.** ⊠ *Av. Marquès de l'Argentera 1, Born-Ribera* Ⓜ *Barceloneta (Metro L4).* **Estació de Passeig de Gràcia.** ⊠ *Passeig de Gràcia/ Carrer Aragó, Eixample* ☎ *912/343–2343 station info* ⊕ *www.adif.es/en* Ⓜ *L2/L3/ L4 Passeig de Gràcia.* **Estació de Sants.** ⊠ *Pl. dels Països Catalans s/n, Les Corts* ☎ *912/243–2343* Ⓜ *L3/L5 Sants Estació.* **Ferrocarrils de la Generalitat de Catalunya (FGC).** ⊠ *Carrer Vergos 44, Sarrià* ☎ *93/3366–3000* ⊕ *www.fgc.cat/en* Ⓜ *Sarrià (FGC).* **RENFE.** ⊠ *Av. de la Ciudad de Barcelona 8, Madrid* ☎ *9/210–9420 for tickets, 912/232–0320 general information* ⊕ *www.renfe.com.*

**INFORMATION AND PASSES Eurail.** ⊕ *www.eurail.com.* **Rail Europe.** ⊕ *www. raileurope.com.*

# Restaurants and Hotels

*Restaurant and hotel reviews have been shortened. For full information, visit Fodors.com.*

| What It Costs in Euros | | | |
|---|---|---|---|
| $ | $$ | $$$ | $$$$ |
| **RESTAURANTS** | | | |
| under €16 | €16–€22 | €23–€29 | over €29 |
| **HOTELS** | | | |
| under €125 | €125–€174 | €175–€225 | over €225 |

# Tours

### ART TOURS

The Ruta del Modernisme (Moderniste Route), a self-guided tour, provides an excellent guidebook (available in English) that interprets 120 Moderniste sights from the Sagrada Família and the Palau de la Música Catalana to Art Nouveau building facades, lampposts, and paving stones. The €18 Guide, sold at the Pavellons Güell and the Institut Municipal del Paisatge Urbà (⌖ Av. Drassanes 6), comes with a book of vouchers good for discounts up to 50% on admission to most of the Moderniste buildings and sites in the Guide in Barcelona and 13 other towns and cities in Catalonia, as well as free guided tours in English at selected Moderniste sights. Check when buying the guide what is on and when, as availability may vary.

The Palau de la Música Catalana offers guided tours in English every hour on the hour from 10 to 3:30. Sagrada Família guided tours cost extra. Casa Milà offers a selection of private experiences, including a guided tour before the house opens to the public and a night tour with dinner. Architect Dominique Blinder of Urban Cultours project specializes in Barcelona's Jewish heritage and explorations of the Barcelona Jewish Quarter but can also provide tours of virtually any architectural aspect of Barcelona.

## CULINARY TOURS

Barcelona's cooking classes have upped their game of late, with traditional, mass-tourism-focused cooking schools making way for a new generation of "slow food" favorites like The Paella Club and Bear on Bike. Jane Gregg, founder of Epicurean Ways, offers gourmet and wine tours of Barcelona and Catalonia. Teresa Parker of Spanish Journeys organizes cooking classes, seasonal specials, custom cultural or culinary tours, corporate cooking retreats, or off-the-beaten-path travel. Canadian-born Marwa Preston of Wanderbeak offers food experiences ranging from Michelin-starred splurges to tapas walks, with just the right mix of food, wine, and local culture.

**CONTACTS Aula Gastronómica.** ⊠ Carrer Sagristans 5, Entresuelo, Barri Gòtic ☎ 93/301–1944, 628–30–1502 mobile ⊕ www.aulagastronomica.com/ cooking-classes Ⓜ Jaume I (Metro L4). **Epicurean Ways.** ☎ 4434/738–2293 in U.S., 636–102–46 in Spain ⊕ www.epicureanways.com. **Wanderbeak.** ⊠ Carrer del Comerç, 29, Barcelona ☎ 93/220-6101 ⊕ www.wanderbeak.com.

## BOAT TOURS

Golondrina harbor boats make short trips from the Portal de la Pau, near the Columbus monument. The fare is €7.70 for a 40-minute "Barcelona Port" tour of the harbor and €15.50 for the "Barcelona Sea" 90-minute ride out past the beaches and up the coast to the Fòrum at the eastern end of Diagonal. Frequency and departure times may vary depending on the season, but the Port tour typically runs hourly from 12:15 am–5:15 pm in spring and summer, and every 30 minutes in July, August, and September, while the Sea tour departs at 12:30 pm daily, all year-round; three times daily (at 12:30, 1:30 and 3:30) in spring and fall, and hourly from 12:30 to 6:30 pm from April to September.

**CONTACTS Las Golondrinas.** ⊠ Pl. Portal de la Pau s/n, Moll de les Drassanes, La Rambla ☎ 93/442–3106 ⊕ lasgolondrinas.com/en Ⓜ Drassanes (Metro L3).

## BUS TOURS

The Bus Turístic double-decker buses (aka Hop On, Hop Off buses) run on three interconnected routes, with 44 stops: an easy way to get around Barcelona and see all the sights. The blue route covers upper Barcelona; the red route tours lower Barcelona; and the green route runs from the Port Olímpic along Barcelona's beaches to the Fòrum at the eastern end of Diagonal (April–October only). The cost is €27 for one day (€36 for two days); onboard or at the ticket booth, with a 10% online purchase discount. There are free audio guides on board, and you receive a booklet with discount vouchers for various attractions. The blue and red routes start at Plaça de Catalunya near Café Zurich. The green route starts at Port Olímpic next to the Hotel Arts. Passengers can jump off and catch a later bus at any stop along the way; some stops are "hubs" where you can switch to a bus on one of the other routes. There's free Wi-Fi on board.

**CONTACTS Julià Travel.** ⊠ *Carrer Balmes 5, Eixample* ☎ *93/402–6900* ⊕ *www. juliatravel.com/destinations/barcelona* Ⓜ *Catalunya, L1/L2 Universitat.*

## WALKING TOURS

Turisme de Barcelona offers weekend walking tours of the Barri Gòtic, the Waterfront, Picasso's Barcelona, Modernisme, and a shopping circuit, in English. Prices range from €18 to €25, with 10% discounts for purchases online. For private tours, Julià Travel leads walks around Barcelona. Tours leave from their offices, but you may be able to arrange a pickup at your hotel. Prices range from around €69 for a private half-day tour, to €239 for a full day, including lunch.

## SEGWAY TOURS

Barcelona Segway Tours, with an office near Arc de Triomf, puts you up on one of its futuristic two-wheelers for a two-hour tour (€49) of the Barri Gòtic, La Rambla, and the seafront; its longer three-hour excursion (€69) starts at Arc de Triomf and takes you to the top of the green mountain of Montjuic. Tours depart daily at 10 am, 12:30, and 4pm. Helmets are provided; children must be more than 10 years of age; learn more at www.barcelonasegwaytour.com.

## Visitor Information

### Turisme de Barcelona

GUIDED TOURS | In addition to being a useful resource for information, tickets, and bookings, Turisme de Barcelona offers daily walking tours of the Barri Gòtic, Picasso's Barcelona, Modernisme, and more. There is also an Easy Walking Tour of the Barri Gòtic, which has been adapted for people with reduced mobility: Departure times for tours in English depend on which of the tours you choose. Book online for a 10% discount. The Picasso tour, which includes the

entry fee for the Museu Picasso, is a great bargain. All tours depart from the Plaça de Catalunya tourist office, except for the Easy Walking Tour, which starts at The Tourist Office in Plaça Sant Jaume. ⊠ *Passatge de la Conceptió 7–9, Eixample* ☎ *93/368–9700* ⊕ *barcelonaturisme. com* ◷ *Closed Sat. and Sun.* Ⓜ *Pl. de Catalunya.*

# La Rambla

The promenade in the heart of premodern Barcelona was originally a watercourse, dry for most of the year, that separated the walled Ciutat Vella from the outlying Raval. In the 14th century, the city walls were extended and the arroyo was filled in, so it gradually became a thoroughfare where peddlers, farmers, and tradesmen hawked their wares. (The watercourse is still there, under the pavement. From time to time a torrential rain will fill it, and the water rises up through the drains.) The poet-playwright Federico García Lorca called this the only street in the world he wished would never end—and in a sense, it doesn't.

Down the watercourse now flows a river of humanity, gathered here and there around the mimes, acrobats, jugglers, musicians, puppeteers, portrait artists, break dancers, rappers, and rockers competing for the crowd's attention. Couples sit at café tables no bigger than tea trays while nimble-footed waiters dodge traffic, bringing food and drink from kitchens. With the din of taxis and motorbikes in the traffic lanes on either side of the promenade, the revelers and rubberneckers, and the Babel of languages, the scene is as animated at 3 am as it is at 3 pm.

Barcelona's most famous boulevard boasts a generous pedestrian strip down the middle and it is a tourist magnet. Much as you may want to avoid the crowds and the tacky, touristy shops and caleries that now cater to the crush of visitors, a stroll here is essential to your Barcelona experience. From the rendez-vous point at the head of La Rambla at Café Zurich to La Boqueria produce market, the Liceu opera house, or La Rambla's lower reaches, there are crowds but also gems along this spinal column of Barcelona street life. Keep a close eye on your valuables, as this part of the city is sadly teeming with pickpockets.

# ◉ Sights

### Carrer dels Escudellers

STREET | Named for the *terrissaires* (earthenware potters) who worked here making *escudellas* (bowls or stew pots), this colorful loop is an interesting subtrip off La Rambla. Go left at Plaça del Teatre and you'll pass the landmark Grill Room at No. 8, an Art Nouveau saloon with graceful wooden decor and an ornate oak bar; next is La Fonda Escudellers, another lovely, glass- and stone-encased dining emporium. (Alas, the food is not especially good at either.)

At Nos. 23–25 is Barcelona's most comprehensive ceramics display, Art Escudellers. Farther down, on the right, is Los Caracoles, once among the most traditional of Barcelona's restaurants and now mainly the choice of tourists with deep pockets. Still, the bar and the walk-through kitchen on the way in are picturesque, as are the dining rooms and the warren of little stairways between them. Another 100 yards down Carrer Escu-dellers is Plaça George Orwell, named for the author of *Homage to Catalonia,* a space created to bring light and air into this somewhat sketchy neighborhood. The little flea market that hums along on Saturday is a great place to browse.

Take a right on the narrow Carrer de la Carabassa—a street best known in days past for its houses of ill fame, and one of the few remaining streets in the city still entirely paved with cobblestones. It

is arched over with two graceful bridges that once connected the houses with their adjacent gardens. At the end of the street, looming atop her own basilica, is Nostra Senyora de la Mercè (Our Lady of Mercy). This giant representation of Barcelona's patron saint is a 20th-century (1940) addition to the 18th-century Esglé-sia de la Mercè; the view of La Mercè gleaming in the sunlight, babe in arms, is one of the Barcelona waterfront's most impressive sights.

As you arrive at Carrer Ample, note the 15th-century door with a winged Sant Miquel Archangel delivering a backhand blow to a scaly Lucifer. It's from the Sant Miquel church, formerly part of City Hall, torn down in the early 19th century. From the Mercè, a walk out Carrer Ample (to the right) leads back to the bottom of La Rambla. ⊠ *Carrer dels Escudellers, Barcelona* Ⓜ *Drassanes.*

### Carrer Petritxol

STREET | Just steps from La Rambla, Car-rer Petritxol is one of Barcelona's most popular streets. Lined with art galleries, *xocolatcríos* (chocolate shops), and stationers, this narrow passageway dates from the 15th century, when it was used as a shortcut through the backyard of a local property owner.

Working up Petritxol from Plaça del Pi, stop to admire the late-17th-century sgraf-fito design (mural ornamentation made by scratching away a plaster surface), some of the city's best, on the facade over the Ganiveteria Roca knife store, *the* place for cutlery in Barcelona. Next on the right, at Petritxol 2 is the 200-year-old Dulcinea, with a portrait of the great Cat-alan playwright Àngel Guimerà (1847–1924) over the fireplace. Drop in for the house specialty, the *suizo* ("Swiss" hot chocolate and whipped cream).

Note the plaque to Àngel Guimerà over No. 4 and Sala Parès at No. 5, founded in 1840, the dean of Barcelona's art galleries, where major figures like Isidre

Barcelona Metro

Nonell, Santiago Rusiñol, and Picasso have shown their work, and its affiliated Galeria Trama, which shows more contemporary work. Look carefully at the "curtains" carved into the wooden door at No. 11 and the floral ornamentation around the edges of the ceiling inside; the store is Granja la Pallaresa, yet another enclave of chocolate and *ensaimada* (a light-looking but deadly sweet Mallorcan pastry, with confectioner's sugar dusted on top). ✉ *Carrer Petrixol, Barcelona* Ⓜ *Liceu, Catalunya.*

### Casa Bruno Cuadros

NOTABLE BUILDING | Like something out of an amusement park, this former umbrella shop was whimsically designed (assembled is more like it) by Josep Vilaseca in 1885. A Chinese dragon with a parasol, Egyptian balconies and galleries, and a Peking lantern all reflect the Eastern style that was very much in vogue at the time of the Universal Exposition of 1888. Now housing a branch office of the Banco Bilbao Vizcaya Artentaria (BBVA), this prankster of a building is much in keeping with Art Nouveau's eclectic playfulness, though it has never been taken very seriously as an expression of Modernisme and is generally omitted from most studies of Art Nouveau architecture. ✉ *La Rambla 82, La Rambla* Ⓜ *Liceu.*

### Església de Betlem

CHURCH | The Church of Bethlehem is one of Barcelona's few baroque buildings, and hulks stodgily on La Rambla just above Rambla de les Flors. Burned out completely at the start of the Civil War in 1936, the church is unremarkable inside; the outside, spruced up, is made of what looks like quilted stone. If you find this less than a must-see, worry not: you have all of Barcelona for company, with the possible exception of Betlem's parishioners. This was where Viceroy Amat claimed the hand of the young virreina-to-be when in 1780 she was left in the lurch by the viceroy's nephew. In

a sense, Betlem has compensated the city with the half century of good works the young widow was able to accomplish with her husband's fortune. ✉ *Carme 2, La Rambla* ☎ *93/318-3823* Ⓜ *Catalunya.*

### Font de Canaletes

FOUNTAIN | This fountain is a key spot in Barcelona, the place where all great *futbol* victories are celebrated by jubilant (and often unruly) Barça fans. It was originally known for the best water in Barcelona, brought in by *canaletes* (small canals) from the mountains. The bronze plaque on the pavement in front of the fountain explains in Catalan that if you drink from these waters, you will fall under Barcelona's spell and are destined to return. ✉ *Rambla de Canaletes s/n, La Rambla* Ⓜ *Catalunya.*

### ★ Gran Teatre del Liceu

NOTABLE BUILDING | Barcelona's opera house has long been considered one of the most beautiful in Europe, a rival to La Scala in Milan. First built in 1848, this cherished cultural landmark was torched in 1861, later bombed by anarchists in 1893, and once again gutted by an accidental fire in early 1994. During that most recent fire, Barcelona's soprano Montserrat Caballé stood on La Rambla in tears as her beloved venue was consumed. Five years later, a restored Liceu, equipped for modern productions, opened anew. Some of the Liceu's most spectacular halls and rooms, including the glittering foyer known as the Saló dels Miralls (Room of Mirrors), were untouched by the fire of 1994, as were those of Spain's oldest social club, El Círculo del Liceu—established in 1847 and restored to its pristine original condition after the fire. ✉ *La Rambla 51–59, La Rambla* ☎ *93/485-9931 premium visit reservations* ⊕ *www.liceubarcelona.cat* Ⓜ *Liceu.*

# La Rambla

**Sights** ▼

1 Carrer dels Escudellers .......... **C5**
2 Carrer Petritxol .......... **C3**
3 Casa Bruno Cuadros .... **C4**
4 Església de Betlem ...... **C3**
5 Font de Canaletes ...... **D2**
6 Gran Teatre del Liceu ... **C4**
7 La Boqueria .............. **C3**
8 Mirador de Colom ...... **B7**
9 Museu Marítim .......... **B7**
10 Palau Güell .............. **C5**
11 Plaça Reial .............. **C5**
12 Port de Barcelona ...... **C7**
13 Portaferrissa Fountain .................. **C3**

**Restaurants** ▼

1 Direkte Boqueria .......... **C4**

**Quick Bites** ▼

1 Cafè de l'Òpera .......... **C4**

**Hotels** ▼

1 Baguès .................... **C3**
2 Hotel DO Plaça Reial .... **C5**
3 Hotel 1898 ................ **C3**
4 Hotel Pulitzer ............. **C1**
5 Le Méridien Barcelona ................ **C2**

Visit La Boqueria market early (it opens at 8 am) to avoid the crowds as you discover all this colorful institution has to offer.

## ★ La Boqueria

**MARKET** | Barcelona's most spectacular food market, also known as the Mercat de Sant Josep, is an explosion of life and color. As you turn in from La Rambla, you're greeted by bar-restaurants serving tapas at counters and stall after stall selling fruit, herbs, veggies, nuts, candied preserves, cheese, ham, fish, and poultry. Under a Moderniste hangar of wrought-iron girders and stained glass, the market occupies a Neoclassical square built in 1840. Highlights include the sunny greengrocer's market outside, along with Pinotxo (Pinocchio), just inside to the right, which serves some of the best food in Barcelona. The Kiosko Universal and Quim de la Boqueria both offer delicious alternatives. Don't miss the *fruits del bosc* (fruits of the forest) stand at the back of La Boqueria, with its display of wild mushrooms, herbs, nuts, and berries. To avoid the worst of the crowds, visit before 8 am or after 5 pm. ⊠ *La Rambla 91, La Rambla* ☎ *93/413–2345 market telephone, 93/304–0270 The Traders Association telephone* ⊕ *www.boqueria.info* ⊗ *Closed Sun.* Ⓜ *Liceu.*

**Mirador de Colom** (*Columbus Monument*)
**VIEWPOINT** | This Barcelona landmark to Christopher Columbus sits grandly at the foot of La Rambla along the wide harbor-front promenade of Passeig de Colom, not far from the very shipyards (Drassanes Reials) that constructed two of the ships of his tiny but immortal fleet. Standing atop the 150-foot-high iron column—the base of which is aswirl with gesticulating angels—Columbus seems to be looking out at "that far-distant shore" he discovered; in fact he's pointing, with his 18-inch-long finger, in the general direction of Sicily. For a bird's-eye view of La Rambla and the port, take the elevator to the small viewing platform (*mirador*) at the top of the column. The entrance is on the harbor side. ⊠ *Pl. Portal de la Pau s/n, Port Olímpic* ☎ *93/285–3834* 🎫 *€6* ⟲ *Last elevator ride is at 8 pm* Ⓜ *Drassanes.*

A shipshape collection of nautical wonders is on display at the Museu Marítim.

### ★ Museu Marítim

**HISTORY MUSEUM | FAMILY |** This superb museum is housed in the 13th-century Drassanes Reials (Royal Shipyards), at the foot of La Rambla adjacent to the harborfront. This vast covered complex launched the ships of Catalonia's powerful Mediterranean fleet directly from its yards into the port. Today, these are the world's largest and best-preserved medieval shipyards. On the Avinguda del Paral·lel side of Drassanes is a completely intact section of the 14th- to 15th-century walls—Barcelona's third and final ramparts—that encircled El Raval along the Paral·lel and the Rondas de Sant Pau, Sant Antoni, and Universitat. Though the shipyards seem more like a cathedral than a naval construction site, the Maritime Museum is filled with vessels, including a spectacular collection of ship models. Headphones and infrared pointers provide a first-rate self-guided tour. The cafeteria-restaurant Norai, open daily 9 am to 8 pm offers dining in a setting of medieval elegance, and has a charming terrace. ✉ *Av. de les Drassanes s/n, La Rambla* ☎ *93/342–9920* ⊕ *www.mmb.cat/en* ✉ *€10 (includes admission to Santa Eulàlia clipper); free Sun. after 3* ⊙ *Santa Eulàlia closed Mon.* Ⓜ *Drassanes.*

### ★ Palau Güell

**HISTORIC HOME |** Gaudí built this mansion in 1886–90 for textile baron Count Eusebi de Güell Bacigalupi, his most important patron. The dark facade is a dramatic foil for the brilliance of the inside, where spear-shape Art Nouveau columns frame the windows, rising to support a series of detailed and elaborately carved wood ceilings. The basement stables are famous for the "fungiform" (mushroom-like) columns carrying the weight of the whole building. Don't miss the figures of the faithful hounds, with the rings in their mouths for hitching horses, or the wooden bricks laid down in lieu of cobblestones in the entryway upstairs. The dining room is dominated by an Art Nouveau fireplace in the shape of a deeply curving horseshoe arch and wall with floral and animal motifs. Gaudí is most himself on the roof, where his playful, polychrome ceramic chimneys seem like preludes to later works like the Park Güell and La Pedrera. ⊠ *Nou de la Rambla 3–5, La Rambla* ☏ *93/472–5775,* ⊕ *www.palauguell.cat/en* ⊡ *€12 (€9 for students); free 1st Sun. of month for tickets purchased online* ⊗ *Closed Mon.* ☞ *Guided tours (1 hr) in English Sat. at 10:30 am at no additional cost* Ⓜ *Drassanes, Liceu.*

### ★ Plaça Reial

**PLAZA/SQUARE** | Nobel Prize–winning novelist Gabriel García Márquez, architect and urban planner Oriol Bohigas, and Pasqual Maragall, former president of the Catalonian Generalitat, are among the many famous people said to have acquired apartments overlooking this elegant square, a chiaroscuro masterpiece in which neoclassical symmetry clashes with big-city street funk. Plaça Reial is bordered by stately ocher facades with balconies overlooking the wrought-iron Fountain of the Three Graces, and an array of lampposts designed by Gaudí in 1879. Cafés and restaurants line the square. Plaça Reial is most colorful on Sunday morning, when collectors gather to trade stamps and coins; after dark it's a center of downtown nightlife for the jazz-minded, the young, and the adventurous (it's best to be streetwise touring this area in the late hours). ⊠ *Plaça Reial, La Rambla* Ⓜ *Liceu.*

### Port de Barcelona

**MARINA/PIER** | Beyond the Columbus monument—behind the ornate Duana (now the Barcelona Port Authority headquarters)—is La Rambla de Mar, a boardwalk with a drawbridge designed to allow boats into and out of the inner harbor. La Rambla de Mar extends out to the Moll d'Espanya, with its ultra-touristy Maremagnum shopping center (open on Sunday, unusual for Barcelona) and the excellent Aquarium. Next to the Duana you can board a Golondrina boat for a tour of the port and the waterfront or, from the Moll de Barcelona on the right, take a cable car to Montjuïc or Barceloneta. Trasmediterránea and Baleària passenger ferries leave for Italy and the Balearic Islands from the Moll de Barcelona; at the end of the quay is Barcelona's World Trade Center and the Eurostars Grand Marina Hotel. ⊠ *Port Olímpic* Ⓜ *Drassanes.*

### Portaferrissa Fountain

**FOUNTAIN** | Both the fountain and the ceramic representation of Barcelona's second set of walls and the early Rambla are worth studying carefully. If you can imagine pulling out the left side of the ceramic scene and looking broadside at the amber yellow 13th-century walls that ran down this side of the Rambla, you will see a clear picture of what this spot looked like in medieval times. The sandy Rambla ran along outside the walls, while the portal looked down through the ramparts into the city. As the inscription on the fountain explains, the Porta Ferrica, or Iron Door, was named for the iron measuring stick attached to the wood and used in the 13th and 14th centuries to establish a unified standard for measuring goods. The fountain itself dates to 1680; the ceramic tiles are 20th century. ⊠ *Portaferrissa 2, La Rambla* Ⓜ *Liceu, Catalunya.*

## 🍽 Restaurants

### Direkte Boqueria

**$$$$ | CATALAN** | Local gourmands pilgrimage to this tiny, unassuming-looking bar on the edge of the famous Boquería market, where Catalan chef Arnau Muñío flexes his culinary chops in full view of the diners at his chef's-table-style counter. There are two tasting menus, one long, one short, both of which showcase Muñío's unique approach

# Barcelona's Lovers' Day

One of the best days to spend in Barcelona is April 23: St. George's Day, La Diada de Sant Jordi, Barcelona's "Valentine's Day." A day so sweet and playful, so goofy and romantic, that the whole of Catalonia goes giddy from dawn to dusk.

Legend has it that the patron saint of Catalonia, the knight-errant St. George (Sant Jordi in Catalan) slew a dragon that was about to devour a beautiful princess in the little village of Montblanc, south of Barcelona. From the dragon's blood sprouted a rosebush, from which the hero plucked the prettiest blossom for the princess. Hence the traditional Rose Festival celebrated in Barcelona since the Middle Ages, to honor chivalry and romantic love, and a day for men to present their true loves with roses. In 1923 the festival merged with International Book Day to mark the anniversary of the all-but-simultaneous deaths of Miguel de Cervantes and William Shakespeare, on April 23, 1616; it then became the custom for the ladies to present their flower-bearing swains with a book in return.

Close to 7 million roses and close to 20 million euros worth of books (reportedly more than the rest of the year combined) are sold in Catalonia on Sant Jordi's Day. In Barcelona, bookstalls run the length of nearly every major thoroughfare, and although it's an official workday, nearly everybody manages to duck out for at least a while and go browsing. There is a 24-hour reading of *Don Quixote*. Authors come to bookstalls to sign their works. Given Barcelona's importance as a publishing capital, the literary side of the holiday gets special attention.

A Roman soldier martyred for his Christian beliefs in the 4th century, St. George is venerated as the patron saint of 15 European countries—England, Greece, and Romania among them. Images of St. George are everywhere in Barcelona—most notably, perhaps, on the facade of the Catalonian seat of government, the Generalitat. Art Nouveau sculptor Eusebi Arnau depicted Sant Jordi skewering the unlucky dragon on the facade of the Casa Amatller, and on the corner of Els Quatre Gats café. Gaudí referenced the story with an entire building, the Casa Batlló, with the saint's cross implanted on the scaly roof and the skulls and bones of the dragon's victims framing the windows.

Sant Jordi's Day roses are tied with a spike of wheat (for his association with springtime and fertility) and a little red and yellow *senyera*, the Catalonian flag.

In Sarrià there are displays of 45 varieties of rose, representing 45 different kinds of love, from impossible to unrequited, from platonic to filial and maternal. In the Plaça Sant Jaume the Generalitat, its patio filled with roses, opens its doors to the public. Choral groups sing love songs in the Barri Gòtic; jazz combos play in Plaça del Pi. La Rambla is packed solid from the Diagonal to the Mediterranean, with barcelonins basking in the warmth of spring and romance. Rare is the woman anywhere in town without a rose in hand, bound with a red-and-yellow ribbon that says "*t'estimo*": I love you.

to Catalan-Asian fusion food. **Known for:** need to book ahead; Asian-Catalan fusion; accessible fine dining. $ *Average main: €54* ⊠ *Cabres 13, La Rambla* ☎ *93/114–6939* ⊕ *www.direkte.cat* ⊙ *Closed Sun.* Ⓜ *Liceu.*

## ☕ Coffee and Quick Bites

### Cafè de l'Òpera

$ | **CAFÉ** | Directly across from the Liceu opera house, this high-ceiling Art Nouveau café has welcomed operagoers and performers for more than 100 years. It's a central point on the Rambla tourist traffic pattern, so locals are increasingly hard to find, but the café has hung onto its atmosphere of faded glory nonetheless. **Known for:** late-night hours; good for a drink; Art Nouveau decor. $ *Average main: €14* ⊠ *La Rambla 74, La Rambla* ☎ *93/317–7585* ⊕ *www.cafeoperabcn.com* Ⓜ *Liceu.*

##  Hotels

### Bagués

$$$ | **HOTEL** | The luxury of the Eixample has worked its way down to La Rambla, as this boutique gem (formerly the shop and atelier of the well-known Art Nouveau jeweler of the same name) bears ample witness. **Pros:** steps from the opera house; free entrance to the Egyptian Museum of Barcelona; view of the cathedral and port from the rooftop terrace. **Cons:** street-facing rooms can be noisy; hectic location; rooms a bit small for the price. $ *Rooms from: €220* ⊠ *La Rambla 105, La Rambla* ☎ *93/343–5000* ⊕ *www.hotelbagues.com* 🛏 *31 rooms* ❌ *No Meals* Ⓜ *Catalunya, Liceu.*

### Hotel DO Plaça Reial

$$$$ | **HOTEL** | Just at the entrance to the neoclassical Plaça Reial, this charming boutique hotel—with its three separate dining areas—is a find for lovers of food and tasteful design. **Pros:** very central location; 24-hour room service;

contactless check-in. **Cons:** street noise discernible in lower rooms; area can get busy; neighborhood can be rowdy at night. $ *Rooms from: €233* ⊠ *Pl. Reial 1, La Rambla* ☎ *61/856–7874* ⊕ *sonder.com* 🛏 *18 rooms* ❌ *No Meals* Ⓜ *Liceu.*

### Hotel 1898

$$$ | **HOTEL** | Overlooking La Rambla, this imposing mansion (once the headquarters of the Compañía General de Tabacos de Filipinas) couldn't be better located for anyone who likes to be right in the thick of things—especially for opera fans, with the Liceu just around the corner. **Pros:** impeccable service; historic spaces plus modern amenities like a spa and roof deck; ideal location for exploring the Barri Gòtic. **Cons:** some street noise from the Rambla in lower rooms; some guests complain about water pressure; subway rumble discernible in lower rooms on the Rambla side. $ *Rooms from: €200* ⊠ *La Rambla 109, La Rambla* ☎ *93/552–9552* ⊕ *www.hotel1898.com* 🛏 *169 rooms* ❌ *No Meals* Ⓜ *Catalunya, Liceu.*

### Hotel Pulitzer

$$ | **HOTEL** | Hotel Pulitzer is an oasis of calm and appealingly located for those scouring the area's shops for the latest trends. **Pros:** hidden gem for this area; rooftop is a Barcelona hot spot; good value. **Cons:** some rooms could do with an upgrade; no gym, pool, or spa; crowded part of town. $ *Rooms from: €167* ⊠ *Bergara 8, La Rambla* ☎ *93/481-6767* ⊕ *www.hotelpulitzer.es/en* 🛏 *91 rooms* ❌ *No Meals* Ⓜ *Catalunya.*

### Le Méridien Barcelona

$$$$ | **HOTEL** | There's no dearth of hotels along La Rambla in the heart of the city, but few rival the upscale Le Méridien, popular with businesspeople and tourists alike for its suites overlooking the promenade and cozy amenities. **Pros:** central location; Mediterranean suites have large private terraces; soaker tubs in deluxe rooms. **Cons:** slightly sketchy location; rooms small for the price; no

pool. ⑤ *Rooms from: €250* ✉ *La Rambla 111, La Rambla* ☎ *93/318–6200* ⊕ *www. marriott.com/hotels/travel/bcnmd-le-meridien-barcelona* ⇄ *231 rooms* ⦿| *No Meals* Ⓜ *Catalunya, Liceu.*

##  Nightlife

The liveliest pedestrian promenade in the city bustles with a dizzying array of tourist-baiting shops, eateries, and arched paths to Plaça Reial's euphoric nightlife scene. Casual and unpretentious, the scene erupts nightly with a parade of rambunctious crowds of expats, curious interlopers, and assorted celebrations.

### BARS
#### Boadas
COCKTAIL LOUNGES | Barcelona's oldest cocktail bar opened its doors in 1933 and quickly gained a reputation as the only place to enjoy a genuine mojito. The faithful—who still include a few of the city's luminaries—have been flocking ever since, despite the bar's decidedly lackluster decor. The space has the look and feel of an old-fashioned private club and is still the spot to watch old-school barmen in dapper duds mixing drinks the way tradition dictates. ✉ *Tallers 1, La Rambla* ☎ *93/318–9592* ⊕ *boadascocktails.com* Ⓜ *Catalunya.*

#### Jamboree-Jazz and Dance-Club
LIVE MUSIC | This legendary nightspot has hosted some of the world's most influential jazz musicians since its opening in 1960. Decades later, the club continues to offer two nightly shows and remains a notable haven for new generations of jazz and blues aficionados. After the last performance, the spot transforms into a late-night dance club playing soul, hip-hop, and R&B. ✉ *Pl. Reial 17, La Rambla* ☎ *93/304–1210* ⊕ *www.jamboreejazz.com/en* Ⓜ *Liceu.*

# Barri Gòtic

A labyrinth of medieval buildings, squares, and narrow cobblestone streets, the Barri Gòtic comprises the area around the Catedral de la Seu, built over Roman ruins you can still visit and filled with the Gothic structures that marked the zenith of Barcelona's power in the 15th century. On certain corners you feel as if you're making a genuine excursion back in time.

The Barri Gòtic rests squarely atop the first Roman settlement. Sometimes referred to as the *rovell d'ou* (the yolk of the egg), this high ground the Romans called Mons Taber coincides almost exactly with the early 1st- to 4th-century fortified town of Barcino. Sights to see here include the Plaça del Rei, the remains of Roman Barcino underground beneath the Museum of the History of the City, the Plaça Sant Jaume and the area around the onetime Roman Forum, the medieval Jewish Quarter, and the ancient Plaça Sant Just.

## ◉ Sights

### Ajuntament de Barcelona
HISTORIC SIGHT | The 15th-century city hall on Plaça Sant Jaume faces the Palau de la Generalitat, with its mid-18th-century neoclassical facade, across the square once occupied by the Roman Forum. The Ajuntament is a rich repository of sculpture and painting by the great Catalan masters, from Marès to Gargallo to Clarà, from Subirachs to Miró and Llimona. Inside is the famous Saló de Cent, from which the Consell de Cent, Europe's oldest democratic parliament, governed Barcelona between 1373 and 1714. The Saló de les Croniques (Hall of Chronicles) is decorated with Josep Maria Sert's immense black-and-burnished-gold murals (1928) depicting the early-14th-century Catalan campaign

In Byzantium and Greece under the command of Roger de Flor. The city hall is open to visitors on Sunday, with self-guided visits in English hosted at 10am (reserve online). Virtual 360° tours are available at any time. ⊠ *Pl. Sant Jaume 1, Barri Gòtic* ☎ *93/402–7000* ⊕ *ajuntament.barcelona.cat/en* ⊠ *Free* Ⓜ *Jaume I, Liceu.*

### Baixada de Santa Eulàlia
RELIGIOUS BUILDING | Down Carrer Sant Sever from the side door of the cathedral cloister, past Carrer Salomó ben Adret and the Església de Sant Sever, is a tiny shrine, in an alcove overhead, dedicated to the 4th-century martyr Santa Eulàlia, former patron saint of the city (before she was replaced by current patron saint Mare de Deu de la Mercè). Down this hill, or *baixada* (descent), Eulàlia was rolled in a barrel filled with—as the Jacint Verdaguer verse in ceramic tile on the wall reads—*glavis i ganivets de dos talls* (swords and double-edged knives), the final of the 13 tortures to which she was subjected before her crucifixion at Plaça del Pedró. ⊠ *Carrer Sant Sever s/n, Barri Gòtic* Ⓜ *Liceu, Jaume I.*

### Casa de l'Ardiaca (*Archdeacon's House*)
NOTABLE BUILDING | The interior of this 15th-century building, home of the Municipal Archives (upstairs), has superb views of the remains of the 4th-century Roman watchtowers and walls. Look at the Montjuïc sandstone carefully, and you will see blocks taken from other buildings carved and beveled into decorative shapes, proof of the haste of the Romans to fortify the site as the Visigoths approached from the north, when the Pax Romana collapsed. In the center of the lovely courtyard here, across from the Santa Llúcia chapel, is a fountain; on the day of Corpus Christi in June the fountain impressively supports *l'ou com balla,* or "the dancing egg," a Barcelona tradition in which eggs are set to bobbing atop jets of water in various

places around the city. ⊠ *Santa Llúcia 1, Barri Gòtic* ☎ *93/256–2255 Barcelona City Archive* ⊕ *ajuntament.barcelona.cat/ arxiumunicipal/arxiuhistoric/ca* ⊗ *Closed Sun.* Ⓜ *Jaume I, Liceu.*

### Columnes del Temple d'August (*Columns of the Temple of Augustus*)
RUINS | The highest point in Roman Barcelona is marked with a circular millstone at the entrance to the Centre Excursionista de Catalunya, a club dedicated to exploring the mountains and highlands of Catalonia on foot and on skis. Inside the entryway on the right are some of the best-preserved 1st- and 2nd-century Corinthian Roman columns in Europe. Massive, fluted, and crowned with the typical Corinthian acanthus leaves in two distinct rows under eight fluted sheaths, these columns remain only because Barcelona's early Christians elected, atypically, not to build their cathedral over the site of the previous temple. The Temple of Augustus, dedicated to the Roman emperor, occupied the northwest corner of the Roman Forum, which coincided approximately with today's Plaça Sant Jaume. ⊠ *Centre Excursionista de Catalunya, Carrer Paradís 10, Barri Gòtic* ☎ *93/315–2311 Centre Excursionista de Catalunya* ⊕ *ajuntament.barcelona.cat/ museuhistoria/ca/muhba-temple-daugust* Ⓜ *Jaume I.*

### Generalitat de Catalunya
NOTABLE BUILDING | Opposite city hall, the Palau de la Generalitat is the seat of the autonomous Catalan government. Seen through the front windows of this ornate 15th-century palace, the gilded ceiling of the Saló de Sant Jordi (St. George's Hall), named for Catalonia's dragon-slaying patron saint, gives an idea of the lavish decor within. Carrer del Bisbe, running along the right side of the building from the square to the cathedral, offers a favorite photo op: the gargoyle-bedecked Gothic bridge overhead, connecting the Generalitat to the building across

## Sights ▼

1  Ajuntament de Barcelona ......... E6
2  Baixada de Santa Eulàlia ......... D5
3  Casa de l'Ardiaca .................. E5
4  Columnes del Temple d'August ... E6
5  Generalitat de Catalunya ......... G1
6  La Casa Martí–Els Quatre Gats ... E3
7  La Catedral de Barcelona ......... E5
8  Museu d'Història de
   Barcelona (MUHBA) ............... F6
9  Palau del Lloctinent ............... F5
10  Plaça de Garriga i Bachs ......... E5
11  Plaça del Rei ...................... F5
12  Plaça Sant Felip Neri ............. D5
13  Plaça Sant Jaume ................. E6
14  Plaça Sant Just .................... E7
15  Reial Cercle Artístic ............... E4

## Restaurants ▼

1  Caelis ............................... F3
2  Els Quatre Gats .................... E3
3  Koy Shunka ......................... F4
4  La Alcoba Azul ..................... D5
5  Pla B ................................ E7
6  Restaurante Informal .............. E9

## Quick Bites ▼

1  Irati Taverna Basca ................ C5

## Hotels ▼

1  Aral Aparthotel 4*S ............... D7
2  Duquesa de Cardona .............. E9
3  Hotel Catalonia
   Portal de l'Àngel .................. E3
4  Hotel Neri .......................... D5
5  Kimpton Vividora Hotel ........... D3
6  Mercer Hotel Barcelona ........... F7
7  Ohla Barcelona .................... F3
8  The Serras ......................... E9

The ornate Gothic interior of the Catedral de la Seu is always enclosed in shadows, even at high noon.

the street. The Generalitat opens to the public on the second and fourth weekends of the month, with free one-hour guided tours in English (request in advance), through the Generalitat website. ✉ Pl. de Sant Jaume 4, Barri Gòtic ☎ 93/402–4600 ⊕ www.gencat.cat 🎫 Free Ⓜ Jaume I, Liceu.

### La Casa Martí—Els Quatre Gats

**NOTABLE BUILDING** | Built by Josep Puig i Cadafalch for the Martí family, this Art Nouveau house was the fountainhead of bohemianism in Barcelona. It was here in 1897 that four friends, notable dandies all—Ramon Casas, Pere Romeu, Santiago Rusiñol, and Miguel Utrillo—started a café called the Quatre Gats (Four Cats), meaning to make it *the* place for artists and art lovers to gather. (One of their wisest decisions was to mount a show, in February 1900, for an up-and-coming young painter named Pablo Picasso.) The exterior was decorated with figures by sculptor Eusebi Arnau (1864–1934). Inside, Els Quatre Gats hasn't changed one iota: pride of place goes to the Casas self-portait, smoking his pipe, comically teamed up on a tandem bicycle with Romeu. Drop in for a café con leche and you just might end up seated in Picasso's chair. ✉ Montsió 3 bis, Barri Gòtic ☎ 93/302–4140 ⊕ www.4gats.com Ⓜ Catalunya, Jaume I, Urquinaona.

### ★ La Catedral de Barcelona (La Catedral de Santa Creu i Santa Eulàlia)

**CHURCH** | Barcelona's cathedral is a repository of centuries of the city's history and legend—although as a work of architecture visitors might find it a bit of a disappointment. Don't miss the beautifully carved choir stalls of the Knights of the Golden Fleece; the intricately and elaborately sculpted organ loft over the door out to Plaça Sant Iu; the series of 60-odd wood sculptures of evangelical figures along the exterior lateral walls of the choir; and, in the crypt, the tomb of Santa Eulàlia. The leafy, palm tree–shaded cloister surrounds a tropical garden and a pool populated by 13 snow-white geese, one for each of the tortures inflicted upon St. Eulàlia in an effort to break her faith. In front of the cathedral is the grand square of Plaça de la Seu, where on occasion, barcelonins gather to dance the *sardana*, the circular folk dance. ⊠ *Pl. de la Seu s/n, Barri Gòtic* ☎ *93/342–8262* ⊕ *www. catedralbcn.org* ⊠ *Free for worshippers; cultural/tourist visits €9 (includes cathedral, cloister, roof, and choir); Sunday tickets €15 and include entrance to the museum.* Ⓜ *Jaume I.*

★ **Museu d'Història de Barcelona (MUHBA)** (*Museum of the History of Barcelona*) HISTORY MUSEUM | This fascinating museum just off Plaça del Rei traces Barcelona's evolution from its first Iberian settlement through its Roman and Visigothic ages and beyond. The Romans took the city during the Punic Wars, and you can tour underground remains of their Colonia Favencia Iulia Augusta Paterna Barcino (Favored Colony of the Father Julius Augustus Barcino) via metal walkways. Some 43,000 square feet of archaeological artifacts, from the walls of houses, to mosaics and fluted columns, workshops (for pressing olive oil and salted fish paste), and street systems, can be found in large part beneath the plaça. See how the Visigoths and their descendants built the early medieval walls on top of these ruins, recycling chunks of Roman stone and concrete, bits of columns, and even headstones. In the ground-floor gallery is a striking collection of marble busts and funerary urns discovered in the course of the excavations. Guided tours are available in English at 10:30 am daily, but have to be reserved in advance. ⊠ *Palau Padellàs, Pl. del Rei s/n, Barri Gòtic* ☎ *93/256–2100* ⊕ *www.barcelona.cat/museuhistoria/en* ⊠ *From €7; free with Barcelona Card, Sat. and the first Sun. of month* ⊗ *Closed Mon.* Ⓜ *Jaume I.*

**Palau del Lloctinent** (*Lieutenant's Palace*) CASTLE/PALACE | The three facades of the Palau face Carrer dels Comtes de Barcelona on the cathedral side, the Baixada de Santa Clara, and Plaça del Rei. Typical of late Gothic early Renaissance Catalan design, it was constructed by Antoni Carbonell between 1549 and 1557, and remains one of the Gothic Quarter's most graceful buildings. The heavy stone arches over the entry, the central patio, and the intricately coffered wooden roof over the stairs are all good examples of noble 16th-century architecture. The door on the stairway is a 1975 Josep Maria Subirachs work portraying scenes from the life of Sant Jordi and the history of Catalonia. The Palau del Lloctinent was inhabited by the king's official emissary or viceroy to Barcelona during the 16th and 17th centuries; it now houses the historical materials of the Archivo de la Corona de Aragón (Archive of the Crown of Aragon), and offers an excellent exhibit on the life and times of Jaume I, one of early Catalonia's most important figures. The patio also occasionally hosts early-music concerts, and during the Corpus Christi celebration is one of the main venues for the ou com balla, when an egg "dances" on the fountain amid an elaborate floral display. ⊠ *Carrer dels Comtes 2, Barri Gòtic* ☎ *93/485–4285 archives office* Ⓜ *Jaume I.*

**Plaça de Garriga i Bachs**
PLAZA/SQUARE | Ceramic murals depicting executions of heroes of the Catalan resistance to Napoleonic troops in 1809 flank this little space just outside the cloister of La Catedral de Barcelona. The first three scenes show the five resistance leaders waiting their turns to be garroted or hanged (the *garrote vil*, or vile garrote, was reserved for the clergymen, as hanging was considered a lower and less-humane form of execution). The fourth scene depicts the surrender of three agitators who attempted to rally a general Barcelona uprising to save the first five by ringing the cathedral bells. The three are seen here, pale and exhausted after 72 hours of hiding in the organ, surrendering after being promised amnesty by the French. All three were subsequently executed. The bronze

statue of the five martyred insurgents (1929), in the center of the monument, is by the Moderniste sculptor Josep Llimona, whose prolific work in Barcelona also includes the frieze on the Arc de Triomf and the equestrian statue of Count Ramon Berenguer III (1068–1131) in the Plaça de Ramon Berenguer el Gran, between Via Laietana and the Cathedral. ⊠ *Pl. de Garriga i Bachs, Barri Gòtic* Ⓜ *Jaume I.*

### ★ Plaça del Rei

**PLAZA/SQUARE** | This little square is a compact a nexus of history. Long held to be the scene of Columbus's triumphal return from his first voyage to the New World—the precise spot where Ferdinand and Isabella received him is purportedly on the stairs fanning out from the corner of the square—the Palau Reial Major (admission included in the €7 entrance fee for the Museu d'Història de Barcelona; closed Monday) was the official royal residence in Barcelona. The main room is the Saló del Tinell, a magnificent banquet hall built in 1362. To the left is the Palau del Lloctinent (Lieutenant's Palace); towering overhead in the corner is the dark 15th-century Torre Mirador del Rei Martí (King Martin's Watchtower). ⊠ *Pl. del Rei s/n, Barri Gòtic* Ⓜ *Jaume I.*

### ★ Plaça Sant Felip Neri

**PLAZA/SQUARE** | A tiny square just behind Plaça de Garriga Bachs off the side of the cloister of La Catedral de Barcelona, this was once a burial ground for Barcelona's executed heroes and villains, before all church graveyards were moved to the south side of Montjuïc, the present site of the municipal cemetery. The church of San Felip Neri here is a frequent venue for classical concerts. On January 30th, 1938, one of Franco's bombs fell in the square, taking the lives of 42 people, most of whom were children from the School of Sant Philip Neri. Fragments of a bomb made the pockmarks that are still visible on the walls of the church. These days, the schoolchildren still play in the square, which is cherished by locals for its silence and serenity (at least when the children are indoors), despite its tragic history. ⊠ *Pl. Sant Felip Neri, Barri Gòtic* Ⓜ *Jaume I, Liceu.*

### Plaça Sant Jaume

**PLAZA/SQUARE** | Facing each other across this oldest epicenter of Barcelona (and often on politically opposite sides as well) are the seat of Catalonia's regional government, the Generalitat de Catalunya, in the Palau de La Generalitat, and the City Hall, the Ajuntament de Barcelona, in the Casa de la Ciutat. This square was the site of the Roman forum 2,000 years ago, though subsequent construction filled the space with buildings. The square was cleared in the 1840s, but the two imposing government buildings are actually much older: the Ajuntament dates from the 14th century, and the Generalitat was built between the 15th and mid-17th century. Guided tours are temporarily suspended; check for availability. ⊠ *Pl. Sant Jaume, Barri Gòtic* Ⓜ *Jaume I.*

### Plaça Sant Just

**PLAZA/SQUARE** | To the left of city hall, down Carrer Hèrcules (named for the mythical founder of Barcelona) are this square and the site of the Església de Sant Just i Pastor, one of the city's oldest Christian churches. Although the present structure dates from 1342, and nothing remains of the original church, founded in 801 by King Louis the Pious, early Christian catacombs are reported to have been found beneath the plaça. The Gothic fountain was built in 1367 by the patrician Joan Fiveller, then the city's Chief Minister. (Fiveller's major claim to fame was to have discovered a spring in the Collserola hills and had the water piped straight to Barcelona.) The fountain in the square bears an image of St. Just, and the city and sovereign count-kings' coats of arms, along with a pair of falcons. The entryway and courtyard to the left of Carrer Bisbe Caçador are for the Palau Moixó, the town house of an important

# El Call: The Jewish Quarter

Barcelona's Jewish Quarter, El Call (a name derived from the Hebrew word *qahal*, or "meeting place"), is just to the Rambla side of the Palau de la Generalitat. Carrer del Call, Carrer de Salomó ben Adret, Carrer de Marlet, and Arc de Sant Ramón del Call mark the heart of the medieval ghetto. Confined by law to this area at the end of the 7th century (one reason the streets in Calls or Aljamas were so narrow was that their inhabitants could only build into the streets for more space), Barcelona's Jews were the private bankers to Catalonia's sovereign counts (only Jews could legally lend money). The Jewish community also produced many leading physicians, translators, and scholars in medieval Barcelona, largely because the Jewish faith rested on extensive Talmudic and textual study, thus promoting a high degree of literacy. The reproduction of a plaque bearing Hebrew text on the corner of Carrer de Marlet and Arc de Sant Ramón del Call was the only physical reminder of the Jewish

presence here until the medieval synagogue reopened as a historical site in 2003.

In 2018, the name of Carrer de Sant Domènec was changed to Carrer de Ben Salomo Ben Adret to commemorate the 1391 attack on the Jewish community, in which 300 people were murdered on the feast day of Saint Dominic. The new name pays homage to Salomó ben Adret, a distinguished rabbi and leader of Catalan Judaism who served as an advisor to three monarchs.

The story of Barcelona's Jewish community came to a bloody end in August 1391, when during a time of famine and pestilence a nationwide outbreak of anti-Semitic violence reached Barcelona, with catastrophic results: nearly the entire Jewish population was murdered or forced to convert to Christianity. This resulted in a centuries-long end to public Jewish life in the city.

early Barcelona family; down Carrer Bisbe Caçador is the Acadèmia de Bones Lletres, the Catalan Academy of Arts and Letters. The church is dedicated to the boy martyrs Just and Pastor; the Latin inscription over the door translates into English as "Our pious patron is the black and beautiful Virgin, together with the sainted children Just and Pastore." ⊠ *Pl. Sant Just, Barri Gòtic* Ⓜ *Jaume I.*

### Reial Cercle Artístic

**ART MUSEUM** | This private fine-arts society, at the bottom of Portal de l'Angel, where it divides and leads off left to the Cathedral, has two art galleries (one with a permanent collection of works by Salvador Dalí; the other, upstairs, for themed exhibitions), as well as a restaurant and

bar open to the public. It also offers drawing and painting classes and occasional film showings and concerts. Note the elegant Gothic details of the main entrance, with its heavy keystone arch, the stone carvings inside to the right in the Sala Güell, and the stairway sculptures. The El Cercle restaurant upstairs has an intimate feel, though the service can be inconsistent; best option here is a drink or a light lunch on the terrace, overlooking the passing throngs. ⊠ *Carrer dels Arcs 5, Barri Gòtic* ☎ *93/318–7866, 93/318–1774 Dalí collection* ⊕ *www. reialcercleartistic.cat* ⊠ *€10 to Dalí collection* ☉ *Restaurant closed Sun. and Mon.* Ⓜ *Catalunya, Jaume I.*

## Did You Know?

The Barri Gòtic actually sits on top of the first Roman settlement. Roman walls are visible around the edges of the neighborhood.

# 🍴 Restaurants

## ★ Caelis

$$$$ | CATALAN | This restaurant takes contemporary decor and fine-dining style and adds the pizzazz of open-kitchen cooking. It's known for its decadent tastings menus, and the star dish is a rich *mar i muntanya* macaroni with lobster, foie gras, and artichoke. **Known for:** Michelin star; tasting menus for carnivores and vegetarians; lunchtime menu option. ⑤ *Average main: €98* ✉ *Via Laietana 49, Barri Gòtic* ✢ *Inside Hotel Ohla Barcelona* ☎ *93/510–1205* ⊕ *www.caelis.com* ☾ *Closed Sun.–Tues.* Ⓜ *Urquinaona.*

## Els Quatre Gats

$$ | CATALAN | "The Four Cats" was founded in 1897 by a quartet of Moderniste artists—the bohemians of their day—whose work still graces the walls, and the building, Casa Martí (1896), by Modernista master Josep Puig i Cadafalch with sculptural detail by Eusebi Arnau, is a treat in itself. The restaurant in back offers a range of traditional Catalan dishes, but the cooking is uninspired and overpriced so stick to the front room café, where you can linger over a drink, order some of the simpler offerings like *pa de coca* (thin country flatbreads with tomato and olive oil), cheese, cured ham, or *pebrots de Padrón* (fried green peppers), and enjoy a bit of local cultural history. **Known for:** keep a sharp eye on your valuables; Picasso's first exhibition was held here in 1899; it's about the history, not the food. ⑤ *Average main: €20* ✉ *Montsió 3, Barri Gòtic* ☎ *93/302–4140* ⊕ *www.4gats.com* Ⓜ *Catalunya, Urquinaona.*

## Koy Shunka

$$$$ | JAPANESE | The Japanese-Chinese team of master chefs Hideki Matsuhisa and Xu Zhangchao received a Michelin star for their tribute to Asian fusion cooking based on products from the Catalan larder. Dishes vary with the season but may include standouts such as *berberechos en salsa de sake* (cockles in sake sauce), *cerdo ibérico con ciruelas* (Ibérico pork with plums), and *ventresca de atun* (tuna belly with grated tomato and lemon) are several of the infinite variations on the Asia-meets-Catalonia theme in this sleek, contemporary setting. **Known for:** tasting menus only; not to be confused with the team's less adventurous Shunka restaurant nearby; inventive fusion cuisine. ⑤ *Average main: €110* ✉ *Copons 7, Barri Gòtic* ☎ *93/412–7939* ⊕ *www.koyshunka.com* ☾ *Closed Mon., Tues., 3 wks in Aug., and 2 wks at Christmas. No dinner Sun.* Ⓜ *Urquinaona.*

## ★ La Alcoba Azul

$$ | TAPAS | One of Barcelona's most beloved bars, La Alcoba Azul offers a wide selection of tapas with a full-on immersive atmosphere. The decor reflects the Moorish influence of Andalucía, mixed with the quirkiness of the original owners so you'll get illuminated lanterns and broken birdcages hang from the ceiling, while a years-old candle burns in a corner. **Known for:** selection of tapas-sized tostas (open-faced toasted sandwiches); the cod carpaccio is a must-try; wonderfully quirky decor. ⑤ *Average main: €18* ✉ *Salomó ben Adret 14, Barri Gòtic* ☎ *93/302–8141* ⊕ *laalcobaazul.com/en* Ⓜ *Liceu, Jaume I.*

## Pla B

$$ | CATALAN | Filled with couples night after night, this candle-lit dining spot is an atmospheric spot that plays up the room's ancient stone, brick, and wood. The cuisine is light and contemporary, featuring inventive salads and fresh seafood, as well as options for vegetarians and vegans. **Known for:** lunch set menu; extensive wine list; romantic ambience. ⑤ *Average main: €18* ✉ *Bellafila 5, Barri Gòtic* ☎ *93/412–6552* ⊕ *www.restaurant-pla.cat* Ⓜ *Jaume I.*

# A Primer on Barcelona's Cuisine

Menus in Catalan are as musical as they are aromatic, with rare ingredients such as *salicornia* (seawort, or sea asparagus) with *bacalao* (cod), or fragrant wild mushrooms such as *rossinyols* (chanterelles) and *moixernons* (St. George's mushroom) accompanying dishes like *mandonguilles amb sepia* (meatballs with cuttlefish).

Four sauces grace the Catalan table: *sofregit* (fried onion, tomato, and garlic—a base for nearly everything); *samfaina* (a ratatouille-like sofregit with eggplant and sweet red peppers); *picada* (garlic, almonds, bread crumbs, olive oil, pine nuts, parsley, saffron, or chocolate); and *allioli* (pounded garlic and virgin olive oil).

The three *e*'s deserve a place in any Catalan culinary anthology: *escalibada* (roasted red peppers, eggplants, and tomatoes served in garlic and olive oil); *esqueixada* (shredded salt-cod salad served raw with onions, peppers, olives, beans, olive oil, and vinegar); and *escudella* (a winter stew of meats and vegetables with noodles and beans).

Universal specialties are *pa amb tomaquet* (toasted bread with squeezed tomato and olive oil), *espinaques a la catalana* (spinach cooked with raisins, garlic, and pine nuts), and *botifarra amb mongetes* (pork sausage with white beans).

The *mar i muntanya* (Catalan "surf 'n' turf") has been a standard since Roman times. Rice dishes are simply called *arròs*, and range from standard seafood paella to the *arròs a banda* (paella with shelled prawns, shrimp, and mussels), to *arròs negre* (paella cooked in cuttlefish ink) or *arròs caldós* (a brothy risotto-like dish often made with lobster). *Fideuà* is a paella made of vermicelli noodles, not rice.

Fresh fish such as *llobarro* (sea bass, *lubina* in Spanish) or *dorada* (gilthead bream) cooked *a la sal* (in a shell of salt) are standards, as are grilled *llenguado* (sole) and *rodaballo* (turbot). Duck, goose, chicken, and rabbit frequent Catalan menus, as do *cabrit* (kid or baby goat), *xai* (lamb), *porc* (pork), *vedella* (veal), and *bou* (beef). Finally come the two Catalan classic desserts, *mel i mató* (honey and fresh cream cheese) and *crema catalana* (a crème brûlée–like custard with a caramelized glaze).

A typical session *à table* in Barcelona might begin with *pica-pica* (hors d'oeuvres), a variety of delicacies such as *jamón ibérico de bellota* (acorn-fed ham), *xipirones* (baby squid), *pimientos de Padrón* (green peppers, some spicy), or *bunyols de bacallà* (cod fritters or croquettes), and pa amb tomaquet. From here you can order a starter such as *canelones* (cannelloni) or you can go straight to your main course.

★ **Restaurante Informal**

$$$ | CATALAN | On the ground floor of the The Serras hotel, local star chef Marc Gascons has outdone himself with this superb bistro-style restaurant that serves upscale takes on tapas and modern twists on traditional Catalan food. The menu is like a hip, contemporary version of what a Barcelona grandma would serve for Sunday dinner. **Known for:** Michelin-starred chef; creative patatas bravas; contemporary twist on Catalan classics. ⓢ *Average main: €25* ⊠ *Passeig de Colom 9, Barri Gòtic* ☎ *93/169–1869* ⊕ *restauranteinformal.com/en* ⊗ *Closed Mon. and Tues.* Ⓜ *Barceloneta.*

## ☕ Coffee and Quick Bites

### Irati Taverna Basca

$$ | BASQUE | There's only one drawback to this lively Basque bar between Plaça del Pi and La Rambla: it's narrow at the street end, and harder to squeeze into than the metro at rush hour. Skip the pintxos (typical of San Sebastian) on the bar and opt instead for the plates brought out piping-hot from the kitchen. **Known for:** dinner and lunch are served, but it's more fun for tapas; refreshing Txakoli sparkling wine; bustling atmosphere. $ *Average main: €20* ⊠ *Cardenal Casañas 17, Barri Gòtic* ☎ *93/302–3084* ⊕ *gruposagardi.com/restaurante/irati-taverna-basca* Ⓜ *Liceu.*

## 🛏 Hotels

### Arai Aparthotel 4*S

$$$$ | HOTEL | FAMILY | You couldn't ask for a more convenient location from which to explore Barcelona's Barri Gòtic—or for a lodging more elegant—than one of the aparthotel suites in this stunning restoration. **Pros:** warm and attentive service; free admission to Egyptian Museum of Barcelona; historic character retained in former palace. **Cons:** rooms on the top floor lack historic charm; on busy street; seedy area. $ *Rooms from: €273* ⊠ *Avinyó 30, Barri Gòtic* ☎ *93/320–3950* ⊕ *www.hotelarai.com* ⇌ *31 rooms* ⦿ *No Meals* Ⓜ *Liceu.*

### Duquesa de Cardona

$$$$ | HOTEL | A 16th-century town house, built when the Passeig de Colom in front was lined with the summer homes of the nobility, houses this waterfront hotel a five-minute walk from everything in the Barri Gòtic and Barceloneta and a 30-minute walk from the Eixample. **Pros:** pillow menu; room service until 10:30 pm; dreamy location. **Cons:** pricey for a four-star; no spa; rooms on the small side. $ *Rooms from: €230* ⊠ *Passeig de Colom 12, Barri Gòtic* ☎ *93/268–9090*

⊕ *www.hduquesadecardona.com* ⇌ *64 rooms* ⦿ *No Meals* Ⓜ *Barceloneta, Drassanes.*

### Hotel Catalonia Portal de l'Àngel

$ | HOTEL | Converted in 1998 from a historic stately home dating back to 1825, the Catalonia Portal d'Angel beckons with its neoclassic facade and original grand marble staircase. **Pros:** great location; pleasant breakfast pavilion in the garden; includes walking tours of the Old City and the Eixample. **Cons:** could use an all-around refresh; faces busy pedestrian mall; small rooms. $ *Rooms from: €108* ⊠ *Av. Portal d'Angel 17, Barri Gòtic* ☎ *93/318–4141* ⊕ *www.cataloniahotels.com/en/hotel/catalonia-portal-del-angel* ⇌ *83 rooms* ⦿ *No Meals* Ⓜ *Catalunya.*

### ★ Hotel Neri

$$$$ | HOTEL | Just steps from the cathedral, in the heart of the city's old Jewish Quarter, this elegant, upscale, boutique hotel, part of the prestigious Relais & Chateaux hotel group, marries ancient and avant-garde designs. **Pros:** ideal, central location (in the middle of Barri Gòtic); very professional reception and staff; set in a restored medieval palace. **Cons:** very pricey; limited loungers by the rooftop pool; noisy on summer nights and school days. $ *Rooms from: €374* ⊠ *Sant Sever 5, Barri Gòtic* ☎ *93/304–0655* ⊕ *www.hotelneri.com/en* ⇌ *28 rooms* ⦿ *No Meals* Ⓜ *Jaume I, Liceu.*

### ★ Kimpton Vividora Hotel

$$$$ | HOTEL | Every Kimpton hotel is designed to reflect the character of the city it inhabits and, in the case of Kimpton Vividora, that means Mediterranean blues and earthy terra-cotta hues mixed with bright splashes of color and a lush rooftop terrace with stunning views. **Pros:** rooftop bar with great views; a design-lover's dream; local partnerships sourced for toiletries, tea and coffee. **Cons:** no parking available; not all rooms have city views; touristy area (but on a quiet side street). $ *Rooms from: €285*

✉ Duc 15, Barri Gòtic ☎ 93/642–5400 ⊕ kimptonvividorahotel.com/en ⇆ 156 rooms ⍾⃞ No Meals Ⓜ Catalunya.

**Mercer Hotel Barcelona**

$$$$ | **HOTEL** | On a narrow side street near Plaça Sant Jaume, this romantic boutique hotel, a medieval town house, is among the most spectacular examples of Barcelona's signature genius for the redesign and rebirth of historical properties. **Pros:** in the heart of the Old City; breakfast in glassed-in patio with orange trees; comfortable rooftop terrace with a larger than usual pool and (in season) a bar-café. **Cons:** expensive breakfast; no gym or spa; very pricey. ⑤ *Rooms from:* €437 ✉ Carrer dels Lledó 5, Barri Gòtic ☎ 93/310–7480 ⊕ www.mercerbarcelona.com/en ⇆ 28 rooms ⍾⃞ No Meals Ⓜ Jaume I.

**Ohla Barcelona**

$$$$ | **HOTEL** | One of Barcelona's top design hotels (also with incredible food), the Ohla has a neoclassical exterior (not counting the playful eyeballs stuck to the facade) that belies its avant-garde interior, full of witty, design-conscious touches. **Pros:** rooftop terrace and pool; high-end wines at Vistro49; remarkable restaurant Caelis on-site. **Cons:** some rooms are small; uncomfortable furniture in lobby; adjacent to noisy Via Laietana. ⑤ *Rooms from:* €239 ✉ Via Laietana 49, Barri Gòtic ☎ 93/341–5050 ⊕ www.ohlabarcelona.com ⇆ 74 rooms ⍾⃞ Free Breakfast Ⓜ Urquinaona.

**The Serras**

$$$$ | **HOTEL** | If you're looking for an ultra-exclusive boutique hotel that offers superb comfort, discretion, and excellent facilities, then this is it. **Pros:** dreamy rooftop terrace with show-stopping views; excellent restaurant Informal; outstanding, personalized service. **Cons:** rooms on the smaller side; hard on the budget; no sauna or spa. ⑤ *Rooms from:* €395 ✉ Passeig Colom 9, Barri Gòtic

☎ 93/169–1868 ⊕ www.hoteltheserras-barcelona.com ⇆ 28 rooms ⍾⃞ No Meals Ⓜ Barceloneta, Drassanes.

## Ⓨ Nightlife

Medieval Barri Gòtic is a wanderer's paradise filled with ancient winding streets, majestic squares, and myriad period-perfect wine bars and dimly lighted pubs found in the hidden corners of labyrinthine alleyways.

### BARS
**El Paraigua**

**COCKTAIL LOUNGES** | This restaurant's stunning Moderniste facade, an exquisite vintage cash register, and other delicate reminders of its former incarnation as a turn-of-the-20th-century umbrella shop—is usually enough to lure newcomers inside for a closer look but for fun-loving night owls, the real attraction is downstairs in the exposed-brick cocktail club, a former convent basement offering first-rate cocktails and often live music. ✉ Carrer del Pas de l'Ensenyança 2, Barri Gòtic ☎ 93/317–1479 ⊕ www.elparaigua.com Ⓜ Jaume I.

**Harlem Jazz Club**

**LIVE MUSIC** | Located on a rare tree-lined street with twinkling lights, this club attracts patrons of all ages and musical tastes for live Cuban salsa, swing, and reggae alongside creative cocktails in a relaxed and friendly atmosphere. Most concerts start around 10 or 11 pm. ✉ Comtessa de Sobradiel 8, Barri Gòtic ☎ 93/310–0755 ⊕ www.harlemjazzclub.es Ⓜ Jaume I, Liceu.

**La Vinateria del Call**

**WINE BARS** | In the heart of Barcelona's former Jewish Quarter, this rustic charmer serves a wide variety of hearty national wines paired with regional cheeses, meats, and tapas. The antique carved-wood furnishings and candlelit setting makes for an atmospheric respite from the area's chaotic pace. M Salomo ben Adret 9, Barri Gòtic ☎ 93/302–6092 ⊕ www.lavinateriadelcall.com M Jaume I, Liceu.

### Ocaña

**BARS** | In a trio of ancient mansions on buzzy Plaça Reial's southern flank, this venue is dedicated to Jose Peréz Ocaña, a cross-dressing artist, LGBTQ activist, proud bohemian, and dominating figure of Barcelona's post-Franco, alternative-culture explosion. Ocaña also has an adjoining Mediterranean restaurant; a sizable café bar, club, and cocktail lounge; and the fiercest drag queen hostesses on the square. ⊠ Pl. Reial 13–15, Barri Gòtic ☎ 93/676–4814 ⊕ www.ocana.cat M Drassanes.

## Performing Arts

### FLAMENCO

Barcelona's flamenco scene is surprisingly vibrant for a culture so far removed from Andalusia. Los Tarantos, in Plaça Reial, is a must for its authentic flamenco performances.

### ★ Los Tarantos

**FOLK/TRADITIONAL DANCE** | Open since 1963, this small basement spot is the oldest tablao flamenco in Barcelona. It spotlights some of Andalusia's best flamenco in 40-minute shows of dance, percussion, and song. These shows are a good intro to the art, and feel much less touristy than most standard flamenco fare. Shows are daily and it's best to reserve online. ⊠ Pl. Reial 17, Barri Gòtic ☎ 93/304–1210 ⊕ www.tarantosbarcelona.com/en M Liceu.

## Shopping

The Barri Gòtic was built on trade and cottage industries, and there are plenty of nimble fingers producing artisan goods in the old-world shops along its stone streets. Start at the cathedral and work your way outward.

## Catalan Flamenco

Barcelona has a burgeoning and erudite flamenco scene, even if the dance is imported from Andalusia. For the best flamenco in Barcelona, consult listings and concierges and don't be put off if the venue seems touristy—these venues often book the best artists. Barcelona-born *cantaors* (flamenco singers) include Mayte Martín and Miguel Poveda. Keep an eye on the billboards also for names like Estrella Morente (also a flamenco singer) and Chano Domínguez, a pianist who often appears at the Barcelona Jazz Festival.

### ART GALLERIES

#### Sala Parès

**ART GALLERY** | The dean of the city's art galleries is also the oldest one in Spain. It opened in 1040 as an art-supplies shop; as a gallery, it dates from 1877 and has shown every Barcelona artist of note since. Picasso, Dalí, and Miró exhibited their work here, as did Rusiñol before them. Nowadays, artists like Magí Puig and Carlos Morago get pride of place. ⊠ Petritxol 5, Barri Gòtic ☎ 93/318–7020 ⊕ salapares.com ۩ Closed Sun. and Mon. M Liceu, Catalunya.

### CERAMICS AND GLASSWARE

#### ★ Art Escudellers

**CERAMICS** | Ceramic pieces from all over Spain are on display at this large store across the street from the restaurant Los Caracoles; more than 140 different artisans are represented, with maps showing what part of Spain the work is from. There are several other branches of Art Escudellers in the old city. ⊠ Escudellers 23, Barri Gòtic ☎ 93/412–6801 ⊕ www.artescudellers.com M Liceu, Drassanes.

## CLOTHING

### ★ L'Arca

**MIXED CLOTHING** | This family-owned (and women-owned) store sells vintage clothing, fabrics, jewelry, and accessories, with a focus on wedding dresses, veils, and lace. Despite the found-object attitude and ambience of the place, they're not giving away these vintage baubles, so don't be surprised at the hefty price tags. You'll also find a collection of their own bridal gowns, newly made but in romantic, old-fashioned styles. Notably, the shop supplied many costumes and props for the filming of *Titanic*. ⊠ *Banys Nous 20, Barri Gòtic* ☎ *93/302–1598* ⊕ *larcabarcelona.com* Ⓜ *Liceu.*

### Sombrereria Obach

**HATS & GLOVES** | This hat shop is as much part of the Barri Gòtic's landscape as any of its medieval churches. It occupies a busy corner in El Call (the old Jewish district) and has curved glass windows with displays of timeless, classic hats—from traditional Basque berets to Stetsons and Panamas—that have been dressing heads in Barcelona since 1924. ⊠ *Call 2, Barri Gòtic* ☎ *93/318–4094* ⊕ *www.sombrereriaobach.com* Ⓜ *Liceu, Jaume I.*

## FOOD

### Caelum

**FOOD** | At the corner of Carrer de la Palla and Banys Nous, this café and shop sells wine and foodstuffs such as honey, biscuits, chocolates, and preserves made in convents and monasteries all over Spain. You can pop in to pick up an exquisitely packaged pot of jam, or linger over pastries and coffee in the tearoom. ⊠ *Palla 8, Barri Gòtic* ☎ *93/302–6993* Ⓜ *Liceu, Jaume I.*

### La Casa del Bacalao

**FOOD** | As you can guess from the name, which is decorated with cod-fishing memorabilia, this shop specializes in bacalao—salted and dried salt cod, whichis used in a wide range of Catalan recipes (such as *esqueixada*, in which shredded strips of raw salt cod are served in a marinade of oil and vinegar). Slabs of bacalao can be vacuum-packed for portability, and there are lots of recipe books if you're looking for inspiration. ⊠ *Moles 11, just off Portal de l'Àngel, Barri Gòtic* ☎ *93/301–6539* ⊕ *lacasadelbacalao.es* Ⓜ *Catalunya.*

## GIFTS AND SOUVENIRS

### Centre d'Artesania Catalunya

**CRAFTS** | In 2010 the Catalan government created the registered trademark Empremtes de Catalunya to represent Catalan artisans and to make sure that visitors get the real deal when buying what they believe to be genuine products. The official shop now sells jewelry re-created from eras dating back to pre-Roman times, Gaudí-inspired sculptures, traditional Cava mugs, and some bravely avant-garde objects from young artisans—all officially sanctioned as fit to represent the city. ⊠ *Banys Nous 11, Barri Gòtic* ☎ *93/467–4660* ⊕ *ccam.gencat.cat/ca/inici* Ⓜ *Liceu, Jaume I.*

### Cereria Subirà

**CRAFTS** | Known as the city's oldest shop, having remained open since 1761 (though it was not always a candle store), this "waxery" (*cereria*) offers candles in all sizes and shapes, ranging from wild mushrooms to the Montserrat massif, home of the Benedictine abbey. ⊠ *Baixada de la Llibreteria 7, Barri Gòtic* ☎ *93/315–2606* ⊕ *cereriasubira.cat/en* Ⓜ *Jaume I.*

## MARKETS

### Mercat Gòtic

**MARKET** | A browser's bonanza, this interesting if somewhat pricey Thursday market (10 am–8 pm) for antique clothing, jewelry, and art occupies the plaza in front of the cathedral. In December, a Christmas market takes over the space. Most stalls aren't open during the vacation month of August. ⊠ *Av. Plaça de la Catedral, Barri Gòtic* ⊕ *www.mercatgoticbcn.com* Ⓜ *Jaume I.*

## SHOES

### ★ La Manual Alpargatera

**SHOES** | If you appreciate old-school craftsmanship in footwear and reasonable prices, visit this boutique just off Carrer Ferran. Handmade rope-sole sandals and espadrilles are the specialty, and this shop has sold them to everyone—including the pope. The flat, beribboned espadrilles model used for dancing the *sardana* is available, as are fashionable wedge heels with peep toes and comfy slippers. The price of a pair of espadrilles here start at $22, which is far less than the same quality shoes in the United States. They offer free shipping outside of Spain on orders of €250 or more.
✉ *Avinyó 7, Barri Gòtic* ☎ *93/301–0172* ⊕ *lamanual.com/en* Ⓜ *Liceu, Jaume I.*

# El Raval

El Raval (from *arrabal*, meaning "suburb" or "slum") is the area to the west of La Rambla, on the right as you walk toward the port. Originally a rough quarter outside the second set of city walls that ran down the left side of La Rambla, El Raval was once notorious for its Barri Xinès (or Barrio Chino) red-light district, the lurid attractions of which are known to have fascinated a young Pablo Picasso.

Gypsies, acrobats, prostitutes, and *saltimbanques* (clowns and circus performers) who made this area their home soon found immortality in the many canvases Picasso painted of them during his Blue Period. It was the ladies of the night on Carrer Avinyó, not far from the Barri Xinès, who may have inspired one of the 20th-century's most famous paintings, Picasso's *Les Demoiselles d'Avignon,* an important milestone on the road to Cubism. Not bad for a city slum.

El Raval, though still rough-and-tumble, has been gentrified and much improved since 1980, largely as a result of the construction of the Museu d'Art Contemporani de Barcelona (MACBA) and other cultural institutions nearby, such as the Centre de Cultura Contemporània (CCCB), Filmoteca, and the Convent dels Àngels. La Rambla del Raval has been opened up between Carrer de l'Hospital and Drassanes, bringing light and air into the streets of the Raval for the first time in a thousand years. The medieval Hospital de la Santa Creu, Plaça del Pedró, the Mercat de Sant Antoni, and Sant Pau del Camp are highlights of this funky, rough-edged part of Barcelona.

## ⊙ Sights

### ★ Antic Hospital de la Santa Creu i Sant Pau

**HISTORIC SIGHT** | Founded in the 10th century as one of Europe's earliest medical facilities, the mostly 15th- and 16th-century complex contains some of Barcelona's most impressive Gothic architecture. From the grand entrance, the first building on the left is the 18th-century Reial Acadèmia de Cirurgia i Medicina (Royal Academy of Surgery and Medicine); the surgical amphitheater is kept just as it was in the days when students learned by observing dissections.

Through a gate to the left of the Casa de Convalescència is the garden-courtyard of the hospital complex, the Jardins de Rubió i Lluc, centered on a baroque cross and lined with orange trees. On the right is the Biblioteca Nacional de Catalunya, Catalonia's national library. The library is spectacular: two parallel halls—once the core of the hospital—230 feet long, with towering Gothic arches and vaulted ceilings, designed in the 15th century by the architect of the church of Santa Maria del Pi, Guillem Abiell. This was the hospital where Antoni Gaudí was taken, unrecognized and assumed to be a pauper, after he was struck by a trolley on June 7, 1926. ✉ *Hospital 56 (or Carme 45), El Raval* ☎ *93/317–1686 Reial Acadèmia de Medicina, 93/270–2300 Biblioteca de*

# El Raval

Gran Via de les Corts Catalanes

Universitat
Plaça de la Universitat
Ronda Universitat

SANT ANTONI

Carrer de Sepúlveda
Carrer de Floridablanca
Carrer de Tamarit
Carrer de Manso
Carrer Parlament
C. del Marquès de Campo Sagrado
Carrer Aldana

Sant Antoni

Ronda de Sant Antoni
Carrer Valldenzella
Carrer del Tigre
Carrer de la Paloma
Carrer d Ferlandina
C. Guitré
C. d. Peu de la Creu
C. del Carme

EL RAVAL

Carrer d. St. Antoni Abat
Carrer de la Cera
C. Vistalegre
Carrer de l'Aurura
Carrer de Sant Pacià
Carrer Lleialtat
Carrer Santa Elena

BARRI XINÈS

C. de Sant Pau
Carrer de les Tàpies
Carrer Nou de la Rambla

Av. del Paral·lel

Carrer del Carme
Carrer Hospital
Sant Rafael
Sant Josep Oriol
Carrer de Sant Pau
Carrer de Marquès de Barbera
Carrer Nou de la Rambla
Arc de Teatre

Liceu

LA RAMBLA

Plaça Reial

Carrer Pintor Fortunvy
Carrer Elisabets

Ronda de Sant Antoni

0    200 yards
0    200 m

## KEY

- **1** Sights
- **1** Restaurants
- **1** Quick Bites
- **1** Hotels
- Ⓜ Metro Stops

## Sights ▼

1 Antic Hospital de la Santa
  Creu i Sant Pau ......... **D5**
2 Centre de Cultura
  Contemporània de
  Barcelona (CCCB) ...... **D2**
3 Museu d'Art Contemporani
  de Barcelona (MACBA) **D3**
4 Plaça del Pedró .......... **C4**
5 Sant Pau del Camp ..... **B6**

## Restaurants ▼

1 Bar Cañete .............. **E6**
2 Ca l'Estevet............. **C2**
3 Ca l'Isidre ............... **B6**
4 Cera 23.................. **B4**
5 Dos Pebrots ............ **D3**
6 Fonda España ........... **E6**
7 Frankie Gallo
  Cha Cha Cha............ **D6**
8 Suculent ................. **C6**
9 Trópico................... **C6**

## Quick Bites ▼

1 Bar Central .............. **E3**

## Hotels ▼

1 Casa Camper
  Barcelona ............... **E3**
2 Hotel España ........... **E6**

Catalunya ⊕ www.bno.cat ⏲ C10 (Reial Acadèmia do Medicina de Catalunya tour) ⊘ Reial Acadèmia de Medicina de Catalunya: Closed Sun.–Tues., Thurs., and Fri; Biblioteca de Catalunya and Capella: Closed Sun. Ⓜ Liceu.

## Centre de Cultura Contemporània de Barcelona (CCCB) (CCCB)

ARTS CENTER | Just next door to the MACBA, this multidisciplinary gallery, lecture hall, and concert and exhibition space offers a year-round program of cultural events and projects. The center also has a remarkable film archive of historic shorts and documentaries, free to the public. Housed in the restored and renovated Casa de la Caritat, a former medieval convent and hospital, the CCCB, like the Palau de la Música Catalana, is one of the city's shining examples of contemporary flare added to traditional architecture and design. A smoked-glass wall on the right side of the patio, designed by architects Albert Villaplana and Helio Piñon, reflects out over the rooftops of El Raval to Montjuïc and the Mediterranean beyond. ⊠ Montalegre 5, El Raval ☎ 93/306 1100 ⊕ www.cccb. org ⏲ Exhibitions €6; Sun. 3–8, free (pre-book online). Admission to CCCB Film Archive is free with previous reservation ⊘ Closed Mon. Ⓜ Universitat, Catalunya.

## ★ Museu d'Art Contemporani de Barcelona (MACBA) (MACBA Museum of Contemporary Art Barcelona)

ART MUSEUM | FAMILY | Designed by American architect Richard Meier in 1992, this gleaming explosion of light and geometry in El Raval houses a permanent collection of contemporary art, and also regularly mounts special temporary exhibitions. Meier gives a nod to Gaudí (with the Pedrera-like wave on one end of the main facade), but his minimalist building otherwise looks unfinished.

That said, the MACBA is unarguably an important addition to the cultural capital of this once-shabby neighborhood. The MACBA's 20th-century art collection (Calder, Rauschenberg, Oteiza, Chillida, Tàpies) is excellent, while the free app offers a useful introduction to the philosophical foundations of contemporary art as well as the pieces themselves. The museum also offers wonderful workshops and activities for kids. ⊠ Pl. dels Àngels 1, El Raval ☎ 93/412–0810 ⊕ www.macba.cat ⏲ €11, free Sat. after 4 ⊘ Closed Tues. Ⓜ Universitat, Catalunya.

## Plaça del Pedró

PLAZA/SQUARE | This landmark in medieval Barcelona was the dividing point where ecclesiastical and secular paths parted. The high road, Carrer del Carme, leads to the cathedral and the seat of the bishopric; the low road, Carrer de l'Hospital, heads down to the medieval hospital and the Boqueria market, a clear choice between body and soul. Named for a stone pillar, or pedró (large stone), marking the fork in the road, the square became a cherished landmark for Barcelona Christians after Santa Eulàlia, co-patron of Barcelona, was crucified there in the 4th century after suffering the legendary 13 ordeals designed to persuade her to renounce her faith—which, of course, she heroically refused to do. As the story goes, an overnight snowfall chastely covered her nakedness with virgin snow. The present version of Eulàlia and her cross was sculpted by Barcelona artist Frederic Marès and erected in 1951. The bell tower and vacant alcove at the base of the triangular square belong to the **Capella de Sant Llàtzer** church, originally built in the open fields in the mid-12th century and used as a leper hospital and place of worship after the 15th century when Sant Llàtzer (St. Lazarus) was officially named patron saint of lepers. Flanked by two ordinary apartment buildings, the Sant Llàtzer chapel has a tiny antique patio and apse visible from the short Carrer de Sant Llàtzer, which cuts behind the church between Carrer del Carme and Carrer Hospital. ⊠ Pl. del Pedró, El Raval Ⓜ Sant Antoni.

### ★ Sant Pau del Camp

CHURCH | Barcelona's oldest church was originally outside the city walls (*del camp* means "in the fields") and was a Roman cemetery as far back as the 2nd century, according to archaeological evidence. What you see now was built in 1127 and is the earliest Romanesque structure in Barcelona. Elements of the church—the classical marble capitals atop the columns in the main entry—are thought to be from the 6th and 7th centuries. The hulking, mastodonic shape of the church is a reminder of the church's defensive posture in the face of intermittent Roman persecution and, later, Moorish invasions and sackings. Check for musical performances here, as the church is an acoustical gem. The tiny cloister is Sant Pau del Camp's best feature and one of Barcelona's semisecret treasures. ⊠ *Sant Pau 101, El Raval* ☎ *93/441–0001* ⊕ *stpaudelcamp.blogspot.com* 🎟 *Free when Masses are celebrated; entrance €5, guided tours €9 (Sat. at 1pm)* ☯ *Cloister closed Sun. during Mass; no tours in mid-Aug.* Ⓜ *Paral·lel.*

## 🍴 Restaurants

### ★ Bar Cañete

$$ | TAPAS | This spot just around the corner from the Liceu opera house is one of Barcelona's best tapas restaurants, with a long bar overlooking the burners and part of the kitchen that leads down to the 20-seat communal tasting table at the end of the room. Specialists in Ibérico products, they serve obscure cuts of Ibérico pork, such as *pluma ibérica* and *secreto ibérico* (nuggets of meat found on the inside of the shoulder blade and much-prized by Ibérico fanatics), though the real highlight of the menu is the market-fresh seafood that ranges from oysters, to grilled baby scallops and house special dishes like the baby squid (*chipirones*) with white Santa Pau beans. **Known for:** fresh seafood; superb tapas; boisterous atmosphere. ⑤ *Average main:*

*€18* ⊠ *Unió 17, El Raval* ☎ *93/270–3458* ⊕ *www.barcanete.com/en* Ⓜ *Liceu.*

### Ca l'Estevet

$$ | CATALAN | This restaurant has been serving old-school Catalan cuisine to local and loyal customers since 1940 (and under a different name for 50 years before that), and the practice has been made perfect. Standouts include *butifarra* sausage with spinach and chickpeas, meatballs with squid and shrimp, or veal stew with wild mushrooms. **Known for:** historic location; large, hearty portions; Catalan specialties. ⑤ *Average main: €16* ⊠ *Valldonzella 46, El Raval* ☎ *93/301–2939* ⊕ *www.restauranteste-vet.com* ☯ *No dinner Sun. and Mon.* Ⓜ *Universitat.*

### Ca l'Isidre

$$$$ | CATALAN | Since the early 1970s, Ca l'Isidre has elevated simplicity to the level of the spectacular, with traditional Catalan dishes prepared to an extraordinarily high standard (and at a rather high price tag by Barcelona standards). Ignore the menu—just follow the recommendations and order whatever's in season. **Known for:** art collection; locally sourced produce; once frequented by Miró and Dalí, whose work is on the walls, as well as current celebrities and politicians. ⑤ *Average main: €32* ⊠ *Flors 12, El Raval* ☎ *93/441–1139* ⊕ *www.calisidre.com* ☯ *Closed Mon., and 1st 2 wks of Aug.; No dinner Tues., Wed., Sun.* Ⓜ *Paral·lel.*

### Cera 23

$$ | SPANISH | A gem among a crop of modern restaurants putting the razzle back into the run-down Raval, Cera 23 offers a winning combination of great service and robust cooking in a fun, friendly setting; stand at the bar and enjoy a blackberry mojito while you wait for your table. The focus of the dining area is the open kitchen, so guests can watch the cooks create contemporary presentations of traditional Spanish dishes. **Known for:** exceptional service; slow-cooked

One of the earliest medical complexes in Europe is the Antic Hospital de la Santa Creu i Sant Pau.

pork ribs with honey and soy sauce; "volcano" of black rice. $ *Average main: €15* ☒ *Cera 23, El Raval* ☎ *93/442–0808* ⊕ *www.cera23.com* ☾ *Closed Wed. and Thurs. No lunch* Ⓜ *Sant Antoni.*

### Dos Pebrots

$$ | **MEDITERRANEAN** | Albert Raurich of the upscale Dos Palillos restaurant, transformed his favorite neighborhood haunt, Bar Raval, into a cutting-edge tapas bar that explores the history of Mediterranean cuisine. The gleaming makeover hasn't robbed the space of its old-town feel, though, thanks to little touches like the restored original facade and vintage cutlery. **Known for:** restored original exterior; unusual ingredients; unique tapas. $ *Average main: €20* ☒ *Doctor Dou 19, El Raval* ☎ *93/853–9598* ⊕ *www.dospebrots.com* ☾ *Closed Mon. and Tues., and 2 wks at Christmas* Ⓜ *Catalunya.*

### ★ Fonda España

$$$ | **CATALAN** | The sumptuous glory of this restored late-19th-century Art Nouveau dining room has food to match, courtesy of chef German Espinosa, who spent many years working under superstar Martín Berasategui. **Known for:** the tasting menus; satisfying traditional dishes; Art Nouveau decor. $ *Average main: €23* ☒ *Hotel España, Sant Pau 9, El Raval* ☎ *93/550–0010* ⊕ *www.hotelespanya.com* ☾ *Closed Mon.–Wed. and Aug. No dinner Sun.* Ⓜ *Liceu.*

### Frankie Gallo Cha Cha Cha

$ | **PIZZA** | There are days when only a pizza will do and this might be the best spot in Barcelona to satisfy the craving, with a combination of wood-fired sourdough pizzas, craft beer, top-notch artisanal ingredients, and a buzzing atmosphere. The eggplant parmigiana pizza is a best seller, as is the tiramisú for dessert. **Known for:** eggplant parmigiana pizza; great atmosphere; some of the best pizza joint in town. $ *Average main: €13* ☒ *Marquès de Barberà, 15, El Raval* ☎ *93/159–4250* ⊕ *frankiegallochachacha.com* ☾ *Closed Mon.* Ⓜ *Drassanes.*

### ★ Suculent

$$ | CATALAN | This is a strong contender for the crown of Barcelona's best bistro, where chef Toni Romero turns out Catalan tapas and dishes that have roots in rustic classics but reach high modern standards of execution. The name is a twist on the Catalan *sucar lent* (to dip slowly), and excellent bread is duly provided to soak up the sauces, which you won't want to let go to waste. **Known for:** big, bold flavors; must-try steak tartare on marrow bone; set menus but à la carte available at the bar. ⓢ *Average main: €18* ✉ *Rambla del Raval 45, El Raval* ☎ *93/443–6579* ⊕ *www.suculent. com* ☾ *Closed Sat. and Sun.* Ⓜ *Liceu.*

### ★ Trópico

$ | LATIN AMERICAN | This lively brunch spot is a breath of fresh air in a neighborhood perhaps best described as "up and coming." The name "trópico" (or tropical) refers to both the bright decor and the menu that takes inspiration from the tastes of the tropics—from Colombian *arepas* to Brazilian chicken *coxinhas*, Thai dragon fruit smoothies, Peruvian *ají*, and Indian-style curries. Founders Leonardo Tristancho from Colombia and Rodrigo Marco from Brazil have created a space that reflects their love of vibrant, unapologetic flavors, blended with all the warmth of Latin hospitality. **Known for:** Colombian arepas; Latin hospitality; vibrant decor and atmosphere. ⓢ *Average main: €14* ✉ *Marquès de Barberà 24, El Raval* ☎ *93/667–7552* ⊕ *www.tropicobcn.com* Ⓜ *Drassanes.*

## ☕ Coffee and Quick Bites

### Bar Central

$ | CAFÉ | If you're looking for a calm respite in which to enjoy a mid-morning coffee or a laid-back lunch, you can't beat a patio table at this café in the lush gardens of Casa de la Misericòrdia (a former orphanage), replete with palm trees, ferns, moss, and a small waterfall that mutes the street noise. In the evening, twinkling lights add a touch of romance to the already magical space. **Known for:** quiet surroundings; romantic ambience in the evening; good croissants. ⓢ *Average main: €12* ✉ *d'Elisabets 6, El Raval* ☎ *93/270–3314* ⊕ *barcentral. bar* Ⓜ *Catalunya.*

## 🛏 Hotels

### Casa Camper Barcelona

$$$ | HOTEL | A marriage between the Camper footwear empire and the (now defunct) Vinçon design store produced this 21st-century hotel halfway between La Rambla and the MACBA (Barcelona Museum of Contemporary Art), with a focus on sustainability (think solar panels and water recycling). **Pros:** great breakfast with dishes cooked to order; complimentary 24-hour snack bar; just steps from the MACBA and the Boqueria. **Cons:** no in-room minibar; extra per person charge for children over three years old; expensive for what you get. ⓢ *Rooms from: €220* ✉ *Elisabets 11, El Raval* ☎ *93/342–6280* ⊕ *www.casacamper.com* ⟿ *40 rooms* ⦿| *Free Breakfast* Ⓜ *Catalunya, Liceu.*

### ★ Hotel España

$$ | HOTEL | This beautifully renovated Art Nouveau gem is the second oldest (after the nearby Sant Agustí) and among the best of Barcelona's smaller hotels. **Pros:** near Liceu opera house and La Rambla; lavish breakfast; alabaster fireplace in the bar lounge. **Cons:** rooftop has restricted views; could use a refresh; lower rooms facing Carrer Sant Pau get some street noise. ⓢ *Rooms from: €160* ✉ *Sant Pau 9–11, El Raval* ☎ *93/550–0000* ⊕ *www. hotelespanya.com* ⟿ *83 rooms* ⦿| *No Meals* Ⓜ *Liceu.*

## 🌙 Nightlife

El Raval has slowly evolved from a forgotten, seedy no-man's-land into one of the choicest districts to enjoy provocative modern art and a pulsating, boho-glam party scene. Though not to everyone's taste, hippie students, tattooed misfits, artists, and more recently trend-seeking nomads routinely bar crawl up and down a stretch of nightlife-friendly streets (Joaquin Costa is one) featuring a wide assortment of divey dens, music bars, pubs, and funky *coctelerias*.

## BARS
### Ambar
**BARS** | Right off the tree-lined Rambla del Raval, the clientele at this popular watering hole is as colorful as the snazzy, red-quilted bar and moody green-blue lighting: expat students and pierced young artists rub shoulders with visiting rabble-rousers warming up for a wild night out. With its basic menu of classic cocktails and long drinks, the main attraction is arguably the space itself—the epitome of shabby chic (with an emphasis on shabby) with its calculated mix of modern and retro. ⊠ *Sant Pau 77, El Raval* ☎ *93/441-3725.*

### Casa Almirall
**BARS** | The twisted wooden fronds framing the bar's mirror, an 1888 vintage bar-top iron statue of a muse, and Art Nouveau touches such as curvy door handles make this one of the most atmospheric bars in Barcelona. It's also the second oldest, dating from 1860. (The oldest is the Marsella, another Raval favorite.) It's a good spot for evening drinks after hitting the nearby MACBA (Museu d'Art Contemporani de Barcelona) or for a pre-lunch *vermut* (vermouth) on weekends. ⊠ *Joaquín Costa 33, El Raval* ☎ *93/318-9917* ⊕ *www.casaalmirall.com/en* Ⓜ *Universitat.*

### La Confitería
**BARS** | In a former pastry shop, this vintage bar has retained so much of the 19th-century Moderniste facade and interior touches (onetime cake display cases are now filled with period memorabilia) that visitors might experience the sensation of time standing still. Divided into two equally inviting spaces, the front

is usually packed with regulars, while the granite-and-metal tables in the back are popular with couples. ⊠ *Sant Pau 128, El Raval* ☎ *93/140-5435* ⊕ *www.confiteria. cat* Ⓜ *Paral·lel.*

### Marsella
**BARS** | Inaugurated in 1820, this historic venue, a favored haunt for artistic notables such as Gaudí, Picasso, and Hemingway, has remained remarkably unchanged since its celebrated heyday. The chipped paint on the walls and ceiling, cracked marble tables, and elaborate spiderwebs on chandeliers and bottles all add to the charm, but the main reason patrons linger is one special shot: Marsella is one of few establishments serving homemade absinthe (*absenta* in Spanish), a potent aniseed-flavored spirit meant to be savored and rumored to enhance productivity. ⊠ *Sant Pau 65, El Raval* ☎ *93/442-7263* ⊕ *www.facebook. com/Bar-Marsella-148097715525039* Ⓜ *Liceu.*

### Sala Apolo
**DANCE CLUBS** | Set across three levels and multiple rooms, Sala Apolo offers a variety of house/techno nights and intimate live music concerts. Two Sunday afternoons a month, it turns into Barcelona's hottest LGBTQ destination, playing host to the immensely popular Churros con Chocolate and VenTú! tea dances. ⊠ *Nou de la Rambla, 113, El Raval* ☎ *93/441-4001* ⊕ *www.sala-apolo.com* Ⓜ *Paral·lel.*

### 33/45
**BARS** | From the street, this indie-cool spot might seem too brightly lighted for gritty-glam Raval, but the mismatched sofas with oversize pillows and the eclectic selection of flavored gins, tequila blends, and imported beer attracts a steady flow of lounge lizards. ⊠ *Joaquin Costa 4, El Raval* ☎ *93/187-4138* ⊕ *www.3345.es* Ⓜ *Sant Antoni.*

### Two Schmucks
**BARS** | One of the Barcelona cocktail bars to make it onto the "World's 50

Best Bars" list, Two Schmucks is the kind of fun-filled neighborhood bar that's hard to resist. The vibe is laid-back, but never boring, and it's spawned spin-offs Two Schmucks on a Terrace and the rock-'n'-roller Lucky Schmuck, also in Raval. ⊠ *Joaquín Costa 52, El Raval* ☎ *67/448–0073* ⊕ *www.two-schmucks. com* Ⓜ *Universitat.*

## MUSIC CLUBS: JAZZ AND BLUES
### Jazz Sí Club
LIVE MUSIC | Run by the Barcelona contemporary music school next door, this workshop and (during the day) café is a forum for musicians, teachers, and fans to listen to and debate their art. Most weeks, the schedule offers jazz on Monday and Wednesday; pop, blues, and rock jam sessions on Tuesday; Cuban salsa on Thursday; flamenco on Friday; and rock and pop on weekends. The small cover charge (€6–€10, depending on which night you visit) includes a drink. Gigs start between 6:30 and 8:45 pm. ⊠ *Requesens 2, El Raval* ☎ *93/329–0020* ⊕ *tallerdemusics.com/en/jazzsi-club* Ⓜ *Sant Antoni.*

## 🛍 Shopping

Shopping in El Raval reflects the district's multicultural and bohemian vibe. Around MACBA (Barcelona Museum of Contemporary Art) you'll find dozens of designer-run start-ups selling fashion, crafts, and housewares, while the edgier southernmost section has an abundance of curious establishments chock-full of ethnic foods (along Calles Hospital and Carme) and vintage clothing (on Calle Riera Baixa).

## BOOKS
### La Central del Raval
BOOKS | This bookstore in the former chapel of the Casa de la Misericòrdia sells books amid stunning architecture and holds regular cultural events. You can sift through books of various genres, from anthropology and architecture to

photography and poetry, and the English-language section showcases both best-sellers and lesser-known works. Behind the bookstore is Bar Central's lush garden restaurant, which is still a bit of a local secret. ⊠ *Elisabets 6, El Raval* ☎ *90/080–2109* ⊕ *www.lacentral.com* Ⓜ *Catalunya.*

## MARKETS
### Flea Market Barcelona
SECOND-HAND | Barcelona's love for retro and vintage reaches its pinnacle twice a month in two different squares. In Plaça Blanquerna, on the second Sunday of the month, Flea Market Barcelona (aka "El Flea") bring together the hipsters and the hippies, the dads and the dealers, who empty out their wardrobes and garages so that you can walk away with art-deco wall clocks or a 1970s hand mixer. Over in Plaça Salvador Seguí, on the first Sunday of the month, is the so-called "Fleadonia." ⊠ *Pl. Blanquerna* ⊕ *fleamarketbcn.com* Ⓜ *Drassanes.*

### Mercat de Sant Antoni
MARKET | A mammoth hangar at the junction of Ronda de Sant Antoni and Comte d'Urgell, designed in 1882 by Antoni Rovira i Trias, the Mercat de Sant Antoni is considered the city's finest example of wrought-iron architecture. The Greek-cross-shaped market covers an entire block on the edge of the Eixample, and some of the best Moderniste stall facades in Barcelona distinguish this exceptional space. Fully functioning as of 2017 after years of painstaking restoration to incorporate medieval archaeological remains underneath, the market is a foodie paradise of fruit, vegetables, fish, cheeses, and more. The indoor food market is closed on Sunday but this is when, in the morning, you can wander the outdoor stalls of the weekly flea market full of stamps and coins, comic books and trading cards, VHS, CDs, vinyl, and vintage clothing. ⊠ *Comte d'Urgell 1, El Raval* ☎ *93/426–3521* ⊕ *www.mercatdesantantoni.com* Ⓜ *Sant Antoni.*

# Sant Pere and Born/La Ribera

Sant Pere, Barcelona's old textile neighborhood, is centered on the church of Sant Pere. A half mile closer to the port, the Barri de la Ribera and the former market of El Born, now known as the Born-Ribera district, were at the center of Catalonia's great maritime and economic expansion of the 13th and 14th centuries. Surrounding the basilica of Santa Maria del Mar, the Born-Ribera area includes Carrer Montcada, lined with 14th- to 18th-century Renaissance palaces; Passeig del Born, where medieval jousts were held; Carrer Flassaders and the area around the early mint; the antiques shop- and restaurant-rich Carrer Banys Vells; Plaça de les Olles; and Pla del Palau, where La Llotja, Barcelona's early maritime exchange, housed the fine-arts school where Picasso, Gaudí, and Domènech i Montaner all studied, as did many more of Barcelona's most important artists and architects.

Long a depressed neighborhood, La Ribera began to experience a revival in the 1980s; now replete with intimate bars, cafés, and trendy boutiques, it continues to enjoy the blessings of gentrification. An open excavation in the center of El Born, the onetime market restored as a multipurpose cultural center, offers a fascinating view of pre-1714 Barcelona, dismantled by the victorious troops of Felipe V at the end of the War of the Spanish Succession. The Passeig del Born, La Rambla of medieval Barcelona, is once again a pleasant leafy promenade.

## ◉ Sights

**Capella d'en Marcús** (*Marcús Chapel*)
CHURCH | This Romanesque hermitage looks as if it had been left behind by some remote order of hermit-monks who meant to take it on a picnic in the Pyrenees. The tiny chapel, possibly—along with Sant Llàtzer—Barcelona's smallest religious structure, and certainly one of its oldest, was originally built in the 12th century on the main Roman road into Barcelona, the one that would become Cardo Maximo just a few hundred yards away as it passed through the walls at Portal de l'Àngel.

Bernat Marcús, a wealthy merchant concerned with public welfare and social issues, built a hospital here for poor travelers; the hospital chapel that bears his name was dedicated to the Mare de Déu de la Guia (Our Lady of the Guide). As a result of its affiliation, combined with its location on the edge of town, the chapel eventually became the headquarters of the Confraria del Correus a Cavall (Brotherhood of the Pony Express), also known as the *troters* (trotters), that made Barcelona the key link in overland mail between the Iberian Peninsula and France. ⊠ *Carders 2 (Placeta d'en Marcús), Born-Ribera* ☎ *93/310–2390* Ⓜ *Jaume I.*

### Carrer Flassaders

STREET | Named for the weavers and blanket makers to whom this street belonged in medieval times, Carrer Flassaders is best approached from Carrer Montcada, at **El Xampanyet**, one of La Ribera's most popular bars for tapas and cava. Duck into the short, dark Carrer Arc de Sant Vicenç. At the end, you'll find yourself face to face with La Seca, what used to be the Royal Mint (officially, the Reial Fàbrica de la Moneda de la Corona d'Aragó), where money was manufactured until the mid-19th century. Coins bearing the inscription, in Castilian, "Principado de Cataluña" (Principality of Catalonia) were made here as late as 1836.

Turn left on Carrer de la Seca to Carrer de la Cirera. Overhead to the left is the image of Santa Maria de Cervelló, one of the patron saints of the Catalan fleet, on the back of the Palau Cervelló on Carrer

Sant Pere and La Ribera

EL FORT PIUS

Antic Estació del Nord

Arc de Triome

Av. Vilanova

Arc de Triome

Parc de l'Estacio del Nord

Carrer des Almogàvers

Carrer de Buenaventura Muñoz

Passeig de Pujades

Av. Meridiana

Parc de la Ciutadella

Universitat Pompeu Fabra

Parlament de Catalunya

Parc Zoològic

Carrer d'Ausiás Marc

Passeig de Saint Joan

C. de Napols

C. de Sicilia

Carrer d'Ali Bei

Carrer de Roger de Flor

Passeig de Lluís companys

Pas-eig de Lluís companys

Carrer de Wellington

Pg. Circumval lació

### Sights ▼

| | | |
|---|---|---|
| 1 | Capella d'un Marcus | D6 |
| 2 | Carrer Flassaders | E6 |
| 3 | La Llotja | A1 |
| 4 | Museu de la Xocolata | F6 |
| 5 | Museu Picasso | D6 |
| 6 | Palau Dalmases | D7 |
| 7 | Palau de la Música Catalana | C3 |
| 8 | Passeig del Born | E7 |
| 9 | Santa Maria del Mar | D7 |

### Restaurants ▼

| | | |
|---|---|---|
| 1 | Bar del Pla | D6 |
| 2 | Bodega La Puntual | D7 |
| 3 | Cal Pep | E8 |
| 4 | Cremat 11 | D6 |
| 5 | El Passadís d'en Pep | D8 |
| 6 | Fismuler | F3 |
| 7 | Le Cucine Mandarosso | C4 |
| 8 | Llamber | F7 |
| 9 | Picnic | F5 |
| 10 | Proper | D7 |
| 11 | Sagardi | C7 |

### Quick Bites ▼

| | | |
|---|---|---|
| 1 | Gocce di Latte | D8 |

### Hotels ▼

| | | |
|---|---|---|
| 1 | The Barcelona EDITION | C5 |
| 2 | Ciutat de Barcelona | E6 |
| 3 | H10 Montcada | C6 |
| 4 | Hotel Rec | F3 |
| 5 | Hotel Yurbban Trafalgar | D3 |

**KEY**

1 Sights
1 Restaurants
1 Quick Bites
1 Hotels
Ⓜ Metro Stops
🛈 Tourist Information

0 — 200 yards

0 — 200 meters

Montcada. Turn right on Carrer de la Cirera, and arrive at the corner of Carrer dels Flassaders. Walk left past several shops. Wander down Flassaders through a gauntlet of elegant clothing, furnishings, and jewelry design boutiques, and you'll pass the main entry to Escenari Joan Brossa at Number 40, with the gigantic Bourbon coat of arms over the imposing archway.

Look up to your right at the corner of the gated Carrer de les Mosques, famous as Barcelona's narrowest street. The mustachioed countenance peering down at you was once a medieval advertisement for a brothel. **Pasteleria Hofmann**, at Number 44, is the excellent pastry shop (don't pass up the mascarpone croissants) of famous Barcelona chef, the late Mey Hofmann, whose cooking school is over on nearby Carrer Argenteria. A right on Passeig del Born will take you back to Santa Maria del Mar. ⊠ *Flassaders, Born-Ribera* Ⓜ *Jaume I.*

**La Llotja** (*Maritime Exchange*)
NOTABLE BUILDING | Barcelona's maritime trade center, the Casa Llotja de Mar, was designed to be the city's finest example of civil architecture, built in the Catalan Gothic style between 1380 and 1392. At the end of the 18th century, the facades were (tragically) covered in the neoclassical uniformity of the time, but the interior, the great Saló Gòtic (Gothic Hall), remained unaltered, and was a grand venue for balls throughout the 19th century. The hall, with its graceful arches and columns and floors of light Carrara and dark Genovese marble, has now been brilliantly restored. The building, which is not typically open to the general public, now houses the Barcelona Chamber of Commerce. The Reial Acadèmia Catalana de Belles Arts de Sant Jordi (Royal Catalan Academy of Fine Arts of St. George) still has its seat in the Llotja, and its museum is one of Barcelona's semisecret collections of art, from medieval paintings by unknown artists to modern works by members of the Academy itself.

■ TIP➜ **To slip into the Saló Gòti, walk down the stairs from the museum to the second floor, then take the marble staircase down and turn right.** ⊠ *Casa Llotja, Passeig d'Isabel II 1, Born-Ribera* ☎ *93/319–2432 Reial Acadèmia, 670/466260 guided visits to museum* ⊕ *www.racba.org* 🎦 *Guided tours €12 (English tours Sat. at 11 am)* Ⓜ *L4 Barceloneta.*

**Museu de la Xocolata** (*Museum of Chocolate*)
OTHER MUSEUM | FAMILY | The elaborate, painstakingly detailed chocolate sculptures, which have included everything from La Sagrada Família to Don Quixote's windmills, delight both youthful and adult visitors to this museum, set in an imposing 18th-century former monastery and developed by the Barcelona Provincial Confectionery Guild. Other exhibits here touch on Barcelona's centuries-old love affair with chocolate, the introduction of chocolate to Europe by Spanish explorers from the Maya and Aztec cultures in the New World, and both vintage and current machinery and tools used to create this sweet delicacy.

The "Bean To Bar" experience showcases the full production process for making artisanal chocolate using traceable cocoa from different parts of the world. You can buy the finished products, including boxes and bars of chocolate, in the museum shop. The beautiful café offers rich hot and cold chocolate drinks and house-made cakes and pastries. Tasting sessions and classes on making chocolate are offered, too. ⊠ *Comerç 36, Born-Ribera* ☎ *93/268–7878* ⊕ *www. museuxocolata.cat* 🎦 *€6* ⊙ *Closed Mon.* Ⓜ *L4 Jaume 1, L1 Arc de Triomf.*

★ **Museu Picasso** (*Picasso Museum*)
ART MUSEUM | The Picasso Museum is housed in five adjoining palaces on Carrer Montcada, a street known for Barcelona's most elegant medieval mansions.

Picasso spent his key formative years in Barcelona (1895–1904), and although this collection doesn't include a significant number of the artist's most famous paintings, it is strong on his early work, showcasing the link between Picasso and Barcelona. Displays include childhood sketches, works from Picasso's Rose and Blue periods, and the many famous 1950s Cubist variations on Velázquez's *Las Meninas* (in Rooms 12–16). The lower-floor sketches, oils, and schoolboy caricatures and drawings from Picasso's early years in A Coruña are perhaps the most fascinating part, showing the facility the artist seemed to possess almost from the cradle. On the second floor are works from his Blue Period in Paris, a time of loneliness, cold, and hunger for the artist. ■**TIP→ Admission is free the first Sunday of the month and every Thursday from 4 p.m. Book online or arrive early to avoid the long lines and crowds.** ⊠ *Montcada 15–19, Born-Ribera* ☎ *93/256–3000, 93/256–3022 guided tour and group reservations* ⊕ *www.museupicasso.bcn.cat* ≅ *€12; free Thurs. from 4 pm, and 1st Sun. of month. Tours €6* ⊘ *Closed Mon.* ☞ *Guided tours of permanent collection (in English) are Sun. at 11* Ⓜ *L4 Jaume I, L1 Arc de Triomf.*

### Palau Dalmases
**NOTABLE BUILDING** | If you can get through the massive wooden gates that open onto Carrer Montcada (at the moment, the only opportunity is when the first-floor café-theater, Espai Barroc, is open), you'll find yourself in Barcelona's best 17th-century Renaissance courtyard, built into a former 15th-century Gothic palace. Note the door knockers up at horseback level, and then study the frieze—featuring *The Rape of Europa*—that runs up the stone railing of the elegant stairway at the end of the patio. It's a festive abduction: Neptune's chariot, cherubs, naiads, dancers, tritons, and musicians accompany Zeus, in the form of a bull, as he carries poor Europa up the stairs and off to Crete. The stone carvings in the courtyard, the 15th-century Gothic chapel, with its reliefs of angelic musicians, and the vaulting in the reception hall and salon, are all that remain of the original 15th-century palace. ⊠ *Montcada 20, Born-Ribera* ☎ *66/076–9865 Espai Barroc* ⊕ *www.flamencopalaudalmases.com* ≅ *Shows from €25 (includes 1 drink)* Ⓜ *L4 Jaume I.*

### ★ Palau de la Música Catalana
**NOTABLE BUILDING** | One of the world's most extraordinary music halls, with facades that are a riot of color and form, the Music Palace is a landmark of Carrer Amadeus Vives, set just across Via Laietana, a 10-minute walk from Plaça de Catalunya. The Palau is a flamboyant tour de force designed in 1908 by Lluís Domènech i Montaner. Originally conceived by the Orfeó Català musical society as a vindication of the importance of music at a popular level—as opposed to the Liceu opera house's identification with the Catalan aristocracy—the Palau was for many decades an opposing crosstown force with the Liceu. The exterior is remarkable in itself. The Miquel Blay sculptural group is Catalonia's popular music come to life, with everyone included from St. George the dragonslayer to women and children, fishermen, and every strain and strata of popular life and music. Inside, the decor assaults your senses before the first note of music is ever played, be it by a chamber orchestra, a renowned piano soloist, a gospel choir, or an Afro-Cuban combo. ⊠ *Palau de la Música 4–6, Born-Ribera* ☎ *93/295–7200, 90/247–5485 box office* ⊕ *www.palaumusica.cat/en* ≅ *Standard guided tour €18* Ⓜ *L1/L4 Urquinaona.*

### ★ Passeig del Born
**PLAZA/SQUARE** | Once the site of medieval jousts and the Inquisition's autos-da-fé, the passeig, at the end of Carrer Montcada behind the church of Santa Maria del Mar, was early Barcelona's most important square. Late-night cocktail bars and small restaurants with tiny spiral

stairways now line the narrow, elongated plaza. Walk down to the Born—a great iron hangar, that was once a produce market designed by Josep Fontseré and in the Plaça Comercial, across from the end of the promenade. The initial stages of the construction of a public library here uncovered the remains of the lost city of 1714, complete with blackened fireplaces, taverns, wells, and the canal that brought water into the city. The streets of the 14th- to 18th-century Born-Ribera now lie open in the sunken central square of the old market; around it, at ground level, are a number of new, multifunctional, exhibition and performance spaces. ☒ *Passeig del Born, Born-Ribera* ☏ *93/256–6851 El Born Centre de Cultura i Memòria* ⊕ *elbornculturaimemoria.barcelona.cat* Ⓜ *L4 Jaume I/Barceloneta.*

### ★ Santa Maria del Mar

CHURCH | The most beautiful example of early Catalan Gothic architecture, Santa Maria del Mar is extraordinary for its unbroken lines and elegance, and the lightness of the interior is especially surprising considering the blocky exterior. The site was home to a Christian cult from the late 3rd century. Built by mere stonemasons who chose, fitted, and carved each stone hauled down from a Montjuïc quarry, the church is breathtakingly and nearly hypnotically symmetrical. The medieval numerological symbol for the Virgin Mary, the number eight (or multiples thereof) runs through every element of the basilica: the 16 octagonal pillars are 2 meters in diameter and spread out into rib vaulting arches at a height of 16 meters; the painted keystones at the apex of the arches are 32 meters from the floor; and the central nave is twice as wide as the lateral naves (8 meters each). Although anticlerical anarchists burned the basilica in 1936, it was restored after the end of the Spanish Civil War by Bauhaus-trained architects. ☒ *Pl. de Santa Maria 1, Born-Ribera* ☏ *93/310–2390* ⊕ *www.santamariadelmarbarcelona.org* ☒ *From €5* Ⓜ *L4 Jaume I.*

## 🍴 Restaurants

### ★ Bar del Pla

$ | CATALAN | Specializing in Catalan bar food and local, organic, biodynamic, and natural wine, this sometimes-rowdy bar may not look like much from the outside but the hordes of people waiting to be seated give it away. Top choices include the mushroom carpaccio with wasabi vinaigrette and strawberries, the black squid-ink croquettes and the spicy *patatas bravas*. **Known for:** totally on-trend despite the old-school appearance; excellent tapas; Catalan natural wines. ⑤ *Average main: €15* ☒ *Montcada 2, Born-Ribera* ☏ *93/268–3003* ⊕ *www.bardelpla.cat* ⊙ *Closed Sun.* Ⓜ *Jaume I L4.*

### ★ Bodega La Puntual

$$ | CATALAN | Just down the road from the Picasso Museum, Bodega La Puntual might look like a tourist trap, but it's a classic, specializing in hearty portions of Catalan fare, made from seasonal, locally sourced produce. Top menu choices include the fresh marinated anchovies, the plate of premium hand-cut Iberian *jamón*, and *trinxat*: a traditional Catalan dish made with potatoes, cabbage, and pork meat, served with a fried egg. **Known for:** great for lunch after the Picasso Museum; seasonal, locally sourced ingredients; traditional Catalan food. ⑤ *Average main: €22* ☒ *Montcada 22, Born-Ribera* ☏ *93/310–3545* ⊕ *grupovarela.es/bodega-la-puntual-barcelona* Ⓜ *Jaume I L4.*

### ★ Cal Pep

$$ | TAPAS | It's has been in a permanent feeding frenzy for more than 30 years, intensified by hordes of tourists, but this loud, hectic bar manages to keep delivering the very highest quality tapas, year in year out. Be prepared to wait up to an hour for a place at the counter; reservations for the tables in the tiny back room and on the outdoor terrace are accepted, but the counter is where the action is. **Known for:** lively counter scene;

delicious tortilla de patatas; excellent fish fry. $ *Average main: €20* ⊠ *Pl. de les Olles 8, Born-Ribera* ☎ *93/310–7961* ⊕ *www.calpep.com* ⊗ *Closed Sun. and 3 wks in Aug. No lunch Mon.* Ⓜ *Jaume I, Barceloneta.*

### Cremat 11

$ | **FRENCH FUSION** | Brunch spots may be ten a penny these days but few can compete with the superb, French-owned Cremat 11, almost hidden down this tiny street behind the Picasso Museum. The dining room is small but cozy, and there is also a shady outdoor patio on what is arguably one of the prettiest squares in the city. **Known for:** killer cocktails; steak and eggs; leafy patio on a pretty square. $ *Average main: €12* ⊠ *Cremat Gran 11, Born-Ribera* ☎ *682/038377* ⊕ *cremat11. business.site* ⊗ *Closed Tues. and Wed.* Ⓜ *Jaume I L4.*

### El Passadís d'en Pep

$$$$ | **SEAFOOD** | Hidden away at the end of a narrow unmarked passageway off the Pla del Palau, near the Santa Maria del Mar church, this restaurant is a favorite with well-heeled and well-fed gourmands who tuck in their napkins before devouring some of the city's best traditional seafood dishes. Don't bother asking for a menu—there isn't one (although you can prebook a set menu in advance online if you prefer), rather, you can either place yourself completely in the hands of the team, or tell your server what your budget is (starting from €50 per person). **Known for:** no actual menu; tapas served in rapid-fire succession; fresh seafood and Iberian ham. $ *Average main: €50* ⊠ *Pl. del Palau 2, Born-Ribera* ☎ *93/310–1021* ⊕ *www.passadis.com* ⊗ *Closed Sun., public holidays, and 3 wks in Aug.* Ⓜ *Jaume I.*

### Fismuler

$$$ | **SPANISH** | The cosmopolitan crowd here doesn't just come for hip vibe and stylish decor: Fismuler Barcelona re-creates its Madrid-based mother-ship's precise, market-based cooking and adds interesting local touches. Star dishes include a translucent, semi-cured carpaccio of gilthead bream with grapes and almonds, and an unctuous, complex cheesecake that tastes more like cheese than cake and is an utterly sinful, gooey delight. **Known for:** killer cheesecake; inventive cooking; trendy atmosphere. $ *Average main: €25* ⊠ *Rec Comtal 17, Born-Ribera* ☎ *93/514–0050* ⊕ *www. fismuler.com* Ⓜ *Arc de Triomf.*

### Le Cucine Mandarosso

$$ | **ITALIAN** | This no-frills, big-flavor southern-Italian restaurant near the Via Laietana is a favorite with locals for its friendly prices, boisterous atmosphere, and generous portions of burrata, lasagne, ragù, carbonara, and so on, featuring authentic ingredients from the in-store deli. Leave room for the excellent tiramisu. **Known for:** great homemade pastas; hidden gem; always packed. $ *Average main: €15* ⊠ *Verdaguer i Callís 4, Born-Ribera* ☎ *93/269–0780* ⊕ *www. lecucinemandarosso.com* ⊗ *Closed Mon.* Ⓜ *Urquinaona.*

### Llamber

$$ | **TAPAS** | This dapper, friendly space attracts a crowd with its excellent wine list and the well-crafted tapas based on classic Catalan and Asturian recipes, as interpreted by chef Francisco Heras, who has earned his chops in Spain's top restaurants. Consider the pig's trotters with rice, and potatoes stuffed with Cabrales cheese and hazelnut praline. **Known for:** good option for late-night eats; pig's trotters with rice; well-crafted tapas. $ *Average main: €18* ⊠ *Fusina 5, Born-Ribera* ☎ *93/319–6250* ⊕ *www. llamber.com* Ⓜ *Jaume 1.*

### ★ Picnic

$ | **LATIN AMERICAN** | Between the buzzing indoor dining room, the breezy outdoor patio, and the strongest Bloody Mary game in town, there's a reason why Picnic has reigned supreme on the Barcelona brunch scene for more than a decade. House specials include the

quinoa and potato hash browns, the fried green tomatoes with feta and fresh corn salsa, and, of course, the killer eggs Benedict. **Known for:** top brunch choice in town; the Bloody Marys; breezy outdoor patio. $ *Average main: €12* ✉ *Comerç 1, Born-Ribera* ☎ *93/511–6661* ⊕ *www. picnic-restaurant.com* Ⓜ *Arc de Triomf L1.*

**Proper**

$$ | **ARGENTINE** | The menu at this "gastronomic tavern" run by Argentinian chef Augusto Mayer is simple and affordable, with unfussy dishes of local, seasonal produce, mostly prepared in the wood-fired oven and meant for sharing. The steak is outstanding, of course, but other, more delicate choices are also worth exploring, like the eggplant with ricotta, figs, and lemon preserves or the tuna confit with kefir tartar sauce. **Known for:** wood-fired oven; local produce; Argentinian-style steak. $ *Average main: €20* ✉ *Banys Vells 20, Born-Ribera* ☎ *93/295– 5307* ⊕ *www.properbcn.com* ☽ *Closed Sun. and Mon. No lunch.* Ⓜ *Jaume I L4.*

**Sagardi**

$$ | **BASQUE** | **FAMILY** | An attractive wood-and-stone cider-house replica, Sagardi piles the counter with a dazzling variety of cold Basque-style pintxos served on toothpicks; even better, though, are the hot offerings from the kitchen. The restaurant in back serves Basque delicacies like veal sweetbreads with artichokes and *txuletas de buey* (beef steaks) grilled over coals. **Known for:** busy outdoor patio; veal sweetbreads and steak; multiple locations, all equally good. $ *Average main: €22* ✉ *Argenteria 62, Born-Ribera* ☎ *93/319–9993* ⊕ *www.gruposagardi. com* Ⓜ *Jaume I.*

## ☕ Coffee and Quick Bites

### ★ Gocce di Latte

$ | **ICE CREAM** | If you're looking to freshen up after a long, sweaty day of sightseeing, this artisanal Italian-owned *gelateria* is just the ticket. In addition to a broad

range of dairy-based flavors, there are plant-based options and fresh-fruit sorbets, plus gluten-free cones. **Known for:** open until midnight; dairy-free options, like vegan dark chocolate; Italian-style gelato. $ *Average main: €6* ✉ *Pla de Palau 4, Born-Ribera* ☎ *61/798–6186* ⊕ *www.facebook.com/heladeriagoc-cedilatte* Ⓜ *Barceloneta L4.*

## 🛏 Hotels

### ★ The Barcelona EDITION

$$$$ | **HOTEL** | The Edition hotels are known for their sleek, minimalist design and top-notch food and drink options and the Barcelona outpost adds a breezy 10th-floor terrace with sweeping views. **Pros:** excellent service; great food and drink options; dreamy views from the rooftop. **Cons:** tiny swimming pool; only upgraded rooms have balconies; pricey. $ *Rooms from: €380* ✉ *Av. de Francesc Cambó 14, Born-Ribera* ☎ *93/626–3330* ⊕ *www.editionhotels.com/es/barcelona* ⊷ *100 rooms* ⦿ *No Meals* Ⓜ *Jaume I L4.*

### Ciutat de Barcelona

$$ | **HOTEL** | Ciutat de Barcelona is a no-frills hotel with a bit of an edge, in the trendy El Born quarter of the Old City. **Pros:** close to Picasso Museum, Santa Maria del Mar, and the Gothic quarter; decent value for price; friendly, helpful staff. **Cons:** somewhat sketchy neighborhood; Carrer Princesa gets a lot of pedestrian traffic; no spa, gym, or sauna. $ *Rooms from: €150* ✉ *Princesa 35, Born-Ribera* ☎ *93/269–7475* ⊕ *www. ciutatbarcelona.com* ⊷ *78 rooms* ⦿ *No Meals* Ⓜ *L4 Jaume I.*

### H10 Montcada

$$ | **HOTEL** | A short walk from the attractions of the Gothic Quarter and the Born-Ribera district, the Montcada is a good choice for comfort and convenience. **Pros:** inviting rooftop deck with Jacuzzi; pleasant breakfast room; great location. **Cons:** no pool or spa; bed lighting could improve; a bit pricey for what it

is, $ *Rooms from: €180* ⊠ *Via Laietana 24, Born-Ribera* ☎ *93/268–8570* ⊕ *www. h10hotels.com* ⇨ *80 rooms* ⏀ *No Meals* Ⓜ *Jaume I.*

### ★ Hotel Rec

$ | HOTEL | Within an easy stroll of many of Barcelona's best restaurants and top sights, this is an affordable urban adults-only hotel in an unbeatable location. **Pros:** great value; great location; top restaurant downstairs. **Cons:** rooms on the small side; area can be sketchy at night; noisy street outside. $ *Rooms from: €99* ⊠ *Rec Comtal 17–19, Sant Pere* ☎ *93/556–9960* ⊕ *www.hotelrecbarcelona.com* ⇨ *99 rooms* ⏀ *No Meals* Ⓜ *Arc de Triomf L1.*

### Hotel Yurbban Trafalgar

$$ | HOTEL | Guests and locals alike rave about the rooftop terrace at the Yurbban Trafalgar, and with good reason: the panoramic view is hands down one of the best in the city at this hip, casual hotel, which offers some of the best value accommodation in the city. **Pros:** superb rooftop terrace; outstanding breakfast; spa access at next-door property. **Cons:** small shower stalls; room service ends at 11 pm; small, basic rooms. $ *Rooms from: €144* ⊠ *Trafalgar 30, Eixample Dreta* ☎ *93/268–0727* ⊕ *yurbban.com/en* ⇨ *56 rooms* ⏀ *No Meals* Ⓜ *L1/L3 Urquinaona.*

## 🅨 Nightlife

Nightlife in La Ribera tends to be laid-back, in keeping with the rather tranquil, medieval architectural surroundings. El Born is more eclectic, with bars and lounge spots specializing in everything from craft beer to organic wines.

### BARS

#### Ale&Hop

BREWPUBS | A slick microbrewery with exposed brick walls and indie beats, Ale&Hop was a trailblazer in the city's craft-beer-bar invasion. There are plenty of artisanal brews, plus wine

and vegetarian snacks. ⊠ *Basses de Sant Pere 10, Sant Pere* ☎ *93/126–9094* ⊕ *www.facebook.com/aleandhop* Ⓜ *Arc de Triomf.*

### ★ Eldiset

WINE BARS | Specializing in local wine from Catalonia, this charming wine bar—an escape from the rowdy watering holes in nearby Passeig del Born and Plaça Comercial—also has an impressive food menu. ⊠ *Antic de Sant Joan 3, Born-Ribera* ☎ *93/268–1987* ⊕ *www.facebook.com/eldiset* Ⓜ *Barceloneta L4.*

### La Vinya del Senyor

WINE BARS | Ambitiously named "The Lord's Vineyard," this romantic wine bar directly across from the entrance to the Santa Maria del Mar has an extensive wine list featuring more than 350 wines by the bottle, and a rotating selection of 20 by the glass. Watch your step on the rickety ladder leading to the pint-size mezzanine. ⊠ *Pl. de Santa Maria 5, Born-Ribera* ☎ *93/310–3379* ⊕ *www.lavinyadelsenyor.es* Ⓜ *Jaume I.*

### Paradiso

COCKTAIL LOUNGES | Hidden behind the fridge door in an unassuming-looking pastrami bar, this speakeasy is one of the city's worst-kept secrets. Cocktail maestro Giacomo Giannotti's creations are works of art, bursting with fire, smoke, and dry ice. And they taste absolutely delicious. Prepare to stand in line for up to an hour to get in. ⊠ *Rera Palau 4, Born-Ribera* ☎ ⊕ *paradiso.cat/en* Ⓜ *Barceloneta L4.*

### Paspartú

COCKTAIL LOUNGES | Dark and inviting, the bar stocks 25 gin flavors and has plenty of comfortable seating in which to try them. ⊠ *Basses de Sant Pere 12, Barcelona* ☎ *699/546252* ⊕ *www.facebook.com/paspartubar* Ⓜ *Arc de Triomf.*

### Rubí Bar

BARS | The whimsical apothecary-like spirits cabinet, exposed-stone wall, and dramatic red lighting will be the first things to catch your eye, but the relaxed atmosphere and inventive selection of cocktails bring locals and expats back again and again. Check out the choice of home-brewed flavored gins tantalizingly displayed on the bar shelves in hand-labeled bottles. ⊠ *Banys Vells 6, Born-Ribera* ☎ *697/673802* Ⓜ *Jaume I.*

## 🎭 Performing Arts

**La Puntual** (*Putxinel·lis de Barcelona*) THEATER | FAMILY | As one of the city's pioneering puppet (in Catalan, *putxinel·li*) theaters, this beloved venue features entertaining marionette, puppet, and shadow puppet performances. Weekend matinee performances are major kid magnets and tend to sell out fast, so arrive early or reserve a ticket in advance online. ⊠ *Allada Vermell 15, Born-Ribera* ☎ *639/305353* ⊕ *www.lapuntual.info* ☞ *From €9* Ⓜ *Jaume I.*

## 🛍 Shopping

The Ribera and Born neighborhoods have some of Barcelona's best shopping. Interior design and clothing shops are the main draw, especially along Carrer Argenteria, Plaça de Santa Maria, and Carrer Banys Vells.

### CERAMICS AND GLASSWARE
**Baraka**
CRAFTS | Barcelona's prime purveyor of Moroccan goods, ceramics chief among them, the wares here are generally of good price and great quality. Other African countries are represented, too, such as spectacular busts covered in tiny beads from Cameroon. ⊠ *Canvis Vells 2, Born-Ribera* ☎ *93/268–4220* ⊕ *www. barakaweb.com* Ⓜ *Jaume I.*

### CLOTHING
**El Ganso**
MIXED CLOTHING | Who would have thought that two Madrid-born brothers could out-Brit the Brits? One of Spain's more recent fashion success stories, El

Ganso makes very appealing preppy-inspired men's, women's, and children's wear—striped blazers, pleated skirts, and tailored suits made for upper-class frolics. ⊠ *Rambla de Catalunya, 116, Eixample* ☎ *93/368–2069* ⊕ *www.elganso.com* Ⓜ *Diagonal.*

★ **Ivori**
MIXED CLOTHING | This ultra-chic clothing store stocks both men's and women's clothing and accessories, all made by young Catalan designers. A labor of love that is spearheaded by local designer Carola Alexandre, who sells her own designs as well as pieces by the likes of Name BCN, Lubochka, and Mus Roew. ⊠ *Mirallers, 7, Born-Ribera* ☎ *93/137–0264* ⊕ *www.ivoribarcelona. com* Ⓜ *Jaume 1, L4.*

**La Comercial**
MIXED CLOTHING | This mini-agglomeration of boutiques spreads out over three streets, together defining El Born's penchant for the achingly à la mode. Menswear can be found at Bonaire 7, Rec 73 and 75, with the latter entirely dedicated to the natty threads of U.K. designer Paul Smith. Women can choose from predominantly French designers such as Isabel Marant and Sonia Rykiel at Rec 52. ⊠ *Rec 52–75, Carrer Rec, Born-Ribera* ☎ *93/319–3463* ⊕ *www.lacomercial.info/ en* Ⓜ *Jaume I.*

### FOOD
★ **Casa Gispert**
FOOD | This shop is one of the most aromatic and picturesque in Barcelona, bursting with teas, coffees, spices, saffron, chocolates, and nuts. The star is an almond-roasting stove in the back of the store—purportedly the oldest in Europe, dating from 1851 like the store itself, so make sure to pick up a bag of freshly roasted nuts to take with you. ⊠ *Sombrerers 23, Born-Ribera* ☎ *93/319–7535* ⊕ *www.casagispert.com* Ⓜ *Jaume I.*

## Demasié

**FOOD** | The shop's motto, "galetes Exa-geradament Bones" (biscuits that are exaggeratedly good) may seem like a bit of hype, but these rich colorful cookies are exceptionally tasty. They are best enjoyed with a cup of coffee at the bar inside, or you can have them wrapped up in a pretty duck-egg-blue box to take home with you. ⊠ *Princesa 28, Born-Ribera* ☎ *93/269–1180* ⊕ *www.demasie.es* Ⓜ *Jaume I.*

## ★ El Magnífico

**FOOD** | Just up the street from Santa Maria del Mar, this coffee emporium is famous for its sacks of coffee beans from all over the globe and is said to serve the best cup of coffee in Barcelona, also available to go. El Magnífico's best-kept secret is its nearby "Mag by El Magnífico" coffee shop, open Friday through Sunday only (⊠ *Carrer de Grunyí 10*). ⊠ *Argenteria 64, Born-Ribera* ☎ *93/319–3975* ⊕ *www.cafeselmagnifico.com* Ⓜ *Jaume I.*

## La Botifarreria de Santa Maria

**FOOD** | This busy emporium next to the church of Santa Maria del Mar stocks excellent cheeses, hams, pâtés, and homemade *sobrassadas* (pork pâté with paprika). Catalan botifarra sausage is the main item here, with a wide range of varieties, including egg sausage for meatless Lent and sausage stuffed with spinach, asparagus, cider, cinnamon, and Cabrales cheese. ⊠ *Santa Maria 4, Born-Ribera* ☎ *93/319–9123* ⊕ *www.labotifarreria.com* Ⓜ *Jaume I.*

## ★ Pastelería Hofmann

**$** | **BAKERY** | The late Mey Hofmann, a constellation in Barcelona's gourmet galaxy for the last three decades through her restaurant and cooking courses, established this sideline dedicated exclusively to pastry. Everything from the lightest, flakiest croissants to the cakes, tarts, and ice creams are about as good they get in this legendary sweets emporium. **Known for:** croissants filled with mascarpone or almond cream; tiny shop; legendary pastry shop. **$** *Average main: €8* ⊠ *Flassaders 44, Born-Ribera* ☎ *93/268–8221* ⊕ *www.hofmann-bcn.com* Ⓜ *Jaume I.*

## ★ Vila Viniteca

**WINE/SPIRITS** | Near Santa Maria del Mar, this is perhaps the best wine treasury in Barcelona, with a truly massive catalog, tastings, courses, and events, including a hugely popular street party to welcome in new-harvest wines (usually late October or early November). Under the same ownership, the tiny grocery store next door offers exquisite artisanal cheeses ranging from French goat cheese to Extremadura's famous *Torta del Casar*. There are a few tables inside, and, for a corkage fee, you can enjoy a bottle of wine together with a tasting platter. ⊠ *Agullers 7–9, Born-Ribera* ☎ *9390/777–7017* ⊕ *www.vilaviniteca.es* Ⓜ *Jaume I.*

## GIFTS AND SOUVENIRS

### Natura

**CRAFTS** | The Spanish Natura chain has branches around the city and stocks a good selection of global crafts, including incense, clothing, tapestries, candles, shoes, gadgets, and surprises of all kinds. ⊠ *Argenteria 78, Born-Ribera* ☎ *93/268–2525* ⊕ *www.naturaselection.com* Ⓜ *Jaume I.*

# La Ciutadella and Barceloneta

Barceloneta and La Ciutadella fit together historically. In the early 18th century, some 1,000 houses in the Barrio de la Ribera, then the waterfront neighborhood around Plaça del Born, were ordered torn down, to create fields of fire for the cannon of La Ciutadella, the newly built fortress that kept watch over the rebellious Catalans. Barceloneta, then a marshy wetland, was filled in and developed almost four decades later, in

## Sights ▼

| | | |
|---|---|---|
| 1 | Arc de Triomf | F1 |
| 2 | Ciutadella Park | G1 |
| 3 | El Transbordador Aeri del Port... | B7 |
| 4 | Estació de França | E3 |
| 5 | Museu del Disseny de Barcelona | H1 |
| 6 | Museu d'Història de Catalunya | D4 |
| 7 | Parlament de Catalunya | G2 |
| 8 | Port Olímpic | J5 |
| 9 | Port Vell | D4 |
| 10 | Sant Miquel del Port | E5 |

## Restaurants ▼

| | | |
|---|---|---|
| 1 | Agua | H5 |
| 2 | Barceloneta | C6 |
| 3 | Camping Mar | A9 |
| 4 | Can Majó | E6 |
| 5 | Can Solé | D5 |
| 6 | 1881 Per Sagardi | D4 |
| 7 | El 58 | J2 |
| 8 | Els Tres Porquets | H1 |
| 9 | Enoteca Paco Pérez | I5 |
| 10 | Green Spot | D3 |
| 11 | La Cova Fumada | D5 |
| 12 | L' Artesana Poblenou | J1 |

## Quick Bites ▼

| | | |
|---|---|---|
| 1 | The Cake Man Bakery | J3 |
| 2 | El Vaso de Oro | E4 |

## Hotels ▼

| | | |
|---|---|---|
| 1 | Hotel Arts Barcelona | I5 |
| 2 | Motel One Barcelona-Ciutadella | G1 |
| 3 | W Barcelona | A9 |

**KEY**

- 🄋 Sights
- 🄋 Restaurants
- 🄋 Quick Bites
- 🄋 Hotels
- Ⓜ Metro Stops

1753, to house the families who had lost homes in La Ribera.

Open water in Roman times, and gradually silted in only after the 15th-century construction of the port, it became Barcelona's fishermen's and stevedores' quarter. Eventually it became a sort of a safety valve, a little fishing village next door where locals could go to escape the formalities and constraints of city life, for a Sunday seafood lunch on the beach and a stroll through what felt like a freer world. With its tiny original apartment blocks, and its checkered history, Barceloneta maintains its spontaneous, carefree flavor.

## ◎ Sights

### Arc de Triomf

NOTABLE BUILDING | This exposed-redbrick arch was built by Josep Vilaseca as the grand entrance for the 1888 Universal Exhibition. Similar in size and sense to the traditional triumphal arches of ancient Rome, this one refers to no specific military triumph anyone can recall. In fact, Catalonia's last military triumph of note may have been Jaume I el Conqueridor's 1229 conquest of the Moors in Mallorca—as suggested by the bats (always part of Jaume I's coat of arms) on either side of the arch itself. The Josep Reynés sculptures adorning the structure represent Barcelona hosting visitors to the exhibition on the western side (front), while the Josep Llimona sculptures on the eastern side depict the prizes being given to its outstanding contributors. ⊠ Passeig de Sant Joan, La Ciutadella Ⓜ L1 Arc de Triomf.

★ **Ciutadella Park** (Parc de la Ciutadella) CITY PARK | FAMILY | Once a fortress designed to consolidate Madrid's military occupation of Barcelona, the Ciutadella is now the city's main downtown park. The clearing dates from shortly after the War of the Spanish Succession in the early 18th century, when Felipe V demolished some 1,000 houses in what was then the Barri de la Ribera to build a fortress and barracks for his soldiers and a glacis (open space) between rebellious Barcelona and his artillery positions. The fortress walls were pulled down in 1868 and replaced by gardens laid out by Josep Fontseré. In 1888 the park was the site of the Universal Exposition that put Barcelona on the map as a truly European city. ⊠ Passeig de Picasso 21, La Ciutadella Ⓜ L4 Barceloneta, Ciutadella–Vila Olímpica, L1 Arc de Triomf.

**El Transbordador Aeri del Port** (Port Cable Car)
TRANSPORTATION | FAMILY | This hair-raising cable-car ride over the Barcelona harbor, from Barceloneta to Montjuïc hill, is a serious adrenaline rush. Swaying 100 feet or so in the air, the windowed gondola, which holds 19 people, travels the mile-long route in about 10 minutes—every one of them packed with fabulous bird's-eye views. Cable-car access is from both ends, though most people leave from the Torre de San Sebastián (San Sebastian tower) in Barceloneta heading to the Torre de Miramar on Montjuïc.
■TIP➜ The Torre de Altamar restaurant in the tower at the Barceloneta end serves excellent food and wine. ⊠ Passeig Joan de Borbó 88, Barceloneta ☎ 93/430–4716 ⊕ www.telefericodebarcelona.com ⊡ €11 one-way; €16.50 round-trip Ⓜ Barceloneta.

### Estació de França

TRAIN/TRAIN STATION | Barcelona's main railroad station until about 1980, and still in use, the elegant Estació de França is outside the west gate of the Ciutadella. Rebuilt in 1929 for the International Exhibition and restored in 1992 for the Olympics, this mid-19th-century building overshadows Estació de Sants, the city's main intercity and international terminus. The marble and bronze, the Moderniste decorative details, and the delicate

Formerly an obsolete harbor, Port Vell is a modern yacht-basin and lively entertainment center.

tracery of its wrought-iron roof girders make this one of the most beautiful buildings of its kind. Stop in for a sense of the bygone romance of European travel. ⊠ *Av. Marquès de l'Argentera s/n, La Ciutadella* ☎ *902/320–230 RENFE office* Ⓜ *L4 Barceloneta.*

★ **Museu del Disseny de Barcelona** (*Design Museum of Barcelona*)
**ARTS CENTER** | This eye-catching center for design is home to six permanent collections featuring textiles, historical clothing, haute couture, ceramics, decorative arts, and graphic design. The product design and modern and contemporary furniture collections are particularly outstanding. Temporary exhibits run the gamut, and the building itself, by MBM Arquitectes (Oriol Bohigas, doyen of the firm), was the prime mover in much of Barcelona's makeover for the 1992 Olympics), juts out like a multistoried wedge into the Plaça de les Glòries. ⊠ *Pl. de les Glòries Catalans 37–8, Poblenou* ☎ *93/256–6800* ⊕ *www.museudeldisseny.cat* ⊠ *€6;*

free Sun. 3–8 and all day 1st Sun. every month; temporary exhibit cost varies ☉ Closed Mon. Ⓜ L1 Glòries, Glòries (Tram).

**Museu d'Història de Catalunya** (*Museum of the History of Catalonia*)
**HISTORY MUSEUM** | Established in what used to be a port warehouse, this state-of-the-art interactive museum makes you part of Catalonian history, from prehistoric times to the contemporary democratic era. After centuries of "official" Catalan history dictated from Madrid (from 1714 until the mid-19th century Renaixença, and from 1939 to 1975), this offers an opportunity to revisit Catalonia's autobiography. Audioguides are available in English. The rooftop restaurant (1881 Per Sagardi) has fabulous harbor views. ⊠ *Pl. de Pau Vila 3, Barceloneta* ☎ *93/254–700* ⊕ *www.mhcat.cat* ⊠ *From €6 (free on the first Sun. of every month, 10 am–2:30 pm)* ☉ *Closed Sun. afternoon and Mon.* Ⓜ *L4 Barceloneta.*

## Parlament de Catalunya

NOTABLE BUILDING | Once the arsenal for the Ciutadella—as evidenced by the thickness of the building's walls—this is the only surviving remnant of Felipe V's fortress. For a time it housed the city's museum of modern art, before it was repurposed to house the unicameral Catalan Parliament. Under Franco, the Generalitat—the regional government—was suppressed, and the Hall of Deputies was shut fast for 37 years. Book a free 45-minute guided tour (Mon.–Fri.) of the building via the website at least two days in advance; it includes the grand "Salon Rose," which is worth a visit in itself. ✉ Pl. de Joan Fiveller, Parc de la Ciutadella s/n, La Ciutadella ☎ 93/304–6645 ⊕ www.parlament.cat ⊆ Free Ⓜ L4 Ciutadella/Vila Olímpica.

## Port Olímpic

MARINA/PIER | The Olympic Port is 2 km (1 mile) up the beach from Barceloneta and is marked by the mammoth shimmering goldfish sculpture by starchitect Frank Gehry, with the towering five-star Hotel Arts just behind. A swath of swanky beachfront nightclubs line the promenade here and farther up is a marina packed with oversized yachts. Much of the area is undergoing a significant overhaul, with renovations scheduled to last into 2023. These include a reimagining of the various docks and piers to make them more accessible to the public and replacing the glut of seedy bars along the Moll de Mestral with a wider variety of businesses. ✉ Port Olímpic, Port Olímpic ⊕ www.portolimpic.barcelona/ca Ⓜ Ciutadella/Vila Olímpica.

## Port Vell (Old Port)

MARINA/PIER | FAMILY | From Pla del Palau, cross to the edge of the port, where the Moll d'Espanya, the Moll de la Fusta, and the Moll de Barceloneta meet (Moll means docks). Just beyond the colorful Roy Lichtenstein sculpture, the modern Port Vell complex—home to the aquarium and Maremagnum shopping mall—stretches seaward to the right on the Moll d'Espanya. The Palau de Mar, with rows of pricey, tourist-oriented quayside terrace restaurants (La Gavina or Merendero de la Mari are okay if you must), stretches down along the Moll de Barceloneta to the left. The rather soulless Maremagnum complex is noteworthy if only for being one of very few shopping options that remains open on Sunday. ✉ Port Vell, Barceloneta Ⓜ L4 Barceloneta.

## Sant Miquel del Port

CHURCH | Have a close look at this baroque church with its modern (1992), pseudo-bodybuilder version of the winged archangel Michael himself, complete with sword and chain, in the alcove on the facade. (The figure is a replica; the original was destroyed in 1936.) One of the first buildings to be completed in Barceloneta, Sant Miquel del Port was begun in 1753 and finished by 1755 under the direction of architect Damià Ribes. Due to strict orders to keep Barceloneta low enough to fire La Ciutadella's cannon over, Sant Miquel del Port had no bell tower and only a small cupola until Elies Rogent added a new one in 1853. Interesting to note are the metopes: palm-sized gilt bas-relief sculptures around the interior cornice and repeated outside at the top of the facade. These 74 Latin-inscribed allegories each allude to different attributes of St. Michael. For example, the image of a boat and the Latin inscription "iam in tuto" (finally safe), alludes to the saint's protection against the perils of the sea. ✉ Carrer de Sant Miquel 39, Barceloneta ☎ 93/221–6550 ⊕ santmiqueldelport.org Ⓜ L4 Barceloneta.

## 🏖 Beaches

### Platja de la Barceloneta

BEACH | FAMILY | Reached by walking down Passeig Joan de Borbó and turning left at Plaça del Mar, the adjacent beaches of Barceloneta and Sant Miquel aro the easiest to get to and hence the busiest—though they're also the most fun for people-watching. Note that itinerant beach vendors can be a nuisance, and pickpocketing has become increasingly problematic in recent years. The calm waters are easy for swimming, and there are several companies that provide surfing and paddle board rentals and lessons. Take note of Rebecca Horn's contemporary sculpture of towering, rusting cubes, *L'Estel Ferit*, a popular meeting spot on Sant Miquel beach. **Amenities:** food and drink; lifeguards; showers; toilets; water sports. **Best for:** partiers; swimming; walking; paddle boarding; surfing (mostly in winter). ✉ *Passeig Marítim de la Barceloneta s/n, Barceloneta* Ⓜ *Ciutadella/Vila Olímpica.*

### Platja de la Mar Bella

BEACH | Closest to the Poblenou metro stop, this is a thriving gay enclave and the unofficial nudist beach of Barcelona (although clothed bathers are welcome, too). The water-sports center Base Nàutica de la Mar Bella rents equipment for sailing, surfing, and windsurfing. Outfitted with showers, drinking fountains, and a children's play area, La Mar Bella also has lifeguards who warn against swimming near the breakwater. **Amenities:** food and drink; lifeguards; showers; toilets; water sports. **Best for:** partiers; nudists; LGBTQ beachgoers; swimming; windsurfing. ✉ *Passeig Marítim del Bogatell, Poblenou* Ⓜ *Poblenou.*

### Platja de la Nova Icària

BEACH | FAMILY | One of Barcelona's most popular beaches, this strand is just east of Port Olímpic, with a full range of entertainment and refreshment venues close at hand. The wide beach is directly across from the neighborhood built as the residential Olympic Village for Barcelona's 1992 Olympic Games, an interesting housing project that has now become a popular residential neighborhood. Vendors prowl the sand, offering everything from sunglasses to cold

drinks to massages. Pickpocketing has been an issue here, too, so keep an eye on your belongings. **Amenities:** food and drink; lifeguards; showers; toilets; water sports. **Best for:** partiers; swimming; walking; windsurfing. ✉ *Passeig Marítim del Port Olímpic s/n, Port Olímpic* Ⓜ *Ciutadella/Vila Olímpic.*

### Platja de Sant Sebastià

BEACH | Barceloneta's most southwestern platja (at the very end of Passeig Joan de Borbó), Sant Sebastià is the oldest and most historic of the city beaches; it was here that 19th-century locals cavorted in bloomers and bathing costumes. Despite repeated attempts to "clean up" Sant Sebastià, it remains a popular unofficial nudist spot. The famous sail-shaped W Barcelona hotel stands at the far south end. **Amenities:** food and drink; lifeguards; showers; toilets. **Best for:** partiers; swimming. ✉ *Passeig Marítim de la Barceloneta s/n, Barceloneta* Ⓜ *Barceloneta.*

## 🍴 Restaurants

Barceloneta and the Port Olímpic (Olympic Port) have little in common beyond their seaside location. Port Olímpic is a massive-scaled, modern environment, while Barceloneta has retained its traditional character as a blue-collar neighborhood, even if few fishermen live here now. Decades-old family restaurants and tourist traps can look similar from the street; a telltale sign of unreliable establishments is the presence of hard-selling waiters outside, aggressively courting passing customers.

East of the Eixample and extending to the sea just beyond Port Olímpic, Poblenou's formerly rough-around-the-edges neighborhood with a historical heart has lately seen an influx of edgy art studios, design shops, and a few hip restaurants—many of these spaces are installed in converted warehouses.

## Agua

$$ | MEDITERRANEAN | Hit Agua's beach-front terrace on warm summer nights and sunny winter days, or just catch rays inside through immense windows; either way you'll have a prime spot for people-watching and fresh seafood-eating. Expect good-if-not-spectacular fare and hit-or-miss service at this popular tourist favorite. **Known for:** popular tourist spot; beachfront location; fresh seafood. ⑤ *Average main: €21* ✉ *Passeig Marítim de la Barceloneta 30, Port Olímpic* ☎ *93/225–1272* ⊕ *restauranteagua.com* Ⓜ *Ciutadella–Vila Olímpica.*

## Barceloneta

$$$ | SEAFOOD | This restaurant in an enormous riverboat-like building at the end of the yacht marina in Barceloneta is geared for high-volume business, but the paellas and grilled fish dishes are reliably excellent. The hundreds of fellow diners make the place feel like a cheerful celebration. **Known for:** fresh grilled fish; excellent rice and paella; lively waterside spot. ⑤ *Average main: €27* ✉ *Escar 22, Moll de Pescadors, Barceloneta* ☎ *93/221–2111* ⊕ *www.restaurantbarceloneta.com* Ⓜ *Barceloneta.*

## Camping Mar

$$ | MEDITERRANEAN | Slightly hidden in the exclusive yachting marina behind the W Barcelona hotel, this is a restaurant that only attracts those in the know, which might explain why it is largely devoid of tourists. The menu includes healthy starters like red tuna and eggplant tartare and grilled avocado salad, and there's a nice selection of both seafood- and meat-based paellas. **Known for:** paellas; healthy options; hidden gem. ⑤ *Average main: €21* ✉ *Pg. Joan de Borbó 103, Marina Vela, Barceloneta* ☎ *93/408–8901* ⊕ *www.encompaniadelobos.com/en/camping-mar* ☾ *Closed Mon.–Wed.* Ⓜ *Barceloneta.*

## Can Majó

$$ | SEAFOOD | FAMILY | Can Majó doesn't consistently reach the standards that once made it famous but the food is still a notch above most of the touristy haunts nearby. Specialties include *caldero de bogavante* (a cross between paella and lobster bouillabaisse) and *suquet* (fish stewed in its own juices), and the terrace overlooking Barceloneta Beach is a pleasantly upscale alternative to the surrounding beach bars. **Known for:** excellent paella; fish dishes; terrace overlooking the Mediterranean. ⑤ *Average main: €22* ✉ *Emília Llorca Martín 23, (also an entrance at Carrer de l'Almirall Aixada, 23), Barceloneta* ☎ *93/221–5455* ⊕ *www.canmajo.es* ☾ *Closed Mon; No dinner Tues., Wed., and Sun.* Ⓜ *Barceloneta.*

## Can Solé

$$$$ | SEAFOOD | With no sea views or terrace to attract diners, Can Solé has to rely on its reputation as one of Barceloneta's best options for seafood. Faded photos of half-forgotten local celebrities line the walls of this nearly 120-year-old establishment, but there's nothing out-of-date about the exquisitely fresh seafood. **Known for:** historical atmosphere; traditional Spanish rice dishes; fresh fish daily. ⑤ *Average main: €30* ✉ *Sant Carles 4, Barceloneta* ☎ *93/221–5012* ⊕ *restaurant-cansole.com* ☾ *Closed Mon. No dinner Sun.* Ⓜ *Barceloneta.*

## 1881 per Sagardi

$$$ | MEDITERRANEAN | Enjoy fabulous views of yachts sailing out into the glittering Mediterranean while dining on fresh seafood—caught by local fisherman or sourced at the Barceloneta market—and expertly prepared on the wood-fired grill. This stylish restaurant is perched atop a renovated warehouse that now houses the Museum of the History of Catalonia. **Known for:** locally sourced seafood; all-day kitchen; terrace with great harbor and city views. ⑤ *Average main: €24* ✉ *Pl. de Pau Vila 3, Barceloneta*

# La Barceloneta, Land of Paella

Paella is Valencian, not Catalan, but it's typical for Barcelona families to go out for paella in Barceloneta on Sunday. Paella *de marisco*, or rice with mixed seafood (usually clams, mussels, octopus, and prawns) is the most popular, though you can also find meat and vegetarian versions. You'll generally see paella listed under rice dishes, which include many variations like *arroz negro* (black rice), cooked in squid ink, and *arroz caldoso*, a soupier rice. Catalan *fideuá* is made with vermicelli noodles mixed with the standard paella ingredients. Paella is for a minimum of two diners—it's usually enough for three. Don't go to any place where they have a photo of paella on a menu outside—it's a sure sign that the dish isn't made in-house.

☎ 93/221–0050 ⊕ www.gruposagardi. com Ⓜ Barceloneta.

## ★ El 58

$$ | TAPAS | A long list of seasonal Mediterranean small plates, ranging from coal-grilled octopus to vegetarian risotto to traditional Catalan sausage stew, is chalked up on the boards here each day. Inside it's casually hip, with exposed brick walls and vintage furniture; there's a small back patio for al fresco dining as well as tables out front on the Rambla del Poblenou for excellent people-watching. **Known for:** wide range of tapas; charming back patio; nicely presented dishes. $ *Average main: €20* ✉ Rambla del Poblenou 58, Poblenou ☎ 93/601–3903 ⊕ facebook.com/el58poblenou ☉ Closed Sun. Ⓜ Poblenou.

## Els Tres Porquets

$$ | TAPAS | Tucked behind the modern outdoor Glòries shopping mall, Els Tres Porquets (The Three Little Pigs) packs in foodies and bon vivants with a wide range of seasonal tapas and small dishes. The interesting wine list includes lesser-known but noteworthy selections from Spain and around the world. **Known for:** interesting wine list; delicious cheeses; Iberian specialties. $ *Average main: €16* ✉ Rambla del Poblenou 165, Poblenou ☎ 93/300–8750 ⊕ www.elstresporquets. es ☉ Closed Sun. Ⓜ Glòries, Clot.

## ★ Enoteca Paco Pérez

$$$$ | MEDITERRANEAN | The sleek white-on-white dining room sets the tone for chef Pérez's contemporary take on Mediterranean cuisine. Tasting menus present around a dozen courses, most with a seasonal, seafood-centric focus, like a sea cucumber pasta with bone marrow and young artichokes. **Known for:** creative wine list; tasting menus; two-Michelin-starred cuisine. $ *Average main: €196* ✉ Hotel Arts, Carrer de la Marina 19-21, Port Olímpic ☎ 93/221–1000 ⊕ enoteca-pacoperez.com/en ☉ Closed Mon. and Tues. No dinner Sun. and Wed. Special €95 lunch menu available Sun. and Wed. only Ⓜ Ciutadella–Vila Olímpica.

## Green Spot

$$ | VEGETARIAN | The vegan and vegetarian options in Barcelona have improved remarkably in recent years, led by the likes of Green Spot, with its extensive menu of flavor-packed plant-based dishes designed to please non-meat-eaters and carnivores alike. The dining room's pale oak paneling elegantly frames an open kitchen and airy dining room. **Known for:** stylish space; craft beer and natural wine; vegan and vegetarian pizzas. $ *Average main: €16* ✉ Reina Cristina 12, Barceloneta ☎ 93/802–5565 ⊕ www.encompaniadelobos.com/the-green-spot/ Ⓜ Barceloneta.

### ★ La Cova Fumada

$ | TAPAS | There's no glitz, no glamour, and not even a sign outside, but the battered wooden doors of this old, family-owned tavern hide a tapas bar to be treasured. Loyal customers and hordes of tourists queue for the market-fresh seafood, served from the furiously busy kitchen. **Known for:** lunch only; "bomba" (fried potato croquette); blink and you'll miss it. $ Average main: €12 ⊠ Baluard 56, Barceloneta ☎ 93/221–4061 ⊘ Closed Sun. Ⓜ Barceloneta.

### L'Artesana Poblenou

$$ | TAPAS | A top-notch natural wine list and an ever-changing menu of inventive tapas like pumpkin-ginger soup, cuttlefish "meatballs," and fig pastry with yogurt draw a devoted local crowd to this casual neighborhood eatery. **Known for:** well-priced menu del dia (around €13); local favorite; excellent croquetas. $ Average main: €20 ⊠ Sant Joan de Malta 148, Poblenou ☎ 93/002–2039 ⊕ l-artesana-poblenou.negocio.site ⊘ Closed Sun. and Mon. Ⓜ Poblenou, Pere IV (Tram).

## ☕ Coffee and Quick Bites

### ★ The Cake Man Bakery

$ | BAKERY | This Poblenou bakery's ever-changing selection of delectable homemade cakes, tarts, and cookies—including many vegan and gluten-free options—hits the sweet spot. The Saturday-only brunch features savory egg sandwiches served on house-baked brioche buns. **Known for:** English- and Australian-style baked goods; seasonal specialties; Saturday brunch. $ Average main: €4 ⊠ Amistat 18, Poblenou ☎ 66/440–5965 ⊕ the-cake-man-bakery.business.site ⊘ Closed Sun. and Mon. Ⓜ Poblenou.

### ★ El Vaso de Oro

$$ | TAPAS | A favorite with visiting gourmands, this often-overcrowded little counter serves some of the best beer and tapas in town. The house-brewed artisanal draft beer—named after the Fort family who owns and runs the bar—is drawn and served with loving care by veteran, epauletted waiters who have it down to a fine art. **Known for:** beef fillet is a favorite; stand-up dining; old-school service. $ Average main: €15 ⊠ Balboa 6, Barceloneta ☎ 93/319–3098 Ⓜ Barceloneta.

## 🛏 Hotels

### ★ Hotel Arts Barcelona

$$$$ | HOTEL | This luxurious Ritz-Carlton-owned, 44-story hotel is just steps from the beach and all the nightlife of Port Olímpic. **Pros:** superb restaurant on-site; seafront pool area with loungers; fantastic views from rooms, especially on higher floors. **Cons:** reception area can get quite busy; very pricey; far from the city center. $ Rooms from: €420 ⊠ Carrer de la Marina 19–21, Port Olímpic ☎ 93/221–1000 ⊕ www.hotelartsbarcelona.com ⇨ 483 rooms ⦾ No Meals Ⓜ L4 Ciutadella–Vila Olímpica.

### Motel One Barcelona-Ciutadella

$ | HOTEL | This stylish budget hotel fits the bill for well-designed, no-frills accommodations in a great location. **Pros:** great value; optimal location for exploring the city; rooftop terrace and bar. **Cons:** no pool, gym, or spa; no minibars; rooms are very small. $ Rooms from: €99 ⊠ Passeig de Pujades 11–13, La Ciutadella ☎ 93/626–1900 ⊕ www.motel-one.com ⇨ 301 rooms ⦾ No Meals Ⓜ Arc de Triomf, Wellington (Tram).

### W Barcelona

$$$$ | RESORT | The city's only true beachfront hotel, this towering sail-shape monolith is more of a self-contained urban resort, with multiple restaurants and bars, indoor and outdoor pools, lounge decks, plus a sprawling spa and gym—and just about every space has sea views. **Pros:** unrivaled views; beachfront setting; multiple bars and restaurants on-site. **Cons:** pricey rates; loud music

in public areas, far from public transportation. ⬦ *Rooms from: €400* ✉ *Pl. de la Rosa del Vents 1, Barcelona* ☎ *93/295–2800* ⊕ *www.marriott.com* ↝ *473 rooms* ⦿ *No Meals* Ⓜ *L4 Barceloneta.*

## ▼ Nightlife

The stretch of seaside between Port Vell and Port Olímpic is bursting with Barceloneta's lively *chiringuitos* (beach shacks), laid-back bars, and terraced seafood restaurants. In sharp contrast, Port Olímpic's posh nightclub scene caters to a mixed international bag of partygoers, ages 21 and over.

Once the city's central industrial hub, Poblenou's contrasting faces—a quaint tree-lined rambla surrounded by vast warehouse spaces and ultramodern edifices—has become Barcelona's hippest enclave. Once-abandoned spaces have been renovated into chic artists' lofts, while vintage shops and nondescript restaurants are now enjoying new lives as retro bars and lounges.

### BARS

#### ★ Balius Bar

COCKTAIL LOUNGES | Sporting the original sign and glass shelving of the pharmacy that once stood here, Balius Bar has retro-chic decor, great music (check out the live jazz sessions on Sunday evenings), and top-notch cocktails. ✉ *Pujades 196, Poblenou* ☎ *93/315–8650* ⊕ *baliusbar. com* Ⓜ *Poblenou.*

#### La Cervecita Nuestra de Cada Día

BREWPUBS | A must for craft beer lovers, this modern high-ceilinged bar and shop is filled to the brim with more than 200 international craft brands plus around 15 rotating artisanal beers on tap. Claim your spot early as regulars routinely dominate the seating at the long bar or the cozy corner tables up front. ✉ *Llull 184, Poblenou* ☎ *616/318–430* ⊕ *www. facebook.com/Lacervecitanuestradeca-dadia* Ⓜ *Llacuna.*

#### Madame George

COCKTAIL LOUNGES | Everything about this stylish bar is a happy contradiction: the chandeliered space has large gilded mirrors and polished chocolate brown stools that curiously complement the rickety antiques and quirky touches (check out the bathtub sofa in the back room). Cocktails run the full gamut from classic to creative. ✉ *Pujades 179, Poblenou* ☎ *93/500–5151* ⊕ *www.madamegeorge-bar.com* Ⓜ *Poblenou.*

#### Més de Vi

WINE BARS | The brainchild of two Catalan sommeliers, Més de Vi is a chic wine bar with a purpose: to educate visitors on the art of Spanish wines, with a particular focus on regional vintages. There are plenty of seating options: a tasting table for serious aficionados, romantic tête-à-tête tables, and a bar area for socializing. ✉ *Marià Aguiló 123, Poblenou* ☎ *93/007–9151* ⊕ *www.restaurantemesdevi.es/en* Ⓜ *Poblenou.*

# The Eixample

The Eixample (ay-shompla) is an open-air Moderniste museum. Designed as a grid, in the best Cartesian tradition, the Eixample is oddly difficult to find your way around in; the builders seldom numbered the buildings and declined to alphabetize the streets, and even Barcelona residents can get lost in it. The easiest orientation to grasp is the basic division between the well-to-do Dreta, to the right of Rambla Catalunya looking inland, and the more working-class Ezquerra to the left. Eixample locations are also either *mar* (on the ocean side of the street) or *muntanya* (facing the mountains). Another useful rule of thumb is that a downhill slant generally leads to the sea, while an uphill slant will take you to the mountains.

The Eixample

## Sights ▼

1 Casa Amatller ............ **F5**
2 Casa Batlló ............... **F5**
3 Casa Calvet ............. **G7**
4 Casa de les Punxes ..... **G3**
5 Casa Golferichs ......... **A6**
6 Casa Milà ................. **F4**
7 Fundació
  Antoni Tàpies ............. **F5**
8 Museu del Modernisme
  de Barcelona ............. **E6**
9 Passatge Permanyer ... **G6**
10 Recinte Modernista
   de Sant Pau ............... **I2**
11 Temple Expiatori de la
   Sagrada Família .......... **I4**

## Restaurants ▼

1 Bar Mut ................. **G3**
2 Benzina ................. **A9**
3 Besta .................... **D4**
4 Betlem ................... **H6**
5 Cinc Sentits ............. **A7**
6 Ciudad Condal ........... **F6**
7 Cruix .................... **A7**
8 Disfrutar ................ **B4**
9 Embat ................... **II4**
10 Honest Greens ........... **E7**
11 La Real
   Hamburgueseria ........ **G5**
12 La Taverna del Clínic ... **B3**
13 Lasarte ................... **F4**
14 Manairó .................. **I6**
15 Moments ................. **F6**
16 Sartoria Panatieri ....... **G4**
17 Slow & Low .............. **A7**
18 Xerta .................... **E3**

## Quick Bites ▼

1 DeLaCrem ................ **D6**
2 L'Atelier ................. **A6**

## Hotels ▼

1 Alexandra
  Barcelona Hotel ......... **F4**
2 Alma Hotel
  Barcelona ................ **F4**
3 The Corner Hotel ........ **C4**
4 Hotel Astoria ............ **D2**
5 Hotel Claris Grand
  Luxe Barcelona ......... **G5**
6 Hotel El Palace
  Barcelona ............... **G7**
7 Majestic
  Hotel & Spa .............. **H8**
8 Mandarin Oriental
  Barcelona ................ **F6**
9 ME Barcelona ............ **F7**
10 Monument Hotel ......... **F4**
11 Ohla Eixample ............ **E3**
12 Radisson Blu Hotel
   1882 ..................... **I3**
13 Sir Victor Hotel .......... **F3**
14 SixtyTwo Hotel .......... **F5**
15 yök Casa + Cultura ...... **H8**
16 Yurbban Passage
   Hotel & Spa .............. **G8**

# 👁 Sights

## Casa Amatller

**HISTORIC HOME** | The neo-Gothic Casa Amatller was built by Josep Puig i Cadafalch in 1900, when the architect was 33 years old. Puig i Cadafalch's architectural historicism sought to recover Catalonia's proud past, in combination with eclectic elements from Flemish and Dutch architectural motifs. Note the Eusebi Arnau sculptures—especially his St. George and the Dragon, and the figures of a drummer with his dancing bear. The first-floor apartment, where the Amatller family lived, is a museum, with the original furniture and decor (self-guided tours are available with an English audioguide). Admission is discounted if booked online. ✉ *Passeig de Gràcia 41, Eixample Dreta* ☎ *93/216–0175* ⊕ *amatller.org/en* ✉ *From €19* ☞ *15% admission discount if you book online through the website* Ⓜ *L2/L3/L5 Passeig de Gràcia, FGC Provença.*

## ★ Casa Batlló

**HISTORIC HOME** | **FAMILY** | Gaudí at his most spectacular, the Casa Batlló is actually a makeover: it was originally built in 1877 by one of Gaudí's teachers, Emili Sala Cortés, and acquired by the Batlló family in 1900. Batlló wanted to tear down the undistinguished Sala building and start over, but Gaudí persuaded him to remodel the facade and the interior, and the result is astonishing. The facade—with its rainbow of colored glass and *trencadís* (polychromatic tile fragments) and the toothy masks of the wrought-iron balconies projecting outward toward the street—is an irresistible photo op. Nationalist symbolism is at work here: the scaly roof line represents the Dragon of Evil impaled on St. George's cross, and the skulls and bones on the balconies are the dragon's victims, allusions to medieval Catalonia's code of chivalry and religious piety. The fully restored house is packed with state-of-the-art technologies, including immersive rooms, surprising audiovisual productions and an intelligent audio guide available in 15 languages. Children can enjoy an Augmented Reality SmartGuide: a fun, interactive way to discover the genius of Gaudí. From May to October, finish your visit with a magical open-air concert on the roof (starts at 8 pm) and a drink. ✉ *Passeig de Gràcia 43, Eixample Dreta* ☎ *93/216–0306* ⊕ *www.casabatllo.es* ✉ *From €35* Ⓜ *L2/L3/L4 Passeig de Gràcia, FGC Provença.*

## Casa Calvet

**NOTABLE BUILDING** | This exquisite but more conventional town house (for Gaudí, anyway) was the architect's first commission in the Eixample (the second was the dragon-like Casa Batlló, and the third, and last—he was never asked to do another—was the stone quarry–esque Casa Milà). Peaked with baroque scroll gables over the unadorned (no ceramics, no color, no sculpted ripples) Montjuïc sandstone facade, Casa Calvet compensates for its structural conservatism with its Art Nouveau details, from the door handles to the benches, chairs, vestibule, and spectacular glass-and-wood elevator. The only part of the building accessible to visitors is the ground-floor China Crown restaurant, originally the suite of offices for Calvet's textile company, with its exuberant Moderniste decor. ✉ *Carrer Casp 48, Eixample Dreta* ☎ *93/315 8095 (China Crown restaurant)* Ⓜ *L1/L4 Urquinaona.*

## Casa de les Punxes (*House of the Spikes*)

**NOTABLE BUILDING** | Also known as Casa Terrades for the family that owned the house and commissioned Puig i Cadafalch to build it, this extraordinary cluster of six conical towers ending in impossibly sharp needles is another of Puig i Cadafalch's inspirations, this one rooted in the Gothic architecture of northern European countries. One of the few freestanding Eixample buildings, visible from 360 degrees, this ersatz Bavarian or Danish castle in downtown Barcelona is composed entirely of private apartments, some of them built into the conical towers themselves on three circular levels, connected by spiral stairways. Casa de les Punxes currently functions as a co-working space and is not open to visitors. ✉ *Av. Diagonal 420, Eixample Dreta* ☎ *93/018–5242* ⊕ *www.barcelona. de/en/barcelona-casa-de-les-punxes.html* Ⓜ *L4/L5 Verdaguer, L3/L5 Diagonal.*

**Casa Golferichs** (*Golferichs Civic Center*) HISTORIC HOME | Gaudí disciple Joan Rubió i Bellver built this extraordinary house, known as El Xalet (The Chalet), for the Golferichs family when he was only 30. The rambling wooden eaves and gables of the exterior enclose a cozy and comfortable dark-wood-lined interior with a pronounced verticality. The top floor, with its rich wood beams and cerulean walls, is often used for intimate concerts; the ground floor exhibits paintings and photographs. The building serves now as the quarters of the Golferichs Centre Civic, which offers local residents a range of conferences and discussions, exhibitions and adult education courses, and organizes various thematic walking tours of the city. ✉ *Gran Via 491, Eixample Esquerra* ☎ *93/323–7790* ⊕ *www. golferichs.org* ⊘ *Closed Sat.–Sun.* Ⓜ *L1 Rocafort, Urgell.*

★ **Casa Milà**
NOTABLE BUILDING | Usually referred to as *La Pedrera* (The Stone Quarry), with a curving stone facade that undulates around the corner of the block, this building, unveiled in 1910, is one of Gaudí's most celebrated yet initially reviled designs. Seemingly defying the laws of gravity, the exterior has no straight lines, and is adorned with winding balconies covered with wrought-iron foliage sculpted by Josep Maria Jujol. Gaudí's rooftop chimney park, alternately interpreted as veiled Saharan women or helmeted warriors, is as spectacular as anything in Barcelona, especially in late afternoon when the sunlight slants over the city into the Mediterranean. Inside, the handsome Àtic de la Balena (Whale Attic) has excellent critical displays of

Gaudí's works from all over Spain. The Pis dels veïns (Tenants' Apartment) is an interesting look into the life of a family that lived in La Pedrera in the early 20th century. Entrance lines can be long; book ahead for tours. ✉ *Passeig de Gràcia 92, Eixample Dreta* ☎ *93/214–2576* ⊕ *www. lapedrera.com/en* ✉ *From €24* Ⓜ *L2/L3/ L5 Diagonal, FGC Provença.*

**Fundació Antoni Tàpies**
ART MUSEUM | This foundation created in 1984 by Catalonia's then-most important living artist, Antoni Tàpies, continues to promote the work of important Catalan artists and writers. Tàpies, who died in 2012, was an abstract painter who was influenced by surrealism, and his passion for art and literature still echoes in the halls of this enchanting Modernist building by esteemed architect Domènech i Montaner. There are thought-provoking temporary exhibitions, a comprehensive lecture series, and film screenings. The modern split-level gallery also has a bookstore that's strong on Tàpies, Asian art, and Barcelona art and architecture. ✉ *Carrer Aragó 255, Eixample Esquerra* ☎ *93/487–0315* ⊕ *www.fundaciotapies. org* ✉ *€8* ⊘ *Closed Sun. afternoon and Mon.* Ⓜ *L2/L3/L4 Passeig de Gràcia.*

**Museu del Modernisme de Barcelona** (*Museum of Catalan Modernism: MMBCN*)
ART MUSEUM | Though often unjustly bypassed in favor of rival displays in the Casa Milà, Casa Batlló, and the DHUB Design Museum in Plaça de les Glòries, this museum houses a small but rich collection of Moderniste furnishings, paintings and posters, sculpture (including works by Josep Limona), and decorative arts. Don't miss the section devoted to Gaudí-designed furniture. ✉ *Carrer Balmes 48, Eixample Esquerra* ☎ *93/272–2896* ⊕ *www.gothsland.com* ✉ *€12* ⊘ *Closed Sun.* Ⓜ *L1/L2 Universitat.*

## Passatge Permanyer

STREET | Cutting through the middle of the block bordered by Pau Claris, Roger de Llúria, Consell de Cent, and Diputació, this charming, leafy mid-Eixample sanctuary is one of 46 passatges (alleys or passageways) that cut through the blocks of this gridlike area. Once an aristocratic enclave and hideaway for pianist Carles Vidiella and poet, musician, and illustrator Apel·les Mestre, Passatge Permanyer is, along with the nearby Passatge Méndez Vigo, the best of these through-the-looking-glass downtown Barcelona alleyways. ⊠ Passatge Permanyer, Eixample Dreta Ⓜ L2/L3/L4 Passeig de Gràcia.

## ★ Recinte Modernista de Sant Pau

NOTABLE BUILDING | Set in what was one of the most beautiful public projects in the world—the Hospital de Sant Pau—the Sant Pau Art Nouveau Site is, sadly, no longer a hospital, but it is a UNESCO World Heritage site that's extraordinary in its setting, style, and the idea that inspired it. Architect Lluis Domènech i Montaner believed that trees, flowers, and fresh air were likely to help people recover from what ailed them more than anything doctors could do in emotionally sterile surroundings. The hospital wards were set among gardens, their brick facades topped with polychrome ceramic tile roofs in extravagant shapes and details. Domènech also believed in the therapeutic properties of form and color, and decorated the hospital with Eusebi Arnau sculptures and colorful mosaics, replete with motifs of hope and healing and healthy growth. The center offers self-guided tours with audio guides in the form of an app that can be downloaded to your personal devices, for maximum safety and hygiene. ⊠ Carrer Sant Antoni Maria Claret 167, Eixample Dreta ☎ 93/553–7801 ⊕ www.santpaubarcelona.org/en ⊠ From €15; free 1st Sun. of month Ⓜ L5 Sant Pau/Dos de Maig.

## ★ Temple Expiatori de la Sagrada Família

NOTABLE BUILDING | Barcelona's most emblematic architectural icon, Antoni Gaudí's Sagrada Família, is still under construction close to 140 years after it was begun. This striking and surreal creation was conceived as a gigantic representation of the entire history of Christianity. Begun in 1882 under architect Francisco de Paula del Villar and passed on in 1883 to Gaudí (until his death in 1926), the church is now in the final stage of construction. No building in Barcelona and few in the world are more deserving of the investment of a few hours to the better part of a day. The apse of the basilica, consecrated by Pope Benedict XVI in 2010, has space for close to 15,000 people and a choir loft for 1,500. The towers include those dedicated to the four evangelists—Matthew, Mark, Luke, and John—and the highest of all, dedicated to Christ the Savior. Once completed, the great central tower and dome, resting on four immense columns of Iranian porphyry, considered the hardest of all stones, will soar to a height of 564 feet, making the Sagrada Família Barcelona's tallest building. Prior to the outbreak of the COVID-19 pandemic, the Sagrada Família was due to be completed by 2026, the 100th anniversary of Gaudí's death, after 144 years of construction. A new official date is yet to be announced. Take an elevator up the bell towers for spectacular views. The museum displays Gaudí's scale models and photographs showing the progress of construction. The architect is buried to the left of the altar in the crypt.

■TIP→ Lines to enter the church can stretch around the block. Buy your tickets online, with a reserved time of entry, and jump the queue. ⊠ Pl. de la Sagrada Família, Carrer Mallorca 401, Eixample Dreta ☎ 93/207–3031, 93/208–0414 visitor info ⊕ sagradafamilia.org ⊠ From €26 Ⓜ L2/L5 Sagrada Família.

Continued on page 464

# TEMPLE EXPIATORI DE LA
# SAGRADA FAMÍLIA

Antoni Gaudí's striking and surreal masterpiece was conceived as nothing short of a Bible in stone, an arresting representation of the history of Christianity. Today, this Roman Catholic church is Barcelona's most emblematic architectural icon. Looming over the city like a manmade massif of grottoes and peaks, La Sagrada Família strains skyward in piles of stalagmites. Construction is ongoing and continues to stretch toward the heavens.

## CONSTRUCTION, PAST AND PRESENT

"My client is not in a hurry," was Gaudí's reply to anyone curious about his project's timetable . . . good thing, too, because La Sagrada Família was begun in 1882 under architect Francesc Villar, passed on in 1891 to Gaudí, and is still thought to be several years from completion. Gaudí added Art Nouveau touches to the crypt and, in 1883, started the Nativity facade. Conceived as a symbolic construct encompassing the complete story and scope of the Christian faith, the church was intended by Gaudí to impress the viewer with the full sweep and force of the Gospel. At the time of his death in 1926 only one tower of the Nativity facade had been completed.

By 2026, the 100th anniversary of Gaudí's death, after 144 years of construction in the tradition of the great medieval and Renaissance cathedrals of Europe, La Sagrada Família may well be complete enough to call finished. Architect Jordi Bonet continues in the footsteps of his father, architect Lluís Bonet, to make Gaudí's vision complete as he has since the 1980s.

(left) Sagrada Família interior. (top) Shepherds gather to witness the birth of Christ in the Nativity facade.

# BIBLE STUDIES IN STONE: THE FACADES

Gaudí's plans called for three immense facades. The northeast-facing **Nativity facade** and the southwest-facing **Passion facade** are complete. The much larger southeast-facing **Glory facade,** the building's main entry, is still under construction. The final church will have 18 towers: The four **bell towers** over each facade represent the 12 apostles; the four **larger towers** represent the evangelists Mark, Matthew, John, and Luke; the **second-highest tower** in the reredos behind the altar honors the Virgin Mary; and, in the center, the **Torre del Salvador** (Tower of the Savior) will soar to a height of 564 feet.

## THE NATIVITY FACADE

Built during Gaudí's lifetime, this facade displays his vision and sculptural style, the organic or so-called "melting wax" look that has become his signature. The facade is crowned by **four bell towers,** representing the apostles Barnabas, Jude, Simon, and Matthew and divided into three sections around the doors of **Charity** in the center, **Faith** on the right, and **Hope** on the left.

(left) The ornamental Nativity facade. (above, top right) The Portal of Charity. (above, center right) The spiraling staircase. (above, bottom right) A decorative cross.

The focal point in the Nativity facade: Joseph and Mary presenting the infant Jesus.

Over the central **Portal of Charity** is the birth of Christ, with a representation of the Annunciation overhead in an ice grotto, another natural element. Above that are the signs of the zodiac for the Christmas sky at Bethlehem, with two babies representing the Gemini and the horns of a bull for Taurus. The evergreen cypress tree rising above symbolizes eternity, with the white doves as souls seeking life everlasting.

The **Portal of Faith** on the right shows Christ preaching as a youth. Higher up are the Eucharistic symbols of grapes and wheat and a hand and eye, symbols of divine Providence.

The **Portal of Hope** on the left shows a series of biblical scenes including the slaughter of the innocents, the flight into Egypt, Joseph surrounded by his carpenter's tools looking down at his infant son, and the marriage of Joseph and Mary with Mary's parents, Joaquin and Anna, looking on. Above is a boat, representing the Church, piloted by Joseph, with the Holy Spirit represented as a dove.

## THE PASSION FACADE

On the **Passion facade**, Gaudí intended to dramatize the abyss between the birth of a child and the death of a man. In 1986, Josep Maria Subirachs, an artist known for his atheism and his hard-edged and geometrical sculptural style, was commissioned to finish the Passion facade. The contrast is sharp, in content and in sculptural style, between this facade and the Nativity facade. Framed by leaning columns of tibia-like bones, the Passion facade illustrates the last days of Christ and his Resurrection. The scenes are laid out chronologically in an S-shape path beginning at the bottom left and ending at the upper right.

At bottom left is the **Last Supper**, the disciples' faces contorted in confusion and anguish, most of all Judas clutching his bag of money behind his back over a reclining hound, the contrasting symbol of fidelity. To the right is the Garden of Gethsemane and Peter awakening, followed by the **Kiss of Judas.**

Judas kissing Jesus while a cryptogram behind contains a numerical combination adding up to 33, the age of Christ's death.

The stark, geometric Passion facade.

To the right of the door is **Peter's Third Denial** of Christ "ere the cock crows." Farther to the right are **Pontius Pilate and Jesus** with the crown of thorns.

Above on the second tier are the **Three Marys** and Simon helping Jesus lift the cross. Over the center, **Jesus carries the cross.** To the left, Gaudí himself is portrayed, pencil in hand, the evangelist in stone, while farther left a **mounted centurion** pierces the side of the church with his spear, the church representing the body of Christ. At the top left, **soldiers gamble for Christ's clothing** while at the top center is the **crucifixion**, featuring Subirachs's controversial (in 1971 when it was unveiled) naked and anatomically complete Christ. Finally to the right, Peter and Mary grieve at **Christ's entombment**, an egg overhead symbolizing rebirth and the resurrection. At a height of 148 feet are the four Apostles on their bell towers. Bartholomew, on the left, looks upward toward the 26-foot risen Christ between the four bell towers at a height of 198 feet.

## THE GLORY FACADE

The Glory facade, still under construction, will have a wide stairway and esplanade or porch leading up to three portals dedicated, as in the other facades, to Charity, Faith, and Hope. The doors are inscribed with the Lord's Prayer in bronze in 50 languages, with the Catalan version in the center in relief. Carrer Mallorca will be routed underground, and the entire city block across the street will be razed to make space for the esplanade and park. Present predictions are between 2026 and 2030 for the completion of this phase, but progress has slowed due to Covid.

The Glory facade

# THE INTERIOR: "TEMPLE OF HARMONIOUS LIGHT"

(top) Above the altar, supporting columns form a canopy of light. (below) Towering columns and stained-glass windows keep the interior bright.

Until 2010, La Sagrada Família was able to be adequately appreciated without going inside. But since the interior was completed for the Papal consecration, it's become Barcelona's most stunning space, comparable to the breathtaking upsweep of the finest soaring Gothic architecture but higher, brighter, and carved in a dazzling fusion of hard-edged Subirachs over organic Gaudí.

## DESIGN

The floor plan for the church is laid out in the form of a **Latin cross** with five longitudinal naves intersected by three transepts. The **apse** has space for 15,000 people, a choir loft for 1,500, and is large enough to encompass the entire Santa Maria del Mar basilica. From the Glory Façade, the Baptistry Chapel is to the left and the Chapel of the Sacrament and Penitence is to the right. The Chapel of the Assumption is at the back of the apse. Over the main altar is the figure of the crucified Christ, suspended in mid-air under a diaphanous canopy.

## LIGHT

The basilica's main nave and the apse create an immense, immaculate space culminating in the highest point: the main alter's hyperboloid skylight 75 meters (250 feet) above the floor. The vaulting is perforated with 288 skylights admitting abundant light. The sharp-edged, treelike leaning columns shape the interior spaces and will support the six towers being built above them. Vaults are decorated with green and gold Venetian mosaics that diffuse the light as if they were leaves in a forest, making the basilica, in the words of Gaudí, "the temple of harmonious light."

# 🍴 Restaurants

The sprawling blocks of the Eixample contain Barcelona's finest selection of restaurants, from upscale and elegant traditional cuisine in Modernist houses to high-concept fare in sleek minimalist-experimental spaces.

### ★ Bar Mut

$$$ | CATALAN | Just above Diagonal, this elegant retro space serves first-rate products ranging from wild sea bass to the best Ibérico hams. Crowded, noisy, chaotic, delicious—it's everything a great tapas bar or restaurant should be. **Known for:** snacks at nearby spin-off Entrepanes Diaz; great wine list; upmarket tapas. $ *Average main: €26* ✉ *Pau Claris 192, Eixample Dreta* ☎ *93/217–4338* ⊕ *www. barmut.com* ⊘ *Closed Mon.* Ⓜ *Diagonal.*

### ★ Benzina

$$ | ITALIAN | Named for the car-mechanic shop that once stood here, Benzina blends industrial-chic elements with splashes of color and excellent music (on vinyl, naturally) to create a hip but cozy Italian restaurant. The food, however, is center stage: the freshly made pasta is among the best in the city, and other must-eats include the melt-in-the-mouth eggplant parmigiana with Parmesan ice cream and the *fritto misto* of calamari, shrimp, and fresh anchovies with curry mayo. **Known for:** chic decor; "Sferamisu" chocolate bomb of deconstructed tiramisú; best spaghetti carbonara in the city. $ *Average main: €18* ✉ *Passatge Pere Calders 6, Sant Antoni* ☎ *93/659– 5583* ⊕ *www.benzina.es* ⊘ *Closed Mon.– Tues., No lunch Wed.–Thur.* Ⓜ *Poble Sec.*

### ★ Besta

$$ | CATALAN | The atmosphere is relaxed but sophisticated and the constantly changing menu is a melting pot of seasonal produce from the Spanish regions of Catalonia and Galicia. Freshly caught fish and seafood take pride of place, as do the seasonal vegetables. **Known for:** cosmopolitan vibe; seafood dishes; Catalan-Galician cuisine. $ *Average main: €20* ✉ *Aribau 106, Eixample* ☎ *93/019–8294* ⊕ *bestabarcelona.com* ⊘ *Closed Tues.– Wed. No dinner Mon.* Ⓜ *Universitat L1, L2.*

### ★ Betlem

$$ | CATALAN | Set In a charming Moderniste space dating back to 1892, this bar hits the perfect balance of quality, price, service, and ambiance. The menu mixes classic dishes like deep-fried calamari and spicy *patatas bravas,* with house specials like the steak tartare and show-stopping omelet with black pudding (or *butifarra negra*) and seasonal mushrooms. **Known for:** Moderniste interior; sunny terrace; omelet with black pudding and mushrooms. $ *Average main: €15* ✉ *Girona 70, Eixample* ☎ *93/265–5105* Ⓜ *Girona L4.*

### Cinc Sentits

$$$$ | CATALAN | Obsessively local, scrupulously sourced, and masterfully cooked, the dishes of Catalan-Canadian chef Jordi Artal put the spotlight on the region's finest ingredients in an intimate, sophisticated setting. It's hard to believe that this garlanded restaurant is Jordi's first, but there's no arguing with the evidence of your *cinc sentits* (five senses). **Known for:** tasting menu only; awarded two Michelin stars; excellent chef. $ *Average main: €139* ✉ *Entença 60, Eixample Esquerra* ☎ *93/323–9490* ⊕ *cincsentits.com* ⊘ *Closed Sun., Mon., and public holidays* Ⓜ *Provença.*

### Ciudad Condal

$$ | TAPAS | FAMILY | At the bottom of Rambla de Catalunya, this scaled-up tapas bar draws a throng of mostly international clients and has tables outside on this busy part-pedestrianized street all year round. The *solomillo* (miniature beef fillet) is a winner here, as is the *broqueta d'escamarlans* (brochette of jumbo shrimp). **Known for:** reliable quality; central location; long wait times. $ *Average*

main: €15 ✉ Rambla de Catalunya 18, Eixample ☎ 93/318–1997 ⊕ ciudadcondal. cat Ⓜ Passeig de Gràcia, Catalunya.

### ★ Cruix

$$$ | CATALAN | With an eight-course tasting menu priced at just €35, Cruix is the fine-dining restaurant for people who don't want to spend 200 euros on a meal. Everything here is laid-back and unpretentious, including the exposed-brick interior, but the quality speaks to the Chef Miquel Pardo's pedigree: he worked under Spanish superstar chefs like Albert Adrià and Jordi Cruz before opening Cruix in 2017. **Known for:** excellent rice with shrimp and garlic; creative food; fine dining on a budget. $ Average main: €28 ✉ Entença 57, Eixample ☎ 93/525–2318 ⊕ www.cruixrestaurant. com ⊘ Closed Mon. and Tues. No dinner Sun. Ⓜ Rocafort L1.

### ★ Disfrutar

$$$$ | ECLECTIC | Three former head chefs from the now-closed "World's Best Restaurant" El Bulli combined their considerable talents to create this roller-coaster ride of culinary fun (the word "disfrutar" is Spanish for "to enjoy") spotlighting tasting menus of dazzling inventiveness and good taste. Bowls are swirled to reveal beetroot meringues emerging from sesame-seed "earth" (the seeds are made to look like soil), and jellied truffle-and-egg tempura hit the bull's-eye of pure pleasure; desserts are otherworldly. **Known for:** surprisingly accessible wine list; tasting menus only; inventive food. $ Average main: €210 ✉ Villarroel 163, Eixample Esquerra ☎ 93/348–6896 ⊕ www.disfrutarbarcelona.com ⊘ Closed Sat.–Sun., 2 wks in Aug., and 1 wk after Christmas Ⓜ Hospital Clínic.

### Embat

$$ | CATALAN | An *embat* is a puff of wind in Catalan, and this little bistro is a breath of fresh air in the sometimes stuffy Eixample. The highly affordable market cuisine is always impeccably fresh and freshly conceived, from the great-value three-course lunch selection to the more elaborate evening menu. **Known for:** market-fresh Catalan dishes; stylish minimalist interior; modern, unfussy fare. $ Average main: €17 ✉ Mallorca 304, Eixample Dreta ☎ 93/458–0855 ⊕ embatrestaurant.com ⊘ Closed Mon. No dinner Sun. and Tues. Ⓜ Verdaguer.

### Honest Greens

$$ | VEGETARIAN | There are a few fish and meat options on the menu but most visitors skip the animal proteins and opt for the impressive selection of plant-based foods. Delicious salads, tasty vegetarian curries, and fresh grilled vegetables are a hit with the health-conscious and the vegan desserts are even tastier than regular versions. **Known for:** several outposts around the city; great desserts; healthy but delicous food. $ Average main: €18 ✉ Rambla de Catalunya 3, Eixample ☎ 93/122–7664 ⊕ honestgreens.com/en Ⓜ Catalunya L1, L3.

### La Real Hamburguesería

$ | BURGER | If you're jonesing for a burger, this laid-back, Venezuelan-owned fast-food spot is the place to go. The burgers are great, of course, but so are sides like deep-fried cheese sticks (*tequeños*) with sweet chili sauce. **Known for:** vegan and vegetarian options available; Latin-American-style sides; small outdoor terrace. $ Average main: €14 ✉ València 285, Tienda 03, Eixample ☎ 93/832–8694 ⊕ larealbcn.com Ⓜ Girona L4.

### La Taverna del Clínic

$$ | CATALAN | Just outside the main entrance to Barcelona's largest hospital (Hospital Clínic), La Taverna del Clínic is a place you would (hopefully) never stumble upon by accident, but discerning locals and serious food lovers know this is a great spot for modern twist on classic Catalan fare. The truffle cannelloni is especially good, as is the *patatas bravas*. **Known for:** sunny outdoor patio; good wine list; contemporary tapas.

⑤ *Average main: €20* ✉ *Rosselló 155, Eixample Esquerra* ☎ *93/410–4221* ⊕ *www.latavernadelclinic.com* ◷ *Closed Sun.* Ⓜ *Hospital Clinic.*

### ★ Lasarte

**$$$$** | **BASQUE** | While Martin Berasategui, one of San Sebastián's corps of master chefs, no longer runs the day-to-day operations of this Barcelona kitchen (it's in the capable hands of chef Paolo Casagrande) the restaurant continues to be a culinary triumph. Expect an eclectic selection of Basque, Mediterranean, and off-the-map creations, a hefty bill, and fierce perfectionism apparent in every dish. **Known for:** heavenly grilled pigeon; magnificent tasting menu; inventive cuisine at one of the best restaurants in Barcelona. ⑤ *Average main: €70* ✉ *Mallorca 259, Eixample* ☎ *93/445–3242* ⊕ *www.restaurantlasarte.com* ◷ *Closed Sun., Mon., Tues., 2 wks in Jan., 1 wk at Easter, and 3 wks in Aug./Sept.* Ⓜ *Diagonal, Passeig de Gràcia, Provença (FGC).*

### Manairó

**$$$** | **CATALAN** | A *manairó* is a mysterious Pyrenean elf, and Jordi Herrera may be the culinary version: his ingenious cooking methods—such as filet mignon *al faquir* (heated from within on red-hot spikes) or blowtorched on a homemade centrifuge—may seem eccentric but produce undeniably good results. Melt-in-your-mouth meat dishes form the centerpiece of Manairó's menus, but they are ably supported by a bonanza of bold and confident creations that aren't frightened of big flavors. **Known for:** food that's fun to look at and even better to eat; delicious meat dishes; innovative contemporary cuisine. ⑤ *Average main: €26* ✉ *Diputació 424, Eixample Dreta* ☎ *93/231–0057* ⊕ *www.manairo.com* ◷ *Closed Sun., Mon., and 1st wk of Jan.* Ⓜ *Monumental.*

### ★ Moments

**$$$$** | **CATALAN** | Inside the ultrasleek Hotel Mandarin Oriental Barcelona, this restaurant, with food by Raül Balam and his mother—the legendary Carme Ruscalleda—lives up to its stellar pedigree, with original preparations that draw on deep wells of Catalan culinary traditions. Dishes display a masterful lightness of touch and come to the table so exquisitely presented that putting a fork into them feels almost like wanton vandalism; the reward, however, is sublime, with treasures of taste revealed in every astonishing bite. **Known for:** outstanding wine list; tasting menus are the only option; chef's table in the kitchen. ⑤ *Average main: €189* ✉ *Passeig de Gràcia 38–40, Eixample Dreta* ☎ *93/151–8781* ⊕ *www.mandarinoriental.com* ◷ *Closed Mon.–Wed. and 2 wks in Jan. No dinner Sun., no lunch Thurs.–Fri.* Ⓜ *Passeig de Gràcia.*

### Sartoria Panatieri

**$** | **PIZZA** | "Farm to pizza" is the tagline at this urban chic pizzeria specializing in home-cured artisanal charcuteries and pizzas made in a wood-fired oven. The dough for the Neapolitan-style pizzas is made with organic hand-milled flour, and all the ingredients are fresh, organic, seasonal, and local (some are grown on-site at the restaurant). **Known for:** chic crowd; Neapolitan-style pizza made in a wood-fired oven; home-cured artisanal charcuteries. ⑤ *Average main: €14* ✉ *Provença 330, Eixample* ☎ *93/105–5795* ⊕ *www.sartoriapanatieri.com* Ⓜ *Diagonal L3, L5.*

### ★ Slow & Low

**$$$$** | **FUSION** | The energetic young team behind Slow & Low is a blend of many different cultures and it shows in the menu, which combines Mediterranean, Mexican, Peruvian, and even some Southeast Asian influences. Better still, they make it look effortless in standout dishes like a green curry with seasonal green peas and Basque-style *pil-pil* code tripe, or the Mediterranean red shrimp Thai salad with som tam sorbet. **Known for:** creative tasting menu; young, international team; fresh seafood and seasonal veggies. ⑤ *Average main: €72* ✉ *Comte*

Borroll, 110, Sant Antoni ☎ 93/525–4512 ⊕ slowandlowbcn.com ⊕ Closed Sun. and Mon. Ⓜ Urgell L1.

### ★ Xerta

$$$$ | CATALAN | Much of Xerta's menu is the expected swanky fine-dining fare, but stand-out options use unique produce from the deltas and rivers of the Terres de l'Ebre region, such as sweet miniature *canyuts* (razor clams), oysters, and fresh eel. The superb weekday four-course lunch menu is a steal at €42. **Known for:** midweek lunch menu; outstanding seafood and rice dishes; regional produce. Ⓢ *Average main: €55* ✉ Ohla Eixample hotel, Còrsega 289, Eixample ☎ 9393/737–9080 ⊕ www. xertarestaurant.com ⊙ Closed Sun. and Mon. Ⓜ Provença.

### ☕ Coffee and Quick Bites

### ★ DeLaCrem

$ | ICE CREAM | For a cool pick-me-up on a hot Barcelona afternoon, you can't beat the seasonal, locally sourced, Italian-style ice cream from DeLaCrem. Expect classics like vanilla, chocolate, and dulce de leche as well as more unconventional combinations like mandarin and orange blossom yogurt, pear and Parmesan, or pumpkin and toasted butter. **Known for:** pumpkin and toasted butter gelato; unconventional flavors; Italian-style ice cream. Ⓢ *Average main: €5* ✉ Enric Granados,15, Eixample ☎ 93/004–1093 ⊕ delacrem.cat Ⓜ Universitat L1, L2.

### ★ L' Atelier

$ | BAKERY | This superb café, bakery, and pastry school has set a new standard for sweet treats in the city. The glazed cinnamon rolls are a standout, as is the to-die-for brioche filled with red berries and mascarpone, while the fresh croissant cone overflowing with soft-serve ice cream, praline, and salted caramel is a rare thing of great beauty. **Known for:** there are a few tables to eat at; creative desserts; breakfast pastries. Ⓢ *Average*

main: €10 ✉ Viladomat 140, Eixample ☎ 93/828–7373 ⊕ latelierbarcelona.com ⊙ Closed Sun. afternoon Ⓜ Urgell L1.

## 🛏 Hotels

### ★ Alexandra Barcelona Hotel

$$$ | HOTEL | FAMILY | Part of Hilton's upscale Curio Collection, the real draw about the Hotel Alexandra are the spectacular—and surprisingly affordable—suites with private terraces. **Pros:** relatively affordable; on-site restaurant serves some of the the best steak in town; great-value suites have terraces and outdoor tubs. **Cons:** doesn't have much local character; standard rooms on the small side; interior is rather dark. Ⓢ *Rooms from: €207* ✉ Mallorca 251, Eixample ☎ 93/467–7166 ⊕ www.hilton. com/en/hotels/bcnmaqq-alexandra-barcelona-hotel ⤳ 116 ❖ No Meals Ⓜ Diagonal L3, L5.

### ★ Alma Hotel Barcelona

$$$$ | HOTEL | The facade recalls the Moderniste origins of this wonderful building but the redesigned inside spaces make the Alma one of Barcelona's sleekest mid-Eixample hotels. **Pros:** impressive design; gorgeous garden with a restaurant; no keys or cards; you access your room with your fingerprint (taken when you check in). **Cons:** budget-stretching room rates; no outdoor pool; pricey breakfast. Ⓢ *Rooms from: €312* ✉ Carrer Mallorca 271, Eixample ☎ 93/216–4490 ⊕ www.almahotels.com ⤳ 72 rooms ❖ No Meals Ⓜ L3/L5 Diagonal, L4 Girona, FGC Provença.

### The Corner Hotel

$$ | HOTEL | This hip hotel, positioned (yes, you guessed it) on a corner, has been fashioned from a handsome, turn-of-the-century building within a few blocks of Gaudí's key sights on Passeig de Gràcia. **Pros:** walking distance to Passeig de Gràcia; cool decor; rooftop terrace with great views. **Cons:** breakfast expensive for what you get; interior-facing rooms

lack natural light; common areas can get rather busy. $ *Rooms from: €154* ✉ *Mallorca 178, Eixample Esquerra* ☎ *93/554–2400* ⊕ *www.thecornerhotel-barcelona.com* ⇆ *72 rooms* ⦿ *No Meals* Ⓜ *FGC Provença; L5 Hospital Clinic.*

### Hotel Astoria
$ | HOTEL | Three blocks west of Rambla Catalunya, near the upper middle of the Eixample, this renovated classic property, part of the Derby Hotels Collection group of fabulous artistic restorations, is a treasure for the budget-minded. **Pros:** convenient location; excellent value for price; free entrance to the Egyptian Museum of Barcelona. **Cons:** limited gym facilities; rooms on lower floors on the street side can be noisy; rooftop terrace pool is small. $ *Rooms from: €114* ✉ *Carrer Paris 203, Eixample Esquerra* ☎ *93/209–8311* ⊕ *www.derbyhotels.es/en/hotels/astoria-hotel* ⇆ *117 rooms* ⦿ *No Meals* Ⓜ *Provença (FGC), L3/L5 Diagonal.*

### Hotel Claris Grand Luxe Barcelona
$$$$ | HOTEL | In the heart of Eixample and within walking distance of most of the city, the legendary Hotel Claris, with its vast collection of antiques, is an icon of design, tradition, and connoisseurship. **Pros:** impressive design and antiques collection; Mayan Secret Spa with temazcal and pure chocolate skin treatment; rooms in a variety of styles. **Cons:** basic ("Superior") rooms small for the price; rooftop terrace noise at night can reach down into sixth-floor rooms; capacity bookings can sometimes overwhelm the staff. $ *Rooms from: €250* ✉ *Carrer Pau Claris 150, Eixample Dreta* ☎ *93/487–6262* ⊕ *www.hotelclaris.com* ⇆ *124 rooms* ⦿ *No Meals* Ⓜ *L2/L3/L4 Passeig de Gràcia.*

### ★ Hotel El Palace Barcelona
$$$$ | HOTEL | Founded in 1919 by Caesar Ritz, the original Ritz (the grande dame of Barcelona hotels) was renamed in 2005 but kept its lavish, timeless style intact blending its grand style with contemporary experiences, from the liveried doorman in top hat and lobby's massive crystal chandelier to seasonal immersive pop-up experiences on the seventh floor rooftop garden. **Pros:** historic granddame luxury; Mayan-style sauna in the award-winning spa; legendary cocktail bar. **Cons:** formal atmosphere; painfully pricey; may feel slightly intimidating. $ *Rooms from: €339* ✉ *Gran Vía de les Corts Catalanes 668, Eixample Dreta* ☎ *93/510–1130* ⊕ *www.hotelpalacebarcelona.com* ⇆ *120 rooms* ⦿ *No Meals* Ⓜ *L2/L3/L4 Passeig de Gràcia.*

### ★ Majestic Hotel & Spa
$$$$ | HOTEL | With an unbeatable location on Barcelona's most stylish boulevard—steps from Gaudí's La Pedrera and near the area's swankiest shops—and a stunning rooftop terrace with killer views of the city's landmarks, this hotel is a near-perfect place to stay. **Pros:** very good restaurant and spa; superb, personalized service; beloved city landmark with interesting history. **Cons:** street outside often bustling; pricey but excellent buffet breakfast; some standard rooms a bit small for the price. $ *Rooms from: €323* ✉ *Passeig de Gràcia 68-70, Eixample Dreta* ☎ *93/488–1717* ⊕ *majestichotelgroup.com/en/barcelona/hotel-majestic* ⇆ *275 rooms* ⦿ *No Meals* Ⓜ *L2/L3/L4 Passeig de Gràcia, Provença (FGC).*

### ★ Mandarin Oriental Barcelona
$$$$ | HOTEL | A carpeted ramp leading from the elegant Passeig de Gràcia lends this hotel the air of a privileged—and pricey—inner sanctum. **Pros:** outstanding Moments restaurant; exceptional, discreet service; babysitters and parties for the kids, on request. **Cons:** painfully expensive; Wi-Fi free in rooms only if booked online; lower room categories small for a five-star accommodation. $ *Rooms from: €475* ✉ *Passeig de Gràcia 38–40, Eixample Dreta* ☎ *93/151–8888* ⊕ *www.mandarinoriental.com/barcelona* ⇆ *120 rooms* ⦿ *No Meals* Ⓜ *L2/L3/L4 Passeig de Gràcia, L3/L5 Diagonal, Provença (FGC).*

## ★ ME Barcelona

$$$$ | HOTEL |"Location, location, location" has become such an overused trope but, in the case of the ultra-swanky ME Barcelona, it simply can't be denied. **Pros:** spacious rooftop and heated year-round pool; strong sustainability profile; unbeatable central location. **Cons:** a bit pricey; far from the beach; rooms don't have balconies. ⑤ *Rooms from: €350 ⊠ Casp 1–13, Eixample Dreta* ☎ *93/122–8278* ⊕ *www.melia.com/en/hotels/spain/barcelona/me-barcelona* ☞ *164 rooms* ¡◎¡ *No Meals* Ⓜ *Catalunya L1, L3.*

## ★ Monument Hotel

$$$$ | HOTEL | Originally the home of Enric Battló, a brother of the textile magnate who commissioned Gaudí to redesign the Moderniste masterpiece Casa Battló, and a minute's walk away on the Passeig de Gràcia, the historic 1898 building that houses the Monument went through several incarnations before it was transformed into the elegant upmarket hotel it is today. **Pros:** superbly professional multilingual staff; outstanding dining options; ideal mid-Eixample location. **Cons:** pricey breakfast; most "junior suites" are in effect large doubles with seating areas; hard on the budget. ⑤ *Rooms from: €280 ⊠ Passeig de Gràcia 75, Eixample* ☎ *93/548–2000* ⊕ *www.monumenthotel.com* ☞ *158 rooms* ¡◎¡ *No Meals* Ⓜ *L3/L5 Diagonal, Provença (FGC).*

## Ohla Eixample

$$$$ | HOTEL | With its location just off Passeig de Gràcia and Rambla de Catalunya, Ohla Eixample is ideally situated for designer shopping and gawking at Gaudí, but it's still within easy reach of the Ciutat Vella and the beach. **Pros:** outstanding food; sleek design; well located for shopping and Gaudí. **Cons:** lack of privacy with open plan room/shower; more modern than cozy; a bit far from the Old Town. ⑤ *Rooms from: €239 ⊠ Còrsega 289, Eixample* ☎ *93/737–7977* ⊕ *www.ohlaeixample.com/en* ☞ *94 rooms* ¡◎¡ *Free Breakfast* Ⓜ *Diagonal L3, L5.*

## ★ Radisson Blu Hotel 1882

$$$ | HOTEL | Just a few minutes' walk from Gaudí's unfinished masterpiece, la Sagrada Família, this eco-conscious hotel may be named for the year in which work on that project began but the feel is distinctly contemporary. **Pros:** private parking (at a cost); strong sustainability profile; affordable designer hotel. **Cons:** no bar on the rooftop; no restaurant (except breakfast); quite far from downtown attractions and beaches. ⑤ *Rooms from: €208 ⊠ Còrsega 482, Barcelona* ☎ *93/347–8486* ⊕ *www.hotelbarcelona1882.com* ☞ *182 rooms* ¡◎¡ *No Meals* Ⓜ *Sagrada Familia L2, L5.*

## Sir Victor Hotel

$$$$ | HOTEL | Named after Catalan poet and playwright Caterina Albert i Paradís, who became a prominent member of the Modernisme movement under her pseudonym Victor Català, the uptown, upmarket Sir Victor Hotel will appeal to design lovers with its modern, ultra-elegant look. **Pros:** on-point design; rooftop overlooking La Pedrera; excellent food and drinks. **Cons:** expensive public parking; standard rooms on the small side; quite pricey. ⑤ *Rooms from: €246 ⊠ Rosselló 265, Eixample* ☎ *93/271–1244* ⊕ *www.sirhotels.com/en/victor* ☞ *91 rooms* ¡◎¡ *No Meals* Ⓜ *Diagonal L3, L5.*

## SixtyTwo Hotel

$$$ | HOTEL | Across from Gaudí's Casa Batlló and just down Passeig de Gràcia from his Casa Milà (La Pedrera), this boutique hotel is surrounded by Barcelona's top shopping addresses and leading restaurants. **Pros:** ideal location; good deals on parking; free coffee, tea, and snacks in the lounge, 24/7. **Cons:** noise can be an issue in lower-level rooms; no pool, gym, or spa; some rooms a bit small. ⑤ *Rooms from: €185 ⊠ Passeig de Gràcia 62, Eixample Dreta* ☎ *93/272–4180* ⊕ *www.sixtytwohotel.com* ☞ *44 rooms* ¡◎¡ *No Meals* Ⓜ *L2/L3/L4 Passeig de Gràcia.*

## yök Casa + Cultura

$$$ | APARTMENT | Ideally located at the edge of the Eixample and Sant Pere neighborhoods, yök is made up of only three renovated boutique apartments that date back to 1900 and the time of the Catalan Moderniste movement. **Pros:** sleek design; great option for families or groups; stunning rooftop. **Cons:** minimum two-night stay; no pool or spa; no restaurant. $ *Rooms from: €210* ✉ *Trafalgar 39, Eixample* ☎ *64/062–5313* ⊕ *www.helloyok.com* ↪ *3 apartments* ⍾ *No Meals* Ⓜ *Arc de Triomf L1.*

## ★ Yurbban Passage Hotel & Spa

$$$ | HOTEL | On the edge of the hip Sant Pere neighborhood, right where it meets the Eixample, this is the more sophisticated sister property to the Yurbban Trafalgar next door. **Pros:** good value; rooftop with views and a pool; outstanding spa. **Cons:** small rooftop pool; area can be a bit sketchy at night; no parking. $ *Rooms from: €214* ✉ *Trafalgar 26, Eixample* ☎ *93/882–8977* ⊕ *www.yurbbanpassage.com* ↪ *60 rooms* ⍾ *No Meals* Ⓜ *Urquinaona L1, L4.*

#  Nightlife

Barcelona's vast L'Eixample district is the largest and most diverse nightlife destination in town.

## BARS

### ★ Banker's Bar

COCKTAIL LOUNGES | With decor details from its past life as a bank (like the safety deposit boxes on the wall), the swank cocktail bar of the Mandarin Oriental Hotel lounge is an atmospheric spot for an opulent night out. There's an "East meets West" menu for classic cocktail favorites—the Banker's Martini is the house specialty—and light food. DJs play mellow jazz, swing, and blues tunes on weekends. ✉ *Hotel Mandarin Oriental, Passeig de Gràcia 38–40, Eixample Dreta* ☎ *93/151–8782* ⊕ *www.mandarinoriental.es/barcelona* Ⓜ *Passeig de Gràcia.*

## Dry Martini

COCKTAIL LOUNGES | An homage to the traditional English martini bar of decades past, this stately spot by local mixology maestro Javier de las Muelas is paradise for cocktail aficionados seeking expertly mixed drinks. ✉ *Aribau 162, Eixample Esquerra* ☎ *93/217–5072* ⊕ *www.drymartiniorg.com* Ⓜ *Provença.*

## Jonny Aldana

BARS | This cheery technicolor bar-resto, featuring a tiled facade and open-window bar with stools inside and out, is bursting with 1950s iconography. Wines are sold by the glass and beer is served from the tap, but it's the superb vermouths and cocktails combined with vegetarian tapas that keep patrons coming back. ✉ *Aldana 9, Sant Antoni* ☎ *93/250–7005* ⊕ *www.jonnyaldana.com* Ⓜ *Paral·lel.*

## Les Gens que J'aime

COCKTAIL LOUNGES | Bohemia meets the Moulin Rouge at this intimate, below-street-level bordello-inspired bar with turn-of-the-20th-century memorabilia like fringed lampshades, faded period portraits, and comfy wicker sofas cushioned with lush red velvet. There's usually jazz playing in this laid-back spot where guests linger over reasonably priced cocktails (whiskey sours are popular). ✉ *València 286, bajos, Eixample Dreta* ☎ *93/215–6879* ⊕ *www.lesgensquejaime.com* Ⓜ *Passeig de Gràcia.*

## Milano

LIVE MUSIC | For more than a decade, this "secret" basement bar, in an area otherwise dominated by student pubs and tourist traps, has had a rotating line-up of international acts including blues, soul, jazz, flamenco, swing, and pop. The space resembles a 1940s cabaret, with a brass bar, spot-lit photos of previous acts, and red banquette-style seating. ✉ *Ronda Universitat 35, Eixample Esquerra* ☎ *93/112–7150* ⊕ *www.camparimilano.com/en* Ⓜ *Catalunya, Universitat.*

### ★ Morro Fi

BARS | Opened by a trio of vermouth aficionados, Morro Fi (loosely translates as "refined palate") began as a food blog that morphed into a bar determined to educate people about enjoying vermouth (they even produce their own brand) with select tapas. The result? Locals and the odd expat routinely spilling out into the streets, drink in hand while indie music blares. ⊠ Consell de Cent 171, Eixample Esquerra ⊕ www.morrofi.cat Ⓜ Urgell.

### ★ Pepa Bar a Vins

WINE BARS | When it comes to wine, the team at Pepa really know their grapes, and they excel with natural wines, though there's also vermouth and artisanal beer if you're in the mood for that. The food is excellent, too, and it's all served in an old converted library. ⊠ Aribau 41, Eixample ☎ 93/611–1885 Ⓜ Universitat L1, L2.

### Senyor Vermut

BARS | This snazzy, high-ceilinged ver-muteria has guests lining up to sample a generous selection of more than 40 vermuts served with traditional tapas. From bitter to earthy or aged in a barrel, the classic aperitif is the star attraction though other offerings include wine, beer, and juices. ⊠ Carrer de Provença 85, Eixample Esquerra ☎ 93/532–8865 Ⓜ Entença.

### SIPS

COCKTAIL LOUNGES | Perhaps more akin to a laboratory than a cocktail bar, SIPS draws from a menu influenced by seasonal ingredients and uses state-of-the-art techniques to mix a range of classic recipes and signature concoctions. ⊠ Muntaner 108, Eixample ☎ 61/964–1402 ⊕ sips.barcelona Ⓜ Hospital Clínic L5.

### Solange Cocktails and Luxury Spirits

COCKTAIL LOUNGES | This sleek, luxurious lounge space is named after Solange Dimitrios, 007's original Bond girl, and the homage includes signature cocktails that reference Bond films, characters, and even a "secret mission" concoction for the more daring. ⊠ Aribau 143, Eixample Esquerra ☎ 93/164–3625 ⊕ www.solangecocktail.com Ⓜ Hospital Clínic, Diagonal.

### Xixbar

COCKTAIL LOUNGES | The interior of this Alice in Wonderland–like venue of checkered half-walls, a marble bar, and contemporary objets d'art rarely seen on ceilings is the first clue that you've landed somewhere special. Beyond that, with 50-plus flavors of gins and infusions, and a lounge-friendly 3 am last call on weekends, Xix turns conventional cocktail drinkers into card-carrying gin lovers. ⊠ Rocafort 19, Sant Antoni ☎ 93/423–4314 ⊕ www.xixbar.com Ⓜ Poble Sec.

## 🎭 Performing Arts

### THEATER

#### Teatre Nacional de Catalunya

ARTS CENTER | This grandiose glass-enclosed classical theater was designed by Ricardo Bofill, architect of Barcelona's airport and the sail-shaped W Barcelona hotel. Programs cover everything from Shakespeare to avant-garde theater. Most productions, as the name suggests, are in Catalan but beautiful to witness all the same. ⊠ Plaça de les Arts 1, Eixample Dreta ☎ 93/306–5700 ⊕ www.tnc.cat Ⓜ Glóries, Monumental.

#### Teatre Tívoli

THEATER | FAMILY | One of the city's most beloved traditional theater and dance venues, the century-old Tívoli has staged timeless classics and has hosted everyone from the Ballet Nacional de Cuba to flamenco and teeny-bopper treats. ⊠ Casp 8, Eixample Dreta ☎ 93/215–9570 ⊕ www.grupbalana.com Ⓜ Catalunya.

# Gràcia

Once it's own village, Gràcia has become Barcelona's bohemian neighborhood, filled with trendy bars and restaurants, outdoor cafés, gourmet shops, artists studios, and designer boutiques. This is where Barcelona's young, creative crowd comes to party and hang out. The area begins at Gaudí's playful Park Güell and continues past his first commissioned house, Casa Vicens.

## ◉ Sights

### ★ Casa Vicens

HISTORIC HOME | Antoni Gaudí's first important commission as a young architect began in 1883 and finished in 1885. For this house Gaudí still used his traditional architect's tools, particularly the T square. The historical eclecticism (that is, borrowing freely from past architectural styles around the world) of the early Art Nouveau movement is evident in the Orientalist themes and Mudejar (Moorish-inspired) motifs lavished throughout the design.

The client, Don Manuel Vicens Montaner, a stock and currency broker, entrusted the young architect with designing his summer garden home in the former village of Gràcia. Casa Vicens stands out for its polychromatic façade, made with green and white checkered tiles, in combination with tiles with floral patterns. ⊠ Carrer de les Carolines 20–26, Gràcia 🕾 93/271–1064 ⊕ www.casavicens.org 🎫 €16 Ⓜ Fontana, Lesseps.

### Casa-Museu Gaudí

HISTORIC HOME | Up the steps of Park Güell and to the right is the whimsical Alice-in-Wonderland-esque house where Gaudí lived with his niece from 1906 until 1925. Now a small museum, exhibits include Gaudí-designed furniture and decorations, drawings, and portraits and busts of the architect. Stop by if you are in the park, but the museum is not worth travelling far for. Note that the museum is not included in the admission fee for Park Güell. Additionally, the museum closed during Covid and at the time of writing it was not clear when it will reopen. ⊠ Park Güell, Carretera del Carmel 23A, Gràcia 🕾 93/208–0414 Ticket information ⊕ sagradafamilia.org/casa-museu-gaudi 🎫 €5.50 Ⓜ Lesseps, Vallcarca.

### Gran de Gràcia

STREET | This highly trafficked central artery and shopping thoroughfare running up through Gràcia is lined with buildings of great artistic and architectural interest, beginning with the hotel Casa Fuster, built between 1908 and 1911 by Palau de la Música Catalana architect Lluís Domènech i Montaner in collaboration with his son Pere Domènech i Roure. As you move up Gran de Gràcia, probable Francesc Berenguer buildings can be identified at No. 15; No. 23, with its scrolled cornice; and Nos. 35, 49, 51, 61, and 77. Officially attributed to a series of architects—Berenguer lacked a formal degree, having left architecture school to become Gaudí's "right hand"—these Moderniste masterworks have long inspired debate over Berenguer's role. ⊠ Gran de Gràcia, Gràcia Ⓜ Fontana, Lesseps, Gràcia (FGC).

### Mercat de la Llibertat

MARKET | Far more manageable—both in size and crowds—than Boqueria market, this landmark iron-and-brick structure nonetheless impresses with its high ceilings and ornamental elements. Built between 1888 and 1893 by Catalan architect Miquel Pascual i Tintorer in collaboration with Francesc Berenguer, it features wonderful decorative elements, like the swans swimming along the roof line and the snails surrounding Gràcia's coat of arms. ⊠ Pl. Llibertat 27, Gràcia ⊕ www.bcn.es/mercatsmunicipals ⊘ Closed Sun. Ⓜ Fontana, Gràcia (FGC).

# Gràcia

## Sights ▼
1 Casa Vicens ............. **B2**
2 Casa-Museu Gaudí...... **E1**
3 Gran de Gràcia .......... **B3**
4 Mercat de la
  Llibertat .................. **B4**
5 Park Güell ................ **E1**

6 Plaça de la Vila
  de Gràcia ................ **B4**
7 Plaça de la Virreina..... **D3**
8 Plaça del Diamant ....... **C3**
9 Plaça Rovira i Trias ..... **E2**

## Restaurants ▼
1 Berbena.................. **A5**
2 La Panxa del Bisbe ...... **E2**
3 La Pepita................. **C5**
4 Platerets ................. **D5**

## Quick Bites ▼
1 Nabucco Tiramisu ....... **C4**

## Hotels ▼
1 Hotel Casa Fuster....... **B5**
2 Seventy Barcelona ...... **C6**

**KEY**

- 1 Sights
- 1 Restaurants
- 1 Quick Bites
- 1 Hotels
- Ⓜ Metro Stops
- 🛈 Tourist Information

## ★ Park Güell

CITY PARK | FAMILY | Alternately shady, green, floral, or sunny, this park is one of Gaudí's, and Barcelona's, most visited venues. Named for and commissioned by Gaudí's main patron, Count Eusebi Güell, it was originally intended as a gated residential community based on the English Garden City model, with a covered marketplace. The pillars of the market support the main public square above it, where impromptu dances and plays were performed. Gaudí highlights include the gingerbread gatehouses; the Casa-Museu Gaudí, where the architect lived; the Room of a Hundred Columns; and the fabulous serpentine polychrome bench that snakes along the main square by Gaudí assistant Josep Maria. Visitors must pay an entrance fee to the "monumental area," where the main attractions are located; the rest of the park remains free to enter. Tickets should be booked online up to three months in advance. ✉ Carretera del Carmel, 23, Gràcia ☎ 93/409–1830 ⊕ parkguell.barcelona/en ☞ €10 ☞ Tickets have set entry times. Ⓜ Lessops, Vallcarca.

## Plaça de la Vila de Gràcia

PLAZA/SQUARE | Originally named (until 2009) for the memorable Gràcia mayor Francesc Rius i Taulet, this is the barrio's most emblematic and historic square, marked by the handsome clock tower in its center. The tower, unveiled in 1864, is just over 110 feet tall. It has water fountains around its base, royal Bourbon crests over the fountains, and an iron balustrade atop the octagonal brick shaft stretching up to the clock and belfry. The symbol of Gràcia, the clock tower was bombarded by federal troops when Gràcia attempted to secede from the Spanish state during the 1870s. The Gràcia Casa de la Vila (town hall) at the lower end of the square is another building by Gaudí's assistant Francesc Berenguer. ✉ Pl. de la Vila de Gràcia, Gràcia Ⓜ Fontana, Gràcia (FGC).

## ★ Plaça de la Virreina

PLAZA/SQUARE | The much-damaged and oft-restored church of Sant Joan de Gràcia anchors this lovely square where the Palau de la Virreina once stood; it was the summer residence of the same virreina (wife, or in this case, widow of a viceroy) whose 18th-century palace, the Palau de la Virreina, stands on the Rambla. The story of La Virreina, a young noblewoman widowed at an early age by the death of the elderly viceroy of Peru, is symbolized in the bronze sculpture atop the fountain in the center of the square: it portrays Ruth of the Old Testament, represented carrying the sheaves of wheat she was gathering when she learned of the death of her husband, Boaz. Ruth is the Old Testament paradigm of wifely fidelity to her husband's clan, a parallel to La Virreina—who spent her life doing good deeds with her husband's fortune. The rectorial residence at the back of the church is the work of Gaudí's perennial assistant and right-hand man Francesc Berenguer. ✉ Pl. de la Virreina, Gràcia Ⓜ Joanic, Fontana.

## Plaça del Diamant

PLAZA/SQUARE | This little square is of enormous sentimental importance in Barcelona as the site of the opening and closing scenes of 20th-century Catalan writer Mercé Rodoreda's famous 1962 novel La Plaça del Diamant. Translated by the late American poet David Rosenthal as The Time of the Doves, it is the most widely translated and published Catalan novel of all time: a tender yet brutal story of a young woman devoured by the Spanish Civil War and, in a larger sense, by life itself. The bronze birds represent the pigeons that Colometa spent her life obsessively breeding; the male figure on the left pierced by bolts of steel is Quimet, her first love and husband, whom she met at a dance in this square and later lost in the war. ✉ Pl. del Diamant, Barcelona Ⓜ Fontana.

## ★ Plaça Rovira i Trias

PLAZA/SQUARE | This charming little square and the story of Antoni Rovira i Trias shed much light on the true nature of Barcelona's eternal struggle with Madrid and Spanish central authority. Take a careful look at the map of Barcelona positioned at the feet of the bronze statue of the architect, who is seated on the bench, and you'll see a vision of what the city might have looked like if Madrid's (and the Spanish army's) candidate for the design of the Eixample, Ildefons Cerdà, had not been imposed over the plan devised by Rovira i Trias, the legitimate winner of the open competition for the commission. Rovira i Trias's plan shows an astral design radiating out from a central square while Cerdà's design established the emblematic uniformed blocks and wide boulevards that Eixample is known for. ⊠ Pl. Rovira i Trias, Gràcia Ⓜ Joanic.

## 🍴 Restaurants

This lively and intimate neighborhood is home to many of Barcelona's artists, musicians, and actors. The bohemian atmosphere is reflected in an eclectic collection of restaurants encompassing everything from street food and affordable ethnic cuisine to thoroughly sophisticated dining.

### Berbena

$$ | CATALAN | One of the first things you'll notice here is the scent of freshly baked bread, then you'll take in the open kitchen and cozy, ultra-contemporary interior, with oversized windows facing the street. The chef's modern spin on Catalan cuisine features Peruvian and Asian influences, and the dishes are made almost exclusively using locally sourced organic products. Known for: excellent selection of cheeses; interesting natural wines; seasonal, organic food. ⑤ Average main: €18 ⊠ Minerva 6, Gràcia ☎ 93/801–5987 ⊕ berbenabcn.com ⊘ Closed Sun. and Mon. Ⓜ Diagonal.

### La Panxa del Bisbe

$$ | TAPAS | Literally "The Bishop's Belly," this casual spot achieves a rare feat: putting modern international twists on Mediterranean cuisine without ruining it. La Panxa is a bit off the beaten path and thrives on a steady stream of repeat customers, who come for superb tapas and the restaurant's own craft beer on tap. Known for: affordable tasting menu; great tapas; good stop on way back from Park Güell. ⑤ Average main: €18 ⊠ Torrent de les Flors 158, Gràcia ☎ 93/213–7049 ⊘ Closed Sun. and Mon. Ⓜ Lesseps.

### ★ La Pepita

$$ | TAPAS | Don't be distracted by the graffitied walls and highly Instagrammable dishes: the innovative tapas at La Pepita lives up to the hipster hype. The room is dominated by long marble-topped bar—there are only a handful of tables in the narrow space—so it's best for couples or small groups. Known for: Spanish fried eggs and potatoes with foie gras; popcorn-topped ice cream; shrimp croquetas. ⑤ Average main: €20 ⊠ Còrsega 343, Gràcia ☎ 93/238–4893 ⊕ www.lapepitabcn.com Ⓜ Diagonal.

### Platerets

$$ | INTERNATIONAL | Seasonal Catalan cuisine with an Asian bent is the theme at this sleek, minimalist dining space, featuring high ceilings and large picture windows. Along with traditional tortillas and croquetas, the menu offers a variety of Asian-inspired bowls and small plates, such as crispy pork with tonkatsu sauce. Known for: Asian-style bowls; eggplant tempura with honey and lime; good options for vegans and vegetarians. ⑤ Average main: €22 ⊠ Milà i Fontanals 29, Gràcia ☎ 93/463–6585 ⊕ www.platerets.com ⊘ Closed Sun. and Mon. Ⓜ Verdaguer.

##  Coffee and Quick Bites

### ★ Nabucco Tiramisu

**$ | ITALIAN |** Top-notch coffee, homemade pastries and cakes, and healthy fare like avocado toast make this organic café a particularly bustling spot at breakfast. For lunch or a casual dinner, there's a long list of panini sandwiches, as well as excellent quiches and Italian-inspired salads. **Known for:** terrace seating right on the plaza; healthy menu; great coffee. ⑤ *Average main: €6* ⊠ *Pl. de la Vila de Gràcia 8, Gràcia* ☎ *93/217–6101* ⊕ *nabuccotiramisu.com* Ⓜ *Fontana, Gràcia (FGC).*

## 🛏 Hotels

### Hotel Casa Fuster

**$$$$ | HOTEL |** This luxury hotel offers one of two chances (the other is the Hotel España) to stay in a Modernist masterpiece designed by Lluís Domènech i Montaner, architect of the iconic Palau de la Música Catalana. **Pros:** well situated for exploring both Gràcia and the Eixample; sprawling rooftop terrace with city and mountain views; large rooms with luxury-level amenities. **Cons:** service can be a bit stiff; maybe too much Modernism for some; rooms facing Passeig de Gràcia could use better soundproofing. ⑤ *Rooms from: €300* ⊠ *Passeig de Gràcia 132, Gràcia* ☎ *93/255–3000* ⊕ *www.hotelcasafuster.com* ⤴ *105 rooms* ⦿ *No Meals* Ⓜ *Diagonal.*

### ★ Seventy Barcelona

**$$ | HOTEL |** On the southern border of Gràcia, a short stroll to the Passeig de Gràcia, this boutique hotel is in an ideal spot for travelers who like to be close to the action, without being in the thick of it. **Pros:** good location; good quality for the price; thoughtful staff. **Cons:** busy street outside; outdoor pool is small; few rooms with patios or balconies. ⑤ *Rooms from: €160* ⊠ *Còrsega 344–352, Barcelona* ☎ *93/012–1270* ⊕ *www.seventybarcelona.com* ⤴ *145 rooms* ⦿ *No Meals* Ⓜ *Diagonal.*

## 🛍 Shopping

### Anna Povo

**WOMEN'S CLOTHING |** Look for an elegant and innovative selection of relaxed knits, coats, and dresses at this stylish boutique. Anna Povo's designs tend to sleek and minimalist, in cool tones of gray and beige. ⊠ *Providència 75, Gràcia* ☎ *93/319–3561* ⊕ *www.annapovo.com* Ⓜ *Joanic.*

# Upper Barcelona: Sarrià and Pedralbes

Sarrià was originally a country village, overlooking Barcelona from the foothills of the Collserola. Eventually absorbed by the westward-expanding city, the village, 15 minutes by FGC commuter train from Plaça de Catalunya, has become a unique neighborhood made up of old-timers who speak only Catalan; writers, artists, and other creatives; gourmet shops and upscale restaurants; and expats, who prize the neighborhood for its proximity to the international schools.

Cross Avinguda Foix from Sarrià and you're in Pedralbes—the wealthiest residential neighborhood in the city. (Many of the F.C. Barcelona superstars have their multimillion-euro homes here, and the exclusive Real Club de Tenis de Barcelona is close by.) The centerpiece of this district is the 14th-century Monestir (Monastery) de Pedralbes; other points of interest include Gaudí's Pavellons de la Finca Güell, and the gardens of the Palau Reial de Pedralbes, a 20-minute walk downhill from the monastery.

## 👁 Sights

### Col·legi de les Teresianes

**NOTABLE BUILDING |** Built for the Reverend Mothers of St. Theresa in 1889, when Gaudí was still occasionally using straight lines, this former operating school has

# Upper Barcelona: Sarrià and Pedralbes

Reina Elisenda

Plaça Pedralbes

Plaça Jaume Ii

Canet

PEDRALBES

Sarrià

Plaça Sant Vicens

SARRIÀ

Plaça D'ertós

Tres Torres

Jardins De La Villa Amelia

Palau Reial

AREA DIAGONAL

Plaça Pius Xii

Maria Cristina

La Bonanova

Plaça de la Reina María Cristina

Jardins D'eduard Marquina

LES CORTS

Les Corts

Travessera de les Corts

Plaça del Centre

**KEY**

- ❶ Sights
- ❶ Restaurants
- ❶ Hotels
- Ⓜ Metro Stops
- FGC Stops

| 0 | 300 yards |
| 0 | 300 meters |

**Sights** ▼

1 Col·legi de les Teresianes................. **E4**
2 Pavellons de la Finca Güell–Càtedra Gaudí ... **A4**
3 Real Monestir de Santa Maria de Pedralbes .... **A1**
4 Sarrià..................... **C1**
5 Tibidabo.................. **C1**
6 Torre Bellesguard........ **E2**

**Restaurants** ▼

1 ABaC..................... **E2**
2 Bar Tomás de Sarrià..... **C2**
3 Coure...................... **E6**
4 Gouthier.................. **C3**
5 Hisop ...................... **E6**
6 Silvestre ................. **E4**
7 Tram-Tram................ **C1**
8 Via Veneto ............... **E6**

**Hotels** ▼

1 Primero Primera ......... **E3**
2 Vilana Hotel .............. **E2**

upper floors that are reminiscent of Berenguer's apartment at Carrer de l'Or 44, with its steep peaks and verticality. Hired to take over for another architect, Gaudí found his freedom of movement limited in this project. The dominant theme is the architect's use of steep, narrow catenary arches and Mudejar exposed-brick pillars. The most striking effects are on the second floor, where two rows of a dozen catenary arches run the width of the building, each of them unique, because, as Gaudí explained, no two things in nature are identical. The brick columns are crowned with T-shaped brick capitals (for St. Theresa). ⊠ *Ganduxer 85, Sant Gervasi* 🕾 *93/212–3354* ⊕ *ganduxer.escolateresiana.com* ⊘ *Closed Sat. and Sun.* Ⓜ *La Bonanova, Les Tres Torres (FGC).*

### ★ Real Monestir de Santa Maria de Pedralbes

**RELIGIOUS BUILDING** | This marvel of a monastery, named for its original white stones (*pedres albes, from the Latin pet-ras albas* ), is really a convent, founded in 1326 for the Franciscan order of Poor Clares by Reina (Queen) Elisenda. The three-story Gothic cloister, one of the finest in Europe, surrounds a lush garden. The day cells, where the nuns spend their mornings praying, sewing, and studying, circle the arcaded courtyard.

The Capella de Sant Miquel, just to the right of the entrance, has murals painted in 1346 by Catalan master Ferrer Bassa. Look for the letters spelling out " *No m'oblidi/ digui-li a Joan/ a quatre de setembre de 1415"* ("Do not forget me / tell John / September 4, 1415") scratched between the figures of St. Francis and St. Clare (with book and quill). While the true meaning of the message is unknown, one theory is that it was written by a brokenhearted novice. The nuns' upstairs dormitory contains the convent's treasures: paintings, liturgical objects, and seven centuries of artistic and cultural patrimony. ⊠ *Baixada del*

*Monestir 9, Pedralbes* 🕾 *93/256–3434* ⊕ *monestirpedralbes.bcn.cat/en* 🖃 *€5; free for visitors under 16, and with the Barcelona Card; free Sun. after 3 pm, and 1st Sun. of every month* ☉ *Closed Mon.* Ⓜ *Reina Elisenda (FGC).*

### Pavellons de la Finca Güell–Càtedra Gaudí

**NOTABLE BUILDING** | Work on the Finca began in 1883 as an extension of Count Eusebi Güell's family estate. Gaudí, the count's architect of choice, was commissioned to do the gardens and the two entrance pavilions (1884–87); the rest of the project was never finished. The Pavellons (pavilions) now belong to the University of Barcelona, which has handed them over to the Municipal Institute for Urban Landscape (IMPUiQV) for ten years (2015–2024). During this period, IMPUiQV will carry out a comprehensive restoration of Gaudí's work. Depending on the state of the renovation work, the complex may be open for group visits, heritage visits, as well as cultural and educational activities but will largely remain closed. The fierce wrought-iron dragon gate is Gaudí's reference to the Garden of the Hesperides, as described by national poet Jacint Verdaguer's epic poem *L'Atlàntida* (1877)—the *Iliad* of Catalonia's historic-mythic origins. ■**TIP→ Entrance is by appointment only.** ⊠ *Av. Pedralbes 7, Pedralbes* 🕾 *93/317–7652* Ⓜ *Palau Reial (Metro L3).*

### Sarrià

**NEIGHBORHOOD** | Sarrià was originally a cluster of farms and country houses, a village that was once dismissively described as nothing but "winds, brooks, and convents." Today, this quiet enclave is now a prime residential neighborhood overlooking Barcelona from the hills.

Start an exploration at the main square, the Plaça de Sarrià—the site of Tuesday antique and bric-a-brac markets; Sunday morning sardana dances; Christmas pageants; and concerts, book fairs, and artisanal food and wine events at various times during the year. The 10th-century

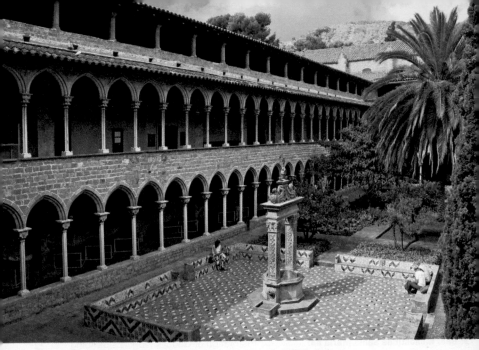

A quiet space for reflection: the courtyard of the Monestir de Pedralbes

Romanesque Church of Sant Vicenç dominates the square, and its bell tower, illuminated on weekend nights, is truly impressive. Across Passeig de la Reina Elisenda from the church is the 100-year-old Moderniste Mercat de Sarrià. Allow a few hours to wander the surrounding streets and to stop at Sarrià's famous Foix pastry shops. ⊠ *Sarrià.*

### Tibidabo

**VIEWPOINT | FAMILY |** One of Barcelona's two promontories bears a distinctive name, generally translated as "To Thee I Will Give." It refers to the Catalan legend that this was the spot from which Satan tempted Christ with all the riches of the Earth below (namely, Barcelona). On a clear day, the views from this 1,789-foot peak are legendary.

Tibidabo's skyline is marked by a neo-Gothic church, the work of Enric Sagnier in 1902, and—off to one side, near the village of Vallvidrera—the 854-foot communications tower, the Torre de Collserola, designed by Sir Norman Foster. If you're with kids, take the San Francisco–style Tramvía Blau (Blue Trolley) from Plaça Kennedy to the overlook at the top, and transfer to the funicular to the 100-year-old amusement park at the summit. ⊠ *Pl. Tibidabo 3–4, Tibidabo* ☎ *93/211–7942 amusement park* ⊕ *www.tibidabo.cat* ✉ *Amusement park €28.50* Ⓜ *Av. Tibidabo (FGC L7), then Tramvía Blau or Bus #196.*

### ★ Torre Bellesguard

**HISTORIC HOME |** For an extraordinary Gaudí experience, visit this private residence. It was built between 1900 and 1909 over the ruins of the summer palace of the last of the sovereign count-kings of the Catalonia-Aragon, Martí I l'Humà (Martin I the Humane), whose reign ended in 1410. In homage to this medieval history, Gaudí endowed the house with a tower, gargoyles, and crenellated battlements. The rest—the catenary arches, the trencadís in the facade, the stained-glass windows—is pure Art Nouveau. Guided tours in English available every day at 11 am and 1 pm. The visit includes access to the roof, which Gaudí designed to resemble a dragon, along with the gardens, patio, and stables.

**■TIP→** Reservations are required for the highly recommended guided tour (reserva@ bellesguardgaudi.com). ⊠ *Carrer Bellesguard 16–20, Sant Gervasi* ☎ *93/250–4093* ⊕ *www.bellesguardgaudi.com* 🎫 *Guided tour €10 (children under 8 free)* 🕐 *Closed Mon.* Ⓜ *Av. Tibidabo (FGC).*

## 🍴 Restaurants

Take an excursion to the upper reaches of town for an excellent selection of bars, cafés, and restaurants, along with cool summer evening breezes and a sense of well-heeled village life.

### ABaC

**$$$$ | CONTEMPORARY |** Chef Jordi Cruz is a celebrity in Spain, and pulls out all the stops with a panoply of artfully-presented dishes that vary from season to season; no expense or effort is ever spared. ABaC is open only for dinner, and serves only a set tasting menu, which you can request with or without paired wines. **Known for:** elegant setting in a boutique hotel; creative in-season dishes; celebrity chef. ⑤ *Average main: €250* ⊠ *Av. del Tibidabo 1–7, Tibidabo* ☎ *93/319–6600* ⊕ *www. abacrestaurant.com/en* Ⓜ *Tibidabo.*

### Bar Tomás de Sarrià

**$ | TAPAS |** Famous for its *patatas bravas amb allioli* (potatoes with fiery hot sauce and allioli, an emulsion of crushed garlic and olive oil), accompanied by freezing mugs of San Miguel beer, this old-fashioned Sarrià classic is worth seeking out. You'll have to elbow your way to a tiny table and shout to be heard over the hubbub, but the effort is richly rewarding. **Known for:** sidewalk tables for snacking alfresco; noisy, friendly neighborhood vibe; selection of tapas. ⑤ *Average main: €8* ⊠ *Major de Sarrià 49, Sarrià* ☎ *93/203–1077* ⊕ *www.eltomasdesarria. com* 🕐 *Closed Sun. and part of Aug.* Ⓜ *Sarrià (FGC).*

### Coure

**$$$ | MEDITERRANEAN |** *Cuina d'autor* is a Catalan phrase for chef-led original cooking, and that is exactly what you get in this smart subterranean space on restaurant-centric Passatge Marimón, just above the Diagonal thoroughfare. The upstairs bar gets busy with a post-work crowd of food-loving locals, but downstairs is a cool, minimalist restaurant. **Known for:** sushi bar-style counter seating with view of the kitchen; artistic presentation; tasting menu with wine pairing. ⑤ *Average main: €23* ⊠ *Passatge Marimón 20, Sant Gervasi* ☎ *93/200–7532* 🕐 *Closed Sun. and Mon., and 3 wks in Aug.* Ⓜ *Diagonal.*

### Gouthier

**$$ | SEAFOOD |** Weather permitting, this French-inspired oyster bar puts tables and banquettes out in the Plaça Sant Vicenç, arguably the prettiest square in Sarrià. Make your choice among 12 varieties of oysters—especially the plump sweet ones from Normandy—shucked and served fresh with rye bread and pats of French butter, as well as other more elaborate tapas dishes. **Known for:** pleasant terrace; good wine list; Spanish oysters from the Delta de l'Ebro. ⑤ *Average main: €18* ⊠ *Mañé i Flaquer 8, Sarrià* ✛ *Located on Pl. Vicenç de Sarrià* ☎ *93/205–9969* ⊕ *www.gouthier. es* 🕐 *Closed Sun. No lunch Tues.–Thurs.* Ⓜ *Sarrià (FGC).*

### Hisop

**$$$ | CATALAN |** The interior design of Oriol Ivern's small restaurant is minimalist, but his cooking is intricate—and wonderful. This is budget-conscious fine dining that avoids exotic ingredients but lifts local dishes to exciting new heights; the menu changes four times a year to take advantage of what's best in season. **Known for:** local, seasonal ingredients; extensive well-chosen wine list; great value tasting menu. ⑤ *Average main: €27* ⊠ *Passatge de Marimón 9, Sant*

*Gervasi* ☎ *93/241–3233* ⊕ *www.hisop. com* ⊘ *Closed Sun. and 1st wk of Jan.* Ⓜ *Diagonal.*

### Silvestre

$$ | CATALAN | A graceful and easygoing mainstay in Barcelona's culinary landscape, this restaurant serves modern market cuisine to discerning diners. Pay particular attention to Silvestre's impeccable tuna tartare, the scallops with shiitake mushrooms, or ragout of oxtail in red wine. **Known for:** intimate ambiance; the tuna tartare; well-chosen house wines. ⑤ *Average main: €16* ✉ *Santaló 101, Sant Gervasi* ☎ *93/241–4031* ⊕ *www.restaurante-silvestre.com* ⊘ *Closed 3 wks in Aug. No lunch weekends* Ⓜ *Muntaner (FGC).*

### Tram-Tram

$$$ | MEDITERRANEAN | Above Reina Elisenda on Sarrià's main drag, this restaurant is a Barcelona classic, known for using local fresh products and artful presentation. Pride of place on the à la carte menu (alas, there's no prix fixe lunch) goes to dishes like *fondant de cordero lechal* (milk-fed baby lamb) and *bacalao* (cod) with ratatouille. **Known for:** excellent Spanish omelet; pleasant interior garden patio; affordable menú de degustació (tasting menu). ⑤ *Average main: €26* ✉ *Major de Sarrià 121, Sarrià* ☎ *93/204–8518* ⊕ *tram-tram.com* ⊘ *Closed Mon.–Tues. and 2 wks in Aug. No dinner Sun.* Ⓜ *Sarrià (FGC).*

### ★ Via Veneto

$$$$ | MEDITERRANEAN | Open since 1967, this elegant, family-owned temple of fine Catalan dining was a favorite of Salvador Dalí and now attracts local sports stars and politicians. The menu is a mix of contemporary offerings punctuated by old-school classics, and you can trust the expert sommelier to guide you through the daunting 10,000-bottle-strong wine list. **Known for:** theatrical presentation of roast baby duck; tasting menu; celebrity clientele. ⑤ *Average main: €38* ✉ *Ganduxer 10, Sant Gervasi* ☎ *93/200–7244*

⊕ *www.viavenetobarcelona.com* ⊘ *Closed Sun. and Aug. No lunch Sat.* Ⓜ *La Bonanova (FGC), Maria Cristina (Metro L3).*

## 🛏 Hotels

### Primero Primera

$$ | HOTEL | FAMILY | The Perez family converted their apartment building on a leafy side street in the quiet, upscale, residential neighborhood of Tres Torres and opened it as an exquisitely designed, homey boutique hotel. **Pros:** retro-modern ambience; private parking; restaurant Planta Baja ($) open to the public. **Cons:** no spa; very small pool; bit of a distance to public transportation. ⑤ *Rooms from: €180* ✉ *Doctor Carulla 25–29, Sant Gervasi* ☎ *93/417–5600* ⊕ *www. primeroprimera.com* ⇆ *30 rooms* Ⓜ *Tres Torres (FGC).*

### Vilana Hotel

$ | HOTEL | In an upscale residential neighborhood above Passeig de la Bonanova, this boutique accommodation can ease some of the budgetary strains of coming to a prime tourist destination. **Pros:** quiet surroundings; pleasant, attentive English-speaking staff; large, sunlit rooms. **Cons:** room service closes at 10:30; small gym, but no pool or spa; €25/day parking fee. ⑤ *Rooms from: €80* ✉ *Vilana 7, Sant Gervasi* ☎ *93/434–0363* ⊕ *vilanahotel. com* ⇆ *22 rooms* Ⓜ *Sarrià (FGC).*

## 🏃 Activities

### SOCCER

#### ★ Camp Nou: Futbol Club Barcelona

SOCCER | Founded in 1899, FC Barcelona won its third European Championship in 2009, along with the Liga championship, and its 27th Copa del Rey (King's Cup)—Spain's first-ever *triplete*—and did it again in 2015. Even more impressive was its razzle-dazzle style of soccer, rarely seen in the age of cynical defensive lockdowns and muscular British-style play. Barça, as the club is known, is Real Madrid's nemesis (and vice versa) and a sociological and historical phenomenon of deep significance in Catalonia.

Note that renovations—begun in 2022 and ongoing through 2025 or 2026—to Camp Nou will no doubt disrupt the daily stadium tours and access to the team's very popular museum. Do check on their status, however, as both the tours and the museum are absolute musts for *futbol* fans.

And don't give up on trying to see a Barça match. During the main construction works (the 2023–24 season and possibly beyond), the team will play its home games at the Olympic Stadium in Montjuïc. Check schedules and buy tickets online through the FC Barcelona website. Ticketmaster (⊕ *www.ticketmaster.es*) or Entradas (⊕ *www.entradas.es*) also sell tickets. ⊠ *Camp Nou, Aristides Maillol 12, Les Corts* ☎ *902/189900* ⊕ *www. fcbarcelona.com* Ⓜ *Collblanc, Palau Reial (Metro Line 5)*.

# Montjuïc and Poble Sec

A bit remote from the hustle and bustle of Barcelona street life, Montjuïc more than justifies a day or two of exploring. It's easy to take buses within Montjuïc to get from sight to sight.

## ⊙ Sights

### ★ CaixaForum Barcelona
ARTS CENTER | The 1911 Casaramona textile factory, a neo-Mudejar Art Nouveau masterpiece by Josep Puig i Cadafalch (architect of Casa de les Punxes, Casa Amatller, and Casa Quadras), is now a center for temporary art exhibits, as well as concerts, live performances, and other cultural events. The original brickwork is spectacular, while a 2002 restoration added sleek white modern entryway designed by Japanese architect Arata Isozaki, also responsible for the nearby

Palau Sant Jordi. ⊠ *Av. Francesc Ferrer i Guàrdia 6–8, Montjuïc* ☎ *93/476–8600* ⊕ *caixaforum.org/es/barcelona* ⊠ €6 Ⓜ *Pl. Espanya*.

### Castell de Montjuïc
CASTLE/PALACE | FAMILY | Built in 1640 by rebels against Felipe IV, the castle has had a dark history as a symbol of Barcelona's military domination by foreign powers, usually the Spanish army. The fortress was stormed several times, most famously in 1705 by Lord Peterborough for Archduke Carlos of Austria. In 1808, during the Peninsular War, it was seized by the French under General Dufresne. During an 1842 civil disturbance, Barcelona was bombed from its heights by a Spanish artillery battery. After the 1936–39 civil war, the castle was used as a dungeon for political prisoners. Lluís Companys, president of the Generalitat de Catalunya during the civil war, was executed by firing squad here on October 14, 1940. In 2007 the fortress was formally ceded back to Barcelona.

An excellent visitor center highlights the history of the castle throughout the ages; other spaces are given over to temporary exhibits. The various terraces offer fantastic panoramic views over the city and out to sea. The moat, which contains attractive gardens, is the site of the popular summer Sala Montjuic Open Air Cinema (⊕ *www.salamontjuic. org*), screening original versions of classic films with live music concerts before the showings. ⊠ *Ctra. de Montjuïc 66, Montjuïc* ☎ *93/256–4440* ⊕ *ajuntament. barcelona.cat/castelldemontjuic/en* ⊠ €5 (free Sun. from 3 pm) Ⓜ *Paral·lel and Funicular*.

### Estadi Olímpic Lluís Companys (*Olympic Stadium*)
HISTORIC SIGHT | FAMILY | The Olympic Stadium was originally built for the International Exhibition of 1929, with the idea that Barcelona would then host the 1936 Olympics (ultimately staged in Hitler's Berlin). After failing twice to

# Montjuïc and Poble Sec

**KEY**

- 🔵 Sights
- 🔴 Restaurants
- 🟢 Hotels
- Ⓜ Metro Stops
- 🈺 Tourist Information

## Sights ▼

1 CaixaForum Barcelona ............... **B2**
2 Castell de Montjuïc ...... **C7**
3 Estadi Olímpic Lluís Companys ............... **A4**
4 Fundació Joan Miró ..... **C4**
5 Mies van der Rohe Pavilion ................... **B2**
6 Museu d'Arqueologia de Catalunya ............. **C4**
7 Museu Nacional d'Art de Catalunya ...... **B3**
8 Plaça d'Espanya ......... **C1**
9 Poble Espanyol .......... **A2**

## Restaurants ▼

1 La Platilleria ............. **E4**
2 Quimet & Quimet ........ **E4**

## Quick Bites ▼

1 La Fabrique .............. **D3**

## Hotels ▼

1 Hotel Brummell .......... **E5**
2 Hotel Grums .............. **E6**

win the nomination, the city celebrated the attainment of its long-cherished goal by renovating the semi-derelict stadium—preserving the original facade and shell—in time for 1992, providing seating for 60,000.

Though you can view the stadium for free from the entrance area, the field and indoor areas are not normally open to the public. That said, tickets to a Barcelona Football Club (⊕ www.fcbarcelona.com) match will get you in. The beloved team will be playing its home games here while Camp Nou undergoes a multiyear renovation (starting in 2022).

The nearby Museu Olímpic i de l'Esport, a museum about the Olympic movement in Barcelona, shows audiovisual replays from the 1992 Olympics, and provides interactive simulations for visitors to experience the training and competition of Olympic athletes. An information center traces the history of the modern Olympics from Athens in 1896 to the present. Next door and just downhill stands the futuristic Palau Sant Jordi sports and concert arena, designed by the noted Japanese architect Arata Isozaki. ⊠ Passeig Olímpic, 15–17, Montjuïc ☎ 93/426–2089 Estadi Olímpic, 93/292–5379 Museu Olímpica ⊕ www. estadiolimpic.cat (stadium); www.museuolimpicbcn.cat/en (museum) ⊠ Stadium is free, museum €5.80 ⊗ Museum closed Mon. Ⓜ Pl. Espanya.

★ **Fundació Joan Miró**
ART MUSEUM | The masterpieces by native Barcelona artist Joan Miró (1893–1983) on display at this museum include paintings, sculpture, and textile works from all periods of his life. They coexist with temporary exhibitions of 20th and 21st century artists, and, in the newer Espai 13 space, cutting-edge contemporary art.

The airy white building, with panoramic views north over Barcelona, was designed by the artist's close friend and collaborator Josep Lluís Sert and opened

in 1975. Extensions were added by Sert's pupil Jaume Freixa in 1988 and 2000. Miró's playful and colorful style, filled with Mediterranean light and humor, seems a perfect match for the surroundings. Various patios, as well as the roof terrace, are home to notable Miró sculptures, including the bronze *Sun, Moon and one Star* with a dramatic backdrop of the city. The artist rests in the cemetery on Montjuïc's southern slopes. ⊠ Parc de Montjuïc s/n, Parc de Montjuïc, Montjuïc ⊹ Bus stop Fundació Joan Miró ☎ 93/443–9470 ⊕ www.fmirobcn. org ⊠ €13 ⊗ Closed Mon.–Wed. Ⓜ Pl. Espanya, Paral·lel then Funicular.

## Mies van der Rohe Pavilion
NOTABLE BUILDING | One of the masterpieces of the Bauhaus School, the legendary Pavelló Mies van der Rohe—the German contribution to the 1929 International Exhibition, reassembled between 1983 and 1986—remains a stunning "less is more" study in interlocking planes of white marble, green onyx, and glass. In effect, it is Barcelona's aesthetic opposite to the flamboyant Art Nouveau/Modernisme of Gaudí and his contemporaries.

Note the mirror play of the black carpet inside the pavilion with the reflecting pool outside, and the iconic Barcelona chair designed by Ludwig Mies van der Rohe (1886–1969) and Lilly Reich (1885–1947). Reproductions have graced modern interiors around the world for decades. ⊠ Av. Francesc Ferrer i Guàrdia 7, Montjuïc ☎ 93/215–1011 ⊕ miesbcn. com ⊠ €8 Ⓜ Pl. Espanya.

## Museu d'Arqueologia de Catalunya
HISTORY MUSEUM | Just downhill to the right of the Palau Nacional, the Museum of Archaeology holds important finds from the Greek ruins at Empúries, on the Costa Brava. These are shown alongside fascinating objects from, and explanations of, megalithic Spain. ⊠ Passeig Santa Madrona 39–41, Montjuïc

☎ 93/423–2149 ⊕ www.mac.cat ⛁ €6; free first Sun. of month ☾ Closed Sun. afternoon and Mon. Ⓜ Pl. Espanya.

★ **Museu Nacional d'Art de Catalunya** (National Art Museum of Catalonia, MNAC)
ART MUSEUM | Housed in the imposingly domed, towered, frescoed, and columned Palau Nacional, built in 1929 as the centerpiece of the International Exposition, this superb museum was renovated between 1985 and 1992 by Gae Aulenti, architect of the Musée d'Orsay in Paris. In 2004, the museum's four holdings (Romanesque, Gothic, the photography collection, and the Cambó Collection—an eclectic trove, including a Goya, donated by Francesc Cambó) were joined by the 19th- and 20th-century collection of Catalan Impressionist and Moderniste painters. With this influx of artistic treasure, the Museu Nacional has become Catalonia's grand central museum.

Pride of place goes to the Romanesque exhibition, the world's finest collection of Romanesque frescoes, altarpieces, and wood carvings, most of them rescued from chapels in the Pyrenees during the 1920s to save them from deterioration, theft, and art dealers. Many, such as the famous Cristo de Taüll fresco (from the church of Sant Climent de Taüll in Taüll), have been painstakingly removed from crumbling walls of abandoned sites and remounted on ingenious frames that exactly reproduce the contours of their original settings. The stunning central hall of the museum contains an enormous pillared and frescoed cupola. ✉ Palau Nacional, Parc de Montjuïc s/n, Montjuïc ☎ 93/622–0360 ⊕ www.museunacional. cat ⛁ From €12 (valid for day of purchase and 1 other day in same month); free Sat. after 3 pm and 1st Sun. of month ☾ Closed Mon. Ⓜ Pl. Espanya.

**Plaça d'Espanya**
PLAZA/SQUARE | This busy circle is a good place to avoid, but you'll probably need to cross it to get to the National Art Museum of Catalonia and other nearby Montjuïc attractions. It's dominated by the so-called Venetian Towers, built as the grand entrance to the 1929 International Exposition. They flank the lower end of the Avinguda Maria Cristina (the buildings on both sides are important venues for the trade fairs and industrial expositions that regularly descend on Barcelona).

At the far end is the Font Màgica (the Magic Fountain), which was created by Josep Maria Jujol, the Gaudí collaborator who designed the curvy and colorful benches in Park Güell, and which has a spectacular nighttime display of lights and music. The sculptures are by Miquel Blay, one of the master artists and craftsmen who put together the Palau de la Música. On the opposite side of the circle from the Towers, the neo-Mudejar bullring, Les Arenes, is now a multilevel shopping mall. ✉ Pl. Espanya, Sants Ⓜ Pl. Espanya.

**Poble Espanyol** (Spanish Village)
MUSEUM VILLAGE | FAMILY | Created for the 1929 International Exhibition, this faux Spanish village is a sort of open-air architectural museum, with 117 faithful replicas to scale of regional building styles, from an Aragonese Gothic-Mudejar bell tower to the tower walls of Ávila, drawn from all over Spain. The ground-floor spaces are devoted to boutiques, cafés and restaurants, workshops, and artist studios.

The liveliest time to come is at night, and a reservation at one of the half dozen restaurants gets you in for free, as does the purchase of a ticket for either of the two nightclubs or the Tablao del Carmen flamenco show. Its main square also functions as a concert venue, hosting well-known international bands like Bad Religion and Wilco. ✉ Av. Francesc Ferrer

Find replicas of buildings from all over Spain and see craftspeople at work in the Spanish village, at the foot of Montjuïc.

*i Guàrdia 13, Montjuïc* ☎ *93/508–6300* ⊕ *www.poble-espanyol.com* 🎫 *€14 (€11.20 online); after 8 pm €7* Ⓜ *Pl. Espanya.*

## 🍴 Restaurants

### ★ La Platilleria

$$ | TAPAS | Standards like Ibérico ham and *patatas bravas* are on offer at this snug tapas bar, but it's the rotating selection of seasonal small plates that really make it worth a visit. There's no menu; a chalkboard brought to your table lists the main ingredient—cod, pork rib, sweetbreads, for example—and friendly servers will explain the daily preparation for each. **Known for:** seasonal small plates; friendly service; nice selection of Catalan wines by the glass. $ *Average main: €20* ✉ *Roser 82, Poble Sec* ☎ *93/463–5401* 🕐 *Closed Sun.–Tues.* Ⓜ *Paral·lel.*

### Quimet & Quimet

$$ | TAPAS | The secret is out about this tiny, century-plus-old tapas bar, which has become so overrun with visitors in recent years that locals have mostly started steering clear. Nevertheless, it's an atmospheric place, and the innovative tapas—largely made using *conservas* (canned and tinned foods)—are still well worth the visit. **Known for:** arrive early to avoid the crowds; classic foodie haunt; local wines. $ *Average main: €15* ✉ *Poeta Cabanyes 25, Poble Sec* ☎ *93/442–3142* ⊕ *www.quimetquimet. com* 🕐 *Closed Sun.* Ⓜ *Paral·lel.*

## ☕ Coffee and Quick Bites

### La Fabrique

$ | BAKERY | Delicious artisanal breads and pastries are baked fresh every day at this patisserie, with different breads available on different days. Their almond croissant is the best in town. **Known for:** organic breads and pastries; croissants; daily bread specials. $ *Average main: €3* ✉ *Radas 35, Poble Sec* ☎ *93/443–1023* ⊕ *lafabrique.cat* 🚶 *Takeaway only* Ⓜ *Poble Sec.*

# 🛏 Hotels

## Hotel Brummell

$$ | HOTEL | The rustic-chic lobby with work by local artists sets the tone at this stylish boutique hotel. Along with a small downstairs bar, there's a lovely deck with a narrow plunge pool, sauna, and herb garden. **Pros:** young, friendly international staff; free yoga classes at nearby studio; chic design. **Cons:** no minibar; an uphill walk from closest metro; slightly off the beaten track. ⑤ *Rooms from: €160* ✉ *Nou de la Rambla 174, Poble Sec* ☎ *93/125–8622* ⊕ *www.hotelbrummell.com* ⌁ *20 rooms* ⧉ *No Meals* Ⓜ *Paral·lel.*

## Hotel Grums

$$$ | HOTEL | FAMILY | This pleasant boutique hotel is close to the port—convenient for cruise ship visitors—and has easy access to the museums and gardens of Montjuïc. **Pros:** quiet location; good for families; well-equipped spa with Jacuzzi and sauna. **Cons:** far from Eixample attractions; extra charges for the spa; rooms are on the small side. ⑤ *Rooms from: €177* ✉ *Carrer Palaudaries 26, Poble Sec* ☎ *93/442066* ⊕ *www.hotelgrumsbarcelona.com* ⌁ *78 rooms* ⧉ *No Meals* Ⓜ *Paral·lel.*

# 🍸 Nightlife

Poble Sec, a stone's throw from L'Eixample district, has an eclectic collection of fashionable cafés, bars, and eateries.

## BARS

### Celler Cal Marino

WINE BARS | Rustic and charming with an arched, brick-wall, barrel tables, and rows of multicolor *sifón* fizzy-water bottles, this homey venue serves wine by the glass or liter (for takeaway) from the wine cellar, artisanal beers, and vermouth paired with homemade tapas. ✉ *Margarit 54, Poble Sec* ⊕ *calmarino.tumblr.com* Ⓜ *Poble Sec, Paral·lel.*

### Lilith & Sons

COCKTAIL LOUNGES | Come to this corner bar for inventive, beautifully executed, seasonal craft cocktails like the Blood Muse, an umami twist on the classic Negroni, with soy sauce, balsamic vinegar, and a garnish of nori seaweed. ✉ *Fontrodona 23, Poble Sec* ☎ *63/372-2120* ⊕ *www.lilithandsons.com* Ⓜ *Paral·lel.*

# 🎭 Performing Arts

## FLAMENCO

### El Tablao de Carmen

FOLK/TRADITIONAL DANCE | Large tour groups come to this venerable flamenco dinner-theater venue in the Poble Espanyol named after, and dedicated to, the legendary dancer Carmen Amaya. Die-hard flamenco aficionados might dismiss the ensembles that perform here as a tad touristy, but the dancers, singers, and guitarists are pros. Visitors can enjoy one of the two nightly performances over a drink or over their choice of a prix-fixe meal, with prices ranging from €45 to €154. Reservations are recommended. Dinner shows are held daily at 6 pm and 8:30 pm. ✉ *Poble Espanyol, Av. Francesc Ferrer i Guàrdia 13, Montjuïc* ☎ *93/325–6895* ⊕ *www.tablaodecarmen. com* ▱ *Starting from €45 for a flamenco show and a drink* Ⓜ *Pl. Espanya.*

Chapter 9

# CATALONIA, VALENCIA, AND THE COSTA BLANCA

Updated by
Jennifer Ceaser

| ⊙ Sights | 🍴 Restaurants | 🛏 Hotels | 🛍 Shopping | 🍸 Nightlife |
|----------|---------------|----------|------------|-------------|
| ★★★★☆ | ★★★★★ | ★★★☆☆ | ★★☆☆☆ | ★★★☆☆ |

# WELCOME TO CATALONIA, VALENCIA, AND THE COSTA BLANCA

## TOP REASONS TO GO

★ **Girona:** Explore a town where monuments of Christian, Jewish, and Islamic cultures have coexisted for centuries and are just steps apart.

★ **Valencia:** Discover a treasure trove of museums, concert halls, riverfront parks, and architecture old and new in Spain's third-largest city.

★ **Great restaurants:** Foodies argue that the fountainhead of creative gastronomy has moved from France to Spain—and in particular to the great restaurants of the Empordà and Costa Brava.

★ **Dalí's home and museum:** "Surreal" doesn't begin to describe the Teatre-Museu Dalí in Figueres or the artist's eccentric home in Portlligat.

★ **Beaches:** From the Costa Brava, with its secluded beaches framed by dramatic rocky cliffs, down to the wide, golden strands of the Costa Daurada, some of the country's most spectacular beaches dot the Catalan coast.

Year-round, Catalonia is the most visited of Spain's autonomous communities. In summer, the rugged Costa Brava and the Costa Daurada's sandy beaches are havens for sun-worshippers, while its mountainous interior hides medieval wonders. Excellent rail, air, and highway connections link Catalonia to Valencia, its neighbor to the south.

1 Girona

2 Figueres

3 Besalú

4 Tossa de Mar

5 Sant Feliu de Guixols

6 S'Agaró

7 Calella de Palafrugell and Around

8 Begur and Around

9 Cadaqués and Around

10 Montserrat

11 Sitges

12 Santes Creus

13 Santa Maria de Poblet

14 Tarragona

15 Valencia

16 Albufera Nature Park

17 Dénia

18 Calpe

19 Altea

20 Alicante

# EATING AND DRINKING WELL IN CATALONIA AND VALENCIA

Paella valenciana in a classic paella pan.

Cuisine in both Catalonia and Valencia runs the gamut of classic Mediterranean fare, with paella being one of the most renowned and popular dishes. Fish preparations are similar along the coast, though inland favorites vary from place to place.

The grassy meadows of Catalonia's northern Alt Empordà region put quality beef on local tables; from the Costa Brava comes fine seafood, such as anchovies from L'Escala and *gambas* (prawns) from Palamós, both deservedly famous. *Romesco*—a blend of almonds, peppers, garlic, and olive oil—is used as a vegetable, fish, and seafood sauce in Tarragona, especially during the *calçotadas* (spring onion feasts). *Allioli*, garlicky mayonnaise, is another popular topping. The Ebro Delta is renowned for fresh fish, oysters, and eels, as well as *rossejat* (fried rice in a fish broth). Valencia and the Mediterranean coast are the homeland of *paella valenciana*. *Arròs a banda* is a variant in which the fish and rice are cooked separately.

## CALÇOTS

The *calçot* is a sweet spring onion developed by a 19th-century farmer who discovered how to extend the edible portion by packing soil around the base. It is grilled on a barbecue, then peeled and dipped into romesco sauce. In January, the town of Valls holds a *calçotada* where upward of 30,000 people gather for meals of onions, sausage, lamb chops, and red wine.

## RICE

Paella valenciana is one of Spain's most famous gastronomic contributions. A simple country dish dating to the early 18th century, "paella" refers to the wide frying pan with short, sturdy handles that's used to cook the rice. Anything fresh from the fields that day, along with rice and olive oil, traditionally went into the pan, but paella valenciana has particular ingredients: short-grain rice, chicken, rabbit, *garrofó* (a local legume), tomatoes, green beans, sweet peppers, olive oil, and saffron. *Paella marinera* (seafood paella) is a different story: rice, cuttlefish, squid, mussels, shrimp, prawns, lobster, clams, garlic, olive oil, sweet paprika, and saffron, all stewed in fish broth. Other paella variations include *paella negra* or *arròs negre*, a black rice dish made with squid ink, and *fideuà,* made with short noodles instead of rice.

Fresh calçots

## SEAFOOD STEWS

*Sèpia amb pèsols* is a vegetable and seafood *mar i muntanya* ("surf and turf") beloved on the Costa Brava: cuttlefish and peas are stewed with potatoes, garlic, onions, tomatoes, and a splash of wine. The *picadillo*—the finishing touches of flavors and textures—includes parsley, black pepper, fried bread, pine nuts, olive oil, and salt. *Es niu* ("the nest") of game fowl,

cod, tripe, cuttlefish, pork, and rabbit is another Costa Brava favorite. Stewed for a good five hours, this is a much-celebrated wintertime classic. You'll also find *suquet de peix,* a potato-based fish stew, at restaurants along the Costa Brava.

## FRUITS AND VEGETABLES

Valencia and the eastern Levante region have long been famous as Spain's *huerta,* or garden. The alluvial soil of the littoral produces an abundance of everything from tomatoes to asparagus, peppers, chard, spinach, onions, artichokes, cucumbers, and the whole range of Mediterranean bounty. Valencia is also the country's largest producer of oranges. Catalonia's Maresme and Empordà regions are also fruit and vegetable centers, making this coastline a cornucopia of fresh produce.

## WINES

The Penedès wine region west of Barcelona has been joined by new wine Denominations of Origin from all over Catalonia. Alt Camp, Tarragona, Priorat, Montsant, Costers del Segre, Pla de Bages, Alella, and Empordà all produce excellent reds and whites to join Catalonia's sparkling cava on local wine lists. The rich, full-bodied reds of Montsant and Priorat, especially, are among the best in Spain.

Suquet of fish, potatoes, onions, and tomatoes.

The long curve of the Mediterranean from the French border to Cabo Cervera below Alicante encompasses the two autonomous communities of Catalonia and Valencia, with the country's second- and third-largest cities (Barcelona and Valencia, respectively). Rivals in many respects, the two communities share a language, history, and culture that set them apart from the rest of Spain.

Girona is the gateway to Northern Catalonia's attractions—the Pyrenees, the volcanic region of La Garrotxa, and the beaches of rugged Costa Brava. The region is memorable for the soft, green hills of the Empordà farm country and the Alberes mountain range at the eastern end of the Pyrenees. Across the landscape are *masías* (farmhouses) with staggered-stone roofs and square towers that make them look like fortresses. Even the tiniest village has its church, arcaded square, and *rambla,* where villagers take their evening *paseo* (stroll).

Over the years these Mediterranean shores entertained Phoenician, Greek, Carthaginian, and Roman visitors; the Romans stayed several centuries and left archaeological remains all the way down the coast, particularly in Tarragona, the capital of Rome's Spanish empire by 218 BC.

The province of Valencia was incorporated into the Kingdom of Aragón, Catalonia's medieval Mediterranean empire, when it was conquered by Jaume I in the 13th century. Along with Catalonia, Valencia became part of the united Spanish state in the 15th century, but defenders of its separate cultural and linguistic identity still resent the centuries of Catalan domination. The Catalan language prevails in Catalonia, but Valenciano—a dialect of Catalan—is spoken and used on street signs in the Valencian provinces.

The coastal farmland and beaches that attracted the ancients now call to modern-day tourists, and in parts, a number of "mass-tourism" resorts have marred the shore. Inland, however, local culture survives intact. The rugged and beautiful territory is dotted with small fortified towns, several of which bear the name of Spain's 11th-century national hero, El Cid, commemorating the battles he fought here against the Moors some 900 years ago.

## MAJOR REGIONS
For many, **Northern Catalonia** is one of the top reasons to visit Spain. The historic center of Girona, its principal city, is a labyrinth of climbing cobblestone streets and staircases, with remarkable Gothic

and Romanesque buildings at every turn. El Call, the Jewish Quarter, is one of the best-preserved areas of its kind in Europe, and the Gothic cathedral is an architectural masterpiece. Streets in the modern part of the city are lined with smart shops and boutiques, and the overall quality of life in Girona is considered among the best in Spain.

Nearby is Figueres, an unremarkable town made exceptional by the Dalí Museum. Lesser known are the medieval towns in and around the volcanic (now extinct) area of La Garrotxa: the most charming is Besalú, a picture-perfect Romanesque village on a bluff overlooking the Riu Fluvià.

The **Costa Brava** (Wild Coast) is a nearly unbroken series of sheer rock cliffs dropping down to clear blue-green waters, punctuated by innumerable coves and tiny beaches on narrow inlets, called *calas*. It basically begins at Blanes and continues north along 135 km (84 miles) of coastline to the French border at Portbou.

Although the area does have spots of real-estate excess, the rocky terrain of many pockets (Tossa de Mar, Begur, and Cadaqués) has discouraged overbuilding. On a good day here, the luminous blue of the sea contrasts with red-brown headlands and cliffs, and the distant lights of fishing boats reflect on wine-colored waters at dusk. Stands of pine trees veil the footpaths to the many secluded coves and little patches of sand—often, the only access is by boat.

**Southern Catalonia** is home to the long, wide sand beaches of the Costa Daurada (Golden Coast) and the lively seaside town of Sitges. The region's principal city, Tarragona, brims with magnificent Roman-era sites. Inland, the Cistercian monasteries of Santes Creus and Santa Maria de Poblet impress, while Montserrat, home to the shrine of La Moreneta

(the Black Virgin of Montserrat), is one of most popular day trips from Barcelona.

Farther south lies **Valencia**, Spain's third-largest city and the capital of its region and province, equidistant from Barcelona and Madrid. For a day trip there's the Albufera, a scenic coastal wetland teeming with native wildlife, especially migratory birds.

The **Costa Blanca** (White Coast) begins at Dénia, south of Valencia, and stretches down roughly to Torrevieja, below Alicante. It's best known for its magical vacation combo of sand, sea, and sun, with popular beaches and more secluded coves and stretches of sand. Alicante itself has two long beaches, a charming old quarter, and mild weather most of the year.

# Planning

## When to Go

Come for the beaches in the hot summer months, but expect crowds and serious heat—in some places up to 40°C (104°F). The Mediterranean coast is more comfortable in May and September.

Winter travel in the region has its advantages: Valencia still has plenty of sunshine, and if you're visiting villages and wineries in the countryside, you might have the place all to yourself. Note that many restaurants and hotels outside the major towns may close on weekdays or longer in winter, so call ahead. Many museums and sights also close early in winter.

The Costa Brava, Costa Daurada, and Costa Blanca beach areas get hot and crowded in summer, and accommodations are at a premium. In contrast, spring is mild and an excellent time to tour the region, particularly the rural areas.

# Planning Your Time

Northeast of Barcelona, the beautiful town of Girona is easily reachable from the city by train in under an hour. Nearby Figueres is a must if you want to see the Teatre-Museu Dalí. Girona makes an excellent base from which to explore La Garrotxa and the Costa Brava—for that, you'll need to rent a car.

Trains and buses from Barcelona service the beaches and seaside towns of the Costa Daurada, including Castelldefels, Altafulla, and Sitges, which can be reached in as little as a half-hour. Tarragona, less than one hour from Barcelona by train or a 1½-hour drive, is worth allotting a couple of days to explore its Roman wonders on foot.

Valencia is less than three hours by express train from Barcelona. Historic Valencia and the Santiago Calatrava–designed City of Arts and Sciences complex can be covered in two days, but stay longer and indulge in the city's food and explore the nightlife in the Barrio del Carmen.

Travel agencies in Alicante can arrange tours of the city and bus and train tours to Guadalest, the Algar waterfalls, the Peñón de Ifach (Calpe) on the Costa Blanca, and inland to Elche.

## FESTIVALS
In Valencia, **Las Fallas** fiestas begin March 1 and reach a climax between March 15 and El Día de San José (St. Joseph's Day) on March 19, Father's Day in Spain. Las Fallas originated from St. Joseph's role as patron saint of carpenters; in medieval times, carpenters' guilds celebrated the arrival of spring by cleaning out their shops and making bonfires with scraps of wood.

These days, it's a 19-day celebration ending with fireworks, floats, carnival processions, and bullfights. On March 19, huge wood and papier-mâché effigies of political figures and other personalities (the result of a year's work by local community groups) are torched to end the fiestas.

# Getting Here and Around

## AIR
El Prat de Llobregat in Barcelona is the main international airport for the Costa Brava. Girona is the closest airport to the region, with bus connections directly into the city and to Barcelona. Valencia has an international airport with direct flights to London, Paris, Brussels, Lisbon, Zurich, and Milan as well as regional flights from Barcelona, Madrid, Málaga, and other cities in Spain. There is a regional airport in Alicante serving the Valencian region and Murcia.

## BOAT
Short-cruise lines along the coast offer the chance to view the Costa Brava from the sea. Plan to spend around €25, depending on the length of the cruise. Many longer cruises include a stop en route for a swim. Nautilus is one such outfit, offering a variety of excursions, including ones to the Medes Islands underwater park in a glass-keel boat. The cost is around €22. Boats run daily April–October and weekends November–March.

**BOAT AND FERRY INFORMATION**
**Nautilus.** ✉ *Passeig Marítim 23, L'Estartit* ☎ *972/751489* ⊕ *www.nautilus.es.*

## BUS
Private companies run buses down the coast and from Madrid to Valencia, and to Alicante. ALSA is the main bus line in this region; check local tourist offices for schedules. Sarfa operates limited bus service from the Barcelona airport to many towns along the Costa Brava including Sant Feliu de Guixols, Platja d'Aro, Palamos, Palafrugell, and Begur. Sagalés mainly services Girona, Lleida, and the Costa Brava, and runs buses

between the Girona and Barcelona airports.

**CONTACTS ALSA.** ☎ *902/422242* ⊕ *www. alsa.es.* **Moventis Sarfa.** ⊠ *Barcelona* ☎ *902/302025* ⊕ *compras.movent-is.es/online.* **Sagalés.** ⊠ *Barcelona* ☎ *902/130014 tickets* ⊕ *www.sagales. com.* **Sagalés AirportLine.** ☎ *902/130014* ⊕ *www.sagalesairportline.com.*

## CAR

A car is necessary for explorations inland and is far more convenient for reaching locations on the Costa Brava, where drives are scenic, though coastal roads can have a lot of twists and turns. Catalonia and Valencia have excellent roads; the only drawbacks are the high cost of fuel and the high tolls on the *autopistas* (highways, usually designated by the letters "AP"). The national roads (starting with the letter N) can get clogged, however, so you're often better off on toll roads if your time is limited.

## TRAIN

Most of the Costa Brava is not served directly by railroad. A local line runs up the coast from Barcelona to Blanes, then turns inland and connects at Maçanet-Massanes with the main line up to France. Direct trains stop only at major connections, such as Girona, Llançà, and Figueres.

By contrast, a train line runs from Barcelona south along the coast, making it easy to reach many of the Costa Daurada's main seaside towns.

Keep in mind that some cities—including Tarragona and Valencia—have two train stations; one serving high-speed trains and located outside the city center, and one in the city center serving slower (and usually less expensive) regional trains.

From Barcelona to Tarragona, there are trains running approximately every 15 minutes. Regional trains take just over an hour and stop at the Tarragona station in the city center; direct high-speed trains cut that time in half, arriving at Camp de Tarragona station, a 10-minute taxi ride to the center.

Express trains reach Valencia from all over Spain, arriving at the Joaquin Sorolla station; from there, a shuttle bus takes you to the Estación del Norte, the terminus in the center of town, for local connections. From Barcelona there are 15 trains a day, including the fast train Euromed, which takes 2 hours 40 minutes. There are 22 daily trains to Valencia from Madrid; the high-speed train takes about 1 hour 40 minutes.

For the Costa Blanca, the rail hub is Alicante.

**CONTACTS RENFE.** ☎ *912/320320* ⊕ *www.renfe.com.*

# Farmhouse Stays in Catalonia

Dotted throughout Catalonia are farmhouses (*casas rurales* in Spanish, and *cases de pagès* or *masíes* in Catalan), where you can spend a weekend or longer. Accommodations vary from small rustic homes to spacious luxurious farmhouses with fireplaces and pools. Stay in a guest room at a bed-and-breakfast, or rent an entire house and do your own cooking. Most tourist offices, including the main Catalonia Tourist Office, have information and listings. Several organizations in Spain have detailed listings and descriptions of Catalonia's farmhouses.

**CONTACTS Agroturisme.** ☎ *932/680900* ⊕ *www.agroturisme.cat.* **Cases Rurals.** ☎ *660/576834* ⊕ *www.casesrurals.com.*

# Restaurants

The region has several internationally acclaimed restaurants, but they aren't the only options when it comes to dining well. From traditional paella in a family-run restaurant to tapas at a *chiringuito* (beach shack) with tables on the sand, there are many ways to enjoy the gourmet delights.

Catalonia's eateries are deservedly famous. Girona's El Celler de Can Roca was voted Best Restaurant in the World multiple times in recent years in the annual critics' poll conducted by British magazine *Restaurant,* and a host of other first-rate establishments continue to offer inspiring fine dining in Catalonia.

Valencia is fast becoming one of Spain's culinary hot spots, counting eight Michelin-starred restaurants in 2022, including the two-starred El Poblet from chef Quique Dacosta, whose three-starred eponymous establishment in Dénia is a Costa Blanca must.

*Restaurant reviews have been shortened. For full information, visit Fodors.com. Restaurant prices are the average cost of a main course at dinner or, if dinner is not served, at lunch.*

## Hotels

Lodgings on the Costa Brava, Costa Daurada, and Costa Blanca range from the finest hotels to spartan pensions. If you plan to visit during the high season (July and August), be sure to book reservations well in advance at almost any hotel in these areas; Costa Brava, in particular, is one of the most popular summer resort areas in Spain. Note that many hotels in resort towns are closed for all or part of the winter season (November–March).

*Hotel reviews have been shortened. For full information, visit Fodors.com. Hotel prices are the lowest cost of a standard double room in high season.*

| What It Costs in Euros | | | |
|---|---|---|---|
| $ | $$ | $$$ | $$$$ |
| **RESTAURANTS** | | | |
| under €12 | €12–€17 | €18–€22 | over €22 |
| **HOTELS** | | | |
| under €90 | €90– €125 | €126– €180 | over €180 |

## Girona

*97 km (60 miles) northeast of Barcelona.*

At the confluence of four rivers, Northern Catalonia's Girona (population: 104,000) keeps intact the magic of its historic past. With its ancient city walls and soaring Gothic cathedral (which made an appearance in *Game of Thrones*), it resembles a vision from the Middle Ages.

Today, as a university center, Girona combines past and vibrant present: art galleries, chic cafés, and trendy boutiques have set up shop in many of the restored buildings of the old quarter, known as the Força Vella (Old Fortress), which is on the east side of the Riu Onyar (Onyar River). Built on the side of the mountain, it presents a tightly packed labyrinth of medieval buildings and monuments on narrow cobblestone streets with connecting stairways. You can still see vestiges of the Iberian and Roman walls in the cathedral square and in the patio of the old university. In the central quarter is El Call, one of Europe's best-preserved medieval (12th- to 15th-century) Jewish communities and an important center of Kabbalistic studies.

The main street of the Força Vella is Carrer de la Força, which follows the old Via Augusta, the Roman road that connected Rome with its provinces.

# Costa Brava, Costa Blanca and Costa Daurada Beaches

## Costa Brava Beaches

The beaches on the Costa Brava range from stretches of fine white sand to rocky coves and inlets; summer vacationers flock to **Tossa de Mar, Roses, Begur,** and **Calella de Palafrugell**; in all but the busiest weeks of July and August, the tucked-away coves of **Cap de Creus National Park** are oases of peace and privacy.

## Costa Blanca Beaches

The southeastern coastline of the Costa Blanca varies from the long stretches of sand dunes north of **Dénia** and south of **Alicante** to the coves and crescents in between. The benign climate permits lounging on the beach at least eight months of the year. **Altea**, popular with families, is busy and pebbly, but the old town has retained a traditional pueblo feel with narrow cobbled streets and attractive squares. **Calpe**'s beaches have the scenic advantage of the sheer outcrop Peñón de Ifach (Cliff of Ifach), which stands guard over stretches of sand to either side. Dénia has family-friendly beaches to the north, where children paddle in relatively shallow waters, and rocky inlets to the south.

## Costa Daurada Beaches

The Costa Daurada (Costa Dorada in Spanish) begins southwest of Barcelona and continues through the Tarragona province and down to L'Ampolla. It's characterized by wide, long, golden-sand beaches—those of **Castelldefels** (technically in neighboring Costa Garraf) and **Altafulla** are popular with day-trippers from Barcelona—interspersed with rocky coves that can be reached only on foot. **Sitges** is one of this coast's brightest stars, with its mix of great beaches, historical architecture, and a heady party scene. Southwest of Tarragona lies the mega-resort town of **Salou** and the quainter beaches of **Cambrils**.

Explore Girona on foot to discover many of its delights. One of Girona's treasures is its setting, high above where the Onyar merges with the Ter; the latter flows from a mountain waterfall that can be glimpsed in a gorge above the town. Walk first along the west bank of the Onyar, between the train trestle and the Plaça de la Independència, to admire the classic view of the old town, with its multicolored riverfront facades. Note how many of the windows and balconies are adorned with fretwork grilles of embossed wood or delicate iron tracery.

Cross Pont de Sant Agustí over to the old quarter from under the arcades in the corner of Plaça de la Independència and find your way to the Punt de Benvinguda tourist office, to the right at Rambla Llibertat 1. Work your way up through the labyrinth of steep streets, using the cathedral's huge baroque facade as a guide. Try to be in Girona during the second week of May, when the streets of the old quarter are festooned with the flowers of spring during the Girona Flower Festival.

### GETTING HERE AND AROUND

More than 20 trains run daily from Barcelona to Girona (continuing on to the French border). Regional trains, which take between one and two hours, can be picked up from a number of stations in Barcelona, while the high-speed AVE train service is a convenient option, running from Barcelona Sants station to

## Northern Catalonia and the Costa Brava

Girona in under 40 minutes (it's advisable to prebook the AVE). Tickets are around €35 round-trip. The train station is about a 20-minute walk from the old quarter; alternatively, taxis can be picked up in front of the train station on arrival.

Far less efficient Sagalés buses run from Barcelona's El Prat de Llobregat airport and Estació del Nord, in the center of Barcelona, to Girona city bus station, with a stop at the Girona Airport. They take an average of 75 minutes and cost €15 one-way, €24 round-trip.

Getting around the city is easiest on foot or by taxi. Several bridges connect the historic old quarter with the more modern town across the river.

**CONTACTS Sagalés.** ☒ *Girona* ☎ *902/130014* ⊕ *www.sagales.com.*

### DISCOUNTS AND DEALS

GironaMuseus (⊕ *museus.girona.cat*) offers discounted admission to six city museums after paying full price for the first museum. ■**TIP→ Some museums are free on the first Sunday of every month.** Check the tourist office or at the Punt de Benvinguda welcome center, which can also arrange guided tours.

### VISITOR INFORMATION
**VISITOR INFORMATION Girona Office of Tourism.** ☒ *Rambla de la Llibertat 1, Girona* ☎ *972/010001* ⊕ *www.girona.cat/ turisme.* **Punt de Benvinguda.** ☒ *Berenguer Carnicer 3, Girona* ☎ *972/011669* ⊕ *www. girona.cat/turisme.*

# ⊙ Sights

**Banys Arabs** (*Arab Baths*)

HISTORIC SIGHT | A misnomer, the Banys Arabs were actually built by Morisco craftsmen (workers of Moorish descent) in the late 12th century, long after Girona's Islamic occupation (714–797) had ended. Following the old Roman model that had disappeared in the West, the custom of bathing publicly may have been brought back from the Holy Land with the Crusaders. These baths are sectioned off into three rooms in descending order: a *frigidarium*, or cold bath, a square room with a central octagonal pool and a skylight with cupola held up by two stories of eight fine columns; a *tepidarium*, or warm bath; and a *caldarium*, or steam room, beneath which is a chamber where a fire was kept burning. Here the inhabitants of old Girona came to relax, exchange gossip, or do business. ✉ *Carrer Ferran el Catòlic s/n, Girona* ☎ *972/190969* ⊕ *www.banys-arabs.cat* 🎟 *€3.*

**Basílica de Sant Feliu**

CHURCH | One of Girona's most beloved churches and its first cathedral until the 10th century, Sant Feliu was repeatedly rebuilt and altered over four centuries and stands today as an amalgam of Romanesque columns, a Gothic nave, and a baroque facade. The vast bulk of this structure is landmarked by one of Girona's most distinctive belfries, topped by eight pinnacles. The basilica was founded over the tomb of St. Felix of Africa, a martyr under the Roman emperor Diocletian. ✉ *Pujada de Sant Feliu 29, Girona* ☎ *972/201407* ⊕ *www. catedraldegirona.cat* 🎟 *€7 (includes Girona Cathedral).*

★ **Catedral de Girona** (*Girona Cathedral*)

CHURCH | At the heart of the Força Vella, the cathedral looms above 90 steps and is famous for its nave—at 75 feet, the widest in the world and the epitome of the spatial ideal of Catalan Gothic architects. Since Charlemagne founded the original church in the 8th century, it has been through many fires and renovations.

Take in the rococo-era facade, "eloquent as organ music" and impressive flight of 17th-century stairs, which rises from its own *plaça*. Inside, three smaller naves were compressed into one gigantic hall by the famed architect Guillermo Bofill in 1416. The change was typical of Catalan Gothic "hall" churches, and it was done to facilitate preaching to crowds. Note the famous silver canopy, or *baldaquí* (baldachin). The oldest part of the cathedral is the 11th-century Romanesque Torre de Carlemany (Charlemagne Tower).

The cathedral's exquisite 12th-century cloister has an obvious affinity with the cloisters in the Roussillon area of France. Inside the Treasury there's a variety of precious objects. They include a 10th-century copy of Beatus's manuscript *Commentary on the Apocalypse* (illuminated in the dramatically primitive Mozarabic style), the Bible of Emperor Charles V, and the celebrated *Tapís de la Creació* (*Tapestry of the Creation*), considered by most experts to be the finest tapestry surviving from the Romanesque era. ✉ *Pl. de la Catedral s/n, Girona* ☎ *972/427189* ⊕ *www.catedraldegirona. cat* 🎟 *€7 (includes Basílica de Sant Feliu).*

★ **El Call** (*Jewish Quarter*)

HISTORIC DISTRICT | Girona is especially noted for its 12th-century Jewish Quarter, El Call, which branches off Carrer de la Força, south of the Plaça Catedral. The quarter is a network of lanes that crisscross above one another, and houses built atop each other in disorderly fashion along narrow stone medieval streets. The earliest presence of Jews in Girona is uncertain, but the first historical mention dates from 982. This once-prosperous community—one of the most flourishing in Europe during the Middle Ages—was, at its height, a leading center of Kabbalistic learning. ✉ *Girona.*

There's more to Girona's cathedral than the 90 steps to get to it; inside there's much to see, including the Treasury.

### Monestir de Sant Pere de Galligants

RELIGIOUS BUILDING | The church of St. Peter, across the Galligants River, was finished in 1131, and is notable for its octagonal Romanesque belfry and the finely detailed capitals atop the columns in the cloister. It now houses the **Museu Arqueològic** (Museum of Archaeology), which documents the region's history since Paleolithic times and includes some artifacts from Roman times. ⊠ *Santa Llúcia 8, Girona* ☎ *972/202632* ⊕ *www. macgirona.cat* 🖾 *€6* ⊘ *Closed Mon.*

### Museu d'Art

ART MUSEUM | The Episcopal Palace near the cathedral contains the wide-ranging collections of Girona's main art museum. On display is everything from superb Romanesque *majestats* (carved wood figures of Christ) to reliquaries from Sant Pere de Rodes, illuminated 12th-century manuscripts, and works of the 20th-century Olot school of landscape painting. ⊠ *Pujada de la Catedral 12, Girona* ☎ *972/203834* ⊕ *museuart.cat* 🖾 *€6* ⊘ *Closed Mon.*

### Museu d'Història de Girona (*Girona History Museum*)

HISTORY MUSEUM | From pre-Roman objects to paintings and drawings from the notorious siege at the hands of Napoleonic troops, to the early municipal lighting system and the medieval printing press, artifacts from Girona's long and embattled past are exhibited in this fascinating museum. Rooms organized chronologically and by theme educate visitors on the ways the city has developed. ⊠ *Carrer de la Força 27, Girona* ☎ *972/222229* ⊕ *www.girona. cat/museuhistoria* 🖾 *€4; free 1st Sun. of month* ⊘ *Closed Mon.*

### ★ Museu d'Història dels Jueus (*Museum of Jewish History*)

HISTORY MUSEUM | Housed in a former synagogue, this museum examines the history, daily life, and artistic and cultural traditions of Catalonia's Jewish communities in medieval times, with a focus on Girona. A highlight is the 21 stone tablets, one of the finest collections in the world of medieval Jewish funerary slabs. These came from the old Jewish cemetery of Montjuïc, revealed when the railroad between Barcelona and France was laid out in the 19th century.

The museum organizes conferences, exhibitions, and seminars. It also contains the Institut d'Estudis Nahmànides, with an extensive library of Judaica. ☒ *Carrer de la Força 8, Girona* ☎ *972/216761* ⊕ *www.girona.cat/call/ eng/museu.php* ☒ *€4.*

### Passeig Arqueològic

**HISTORIC SIGHT** | The landscaped gardens of this stepped archaeological walk are below the Força Vella's restored Carolingian walls (which you can walk, in parts) and enjoy superlative views of the city from belvederes and watchtowers. From there, climb through the Jardins de la Francesa to the highest ramparts for a view of the cathedral's 11th-century Torre de Carlemany. ☒ *Girona.*

## 🍴 Restaurants

### Café le Bistrot

$ | **CATALAN** | This bistro's menu includes a 20-strong list of Catalan-style pizzas, served on peasant bread and incorporating regional ingredients like *botifarra* (sausage) and seasonal mushrooms. The delightful terrace is situated below a flight of stone stairs leading to the 17th-century Sant Martí church. **Known for:** affordable pizzas; lovely terrace; regional cheese plate. ⑤ *Average main: €10* ☒ *Pujada de Sant Domènec 4, Girona* ☎ *972/218803* ⊕ *lebistrot.cat.*

### Cal Ros

$$$$ | **CATALAN** | Tucked under the arcades just behind the north end of Plaça de la Llibertat, this restaurant combines ancient stone arches with crisp, contemporary furnishings and cheerful lighting. The menu changes regularly, featuring organically raised local produce in season, and fresh fish in updated versions of traditional Catalan cuisine. **Known for:** traditional cuisine with a modern spin;

atmospheric setting; rice dishes. ⑤ *Average main: €24* ☒ *Carrer Cort Reial 9, Girona* ☎ *972/219176* ⊗ *Closed Mon. and Tues. No dinner Sun.*

### ★ El Celler de Can Roca

$$$$ | **CONTEMPORARY** | Holder of three Michelin stars since 2009, El Celler de Can Roca, helmed by the Roca brothers—Joan, Josep, and Jordi—is a life-changing culinary experience. Its two tasting menus, ranging from 14 to 22 courses and priced in the €200 range, feature wildly inventive dishes and daring presentations. **Known for:** reservations required many months or even a year ahead; expansive wine list; considered one of the best restaurants in the world. ⑤ *Average main: €200* ☒ *Can Sunyer 48, Girona* ☎ *972/222157* ⊕ *cellercanroca. com* ⊗ *Closed Sun. and Mon., Easter and Christmas holidays, and most of Aug. No lunch Tues.*

### La Fabrica

$ | **CAFÉ** | Owned by a professional cyclist and decorated with an abundance of bike memorabilia, this inviting cafe serves healthy, organic breakfasts and lunches—avocado toast, egg dishes, quinoa bowls—along with superb locally roasted coffee. It's a popular fuel-up stop for local cyclists. **Known for:** vegan options; excellent coffee; healthy breakfast and lunch bowls. ⑤ *Average main: €9* ☒ *Carrer de la Llebre 3, Girona* ☎ *872/000273* ⊕ *www. lafabricagirona.com* ⊗ *No dinner.*

### Mimolet

$$ | **CATALAN** | Contemporary architecture and cuisine in the old part of Girona make for interesting dining at this sleek, streamlined restaurant. Grilled eel and pepper rice and *fideuà* with shrimp in a seafood emulsion are typical dishes, and there's a frequently changing five- and 10-course tasting menu. **Known for:** tasting menu of seasonal dishes; local oysters on the half-shell; good wine list. ⑤ *Average main: €21* ☒ *Pou Rodó 12, Girona* ☎ *972/297973* ⊕ *www.mimolet. cat* ⊗ *Closed Mon.*

With its picturesque rivers, Girona is often called the Spanish Venice.

### Rocambolesc

**$ | ICE CREAM | FAMILY |** Not your average ice-cream parlor, this to-go spot is the brainchild of master confectioner Jordi Roca, of El Celler de Can Roca fame. Exquisite *helados*, fanciful toppings, and popsicles in the shape of Girona's famous climbing bear are just some of the treats you'll find here. **Known for:** molded popsicles; fun toppings; excellent ice cream. *⑤ Average main: €5 ⊠ Carrer Santa Clara 50, Girona ☏ 972/416667 ⊕ www.rocambolesc.com.*

## 🛏 Hotels

### Casa Cacao

**$$$$ | HOTEL |** The first hotel from the three-Michelin-starred Roca Brothers occupies a historic building in the medieval center. **Pros:** large rooms; excellent location in the medieval center; gourmet breakfast included. **Cons:** rooms are pricey; smaller rooms lack views; parking is extra. *⑤ Rooms from: €250 ⊠ Carrer Ginesta 2, Girona ☏ 972/282828*

⊕ *hotelcasacacao.com ⤴ 15 suites* ⑩ *Free Breakfast.*

### Hotel Peninsular

**$ | HOTEL |** In a handsomely restored 19th-century building across the Onyar River, with views into Girona's historic Força Vella, this modest hotel occupies a strategic spot at the end of the Pont de Pedra (Stone Bridge), a Girona landmark in the center of the shopping district. **Pros:** good location at the hub of Girona life; friendly staff; near the stop for the bus from Girona airport. **Cons:** no frills; basic decor; smallish rooms. *⑤ Rooms from: €90 ⊠ Carrer Nou 3, Av. Sant Francesc 6, Girona ☏ 972/203800 ⊕ www. hotelpeninsulargirona.com ⤴ 48 rooms* ⑩ *No Meals.*

## 🍸 Nightlife

Girona is a university town, so the night scene is especially lively during the school year. In the labyrinth of small streets throughout the pedestrianized Barri Vell (Old Town), several *vermuterias* (vermouth-focused bars), wine bars, and affable taverns provide entertainment as night falls.

### Sunset Jazz Club

**LIVE MUSIC** | As the evening develops, drop into the Sunset Jazz Club to catch some live jazz by national and international artists in a softly lit, buzzing venue with exposed brick walls and dark furnishings. ⊠ *Calle Jaume Pons i Martí 12, Girona* ☎ *872/080145* ⊕ *www.sunsetjazz-club. com.*

##  Shopping

### CRAFTS
**Recorda-te'n**

**SOUVENIRS** | Local crafts, from wood puzzles of the Girona Cathedral to ceramic versions of the city's famous colorful houses along the Onyar River, are for sale at this small shop on Carrer de la Força, in the heart of the old quarter. ⊠ *Carrer de la Força 2, Girona* ☎ *972/227890* ⊕ *recordaten.cat.*

### FOOD, CANDY, AND WINE
**Gluki**

**CHOCOLATE** | This Olot-based chocolatier and confectioner has been in business since 1870. ⊠ *Carrer Nou 9, Girona* ☎ *972/201989* ⊕ *www.gluki.cat.*

**La Simfonia**

**WINE/SPIRITS** | At this relaxed wine shop that has a small restaurant, you can get a tour through a stellar range of regional wines (and cheeses)—and sample before you buy. ⊠ *Pl. de l'Oli 6, Girona* ☎ *972/411253* ⊕ *www.lasimfonia.com.*

### JEWELRY
**Baobab**

**JEWELRY & WATCHES** | A lot of designer Anna Casal's original jewelry seems at first sight to be rough-hewn; it takes a second careful look to realize how sophisticated it really is. This shop doubles as her studio. ⊠ *Carrer de les Hortes 18, Girona* ☎ *972/410227* ⊕ *baobabjoieriagirona.blogspot.com.*

# Figueres

*37 km (23 miles) north of Girona.*

Figueres is the capital of the *comarca* (county) of the Alt Empordà, the bustling county seat of this predominantly agricultural region. People come from the surrounding area to shop at its many stores and stock up on farm equipment and supplies. Thursday is market day, and farmers gather at the top of La Rambla to do business and gossip while taking refreshments at cafés.

What brings the tourists to Figueres in droves, however, has little to do with agriculture and everything to do with Salvador Dalí's jaw-droppingly surreal "theater-museum"—one of the most visited museums in Spain.

### GETTING HERE AND AROUND
There's regular regional train service from Barcelona to Figueres and the trip takes about two hours. (The high-speed train is half that, but you'll have to take a shuttle from the Figueres Vilafant station, which is outside the city.)

Local buses are also frequent, especially from Cadaqués, which is about an hour away, with more than eight scheduled daily. If you're driving, take the AP7 north from Girona. The town is small enough to explore on foot.

### VISITOR INFORMATION
**CONTACTS Figueres.** ⊠ *Pl. de l'Escorxador 2, Figueres* ☎ *972/503155* ⊕ *en. visitfigueres.cat.*

## ◉ Sights

**Castell de Sant Ferran** (*Sant Ferran Castle*)
**CASTLE/PALACE** | Just a minute's drive northwest of Figueres is this imposing 18th-century fortified castle, one of the largest in Europe—only when you start exploring can you appreciate how immense it is. The parade grounds extend for acres, and the arcaded stables

# Figueres's Famous Son

With a painterly technique that rivaled that of Jan van Eyck, a flair for publicity so aggressive it would have put P. T. Barnum to shame, and a penchant for the shocking (he loved telling people Barcelona's historic Barri Gòtic should be knocked down), artist Salvador Dalí, whose most lasting image may be the melting watches in his iconic 1931 painting *The Persistence of Memory*, enters art history as one of the foremost proponents of surrealism, the movement launched in the 1920s by André Breton. The artist, who was born in Figueres and died there in 1989, decided to create a museum-monument to himself during the last two decades of his life. Dalí often frequented the Cafeteria Astòria at the top of La Rambla (still the center of social life in Figueres), signing autographs for tourists or just being Dalí: he once walked down the street with a French omelet in his breast pocket instead of a handkerchief.

can hold more than 500 horses; the perimeter is roughly 4 km (2½ miles around). This castle was the site of the last official meeting of the Republican parliament (on February 1, 1939) before it surrendered to Franco's forces. Ironically, it was here that Lieutenant Colonel Antonio Tejero was imprisoned after his failed 1981 coup d'état in Madrid.

■TIP→ Call ahead and arrange for the two-hour Catedral de l'Aiguas guided tour in English (€15), which includes a trip through the castle's subterranean water system by Zodiac pontoon boat. ⊠ *Pujada del Castell s/n, Figueres* ☎ *972/506094* ⊕ *castell-santferran.com* 🖅 *€4* ⊘ *Closed Mon.*

### Museu del Joguet de Catalunya (*Toy Museum*)

**OTHER MUSEUM | FAMILY |** Hundreds of antique dolls and toys are on display here—including collections owned by, among others, Salvador Dalí, Federico García Lorca, and Joan Miró. The museum also hosts Catalonia's only *caganer* exhibit. These playful little figures answering nature's call have long had a special spot in the Catalan *pessebre* (Nativity scene). Farmers are the most traditional figures, squatting discreetly behind the animals, but these days you'll find Barça soccer players and politicians,

too. ⊠ *Carrer de Sant Pere 1, Figueres* ☎ *972/504585* ⊕ *www.mjc.cat* 🖅 *€7* ⊘ *Closed Sun. and Mon.*

### ★ Teatre-Museu Dalí (*Dalí Theater Museum*)

**ART MUSEUM |** "Museum" was not a big enough word for Dalí, so he christened his monument a theater. In fact, the building was once the Força Vella theater, reduced to a ruin in the Spanish Civil War. Now topped with a glass geodesic dome and studded with Dalí's iconic egg shapes, the multilevel structure pays homage to his fertile imagination and artistic creativity. It includes gardens, ramps, and a spectacular drop cloth Dalí painted for Les Ballets de Monte Carlo. Don't look for his greatest paintings here, although there are some memorable images, including *Gala at the Mediterranean*, which takes the body of Gala (Dalí's wife) and morphs it into the image of Abraham Lincoln once you look through coin-operated viewfinders.

The sideshow theme continues with other coin-operated pieces, including *Taxi Plujós* (*Rainy Taxi*), in which water gushes over the snail-covered occupants sitting in a Cadillac once owned by Al Capone, or *Sala de Mae West*, a trompe-l'oeil vision in which a pink sofa, two

The Dalí Museum in Figueres is itself a work of art. Note the eggs on the exterior: they're a common image in the artist's work.

fireplaces, and two paintings morph into the face of the onetime Hollywood sex symbol. Fittingly, another "exhibit" on view is Dalí's own crypt. ⊠ *Pl, Gala-Salvador Dalí 5, Figueres* ☎ *972/677500* ⊕ *www.salvador-dali.org* ✉ *€15* ☾ *Closed Mon. except July and Aug. and public holidays.*

##  Restaurants

### Bocam

**$$ | SPANISH |** This stylish restaurant, just around the corner from the Dalí Theatre-Museum, focuses on seasonal Empordà ingredients from the Pyrenees and the Mediterranean. Look for classic Catalan fare like prawn and cuttlefish fideuá alongside more modern dishes such as tuna tataki with black garlic. **Known for:** seasonal ingredients; pleasant terrace; local Empordà wines. ⑤ *Average main. €17* ⊠ *Carrer de la Jonquera 18, Figueres* ☎ *972/539494* ⊕ *bocam.cat/ca/inici/* ☾ *Closed Mon. No dinner Sun.*

### ★ El Motel

**$$$$ | CATALAN |** Just 1½ km (1 mile) north of town, this restaurant—housed within a rather nondescript hotel—has been hailed as the birthplace of modern Catalan cuisine and is a beacon for gourmands. The hyper-local menu changes with the seasons and features such dishes as eggplant with anchovies from Cadaqués, black truffle risotto, and a vanilla tart topped with strawberries from nearby Vilafant. **Known for:** impeccable service; marvelous cheese selection; historic culinary destination. ⑤ *Average main: €29* ⊠ *inside Hotel Empordà, Av. Salvador Dalí i Domènech 170, Figueres* ☎ *972/500562* ⊕ *www.elmotelrestaurant.com.*

## Hotels

### Hotel Duràn

**$ | HOTEL |** Dalí had his own private dining room in this former stagecoach relay station, though the guest rooms, refurbished in bland pale-wood tones

# Dali's Castle

**Castell Gala Dalí - Púbol.** The third point of the Dalí triangle (along with the Teatre-Museu Dalí and Casa Salvador Dalí - Portlligat, his summer house) is the medieval castle of Púbol, where the artist's wife and perennial model, Gala, is buried in the crypt. During the 1970s this was Gala's residence, though Dalí also lived here in the early 1980s. It contains paintings and drawings, Gala's haute-couture dresses, and other objects chosen by the couple. It's also a chance to wander through another Daliesque landscape, with lush gardens, fountains decorated with masks of Richard Wagner (the couple's favorite composer), and distinctive elephants with giraffe's legs and claw feet. Púbol, a small village roughly between Girona and Figueres, is near the C66. If you are traveling by train, get off at the Flaçà station on the Barcelona–Portbou line; take a taxi 4 km (2½ miles) to Púbol. ⊠ *Púbol-la Pera, Púbol* ☎ *972/488655* ⊕ *www.salvador-dali.org* ✉ *€8* ⊙ *Hours and opening days vary month to month* ⚲ *Booking tickets in advance (online) is essential.*

and standard contemporary furnishings, offset the hotel's historic 19th-century exterior. **Pros:** good central location; family-friendly; dining room has pictures of Dalí. **Cons:** somewhat erratic service; parking inconvenient and an extra charge; rooms lack character. ⑤ *Rooms from: €85* ⊠ *Carrer Lasauca 5, Figueres* ☎ *972/501250* ⊕ *www.hotelduran.com* ⟿ *65 rooms* ⦿❘ *No Meals.*

# Besalú

*34 km (21 miles) northwest of Girona, 25 km (15 miles) west of Figueres.*

Besalú is one of the best-preserved medieval towns in Catalonia. Among its main sights are the 12th-century Romanesque fortified bridge over the Riu Fluvià; two churches—Sant Vicenç (set on an attractive, café-lined plaza) and Sant Pere; and the ruins of the convent of Santa Maria on the hill above town.

## GETTING HERE AND AROUND

With a population of less than 2,500, the village is easily small enough to stroll through—restaurants and sights are within walking distance of each other.

There is bus service to Besalú from Figueres and Girona.

## VISITOR INFORMATION

**CONTACTS Besalú Tourist Office.** ⊠ *Carrer del Pont Vell 1, Besalú* ☎ *972/591240* ⊕ *www.besalu.cat.*

## ◉ Sights

### Església de Sant Pere

CHURCH | This 12th-century Romanesque church is part of a 10th-century monastery, still in an excellent state of preservation. It's set on the town's main plaza, Sant Pere, with many cafes and terraces. ⊠ *Pl. de Sant Pere s/n, Besalú.*

### Església de Sant Vicenç

CHURCH | Founded in 977, this pre-Romanesque gem contains the relics of St. Vincent as well as the tomb of its benefactor, Pere de Rovira. La Capella de la Veracreu (Chapel of the True Cross) displays a reproduction of an alleged fragment of the True Cross brought from Rome by Bernat Tallafer in 977 and stolen in 1899. ⊠ *Pl. Sant Vicenç s/n, Besalú.*

### Jewish Ritual Bath

RUINS | The remains of this 13th-century *mikvah*, or Jewish ritual bath, were

Besalú contains astonishingly well-preserved medieval buildings.

discovered in the 1960s; it's one of the few surviving in Spain. A stone stairway leads down into the chamber where the water was drawn from the river, but little else indicates the role that the baths played in the medieval Jewish community. Access is by guided tour only (organized through the tourist office). ✉ *Calle de Pont Vell 1, Besalú* 🕾 *972/591240 tourist office* 🔲 *€2.50* 🕒 *Admission by guided tour only, Jul.–Sept., Tues. 11 am (in English)* ⚠ *Reservations essential.*

## Pont Fortificat

**BRIDGE** | The town's most emblematic feature is this Romanesque 11th-century fortified bridge with crenellated battlements spanning the Riu Fluvià. ✉ *Carrer del Pont, Besalú.*

## Santa Maria de Besalú

**RUINS** | The ruins of the 13th-century Santa Maria Convent, on a hill just outside of town, make a good walk and offer a panoramic view over Besalú. ✉ *Besalú.*

## 🍴 Restaurants

### ★ Restaurant Pont Vell

**$$$$ | CATALAN** | Book in advance for a table on the romantic riverfront terrace and you'll be rewarded with exceptional views of Besalu's medieval bridge. The prix-fixe menu changes monthly and offers a wide array of traditional Catalan dishes of superb quality, with seasonal ingredients sourced from the nearby Banyols market. **Known for:** warm, friendly service; seasonal menu; terrace with views. 🖻 *Average main: €38* ✉ *Pont Vell 24, Besalú* 🕾 *972/591027* ⊕ *www.restaurantpontvell. com* 🕒 *Closed Mon. and Tues. No dinner Sun. Fri. and Sat. dinner only in winter.*

# Tossa de Mar

*80 km (50 miles) northeast of Barcelona, 41 km (25 miles) south of Girona.*

Christened "Blue Paradise" by painter Marc Chagall, who summered here for four decades, Tossa's pristine beaches

are among Catalonia's best. Set around a gorgeous bay, It's comprised of the the Vila Vella (Old Town) and the Vila Nova (New Town). The Vila Vella is a lovely district open to the sea and threaded by steep cobblestone streets with many restored buildings.

Ava Gardner filmed the 1951 British drama *Pandora and the Flying Dutchman* here (a statue dedicated to her stands on a terrace on the medieval walls). Things may have changed since those days, but this beautiful village retains much of the unspoiled magic of its past. The primary beach at Tossa de Mar is the Platja Gran (Big Beach) in front of the town beneath the walls, and just next to it is Mar Menuda (Little Sea), where the small, colorfully painted fishing boats—maybe the same ones that caught your dinner—pull up onto the beach.

The beaches and town are a magnet for vacationers in July and August. Out of season, it's far more sedate, but the mild temperatures make it an ideal stop for coastal strolls.

### GETTING HERE AND AROUND
By car, the fastest way to Costa Brava's Tossa de Mar from Barcelona is to drive up the inland C-33 tollway toward Girona, then take Sortida 10 (Exit 9A). The C-32 can also get you there in a similar length of time. Direct buses from Barcelona's Estació del Nord run regularly and take about 1 1/4 hours. The main bus station (as well as the local tourist office inside the station) is on Plaça de les Nacions Sense Estat.

##  Sights

### Museu Municipal
ART MUSEUM | In a lovingly restored 14th-century house, this museum is said to be Catalonia's first dedicated to modern art. It is home to one of the only three Chagall paintings in Spain, *Celestial Violinist.* ⊠ Pl. Pintor Roig i Soler 1, Tossa

de Mar 972/340709 €3 Closed Mon.

### Vila Vella and Castillo de Tossa de Mar
HISTORIC DISTRICT | Listed as a national artistic-historic monument in 1931, Tossa de Mar's Vila Vella (Old Town) is the only remaining example of a fortified medieval town in Catalonia. Set high above the town on a promontory, the Old Town is presided over by the ramparts and towers of the 13th-century Castillo de Tossa de Mar, and is a steep yet worthy climb up from the main town, accessed from the western side of Platja Gran Tossa de Mar (Playa Grande).

The cliff-top views, particularly at sunset, are remarkable, and the labyrinth of narrow, cobblestone lanes lined with ancient houses (some dating back to the 14th century) is a delight to explore at a leisurely pace. ■TIP→ Bar del Far de Tossa, near the lighthouse, has some of the best views in town, plus drinks, snacks, and light meals. ⊠ Tossa de Mar.

## Beaches

### Mar Menuda (*Little Sea*)
BEACH | FAMILY | Just north of the town center, this small sandy crescent is a pleasant Blue Flag beach that's popular with local families. The sand is coarse, but the calm, shallow waters make it ideal for children. Fishing boats bob peacefully in the water nearby after completing their morning's work. At the top of the beach there is a second cove called La Banyera de Ses Dones (the women's bathtub), which provides ideal conditions for diving, though if the sea is not calm, it is dangerous for swimmers. By day there is little natural shade, so bring adequate sunblock and an umbrella if you plan a long beach session. It gets extremely busy in high season. **Amenities:** none. **Best for:** snorkeling; sunset; swimming. ⊠ Av. Mar Menuda, Tossa de Mar.

## Platja Gran (*Big Beach*)

**BEACH | FAMILY |** Sweeping past the Vila Vella, this well-maintained, soft-sand Blue Flag beach runs along the front of town to meet the base of the Cap de Tossa. One of the most photographed coastlines in this area of Spain, it is also, at the height of summer, one of the busiest. Conditions are normally fine for swimming (any warnings are announced via loudspeaker). Running behind the beach, there is no shortage of cafés and kiosks selling ice cream and snacks. There is no natural shade, but you can rent deck chairs and umbrellas. **Amenities:** food and drink; lifeguards; showers; toilets; water sports. **Best for:** snorkeling; sunset; swimming. ✉ *Av. de sa Palma, Tossa de Mar.*

# 🍴 Restaurants

### La Cuina de Can Simon

**$$$$ | CATALAN |** Elegantly rustic, this restaurant beside Tossa de Mar's medieval walls serves classical Catalan cuisine from the sea, including lobster rice, and the mountains, such as a traditional mixed-meat stew. A tapas tasting menu (€98) lets you sample a bit of everything. **Known for:** welcoming tapa and cava upon entrance; seasonal menu; top-notch service. ⑤ *Average main: €32* ✉ *Carrer del Portal 24, Tossa de Mar* ☎ *972/341269* ⊕ *cuinacansimon.com* ⊗ *Closed Mon. No dinner Sun.*

### Restaurant Minerva

**$$$ | SEAFOOD |** Dine on fresh seafood and paella on the terrace with fabulous views of the sea and the castle beyond. **Known for:** fresh fish; great views from the terrace; seafood paella. ⑤ *Average main: €22* ✉ *Carrer Sant Ramon de Penyafort 7, Tossa de Mar* ☎ *972/340939* ⊕ *restaurantminerva.es* ⊗ *Closed Wed.*

# 🛏 Hotels

### Hotel Capri

**$$ | HOTEL | FAMILY |** Located on the beach, this hotel is in hailing distance of the old quarter in the medieval fortress; rooms are simple, and those with sea views have private terraces. **Pros:** family-friendly option; good value; great location. **Cons:** no private parking; minimal amenities; rooms are small. ⑤ *Rooms from: €110* ✉ *Passeig del Mar 17, Tossa de Mar* ☎ *972/340358* ⊕ *www.hotelcapritossa. com* ⊗ *Closed Nov.–Feb.* ⇌ *24 rooms* 🍽 *Free Breakfast.*

### ★ Hotel Diana

**$$$ | HOTEL |** Built in 1906 by architect Antoni de Falguera i Sivilla, disciple of Antoni Gaudí, this Moderniste gem sits on the square in the heart of the Vila Vella, steps from the beach. **Pros:** attentive service; Moderniste touches; ideal location, with sea views. **Cons:** some rooms are small; room rates unpredictable; minimal amenities. ⑤ *Rooms from: €176* ✉ *Pl. de Espanya 6, Tossa de Mar* ☎ *972/341886* ⊕ *www.hotelesdante.com* ⊗ *Closed Nov.–Apr.* ⇌ *21 rooms* 🍽 *Free Breakfast.*

# Sant Feliu de Guixols

*23 km (14 miles) northeast of Tossa de Mar.*

Sant Feliu de Guixols is set on a small bay with Moderniste mansions lining the seafront promenade, recalling a time when the cork industry made this one of the wealthier towns on the coast. In front of them, a long crescent beach of fine white sand leads around to the fishing harbor at its north end. Behind the promenade, a well-preserved old quarter of narrow streets and squares leads to a 10th-century gateway with horseshoe arches (all that remains of a pre-Romanesque monastery); also here is a church that combines Romanesque, Gothic, and baroque styles. Nearby, the iron-structured indoor market, which dates back to the 1930s, sells fresh local produce, with colorful stalls often overflowing onto the Plaça del Mercat in front.

## GETTING HERE AND AROUND

To get here, take the C65 from Tossa de Mar—though adventurous souls might prefer the harrowing hairpin curves of the G1-682 coastal road.

##  Sights

### Museu d'Història de Sant Feliu de Guíxols

HISTORY MUSEUM | Inside the Romanesque Benedictine monastery is this museum, which contains interesting exhibits about the town's cork and fishing trades, and displays local archaeological finds. ⌂ *Pl. del Monestir s/n, Sant Feliu de Guixols* ☎ *972/821575* ⊕ *www.museu.guixols.cat* ⊠ *€2* ⊙ *Closed Mon.*

##  Restaurants

### Can Segura

$$ | CATALAN | Half a block in from the beach at Sant Feliu de Guixols, this restaurant serves house-cooked seafood and upland specialties. The *pimientos de piquillos rellenos de brandada* (sweet red peppers stuffed with codfish mousse) are first-rate, as are the rice dishes. **Known for:** excellent rice dishes; daily menu specials; first-rate seafood. ⑤ *Average main: €15* ⊠ *Carrer de Sant Pere 11, Sant Feliu de Guixols* ☎ *972/321009* ⊕ *cansegurahotel.com/en/restaurant.*

### Hotel Restaurant Sant Pol

$$$ | SPANISH | This casual restaurant with a beachfront terrace serves fresh seafood and rice dishes, plus an affordable three-course lunch menu (€16.50). **Known for:** paella and fideuà; sea views; local fish. ⑤ *Average main: €22* ⊠ *Passeig de Sant Pol 125, Sant Feliu de Guixols* ☎ *972/321070* ⊕ *www.hotelsantpol.com* ⊙ *Closed Thurs.*

## Hotels

### Hostal del Sol

$$ | HOTEL | FAMILY | Once the summer home of a wealthy family, this Moderniste hotel has a grand stone stairway and medieval-style tower, as well as a garden and a lawn where you can relax by the pool. **Pros:** family-friendly option; good breakfast; good value. **Cons:** on a busy road; far from the beach; bathrooms a bit claustrophobic. ⑤ *Rooms from: €120* ⊠ *Ctra. a Palamós 194, Sant Feliu de Guixols* ☎ *972/320193* ⊕ *www.hostaldelsol.cat/en* ⊙ *Closed mid-Oct.–Easter* ⊐ *41 rooms* ⦿ *Free Breakfast.*

# S'Agaró

*3 km (2 miles) north of Sant Feliu de Guíxols.*

S'Agaró is an elegant gated community on a rocky point at the north end of the cove. The 30-minute walk along the sea wall from Hostal de La Gavina to Sa Conca Beach is a delight, and the one-hour hike from Sant Pol Beach over to Sant Feliu de Guíxols offers views of the Costa Brava at its best.

##  Restaurants

### Villa Mas

$$$$ | CATALAN | Set in a Moderniste villa with a lovely turn-of-the-20th-century zinc bar, this restaurant serves typical Catalan and seasonal Mediterranean dishes like *arròs a la cassola* (deep-dish rice) with shrimp brought fresh off the boats in Palamos, just up the coast. The terrace is a popular spot just across the road from the beach. **Known for:** fresh seafood catches; across from beach; terrace dining. ⑤ *Average main: €28* ⊠ *Passeig de Sant Pol 95, S'Agaró* ☎ *972/822526* ⊕ *www.restaurantvillamas.com* ⊙ *Closed Mon. and Tues. No dinner Sun.*

## Hotels

### ★ Hostal de la Gavina

$$$$ | HOTEL | Opened in 1932 by farmer-turned-entrepreneur Josep Ensesa, the original hotel grew from a cluster of country villas into a sprawling complex

of buildings of extraordinary splendor that have attracted celebrity guests from Orson Welles and Ava Gardner to Sean Connery. **Pros:** museum-quality furnishings; sea views, including from pool and terrace; impeccable service and amenities. **Cons:** expensive restaurant; walls are thin; hard on the budget. ⑤ *Rooms from: €490* ✉ *Pl. Roserar s/n, S'Agaró* ☎ *972/321100* ⊕ *www.lagavina. com* ⊗ *Closed Nov.–Easter* ⇄ *74 rooms* ⦿❘ *Free Breakfast.*

### S'Agaró Hotel Wellness & Spa

$$ | HOTEL | FAMILY | Surrounded by gardens with the Sant Pol Beach just below, this elegant, family-friendly property features a modern spa with an indoor pool and an outdoor pool with views of the sea. **Pros:** kid-friendly accommodations; beautiful gardens; all rooms have terraces. **Cons:** popular hotel for weddings and conventions; rooms could be better soundproofed; charge to use spa. ⑤ *Rooms from: €120* ✉ *Platja de Sant Pol s/n, S'Agaró* ☎ *972/325200* ⊕ *www. sagarohotel.com* ⇄ *95 rooms* ⦿❘ *Free Breakfast.*

# Calella de Palafrugell and Around

*25 km (15½ miles) north of S'Agaró.*

Up the coast from S'Agaró, the C31 brings you to Palafrugell; to the east are some of the prettiest, least developed inlets of the Costa Brava. One road leads to **Llafranc,** a small port with waterfront hotels and restaurants, and forks right to the fishing village of **Calella de Palafrugell,** known for its July habaneras festival. (The *habanera* is a form of Cuban dance music brought to Europe by Catalan sailors in the late 19th century; it still enjoys a nostalgic cachet here.) Just south is the panoramic promontory of **Cap Roig,** with views of the barren Formigues Isles.

North along the coast lies **Tamariu,** a largely unspoiled former fishing village backed by simple whitewashed houses and a small strip of seafood restaurants that hug the shoreline, is reached by descending a vertiginous road set between mountains and pine forests.

## 🍴 Restaurants

### ★ Pa i Raïm

$$$ | CATALAN | "Bread and Grapes" in Catalan, Pa i Raïm is an excellent restaurant set in writer Josep Pla's ancestral family home in Palafrugell. It has one rustic dining room as well as another in a glassed-in winter garden, plus a leafy terrace, which is the place to be in summer. **Known for:** garden terrace; traditional and contemporary menu; grilled whole fish. ⑤ *Average main: €20* ✉ *Torres i Jonama 56, Palafrugell* ☎ *972/447278* ⊕ *www. pairaim.com* ⊗ *Closed Mon. No dinner Sun.–Thurs.*

## 🛏 Hotels

### Hotel Llevant

$$$ | HOTEL | This charming family-run boutique hotel in the village of Llafranc sits just across from the main beach. **Pros:** friendly service; seaside location; heated outdoor pool. **Cons:** rooms facing the street can be noisy; petite rooms; rates soar in summer. ⑤ *Rooms from: €170* ✉ *Pere Pascuet 3, Llafranc* ☎ *972/300366* ⊕ *www.hotel-llevant.com* ⇄ *24 rooms* ⦿❘ *No Meals.*

### Hotel-Restaurant El Far

$$$$ | B&B/INN | FAMILY | Rooms in this 17th-century hermitage attached to a 15th-century watchtower have original vaulted ceilings, hardwood floors, and interiors accented with floral prints; the larger doubles and the suite can accommodate extra beds for children. **Pros:** friendly service; spectacular views of bay; graceful architecture. **Cons:** need car; pricey for what you get; a bit of a distance from the beach. ⑤ *Rooms from:*

*€330 ⊠ Muntanya de Sant Sebastia, Carrer Urugual s/n, Llatranc ☎ 972/301639 ⊕ www.hotelelfar.com/en �ъл 9 rooms ¶◎¶ Free Breakfast.*

# Begur and Around

*11 km (7 miles) north of Calella de Palafrugell.*

Carved into a hillside above the Costa Brava, Begur is an enchanting maze of steep, narrow streets lined with lavish 19th-century Spanish Colonial mansions, now housing smart restaurants, shops, and boutique hotels. The crumbling ruins of the 11th-century hilltop fortress lord over the town below, and offer magnificent panoramic views of the Mediterranean sea.

From Begur, go east through the calas or take the inland route past the rose-color stone houses and ramparts of the restored medieval town of **Pals.** Nearby **Peratallada** is another medieval fortified town with an 11th-century castle, tower, and palace. The name is derived from *pedra tallada,* meaning "carved stone," and behind its well-preserved walls is a maze of narrow streets and ivy-covered houses built from stone that was carved from the moat, which still encircles the town. In the center, the arcaded Plaça de les Voltes is alive with restaurants, shops, and cafés.

North of Pals there are signs for **Ullastret,** an Iberian village dating to the 5th century BC. **L'Estartit** is the jumping-off point for the spectacular natural park surrounding the **Medes Islands,** famous for its protected marine life and consequently for diving and underwater photography.

 Sights

### Beaches

BEACH | The Begur coast is dotted with idyllic swimming coves and sandy beaches, from the northernmost Platja del Racó south to Aiguablava, its loveliest strand, framed by rugged cliffs and pine trees. Parking can be limited, so it's best to take advantage of the shuttle bus that leaves from Begur's Plaça Forgas, near the main tourist office, and drops you at the three main beaches: Sa Tuna, Sa Riera, and Aiguablava. A coastal footpath, the Camí de Ronda, links many of the beaches and coves. ⊠ *Sa Tuna, Begur.*

### Empúries

RUINS | The Greco-Roman ruins here are Catalonia's most important archaeological site, and this port is one of the most monumental ancient engineering feats on the Iberian Peninsula. As the Greeks' original point of arrival in Spain, Empúries was also where the Olympic Flame entered Spain for Barcelona's 1992 Olympic Games. ⊠ *Puig i Cadafalch s/n ☎ 972/770208 ⊕ www.macempuries. cat ☞ €6.*

## 🍴 Restaurants

### ★ Hostal Restaurant Sa Rascassa

$$$ | SPANISH | Dine on fresh seafood, grilled meats, and pasta on the tranquil, tree-shaded patio or inside the rustic-chic dining room. From here, it's a short stroll to the secluded Aiguafreda swimming cove. **Known for:** variety of seafood tapas; attractive patio; grilled specialties. ⑤ *Average main: €20 ⊠ Cala Aiguafreda 3, Begur ☎ 972/622845 ⊕ hostalsarascassa. com ⊗ Closed Tues. and Nov.–Mar.*

### Restaurant Ibèric

$$$ | CATALAN | This excellent pocket of authentic Costa Brava cuisine serves everything from snails to wild boar in season. Wild mushrooms scrambled with eggs or stewed with hare are specialties. **Known for:** excellent local wine list; lovely terrace; eclectic cuisine. ⑤ *Average main: €20 ⊠ Carrer Valls 11, Ullastret ☎ 972/757108 ⊕ www.restaurantiberic.com ⊗ Closed Mon. No dinner Sun.–Thurs.*

##  Hotels

### ★ Hotel Aigua Blava

**$$$$ | HOTEL | FAMILY |** What began as a small hostel in the 1920s is now a sprawling luxury hotel, run by the fourth generation of the same family. **Pros:** impeccable service; private playground; gardens and pleasant patios at every turn. **Cons:** expensive restaurant; no beach in the inlet; no elevator. ⑤ *Rooms from: €200 ⊠ Platja de Fornells s/n, Begur ☎ 972/622058 ⊕ www.aiguablava.com ☉ Closed Nov.–mid-Apr. ⇌ 85 rooms ⊙⧵ Free Breakfast.*

### La Bionda

**$$$ | HOTEL |** Located in Begur's medieval old town, this eco-friendly boutique hotel embraces the building's 17th-century architecture while introducing modern elements, like a greenhouse-style breakfast room. **Pros:** beautifully designed interiors; medieval center location; rooftop hot tub. **Cons:** rooms are on the smaller side; far from the beaches; parking is off-site. ⑤ *Rooms from: €175 ⊠ Carrer Francesc Forgas 1, Begur ☎ 621/315283 ⊕ labiondabegur.com ⇌ 8 rooms ⊙⧵ Free Breakfast.*

# Cadaqués and Around

*70 km (43 miles) north of Begur.*

Spain's easternmost town, Cadaqués, still has the whitewashed charm that transformed this fishing village into an international artists' haunt in the early 20th century. Salvador Dalí's house, now a museum, is at Portlligat, a 15-minute walk north of town.

## ◉ Sights

### ★ Cap de Creus

**NATURE SIGHT |** North of Cadaqués, Spain's easternmost point is a fundamental pilgrimage, if only for the symbolic geographical rush. The hike out to the lighthouse—through rosemary, thyme, and the salt air of the Mediterranean—is unforgettable. The Pyrenees officially end (or rise) here. New Year's Day finds mobs of revelers awaiting the first emergence of the "new" sun from the Mediterranean.

Gaze down at heart-pounding views of the craggy coast and crashing waves with a warm mug of coffee in hand or fine fare on the table at Bar Restaurant Cap de Creus, which sits on a rocky crag above the Cap de Creus. On a summer evening, you may be lucky and stumble upon some live music on the terrace. ⊠ *Carrer de Cadaqués al Cap de Creus.*

### ★ Casa Salvador Dalí - Portlligat

**HISTORIC HOME |** This was Dalí's summerhouse and a site long associated with the artist's notorious frolics with everyone from poets Federico García Lorca and Paul Eluard to filmmaker Luis Buñuel. Filled with bits of the surrealist's daily life, it's an important point in the "Dalí triangle," completed by the castle at Púbol and the Teatre-Museu Dalí in Figueres.

You can get here by a 3-km (2-mile) walk north along the beach from Cadaqués. Only small groups of visitors are admitted at any given time, and advance reservations are required. ⊠ *Portlligat s/n, Cadaqués ☎ 972/251015 ⊕ www.salvador-dali.org ☜ €14; advance reservations required ☉ Closed Mon. Nov.–Mar. ⚠ Reservations essential.*

### ★ Sant Pere de Rodes

**HISTORIC SIGHT |** The monastery of Sant Pere de Rodes, 7 km (4½ miles) by car (plus a 20-minute walk) above the pretty fishing village of El Port de la Selva, is a spectacular site. Built in the 10th and 11th centuries by Benedictine monks—and sacked and plundered repeatedly since—this restored Romanesque monolith commands a breathtaking panorama of the Pyrenees, the Empordà plain, the sweeping curve of the Bay of Roses, and Cap de Creus. (Topping off the grand trek

The popular harbor of Cadaqués

across the Pyrenees, Cap de Creus is a spectacular six-hour walk from here on the well-marked GR11 trail.)

**■ TIP→ In July and August, the monastery is the setting for the annual Festival Sant Pere (www.festivalsantpere.com), drawing top-tier classical musicians from all over the world. Find event listings online (in Catalan); phone for reservations or to book a post-concert dinner in the monastery's refectory-style restaurant (972/194233).**

✉ Camí del Monestir s/n, El Porte de la Selva ☎ 972/387559 ⊕ patrimoni.gencat.cat/en/monuments ⊠ €6 ۞ Closed Mon.

## 🍴 Restaurants

### ★ Casa Anita

$$$$ | SEAFOOD | Simple, fresh, and generous dishes are the draw at this informal little eatery, an institution in Cadaqués. Tables are shared, and there is no menu; the staff recite the offerings of the day, which might include local prawns and sardines *a la plancha* (grilled), mussels, and sea bass. **Known for:** convivial atmosphere; regional wines; no menu. ⑤ Average main: €30 ✉ Carrer Miquel Rosset 16, Cadaqués ☎ 972/258471 ⊕ www.facebook.com/vipcasaanita ۞ Closed Mon.

### Compartir

$$$$ | CATALAN | The word "compartir" means "to share" and this excellent restaurant bases its menu on a small-plate sharing approach that has been taken to another level by the culinary team of Mateu Casañas, Oriol Castro, and Eduard Xatruch (who also run Barcelona's two-Michelin-starred Disfrutar). Each dish is served by attentive staff within an 18th-century courtyard. **Known for:** beautiful courtyard setting; creative gastronomy; sharing plates. ⑤ Average main: €24 ✉ Riera Sant Vicenç s/n, Cadaqués ☎ 972/258482 ⊕ www.compartir-cadaques.com ۞ Closed Sun. and Mon.

### Restaurant Can Rafa

$$$$ | SEAFOOD | With picture-perfect views of the Cadaqués seafront, this restaurant's terrace is always packed. Check the chalkboard for the day's offerings,

which overwhelmingly focus on local seafood and seafood-based rice dishes. **Known for:** seaside location; excellent wine list; local seafood. $ *Average main: €24 ⊠ Plaça del Passeig 7, Cadaqués* ☎ *972/159401* ⊕ *martinfaixo.com/en/ can-rafa.html* ☉ *No dinner Sun. Winter openings times vary.*

## 🛏 Hotels

### Hotel Llané Petit

$$$ | HOTEL | This small, typically Mediterranean bay-side hotel has a quiet location, a 10-minute seafront amble from Cadaqués center. **Pros:** semiprivate beach next to hotel; outdoor pool; free Wi-Fi. **Cons:** some soundproofing issues; somewhat lightweight beds and furnishings; small rooms. $ *Rooms from: €176 ⊠ Doctor Bartolmeus 37, Cadaqués* ☎ *972/251020* ⊕ *www.llanepetit.com* ☉ *Closed Nov.–Mar.* ⇆ *37 rooms* ⊙I *Free Breakfast.*

### Hotel Playa Sol

$$$$ | HOTEL | FAMILY | In business for more than 50 years, this hotel on the cove of Es Pianc is just a five-minute walk from Cadaqués's center and is a good option for families, with its dedicated family rooms, pool, and bike rental. **Pros:** attentive, friendly service; great views; family-friendly. **Cons:** small rooms; rooms with balcony and sea views are harder to book; pricey rates in summer. $ *Rooms from: €250 ⊠ Platja Pianc 3, Cadaqués* ☎ *972/258100* ⊕ *www.playasol.com* ☉ *Closed Nov.–mid-Feb.* ⇆ *48 rooms* ⊙I *No Meals.*

## Montserrat

*50 km (31 miles) west of Barcelona.*

An easy side trip from Barcelona is a visit to the dramatic, sawtooth peaks of Montserrat, where the shrine of La Moreneta (the Black Virgin of Montserrat) sits. Montserrat is as memorable for its strange topography as it is for its religious treasures. The views over the mountains that stretch all the way to the Mediterranean and, on a clear day, to the Pyrenees, are breathtaking, and the rugged, boulder-strewn terrain makes for exhilarating walks and hikes.

### GETTING HERE AND AROUND

The easiest way to get to Montserrat from Barcelona is by train. Take the FGC (Ferrocarriles) from the Plaça d'Espanya metro station, connecting with either the cable car at Aeri Montserrat or with the rack railway (Cremallera) at Monistrol Montserrat. There are combination tickets sold at the station. Both the cable car and rack railway take 15 minutes and depart about every every 20 minutes. Once you arrive at the monastery, several funiculars can take you farther up the mountain. By car from Barcelona, follow the A2/A7 autopista on the upper ring road (Ronda de Dalt), or from the western end of the Diagonal as far as Salida 25 to Martorell. Bypass this industrial center and follow signs to Montserrat.

## ◉ Sights

### ★ La Moreneta

RELIGIOUS BUILDING | The shrine of La Moreneta, one of Catalonia's patron saints, resides in a Benedictine monastery high in the Serra de Montserrat, surrounded by—and dwarfed by the grandeur of—sheer, jagged peaks. The crests above the monastic complex bristle with chapels and hermitages. The shrine and its setting have given rise to countless legends about what happened here: St. Peter left a statue of the Virgin Mary carved by St. Luke, Parsifal found the Holy Grail, and Wagner (who wrote the opera *Parsifal*) sought musical inspiration.

The shrine is world famous and one of Catalonia's spiritual sanctuaries, and not just for the monks who reside here—honeymooning couples flock here by the thousands seeking La Moreneta's blessing on their marriages, and twice a year, on April 27 and September 8, the diminutive statue of Montserrat's Black Virgin becomes the object of one of Spain's greatest pilgrimages. Only the basilica and museum are regularly open to the public. ■TIP→ The famous Escolania de Montserrat boys' choir sings the Salve and Virulai from the liturgy weekdays at 1 pm and Sunday at noon. ⊠ *Montserrat* ☎ *93/8777777* ⊕ *www.montserratvisita. com* ✉ *€16 sanctuary, audio guide, museum, and audiovisual presentation.*

# Sitges

*43 km (27 miles) southwest of Barcelona.*

Sitges is the prettiest and most popular resort in Barcelona's immediate environs, with excellent beaches and a whitewashed and flowery old quarter. It's also one of Europe's premier gay resorts. From April through September, and on sunny, warm weekends year-round, its wide, sandy beaches swell with tourists and local day-trippers.

On the eastern end of the strand is an alabaster statue of the 16th-century painter El Greco, usually associated with Toledo, where he spent most of his professional career. The artist Santiago Rusiñol is responsible for this surprise; he was such a Greco fan that he not only installed two of his paintings in his Museu del Cau Ferrat but also had this sculpture planted on the beach.

Two nearby Cistercian monasteries to the west of Sitges, Santes Creus and Santa Maria de Poblet, can be seen in a day—provided you have a car.

## GETTING HERE AND AROUND

There's regular train service from all three Barcelona stations to Sitges. The journey takes about 40 minutes (€4.10 each way). It's about a 10-minute walk to the nearest beach from the station.

Buses, roughly the same price, run at least hourly from Plaza Espanya and take about 45 minutes, depending how many stops they make. If you're driving, head south on the C32; for more dramatic vistas, take the C31 coastal road.

## ⊙ Sights

### Beaches

**BEACH | FAMILY** | Sitges's coastline counts around 18 beaches, with many being easily accessible by foot from the old town. The most central, and hence the busiest, are Ribera and Fragata. Neighboring Bassa Rodona is a popular gay beach. Quieter, more family-friendly beaches are Sant Sebastià, to the east, which also has a large playground, and at the far western edge, Terramar, with a swimming cove that allows for calm, protected swimming. ⊠ *Sitges.*

### Museu de Maricel

**ART MUSEUM** | American industrialist Charles Deering's magnificent early 20th-century palace, perched on a cliff overlooking the Mediterranean, is home to this eclectic collection that spans 10 centuries. It includes Romanesque and Gothic altarpieces, paintings from the Neoclassic period, and Modernisme works by artists linked to Sitges. It's worth a visit if only to see the dedicated sculpture room, with *noucentista* sculptures by Joan Rebull framed by enormous windows offering jaw-dropping views of crashing waves below. ⊠ *Carrer Fonollar s/n, Sitges* ☎ *938/940364* ⊕ *museusdesitges.cat/en* ✉ *€10, includes Museu del Cau Ferrat* ☉ *Closed Mon.*

### ★ Museu del Cau Ferrat

**ART MUSEUM** | This is the most interesting museum in Sitges, established by the bohemian artist and cofounder of El Quatre Gats café in Barcelona, Santiago Rusiñol (1861–1931), and containing some of his own paintings together with works by El Greco and Picasso. Connoisseurs of wrought iron will love

Whitewashed buildings dominate the landscape in Sitges.

the beautiful collection of *cruces termi-nales*, crosses that once marked town boundaries. ✉ *Carrer Fonollar 6, Sitges* ☎ *938/940364* ⊕ *www.museusdesitges. com* 🎟 *€10, includes Museu del Maricel* 🕒 *Closed Mon.*

### Passeig Maritim

**PROMENADE** | A focal point of Sitges life, this 1½-mile-long esplanade is an iconic pedestrianized promenade that sweeps along the bay of Sitges. It's backed by upmarket villas, boutique hotels, restaurants, and bars. ✉ *Passeig Maritim, Sitges.*

## 🍴 Restaurants

### Chiringuito

**$$$** | **TAPAS** | Spelled with a capital C, this legendary seaside spot opened in 1913 and spawned the term that's given to similar bars dotting the Spanish coast. There's nothing particularly outstanding about the food—typical seafood tapas, much of it fried—but the waterfront ter-race is ideal for soaking up the sun and more than a century of history. **Known for:** sea views; so-so food; historical eatery. 💲 *Average main: €18* ✉ *Passeig de la Ribera 31, Sitges* ☎ *938/947596* ⊕ *www. facebook.com/chiringuitositges.*

### ★ El Cable

**$$** | **TAPAS** | There's almost always a line outside this old-school, family-owned tapas bar, a local favorite since its found-ing in 1940. If you can't get a table, sidle up to the long wood bar, choose from the display of bite-sized, toothpick-speared *pintxos*, and eat them standing, just like a local. **Known for:** patatas bravas; inexpen-sive food and drink; variety of pintxos. 💲 *Average main: €12* ✉ *Carrer Barcelona 1, Sitges* ☎ *938/948761* ⊕ *www.elcable. cat.*

### Vivero

**$$$** | **SEAFOOD** | Carved into a rocky point above Playa San Sebastiá, the multi-level Vivero is actually three distinct spaces: a casual, alfresco tapas spot up top; a swankier "beach club" at the bottom; and sandwiched between is a bi-level indoor/outdoor restaurant, with a wide variety of seafood dishes and paellas. Whichever you choose, the real reason to come is for the magnificent views, especially at sunset. **Known for:** outdoor dining; several spaces with different vibes; wonderful sea views. $ Average main: €22 ⊠ Passeig Balmins s/n, Playa San Sebastián, Sitges ☎ 938/942149 ⊕ www.elviverositges.com ⊗ No dinner.

##  Hotels

### ★ ME Sitges Terramar
**$$$$ | HOTEL |** From the buzzy rooftop with cocktails and street food to the superb seaside restaurant to the beach club where you can lounge in a hammock with your toes in the sand, this beachfront hotel is one of Sitges' top stays. **Pros:** excellent dining and drinking options; seaside location; organic spa with vegan products. **Cons:** a half-hour walk to town center; some amenities are only open seasonally; no restaurants nearby. $ Rooms from: €200 ⊠ Passeig Marítim 80, Sitges ☎ 938/940050 ⊕ www.mebymelia.com ⇥ 213 rooms �*⊙*| No Meals.

### Meliá Sitges
**$$$ | HOTEL | FAMILY |** Set on a hilltop in a peaceful residential area, this hotel offers bright, spacious, contemporary rooms with furnished balconies—many of which have sea views. **Pros:** wide variety of room/bed configurations; all rooms have balconies; family-friendly with kids' amenities. **Cons:** a 15-minute walk to town; somewhat corporate in feel; common areas could use a refresh. $ Rooms from: €150 ⊠ Carrer de Joan Salvat Papasseit 38, Sitges ☎ 938/110811 ⊕ www.melia.com ⇥ 307 rooms ⊙| No Meals.

## ⊻ Nightlife

Much of Sitges' nightlife revolves around gay bars and dance clubs, with a high concentration along Carrer Sant Bonaventura, Carrer de Joan Tarrida, Carrer

Bonaire, and Carrer Primer de Maig (aka the Street of Sin). Some are hard-core leather and biker bars, while others have a more straight-friendly vibe. Keep in mind that most don't open until 11 pm.

### El Gin Tub
**COCKTAIL LOUNGES |** Head down a flight of stairs to this underground speakeasy, decorated in a Victorian style and featuring a menu of classic cocktails—many made with house-infused gin. There's live music and burlesque nearly every night. ⊠ Calle Parellades 43, Sitges ☎ 65/600693 ⊕ elgintub.com.

### Pub Voramar
**BARS |** Nautical knick-knacks line every square inch of this cozy tavern, which dates back to 1956. A small terrace overlooks Sant Sebastià beach. ⊠ Port Alegre 55, Sitges ☎ 938/944403.

# Santes Creus

95 km (59 miles) west of Barcelona.

Head inland and you discover how much the art and architecture—the very tone of Catalan culture—owes to its medieval religious heritage. Monolithic Romanesque architecture and beautiful cloisters characterize the Cistercian monastery of Santes Creus.

## GETTING HERE AND AROUND
It's a 1¼-hour drive to Santes Creus from Barcelona via the AP-7, followed by the AP-2 (Lleida), C51 and TP2002. From Sitges, it's 45 minutes; take the C32 west to the AP-7 and follow the above directions.

## ⊙ Sights

### Santes Creus
**RELIGIOUS BUILDING |** Founded in 1158 on the banks of the Gaià River, Santes Creus is one of Catalonia's largest and best-preserved Cistercian monasteries. Its otherwise austere church features glorious

Cistercian and Gothic stained-glass windows and the royal tombs of King Peter III and James II and his wife Blanche of Anjou of the Kingdom of Aragón. Other highlights include the ornate 14th-century Gothic cloisters. ⊠ *Pl. Jaume el Just s/n, Santes Creus* ☎ *977/638329* ⊕ *patrimoni. gencat.cat/en/monuments/monuments/ royal-monastery-of-santes-creus* ⌨ *€6* ⊙ *Closed Mon.*

# Santa Maria de Poblet

*8 km (5 miles) west of Santes Creus.*

This splendid Cistercian monastery, located at the foot of the Prades Mountains, is one of the great masterpieces of Spanish monastic architecture. Declared a UNESCO World Heritage Site, the cloister is a stunning combination of lightness and size, and on sunny days the shadows on the yellow sandstone are extraordinary.

## GETTING HERE AND AROUND

From Barcelona to Poblet, it's a 1½-hour drive via the AP7 and AP2, or about one hour from Sitges, via the C32 and AP-2 (Exit 9 when coming from Sitges).

## ⊙ Sights

### ★ Monasterio de Santa María de Poblet

RELIGIOUS BUILDING | Founded in 1150 by Ramón Berenguer IV in gratitude for the Christian Reconquest, the monastery first housed a dozen Cistercians from Narbonne. Later, the Crown of Aragón used Santa Maria de Poblet for religious retreats and burials. The building was damaged in an 1836 anticlerical revolt, and monks of the reformed Cistercian Order have managed the difficult task of restoration since 1940. Today, a community of 25 monks and novices still pray before the splendid retable over the tombs of Aragonese rulers, restored to their former glory by sculptor Frederic Marès. ⊠ *Off AP-2 (Exit 9 from*

---

## Celebrated Onions 🍽

**Valls.** This town, famous for its early spring *calçotada* (onion feast) held on the last Sunday of January, is 10 km (6 miles) from Santes Creus and 15 km (9 miles) from Poblet. Even if you miss the big day, calçots are served November through April at rustic farmhouses such as Cal Ganxo in nearby Masmolets (⊠ *Carrer de la Font F 14* ☎ *977/605960*).

---

*Barcelona, Exit 8 from Lleida), Pl. Corona de Aragón 11* ☎ *977/870089* ⊕ *www. poblet.cat* ⌨ *€8.50.*

# Tarragona

*98 km (61 miles) southwest of Barcelona, 251 km (156 miles) northeast of Valencia.*

Tarragona, the principal town of southern Catalonia, today is a vibrant center of culture and art, a busy fishing and shipping port, and a natural jumping-off point for the towns and pristine beaches of Sitges and the Costa Daurada, 216 km (134 miles) of coastline. However, in Roman times, Tarragona was one of the finest and most important outposts of the Empire, and was famous for its wine even before that. The town's population was the first *gens togata* (literally, the toga-clad people) in Spain, which conferred on them equality with the citizens of Rome. Its vast Roman remains, chief among them the Circus Maximus, bear witness to Tarragona's grandeur, and to this the Middle Ages added wonderful city walls and citadels. Due to its Roman remains and medieval Christian monuments, Tarragona has been designated a UNESCO World Heritage Site.

Though modern, Tarragona has preserved its heritage superbly. Stroll along the town's cliff-side perimeter and you'll see why the Romans set up shop here: Tarragona is strategically positioned at the center of a broad, open bay, with an unobstructed view of the sea. As capital of the Roman province of Hispania Tarraconensis (from 218 BC), Tarraco (as it was then called) formed the empire's principal stronghold in Spain. St. Paul preached here in AD 58, and Tarragona became the seat of the Christian church in Spain until it was superseded by Toledo in the 11th century.

If you're entering the city en route from Barcelona, you'll pass the **Triumphal Arch of Berà**, dating from the 3rd century BC, 19 km (12 miles) north of Tarragona; and from the Lleida (Lérida) autopista, you can see the 1st-century **Roman aqueduct** that helped carry fresh water 32 km (20 miles) from the Gaià River. Tarragona is divided clearly into old and new by Rambla Vella; the old town and most of the Roman remains are to the north, while modern Tarragona spreads out to the south. Start your visit at acacia-lined Rambla Nova, at the end of which is a balcony overlooking the sea, the **Balcó del Mediterràni**. Then walk uphill along Passeig de les Palmeres and look below to view the ancient amphitheater in all its glory.

### GETTING HERE AND AROUND

Tarragona is well connected by train. From Barcelona, direct high-speed trains take about 35 minutes, arriving at Camp de Tarragona station, a 10-minute taxi ride to the center. Slower regional trains take about 1 hour 15 minutes but do stop in the city center. Tickets start at €8.05. There is also regular train service from other major cities, including Madrid.

Buses are frequent between Barcelona and Tarragona—7 to 10 leave Barcelona's Estació del Nord for Tarragona every day. Connections between Tarragona and Valencia are frequent, too. There are also

bus connections with the main Andalusian cities, plus Alicante and Madrid.

Tours of the cathedral and archaeological sites are organized by the tourist office, located just below the cathedral.

### VISITOR INFORMATION

**CONTACTS Visitor Information Tarragona.** ⊠ Carrer Major 37, Tarragona ☎ 977/250795 ⊕ www.tarragonaturisme. cat/en.

## ⊙ Sights

### Amphitheater

**RUINS** | Tarragona, the Emperor Augustus's favorite winter resort, had arguably the finest amphitheater in Roman Iberia, built in the 2nd century AD for gladiatorial and other contests. The remains have a spectacular view of the sea. You're free to wander through the access tunnels and along the tiers of seats. In the center of the theater are the remains of two superimposed churches, the earlier of which was a Visigothic basilica built to mark the bloody martyrdom of St. Fructuós and his deacons in AD 259. ⊠ Parc de l'Amphiteatre Roma s/n, Tarragona ☎ 977/242579 ⊕ www.tarragona.cat/ patrimoni/museu-historia ☜ €3.30 (joint entry with 4 monuments, €7.40; all monuments €11.05) ۞ Closed Mon.

### Casa Castellarnau

**HISTORY MUSEUM** | The headquarters of the city's Museu d'Història (History Museum), with plans showing the evolution of the city, this Gothic palauet (town house) built by Tarragona nobility in the 18th century includes stunning furnishings from the 18th and 19th centuries. The last member of the Castellarnau family vacated the house in 1954. The museum's highlight is the Hippolytus Sarcophagus, which bears a bas-relief depicting the legend of Hippolytus and Fraeda. ⊠ Carrer dels Cavallers 14, Tarragona ☎ 977/242220 ⊕ www.tarragona. cat/patrimoni/museu-historia ☜ €3.30

*(joint entry with 4 monuments, €7.40; all monuments €11.05)* ⊙ *Closed Mon.*

### Catedral

**RELIGIOUS BUILDING** | Built between the 12th and 14th centuries on the site of a Roman temple and a mosque, this cathedral shows the transition from Romanesque to Gothic style. The initial rounded placidity of the Romanesque apse gave way to the spiky restlessness of the Gothic—the result is somewhat confusing.

The main attraction here is the 15th-century Gothic alabaster altarpiece of Sant Tecla by Pere Joan, a richly detailed depiction of the life of Tarragona's patron saint. Converted by Sant Paul and subsequently persecuted by local pagans, Sant Tecla was repeatedly saved from demise through divine intervention. ⊠ *Pl. de la Seu s/n, Tarragona* ☎ *977/226935* ⊕ *www.catedraldetarragona.com* ☑ *€5 (cathedral and museum)* ⊙ *Closed Sun. mid-Sept.–mid-Jun.*

### Circ Romà *(Roman Circus)*

**RUINS** | Students have excavated the vaults of the 1st-century AD Roman arena, near the amphitheater. The plans just inside the gate show that the vaults now visible formed only a small corner of a vast space (350 yards long), where 23,000 spectators gathered to watch chariot races. As medieval Tarragona grew, the city gradually engulfed the circus. ⊠ *Rambla Vella 2, Tarragona* ☎ *977/221736* ⊕ *www.tarragona.cat/ patrimoni/museu-historia* ☑ *€3.30 (joint entry with 4 monuments, €7.40; all monuments €11.05)* ⊙ *Closed Mon.*

### El Serrallo

**NEIGHBORHOOD** | The always-entertaining fishing quarter and harbor are below the city near the bus station and the mouth of the Francolí River. Restaurants in the port, such as the popular El Pòsit del Serrallo (Moll des Pescadors 25), offer fresh fish in a rollicking environment. ⊠ *Tarragona.*

### Museu Paleocristià i Necrópolis *(Early-Christian Museum and Necropolis)*

**RUINS** | Just uphill from the fish market are this early Christian necropolis and museum. In 1923, the remains of a burial ground were discovered during the construction of a tobacco factory. The excavations on display—more than 2,000 tombs, sarcophagi, and funeral objects—allow visitors a fascinating insight into Roman funeral practices and rituals. ⊠ *Av. Ramon y Cajal 84, Tarragona* ☎ *977/251515* ⊕ *www.mnat.cat/ museu-i-necropolis-paleocristians* ☑ *€4* ⊙ *Closed Mon.*

### Passeig Arqueològic

**PROMENADE** | A 1½-km (1-mile) circular path skirting the surviving section of the 3rd-century-BC Ibero-Roman ramparts, this walkway was built on even earlier walls of giant rocks. On the other side of the path is a glacis, a fortification added by English military engineers in 1707 during the War of the Spanish Succession. Look for the rusted bronze of Romulus and Remus. ⊠ *Access from Via de l'Imperi Romà, Tarragona.*

### Praetorium

**RUINS** | This towering building was Augustus's town house, and is reputed to be the birthplace of Pontius Pilate. Its Gothic appearance is the result of extensive alterations in the Middle Ages, when it housed the kings of Catalonia and Aragón during their visits to Tarragona. ⊠ *Pl. del Rei, Tarragona* ☎ *977/221736* ⊕ *www. tarragona.cat/patrimoni/museu-historia* ☑ *€3.30 (joint entry with 4 monuments, €7.40; all monuments €11.05)* ⊙ *Closed Mon.*

## 🍴 Restaurants

### Arcs

**$$$ | CATALAN** | Stone arches dating from the 14th-century frame the tables at this atmospheric restaurant in the historical Part Alta. The cooking is smart and modern, with a focus on seasonal, local ingredients, like the crispy veal canneloni topped with a reduction of Priorat, an intense red wine from the Tarragona province. **Known for:** innovative cooking; great service; dramatic setting. $ *Average main: €20 ⊠ Carrer Misser Sitges 13, Tarragona ☎ 977/218040 ⊕ restaurantarcs.com ⊗ Closed Mon. No dinner Sun.–Wed.*

### Les Coques

**$$$** | **CATALAN** | If you have time for only one meal in the city, take it at this elegant little restaurant in the heart of historic Tarragona. The menu is bursting with both mountain and Mediterranean fare, and the prix fixe lunch is a bargain at €19. **Known for:** good wine list; good-value prix fixe lunch; mountain fare. $ *Average main: €22 ⊠ Carrer Sant Llorenç 15, Tarragona ☎ 977/228300 ⊕ www.les-coques.com ⊗ Closed Mon. No dinner Sun.–Thurs.*

 **Hotels**

### Hotel Plaça de la Font

**$** | **HOTEL** | The central location and the cute rooms at this budget choice just off the Rambla Vella in the Plaça de la Font make for a practical base for exploring downtown Tarragona. **Pros:** easy on the budget; nearby public parking lot; comfortable, charming rooms. **Cons:** basic facilities; rooms with balconies can be noisy on weekends; rooms are on the small side. $ *Rooms from: €78 ⊠ Pl. de la Font 26, Tarragona ☎ 977/240882 ⊕ www.hotelpdelafont.com ⌁ 20 rooms ⦿ No Meals.*

### ⦿ Nightlife

Nightlife in Tarragona takes two forms: older and quieter in the upper city, younger and more raucous down below. There are some lovely rustic bars and wine bars in the *casco antiguo*, the upper section of Old Tarragona, around Plaça del Forum and Carrer de Santa Anna. Port Esportiu, a pleasure-boat harbor separate from the

working port, has another row of dining and dancing establishments; young people flock here on weekends and summer nights.

### El Korxo

**WINE BARS** | This popular, cozy wine bar, with chunky wooden tables, subdued lighting, and quirky creative details, offers its clientele a taste of different wines from around Spain, as well as craft beers, charcuterie and cheeses, and other light snacks. ⊠ *Santa Anna 6, Tarragona ☎ 692/460018 ⊕ www.facebook.com/korxo.vinsitapes/.*

### 🛍 Shopping

### Carrer Major

**ANTIQUES & COLLECTIBLES** | You have to bargain hard but Carrer Major has some exciting antiques stores. They're worth a thorough rummage, as the gems tend to be hidden. ⊠ *Carrer Major, Tarragona.*

# Valencia

*351 km (218 miles) southwest of Barcelona, 357 km (222 miles) southeast of Madrid.*

Valencia, Spain's third-largest municipality, is a proud city with a thriving nightlife and restaurant scene, quality museums, and spectacular contemporary architecture, juxtaposed with a thoroughly charming historic quarter. During the civil war, it was the last seat of the Republican Loyalist government (1935–36), holding out against Franco's National forces until the country fell to 40 years of dictatorship. Today it represents the essence of contemporary Spain—daring design and architecture along with experimental cuisine—but remains deeply conservative and proud of its traditions. Although it faces the Mediterranean, Valencia's history and geography have been defined most significantly by the Turia River and the fertile huerta that surrounds it.

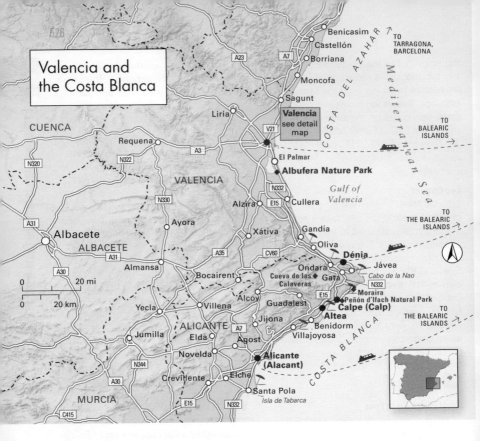

## Valencia and the Costa Blanca

The city has been fiercely contested ever since it was founded by the Greeks. El Cid captured Valencia from the Moors in 1094 and won his strangest victory here in 1099: he died in the battle, but his corpse was strapped into his saddle and so frightened the besieging Moors that it caused their complete defeat. In 1102 El Cid's widow, Jimena, was forced to return the city to Moorish rule; Jaume I finally drove them out in 1238. Modern Valencia was best known for its frequent disastrous floods until the Turia River was diverted to the south in the late 1950s. Since then the city has been on a steady course of urban beautification. The lovely bridges that once spanned the Turia look equally graceful spanning a wandering municipal park, and the spectacularly futuristic Ciutat de les Arts i les Ciències (City of Arts and Sciences), most of it designed by Valencia-born architect

Santiago Calatrava, has at last created an exciting architectural link between this river town and the Mediterranean. If you're in Valencia, an excursion to Albufera Nature Park (which is said to be the birthplace of paella) is a worthwhile day trip.

## GETTING HERE AND AROUND
By car, Valencia is about 3½ hours from Madrid via the A3 motorway, and about the same from Barcelona on the AP-7 toll road. Valencia is well connected by bus and train, with regular service to and from cities throughout the country, including 10 daily AVE high-speed express trains from Madrid, making the trip in 1 hour 40 minutes, and six express trains (Euromed and ALVIA) daily from Barcelona, taking 2 hours 40 minutes. Valencia's bus station is across the river from the old town; frequent buses make

the four-hour trip from Madrid and the five-hour trip from Barcelona. Dozens of airlines, large and small, serve Valencia airport, connecting the city with cities throughout Spain and the rest of Europe.

Once you're here, the city has an efficient network of bus, tram, and metro service. For timetables and more information, stop by a local tourist office. There are six of them throughout the city, including at the airport, the Joaquín Sorolla train station, and city hall.

### BUS CONTACT Valencia Bus Station.
⊠ *Carrer de Menendez Pidal 11, Valencia* ☎ *963/466266.*

## FESTIVALS
### Gran Fira de València (Great Valencia Fair)
ARTS FESTIVALS | Valencia's monthlong festival, in July, celebrates theater, film, dance, and music. Check the website for the latest updates. ⊠ *Valencia* ⊕ *gran-firavalencia.com.*

### ★ Las Fallas
FESTIVALS | If you want nonstop nightlife at its frenzied best, come during the climactic days of Las Fallas, March 15–19 (the festival begins March 1), when revelers throng the streets to see the gargantuan *ninots,* effigies made of wood, paper, and plaster depicting satirical scenes and famous people. Last call at many bars and clubs isn't until the wee hours, if at all. On the last night, all the effigies but one (the winner is spared) are burned to the ground during La Crema, and it seems as though the entire city is ablaze. ⊠ *Valencia* ⊕ *www. visitvalencia.com.*

## TOURS
### Valencia Bus Turístic
BUS TOURS | FAMILY | Valencia's double-decker tourist bus allows you to hop on and hop off as you please, while audio commentary introduces the city's history and highlights. It runs daily, from approximately 10–9 (hours vary depending on the season), and departs every 20–30 minutes from 17 boarding points.

The cost of the 24- and 48-hour tickets are €19 and €20, respectively. The same company also offers a two-hour guided trip (€19) to Albufera Nature Park, including an excursion by boat through the wetlands, departing from the Plaza de la Reina. ⊠ *Valencia* ☎ *699/982514* ⊕ *www. valenciabusturistic.com* ☒ *From €17.*

## VISITOR INFORMATION
**CONTACTS Valencia Tourist Office.**
⊠ *Pl. del Ayuntamiento 1, Valencia* ☎ *963/524908* ⊕ *www.visitvalencia.com.*

## ◉ Sights

### Casa Museo José Benlliure
ART MUSEUM | The modern Valencian painter and sculptor José Benlliure (1858–1937) is known for his intimate portraits and massive historical and religious paintings, many of which hang in Valencia's Museo de Bellas Artes (Museum of Fine Arts). Here in his elegant house and studio are 50 of his works, including paintings, ceramics, sculptures, and drawings. Also on display are works by his son, Pepino, who painted in the small, flower-filled garden in the back of the house, and iconographic sculptures by Benlliure's brother, the well-known sculptor Mariano Benlliure. ⊠ *Calle Blanquerías 23, Valencia* ☎ *963/911662* ☒ *€2; free Sun.* ☉ *Closed Mon.*

### ★ Catedral de Valencia
CHURCH | Valencia's 13th- to 15th-century cathedral is the heart of the city. The building has three portals—Romanesque, Gothic, and rococo. Inside, Renaissance and baroque marble were removed to restore the original Gothic style, as is now the trend in Spanish churches. The Capilla del Santo Cáliz (Chapel of the Holy Chalice) displays a purple agate vessel purported to be the Holy Grail (Christ's cup at the Last Supper) and thought to have been brought to Spain in the 4th century. Behind the altar is the left arm of St. Vincent, martyred in Valencia in 304.

Valencia's L'Oceanogràfic (Ciutat de les Arts i les Ciènces) has amazing exhibits, as well as an underwater restaurant.

Stars of the cathedral museum are Goya's two famous paintings of St. Francis de Borja, Duke of Gandia. Left of the entrance is the octagonal tower El Miguelete, which you can climb (207 steps) to the top (entry, €2): the roofs of the old town create a kaleidoscope of orange and brown terra-cotta, with the sea in the background. ⊠ *Pl. de l'Almoina, s/n, Ciutat Vella* ☎ *963/918127* ⊕ *www.catedraldevalencia.es* ⊠ *€8, includes audio guide.*

### ★ Centre del Carme Cultura Contemporánia (CCCC)

ARTS CENTER | Occupying a 13th-century Cistercian monastery in the old city's bohemian Carmen quarter, this arts center showcases contemporary art juxtaposed against a historical setting. Rotating exhibitions featuring paintings, sculpture, and video installations take place in marvelously dramatic spaces, including a 13th-century monks' dormitory and an ancient Gothic cloister. ⊠ *Carrer del Museu 2, El Carmen* ☎ *961/922640* ⊕ *www.consorcimuseus.gva.es* ⊠ *Free* ⊙ *Closed Mon.*

### ★ Ciutat de les Arts i les Ciències (*City of Arts and Sciences*)

SCIENCE MUSEUM | FAMILY | Designed mainly by native son Santiago Calatrava, this sprawling futuristic complex is the home of Valencia's Museu de les Ciències (Science Museum), Hemisfèric (Hemispheric Planetarium), Oceanogràfic (Oceanographic Park), and Palau de les Arts (Palace of the Arts, an opera house and cultural center). With resplendent buildings resembling crustaceans, the Ciutat is a favorite of architecture buffs and curious kids.

The Science Museum has soaring platforms filled with lasers, holograms, simulators, hands-on experiments, and a swell "zero gravity" exhibition on space exploration. The eye-shaped planetarium projects 3-D virtual voyages on its huge IMAX screen. At Oceanogràfic (the work of architect Felix Candela), home to the largest aquarium in Europe, you can take a submarine ride through a coastal marine habitat. ✉ *Av. del Profesor López Piñero 7, Valencia* ☎ *961/974686* ⊕ *www.cac.es* ✉ *Science Museum €8, Oceanogràfic €32, Hemisfèric €8. Combined ticket €39.*

### Institut Valencià d'Art Modern (IVAM)

**ART MUSEUM** | Dedicated to modern and contemporary art, this blocky building on the edge of the old city—where the riverbed makes a loop—houses a permanent collection of 20th-century avant-garde painting, European Informalism (including the Spanish artists Antonio Saura, Antoni Tàpies, and Eduardo Chillida), pop art, and photography. Note that, during recent renovations (slated to end in early 2023), the permanent collection was being temporarily housed in Alicante, so only a small portion of the museum was open and entrance was free. Check on the status of the renovations and admission fees before visiting. ✉ *Carrer de Guillem de Castro 118, Ciutat Vella* ☎ *963/176600* ⊕ *www.ivam.es* ⊘ *Closed Mon.* Ⓜ *Line 1.*

### Lonja de la Seda (*Silk Exchange*)

**NOTABLE BUILDING** | On the Plaza del Mercado, this 15th-century building is a product of Valencia's golden age, when the city's prosperity as one of the capitals of the Corona de Aragón made it a leading European commercial and artistic center. The Lonja, a UNESCO World Heritage Site, was constructed as an expression of this splendor and is widely regarded as one of Spain's finest civil Gothic buildings. Its facade is decorated with ghoulish gargoyles, complemented inside by the high vaulting and slender helicoidal (twisted) columns of the cavernous Contract Hall, one of the building's three separate sections. The upper level of the Pavilion of the Consulate of the Sea is particularly impressive, with its ornate 15th-century wood ceiling. ✉ *Lonja 2, Ciutat Vella* ☎ *962/084153* ✉ *€2; free Sun.* ⊘ *Closed Mon.*

### ★ Mercado Central (*Central Market*)

**MARKET** | This bustling food market (at nearly 88,000 square feet, one of the largest in Europe) is open from 7:30 am to 3 pm, Monday through Saturday. Locals and visitors alike line up at its more than 1,200 colorful stalls to shop for fruit, vegetables, meat, fish, and confectionery. Hop on a stool at The Central Bar, located in the heart of the throng, and taste award-winning chef Ricard Camarena's casual yet no less tasty take on tapas and *bocadillos* (sandwiches), while enjoying front-row-seat viewing of the action. ✉ *Pl. Ciudad de Brujas s/n, Valencia* ☎ *963/829100* ⊕ *www.mercadocentralvalencia.es* ⊘ *Closed Sun.*

### ★ Museo de Bellas Artes (*Museum of Fine Arts*)

**ART MUSEUM** | Valencia was a thriving center of artistic activity in the 15th century—one reason that the city's Museum of Fine Arts, with its lovely palm-shaded cloister, is among the best in Spain. Its permanent collection includes many of the finest paintings by Jacomart and Juan Reixach, members of the group known as the Valencian Primitives, as well as work by Hieronymus Bosch—or El Bosco, as they call him here. The ground floor has a number of brooding, 17th-century Tenebrist masterpieces by Francisco Ribalta and his pupil José Ribera, a Diego Velázquez self-portrait, and a room devoted to Goya.

The museum is at the edge of the Jardines del Real (Royal Gardens; open daily 8–dusk), with its fountains, rose gardens, tree-lined avenues, and small zoo. To get here, cross the old riverbed by the Puente de la Trinidad (Trinity Bridge) to the north bank. ✉ *Calle Sant Pius V 9, Trinitat* ☎ *963/870300* ⊕ *www.museobellasartesvalencia.gva.es* ✉ *Free* ⊘ *Closed Mon.*

### Palacio del Marqués de Dos Aguas (*Ceramics Museum*)

**HISTORY MUSEUM** | Since 1954, this palace has housed the Museo Nacional de

# Valencia

## KEY

- **1** Exploring Sights
- **1** Restaurants
- **1** Hotels

## Sights ▼

1  Casa Museo José
   Benlliure ................. **B1**
2  Catedral de Valencia .... **C3**
3  Centre del Carme
   Cultura Contemporánia
   (CCCC).................... **B1**
4  Ciutat de les Arts i les
   Ciències................... **E7**
5  Institut Valencià d'Art
   Modern (IVAM) .......... **A1**
6  Lonja de la Seda ........ **B3**
7  Mercado Central........ **B4**
8  Museo de Bellas
   Artes .................... **D1**
9  Palacio del Marqués
   de Dos Aguas ............ **C4**
10 Palau de la
   Generalitat............... **C2**
11 Real Colegio de
   Corpus Christi ........... **D4**
12 San Nicolás ............. **B3**

## Restaurants ▼

1  La Pepica ................. **E6**
2  La Riuà .................. **D3**
3  Tinto Fino Ultramarino... **C3**

## Hotels ▼

1  Ad Hoc Monumental ... **D2**
2  Caro Hotel .............. **D2**
3  Palau de la Mar.......... **E6**
4  SH Inglés ................ **D4**
5  Westin Valencia ......... **E6**

Cerámica, with a magnificent collection of local and artisanal ceramics from ancient Greek, Iberian, and Roman times through the 20th century. The selection of traditional Valencian ceramics is especially noteworthy (look for the Valencian kitchen on the second floor).

The building itself, near Plaza Patriarca, has gone through many changes over the years and now has elements of several architectural styles, including a fascinating baroque alabaster facade. Embellished with carvings of fruits and vegetables, the facade was designed in 1740 by Ignacio Vergara. It centers on the two voluptuous male figures representing the Dos Aguas (Two Waters), a reference to Valencia's two main rivers and the origin of the noble title of the Marqués de Dos Aguas. ⊠ *Rinconada Federico García Sanchiz 6, Valencia* ☏ *963/516392* ⌨ *€3; free Sat. 4–8 and Sun.* ⊘ *Closed Mon.*

### Palau de la Generalitat

**NOTABLE BUILDING** | On the left side of the Plaza de la Virgen, fronted by orange trees and box hedges, is this elegant facade. The Gothic building was once the home of the Cortes Valencianas (Valencian Parliament), until it was suppressed by Felipe V for supporting the losing side during the 1700–14 War of the Spanish Succession. The two *salones* (reception rooms) in the older of the two towers have superb woodwork on the ceilings. Don't miss the Salon de los Reyes, a long corridor lined with portraits of Valencia's kings through the ages; 30-minute weekday guided tours (required) are available by calling or emailing (*protocolo. visitaspalau@gva.es*) in advance. ⊠ *Calle Caballeros 2, Valencia* ☏ *963/424636* ⊘ *Closed weekends.*

### Real Colegio Seminario de Corpus Christi

**RELIGIOUS BUILDING** | This seminary, with its church, cloister, and library, is the crown jewel of Valencia's Renaissance architecture. Founded by San Juan de Ribera in the 16th century, it has a lovely Renaissance patio and an ornate church, and its museum—Museum of the Patriarch—holds artworks by Juan de Juanes, Francisco Ribalta, and El Greco. ⊠ *Calle de la Nave 1, Casco Antiguo* ☏ *963/514176* ⊕ *www.seminariocorpuschristi.org* ⌨ *€5.*

### San Nicolás

**CHURCH** | A small plaza contains Valencia's oldest church (dating to the 13th century), once the parish of the Borgia Pope Calixtus III. The first portal you come to, with a tacked-on, rococo bas-relief of the Virgin Mary with cherubs, hints at what's inside: every inch of the originally Gothic church is covered with exuberant ornamentation. ⊠ *Calle Caballeros 35, Casco Antiguo* ☏ *963/913317* ⊕ *www. sannicolasvalencia.com* ⌨ *€7* ⊘ *Closed Mon.*

##  Beaches

### Playa de las Arenas

**BEACH** | This wide (nearly 450 feet) and popular grand municipal beach stretches north from the port and the America's Cup marina more than a kilometer (½ mile) before it gives way to the even busier and livelier Platja de Malvarossa. The Paseo Marítimo promenade runs the length of the beach and is lined with restaurants and hotels. There's no shade anywhere, but the fine golden sand is kept pristine and the water is calm and shallow. **Amenities:** food and drink; lifeguards; showers; toilets; water sports. **Best for:** sunset; swimming; walking; windsurfing. ⊠ *Valencia* ⊕ *www.playadelasarenas.com/en.*

## Restaurants

### La Pepica

**$$$** | **SPANISH** | Locals regard this bustling, informal restaurant, on the promenade at El Cabanyal beach, as the best in town for seafood paella. Founded in 1898, the walls of the establishment are covered with signed pictures of appreciative visitors, from Ernest Hemingway to

## Did You Know?

Valencia's March festival, Las Fallas, is a fabulous 19-day celebration. means "bonfires," and a highlight of the party is when the larger-than-life papier-mâché effigies of various celebrities and political figures are torched to end the festival.

King Juan Carlos and the royal family. **Known for:** historic locale; sea views; locally revered seafood paella. $ *Average main: €20* ✉ *Av. Neptuno 6, Valencia* ☎ *963/710366* ⊕ *www.lapepica.com* ☾ *Closed Mon. Closed evenings except Fri. and Sat. in Dec. and Jan.*

### La Riuà

$$ | SPANISH | A favorite of Valencia's well connected and well-to-do since 1982, this family-run restaurant a few steps from the Plaza de la Reina specializes in seafood dishes like *anguilas* (eels) prepared with *all i pebre* (garlic and pepper), *parrillada de pescado* (selection of freshly grilled fish), and traditional paellas. Lunch begins at 2 and not a moment before. **Known for:** longtime family-run establishment; award-winning dining; specialty eel dish. $ *Average main: €16* ✉ *Calle del Mar 27, Valencia* ☎ *963/914571* ⊕ *www. lariua.com* ☾ *Closed Mon. and Wed. No dinner Tues. and Sun.*

### Tinto Fino Ultramarino

$$$ | ITALIAN | A few steps from the Plaza de la Reina, this cozy spots blends the concept of a tapas bar with that of an Italian wine bar, with dishes like oxtail cannelloni, eggplant "meatballs," and classic lasagna served small plates-style. There's a fantastic list of Valencian, Spanish, and Italian wines, with many available by the glass. **Known for:** tapas-style Italian dishes; friendly service; Valencian wines by the glass. $ *Average main: €20* ✉ *Carrer de la Corretgeria 38, Ciutat Vella* ☎ *963/154599* ⊕ *www.facebook.com/TintoFinoUltramarino* ☾ *No lunch weekdays.*

## 🛏 Hotels

### Ad Hoc Monumental

$$ | HOTEL | This nicely designed 19th-century town house sits on a quiet street at the edge of the old city, a minute's walk from the Plaza Almoina and the cathedral in one direction, and steps from the Turia gardens in the other. **Pros:** close to sights but quiet; great value; courteous, helpful

staff. **Cons:** small rooms; not especially family-oriented; parking can be a nightmare. $ *Rooms from: €90* ✉ *Carrer Boix 4, Ciutat Vella* ☎ *963/919140* ⊕ *www. adhochoteles.com* ⤳ *28 rooms* ⦿| *No Meals.*

### ★ Caro Hotel

$$$$ | HOTEL | Set in a former palace and fusing ancient remnants—including sections of the city's original medieval walls—with sophisticated, contemporary design, this boutique hotel offers a quiet yet central location to explore the old town. **Pros:** close to central attractions; unique, stylish design; excellent breakfast (€22). **Cons:** some rooms are on the smaller side; minimalist design may not appeal to all; tall guests should avoid upper-floor rooms with sloped ceilings. $ *Rooms from: €200* ✉ *Carrer de l'Almirall 14, Ciutat Vella* ☎ *963/059000* ⊕ *www.carohotel.com* ⤳ *26 rooms* ⦿| *No Meals.*

### Palau de la Mar

$$$$ | HOTEL | In a restored 19th-century palace, this boutique hotel looks out at the Porta de La Mar, which marked the entry to the old walled quarter of Valencia. **Pros:** big bathrooms with double sinks; courtyard and garden; great location near the sights and shops. **Cons:** small gym; rooms overlooking road can be noisy; top-floor rooms have low, slanted ceilings. $ *Rooms from: €240* ✉ *Av. Navarro Reverter 14, Ciutat Vella* ☎ *963/162884* ⊕ *www.hospes.com/en/palau-mar* ⤳ *66 rooms* ⦿| *Free Breakfast.*

### SH Inglés

$$ | HOTEL | This nicely designed boutique hotel, located in a renovated 18th-century building, features a wide variety of layouts in its 63 rooms. **Pros:** attractive design; central location; friendly service. **Cons:** rooms at the front have street noise; little soundproofing between rooms; beds are small. $ *Rooms from: €110* ✉ *Carrer del Marquès de Dos Aigües 6, Ciutat Vella* ☎ *963/516426*

⊕ www.sh-hoteles.com ⤳ 63 rooms ⏀ No Meals.

### Westin Valencia

$$$$ | HOTEL | Set in 1917 building in a quiet area of the city, this stately hotel features an enormous, lushly planted interior garden surrounded by dining terraces of its three restaurants. **Pros:** professional multilingual staff; large rooms; beautiful courtyard garden. **Cons:** surrounding area not particularly interesting; 20-minute walk to the old town; rooms could use a refresh. ⑤ Rooms from: €250 ⊠ Av. Amadeo de Saboya 16, Pl. del Reial ☎ 963/625900 ⊕ www.marriott.com ⤳ 135 rooms ⏀ No Meals.

## 🍸 Nightlife

Valencianos have perfected the art of doing without sleep. Nightlife in the old town centers on Barrio del Carmen, a lively web of streets that unfolds north of Plaza del Mercado. Popular bars and pubs dot Calle Caballeros, starting at Plaza de la Virgen; the Plaza del Tossal also has some buzzy cafés, as does Calle Alta, off Plaza San Jaime.

The newest, hippest district is Russafa (Ruzafa in Spanish), where on any given night, a trendy, mostly younger crowd hops among its many bars, restaurants, and café terraces. Most can be found along the main thoroughfare, Calle de Ruzafa, and the surrounding streets of Cadiz, Sueca, and Literat Azorín.

Check out the English-language nightlife and culture website 24/7 Valencia (⊕ www.247valencia.com) to see the latest on what's happening in the city.

### BARS AND CAFÉS

#### Café de las Horas

BARS | This surreal bordello-style bar is an institution for Valencia's signature cocktail, Agua de Valencia (a syrupy blend of cava or Champagne, orange juice, vodka, and gin). The bar's warm atmosphere and convivial vibe are perfect for whiling away the hours at the start (or end) of the night. ⊠ Calle Conde de Almodóvar 1, Valencia ☎ 963/917336 ⊕ cafedelashoras.com.

### ★ La Fabrica de Hielo

BARS | A former ice factory on Cabanyal Beach has been transformed into this industrial-chic drinking spot, complete with soaring ceilings, exposed brick walls, and vintage furnishings. Inexpensive drinks and bar food and a seaside terrace attract a trendy crowd, as does the free live music most nights. ⊠ C. de Pavia 37, Trinitat ☎ 963/682619 ⊕ www.lafabricadehielo.net.

### Mes Amours

WINE BARS | A more sedate entry in the Russafa district's buzzy nightlife scene, this wine bar specializes in natural wines from small producers, mainly from Spain and France. Inside is charmingly retro, while a nice-sized corner terrace lets you soak in the lively street life. ⊠ Carrer de la Reina Doña Maria 1, Eixample ☎ 611/349008 ⊕ www.mesamours.es.

### MUSIC CLUBS

#### Jimmy Glass Jazz Bar

LIVE MUSIC | Aficionados of modern jazz gather at this bar, which books an impressive range of local and international combos and soloists. Opening times vary according to the performance schedule, with up to four shows on different nights each week. ⊠ Carrer Baja 28, El Carmen ⊕ www.jimmyglassjazz.net.

## 🎭 Performing Arts

### MUSIC

#### Palau de la Música

PERFORMANCE VENUE | On one of the nicest stretches of the Turia riverbed is this huge glass vault, Valencia's main concert venue. Home of the Orquesta de Valencia, the main hall also hosts touring performers from around the world, including chamber and youth orchestras, opera, and an excellent concert series featuring early, baroque, and classical music. ⌖ *Passeig de l'Albereda 30, Valencia* ☎ *963/375020* ⊕ *www.palauvalencia. com.*

## 🛍 Shopping

### Plaza Redonda

**MARKET** | A few steps from the cathedral, off the upper end of Calle San Vicente Mártir, the restored Plaza Redonda ("Round Square") is lined with stalls selling all sorts of souvenirs and traditional crafts. ⌖ *Pl. Redonda, El Carmen.*

### Undërwood

**MIXED CLOTHING** | An ever-changing selection of cool designs emblazon the t-shirts and hoodies of this independently owned shop, which produces all of its eco-friendly fashions locally. ⌖ *C. del Trench 16, Ciutat Vella* ☎ *644/612146* ⊕ *underwoodpeople.com.*

## Albufera Nature Park

*11 km (7 miles) south of Valencia.*

South of Valencia, Albufera Nature Park is one of Spain's most spectacular wetland areas. Home to the largest freshwater lagoon on the peninsula, this protected area and bird-watcher's paradise is bursting with unusual flora and fauna, such as rare species of wading birds. Encircled by a tranquil backdrop of rice fields, it's no surprise that the villages that dot this picturesque place have some of the best options in the region for trying classic Valencian paella or *arròs a banda* (rice cooked in fish stock).

### GETTING HERE AND AROUND

From Valencia, buses 24 and 25 depart for El Palmar; get off at the Pinars-Carretera del Palmar stop, about a 45-minute ride. From there, it's a short walk to the Centre d'Interpretació Raco de l'Olla, the park's information center, which provides maps, guides, and tour arrangements. It's open daily from 9 am–2 pm.

## 👁 Sights

### ★ Albufera Nature Park

**NATURE PRESERVE** | This beautiful freshwater lagoon was named by Moorish poets—*albufera* means "the sun's mirror." The park is a nesting site for more than 300 bird species, including herons, terns, egrets, ducks, and flamingos. Bird-watching companies offer boat rides all along the Albufera. You can also explore the park on foot or by bike. ⌖ *Ctra. de El Palmar s/n, El Palmar* ✛ *Carrer de Vicente Baldoví s/n* ☎ *963/868050* ⊕ *parquesnaturales.gva.es* 🎟 *Free.*

### El Palmar

**TOWN** | This is the major village in the area, with streets lined with restaurants specializing in various types of paella. The most traditional kind is made with rabbit or game birds, though seafood is also popular. ⌖ *El Palmar.*

## 🍴 Restaurants

### Maribel Arroceria

**$$ | SPANISH** | So tasty is the paella here that even Valencianos regularly travel out of the city to Maribel Arroceria, off the main drag in El Palmar. Sit surrounded by the rice fields of Albufera Nature Park, either in the contemporary, air-conditioned dining room or outside at pavement tables overlooking the canal. **Known for:** canal seating; fresh whole fish; paella and fideuà. ⑤ *Average main: €17* ⌖ *Carrer de Francisco Monleón 5, El Palmar* ☎ *961/620060* ⊕ *www.arroceriamaribel. com* 🕤 *Closed Wed. No dinner.*

## Dénia

The stretch of coastline known as the Costa Blanca (White Coast) begins at Dénia, south of Valencia. Dénia is the port of departure on the Costa Blanca for the ferries to Ibiza, Formentera, and Mallorca—but if you're on your way to or from the islands, stay a night in the lovely

Dénia's massive fort overlooks the harbor and provides a dramatic element to the skyline, with the Montgü mountains in the background.

little town in the shadow of a dramatic cliff-top fortress. Or, spend a few hours wandering in the Baix la Mar, the old fishermen's quarter with its brightly painted houses, and exploring the historic town center. The town has become something of a culinary hot spot and is home to award-winning restaurants, which for its compact size is something of an achievement.

### GETTING HERE AND AROUND
Dénia is linked to other Costa Blanca destinations via Line 1 of the Alicante–Benidorm narrow-gauge TRAM train. There's also regular bus service from major towns and cities, including Madrid (7¼–9 hours) and Valencia (1¾–2½ hours). Local buses can get you around all of the Costa Blanca communities.

The Playa del Arenal, a tiny bay cut into the larger one, is worth a visit in summer. You can reach it via the coastal road (CV736) between Dénia and Jávea.

**VISITOR INFORMATION**
**CONTACTS Visitor Information Dénia.** ⊠ *Pl. Oculista Buigues 9, Dénia* ☎ *966/422367* ⊕ *www.denia.net.*

## 👁 Sights

### Castillo de Dénia
**CASTLE/PALACE** | The most interesting architectural attraction here is the castle overlooking the town, and the Palau del Governador (Governor's Palace) inside. On the site of an 11th-century Moorish fortress, the Renaissance-era palace was built in the 17th century and was later demolished. The fortress has an interesting archaeological museum as well as the remains of a Renaissance bastion and a Moorish portal with a lovely horseshoe arch. ⊠ *Av. del Cid–Calle San Francisco s/n, Dénia* ☎ *966/422367* 💶 *€3 (includes entrance to archaeological museum).*

**Cueva de las Calaveras** (*Cave of the Skulls*)

CAVE | FAMILY | About 15 km (9 miles) inland from Dénia, this 400-yard-long cave was named for the 12 Moorish skulls found here when it was discovered in 1768. The cave of stalactites and stalagmites has a dome rising to more than 60 feet and leads to an underground lake. ⊠ *Ctra. Benidoleig–Pedreguera, Km 1.5, Benidoleig* ☎ *966/404235* ⊕ *www.cuevadelascalaveras.com* ⚑ *€4.*

##  Restaurants

### El Raset

$$$ | SEAFOOD | Across the harbor, this Valencian favorite has been serving traditional cuisine with a modern twist for more than 30 years. From a terrace with views of the water you can choose from an array of excellent seafood dishes, including house specialties such as *arroz en caldero* (rice with monkfish, lobster, or prawns) and *gambas rojas* (local red prawns). À la carte dining can be expensive, while set menus are easier on your wallet. **Known for:** tasty paella; reasonably priced set menus; excellent seafood dishes. ⑤ *Average main: €20* ⊠ *Calle Bellavista 7, Dénia* ☎ *965/785040* ⊕ *www.grupoelraset.com.*

## Hotels

### ★ Art Boutique Hotel Chamarel

$$$ | B&B/INN | Ask the staff and they'll tell you that *chamarel* means a "mixture of colors," and this hotel brimming with charm, built as a grand family home in 1840, is certainly an eccentric blend of styles, cultures, periods, and personalities. **Pros:** friendly, helpful staff; interior courtyard; individual attention. **Cons:** rooms over the street are noisy; not on the beach; minimum stay required. ⑤ *Rooms from: €150* ⊠ *Calle Cavallers 3, Dénia* ☎ *966/435007* ⊕ *www.hotelchamarel.com* ⇌ *15 rooms* ⱺⵊ *Free Breakfast.*

### ★ Hostal Loreto

$ | HOTEL | Travelers on tight budgets will appreciate this basic yet impeccable lodging, set in a former nunnery and located on a central pedestrian street in the historic quarter just steps from the Town Hall. **Pros:** great central location; roof terrace; good value. **Cons:** rooms can be dark; dated room decor; no elevator. ⑤ *Rooms from: €82* ⊠ *Calle Loreto 12, Dénia* ☎ *966/435419* ⊕ *www.hostalloreto.com* ⇌ *43 rooms* ⱺⵊ *Free Breakfast.*

# Calpe (Calp)

*35 km (22 miles) south of Dénia.*

Calpe has an ancient history, as it was chosen by the Phoenicians, Greeks, Romans, and Moors as a strategic point from which to plant their Iberian settlements. The real-estate developers were the latest to descend upon it: much of Calpe today is overbuilt with high-rise resorts and *urbanizaciónes.* But the old town is a delightful maze of narrow streets and small squares, archways and cul-de-sacs, with houses painted in Mediterranean blue, red, ocher, and sandstone; wherever there's a broad expanse of building wall, you'll likely discover a mural. Calpe is a delightful place to wander.

## GETTING HERE AND AROUND

The narrow-gauge TRAM railway from Dénia to Alicante also serves Calpe, as do local buses.

## VISITOR INFORMATION

CONTACTS **Visitor Information Calpe.** ⊠ *Av. Ejércitos Españoles 44, Calp* ☎ *965/836920* ⊕ *www.calpe.es.*

## Sights

### Fish Market

MARKET | The fishing industry is still very important in Calpe, and every evening the fishing boats return to port with their catch. The subsequent auction at the fish market can be watched from the walkway of La Lonja de Calpe. ⊠ *Port, Calp* ⊗ *Closed weekends.*

### Peñón d'Ifach Natural Park

**NATURE SIGHT** | The landscape of Calpe is dominated by this huge calcareous rock more than 1,100 yards long, 1,090 feet high, and joined to the mainland by a narrow isthmus. The area is rich in flora and fauna, with more than 300 species of plants and 80 species of land and marine birds. A visit to the top is not for the fainthearted; wear shoes with traction for the hike, which includes a trip through a tunnel to the summit. The views are spectacular, reaching to the island of Ibiza on a clear day. ⊠ *Calp* ⊕ *parquesnaturales.gva.es.*

 **Restaurants**

### Patio de la Fuente

**$$$ | MEDITERRANEAN** | In an intimate little space with wicker chairs and pale mauve walls, this restaurant in the old town serves a bargain Mediterranean three-course prix fixe dinner, wine included; you can also order à la carte. In summer, dine on the comfortable patio out back. **Known for:** house-made Scotch eggs; good-value three-course dinner; outdoor dining. ⑤ *Average main: €18* ⊠ *Carrer Dos de Mayo 16, Calp* ☎ *965/831695* ⊕ *www.patiodelafuente.com* ⊗ *Closed Sun. and Mon.*

 **Hotels**

### Pensión el Hidalgo

**$ | B&B/INN** | This family-run pension near the beach has small but cozy rooms with a friendly, easygoing feel, and several have private balconies overlooking the Mediterranean. **Pros:** beachfront location; breakfast terrace with sea views; reasonable prices. **Cons:** snug rooms; you must book far ahead in summer; basic design. ⑤ *Rooms from: €70* ⊠ *Av. Rosa de los Vientos 19, Calp* ☎ *965/839862* ⊕ *pensionelhidalgo.es* ⤳ *9 rooms* ❄️ *No Meals.*

## 🏃 Activities

### Mundo Marino

**BOATING | FAMILY** | Choose from a wide range of sailing trips, including cruises up and down the coast, and sunset trips with a glass of cava. Glass-bottom boats make it easy to observe the abundant marine life. ⊠ *Puerto Pesquero, Calp* ☎ *966/423066* ⊕ *www.mundomarino.es.*

# Altea

*11 km (7 miles) southwest of Calpe.*

Perched on a hill overlooking a bustling beachfront, Altea (unlike some of its neighboring towns) has retained much of its original charm, with an atmospheric old quarter laced with narrow cobblestone streets and stairways, and gleaming white houses. At the center is the striking church of Nuestra Señora del Consuelo, with its blue ceramic-tile dome, and the Plaza de la Iglesia in front.

### GETTING HERE AND AROUND

Also on the Dénia–Alicante narrow-gauge TRAM train route, Altea is served by local buses, with connections to major towns and cities. The old quarter is mainly pedestrianized.

### VISITOR INFORMATION

**CONTACTS Visitor Information Altea.**
⊠ *Calle Sant Pere 14, Altea* ☎ *965/844114* ⊕ *www.visitaltea.es.*

## 🍴 Restaurants

### La Costera

**$$$ | FRENCH** | This popular restaurant focuses on fine French fare, with such specialties as house-made foie gras, fillet of turbot, and beef entrecôte. There's also a variety of game in season, including venison and partridge. **Known for:** French specialties; in-season game; bucolic outdoor terrace. ⑤ *Average main: €22* ⊠ *Costera Mestre de Música 8, Altea* ☎ *965/840230* ⊕ *www.altealacostera.*

*com* 🕐 *Closed Mon. and Tues. No lunch weekdays. No dinner Sun.*

### Oustau de Altea

$$ | EUROPEAN | In one of the prettiest corners of Altea's old town, this eatery was formerly a cloister and a school. Today the dining room and terrace combine contemporary design gracefully juxtaposed with a rustic setting, and the restaurant is known for serving polished international cuisine with French flair. **Known for:** prix-fixe menu (€45) includes bottle of wine; dishes named after classic films; French-style cuisine. ⑤ *Average main: €16* ⊠ *Calle Mayor 5, Casco Antiguo* ☎ *965/842078* ⊕ *www.oustau.com* 🕐 *Closed Mon. and Feb.–mid-Mar.*

## 🛏 Hotels

### Hostal Fornet

$ | HOTEL | The pièce de résistance at this simple, pleasant hotel, at the highest point of Altea's historic center, is the roof terrace with its stunning view; from here, you look out over the church's distinctive blue-tiled cupola and the surrounding tangle of streets, with a Mediterranean backdrop. **Pros:** lovely views; multilingual owners; top value. **Cons:** door is locked when reception is not staffed, and you have to call to be let in; small rooms; no pool or beach. ⑤ *Rooms from: €55* ⊠ *Calle Beniardá 1, Casco Antiguo* ☎ *965/843005* ⊕ *web.hostalfornetaltea.com* 🔄 *23 rooms* ⦿ *No Meals.*

# Alicante (Alacant)

*183 km (114 miles) south of Valencia, 52 km (32 miles) south of Altea.*

The Greeks called it Akra Leuka (White Summit) and the Romans named it Lucentum (City of Light). A crossroads for inland and coastal routes since ancient times, Alicante has always been known for its luminous skies. The city is dominated by the 16th-century grande dame castle, **Castillo de Santa Bárbara,** a top attraction. The best approach is via the elevator cut deep into the mountainside.

Also memorable is Alicante's grand **Esplanada,** lined with date palms. Directly under the castle is the city beach, the Playa del Postiguet, but the city's pride is the long, curved Playa de San Juan, which runs north from the Cap de l'Horta to El Campello.

## GETTING HERE AND AROUND

Alicante has two train stations: the main Estación de Madrid and the local Estación de la Marina, from which the local FGV line runs along the Costa Blanca from Alicante to Dénia. Playa Postiguet can be reached by several buses from downtown, including 21 and 22.

The slower narrow-gauge TRAM train goes from the city center on the beach to El Campello. From the same open-air station in Alicante, the Line 1 train departs to Benidorm, with connections on to Altea, Calpe, and Dénia.

## VISITOR INFORMATION

**CONTACTS Tourist Information Alicante.** ⊠ *Muelle Levante 6, Alicante* ☎ *965/177201* ⊕ *www.alicanteturismo.com.* **TRAM.** ⊠ *Alicante-Luceros, Alicante* ☎ *900/720472* ⊕ *www.tramalicante.es.*

## 👁 Sights

### Ayuntamiento

NOTABLE BUILDING | Constructed between 1696 and 1780, the town hall is a beautiful example of baroque civic architecture. Inside, a gold sculpture by Salvador Dalí of San Juan Bautista holding the famous cross and shell rises to the second floor in the stairwell. Ask gate officials for permission to explore the ornate halls and rococo chapel on the first floor. Look for the plaque on the first step of the staircase that indicates the exact sea level, used to define the rest of Spain's altitudes "above sea level." ⊠ *Pl. de*

Alicante's Esplanada de España, lined with date palms, is the perfect place for a stroll. The municipal brass band offers concerts on the bandstand of the Esplanada on Sunday evenings in July and August.

*Ayuntamiento, Alicante* ☎ *966/900886* 🖾 *Free* 🕙 *Closed weekends.*

### Basílica de Santa María

**CHURCH** | Constructed in a Gothic style over the city's main mosque between the 14th and 16th century, this is Alicante's oldest house of worship. The main door is flanked by beautiful baroque stonework by Juan Bautista Borja, and the interior highlights are the golden rococo high altar, a Gothic image in stone of St. Mary, and a sculpture of Sts. Juanes by Rodrigo de Osona. ⊠ *Pl. de Santa María 1, Alicante* ☎ *965/177201 tourist office (for information)* 🕙 *Closing times can vary due to religious services.*

### ★ Castillo de Santa Bárbara (*Santa Barbara Castle*)

**CASTLE/PALACE** | One of the largest existing medieval fortresses in Europe, Castillo de Santa Bárbara sits atop 545-foot-tall Monte Benacantil. From this strategic position you can gaze out over the city, the sea, and the whole Alicante plain for many miles. Remains from civilizations dating from the Bronze Age onward have been found here; the oldest parts of the castle, at the highest level, are from the 9th through 13th conturioc.

The castle also houses the Museo de la Ciudad de Alicante (MUSA), which uses audiovisual presentations and archaeological finds to tell the story of Alicante, its people, and the city's enduring relationship with the sea. ⊠ *Monte Benacantil s/n, Alicante* ☎ *965/152969* ⊕ *www. castillodesantabarbara.com* 🖾 *Castle and museum free.*

### Concatedral de San Nicolás de Bari

**CHURCH** | Built between 1616 and 1662 on the site of a former mosque, this church (called a *con*catedral because it shares the seat of the bishopric with the Concatedral de Orihuela) has an austere facade designed by Agustín Bernardino, a disciple of the great Spanish architect Juan de Herrera. Inside, it's dominated by a dome nearly 150 feet high, a pretty cloister, and a lavish baroque side chapel, the Santísima Sacramento, with an elaborate sculptured stone dome of its own. Its name comes from the day that Alicante was reconquered (December 6, 1248) from the Moors, the feast day of San Nicolás. ⊠ *Pl. Abad Penalva 2, Alicante* ☏ *965/212662* ⊕ *concatedralalicante.com* ⊠ *Free.*

**Museo Arqueológico de Alicante**
HISTORY MUSEUM | Inside the old hospital of San Juan de Dios, the MARQ has a collection of artifacts from the Alicante region dating from the Paleolithic era to modern times, with a particular emphasis on Iberian art. ⊠ *Pl. Dr. Gómez Ulla s/n, Alicante* ☏ *965/149000* ⊕ *www.marqalicante.com* ⊠ *€3* ⊗ *Closed Mon.*

## 🍴 Restaurants

**El Buen Comer**
$$ | SPANISH | On the edge of the old town, this relaxed bi-level restaurant serves enticing dishes in plentiful portions. Downstairs, indulge in tapas and simpler dishes, or head to the fancier dining space upstairs for specialties like roast suckling pig, lamb chops, and sea bass baked in rock salt. **Known for:** specialty meat and seafood dishes; well-priced prix-fixe menus; rice dishes. ⑤ *Average main: €15* ⊠ *Calle Mayor 8, Alicante* ☏ *965/213103* ⊕ *www.elbuencomer.es* ⊗ *Closed Tues.*

**La Taberna del Gourmet**
$$$ | TAPAS | This wine bar and restaurant in the heart of the *casco antiguo* (old town) earns high marks from locals and international visitors alike. There's a wide selection of montaditos (sandwiches), paella, and fresh seafood tapas—oysters, mussels, razor clams—complemented by a well-chosen list of Spanish wines. **Known for:** reservations essential; tapas tasting menu (€30); excellent wine list. ⑤ *Average main: €20* ⊠ *Calle San Fernando 10, Alicante* ☏ *965/204233* ⊕ *www.latabernadelgourmet.com.*

**Nou Manolín**
$$$$ | SPANISH | An Alicante institution, this inviting exposed-brick and wood-lined restaurant is very popular with locals, who come for the excellent-value tapas, market produce, and freshly caught fish, a tribute to the city's enduring relationship with the sea. **Known for:** buzzy atmsophere; authentic local vibe; market-fresh produce and fish. ⑤ *Average main: €25* ⊠ *Calle Villegas 3, Alicante* ☏ *965/616425* ⊕ *www.grupogastronou.com* ⊗ *No dinner Sun.*

## 🛏 Hotels

**Hotel Les Monges Palace Boutique**
$ | HOTEL | In a restored 1912 building, this family-run hotel in central *casco antiguo* features lovingly preserved exposed stone walls, ceramic tile floors, and rooms furnished with eccentric artwork and quirky charm. **Pros:** personalized service; lots of character; rooftop terrace with castle views. **Cons:** bathrooms in standard rooms are small; must book well in advance; the newer, modern part is not as atmospheric. ⑤ *Rooms from: €75* ⊠ *Calle San Agustín 4, Alicante* ☏ *965/215046* ⊠ *24 rooms* ⑩ *Free Breakfast.*

## ▼ Nightlife

El Barrio, the old quarter west of Rambla de Méndez Núñez, is the prime nightlife area of Alicante, with music bars and discos every couple of steps. In summer, or after 3 am, the liveliest places are along the water, on Ruta del Puerto and Ruta de la Madera.

## 🛍 Shopping

**Mercado Central**
MARKET | Bulging with fish, vegetables, and other local items, this is the place to stop by and discover Alicante's fresh produce, traded from this Moderniste-inspired building since 1921. ⊠ *Av. Alfonso el Sabio 10, Alicante.*

# Chapter 10

# IBIZA AND THE BALEARIC ISLANDS

Updated by
Elizabeth Prosser

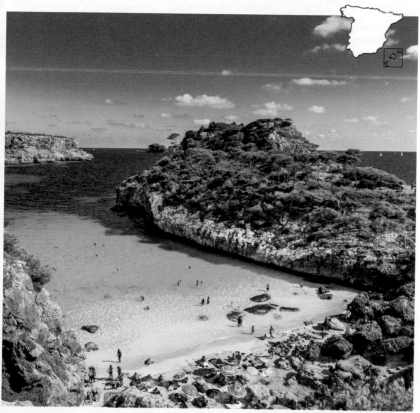

👁 **Sights**　　🍴 **Restaurants**　　🛏 **Hotels**　　🛍 **Shopping**　　🍸 **Nightlife**
★★★☆☆　　★★★★☆　　★★★★☆　　★★★☆☆　　★★★☆☆

# WELCOME TO
# IBIZA AND THE BALEARIC ISLANDS

## TOP REASONS TO GO

★ **Pamper yourself:**
Luxurious boutique hotels on restored and redesigned rural estates are *the* hip places to stay in the Balearics. Many have their own holistic spas: restore and redesign yourself at one of them.

★ **Enjoy seafood delicacies:** Seafood specialties come straight from the boat to portside restaurants all over the islands.

★ **Party hard:** Ibiza's summer club scene is the biggest, wildest, and glitziest in the world.

★ **Take in the gorgeous views:** The *miradores* (viewpoints) of Mallorca's Tramuntana, along the road from Valldemossa to Sóller, highlight the most spectacular seacoast in the Mediterranean.

★ **Discover Palma:**
Capital of the Balearics, Palma is one of the great unsung cities of the Mediterranean—a showcase of medieval and modern architecture, a venue for art and music, a mecca for sailors, and a killer place to shop for shoes.

The Balearic Islands lie 80–305 km (50–190 miles) off the Spanish mainland, roughly between Valencia and Barcelona. In the center, Mallorca, with its rolling eastern plains and mountainous northwest, is the largest of the group. Menorca, its closest neighbor, is virtually flat; but like Ibiza and tiny Formentera to the west, it has a rugged coastline of small inlets and sandy beaches.

**1 Ibiza.** Sleepy from November to May, the island is Party Central in midsummer for retro hippies and nonstop clubbers. Dalt Vila, the medieval quarter of Eivissa, the capital, on the hill overlooking the town, is a UNESCO World Heritage Site.

**2 Formentera.**
Day-trippers from Ibiza chill out on this (comparatively) quiet little island with long stretches of protected beach.

**3 Mallorca.** Palma, the island's capital, is a trove of art and architectural gems. The Tramuntana, in the northwest, is a region of forested peaks and steep sea cliffs that few landscapes in the world can match.

**4 Menorca.** Mahón, the capital city, commands the largest and deepest harbor in the Mediterranean. Many of the houses above the port date to the 18th-century occupation by the British Navy.

0   20 mi

0   20 km

MENORCA   Fornells

Cap de Formentor

Ciutadella   4 Alaior

Cap d'Artrutx   Mahón
(Maó)

Pollença

Sóller   Alcudia

Valldemossa   Artà

SIERRA DE TRAMUNTANA   Inca   Coves d'Arta

MALLORCA

3

Andraitx   Manacor

Palma   Montuïri

Lluchmayor

Santanyi

Cap de ses Salines

CABRERA

Mediterranean Sea

Sant
Joan

Sant
ntoni   Santa Eulària
des Riu

Ibiza   1
(Eivissa)   IRIZA

San Francisco Javier

Cap de
Barbería   2

FORMENTERA

# EATING AND DRINKING WELL IN THE BALEARIC ISLANDS

Tumbet is a traditional vegetable dish, served in a clay pot.

Mediterranean islands should guarantee great seafood—and the Balearics deliver, with superb products from the crystalline waters surrounding the archipelago. Inland farms supply free-range beef, lamb, goat, and cheese.

Ibiza's fishermen head out to the tiny inlets for sea bass and bream, which are served in beach shacks celebrated for *bullit de peix* (fish casserole), *guisat* (fish and shellfish stew), and *burrida de ratjada* (ray with almonds). Beyond the great seafood, there are tradition-al farm dishes that include *sofrit pagès* (lamb or chicken with potatoes and red peppers), *botifarron* (blood sausage), and *rostit* (oven-roasted pork). Mallorcans love their *sopas de peix* (fish soup) and their *panades de peix* (fish-filled pastries), while Menorca's harbor restaurants are famous for *llagosta* (spiny lobster), grilled or served as part of a *caldereta*—a soupy stew. Interestingly, mayonnaise is widely believed to have been invented by the French in Mahón, Menorca, after they took the port from the British in 1756.

## BALEARIC ALMONDS

Almonds are omnipresent in the Balearics, used in sweets, sauces, and seafood recipes. Typically used in the *picada*—the ground nuts, spices, and herbs on the surface of a dish—almonds are essential to the Balearic economy. After a 19th-century phylloxera plague decimated Balearic vineyards, almond trees replaced vines and the almond crop became a staple. In February, Mallorca is awash with a delicate white blanket of almond tree blossoms.

## VEGETABLES

The *tumbet mallorquin* is a classic Balearic dish made of layers of fried zucchini, bell peppers, potatoes, and eggplant with tomato sauce between each layer. It's served piping hot in individual earthenware casseroles.

## SEAFOOD

There are several seafood dishes to look out for in the Balearics. *Burrida de ratjada* is boiled ray baked between layers of potato with almonds. The *picada* covering the ray during the baking includes almonds, garlic, egg, a slice of fried bread, parsley, salt, pepper, and olive oil. *Caldereta de llagosta* (spiny lobster soup) is a quintessential Menorcan staple sometimes said to be authentic only if the Menorcan spiny lobster is used. *Guisat de marisc* (shellfish stew) is an Ibiza stew of fish and shellfish cooked with a base of onions, potatoes, peppers, and olive oil. Nearly any seafood from the waters around Ibiza may well end up in this staple.

## PORK

*Rostit* is baked in the oven with liver, eggs, bread, apples, and plums. *Sobrasada* (finely ground pork seasoned with sweet red paprika and stuffed in a sausage skin) is one of Mallorca's two most delectable food products (the other is the *ensaïmada,* a

Clams are one of the many seafood options you'll find in the Balearics.

sweet spiral pastry made with *saïm,* or lard). Sobrasada originated in Italy but became popular in Mallorca during the 16th century.

## MENORCAN CHEESE

Mahón cheese is a Balearic trademark, and Menorca has a *denominación de origen* (D.O.), one of the 12 officially designated cheese-producing regions in Spain. The *curado* (fully cured) cheese is the tastiest.

## WINE

With just 2,500 acres of vineyards (down from 75,000 in 1891), Mallorca's two D.O. wine regions—Binissalem, near Palma, and Pla i Llevant on the eastern side of the island—will likely remain under the radar to the rest of the world. While you're here, though, treat yourself to a Torre des Canonge white, a fresh, full, fruity wine, or a red Ribas de Cabrera from the oldest vineyard on the island, Hereus de Ribas in Binissalem, founded in 1711. Viticulture on Menorca went virtually extinct with the reversion of the island to Spain after its 18th-century British occupation, but since the last half of the 20th century, a handful of ambitious, serious winemakers—mainly in the area of Sant Lluís—has emerged to put the local product back on the map.

Local cheese from Menorca.

# BEST BEACHES OF THE BALEARICS

Ibiza is "Party Island," and its beaches get crowded.

When it comes to oceanfront property, the Balearic Islands have vast and varied resources: everything from long sweeps of beach on sheltered bays to tiny crescents of sand in rocky inlets and coves called *calas*, some so isolated you can reach them only by boat.

Many of the Balearic beaches, like their counterparts on the mainland coasts, have become destinations for communities of holiday chalets and retirement homes, usually called *urbanizaciónes,* their waterfronts lined with the inevitable shopping centers and pizza joints—skip these and head to the simpler and smaller beaches in or adjoining the Balearics' admirable number of nature reserves. Granted you'll find few or no services, and be warned that smaller beaches mean crowds in July and August, but these are the Balearics' best destinations for sun and sand. The local authorities protect these are-as more rigorously than they do those on the mainland, and the beaches are gems.

## BEACH AMENITIES

Be prepared: services at many of the smaller Balearic beaches are minimal or nonexistent. If you want a deck chair or something to eat or drink, bring it with you or make sure to ask around to see if your chosen secluded inlet has at least a *chiringuito*: a waterfront shack where the food is likely to feature what the fisherman pulled in that morning.

## SES SALINES, IBIZA

Easy to reach from Eivissa, Ibiza's capital, this is one of the most popular beaches on the island, but the setting—in a protected natural park area—has been spared overdevelopment. The beach is relatively narrow, but the fine golden sand stretches more than a kilometer along the curve of Ibiza's southernmost bay. Two other great choices, on the east coast, are Cala Mastella, a tiny cove tucked away in a pine woods where a kiosk on the wharf serves the fresh catch of the day, and Cala Llenya, a family-friendly beach in a protected bay with shallow water.

The benefits of the popular beaches are their ample amenities.

## BENIRRÁS, IBIZA

Benirrás is a small cove tucked away on Ibiza's northern coast backed by pine-clad hills. Known for its sunsets and laid-back vibe, it's popular with artists and hippies. Every Sunday at sunset, drummers gather to form ritualistic drum circles, one of the island's most popular events. On other days, it's a peaceful stretch of soft sand with calm water to spend a few hours.

## PLAYA DE SES ILLETES, FORMENTERA

The closest beach to the port at La Sabina, where the ferries come in from Ibiza, Ses Illetes is Formentera's preeminent party scene: some 3 km (2 miles)

of fine white sand with beach bars and snack shacks, and Jet Skis and windsurfing gear for rent.

## ES TRENC, MALLORCA

One of the few long beaches on the island that's been spared resort development, this pristine 3-km (2-mile) stretch of soft, white sand southeast of Palma, near Colònia Sant Jordi, is a favorite with nude bathers—who stay mainly at the west end—and day-trippers who arrive by boat. The water is crystal-clear blue and shallow for some distance out. The 10-km (6-mile) walk along the beach from Colònia Sant Jordi to the Cap Salines lighthouse is one of Mallorca's treasures.

## CALA MACARELLA/CALA MACARELLETA, MENORCA

This pair of beautiful, secluded coves edged with pines is about a 20-minute walk through the woods from the more developed beach at Santa Galdana, on Menorca's south coast. Macarella is the larger and busier of the two; Macarelleta, a few minutes farther west along the path, is popular with nude bathers and boating parties. Cala Pregonda, on the north coast, is a lovely crescent cove with pine and tamarisk trees behind and dramatic rock formations at both ends.

For peace and quiet, head to Macarella on Mallorca.

Could anything go wrong in a destination that gets, on average, 300 days of sunshine a year? True, the water is only warm enough for a dip May–October, but the climate does seem to give the residents of the Balearics a sunny disposition year-round. They are a remarkably hospitable people, not merely because tourism accounts for such a large chunk of their economy, but because history and geography have combined to put them in the crossroads of so much Mediterranean trade and traffic.

The Balearic Islands were outposts, successively, of the Phoenician, Carthaginian, and Roman empires before the Moors invaded in 902 and took possession for some 300 years. In 1235, Jaume I of Aragón ousted the Moors, and the islands became part of the independent kingdom of Mallorca until 1343, when they returned to the Crown of Aragón under Pedro IV. With the marriage of Isabella of Castile to Ferdinand of Aragón in 1469, the Balearics were joined to a united Spain. Great Britain occupied Menorca in 1704, during the War of the Spanish Succession, to secure the superb natural harbor of Mahón as a naval base, but returned it to Spain in 1802 under the Treaty of Amiens.

During the Spanish Civil War, Menorca remained loyal to Spain's democratically elected Republican government, while Mallorca and Ibiza sided with Francisco Franco's insurgents. Mallorca then became a base for Italian air strikes against the Republican holdouts in Barcelona. This topic is still broached delicately on the islands; they remain fiercely independent of one another in many ways. Even Mahón and Ciutadella, at opposite ends of Menorca—all of 44 km (27 miles) apart—remain estranged over differences dating to that war.

The tourist boom, which began during Franco's regime (1939–75), turned great stretches of Mallorca's and Ibiza's coastlines into strips of high-rise hotels, fast-food restaurants, and discos.

# Planning

## When to Go

July and August are peak season in the Balearics; it's hot, and even the most secluded beaches are crowded. Weatherwise, May and October are ideal, with June and September just behind. Winter is quiet; it's too cold for the beach but fine for hiking, golfing, and exploring—though on Menorca the winter winds are notoriously fierce. The clubbing season on Ibiza begins in June.

Note: between November and March or April many hotels and restaurants are closed for their own vacations or seasonal repairs.

## Planning Your Time

Most European visitors to the Balearics pick one island and stick with it, but you could easily see all three. Start in Mallorca with **Palma**. Begin early at the cathedral and explore the Llotja, the Almudaina palace, and the Plaça Major. The churches of Santa Eulàlia and Sant Francesc and the Arab Baths are a must. Staying overnight in Palma means you can sample the nightlife and have time to visit the museums.

Take the old train to **Sóller** and rent a car for a trip over the Sierra de Tramuntana to **Deià, Son Marroig,** and **Valldemossa.** The roads are twisty, so give yourself a full day. Spend the night in Sóller, and you can drive from there in less than an hour via **Lluc** and **Pollentia** to the Roman and Moorish ruins at **Alcúdia.**

By fast ferry it's just over three hours from Port d'Alcúdia to **Ciutadella,** on Menorca; the port, the **cathedral,** and the narrow streets of the old city can be explored in half a day. Make your way across the island to **Mahón,** and devote an afternoon to the highlights there.

From Mahón, you can take a 30-minute interisland flight to **Eivissa.** On Ibiza, plan a full day for the UNESCO World Heritage Site **Dalt Vila** and the shops of **Sa Penya,** and the better part of another for **Santa Gertrudis** and the north coast. If you've come to Ibiza to party, of course, time has no meaning.

## Getting Here and Around

### AIR

The easiest way to reach Mallorca, Menorca, and Ibiza is to fly. Each of the three islands is served by an international airport, all of them within 15–20 minutes by car or bus from their respective capital cities. There are daily domestic connections to each from Barcelona (about 50 minutes), Madrid, and Valencia; no-frills and charter operators fly to Eivissa, Palma, and Mahón from many European cities, especially during the summer. There are also flights between the islands. Book early in high season.

### BIKE

The Balearic Islands—especially Ibiza and Formentera—are ideal for exploration by bicycle. Ibiza is relatively flat and easy to negotiate, though side roads can be in poor repair. Formentera is level, too, with bicycle lanes on all connecting roads. Parts of Mallorca are quite mountainous, with challenging climbs through spectacular scenery; along some country roads, there are designated bike lanes. Bicycles are easy to rent, and tourist offices have details of recommended routes. Menorca is relatively flat, with lots of roads that wander through pastureland and olive groves to small coves and inlets.

### BOAT AND FERRY

*From Barcelona:* The Acciona Trasmediterránea and Balearia car ferries serve Ibiza, Mallorca, and Menorca from Barcelona. The most romantic way to get to the Balearic Islands is by overnight ferry from Barcelona to Palma, sailing (depending on the line and the season) between 11 and 11:30 pm; you can watch the lights of Barcelona sinking into the horizon for hours—and when you arrive in Palma, around 7 am, see the spires of the cathedral bathed in the morning sun. Overnight ferries have lounges and private cabins. Round-trip fares vary with the line, the season, and points of departure and destination but from Barcelona start from as low as €45 for lounge seats or €150 per person for a double cabin (tax included).

Faster ferries operated by Balearia, with passenger lounges only, speed from Barcelona to Eivissa (Ibiza), to Palma and Alcúdia (Mallorca), and to Mahón (Menorca). Depending on the destination, the trip takes between three and six hours.

*From Valencia:* Acciona Trasmediterránea ferries leave Valencia late at night for Ibiza, arriving early in the morning. Balearia fast ferries (no vehicles) leave Valencia for Sant Antoni on Ibiza in the late afternoon, making the crossing in about 2½ hours. Acciona Trasmediterránea and Balearia have services from Valencia to Mallorca, and Trasmediterránea also runs a service to Mahón (Menorca). Departure days and times vary with the season, with service more frequent in summer.

*From Dénia:* Balearia runs a daily three-hour fast ferry service for passengers and cars between Dénia and Ibiza, another between Dénia and Formentera, and a similar eight-hour service between Dénia and Palma on weekends.

*Interisland:* Daily fast ferries connect Ibiza and Palma; one-way fares run €66–€81, depending on the type of accommodations. The Pitiusa and Trasmapi lines offer frequent fast ferry and hydrofoil service between Ibiza and Formentera (€22.50 one way, €40–€50 round trip). Daily ferries connect Alcúdia (Mallorca) and Ciutadella (Menorca) in three to four hours, depending on the weather; a hydrofoil makes the journey in about an hour.

**BOAT AND FERRY CONTACTS Acciona Trasmediterránea.** ☎ *90202/454645* ⊕ *www.trasmediterranea.es/en.* **Balearia.** ☎ *991202/660215* ⊕ *www.balearia. com.* **Mediterranea Pitiusa.** ✉ *Eivissa* ☎ *609/741067 reservations, 971/314461 Eivissa ticket office* ⊕ *www.mediterraneapitiusa.com.* **Trasmapi.** ✉ *Eivissa* ☎ *971/314433 information, 971/310711 Eivissa ticket office* ⊕ *www.trasmapi. com.*

## BUS

There is bus service on all the islands, though it's not extensive, especially on Formentera. ⇨ *Check each island's Getting Here and Around section for details.*

## CAR

Ibiza is best explored by car or motor scooter: many of the beaches lie at the end of rough, unpaved roads. Tiny Formentera can almost be covered on foot, but renting a car or a scooter at La Sabina is a time-saver. A car is essential if you want to beach-hop on Mallorca or Menorca and explore beyond the main cities and resorts.

## TAXI

On Ibiza, taxis are available at the airport and in Eivissa, Figueretas, Santa Eulàlia, and Sant Antoni. On Formentera, there are taxis in La Sabina and Es Pujols. Legal taxis on Ibiza and Formentera are metered, but it's a good idea to get a rough estimate of the fare from the driver before you climb aboard. Taxis in Palma are metered. For trips beyond the city, charges are posted at the taxi stands. On Menorca, you can pick up a taxi at the airport or in Mahón or Ciutadella.

## TRAIN

The public Ferrocarriles de Mallorca railroad track connects Palma and Inca, with stops at about half a dozen villages en route.

A journey on the privately owned Palma–Sóller railroad is a must: completed in 1912, it still uses the carriages from that era. The train trundles across the plain to

Bunyola, then winds through tremendous mountain scenery to emerge high above Sóller. An ancient tram connects the Sóller terminus to Port de Sóller, leaving every hour on the hour 8–5; the Palma terminal is near the corner of the Plaça d'Espanya, on Calle Eusebio Estada next to the Inca train station.

# Restaurants

On the Balearic Islands many restaurants tend to have short business seasons. This is less true of Mallorca, but on Menorca, Ibiza, and especially on Formentera, it might be May (or later) before the shutters are removed from that great seafood shack you've heard so much about. Really fine dining experiences are in limited supply on most of the islands, although this tide is turning, especially in cosmopolitan Palma de Mallorca. In the popular beach resorts, the promenades can seem overrun with paella and pizza joints. Away from the water, however, there are exceptional meals to be had—and the seafood couldn't be any fresher.

*Restaurant reviews have been shortened. For full information, visit Fodors.com.*

# Hotels

Many hotels on the islands include a continental or full buffet breakfast in the room rate.

### IBIZA
Ibiza's high-rise resort hotels and holiday apartments are mainly in Sant Antoni, Talamanca, Ses Figueretes, and Playa d'en Bossa. Overbuilt Sant Antoni has little but its beach to recommend it. Playa d'en Bossa, close to Eivissa, is prettier but lies under a flight path. To get off the beaten track and into the island's largely pristine interior, look for *agroturismo* lodgings in Els Amunts (the Uplands) and in villages such as Santa Gertrudis or Sant Miquel de Balanzat.

### FORMENTERA
If July and August are the only months you can visit, reserve well in advance. Accommodations on Formentera, the best of them on the south Platja de Mitjorn coast, tend to be small private properties converted to studio apartment complexes rather than megahotels.

### MALLORCA
Mallorca's large-scale resorts—more than 1,500 of them—are concentrated mainly on the southern coast and primarily serve the package-tour industry. Perhaps the best accommodations on the island are the number of grand old country estates and town houses that have been converted into boutique hotels, ranging from simple and relatively inexpensive agroturismos to stunning outposts of luxury. Palma also boasts an excellent selection of thoughtfully designed boutique hotels.

### MENORCA
Aside from a few hotels and hostels in Mahón and Ciutadella, almost all of Menorca's tourist lodgings are in beach resorts. As on the other islands, many of these are fully reserved by travel operators in the high season and often require a week's minimum stay, so it's generally most economical to book a package that combines airfare and accommodations. Or inquire at the tourist office about boutique and country hotels, especially in and around Sant Lluís.

*Hotel reviews have been shortened. For full information, visit Fodors.com.*

| What It Costs in Euros | | | |
|---|---|---|---|
| **$** | **$$** | **$$$** | **$$$$** |
| **RESTAURANTS** | | | |
| under €12 | €12–€17 | €18–€22 | over €22 |
| **HOTELS** | | | |
| under €90 | €90–€125 | €126–€180 | over €180 |

# Tours

Ibiza resorts run trips to neighboring beaches and to smaller islands. Trips from Ibiza to Formentera include an escorted bus tour. In Sant Antoni, there are a number of tour organizers to choose from.

Most Mallorca hotels and resorts offer guided tours. Typical itineraries are the Caves of Artà or Drac, on the east coast, including the nearby Auto Safari Park and an artificial-pearl factory in Manacor; the Chopin museum in the old monastery at Valldemossa, returning through the writers' and artists' village of Deià; the port of Sóller and the Arab gardens at Alfàbia; the Thursday market and leather factories in Inca; Port de Pollença; Cap de Formentor; and the northern beaches.

### Excursions a Cabrera

BOAT TOURS | Several options are available for visits to Cabrera, from a three-hour sunset tour, including sparkling wine and dessert, to a daylong tour, with time to explore independently. One option for this is to take a self-guided tour of the island's underwater ecosystem—using a mask and snorkel with their own sound system; the recording explains the main points of interest as you swim. Boats generally depart from Colònia Sant Jordi, 47 km (29 miles) southeast of Palma. You can buy tickets on the dock at Carrer Babriel Roca or online. ✉ *Carrer de Dofi 11, Colònia de Sant Jordi* ☎ *971/649034* ⊕ *www.excursionsacabrera.es* ✆ *From €40.*

### Yellow Catamarans

BOAT TOURS | On Menorca, sightseeing trips on glass-bottom catamarans leave Mahón's harbor from the quayside near the Xoriguer gin factory. Departure times vary; check with the tourist information office on the Moll de Ponent, at the foot of the winding stairs from the old city to the harbor. ✉ *Moll de Llevant 12, Mahón* ☎ *971/352307, 639/676351 for*

*reservations* ⊕ *www.yellowcatamarans. com* ✆ *From €12.50* ⊘ *Closed Sun. mid-July–mid Sept.*

# Ibiza

Tranquil countryside, secluded coves, and intimate luxury lodging to the north; sandy beaches and party venues by the score to the south; a capital crowned with a historic UNESCO World Heritage Site, and laid-back (and English-speaking) hospitality islandwide—Ibiza is a vacation destination not to be missed. Settled by the Carthaginians in the 5th century BC, Ibiza has seen successive waves of invasion and occupation, the latest of which began in the 1960s, when it became a tourist destination. With a full-time population of barely 140,000, it now gets some 2 million visitors a year. It's blessed with beaches—56 of them, by one count—and also has the world's largest nightclub. About a quarter of the people who live on Ibiza year-round are expats.

October through April, the pace of life here is decidedly slow, and many of the island's hotels and restaurants are closed. In the 1960s and early 1970s, Ibiza was discovered by sun-seeking hippies and eventually emerged as an icon of counterculture chic. Ibizans were—and still are—friendly to and tolerant of their eccentric visitors. In the late 1980s and 1990s, club culture took over. Young ravers flocked here from all over the world to dance all night and pack the sands of built-up beach resorts like Sant Antoni. That party-hearty Ibiza is still alive and well, but a new wave of luxury rural hotels, offering oases of peace and privacy, with spas and high-end restaurants, marks the most recent transformation of the island into a venue for more upscale tourism. In fact, it is entirely feasible to spend time on Ibiza and not see any evidence of the clubbing and nightlife scene for which it is so famous.

## GETTING HERE AND AROUND

Ibiza is a 55-minute flight or a nine-hour ferry ride from Barcelona.

Ibizabus serves the island. Buses run to Sant Antoni every 15–30 minutes 7:30 am–midnight (until 10:30 pm November–May) from the bus station on Avenida d'Isidor Macabich in Eivissa, and to Santa Eulàlia every half hour 6:50 am–11:30 pm Monday–Saturday (until 10:30 November–April), with late buses on Saturday in the summer party season at midnight, 1, and 2 am; Sunday service is hourly 7:30 am–11:30 pm (until 10:30 pm November–April). Buses to other parts of the island are less frequent, as is the cross-island bus between Sant Antoni and Santa Eulàlia.

On Ibiza, a six-lane divided highway connects the capital with the airport and Sant Antoni. Traffic circles and one-way streets make it a bit confusing to get in and out of Eivissa, but out in the countryside driving is easy and in most cases is the only way of getting to some of the island's smaller coves and beaches.

**BUS CONTACT Ibizabus.** ⊠ *Eivissa* 🕾 *971/340382, 600/482972 for Discobus* ⊕ *www.ibizabus.com.*

**TAXI CONTACTS Cooperativa Limitada de Taxis de Sant Antoni.** ⊠ *Carrer del Progrés, San Antoní* 🕾 *971/343764.* **Radio-Taxi.** ⊠ *Eivissa* 🕾 *971/398483.*

# Eivissa (Ibiza Town)

Hedonistic and historic, Eivissa (Ibiza, in Castilian) is a city jam-packed with cafés, nightspots, and trendy shops; looming over it are the massive stone walls of **Dalt Vila**—the medieval city declared a UNESCO World Heritage Site in 1999—and its Gothic cathedral. Squeezed between the north walls of the old city and the harbor is **Sa Penya**, a long labyrinth of stone-paved streets with some of the city's best offbeat shopping, snacking, and exploring.

## TOURS
### Dalt Vila Tours

**SPECIAL-INTEREST TOURS | FAMILY |** This 75-minute dramatized tour of Dalt Vila departs from the Portal de Ses Taules, at the foot of the walls. Three performers in period costume enact a legendary 15th-century love story as they move through the medieval scenes. Reservations are essential. The tour is in Spanish, though English speakers can be accommodated for groups of 10 or more. Confirm timetables at the Tourist Office. ⊠ *Portal de Ses Taules, Dalt Vila* 🕾 *971/399232* 🎫 *From €10.*

## VISITOR INFORMATION
### Ibiza Tourist Office

⊠ *Pl. de la Catedral s/n, Dalt Vila* 🕾 *971/399232* ⊕ *tourism.eivissa.es.*

#  Sights

### Bastió Promenade

**PROMENADE |** The Bastio Sant Bernat stone edifice is one of the oldest bastions in the Balearic Islands, harkening back to when inhabitants feared attacks from pirates. From here a promenade with stunning sea views runs west to the bastions of Sant Jordi and Sant Jaume, past the Castell—a fortress formerly used as an army barracks. In 2007 work began to transform the fortress into a luxury parador, but archaeological discoveries under the worksite have delayed the reconstruction indefinitely. The promenade ends at the steps to the Portal Nou (New Gate). ⊠ *Carrer Portal Nou, Eivissa.*

### Cathedral

**CHURCH |** Built on a site used for temples and other religious buildings since the time of the Phoenicians, Ibiza's cathedral has a Gothic tower and a baroque nave and a small museum of religious art and artifacts. It was built in the 13th and 14th centuries and renovated in the 18th century. ⊠ *Pl. de la Catedral s/n, Dalt Vila* 🕾 *971/312773* 🎫 *Museum €1.*

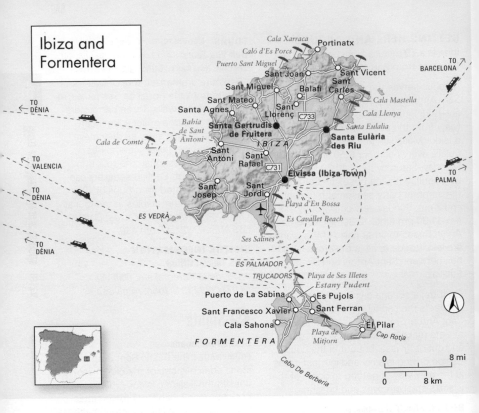

Ibiza and
Formentera

Cala Xarraca
Portinatx
Caló d'Es Porcs
Puerto Sant Miguel
Sant Joan
Sant Vicent
TO
BARCELONA
Sant Miguel
Balafi
Sant Carles
Sant Mateo
Cala Mastella
TO
DÉNIA
Santa Agnes
Sant Llorenç
C733
Cala Llenya
Babía de Sant Antoni
Santa Gertrudis de Fruitera
Santa Eulalia
Cala de Comte
IBIZA
Santa Eulària des Riu
Sant Antoni
Sant Rafael
C731
TO
VALENCIA
Elvissa (Ibiza Town)
TO
PALMA
TO
DÉNIA
Sant Josep
Sant Jordi
Playa d'En Bossa
ES VEDRÀ
Es Cavallet Beach
Ses Salines
TO
DÉNIA
ES PALMADOR
TRUCADORS
Playa de Ses Illetes
Estany Pudent
Puerto de La Sabina
Es Pujols
Sant Francesco Xavier
Sant Ferran
Cala Sahona
El Pilar
FORMENTERA
Playa de Mitjorn
Cap Rotja
Cabo De Berberia

0        8 mi

0        8 km

## Centre d'Interpretació Madina Yabisa

HISTORY MUSEUM | A few steps from the cathedral, this small center has a fascinating collection of audiovisual materials and exhibits on the period when the Moors ruled the island. ⊠ *Carrer Major 2, Dalt Vila* ☎ *971/392390* 🎫 *€2* ⊘ *Closed Mon.*

## Museu d'Art Contemporani

ART MUSEUM | Just inside the old city portal arch, this museum houses a collection of paintings, sculpture, and photography from 1959 to the present. The scope of the collection is international, but the emphasis is on artists who were born or lived in Ibiza during their careers. There isn't much explanatory material in English, however. There is also an underground archaeological site in the basement, some of which dates back as far as the 6th century BC. ⊠ *Ronda Narcís Puget s/n, Dalt Vila* ☎ *971/302723* ⊕ *www.mace.eivissa.es* 🎫 *Free* ⊘ *Closed Mon.*

## Sant Domingo

CHURCH | The roof of this 17th-century church is an irregular arrangement of tile domes. It is worth visiting for the fresco paintings on the main nave, created by the Mallorcan painter Matas in 1884, and for the chapels. The nearby *ajuntament* (town hall) is housed in the former monastery of the church. ⊠ *Carrer General Balanzat 6, Dalt Vila* ⊘ *Closed Mon.*

## 🏖 Beaches

### Es Cavellet Beach

BEACH | This wild stretch of white sand hugged by turquoise waves is popular with nudist sunbathers and can be reached on foot from Ses Salines beach

(20-minute walk). By car it's a 10-km (6-mile) drive from Eivissa, through the salt flats. Parts are backed by sand dunes, and on a clear day it serves up views of Eivissa and Formentera. El Chiringuito bar and restaurant, one of Ibiza's favorite waterfront beach bars, is known for its relaxed vibe, good food and cocktails, and its lively season-opening and season-closing parties. **Amenities:** food and drink; parking (fee); showers. **Best for:** nudists; swimming. ⊠ *Sant Josep de sa Talaia.*

### Ses Salines

BEACH | Very much a place to see and be seen, the beach at Ses Salines is a mile-long narrow crescent of golden sand about 10 minutes' drive from Eivissa, in a wildlife conservation area. Trendy restaurants and bars, like the Jockey Club and Malibu, bring drinks to you on the sand and have DJs for the season, keeping the beat in the air all day long. The beach has different areas: glitterati in one zone, naturists in another, gay couples in another. There are no nearby shops, but the commercial vacuum is filled by vendors of bags, sunglasses, fruit drinks, and so on, who can be irritating. The sea is shallow, with a gradual drop-off, but on a windy day breakers are good enough to surf. **Amenities:** food and drink; lifeguards; parking (fee); showers; toilets; water sports. **Best for:** nudists; partiers; swimming; windsurfing. ⊠ *Eivissa ✈ 10 km (6 miles) west on E20 ring road from Eivissa toward airport, then south on PM802 local road to beach.*

##  Restaurants

### Es Boldado

$$$$ | MEDITERRANEAN | The real magic of Ibiza can only be discovered when you head off the beaten track, and Es Boldado proves it. Getting here requires a bumpy ride down a dirt track off the main road that links Sant Josep de la Talaia with the beautiful beaches at Cala d'Hort, but the reward more than makes

up for it. **Known for:** incredible views of the Es Vedra islands; seafood paella; off the beaten path. $ *Average main: €28* ⊠ *Playa Cala d'Hort, 07830, Sant Josep de Sa Talaia* ☎ *626/494537* ⊕ *esboldadoibiza.com.*

### Restaurante Jardín La Brasa

$$$$ | MEDITERRANEAN | A perennial favorite, La Brasa is tucked down a side street close to the walls of the Dalt Vila. Here you can dine on traditional Ibizan cuisine, such as barbecued entrecôte steak, lamb chops, or grilled squid, within a tree-filled courtyard lit by fairy lights and candles—a haven from the bustling surroundings. **Known for:** reservations needed in high season; courtyard setting; grilled meat. $ *Average main: €25* ⊠ *Carrer de Pere Sala 3, Eivissa* ☎ *971/301202* ⊕ *www.labrasaibiza.com.*

## 🛏 Hotels

### La Ventana

$$$ | B&B/INN | Inside the medieval walls, this intimate hillside hotel has fine views of the old town and the harbor from some of the rooms. **Pros:** historic setting; roof terrace; good value. **Cons:** surroundings can be noisy until late; lots of stairs to climb, especially if you want a room with a view; rooms are small. $ *Rooms from: €141* ⊠ *Sa Carrossa 13, Eivissa* ☎ *971/390857* ⊕ *en.laventanaibiza.com* ⇌ *12 rooms, 2 suites* ⦿ *No Meals.*

### MIM Ibiza Es Vivé

$$$$ | HOTEL | Owned by F.C. Barcelona soccer superstar Lionel Messi, MIM has a stylish, upbeat vibe and a location convenient to both Eivissa old town and Figueretas beach. **Pros:** great pool area; well located for the old town and the beach; views from the roof terrace. **Cons:** some balconies don't have any views; adults only; rooms on the small side. $ *Rooms from: €359* ⊠ *Carrer de Carles Roman Ferrer 8, Dalt Vila* ☎ *971/301902* ⊕ *mimhotels.com/es/ibiza/hotel-mim-ibiza* ⇌ *53 rooms* ⦿ *Free Breakfast.*

An evening stroll among the shops in Eivissa

# Ⓨ Nightlife

Ibiza's discos are famous throughout Europe. Keep your eyes open during the day for free invitations handed out on the street—these can save you expensive entry fees. Between June and September, an all-night "Discobus" service (☎ 600/482972) runs between Eivissa, Sant Antoni, Santa Eulàlia/Es Canar, Playa d'En Bossa, and the major party venues. The cost is €3 for one ride, €12 for a five-trip ticket.

## BARS AND GATHERING PLACES
### Calle Santa Creu

**GATHERING PLACES | FAMILY |** Hidden behind the walls of the Dalt Vila, this narrow lane is lined with bustling eateries. It's at its most atmospheric in the evening, when you can enjoy a candlelit dinner on the cobblestones as the world slowly saunters past. ✉ *Santa Creu, Dalt Vila.*

### Carrer de la Mare de Déu (Calle de la Virgen) (*Calle de la Virgen*)

**GATHERING PLACES |** Gay nightlife converges on this street in Sa Penya. ✉ *Mare de Déu, Eivissa.*

### Sunset Ashram

**BARS |** There are many places to take in a spectacular sunset in Ibiza, but this one ranks as one of the White Isle's top spots. Set above a beautiful stretch of unspoiled coastline, boho Sunset Ashram mixes beach casual with ambient music, tasty cocktails, and unobstructed panoramic views of the golden hour. Dinner is also served here (reservations essential). ✉ *Cala Conta s/n, San Agustin des Vedra* ☎ *661/347222* ⊕ *www.sunsetashram. com/en.*

## DANCE CLUBS
### Amnesia

**DANCE CLUBS |** This popular club in San Rafael opened in 1980 and it's still going strong, with several ample dance floors that throb to house and funk. Like most of the clubs on the island, it opens for the season around the end of May, with a gala bash. ⊠ *Ctra. Eivissa–Sant Antoni, Km 5, San Rafael* ☎ *971/198041* ⊕ *www. amnesia.es.*

### Keeper

**DANCE CLUBS** | Clubbers start the evening here, where there's no cover and the action starts at 11 pm. The indoor space at Keeper can get a bit cramped, but out on the terrace freedom reigns. ⊠ *Marina Botafoch, Paseo Juan Carlos I s/n, Ibiza Nueva* ☎ *971/310509.*

### Pacha

**DANCE CLUBS** | A young, international crowd gathers after 2 am at the flagship venue of this club empire, where each of the five rooms offers a different style, including techno, house music, R&B, and hip-hop. ⊠ *Av. 8 de Agosto s/n, Eivissa* ☎ *971/313600* ⊕ *www.pacha.com.*

## 🛍 Shopping

Although the Sa Penya area of Eivissa still has a few designer boutiques, much of the area is now given over to the so-called hippie market, with stalls selling clothing and crafts of all sorts May–October. Browse Avenida Bartolomeu Rosselló and the main square of Dalt Vila for casual clothes and accessories.

### Divina

**MIXED CLOTHING** | With no shortage of shops in Eivissa selling clothing in the classic white Ibiza style, Divina stands out for its range of clothes for kids and its modest selection of real Panama hats. ⊠ *Pl. de la Vila 17, Dalt Vila* ☎ *971/301157.*

### Enotecum

**WINE/SPIRITS** | This store has a good range of wines, including labels produced in the Balearics, and spirits. ⊠ *Av. d'Isidoro Macabich 36, Eivissa* ☎ *971/399167* ⊕ *www.enotecum.com* ☉ *Closed Sun.*

## 🏃 Activities

### BOATING
#### Coral Yachting

**BOATING** | You can charter all sorts of power craft, sailboats (small and large), and catamarans here, by the day or by the week, with or without a skipper. ⊠ *Marina Botafoc, Local 323–324, Eivissa* ☎ *971/313926* ⊕ *www.coralyachting. com.*

### HORSEBACK RIDING
#### Can Mayans

**HORSEBACK RIDING** | Hire horses here for rides along the coast and inland. Can Mayans has a riding school and a gentle touch with beginners. ⊠ *Ctra. Santa Gertrudis–Sant Lorenç, Km 4, San Lorenzo de Balafia* ☎ *690/922144* ⊕ *www. canmayans.es.*

### SCUBA DIVING
#### Active Dive

**DIVING & SNORKELING** | Instruction and guided dives, as well as kayaking, parasailing, and boat rentals are available here. ⊠ *Surf Lounge Ibiza, Calle des Molí 10, Sant Antoni* ☎ *618/796358* ⊕ *www. active-dive.com.*

#### Arenal Diving

**SCUBA DIVING** | Book lessons and dives here, from beginner level to advanced, with PADI-trained instructors and guides. ⊠ *Av. Doctor Fleming 16, Sant Antoni* ☎ *633/078412* ⊕ *www.arenaldiving.com.*

#### Sea Horse Scuba Diving Centre

**SCUBA DIVING** | A short distance from Sant Antoni, this aquatic center offers basic scuba training as well as excursions to spectacular nearby dive sites, especially the Cala d'Hort Marine Nature Reserve and the Pillars of Hercules underwater caves. ⊠ *Edificio Yais 5, Calle Vizcaya 8, Playa Port des Torrent, Sant Josep de sa Talaia* ☎ *629/349499* ⊕ *www.seahorse-divingibiza.net.*

## TENNIS
### Ibiza Club de Campo
TENNIS | With six clay courts, seven courts for padel tennis (a racquet sport that's like a mix between tennis and squash and typically played in doubles), a 25-meter pool, and a gym, this is the best-equipped club on the island. Nonresidents and nonmembers can play tennis for €10 or padel from €7 per hour per person. ✉ *Ctra. Ibiza–Sant Josep, Km 2.5, Sant Josep de sa Talaia* ☎ *971/303030* ⊕ *www.ibizaclubdecampo.es* 🎾 *From €7/hr.*

# Santa Eulària des Riu

*15 km (9 miles) northeast of Eivissa.*

At the edge of this town on the island's eastern coast, to the right below the road, a Roman bridge crosses what some claim is the only permanent river in the Balearics (hence *des Riu*, or "of the river"). The town itself follows the curve of a long sandy beach, a few blocks deep with restaurants, shops, and vacation apartments. From here it's a 10-minute drive to Sant Carles and the open-air hippie market, Las Dalias, held there every Saturday and Sunday. The popular Las Dalias night market offers shopping with live music, food, and drinks and runs from June to September, every Sunday, Monday, and Tuesday.

### GETTING HERE AND AROUND
By car, take the PM-801 from Eivissa. From May to October, buses run from Eivissa more or less every half hour Monday–Saturday and every hour on Sunday. Service is less frequent the rest of the year.

### VISITOR INFORMATION
CONTACTS **Santa Eularia des Riu.** ✉ *Carrer Mariano Riquer Wallis 4, Santa Eulària des Riu* ☎ *971/330728* ⊕ *www.visitsantaeulalia.com.*

## 🍴 Restaurants

### Hoyo 19
$$$ | MEDITERRANEAN | FAMILY | Hoyo 19 (or Hole 19) overlooks the golf course, but locals come here to enjoy the serenity and beautiful green setting, just a 10-minute drive from Santa Eulària. Open all year-round, from breakfast on, the menu focuses on Mediterranean haute cuisine, with superb rice dishes cooked over a wood fire and excellent locally sourced meat and fish options. **Known for:** patios overlooking the golf course; rice dishes cooked over a wood fire; peaceful setting. ⑤ *Average main: €18* ✉ *Golf Ibiza, Ctra. Jesús a Cala Llonga, s/n, Santa Eulària des Riu* ☎ *971/196052* ⊕ *www.golfibiza.com/restaurante.*

### Oleoteca Ses Escoles
$$$ | MEDITERRANEAN | Chef-owner Miguel Llabres honed his craft at starred restaurants in Mallorca and opened here in 2014, to local acclaim. He keeps the menu short and focuses on garden-fresh seasonal vegetables and free-range local meats. **Known for:** Ibizan potato salad; gourmet shop; free-range local meats. ⑤ *Average main: €22* ✉ *Crtra Ibiza-Portinatx KM 9.8, Sant Joan de Labritja* ☎ *871/870229* ⊕ *www.sesescoles.com* ⊘ *Closed Mon.*

## 🛏 Hotels

### Can Curreu
$$$$ | B&B/INN | The traditional architecture here, reminiscent of a Greek island village, features a cluster of low, whitewashed buildings—and each room has one of these buildings to itself, with a private patio artfully separated from its neighbors. **Pros:** friendly, efficient staff; luxurious spa; horseback riding stables. **Cons:** patchy Wi-Fi; bit of a drive to the nearest beaches; pricey. ⑤ *Rooms from: €358* ✉ *Ctra. de Sant Carles, Km 12, Santa Eulària des Riu* ☎ *971/335280* ⊕ *www.cancurreu.com* 🛏 *18 rooms* ⑩ *Free Breakfast.*

## ★ Can Gall

**$$$$ | B&B/INN |** Santi Mari Ferrer remade his family's *finca* (farmhouse), with its massive stone walls and native savina wood beams, into one of the island's friendliest and most comfortable country inns. **Pros:** family-friendly; poolside pergola for events and yoga sessions; oasis of quiet. **Cons:** often booked out for weddings; some private terraces a bit small; 15-minute drive to beaches. $ *Rooms from: €230* ✉ *Ctra. Sant Joan, Km 17.2, San Lorenzo de Balafia* ☎ *971/337031, 670/876054* ⊕ *www.cangall.com* ⤙ *2 rooms, 9 suites* ❖❖ *Free Breakfast.*

### Hostal Yebisah

**$$ | HOTEL |** Longtime residents and civic boosters Toni and Tanya Molio are the owners of this simple lodging on the promenade in the heart of town. **Pros:** friendly service; good value; ideal location. **Cons:** best rates only for minimum booking of four nights; minimal amenities; bathrooms a bit cramped. $ *Rooms from: €105* ✉ *Paseo S'Alamera 13, Santa Eulària des Riu* ☎ *971/330160* ⊕ *www. hostalyebisah.com* ◷ *Closed Nov.–Apr.* ⤙ *26 rooms* ❖❖ *No Meals.*

### W Ibiza

**$$$$ | HOTEL |** Bright, vibrant, and bursting with color, the W Ibiza encapsulates the lively, hedonistic spirit of Ibiza. **Pros:** beachfront location; ultraplush signature W beds; excellent spa and wellness center. **Cons:** more modern than cozy; rather pricey; attracts the party crowd and can get noisy. $ *Rooms from: €540* ✉ *Carrer Ricardo Curtoys Gotarredona 37, Santa Eulària des Riu* ☎ *871/556888* ⊕ *www.marriott.com/hotels/travel/ibzwh-w-ibiza* ⤙ *162 rooms* ❖❖ *No Meals.*

 **Activities**

## BICYCLING

### Kandani

**BIKING |** Bicycle rentals start at €15 for one day or €10 per day for week-long rentals, and accessories are also available, as are guided cycling tours. ✉ *Carrer César Puget Riquer 27, Santa Eulària des Riu* ☎ *971/339264* ⊕ *www. kandani.es* ✉ *From €15.*

## DIVING

### Divestar Ibiza

**SCUBA DIVING |** This is one of the best-equipped and best-staffed diving centers on the island, for beginners and experienced PADI-qualified divers alike. ✉ *Playa Cala Martina s/n, Santa Eulària des Riu* ☎ *971/336726* ⊕ *www.divestar-ibiza.com.*

### Subfari

**SCUBA DIVING |** This is one of the best places to come for diving off the north coast of the island. ✉ *Puerto de Portinatx s/n, Sant Joan de Labritja* ⟴ *22 km (14 miles) north via C733* ☎ *971/337558, 677/466040* ⊕ *www.subfari.es.*

## GOLF

### Club de Golf Ibiza

**GOLF |** Ibiza's only golf club combines the 9 holes at the Club Roca Llisa resort complex (Course II) with the newer and more challenging 18-hole Course I nearby. Fairway maintenance on Course II leaves a bit to be desired. ✉ *Ctra. Jesús–Cala Llonga s/n, Santa Eulària des Riu* ☎ *971/196052* ⊕ *www.golfibiza.com/en* ✉ *Course I, €98; Course II, €65* ⚑ *Course I: 18 holes, 6561 yards, par 72; Course II: 9 holes, 6265 yards (2 rounds), par 71.*

# Santa Gertrudis de Fruitera

*15 km (9 miles) north of Eivissa.*

Blink and you miss it: that's true of most of the small towns in the island's interior and especially so of Santa Gertrudis. It's not much more than a bend in the road, but it's worth a look. The brick-paved town square is closed to vehicle traffic—perfect for the sidewalk cafés and boutique stores. From here, you are only a few minutes' drive from some of the island's best resort hotels and spas and the most beautiful secluded northern

10

Ibiza and the Balearic Islands IBIZA

coves and beaches: **S'Illa des Bosc, Benirrás** (where they have drum circles to salute the setting sun), **S'Illot des Renclí, Portinatx,** and **Caló d'En Serra.** Artists and expats like it here: they've given the town an appeal that now makes for listings of half a million dollars or more for a modest two-bedroom house.

### GETTING HERE AND AROUND

By car, take the El-400 from Eivissa. Buses run from Eivissa more or less seven times a day on weekdays and less frequently on weekends (check ⊕ ibiza-bus.com).

##  Restaurants

### Can Caus

$$ | **SPANISH** | **FAMILY** | Ibiza might pride itself on its seafood, but there comes a time for meat and potatoes. When that time comes, take the 20-minute drive to the outskirts of Santa Gertrudis to this family-style roadside restaurant where you can feast on skewers of barbecued *sobrasada* (sausage), goat chops, and lamb kebabs. **Known for:** Ibizan home cooking; local vibe; grilled meats. ⑤ *Average main: €16* ⊠ *Ctra. Sant Miquel, Km 3.5, Santa Gertrudis* ☎ *971/197516* ⊕ *www.cancaus.com* ⊙ *Closed Mon. and in low season (varies).*

### La Paloma

$$$ | **MEDITERRANEAN** | Channeling that Ibiza-boho vibe, La Paloma feels like a refuge for artists and hippies, nestled amid the shady overhang of orange and lemon trees. The eclectic menu often features crunchy salads, Middle Eastern– and North African–inspired dishes, fish, and homemade pasta (the chef is Italian and many of the ingredients come directly from there). **Known for:** organic dishes and fresh salads; peaceful setting with beautiful views; large shaded terrace amid a lemon and orange grove. ⑤ *Average main: €22* ⊠ *Carrer Can Pou 4, Sant Joan de Labritja* ✛ *7 km (4½*

*miles) from Santa Gertrudis de Fruitera* ☎ *971/325543* ⊕ *www.palomaibiza.com.*

## 🛏 Hotels

### Atzaró

$$$$ | **HOTEL** | Ibiza may be best known as a magnet for the international jet set, but there's also a quieter, more sophisticated side to the island, which can be found at this hotel on a 13-hectare orange farm. **Pros:** exclusive rural hideaway; 140-foot outdoor freshwater pool; farm-to-table dining. **Cons:** minimum stay five nights in high season; service can be a tad slow; very pricey. ⑤ *Rooms from: €545* ⊠ *Ctra. Sant Joan Km 15, Santa Gertrudis* ☎ *971/338838* ⊕ *www.atzaro.com* ⊙ *Closed Nov.–Mar.* ↝ *24 rooms* ⦿ *Free Breakfast.*

### ★ Cas Gasi

$$$$ | **B&B/INN** | A countryside setting on a hillside overlooking a valley makes this lovely late-19th-century manor house a quiet escape in a lively destination, with photo-ready views of Ibiza's only mountain (1,567-foot Sa Talaiassa). **Pros:** attentive personal service; excellent breakfast; peace and quiet. **Cons:** very expensive; not geared to families; minimum stay required in July and August. ⑤ *Rooms from: €575* ⊠ *Cami Vell a Sant Mateu s/n, Santa Gertrudis* ☎ *971/197700* ⊕ *www.casgasi.com* ↝ *9 rooms, 1 suite* ⦿ *Free Breakfast.*

## 🛍 Shopping

### te Cuero

**LEATHER GOODS** | This store specializes in hand-tooled leather bags and belts with great designer buckles, boots, and sandals. ⊠ *Pl. de la Iglesia 6, Santa Gertrudis* ☎ *971/197100* ⊕ *www.tecueroibiza.com* ⊙ *Closed weekends and Dec.–Mar.*

# Formentera

Environmental protection laws shield much of Formentera, making it a calm respite from neighboring Ibiza's dance-until-you-drop madness. Though it does get crowded in the summer, the island's long, white-sand beaches are among the finest in the Mediterranean; inland, you can explore quiet country roads by bicycle in relative solitude.

From the port at La Savina, it's only 3 km (2 miles) to Formentera's capital, **Sant Francesc Xavier,** a few yards off the main road. There's an active hippie market in the small plaza in front of the church. At the main road, turn right toward Sant Ferran, 2 km (1 mile) away. Beyond Sant Ferran the road continues for 7 km (4 miles) along a narrow isthmus, staying slightly closer to the rougher northern side, where the waves and rocks keep yachts—and thus much of the tourist trade—away.

The plateau on the island's east side ends at the lighthouse **Faro de la Mola.** Nearby is a **monument to Jules Verne,** who set part of his 1877 novel *Hector Servadac* (published in English as *Off on a Comet*) in Formentera. The rocks around the lighthouse are carpeted with purple thyme and sea holly in spring and fall.

Back on the main road, turn right at Sant Ferran toward Es Pujols. The few hotels here are the closest Formentera comes to beach resorts, even if the beach is not the best. Beyond Es Pujols the road skirts **Estany Pudent,** one of two lagoons that almost enclose La Savina. Salt was once extracted from Pudent, hence its name, which means "stinking pond," although the pond now smells fine. At the northern tip of Pudent, a road to the right leads to a footpath that runs the length of **Trucadors,** a narrow sand spit. The long, windswept beaches here are excellent.

## GETTING HERE AND AROUND

Formentera is a one-hour ferry ride from Ibiza or 25 minutes on the jet ferry. Baleària operates ferry services to Formentera from Ibiza and Dénia, the nearest landfall on the Spanish mainland.

On Ibiza, you can also take ferries from Santa Eulària and Sant Antoni to La Savina, as well as numerous ferries to the coves and calas on the east and west coasts of the island. Day-trippers can travel to Formentera for a few hours in the sun before heading back to Ibiza to plug into the nightlife.

A very limited bus service connects Formentera's villages, shrinking to one bus each way between San Francisco and Pilar on Saturday and disappearing altogether on Sunday and holidays.

**FERRY CONTACTS Baleària.** ⊕ *www.balearia.com.*

**TAXI CONTACTS Parada de Taxis La Savina.** ✉ *Ctra. Savina-es Pujols, KM 3, La Savina* ☎ *971/322002.*

## VISITOR INFORMATION

**CONTACTS Formentera Tourist Office.** ✉ *Estación Marítima s/n, La Savina* ☎ *971/322057.*

## ⊕ Beaches

### ★ Playa de Ses Illetes

**BEACH** | The closest beach to the port at La Savina is an exquisitely beautiful string of dunes stretching to the tip of the Trucador Peninsula at Es Pau. Collectively called Ses Illetes, they form part of a national park and are consistently voted as among the five best beaches in the world. Ibiza clubbers like to take the fast ferry over from Eivissa after a long night and chill out here, tapping the sun for the energy to party again. The water is fairly shallow and the meadows of seagrass in it shelter colorful varieties of small fish; the fairly constant breezes are good for windsurfing. Nude and topless sunbathing raises no eyebrows anywhere along the dunes. Be warned: there's no shade here at all, and rented umbrellas fetch premium prices. **Amenities:** food and drink; lifeguards; showers; toilets; water sports. **Best for:** nudists; snorkeling; swimming; windsurfing. ⊠ *La Savina* ✛ *4 km (2½ miles) north of La Savina.*

 **Hotels**

### Can Aisha

$$$$ | **B&B/INN** | With only five apartments, this converted stone farmhouse can feel like a family compound, especially when everyone is gathered on the sundeck or around the communal barbecue. **Pros:** all apartments have private terraces; kitchenettes with basic equipment; shops and restaurants nearby. **Cons:** often booked out; short season; no kids and no pets. ⑤ *Rooms from: €260* ⊠ *Venda de Sa Punta 3205, Es Pujols* ☎ *616/654982* ⊕ *www.canaisha.com* ⊘ *Closed roughly Oct.–May* ⇆ *5 apartments* ⍩ *Free Breakfast.*

### Casa Pacha

$$$$ | **HOTEL** | Legendary nightlife brand Pacha's hotel brings "barefoot simplicity and understated comfort" to Ibiza's laid-back sister island of Formentera. **Pros:** unbeatable beachfront location; yoga classes overlooking the sea; free parking. **Cons:** minimum two-night stay in high season; rather expensive; limited facilities nearby. ⑤ *Rooms from: €600* ⊠ *Camí es Arenals, Km.11, Formentor* ☎ *971/313535* ⊕ *casapacha.com* ⊘ *Closed Oct.–May* ⇆ *14 rooms* ⍩ *Free Breakfast.*

### 🛍 Shopping

The island of Formentera has three main crafts markets: El Pilar, San Françesc Xavier, and Es Pujols. Stores and workshops sell handmade items, including ceramics, jewelry, and leather goods. El Pilar's crafts market draws shoppers on Sunday and Wednesday from May to mid-October. May through mid-October, crafts are sold in the morning at the San Françesc Xavier market and in the evening in Es Pujols from May to September.

# Mallorca

Saddle-shape Mallorca is more than five times the size of Menorca or Ibiza. The Sierra de Tramuntana, a dramatic mountain range soaring to nearly 5,000 feet, runs the length of its northwest coast, and a ridge of hills borders the southeast shores; between the two lies a flat plain that in early spring becomes a sea of almond blossoms, the so-called snow of Mallorca. The island draws close to 14 million visitors a year, many of them bound for summer vacation packages in the coastal resorts. The beaches are beautiful, but save time for the charms of the northwest and the interior: caves, bird sanctuaries, monasteries and medieval towns, local museums, outdoor cafés, and village markets.

### GETTING HERE AND AROUND

From Barcelona, Palma de Mallorca is a 50-minute flight, an 8-hour overnight ferry, or a 4½-hour catamaran journey.

If you're traveling by car, Mallorca's main roads are well surfaced, and a four-lane, 25-km (15-mile) motorway penetrates deep into the island between Palma and Inca. The Vía Cintura (Ma-20), an efficient beltway, rings Palma. For destinations in the north and west, follow the "Andratx" and "Oeste" signs on the beltway; for the south and east, follow the "Este" signs. Driving in the mountains that parallel the northwest coast and descend to a corniche (cliff-side road) is a different matter; you'll be slowed not only by the narrow winding roads but also by tremendous views, tourist traffic, and groups of cyclists.

## VISITOR INFORMATION

**CONTACTS Oficina de Turismo de Mallorca.** ✉ *Son Sant Joan s/n, Palma* ☎ *971/789556* ⊕ *www.infomallorca.net.*

# Palma de Mallorca

If you look north of the cathedral (La Seu, or the seat of the bishopric, to Mallorcans) on a map of the city of Palma, you can see around the Plaça Santa Eulàlia a jumble of tiny streets that made up the earliest settlement. Farther out, a ring of wide boulevards traces the fortifications built by the Moors to defend the larger city that emerged by the 12th century. The zigzags mark the bastions that jutted out at regular intervals. By the end of the 19th century, most of the walls had been demolished; the only place where you can still see the massive defenses is at Ses Voltes, along the seafront west of the cathedral.

A *torrent* (streambed) used to run through the middle of the old city, dry for most of the year but often a raging flood in the rainy season. In the 17th century it was diverted to the east, along the moat that ran outside the city walls. Two of Palma's main arteries, La Rambla and the Passeig des Born, now follow the stream's natural course. The traditional evening paseo takes place on the bustling Born.

If you come to Palma by car, park in the garage beneath the Parc de la Mar (the ramp is just off the highway from the airport, as you reach the cathedral) and stroll along the park. Beside it run the huge bastions guarding the Palau Reial de l'Almudaina; the cathedral, golden and massive, rises beyond. Where you exit the garage, there's a **ceramic mural** by the late Catalan artist and Mallorca resident Joan Miró, facing the cathedral across the pool that runs the length of the park.

If you begin early enough, a walk along the ramparts at Ses Voltes from the mirador beside the cathedral is spectacular. The first rays of the sun turn the upper pinnacles of La Seu bright gold and then begin to work their way down the sandstone walls. From the Parc de la Mar, follow Avinguda Antoni Maura past the steps to the palace. Just below the Plaça de la Reina, where the **Passeig des Born** begins, turn left on Carrer de la Boteria into the Plaça de la Llotja. (If the Llotja itself is open, don't miss a chance to visit—it's the Mediterranean's finest Gothic-style civic building.) From there stroll through the Plaça Drassana to the **Museu d'Es Baluard,** at the end of Carrer Sant Pere. Retrace your steps to Avinguda Antoni Maura. Walk up the Passeig des Born to Plaça Joan Carles I, then right on Avenida de La Unió.

## GETTING HERE AND AROUND

Palma's Empresa Municipal de Transports (EMT) runs 65 bus lines and a tourist train in and around the Mallorcan capital. Most buses leave from the Intermodal station, next to the Inca railroad terminus on the Plaça d'Espanya; city buses leave from the ground floor, while intercity buses leave from the underground level. The tourist office on the Plaça d'Espanya has schedules. Bus A1 connects the airport with the city center and the port; No. 2 circumnavigates the historic city center; No. 20 connect the city center with the Porto Pi commercial center; No. 46 goes to the Fundació Pilar i Joan Miró, and Bus A2 connects S'Arenal with the airport. The fare for a single local ride is €2; to the airport it's €5.

You can hire a horse-drawn carriage with driver at the bottom of the Born, and also on Avinguda Antonio Maura, in the nearby cathedral square, and on the Plaça d'Espanya, at the side farthest from the train station. A tour of the city costs €30 for a half hour, €45 for 45 minutes, €60 for an hour.

■TIP→ **Haggle firmly, and the driver might come down a bit off the posted fare.**

Boats from Palma to neighboring beach resorts leave from the jetty opposite the Auditorium, on the Passeig Marítim. The tourist office has a schedule.

**BUS INFORMATION Empresa Municipal de Transports.** ⊠ *Calle Josep Anselm Clavé 5, Palma* ☎ *971/214444* ⊕ *www.emtpalma. cat.*

**BUS STATION Estació Intermodal.** ⊠ *Pl. d'Espanya s/n, Palma* ☎ *971/177777* ⊕ *www.tib.org.*

**TAXI INFORMATION Radio-Taxi Ciutat.** ⊠ *Francesc Sancho 7, Palma* ☎ *971/201212* ⊕ *www.radiotaxiciutat. com.*

**VISITOR INFORMATION CONTACTS Oficine d'Informació Turística.** ⊠ *Pl. de la Reina 2, Palma* ☎ *971/173990* ⊕ *www.infomallorca.net.*

## TOURS
### City Sightseeing

BUS TOURS | The open-top City Sightseeing bus leaves from behind the Palau de la Aludaina every 20–25 minutes starting at 9:30 am and makes 20 stops throughout the town, including La Rambla, the Passeig Marítim, and the Castell de Bellver. Tickets are valid for 24 or 48 hours, and you can get on and off as many times as you wish. All Palma tourist offices have details. ⊠ *Passeig Maritim 16, Palma* ⊕ *city-sightseeing-spain.com/en/25/palma-de-mallorca* 🎫 *From €18.*

## ◉ Sights

### Ajuntament (*Town Hall*)
GOVERNMENT BUILDING | Along Carrer Colom is the 17th-century *ajuntament* (town hall). Stop in to see the collection of *gigantes*, the huge painted and

costumed mannequins paraded through the streets during festivals, which are on display in the lobby. The olive tree on the right side of the square is one of Mallorca's so-called *olivos milenarios*—purported to be more than 1,000 years old. The adjacent building is the Palau del Consell, the headquarters of the island's government, a late-19th-century building on the site of a medieval prison. The *palau* (palace) has its own collection of gigantes and an impressive stained-glass window over the ornate stone staircase; visits inside can be arranged by appointment (*visites@conselldemallorca. net*). ⊠ *Pl. Cort 1, Centro* ☎ *971/225900* ⊕ *www.palma.cat.*

### Banys Arabs (*Arab Baths*)

**RUINS** | One of Palma's oldest monuments, the 10th-century public bathhouse has a wonderful walled garden of palms and lemon trees. In its day, it was not merely a place to bathe but a social institution where you could soak, relax, and gossip with your neighbors. ⊠ *Carrer Can Serra 7, Centro* ☎ *637/046534* ⌲ *€3.*

### Bodega Antonio Nadal Ros (*Viñas de Son Roig*)

**WINERY** | Binissalem, about a half-hour drive (25 km [15 miles]) from Palma, is the center of one of the island's two D.O.-registered wine regions and has a riotous harvest festival in mid-September, when surplus grapes are dumped by the truckload for participants to fling at each other. Some of Mallorca's best wineries are here, many of them open for tastings and tours. This winery is hard to find, but it's worth a detour, especially for its award-winning red Tres Uvas, a rich blend of Cabernet Sauvignon and Tempranillo, easy on the palate. It's open for tours and tastings, but call ahead on weekends. ⊠ *C. de Son Roig s/n, Binissalem* ☎ *630/914511* ⊕ *www.antonionadalros. com* ⌲ *From €25.*

### Bodegas José Ferrer

**WINERY** | One of the largest of Mallorca's wineries, Bodegas José Ferrer can be visited for tastings. Ferrer wines consistently do well at international competitions in France and Germany; Pedra de Binissalem, their ecological red, is a subtle blend of Cabernet Sauvignon and the local varietal Manto Negro—well worth a try. ⊠ *Carrer del Conquistador 103, Binissalem* ☎ *971/100100* ⊕ *www. vinosferrer.com* ⌲ *From €15.*

### Caixa Forum (*Grand Hotel*)

**NOTABLE BUILDING** | Built between 1901 and 1903 by Luis Domènech i Montaner, originator of Barcelona's Palau de la Música Catalana, this former hotel has an alabaster facade sculpted like a wedding cake, with floral motifs, angelic heads, and coats of arms. The original interiors are gone, however. The building is owned and used by the Fundació La Caixa, a cultural and social organization funded by the region's largest bank. Don't miss the permanent exhibit of paintings by the Mallorcan impressionist Hermenegildo Anglada Camarasa. ⊠ *Pl. Weyler 3, Centro* ☎ *971/178512* ⊕ *caixaforum.org/es/ palma* ⌲ *€6* ⊘ *Closed Dec. 25–Jan. 6.*

### Can Corbella

**NOTABLE BUILDING** | This gem of Palma's early Moderniste architecture, designed in the 1890s by Nicolás Lliteras, is on the corner of Carrer de Jaume II. ⊠ *Pl. Cort, Centro.*

### Can Forteza Rei

**NOTABLE BUILDING** | Designed by Lluís Forteza Rei in 1909, this Art Nouveau delight has twisted wrought-iron railings and surfaces inlaid with bits of polychrome tile, which are signature touches of Antoni Gaudí and his contemporaries. A wonderful carved stone face in a painful grimace, flanked by dragons, ironically frames the stained-glass windows of a third-floor dental clinic. There's a chocolate shop on the ground floor. ⊠ *Pl. Marqués Palmer 1, Centro.*

### Castell de Bellver (*Bellver Castle*)

**CASTLE/PALACE** | Overlooking the city and the bay from a hillside, the castle

Cathedral of Palma de Mallorca

was built at the beginning of the 14th century in Gothic style but with a circular design—the only one of its kind in Spain. It houses an archaeological museum of the history of Mallorca and a small collection of classical sculpture. The Bus Turistic 50 and the EMT municipal buses Nos. 4, 20, and 46 all stop a 20-minute walk from the entrance. In summer, there are classical music concerts in the courtyard, performed by the Ciutat de Palma Symphony Orchestra. ⊠ *Carrer de Camilo José Cela s/n, Palma* ☎ *971/735065, 971/225900 concerts box office* ⊕ *castelldebellver.palma.cat* ✉ *€4 (free Sun.)* ⊘ *Closed Mon.*

★ **Catedral de Mallorca** (*La Seu*)
CHURCH | Palma's cathedral is an architectural wonder that took almost 400 years to build. Begun in 1230, the wide expanse of the nave is supported by 14 70-foot-tall columns that fan out at the top like palm trees. The nave is dominated by an immense rose window, 40 feet in diameter, dating to 1370. Over the main altar (consecrated in 1346) is

the surrealistic *baldoquí* (baldachin) by Antoni Gaudí, completed in 1912. This enormous canopy, with lamps suspended from it like elements of a mobile, rises to a Crucifixion scene at the top. To the right, in the Chapel of the Santísimo, is an equally remarkable 2007 work by the sculptor Miquel Barceló: a painted ceramic tableau covering the walls like a skin.

■ TIP➔ **From April through October you can take a guided tour of the bell tower and the cathedral's terraces overlooking panoramic views of the city. Reservations must be made in advance on the website.** ⊠ *Pl. Almoina s/n, Centro* ☎ *971/713133* ⊕ *www.catedraldemallorca.org* ✉ *€9* ⊘ *Closed Sun.*

★ **Museu d'Es Baluard** (*Museum of Modern and Contemporary Art of Palma*)
ART MUSEUM | West of the city center, this museum rises on a long-neglected archaeological site, parts of which date back to the 12th century. The building itself is an outstanding convergence of old and new: the exhibition space uses the surviving 16th-century perimeter

# Illa de Cabrera

Off the south coast of Mallorca, this verdant isle is one of the last unspoiled places in the Mediterranean—the largest of the 19 islands of the Cabrera Archipelago. To protect its dramatic landscape, varied wildlife, and lush vegetation, it was declared a national park in 1991. Throughout its history, Cabrera has had its share of visitors, from the Romans to the Arabs. The only intact historical remains are those of a 14th-century castle overlooking the harbor. Tours are operated daily by the Marcabrera company (⊕ www.marcabrera.com). Boats depart from Colònia Sant Jordi, 47 km (29 miles) southeast of Palma. Full-day trips (times vary), with a stop to swim or snorkel in the Cueva Azul (Blue Cave), start from €51; two-hour excursions by speedboat, leaving three times a day, are €55.

walls of the fortified city, including a stone courtyard facing the sea and a promenade along the ramparts. There are three floors of galleries, and the collection includes work by Miró, Picasso, and Antoni Tàpies, among other major artists. To get here, take the narrow Carrer de Sant Pere through the old fishermen's quarter, from Plaça de la Drassana. ⊠ Pl. Porta de Santa Catalina 10, Palma ☎ 971/908200 ⊕ www.esbaluard.org/en ☜ €6 ☾ Closed Mon.

**Museu Fundació Pilar y Joan Miró** (*Pilar and Joan Miró Foundation Museum*)
ART MUSEUM | The permanent collection here includes many drawings and studies by the Catalan artist, who spent his last years on Mallorca, but it exhibits far fewer finished paintings and sculptures than the Fundació Miró in Barcelona. While the exhibits are fairly limited, the setting and views of Palma are worth the detour. ⊠ Saridakis 29, Palma ☎ 971/701420 ⊕ www.miromallorca.com ☜ €7.50 ☾ Closed Mon.

**Museu Fundación Juan March**
ART MUSEUM | A few steps from the north archway of the Plaça Major is the Museu Fundación Juan March. This fine little museum was established to display what had been a private collection of modern Spanish art. The building itself was a sumptuous private home built in the 18th century. The second and third floors were redesigned to accommodate a series of small galleries, with one or two works at most—by Pablo Picasso, Joan Miró, Juan Gris, Salvador Dalí, Antoni Tàpies, and Miquel Barceló, among others—on each wall. ⊠ Sant Miquel 11, Centro ☎ 971/713515 ⊕ www.march.es/arte/palma ☜ Free ☾ Closed Sun.

**Palau Reial de l'Almudaina** (*Royal Palace of La Almudaina*)
CASTLE/PALACE | Opposite Palma's cathedral, this palace was originally an Arab citadel, then became the residence of the ruling house during the Middle Ages. It's now a military headquarters and the king's official residence when he's in Mallorca. Guided tours generally depart hourly during open hours and cost €2.

■ TIP→ Try to catch the changing of the Honor Guard ceremony, which takes place in front of the palace at noon on the last Saturday of the month (except July and August). ⊠ Carrer Palau Reial s/n, Centro ☎ 902/044454 ⊕ www.patrimonionacional.es/visita/palacio-real-de-la-almudaina ☜ €7 (Free Wed. and Sun. afternoons) ☾ Closed Mon.

**Passeig des Born**
PROMENADE | While it's known as one of the best streets in Palma to hit the

shops, this tree-lined promenade is also a favored place to *pasear* (stroll), lined with palatial-style stone residences (most of which have now been converted into hotels and shops) and busy café-terraces. Bar Bosch, straddling Passeig des Born and Plaça Rei Joan Carles I, has been a key gathering point for locals since 1936. ⊠ *Passeig des Born, Palma.*

### Plaça Major

PLAZA/SQUARE | A crafts market fills this elegant neoclassical space from 10–2 on Monday, Tuesday, Friday, and Saturday mornings during most of the year. Until 1838, this was the local headquarters of the Inquisition. A flight of steps on the east side of the Plaça Major leads down to Las Ramblas, a pleasant promenade lined with flower stalls. ⊠ *Centro.*

### Sa Llotja (*Exchange*)

NOTABLE BUILDING | On the seafront west of the Plaça de la Reina, the 15th-century Llotja connects via an interior courtyard to the Consolat de Mar (Maritime Consulate). With its decorative turrets, pointed battlements, fluted pillars, and Gothic stained-glass windows—part fortress, part church—it attests to the wealth Mallorca achieved in its heyday as a Mediterranean trading power. The interior (the Merchants' Chamber) often hosts free art exhibitions. ⊠ *Pl. Llotja 5, Palma* ⊠ *Free* ⊘ *Closed Mon.*

### Sant Francesc

CHURCH | The 13th-century monastery church of Sant Francesc was established by Jaume II when his eldest son took monastic orders and gave up rights to the throne. Fra Junípero Serra, the missionary who founded San Francisco, California, was later educated here; his statue stands to the left of the main entrance. The basilica houses the tomb of eminent 13th-century scholar Ramón Llull. The cloisters (enter via the side door, on the right) are especially beautiful and peaceful. The €5 entrance fee includes entrance to five other churches. ⊠ *Pl. Sant Francesc 7, Centro*

## Cuevas del Drach ◉

Mallorca's "Dragon Caves" are four large caves that reach a depth of 80 feet below the surface, one of the largest underground lakes in the world, and a dazzling array of stalagmites and stalactites that form identifiable shapes such as the Virgin of the Cave, the Buddha, and the Valley of Montserrat. The hour-long tour includes a visit to the caves, an optional boat trip across Lake Martel, and a short classical music concert performed on the lake by musicians in an illuminated boat. For more info check ⊕ www. cuevasdeldrach.com/en.

☏ *971/712695* ⊕ *www.spiritualmallorca. com* ⊠ *€5* ⊘ *Closed Sun.*

### Santa Eulàlia

CHURCH | Carrer de la Cadena leads to this imposing Gothic church, where, in 1435, 200 Jews were forced to convert to Christianity after their rabbis were threatened with being burned at the stake. ⊠ *Pl. Santa Eulalia 2, Centro* ☏ *971/714625* ⊠ *Free.*

### Teatre Principal

NOTABLE BUILDING | Take time to appreciate the neoclassical symmetry of this theater, Palma's chief venue for classical music. The opera season here usually runs mid-March–June. ⊠ *Carrer de la Riera 2, Centro* ☏ *971/219700 information, 971/219696 tickets* ⊕ *teatreprincipal. com* ⊠ *Performances vary.*

## ⊕ Beaches

### Es Trenc

BEACH | FAMILY | Even though it's nearly an hour's drive from Palma, this pristine 2-km (1-mile) stretch of fine white sand on Mallorca's southern coast, much longer than it is wide, is one of the most popular beaches on the island—arrive late in summer, and you'll be hard-pressed to find a space to stretch out. At times the water can be a bit choppy, and there are occasional patches of seaweed—but otherwise the clear, clean water slopes off gently from the shore for some 30 feet, making it ideal for families with younger kids. Es Trenc is in a protected natural area free of hotels and other developments, which makes for good bird-watching. Naturists lay their claim to part of the beach's eastern end. **Amenities:** food and drink; lifeguards; parking (fee); toilets. **Best for:** nudists; partiers; swimming; walking. ✉ *MA6040, Colònia de Sant Jordi ✛ 10 km (6 miles) south of Campos, 6½ km (4 miles) east of Colònia Sant Jordi.*

## 🍴 Restaurants

### ★ Adrian Quetglas Restaurant
$$$$ | SPANISH | Adrián Quetglas, an Argentinian-born chef of Mallorcan descent, cooked in some of the finest kitchens in London, Paris, and Moscow before he returned to Mallorca in 2015 to launch this solo venture. Despite having been awarded a Michelin star, Quetglas remains committed to the democratization of fine dining and to delivering the pleasure of high-end gastronomy to a wider audience. **Known for:** emerging Michelin-starred chef; accessible fine dining; lunchtime tasting menu only €45. $ *Average main: €75* ✉ *Passeig de Mallorca 20, Centro* 🕾 *971/781119* ⊕ *adrianquetglas.es* ⊘ *Closed Sun. and Mon.*

### Botànic
$$$ | MEDITERRANEAN | In the leafy garden of the Can Bordoy boutique hotel, Botànic is a plant-forward restaurant that also features locally sourced meat and fish. The menu is inspired by the cuisines of **Known for:** lovely patio; healthy and flavor-packed dishes; seasonal, local produce. $ *Average main: €18* ✉ *Forn*

*de la Glória 14, Centro* 🕾 *971/760550* ⊕ *canbordoy.com/botanic.*

### ★ DINS Santi Taura
$$$$ | CATALAN | Local culinary wunderkind Santi Taura is using his eponymous restaurant in the El Llorenç Parc de la Mar hotel to explore historical recipes of the island, served in an ultrachic, contemporary setting. Some of the most emblematic dishes include *panada de peix de roca*—a "Mallorcan dim sum" of rock fish pie, believed to be one of the oldest recipes on the island—and a dish of rabbit with lobster, which combines the sea and the mountains. **Known for:** traditional Mallorcan rock fish pie; bar seating lets you see the chef at work; local Michelin-starred chef. $ *Average main: €95* ✉ *Pl. de Llorenç Villalonga 4, Centro* 🕾 *656/738214* ⊕ *www.dinssantitaura.com.*

### Forn de Sant Joan
$$$$ | MEDITERRANEAN | This former bakery turned restaurant (*forn* means "bakery" or "oven" in Mallorquin) dates back to the 19th century and features exposed brick walls, colorful floor tiles, modern art, and picture-perfect Mediterranean tapas. There's a cocktail bar on the ground floor that overlooks the street, and one of the three distinct dining areas is the area where bread dough was once prepared. **Known for:** cocktail bar; elevated tapas and Mediterranean dishes; former 19th-century bakery. $ *Average main: €26* ✉ *Carrer de Sant Joan 4, Palma* 🕾 *971/728422* ⊕ *www.forndesantjoan.com.*

## ☕ Coffee and Quick Bites

### Café La Lonja (*Sa Llotja*)
$ | TAPAS | A great spot for coffee or a G&T, this is a classic establishment in the old fishermen's neighborhood. Both the sunny terrace in front and the bar inside are excellent places for drinks and sandwiches. **Known for:** a great pit stop; terrace with views of the Llotja; coffee

and snacks. $ *Average main: €9* ✉ *Carrer Sa Lonja del Mar 2, Palma* ☎ *971/722799* 🌐 *cafelalonja.com* ⊘ *Closed Mon.*

## 🛏 Hotels

### ★ Calatrava

$$$$ | HOTEL | FAMILY | In a 19th-century building on a quiet square in the old town, Calatrava is one of the many historic buildings that have been converted into elegant boutique hotels in recent years. **Pros:** great old-town location; drinks and breakfast served on the rooftop with sea views; spacious rooms. **Cons:** limited breakfast options; arriving by car is tricky and parking is expensive; no pool or gym. $ *Rooms from: €458* ✉ *Pl. de Llorenç Villalonga 8, Centro* ☎ *971/728110* 🌐 *www.calatravahotel.com* ⤵ *16 rooms* �“❘ *Free Breakfast.*

### ★ Cap Rocat

$$$$ | HOTEL | What was once a 19th-century military fortress has been converted into one of Mallorca's—and arguably Europe's—most distinctive hotels, on a rocky outcrop some 25 minutes from Palma. **Pros:** stunning backdrop; impeccable service; superb cuisine. **Cons:** sky-high prices; lacks a sandy beach; isolated from the bustle—and nightlife. $ *Rooms from: €500* ✉ *Ctra. de Enderrocat s/n, Cala Blava* ☎ *971/747878* 🌐 *www.caprocat.com/en* ⊘ *Closed Nov.–mid-Mar.* ⤵ *30 rooms* ❘❝❘ *Free Breakfast.*

### Castillo Hotel Son Vida

$$$$ | HOTEL | This lovely hotel in a 13th-century estate is a 10-minute drive from Palma, with a number of golf courses in the vicinity. **Pros:** heaven for golfers; outstanding service; set in a quiet green area but still close to Palma. **Cons:** adults only; eating off-site requires a cab ride or a rental car; rooms are a little dated. $ *Rooms from: €380* ✉ *Carrer de Raixa 2, Ponent* ☎ *971/493493* 🌐 *www.castillohotelsonvida.com* ⤵ *164 rooms* ❘❝❘ *Free Breakfast.*

### ★ El Llorenç Parc de la Mar

$$$$ | HOTEL | Recent years have seen a number of high-end boutique hotels opening in Palma de Mallorca, none more fabulous than El Llorenç Parc de la Mar. The setting, on a quiet square in the historic Calatrava neighborhood, is ideal for exploring the prettiest parts of Palma on foot. **Pros:** incredible split-level rooftop terrace; personalized service; Michelin-starred restaurant. **Cons:** rooms on the small side; adults only; tricky to get to by car. $ *Rooms from: €425* ✉ *Pl. de Llorenç Villalonga 4, Centro* ☎ *971/677770* 🌐 *www.elllorenc.com/en* ⤵ *33 rooms* ❘❝❘ *Free Breakfast.*

### Finca Serena

$$$$ | HOTEL | Rural retreats don't get much more chic or more beautiful than Finca Serena. **Pros:** rural-chic charm; very relaxing; lovely pool area. **Cons:** watch out for creepy-crawlies; service can be a bit wobbly; extremely pricey. $ *Rooms from: €660* ✉ *Ma-3200, Km 3* ☎ *971/181758* 🌐 *www.fincaserenamallorca.com/en* ⤵ *25 rooms* ❘❝❘ *Free Breakfast.*

### Hostal Apuntadores

$$$ | HOTEL | A favorite among budget travelers, this lodging in the heart of the old town, within strolling distance of the bustling Passeig des Born, has a rooftop terrace with arguably the city's best view—overlooking the cathedral and the sea. **Pros:** good value; some rooms have balconies; rooms have a/c and heat. **Cons:** basic decor; the cheapest rooms share bathrooms; can be noisy. $ *Rooms from: €135* ✉ *Carrer Apuntadores 8, Centro* ☎ *971/713491* 🌐 *www.apuntadoreshostal.com* ⤵ *28 rooms* ❘❝❘ *No Meals.*

### ★ M House

$$$$ | HOTEL | With an enviable location in Palma's old town, close to the cathedral and some of the best shopping in the city, M House is a true urban oasis. **Pros:** trendy vibe; private parking available for €12/day; personalized service. **Cons:** not all rooms have a terrace; very tight parking spots; small swimming pool.

$ Rooms from: €245 ⊠ Camer de Can Miquel 14, Centre ☎ 971/269600 ⊕ www.mhousehotel.com ➔ 37 rooms ❏ Free Breakfast.

## Nightlife

Mallorca's nightlife is never hard to find. Many of the hot spots are concentrated 6 km (4 miles) west of Palma at **Punta Portals,** in Portals Nous, where the royal yacht is moored when former king Juan Carlos I comes to Mallorca in early August for the Copa del Rey international regatta. Another major area is **Avinguda Gabriel Roca.** This section of the Passeig Marítim holds many taverns, pubs, and clubs. The network of streets in the old town, around Carrer Apuntadores, is also prime barhopping territory.

### BARS AND CAFÉS
### ★ Bar Abaco

BARS | The over-the-top baroque exuberance of this bar sets it apart from its humble setting. There are urns and baskets of fresh flowers and fruit tumbling out on to the floor, stone pillars and vaulted ceilings, tall candles, and ambient opera music. Be warned: Abaco's signature cocktails are pricey. ⊠ Carrer de Sant Joan 1, Palma ☎ 971/714939 ⊕ www. bar-abaco.es.

### Carrer dels Apuntadors

GATHERING PLACES | On the west side of Passeig des Born in the old town, this street is lined with casual bars and cafés that appeal to night owls in their twenties and thirties. On the weekend, you can often come across impromptu live rock and pop performed on small stages. ⊠ Carrer dels Apuntadors, Palma.

### Plaça de la Llotja

GATHERING PLACES | This square, along with the surrounding streets, is the place to go for copas (drinking, tapas sampling, and general carousing). ⊠ Plaça de la Llotja, Palma.

### ★ Wineing

WINE BARS | Tucked down Carrer dels Apuntadors, Wineing is a great place to try wines from across the island and beyond. There's a credit-card-operated system that dispenses small tastings (or larger glasses, if you feel inclined), plus a menu of tapas, cheese platters, and grilled meats for sharing. ⊠ Calle Apuntadores 24, Palma ☎ 971/214011 ⊕ www. wineing.es.

## Shopping

Mallorca's specialties are shoes and leather clothing, utensils carved from olive wood, porcelain and handblown glass, and artificial pearls. Look for designer fashions on the **Passeig des Born** and for antiques on **Costa de la Pols,** a narrow little street near the Plaça Riera. The **Plaça Major** has a modest crafts market on Monday, Tuesday, Friday, and Saturday 10–2. During summer, there's a crafts market on the seafront at Sa Llotja. Palma has a range of food markets, including Mercat de l'Olivar, where you can browse stalls piled high with local produce, meat, and fish. Head to the fish section to sample the goods.

Many of Palma's best shoe shops are on Avenida Rei Jaime III, between the Plaça Joan Carles I and Passeig Mallorca.

### FOOD
### Colmado Santo Domingo

FOOD | This is a wonderful little shop for the artisanal food specialties of Mallorca: sobrasada of black pork, sausages of all sorts, cheeses, jams, honeys, and preserves. ⊠ Carrer Santo Domingo 1, Centro ☎ 971/714887 ⊕ www.colmadosantodomingo.com ⊗ Closed Sun.

### GLASS AND CERAMICS
### Gordiola

GLASSWARE | Glassmakers since 1719, Gordiola has a factory showroom in Algaida and a museum, on the Palma–Manacor road, where you can watch the glass being blown and even try your hand at making a piece. There is also a shop in the center of Palma on Carrer de la Victoria, 2. ⊠ *Ctra. Palma–Manacor, Km 19, Algaida* ☎ *971/665046* ⊕ *www.gordiola. com* ⊘ *Closed Sun.*

## MARKETS
### Mercat de Sineu

MARKET | The island's biggest market takes place every Wednesday, 8 am to 1:30 pm, in the town of Sineu, 34 km (21 miles) east of Palma. The market, among the island's oldest, dates back to the 14th century, when livestock was auctioned—a practice that continues to this day. Come early if you want to see the auction, which takes place in and around the main square. Local crafts and produce, plants and flowers, clothing, and leather goods are traded throughout the village along the labyrinth of narrow streets, which can get very busy. ⊠ *Pl. Es Fossar.*

## SHOES AND LEATHER GOODS
### Alpargatería La Concepción

SHOES | Mallorca's most popular footwear is the simple, comfortable slip-on espadrille (usually with a leather front over the first half of the foot and a strap across the back of the ankle). Look for a pair here. ⊠ *Carrer de la Concepción 17, Palma* ☎ *971/710709* ⊕ *www.zapateria-mallorca.com* ⊘ *Closed Sun.*

### Lottusse

LEATHER GOODS | Shop here for high-end shoes, leather coats, and accessories. ⊠ *Av. Jaume III 2, Palma* ☎ *971/710203* ⊕ *www.lottusse.com* ⊘ *Closed Sun.*

# Activities

## BALLOONING
### Mallorca Balloons

BALLOONING | For spectacular views of the island, float up in a hot-air balloon, which lifts off daily, weather permitting, at sunrise and sunset. Call for a reservation. ⊠ *Carrer del Pare Francesc Molina, 33, Manacor* ☎ *971/596969* ⊕ *www.*

*mallorcaballoons.com* ✉ *1-hr flights from €170 per person.*

## BICYCLING

With long, flat stretches and heart-pounding climbs, Mallorca's 675 km (420 miles) of rural roads adapted for cycling make the sport the most popular on the island; many European professional teams train here. Tourist-board offices have excellent leaflets on bike routes with maps, details about the terrain, sights, and distances. The company below can rent you bikes for exploring Palma and beyond.

### Palma on Bike

BIKING | This bike-rental shop, just below the Plaça de la Reina in Palma, is open daily and organizes both city bike tours and road bike tours through the Tramuntana Mountains. ⊠ *Av. Antoni Maura 10, Centro* ☎ *971/718062* ⊕ *www.palmaonbike.com.*

## BIRD-WATCHING

Mallorca has two notable nature reserves: Sa Dragonera and S'Albufera de Mallorca.

### Sa Dragonera

BIRD WATCHING | This island and its large colony of sea falcons are accessible by boat from Sant Elm, at the western tip of Mallorca. The boats, run by the operator Cruceros Margarita, leave from the port of Sant Elm with several sailings a day, mainly in the mornings. ⊠ *Sant Elm* ☎ *638/779001 for Cruceros Margarita* ⊕ *www.crucerosmargarita.com* ✉ *Boat €15.*

### S'Albufera de Mallorca

BIRD WATCHING | This is the largest wetlands zone in Mallorca. ⊠ *Ctra. Port d'Alcúdia–Ca'n Picafort, Alcúdia* ☎ *971/177639* ⊕ *en.balearsnatura.com/parque_natural/parc-natural-de-sal-bufera-de-mallorca* ⌂ *Stop at Centre de Recepció (Reception Center) sa Roca for permission to enter park.*

Mallorca is a popular place for cyclists, and many European professionals train here.

## GOLF

Mallorca has more than 20 18-hole golf courses, among them PGA championship venues of fiendish difficulty. The Federación Balear de Golf (Balearic Golf Federation) can provide more information.

### Canyamel Golf

GOLF | This club, some 64 km (40 miles) from Palma, at the far eastern tip of the island, has wonderful views of the sea. Fans of the club say the 475-yard 13th hole (par 5) is a heartbreaker. ⊠ Av. d'Es Cap Vermell s/n, Capdepera ☎ 971/841313 ⊕ www.canyamelgolf.com ⊠ €83–€105 for 18 holes, depending on the season ⚐ 18 holes, 6562 yards, par 73.

### ★ Golf Alcanada

GOLF | This 18-hole course, designed by Robert Trent Jones Jr., is widely regarded as the best club on the island, with spectacular views of the bay and lighthouse. ⊠ Ctra. del Faro s/n, Alcúdia ☎ 971/549560 ⊕ www.golf-alcanada.com/en ⊠ From €105 for 18 holes, from €62 for 9 holes (depending on season) ⚐ 18 holes, 7107 yards, par 72.

## HIKING

Mallorca is excellent for hiking. In the Sierra de Tramuntana, you can easily arrange to trek one way and take a boat, bus, or train back. Ask the tourist office for detailed maps and itineraries.

### Grup Excursionista de Mallorca (Mallorcan Hiking Association)

HIKING & WALKING | This association can provide hiking information. ⊠ Carrer dels Horts 1, Palma ☎ 971/718823 ⊕ www.gemweb.org.

## SAILING

### Cruesa Mallorca Yacht Charter

SAILING | A wide range of yachts, cruisers, and catamarans are available for rent here, by the day or the week. In high season, only full-week rentals from Saturday to Friday are available. ⊠ Carrer Magalhaes 12, Palma ☎ 971/282821 ⊕ www.cruesa.com/en ⊠ From €900 per week.

**Federación Balear de Vela** (*Balearic Sailing Federation*)

SAILING | For information on sailing, contact the federation. ✉ *Edificio Palma Arena, Av. Uruguay s/n, Palma* ☎ *971/402412* ⊕ *www.federacionbalearvela.org.*

## SCUBA DIVING

**Big Blue**

SCUBA DIVING | This dive center, next to the Alua Hawaii hotel on the beach boardwalk in Palmanova, offers PADI-certified courses for beginners (€269), including two dives with full equipment (tanks, wet suits, regulators, masks, and fins). ✉ *Carrer Martin Ros Garcia 6, Palmanova* ☎ *971/681686* ⊕ *www.bigbluediving.net.*

## TENNIS

Tennis is very popular here—the more so for world champion Rafael Nadal being a Mallorcan. There are courts at many hotels and private clubs, and tennis schools as well. The Federació de Tennis de les Illes Balears (Balearics Tennis Federation) can provide information about playing in the area.

**Federació de Tennis de les Illes Balears** (*Balearic Tennis Federation*)

TENNIS | The Balearic Tennis Federation (FTIB) provides information about tennis in Mallorca, Menorca, Ibiza, and Formentera, where a wide range of clubs combine tennis and leisure activities for everything from beginners to professional players, as well as for families. ✉ *Edificio Palma Arena, Calle Uruguay s/n, Palma* ☎ *971/720956* ⊕ *www.ftib.es/es/welcome.*

# Valldemossa

*18 km (11 miles) north of Palma.*

The jumping-off point for a drive up the spectacular coast of the Tramuntana, this pretty little town, north of Palma, is famous for the vast complex of the Reial Cartuja monastery. Surrounded by natural beauty and stunning views, Chopin spent the winter of 1838 here with George Sand. As most tourists tend to bus in during the day for a few hours and leave, it is worth spending an evening in Valldemossa to soak up the true atmosphere of this beautiful village. At sundown, the quiet streets and plaças are a delight to wander through, flanked by sandy stone houses with green shutters and overflowing plant pots. A classical music festival paying tribute to Chopin (among other composers) is held every August, with most performances taking place in the Reial Cartuja monastery.

## GETTING HERE AND AROUND

Valldemossa is a 30-minute drive from Palma on the MA-1110. Regular bus service from the Plaça d'Espanya in Palma gets you to Valldemossa in about a half hour.

## VISITOR INFORMATION

**CONTACTS Valldemossa Tourist Office.** ✉ *Av. de Palma 7, Valldemossa* ☎ *971/612019.*

## ◉ Sights

★ **Cartoixa de Valldemossa** (*Royal Carthusian Monastery*)

NOTABLE BUILDING | Originally built as a palace in 1309, the monastery was founded in 1399, but after the monks were expelled in 1835, it acquired a new lease on life by offering apartments to travelers. The most famous lodgers were Frédéric Chopin and his lover, the Baroness Amandine Dupin, the French novelist better known by her pseudonym, George Sand. The two spent three difficult months here in the cold, damp winter of 1838–39.

In the church, note the frescoes above the nave—the monk who painted them was Goya's brother-in-law. The pharmacy, made by the monks in 1723, is almost completely preserved. A long corridor leads to the apartments, furnished in period style, occupied by Chopin and Sand (the piano is original). Nearby, another set of apartments houses the local museum, with mementos of Archduke Luis Salvador and a collection of old printing blocks. From here you return to the ornately furnished King Sancho's palace, a group of rooms originally built by King Jaume II for his son. The tourist office, in Valldemossa's main plaza, sells a ticket good for all of the monastery's attractions. ⊠ *Pl. de la Cartuja s/n, Valldemossa* ☎ *971/612106* ⊕ *www.cartoixadevalldemossa.com/en* ✉ *€9.50* ⦸ *Closed Sun.*

##  Hotels

### ★ Mirabó de Valldemossa

$$$$ | **B&B/INN** | At the far end of a winding dirt road in the hills overlooking the Real Cartuja, across the valley of Valldemossa, this luxurious little agroturismo is a romantic hideaway that's hard to reach and even harder to tear yourself away from. **Pros:** friendly personal service; incredible views; peace and quiet. **Cons:** those low stone doorways can be a headache; no gym or spa; no restaurants nearby. |$| *Rooms from: €330* ⊠ *Ctra. Valldemossa, Km 15.950, Valldemossa* ☎ *661/285215* ⊕ *mirabo.es/en* ⬧ *9 rooms* ⦿ *Free Breakfast.*

# Deià

*9 km (5½ miles) southwest of Sóller.*

Deià is perhaps best known as the adopted home of the English poet and writer Robert Graves, who lived here off and on from 1929 until his death in 1985. His grave can be found in the small cemetery at the top of the village. Deià is still a favorite haunt of writers and artists, including Graves's son Tomás—author of *Pa amb Oli* (*Bread and Olive Oil*), a guide to Mallorcan cooking—and British painter David Templeton. Ava Gardner lived here for a time; so, briefly, did Picasso. The setting is unbeatable—all around Deià rise the steep cliffs of the Sierra de

Tramuntana. There's live jazz on summer evenings, and on warm afternoons literati gather at the beach bar in the rocky cove at Cala de Deià, 2 km (1 mile) downhill from the village. Walk up the narrow street to the village church; the small **cemetery** behind it affords views of mountains terraced with olive trees and of the coves below. It's a fitting spot for Graves's final resting place, in a quiet corner.

About 4 km (2½ miles) west of Deià is **Son Marroig,** a former estate of Austrian archduke Luis Salvador (1847–1915), which is now preserved as a museum, with a lovely garden and stunning coastal views. If you're driving, the best way to reach Son Marroig is the twisty MA10.

### GETTING HERE AND AROUND

The Palma–Port de Sóller bus (€4.35) passes through Deià six times daily in each direction Monday–Saturday, five times on Sunday. Taxis to Deià from Palma cost €45 by day, €50 at night; from the airport the fares are €50/€55, and from Sóller €22/€24. Intrepid hikers can walk from Deià through the mountains to Sóller, on a trail of moderate difficulty, in about 2½ hours.

## ◉ Sights

### Ca N'Alluny (La Casa de Robert Graves) (*La Casa de Robert Graves*)

**HISTORIC HOME** | The Fundació Robert Graves opened this museum dedicated to Deià's most famous resident in the house he built in 1932. The seaside house is something of a shrine: Graves's furniture and books, personal effects, and the press he used to print many of his works are all preserved. ⊠ *Ctra. Deià-Sóller s/n, Deià* ☎ *971/636185* ⊕ *www.lacasaderobertgraves.org/en* ✉ *€7* ⦸ *Closed Sun.*

### Monestir de Miramar

**VIEWPOINT** | On the road south from Deià to Valldemossa, this monastery was founded in 1276 by Ramón Llull, who established a school of Asian languages here. It was bought in 1872 by the archduke Luis Salvador and restored as a mirador. Explore the garden and the tiny cloister, then walk through the olive groves to a spectacular lookout. ⊠ *Diseminado Miramar 1, Ctra. Deià–Valldemossa (MA10), Km 67.5, Deià* ☎ *971/616073* ⊕ *www.monestirdemiramar.es* 🖾 *€4* ⊘ *Closed Sun.*

## Son Marroig

**HISTORIC HOME** | This estate belonged to Austrian archduke Luis Salvador, who arrived here as a young man and fell in love with the place. He acquired huge tracts of land along the northwestern coast, building miradores at the most spectacular points but otherwise leaving the pristine beauty intact. Below the mirador, you can see Sa Foradada, a rock peninsula pierced by a huge archway, where the archduke moored his yacht. Now a museum, the estate house contains the archduke's collections of Mediterranean pottery and ceramics, Mallorcan furniture, and paintings. The garden is especially fine. From May through September, the Deià International Festival holds classical concerts here. ⊠ *Ctra. Deià–Valldemossa (MA10), Km 65, Deià* ☎ *971/639158* ⊕ *www.sonmarroig.com* 🖾 *€4* ⊘ *Closed Sun.*

## ⛱ Beaches

### Cala Deià

**BEACH** | Encircled by high pine-topped cliffs, this rocky cove connects to various coastal walking paths as well as a narrow road that twists its way down from the village. Year-round, clear turquoise water makes it great for snorkeling and swimming. The popular Ca's Patro March restaurant, hewn into the rocks, overhangs the sea and stirring views. Book a table at the water's edge well in advance; it's often booked out days or even weeks in advance. There is also a simple beach bar. **Amenities:** food and drink; parking. **Best for:** snorkeling; swimming. ⊠ *Cala Deià, Deià.*

## 🛏 Hotels

### ★ Belmond La Residencia

$$$$ | **HOTEL** | **FAMILY** | Built around two 16th-century manor houses, with additional buildings blending with the lush surroundings, this exceptional hotel is superbly furnished with Mallorcan antiques, modern canvases, and canopied four-poster beds. **Pros:** impossibly picturesque surroundings; in-house art gallery; private shuttle to the beach. **Cons:** quite far from the beach; tricky to navigate for those with reduced mobility; extremely pricey. $ *Rooms from: €1,109* ⊠ *Son Canals s/n, Deià* ☎ *971/639011* ⊕ *www.belmond.com* ⊘ *Closed mid-Nov.–Mar.* 🛏 *71 rooms, 1 villa* ⏐⊘⏐ *Free Breakfast.*

### ★ Hotel Es Molí

$$$$ | **HOTEL** | A converted 17th-century manor house in the hills above the valley of Deià, this peaceful hotel is known for its traditional sense of luxury. **Pros:** attentive service; chamber music concerts twice a week during the summer; heated pool with spacious terrace. **Cons:** three-night minimum for some stays in high season; short season; steep climb to annex rooms. $ *Rooms from: €297* ⊠ *Ctra. Valldemossa–Deià s/n, Deià* ☎ *971/639000* ⊕ *www.esmoli.com* ⊘ *Closed Nov.–mid-Apr.* 🛏 *87 rooms* ⏐⊘⏐ *Free Breakfast.*

### s'Hotel D'es Puig

$$ | **B&B/INN** | **FAMILY** | This family-run "hotel on the hill" has a back terrace with a lemon-tree garden and a wonderful view of the mountains. **Pros:** peaceful setting; private parking for guests; two pools (one heated). **Cons:** books out quickly; four-night minimum in high season; public spaces can feel a bit cramped. $ *Rooms from: €99* ⊠ *Carrer d'es Puig 4, Deià* ☎ *971/639409, 637/820805* ⊕ *www.hoteldespuig.com* ⊘ *Closed Dec. and Jan.* 🛏 *14 rooms* ⏐⊘⏐ *Free Breakfast.*

# Sóller

*13 km (8 miles) north of Jardins d'Alfàbia, 30 km (19 miles) north of Palma.*

All but the briefest visits to Mallorca should include at least an overnight stay in Sóller, one of the most beautiful towns on the island, with palatial homes built in the 19th and early 20th centuries by the landowners and merchants who thrived on the export of the region's oranges, lemons, and almonds. Many of the buildings here, like the **Church of Sant Bartomeu** and the **Bank of Sóller,** on the Plaça Constitució, and the nearby **Can Prunera,** are gems of the Moderniste style, designed by contemporaries of Antoni Gaudí. The tourist information office in the **town hall,** next to Sant Bartomeu, has a walking-tour map of the important sites.

## GETTING HERE AND AROUND

You can travel in retro style from Palma to Sóller on one of the six daily trains (four daily in February, March, November, and December; €32 round trip) operated by Ferrocarril de Sóller, which depart from Plaça d'Espanya. With a string of wooden rail cars with leather-covered seats dating to 1912, the train trundles along for about an hour, making six stops along the 27-km (17-mile) route; the scenery gets lovely—especially at Bunyola and the Mirador Pujol—as you approach the peaks of the Tramuntana. From the train station in Sóller, a charming old trolley car, called the Tranvía de Sóller, threads its way down through town to the Port de Sóller. The fare is €7 each way. You can also buy a combination round-trip ticket for the train and the trolley for €32. The mountain road between Palma and Sóller is spectacular—lemon and olive trees on stone-walled terraces, farmhouses perched on the edges of forested cliffs—but demanding.

■ TIP→ **If you're driving to Sóller, take the tunnel at Alfabía instead. Save your strength for even better mountain roads ahead.**

**TRAIN AND TROLLEY CONTACT Ferrocarril de Sóller.** ⊠ *Eusebio Estada 1, Palma* ☎ *971/752 051 in Palma, 971/752028 in Palma* ⊕ *www.trendesoller.com.*

**VISITOR INFORMATION CONTACTS Sóller Tourist Office.** ⊠ *Pl. Espanya s/n, Sóller* ☎ *971/638008.*

## ◉ Sights

### Can Prunera

**HISTORIC HOME** | A minute's walk or so from the Plaça de la Constitució, along Sóller's main shopping arcade, brings you to this charming museum, where Moderniste style comes to life. In the lovingly restored family rooms on the first floor of this imposing town house you can see how Sóller's well-to-do embraced the Art Deco style: the ornate furniture and furnishings, the stained glass and ceramic tile, and the carved and painted ceilings all helped announce their status in turn-of-the-century Mallorcan society. Upstairs, Can Prunera also houses a small collection of paintings by early modern masters, among them Man Ray, Santiago Rusiñol, Paul Klee, and Joan Miró. The garden is an open-air museum in its own right, with sculptures by José Siguiri, Josep Sirvent, and other Mallorcan artists. ⊠ *Carrer de la Lluna 86–90, Sóller* ☎ *971/638973* ⊕ *www.canprunera. com* ⊠ *€5* ⊘ *Closed Mon. Nov.–Feb.; Closed Sun. and Mon. Mar.–Oct.*

### Station Building Galleries

**ART MUSEUM** | Maintained by the Fundació Tren de l'Art, these galleries have two small but remarkable collections—one of engravings by Miró, the other of ceramics by Picasso. ⊠ *Soller Railway Station, Pl. Espanya 6, Sóller* ⊠ *Free.*

## ◉ Restaurants

### Neni

$$$ | **ISRAELI** | This Israeli restaurant specializes in healthy bites like hummus and falafel, along with more elaborate dishes

like the excellent lamb ribs with feta. It's all served on a breezy patio overlooking the bay of Sóller. **Known for:** sharing plates; communal tables; terrace with views. ⑤ *Average main: €22* ✉ *Carrer de Migjorn 2, Port de Sóller* ☎ *971/638370* ⊕ *www.nenimallorca.com/en.*

## 🛌 Hotels

### Ca'n Abril

**$$$ | B&B/INN |** About a minute's walk from the main square, this family-friendly boutique hotel is an oasis of quiet in summer, when Sóller gets most of its tourist traffic. **Pros:** friendly service; excellent value; honesty bar. **Cons:** parking off-site (€10 per day); no pool or gym; no elevator. ⑤ *Rooms from: €149* ✉ *Carrer Pastor 26, Sóller* ☎ *971/579419* ⊕ *www. hotelcanabril.com* ⊙ *Closed Nov.–mid-Mar.* 🛏 *10 rooms* ⑩ *Free Breakfast.*

### Ca'n Isabel

**$$$ | B&B/INN |** Just across the tram tracks from the train station, this former home still feels much like a family hideaway. **Pros:** convenient location; pretty gardens; good value. **Cons:** no private parking; no elevator; rooms on the small side. ⑤ *Rooms from: €132* ✉ *Carrer Isabel II 13, Sóller* ☎ *971/638097* ⊕ *www.canisabel.com* ⊙ *Closed Nov.–Feb.* 🛏 *6 rooms* ⑩ *Free Breakfast.*

### Gran Hotel Sóller

**$$$$ | HOTEL |** A former private estate with an imposing Moderniste facade, this is the largest hotel in town. **Pros:** friendly and efficient service in at least five languages; convenient to trams; short walk from town center. **Cons:** functional decor; small pools; pricey for what you get. ⑤ *Rooms from: €215* ✉ *Carrer Romaguera 18, Sóller* ☎ *971/638686* ⊕ *www.granhotelsoller.com* 🛏 *40 rooms* ⑩ *Free Breakfast.*

## Fornalutx 👁

This pretty little mountain village nestled amid lemon and orange groves, 4 km (2½ miles) north of Sóller, is a worthy scenic detour. Much of its appeal emanates from the narrow pedestrianized streets, blond-stone houses speckled with bougainvillea and topped with red-tiled roofs, and the views over the Sóller valley.

## 🏃 Activities

Ten minutes or so from the center of Sóller on the trolley, the beachfront at Port de Sóller offers all sorts of water-based fun.

### Nautic Sóller

**WATER SPORTS |** On the northwest coast at Port de Sóller, this place has sea kayaks and motorboats available for rent. ✉ *Calle de la Marina 4, Port de Sóller* ☎ *609/354132* ⊕ *www.nauticsoller.com.*

## Alcúdia

*54 km (34 miles) northeast of Palma.*

Nothing if not strategic, Alcúdia is the ideal base for exploring Mallorca's north coast, with the 13-km-long (8-mile-long) beach from Port d'Alcúdia to C'an Picafort and the adjacent Playa de Muro, the bird-watchers' paradise in the S'Albufera wetlands, and the spectacular drive along the corniche to Cap de Formentor. The charming little walled town itself is a capsule version of Mallorcan history: the first city here was a Roman settlement, in 123 BC. The Moors reestablished a town here, and after the Reconquest it became a feudal possession of the Knights Templar; the first ring of city walls dates to the early 14th century. Begin your visit at the **Church of Sant Jaume** and

Mallorca's Sierra de Tramuntana provides excellent views for hikers.

walk through the maze of narrow streets inside to the **Porta de Xara,** with its twin crenellated towers.

### GETTING HERE AND AROUND

Porta de Alcúdia, where the ferry arrives from Ciutadella, is a 3-km (2-mile) taxi ride from the center of Alcúdia. There is also direct bus service from Palma.

### VISITOR INFORMATION

**CONTACTS Alcúdia Tourist Office.**
⊠ *Passeig de Pere Ventayol s/n, Alcúdia* ☎ *971/549022* ⊕ *www.alcudiamallorca. com.*

##  Sights

### Ciutat Romana de Pol·lèntia

RUINS | Archaeological remains of the ancient city of Pollentia, which dates to about 100 BC, include La Portella residential area, the Forum, and the 1st-century-AD Roman theater. The Museu Monogràfic de Pollentia has a small collection of statuary and artifacts from the nearby excavations of the Roman capital of the island. ⊠ *Av. dels Prínceps d'Espanya s/n,*

*Alcúdia* ☎ *971/547004* ⊕ *www.pollentia. net* ⊠ *€4, includes museum and archaeological site* ⊙ *Oct.–Apr. closed Sat. and Sun.; May–Sept. closed Mon.*

## Pollença

*8 km (5 miles) from Alcúdia, 50 km (31 miles) from Palma.*

This is a pretty little place, with a history that goes back at least as far as the Roman occupation of the island; the only trace of that period is the stone **Roman Bridge** at the edge of town. In the 13th century, Pollença and much of the land around it was owned by the Knights Templar, who built the imposing church of **Nuestra Senyora de Los Ángeles** on the west side of the present-day Plaça Major. The church looks east to the 1,082-foot peak of the Puig de Maria, with the 15th century sanctuary at the top. The **Calvari** of Pollença is a flight of 365 stone steps to a tiny chapel and a panoramic view as far as Cap de Formentor. There's

a colorful weekly market at the foot of the steps on Sunday mornings.

## GETTING HERE AND AROUND

Pollença is a fairly easy drive from Palma on the MA-13. A few buses each day connect Pollença with Palma and Alcúdia.

## VISITOR INFORMATION

**CONTACTS Pollença Tourist Office.**
✉ Guillen Cifre de Colonya s/n, Pollença ☎ 971/535077.

## FESTIVALS

### Festival de Pollença

**MUSIC** | An acclaimed international music event, this festival is held every year in August. Since its inception, in 1961, it has attracted such performers as Mstislav Rostropovich, Jessye Norman, the St. Petersburg Philharmonic, the Camerata Köln, and the Alban Berg Quartet. Concerts are held in the cloister of the Convent of Sant Domingo. ✉ Pollença ☎ 971/530108 ext. 154 ⊕ www.festivalpollenca.com.

##  Sights

### Cap de Formentor

**SCENIC DRIVE** | The winding road north from Port de Pollença to the tip of the island is spectacular. Stop at the Mirador de la Cruete, where the rocks form deep, narrow inlets of multishaded blue. A stone tower called the Talaia d'Albercutx marks the highest point on the peninsula. Continue on, around hairpin bends—and past superb coastal views—to reach Cala Formentor beach. The drive is certainly not for the fainthearted, but the beach at the end is one of Mallorca's best, with fine white sand and calm turquoise water, backed by a forest of pine trees that offer shade. ✉ Formentor.

##  Hotels

### Agroturisme Can Beneït

$$$$ | **HOTEL** | Local hospitality expert Toni Duran converted this 200-acre farm, complete with a converted medieval farmhouse and a century-old olive oil mill, into a cozy boutique hotel. **Pros:** pure relaxation in Mallorca's rural heartland; olive oil made on-site; farm-to-table restaurant. **Cons:** three-night minimum stay in high season; quite isolated; books up quickly. ⑤ Rooms from: €340 ✉ Camí de Binibona s/n, Pollença ☎ 871/811871 ⊕ www.fincacanbeneit.com ⤴ 10 rooms ⊗ Free Breakfast.

### Hotel Juma

$$ | **B&B/INN** | This little hotel, which opened in 1907, is on Pollença's main square, making it a good choice for a weekend stay because of the Sunday market that takes place there. **Pros:** great location; good value; tasty breakfast in the bar. **Cons:** basic decor and amenities; rooms overlooking square can be noisy; parking can be a problem. ⑤ Rooms from: €108 ✉ Pl. Major 9, Pollença ☎ 971/535002 ⊕ www.pollensahotels.com ⊙ Closed mid-Nov.–mid-Mar. ⤴ 7 rooms ⊗ Free Breakfast.

### ★ Son Brull Hotel and Spa

$$$$ | **RESORT** | "Oasis" is what springs to mind when driving up through family vineyards to this lovingly restored medieval monastery, reborn as a deluxe resort hotel. **Pros:** charm and sophistication; excellent breakfast included; strategic location for exploring Pollença, Alcúdia, and the S'Albufereta wildlife reserve. **Cons:** no sea view might disappoint some; minimum booking for some arrivals in high season; pricey. ⑤ Rooms from: €630 ✉ Ctra. Palma–Pollença, Pollença ☎ 971/535353 ⊕ www.sonbrull.com ⊙ Closed Dec. and Jan. ⤴ 13 rooms, 10 suites ⊗ Free Breakfast.

## Lluc

20 km (12 miles) southwest of Pollença.

The Santuari de Lluc, which holds the Black Virgin and is a major pilgrimage site, is widely considered Mallorca's spiritual heart.

**GETTING HERE AND AROUND**

The Santuari is about midway between Sóller and Pollença on the hairpin route over the mountains (MA10). Two buses daily connect these towns, stopping in Lluc. Taxi fare from either town is about €35.

#  Sights

### Santuari de Lluc

RELIGIOUS BUILDING | La Moreneta, also known as La Virgen Negra de Lluc (the Black Virgin of Lluc), is a votary statue of the Virgin Mary that's held in a 17th-century church, the center of this sanctuary complex. The museum has an eclectic collection of prehistoric and Roman artifacts, ceramics, paintings, textiles, folk costumes, votive offerings, Nativity scenes, and work by local artists. Between September and June, a children's choir sings psalms in the chapel daily at 1:15 pm, Monday–Saturday, and at 11 am for Sunday Mass. The Christmas Eve performance of the "Cant de la Sibila" ("Song of the Sybil"), based on a medieval prophecy of the end of the world, is an annual choral highlight. ✉ Pl. dels Pelegrins 1, Lluc ☎ 971/871525 ⊕ santuari.lluc.net/en ⛟ €5.

# Menorca

Menorca, the northernmost of the Balearics, is a knobby, cliff-bound plateau with some 193 km (120 miles) of coastline and a central hill called El Toro, from the 1,100-foot summit of which you can see the whole island. Prehistoric monuments—*taulas* (huge stone T-shapes), *talayots* (spiral stone cones), and *navetes* (stone structures shaped like overturned boats)—left by the first Neolithic settlers are all over the island.

Tourism came late to Menorca, which aligned with the Republic in the Spanish Civil War; Franco punished the island by discouraging the investment in infrastructure that fueled the Balearic boom on Mallorca and Ibiza. Menorca has avoided many of the problems of overdevelopment: there are still very few high-rise hotels, and the herringbone road system, with a single central highway, means that each resort is small and separate. There's less to see and do on Menorca, and more unspoiled countryside than on the other Balearics. The island, home to some 220 species of birds and more than 1,000 species of plants, was designated a Biosphere Reserve in 1993. Menorca is where Spanish mainlanders tend to take their families on vacation.

**GETTING HERE AND AROUND**

To get to Menorca from Barcelona take the overnight ferry, or a 40-minute flight. It's around a one-hour ferry ride from Palma.

Several buses a day run the length of Menorca between Mahón and Ciutadella, stopping en route at Alaior, Mercadal, and Ferreries. The bus line Autos Fornells serves the northeast; Transportes Menorca connects Mahón with Ciutadella and with the major beaches and calas around the island. From smaller towns there are daily buses to Mahón and connections to Ciutadella. In summer, regular buses shuttle beachgoers from the west end of Ciutadella's Plaça Explanada to the resorts to the south and west; from Mahón, excursions to Menorca's most remote beaches leave daily from the jetty next to the Nuevo Muelle Comercial.

If you want to beach-hop in Menorca, it's best to have your own transportation, but most of the island's historic sights are in Mahón or Ciutadella, and once you're in town everything is within walking distance. You can see the island's archaeological remains in a day's drive, so you may want to rent a car for just that part of your visit.

# Menorca

0 _____ 6 miles

0 _____ 6 km

**BUS CONTACTS Autocares Torres.** ✉ *Ciuta-della* ☎ *902/075066* ⊕ *www.bus.e-tor-res.net/en.* **Autos Fornells.** ✉ *Mercadal* ☎ *971/154390* ⊕ *www.autosfornells.com.* **Transportes Menorca.** ✉ *Mahón* ☎ *971/360475* ⊕ *www.tmsa.es.*

## Mahón (Maó)

Established as the island's capital in 1722, when the British began their nearly 80-year occupation, Mahón still bears the stamp of its former rulers. The streets nearest the port are lined with four-story Georgian town houses; the Mahónese drink gin and admire Chippendale furniture; and English is widely spoken. The city is quiet for much of the year, but between June and September the waterfront pubs and restaurants swell with foreigners.

### GETTING HERE AND AROUND
There's ferry service here from Mallorca, but it's much less frequent than to Ciutadella. Within Mahón, Autocares Torres has three bus routes around the city and to the airport.

**BUS STATION Estació Autobuses.** ✉ *Carrer Moll de Llevant 1, Mahón* ☎ *971/356050.*

**TAXI CONTACT Radio-Taxi.** ✉ *Mahón* ☎ *971/367111, 971/482222* ⊕ *www.taxismenorca.com.*

### VISITOR INFORMATION
**CONTACTS Aeropuerto de Menorca Tourist Office.** ✉ *Menorca Airport, Mahón* ☎ *971/356944* ⊕ *www.menorca.es.* **Mahón Tourist Office (Port).** ✉ *Moll de Llevant 2, Mahón* ☎ *971/355952* ⊕ *www.menorca.es.*

# ◉ Sights

**Carrer Isabel II**

**STREET** | This street is lined with many Georgian homes. To get here, walk up Carrer d'Alfons III and turn right at the ajuntament. ⊠ *Carrer Isabel II, Mahón.*

**Mercat Des Claustre**

**MARKET** | This church has a fine painted and gilded altarpiece. Adjoining the church are the cloisters, now a market, with stalls selling fresh produce and a variety of local cheeses and sausages. The central courtyard is a venue for cultural events throughout the year. ⊠ *Pl. del Carme, Mahón* ☎ *638/920259* ⊕ *mercat-desclaustre.com.*

**Santa María**

**CHURCH** | This 13th-century church was rebuilt in the 18th century, during the British occupation, and restored again after being sacked during the Spanish Civil War. The church's pride is its 3,006-pipe baroque organ, imported from Austria in 1810. Organ concerts are given Monday to Saturday at 11 am, from May to October. The altar, and the half-domed chapels on either side, have exceptional frescoes. ⊠ *Pl. de la Constitució s/n, Mahón.*

**Teatre Principal**

**NOTABLE BUILDING** | Opera companies from Italy en route to Spain made the Teatre Principal in Mahón their first port of call; if the maonesos gave a production a poor reception, it was cut from the repertoire. Built in 1829, it has five tiers of boxes, plush red seats, and gilded woodwork: La Scala in miniature. Lovingly restored, it still hosts a brief opera season. If you're visiting in the first week of December or the last week of May, buy tickets well in advance. ⊠ *Carrer Costa Deià 40, Mahón* ☎ *971/355603* ⊕ *www.teatremao.com.*

**Torralba d'en Salort**

**RUINS** | Puzzle over Menorca's prehistoric past at this megalithic site with a number of stone constructions, including a massive taula. Behind it, from the top of a stone wall, you can see, in a nearby field, the monolith **Fus de Sa Geganta** (the Giantess's Spindle). ⊠ *Mahón* ✛ *From Mahón, drive west and turn south at Alaior on road to Cala en Porter; it's 2 km (1 mile) ahead at bend in road, marked by an information kiosk on left.*

**Torre d'en Galmés**

**RUINS** | This Talaiotic site between Alaior and Son Bouis comprises a complex set of stone constructions—fortifications, monuments, deep pits of ruined dwellings, huge vertical slabs, and taulas. ⊠ *Alaior* ✛ *Head south toward Son Bou on west side of Alaior and, after about 1 km (½ mile), the 1st fork left leads to ruins* ☎ *971/157800* ⌨ *€3 (Free Mondays).*

# ◉ Beaches

**Cala Galdana**

**BEACH** | **FAMILY** | A small horseshoe curve of fine white sand, framed by almost vertical pine-covered cliffs, is where Menorca's only river, the Agendar, reaches the sea through a long limestone gorge. The surrounding area is under environmental protection—the handful of resort hotels and chalets above the beach (usually booked solid June–September by package-tour operators) were grandfathered in. Cala Galdana is family-friendly in the extreme, with calm, shallow waters, and a nearby water park–playground for the kids. A favorite with Menorcans and visitors alike, it gets really crowded in high season, but a 20-minute walk through the pine forest leads to the otherwise inaccessible little coves of Macarella and Macarelleta, remote beaches popular with naturists and boating parties. **Amenities:** food and drink; lifeguards; showers; water sports. **Best for:** swimming; walking. ⊠ *35 km (21 miles) from Mahón, Ferreries* ✛ *Take ME1 to Ferreries, then head south from there on local ME22.*

# 🍴 Restaurants

### ★ Cap Roig

$$$ | SEAFOOD | A Menorca institution set above Cala Mesquida, a short drive from Mahon, Cap Roig owes its well-deserved fame to the quality of its seafood and the splendor of its views. The mussels from the port of Mahón are excellent, as is the lobster, which can be served grilled, in a stew, or as part of one of the restaurant's celebrated rice dishes or paellas. **Known for:** lobster rice; splendid views; ultrafresh fish and seafood. $ *Average main: €21* ⊠ *Ctra. Sa Mesquida, 13, Maó* ☎ *971/188383* ⊕ *restaurantcaproig.com.*

### El Rais

$$$$ | ECLECTIC | Rice dishes reign supreme at upscale El Rais, but that doesn't mean it's all paella. There are starters like Japanese-style nigiri and red tuna belly with salt-cured yolk and caviar, as well as risottos, soups, and, of course, rice pudding for dessert. **Known for:** excellent shrimp carpaccio; rice in every form; lunch with views of the port. $ *Average main: €25* ⊠ *Moll de Llevant 314, Maó* ☎ *971/362345* ⊕ *www.sesforquilles.com* ☺ *Closed Mon. and Tues.*

### ★ Es Molí de Foc

$$$$ | SPANISH | Originally a flour mill, this is the oldest building in the village of Sant Climent, and both the atmosphere and the food are exceptional. Taste seasonal dishes, which can include prawn carpaccio with cured Mahón cheese and guacamole, black paella with monkfish and squid, and *carrilleras de ternera* (beef cheeks) with potato. **Known for:** rustic local food with style; brewery on-site; summer terrace. $ *Average main: €24* ⊠ *Carrer Sant Llorenç 65, Sant Climent* ⊹ *4 km (2½ miles) southwest of town* ☎ *971/153222* ⊕ *www.esmolidefoc.es* ☺ *Closed Mon.*

# 🛏 Hotels

### Can Alberti

$$$$ | HOTEL | Built in 1740, during the British occupation, this former private residence has been turned into an upscale boutique hotel. **Pros:** great location; beautiful design; walking distance to the port. **Cons:** no pets; no swimming pool; no on-site parking. $ *Rooms from: €300* ⊠ *Carrer Isabel II 9, Mahón* ☎ *971/354210* ⊕ *www.hotelcanalberti. com* ⇨ *15 rooms* ❶ *Free Breakfast.*

### ★ Cristine Bedfor

$$$$ | HOTEL | Set around a pretty swimming pool and a lush garden in the historic center of Mahón, this boutique hotel is named after its owner. **Pros:** gorgeous gardens; plastic-free ethic; good on-site restaurant. **Cons:** parking costs extra; only junior suites have private terraces; small swimming pool. $ *Rooms from: €339* ⊠ *Carrer de la Infanta 17, Maó* ☎ *971/635502* ⊕ *cristinebedforhotel.com* ⇨ *21 rooms* ❶ *Free Breakfast.*

### Hotel Port Mahón

$$$ | HOTEL | This standby may not win many prizes for imaginative design, but it's a solid choice, with rooms with hardwood floors, generic but comfortable furniture, and plenty of closet space. **Pros:** decent value; some rooms have private terraces with impressive views; good buffet breakfast. **Cons:** uninspired design; patchy a/c; pool and garden front on the Passeig Marítim. $ *Rooms from: €175* ⊠ *Av. Port de Maó s/n, Mahón* ☎ *971/362600* ⊕ *www.sethotels.com* ⇨ *82 rooms* ❶ *Free Breakfast.*

### Hotel Rural y Restaurante Biniarroca

$$$$ | B&B/INN | Antique embroidered bed linens, shelves with knickknacks, and comfy chairs—this is an English vision of a peaceful and secluded rural retreat, and its glory is the garden of irises, lavender, and flowering trees. **Pros:** excellent food on-site; peaceful surroundings; some suites have private terraces. **Cons:** adults only; some low ceilings; bit of a drive to

the beach. ⑤ *Rooms from: €250* ⊠ *Cami Vell 57, Sant Lluís* ☎ 971/150059 ⊕ *www. biniarroca.com* ⊘ *Closed Nov.–Easter* ⚲ *18 rooms* ⑩ *Free Breakfast.*

### ★ Jardi de Ses Bruixes Boutique Hotel

$$$$ | **B&B/INN** | Built in 1811 by a Spanish ship captain, this *casa señorial* (town house) in the heart of Mahón was lovingly restored by architect and co-owner Fernando Pons as a boutique hotel. **Pros:** amiable, eager-to-please staff; at-home atmosphere; strategic location. **Cons:** thin walls; bathtubs in the bedrooms sacrifice privacy to design; difficult to reach by car, though there is free public parking a few minutes' walk away. ⑤ *Rooms from: €240* ⊠ *Carrer de San Fernando 26, Maó* ☎ 971/363166 ⊕ *www.hotelsesbruixes. com* ⚲ *16 rooms* ⑩ *Free Breakfast.*

### Sant Joan de Binissaida

$$$$ | **B&B/INN** | An avenue lined with chinaberry and fig trees leads to this lovely restored farmhouse with environmental credentials, including some solar power and organic produce from the farm. **Pros:** vistas clear to the port of Mahón; excellent restaurant; huge pool. **Cons:** short season, with three-night minimum stay in summer; rooms in the annex lack privacy; bit of a drive to the nearest beach. ⑤ *Rooms from: €240* ⊠ *Camí de Binissaida 108, Es Castell* ☎ 971/355598 ⊕ *www.binissaida.com* ⊘ *Closed Nov.– Apr.* ⚲ *15 rooms* ⑩ *Free Breakfast.*

## ▼ Nightlife

### Akelarre Jazz and Dance Club

**LIVE MUSIC** | This stylish bar near the port has a café-terrace downstairs and live jazz and blues on Thursday and Friday nights. It's open year-round 12 pm–1 am and serves tapas and snacks to share in the evening. ⊠ *Moll de Ponent 41–43, Mahón* ☎ 971/368520.

### Casino Sant Climent

**LIVE MUSIC** | From June to September, catch live music on Wednesdays, Fridays, and some Sundays at the Casino bar and restaurant. Book ahead for tables on the terrace. ⊠ *Sant Jaume 4, Sant Climent* ⊹ *4 km (2½ miles) southwest of Mahón* ☎ 971/853722 ⊕ *www.casinosantcliment.com.*

### Cova d'en Xoroi

**DANCE CLUBS** | This might be the hottest spot in Menorca to catch the sun going down, drink in hand, with afternoon chillout events with live music. A 20-minute drive from Mahón in the beach resort of Cala en Porter, this unique spot is in a series of caves in a cliff high above the sea, which, according to local legend, was once the refuge of a castaway Moorish pirate. ⊠ *Carrer de Sa Cova s/n, Cala en Porter* ☎ 971/377236 ⊕ *www. covadenxoroi.com.*

## 🛍 Shopping

Menorca is known for shoes and leather goods, as well as cheese, gin, and wine. Wine was an important part of the Menorcan economy as long ago as the 18th century: the British, who knew a good place to grow grapes when they saw one, planted the island thick with vines. Viticulture was abandoned when Menorca returned to the embrace of Spain, and it has reemerged only in the past few years.

### Boba's

**SHOES** | Duck into the little alley between Carrer Nou and Carrer de l'Angel, and discover the atelier where Llorenç Pons makes his *espardenyes d'autor* (traditional rope-sole sandals) in original and surprising designs. ⊠ *Pont de l'Angel 4, Mahón* ☎ 647/587456 ⊕ *www.bobasmenorca.com* ⊘ *Closed Sun.*

### ★ Bodegas Binifadet

**WINE/SPIRITS** | This is the most promising of the handful of the local wineries, with robust young reds and whites on store shelves all over Menorca. The owners have expanded their product line into sparkling Chardonnay (sold only on the premises), olive oil, jams and conserves, and wine-based soaps and cosmetics. It's well worth a visit, not merely for tastings and guided tours, but also for a meal on the terrace, weather permitting. The kitchen puts an international touch on traditional Menorcan recipes and products; the prix-fixe menu is a great value at €28 for three courses. In midsummer, reservations are a must. You can also simply drop by for a glass of wine on the terrace; the surroundings are picturesque and peaceful. ⊠ *Ctra. Sant Lluís–Es Castell, Km 0.5, Sant Lluís* ☎ *971/150715* ⊕ *www.binifadet.com* ⊘ *Closed Tues.*

**Pons Quintana**

**SHOES** | This showroom has a full-length window overlooking the factory where its very chic women's shoes are made. ⊠ *Carrer Sant Antoni 120, Alaior* ✛ *13 km (8 miles) northeast of Mahón* ☎ *971/371050* ⊕ *www.ponsquintana. com/en* ⊘ *Closed Sun.*

**Xoriguer**

**WINE/SPIRITS** | One gastronomic legacy of the British occupation is gin. At this distillery on Mahón's quayside near the ferry terminal, you can sample various types of gin and buy some to take home. ⊠ *Moll de Ponent 91, Mahón* ☎ *971/362197* ⊕ *www.xoriguer.es* ⊘ *Closed Sun. and Nov.–Apr.*

## 🏃 Activities

### BICYCLING
**Asociación Cicloturista de Menorca**
**BIKING** | Ask here about organized bike tours of the island. ⊠ *Moll de Llevant 173, Mahón* ☎ *971/364816, 610/464816* ⊕ *www.menorcacicloturista.com/en.*

**Bike Menorca**
**BIKING** | You can rent a road bike, mountain bike, or electric bike by the day (from €20) from this full-service outfitter. ⊠ *Av. Francesc Femenias 44, Mahón* ☎ *971/353798* ⊕ *www.bikemenorca.com* ⊘ *Closed Sun.*

### DIVING
The clear Mediterranean waters here are ideal for diving. Equipment and lessons are available at Cala En Bosc, Son Parc, Fornells, Ciutadella, and Cala Tirant, among others.

**Blue Islands Diving**
**DIVING & SNORKELING** | Established in 2009, Blue Islands Diving in Cala Galdana offers diving for all certification levels, including SSI programs and courses, night dives, and snorkeling tours. ⊠ *Passatge Riu 7, Serpentona, Cala Galdana* ☎ *633/563526* ⊕ *www.blueislandsdiving.com.*

### GOLF
**Golf Son Parc**
**GOLF** | Menorca's sole golf course, designed by Dave Thomas, is 9 km (6 miles) east of Mercadal, about a 20-minute drive from Mahón. Rocky bunkers, and the occasional stray peacock on the fairways, make this an interesting and challenging course. The club, open year-round, also has two composition tennis courts and a restaurant. ⊠ *Urbanització Son Parc s/n, Mercadal* ☎ *971/188875* ⊕ *golfsonparcmenorca.com* 🏷 *€32–€50 for 9 holes, €49–€80 for 18 holes, depending on season* 🏌 *18 holes, 5947 yards, par 71.*

### WALKING
In the south, each cove is approached by a *barranca* (ravine or gully), often from several miles inland. The head of **Barranca Algendar** is down a small, unmarked road immediately on the right of the Ferreries–Cala Galdana road; the barranca ends at the local beach resort, and from there you have a lovely walk north along the sea to an unspoiled half moon of sand at **Cala Macarella.** Extend your walk north, if time allows, through the forest along the riding trail to **Cala Turqueta,** where you'll find some of the island's most impressive grottoes.

# Ciutadella

*44 km (27 miles) west of Mahón.*

Ciutadella was Menorca's capital before the British settled in Mahón, and its history is richer. Settled successively by the Phoenicians, Greeks, Carthaginians, and Romans, Ciutadella fell to the Moors in 903 and became a part of the Caliphate of Córdoba until 1287, when Alfonso III of Aragón reconquered it. He gave estates in Ciutadella to nobles who aided him in the battle, and to this day the old historic center of town has a distinctly aristocratic tone. In 1558 a Turkish armada laid siege to Ciutadella, burning the city and enslaving its inhabitants. It was later rebuilt but never quite regained its former stature.

As you arrive via the ME1, the main artery across the island from Mahón, turn left at the second traffic circle and follow the ring road to the Passeig Marítim; at the end, near the **Castell de Sant Nicolau** is a **monument to David Glasgow Farragut,** the first admiral of the U.S. Navy, whose father emigrated from Ciutadella to the United States. From here, take Passeig de Sant Nicolau to the **Plaēa de s'Esplanada** and park near the Plaça d'es Born. Navigate your way from the cathedral through the narrow, medina-like streets of the old town to the 19th century wrought-iron Mercat de Peix speckled in green and white tiles—and a hive of activity. Bar Ulisses does a roaring trade day and night, while providing the perfect people-watching perch.

## GETTING HERE AND AROUND

Autocares Torres has various bus lines (61, 62 64, 65, 66, 68, 69) running between Ciutadella and the beaches and calas near the city.

**BUS CONTACT Autocares Torres.** ⊠ *Ciutadella* ☎ *902/075066* ⊕ *www.bus.e-torres. net/en.*

**BUS STATION Estación de Autobuses de Ciutadella.** ⊠ *Pl. dels Pins 47, Ciutadella* ☎ *93/075066.*

**TAXI CONTACT Radio Taxi Menorca.** ⊠ *Ciutadella* ☎ *971/367111* ⊕ *www. taxismenorca.com/en/home.*

**VISITOR INFORMATION CONTACTS Ciutadella Tourist Office.** ⊠ *Pl. d'es Born 15, Ciutadella* ☎ *971/383724* ⊕ *www.menorca.es.*

## ◉ Sights

### Cathedral

**CHURCH |** Carrer Major leads to this Gothic edifice, which has some beautifully carved choir stalls. The side chapel has round Moorish arches, remnants of the mosque that once stood on this site; the bell tower is a converted minaret. ⊠ *Carrer de Ca'l Bisbe 8, Ciutadella* ☎ *971/380739* ⊕ *bisbatdemenorca.org/ parroquia-de-ntra-senyora-del-roser-la-catedral* 🖾 *€6* 🕙 *Closed Sun.*

### Convento de Sant Agustí *(El Socorro)*

**NOTABLE BUILDING |** Carrer del Seminari is lined on the west side with some of the city's most impressive historic buildings. Among them is this 17th-century convent, which hosts Ciutadella's summer classical music festival (contact *admin@ jjmmciutadella.com* for details) in its lovely cloister, and the Diocesan Museum collection of paintings, archaeological finds, and liturgical objects. The room housing the historical library and archives is especially impressive. ⊠ *Carrer del Seminari 9, Ciutadella* ☎ *971/481297* 🖾 *€6 (includes cathedral).*

### Mirador d'es Port

**VIEWPOINT |** From a passage on the left side of Ciutadella's columned and crenellated ajuntament on the west side of the Born, steps lead up to this lookout. From here you can survey the harbor. ⊠ *Carrer de Portal de Mar 16, Ciutadella.*

Mahón's harbor, just below the main square and lined with restaurants, is perfect for a summer evening stroll.

### Palau Salort

**HISTORIC HOME** | This is the only noble house in Ciutadella that's open to the public, albeit at limited times, and you can view five rooms of the palace and the interior garden. The coats of arms on the ceiling are those of the families Salort (*sal* and *ort*, a salt pit and a garden) and Martorell (a marten). Opening hours are irregular so best to check in advance. ⊠ *Carrer Major des Born 15, Ciutadella* 💷 *€3.*

### Port

**PROMENADE** | Ciutadella's port is accessible from steps that lead down from Carrer Sant Sebastià. The waterfront here is lined with seafood restaurants, some of which burrow into caverns far under the Born. ⊠ *Ciutadella.*

 Beaches

### Cala Macarella and Cala Macaralleta

**SWIMMING** | **FAMILY** | What just might be the two most beautiful of Menorca's small beaches are reachable three ways:

by boat, by car from the Mahón–Ciutadella highway (ME1), or, if you're feeling robust and ambitious, on foot from the little resort town of Cala Galdana. Cala Macarella is a little crescent of white sand lapped by breathtakingly turquoise and blue waters that are calm and shallow and sheltered by rocks on both sides. Remote as it is, it's popular with locals as well as vacationers. A 10-minute walk along the cliffs brings you to the even smaller and more tranquil Cala Macaralleta, where there are no amenities and fewer sunseekers. **Amenities:** food and drink; lifeguards; parking (no fee); toilets. **Best for:** swimming; walking. ⊠ *Urbanització Serpentona, Ciutadella.*

 Restaurants

### Cafe Balear

**$$$$** | **SEAFOOD** | Seafood doesn't get much fresher than here, as the owners' boat docks nearby every day except Sunday. The relaxed atmosphere welcomes either a quick bite or a full dining experience. **Known for:** fresh-off-the-boat catches; port-side location; lobster caldereta. $ *Average main: €25* ⊠ *Pl. de San Juan 15, Ciutadella* ☎ *971/380005* ⊕ *www.cafebalear.com* ☾ *Closed Mon. Oct.–Jun. and Sun. Jul.–Sept. Closed Nov., Dec. and Jan.*

### S'Amarador

**$$$$ | SEAFOOD |** At the foot of the steps that lead down to the port, this restaurant has a café-terrace out front that's perfect for people-watching, drinks, and tapas. Fresh seafood in any form is a sure bet here: try the local John Dory, baked, grilled, or fried with garlic—or splurge on the caldereta (€42 per person). **Known for:** good-value fixed-price lunch menu; flavorsome lobster stew; bustling terrace. $ *Average main: €25* ⊠ *Pere Capllonch 42, Ciutadella* ☎ *971/383524* ⊕ *www. samarador.com.*

### Smoix

**$$$ | MEDITERRANEAN |** Creative, contemporary Menorcan cuisine is the draw here, in an industrial-style setting with a small leafy courtyard and low-key cosmopolitan vibe. Start things off with a local gin, and choose from a menu that is updated seasonally, showcasing regional flavors with contemporary flair. **Known for:** local gin; brochette with chicken, prawns, shiitake mushrooms, and lime; crayfish ravioli. $ *Average main: €21* ⊠ *Av. Jaume I el Conqueridor 38, Ciutadella* ☎ *971/382808* ⊕ *www.smoix.com* ☾ *Closed Mon. No lunch Tues.*

## 🛏 Hotels

### ★ Faustino Gran

**$$$$ | HOTEL |** Occupying several renovated and restored 16th-century palace buildings, Faustino Gran has a simple yet elegant aesthetic. **Pros:** ideally located in Ciutadella; lovely architecture; outstanding service. **Cons:** pool area on the small side; street-facing rooms can be noisy; rather pricey. $ *Rooms from: €490* ⊠ *Carrer de sa Muradeta 22, Ciutadella*

☎ *971/489191* ⊕ *faustinogran.com/en* ⇥ *46 rooms* ⦿ *Free Breakfast.*

### Hotel Rural Sant Ignasi

**$$$$ | B&B/INN | FAMILY |** About 10 minutes by car from the central square, and set in a centuries-old oak forest, this comfortable manor house dates to 1777 and is a favorite with young Spanish families. **Pros:** decent value; tennis and paddle tennis courts; friendly staff. **Cons:** two-night minimum stay in summer; short season; kids in the pool all day. $ *Rooms from: €200* ⊠ *Ronda Norte s/n, Ciutadella* ⊹ *Take Ronda Norte to 2nd traffic circle at Polígono Industrial; just past traffic circle turn left on Son Juaneda and follow signs* ☎ *971/385575* ⊕ *www.santignasi. com* ☾ *Closed Oct.–Apr.* ⇥ *25 rooms* ⦿ *Free Breakfast.*

## 🛍 Shopping

The *polígono industrial* (industrial complex) on the right as you enter Ciutadella has a number of shoe factories, each with a shop. Prices may be the same as in stores, but the selection is wider. In Plaça d'es Born, a market is held on Monday and Friday.

For the best shopping, try the Ses Voltes area, the Es Rodol zone near Plaça Artrutx, and along the Camí de Maó between Plaça Palmeras and Plaça d'es Born.

### Hort Sant Patrici

**FOOD |** This is a good place to buy the tangy, Parmesan-like Mahón cheese. There's a shop, beautiful grounds with a small vineyard, a sculpture garden and botanical garden, and a display of traditional cheese-making techniques and tools. Most weekdays you can watch the cheese being made, and guided tours (by reservation; €8) are available in English every Monday at 10 am. Hort Sant Patrici has its own vineyards and olive trees. ⊠ *Camí Sant Patrici s/n, Ferreries* ⊹ *18 km (11 miles) east of Ciutadella; exit ME1 at 2nd traffic circle after Ferreries onto*

Camí Sant Patrici ☎ 971/373702 ⊕ www.
santpatrici.com ⊗ Closed Sun. in summer, weekends in winter.

### Nadia Rabosio
JEWELRY & WATCHES | This inventive designer has created an original selection of jewelry and hand-painted silks. ⊠ Carrer Santissim 4, Ciutadella ☎ 971/384080 ⊕ www.nadiarabosio.com ⊗ Closed Sun.

# 🏃 Activities

## HORSEBACK RIDING
Horseback riding, breeding, and dressage have been traditions on the island for hundreds of years, and the magnificent black Menorcan horses play an important role, not only as work animals and for sport, but also in shows and colorful local festivals. There are 17 riding clubs on the island, a number of which offer excursions on the rural lanes of the unspoiled countryside. The Camí de Cavalls is a riding route in 20 stages that completely circumnavigates the island. Cavalls Son Angel in Ciutadella and Menorca a Cavall in Cala Galdana organize excursions for adults and children. Son Martorellet, on the road to the beach at Cala Galdana, is a ranch where you can visit the stables and watch dressage training exhibitions every Tuesday and Thursday afternoon; there's an equestrian show in traditional costume on Saturday.

### Cavalls Son Àngel
HORSEBACK RIDING | FAMILY | This equestrian center specializes in excursions along the Cami de Cavalls, the horseback route that circumnavigates the island, with rides that range from one to two hours for beginners (€25–€55) to three- or five-day trips (all year round except July and August). Riders on the longer excursions need to arrange their own overnight accommodations. ⊠ Camí d'Algaiarens s/n, Ciutadella ☎ 609/833902 ⊕ www.cavallssonangel.com 🖃 From €25.

### Menorca a Cavall
HORSEBACK RIDING | FAMILY | Hour-and-a-half-long excursions, along portions of the Camí de Cavalls, are €40 in autumn through spring, €45 in summer. Longer rides run €60–€100, depending on the season. Single- and two-day routes along the south coast of Menorca can also be organized autumn through spring. ⊠ Finca Es Calafat, Ctra. Ferreries–Cala Galdana (ME22), Km 4.3, Ferreries ☎ 971/374637, 685/990545 ⊕ www.menorcaacavall.com 🖃 From €40.

### Son Martorellet
HORSEBACK RIDING | FAMILY | The equestrian performances at the Son Martorellet stables, featuring demonstrations of dressage with the famed Menorcan horses, are offered Thursday evenings. ⊠ Ctra. Ferreries–Cala Galdana, Km 1.7, Ferreries ☎ 639/156851 ⊕ www.sonmartorellet.com.

# El Toro

24 km (15 miles) northwest of Mahón.

The peak of El Toro is Menorca's highest point, at all of 1,175 feet. From the monastery on top you can see the whole island and across the sea to Mallorca.

## GETTING HERE AND AROUND
Follow signs in Es Mercadal, the crossroads at the island's center.

# 🍴 Restaurants

### Es Molí d'es Recó
$$$ | CATALAN | A great place to stop for a lunch of typical local cuisine, this restaurant is in an old windmill at the west end of Es Mercadal, on the ME1 about halfway between Mahón and Ciutadella and about 4 km (2½ miles) from El Toro. Menorcan specialties here include squid stuffed with anglerfish and shrimp, and chicken with centollo (spider crab). **Known for:** sopa menorquina (vegetable soup); pretty terrace; Menorcan

specialties. $ *Average main: €21* ✉ *Carrer Major 53, Mercadal* ☎ *971/375392.*

# Fornells

*35 km (22 miles) northwest of Mahón.*

A little village (full-time population: 500) of whitewashed houses with red-tile roofs, Fornells comes alive in the summer high season, when Spanish and Catalan families arrive in droves to open their holiday chalets at the edge of town and in the nearby beach resorts. The bay—Menorca's second largest and deepest—is good for windsurfing, sailing, and scuba diving. The first fortifications built here to defend the Bay of Fornells from pirates date from 1625.

**GETTING HERE AND AROUND**

Buses leave the Estació Autobusos on Calle José Anselmo Clavé in Mahón for the 50-minute, 40-km (25-mile) trip to Fornells five times daily. By car, it's an easy half-hour drive north on the PM710.

## 🍴 Restaurants

### Ca Na Marga

$$ | STEAKHOUSE | On an island known for its excellent paellas and fresh fish and seafood, Ca Na Marga is famed for its top-quality steak, served with a choice of sauce, including green peppercorn or Mahón cheese sauce. Balearic specialties such as lamb shank with thyme and grilled rabbit are also a good bet. **Known for:** Mediterranean barbecue; "Chuletón" steak; rustic dining room. $ *Average main: €16* ✉ *Carrer de sa Barrera 24, Fornells* ☎ *971/376410* ⊕ *canamarga.com* ☾ *No lunch Wed. Closed Dec.–Apr.*

## 🏃 Activities

### SAILING

Several miles long and a mile wide but with a narrow entrance to the sea and virtually no waves, the Bay of Fornells gives the beginner a feeling of security and the expert plenty of excitement.

### Wind Fornells

SAILING | Here, on the beach just off Carrer del Rosari, you can rent windsurfing boards and dinghies and take lessons, individually or in groups. It's open May–October. ✉ *Ctra. Es Mercadal–Fornells s/n, Mercadal* ☎ *664/335801* ⊕ *www.windfornells.com* ✉ *Windsurfing boards from €33 for 1.5 hrs.*

# Cova des Coloms

*35 km (22 miles) northwest of Mahón.*

There are caverns and grottoes all over the Balearics, some of them justly famous because of their size, spectacular formations, and subterranean pools. This one is well worth a visit.

**GETTING HERE AND AROUND**

Take the road from Ferreries to Es Migjorn Gran, park by the cemetery, and follow the signs on the footpath, about 30 minutes' walk toward the beach at Binigaus. Signs direct you to the gully, where you descend to the cave.

## ◉ Sights

**Cova des Coloms** (*Cave of Pigeons*)

CAVE | This massive cave is the most spectacular on Menorca, with eerie rock formations rising up to a 77-foot-high ceiling. When planning your visit, bear in mind that it's a 30-minute walk each way from the nearest parking place. ✉ *Ferreries* ⊹ *On eastern side of ravine from Es Migjorn Gran to beach.*

# SEVILLE AND AROUND

11

Updated by
Joanna Styles

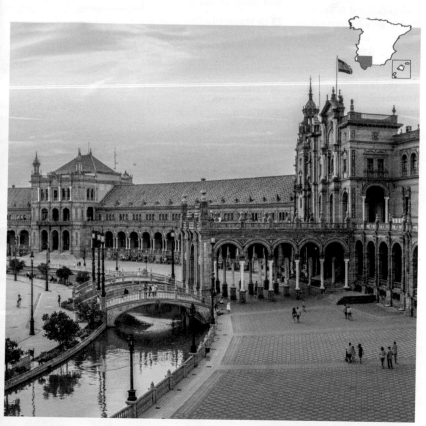

| ⊙ Sights | 🍴 Restaurants | 🛏 Hotels | 🛍 Shopping | 🍸 Nightlife |
|----------|---------------|----------|------------|-------------|
| ★★★★★ | ★★★★★ | ★★★★★ | ★★★★★ | ★★★★☆ |

# WELCOME TO SEVILLE AND AROUND

## TOP REASONS TO GO

★ **The Real Alcázar:** Drink in the sumptuously decorated patios and halls, the heavenly gold ceiling, ornate tile, and lush gardens dotted with pools, palms, and peacocks.

★ **Tour Catedral de Sevilla:** Tour Spain's biggest cathedral (there are 80 chapels) to see Christendom's largest altarpiece.

★ **Live and breathe flamenco:** Tune into Andalusia's soundtrack at one of Seville's many flamenco *tablaos* or spontaneously on any corner in Santa Cruz or Triana.

★ **Feast on tapas:** Make small plates your staples at myriad taverns, traditional and modern, where fine dining comes paired with local wines including sherry.

★ **Shop for tiles:** Learn about the history and process of making Sevillian ceramics in a former factory at the Centro de Cerámica Triana, and shop for beautiful souvenirs.

★ **Linger in the Plaza de España:** Take a leisurely stroll at this magnificent semicircular plaza located in María Luisa Park.

**1 Centro.** The heart of the city's commercial life.

**2 Santa Cruz.** Home to the Real Alcázar and a glorious labyrinth of whitewashed alleys.

**3 El Arenal.** This area includes the Parque Maria Luisa, the Torre de Oro on the river, and many picturesque taverns.

**4 La Macarena.** The city's best churches and convents, pleasant squares, and excellent restaurants are here.

**5 Triana.** Home to the main workshop for Seville's renowned tile ceramicists.

**6 Italica.** Known for the ruins of its Roman city.

**7 Córdoba.** Home to the stunning Mezquita—a must-visit.

**8 Ronda.** Famous for its dramatic escarpments, views, and gorge.

**9 Around Ronda.** Caves, mountain villages, and gorges.

**10 Arcos de la Frontera.** A classic Andalusian pueblo blanco.

**11 Jerez de la Frontera.** The capital of horse culture and sherry.

**12 Cádiz.** So old that Julius Caesar once held public office here.

0     1,000 ft
0     200 m

Calle Torneo

Calle Resolana
C. Becquer
C. Escoberos

Calle Antonio Machín
C. Muñoz León
C. León XIII
Avenida de la Cruz Roja
Calle José María Izquierdo
Calle José Matador
Calle Alemán

LA MACARENA
Calle Relator
C. Lumbreras
Alameda de Hércules
Calle Feria
Calle San Luis
C. Pasaje
Avenida de Miraflores
Avenida de Carretera de Carmona
Calle Carretera de Carmona

Calle Santa Ana
C. Juan Rabadán
C. Pascual de Gayangos
Calle Gelis
Calle Baños
C. San Vicente
C. Miguel Esc.
C. Bachoso
C. Alfonso XII
Calle Castellar
C. San Juan de la Palma
Calle Sol
Calle Soledad Sola
Jardines del Valle
Calle Arroyo
Calle Urquita
Calle San Juan Bosco
Parque Agumoré

Plaza de la Encarnación
C. San Eloy
C. Murillo
C. Zaragoza

C. María Auxiliadora
C. José Laguillo
C. Gonzalo Bilbao
C. Júpiter
Calle Recaredo
C. Juan de Vera
C. Juan Antonio Cavestany

CENTRO

EL ARENAL

Paseo de Cristóbal Colón
TRAM

BARRIO DE SANTA CRUZ

C. Luis Montoto

C. Jiménez Aranda
Avenida de San Francisco Javier
Calle Páramos

Av. de Menéndez Pelayo

Avenida de Málaga

Av. de Eduardo Dato
Nervión M

Puente de San Telmo
M Puerta de Jerez
Calle Bailén
Calle Dos de Mayo
Calle Arfe

M Plaza de Cuba
C. Niebla
Calle Virgen del Valle
Calle Monte Carmelo

Canal de Alfonso XIII

Paseo de las Delicias
Av. de María Luisa

M Prado de San Sebastián
Avenida de Portugal
Prado de San Sebastián
C. Enramadilla
Avenida de la Buhaira
M San Bernardo
Av. Ramón Carande

Parque de María Luisa

PARQUE DE MARÍA LUISA

Virgen de Luján
Fernando IV

# FLAMENCO

## FLAMENCO 101

**Origins:** The music is largely Arabic in its beginnings, but you'll detect echoes of Greek dirges and Jewish chants, with healthy doses of Flemish and traditional Castilian thrown in. Hindu sways, Roman mimes, and other movement informs the dance, but we may never know the specific origins of flamenco. The dance, along with the nomadic Gypsies, spread throughout Andalusia and within a few centuries had developed into many variations and styles, some of them named after the city where they were born (such as *malaguenas* and *sevillanas*) and others taking on the names after people, emotions, or bands. In all, there are more than 50 different styles (or *palos*) of flamenco, four of which are the stylistic pillars others branch off from—differing mainly in rhythm and mood: *toná, soleá, fandango,* and *seguidilla*.

**Clapping and castanets:** The sum of its parts are awe-inspiring, but if you boil it down, flamenco is a combination of music, singing, and dance. Staccato hand-clapping almost sneaks in as a fourth part—the sounds made from all the participants' palms, or *palmas,* is part of the duende—but this element remains more of a connector that all in the performance take part in when their hands are free. Hand-clapping was likely flamenco's original key instrument before the guitar, *cajón* (wooden box used for percussion), and other instruments arrived on the scene. Perhaps the simplest way to augment the clapping is to add a uniquely designed six-string guitar, in which case you've got yourself a *tablao,* or people seated around a singer and clapping. Dance undoubtedly augments the experience, but isn't necessary for a tablao. These exist all throughout Andalusia and are usually private affairs with people who love flamenco. Castanets (or *palillos*) were absorbed by the Phoenician culture and adopted by the Spanish, now part of their own folklore. They accompany other traditional folk dances in Spain and are used pervasively throughout flamenco (though not always present in some forms of dance).

**Flamenco now:** Flamenco's enormous international resurgence has been building for the past few decades. Much of this revival can be attributed to pioneers like legendary singer Camarón de la Isla, guitarist Paco de Lucía, or even outsiders like Miles Davis fusing flamenco with other genres like jazz and rock. Today the most popular flamenco fusion artists include Rosalía and Dellafuente.

## FLAMENCO HEAD TO TOE

Wrists rotate while hands move, articulating each finger individually, curling in and out. The trick is to have it appear like an effortless flourish. Facial expression is considered another tool for the dancer, and it's never plastered on but projected from some deeper place. For women, the hair is usually pulled back in touring flamenco performances in order to give the back row a chance to see more clearly the passionate expressions. In smaller settings like tablaos, hair is usually let down and is supposed to better reveal the beauty of the female form overall. The dancer carries the body in an upright and proud manner: the chest is out, shoulders back. Despite this position, the body should never carry tension—it needs to remain pliable and fluid. With professional dancers, the feet can move so quickly, they blur like hummingbird wings in action. When they move slowly, you can watch the different ways a foot can strike the floor. A *planta* is when the whole foot strikes the floor, as opposed to when the ball of the foot or the heel (*taco*) hits. Each one must be a "clean" strike or the sound will be off.

An exploration of Andalusia must begin with Seville, Spain's fourth-largest city and the place where all romantic images of Andalusia, and Spain, spring vividly to life. Known for steamy-hot summers, delightfully mild winters, its operatic heroine Carmen, and stunning *Game of Thrones* settings, Seville is an enchanting city. Its fabulous food; extraordinary Mudejar, Gothic, and Renaissance architecture; and exotic flamenco rhythms never fail to seduce and charm.

Seville's whitewashed houses, bright with bougainvillea, ocher-color palaces, and baroque facades, have long enchanted both sevillanos and travelers. It's a city for the senses—the fragrance of orange blossom suffuses the air in spring, the sound of flamenco echoes through the alleyways in Triana and Santa Cruz, and views of the great Guadalquivir River accompany you at every turn. This is also a fine city for handsome people—stroll down the swankier pedestrian shopping streets and you can't fail to notice just how good looking everyone is. Aside from being blessed with even features and flashing dark eyes, sevillanos exude a cool sophistication that seems more Catalan than Andalusian.

Seville offers a bewitching mosaic of flamenco, matadors, horses, refreshingly cool patios, and religious fervor. Add to this fine architecture (rich baroque and Renaissance monuments, colonial palaces, and the sumptuous Real Alcázar), plus fine wining and dining, and this city brings vibrant color to any holiday.

At the top of your must-see list sit the Real Alcázar (fortress)—a Mudejar delight whisking you straight to the land of Scheherazade—and the Cathedral, the largest in Spain and topped with the Giralda minaret tower. Continue your architectural feast with one of the city's splendid palaces, excellent museums, and fine churches while taking in Seville's nod to modernity in the Gaudí-style Metropol Parasol, lofty Torre Seville, and the elegant contemporary bridges.

The layout of the historic center of Seville makes exploring easy. The Centro—the central zone around the cathedral, Calle Sierpes, and Plaza Nueva—is splendid and monumental, but it's not where you'll find Seville's greatest charm. El Arenal, home of the Maestranza bullring, the Teatro de la Maestranza concert hall, and a concentration of picturesque taverns, still buzzes the way it must have when stevedores loaded and unloaded ships from the New World. Just southeast of Centro, the medieval Jewish quarter, Barrio de Santa Cruz, is home to the Real Alcázar and a lovely, whitewashed tangle of alleys. The Barrio de la Macarena to the northeast is rich in sights and authentic Seville atmosphere. The fifth and final neighborhood to explore, on the far side of the Río Guadalquivir, is in many ways the best of all: Triana, the traditional habitat for sailors, bullfighters, and flamenco artists, as well as the main workshop for Seville's renowned ceramicists.

Like all Andalusians, the sevillanos know how to party. Highlights of the year come in the Feria de abril, a week of colorful and musical festivities to welcome spring, quickly followed by celebrations marking Pentecost when locals take a pilgrimage to El Rocío on the Atlantic Ocean. Religious fervor comes into its own during Holy Week when thousands of devout locals take part in some of Spain's most famous processions.

Side trips from Seville range from half-day excursions to the Roman Itálica to longer visits to some of Andalusia's finest towns and cities. Nearby Jerez, celebrated for sherry and horses, and Cádiz, a maritime jewel, are both must-sees. Ronda, one of Spain's most beautiful towns, merits a full day, as does Córdoba, whose Moorish mosque ranks as one of the country's most treasured monuments.

# Planning

## When to Go

Visit Seville between October and November or between April and May. It's blisteringly hot in the summer, so spend time in the Pedroches of northern Córdoba province if you plan to visit then. Autumn catches the cities going about their business, the temperatures are moderate, and you will rarely see a line form.

December through March tends to be cool, uncrowded, and quiet, but come spring, it's fiesta time, with Seville's Semana Santa (Holy Week, between Palm Sunday and Easter) the most moving and multitudinous. April showcases whitewashed Andalusia at its floral best, with every patio and facade covered with flowers from bougainvillea to honeysuckle.

## Getting Here and Around

### AIR

Seville's airport is about 7 km (4½ miles) east of the city. There's a bus from the airport to the center of town every half hour daily (5:20 am–1:15 am; €4 one-way, €6 return). Taxi fare from the airport to the city center is around €23 during the day and €26 at night and on Sunday. A number of private companies operate private airport-shuttle services.

### BUS

Seville has two intercity bus stations: Estación Plaza de Armas, the main one, with buses serving Córdoba, Granada, Huelva, and Málaga in Andalusia, plus Madrid and Portugal and other international destinations; and the smaller Estación del Prado de San Sebastián, serving Cádiz and nearby towns and villages.

Seville's urban bus service is efficient and covers the greater city area. Bus Nos. C1, C2, C3, C4, and C5 run circular routes linking the main transportation terminals with the city center. The C1 goes east in a clockwise direction from the Santa Justa train station via Avenida de Carlos V, Avenida de María Luisa, Triana, the Isla de la Cartuja, and Calle de Resolana. The C2 follows the same route in reverse. The C3 runs from the Avenida Menéndez Pelayo to the Puerta de Jerez, Triana, Plaza de Armas, and Calle de Recaredo. The C4 does that route counterclockwise. The C5 runs between Puerta Jerez and Plaza Duque. The tram (called Metro Centro) runs between the San Bernardo station and Plaza Nueva. Buses do not run within the Barrio de Santa Cruz because the streets are too narrow, though they amply serve convenient access points around the periphery of this popular tourist area.

Certain routes operate limited night service from midnight to 2 am Monday through Thursday, with services until 5 am Friday through Sunday. Single rides cost €1.40, but if you're going to be busing a lot, it's more economical to buy a rechargeable multitravel pass (minimum charge is €7), which works out to €0.69 per ride. Special Tarjetas Turísticas (tourist passes) valid for one or three days of unlimited bus travel cost (respectively) €5 and €10. Tickets are sold at newsstands and at the main bus station, Prado de San Sebastián.

**CONTACTS Estación del Prado de San Sebastián.** ⊠ *Calle Vázquez Sagastizábal, El Arenal* ☎ *955/479290.* **Estación Plaza de Armas.** ⊠ *Puente Cristo de la Expiración, Centro* ☎ *955/038665* ⊕ *www.autobusesplazadearmas.es.*

### CAR
Getting in and out of Seville by car isn't difficult, thanks to the SE30 ring road, but getting around in the city by car is problematic. We advise leaving your car at your hotel or in a lot while you're here.

### TAXI
**CONTACTS Radio Taxi Sevilla.** ⊠ *Seville* ☎ *954/580000.*

### TRAIN
Train connections include the high-speed AVE service from Madrid, with a journey time of less than 2½ hours.

**CONTACTS Estación Santa Justa.** ⊠ *Av. Kansas City, El Arenal* ☎ *912/320320.*

### VISITOR INFORMATION
**CONTACTS City of Seville.** ⊠ *Paseo Marqués de Contadero s/n, Barrio de Santa Cruz* ✛ *On waterfront, by Torre de Oro* ☎ *955/471232* ⊕ *www.visitasevilla. es.*

# Restaurants

Eating out is an intrinsic part of the Andalusian lifestyle. Whether it's sharing some tapas with friends over a prelunch drink or a three-course à la carte meal, many Andalusians eat out at some point during the day. Unsurprisingly, there are literally thousands of bars and restaurants throughout the region catering to all budgets and tastes.

At lunchtime, check out the *menús del día* (daily menus) offered by many restaurants, usually three courses and excellent value (expect to pay €8–€15, depending on the type of restaurant and location). Roadside restaurants, known as *ventas*, usually provide good food in generous portions and at reasonable prices. Be aware that many restaurants add a service charge (*cubierto*), which can be as much as €3 per person, and some restaurant prices don't include value-added tax (*impuesto sobre el valor añadido/I.V.A.*) at 10%. Note also that restaurants with tasting menus (*menús de degustación*) usually require everyone at the table to have the menu.

Andalusians tend to eat later than their fellow Spaniards: lunch is 2–4 pm, and dinner starts at 9 pm (10 pm in the summer). In cities, many restaurants are closed Sunday night, and fish restaurants tend to close on Monday; in inland towns and cities, some restaurants close for all of August.

*Restaurant reviews have been shortened. For full information, visit Fodors.com.*

# Hotels

Seville has grand old hotels, such as the Alfonso XIII, and a number of converted former palaces.

In Córdoba, several hotels occupy houses in the old quarter, close to the mosque. Other than during Holy Week and the Festival de los Patios in May, it's easy to find a room in Córdoba.

Rental accommodations bookable on portals such as Airbnb are popular in large towns and cities; double-check reviews before you book.

Not all hotel prices include value-added tax (I.V.A.) and the 10% surcharge may be added to your final bill. Check when you book.

*Hotel reviews have been shortened. For full information, visit Fodors.com.*

## What It Costs in Euros

| $ | $$ | $$$ | $$$$ |
|---|---|---|---|
| **RESTAURANTS** | | | |
| under €15 | €15–€20 | €21–€25 | over €25 |
| **HOTELS** | | | |
| under €100 | €100–€140 | €141–€200 | over €200 |

# Tours

## ★ annie b's Spanish Kitchen

SPECIAL-INTEREST TOURS | Based in Vejer de la Frontera (Cádiz), Scottish-born Annie B offers food and wine experiences, including sherry tours, tuna *almadraba* (an age-old way of trapping) trips, and cooking classes. ✉ *Calle Viñas, 11, Vejer de la Frontera* ☎ *620/560649* ⊕ *www.anniebspain.com* 🖃 *From €155.*

## Azahar Sevilla Tapas Tours

SPECIAL-INTEREST TOURS | Local food and wine expert, and certified sherry educator, Shawn Hennessey leads intimate guided tours around Seville's best tapas bars (traditional and gourmet). Choose from several different options, lunch or evening. ⊕ *azahar-sevilla.com/sevilletapas* 🖃 *From €90.*

## Glovento Sur

AIR EXCURSIONS | Up to five people at a time are taken on balloon trips above Granada, Guadix, and Antequera. ✉ *Placeta Nevot 4, #1A, Granada* ☎ *958/290316* ⊕ *www.gloventosur.com* 🖃 *From €165.*

## Sevilla Bike Tour

BICYCLE TOURS | Guided tours, leaving from the Makinline Shop on Calle Arjona at 10:30 am, take in the major sights of the city and offer interesting stories and insider information along the way. You'll cover about 10 km (6 miles) in three hours. Reservations are required on weekends and recommended on weekdays. ✉ *Calle Arjona 8, Centro* ☎ *954/562625* ⊕ *www.sevillabiketour.com* 🖃 *From €25.*

## Sevilla Walking Tours

WALKING TOURS | Choose one of three walking tours conducted in English: the City Walking Tour, leaving Plaza Nueva from the statue of San Fernando; the Alcázar Tour, leaving Plaza del Triunfo from the central statue; and the Cathedral Tour, also leaving from the

Plaza del Triunfo central statue. ⊠ *Seville* 🕿 *616/501100* ⊕ *sevillawalkingtours.com* 🖃 *From €12.*

**Your First Flamenco Experience**
SPECIAL-INTEREST TOURS | Local dancer Eva Izquierdo from Triana teaches you how to clap in time, and take your first dance steps, in authentic costume, all in an hour. ⊠ *Seville* 🕿 *626/007868* ⊕ *www. ishowusevilla.com* 🖃 *From €23.*

# Centro

The Centro area is the heart of Seville's commercial life. It has bustling shopping streets—several of which are pedestrianized—and leafy squares lined with bars and cafés. The residential streets contain some of the best examples of colonial architecture; noteworthy features include fine facades and roof gables topped with local ceramic tiles. Centro is also home to several of the city's most beautiful churches.

## ◉ Sights

**Ayuntamiento** (*City Hall*)
GOVERNMENT BUILDING | This Diego de Riaño original, built between 1527 and 1564, is in the heart of Seville's commercial center. A 19th-century plateresque facade overlooks the Plaza Nueva. The other side, on the Plaza de San Francisco, is Riaño's work. Visits must be prebooked via the website. ⊠ *Pl. Nueva 1, Centro* 🕿 *955/470243* ⊕ *casaconsistorialse-villa.sacatuentrada.es* 🖃 *€4 (free Sat.)* ⊙ *Closed Fri. and Sun.*

**Calle Sierpes**
STREET | This is Seville's classy main shopping street. Near the southern end, at No. 85, a plaque marks the spot where the Cárcel Real (Royal Prison) once stood. Miguel de Cervantes began writing *Don Quixote* in one of its cells. ⊠ *Calle Sierpes, Centro.*

**★ Catedral de Sevilla**
CHURCH | Seville's cathedral can be described only in superlatives: it's the largest and highest cathedral in Spain, the largest Gothic building in the world, and the world's third-largest church, after St. Peter's in Rome and St. Paul's in London. After Ferdinand III captured Seville from the Moors in 1248, the great mosque begun by Yusuf II in 1171 was reconsecrated to the Virgin Mary and used as a Christian cathedral. In 1401, the people of Seville decided to erect a new cathedral, one that would equal the glory of their great city. They pulled down the old mosque, leaving only its minaret and outer courtyard, and built the existing building in just over a century—a remarkable feat for that time.

Highlights inside include the **Capilla Mayor** (Main Chapel) with a magnificent altarpiece (restored in 2014), the largest in Christendom (65 feet by 43 feet) and depicting some 36 scenes from the life of Christ.

At the south end of the cathedral is the **monument to Christopher Columbus**: his coffin is borne aloft by the four kings representing the medieval kingdoms of Spain: Castile, León, Aragón, and Navarra. At the opposite (north) end, don't miss the **Altar de Plata** (Silver Altar), an 18th-century masterpiece of intricate silversmithing.

In the **Sacristía de los Cálices** (Sacristy of the Chalices) look for Juan Martínez Montañés's wood carving *Crucifixion, Merciful Christ*; Juan de Valdés Leal's *St. Peter Freed by an Angel*; Francisco de Zurbarán's *Virgin and Child*; and Francisco José de Goya y Lucientes's *St. Justa and St. Rufina*. The **Sacristía Mayor** (Main Sacristy) holds the keys to the city, which Seville's Moors and Jews presented to

Seville's cathedral is the largest and tallest cathedral in Spain, the largest Gothic building in the world, and the third-largest church in the world, after St. Peter's in Rome and St. Paul's in London.

their conqueror, Ferdinand III. Finally, in the dome of the **Sala Capitular** (Chapter House), in the cathedral's southeastern corner, is Bartolomé Estéban Murillo's *Immaculate Conception*, painted in 1668.

One of the cathedral's highlights, the **Capilla Real** (Royal Chapel), is concealed behind a ponderous curtain, but you can duck in if you're quick, quiet, and properly dressed (no shorts or sleeveless tops): enter from the Puerta de los Palos, on Plaza Virgen de los Reyes (signposted "Entrada para Culto," or "Entrance for Worship"). Along the sides of the chapel are the tombs of the Beatrix of Swabia, wife of the 13th-century's Ferdinand III, and their son Alfonso X (the Wise); in a silver urn before the high altar rest the relics of Ferdinand III himself, Seville's liberator. Canonized in 1671, he was said to have died from excessive fasting.

Don't forget the **Patio de los Naranjos** (Courtyard of Orange Trees), on the church's northern side, where the fountain in the center was used for ablutions before people entered the original mosque.

The Christians could not bring themselves to destroy the tower when they tore down the mosque, so they incorporated it into their new cathedral. In 1565–68 they added a lantern and belfry to the old minaret and installed 24 bells, one for each of Seville's 24 parishes and the 24 Christian knights who fought with Ferdinand III in the Reconquest. They also added the bronze statue of Faith, which turned as a weather vane (*el giraldillo*, or "something that turns"); thus the whole tower became known as **La Giralda**. With its baroque additions, the slender Giralda rises 322 feet. Inside, instead of steps, 35 sloping ramps—wide enough for two horsemen to pass abreast—climb to a viewing platform 230 feet up. Don't miss the magnificent north facade of the cathedral, housing

## Sights ▼

1 Archivo General de Indias.................... **E6**
2 Ayuntamiento ............ **E5**
3 Basílica de la Macarena ................ **F1**
4 Calle Sierpes ............. **E4**
5 Capilla de los Marineros ................ **C6**
6 Casa de Pilatos ......... **G5**
7 Catedral de Sevilla ...... **E6**
8 Centro de Cerámica Triana ................... **B6**
9 Convento de Santa Paula ............. **G3**
10 Hospital de la Caridad... **E6**
11 Hospital de los Venerables ............... **F6**
12 Iglesia de San Luis de los Franceses ................ **F2**
13 Iglesia del Salvador .... **E5**
14 Isla de La Cartuja ...... **B2**
15 Isla Mágica............... **E1**
16 Jardines de Murillo..... **G7**
17 Juderia (Jewish Quarter)......... **F6**
18 Mercado de Triana ...... **C6**
19 Metropol Parasol ........ **F4**
20 Monasterio de Santa María de las Cuevas .................. **A2**
21 Museo de Artes y Costumbres Populares................. **F9**
22 Museo de Bellas Artes ............. **D4**
23 Museo del Baile Flamenco .......... **F5**
24 Palacio de la Condesa de Lebrija ...... **E4**
25 Palacio de las Dueñas................... **F3**
26 Parque de María Luisa............... **F9**
27 Plaza de España ........ **G8**
28 Plaza de los Refinadores ............. **G6**
29 Plaza de Toros Real Maestranza........ **D6**
30 Real Alcázar............. **F7**
31 San Lorenzo y Jesús del Gran Poder ... **E2**
32 Torre del Oro ............ **D7**
33 University of Seville ..... **F7**

## Restaurants ▼

1 Abantal................... **H5**
2 Bache San Pedro........ **F4**
3 Bar Las Golondrinas.... **B6**
4 Bodeguita Romero...... **D5**
5 Cañabota ................. **E4**
6 Casa Morales ........... **E6**
7 Castizo .................. **D5**
8 De la O .................. **B5**
9 El Pimentón............... **E6**
10 El Pintón .................. **E5**
11 El Rinconcillo........... **G4**
12 Espacio Eslava.......... **D2**
13 La Azotea ................ **D5**
14 La Moneda Casa Inchausti.................. **E6**
15 Palo Cortao.............. **F4**
16 Taberna La Sal ......... **G6**
17 Veganitessen............ **D5**
18 Vinería San Telmo ...... **G6**

## Quick Bites ▼

1 La Campana ............. **E4**

## Hotels ▼

1 Aguilas 5 Sevilla Suites .................... **F5**
2 Casa del Poeta.......... **F6**
3 Corral del Rey ........... **F5**
4 Eurostars Torre Sevilla.................... **A3**
5 Hospes Las Casas del Rey de Baeza........... **G4**
6 Hotel Alfonso XIII ....... **E7**
7 Hotel Amadeus Sevilla................... **F5**
8 Hotel Casa 1800.......... **F6**
9 Hotel Colón Gran Meliá............... **D4**
10 Hotel Monte Triana ..... **A5**
11 Legado Alcázar .......... **E7**
12 Mercer................... **D5**
13 Palacio de Villapanés Hotel......... **G4**
14 Pensión Córdoba ........ **F5**
15 Soho Boutique Catedral.................. **E5**

the **Puerta del Perdón** (Gate of Pardon) entrance to the courtyard. Restored between 2012 and 2015, the brickwork and white plaster on the huge wall strongly reflect the original 12th-century mosque. Admission also includes a visit to the Iglesia del Salvador. ⊠ *Pl. Virgen de los Reyes, Centro* ☎ *954/500528* ⊕ *www.catedraldesevilla.es* 🖭 *€12, free Thurs. from 2:45pm if you book via the website* ⊘ *Closed Sun. mornings.*

**Iglesia de San Luis de los Franceses**

CHURCH | This baroque bonanza of a church, built in 1731 in honor of Louis IX of France, reopened in late 2017 after an extensive restoration. The stunning altarpiece by Pedro Duque Cornejo now gleams in all its former glory along with the ornate ceiling and side chapels. ⊠ *Calle San Luis, Seville* ☎ *954/550207* 🖭 *€4* ⊘ *Closed Mon.*

**Iglesia del Salvador**

CHURCH | Built between 1671 and 1712, the Church of the Savior stands on the site of Seville's first great mosque, remains of which can be seen in its Courtyard of the Orange Trees. Also of note are the sculptures *Jesús de la Pasión* and *St. Christopher* by Martínez Montañés. In 2003 archaeologists discovered an 18th-century burial site here; walkways facilitate visits. ⊠ *Pl. del Salvador, Centro* ☎ *954/211679* 🖭 *€5 (free with Cathedral admission)* ⊘ *Closed Sun.*

**Metropol Parasol**

PLAZA/SQUARE | This huge square, at the west end of Calle Cuna, is home to the world's largest wooden structure, 492 feet long by 230 feet wide. Known in the city as "Las Setas" (The Mushrooms), the piece is actually meant to represent giant trees, and walkways run through the "tree tops" affording great views of the city, especially at sunset. Although it's reminiscent of Gaudí, it was built in 2011. At ground level, the Antiquarium

(€2; closed Mon.) has interesting archaeological remains (mostly Roman), and there's also a large indoor food market. ⊠ *Pl. de la Encarnación, Centro* ☎ *606/635214* 🖭 *€5.*

★ **Palacio de la Condesa de Lebrija**

CASTLE/PALACE | This lovely palace has three ornate patios, including a spectacular courtyard graced by a Roman mosaic taken from the ruins in nearby Itálica, surrounded by Moorish arches and fine *azulejos* (painted tiles). The side rooms house a collection of archaeological items. The second floor contains the family apartments, and visits are by guided tour only. ■TIP→ **It's well worth paying for the second-floor tour, which gives an interesting insight into the collections and the family.** ⊠ *Calle Cuna 8, Centro* ☎ *954/227802* 🖭 *€12.*

**Palacio de las Dueñas**

HISTORIC HOME | The 15th-century home and official residence of the late 18th Duchess of Alba is an oasis of peace and quiet in the bustling city. Set around an ornate patio with Mudejar arches and a central fountain, the house includes antiques and paintings, as well as memorabilia relating to the duchess. Revered in the city and one of Spain's most important noblewomen and society figures, Cayetana de Alba loved bullfighting, flamenco, and ceramics. The visit (first floor only) also includes the stables, gardens (said to have inspired some of Antonio Machado's most famous early verses), and a Gothic chapel. ⊠ *Calle Dueñas 5, Centro* ☎ *954/214828* ⊕ *www.lasduenas. es* 🖭 *€10 (free Mon. 2–2:15pm).*

## 🍴 Restaurants

**Cañabota**

$$$$ | SPANISH | If you fancy treating yourself to some of the best fish in town, head for this modern Michelin-star restaurant just down the road from the Palacio de la Condesa de Lebrija. Seasonal

fish and seafood take center stage; you can see the catch of the day displayed in the window. **Known for:** efficient service; daily specials like marinated sardines; fresh fish and seafood. $ *Average main: €35* ✉ *Calle Orfila 3, Centro* ☎ *954/870 298* ⊕ *canabota.es* ⊗ *Closed Sun. and Mon.*

### Casa Morales

$ | TAPAS | Down a side street off the Avenida de la Constitución, this historic bar (formerly a wine store) takes you back to 19th-century Seville, and it is still run by descendants of the family that established it in 1850. Locals pack the place at lunchtime, when popular dishes include *menudo con garbanzos* (tripe with chickpeas) and *alhóndigas de choco* (cuttlefish croquettes). **Known for:** tripe with chickpeas; wine list; local atmosphere. $ *Average main: €10* ✉ *Calle García de Vinuesa 11, Centro* ☎ *954/221242* ⊗ *No dinner Sun.*

### Castizo

$$ | SPANISH | True tradition (castizo itself) comes into its own at this busy venue serving regional dishes such as *espinacas con garbanzos* (spinach with chickpeas) alongside more modern plates like the popular *coliflor tostada con holandesa trufada* (cauliflower cheese with truffle oil), plus daily fish specials and the rice dish of the day. The open kitchen gives you a frontline view of your meal in the making. **Known for:** open kitchen; daily fish and rice specials; authentic traditional cooking. $ *Average main: €12* ✉ *Calle Zaragoza 6, Centro* ☎ *955/180562* ⊕ *www.barracastizo.es.*

### El Pintón

$$ | FUSION | With a privileged spot a block north from the cathedral, this central restaurant offers two dining spaces: the traditional inside patio, where wood, mirrors, and tasteful lighting create an intimate but airy space, or the pleasant terrace outside. The cuisine combines

---

## Where's Columbus?

Christopher Columbus knew both triumph and disgrace, yet he found no repose—he died, bitterly disillusioned, in Valladolid in 1506. No one knows for certain where he's buried; he was reportedly laid to rest for the first time in the Dominican Republic and then moved over the years to other locations. A portion of his remains can be found in Seville's cathedral.

---

Andalusian dishes with a modern touch, with menu items such as bloody gazpacho, Idiázabal blue cheese risotto, and red tuna tartare. **Known for:** Mediterranean dishes; kitchen open all day; attractive interior. $ *Average main: €16* ✉ *Calle Francos 42, Centro* ☎ *955/075153* ⊕ *elpinton.com.*

### ★ Espacio Eslava

$ | TAPAS | The crowds gathered outside this local favorite off the Alameda de Hercules may be off-putting at first, but the creative, inexpensive tapas (from €4) are well worth the wait—and so is the house specialty, the Basque dessert *sokoa*. Try delicacies like the *cigarro para Bécquer* (cuttlefish in a filo pastry cigar) and *yema sobre bizcocho de boletus* (egg atop a mushroom sponge). ■**TIP**➔ Tables at the tapas bar can't be booked (a call will get you a reservation at the next-door Eslava restaurant); to help avoid a wait, visit between 12:30 and 1:30 pm or between 5 and 8 pm. **Known for:** vegetable strudel; sokoa, a Basque dessert; creative tapas. $ *Average main: €12* ✉ *Calle Eslava 3, Centro* ☎ *954/906568* ⊗ *Closed Mon. No dinner Sun.*

## La Azotea

**$$ | SPANISH |** With a young vibe and a vast and inventive menu (which changes seasonally), this tiny restaurant offers a welcome change from Seville's typical fried fare. The owners' haute-cuisine ambitions are reflected in excellent service and lovingly prepared food—but not in the prices. **Known for:** local vibe; seasonal menu; creative tapas. ⑤ *Average main: €16 ⊠ Calle Conde de Barajas 13, Centro ☎ 955/116748.*

# ☕ Coffee and Quick Bites

### ★ La Campana

**$ | CAFÉ |** Under the gilt-edged ceiling at Seville's most celebrated pastry outlet (founded in 1885), you can enjoy the flanlike *tocino de cielo,* or "heavenly bacon." For breakfast, enjoy a traditional feed of toasted bread with tomato and a strong coffee, served at a standing bar. Prices are reasonable despite its popularity. **Known for:** variety of pastries and desserts; tempting window displays; traditional atmosphere. ⑤ *Average main: €5 ⊠ Calle Sierpes 1, Centro ☎ 954/223570 ⊕ confiterialacampana.com.*

# 🛏 Hotels

### Hospes Las Casas del Rey de Baeza

**$$$$ | HOTEL |** Behind the striking white and ocher facade lies what was once a humble 18th-century corrala, now a pretty hotel combining original features such as teal verandas and rustic elements with modern comforts and fine cuisine. **Pros:** pretty patios; good food; historic touches. **Cons:** slightly out of town; some rooms are dark; rooftop views are ordinary. ⑤ *Rooms from: €250 ⊠ Pl. Jesús de la Redención 2, Centro ☎ 954/561496 ⊕ hospes.com ⟿ 41 rooms ⦿ No Meals.*

### ★ Mercer

**$$$$ | HOTEL |** Housed in a 19th-century mansion, Mercer is one of the city's top boutique hotels, featuring a lofty patio with a fountain, a stunning marble staircase, and a striking geometric chandelier atop a glass gallery. **Pros:** luxury lodging; rooftop terrace with plunge pool; spacious rooms. **Cons:** patio rooms have no views; a little too prim; pricey. ⑤ *Rooms from: €500 ⊠ Calle Castelar 26, Centro ☎ 954/223004 ⊕ www.mercersevilla.com ⟿ 11 rooms ⦿ No Meals.*

### ★ Palacio de Villapanés Hotel

**$$$$ | HOTEL |** This 18th-century palace with elegant updates and stylish contemporary furnishings, marble-columned patios, high ceilings, and a rooftop with terra-cotta-rooftop views, a pool, and bar, is one of the most chic converted-palace accommodations in Seville. **Pros:** local, off-the-beaten path feel; tall windows and high ceilings; oozes style and character. **Cons:** small gym; some rooms are dark; not the most central location. ⑤ *Rooms from: €350 ⊠ Calle Santiago 31, Centro ☎ 650/722265 ⊕ palaciovillapanes.com/en ⟿ 50 rooms ⦿ No Meals.*

### Soho Boutique Catedral

**$$$$ | HOTEL |** Opened in late 2021 in the middle of Seville's pedestrian center, this modern hotel puts you at the heart of the action. **Pros:** spacious rooms; great location; rooftop view of the Giralda. **Cons:** could be too functional for some; street noise in some rooms; limited breakfast. ⑤ *Rooms from: €250 ⊠ Avda. de la Constitución 8, Centro ☎ 854/856059 ⊕ sohohoteles.com ⟿ 62 rooms ⦿ No Meals.*

# 🛍 Shopping

### Ángela y Adela Taller de Diseño

**OTHER SPECIALTY STORE |** Come to this shop for privately fitted and

Seville's grand alcázar is a UNESCO World Heritage Site and an absolute must-see.

custom-made flamenco dresses. ✉ *Calle Chapineros 1, Centro* ☎ *954/227186.*

### Buffuna

**HATS & GLOVES** | This shop carries hand-made hats and caps for all occasions, especially fancy ones. ✉ *Calle Aceituno 6, Centro* ☎ *954/537824* ⊕ *patriciabuffuna. com* ⊙ *Closed weekends.*

### Lola Azahares

**OTHER SPECIALTY STORE** | For flamenco wear, this is one of Seville's most highly regarded stores. ✉ *Calle Cuna 31, Centro* ☎ *954/222912* ⊕ *www.lolaazahares.es.*

### Luisa Perez y Riu

**OTHER SPECIALTY STORE** | Flamenco dresses and all the accessories, designed with a modern touch, are sold at this shop. ✉ *Calle Rivero 9, Centro* ☎ *607/817624* Ⓜ *Puerta de Jerez.*

### Plaza del Duque

**CRAFTS** | A few blocks north of Plaza Nueva, Plaza del Duque has a crafts market Wednesday through Saturday. ✉ *Centro.*

# Barrio de Santa Cruz

The most romantic neighborhood in the city, Santa Cruz offers the visitor quintessential Seville: whitewashed houses with colorful geraniums and bougainvillea cascading down their facades, winding alleyways, and intimate squares scented with orange blossoms in the spring, all lit by old-style lamps at night. This neighborhood is also the busiest and most touristic part of Seville—so stray from the main thoroughfares and lose yourself in the side streets to discover a place where time seems to have stopped and all you hear is birdsong.

## ◉ Sights

### Archivo General de Indias (*Archives of the Indies*)

**HISTORIC SIGHT** | Opened in 1785 in the former Lonja (Merchants' Exchange), this dignified Renaissance building stores a valuable archive of more than 40,000 documents, including drawings, trade documents, plans of South American towns, and even the autographs of Columbus, Magellan, and Cortés. Temporary exhibitions showcase different archives. ⊠ *Av. de la Constitución 3, Barrio de Santa Cruz* ☎ *954/500528* ⬚ *Free* ☾ *Closed Mon.*

### ★ Casa de Pilatos

**HISTORIC HOME** | With its fine patio and superb azulejo decorations, this palace is a beautiful blend of Spanish Mudejar and Renaissance architecture and is considered a prototype of an Andalusian mansion. It was built in the first half of the 16th century by the dukes of Tarifa, ancestors of the present owner, the Duke of Medinaceli. It's known as Pilate's House because Don Fadrique, first marquis of Tarifa, allegedly modeled it on Pontius Pilate's house in Jerusalem, where he had gone on a pilgrimage in 1518. The upstairs apartments, which you can see on a guided tour, have frescoes, paintings, and antique furniture. Admission includes an audio guide in English. ⊠ *Pl. de Pilatos 1, Barrio de Santa Cruz* ☎ *954/225298* ⬚ *From €10.*

### Hospital de los Venerables

**HISTORIC SIGHT** | Once a retirement home for priests, this baroque building has a splendid azulejo patio with an interesting sunken fountain (designed to cope with low water pressure) and an upstairs gallery, but the highlight is the chapel, featuring frescoes by Valdés Leal and sculptures by Pedro Roldán. The building also houses a cultural foundation that organizes on-site art exhibitions. ⊠ *Pl. de los Venerables 8, Barrio de Santa Cruz* ☎ *954/562696* ⬚ *€10, includes audio guide (free Fri. 2–3 pm if you book online)* ☾ *Closed Wed.*

### Jardines de Murillo (*Murillo Gardens*)

**GARDEN** | From the Plaza Santa Cruz you can stroll through these gardens, home to a statue of Christopher Columbus.

In summer there's welcome shade and refreshing fountains. ⊠ *Pl. Santa Cruz, Barrio de Santa Cruz.*

### ★ Juderia (Jewish Quarter)

**HISTORIC DISTRICT** | The twisting alleyways and traditional whitewashed houses add to the tourist charm of this barrio. On some streets, bars alternate with antiques and souvenir shops, but most of the quarter is quiet and residential. On the Plaza Alianza, pause to enjoy the antiques shops and outdoor cafés. In the Plaza de Doña Elvira, with its fountain and azulejo benches, young sevillanos gather to play guitars. Just around the corner from the hospital, at Callejón del Agua and Jope de Rueda, Gioacchino Rossini's Figaro serenaded Rosina on her Plaza Alfaro balcony. Adjoining the Plaza Alfaro, in the Plaza Santa Cruz, flowers and orange trees surround a 17th-century filigree iron cross, which marks the site of the erstwhile church of Santa Cruz, destroyed by Napoléon's general Jean-de-Dieu Soult. ⊠ *Barrio de Santa Cruz.*

### Museo del Baile Flamenco

**OTHER MUSEUM** | This private museum in the heart of Santa Cruz was opened in 2007 by the legendary flamenco dancer Cristina Hoyos and includes audiovisual and multimedia displays briefly explaining the history, culture, and soul of Spanish flamenco. There are also regular classes and shows. ⊠ *Calle Manuel Rojas Marcos 3, Barrio de Santa Cruz* ☎ *954/340311* ⊕ *museodelbaileflamenco. com* ⬚ *€10 museum only; €26 museum and show.*

### Plaza de los Refinadores

**PLAZA/SQUARE** | This shady square filled with palms and orange trees is separated from the Murillo Gardens by an iron grillwork and ringed with stately glass balconies. At its center is a monument to Don Juan Tenorio, the famous Don Juan known for his amorous conquests. ⊠ *Barrio de Santa Cruz.*

## ★ Real Alcázar

CASTLE/PALACE | The Plaza del Triunfo forms the entrance to the Mudejar palace, the official local residence of the king and queen, built by Pedro I (1350–69) on the site of Seville's former Moorish alcázar. Built more than 100 years after the Reconquest of Seville, this isn't a genuine Moorish palace but it's authentic enough—parts of the palace and gardens were recreated as a Dornish palace for the final seasons of *Game of Thrones*, which filmed here in 2015 and 2018.

Entering the alcázar through the Puerta del León (Lion's Gate) and the high, fortified walls, you'll first find yourself in the Patio del León (Courtyard of the Lion). Off to the left are the oldest parts of the building, the 14th-century Sala de Justicia (Hall of Justice) and, next to it, the intimate Patio del Yeso (Courtyard of Plaster), the only extant part of the original 12th-century Almohad Alcázar. Cross the Patio de la Montería (Courtyard of the Hunt) to Pedro's Mudejar palace, arranged around the beautiful Patio de las Doncellas (Court of the Damsels), resplendent with delicately carved stucco. Opening off this patio, the Salón de Embajadores (Hall of the Ambassadors), with its cedar cupola of green, red, and gold, is the most sumptuous hall in the palace. Other royal rooms include the three baths of Pedro's powerful and influential mistress, María de Padilla. María's hold on her royal lover and his courtiers was so great that legend says they all lined up to drink her bathwater. The Patio de las Muñecas (Court of the Dolls) takes its name from two tiny faces carved on the inside of one of its arches.

The Renaissance Palacio de Carlos V is endowed with a rich collection of Flemish tapestries depicting Carlos's victories at Tunis. Upstairs, the Cuarto Real Alto (Royal Chambers where the king and queen stay when they visit) are packed with antiques. In the gardens, inhale the fragrance of jasmine and myrtle, wander among terraces and baths, and peer into the well-stocked goldfish pond. From here, a passageway leads to the Patio de las Banderas (Court of the Flags), which has a classic view of La Giralda. Allow at least two hours for your visit.

■ TIP→ Book your ticket online to avoid long lines, and at least one month in advance to avoid disappointment. If you want to see the Cuarto Real Alto, reserve as far in advance as possible and plan to arrive at least 30 minutes before your allocated time slot. ⊠ *Pl. del Triunfo, Santa Cruz* ☎ *954/502324* ⊕ *www.alcazarsevilla.org* 🎫 *€14, free for last hour of opening on Mon. if you book online; Cuarto Real €5.*

## 🍴 Restaurants

### Abantal

$$$$ | SPANISH | Slightly off the beaten path but worth seeking, chef Julio Fernández's tasting menu takes you on a journey of the senses featuring seemingly ordinary local produce and traditional recipes elevated with unusual textures and preparations. The menu changes with the seasons, but always has nine dishes (€80) or 12 (€100) as well as extra-virgin-olive-oil menus. **Known for:** excellent service; innovative take on dishes; long wine list. ⑤ *Average main: €80* ⊠ *Calle Alcalde José de la Bandera 7, Barrio de Santa Cruz* ☎ *954/540000* ⊕ *www.abantalrestaurante.es* ☾ *Closed Sun., Mon., and Aug.*

### Taberna La Sal

$$ | SPANISH | This cozy restaurant offers an excellent selection of fish and meat dishes. It's renowned for its Almadraba tuna (traditionally hand-lined and caught in Zahara de los Atunes on the Cádiz coast) cooked any which way and always delicious. **Known for:** great choice of tapas; sea anemone risotto; tuna dishes. ⑤ *Average main: €15* ⊠ *Calle Doncellas 8, Santa Cruz* ☎ *954/335846* ⊕ *www.lasalzahara.com* ☾ *Closed Sun.*

### ★ Vineria San Telmo

$$ | SPANISH | Offering dining in a dimly lit dining room or on the street-level terrace, this popular Argentinean-owned restaurant near the touristy alcázar has a menu full of surprises. All dishes—which come as tapas, half portions, or full portions (ideal for sharing)—are superb and sophisticated, especially the eggplant stew with tomato, goat cheese, and smoked salmon; and the curried pumpkin and rocket croquettes. ■TIP→ It can get very crowded and noisy, so it's not always an ideal place for a romantic meal for two. **Known for:** good choice of vegetarian options; extensive choice of Spanish vinos; creative tapas. $ *Average main: €15* ⊠ *Paseo Catalina de Ribera 4, Santa Cruz* ☎ *954/410600* ⊕ *vineriasantelmo. com/en.*

 ## Hotels

### Aguilas 5 Sevilla Suites

$$$$ | HOTEL | If you're looking for a self-catering option in the heart of Santa Cruz, you can't go wrong at this comfortable town house, originally an 18th-century mansion. **Pros:** home-away-from-home vibes; central location; good value for families. **Cons:** parking not nearby; on pricey side for just 2 people; some rooms are dark. $ *Rooms from: €225* ⊠ *Calle Aguilas 5, Barrio de Santa Cruz* ☎ *658/628129* ⊕ *www.aguilas5.com* ⟿ *9 rooms* ❌ *No Meals.*

### Casa del Poeta

$$$$ | HOTEL | Up a narrow alleyway, behind an ordinary facade, a 17th-century palace that was the haunt of Seville's poets at the end of the 19th century is now an oasis of calm. **Pros:** peaceful, central location; rooftop with a view; authentic palatial atmosphere. **Cons:** some rooms are dark; could be too traditional for some; difficult to reach by car (call shortly before arrival for staff to meet you). $ *Rooms from: €275* ⊠ *Calle*

*Don Carlos Alonso Chaparro 3, Santa Cruz* ☎ *954/213868* ⊕ *www.casadelpoeta.es* ⟿ *17 rooms* ❌ *Free Breakfast.*

### Corral del Rey

$$$$ | HOTEL | Southeast Asian and Moroccan decor fuse to perfection throughout this carefully restored 17th-century palace in the heart of Santa Cruz. **Pros:** private and peaceful setting but easy walk to sights; rooftop terrace with plunge pool; meticulously restored 17th-century palace with contemporary updates. **Cons:** some rooms on the small side; based on both sides of small street and some guests have to cross street for breakfast; no direct car access. $ *Rooms from: €300* ⊠ *Calle Corral del Rey 12, Barrio de Santa Cruz* ☎ *954/227116* ⊕ *www. corraldelrey.com* ⟿ *17 rooms* ❌ *Free Breakfast.*

### ★ Hotel Amadeus Sevilla

$$$ | HOTEL | With regular classical concerts, a music room off the central patio, and instruments for guests to use, including pianos in some of the sound-proofed rooms, this 18th-century manor house is ideal for touring professional musicians and music fans in general. **Pros:** small but charming rooms; friendly service; roof terrace. **Cons:** some rooms a little tired; ground-floor rooms can be dark; no direct car access. $ *Rooms from: €150* ⊠ *Calle Farnesio 6, Santa Cruz* ☎ *954/501443* ⊕ *www.hotelamadeussevilla.com* ⟿ *43 rooms* ❌ *No Meals.*

### ★ Hotel Casa 1800

$$$$ | B&B/INN | This classy boutique hotel, in a refurbished 19th-century mansion, is a refuge in bustling Santa Cruz. **Pros:** top-notch amenities; central location; great service. **Cons:** on noisy side street; no restaurant; some rooms small. $ *Rooms from: €275* ⊠ *Calle Rodrigo Caro 6, Santa Cruz* ☎ *954/561800* ⊕ *www.hotelcasa-1800sevilla.com* ⟿ *33 rooms* ❌ *No Meals.*

### Legado Alcázar
**$$$ | HOTEL |** Nestled next to the alcázar—the monument and hotel share walls—this 17th-century noble house offers a tasteful boutique experience in a very quiet corner. **Pros:** very quiet but central location; views of the alcázar; historic features. **Cons:** could be too traditional for some; room size varies; no restaurant on-site. ⑤ *Rooms from: €200* ✉ *Calle Mariana de Pineda 18, Barrio de Santa Cruz* ☎ *954/091818* ⊕ *www.legadoalcazarhotel.com* ⤴ *18 rooms* ⏀ *No Meals.*

### Pensión Córdoba
**$ | HOTEL |** Just a few blocks from the cathedral, nestled in the heart of Santa Cruz, this small, family-run inn is an excellent value. **Pros:** quiet, central location; rooms have a/c; friendly staff. **Cons:** no elevator to second floor; bathrooms need modernizing; no entry after 3 am. ⑤ *Rooms from: €85* ✉ *Calle Farnesio 12, Santa Cruz* ☎ *954/227498* ⤴ *11 rooms* ⏀ *No Meals.*

## ⓨ Nightlife

### EME Catedral Hotel
**CAFÉS |** This rooftop terrace has some of the best views of the cathedral in town. Sip your cocktail to the sound of resident DJs most nights. The terrace is open daily beginning at 1 pm. ✉ *Calle Alemanes 27, Barrio de Santa Cruz* ☎ *954/560000* ⊕ *www.emecatedralhotel.com* Ⓜ *Puerta de Jerez.*

## ⓟ Performing Arts

### FLAMENCO
### ★ La Casa del Flamenco
**FOLK/TRADITIONAL DANCE |** Catch an authentic professional performance in the heart of Santa Cruz on the atmospheric patio of a 15th-century house where the excellent acoustics mean there's no need for microphones or amplifiers. Shows start daily at 5:30 pm and 8:30 pm. ✉ *Calle Ximénez de Enciso 28, Barrio de Santa Cruz* ☎ *954/029999* ⊕ *www.lacasadelflamencosevilla.com* ✉ *From €10.*

### Los Gallos
**FOLK/TRADITIONAL DANCE |** This intimate club in the heart of Santa Cruz attracts mainly tourists. Flamenco performances are entertaining and reasonably authentic. Shows at 7 pm and 8:45 pm daily. ✉ *Pl. Santa Cruz 11, Santa Cruz* ☎ *954/216981* ⊕ *www.tablaolosgallos.com* ✉ *€35.*

## ⓢ Shopping

### Balcris Gallery
**ART GALLERIES |** Artwork by Cristóbal Donaire from nearby Jerez includes multicolored sculptures (bulls, horses, and matadors) and abstract paintings. ✉ *Calle Placentines 1, Barrio de Santa Cruz* ☎ *954/561639* ⊕ *balcris.es* ☉ *Closed Sun.*

### Orange Tree Sevilla
**FOOD |** All those oranges on the trees in the city are put to good use in handmade candies, marmalades, sweetmeats, liqueurs, and beauty products. ✉ *Calle Ximénez de Enciso 22, Barrio de Santa Cruz* ☎ *678/894351* ⊕ *orangetreesevilla.com.*

# El Arenal and Parque María Luisa

Parque María Luisa is part shady, midcity forestland and part monumental esplanade. El Arenal, named for its sandy riverbank soil, was originally a neighborhood of shipbuilders, stevedores, and warehouses. The heart of El Arenal lies between the Puente de San Telmo, just upstream from the Torre de Oro, and the Puente de Isabel II (Puente de Triana). El Arenal extends as far north as Avenida

Alfonso XII to include the Museo de Bellas Artes. Between the park and El Arenal is the university.

## 👁 Sights

### Hospital de la Caridad

HISTORIC SIGHT | Behind the Teatro de la Maestranza is this former almshouse for the sick and elderly, where six paintings by Murillo (1617–82) and two gruesome works by Valdés Leal (1622–90) depicting the Triumph of Death are displayed. The baroque hospital was founded in 1674 by Seville's original Don Juan, Miguel de Mañara (1626–79). A nobleman of licentious character, Mañara was returning one night from a riotous orgy when he had a vision of a funeral procession in which the partly decomposed corpse in the coffin was his own. Accepting the apparition as a sign from God, Mañara devoted his fortune to building this hospital; he is buried before the high altar in the chapel. Admission includes an audio guide (available in English). You can also book guided tours and Gregorian chant concerts. ⊠ Calle Temprado 3, El Arenal ☎ 954/223232 ⊕ www.santa-caridad.es/en 🖾 €8 (free Sun. 4:30–6:30).

### Museo de Artes y Costumbres Populares (Museum of Arts and Traditions)

HISTORY MUSEUM | FAMILY | Among the fascinating items of mainly 19th- and 20th-century Spanish folklore in this museum, in the Mudejar pavilion opposite the Museo Arqueológico, is an impressive Díaz Velázquez collection of lace and embroidery—one of the finest in Europe. There's a reconstruction of a typical late-19th-century Sevillian house on the first floor, while upstairs, exhibits include 18th- and 19th-century court dress, stunning regional folk costumes, religious objects, and musical instruments. In the basement, you can see ceramics, pottery, furniture, and household items from bygone ages. ⊠ Pl. de América 3, El Arenal ☎ 954/721391

⊕ www.museosdeandalucia.es 🖾 €2 🕓 Closed Mon.

### ★ Museo de Bellas Artes (Museum of Fine Arts)

ART MUSEUM | This museum—one of Spain's finest for Spanish art—is in the former convent of La Merced Calzada, most of which dates from the 17th century. The collection includes works by Murillo (the city celebrated the 400th anniversary of his birth in 2018) and the 17th-century Seville school, as well as by Zurbarán, Diego Velázquez, Alonso Cano, Valdés Leal, and El Greco. You will also see outstanding examples of Sevillian Gothic art and baroque religious sculptures in wood (a quintessentially Andalusian art form). In the rooms dedicated to Sevillian art of the 19th and 20th centuries, look for Gonzalo Bilbao's Las Cigarreras, a group portrait of Seville's famous cigar makers. An arts-and-crafts market is held outside the museum on Sunday morning. ⊠ Pl. del Museo 9, El Arenal ☎ 954/786498 ⊕ www.museosdeandalucia.es 🖾 €2 🕓 Closed Mon.

### ★ Parque de María Luisa

CITY PARK | Formerly the garden of the Palacio de San Telmo, this park blends formal design and wild vegetation. In the burst of development that gripped Seville in the 1920s, it was redesigned for the 1929 World's Fair, and the impressive villas you see now are the fair's remaining pavilions, many of them consulates or schools. The old casino holds the Teatro Lope de Vega, which puts on mainly musicals. Note the Anna Huntington statue of El Cid (Rodrigo Díaz de Vivar, 1043–99), who fought both for and against the Muslim rulers during the Reconquest. The statue was presented to Seville by the Massachusetts-born sculptor for the 1929 World's Fair. ⊠ Main entrance, Glorieta San Diego, Parque Maria Luisa.

### Plaza de España

PLAZA/SQUARE | FAMILY | This grandiose half-moon of buildings on the eastern edge of the Parque de María Luisa was Spain's centerpiece pavilion at the 1929 World's Fair. The brightly colored azulejo pictures represent the provinces of Spain, while the four bridges symbolize the medieval kingdoms of the Iberian Peninsula. In fine weather you can rent small boats to row along the arc-shape canal. To escape the crowds and enjoy views of the square from above, pop upstairs. ⊠ *Parque Maria Luisa.*

### Plaza de Toros Real Maestranza (*Royal Maestranza Bullring*)

PLAZA/SQUARE | Sevillanos have spent many a thrilling evening in this bullring, one of the oldest and loveliest plazas de toros in Spain, built between 1760 and 1763. The 20-minute tour (in English) takes in the empty arena, a museum with elaborate costumes and prints, and the chapel where matadors pray before the fight. Bullfights take place in the evening Thursday–Sunday from April through July and in September. Tickets can be booked online or by phone; book well in advance to be sure of a seat. ⊠ *Paseo de Colón 12, El Arenal* ☎ *954/224577 for visits, 954/560759 for bullfights* ⊕ *realmaestranza.com for tours, plazadetorosdelamaestranza. com for tickets* 🎟 *Tours €10 (free Weds. 3:30–7:30 pm).*

### Torre del Oro (*Tower of Gold*)

HISTORIC SIGHT | Built by the Moors in 1220 to complete the city's ramparts, this 12-sided tower on the banks of the Guadalquivir served to close off the harbor when a chain was stretched across the river from its base to a tower on the opposite bank. In 1248, Admiral Ramón de Bonifaz broke through the barrier, and Ferdinand III captured Seville. The tower houses a small naval museum. ⊠ *Paseo Alcalde Marqués de Contadero s/n, El Arenal* ☎ *954/222419* 🎟 *€3 (free Mon.).*

### University of Seville

HISTORIC SIGHT | Fans of Bizet's opera *Carmen* will want to come here, to see where the famous heroine reputedly rolled cigars on her thighs. At the far end of the Jardines de Murillo, opposite Calle San Fernando, stands part of the University of Seville, in what used to be the Real Fábrica de Tabacos (Royal Tobacco Factory). Built in the mid-1700s, the factory employed some 3,000 *cigarreras* (female cigar makers) less than a century later. Free guided tours (book online only) are available on Fridays (9:30 am–12:30 pm and 4–6 pm) and Saturdays (9:30 am–12:30 pm), except in August. ⊠ *Calle San Fernando 4, Parque Maria Luisa* ☎ *954/551052* ⊕ *institucional.us.es* 🎟 *Free* ⊘ *Closed Sun. and Mon.–Thurs. in Aug.*

## 🍴 Restaurants

### Bodeguita Romero

$ | SPANISH | A couple of blocks west of the Cathedral lies one of the city's best-loved tapas venues, usually jam-packed with locals enjoying an aperitif. Established in 1939 and now in its third generation, the bar is most famous for its meat dishes including the *pringá* sandwich (slow-cooked pork, chorizo, and black pudding, in a bun) and pork cheeks. **Known for:** friendly service; delicious house-marinated potatoes; traditional tapas. 🍴 *Average main: €12* ⊠ *Calle Harinas 10, El Arenal* ☎ *954/229556* ⊕ *bodeguitaromero.es* ⊘ *Closed Mon., no dinner Sun.*

### El Pimentón

$ | MEDITERRANEAN | A stone's throw from the cathedral sits this undiscerning eatery famous for its signature *tortitaco* (a shrimp fritter-taco hybrid), paellas, choice of tapas, and value lunch menu (€10.50, weekdays only). The lofty ceilings and bare brick walls are functional rather than inspirational and there's no outside terrace, but the prices, deliciousness, and friendly service more than compensate. **Known for:** tortitaco; value; paellas. ⑤ *Average main: €14 ⊠ Calle García de Vinuesa 29, El Arenal ☎ 954/564032.*

**La Moneda Casa Inchausti**
$$ | SPANISH | Almost within stone's throw of the Giralda, this family-run restaurant has been making a name for itself with fresh fish dishes for over two decades. The owners hail from Sanlúcar de Barrameda downriver, and the ingredients come from their hometown and always include swordfish, sea bass, and anchovies. **Known for:** value tapas; fresh fish; traditional soups and stews. ⑤ *Average main: €15 ⊠ Calle Tomás de Ibarra 10, El Arenal ☎ 954/223642 ⊗ Closed Mon. and August. No dinner Sun.*

**Veganitessen**
$ | VEGETARIAN | If you're a vegan, vegetarian, or flexitarian and finding the meat and fish scene in Seville a bit heavy, head for this bar inside the Mercado del Arenal. It started life as Spain's first vegan bakery in 2009, and since then the menu has grown to encompass breakfast and brunch, plus a long list of 100%-animal-free options to make into burgers, nachos, or wraps. **Known for:** cakes and pastries; good value daily lunch menu; vegan-friendly. ⑤ *Average main: €10 ⊠ Calle Pastor y Landero, Mercado del Arenal, Puesto 32, El Arenal ☎ 611/690463 ⊕ veganitessen.es ⊗ Closed Sun. and Mon. No dinner.*

## 🛏 Hotels

**Hotel Colón Gran Meliá**
$$$$ | HOTEL | Originally opened for 1929's Ibero-American Exposition, this classic hotel retains many original features, including a marble staircase leading up to a central lobby crowned by a magnificent stained-glass dome and crystal chandelier. **Pros:** good central location; some great views; excellent restaurant. **Cons:** pricey; on a busy and noisy street; some rooms overlook air shaft. ⑤ *Rooms from: €350 ⊠ Calle Canalejas 1, El Arenal ☎ 954/505599 ⊕ www.melia.com ⤶ 188 rooms ⦿ No Meals.*

**★ Hotel Alfonso XIII**
$$$$ | HOTEL | Inaugurated by King Alfonso XIII in 1929 when he visited the World's Fair, this grand hotel next to the university is a splendid, historic, Mudejar-style palace, built around a central patio and surrounded by ornate brick arches. **Pros:** both stately and hip; historic surroundings; impeccable service. **Cons:** too sophisticated for some; expensive; a tourist colony. ⑤ *Rooms from: €475 ⊠ Calle San Fernando 2, El Arenal ☎ 954/917000 ⊕ www.hotel-alfonsoxii-seville.com ⤶ 148 rooms ⦿ No Meals.*

## ⊕ Performing Arts

**Teatro de la Maestranza**
OPERA | Long prominent in the opera world, Seville is proud of its opera house. Tickets go quickly, so book well in advance (online is best). ⊠ *Paseo de Colón 22, El Arenal ☎ 954/223344, ⊕ www.teatrodelamaestranza.es.*

**Teatro Lope de Vega**
ARTS CENTERS | Classical music, ballet, and musicals are performed here. Tickets are best booked online. ⊠ *Av. María Luisa s/n, Parque Maria Luisa ☎ 954/472828 for info, 955/472822 for tickets ⊕ www.teatrolopedevega.org.*

## 🛍 Shopping

**Artesanía Textil**
CRAFTS | You can find blankets, shawls, and embroidered tablecloths woven by local artisans at this textile shop. Their products are also available online. ⊠ *Calle García de Vinuesa 33, El Arenal ☎ 954/215088 ⊕ artesania-textil.com.*

**El Postigo**
CRAFTS | This permanent arts-and-crafts market just around the corner from the Cathedral has over 20 stalls and workshops. ⊠ *Calle Arfe s/n, El Arenal.*

# Barrio de la Macarena

This immense neighborhood covers the entire northern half of historic Seville and deserves to be walked many times. Most of the best churches, convents, markets, and squares are concentrated around the center in an area delimited by the Arab ramparts to the north, the Alameda de Hercules to the west, the Santa Catalina church to the south, and the Convento de Santa Paula to the east. The area between the Alameda de Hercules and the Guadalquivir is known to locals as the Barrio de San Lorenzo, a section that's ideal for an evening of tapas grazing.

## ◉ Sights

### Basílica de la Macarena

CHURCH | This church holds Seville's most revered image, the Virgin of Hope—better known as La Macarena. Bedecked with candles and carnations, her cheeks streaming with glass tears, the Macarena steals the show at the procession on Holy Thursday, the highlight of Seville's Semana Santa pageant. The patron of Gypsies and the protector of the matador, her charms are so great that young sevillano bullfighter Joselito spent half his personal fortune buying her emeralds. When he was killed in the ring in 1920, La Macarena was dressed in widow's weeds for a month. The adjacent museum tells the history of Semana Santa traditions through processional and liturgical artifacts amassed by the Brotherhood of La Macarena over four centuries. ⊠ Calle Bécquer 1, La Macarena ☎ 954/901800 ☜ Basilica free, museum €5.

### ★ Convento de Santa Paula

CHURCH | This 15th-century Gothic convent has a fine facade and portico, with ceramic decoration by Nicolaso Pisano. The chapel has some beautiful azulejos and sculptures by Martínez Montañés. It also contains a small museum and a shop selling delicious cakes and jams

made by the nuns. ⊠ Calle Santa Paula 11, La Macarena ☎ 954/540022 ☜ €5 ⊙ Closed weekday afternoons.

### San Lorenzo y Jesús del Gran Poder

CHURCH | This 17th-century church has many fine works by such artists as Martínez Montañés and Francisco Pacheco, but its outstanding piece is Juan de Mesa y Velasco's Jesús del Gran Poder (Christ Omnipotent). ⊠ Pl. San Lorenzo 13, La Macarena ☎ 954/915686 ☜ Free.

## 🍴 Restaurants

### Bache San Pedro

$$ | SPANISH | Barack Obama's chosen spot for tapas when he visited the city in 2019 has outside seating on a small terrace with views of the square or spots inside, where traditional Seville tiles blend perfectly into the sleek industrial vibe. Bringing the taste of Cádiz to Seville, dishes here come as tapas or sharing plates (€3.50–€16) and include croquetas de puchero (stew croquettes), a taco of chicharrones (pork crackling) with Payoyo goat's cheese, and possibly the spiciest patatas bravas (fried potatoes) in town. **Known for:** delicious

desserts; friendly service; innovative cuisine. $ *Average main: €16* ✉ *Pl. Cristo de Burgos 23, Seville* ☎ *954/502934* ⊕ *www.bachesanpedro.com* ⊘ *Closed Mon.*

### El Rinconcillo

$ | SPANISH | Founded in 1670, this lovely spot serves a classic selection of dishes, such as the *pavía de bacalao* (fried bread-ed cod), a superb *salmorejo* (a puree consisting of tomato and bread), and *espinacas con garbanzos*, all in generous portions. The views of Iglesia de Santa Catalina out the front window upstairs are unbeatable, and your bill is chalked up on the wooden counters as you go (tapas are attractively priced from €2.50). **Known for:** views of Iglesia de Santa Catalina; crowds of locals; tapas. $ *Average main: €14* ✉ *Calle Gerona 40, La Macarena* ☎ *954/223183* ⊕ *www.elrinconcillo.es.*

### Palo Cortao

$ | SPANISH | Down an uninspiring side street but with a very quiet terrace with views of San Pedro Church, this bar with stool seating around high tables offers tranquil dining and, most notably, one of the best sherry menus in town. Known as an *abacería* (grocer's store), it serves more than 30 finos, amontillados, and olorosos, plus house-made vermouth on the drinks menu, and each pairs perfectly with a food choice. **Known for:** ajoblanco (cold garlic soup); pairing menu; excellent sherry. $ *Average main: €12* ✉ *Calle Mercedes de Velilla 4, La Macarena* ☎ *649/446120* ⊕ *www.palo-cortao.com* ⊘ *Closed Mon. and Tues. No dinner Sun.*

# Triana

Triana used to be Seville's Gypsy quarter. Today, it has a tranquil, neighborly feel by day and a distinctly flamenco feel at night. Cross over to Triana via the **Puente de Isabel II,** an iron bridge built in 1852 and the first to connect the city's two sections. Start your walk in the **Plaza del Altozano,** the center of the Triana district and traditionally the meeting point for travelers from the south crossing the river to Seville. Admire the facade of the Murillo pharmacy here before walking up **Calle Jacinto.** Look out for the fine **Casa de los Mensaque** (now the district's administrative office and usually open on weekday mornings), home to some of Triana's finest potters and housing some stunning examples of Seville ceramics. Also worth seeking out are the patios at 32, 83–87, and 138 **Calle Alfarería** and at 16 and 19 **Calle Castilla.** They aren't always open, but you can peep through the iron grills. To reach attractions in La Cartuja, take Bus C1.

# ◉ Sights

### Capilla de los Marineros

HISTORIC SIGHT | This seamen's chapel, built in 1759, is one of Triana's most important monuments and home to the Brotherhood of Triana, whose Semana Santa processions are among the most revered in the city. There's also a small museum dedicated to the Brotherhood. ✉ *Calle Pureza 2, Triana* ☎ *954/332645* ✉ *Free, museum €4.*

### Centro de Cerámica Triana (*Ceramics Center*)

ARTS CENTER | With none of the 40 original ceramicists remaining in Triana, this restored factory complete with its orig-inal kilns provides an interesting insight into the neighborhood's tile-making past. Downstairs, an exhibition explains the manufacturing process and the story of ceramics, while upstairs there's a selection of tiles on display. Free guided tours in English. ✉ *Calle Callao 16, Triana* ☎ *954/474293* ⊕ *ceramicatriana.com* ✉ *€3. Free with regular Alcázar ticket.*

### Isla de La Cartuja

ISLAND | Named after its 14th-century Carthusian monastery, this island in the

Guadalquivir River across from northern Seville was the site of the decennial Universal Exposition (Expo) in 1992. The island has the Teatro Central, used for concerts and plays; Parque del Alamillo, Seville's largest and least-known park; and the Estadio Olímpico, a 60,000-seat covered stadium. The best way to get to La Cartuja is by walking across one or both (one each way) of the superb Santiago Calatrava bridges spanning the river. The Puente de la Barqueta crosses to La Cartuja, and downstream the Puente del Alamillo connects the island with Seville. Buses C1 and C2 also serve La Cartuja. ⊠ Triana.

### Isla Mágica

AMUSEMENT PARK/CARNIVAL | FAMILY | The eastern shore of Isla de la Cartuja holds this theme park with more than 20 attractions, including the hair-raising Jaguar roller coaster. Discounts are available online. ⊠ Isla de la Cartuja, Av. de los Descubrimiento s/n, Triana ☎ 954/487030 ⊕ www.islamagica.es ⊠ From €19 ⊙ Closed Nov.–Apr. and weekdays in May, Sept., and Oct.

### Mercado de Triana

MARKET | The small Triana market, which began as an improvised fish market on the banks of the Guadalquivir in the 1830s, is housed in a shiny building next to the bridge and has been given the stamp "Traditional Shopping Center." The vendors sell a colorful mix of food, flowers, cheap fashion, and costume jewelry until 3 pm every day but Sunday. The dozen or so restaurants and bars open daily till late. ⊠ Pl. del Alzotano, Triana ⊕ www.mercadodetrianasevilla.com.

### Monasterio de Santa María de las Cuevas

(Monasterio de La Cartuja)

ART MUSEUM | The 14th-century monastery was regularly visited by Christopher Columbus, who was also buried here for a few years. Part of the building houses the **Centro Andaluz de Arte Contemporáneo,** which has an absorbing collection of contemporary art. ⊠ Isla de la Cartuja, Av. Américo Vespucio, Triana ☎ 955/037070 ⊠ €2 ⊙ Closed Mon.

## 🍴 Restaurants

### Bar Las Golondrinas

$ | SPANISH | Run by the same family for more than 50 years and lavishly decorated in the colorful tiles that pay tribute to the neighborhood's potters, Las Golondrinas is a fixture of Triana life. The staff never change, and neither does the menu—the recipes for the punta de solomillo (sliced sirloin), chipirones (fried baby squid), and caballito de jamón (ham on bread) have been honed to perfection, and they're served as tapas (€3), or raciones, that keep everyone happy. **Known for:** good value; traditional tapas; vibrant atmosphere. ⑤ Average main: €12 ⊠ Calle Antillano Campos 26, Triana ☎ 954/332616.

### De la O

$$ | SPANISH | Tucked away on the riverfront in Triana next to Puente Cristo de la Expiración, this modern venue advocates local produce in traditional Andalusian recipes, showcased in the menu that changes on a weekly basis, along with a long wine list of Andalusian wines. The long, narrow interior has striking wood-paneled walls with a verdant vertical garden in the middle, while outside dining takes in panoramic views of the river on the intimate terrace. **Known for:** dishes presented artistically; waterfront views; quality local produce. ⑤ Average main: €18 ⊠ Paseo de Nuestra Señora de la O 29, Triana ☎ 954/339000 ⊕ www.delaorestaurante.com ⊙ No dinner Sun.–Thurs.

11

Seville and Around TRIANA

# 🛏 Hotels

## Eurostars Torre Sevilla

$$$$ | HOTEL | Andalusia's tallest building, with a 180-meter tower, designed by Cesar Pelli, rises high above the Cartuja area and makes a controversial sight on the city skyline while delivering spectacular views over Seville, Triana, and the river. **Pros:** spectacular views of the city; modern amenities; spacious accommodations. **Cons:** indifferent service at times; elevator system a little confusing; some distance from sights and attractions. ⑤ *Rooms from: €225* ✉ *Calle Gonzalo Jiménez de Quesada 2, Triana* ☎ *954/466022* ⊕ *www.eurostarshotels. com* 🛏 *244 rooms* ⦿ *No Meals.*

## Hotel Monte Triana

$$ | HOTEL | Comfortable, squeaky-clean facilities, and excellent value for the cost are two key reasons for choosing this hotel to the north of the heart of Triana. **Pros:** good value; friendly and helpful staff; private parking. **Cons:** no on-site restaurant; decor too basic for some; 20-minute walk into city center. ⑤ *Rooms from: €130* ✉ *Calle Clara de Jesús Montero 24, Triana* ☎ *954/343111* ⊕ *www.hotelesmonte.com* 🛏 *114 rooms* ⦿ *No Meals.*

# 🎭 Performing Arts

## FLAMENCO

### Lola de los Reyes

FOLK/TRADITIONAL DANCE | This venue in Triana presents reasonably authentic shows and hosts "flamenco afternoons" Thursday through Saturday—check the website for details. Entrance is free, but there's a one-drink minimum. Booking advised. ✉ *Calle Pureza 107, Triana* ☎ *667/631163* ⊕ *www.loladelosreyes.es* Ⓜ *Blas Infante/Parque de los Principes.*

## Teatro Central

ARTS CENTERS | This modern venue on the Isla de la Cartuja stages theater, dance (including flamenco), and classical and contemporary music. Tickets can be bought online or at the ticket office. ✉ *Calle José de Gálvez 6, Triana* ☎ *955/542155 for information* ⊕ *www. teatrocentral.es.*

# 🛍 Shopping

## Potters' District

CERAMICS | Look for traditional azulejo tiles and other ceramics in the Triana potters' district, on Calle Alfarería, Calle Antillano Campos, and Calle Callao such as Cerámica Triana (Calle Callao 14) selling a selection of traditional ceramic items. ✉ *Triana.*

# Itálica

*12 km (7 miles) north of Seville, 1 km (½ mile) beyond Santiponce.*

Neighboring the small town of Santiponce, Itálica is Spain's oldest Roman site and one of its greatest, and it is well worth a visit when you're in Seville. If you're here during August, try to get tickets for the International Dance Festival (festivalitalica.es) held in the ruins.

### GETTING HERE AND AROUND

The M170A bus route runs frequently (weekdays only, 7:40 am–3:25 pm) between the Plaza de Armas bus station in Seville and Itálica. The journey time is 20 minutes. If you have a rental car, you could include a visit to the ruins on your way to Huelva. Allow at least two hours for your visit.

#  Sights

## ★ Itálica

**RUINS** | One of Roman Iberia's most important cities in the 2nd century, with a population of more than 10,000, Itálica today is a monument of Roman ruins. Founded by Scipio Africanus in 205 BC as a home for veteran soldiers, Itálica gave the Roman world two great emperors: Trajan (AD 52–117) and Hadrian (AD 76–138). You can find traces of city streets, cisterns, and the floor plans of several villas, some with mosaic floors, though all the best mosaics and statues have been removed to Seville's Museum of Archaeology. Itálica was abandoned and plundered as a quarry by the Visigoths, who preferred Seville. It fell into decay around AD 700. The remains include the huge, elliptical **amphitheater,** which held 40,000 spectators, a **Roman theater,** and **Roman baths.** The finale for season 7 of *Game of Thrones* was filmed here in 2018. The small visitor center offers information on daily life in the city. ✉ *Av. Extremadura 2, Santiponce* ☎ *600/141767* ⊕ *www.museosdeandalucia.es* ✉ *€2* ⊘ *Closed Mon.*

# Córdoba

*166 km (103 miles) northwest of Granada, 407 km (250 miles) southwest of Madrid, 239 km (143 miles) northeast of Cádiz, 143 km (86 miles) northeast of Seville.*

Strategically located on the north bank of the Guadalquivir River, Córdoba was the Roman and Moorish capital of Spain, and its old quarter, clustered around its famous Mezquita, remains one of the country's grandest and yet most intimate examples of its Moorish heritage. Once a medieval city famed for the peaceful and prosperous coexistence of its three religious cultures—Islamic, Jewish, and Christian—Córdoba is also a perfect analogue for the cultural history of the Iberian Peninsula.

Córdoba today, with its modest population of less than 326,000, offers a cultural depth and intensity—a direct legacy from the great emirs, caliphs, philosophers, physicians, poets, and engineers of the days of the caliphate—that far outstrips the city's current commercial and political power. Its artistic and historical treasures begin with the Mezquita-Catedral (mosque-cathedral), as it is generally called, and continue through the winding, whitewashed streets of the Judería (the medieval Jewish quarter); the jasmine-, geranium-, and orange-blossom-filled patios; the Renaissance palaces; and the two dozen churches, convents, and hermitages, built by Moorish artisans directly over former mosques.

## GETTING HERE AND AROUND

### BIKE

Never designed to support cars, Córdoba's medieval layout is ideal for bicycles, and there's a good network of designated bicycle tracks.

**CONTACTS Rent a Bike Córdoba.** ✉ *Calle Maria Cristina 5, Córdoba* ☎ *957/943700* ⊕ *rentabikecordoba.com.*

### BUS

Córdoba is easily reached by bus from Granada, Málaga, and Seville (lockers are available at the bus station). The city has an extensive public bus network with frequent service. Buses usually start running at 6:30 or 7 am and stop around midnight. You can buy 10-trip passes at newsstands and the bus office in Plaza de Colón. A single-trip fare is €1.30.

Córdoba has organized open-top bus tours of the city that can be booked via the tourist office.

**CONTACTS Córdoba.** ✉ *Glorieta de las Tres Culturas, Córdoba* ☎ *957/404040* ⊕ *www.estacionautobusescordoba.es.*

# Córdoba's History

👁

The Romans invaded Córdoba in 206 BC, later making it the capital of Rome's section of Spain. Nearly 800 years later, the Visigoth king Leovigildus took control, but the tribe was soon supplanted by the Moors, whose emirs and caliphs held court here from the 8th to the early 11th century. At that point Córdoba was one of the greatest centers of art, culture, and learning in the Western world; one of its libraries had a staggering 400,000 volumes. Moors, Christians, and Jews lived together in harmony within Córdoba's walls. In that era, it was considered second in importance only to Constantinople; but in 1009, Prince Muhammad II and Omeyan led a rebellion that broke up the caliphate, leading to power flowing to separate Moorish kingdoms.

Córdoba remained in Moorish hands until it was conquered by King Ferdinand in 1236 and repopulated from the north of Spain. Later, the Catholic monarchs used the city as a base from which to plan the conquest of Granada. In Columbus's time, the Guadalquivir was navigable as far upstream as Córdoba, and great galleons sailed its waters. Today, the river's muddy water and marshy banks evoke little of Córdoba's glorious past, but an old Arab waterfall and the city's bridge—of Roman origin, though much restored by the Arabs and successive generations, most recently in 2012—recall a far grander era.

## CAR
The city's one-way system can be something of a nightmare to navigate, and it's best to park in one of the signposted lots outside the old quarter.

## TAXI
**CONTACTS Radio Taxi.** ✉ *Córdoba* ☎ *957/764444.*

## TRAIN
The city's modern train station is the hub for a comprehensive network of regional trains, with regular high-speed train service to Granada, Seville, Málaga, Madrid, and Barcelona.

**CONTACTS Train Station.** ✉ *Glorieta de las Tres Culturas, Córdoba* ☎ *912/320320.*

## VISITOR INFORMATION
**CONTACTS Tourist Office.** ✉ *Pl. de las Tendillas 5, Centro* ☎ *957/471577* ⊕ *www. turismodecordoba.org.*

## 👁 Sights

**Alcázar de los Reyes Cristianos** (*Fortress of the Christian Monarchs*)
**CASTLE/PALACE** | Built by Alfonso XI in 1328, the alcázar in Córdoba is a Mudejar-style palace with splendid gardens. (The original Moorish alcázar stood beside the Mezquita, on the site of the present Bishop's Palace.) This is where, in the 15th century, the Catholic monarchs held court and launched their conquest of Granada. Boabdil was imprisoned here in 1483, and for nearly 300 years this alcázar served as the Inquisition's base. The most important sights here are the Hall of the Mosaics and a Roman stone sarcophagus from the 2nd or 3rd century. ✉ *Pl. Campo Santo de los Mártires, Judería* ✛ *Next to Guadalquivir River* ⊕ *alcazardelosreyescristianos. cordoba.es* 🖬 *€5* ☾ *Closed Mon.*

### ★ Calleja de las Flores

STREET | A few yards off the northeastern corner of the Mezquita, this tiny street has the prettiest patios, many with ceramics, foliage, and iron grilles. The patios are key to Córdoba's architecture, at least in the old quarter, where life is lived behind sturdy white walls—a legacy of the Moors, who honored both the sanctity of the home and the need to shut out the fierce summer sun. Between the first and second week of May—right after the early May Cruces de Mayo (Crosses of May) competition, when neighborhoods compete at setting up elaborate crosses decorated with flowers and plants—Córdoba throws a Patio Festival, during which private patios are filled with flowers, opened to the public, and judged in a municipal competition. Córdoba's tourist office publishes an itinerary of the best patios in town (downloadable from ⊕ *patios.cordoba. es/en)*—note that most are open only in the mornings on weekdays but all day on weekends. ⊠ *Judería*.

### Casa de Sefarad

HISTORY MUSEUM | This private museum opposite the synagogue is dedicated to the culture of Sephardic Jews in the Mediterranean. Providing a very personal insight, the museum's director leads visitors through the five rooms of the 14th-century house, where displays cover Sephardic domestic life, music, festivities, the history of Córdoba's Jewish district, and finally a collection of contemporary paintings of the women of al-Andalus ("al-Andalus" is Arabic for "Land of the West"). ⊠ *Calle Judíos 17, Judería* ☎ *957/421404* ⊠ *€5* ⊗ *Closed Sun.–Wed.*

### Centro de Creación Contemporánea de Andalucía

ART MUSEUM | Located in a huge Brutalist building whose intricate facade imitates the geometric shapes on the Mezquita stucco work, this center operates primarily as a stage for live art with artists in residence and regular dance performances. It hosts regular exhibitions by contemporary Spanish artists. Every evening at dusk, the exterior facade lights up with artwork, best viewed from the Balcón del Guadalquivir park on the north side of the river. ⊠ *Calle Carmen Olmedo Checa, Sector Sur* ☎ *697/104160* ⊕ *c3a.es* ⊠ *Free* ⊗ *Closed Mon..* Center for Contemporary Creation

### ★ Madinat Al-Zahra (*Medina Azahara*)

RUINS | Built in the foothills of the Sierra Morena by Abd ar-Rahman III (891–961) for his favorite concubine, al-Zahra (the Flower), this once-splendid summer pleasure palace was begun in 936. Historians say it took 10,000 men, 2,600 mules, and 400 camels 25 years to erect this fantasy of 4,300 columns in dazzling pink, green, and white marble and jasper brought from Carthage. A palace, a mosque, luxurious baths, fragrant gardens, fish ponds, an aviary, and a zoo stood on three terraces here, and for around 70 years the Madinat was the de facto capital of al-Andalus, until, in 1013, it was sacked and destroyed by Berber mercenaries. In 1944, the Royal Apartments were rediscovered, and the throne room carefully reconstructed. The outline of the mosque has also been excavated. The only covered part of the site is the Salon de Abd ar-Rahman III (restoration work is due to finish at the end of 2022); the rest is a sprawl of foundations and arches that hint at the splendor of the original city-palace. Begin at the visitor center, which provides background information and a 3-D reconstruction of the city, and continue to the ruins, around 2 km (1 mile) away. You can walk, but it's uphill, so consider taking the shuttle bus, €2.50 or included in the bus ticket (€9) from the Paseo de la Victoria in the city center. Both services run frequently. The tourist office can provide schedule details. Allow 2½ to 3 hours for

**KEY**

- 1 Sights
- 1 Restaurants
- 1 Hotels
- *i* Tourist Information

**Sights** ▼

1 Alcázar de los
  Reyes Cristianos.........**C8**
2 Calleja de las Flores....**D6**
3 Casa de Sefarad........**B6**
4 Centro de Creación
  Contemporánea
  de Andalucía ..........**H9**
5 Madinat Al-Zahra.......**A2**
6 Mezquita.................**D7**
7 Museo Arqueológico....**E5**
8 Museo de
  Bellas Artes .............**G6**
9 Museo Taurino...........**C7**
10 Palacio de Viana........**G1**
11 Plaza de los Dolores.....**E3**
12 Plaza de San Miguel ....**E3**
13 Plaza Santa Marina ....**G1**
14 Puerta de Almodóvar...**B5**
15 San Nicolás
   de la Villa .................**C4**
16 Synagogue ..............**B7**
17 Torre Calahorra ..........**F9**
18 Zoco.......................**C6**

**Restaurants** ▼

1 Amaltea...................**F7**
2 Bodegas Campos.......**H6**
3 Casa Mazal...............**C7**
4 Casa Pepe de la
  Judería...................**D7**
5 El Choco ...................**I4**
6 El Churrasco..............**C6**
7 El Rincón de Carmen....**C6**
8 La Regadera.............**E7**
9 noor .........................**I2**
10 Taberna de
   San Miguel ...............**E3**
11 Taberna La Viuda .......**B9**

**Hotels** ▼

1 Casa de los Azulejos ....**F4**
2 Hospes Palacio
  del Bailío.................**F2**
3 Hotel Balcón
  de Córdoba..............**E6**
4 Hotel Maestre...........**G6**
5 La Llave de la Judería...**C6**
6 NH Collection
  Amistad Córdoba ........**C6**
7 Parador de Córdoba....**A1**
8 Viento 10..................**I5**

your visit. You can visit the ruins at night Tuesday–Saturday between mid-June and mid-September. ⊠ *Ctra. de Palma del Río, Km 5.5, Córdoba* ⊹ *8 km (5 miles) west of Córdoba on C431* ☎ *957/104933* ⊕ *www.museosdeandalucia.es* ☞ *€2* ⊘ *Closed Mon.*

★ **Mezquita** (*Mosque*)

**HISTORIC SIGHT** | Built between the 8th and 10th centuries, Córdoba's mosque is one of the earliest and most beautiful examples of Spanish Islamic architecture. The plain, crenellated exterior walls do little to prepare you for the sublime beauty of the interior. As you enter through the Puerta de las Palmas (Door of the Palms), some 850 columns rise before you in a forest of jasper, marble, granite, and onyx. The pillars are topped by ornate capitals taken from the Visigothic church that was razed to make way for the mosque. Crowning these, red-and-white-stripe arches curve away into the dimness, and the ceiling is of delicately carved tinted cedar. The mezquita has served as a cathedral since 1236, but its origins as a mosque are clear. Built in four stages, it was founded in 785 by Abd ar-Rahman I (756–88) on a site he bought from the Visigoth Christians. He pulled down their church and replaced it with a mosque, one-third the size of the present one, into which he incorporated marble pillars from earlier Roman and Visigothic shrines. Under Abd ar-Rahman II (822–52), the Mezquita held an original copy of the Koran and a bone from the arm of the prophet Mohammed and became a Muslim pilgrimage site second only in importance to Mecca.

Al-Hakam II (961–76) built the beautiful *mihrab* (prayer niche), the mezquita's greatest jewel. Make your way over to the qiblah, the south-facing wall in which this sacred prayer niche was hollowed out. (Muslim law decrees that a mihrab face east, toward Mecca, and that worshippers do likewise when they pray. Because of an error in calculation, this one faces more south than east. Al-Hakam II spent hours agonizing over a means of correcting such a serious mistake, but he was persuaded to let it be.) In front of the mihrab is the *maksoureh*, a kind of anteroom for the caliph and his court; its mosaics and plasterwork make it a masterpiece of Islamic art. A last addition to the mosque as such, the maksoureh was completed around 987 by al-Mansur, who more than doubled its size.

After the Reconquest, the Christians left the mezquita largely undisturbed, dedicating it to the Virgin Mary and using it as a place of Christian worship. The clerics did erect a wall closing off the mosque from its courtyard, which helped dim the interior and thus separate the house of worship from the world outside. In the 13th century, Christians had the Capilla de Villaviciosa built by Moorish craftsmen, its Mudejar architecture blending with the lines of the mosque. Not so the heavy, incongruous baroque structure of the cathedral, sanctioned in the very heart of the mosque by Carlos V in the 1520s. To the emperor's credit, he was supposedly horrified when he came to inspect the new construction, exclaiming to the architects, "To build something ordinary, you have destroyed something that was unique in the world" (not that this sentiment stopped him from tampering with the Alhambra to build his Palacio Carlos V). Rest up and reflect in the Patio de los Naranjos (Orange Court), perfumed in springtime by orange blossoms. The Puerta del Perdón (Gate of Forgiveness), so named because debtors were forgiven here on feast days, is on the north wall of the Orange Court and is the formal entrance to the mosque. The Virgen de los Faroles (Virgin of the Lanterns), a small statue in a niche on the outside wall of the mosque along the north side on Cardenal Herrero, is behind a lantern-hung grille, rather like a lady awaiting a serenade. The Torre del

Córdoba's stunning Mezquita charts the evolution of Western and Islamic architecture over a 1,300-year period.

Alminar, the minaret once used to summon the Muslim faithful to prayer, has a baroque belfry that reopened to visitors in late 2014. Views from the top are well worth the climb, but be aware that It's the equivalent of 12 flights of stairs.

■ TIP→ **Allow a good hour for your visit.** ⊠ *Calle de Torrijos, Judería* ☏ *957/470512* ⊕ *mezquita-catedraldecordoba.es/ en* ⊡ *Mezquita €11, free Mon.–Sat. 8.30–9.30 am, Torre del Alminar €3.*

## Museo Arqueológico

HISTORY MUSEUM | In the heart of the old quarter, this museum is built around a 16th-century mansion and has finds from Córdoba's varied cultural past. You enter via the second floor, which is devoted to prehistoric, Roman, and Moorish exhibits. Highlights include a 1st-century head of Drusus (the son of the Emperor Tiberius) and a marble statue of Aphrodite. The first floor shows finds from Roman and Moorish life in Córdoba including a stunning 2nd-century sculpture of Mithras

killing a bull. Down in the basement you can see the ruins of a Roman theater built in the 1st century AD. The alleys and steps along Altos de Santa Ana make for great wandering. ⊠ *Pl. Jerónimo Paez, Judería* ☏ *957/355517* ⊕ *www.museos- deandalucia.es* ⊡ *€2* ⊘ *Closed Mon.*

## ★ Museo de Bellas Artes

ART MUSEUM | Hard to miss because of its deep-pink facade, Córdoba's Museum of Fine Arts, in a courtyard just off the Plaza del Potro, belongs to a former Charity Hospital. It was founded by Ferdinand and Isabella, who twice received Columbus here. The collection, which includes paintings by Murillo, Valdés Leal, Zurbarán, Goya, and Joaquín Sorolla y Bastida, concentrates on local artists. Highlights are altarpieces from the 14th and 15th centuries and the large collection of prints and drawings, including some by Fortuny, Goya, and Sorolla. ⊠ *Pl. del Potro 1, San Francisco* ☏ *957/103659* ⊕ *www.museosdeandalucia.es* ⊡ *€2* ⊘ *Closed Mon.*

**Museo Taurino** (*Museum of Bullfighting*)
OTHER MUSEUM | Two adjoining mansions
on the Plaza Maimónides (or Plaza de
las Bulas) house this museum, and it's
worth a visit, as much for the chance
to see a restored mansion as for the
posters, Art Nouveau paintings, bulls'
heads, suits of lights (bullfighting outfits),
and memorabilia of famous Córdoban
bullfighters, including the most famous
of all, Manolete. To the surprise of the
nation, Manolete, who was considered
immortal, was killed by a bull in the ring
at Linares in 1947. ⊠ *Pl. de Maimónides
1, Judería* ☎ *957/201056* 💳 *€4 (card
payment only)* ⊗ *Closed Mon.*

**Palacio de Viana**
CASTLE/PALACE | This 17th-century palace
is one of Córdoba's most splendid aristocratic homes. Also known as the **Museo
de los Patios,** it contains 12 interior patios,
each one different; the patios and gardens are planted with cypresses, orange
trees, and myrtles. Inside the building are
a carriage museum, a library, embossed
leather wall hangings, filigree silver, and
grand galleries and staircases. As you
enter, note that the corner column of the
first patio has been removed to allow
the entrance of horse-drawn carriages.
⊠ *Pl. Don Gomé 2, Centro* ☎ *957/496741*
⊕ *palaciodeviana.com* 💳 *From €6*
⊗ *Closed Mon.*

**Plaza de los Dolores**
PLAZA/SQUARE | The 17th-century Conven-
to de Capuchinos surrounds this small
square north of Plaza San Miguel. The
square is where you feel most deeply the
city's languid pace. In its center, a statue
of **Cristo de los Faroles** (Christ of the Lanterns) stands amid eight lanterns hanging
from twisted wrought-iron brackets.
⊠ *Centro.*

**Plaza de San Miguel**
PLAZA/SQUARE | The square and café
terraces around it, and its atmospheric
tavern, Taberna San Miguel–Casa El Pisto,
form one of the city's finest combinations

of art, history, and gastronomy. The San
Miguel church has an interesting facade
with Romanesque doors built around
Mudejar horseshoe arches, and a Mudejar dome inside. ⊠ *Centro.*

**Plaza Santa Marina**
PLAZA/SQUARE | At the edge of the Barrio
de los Toreros, a quarter where many
of Córdoba's famous bullfighters were
born and raised, stands a statue of the
famous bullfighter Manolete (1917–47)
opposite the lovely church of Santa
Marina de Aguas Santas (St. Marina of
Holy Waters), built by Ferdinand III when
he conquered the city in 1236. Not far
from here, on the Plaza de la Lagunilla, is
a bust of Manolete. ⊠ *Centro.*

**Puerta de Almodóvar**
HISTORIC SIGHT | Outside this old Moor-
ish gate at the northern entrance of
the Judería is a statue of **Seneca,** the
Córdoba-born philosopher who rose to
prominence in Nero's court in Rome
and was forced to commit suicide at his
emperor's command. The gate stands at
the top of the narrow and colorful Calle
San Felipe. ⊠ *Judería.*

**San Nicolás de Villa**
CHURCH | This classically dark Spanish
church displays the Mudejar style of
Islamic decoration and art forms. Córdoba's well-kept city park, the pleasant
**Jardines de la Victoria,** with tile benches
and manicured bushes, is a block west.
⊠ *Calle San Felipe, Centro.*

**Synagogue**
HISTORIC SIGHT | The only Jewish temple
in Andalusia to survive the expulsion and
inquisition of the Jews in 1492, Córdoba's synagogue is also one of only three
ancient synagogues left in all of Spain
(the other two are in Toledo). Though it no
longer functions as a place of worship,
it's a treasured symbol for Spain's modern Jewish communities. The outside is
plain, but the inside (restored in 2018),
measuring 23 feet by 21 feet, contains

some exquisite Mudejar stucco tracery. Look for the fine plant motifs and the Hebrew inscription saying that the synagogue was built in 1315. The women's gallery, not open for visits, still stands, and in the east wall is the ark where the sacred scrolls of the Torah were kept. ⊠ *Calle Judíos, Judería* ☎ *957/202928* ⊠ *€1* ⊘ *Closed Mon.*

### Torre Calahorra
**NOTABLE BUILDING** | The tower on the far side of the Puente Romano (Roman Bridge), which was restored in 2008, was built in 1369 to guard the entrance to Córdoba. It now houses the Museo Vivo de Al-Andalus (Arabic for "Land of the West"), with films and audiovisual guides (in English) on Córdoba's history. Climb the narrow staircase to the top of the tower for the view of the Roman bridge and city on the other side of the Guadalquivir. ⊠ *Av. de la Confederación s/n, Sector Sur* ☎ *957/293929* ⊕ *www. torrecalahorra.es* ⊠ *€5, includes audio guide.*

### Zoco
**MARKET** | The Spanish word for the Arab souk (*zoco*) recalls the onetime function of this courtyard near the synagogue. It's now the site of a daily crafts market, where you can see artisans at work, and live music on weekends. ⊠ *Calle Judíos 5, Judería* ☎ *957/204033* ⊠ *Free.*

## 🍴 Restaurants

### Amaltea
**$** | **INTERNATIONAL** | Satisfying vegetarians, vegans, and their meat-eating friends, this organic restaurant includes some meat and fish on the menu. There's a healthy mix of Mexican, Asian, Spanish, and Italian-influenced dishes, including salmon steamed in banana leaves, Raz-el-Hanout lamb wok, and couscous. **Known for:** organic options; inviting interior with relaxed vibe; vegetarian food. ⑤ *Average main: €14* ⊠ *Ronda de Isasa*

10, Centro ☎ 957/491968 ⊘ No dinner Sun. Closed Sun. in summer.

### ★ Bodegas Campos
**$$$** | **SPANISH** | A block east of the Plaza del Potro, this traditional old bodega with high-quality service is the epitome of all that's great about Andalusian cuisine. The dining rooms are in barrel-heavy rustic rooms and leafy traditional patios (take a look at some of the signed barrels—you may recognize a name or two, such as the former U.K. prime minister Tony Blair). **Known for:** excellent tapas bar; regional dishes; bodega setting. ⑤ *Average main: €22* ⊠ *Calle Los Lineros 32, San Pedro* ☎ *957/497500* ⊕ *www. bodegascampos.com.*

### Casa Mazal
**$$** | **ECLECTIC** | In the heart of the Judería, this pretty little restaurant serves a modern interpretation of Sephardic cuisine, with organic dishes that are more exotic than the usual Andalusian fare. The many vegetarian options include gazpacho with mango, and artichoke hearts in saffron sauce; and the *siniya* (trout baked in vine leaves with pomegranate and mint) is delicious. **Known for:** vegetarian dishes; romantic ambience; traditional Sephardic cuisine. ⑤ *Average main: €18* ⊠ *Calle Tomás Conde 3, Judería* ☎ *685/882666* ⊘ *Closed Wed.*

### Casa Pepe de la Judería
**$$$** | **SPANISH** | Geared toward a tourist clientele, this place is always packed, noisy, and fun, and there is live Spanish guitar music on the roof terrace most summer nights. Antiques and some wonderful old oil paintings fill this three-floor labyrinth of rooms just around the corner from the mosque, near the Judería. **Known for:** live music on the roof terrace in summer; croquetas de jamón; traditional Andalusian food. ⑤ *Average main: €25* ⊠ *Calle Romero 1, off Deanes, Judería* ☎ *957/200744* ⊕ *restaurantecasapepdela-juderia.com.*

A typical Córdoba patio, filled with flowers

### ★ El Choco

**$$$$ | SPANISH |** The city's most exciting restaurant, which has renewed its Michelin star annually since 2012, El Choco has renowned chef Kisko Garcia at the helm whipping up innovative dishes based on his 10 Commandments to preserve good cooking. One of them is that taste always comes first, and that plays out well during a meal at this minimalist restaurant with charcoal-colored walls, glossy parquet floors, and dishes offering new sensations and amazing presentations. **Known for:** innovative presentation; good value Michelin-star tasting menu; creative Andalusian cooking. *$ Average main: €110 ⊠ Compositor Serrano Lucena 14, Centro ☎ 957/264863 ⊕ www. restaurantechoco.es ☉ Closed Mon. and Aug. No dinner Sun.*

### El Churrasco

**$$$ | SPANISH |** The name suggests grilled meat, but this restaurant in the heart of the Judería serves much more. In the colorful bar try tapas (from €3.50) such as the *berenjenas crujientes con salmorejo* (crispy fried eggplant slices with thick gazpacho), while in the restaurant, opt for the supremely fresh grilled fish or the steak, which is the best in town, particularly the namesake *churrasco ibérico* (grilled pork, served here in a spicy tomato-based sauce). **Known for:** alfresco dining; tapas; grilled meat. *$ Average main: €22 ⊠ Calle Romero 16, Judería ☎ 957/290819 ☉ Closed Aug.*

### El Rincón de Carmen

**$ | MEDITERRANEAN |** With the sights of the Judería on the doorstep, this is a good, central spot for a quick bite in a typical Córdoba patio setting that's particularly pretty at night. Tapas and sharing plates make up the menu where star turns come from the *magret de pato* (duck breast) and *saquitos de bacalao con salsa dulce de pimientos* (cod pastries with sweet pepper sauce). **Known for:** saquitos de bacalao (cod pastries); generous portions; attractive patio setting. *$ Average main: €14 ⊠ Calle Romero 4, Judería ☎ 957/291055 ⊕ restauranterincondecarmen.es ☉ Closed Mon. and Tues.*

### Lu Regadera

$$ | SPANISH | It feels as if you could be outside at this bright venue on the river whose fresh interior comes with miniature wall gardens—there's even an herb garden in the middle. Local produce takes center stage on the short menu, where you'll find a mix of traditional and modern dishes including house specials such as wild sea bass ceviche, suckling pig, and cream of lemon. **Known for:** tuna tartare; gardenlike interior; good wine list. $ Average main: €18 ⊠ Ronda de Isasa 10, Judería ☎ 957/101400 ⊕ www.regadera.es.

### ★ noor

$$$$ | SPANISH | One of the few two Michelin-starred venues in Andalusia, noor offers Andalusí cuisine in three tasting menus that explore ingredients before the New World was discovered, during its heyday, and afterwards with a combination of Spanish and New World cuisine. Local chef Paco Morales and team create in the open kitchen while diners sit at very modern tables under a dramatic Arabian nights' ceiling. **Known for:** Arabian nights ambience; destination dining; creative, authentic cuisine. $ Average main: €95 ⊠ Calle Pablo Ruiz Picasso 8, Centro ☎ 957/964055 ⊕ noor-restaurant.es ⊙ Closed Sun.–Tues. and July and Aug.

### Taberna de San Miguel

$ | TAPAS | Just a few minutes' walk from the Plaza de las Tendillas and opposite the lovely San Miguel Church, this popular tapas spot—also known as the Casa el Pisto (Ratatouille House)—was established in 1880. You can choose to squeeze in at the bar and dine on tapas (from €3) or spread out a little more on the patio decked with ceramics and bullfighting memorabilia, where half and full portions are served. **Known for:** patio with bullfighting memorabilia; historic ambience; tapas, including pisto. $ Average main: €12 ⊠ Pl. San Miguel 1, Centro ☎ 957/470166 ⊕ www.casaelpisto.com ⊙ Closed Sun. and Mon.

### Taberna La Viuda

$ | SPANISH | Slightly off the beaten tourist trail and with a lively, local vibe, this tavern-style venue specializes in traditional local cuisine such as salmorejo, flamenquín, and oxtail, but you'll also find creative touches on the menu in the form of tuna marinated in ginger and scrambled eggs with smoked fish and trout roe. Most dishes are available as tapas and half or full plates, and all can be paired with local wines. **Known for:** wine pairings; warm welcome; traditional local food. $ Average main: €10 ⊠ Calle San Basilio 52, Judería ☎ 957/296905.

##  Hotels

### Casa de los Azulejos

$$ | B&B/INN | This 17th-century house still has original details like the majestic vaulted ceilings and, with the use of stunning tiles (azulejos)—hence the name—it mixes Andalusian and Latin American influences. **Pros:** interesting architecture; tropical central patio; homemade breakfast. **Cons:** plunge pool is open only in summer; limited privacy; hyperbusy interior design. $ Rooms from: €100 ⊠ Calle Fernando Colón 5, Centro ☎ 957/470000 ⊕ www.casadelosazulejos.com ⤳ 9 rooms ⊙ Free Breakfast.

### ★ Hospes Palacio del Bailío

$$$$ | HOTEL | One of the city's top lodging options, this tastefully renovated 17th-century mansion is built over the ruins of a Roman house (visible beneath glass floors) in the historic center of town. **Pros:** dazzling interiors; pleasant patio gardens; impeccable comforts. **Cons:** not all rooms have views; pricey; not easy to access by car. $ Rooms from: €275 ⊠ Calle Ramírez de las Casas Deza 10–12, Plaza de la Corredera ☎ 957/498993 ⊕ www.hospes.com/palacio-bailio ⤳ 53 rooms ⊙ No Meals.

### ★ Hotel Balcón de Córdoba

$$$$ | HOTEL | In a tastefully restored 17th-century convent, this boutique hotel has spacious, quiet rooms, and the Mezquita is almost within arm's reach from the rooftop terrace. **Pros:** central location; rooftop views of the Mezquita; historic building. **Cons:** small breakfast area; very quiet; difficult to access by car. ⑤ *Rooms from: €250* ✉ *Calle Encarnación 8, Judería* 🕿 *957/498478* ⊕ *balcondecordoba.com* ✈ *10 rooms* ✵ *Free Breakfast.*

### Hotel Maestre

$ | HOTEL | Around the corner from the Plaza del Potro, this is an affordable hotel in which Castilian-style furniture, gleaming marble, and high-quality oil paintings add elegance to excellent value. **Pros:** good location; helpful reception staff; great value. **Cons:** could be too basic for some; small bathrooms; lots of steps. ⑤ *Rooms from: €65* ✉ *Calle Romero Barros 4–6, San Pedro* 🕿 *957/472410* ⊕ *www.hotelmaestre.com* ✈ *26 rooms* ✵ *No Meals.*

### ★ La Llave de la Judería

$$$ | B&B/INN | This small hotel, occupying a collection of houses just a stone's throw from the mezquita, combines enchanting antique furnishings with modern amenities, but its greatest asset is its exceptionally helpful staff. **Pros:** beautiful interiors; close to the Mezquita; rooms are equipped with computers. **Cons:** dark reception area; direct car access is difficult; rooms facing street can be noisy. ⑤ *Rooms from: €180* ✉ *Calle Romero 38, Judería* 🕿 *957/294808* ⊕ *www.lallavedelajuderia.es* ✈ *8 rooms* ✵ *No Meals.*

### NH Collection Amistad Córdoba

$$$$ | HOTEL | Two 18th-century mansions overlooking Plaza de Maimónides in the heart of the Judería have been melded into a modern business hotel with a cobblestone Mudejar courtyard, carved-wood ceilings, and a plush lounge. **Pros:** pleasant and efficient service; central

# La Noche Blanca del Flamenco

Córdoba has a thriving flamenco scene with the annual highlight in mid-June when the city celebrates La Noche Blanca del Flamenco, an evening and night of free concerts in squares. You can also watch free flamenco at noon on Sundays (except May) in the lovely patio at the Centro Flamenco Forforito (off Plaza del Potro; get in line from 11am to be sure of a seat). ⊕ *ir.cordoba.es/potro*

location; large rooms. **Cons:** a little impersonal; not easy to find; parking is difficult. ⑤ *Rooms from: €230* ✉ *Pl. de Maimónides 3, Judería* 🕿 *957/420335* ⊕ *www.nh-hoteles.com* ✈ *108 rooms* ✵ *No Meals.*

### Parador de Córdoba

$$$ | HOTEL | On the slopes of the Sierra de Córdoba, on the site of Abd ar-Rahman I's 8th-century summer palace, this modern parador has sunny rooms and nice views. **Pros:** wonderful views from south-facing rooms; quality traditional cuisine; sleek interiors. **Cons:** not all rooms have views; far from main sights; characterless modern building. ⑤ *Rooms from: €140* ✉ *Av. de la Arruzafa 39, El Brillante* ✛ *5 km (3 miles) north of city* 🕿 *957/275900* ⊕ *www.parador.es* ✈ *94 rooms* ✵ *No Meals.*

### Viento 10

$$ | HOTEL | Tucked away to the east of the old quarter, but within just 10 minutes' walk of the Mezquita is a quiet, romantic haven, once part of the 17th-century Sacred Martyrs Hospital and whose patio dates back to the 15th century. **Pros:** quiet location; Jacuzzi and sauna;

excellent service. **Cons:** not easy to find; a little plain; some walking distance to the main monuments. $ *Rooms from: €120* ✉ *Calle Ronquillo Briceño 10, San Pedro* ☎ *957/764960* ⊕ *www.hotelviento10.es* 🛏 *8 rooms* ⦿| *No Meals.*

##  Nightlife

### Bodega Guzman
**BARS** | For some traditional tipple, check out this atmospheric bodega near the old synagogue. Its sherries are served straight from the barrel in a room that doubles as a bullfighting museum. ✉ *Calle de los Judios 6, Judería* ☎.

### Café Málaga
**LIVE MUSIC** | A block from Plaza de las Tendillas, this is a laid-back hangout for jazz and flamenco aficionados. There's live music most days with regular flamenco nights. ✉ *Calle Málaga 3, Centro* ☎ *957/474107.*

##  Performing Arts

### FLAMENCO
#### Tablao El Cardenal
**FOLK/TRADITIONAL DANCE** | Córdoba's most famous flamenco club offers performances by established artists on a pleasant open-air patio. Admission is €23 (including a drink), and the 90-minute shows take place Monday through Thursday at 8:30 pm and on Friday and Saturday at 9. Book by phone or the website (in Spanish only). ✉ *Calle Buen Pastor 2, Judería* ☎ *619/217922* ⊕ *tablaocardenal.es* 🛒 *€23* ⊘ *Closed Sun.*

##  Shopping

### Meryan
**LEATHER GOODS** | This is one of Córdoba's best workshops for embossed leather. ✉ *Calleja de las Flores 2, Judería* ☎ *957/475902* ⊕ *www.meryancor.com.*

# Ronda

*147 km (91 miles) southeast of Seville, 61 km (38 miles) northwest of Marbella.*

Ronda, one of the oldest towns in Spain, is known for its spectacular position and views. Secure in its mountain fastness on a rock high over the Río Guadalevín, the town was a stronghold for the legendary Andalusian bandits who held court here from the 18th to the early 20th century. Ronda's most dramatic element is its ravine (360 feet deep and 210 feet across)—known as **El Tajo**—which divides La Ciudad, the old Moorish town, from El Mercadillo, the "new town," which sprang up after the Christian Reconquest of 1485. Tour buses roll in daily with sightseers from the coast 49 km (30 miles) away, and on weekends affluent sevillanos flock to their second homes here. Stay overnight midweek to see this noble town's true colors.

In the lowest part of town, known as El Barrio, you can see parts of the old walls, including the 13th-century Puerta de Almocobar and the 16th-century Puerta de Carlos V. From here, the main road climbs past the Iglesia del Espíritu Santo (Church of the Holy Spirit) and up into the heart of town.

### GETTING HERE AND AROUND
The most attractive approach is from the south. The winding but well-maintained A376 from San Pedro de Alcántara, on the Costa del Sol, travels north up through the mountains of the Serranía de Ronda. But you can also drive here from Seville via Utrera; it's a pleasant drive of a little less than two hours. At least six daily buses run here from Marbella, six from Málaga, and seven from Seville.

### VISITOR INFORMATION
**CONTACTS Ronda.** ✉ *Paseo de Blas Infante s/n, Ronda* ☎ *952/187119* ⊕ *www.turismoderonda.es.*

# ⊙ Sights

## Alameda del Tajo

CITY PARK | Beyond the bullring in El Mercadillo, you can relax in these shady gardens, one of the loveliest spots in Ronda. At the end of the gardens, a balcony protrudes from the face of the cliff, offering a vertigo-inducing view of the valley below. Stroll along the cliff-top walk to the Reina Victoria hotel, built by British settlers from Gibraltar at the turn of the 20th century as a fashionable rest stop on the Algeciras–Bobadilla rail line. ⊠ *Paseo Hemingway, Ronda.*

## Baños Arabes (*Arab Baths*)

RUINS | The excavated remains of the Arab Baths date from Ronda's tenure as capital of a Moorish *taifa* (kingdom). The star-shape vents in the roof are an inferior imitation of the ceiling of the beautiful bathhouse in Granada's Alhambra. The baths are beneath the Puente Árabe (Arab Bridge) in a ravine below the Palacio del Marqués de Salvatierra. ⊠ *Calle San Miguel, Ronda* ☎ *656/950937* ☜ *€5.*

## Juan Peña El Lebrijano

BRIDGE | Immediately south of the Plaza de España, this is Ronda's most famous bridge (also known as the Puente Nuevo, or New Bridge), an architectural marvel built between 1755 and 1793. The bridge's lantern-lit parapet offers dizzying views of the awesome gorge. Just how many people have met their ends here nobody knows, but the architect of the Puente Nuevo fell to his own death while inspecting work on the bridge. During the civil war, hundreds of victims were hurled from it. ⊠ *Ronda.*

## Palacio de Mondragón (*Palace of Mondragón*)

HISTORY MUSEUM | This stone palace with twin Mudejar towers was probably the residence of Ronda's Moorish kings. Ferdinand and Isabella appropriated it after their victory in 1485. Today it's the museum of Ronda, and you can wander through the patios, with their brick arches and delicate Mudejar-stucco tracery, and admire the mosaics and *artesonado* (coffered) ceiling. The second floor holds a small museum with archaeological items found near Ronda, plus the reproduction of a dolmen, a prehistoric stone monument. ⊠ *Pl. Mondragón, Ronda* ☎ *952/870818* ☜ *€4.*

## Plaza de Toros

SPORTS VENUE | The main sight in Ronda's commercial center, El Mercadillo, is the bullring. Pedro Romero (1754–1839), the father of modern bullfighting and Ronda's most famous native son, is said to have killed 5,600 bulls here during his career. In the museum beneath the plaza you can see posters for Ronda's very first bullfights, held here in 1785. The plaza was once owned by the late bullfighter Antonio Ordóñez, on whose nearby ranch Orson Welles's ashes were scattered—indeed, the ring has become a favorite of filmmakers. Every September, the bullring is the scene of Ronda's "corridas goyescas," named after Francisco Goya, whose *tauromaquias* (bullfighting sketches) were inspired by Romero's skill and art. The participants and the dignitaries in the audience don the costumes of Goya's time for the occasion. ⊠ *Calle Virgen de la Paz, Ronda* ☎ *952/871539* ⊕ *www.rmcr.org* ☜ *€8 for entry and museum.*

## Santa María la Mayor

CHURCH | This collegiate church, which serves as Ronda's cathedral, has roots in Moorish times: originally the Great Mosque of Ronda, the tower and adjacent galleries, built for viewing festivities in the square, retain their Islamic design. After the mosque was destroyed (when the Moors were overthrown), it was rebuilt as a church and dedicated to the Virgen de la Encarnación after the Reconquest. The naves are late Gothic, and the main altar is heavy with baroque gold leaf. A visit to the rooftop walkway offers lovely views of the town and surroundings. The church is around the corner from the remains of a mosque,

Andalusia's classic pueblos blancos look like Picasso paintings come to life.

Minarete Árabe (Moorish Minaret) at the end of the Marqués de Salvatierra. ⊠ *Pl. Duquesa de Parcent, Ronda* 🎫 *€5.*

## 🍴 Restaurants

### ★ Entre Vinos

**$** | **TAPAS** | Just off the main road opposite the Hotel Colón, this small and cozy bar has established itself as one of Ronda's best for tapas, wine, and artisan beer. Local Ronda wines are a specialty here— in fact, they're the only ones available, although with more than 100 on the wine list, you'll be spoiled for choice; ask the waiter for recommendations and which tapas to pair them with. **Known for:** bodega (winery) atmosphere; gourmet tapas; Ronda wines. ⑤ *Average main: €8* ⊠ *Calle Pozo 2, Ronda* 🕾 *672/284146* ⊘ *Closed Sun. and Mon.*

### Pedro Romero

**$$** | **SPANISH** | Named for the father of modern bullfighting, this restaurant opposite the bullring is packed with bullfight paraphernalia and photos of previous diners who include Ernest Hemingway and Orson Welles. Mounted bulls' heads peer down at you as you eat *choricitos al vino blanco de Ronda* (small sausages in Ronda white wine), *rabo de toro Pedro Romero* (slow-cooked oxtail stew with herbs), or *paté de perdiz* (partridge paté). **Known for:** friendly service; bullfighting decor; traditional Ronda cooking. ⑤ *Average main: €18* ⊠ *Calle Virgen de la Paz 18, Ronda* 🕾 *952/871110* ⊕ *www. rpedroromero.com* ⊘ *Closed Tues., no dinner Sun. or Weds.*

## 🛏 Hotels

### Alavera de los Baños

**$$** | **B&B/INN** | Fittingly, given its location next to the Moorish baths, this small, German-run hotel—which was used as a backdrop for the film *Carmen*—has an Arabian theme throughout. **Pros:** atmospheric and historic; first-floor rooms have their own terraces; owners speak several languages. **Cons:** small bathrooms; steep climb into town; 2-night minimum stay most weekends. ⑤ *Rooms from:*

€120 ⊠ *Calle San Miguel s/n, Ronda*
☎ *952/879143* ⊕ *www.alaveradelos-*
*banos.com* ◷ *Closed Dec.–mid-Feb.*
⊏⟩ *11 rooms* ⦿❙ *Free Breakfast.*

### Hotel Montelirio
**$$$ | B&B/INN** | The 18th-century mansion
of the Count of Montelirio, perched over
the deep plunge to El Tajo, has been
carefully refurbished, maintaining some
original features, but the highlight is
the breathtaking view over the valley.
**Pros:** valley views; Turkish bath and open
fireplace make it great for winter; historic
building. **Cons:** could be too stuffy for
some; parking limited; some rooms
have windows to the street. ⑤ *Rooms
from: €160* ⊠ *Calle Tenorio 8, Ronda*
☎ *952/873855* ⊕ *www.hotelmontelirio.
com* ⊏⟩ *15 rooms* ⦿❙ *No Meals.*

# Around Ronda: Caves, Romans, and Pueblos Blancos

This area of spectacular gorges, remote
mountain villages, and ancient caves is
fascinating to explore and a dramatic
contrast to the clamor and crowds of the
nearby Costa del Sol.

Public transportation is very poor in these
parts. Your best bet is to visit by car—the
area is a short drive from Ronda.

## ◉ Sights

### ★ Acinipo
**RUINS** | Old Ronda, 20 km (12 miles) north
of Ronda, is the site of this old Roman
settlement, a thriving town in the 1st
century AD that was abandoned for
reasons that still baffle historians. Today
it's a windswept hillside with piles of
stones, the foundations of a few Roman
houses, and what remains of a theater.
Views across the Ronda plains and to the

surrounding mountains are spectacular.
The site's opening hours vary depending
on staff availability and excavations—
check with the Ronda tourist office by
phone before visiting. ⊠ *Ronda* ✛ *Take
A376 toward Algodonales; turnoff for
ruins is 9 km (5 miles) from Ronda on
MA449* ☎ *951/041452* ⊠ *Free.*

### Cueva de la Pileta (*Pileta Cave*)
**CAVE** | At this site 20 km (12 miles) west
of Ronda, a Spanish guide (who speaks
some English) will hand you a paraffin
lamp and lead you on a roughly 60-minute
walk that reveals prehistoric wall paintings of bison, deer, and horses outlined
in black, red, and ocher. One highlight
is the Cámara del Pescado (Chamber of
the Fish), whose drawing of a huge fish
is thought to be 15,000 years old. Tours
take place on the hour and last around
an hour. To book, phone between 10 am
and 1 pm only. ⊠ *Benaoján* ✛ *Drive west
from Ronda on A374 and take left exit for
village of Benaoján from where caves are
well signposted* ☎ *677/610500* ⊠ *€10.*

### Olvera
**TOWN** | Here, 13 km (8 miles) north of
Setenil, two imposing silhouettes dominate the crest of the hill: the 11th-century
castle Vallehermoso, a legacy of the
Moors, and the neoclassical church of La
Encarnación, reconstructed in the 19th
century on the foundations of the old
mosque. ⊠ *Cádiz.*

### Setenil de las Bodegas
**TOWN** | This small city, in a cleft in the
rock cut by the Río Guadalporcín, is 8 km
(5 miles) north of Acinipo. The streets
resemble long, narrow caves, and on
many houses the roof is formed by a
projecting ledge of heavy rock. ⊠ *Cádiz.*

### Zahara de la Sierra
**TOWN** | A solitary watchtower dominates
a crag above this village, its outline
visible for miles around. The tower is all
that remains of a Moorish castle where
King Alfonso X once fought the emir of

Riders fill the streets during Jerez's Feria del Caballo (Horse Fair) in early May.

Morocco; the building remained a Moorish stronghold until it fell to the Christians in 1470. Along the streets you can see door knockers fashioned like the hand of Fatima: the fingers represent the five laws of the Koran and are meant to ward off evil. ⊠ *Cádiz* ⊹ *From Olvera, drive 21 km (13 miles) southwest to the village of Algodonales, then south on A376 for 5 km (3 miles).*

# Arcos de la Frontera

*31 km (19 miles) east of Jerez.*

Its narrow and steep cobblestone streets, whitewashed houses, and finely crafted wrought-iron window grilles make Arcos the quintessential Andalusian pueblo blanco. Make your way to the main square, the **Plaza de España**, the highest point in the village; one side of the square is open, and a balcony at the edge of the cliff offers views of the Guadalete Valley. On the opposite end is the church of **Santa María de la Asunción**, a fascinating blend of architectural styles—Romanesque, Gothic, and Mudejar—with a plateresque doorway, a Renaissance retablo, and a 17th-century baroque choir. The *ayuntamiento* (town hall) stands at the foot of the old castle walls on the northern side of the square; across is the Casa del Corregidor, onetime residence of the governor and now a parador. Arcos is the westernmost of the 19 pueblos blancos dotted around the Sierra de Cádiz.

## GETTING HERE AND AROUND
Arcos is best reached by private car, but there are frequent bus services here from Cádiz, Jerez, and Seville on weekdays. Weekend services are less frequent.

## VISITOR INFORMATION
**CONTACTS Arcos de la Frontera.** ⊠ *Cuesta de Belén 5, Arcos de la Frontera* ☎ *956/702264* ⊕ *www.turismoarcos. com.*

# 🍴 Restaurants

## Gastrobar El Retablo

$ | SPANISH | Traditional Andalusian cuisine comes in generous portions (tapas and sharing plates) at this popular venue with a small terrace opposite the Iglesia de Santa María. Stars on the menu include *carrillada de cerdo* (pork cheeks), *bacalao con puré de guisantes* (cod with pea puree), and *arroz con leche* (rice pudding). **Known for:** generous portions; octopus; friendly service. ⑤ *Average main: €12* ✉ *Calle Dean Espinosa 6, Arcos de la Frontera* ☎ *856/041614* ⊘ *Closed Tues.*

## Restaurante Aljibe

$$ | FUSION | Local cooking meets Moroccan cuisine on one of the best fusion menus in the province at this venue with small dining spaces and an Arabian theme. White prawns, *ensalada de higos y payoyo* (fig and goat cheese salad), and *alcachofas con almejas* (artichokes with clams) sit perfectly next to *pastela* (game pie) and couscous dishes. **Known for:** Moroccan sweets for dessert; good service with a smile; Andalusian-Moroccan fusion. ⑤ *Average main: €15* ✉ *Cuesta del Belén 10, Arcos de la Frontera* ☎ *622/836527.*

# 🛏 Hotels

## ★ El Convento

$ | B&B/INN | Perched atop the cliff behind the town parador, this tiny hotel in a former 17th-century convent shares the amazing view of another hotel in town, its swish neighbor (La Casa Grande). **Pros:** picturesque location; value; intimacy. **Cons:** no restaurant; lots of stairs; small spaces. ⑤ *Rooms from: €65* ✉ *Calle Maldonado 2, Arcos de la Frontera* ☎ *956/702333* ⊕ *www.hotelelconvento.es* ⊘ *Closed Jan. and Feb.* ⤴ *13 rooms* ◉| *Free Breakfast.*

## ★ La Casa Grande

$ | B&B/INN | Built in 1729, this extraordinary mansion encircles a central patio with lush vegetation and is perched on the edge of the 400-foot cliff to which Arcos de la Frontera clings. **Pros:** attentive owner; amazing views; impeccable aesthetics. **Cons:** bathrooms lack privacy; long climb to the top floor; inconvenient parking. ⑤ *Rooms from: €90* ✉ *Calle Maldonado 10, Arcos de la Frontera* ☎ *956/703930* ⊕ *www.lacasagrande.net* ⤴ *7 rooms* ◉| *No Meals.*

## Parador Casa del Corregidor

$$$ | HOTEL | Expect a spectacular view from the terrace, as this parador clings to the cliffside, overlooking the rolling valley of the Río Guadalete. **Pros:** gorgeous views from certain rooms; good restaurant; elegant interiors. **Cons:** not all rooms have views; expensive bar and cafeteria; a little tired. ⑤ *Rooms from: €170* ✉ *Pl. del Cabildo s/n, Arcos de la Frontera* ☎ *956/700500* ⊕ *www.parador.es* ⤴ *24 rooms* ◉| *No Meals.*

# Jerez de la Frontera

*97 km (60 miles) south of Seville.*

Jerez, world headquarters for sherry, is surrounded by vineyards of chalky soil, producing palomino and Pedro Ximénez grapes that have funded a host of churches and noble mansions. Names such as González Byass, Domecq, Harvey, and Sandeman are inextricably linked with Jerez. The word "sherry," first used in Great Britain in 1608, is an English corruption of the town's old Moorish name, Xeres. Both sherry and thoroughbred horses (the city was European Capital of Horses in 2018) are the domain of Jerez's Anglo-Spanish aristocracy, whose Catholic ancestors came here from England centuries ago. At any given time, more than half a million barrels of sherry are maturing in Jerez's vast aboveground cellars.

## GETTING HERE AND AROUND

Jerez is a short way from Seville with frequent daily trains (journey time is around an hour) and buses (1 hour 15 minutes), fewer on weekends. If you're traveling to the city by car, park in one of the city-center lots or at your hotel as street parking is difficult. Jerez Airport is small and served by a number of flights to destinations in northern Europe and within Spain.

**AIRPORT Jerez de la Frontera Airport.** ⊠ *Ctra. N-IV, Km 628.5, Jerez de la Frontera* ☎ *956/150000* ⊕ *www.aena.es.*

**BUS STATION Jerez de la Frontera.** ⊠ *Pl. de la Estación, Jerez de la Frontera* ☎ *956/149990.*

**TAXI CONTACT Tele Taxi.** ⊠ *Jerez de la Frontera* ☎ *956/344860, 956/329396.*

**TRAIN STATION Jerez de la Frontera.** ⊠ *Pl. de la Estación s/n, off Calle Diego Fernández Herrera, Jerez de la Frontera* ☎ *912/320320.*

## VISITOR INFORMATION

**CONTACTS Jerez de la Frontera.** ⊠ *Pl. del Arenal, Jerez de la Frontera* ☎ *956/149863* ⊕ *www.turismojerez.com.*

# ◉ Sights

### Alcázar

**CASTLE/PALACE** | Once the residence of the caliph of Seville, the 12th-century alcázar in Jerez de la Frontera and its small, octagonal mosque and baths were built for the Moorish governor's private use. The baths have three sections: the *sala fría* (cold room), the larger *sala templada* (warm room), and the *sala caliente* (hot room) for steam baths. In the midst of it all is the 17th-century Palacio de Villavicencio, built on the site of the original Moorish palace. A camera obscura, a lens-and-mirrors device that projects the outdoors onto a large indoor screen, offers a 360-degree view of Jerez. ⊠ *Calle Alameda Vieja, Jerez de la Frontera* ☎ *956/149955* 💷 *From €5,*

free Mon. *(1:30–2:30 pm Nov.  Mar.;  4:30–5:30 pm April–Oct.).*

### ★ Bodegas Tradición

**WINERY** | Tucked away on the north side of the old quarter and founded in 1998, this is one of the youngest bodegas, but it has the oldest sherry. The five types sit in the casks for at least 20 years—most for longer. Visits (book in advance by phone or email) include a tour of the winery, a lesson in how to pair each sherry type, and a tour of the unique Spanish art collection that includes works by El Greco, Zurburán, Goya, and Velázquez. ⊠ *Pl. de los Cordobeses 3, Jerez de la Frontera* ☎ *956/168628* ⊕ *www.bodegastradicion. es* 💷 *€40.*

### Catedral de Jerez

**CHURCH** | Across from the alcázar and around the corner from the González Byass winery, the cathedral has an octagonal cupola and a separate bell tower, as well as Zurbarán's canvas *La Virgen Niña Meditando* (*The Virgin as a Young Girl*). ⊠ *Pl. de la Encarnación, Jerez de la Frontera* ☎ *956/169059* 💷 *From €6* ⊙ *Closed Sun. mornings.*

### González Byass

**WINERY** | Home of the famous Tío Pepe with its signature logo of a sherry bottle dressed as a man with a guitar, this is one of the most commercial bodegas, dating back to 1835. The tour (in English) is well organized and includes La Concha, an open-air aging cellar designed by Gustave Eiffel. ⊠ *Calle Manuel María González, Jerez de la Frontera* ☎ *956/357016* ⊕ *www.gonzalezbyass. com* 💷 *From €20.*

### Museo Arqueológico

**HISTORY MUSEUM** | Diving into the maze of streets that form the scruffy San Mateo neighborhood east of the town center, you come to one of Andalusia's best archaeological museums. The collection is strongest on the pre-Roman period, and the star item, found near Jerez, is a Greek helmet dating from the 7th

# Winery Tours in Jerez

On a bodega visit, you'll learn about the solera method of blending old wine with new, and the importance of the *flor* (yeast that forms on the wine as it ages) in determining the kind of sherry.

Phone ahead for an appointment to make sure you join a group that speaks your language. Admission fees start at €12 (more for extra wine tasting or tapas); tours lasting 60–90 minutes go through the aging cellars, with their endless rows of casks. (You won't see the actual fermenting and bottling, which take place in more modern, less romantic plants outside town.) Finally, you'll be invited to sample generous amounts of pale, dry fino; nutty amontillado; rich, deep oloroso; and sweet Pedro Ximénez—and, of course, to purchase a few robustly priced bottles in the winery shop.

century BC. ⊠ *Pl. del Mercado s/n, Jerez de la Frontera* ☎ *956/149560* 🎫 *€5* 🕙 *Closed Sun. and Mon.*

★ **Plaza de la Asunción**
**PLAZA/SQUARE** | Here on one of Jerez's most intimate squares you can find the Mudejar church of **San Dionisio,** patron saint of the city, (open 10–noon Monday–Thursday) and the ornate *cabildo municipal* (city hall), with a lovely plateresque facade dating to 1575. ⊠ *Jerez de la Frontera* 🎫 *Free* 🕙 *Church closed for touring Fri.–Sun.*

★ **Real Escuela Andaluza del Arte Ecuestre**
(*Royal Andalusian School of Equestrian Art*)
**SPORTS VENUE | FAMILY** | This prestigious school operates on the grounds of the Recreo de las Cadenas, a 19th-century palace. The school was masterminded by Álvaro Domecq in the 1970s, and at noon every Tuesday and Thursday (Thursday only in January and February) as well as each Friday August through October, the Cartujana horses—a cross between the native Andalusian workhorse and the Arabian—and skilled riders in 18th-century riding costume demonstrate intricate dressage techniques and jumping in the spectacular show *Cómo Bailan los Caballos Andaluces* (roughly, the *Dancing Horses of Andalusia*). ■**TIP➜** Reservations are essential.

The price of admission depends on how close to the arena you sit; the first two rows are the priciest. At certain other times you can visit the museum, stables, and tack room and watch the horses being schooled. ⊠ *Av. Duque de Abrantes, Jerez de la Frontera* ☎ *956/319635* ⊕ *www.realescuela.org* 🎫 *From €23.*

**San Miguel**
**CHURCH** | One block from the Plaza del Arenal, near the alcázar, stands the church of San Miguel. Built over the 15th and 16th centuries, its interior illustrates the evolution of Gothic architecture, with various styles mixed into the design. ⊠ *Pl. de San Miguel, Jerez de la Frontera* ☎ *662/187511* 🎫 *€4* 🕙 *Closed Sun.*

**Sandeman**
**WINERY** | The Sandeman brand of sherry is known for its dashing man-in-a-cape logo. Tours of the sherry bodegas in Jerez give you some insight into his history and let you visit the cellars. Some visitors purchase tapas to have with their sherry tastings. There is also a museum and shop on-site. ⊠ *Calle Pizarro 10, Jerez de la Frontera* ☎ *956/151552* ⊕ *www.sandeman.com/visit-us/jerez/sherry-bodegas* 🎫 *From €12.*

Just about the whole city turns out for Jerez's Feria del Caballo, and traditional Andalusian costumes are a common sight.

## Yeguada de la Cartuja

**FARM/RANCH** | This farm just outside Jerez de la Frontera specializes in Carthusian horses. In the 15th century, a Carthusian monastery on this site started the breed for which Jerez and the rest of Spain are now famous. Visits are on Saturdays at 11 am and include a full tour of the stables and training areas and a show. Book ahead. ✉ *Finca Fuente El Suero, Ctra. Medina–El Portal, Km 6.5, Jerez de la Frontera* ☎ *956/162809* ⊕ *www.yeguada-cartuja.com* 🎫 *From €17.*

## 🍴 Restaurants

### ★ Albores

**$$** | **SPANISH** | Opposite the city hall, this busy restaurant with swift service has pleasant outdoor seating under orange trees and a modern interior with low lighting, and serves innovative, modern dishes with a traditional base. The menu is extensive and changes often, although must-try staples include *barriga de atún con salsa de soja y mermelada de tomate* (tuna belly with soy sauce and tomato jam) and *Retinta* beef. **Known for:** desserts; generous portions (sharing is encouraged; half portions also available); tuna cooked any which way. ⑤ *Average main: €15* ✉ *Calle Consistorio 12, Jerez de la Frontera* ☎ *956/320266* ⊕ *www. restaurantealbores.com.*

### Atuvera

**$** | **FUSION** | Some of the most colorful meals in Andalusia are served inside what were once the stables of a 16th-century palace. Fresh local produce is used to fuse Asian and Mexican flavors in what locals describe as a vibrant explosion of taste. **Known for:** friendly service; nice terrace; fusion cooking. ⑤ *Average main: €10* ✉ *Calle Ramón de Cala 13, Jerez de la Frontera* ☎ *675/548584* ⊕ *atuverajerez.com* 🕐 *Closed Mon.–Weds.*

## Bar Juanito

$ | SPANISH | Traditional bars don't come more authentic than Bar Juanito, which has been serving local dishes for more than 70 years and pairs everything, of course, with sherry. You can eat standing at the bar or seated in the pleasant patio restaurant, where there's often live music on Saturday. **Known for:** pork-based stew; artichoke dishes in season (early spring); wide range of sharing plates. $ *Average main: €12* ⊠ *Calle Pescadería Vieja 8–10, Jerez de la Frontera* ☎ *956/334838.*

## ★ La Carboná

$$$ | SPANISH | In a former bodega, this eatery has a rustic atmosphere with arches, wooden beams, and a fireplace for winter nights, and in summer you can often enjoy live music and sometimes flamenco dancing while you dine. The chef has worked at several top restaurants, and his menu includes traditional grilled meats as well as innovative twists on classic dishes, such as Iberian ham croquettes with curry and Amontillado mayo or *rodaballo con velouté de palo cortado* (skate with sherry velouté). **Known for:** innovative dishes; bodega setting; multiple-course sherry-tasting menu. $ *Average main: €24* ⊠ *Calle San Francisco de Paula 2, Jerez de la Frontera* ☎ *956/347475* ☾ *No dinner Mon. Closed Tues. and July.*

## Venta Esteban

$$ | SPANISH | FAMILY | This restaurant is slightly off the beaten track, but well worth seeking out for traditional Jerez cuisine in a pleasant setting. Choose tapas in the bar or à la carte in the spacious and airy dining rooms. **Known for:** homemade custard; traditional stews; seafood. $ *Average main: €18* ⊠ *Colonia de Caulina C.11–03, Jerez de la Frontera* ✛ *Just off Seville hwy. exit* ☎ *956/316067* ⊕ *www.restauranteventaesteban.es.*

# 🛏 Hotels

## ★ Casa Palacio Maria Luisa

$$$$ | HOTEL | Once home to Jerez's gentlemen's club (known as the Casino) and a symbol of the city's sherry heyday, this restored 19th-century mansion is the most comfortable luxury hotel and the only five-star grand-luxe hotel in town. **Pros:** beautifully designed, über-comfortable rooms; lovely outside terrace; excellent service. **Cons:** might be too grandiose for some; expensive breakfast; small pool. $ *Rooms from: €320* ⊠ *Calle Tornería 22, Jerez de la Frontera* ☎ *956/926263* ⊕ *casapalaciomarialuisa. com* ⇆ *21 rooms* ⧓ *No Meals.*

## Hotel Doña Blanca

$ | HOTEL | Slightly off the main tourist route but still within easy walking distance to attractions, this traditional town-house hotel offers spacious accommodations with some of the best prices in the city. **Pros:** private terrace in some rooms; generously sized rooms; great value. **Cons:** might be too basic for some; not right in the city center; some street noise at night. $ *Rooms from: €60* ⊠ *Calle Bodegas 11, Jerez de la Frontera* ☎ *956/348761* ⊕ *www.hoteldonablanca. com* ⇆ *30 rooms* ⧓ *No Meals.*

## Hotel Jerez & Spa

$$ | B&B/INN | Tastefully furnished, this hacienda-style hotel offers luxury on the outskirts of town. **Pros:** elegant gardens; saltwater swimming pool; Italian restaurant on-site. **Cons:** breakfast is average; some areas need updating; outside of town center. $ *Rooms from: €120* ⊠ *Av. de la Cruz Roja 7, Jerez de la Frontera* ☎ *956/153100* ⊕ *www.hace.es* ⇆ *15 rooms* ⧓ *No Meals.*

## Hotel YIT Casa Grande

$ | HOTEL | This cozy hotel, right in the city center with all the main attractions on its doorstep, comes complete with its original 1920s Art Nouveau design and period antiques. **Pros:** central location; roof terrace; personalized service. **Cons:** some

Cádiz's majestic cathedral, as seen from the Plaza de la Catedral

rooms have street noise; decor might not appeal to everyone; some rooms are dark. $ *Rooms from: €80* ✉ *Pl. de las Angustias 3, Jerez de la Frontera* ☎ *956/345070* ⊕ *www.hotelcasagrandejerez.com* ⇱ *15 rooms* ○ *No Meals.*

# Cádiz

*32 km (20 miles) southwest of Jerez, 149 km (93 miles) southwest of Seville.*

With the Atlantic Ocean on three sides, Cádiz is a bustling town that's been shaped by a variety of cultures and has the varied architecture to prove it. Founded as Gadir by Phoenician traders in 1100 BC, Cádiz claims to be the oldest continuously inhabited city in the Western world. Hannibal lived in Cádiz for a time, Julius Caesar first held public office here, and Columbus set out from here on his second voyage, after which the city became the home base of the Spanish fleet. In the 18th century, when the Guadalquivir silted up, Cádiz monopolized New World trade and became the wealthiest port in Western Europe. Most of its buildings—including the cathedral, built in part with wealth generated by gold and silver from the New World—date from this period. The old city is African in appearance and immensely intriguing—a cluster of narrow streets opening onto charming small squares. The golden cupola of the cathedral looms above low white houses, and the whole place has a slightly dilapidated air. Spaniards flock here in February to revel in the carnival celebrations, and ever more cruise ships visit the harbor, but in general it's not too touristy.

## GETTING HERE AND AROUND

Every day, around 15 local trains connect Cádiz with Seville, Puerto de Santa María, and Jerez. The city has two bus stations. The main one, run by Comes, serves most destinations in Andalusia and farther afield; the other, run by Socibus, serves Córdoba and Madrid. There are buses to and from Sanlúcar de Barrameda (8 on weekdays), Arcos de la

Frontera (2 daily), and the Costa del Sol (via Seville, 2 daily). Cádiz is easy to get to and navigate by car. Once there, the old city is easily explored on foot.

**BUS STATION Cádiz–Estación de Autobuses Comes.** ✉ *Pl. de Sevilla, Cádiz* ☎ *956/807059.* **Cádiz-Estación de Autobuses Socibus.** ✉ *Av. Astilleros s/n, Cádiz* ☎ *956/257415.*

**TAXI CONTACT Radiotaxi.** ✉ *Cádiz* ☎ *956/212121.*

**TRAIN STATION Cádiz.** ✉ *Pl. de Sevilla s/n, Cádiz* ☎ *912/320320.*

**VISITOR INFORMATION**
**CONTACTS Local Tourist Office.** ✉ *Paseo de Canalejas, Cádiz* ☎ *956/241001* ⊕ *turismo.cadiz.es.* **Regional Tourist Office.** ✉ *Av. Ramón de Carranza s/n, Cádiz* ☎ *956/203191* ⊕ *www.cadizturismo.com.*

##  Sights

### Cádiz Cathedral

CHURCH | Five blocks southeast of the Torre Tavira are the gold dome and baroque facade of Cádiz's cathedral, which offers views from atop the Clock Tower (*Torre del Reloj*) that make the climb to the top worth it. Building was begun in 1722, when the city was at the height of its power. Cádiz-born composer Manuel de Falla, who died in 1946, is buried in the crypt. The museum, on Calle Acero, displays gold, silver, and jewels from the New World, as well as Enrique de Arfe's processional cross, which is carried in the annual Corpus Christi parades. The cathedral is known as the New Cathedral because it supplanted the original, neighboring, 13th-century structure, which was destroyed by the British in 1592, rebuilt, and rechristened the church of Santa Cruz when the New Cathedral came along. ✉ *Pl. Catedral, Cádiz* ☎ *956/286154* 🎫 *€7* 🕓 *Closed Sun. morning.*

### Gran Teatro Manuel de Falla

HISTORIC SIGHT | Four blocks west of Santa Inés is the Plaza Manuel de Falla, overlooked by this amazing neo-Mudejar redbrick building. The classic interior is impressive as well—try to attend a performance. ✉ *Pl. Manuel de Falla, Cádiz* ☎ *956/220828.*

### Museo de Cádiz (*Provincial Museum*)

HISTORY MUSEUM | On the east side of the Plaza de Mina is Cádiz's provincial museum. Notable pieces include works by Murillo and Alonso Cano as well as the *Four Evangelists* and a set of saints by Zurbarán. The archaeological section contains two extraordinary marble Phoenician sarcophagi from the time of this ancient city's birth. ✉ *Pl. de Mina, Cádiz* ☎ *856/105023* 🎫 *€2* 🕓 *Closed Sun. afternoon and Mon.*

### Museo de las Cortes

HISTORY MUSEUM | Next door to the Oratorio de San Felipe Neri, this small but pleasant museum has a 19th-century mural depicting the establishment of the Constitution of 1812. Its real showpiece, however, is a 1779 ivory-and-mahogany model of Cádiz, with all of the city's streets and buildings in minute detail, looking much as they do now. ✉ *Calle Santa Inés 9, Cádiz* ☎ *956/221788* 🎫 *Free* 🕓 *Closed weekends.*

### Oratorio de la Santa Cueva

RELIGIOUS BUILDING | A few blocks east of the Plaza de Mina, next door to the Iglesia del Rosario, this oval 18th-century chapel has three frescoes by Goya. On Good Friday, the *Sermon of the Seven Words* is read and Haydn's *Seven Last Words* played. ✉ *Calle Rosario 10, Cádiz* ☎ *956/222262* 🎫 *€4 (free Sun.)* 🕓 *Closed Mon.*

### Oratorio de San Felipe Neri

RELIGIOUS BUILDING | A walk up Calle San José from the Plaza de Mina will bring you to this church, where Spain's first liberal constitution (known affectionately as La Pepa) was declared in

1812. It was here, too, that the Cortes (Parliament) of Cádiz met when the rest of Spain was subjected to the rule of Napoléon's brother, Joseph Bonaparte (more popularly known as Pepe Botella, for his love of the bottle). On the main altar is an *Immaculate Conception* by Murillo, the great sevillano artist who in 1682 fell to his death from a scaffold while working on his *Mystic Marriage of St. Catherine* in Cádiz's Chapel of Santa Catalina. You can hear Mass in Latin on Sunday at noon. ⊠ *Calle Santa Inés 38, Cádiz* ☎ *662/642233* ☞ *€4* ☺ *Closed Sun. and Mon.*

### Plaza San Francisco

**STREET** | Near the ayuntamiento is this pretty square surrounded by white-and-yellow houses and filled with orange trees and elegant street lamps. It's especially lively during the evening paseo. ⊠ *Cádiz.*

### Roman Theater

**RUINS** | Next door to the church of Santa Cruz are the remains of a 1st-century-BC Roman theater, one of the oldest and largest in Spain. The stage is unexcavated (it lies under nearby houses), but you can visit the entrance and large seating area as well as the visitor center. ⊠ *Calle Mesón 11–13, Barrio del Pópulo* ☞ *Free* ☺ *Closed Sun. afternoon and 1st Mon. of month.*

### ★ Torre Tavira

**NOTABLE BUILDING | FAMILY** | At 150 feet, this watchtower is the highest point in the old city. More than a hundred such structures were used by Cádiz ship owners to spot their arriving fleets. A camera obscura gives a good overview of the city and its monuments; the last show is a half hour before closing time. ⊠ *Calle Marqués del Real Tesoro 10, Cádiz* ☎ *956/212910* ⊕ *www.torretavira.com/en* ☞ *€7* ♿ *Visits by reservation only.*

### Yacimiento Arqueológico Gadir

**RUINS** | Few Phoenician settlements have survived intact, but excavations underneath the Puppet Museum revealed some of the best-preserved ruins in Southern Europe. You can visit the 9th-century BC remains and discover eight houses along two cobbled streets complete with animal hoofprints encased in mud and clay. The site also has the remains of a Roman fish-preserving factory with saltwater pools. ⊠ *Calle San Miguel 15, Cádiz* ☎ *956/226337* ☞ *Free* ☺ *Closed Sun. afternoon and Mon.*

## 🍴 Restaurants

### ★ Casa Manteca

**$ | SPANISH |** Cádiz's most quintessentially Andalusian tavern is in the neighborhood of La Viña, named for the vineyard that once grew here. *Chacina* (Iberian ham or sausage) and *chicharrones de Cádiz* (cold pork) served on waxed paper and washed down with *manzanilla* (sherry from Sanlúcar de Barrameda) are standard fare at the low wooden counter that has served bullfighters and flamenco singers, as well as dignitaries from around the world, since 1953. **Known for:** manzanilla sherry; delicious cold cuts; atmospheric interior. $ *Average main: €10* ⊠ *Corralón de los Carros 66, Cádiz* ☎ *956/213603.*

### Código de Barra

**$$$$ | SPANISH |** Local produce comes under the Dutch microscope at one of the most innovative dining venues in Cádiz, under the direction of chef Léon Griffioen. With just eight tables and in minimalist surroundings, the restaurant, decked in black and gray, offers a tasting menu (€50 for nine dishes, €60 for 12; pairing options available) that comes with several surprises including an "olive" and 'deconstructed' tortillitas de camarones—it's one explosion of flavor after another. **Known for:** good and long wine list (ask the staff for pairing suggestions); excellent-value tasting menus; creative take on traditional local cuisine. $ *Average main: €50* ⊠ *Pl. Candelaria 12, Cádiz* ☎ *635/533303* ☺ *Closed Sun.*

### La Candela

$ | SPANISH | A block north of Plaza Candelaria and on one of Cádiz's narrow pedestrian streets, La Candela is a good place to try local fare with a modern twist. The salmorejo comes baked with pork loin tartare, the pork cheeks are melt-in-the-mouth tender, and several dishes come tempura-style or have South American touches such as the sea bass ceviche with tiger's milk and mango. **Known for:** Spanish-Asian fusion food; homemade cheesecake; tapas. ⑤ *Average main: €10* ⊠ *Calle Feduchy 1, Cádiz* ☎ *956/221822* ⊕ *www.lacandelatapasbar.com.*

### Mercado Central de Abastos

$ | SPANISH | With over 170 stalls of fresh produce, Cádiz's main market provides a real insight into the types of local fish and seafood, and seasonal treats. It also has a *rincón gastronómico* (gastro-corner) with several stalls serving dishes based on the produce available in the market. **Known for:** fresh produce; wide choice of quick bites; informal atmosphere. ⑤ *Average main: €10* ⊠ *Pl. de la Libertad, Cádiz* ⊙ *No dinner Sun. Closed Mon.*

## 🛏 Hotels

### Hotel Argantonio

$$ | HOTEL | This small, family-run hotel in the historic center of town combines traditional style and modern amenities. **Pros:** friendly and helpful staff; good-size bathrooms; great location. **Cons:** not easy to find; street-facing rooms can be noisy; rooms in the original building on the small side. ⑤ *Rooms from: €140* ⊠ *Calle Argantonio 3, Cádiz* ☎ *956/211640* ⊕ *www.hotelargantonio.com* ⇔ *17 rooms* ¶◯l *No Meals.*

### Hotel Patagonia Sur

$$$ | HOTEL | With a handy central location just two blocks from the cathedral, this modern hotel offers functional and inexpensive lodging, especially during low season. **Pros:** central location; top-floor rooms have a private terrace; good value. **Cons:** two-night minimum stay in summer; street noise can be intrusive; small rooms. ⑤ *Rooms from: €160* ⊠ *Calle Cobos 11, Cádiz* ☎ *856/174647* ⊕ *www.hotelpatagoniasur.es* ⇔ *16 rooms* ¶◯l *No Meals.*

### Parador de Cádiz

$$$$ | HOTEL | With a privileged position overlooking the bay, this parador has spacious public areas and large modern rooms, most with balconies facing the sea. **Pros:** great views of the bay; bright and cheerful; pool. **Cons:** lacks historic appeal of other paradores; very quiet in the off-season; expensive parking. ⑤ *Rooms from: €300* ⊠ *Av. Duque de Nájera 9, Cádiz* ☎ *956/226905* ⊕ *www.parador.es/en/paradores/parador-de-cadiz* ⇔ *124 rooms* ¶◯l *No Meals.*

# GRANADA AND AROUND

12

Updated by
Joanna Styles

| 👁 Sights | 🍴 Restaurants | 🛏 Hotels | 🛍 Shopping | 🍸 Nightlife |
|-----------|----------------|-----------|-------------|--------------|
| ★★★★★ | ★★★★☆ | ★★★★☆ | ★★★★☆ | ★★★★☆ |

# WELCOME TO GRANADA AND AROUND

## TOP REASONS TO GO

★ **Be seduced by the Alhambra:** Marvel at this extraordinary Moorish delight, a fortress-palace whose patios, courtyards, halls, baths, and gardens rank among the most magnificent in the world.

★ **Lose yourself in time:** Stroll the cobbled alleyways of the Albayzín, the ancient Arab quarter, with its whitewashed facades, churches, convents, and simply stunning views to the Alhambra and the snow-capped Sierra Nevada beyond.

★ **Admire their resting places:** Visit the Capilla Real with the tombs of Spain's greatest monarchs, Isabella and Ferdinand, under whose watch modern day Spain was born and the New World discovered.

★ **Experience the real thing:** Tour the colorful Gypsy caves in Sacromonte and take in a finger-clicking, foot-tapping flamenco show.

★ **Taste the tapas:** Enjoy a complimentary tapa with your drink at any bar in Granada, often more of a mini-meal than a mere mouthful.

Granada is compact and easy to navigate, with the exception of the Albayzín, whose charm lies in losing yourself in the maze of alleyways. Outside the center, prepare for some serious walking in hilly terrain (often on cobbled streets) or take taxis or buses.

**1 La Alhambra.** Perched on a verdant hill and home to Spain's greatest monument, La Alhambra stands tall over the city, offering panoramic views plus some fine hotels.

**2 Realejo.** Beneath La Alhambra, narrow cobbled streets and pleasant squares are home to fine palaces and mansions as well as bustling bars and restaurants.

**3 Sacromonte.** Hilly and riddled with caverns, Sacromonte is the heart of Granada's Gypsy community and its flamenco spirit.

**4 Albayzín.** Occupying the hillside opposite La Alhambra, the ancient Moorish quarter offers a labyrinth of white-washed alleyways, churches, squares with panoramic views, and boutique hotels and restaurants.

**5 Centro.** Flat and bustling, the center houses commercial Granada with its main shopping streets, leafy squares, and fine architecture including the Cathedral and Capilla Real.

**6 Priego de Córdoba.** An olive farming town famous for its mansions and baroque churches.

**7 Baeza.** One of the best-preserved old towns in Spain.

**8 Ubeda.** Slightly larger than Baeza, this town is known for its architecture, artisan crafts, and olive groves. Shop for all your souvenirs here.

**9 The Sierra Nevada.** You'll find stunning mountain views and Europe's southernmost ski resort about 45 minutes from Granada.

**10 The Alpujarras.** The southern slopes of the Sierra Nevada have long been loved by artists and writers for their remoteness and stunning views.

**11 Huerta de San Vicente.** Lorca's summer home is now a museum and a must-visit for fans of the poet.

Córdoba  Jaén
**6** Priego
de Córdoba  Baeza **8**
**7** Úbeda
**11**
GRANADA **9** Sierra Nevada
**10** The Alpujarras
Málaga  Almería
*Mediterranean Sea*

ALBAYZÍN
**4**

*Carretera de Murcia*

*Cuesta Alhacaba*

SACROMONTE
**3**

*Rio Darro*

0          1,000 ft
0      200 m

Calle Gran Vía de Colón

C. Zenete

C. San Juan de los Reyes

C. Carrera del Darro

C. Elvira

C. Arandas

C. San Jerónimo

C. Cárcel Baja

C. Cárcel Baja

LA
ALHAMBRA
**1**

CENTRO
**5**

C. Reyes Católicos

C. Reyes Católicos

C. Mesones

C. Alhóndiga

Calle Elvira

REALEJO
**2**

Calle Pavaneras

Calle Alvas

Calle San Matías

Ángel

C. Angel Ganivet

Recogidas

C. Acera del Darro

Calle de San Antón

C. Molinos

C. Santiago

C. Paseo Seco de Lucena

Carmen
de los Mártires

C. Mirasol

C. Carrera de la Virgen

C. Castañeda

Calle San Isidro

Paseo de la Bomba

# EATING AND DRINKING WELL IN ANDALUSIA

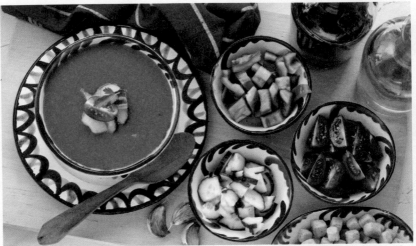

A cool bowl of gazpacho, with accompaniments.

Andalusian cuisine, as diverse as the geography of seacoast, farmland, and mountains, is held together by its Moorish aromas. Cumin seed and other Arabian spices, along with salty-sweet combinations, are ubiquitous.

The eight Andalusian provinces cover a wide geographical and culinary spectrum. Superb seafood is center stage in Cádiz, Puerto de Santa María, and Sanlúcar de Barrameda. *Jamón ibérico de bellota* (Iberian acorn-fed ham) and other Iberian pork products rule from the Sierra de Aracena in Huelva to the Pedroches Mountains north of Córdoba. In Seville, look for products from the Guadalquivir estuary, the Sierra, and the rich Campiña farmland, all prepared with great creativity. In Córdoba, try *salmorejo cordobés* (a thick gazpacho), *rabo de toro* (oxtail stew), or representatives of the salty-sweet legacy from Córdoba's Moorish heritage such as *cordero con miel* (lamb with honey). Spicy *crema de almendras* (almond soup) is a Granada favorite along with *habas con jamón* (broad beans with ham) from the Alpujarran village of Trevélez.

## SHERRY

Dry sherry from Jerez de la Frontera (fino) and from Sanlúcar de Barrameda (manzanilla) share honors as favorite tapas accompaniments. Manzanilla, the more popular choice, is fresher and more delicate, with a slight marine tang. Both are the preferred drinks at Andalusian *ferias* (fairs), particularly in Seville in April and Jerez de la Frontera in May.

## COLD VEGETABLE SOUPS

Spain's most popular contribution to world gastronomy after paella may well be gazpacho, a simple peasant soup served cold and filled with scraps and garden ingredients. Tomatoes, cucumber, garlic, oil, bread, and chopped peppers are the ingredients, and side plates of chopped onion, peppers, garlic, tomatoes, and croutons accompany, to be added to taste. *Salmorejo cordobés*, a thicker cold vegetable soup with the same ingredients but a different consistency, is used to accompany tapas.

## MOORISH FLAVORS

Andalusia's 781-year sojourn at the heart of Al-Andalus, the Moorish empire on the Iberian Peninsula, left as many tastes and aromas as mosques and fortresses. Cumin-laced *boquerones en adobo* (marinated anchovies) or the salty-sweet *cordero con miel* are two examples, along with coriander-spiked *espinacas con garbanzos* (spinach with garbanzo beans) and *perdiz con dátiles y almendras* (partridge stewed with dates and almonds). Desserts especially reflect the Moorish legacy in morsels such as *pestiños*, cylinders or twists of fried dough in anise-honey syrup.

Crispy fried fish are an Andalusian delicacy.

## FRIED FISH

Andalusia is famous for its fried fish, from *pescaito frito* (fried whitebait) to *calamares fritos* (fried squid rings). Andalusians are masters of deep-frying techniques using very hot olive and vegetable oils that produce peerlessly crisp, dry *frituras* (fried seafood); much of Andalusia's finest tapas repertory is known for being served piping hot and crunchy. Look for *tortillita de camarones*, a delicate lacework of tiny fried shrimp.

## STEWS

*Guisos* are combinations of vegetables, with or without meat, cooked slowly over low heat. *Rabo de toro* is a favorite throughout Andalusia, though Córdoba claims the origin of this dark and delicious stew made from the tail of a fighting bull. The segments of tail are cleaned, browned, and set aside before leeks, onions, carrots, garlic, and bay leaves are stewed in the same pan. Cloves, salt, pepper, a liter of wine, and a half liter of beef broth are added to the stew with the meat, and they're all simmered for two to three hours until the meat is falling off the bone and thoroughly tenderized. *Alboronía,* also known as *pisto andaluz,* is a traditional stew of eggplant, bell peppers, and zucchini.

Fried calamari with lemon.

Nestling below the perennially snow-capped Sierra Nevada and rising majestically from a vast fertile place, Granada proudly offers visitors two jewels in Andalusia's crown: the Alhambra and the tomb of the Catholic Monarchs. The two aesthetics, Moorish and Christian, pervade the entire city in its architecture, cuisine, handicrafts, and people.

The kingdom of Granada dates back to 1013, when it was founded by the Moorish Nasrid dynasty, under whose reign the city prospered as one of the richest in Spain for over four centuries. In 1491, split by internal squabbles, Boabdil, the "Rey Chico" (Boy King) gave Ferdinand of Aragón his opportunity to claim Granada for Castille. Spurred by Isabella's religious fanaticism, he laid siege to the city for seven months, and on January 2, 1492, Boabdil was forced to surrender the keys of the city.

Granada perches on three hills: the reddish Alhambra palace dominates the trio and the city skyline; on the opposite side across the small Darro River sprawls the Albayzín, Granada's historic Moorish quarter where time seems to have come to a standstill; and on the third hill sits the Sacromonte, studded with ancient caves and home to the city's Gypsies and flamenco.

All three areas are well worth exploring. The Alhambra ranks as the top must-see and merits a whole day of your visit. If your stay is longer, aim to tour the palace at night too. The Albayzín is an area best appreciated by a leisurely stroll and Sacromonte is an interesting detour before you descend the hills to the historic center below.

The maze of streets that make up the center harbor a bustling hub of commercial activity, yet another legacy of Granada's Moorish past. The main shopping streets, centering on the Puerta Real, are the Gran Vía de Colón, Reyes Católicos, Zacatín, and Recogidas. Most antiques shops are on Cuesta de Elvira and Alcaicería—off Reyes Católicos. Cuesta de Gomérez, on the way up to the Alhambra, also has several handicrafts shops and guitar workshops. Handicrafts have a distinct Moorish air, present in the ceramics, marquetry (especially the *taraceas*, wooden boxes with inlaid tiles on their lids), woven textiles, and silver-, brass-, and copper-ware.

Side trips from Granada give you the chance to experience some of the finest towns in eastern Andalusia. In the rolling olive groves and high mountains, you'll find gems such as Priego de Córdoba, home to some of the region's most impressive Baroque churches; Baeza and Úbeda, both with exceptional examples of Renaissance architecture; the Sierra Nevada, a paradise for mountain walkers and climbers; and the Alpujarras, one of Andalusia's most scenic mountain regions, dotted with white villages.

# Planning

## When to Go

The best months to go are October and November and April and May. It's blisteringly hot in the summer; if that's your only chance to come, plan on visiting Granada's Sierra Nevada to beat the heat. Autumn catches the cities going about their business, the temperatures are moderate, and you will rarely see a line form.

## Getting Here and Around

### AIR

Four daily flights connect Granada with Madrid and three connect it with Barcelona.

**CONTACTS Aeropuerto de Granada.** (*Aeropuerto Federico García Lorca*) ✉ *Granada* ☎ *902/404704.*

### BUS

Granada's main bus station is at Carretera de Jaén, 3 km (2 miles) northwest of the center of town beyond the end of Avenida de Madrid. Most buses operate from here, except for buses to nearby destinations such as Fuentevaqueros, Viznar, and some buses to Sierra Nevada, which leave from the city center's Plaza del Triunfo near the RENFE station. Luggage lockers (*la consigna*) are available at the main bus and train stations, and

you can also leave your luggage at City Locker (✉ *Carrera del Darro 3*) and Locker in the City (✉ *Pasaje Conde Alcalá 1*).

Autocares Tocina operates buses between Granada and the Sierra Nevada. ALSA buses run to and from Las Alpujarras (3 times daily), Córdoba (6 times daily), Seville (6 times daily), Málaga (20 times daily), and Jaén, Baeza, Úbeda, Cazorla, Almería, Almuñécar, and Nerja (several times daily).

In Granada, airport buses (€3) run between the center of town and the airport, leaving roughly every hour 7 am–8 pm from the Palacio de Congresos and making a few other stops along the way to the airport. Times are listed at the bus stop.

Granada has an extensive public bus network within the city. You can buy 5-, 10-, and 20-trip discount passes on the buses and at newsstands. The single-trip fare is €1.40. Granada Cards include bus trips plus guaranteed tickets for the Alhambra and other main monuments (without having to wait in lines). The card costs from €37, saving at least a third on regular prices. You can purchase the cards online via (⊕ *www.granadatur.com/granada-card*) or by phone (☎ *858/889990, daily 9–8*) in advance of your visit; you can download them on your cell phone, or print at home or at the tourist office.

**CONTACTS ALSA.** ☎ *902/422242* ⊕ *www.alsa.es.* **Granada Bus Station.** ✉ *Ctra. Jaén, Granada* ☎ *902/422242.*

### CAR

With the exception of parts of the Alpujarras, most roads in this region are smooth, and touring by car is one of the most enjoyable ways to see the countryside. Local tourist offices can advise about scenic drives. One good route heads northwest from Seville on the A66 passing through stunning scenery; turn northeast on the A461 to Santa Olalla de Cala to the village of Zufre, dramatically set at the edge of a gorge. Backtrack and continue on to Aracena. Return via the Minas de Riotinto (signposted from Aracena), which will bring you back to the A66 heading east to Seville.

### TAXI

Taxis are plentiful and may be hailed on the street or from specified taxi stands. Fares are reasonable, and meters are strictly used; the minimum fare is about €4. You are not required to tip taxi drivers, although rounding off the amount is appreciated. Uber is available in Granada and Baeza.

Expect to pay around €20–€25 for cab fare from the airport to the city center.

**CONTACTS Taxi Genil.** ☒ *Granada* ☏ *958/132323.* **Pide Taxi Granada.** ☒ *Granada* ☏ *958/280000.*

### TRAIN

There are regular trains from Seville and Almería, and a twice-daily fast service from Málaga, taking 70 minutes. A faster service to Seville (2 hours 20 minutes) is expected to come into service in early 2023 when trains to Málaga will take 10 minutes less. There are a couple of daily trains from Madrid, Valencia, and Barcelona.

**CONTACTS Train Station.** ☒ *Av. de los Andaluces, Granada* ☏ *912/320320.*

## Restaurants

Eating out is an intrinsic part of the Andalusian lifestyle. Whether it's sharing some tapas with friends over a pre-lunch drink or a three-course à la carte meal, many Andalusians eat out at some point during the day. Unsurprisingly, there are literally thousands of bars and restaurants throughout the region catering to all budgets and tastes. Note that bars in Granada tend to serve a free tapa with every drink.

At lunchtime, check out the *menús del día* (daily menus) offered by many restaurants, usually three courses and excellent value (expect to pay €8–€15, depending on the type of restaurant and location). Roadside restaurants, known as *ventas*, usually provide good food in generous portions and at reasonable prices. Be aware that many restaurants add a service charge (*cubierto*), which can be as much as €3 per person, and some restaurant prices don't include value-added tax (*impuesto sobre el valor añadido/I.V.A.*) at 10%. Note also that restaurants with tasting menus (*menús de degustación*) usually require everyone at the table to have the menu.

Andalusians tend to eat later than their fellow Spaniards: lunch is 2–4 pm, and dinner starts at 9 pm (10 pm in the summer). In cities, many restaurants are closed Sunday night, and fish restaurants tend to close on Monday; in inland towns and cities, some restaurants close for all of August.

*Restaurant reviews have been shortened. For full information, visit Fodors. com.*

## Hotels

The Parador de Granada, next to the Alhambra, is a magnificent way to enjoy Granada. Hotels on the Alhambra hill, especially the parador, must be reserved far in advance. Lodging establishments in Granada's city center, around the Puerta Real and Acera del Darro, can be unbelievably noisy, so if you're staying there, ask for a room toward the back. Though Granada has plenty of hotels, it can be difficult to find lodging during peak tourist season (Easter through late October).

Rental accommodations bookable on portals such as Airbnb are popular in large towns and cities, although quality varies so double-check reviews before you book.

Not all hotel prices include value-added tax (I.V.A.) and the 10% surcharge may be added to your final bill. Check when you book.

*Hotel reviews have been shortened. For full information, visit Fodors.com.*

## What It Costs in Euros

|  | $ | $$ | $$$ | $$$$ |
|---|---|---|---|---|
| RESTAURANTS | | | | |
|  | under €12 | €12–€17 | €18–€22 | over €22 |
| HOTELS | | | | |
|  | under €90 | €90–€125 | €126–€180 | over €180 |

# Tours

### Riding Andalucia
SPECIAL-INTEREST TOURS | This is an established Alpujarras equestrian agency that organizes horseback riding in the Sierra Nevada. ⊠ *C. Ermita, Bubión* ☎ *958/763135* ⊕ *www.ridingandalucia. com* ⊠ *Rides from €30, tours from €810.*

### Cycling Country
BICYCLE TOURS | For information about cycling tours around Granada (Andalusia and Spain), 1–10 days long, contact this company, run by husband-and-wife team Geoff Norris and Maggi Jones in a town about 55 km (33 miles) away. ⊠ *Calle Salmerones 18, Alhama de Granada* ☎ *958/360655* ⊕ *www.cyclingcountry. com* ⊠ *From €50.*

### Glovento Sur
AIR EXCURSIONS | Up to five people at a time are taken on balloon trips above Granada, Guadix, and Antequera. ⊠ *Placeta Nevot 4, #1A, Granada* ☎ *958/290316* ⊕ *www.gloventosur.com* ⊠ *From €165.*

### Granada Tapas Tours
GUIDED TOURS | Long-time British resident Gayle Mackie offers a range of tapas tours lasting up to three hours. ⊠ *Granada* ☎ *619/444984* ⊕ *www.granadata-pastours.com* ⊠ *From €50, including 6 tapas.*

### Nevadensis
GUIDED TOURS | Based in the Alpujarras, Nevadensis leads guided hiking, climbing, and skiing tours of the Sierra Nevada. Note that prices are per group. ⊠ *Pl. de la Libertad, Pampaneira* ☎ *659/109662* ⊕ *www.nevadensis.com* ⊠ *From €150.*

# Visitor Information

CONTACTS Municipal Tourist Office. ⊠ *Pl. del Carmen 9, Centro* ☎ *958/248280* ⊕ *www.granadatur.com.* Provincial Tourist Office. ⊠ *Plaza de Santa Ana, Centro* ☎ *958/575202* ⊕ *www.turgranada.es.*

# La Alhambra

## ⊙ Sights

### ★ Alhambra
CASTLE/PALACE | With more than 2.7 million visitors a year, the Alhambra is Spain's most popular attraction. This sprawling palace-fortress was the last bastion of the 800-year Moorish presence on the Iberian Peninsula. Composed of royal residential quarters, court chambers, baths, and gardens, surrounded by defense towers and massive walls, the Alhambra is an architectural gem. The courtyards, patios, and halls offer an ethereal maze of Moorish arches, columns, and domes containing intricate stucco carvings and patterned ceramic tiling. The heart of the Alhambra, the Palacios Nazaríes contain delicate apartments, lazy fountains, and tranquil pools, and are divided into three sections: the *mexuar*, where business, government, and palace administration were headquartered; the *serrallo*, state rooms where the sultans

# Granada

**Sights** ▼

1 Abadía del
   Sacromonte .............. **I3**
2 Alhambra ................. **F6**
3 Capilla Real.............. **C6**
4 Carmen de los
   Mártires................... **F7**
5 Casa de los Pisa ........ **D5**
6 Casa de los Tiros........ **D6**
7 Casa-Museo de
   Manuel de Falla......... **F7**
8 Cathedral ................. **C6**
9 Centro José Guerrero... **C6**
10 Corral del Carbón........ **C6**
11 El Bañuelo ............... **D5**
12 El Cuarto Real ........... **D7**
13 Fundación
   Rodríguez-Acosta /
   Instituto
   Gómez-Moreno .......... **E6**
14 Museo Cuevas del
   Sacromonte ............. **G3**
15 Paseo Padre Manjón.... **E5**

**Restaurants** ▼

1 Bar Los Diamantes ..... **D6**
2 Bodegas Castañeda..... **C5**
3 Café Botánico........... **B5**
4 Damasqueros ........... **D6**
5 El Mercader.............. **C5**
6 El Trillo .................. **D4**
7 hicuri ..................... **D6**
8 La Bodega de
   Antonio.................. **A6**
9 La Brujidera .............. **C6**
10 Oliver..................... **B6**
11 Om-Kalsum.............. **A6**
12 Paprika................... **C4**
13 Pastelería
   López-Mezquita.......... **C6**
14 Ruta del Azafrán ........ **E5**
15 Tinta Fina ................ **C7**

**Hotels** ▼

1 Carmen de la
   Alcubilla del Caracol .... **E6**
2 Casa Morisca ............ **F4**
3 Gar Anat Hotel
   Boutique .................. **C6**
4 Hospes Palacio
   de los Patos ............. **A7**
5 Hostal Rodri ............. **B5**
6 Hotel Alhambra
   Palace..................... **E6**
7 Hotel Casa 1800......... **D5**
8 Hotel Palacio
   Santa Inés ............... **D5**
9 Hotel Párraga Siete .... **B7**
10 Palacio
   de los Navas ............. **C7**
11 Parador de Granada..... **F6**

Calle Siete Cuestas

Camino del Sacromonte

Darro

|   | 0 | | 1,000 ft |
|---|---|---|---|
|   | 0 | 200 m | |

Camino de la Silla del Moro

Carmen
de los
Mártires

Paseo de la Sabica

Av. Santa María de la Alhambra

Paseo de las Palmas

**Carretera de la Sierra**

**KEY**

🔴 Sights

🔴 Restaurants

🔴 Hotels

G   H   I

held court; and the harem. The beautiful Sala de los Abencerrajes (Hall of the Moors) has a fabulous, ornate ceiling and star-shape cupola reflected in the pool below. ✉ *Cuesta de Gomérez, Alhambra* ☎ *858/889002 tickets, 958/027971 information* ⊕ *tickets.alhambra-patronato. es/en* ☞ *From €2, Museo de la Alhambra and Palacio de Carlos V free* ☉ *Museo de Bellas Artes and Museo de la Alhambra closed Mon.*

### Carmen de los Mártires

HISTORIC HOME | Up the hill from the Hotel Alhambra Palace, this turn-of-the-20th-century *carmen* (private villa) and its gardens—the only area open to tourists—are like a Generalife (the Alhambra summer palace) in miniature. ✉ *Paseo de los Mártires, Alhambra* ☎ *958/849103* ☞ *Free.*

### Casa-Museo de Manuel de Falla

HISTORIC HOME | The composer Manuel de Falla (1876–1946) lived and worked for many years in this rustic house tucked into a charming hillside lane with lovely views of the Alpujarras. In 1986, Granada paid homage to him by naming its new concert hall (down the street from the Carmen de los Mártires) the Auditorio Manuel de Falla—from this institution, fittingly, you have a view of his little white house. Note the bust in the small garden: it's placed where the composer once sat to enjoy the sweeping vista. ✉ *Calle Antequeruela Alta 11, Alhambra* ☎ *958/222189* ☞ *€3* ☉ *Closed Mon.*

## 🛏 Hotels

### ★ Carmen de la Alcubilla del Caracol

$$$ | B&B/INN | In a traditional *granadino* villa on the slopes of the Alhambra, this privately run lodging is one of Granada's most stylish hotels. **Pros:** great views; walking distance to the Alhambra; bright, airy rooms. **Cons:** parking difficult; slightly out of town; tough climb in hot weather.

⑤ *Rooms from: €150* ✉ *Calle Aire Alta 12, Alhambra* ☎ *958/215551* ⊕ *www.alcubilladelcaracol.com* ☉ *Closed mid-July–Aug.* ⇗ *7 rooms* ⑂ *No Meals.*

### Hotel Alhambra Palace

$$$$ | HOTEL | Built by a local duke in 1910, this neo-Moorish hotel is on leafy grounds at the back of the Alhambra hill, and has a very *Arabian Nights* interior (think orange-and-brown overtones, multicolor tiles, and Moorish-style arches and pillars). **Pros:** bird's-eye views; historical ambiance; location near the Alhambra. **Cons:** some rooms look a little tired; standard rooms on the small side; steep climb up from Granada. ⑤ *Rooms from: €250* ✉ *Pl. Arquitecto García de Paredes 1, Alhambra* ☎ *958/221468* ⊕ *www.h-alhambrapalace.es* ⇗ *126 rooms* ⑂ *No Meals.*

### ★ Parador de Granada

$$$$ | HOTEL | This is Spain's most expensive and most popular parador, right within the walls of the Alhambra. **Pros:** good location for the Alhambra; garden restaurant; lovely interiors. **Cons:** very expensive; removed from city life; no views in some rooms. ⑤ *Rooms from: €400* ✉ *Calle Real de la Alhambra, Alhambra* ☎ *958/221440* ⊕ *www.paradorsofspain.com* ⇗ *40 rooms* ⑂ *No Meals.*

## 👜 Shopping

### Tienda Libreria de la Alhambra (*Alhambra Shop and Bookshop*)

SOUVENIRS | Packed with exquisite artisan and design objects, all Alhambra-themed, and an extensive range of history and art books, the official Alhambra shop makes a great place to shop for souvenirs and presents. Shipping service available from the shop or online. ✉ *Calle Reyes Católicos 40, Centro* ⊕ *alhambratienda.es.*

*Continued on page 668*

# ALHAMBRA: PALACE-FORTRESS

 Floating mirage-like on its promontory overlooking Granada, the mighty and mysterious Alhambra shimmers vermilion in the clear mountain air, with the white peaks of the Sierra Nevada rising behind it. This sprawling palace-fortress, named from the Arabic for "red citadel" (*al-Qal'ah al-Hamra*), was the last bastion of the 800-year Moorish presence on the Iberian Peninsula. Composed of royal residential quarters, court chambers, baths, and gardens, surrounded by defense towers and massive walls, the Alhambra is an architectual gem where Moorish kings worked and played—and murdered their enemies.

**LOOK UP**

Among the stylistic elements you can see in the Alhambra are **Arabesque** geometrical designs, and elaborate **Mocárabe** arches.

Built of perishable materials, the Alhambra was meant to be forever replenished and replaced by succeeding generations. The Patio de los Leones' (above) has recently been restored to its original appearance.

## INSIDE THE FORTRESS

More than 3 million annual visitors come to the Alhambra today, making it Spain's top attraction. Vistors revel in the palace's architectural wonders, most of which had to be restored after the alterations made after the Christian reconquest of southern Spain in 1492 and the damage from an 1821 earthquake. Incidentally, Napoléon's troops commandeered the site in 1812 with intent to level it but their attempts were foiled.

The courtyards, patios, and halls offer an ethereal maze of Moorish arches, columns, and domes containing intricate stucco carvings and patterned ceramic tiling. The intimate arcades, fountains, and light-reflecting pools throughout are identified in the ornamental inscriptions as physical renderings of paradise taken from the Koran and Islamic poetry. The contemporary visitor to this dreamlike space feels the fleeting embrace of a culture that brought its light to a world emerging from medieval darkness.

## ARCHITECTURAL TERMS

**Arabesque:** An ornament or decorative style that employs flower, foliage, or fruit, and sometimes geometrical, animal, and figural outlines to produce an intricate pattern of interlaced lines.

**Mocárabe:** A decorative element of carved wood or plaster based on juxtaposed and hanging prisms resembling stalactites. Sometimes called *muquarna* (honeycomb vaulting), the impression is similar to a beehive and the "honey" has been described as light.

**Mozárabe:** Sometimes confused with Mocárabe, the term Mozárabe refers to Christians living in Moorish Spain. Thus, Christian artistic styles or recourses in Moorish architecture (such

as the paintings in the Sala de los Reyes) are also identified as *mozárabe*, or, in English, mozarabic.

**Mudéjar:** This word refers to Moors living in Christian Spain. Moorish artistic elements in Christian architecture, such as horseshoe arches in a church, also are referred to as Mudéjar.

# ALHAMBRA'S ARCHITECTURAL HIGHLIGHTS

The **columns** used in the construction of the Alhambra are unique, with extraordinarily slender cylindrical shafts, concave base moldings, and carved rings decorating the upper extremities. The capitals have simple cylindrical bases under prism-shaped heads decorated in a variety of vegetal motifs. Nearly all of these columns support false arches constructed purely for decorative purposes. The 124 columns surrounding the Patio de los Leones (Court of the Lions) are the best examples.

**Cursive epigraphy** is used to quote the Koran and Arabic poems. Considered the finest example of this are the Ibn-Zamrak verses that decorate the walls of the Sala de las Dos Hermanas.

**Glazed ceramic tiles** covered with geometrical patterns in primary colors cover the walls of the Alhambra with a profusion of styles and shapes. Red, blue, and yellow are the colors of magic in Sufi tradition, while green is the life-giving color of Islam.

The **horseshoe arch**, widening before rounding off with lower ends extending around the circle until they begin to converge, was the quintessential Moorish architectural innovation, used not only for aesthetic and decorative purposes but because it allowed greater height than the classical, semicircular arch inherited from the Greeks and Romans. The horseshoe arch also had a mystical significance in recalling the shape of the *mihrab*, the prayer niche in the *qibla* wall of a mosque indicating the direction of prayer and suggesting a door to Mecca or to paradise. Horseshoe arches and arcades are found throughout the Alhambra.

The Koran describes paradise as "gardens underneath which rivers flow," and **water** is used as a practical and ornamental architectural element throughout the Alhambra. Whether used musically, as in the canals in the Patio de los Leones or visually, as in the reflecting pool of the Patio de los Arrayanes, water is used to enhance light, enlarge spaces, or provide musical background for a desert culture in love with the beauty and oasis-like properties of hydraulics in all its forms.

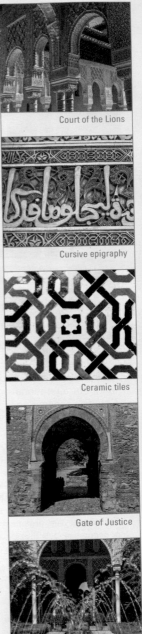

Court of the Lions

Cursive epigraphy

Ceramic tiles

Gate of Justice

Alhambra fountains

The Alcazaba was built chiefly by Nasrid kings in the 1300s.

## LAY OF THE LAND

The complex has three main parts: the Alcazaba, the Palacio Nazaríes (Nasrid Royal Palace), and the Generalife. Across from the main entrance is the original fortress, the **Alcazaba**. Here, the watchtower's great bell was once used to announce the opening and closing of the irrigation system on Granada's great plain.

A wisteria-covered walkway leads to the heart of the Alhambra, the **Palacios Nazaríes**. Here, delicate apartments, lazy fountains, and tranquil pools contrast vividly with the hulking fortifications outside. It is divided into three sections: the *mexuar*, where business, government, and palace administration were headquartered; the *serrallo*, a series of state rooms where the sultans held court and entertained their ambassadors; and the *harem*, which in its time was entered only by the sultan, his family, and their most trusted servants, most of them eunuchs. Nearby is the Renaissance **Palacio de Carlos V** (Palace of Charles V), featuring a perfectly square exterior but a circular interior courtyard. Designed by Pedro Machuca, a pupil of Michelangelo, it is where the sultan's private apartments once stood. Part of the building houses the free **Museo de la Alhambra**, devoted to Islamic art. Upstairs is the more modest **Museo de Bellas Artes**.

Over on Cerro del Sol (Hill of the Sun) is **Generalife**, the ancient summer palace of the Nasrid kings.

## TIMELINE

**1238** First Nasrid king, Ibn el-Ahmar, begins Alhambra.

**1391** Nasrid Palaces is completed.

**1492** Boabdil surrenders Granada to Ferdinand and Isabella, parents of King Henry VIII's first wife, Catherine of Aragon.

**1524** Carlos V begins Renaissance Palace.

**1812** Napoléonic troops arrive with plans to destroy Alhambra.

**1814** The Duke of Wellington sojourns here to escape the pressures of the Peninsular War.

**1829** Washington Irving lives on the premises and writes Tales of the *Alhambra*, reviving interest in the crumbling palace.

**1862** Granada municipality begins Alhambra restoration that continues to this day.

# ALHAMBRA'S PASSAGES OF TIME

From Columbus's commissioning to a bloody murder, historic events as well as everyday affairs happened between these walls.

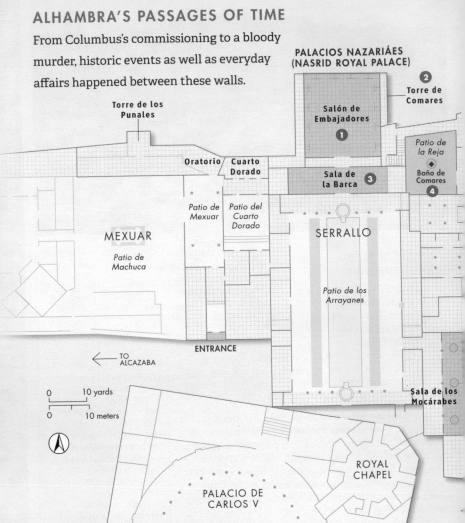

Tower of Comares and Patio de los Arrayanes

**❶** In **El Salón de Embajadores**, Boabdil drew up his terms of surrender, and Christopher Columbus secured royal support for his historic voyage in 1492. The carved wooden ceiling is a portrayal of the seven Islamic heavens, with six rows of stars topped by a seventh-heaven cupulino or micro-cupola.

**❷** **Torre de Comares**, a lookout in the corner of this hall is where Carlos V uttered his famous line, "Ill-fated the man who lost all this."

**❸** Mistakenly named from the Arabic word *baraka* (divine blessing), **Sala de la Barca** has a carved wooden ceiling often described as an inverted boat.

Sala de los Reyes

**7** Shhh, don't tell a secret here. In the Sala de los Ajimeces, a whisper in one corner can be clearly heard from the opposite corner.

**8** In the Sala de las Dos Hermanas, twin slabs of marble embedded in the floor are the "sisters," though Washington Irving preferred the story of a pair of captive Moorish beauties.

**9** In the Patio de Los Leones (Court of the Lions), a dozen crudely crafted lions (restored to their former glory in 2012) support the fountain at the center of this elegant courtyard, representing the signs of the zodiac sending water to the four corners.

**10** In the Sala de los Abencerrajes, Muley Hacen (father of Boabdil) murdered the male members of the Abencerraje family in revenge for their chief's seduction of his daughter Zoraya. The rusty stains in the fountain are said to be bloodstains left by the pile of Abencerraje heads.

The star-shaped cupola, reflected in the pool, is considered the Alhambra's most beautiful example of stalactite or honeycomb vaulting. The octagonal dome over the room is best viewed at sunset when the 16 small windows atop the dome admit sharp, low sunlight that refracts kaleidoscopically through the beehive-like prisms.

**11** In the Sala de los Reyes, the ceiling painting depicts the first 10 Nasrid rulers. It was painted by a Christian artist since Islamic artists were not allowed to usurp divine power by creating human or animal figures.

The overhead painting of the knight rescuing his lady from a savage man portrays chivalry, a concept introduced to Europe by Arabic poets.

**12** The terraces of Generalife grant incomparable views of the city.

Generalife gardens

Peinador de la Reina **5**

Apartamientos de Carlos V

Patio de Lindaraja

HAREM

**6** Mirador de Daraxa

Sala de las Dos Hermanas **8**

Sala de los Ajimeces **7**

Patio de los Leones

**9**

Sala de los Reyes **11**

Cistern

Sala de los Abencerrajes **10**

TO JARDINES DEL PARTAL, GENERALIFE **12** →

**4** The Baño de Comares is where the sultan's favorites luxuriated in brightly tiled pools beneath star-shape pinpoints of light from the ceiling above.

**5** El Peinador de la Reina, a nine-foot-square room atop a small tower was the Sultana's boudoir. The perforated marble slab was used to infiltrate perfumes while the queen performed her toilette. Washington Irving wrote his *Tales of the Alhambra* in this romantic tree-house-like perch.

**6** Sultana Zoraya often found refuge in this charming little balcony (Mirador de Daraxa) overlooking the Lindaraja garden.

# Realejo

## 👁 Sights

### Casa de los Tiros

**HISTORIC HOME** | This 16th-century palace, adorned with the coat of arms of the Grana Venegas family who owned it, was named House of the Shots for the musket barrels that protrude from its facade. The stairs to the upper-floor displays are flanked by portraits of miserable-looking Spanish royals, from Ferdinand and Isabella to Felipe IV. The highlight is the carved wooden ceiling in the Cuadra Dorada (Hall of Gold), adorned with gilded lettering and portraits of royals and knights. Old lithographs, engravings, and photographs show life in Granada in the 19th and early 20th centuries. ✉ *Calle Pavaneras 19, Realejo-San Matías* ☎ *600/143175* 🖥 *€2* ⊙ *Closed Mon.*

### El Cuarto Real

**NOTABLE BUILDING** | Just a block away from Casa de los Tiros is the beautifully restored El Cuarto Real, a 13th-century Nasrid palace which has decorations almost identical to the Alhambra. Only the fortified tower remains standing with its exquisite *qubba* (reception room) with stunning walls and ceiling motifs. The adjoining modern extension houses temporary art exhibitions, and the formal gardens make a peaceful place to rest. ✉ *Pl. de los Campos 6, Realejo-San Matías* ☎ *958/849111* 🖥 *€2* ⊙ *Closed Sun. afternoon and Mon.*

### Fundación Rodríguez-Acosta/Instituto Gómez-Moreno

**ARTS CENTER** | This nonprofit organization was founded at the behest of the painter José Marí Rodríguez-Acosta. Inside a typical *carmen*, it houses works of art, archaeological finds, and a library collected by the Granada-born scholar Manuel Gómez-Moreno Martínez. Other exhibits include valuable and unique objects from Asian cultures and the prehistoric and classical eras. ✉ *Callejón Niño del Rollo 8, Realejo-San Matías* ☎ *958/227497* ⊕ *www.fundacionrodriguezacosta.com* 🖥 *From €5* ⊙ *Closed afternoons.*

## 🍴 Restaurants

### ★ Damasqueros

**$$$$** | **SPANISH** | The modern, wood-paneled dining room and warm lighting form the perfect setting for the creative Andalusian cuisine cooked here by local chef Lola Marín, who learned her trade with some of Spain's top chefs, such as Martín Berasategui. The tasting menu changes weekly and always includes in-season produce in its six courses (cold and hot starters, fish, meat, and dessert). **Known for:** service; wine pairing; fresh local produce. 💲 *Average main: €52* ✉ *Calle Damasqueros 3, Realejo-San Matías* ☎ *958/210550* ⊕ *www.damasqueros.com* ⊙ *Closed Mon. No dinner Sun.*

### hicuri

**$** | **VEGETARIAN** | Even if you aren't a vegan, the plant-based menu won't disappoint at this quirky restaurant, just a block east of Casa de los Tiros. You'll find a good choice of food—there are even four types of vegan burgers with hand-cut French fries—while firm favorites with regulars include the vegetable lasagna and Cordon Bleu seitan. **Known for:** lunchtime menu; quirky artwork; choice of vegan food. 💲 *Average main: €10* ✉ *Plaza de los Girones 4, Realejo-San Matías* ☎ *858/987473* ⊕ *restaurantehicuriartvegan.com* ⊙ *Closed Sun.*

## 🛏 Hotels

### Gar Anat Hotel Boutique

**$$** | **HOTEL** | Once a humble hostel on the Granada leg of the Camino de Santiago pilgrimage route, the 17th-century restored palace now offers stylish boutique accommodation. **Pros:** eclectic decor; generous breakfast; central location. **Cons:** slight challenge to find by car; some rooms small and dark; street noise can be intrusive. $ *Rooms from: €110* ⊠ *Placeta de Peregrinos 2, Realejo-San Matías* ☎ *958/225528* ⊕ *www.hotelgaranat.com* ⇔ *15 rooms* ⦿ *No Meals.*

# Sacromonte

The third of Granada's three hills, the Sacromonte rises behind the Albayzín and is covered with prickly pear cacti and riddled with caverns. The Sacromonte has long been notorious as a domain of Granada's Gypsies and thus a den of thieves and scam artists, but its reputation is largely undeserved. The quarter is more like a quiet Andalusian *pueblo* (village) than a rough neighborhood.

Many of the quarter's colorful *cuevas* (caves) have been restored as middle-class homes, and some of the old spirit lives on in a handful of *zambras* (flamenco performances in caves, which are garishly decorated with brass plates and cooking utensils). These shows differ from formal flamenco shows in that the performers mingle with you, usually dragging one or two onlookers onto the floor for an improvised dance lesson. Ask your hotel to book you a spot on a *cueva* tour, which usually includes a walk through the neighboring Albayzín and a drink at a tapas bar in addition to the zambra.

## ◉ Sights

### Abadía de Sacromonte

CAVE | The caverns on Sacromonte are thought to have sheltered early Christians. In the 15th century, treasure hunters found bones inside and assumed they belonged to San Cecilio, the city's patron saint. Thus, the hill was sanctified—*sacro monte* (holy mountain)—and

this abbey was built on its summit. Audio guides are available in English. ⊠ *C. del Sacromonte, Sacromonte* ☎ *958/221445* ⊕ *sacromonteabbey.com* ⊠ *From €5.*

### Museo Cuevas del Sacromonte

OTHER MUSEUM | The ethnographical museum here shows how people lived in this area, and elsewhere in this interesting complex looks at Granada's flora and fauna. During the summer months, there are live flamenco concerts. Tours available in English.

⚠ **It's a steep walk to reach the center, even if you take Bus No. C2 (from Plaza Nueva) to shorten the distance.** ⊠ *Barranco de los Negros, Sacromonte* ☎ *958/215120* ⊕ *http://sacromontegranada.com/* ⊠ *€5.*

# Albayzín

Covering a hill of its own, across the Darro ravine from the Alhambra, this ancient Moorish neighborhood is a mix of dilapidated white houses and immaculate *carmenes* (private villas). It was founded in 1228 by Moors who had fled Baeza after Ferdinand III captured the city. Full of cobblestone alleyways and secret corners, the Albayzín guards its old Moorish roots jealously, though its 30 mosques were converted to baroque churches long ago. A stretch of the Moors' original city wall runs beside the ridge called the **Cuesta de la Alhacaba.**

If you're walking—the best way to explore—you can enter the Albayzín from either the Cuesta de Elvira or the Plaza Nueva. Alternatively, on foot or by taxi (parking is impossible), begin in the Plaza Santa Ana and follow the Carrera del Darro, Paseo Padre Manjón, and Cuesta del Chapíz. One of the highest points in the quarter, the plaza in front of the church of San Nicolás (*€3*)—the **Mirador de San Nicolás**—has one of the finest views in all of Granada: on the hill opposite, the turrets and towers of the Alhambra form a dramatic silhouette against the snowy peaks of the Sierra Nevada. The sight is most magical at dawn, dusk, and on nights when the Alhambra is floodlighted. Take note of the mosque just next to the church—views of the Alhambra from the mosque gardens are just as good as those from the Mirador de San Nicolás and a lot less crowded. Interestingly, given the area's Moorish history, the two sloping, narrow streets of Calderería Nueva and Calderería Vieja that meet at the top by the Iglesia San Gregorio have developed into something of a North African bazaar, full of shops and vendors selling clothes, bags, crafts, and trinkets. The numerous little teahouses and restaurants here have a decidedly Moroccan flavor.

■TIP→ **Many of the streets are cobbled so wear sturdy footwear with thick soles.**

## 👁 Sights

### Casa de los Pisa
**HISTORIC HOME** | Originally built in 1494 for the Pisa family, the claim to fame of this house is its relationship to San Juan de Dios, who came to Granada in 1538 and founded a charity hospital to take care of the poor. Befriended by the Pisa family, he was taken into their home when he fell ill in February 1550. A month later, he died there, at the age of 55. Since that time, devotees of the saint have traveled from around the world to this house with a stone Gothic facade, now run by the Hospital Order of St. John. Inside are numerous pieces of jewelry, furniture, priceless religious works of art, and an extensive collection of paintings and sculptures depicting St. John. ⊠ *Calle Convalecencia 1, Albaicín* 🕾 *958/222144* 🎫 *€3* 🕙 *Closed Sun. and afternoons.*

### El Bañuelo (*Little Bath House*)
**HISTORIC SIGHT** | These 11th-century Arab steam baths might be a little dark and dank now, but try to imagine them some

900 years ago, filled with Moorish beauties. Back then, the dull brick walls were backed by bright ceramic tiles, tapestries, and rugs. Light comes in through star-shape vents in the ceiling, à la the bathhouse in the Alhambra. ⊠ *Carrera del Darro 31, Albaicín* 🕾 *958/229738* 🎫 *€5 (ticket includes admission to Dar al-Horra).*

### Paseo Padre Manjón
**STREET** | Along the Río Darro, this paseo is also known as the Paseo de los Tristes (Promenade of the Sad Ones) because funeral processions once passed this way. The cafés and bars here are a good place for a coffee break. The park, dappled with wisteria-covered pergolas, fountains, and stone walkways, has a stunning view of the Alhambra's northern side. ⊠ *Albaicín.*

## 🍴 Restaurants

### El Mercader
**$$$** | **INTERNATIONAL** | Eclectic décor and innovative food are on offer at this cozy venue, off Plaza Nueva whose chef, Nuria de la Torre, won the local Culinary Masters competition in 2021. Her menu takes seasonal ingredients as its base while dishes combine local staples with unusual partners. **Known for:** innovative dishes; fun decor; attentive service. 🖇 *Average main: €20* ⊠ *Calle Imprenta 4, Centro* 🕾 *633/790440* 🕙 *Closed Mon. and Tues.*

### ★ El Trillo
**$$$** | **SPANISH** | Tucked away in the warren of alleyways in a restored Albayzín villa, this lovely restaurant offers perhaps the best food in the area. There's a formal dining room, outside garden with pear and quince trees, plus a roof terrace with Alhambra views. **Known for:** rice with wild boar; views of the Alhambra; fine dining. 🖇 *Average main: €20* ⊠ *Callejón del Aljibe del Trillo 3, Albaicín* 🕾 *958/225182* ⊕ *www.restaurante-eltrillo.com* 🕙 *Closed Tues.*

### Paprika

$$ | VEGETARIAN | Inside a pretty brick building and with an informal terrace sprawling over the wide steps of the Cuesta de Abarqueros, Paprika offer unpretentious vegan food. Most ingredients and wines are organic, and dishes include salads, stir-fries, and curries, such as Thai curry with tofu, coconut, and green curry sauce. **Known for:** organic ingredients; value plate of the day; choice of vegan food. ⑤ *Average main: €12* ✉ *Cuesta de Abarqueros 3, Albaicín* ☎ *958/804785* ⊕ *www.paprika-granada. com.*

### Ruta del Azafrán

$$ | SPANISH | A charming surprise nestled at the foot of the Albayzín by the Darro—this sleek contemporary space in the shadow of the Alhambra offers a selection of specialties. The menu is interesting and diverse and includes dishes like tuna *tataki* (a method of pounding fish in Japanese cuisine) with apple chutney and several different couscous dishes. **Known for:** tasting menus; views of the Alhambra, especially at night; international dishes. ⑤ *Average main: €16* ✉ *Paseo de los Tristes 1, Albaicín* ☎ *958/226882* ⊕ *rutadelazafran.com.*

## 🛏 Hotels

### ★ Casa Morisca

$$$ | B&B/INN | The architect who owns this 15th-century building transformed it into a hotel so distinctive that he received Spain's National Restoration Award for his preservation of original architectural elements, including barrel-vaulted brickwork, wooden ceilings, and the original pool. **Pros:** historic location; easy parking; award-winning design. **Cons:** slightly out of the town center; no restaurant on-site; stuffy interior rooms. ⑤ *Rooms from: €140* ✉ *Cuesta de la Victoria 9, Albaicín* ☎ *958/221100* ⊕ *www.hotelcasamorisca. com* ⇆ *14 rooms* ⦿ *No Meals.*

### Hotel Casa 1800

$$$ | HOTEL | A stone's throw from the Paseo de los Tristes, this restored 17th-century mansion has a fine, tiered patio. **Pros:** historic building; walking distance to most sights; deluxe suite has balcony with views of the Alhambra. **Cons:** no bar; rooms are small (but comfortable); on a street that doesn't permit cars. ⑤ *Rooms from: €150* ✉ *Calle Benalua 11, Albaicín* ☎ *958/210700* ⊕ *www. hotelcasa1800granada.com* ⇆ *25 rooms* ⦿ *No Meals.*

### Hotel Palacio Santa Inés

$$ | HOTEL | It's not often you get to stay in a 16th-century palace—and this one has a stunning location in the heart of the Albayzín. **Pros:** perfect location for exploring the Albayzín; some rooms have Alhambra views; quirky interiors. **Cons:** communal areas a little tired; some rooms rather dark; can't get there by car. ⑤ *Rooms from: €125* ✉ *Cuesta de Santa Inés 9, Albaicín* ☎ *958/222362* ⊕ *www. palaciosantaines.es* ⇆ *35 rooms* ⦿ *No Meals.*

## 🎭 Performing Arts

### FLAMENCO

#### Cueva de la Rocío

FOLK/TRADITIONAL DANCE | This is a good spot for authentic flamenco shows, staged nightly at 8, 9, 10, and 11. ✉ *C. del Sacromonte 70, Albaicín* ☎ *958/227129* ⊕ *cuevarocio.es* 🎟 *From €15.*

#### El Templo del Flamenco

FOLK/TRADITIONAL DANCE | Slightly off the beaten track (take a taxi to get here) and less touristy because of it, this venue has shows at 8 and 10 daily. ✉ *Calle Parnaleros Alto 41, Albaicín* ☎ *622/500052 Tickets, 654/373136 Information* ⊕ *eltemplodelflamenco.com/en* 🎟 *From €15.*

#### Jardines de Zoraya

FOLK/TRADITIONAL DANCE | This show doesn't take place in a cave, but the music and dance are some of the most authentic available. Daily flamenco shows are at 5.30, 8, and 10:30 pm. ✉ *Calle Panaderos 32, Albaicín* ☏ *958/206266* ⊕ *www.jardinesdezoraya.com* 🍴 *From €25.*

# Centro

## 👁 Sights

**Capilla Real** (*Royal Chapel*)
RELIGIOUS BUILDING | Catholic monarchs Isabella of Castile and Ferdinand of Aragón are buried at this shrine. When Isabella died in 1504, her body was first laid to rest in the Convent of San Francisco. The architect Enrique Egas began work on the Royal Chapel in 1506 and completed it 15 years later, creating a masterpiece of the ornate Gothic style now known in Spain as Isabelline. In 1521, Isabella's body was transferred to the Royal Chapel crypt, joined by that of her husband, Ferdinand, and later her daughter, Juana la Loca (Joanna the Mad); son-in-law, Felipe el Hermoso (Philip the Handsome); and Prince Felipe of Asturias. The **crypt** containing the coffins is simple, but it's topped by elaborate marble tombs showing Ferdinand and Isabella lying side by side. The **altarpiece** comprises 34 carved panels depicting religious and historical scenes. The **sacristy** holds Ferdinand's sword, Isabella's crown and scepter, and a fine collection of Flemish paintings once owned by Isabella. ✉ *Calle Oficios, Centro* ☏ *958/227848* ⊕ *www.capillareal-granada.com* 🍴 *€5.*

**Cathedral**
RELIGIOUS BUILDING | Carlos V commissioned the cathedral in 1521 because he considered the Capilla Real "too small for so much glory" and wanted to house his illustrious late grandparents someplace more worthy. Carlos undoubtedly had great intentions, as the cathedral was created by some of the finest architects of its time: Enrique Egas, Diego de Siloé, Alonso Cano, and sculptor Juan de Mena. Alas, his ambitions came to little, for the cathedral is a grand and gloomy monument, not completed until 1714 and never used as the crypt for his grandparents (or parents). Enter through a small door at the back, off the Gran Vía. Old hymnals are displayed throughout, and there's a museum, which includes a 14th-century gold-and-silver monstrance given to the city by Queen Isabella. ✉ *Gran Vía, Centro* ☏ *958/222959* 🍴 *€5 (including audio guide)* ☽ *Closed Sun. morning.*

**Centro José Guerrero**
ART GALLERY | Just across a lane from the cathedral and Capilla Real, this building houses colorful modern paintings by José Guerrero. Born in Granada in 1914, Guerrero traveled throughout Europe and lived in New York in the 1950s before returning to Spain. The center also runs excellent temporary contemporary art shows. ✉ *Calle Oficios 8, Centro* ☏ *958/225185* ⊕ *www.centroguerrero. es* 🍴 *Free* ☽ *Closed Sun. afternoon and Mon.*

**Corral del Carbón** (*Coal House*)
HISTORIC SIGHT | This building was used to store coal in the 19th century, but its history is much longer. Dating to the 14th century, it was used by Moorish merchants as a lodging house, and then by Christians as a theater. It's one of the oldest Moorish buildings in the city and the only Arab structure of its kind in Spain. ✉ *Calle Mariana Pineda, Centro* 🍴 *Free.*

## 🍴 Restaurants

**Bar Los Diamantes**
$$ | TAPAS | This lively bar (with a sister branch on Plaza Nueva) is a big favorite with locals and draws crowds whatever the time of year. Specialties include fried fish and seafood—try the *surtido*

*de pescado* (assortment of fried fish) to sample the best as well as *sesos* (fried lambs' brains). **Known for:** busy atmosphere; generous free tapa with first drink; fried fish. $ *Average main: €15* ⊠ *Plaza Bibrambla 2, Centro* ☎ *958/348255* ⊕ *www.barlosdiamantes.com.*

### Bodegas Castañeda

$$$ | SPANISH | A block from the cathedral across Gran Vía, this is a delightfully typical Granada bodega with low ceilings and dark wood furniture. In addition to the wines, specialties here are plates of cheese, pâté, and *embutidos* (cold meats). **Known for:** Spanish tortilla with creamy aioli; atmospheric bar; tapas. $ *Average main: €18* ⊠ *Calle Almireceros 1–3, Centro* ☎ *958/215464.*

### ★ Café Botánico

$$ | TAPAS | Southeast of Granada's cathedral, this is modern hot spot is a world apart from Granada's usual traditional tapas bar. It attracts an eclectic crowd of students, families, and businesspeople for a diverse, international menu, including Mexican fajitas, poke bowls, and Thai cod all sitting side by side. **Known for:** homemade desserts; good-value lunch deal; international menu. $ *Average main: €15* ⊠ *Calle Málaga 3, Centro* ☎ *958/271598.*

### La Bodega de Antonio

$$ | SPANISH | Just off Calle Puentezuelas, this authentic patio complete with original pillars provides a cozy vibe. Specials include the house cod (with prawns and clams) and Galician-style octopus, best enjoyed with a *cerdito* (a "little pig" ceramic jug of sweet white wine, so named for its snout pourer). **Known for:** Galician-style octopus; choice of croquettes; generous portions. $ *Average main: €14* ⊠ *Calle Jardines 4, Centro* ☎ *958/252275* ⊙ *Closed Wed. and Aug.*

### ★ La Brujidera

$$ | TAPAS | Also known simply as Casa de Vinos (Wine House), this place, up a pedestrian street just behind Plaza Nueva, is a must for Spanish wine lovers. The cozy interior is reminiscent of a ship's cabin, with wood paneling lining the walls, along with bottles of more than 150 Spanish wines. **Known for:** vermouth and sherries on tap; meat and cheese boards; long wine list. $ *Average main: €12* ⊠ *Monjas del Carmen 2, Centro* ☎ *687/851507* ⊙ *Closed 1 wk in Feb.*

### Oliver

$$$ | SPANISH | The interior may look a bit bare, but whatever this fish restaurant lacks in warmth it makes up for with the food. It serves simple but high-quality dishes like grilled mullet, dorado baked in salt, prawns with garlic, and monkfish in saffron sauce. **Known for:** migas (fried bread crumbs); fresh fish; tapas bar. $ *Average main: €18* ⊠ *Pl. Pescadería 12, Centro* ☎ *958/262200* ⊕ *restauranteoliver.com* ⊙ *Closed Sun.*

### Om-Kalsum

$ | MOROCCAN | The Moroccan tapas at this small and bustling venue make a pleasant change from the traditional local fare. Tagine, couscous, and kefta are all menu staples where you'll also find a selection of Middle Eastern dishes, also available in vegetarian versions. **Known for:** lively atmosphere; selection of tapas; Moroccan tapas. $ *Average main: €8* ⊠ *Calle Jardines 17, Centro* ⊙ *Closed Sun.*

### Pastelería López-Mezquita

$ | SPANISH | Sweet and savory treats come into their own at this family-owned business in the city center. Top of the specialty list are *piononos* (sponge bites filled with caramel and custard) and *pastela* (Moroccan chicken pie). **Known for:** pastela; cakes and cookies; piononos (sponge bites with custard). $ *Average main: €5* ⊠ *Calle Reyes Católicos 39, Centro* ☎ *958/221205* ⊙ *Closed Sun. afternoon.*

## Tinta Fina

$$$ | SPANISH | Underneath the arches just off Puerta Real, this modern bar and restaurant has a reputation for being one of Granada's most chic venues. It's known for fresh seafood, including oysters and red shrimp, though generous portions of char-grilled steaks, steak tartare, and fresh foie gras are a hit with carnivores. **Known for:** chic atmosphere; cocktail and G&T menus; seafood. $ *Average main: €20* ✉ *Calle Angel Ganivet 5, Centro* ☎ *958/100041* ⊕ *www.tintafinarestaurante.com.*

 Hotels

## Hospes Palacio de los Patos

$$$$ | HOTEL | This beautifully restored palace is unmissable, sitting proudly on its own in the middle of one of Granada's busiest shopping streets. **Pros:** central location; great spa and restaurant; historic setting. **Cons:** some rooms are at street level; some street noise; parking not included. $ *Rooms from: €250* ✉ *Calle Solarillo de Gracia 1, Centro* ☎ *958/535790* ⊕ *www.hospes.com* ⮑ *40 rooms* ꙴ *No Meals.*

## ★ Hostal Rodri

$ | HOTEL | This comfortable and quiet hotel lies conveniently off Plaza de la Trinidad near the cathedral and is a good option for cheaper lodging in a city with so many upscale accommodations. **Pros:** central location; value; clean, comfortable rooms. **Cons:** could be too basic for some; no breakfast on site; some rooms on small side. $ *Rooms from: €50* ✉ *Calle Laurel de las Tablas 9, Centro* ☎ *958/288043* ⊕ *www.hostalrodri.com* ⮑ *10 rooms* ꙴ *No Meals.*

## Hotel Párraga Siete

$ | HOTEL | This family-run hotel in the heart of the old quarter within easy walking distance of sights and restaurants offers excellent value and amenities superior to its official two-star rating. **Pros:** central, quiet location; easy nearby parking; good on-site restaurant. **Cons:** no historic character; interiors might be too sparse for some; some rooms are very small. $ *Rooms from: €80* ✉ *Calle Párraga 7, Centro* ☎ *958/264227* ⊕ *www.hotelparragasiete.com* ⮑ *20 rooms* ꙴ *No Meals.*

## Palacio de los Navas

$$$ | B&B/INN | In the center of the city, this palace was built by aristocrat Francisco Navas in the 16th century and it later became the Casa de Moneda (the Mint); its original architectural features blend well with modern ones. **Pros:** great location; rooms are set around a beautiful interior patio; peaceful oasis during the day. **Cons:** breakfast uninspiring; can be noisy at night; parking difficult. $ *Rooms from: €130* ✉ *Calle Navas 1, Centro* ☎ *958/215760* ⊕ *www.hotelpalaciodelosnavas.com* ⮑ *19 rooms* ꙴ *No Meals.*

Ⓨ Nightlife

## Bohemia Jazz Café

LIVE MUSIC | This atmospheric jazz bar has piano performances and occasional live bands, Tuesday through Sunday. ✉ *Pl. de los Lobos 11, Centro.*

Ⓢ Shopping

## Artesanías González

CRAFTS | Not far from La Alhambra, this is one of the best and longest-established places to buy inlaid wood *taracea* on handmade chessboards, boxes, side tables, and coasters. ✉ *Cuesta de Gomérez 12, Centro* ☎ *657/987239.*

# Outskirts of Granada

Ⓞ Sights

## Casa-Museo Federico García Lorca

HISTORIC HOME | Granada's most famous native son, the poet Federico García Lorca, gets his due here, in the middle of a park devoted to him on the southern fringe of the city. Lorca's onetime summer home, **La Huerta de San Vicente,** is now a museum (guided tours only)—run by his niece Laura García Lorca—with such artifacts as his beloved piano and changing exhibits on specific aspects of his life. ⊠ *Parque García Lorca, Virgen Blanca, Arabial* ☎ *958/258466* ⊕ *www. huertadesanvicente.com* 🎫 *€3 (free Wed.)* ⊘ *Closed Mon.*

## Monasterio de la Cartuja

RELIGIOUS BUILDING | The exterior of this Carthusian monastery in northern Granada is sober and monolithic, but inside are twisted, multicolor marble columns; a profusion of gold, silver, tortoiseshell, and ivory; intricate stucco; and the extravagant sacristy—it's easy to see why it has been called the Christian answer to the Alhambra. Among its wonders are the trompe l'oeil spikes, shadows and all, in the Sanchez Cotan cross over the *Last Supper* painting at the west end of the refectory. It was begun in 1506 and moved to its present site in 1516, though construction continued for the next 300 years. If you're lucky, you may see small birds attempting to land on these faux perches. You can reach it by Bus No. N7. ⊠ *C. de Alfacar, Cartuja* ☎ *958/161932* 🎫 *€5.*

## Parque de las Ciencias (*Science Park*)

SCIENCE MUSEUM | FAMILY | Across from Granada's convention center and easily reached on Bus No. C4, this science museum is one of the most visited in museums Andalusia. It has a planetarium and interactive demonstrations of scientific experiments. The 165-foot observation tower has views to the south and west. ⊠ *Av. del Mediterráneo s/n, Zaidín*

958/131900 ⊕ www.parqueciencias. com ✉ From €7 🕙 Closed Mon.

## 🍴 Restaurants

### Restaurante Arriaga

$$$$ | **BASQUE** | Run by Basque chef Álvaro Arriaga, this restaurant sits on the top floor of the Museo de la Memoria de Andalucía just outside the city (it's well worth the taxi drive) and has panoramic views of Granada with the Sierra Nevada behind. Choose from two tasting menus (€75 for six dishes and €90 for nine dishes), both with one surprise after another and available with Andalusian wine pairing. **Known for:** panoramic views of Granada; culinary surprises (the menu starts with dessert!); tasting menus. Ⓢ *Average main: €75* ⊠ *Av. de las Ciencias 2, Armilla* 958/132619 ⊕ *www. restaurantearriaga.com* 🕙 *Closed Mon., no dinner Sun. or Tues.*

# Priego de Córdoba

*103 km (64 miles) southeast of Córdoba, 25 km (15 miles) southeast of Zuheros.*

The jewel of Córdoba's countryside is Priego de Córdoba, a town of 22,500 inhabitants at the foot of Monte Tinosa. Wander down Calle del Río, opposite the town hall, to see 18th-century mansions, once the homes of silk merchants. At the end of the street is the Fuente del Rey (King's Fountain), with some 130 water jets, built in 1803. Don't miss the lavish baroque churches of La Asunción and La Aurora or the Barrio de la Villa, an old Moorish quarter with a maze of narrow streets of white-walled buildings. If you plan to visit several monuments, buy the Bono turístico (€5) to save on admission prices.

## GETTING HERE AND AROUND

Priego has reasonable bus service from Córdoba (2½ hours) and Granada (1½ hours), although your best bet is to visit by car en route to either of these cities. Once there, it's perfect for pedestrian exploration.

## VISITOR INFORMATION

**CONTACTS Priego de Córdoba.** ⊠ *Pl. de la Constitución 3, Priego de Córdoba* 957/700625 ⊕ *www.turismodepriego. com.*

## 🍴 Restaurants

### La Pianola (*Casa Pepe*)

$ | **SPANISH** | Expect cheap, cheerful, and lively dining at this small venue, a couple of blocks south of the castle and usually packed with locals. On the menu are usual Córdoba staples including oxtail, but the specialties here are the *saquito de boletus* (mushroom pastry) and *carrillada de cerdo* (roast pork cheek). **Known for:** delicious French toast for dessert; good tapas; value dining. Ⓢ *Average main: €10* ⊠ *Calle Obispo Caballero 6, Priego de Córdoba* 957/700409 🕙 *Closed Mon.*

## 🛏 Hotels

### Casa Baños de la Villa

$$$ | **HOTEL** | Tucked at the heart of Priego's bright white center, this boutique hotel offers an oasis of peace and quiet, plus the chance to enjoy the in-house spa pool and Turkish bath (included in the price). **Pros:** central location; in-house spa; friendly hosts. **Cons:** no exterior views from rooms; some might find the decor a little brash; monotonous breakfast. Ⓢ *Rooms from: €130* ⊠ *Calle Real 63, Priego de Córdoba* 957/547274 ⊕ *www.casabanosdelavilla.com* ⇱ 9 *rooms* ⦿| *Free Breakfast.*

### Hotel-Museo Patria Chica

$$ | **HOTEL** | This charming hotel in a fully restored 19th-century mansion has so

many antiques and memorabilia that the term "hotel-museum" really does live up to its name. **Pros:** central location; pool and restaurant on-site; period furnishings. **Cons:** small bathrooms; slightly out of the town center; quiet. ⑤ *Rooms from: €120 ⊠ Carrera de las Monjas 47, Priego de Córdoba ☎ 957/058385 ⊕ www. hotelpatriachica.com ⤳ 15 rooms* ⦿| *No Meals.*

# Baeza

*48 km (30 miles) northeast of Jaén on N321.*

The historic town of Baeza, nestled between hills and olive groves, is one of the best-preserved old towns in Spain. Founded by the Romans, it later housed the Visigoths and became the capital of a Moorish taifa, one of some two dozen mini-kingdoms formed after the Ummayad Caliphate was subdivided in 1031. Ferdinand III captured Baeza in 1227, and for the next 200 years it stood on the frontier of the Moorish kingdom of Granada. In the 16th and 17th centuries, local nobles gave the city a wealth of Renaissance palaces.

## GETTING HERE AND AROUND

Frequent buses (10 per day on weekdays, 7 per day on weekends; *ALSA* 902/422242) connect Baeza with Jaén (45 minutes) and Úbeda, although a private car is the best option given the remoteness of the town and that you may want to explore nearby Úbeda on the same day. Baeza is small and flat, and with its sights clustered around the very center it's very easy to explore on foot.

## TOURS

### Semer Guided Tours

**GUIDED TOURS** | Two-and-a-half-hour guided tours around Baeza (in English, minimum two people, Tuesday–Sunday) recount the history, culture, and traditions of the town. Tours of Úbeda are also available, with a discount for combined tours of both towns. ⊠ *Baeza* ☎ *953/757916 ⊕ visitasguiadasubedaybaeza.com* ⤳ *From €13.*

## VISITOR INFORMATION

**CONTACTS Baeza.** ⊠ *Pl. del Pópulo, Baeza* ☎ *953/779982.*

## ◉ Sights

### Ayuntamiento (*Town Hall*)

**GOVERNMENT BUILDING** | Baeza's town hall was designed by cathedral master Andrés de Vandelvira. The facade is ornately decorated with a mix of religious and pagan imagery. Look between the balconies for the coats of arms of Felipe II, the city of Baeza, and the magistrate Juan de Borja. Ask at the tourist office about visits to the *salón de plenos,* a meeting hall with painted, carved woodwork. ⊠ *Pl. Cardenal s/n, Baeza.*

### Baeza Cathedral

**CHURCH** | Originally begun by Ferdinand III on the site of a former mosque, the cathedral was largely rebuilt by Andrés de Vandelvira, architect of Jaén's cathedral, between 1570 and 1593, though the west front has architectural influences from an earlier period. A fine 14th-century rose window crowns the 13th-century Puerta de la Luna (Moon Door). Don't miss the baroque silver monstrance (a vessel in which the consecrated Host is exposed for the adoration of the faithful), which is carried in Baeza's Corpus Christi processions—the piece is kept in a concealed niche behind a painting, but you can see it in all its splendor by putting a coin in a slot to reveal the hiding place. Next to the monstrance is the entrance to the clock tower, where a small donation and a narrow spiral staircase take you to one of the best views of Baeza. The remains of the original mosque are in the cathedral's Gothic cloisters. ⊠ *Pl. de Santa María, Baeza* ☎ *953/744157* ⛭ *€6.*

## Casa del Pópulo

HISTORIC HOME | Located in the central paseo—where the Plaza del Pópulo (or Plaza de los Leones) and Plaza de la Constitución (or Plaza del Mercado Viejo) merge to form a cobblestone square—this graceful town house was built around 1530. The first Mass of the Reconquest was supposedly celebrated on its curved balcony; it now houses Baeza's tourist office. ⊠ *Pl. del Pópulo, Baeza.*

## Convento de San Francisco

HISTORIC SIGHT | This 16th-century convent is one of Vandelvira's religious architectural masterpieces. The building was damaged by the French army and partially destroyed by a light earthquake in the early 1800s, but you can see its restored remains. ⊠ *Calle de San Francisco, Baeza.*

## Museo de Baeza

HISTORY MUSEUM | Tucked away behind the tourist office, the Baeza Museum is in itself a museum piece. Housed in a 15th-century noble palace, the facade and interiors are home to an interesting display of Baeza's history, from Roman remains to more recent religious paintings. ⊠ *Calle Casas Nuevas, Baeza* 🕾 *953/741582* 🖭 *€2* ◴ *Closed Mon.*

## 🍽 Restaurants

### Palacio de Gallego

$$$ | SPANISH | Located next to the cathedral, this is one of the best restaurants in town, known for its barbecue and roasted dishes. If you're not too hungry, enjoy tapas in the bar. **Known for:** outdoor terrace; red tuna steak; barbecue. 🖇 *Average main: €20* ⊠ *Calle Santa Catalina, Baeza* 🕾 *695/117175* ◴ *Closed Tues. No lunch Wed.*

# Úbeda

*9 km (5½ miles) northeast of Baeza on N321.*

Úbeda's *casco antiguo* (old town) is one of the most outstanding enclaves of 16th-century architecture in Spain. It's a stunning surprise in the heart of Jaén's olive groves, set in the shadow of the wild Sierra de Cazorla mountain range. For crafts enthusiasts, this is Andalusia's capital for many kinds of artisan goods. Follow signs to the Zona Monumental, where there are countless Renaissance palaces and stately mansions, though most are closed to the public.

## GETTING HERE AND AROUND

Frequent buses (10 weekdays, 7 weekends; *ALSA* 902/422242) connect Úbeda with Jaén (one hour) and Baeza, although a private car is the best option given the remoteness of the town and that you may want to explore nearby Baeza in the same day. Úbeda's sights are all within easy reach of the center so exploring on foot is easy.

## TOURS

### Semer Guided Tours

⊠ *Calle Juan Montilla 3, Úbeda* 🕾 *953/757916* ⊕ *https://visitasguiadasubedaybaeza.com/.*

## 👁 Sights

### Ayuntamiento Antiguo (*Old Town Hall*)

NOTABLE BUILDING | Begun in the early 16th century but restored as a beautiful arcaded baroque palace in 1680, the former town hall is now a conservatory of music. From the hall's upper balcony, the town council watched celebrations and autos-da-fé ("acts of faith"—executions of heretics sentenced by the Inquisition) in the square below. You can't enter the town hall, but on the north side you can visit the 13th-century church of San Pablo, with an Isabelline south portal. ⊠ *Pl.*

Primero de Mayo, Úbeda ⊕ Off Calle María de Molina ☎ 953/750637 ☞ Church free ☾ Closed Mon.

### Hospital de Santiago

**NOTABLE BUILDING** | Sometimes jokingly called the Escorial of Andalusia (in allusion to Felipe II's monolithic palace and monastery outside Madrid), this is a huge, angular building in the modern section of town and yet another one of Vandelvira's masterpieces in Úbeda. The plain facade is adorned with ceramic medallions, and over the main entrance is a carving of Santiago Matamoros (St. James the Moorslayer) in his traditional horseback pose. Inside are an arcaded patio and a grand staircase. Now a cultural center, it holds many of the events at the Festival of Ubeda, celebrating music and dance in May and June (⊕ www. festivaldeubeda.com). ✉ Av. Cristo Rey, Úbeda ☎ 953/750842 ☞ Free ☾ Closed Sun. in July, and weekends in Aug.

### Sacra Capilla de El Salvador

**RELIGIOUS BUILDING** | The Plaza Vázquez de Molina, in the heart of the casco antiguo, is the site of this building, which is photographed so often that it's become the city's unofficial symbol. It was built by Vandelvira, but he based his design on some 1536 plans by Diego de Siloé, architect of Granada's cathedral. Considered one of the masterpieces of Spanish Renaissance religious art, the chapel was sacked in the frenzy of church burnings at the outbreak of the civil war, but it retains its ornate western facade and altarpiece, which has a rare Berruguete sculpture. ✉ Pl. Vázquez de Molina, Úbeda ☎ 609/279905 ☞ €5 (free Tues.–Thurs at. 10–10.30.

### ★ Sinagoga del Agua

**RELIGIOUS BUILDING** | This 13th-century synagogue counts among Úbeda's most amazing discoveries. Entirely underground and known as the Water Synagogue for the wells and natural spring under the mikvah, it comprises seven areas open to visitors, including the main area of worship, mikvah, women's gallery, and rabbi's quarters. During summer solstice the sun's rays illuminate the stairway, providing the only natural light in the synagogue. ✉ Calle Roque Rosas, Úbeda ☎ 953/758150 ⊕ www. sinagogadelagua.com ☞ €5.

## 🍴 Restaurants

### Asador de Santiago

$$$ | **SPANISH** | At this adventurous restaurant just off the main street, the chef prepares both Spanish classics, like white shrimp from Huelva and slow-roasted local lamb and goat, as well as innovative dishes like sashimi de atún rojo con ajo blanco de piñones (red tuna with pine nut garlic soup) and lomo de ciervo en escabeche (venison steak in pickled sauce). The candle-filled interior is more traditional than the bar and has terra-cotta tiles, dark wood furnishings, and crisp white linens. **Known for:** roast meats; Spanish classics; fine dining. ⑤ Average main: €25 ✉ Av. Cristo Rey 4, Úbeda ☎ 953/750463 ⊕ asadordesantiago.com ☾ No dinner Sun.

### Cantina La Estación

$$$ | **SPANISH** | Meals here, one of Úbeda's top restaurants, are served in a train-carriage interior decorated with railway memorabilia, while tapas reign at an outside terrace and at the bar. This distinctive eatery serves tasting menus and always has a guiso del día (stew of the day) as well as creative dishes like milhojas de cordero con boniato (lamb millefeuille with sweet potato). **Known for:** fun interior; innovative dishes; extensive and reasonably priced wine menu. ⑤ Average main: €18 ✉ Cuesta de la Rodadera 1, Úbeda ☎ 687/777230 ☾ Closed Wed. No dinner Tues. and July.

### Taberna Misa de 12

$$$ | **SPANISH** | This small bar has the best position on the leafy square, one block

from the Plaza del Ayuntamiento, and the pleasant outside terrace is the best place to enjoy the tapas. Despite the tiny kitchen, the menu stretches long and includes glazed artichokes, red tuna tartare, and Iberian pork cuts. **Known for:** outdoor dining; wine list; tapas. ⑤ *Average main: €20* ⊠ *Pl. Primero de Mayo 7, Úbeda* ☎ *622/480049* ⊕ *www.misade12. com* ◑ *Closed Mon.*

## 🛏 Hotels

### ★ Palacio de la Rambla
**$$ | B&B/INN |** In old Úbeda, this stunning 16th-century mansion has been in the same family since it was built—it still hosts the Marquesa de la Rambla when she's in town—and eight of the rooms are available for overnighters. **Pros:** central location; all rooms have access to the garden; elegant style. **Cons:** some areas a little tired; grandiosity not for everyone; not much parking. ⑤ *Rooms from: €125* ⊠ *Pl. del Marqués 1, Úbeda* ☎ *953/750196* ⊕ *www.palaciodelarambla. com* ⌁ *8 rooms* ◎ *Free Breakfast.*

### ★ Parador de Úbeda
**$$$$ | HOTEL |** This splendid parador is in a 16th-century ducal palace in a prime location on the Plaza Vázquez de Molina, next to the Capilla del Salvador. **Pros:** elegant surroundings; excellent restaurant; perfect location. **Cons:** could be too formal for some; church bells in the morning; parking is difficult. ⑤ *Rooms from: €210* ⊠ *Pl. Vázquez de Molina s/n, Úbeda* ☎ *953/750345* ⊕ *www.parador.es* ⌁ *36 rooms* ◎ *No Meals.*

## 🛍 Shopping

### Alfarería Góngora
**CERAMICS |** All kinds of ceramics are sold here. ⊠ *Calle Cuesta de la Merced 32, Úbeda* ☎ *953/754605.*

### Alfarería Tito
**CERAMICS |** The extrovert Juan Tito can often be found at the potter's wheel in his rambling shop, which is packed with ceramics of every size and shape. ⊠ *Pl. del Ayuntamiento 12, Úbeda* ☎ *953/751302* ⊕ *www.alfareriatito.com.*

### Pablo Tito
**CERAMICS |** Clay sculptures of characters from *Don Quixote,* fired by Pablo Tito in an old Moorish-style kiln, are the specialty of this studio and shop (also online). There is also a museum (Monday through Saturday 8–2 and 4–8, Sunday 10–2) on the premises. ⊠ *Calle Valencia 22, Úbeda* ☎ *953/751496* ⊕ *pablotito.es/ tienda.*

# The Sierra Nevada

## 👁 Sights

### Mulhacén
**MOUNTAIN |** To the east of Granada, the mighty Mulhacén, the highest peak in mainland Spain, soars to 11,427 feet. Legend has it that it came by its name when Boabdil, the last Moorish king of Granada, deposed his father, Abul Hassan Ali, and had the body buried at the summit of the mountain so that it couldn't be desecrated. For more information on trails to the two summits, check the National Park Service's site (⊕ www.nevadensis.com). ⊠ *Sierra Nevada.*

### Pico de Veleta
**MOUNTAIN |** Peninsular Spain's second-highest mountain is 11,125 feet high. The view from its summit across the Alpujarras to the sea at distant Motril is stunning, and on a very clear day you can see the coast of North Africa. When the snow melts (July and August) you can drive or take a minibus from the Albergue Universitario (Universitario Mountain

Refuge) to within around 400 yards of the summit—a trail takes you to the top in around 45 minutes.

■TIP→ **It's cold up there, so take a warm jacket and scarf, even if Granada is sizzling hot.** ⊠ *Sierra Nevada.*

## ⚙ Activities

### SKIING

**Estación de Esquí Sierra Nevada**

SNOW SPORTS | FAMILY | Europe's southernmost ski resort is one of its best equipped. At the Pradollano and Borreguiles stations, there's good skiing from December through April or May; each has a special snowboarding circuit, floodlighted night slopes, a children's ski school, and après-ski sun and swimming in the Mediterranean less than an hour away. In winter, buses to Pradollano leave Granada's bus station three times a day on weekdays and four times on weekends and holidays. Tickets are €9 round-trip. As for Borreguiles, you can get there only on skis. There's an information center (⊕ www.sierranevada.es/en) at Plaza de Andalucia 4. ⊠ *Sierra Nevada.*

# The Alpujarras

*Village of Lanjarón: 46 km (29 miles) south of Granada.*

A trip to the Alpujarras, on the southern slopes of the Sierra Nevada, takes you to one of Andalusia's highest, most remote, and most scenic areas, home for decades to painters, writers, and a considerable foreign population. The Alpujarras region was originally populated by Moors fleeing the Christian Reconquest (from Seville after its fall in 1248, then from Granada after 1492). To this day, the Galicians' descendants continue the Moorish custom of weaving rugs and blankets in the traditional Alpujarran colors of red,

green, black, and white, and they sell their crafts in many of the villages. Be on the lookout for handmade basketry and pottery as well.

Houses here are squat and square; they spill down the southern slopes of the Sierra Nevada, bearing a strong resemblance to the Berber homes in the Rif Mountains, just across the Mediterranean in Morocco. If you're driving, the road as far as Lanjarón and Orgiva is smooth sailing; after that come steep, twisting mountain roads with few gas stations. Beyond sightseeing, the area is a haven for outdoor activities such as hiking and horseback riding. Inquire at the **Information Point** at Plaza de la Libertad, at Pampaneira.

## ⊙ Sights

### Lanjarón and Nearby Villages

TOWN | The western entrance to the Alpujarras is some 46 km (29 miles) from Granada at Lanjarón. This spa town is famous for its mineral water, collected from the melting snows of the Sierra Nevada and drunk throughout Spain. Orgiva, the next and largest town in the Alpujarras, has a 17th-century castle. Here you can leave the A348 and follow signs for the villages of the Alpujarras Altas (High Alpujarras), including Pampaneira, Capileira, and especially Trevélez, which lies on the slopes of the Mulhacén at 4,840 feet above sea level. Reward yourself with a plate of the local *jamón serrano*. Trevélez has three levels—the Barrio Alto, Barrio Medio, and Barrio Bajo—and the butchers are concentrated in the lowest section (Bajo). The higher levels have narrow cobblestone streets, whitewashed houses, and shops. ⊠ *Lanjarón.*

# 🛏 Hotels

## Hotel Alcadima

$ | **HOTEL** | **FAMILY** | One of the best-value hotels in the area, this pleasant if unfancy hotel in the rustic spa town of Lanjarón makes a good base for exploring the lower part of the Alpujarras. **Pros:** swimming pool; two-bedroom suites are ideal for families; excellent restaurant. **Cons:** down an unattractive side street; could be too plain for some; Lanjarón isn't the prettiest village in the area. ⑤ *Rooms from:* €65 ✉ *Calle Francisco Tarrega 3, Lanjarón* ☎ *958/770809* ⊕ *www.alcadima.com* 🛏 *45 rooms* ⑩ *No Meals.*

## Los Tinaos

$ | **APARTMENT** | Located on the way to Trevélez, in the pretty whitewashed village of Bubión that almost clings to the mountainside, these comfortable apartments (for two or four people) come squeaky-clean, with open log fires as well as central heating, and sweeping views across the valley. **Pros:** valley views; bar serving locally produced wine; a short walk from Pitres. **Cons:** steep walk down; could be too basic for some; apartments on the small side. ⑤ *Rooms from: €65* ✉ *Calle Parras 2, Bubión* ☎ *958/763217* ⊕ *www.lostinaos.com* 🛏 *10 rooms* ⑩ *No Meals.*

# Chapter 13

# COSTA DEL SOL AND COSTA DE ALMERÍA

13

Updated by
Joanna Styles

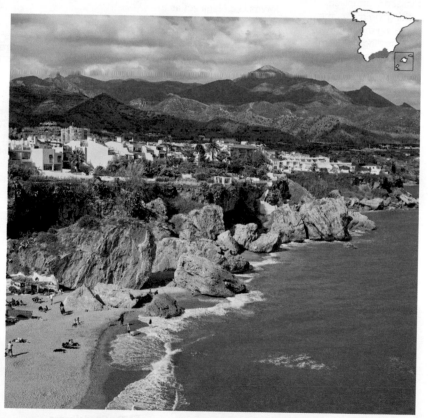

| ⊙ Sights | 🍴 Restaurants | 🛏 Hotels | 🛍 Shopping | ▼ Nightlife |
|---|---|---|---|---|
| ★★★★☆ | ★★★★★ | ★★★★☆ | ★★★★☆ | ★★★☆☆ |

# WELCOME TO COSTA DEL SOL AND COSTA DE ALMERÍA

## TOP REASONS TO GO

★ **Enjoy the sun and sand:** Relax at any of the beaches; they're all free, though in summer there isn't much towel space.

★ **Soak up the atmosphere:** Spend a day in Málaga, Picasso's birthplace, visiting the museums, exploring the old town, and strolling the Palm Walkway in the port.

★ **Check out Puerto Banús:** Wine, dine, and celebrity-watch at the Costa del Sol's most luxurious and sophisticated port town.

★ **Visit Cabo de Gata:** This protected natural reserve is one of the wildest and most beautiful stretches of coast in Spain.

★ **Shop for souvenirs:** Check out the weekly market in one of the Costa resorts to pick up bargain-price souvenirs, including ceramics.

The towns and resorts along the southeastern Spanish coastline vary considerably according to whether they lie to the east or to the west of Málaga. To the east are the Costa de Almería and the Costa Tropical, less developed stretches of coastline. Towns like Nerja act as a gateway to the dramatic mountainous region of La Axarquía. West from Málaga along the Costa del Sol proper, the strip between Torremolinos and Marbella is the most densely populated. Seamless though it may appear, as one resort merges into the next, each town has a distinctive character, with its own sights, charms, and activities.

**1 The Cabo de Gata Nature Reserve.** Wild nature and unspoiled beaches in Spain's most southeasterly corner.

**2 Agua Amarga.** Picturesque fishing resort at the heart of the Cabo de Gata.

**3 Almería.** A vibrant city and one of Spain's top spots for gastronomy.

**4 Almuñécar.** A traditional seaside town with two lovely beaches.

**5 Nerja.** Pretty white town perched on the cliffs

and home to the famous Nerja Caves.

**6 The Axarquía.** High mountains dotted with pretty white villages.

**7 Málaga.** The capital of the Costa del Sol and Spain's Museum City.

**8 Antequera.** A historic town with an impressive list of ancient monuments.

**9 The Guadalhorce Valley.** Home to a

spectacular river gorge and the Caminito del Rey walkway.

**10 Torremolinos.** Bustling resort with excellent beaches.

**11 Fuengirola.** Family-friendly seaside town, popular with expat residents.

**12 Mijas.** Stunning white village with panoramic views over the coastline.

**13 Marbella.** A favorite with the international jet set and a center for glitz and glamour.

**14 Ojén.** Pretty white village and the gateway to some excellent mountain walking.

**15 Estepona.** Attractive resort town famous for its murals and orchids.

**16 Casares.** Spectacular white village perched on a rocky outcrop.

**17 Tarifa.** Europe's kitesurf capital and home to miles of sandy beaches.

**18 Gibraltar.** "The Rock" is an extraordinary combination of Spain and Great Britain, with a fascinating history.

# EATING AND DRINKING WELL ALONG SPAIN'S SOUTHERN COAST

Beachside dining on the Costa del Sol.

Spain's southern coast is known for fresh fish and seafood, grilled or quickly fried in olive oil. Sardines roasted on spits are popular along the Málaga coast, while upland towns offer more robust mountain fare, especially in Almería.

*Chiringuitos,* small shanties along the beaches, are summer-only Costa del Sol restaurants that serve fish fresh off the boats. Málaga is known for seafood restaurants serving *fritura malagueña de pescaíto* (fried fish). In mountain towns, you'll find superb Málaga *chivo malagueño* (goat), often baked and served with garlic; goat and sheep cheeses; wild mushrooms; and game dishes. Almería shares Moorish aromas of cumin and cardamom with its Andalusian sisters to the west but also turns the corner toward its northern neighbor, Murcia, where delicacies such as *mojama* (salt-dried tuna) and *hueva de maruca* (ling roe) have been favorites since Phoenician times. Almería's wealth of vegetables and legumes combine with pork and game products for a rougher, more powerful culinary canon of thick stews and soups.

## TO DRINK

Málaga has long been famous for the sweet Muscatel wine that Russian empress Catherine the Great loved so much she imported it to St. Petersburg duty-free in 1792. In the 18th century, Muscatel was sold medicinally in pharmacies for its curative powers and is still widely produced and often served as accompaniment to dessert or tapas.

## COLD ALMOND AND GARLIC SOUP

*Ajoblanco,* a summer staple in Andalusia, is a refreshing salty-sweet combination. Exquisitely light and sharp, the soup has a surprisingly creamy and fresh taste. Almonds, garlic, hard white bread, olive oil, water, sherry vinegar, and a topping of muscat grapes are standard ingredients.

## FRIED FISH MÁLAGA STYLE

A popular dish along the Costa del Sol and the Costa de Almería, *fritura malagueña de pescaíto* is basically any sort of very small fish—such as anchovies, cuttlefish, baby squid, whitebait, and red mullet—fried in oil so hot that the fish end up crisp and light as a feather. The fish are lightly dusted in white flour, cooked quickly, and drained briefly before arriving piping hot and bone-dry on your plate. For an additional Moorish aroma, fritura masters add powdered cumin to the flour.

## ALMERÍA STEWS

Almería is known for heartier fare than neighboring Málaga. *Puchero de trigo* (wheat and pork stew) is a fortifying winter comfort stew of boiled whole grains of wheat cooked with chickpeas, pork, black sausage, fatback, potatoes, saffron, cumin, and fennel. *Ajo colorao* (also known as *atascaburras*) is

A classic potato-based stew

Sardines being roasted over glowing logs.

another popular stew, which consists of potatoes, dried peppers, vegetables, and fish that are simmered into a thick red-orange stew *de cuchara* (eaten with a spoon). Laced with cumin and garlic and served with thick country bread, it's a stick-to-your-ribs mariner's soup.

## ROASTED SARDINES

Known as *moraga de sardinas,* or *espeto de sardinas,* this method of cooking sardines is popular in the summer along the Pedregalejo and Carihuela beaches east and west of Málaga: the sardines (best eaten May through August) are skewered and extended over logs at an angle so that the fish oils run back down the skewers instead of falling into the coals and causing a conflagration. Fresh fish and cold white wine or beer make this a beautiful and relaxing sunset beach dinner.

## A THOUSAND AND ONE EGGS

In Andalusia and especially along the Costa del Sol, *huevos a la flamenca* (eggs flamenco-style) is a classic dish combining peppers, potatoes, ham, and peas with an egg broken over the top and baked sizzling hot. Other musts: *revuelto de setas y gambas* (scrambled eggs with wild mushrooms and shrimp) and the universal Iberian potato omelet, the *tortilla de patatas.*

# BEST BEACHES OF THE SOUTHERN COAST

One of the many resorts in Torremolinos.

Tourists have been coming to the Costa del Sol since the 1950s, attracted by its magical combination of brochure-blue sea, miles of beaches, and reliably sunny weather.

The beaches here range from the gravel-like shingle in Almuñécar, Nerja, and Málaga to fine, gritty sand from Torremolinos westward. The best (and most crowded) beaches are east of Málaga and those flanking the most popular resorts of Nerja, Torremolinos, Fuengirola, and Marbella. For more secluded beaches, head west of Estepona and past Gibraltar to Tarifa and the Cádiz coast. The beaches change when you hit the Atlantic, becoming appealingly wide with fine golden sand. The winds are usually quite strong here, which means that although you can't read a newspaper while lying out, the conditions for windsurfing and kiteboarding are near perfect.

Beaches are free, and busiest in July, August, and on Sunday May through October when malagueño families arrive for a full day on the beach and lunch at a chiringuito.

## OVER THE TOPLESS

In Spain, as in many parts of Europe, it is perfectly acceptable for women to go topless on the beach, although covering up is the norm at beach bars. There are several nude beaches on the Costas; look for the *playa naturista* sign. The most popular are in Maro (near Nerja), Benalnatura (Benalmádena Costa), Cabo Pino (Marbella), and near Tarifa.

## LA CARIHUELA, TORREMOLI-NOS

This former fishing district of Torremolinos has a wide stretch of beach. The chiringuitos here are some of the best on the Costa, and the promenade, which continues until Benalmádena port, with its striking Asian-inspired architecture and great choice of restaurants and bars, is delightful for strolling.

## CARVAJAL, FUENGIROLA

Backed by low-rise buildings and greenery, the beach here is unspoiled and refreshingly low-key. East of Fuengirola center, the Carvajal beach bars have young crowds, with regular live music in summer. It's also an easily accessible beach on the Málaga–Fuengirola train, with a stop within walking distance of the sand.

## PLAYA LOS LANCES, TARIFA

This white sandy beach is one of the least spoiled in Andalusia. Near lush vegetation, lagoons, and the occasional campground and boho-chic hotel, Tarifa's main beach is famed throughout Europe for its windsurfing and kiteboarding, so expect some real winds: *levante* from the east and *poniente* from the west.

## CABO DE GATA, ALMERÍA

Backed by natural parkland, with volcanic rock formations creating dramatic

Tarifa is known for its wind: great for windsurfing, kiteboarding, and kite flying.

cliffs and secluded bays, Almería's stunning Cabo de Gata coastline includes superb beaches and coves within the protected UNESCO Biosphere Reserve. The fact that most of the beaches here are accessible only via marked footpaths adds to their off-the-beaten-track appeal.

## PUERTO BANÚS, MARBELLA

Looking for action? Some great beach scenes flank the world-famous luxurious port. Puerto Banús is known for its excellent, laid-back Caribbean-style seafood restaurants, good music, and hip, good-looking crowd. Another superb sandy choice are the coves west of the marina, so-called boutique beaches, with club areas and massages available, as well as attractive beaches and tempting shallow waters.

## EL SALADILLO, ESTEPONA

Between Marbella and Estepona (take the Cancelada exit off the A7), this relaxed and inviting beach is not as well known as its glitzier neighbors. It's harder to find, so mainly locals in the know frequent it. There are two popular seafood restaurants here, plus a volleyball net, showers, and sun beds and parasols for rent.

Crashing waves at Cabo de Gata.

With roughly 320 days of sunshine a year, the Costa del Sol well deserves its nickname, "the Sunshine Coast." It's no wonder much of the coast has been built up with resorts and high-rises. Don't despair, though: you can still find some classic Spanish experiences, whether in the old city of Marbella or one of the smaller villages like Casares. And despite the hubbub of high season, visitors can always unwind here, basking or strolling on mile after mile of sandy beach.

Technically, the stretch of Andalusian shore known as the Costa del Sol runs west from the Costa Tropical, near Granada, to the tip of Tarifa, the southernmost point in Europe, just beyond Gibraltar. For most of the Europeans who have flocked here over the past 50 years, though, the Sunshine Coast has been largely restricted to the 70-km (43-mile) sprawl of hotels, vacation villas, golf courses, marinas, and nightclubs between Torremolinos, just west of Málaga, and Estepona, down toward Gibraltar. Since the late 1950s this area has mushroomed from a group of impoverished fishing villages into an overdeveloped seaside playground and retirement haven. The city of Almería and its coastline, the Costa de Almería, is southwest of Granada's Alpujarras region and due east of the Costa Tropical (around 147 km [93 miles] from Almuñécar).

## MAJOR REGIONS

South of Spain's Murcia Coast lie the shores of Andalusia, beginning with the **Costa de Almería.** Several of the coastal towns here, including **Agua Amarga,** have a laid-back charm, with miles of sandy beaches and a refreshing lack of high-rise developments. The mineral riches of the surrounding mountains gave rise to Iberia's first true civilization, whose capital can still be glimpsed in the 4,700-year-old ruins of Los Millares, near the village of Santa Fe de Mondújar. The small towns of Níjar and Sorbas maintain an age-old tradition of pottery making and other crafts, and the western coast of **Almería** has tapped unexpected wealth from a parched land, thanks to modern techniques of growing produce in plastic greenhouses. In contrast to the inhospitable landscape of the mountain-fringed Andarax Valley, the area east of Granada's Alpujarras, near Alhama, has a cool climate and gentle landscape, both conducive to making fine wines.

East of Málaga and west of Almería lies the **Costa Tropical.** Housing developments resemble buildings in Andalusian villages rather than the bland high-rises elsewhere, and its tourist onslaught has been mild. A flourishing farming center, the area earns its keep from tropical fruit, including avocados, mangoes, and pawpaws (also known as custard apples). You may find packed beaches and traffic-choked roads at the height of the season, but for most of the year the Costa Tropical is relatively free of other tourists, if not also devoid of expatriates.

**The Málaga Province,** with the city of **Málaga** and the provincial towns of the upland hills and valleys to the north, creates the kind of contrast that makes travel in Spain so tantalizing. The region's Moorish legacy—tiny streets honeycombing the steamy depths of Málaga, the layout of the farms, and the crops themselves, including olives, grapes, oranges, and lemons—is a unifying visual theme. Ronda and the whitewashed villages of Andalusia behind the Costa del Sol make for one of Spain's most scenic and emblematic driving routes.

To the west of Málaga, along the coast, the sprawling outskirts of **Torremolinos** signal that you're entering the Costa del Sol, with its beaches, high-rise hotels, and serious numbers of tourists. On the far west, you can still discern Estepona's fishing village and Moorish old quarter amid its booming coastal development. Just inland, **Casares** piles whitewashed houses over the bright-blue Mediterranean below.

# Planning

## When to Go

May, June, and September are the best times to visit this coastal area, when there's plenty of sunshine but fewer tourists than in the hottest season of July and August. Winter can have bright sunny days, but you may feel the chill, and many hotels in the lower price bracket have heat for only a few hours a day; you can also expect several days of rain. Holy Week, the week before Easter Sunday, is a fun time to visit to see the religious processions.

## Planning Your Time

Travelers with their own wheels who want a real taste of the area in just a few days could start by exploring the relatively unspoiled villages of the Costa Tropical: wander around quaint Salobreña, then hit the larger coastal resort of Nerja, and head inland for a look around pretty Frigiliana.

Move on to Málaga next; it has lots to offer, including several top art museums, excellent restaurants, and some of the best tapas bars in the province. It's also easy to get to stunning, mountaintop Ronda (*see Chapter 11*), which is also on a bus route.

Hit the coast at Marbella, the Costa del Sol's swankiest resort, and then take a leisurely stroll around Puerto Banús. Next, head west to Gibraltar for a day of shopping and sightseeing before returning to the coast and Torremolinos for a night on the town.

Choose your base carefully, as the various areas here make for very different experiences. Málaga is a vibrant Spanish city, virtually untainted by mass tourism, while Torremolinos is a budget destination catering mostly to the mass market. Fuengirola is quieter, with a large population of middle-aged expatriates; farther west, the Marbella–San Pedro de Alcántara area is more exclusive and expensive.

# Getting Here and Around

## AIR

All flights from the United States to Málaga connect in Madrid. British Airways flies several times daily from London (City, Gatwick, and Heathrow) to Málaga, and the budget airlines easyJet and Ryanair also link the two cities. There are direct flights to Málaga from most other major European cities on Iberia or other airlines. Iberia Express/Vueling has three flights daily from Madrid (1¼ hours), four flights daily from Barcelona (1½ hours), and regular flights from other Spanish cities.

Málaga's Costa del Sol airport is 10 km (6 miles) west of town and is one of Spain's most modern. Trains from the airport into town run every 20 minutes 6:44 am–12:54 am (12 minutes, €1.80) and from the airport to Fuengirola every 20 minutes 5:32 am–11:42 pm (34 minutes, €2.70), stopping at several resorts en route, including Torremolinos and Benalmádena.

From the airport there's also bus service to Málaga every half hour 7 am–midnight (€4). At least 10 daily buses (more frequently July–September) run between the airport and Marbella (45 minutes, from €6.15). Taxi fares from the airport to Málaga, Torremolinos, and other resorts are posted inside the terminal: from the airport to Marbella is about €65, to Torremolinos €20, and to Fuengirola €35. Many of the better hotels and all tour companies will arrange for pickup at the airport. Uber operates from Málaga Airport to Costa del Sol resorts and Cabify from the airport to Málaga city center. Both services are slightly cheaper than

taxis and available via their respective online apps.

**AIRPORT CONTACT Aeropuerto Costa del Sol (AGP).** (Aeropuerto de Málaga) ⊠ Av. Comandante García Morato s/n, Málaga ☎ 913/211000 ⊕ www.aena.es.

## BIKE

The Costa del Sol is famous for its sun and sand, but many people supplement their beach time with mountain-bike forays into the hilly interior, particularly around Ojén, near Marbella, and along the mountain roads around Ronda. One popular route, which affords sweeping vistas, follows the mountain road from Ojén west to Istán. The Costa del Sol's temperate climate is ideal for biking, though it's best not to exert yourself on the trails in July and August, when temperatures soar. There are numerous bike-rental shops in the area, particularly in Marbella, Ronda, and Ojén; many shops also arrange bike excursions. The cost to rent a mountain bike for the day is around €20. Guided bike excursions, which include bikes, support staff, and cars, generally start at about €50 a day.

**BIKE RENTAL CONTACT Bike Tours Malaga.** ⊠ Calle Vendeja 6, Málaga ☎ 650/677063 ⊕ www.biketoursmalaga. com. **Marbella Rent a Bike.** ⊠ Marbella ☎ 952/811062 ⊕ www.marbellarentabike. com.

## BUS

The high-speed AVE train line runs two services daily (70 minutes) between Málaga and Granada, and there's an excellent train service between Málaga and Fuengirola with stops at the airport, Torremolinos and Benalmádena. Frequent buses also connect the Costa del Sol with Granada, and the bus generally offers the best way to get around once you're here. During holidays it's wise to reserve your seat in advance for long-distance travel.

On the Costa del Sol, bus services connect Málaga with Cádiz (two daily),

Córdoba (four daily), Granada (16 daily), and Seville (four daily). In Fuengirola you can catch buses for Mijas, Marbella, Estepona, and Algeciras. Avanzabus serves most of the Costa del Sol including Ronda. ALSA serves Granada, Córdoba, Seville, and Nerja. Damas serves Jerez, and Comes runs services to Cádiz. There are also daily buses between Málaga airport and Granada and Seville.

**BUS CONTACTS ALSA.** ☎ *902/422242* ⊕ *www.alsa.es.* **Avanzabus.** ☎ *912/722832* ⊕ *www.avanzabus.com.* **Comes.** ☎ *956/807059* ⊕ *www.tgcomes. es.* **Damas.** ✉ *Seville* ☎ *959/256900* ⊕ *damas-sa.es.*

## CAR

A car allows you to explore Andalusia's mountain villages. Mountain driving can be hair-raising but is getting better as highways are improved.

Málaga is 536 km (333 miles) from Madrid, taking the A4 to Córdoba, then the A44 to Granada, the A92 to Antequera, and the A45; 162 km (101 miles) from Córdoba via Antequera; 220 km (137 miles) from Seville; and 131 km (81 miles) from Granada by the shortest route of the A92 to Loja, then the A45 to Málaga.

To take a car into Gibraltar you need, in theory, an insurance certificate and a logbook (a certificate of vehicle ownership). In practice, all you need is your passport as well as a valid driving license. Head for the well-signposted multistory parking garage, as street parking on the Rock is scarce.

**NATIONAL CAR-RENTAL AGENCIES Helle Hollis.** ☎ *952/245544* ⊕ *www.hellehollis. com.*

## TAXI

Taxis are plentiful throughout the Costa del Sol and may be hailed on the street or from specified taxi ranks marked "Taxi." Restaurants are usually happy to call a taxi for you, too. Fares are reasonable, and meters are strictly used. You are not required to tip taxi drivers, though rounding up the amount will be appreciated. Uber operates throughout the Costa del Sol, and Cabify services are available in Málaga city and Marbella.

## TRAIN

Málaga is the main rail terminus in the area, with 11 high-speed trains per day from Madrid (2½ to 3 hours, depending on the train). Málaga is also linked by high-speed train with Barcelona (six daily, about 6 hours). Ten daily trains also link Seville with Málaga in just under two hours.

High-speed AVE trains from Granada to Málaga began operation in early 2022, reducing the journey time to 1 hour 10 minutes, although there is just one service in each direction daily. Málaga's train station is a 15-minute walk from the city center, across the river.

RENFE connects Málaga, Torremolinos, and Fuengirola, stopping at the airport and all resorts along the way. The train leaves Málaga every 20 minutes 5:20 am–11:30 pm, and Fuengirola every 20 minutes 6:10 am–12:20 am. For the city center, get off at the last stop. A daily train connects Málaga and Ronda via the dramatic Chorro gorge (2 hours).

# Restaurants

Málaga is best for traditional Spanish cooking, with a wealth of bars and seafood restaurants serving *fritura malagueña*, the city's famous fried seafood. Torremolinos's Carihuela district is also a good destination for lovers of Spanish seafood. The area's resorts serve every conceivable foreign cuisine, from Thai to the Scandinavian smorgasbord. For delicious cheap eats, try the *chiringuitos*. Strung out along the beaches, these summer-only restaurants serve seafood fresh off the boats. Because there are so many foreigners here, meals on the coast are served earlier than elsewhere in Andalusia; most restaurants open at 1 or 1:30 for lunch and 7 or 8 for dinner.

*Restaurant reviews have been shortened. For full information, visit Fodors. com.*

## Hotels

Most hotels on the developed stretch between Torremolinos and Fuengirola offer large, functional rooms near the sea at competitive rates, but the area's popularity as a budget destination means that most such hotels are booked in high season by package-tour operators. Finding a room at Easter, in July and August, or over holiday weekends can be difficult if you haven't reserved in advance. In July and August many hotels require a stay of at least three days. Málaga is an increasingly attractive base for visitors to this corner of Andalusia and has some good hotels. Marbella, meanwhile, has more than its fair share of grand lodgings, including some of Spain's most expensive rooms. Gibraltar's handful of hotels tends to be more expensive than most comparable lodgings in Spain.

There are also apartments and villas for short- or long-term stays, ranging from traditional Andalusian farmhouses to luxury villas. One excellent source for apartment and villa rentals is **Spain Holiday** (☎ *951/204601*, ⊕ *spain-holiday.com*). For Marbella, you can also try **Nordica Rentals** (☎ *952/811552*, ⊕ *nordicamarbella.com*), and, for high-end rentals, **The Luxury Villa Collection** ( *44/203–903–9094 in the UK,* ⊕ *theluxuryvillacollection. com*). Our local writers vet every hotel to recommend the best overnights in each price category, from budget to expensive. Unless otherwise specified, you can expect a private bath, phone, and TV in your room.

*Hotel reviews have been shortened. For full information, visit Fodors.com.*

### What It Costs in Euros

| | $ | $$ | $$$ | $$$$ |
|---|---|---|---|---|
| **RESTAURANTS** | | | | |
| | under €12 | €12–€17 | €18–€22 | over €22 |
| **HOTELS** | | | | |
| | under €90 | €90–€125 | €126–€180 | over €180 |

## Golf in the Sun

Nicknamed the "Costa del Golf," the Sun Coast has over 70 golf courses within putting distance of the Mediterranean. Most of the courses are between Rincón de la Victoria (east of Málaga) and Gibraltar. The best time for golfing is October–June; greens fees are lower in high summer. Check out the comprehensive website ⊕ *golfinspain.com* for up-to-date information.

## Tours

Several companies run one- and two-day excursions from Costa del Sol resorts. You can book with local travel agents and hotels; excursions leave from Málaga, Torremolinos, Fuengirola, Marbella, and Estepona, with prices varying by departure point. Most tours last half a day, and in most cases you can be picked up at your hotel. Popular tours include Málaga, Gibraltar, the Cuevas de Nerja, Mijas, Tangier, and Ronda. The Costa del Sol's varied landscape is also wonderful for hiking and walking, and several companies offer walking or cycling tours.

### TOUR OPERATORS
**John Keo Walking Tours**

WALKING TOURS | This company provides guided walks and hikes around the eastern Costa del Sol. Reservations are essential. ☎ *647/273502* ⊕ *www.hiking-walkingspain.com* ✉ *From €25.*

### Sierra MTB

**BICYCLE TOURS** | A good range of rural and urban guided cycling tours suit all levels. Weekend and weeklong packages, including accommodations and a different bike ride every day, are available in addition to day trips. ✉ *Málaga* ☎ *616/295251* ⊕ *www.sierracycling.com* ✉ *From €90.*

### Viajes Rusadir

**CRUISE EXCURSIONS** | This local firm specializes in Costa del Sol excursions and private tours. ☎ *952/463458* ⊕ *www. viajesrusadir.com* ✉ *From €40.*

### Wild Andalucia

**GUIDED TOURS** | Birdwatching day trips around the province of Málaga at different inland and coastal locations; longer tours to other parts of Andalusia are also available. Prices are per person based on a group of four. ✉ *Málaga* ☎ *650/785926* ⊕ *www.wildandalucia.com* ✉ *From €65.*

## Visitor Information

The official website for the Costa del Sol is ⊕ *www.visitacostadelsol.com.* It has good information on sightseeing and events, guides to towns and villages, and contact details for the regional and local tourist offices, which are listed under their respective towns and cities. Tourist offices are generally open Monday through Saturday 10–7 (until 8 in summer) and Sunday 10–2.

## The Cabo de Gata Nature Reserve

*40 km (25 miles) east of Almería, 86 km (53 miles) south of Mojácar.*

The southeast corner of Spain is one of the country's last unspoiled wildernesses, and much of the coastline is part of a highly protected nature reserve. San José, the largest village, has a pleasant bay, though these days the village has rather outgrown itself and can be very busy in summer. Those preferring smaller, quieter destinations should look farther north, at places such as Agua Amarga, Rodalquilar, and the often-deserted beaches nearby.

### GETTING HERE AND AROUND

You need your own wheels to explore the nature reserve and surrounding villages, including San José. When it's time to hit the beach, Playa de los Genoveses and Playa Monsul, to the south of San José, are some of the best. A rough road follows the coast around the spectacular cape, eventually linking up with the N332 to Almería. Alternatively, follow the signs north for the towns of Níjar (approximately 20 km [12 miles] north) and Sorbas (32 km [20 miles] northeast of Níjar); both towns are famed for their distinctive green-glazed pottery, which you can buy directly from workshops.

 Sights

#### Parque Natural Marítimo y Terrestre Cabo de Gata–Níjar

**NATURE PRESERVE** | Birds are the main attraction at this nature reserve just south of San José; it's home to several species native to Africa, including the *camachuelo trompetero* (large-beaked bullfinch), which is not found anywhere else outside Africa. Check out the Punto de Información visitor center in Rodalquilar, which has an exhibit and information on the region and organizes guided walks and tours of the area. ✉ *Calle Fundición, San José* ✛ *Rodalquilar* ☎ *671/594419* ⊗ *Closed Tues. and Wed.; Jan.—March.*

 Beaches

#### El Playazo

**BEACH** | *Playazo* literally means "one great beach," and this sandy cove is certainly one of the gems in the Cabo de Gata nature reserve. Just a few minutes' drive from the village of Rodalquilar

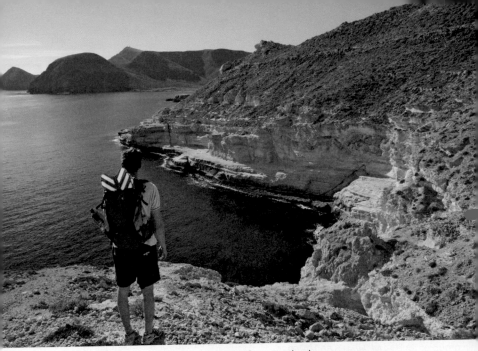

Dramatic views of the coastline from the Cabo de Gata natural park

(once home to Spain's only gold mine), the yellow-sand beach is surrounded by ocher-color volcanic rock; an 18th-century fortress stands at one end. These are sheltered waters, so bathing is safe and warm, and the offshore rocks make for great snorkeling. This beach is deserted during most of the year, and its isolation and lack of amenities mean that even in the summer months you won't come across too many other beachgoers. Although nude bathing isn't officially allowed here, it is tolerated. **Amenities:** none. **Best for:** snorkeling; solitude; sunrise. ⊠ *Rodalquilar, San José.*

### Playa de los Genoveses

BEACH | Named after the Genovese sailors who landed here in 1127 to aid King Alfonso VII, this beach is one of the area's best known and most beautiful. The long, sandy expanse is backed by pines, eucalyptus trees, and low-rising dunes. The sea is shallow, warm, and crystal clear here—snorkeling is popular around the rocks at either end of the cove. Free parking is available late

September through early June; in summer, you must park in nearby San José and take a free shuttle bus to the beach. The beach can also be reached via an easy coastal walk from San José, a 7-km (4½-mile) round trip. The beach has no amenities to speak of, so take plenty of water if it's hot. **Amenities:** parking. **Best for:** snorkeling; solitude; sunset; walking. ⊠ *San José.*

## 🛏 Hotels

### El Faro de los Genoveses

$$$$ | APARTMENT | With panoramic views of San José and the wide bay, these modern self-catering apartments make the most of their elevated position at the far west end of the village. **Pros:** friendly and flexible owners; stunning sea and mountain views; clean and comfortable accommodations. **Cons:** 2-night minimum stay; slightly out of the village; some noise from the bar. ⑤ *Rooms from: €200* ⊠ *Calle La Morra 4, San José* ☎ *679/443934* ⊕ *elfarodelosgenoveses.com* 🛏 *8 apartments* ⑪ *No Meals.*

# Agua Amarga

*22 km (14 miles) north of San José, 55 km (34 miles) east of Almería.*

Like other coastal hamlets, Agua Amarga started out in the 18th century as a tuna-fishing port. These days, as perhaps the most pleasant village on the Cabo de Gata coast, it attracts lots of visitors, although it remains much less developed than San José. One of the coast's best beaches is just to the north: the dramatically named Playa de los Muertos (Beach of the Dead), a long stretch of fine gravel bookended with volcanic outcrops.

## GETTING HERE AND AROUND

If you're driving here from Almería, follow signs to the airport, then continue north on the A7; Agua Amarga is signposted just north of the Parque Natural Cabo de Gata. The village itself is small enough to explore easily on foot.

## 🍴 Restaurants

### La Palmera

**$$$ | SPANISH |** At the far eastern end of the beach, the terrace at this hotel restaurant sits right on the sand; get a table here rather than inside the less impressive dining room. Fresh fish, locally caught and grilled, is the highlight of the menu, which also includes simple salads and plates of fried fish. **Known for:** arroz a banda (rice with fish and aioli); beachfront dining; locally caught fish. ⓢ *Average main: €18* ✉ *Calle Aguada 4, Agua Amarga* ☎ *676/726819* ⊕ *hostalrestaurantelapalmera.net/en* ⊗ *Closed for 6 wks in winter. Call to check.*

##  Hotels

### Hotel El Tío Kiko

**$$$$ | HOTEL |** On a hill to the west of the village, this modern luxury hotel has commanding sea views and is close enough to the main beach to walk (but far enough to enjoy peace and quiet).

**Pros:** ... have balconies, some with hot tubs. **Cons:** 3–4-night stay minimum July–Aug.; could be too quiet for some; up a hill. ⓢ *Rooms from: €200* ✉ *Calle Embarque 12, Agua Amarga* ☎ *950/138080* ⊕ *www.eltiokiko.com* ⮎ *27 rooms* ⊚ *Free Breakfast.*

# Almería

*183 km (114 miles) east of Málaga.*

Warmed by the sunniest climate in Andalusia, Almería is a youthful Mediterranean city, basking in sweeping views of the sea from its coastal perch and close to several excellent beaches. It's also a capital of the grape industry, thanks to its wonderfully mild climate in spring and fall. Rimmed by tree-lined boulevards and some landscaped squares, the city's core is a maze of narrow, winding alleys formed by flat-roofed, distinctly Mudejar houses. Now surrounded by modern apartment blocks, these dazzlingly white older homes continue to give Almería an Andalusian flavor. Barely touched by tourism, this compact city is well worth a visit—allow an overnight stay to take in the main sights en route to or from Cabo de Gata or Málaga. Almería was Gastronomic Capital of Spain in 2019, so be sure to try the local fare and tapas bars, where you'll be offered a free (and usually elaborate) tapa with your drink.

## GETTING HERE AND AROUND

Bus No. 30 (€1.05) runs roughly every 35 minutes 7 am–11 pm from Almería airport to the center of town (Calle del Doctor Gregorio Marañón).

The city center is compact, and most of the main sights are within easy strolling distance of each other.

## VISITOR INFORMATION

**CONTACTS** Almería Visitor Information. ⊠ *Paseo de Almería 12, Almería* ☎ *950/210538* ⊕ *www.turismodealmeria. org.*

# Sights

### Alcazaba

**MILITARY SIGHT** | Dominating the city is this fortress, built by Caliph Abd ar-Rahman I and given a bell tower by Carlos III. From here you have sweeping views of the port and city. Among the ruins of the fortress, which was damaged by earthquakes in 1522 and 1560, are landscaped gardens of rock flowers and cacti. ⊠ *Calle Almanzor, Almería* ☎ *950/801008* ⧠ *Free* ⊙ *Closed Mon.*

### Cathedral

**CHURCH** | Below the *alcazaba* (citadel) is the local cathedral, with buttressed towers that give it the appearance of a castle. It's in Gothic style but with some classical touches around the doors. Guided tours are available, and admission includes a visit to the ecclesiastical museum. ⊠ *Pl. de la Catedral, Almería* ☎ *605/429979* ⧠ *€6.*

### Mercado Central de Almería

**MARKET** | Built in 1892 in a Modernist style, Almería's main market provides a colorful insight into the province's long list of fresh produce. The iron structure, characteristic of late 19th-century buildings, is enclosed by a pretty tiled facade. Don't miss the plaque marking Marie Curie's visit here in 1931. ⊠ *Calle Aguilar de Campo s/n, Almería* ⊙ *Closed Sun.*

### ★ Refugios de la Guerra Civil (*Civil War Shelters*)

**TUNNEL** | Almería, the last bastion of the Republican government during the Spanish Civil War, was hit by 754 bombs launched via air and sea by Nationalist forces. To protect civilians, 4½ km (2¾ miles) of tunnels were built under the city to provide shelter for more than

## Los Millares ◉

This important archaeological site is nearly 2½ km (1½ miles) southwest from the village of Santa Fe de Mondújar and 19 km (12 miles) from Almería. This collection of ruins scattered on a windswept hilltop was the birthplace of civilization in Spain nearly 5,000 years ago. Large tombs show that the community had an advanced society, and the formidable defense walls indicate it had something to protect. A series of concentric fortifications shows that the settlement grew, eventually holding some 2,000 people. The town was inhabited from 2700 to 1800 BC.

34,000 people. About 1 km (½ mile) can now be visited on a guided tour that covers the food stores, sleeping quarters, and an operating theater for the wounded, with its original medical equipment. ⊠ *Pl. Manuel Pérez García s/n, Almería* ☎ *950/268696* ⧠ *€3* ⊙ *Closed Mon.*

# Restaurants

### La Encina

**$$$** | **SPANISH** | This justly popular restaurant is housed in an 1860s building that also incorporates an 11th-century Moorish well. Time may have stood still with the setting, but the cuisine reflects a modern twist on traditional dishes, including seafood mains like *bacalao con cebolla, miel y pasas con crujiente de espinacas* (cod with onion, honey, and raisins) or *rabo de novillo con almendras* (oxtail stew with almonds). **Known for:** bacalao; wine list; creative tapas. **$** *Average main: €18* ⊠ *Calle Marín 3, Almería* ☎ *950/273429* ⊙ *Closed Mon.*

## Valentín

**$$$ | SPANISH |** This popular, central spot serves fine regional specialties, such as *arroz de marisco* (rice with seafood), *cazuela de rape en salsa de almendras* (monkfish stew with almond sauce), and the delicious *kokotxas de bacalao en salsa de ostras* (cod cheeks in oyster sauce). The surroundings are rustic-yet-elegant Andalusian: whitewashed walls, dark wood, and exposed brick. **Known for:** can be hard to get a table; rustic-chic setting; rice dishes. $ *Average main: €21* ✉ *Calle Tenor Iribarne 10, Almería* ☎ *950/264475* ⊙ *Closed Jan.*

 **Hotels**

### Aire Hotel

**$$$ | HOTEL |** In the heart of the old quarter, early-19th-century architecture is paired with comfortable and up-to-date amenities in this boutique hotel with strong design features. **Pros:** central location; views of the Alcazaba at breakfast; some rooms and the terrace have great views. **Cons:** some rooms have no views; street noise in some rooms; in-room showers offer no privacy. $ *Rooms from: €130* ✉ *Pl. de la Constitución 4, Almería* ☎ *950/282096* ⊕ *www.airehotelalmeria.com* ⇆ *22 rooms* ⊠ *No Meals.*

### Hotel Catedral

**$$$ | HOTEL |** In full view of the cathedral, this small hotel combines traditional charm (it has kept many of its original mid-19th-century features, including a stunning arched entryway) with modern elegance. **Pros:** cathedral views; good breakfast; rooftop terrace with plunge pool. **Cons:** cathedral church bells not for everyone; hotel events can be noisy; reception staff could be friendlier. $ *Rooms from: €150* ✉ *Pl. de la Catedral 8, Almería* ☎ *950/278178* ⊕ *www.hotelcatedral.net* ⇆ *20 rooms* ⊠ *No Meals.*

### Nuevo Torreluz Hotel

**$ | HOTEL |** Value is the overriding attraction of this comfortable and elegant modern hotel, which has slick, bright rooms and the kind of amenities you'd expect to come at a higher price. **Pros:** great central location; good value; large rooms. **Cons:** rooms in the main building are more expensive; limited breakfast; no pool. $ *Rooms from: €70* ✉ *Pl. Flores 10, Almería* ☎ *950/234399* ⊕ *www.torreluz.com* ⇆ *98 rooms* ⊠ *No Meals.*

## 🎭 Performing Arts

In Almería, the action is on **Plaza Flores,** moving down to the beach in summer.

### ★ Peña El Taranto

**ARTS CENTERS |** Founded in 1963, this excellent venue (home to the city's Arab water deposits) has been one of the main centers for flamenco in Andalusia, and foot-stomping live flamenco and concerts are performed every two weeks. Check in advance for exact times and dates. ✉ *Calle Tenor Iribame 20, Almería* ☎ *950/235057* ⊕ *www.eltaranto.com.*

# Almuñécar

*85 km (53 miles) east of Málaga.*

This small-time resort with a shingle beach is popular with Spanish and Northern European vacationers. It's been a fishing village since Phoenician times, 3,000 years ago, when it was called Sexi; later, the Moors built a castle here for the treasures of Granada's kings. The road west from Motril and Salobreña passes through what was the empire of the sugar barons, who brought prosperity to Málaga's province in the 19th century: the cane fields now give way to lychees, limes, mangoes, pawpaws, and olives.

The village is actually two, separated by the dramatic rocky headland of Punta de la Mona. To the east is Almuñécar proper,

A religious procession in Almuñécar

and to the west is **La Herradura,** a quiet fishing community. Between the two is the Marina del Este yacht harbor, which, along with La Herradura, is a popular diving center. A renowned jazz festival (⊕ www.jazzgranada.es) takes place annually in July, often showcasing big names.

## GETTING HERE AND AROUND
The A7 runs north of town. There is an efficient bus service to surrounding towns and cities, including Málaga, Granada, Nerja, and, closer afield, La Herradura. Almuñécar's town center is well laid out for strolling, and the local tourist office has information on bicycle and scooter rental.

## VISITOR INFORMATION
**CONTACTS Almuñécar.** ⊠ *Av. de Europa, Almuñecar* ☎ *958/631125* ⊕ *www.visitalmunecar.es.*

## ⊙ Sights

### Castillo de San Miguel (*St. Michael's Castle*)
**CASTLE/PALACE** | A Roman fortress once stood here, later enlarged by the Moors, but the castle's present aspect, crowning the city, owes more to 16th-century additions. The building was bombed during the Peninsular War in the 19th century, and what was left was used as a cemetery until the 1990s. You can wander the ramparts and peer into the dungeon; the skeleton at the bottom is a reproduction of human remains discovered on the spot. ⊠ *Calle San Miguel Bajo, Almuñécar* ☎ *650/027584* ⊠ *€4, includes admission to Cueva de Siete Palacios* ⊗ *Closed Mon.*

### Cueva de Siete Palacios (*Cave of Seven Palaces*)
**OTHER MUSEUM** | Beneath the Castillo de San Miguel is this large, vaulted stone cellar of Roman origin, now Almuñécar's

archaeological museum. The collection is small but interesting, with Phoenician, Roman, and Moorish artifacts.

⊠ *Calle San Miguel Bajo, Almuñécar* 🕾 *958/616131* 🎫 *€4, includes admission to Castillo de San Miguel* ۵ *Closed Mon.*

## 🍴 Restaurants

### ★ FIRMVM

$$$ | SPANISH | One of the eastern Costa del Sol's foodie treats sits in a pleasant central square with its signature ruby-red feature wall. Chef Sergio González combines the best of local produce with more exotic touches to perfection: the venison comes with green pesto and ricotta, and duck, local mango, and shrimp go into the gyozas. **Known for:** good-value tasting menu; attentive and friendly service; creative fusion dishes. ⑤ *Average main: €20* ⊠ *Pl. Damasco 2, Almuñécar* 🕾 *958/633565* ⊕ *restaurantefirmvm.com* ۵ *Closed Mon. No dinner Sun.*

## 🛏 Hotels

### Casablanca

$$ | HOTEL | This quaint family-run hotel comes with a pink-and-white neo-Moorish facade, a choice location next to the beach and near the botanical park, and comfortable rooms that are all different. **Pros:** great location; all rooms have private balconies or views; intimate, family-run atmosphere. **Cons:** only some rooms have sea views; two-night minimum stay in July and August; rooms vary, and some are small. ⑤ *Rooms from: €95* ⊠ *Pl. San Cristóbal 4, Almuñécar* 🕾 *958/635575* ⊕ *www.hotelcasablancaalmunecar.com* 🛏 *39 rooms* 🍽 *No Meals.*

## Salobreña 👁

About 13 km (8 miles) east of Almuñécar, this unspoiled village of near-perpendicular streets and old white houses on a steep hill beneath a Moorish fortress is a true Andalusian *pueblo* (village), separated from the beachfront restaurants and bars in the newer part of town. It's great for a quick visit, and the pebbly beach makes a nice walk. You can reach Salobreña by descending through the mountains from Granada or by continuing west from Almería on the A7.

## Nerja

*52 km (32 miles) east of Málaga, 22 km (14 miles) west of Almuñécar.*

Nerja—the name comes from the Moorish word *narixa,* meaning "abundant springs"—has a large community of expats, who live mainly outside town in *urbanizaciones* ("village" developments). The old village is on a headland above small beaches and rocky coves, which offer reasonable swimming despite the gray, gritty sand. In July and August, Nerja is packed with tourists, but the rest of the year it's a pleasure to wander the old town's narrow streets.

### GETTING HERE AND AROUND

Nerja is a speedy hour's drive east from Málaga on the A7. If you're driving, park in the underground lot just west of the Balcón de Europa (it's signposted) off Calle La Cruz. The town is small enough to explore on foot.

### VISITOR INFORMATION

**CONTACTS Nerja.** ⊠ *Calle Carmen 1, Nerja* 🕾 *952/521531* ⊕ *turismo.nerja.es.*

# Sights

## ★ Balcón de Europa

**PROMENADE | FAMILY |** The highlight of Nerja, this tree-lined promenade is on a promontory just off the central square, with magnificent views of the mountains and sea. You can gaze far off into the horizon using the strategically placed telescopes, or use this as a starting point for a horse-and-carriage clip-clop ride around town. Open-air concerts are held here in July and August. ⊠ *Nerja.*

## Cuevas de Nerja (*Nerja Caves*)

**CAVE |** Between Almuñécar and Nerja, these caves are on a road surrounded by giant cliffs and dramatic seascapes. Signs point to the cave entrance above the village of Maro, 4 km (2½ miles) east of Nerja. Its spires and turrets, created by millennia of dripping water, are now floodlit for better views. One suspended pinnacle, 200 feet long, is the world's largest known stalactite. The cave painting of seals discovered here may be the oldest example of art in existence—and the only one known to have been painted by Neanderthals. The awesome subterranean chambers create an evocative setting for concerts and ballets during the Nerja Festival of Music, held annually in July. There is also a bar-restaurant near the entrance with a spacious dining room that has superb views.

Visits are with self-guided audio tours (available in English). All ticket prices are cheaper online. ⊠ *Maro* ☎ *952/529520* ⊕ *www.cuevadenerja.es* ✆ *€12.*

# Beaches

## Las Alberquillas

**BEACH |** One of the string of coves on the coastline west of Nerja, this beach of gray sand mixed with shingle is backed by pine trees and scrub that perfume the air. Reachable only via a stony track down the cliffs, this protected beach is one of the few on the Costa del Sol to be almost

## Frigiliana

On an inland mountain ridge overlooking the sea, this pretty village has spectacular views and an old quarter of narrow, cobbled streets and dazzling white houses decorated with pots of geraniums. It was the site of one of the last battles between the Christians and the Moors. Frigiliana is a short drive from the highway to the village; if you don't have a car, you can take a bus here from Nerja, which is 8 km (5 miles) away.

completely untouched by tourism. Its moderate waves mean you need to take care when bathing. The snorkeling around the rocks at either end of the beach is among the best in the area. This spot's seclusion makes the beach a favorite with couples and nudists—it's reasonably quiet even at the height of summer. Limited parking is available off the N340 highway, but there are no amenities, so take plenty of water. **Amenities:** none. **Best for:** nudists; snorkeling; solitude. ⊠ *N340, Km 299, Nerja.*

# Restaurants

## ★ Oliva

**$$$$ | MEDITERRANEAN |** Mediterranean cuisine based on fresh, local produce takes center stage at this restaurant, which has both a minimalist, intimate dining room and a pleasant terrace that's heated in winter. Highlights on the seasonal menu (it changes four times a year) include the sole mille-feuille and the pistachio falafel. **Known for:** Iberian pork; wine list; the best innovative cuisine in town. ⑤ *Average main: €25* ⊠ *Pl. de España 2, Nerja* ☎ *952/522988* ⊕ *www.restauranteoliva. com.*

## 🛌 Hotels

### ★ Hotel Carabeo

**$$ | B&B/INN |** Down a side street near the center of town but still near the sea, this British-owned boutique hotel combines a great location and views with comfortable, pleasant rooms. **Pros:** sea views; excellent restaurant; great location. **Cons:** rooms are comfortable but compact; difficult to get a room in high season; not open out of season. ⑤ *Rooms from: €100* ✉ *Calle Hernando de Carabeo 34, Nerja* ☎ *952/525444* ⊕ *www.hotelcarabeo.com* ⊘ *Closed Dec.–Feb.* ⇆ *7 rooms* ⵔ *Free Breakfast.*

# The Axarquía

*Vélez-Málaga: 36 km (22 miles) east of Málaga.*

The Axarquía region stretches from Nerja to Málaga, and the area's charm lies in its mountainous interior, peppered with pueblos, vineyards, and tiny farms. Its coast consists of narrow, pebbly beaches and drab fishing villages on either side of the high-rise resort town of Torre del Mar.

## GETTING HERE AND AROUND

Although bus routes are fairly comprehensive throughout the Axarquía, reaching the smaller villages may involve long delays; renting a car is convenient and lets you get off the beaten track and experience some of the beautiful unspoiled hinterland in this little-known area. The four-lane A7 highway cuts across the region a few miles in from the coast; traffic on the old coastal road (N340) is slower.

## TOURS

### La Rosilla

**SPECIAL-INTEREST TOURS |** Experience local food and culture at a *finca* (traditional estate or ranch) in the heart of the Axarquía. ☎ *659/734401* ⊕ *larosilla-catering.com* ✉ *From €65.*

**VISITOR INFORMATION**
**CONTACTS Cómpeta.** ✉ *Av. de la Constitución, Cómpeta* ☎ *952/553685* ⊕ *www.competa.es.*

## 👁 Sights

### Ruta del Sol y del Vino and Ruta de la Pasa

**TRAIL |** The Axarquía has a number of tourist trails that take in the best of local scenery, history, and culture. Two of the best are the Ruta del Sol y del Vino (Sunshine and Wine Trail), through Algarrobo, Cómpeta (the main wine center), and Nerja; and the Ruta de la Pasa (Raisin Trail), which goes through Moclinejo, El Borge, and Comares. The trails are especially spectacular during the late-summer grape harvest or in late autumn, when the leaves of the vines turn gold. A visit to nearby Macharaviaya (7 km [4 miles] north of Rincón de la Victoria) might lead you to ponder this sleepy village's past glory: in 1776 one of its sons, Bernardo de Gálvez, became the Spanish governor of Louisiana and later fought in the American Revolution (Galveston, Texas, is named for him). Macharaviaya prospered under his heirs and for many years enjoyed a lucrative monopoly on the manufacture of playing cards for South America. Gálvez was named Honorary Citizen of the United States in December 2014, and his portrait now hangs in the Foreign Affairs Committee room in the Capitol. A sculpture of the family around a fountain stands next to Málaga train station. ✉ *Ruta del Sol y del Vino.*

### Vélez-Málaga

**TOWN |** The capital of the Axarquía is a pleasant agricultural town of white houses, mango and avocado orchards, and vineyards. It's worth a half-day trip to see the Thursday market, the Contemporary Art Centre (CAC), the ruins of a Moorish castle, and the church of Santa María la Mayor, built in the Mudejar style on the site of a mosque that was destroyed when the town fell to the Christians in 1487. The town also has a thriving flamenco scene with regular events, usually on Fridays (⊕ www.flamencoabierto.com). ⊠ Vélez-Málaga.

## 🍴 Restaurants

### Venta El Curro

$ | SPANISH | On a river bend between the hamlets of Árchez and Corumbela, this friendly venta offers traditional country cooking at its best. Sit outside on the shady terrace for stunning views of the valley as you dine on generous portions of grilled meats (pork, veal, and chicken) and salads or tapas. ⑤ Average main: €12 ⊠ Ctra de Corumbela 6, Cómpeta ☎ 678/618119 ⊗ Closed Tues.

## 🛏 Hotels

### Hotel Palacio Blanco

$$ | HOTEL | This light and airy boutique hotel is housed in a charmingly restored 18th-century mansion just a short distance from the castle. **Pros:** spacious rooms; central location; rooftop terrace with pool. **Cons:** few facilities; first-floor rooms are a little dark; no on-site parking. ⑤ Rooms from: €95 ⊠ Calle Felix Lomas 4, Vélez-Málaga ☎ 952/549174 ⊕ www.palacioblanco.com ➷ 9 rooms ⑩ No Meals.

# Málaga

*175 km (109 miles) southeast of Córdoba.*

Málaga is one of southern Spain's most welcoming and happening cities, and it more than justifies a visit. Visitor figures soared after the Museo Picasso opened in 2003 and again after a new cruise-ship terminal opened in 2011, and the city has had a well-earned face-lift, with many of its historic buildings restored or undergoing restoration. The area between the river and the port has been transformed into the Soho art district, and since the arrival of three new art museums in 2015, the city has become one of southern Europe's centers for art. Alongside all this rejuvenation, some great shops and lively bars and restaurants have sprung up all over the center.

True, the approach from the airport certainly isn't that pretty, and you'll be greeted by huge 1970s high-rises that march determinedly toward Torremolinos. But don't give up: in its center and eastern suburbs, this city of about 570,000 people is a pleasant port, with ancient streets and lovely villas amid exotic foliage. Blessed with a subtropical climate, it's covered in lush vegetation and averages some 324 days of sunshine a year.

Central Málaga lies between the Río Guadalmedina and the port, and the city's main attractions are all here. The Centro de Arte Contemporáneo (CAC) sits next to the river; to the east lies the Soho district, hoisted from its former seedy red-light reputation to a vibrant cultural hub with galleries and up-and-coming restaurants. Around La Alameda Boulevard (mostly pedestrianized in 2019), with its giant weeping fig trees, is old-town Málaga: elegant squares, pedestrian shopping streets such as Calle Marqués de Larios, and the major monuments, which are often tucked away in labyrinthine alleys.

Eastern Málaga starts with the pleasant suburbs of El Palo and Pedregalejo, once traditional fishing villages. Here you can eat fresh fish in the numerous chiringuitos and stroll Pedregalejo's seafront promenade or the tree-lined streets of El Limonar. A few blocks west is Málaga's bullring, La Malagueta, built in 1874, and Muelle Uno (port-front commercial center), whose striking glass cube is home to the Centre Pompidou. It's great for a drink and for soaking up views of the old quarter.

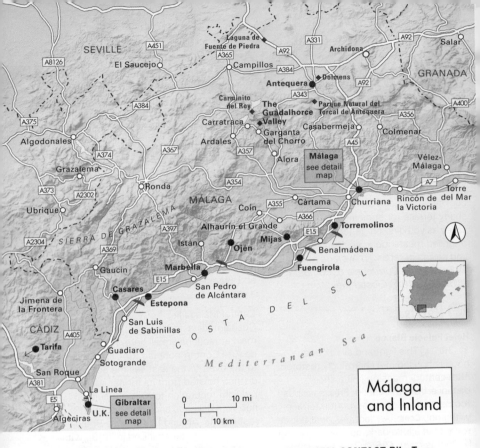

## GETTING HERE AND AROUND

If you're staying at one of the coastal resorts between Málaga and Fuengirola, the easiest way to reach Málaga is via the train (every 20 minutes). If you're driving, there are several well-signposted underground parking lots, and it's not that daunting to negotiate by car. Málaga has two metro lines from the west, and both reach central train and bus stations.

Málaga is mostly flat, so the best way to explore it is on foot or by bike via the good network of designated bike paths. To get an overview of the city in a day, hop on the Málaga Tour City Sightseeing Bus. There is a comprehensive bus network, too, and the tourist office can advise on routes and schedules. Taxis are readily available and Cabify and Uber both operate in Málaga city.

**BIKE RENTAL CONTACT Bike Tours Malaga.** ☒ *Calle Vendeja 6, Málaga* ☎ *650/677063* ⊕ *www.biketoursmalaga. com.*

**BUS CONTACT Málaga Bus Station.** ☒ *Paseo de los Tilos, Málaga* ☎ *952/350061.*

**CAR RENTAL CONTACTS Europcar.** ☒ *, Málaga* ☎ *911/505000* ⊕ *www.europcar. es.* **Niza Cars.** ☒ *, Málaga* ☎ *952/236179* ⊕ *www.nizacars.es.*

**TAXI COMPANY Unitaxi.** ☒ *Málaga* ☎ *952/333333.*

**TRAIN INFORMATION Málaga Train Station.** ☒ *Esplanada de la Estación, Málaga* ☎ *912/320320* ⊕ *www.renfe.com.*

## TOURS
### Málaga Tour City Sightseeing Bus
**BUS TOURS** | This open-top, hop-on hop-off tour bus gives you an overview of

Málaga's main sights in a day, including the Gibralfaro. Buy tickets online ahead of your trip or when you board the bus. ✉ *Málaga* ⊕ *www.city-sightseeing.com* 🚌 *From €25.*

## Spain Food Sherpas
**GUIDED TOURS** | Eat your way around Málaga with the Taste of Tapas Tour or the evening Wine and Tapas Tour with local guides who know their stuff when it comes to the city's culinary culture. ✉ *Málaga* ⊕ *www.spainfoodsherpas.com* 🚌 *From €65.*

## VISITOR INFORMATION
**CONTACTS Guide to Malaga.** ✉ *Málaga* ⊕ *www.guidetomalaga.com.* **Málaga Turismo.** ✉ *Pl. de la Marina, Paseo del Parque, Málaga* 🕿 *951/926620* ⊕ *www.visita.malaga.eu.*

# ◉ Sights

## Alcazaba
**RUINS** | Just beyond the ruins of a Roman theater on Calle Alcazabilla stands Málaga's greatest monument. This fortress was begun in the 8th century, when Málaga was the principal port of the Moorish kingdom, although most of the present structure dates to the 11th century. The inner palace was built between 1057 and 1063, when the Moorish emirs took up residence; Ferdinand and Isabella lived here for a while after conquering the city in 1487. The ruins are dappled with orange trees and bougainvillea and include a small museum; from the highest point you can see over the park and port. ✉ *Málaga* ⊕ *Entrance on Calle Alcazabilla* 🚌 *From €4 (free Sun. from 2 pm).*

## Centre Pompidou Málaga
**ART MUSEUM** | One of the four branches outside France of the Centre Pompidou in Paris opened in March 2015 in the striking glass cube designed by Daniel Buren at Muelle Uno on Málaga port. The museum showcases 20th- and 21st-century modern art, with semi-permanent exhibitions that change every two years and always include works (paintings, sculptures, videos, and installations) by renowned artists such as Accardi, Ernst, Léger, and Matisse. There are also regular temporary exhibitions each year. ✉ *Pasaje Doctor Carrillo Casaux s/n, Málaga* 🕿 *951/926200* ⊕ *www.centrepompidou-malaga.eu* 🚌 *From €7 (free Sun. from 4 pm)* ⊗ *Closed Tues.*

## Centro de Arte Contemporáneo (Contemporary Arts Center)
**ART MUSEUM** | This museum includes photographic studies and paintings, some of them immense. The 7,900 square feet of bright exhibition space is used to showcase ultramodern artistic trends—the four exhibitions feature changing exhibits from the permanent collection, two temporary shows, and one show dedicated to up-and-coming Spanish artists. The gallery attracts world-class modern artists like Phil Frost, KAWS, and Julian Schnabel. Outside, don't miss the giant murals behind the museum painted by the street artists Shepard Fairey (aka Obey) and Doan Stockton (aka D*Face). ✉ *Alemania s/n, Málaga* 🕿 *952/120055* ⊕ *cacmalaga.eu* 🚌 *Free* ⊗ *Closed Mon.*

## Gibralfaro (Fortress)
**VIEWPOINT** | Surrounded by magnificent vistas and floodlit at night, these fortifications were built for Yusuf I in the 14th century; the Moors called them Jebelfaro, from the Arab word for "mount" and the Greek word for "lighthouse," after a beacon that stood here to guide ships into the harbor and warn of pirates. The lighthouse has been succeeded by a small parador. ✉ *Gibralfaro Mountain, Málaga* ⊕ *Drive by way of Calle Victoria, or take Bus 35 (10 departures per day, roughly every 45 mins 10–7) from stop in park near Pl. de la Marina* 🚌 *From €4 (free Sun. from 2 pm).*

## La Concepción
**GARDEN** | This botanical garden was created in 1855 by the daughter of the British consul, who married a Spanish

## Sights ▼

1 Alcazaba ................. **C2**

2 Centre Pompidou
   Málaga ................... **D3**

3 Centro de Arte
   Contemporáneo ......... **B5**

4 Gibralfaro ................ **D2**

5 La Concepción .......... **B3**

6 Málaga Cathedral ....... **C3**

7 Mercado de
   Atarazanas .............. **B3**

8 Museo Carmen
   Thyssen Málaga ........ **B2**

9 Museo Casa Natal
   de Picasso ............... **C2**

10 Museo del Vidrio y
   Cristal ................... **B1**

11 Museo Picasso
   Málaga ................... **C2**

12 Museo Unicaja de
   Artes y Costumbres
   Populares ............... **B3**

13 Palacio Episcopal ........ **C3**

14 Pasaje Chinitas .......... **C2**

## Restaurants ▼

1 Araboka .................. **C3**

2 Chiringuito Maria ....... **A5**

3 Los Patios de Beatas .... **C2**

4 Óleo Restaurante ....... **B4**

5 Restaurante Alexso ..... **C1**

## Hotels ▼

1 El Castillo de
   Santa Catalina .......... **E2**

2 Gran Hotel Miramar ..... **E3**

3 Hotel Castilla
   Guerrero ................. **B4**

4 Parador de Málaga–
   Gibralfaro ................ **E2**

5 Room Mate Larios ...... **B3**

shipping magnate—the captains of the Spaniard's fleet had standing orders to bring back seedlings and cuttings from every "exotic" port of call. The wisteria pergola, in bloom in early April, is one of the highlights. The garden is just off the exit road to Granada—too far to walk, but well worth the cab fare or the bus journey (No. 2 from La Alameda, then a 20-minute walk or on the Málaga Tour Bus) from the city center. ⊠ *Ctra. de las Pedrizas, Km 216, Málaga* 🕾 *951/926180* 🎫 *€6 (free Sun. afternoon, Oct.—March)* ☯ *Closed Mon.*

### Málaga Cathedral

CHURCH | Built between 1528 and 1782, the cathedral is a triumph, although a generally unappreciated one, having been left unfinished when funds ran out. Because it lacks one of its two towers, the building is nicknamed "La Manquita" (the One-Armed Lady). The enclosed choir (restored in 2019), which miraculously survived the burnings of the civil war, is the work of 17th-century artist Pedro de Mena, who carved the wood wafer-thin in some places to express the fold of a robe or shape of a finger. The choir also has a pair of massive 18th-century pipe organs, one of which is still used for the occasional concert. Adjoining the cathedral is a small museum of religious art and artifacts. A walk around the cathedral on Calle Cister will take you to the magnificent Gothic Puerta del Sagrario. A rooftop walkway (guided tours only) gives you stunning views of the ocher domes and the city. ⊠ *Calle Molina Lario, Málaga* 🕾 *640/871711* 🎫 *From €6* ☯ *Closed Sun. morning.*

### Mercado de Atarazanas

MARKET | From the Plaza Felix Saenz, at the southern end of Calle Nueva, turn onto Sagasta to reach the Mercado de Atarazanas. The 19th-century iron structure incorporates the original Puerta de Atarazanas, the exquisitely crafted 14th-century Moorish gate that once connected the city with the port. Don't miss the magnificent stained-glass window depicting highlights of this historic port city as you stroll around the stalls filled with local produce. The bars at the entrance offer good-value tapas, open at lunchtime only. Fish stalls are closed on Monday. ⊠ *Calle Atarazanas, Málaga* ☯ *Closed Sun.*

### Museo Carmen Thyssen Málaga

ART MUSEUM | Like Madrid, Málaga has its own branch of this museum, with more than 200 works from Baroness Thyssen's private collection. Shown in a renovated 16th-century palace, the collection features mainly Spanish paintings from the 19th century but also has work from two great 20th-century artists, Joaquín Sorolla y Bastida and Romero de Torres. The museum also hosts regular exhibitions, concerts, talks, and art workshops. If you're looking for art-based souvenirs and books, the museum shop provides great inspiration and the adjoining café has a good-value lunchtime menu. ⊠ *Calle Compañia 10, Málaga* 🕾 *902/303131* ⊕ *www.carmenthyssen-malaga.org* 🎫 *€10 (free Sun. from 4 pm)* ☯ *Closed Mon.*

### Museo Casa Natal de Picasso (*Picasso's Birthplace*)

ART MUSEUM | Málaga's most famous native son, Pablo Picasso, was born here in 1881. The building has been painted and furnished in the style of the era and houses a permanent exhibition of the artist's early sketches and sculptures, as well as memorabilia, including his christening robe and family photos. ⊠ *Pl. de la Merced 15, Málaga* 🕾 *951/926060* ⊕ *www.fundacionpicasso.malaga.eu* 🎫 *From €3.*

### Museo del Vidrio y Cristal (*Museum of Glass and Crystal*)

ART MUSEUM | More than 3,000 pieces of glass and crystal, lovingly collected by the owner, are displayed throughout this 18th-century mansion, which is a museum piece in its own right. The pieces, whether ancient Egyptian or from

Europe's Lalique and Whitefriars, give a unique insight into man's decorative use of glass. Visits are by guided tour only. ✉ *Plazuela Santísimo Cristo de la Sangre 2, Málaga* ☎ *952/220271* ⊕ *www.museovidrioycristalmalaga.com* ✉ *€7* ⊙ *Closed Mon., and Aug.*

### ★ Museo Picasso Málaga

ART GALLERY | Part of the charm of this art gallery, one of the city's most prestigious museums, is that its small collection is such a family affair. These are the works that Pablo Picasso kept for himself or gave to his family, including the exquisite *Portrait of Lola*, the artist's sister, which he painted when he was 13, and the stunning *Three Graces*. The holdings were largely donated by two family members—Christine and Bernard Ruiz-Picasso, the artist's daughter-in-law and her son. The works are displayed in chronological order according to the periods that marked Picasso's 73-year development as an artist. The museum is housed in a former palace where, during restoration work, Roman and Moorish remains were discovered. These are now on display, together with the permanent collection of Picassos and temporary exhibitions.

■TIP→ **Guided tours in English are available; book at least five days ahead.** ✉ *Calle San Agustín, Málaga* ☎ *952/127600* ⊕ *www.museopicassomalaga.org* ✉ *From €9 (free last 2 hrs on Sun.).*

### Palacio Episcopal (*Bishop's Palace*)

CASTLE/PALACE | Facing the cathedral's main entrance, this is a fine 18th-century mansion with one of the most stunning facades in the city, as well as interesting interior details. Temporary exhibitions, usually with a religious theme, take place regularly. ✉ *Pl. Obispo 6, Málaga* ☎ *951/294051* ✉ *€5.*

### Pasaje Chinitas

STREET | The narrow streets and alleys on each side of Calle Marqués de Larios have charms of their own. The most famous is Pasaje Chinitas, off Plaza

## Something Sweet 🍴

For coffee and cakes, malagueños favor **Lepanto,** the classy shop at ✉ Calle Marqués de Larios 7, where uniform-clad staff serve a variety of pastries, cakes, and other sweets. Just next door at **Casa Mira** is delicious homemade ice cream, and at Christmas, their locally famous *turrón* (nougat) and festive candies.

de la Constitución and named for the notorious Chinitas cabaret here. Peep into the dark, vaulted *bodegas* (wineries) where old men down glasses of *seco añejo* or Málaga Virgen, local wines made from Málaga's muscat grapes. Silversmiths and vendors of religious books and statues ply their trades in shops that have changed little since the early 1900s. Backtrack across Larios, and, in the streets leading to Calle Nueva and Calle San Juan, you can see shoeshine boys, lottery-ticket vendors, street guitarists, and tapas bars serving wine from huge barrels. ✉ *Málaga.*

## 🍴 Restaurants

### Araboka

$$$ | SPANISH | Tucked behind the Picasso Museum, Araboka has a well-deserved reputation as an excellent gastro bar serving Mediterranean dishes made from local produce. Inside, the restaurant is contemporary with low lighting and plant motifs on the walls, and outside there's a pleasant terrace. **Known for:** outdoor terrace; extensive wine list; sharing plates. ⑤ *Average main: €18* ✉ *Calle Pedro de Toledo 4, Málaga* ☎ *952/124671* ⊕ *www.arabokarestaurante.com.*

### Chiringuito Maria

**$$ | SPANISH |** Fresh seafood and crisp fried fish star on the menu at this busy *chiringuito* (beach restaurant) on the western seafront near the tall chimney. Eat inside in nautically themed decor or outside on the terrace on the sand. **Known for:** efficient service; fresh fish and seafood; grilled sardines. ⑤ *Average main: €15* ⊠ *Calle Pacífico 129, Málaga* ☎ *952/245681* ⊘ *Closed Mon. and Feb. No dinner in the winter.*

### ★ Los Patios de Beatas

**$$$ | SPANISH |** Sandwiched between the Museo Picasso and Fundación Picasso is one of Málaga's largest wine collections (there are more than 500 on the list). The two historic mansions that make up this restaurant include an original patio and 17th-century stone wine vats; you can sit on barstools in the beamed tapas section, where the walls are lined with dozens of wine bottles, or dine on the airy patio, which is covered with stained glass. **Known for:** stunning interior; innovative tapas; wine list. ⑤ *Average main: €20* ⊠ *Calle Beatas 43, Málaga* ☎ *952/210350* ⊕ *www.lospatiosdebeatas.com.*

### Óleo Restaurante

**$$$ | INTERNATIONAL |** Attached to the Centro de Arte Contemporáneo, this small restaurant offers a range of Mediterranean dishes and sushi best enjoyed on the riverside terrace. Sharing plates include hummus or Vietnamese rolls with Málaga kid goat; highlights on the main menu are *carrillada ibérica* (stewed Iberian pork), tuna steak, and a long list of sushi. **Known for:** riverside dining; stewed Iberian pork; sushi. ⑤ *Average main: €20* ⊠ *Calle Alemania, Málaga* ✤ *Next to CAC* ☎ *952/219062* ⊕ *www.oleorestaurante. es* ⊘ *Closed Mon.*

### Restaurante Alexso

**$$ | SPANISH |** Chef Jose Antonio Moyano takes traditional Málaga cuisine and gives it an innovative twist in all his dishes. Go for local favorites such as the *fideos tostados con alioli de pimientos asados* (baked pasta with pepper aioli) and the daily stew, or the beetroot carpaccio with smoked eel or the *calamar en crema de guisante* (squid with pea puree). ⑤ *Average main: €15* ⊠ *Calle Mariblanca 10, Málaga* ☎ *952/849558* ⊕ *restaurantealexso.es* ⊘ *Closed Sun. and Mon.*

## 🛏 Hotels

### ★ El Castillo de Santa Catalina

**$$$$ | HOTEL |** Fully restored to its full 1930s neo-Mudejar glory, this castlelike hotel is one of the city's most atmospheric and romantic—a Málaga version of *The Arabian Nights.* **Pros:** panoramic views of Malaga city and bay; peaceful location; historic atmosphere. **Cons:** some distance out of town; could be too quiet for some; occasionally busy with events. ⑤ *Rooms from: €250* ⊠ *Calle Ramos Carrión, 38, Málaga* ☎ *952/212700* ⊕ *www.hotelcastillosantacatalina.com* ⤴ *24 rooms* ⦿ *No Meals.*

### Gran Hotel Miramar

**$$$$ | HOTEL |** Málaga's giant "wedding-cake" palace was opened by King Alfonso XIII in 1926 as one of the city's first hotels and fully restored to its former glory in 2017; if you can't splurge on a room, at least treat yourself to a coffee or cocktail here. **Pros:** most luxurious accommodations in town; stunning interior patio; personal butler service. **Cons:** pricey; short walk from city center; faces a busy road. ⑤ *Rooms from: €325* ⊠ *Paseo de Reding 22, Málaga* ☎ *952/603000* ⊕ *www.granhotelmiramarmalaga.com* ⤴ *190 rooms* ⦿ *No Meals.*

### Hotel Castilla Guerrero

**$$ | HOTEL |** This centrally located and gracious hotel has well-priced rooms that are small but functional, with double glazing to block out any late-night street revelry—those facing the side street or the interior patio are the quietest. **Pros:** great location between the city center and the port; rooms are clean and modern; parking. **Cons:** street noise in some rooms; friendly owners don't speak much English; rooms are small. $ *Rooms from: €100* ⊠ *Calle Córdoba 7, Málaga* ☎ *952/218635* ⊕ *www.hotelcastillaguerrero.com* ↪ *51 rooms* ⦿ *No Meals.*

★ **Parador de Málaga–Gibralfaro**
$$$$ | HOTEL | The attractive rooms at this cozy, gray-stone parador are some of the best in Málaga, with spectacular views of the city and the bay, so reserve well in advance. **Pros:** flawless Málaga-and-Mediterranean vistas from balconies; rooftop pool; popular restaurant. **Cons:** can be very busy; tired communal areas; some distance uphill from town. $ *Rooms from: €230* ⊠ *Monte de Gibralfaro s/n, Málaga* ☎ *952/221902* ⊕ *www.parador.es* ↪ *38 rooms* ⦿ *No Meals.*

**Room Mate Larios**
$$$$ | HOTEL | On the central Plaza de la Constitución, in the middle of a sophisticated shopping area, this elegantly restored 19th-century building holds luxuriously furnished rooms. **Pros:** stylish; rooftop bar with cathedral views; king-size beds. **Cons:** cathedral bells ring every 15 mins (from 7 am to midnight); interior rooms are dark; daytime noise from shopping street. $ *Rooms from: €190* ⊠ *Marqués de Larios 2, Málaga* ☎ *952/222200* ⊕ *www.room-matehotels.com* ↪ *45 rooms* ⦿ *No Meals.*

## 🎭 Performing Arts

Málaga's main nightlife districts are Maestranza, between the bullring and the Paseo Marítimo, and the beachfront in the suburb of Pedregalejo. Central Málaga also has a lively bar scene around the Plaza Uncibay and Plaza de la Merced. Málaga holds a biennial flamenco festival with events throughout the year; the next one is in 2023.

### Teatro Cervantes
CONCERTS | The city's main theater venue offers a year-round program of concerts, flamenco performances, dance, and plays. ⊠ *Calle Ramón Marín s/n, Málaga* ☎ *952/224109* ⊕ *teatrocervantes.com.*

### Teatro del Soho
THEATER | Owned by Antonio Banderas, this modern theater has a varied program of music, flamenco, and plays, plus an annual musical (Dec.–March) starring Banderas himself. ⊠ *Calle Córdoba 13, Málaga* ☎ *952/429173* ⊕ *teatrodelsoho.com.*

# Antequera

*64 km (40 miles) north of Málaga, 87 km (54 miles) northeast of Ronda.*

The town of Antequera holds a surprising number of magnificent baroque monuments (including some 30 churches)—it provides a unique snapshot of a historic Andalusian town, one a world away from the resorts on the Costa del Sol. It became a stronghold of the Moors after their defeat at Córdoba and Seville in the 13th century. Its fall to the Christians in 1410 paved the way for the Reconquest of Granada; the Moors' retreat left a fortress on the town heights.

Next to the town fortress is the former church of **Santa María la Mayor.** Built of sandstone in the 16th century, it has a ribbed vault and is now used as a concert hall. The church of **San Sebastián** has a brick baroque Mudejar tower topped by a winged figure called the Angelote (Big Angel), the symbol of Antequera. The church of **Nuestra Señora del Carmen** (Our Lady of Carmen) has an extraordinary baroque altarpiece that towers to the ceiling. On Thursday, Friday, and Saturday evenings, mid-June–mid-September, many monuments are floodlit and open until late.

### GETTING HERE AND AROUND
There are several daily buses from Málaga and Ronda to Antequera. Drivers will arrive via the A367 and A384 and should head for the underground parking lot on

Calle Diego Ponce in the center of town, which is well signposted. Antequera is small and compact, and most monuments are within easy walking distance, although the castle is up a fairly steep hill. You need a car to visit the Dolmens.

## VISITOR INFORMATION

**CONTACTS Municipal Tourist Office.**
✉ *Calle Encarnación 4, Antequera* ☎ *952/702505* ⊕ *turismo.antequera.es.*

#  Sights

### Archidona

**TOWN** | About 8 km (5 miles) from Antequera's Lovers' Rock, the village of Archidona winds its way up a steep mountain slope beneath the ruins of a Moorish castle. This unspoiled village is worth a detour for its **Plaza Ochavada,** a magnificent 17th-century octagon resplendent with contrasting red and ocher stone. ✉ *A45, Archidona.*

### ★ Dolmens

**RUINS** | These mysterious prehistoric megalithic burial chambers, just outside Antequera, were built some 4,000 years ago out of massive slabs of stone weighing more than 100 tons each. The best-preserved dolmen is La Menga. Declared UNESCO World Heritage Sites in 2016, the Dolmens offer an interesting insight into the area's first inhabitants and their burial customs, well explained at the visitor center. Regular events include Equinox and Solstice meetings, and the MengaStones Festival, June–Sept. Details are available at the tourist office. Note that gates to the dolmens close 30 minutes before closing time. ✉ *Antequera* ⊹ *Signposted off Málaga exit rd.* ☎ *952/712206* 🎫 *Free* ⊙ *Closed Mon.*

### Laguna de Fuente de Piedra

**NATURE PRESERVE** | Europe's major nesting area for the greater flamingo is a shallow saltwater lagoon. In February and March, these birds arrive from Africa by the thousands to breed, returning to Africa in August when the water dries up. Flamingo hatching time is April–June. The visitor center has information on wildlife. Bring binoculars if you have them. Guided tours are available in English (from €9 per person; book ahead online). ✉ *Antequera* ⊹ *10 km (6 miles) northwest of Antequera, off A92 to Seville* ☎ *675/645957* ⊕ *www.visitasfuentepiedra.es* 🎫 *Free.*

### Museo de la Ciudad de Antequera

**ART MUSEUM** | The town's pride and joy is *Efebo,* a beautiful bronze statue of a boy that dates back to Roman times. Standing almost 5 feet high, it's on display along with other ancient, medieval, and Renaissance art and artifacts in this impressive museum. ✉ *Pl. Coso Viejo, Antequera* ☎ *952/708300* ⊕ *turismo. antequera.es* 🎫 *Free* ⊙ *Closed Mon.*

### ★ Parque Natural del Torcal de Antequera

(*El Torcal Nature Park*)
**NATURE SIGHT** | Well-marked walking trails (stay on them) guide you at this park, where you can walk among eerie pillars of pink limestone sculpted by eons of wind and rain. Guided hikes (in Spanish only) can be arranged, as well as stargazing in July and August. The visitor center has a small museum. ✉ *Centro de Visitantes, Antequera* ⊹ *10 km (6 miles) south on Ctra. C3310* ☎ *952/243324* 🎫 *Free.*

# 🍴 Restaurants

### Restaurante Arte de Cozina

**$$$ | SPANISH |** As the name suggests, this cozy restaurant offers art in cooking, and its take on typical local dishes is one of the best in Málaga province. The menu is seasonal with an emphasis on local produce; it might include a selection of *porras* (thick, cold soup) and *choto malagueño* (kid goat in spicy sauce). **Known for:** bienmesabe dessert; kid goat; traditional dishes. **⑤** *Average main: €20* ✉ *Calle Calzada 25, Antequera* ☎ *952/840014* ⊕ *artedecozina.com* ⊙ *No dinner Sun.–Tues.*

##  Hotels

### Parador de Antequera

$$$ | HOTEL | Within a few minutes' walk of the historic center, this parador provides a welcome oasis of calm for relaxing after sightseeing, and panoramic vistas of the Peña de los Enamorados can be seen from the gardens, restaurant, and some rooms. **Pros:** quiet, romantic setting; pool with loungers; views. **Cons:** not all rooms have views; interior design could be too impersonal for some; slightly out of town. $ *Rooms from: €150 ✉ Pl. García del Olmo 2, Antequera* ☎ *952/840261* ⊕ *www.parador.es* ⤳ *58 rooms* ☉ *No Meals.*

# The Guadalhorce Valley

*About 34 km (21 miles) from Antequera, 66 km (11 miles) from Málaga.*

The awe-inspiring **Garganta del Chorro** (Gorge of the Stream) is a deep limestone chasm where the Río Guadalhorce churns and snakes its way some 600 feet below the road. The railroad track that worms in and out of tunnels in the cleft was, amazingly, the main line heading north from Málaga for Bobadilla junction and, eventually, Madrid until the AVE track was built.

North of the gorge, the Guadalhorce has been dammed to form a series of scenic reservoirs surrounded by piney hills, which constitute the **Parque de Ardales** nature area. Informal, open-air restaurants overlook the lakes and a number of picnic spots. Driving along the southern shore of the lake, you reach Ardales and, turning onto the A357, the old spa town of **Carratraca**. Once a favorite watering hole for both Spanish and foreign aristocracy, it has a Moorish-style *ayuntamiento* (town hall) and an unusual polygonal bullring. Today the 1830 guesthouse has been renovated into the luxury Villa Padierna spa hotel. The splendid Roman-style marble-and-tile bathhouse has benefited from extensive restoration.

## GETTING HERE AND AROUND

Coming from Antequera, take the "El Torcal" exit, turning right onto the A343; then from the village of Alora, follow the minor road north. From Málaga go west on the A357 through Cártama, Pizarra, Carratraca, and Ardales. There's also a train (three services daily) from Málaga to El Chorro station, which is handy if you're planning to walk the Caminito del Rey.

## ◉ Sights

### ★ Caminito del Rey

TRAIL | Clinging to the cliff side in the valley, the "King's Walk" is a suspended catwalk built for a visit by King Alfonso XIII at the beginning of the 19th century. It reopened in March 2015 after many years and a €9 million restoration and is now one of the province's main tourist attractions—as well as one of the world's dizziest. No more than 400 visitors are admitted daily for the walk, which includes nearly 3 km (2 miles) on the boardwalk itself and nearly 5 km (3 miles) on the access paths. It takes four to five hours to complete, and it's a one-way walk, so you need to make your own way back to the start point at the visitor center at the Ardales end (shuttle buses offer regular service; check when the last bus leaves and time your walk accordingly). A certain level of fitness is required and the walk is not recommended for young children or anyone who suffers from vertigo.

■ TIP→ This is one of the Costa del Sol's busiest attractions; book well ahead. ✉ *Valle del Guadalhorce* ⊕ *caminitodel-rey.info* 🎟 *From €10* ☉ *Closed Mon.*

Beach umbrellas at the edge of the surf in Torremolinos

# Torremolinos

*11 km (7 miles) west of Málaga, 16 km (10 miles) northeast of Fuengirola, 43 km (27 miles) east of Marbella.*

Torremolinos is all about fun in the sun. It may be more subdued than it was in the action-packed 1960s and '70s, but it remains the gay capital of the Costa del Sol. Scantily attired Northern Europeans of all ages still jam the streets in season, shopping for bargains on Calle San Miguel, downing sangria in the bars of La Nogalera, and congregating in the bars and English pubs. By day, the sunseekers flock to El Bajondillo and La Carihuela beaches, where, in high summer, it's hard to find towel space on the sand.

Torremolinos has two sections. Central Torremolinos is built around the Plaza Costa del Sol, refurbished and fully pedestrianized in 2019; Calle San Miguel, the main shopping street; and the brash Plaza de la Nogalera, which is full of overpriced bars and restaurants. The Pueblo Blanco area, off Calle Casablanca, is more pleasant; and the Cuesta del Tajo, at the far end of Calle San Miguel, winds down a steep slope to El Bajondillo beach. Here, crumbling walls, bougainvillea-clad patios, and old cottages hint at the quiet fishing village of bygone years.

The second, more sedate, section of Torremolinos is La Carihuela. To get here, head west out of town on Avenida Carlota Alessandri and turn left following the signs. This more authentically Spanish area still has a few fishermen's cottages and excellent seafood restaurants. The traffic-free esplanade is pleasant for strolling, especially on a summer evening or Sunday at lunchtime, when it's packed with Spanish families. Just 10 minutes' walk north from the beach is the Parque de la Batería, a very pleasant park with fountains, ornamental gardens, and good views of the sea.

## GETTING HERE AND AROUND

Torremolinos is a short train or bus journey from Málaga. The town itself is mostly flat, except for the steep slope to

El Bajondillo—if you don't want to walk, take the free elevator.

**BUS CONTACT Bus Station.** ⊠ *Calle Hoyo, Torremolinos* ☎ .

**TAXI CONTACT Radio Taxi Torremolinos.** ⊠ *Torremolinos* ☎ *952/380600.*

### VISITOR INFORMATION

**CONTACTS Plaza del Remo.** ⊠ *Pl. del Remo, Torremolinos* ⊹ *At the center of La Carihuela beach on the seafront* ☎ *952/372956* ⊕ *www.turismotorremolinos.es.* **Torremolinos.** ⊠ *Pl. Comunidades Autónomas, Torremolinos* ☎ *952/371909.*

 Beaches

#### La Carihuela

**BEACH | FAMILY |** This 2-km (1-mile) stretch of sand running from the Torremolinos headland to Puerto Marina in Benalmádena is a perennial favorite with Málaga residents as well as visitors. Several hotels, including the Tropicana, flank a beach promenade that's perfect for a stroll, and there are plenty of beach bars where you can rent a lounger and parasol—and also enjoy some of the best pescaíto frito on the coast. The gray sand is cleaned regularly, and the moderate waves make for safe bathing. Towel space (and street parking) is in short supply during the summer months, but outside high season this is a perfect spot for soaking up some winter sunshine. **Amenities:** food and drink; lifeguards (mid-June–mid-September); showers; toilets; water sports. **Best for:** swimming; walking. ⊠ *Torremolinos* ⊹ *West end of town, between center and Puerto Marina.*

 Restaurants

#### Casa Juan Los Mellizos

**$$ | SEAFOOD |** Thanks to the malagueño families who flock here on weekends for the legendary fresh seafood, this restaurant seats 170 inside and 150 outside in an attractive square, one block back from the seafront. Try for a table overlooking

the mermaid fountain. **Known for:** rice dishes; fried fish; zarzuela de marisco (seafood stew). ⑤ *Average main: €15* ⊠ *Pl. San Ginés, La Carihuela, Torremolinos* ☎ *952/373512.*

#### Yate El Cordobes

**$$ | SPANISH |** Ask the locals which beachfront chiringuito they prefer and El Yate will probably be the answer. Run and owned by an affable cordobés family, the menu holds few surprises, but the seafood is freshly caught, and meat and vegetables are top quality. **Known for:** beachside dining; paella; fresh seafood. ⑤ *Average main: €16* ⊠ *Paseo Marítimo Playamar s/n, Torremolinos* ☎ *952/384956* ⊗ *Closed Jan.*

🛏 Hotels

#### Hotel Fénix

**$$$$ | HOTEL |** One of the handful of adults-only hotels here, Hotel Fénix offers easy access to both the city center via the main entrance and El Bajondillo beach (one block away) via the first floor. **Pros:** handy location; sea views; good breakfast. **Cons:** three-night minimum stay in summer; not on the beachfront; some rooms have limited view. ⑤ *Rooms from: €250* ⊠ *Av. de las Mercedes 22, Torremolinos* ☎ *952/051994* ⊕ *www. thepalmexperiencehotels.com* ⤳ *126 rooms* ⑩ *Free Breakfast.*

#### Hotel La Luna Blanca

**$$$ | HOTEL |** A touch of Asia comes to Torremolinos at Spain's only Japanese hotel, tucked away at the western end of the resort and a few minutes' walk from La Carihuela. **Pros:** peaceful; free parking; close to La Carihuela. **Cons:** steep walk back from the beach; three-night minimum stay in July and August; can be difficult to find. ⑤ *Rooms from: €180* ⊠ *Pasaje del Cerrillo 2, Torremolinos* ☎ *952/053711* ⊕ *hotellalunablanca.es* ⤳ *11 rooms* ⑩ *No Meals.*

### Hotel MS Tropicana

$$$ | HOTEL | FAMILY | On the beach at the far end of La Carihuela, in one of the most pleasant parts of Torremolinos, this low-rise resort hotel has a loyal following for its friendly and homey style and comfortable, bright rooms. **Pros:** great for families; has its own beach club; surrounded by bars and restaurants. **Cons:** minimum four-night stay in July and August; some rooms are tired; can be noisy. ⑤ *Rooms from: €165 ⊠ Trópico 6, La Carihuela* ☎ *951/615102* ⊕ *www. hotelmstropicana.com* ↯ *84 rooms* ⦿l *Free Breakfast.*

## ⓨ Nightlife

Most nocturnal action is in the center of Torremolinos, and most of its gay bars are in or around the Plaza de la Nogalera, in the center, just off the Calle San Miguel.

### Parthenon

DANCE CLUBS | One of the longest-established gay bars in Torremolinos has live music and drag shows most nights. Check the club's Facebook page for details. ⊠ *La Nogalera 716, Torremolinos* ☎ *678/479381.*

## 🎭 Performing Arts

### Taberna Flamenca Pepe López

ARTS CENTERS | Many of the better hotels stage flamenco shows, but you may also want to check out this venue, which has shows Thurs.–Sat. throughout the year (call or check the Facebook page to confirm times). ⊠ *Pl. de la Gamba Alegre, Torremolinos* ☎ *952/381284* � *€30.*

# Fuengirola

*16 km (10 miles) west of Torremolinos, 27 km (17 miles) east of Marbella.*

Fuengirola is less frenetic than Torremolinos. Many of its waterfront high-rises

are vacation apartments that cater to budget-minded sunseekers from Northern Europe and, in summer, a large contingent from Córdoba and other parts of Spain. The town is also a haven for British retirees (with plenty of English and Irish pubs to serve them) and a shopping and business center for the rest of the Costa del Sol. The Tuesday market here is the largest on the coast and a major tourist attraction.

**GETTING HERE AND AROUND**
Fuengirola is the last stop on the train line from Málaga. There are also regular buses that leave from Málaga's and Marbella's main bus stations.

**BIKE RENTAL CONTACT Route Electric Bike.** ⊠ *Paseo Marítimo Rey de España 10, Fuengirola* ☎ *951/405150* ⊕ *www. phoenixrentalfuengirola.com.*

**BUS CONTACT Bus Station.** ⊠ *Av. Alfonso XIII 5, Fuengirola* ☎ .

**TAXI CONTACT Radio Taxi Fuengirola.** ⊠ *Fuengirola* ☎ *952/471000.*

**VISITOR INFORMATION
CONTACTS Fuengirola Tourist Office.** ⊠ *Av. Jesús Santos Rein 6, Fuengirola* ☎ *952/467457* ⊕ *turismo.fuengirola.es.*

## ⊙ Sights

### Bioparc Fuengirola

ZOO | FAMILY | In this modern zoo, wildlife live in a cageless environment as close as possible to their natural habitats. The Bioparc is involved in almost 50 international breeding programs for species in danger of extinction and also supports conservation projects in Africa and several prominent ecological initiatives. Four different habitats have been created, and chimpanzees, big cats, and crocodiles may be viewed, together with other mammals such as white tigers and pygmy hippos, as well as reptiles and birds. There are also daily shows and exhibitions, and various places to get refreshments. In July and August the zoo stays open until 11 pm to allow visitors to see the nocturnal animals. ⊠ *Av. José Cela 6, Fuengirola* ☎ *952/666301* ⊕ *www. bioparcfuengirola.es* ⊠ *€23.*

### Castillo de Sohail

CASTLE/PALACE | On the hill at the far west of town is the impressive Castillo de Sohail, built as a fortress against pirate attacks in the 10th century and named for the Moorish term for Fuengirola. Don't miss the views of the valley, sea, and coast from the battlements. Marenostrum festival featuring Spanish and international artists is held here during the summer months (⊕ *marenostrumfuengirola.com*). ⊠ *Calle Tartessos, Fuengirola* ✛ *15-min walk west from center* ☎ *663/996727* ⊠ *Free* ☉ *Closed Mon.*

##  Beaches

### Carvajal

BEACH | FAMILY | Lined with low-rises and plenty of greenery, this urban beach is between Benalmádena and Fuengirola. One of the Costa del Sol's Blue Flag holders (awarded to the cleanest beaches with the best facilities), the 1¼-km (¾-mile) beach has yellow sand and safe swimming conditions, which make it very popular with families. Beach bars rent lounge chairs and umbrellas, and there's regular live music in the summer. Playa Carvajal is packed throughout July and August and most summer weekends, but at any other time this beach is quite quiet. The Benalmádena end has a seafront promenade and street parking, and the Carvajal train station (on the Fuengirola–Málaga line) is just a few yards from the beach. **Amenities:** food and drink; lifeguards (mid-June–mid-September); parking (free); showers; toilets; water sports. **Best for:** sunrise; swimming. ⊠ *N340, Km 214–216, Fuengirola.*

## Restaurants

### Bodega Charolais

$$$ | SPANISH | Andalusian cuisine meets Basque tradition at this authentic restaurant in the heart of the older part of Fuengirola. Dine on fresh local produce either outside on the pleasant corner terrace or inside the rustic dining room. **Known for:** excellent wine list; duck; Basque-Andalusian fusion. $ *Average main: €20* ⊠ *Calle Larga 14, Fuengirola* ☎ *952/475441* ⊕ *www.bodegacharolais. com* ☉ *Closed Wed.*

### Restaurante Bodega La Solera

$$ | SPANISH | Tucked into the elbow of a narrow street near the main church square, this restaurant serves up superb Spanish dishes, including *albóndigas de ibérico en salsa de almendras* (Iberian pork meatballs in almond sauce) and *bacalao frito sobre pisto de verduras* (fried cod on ratatouille). The three-course daily menu with a half bottle of wine (€19.50) offers a wide range of choices. **Known for:** wine selection; good-value daily menu; Iberian pork meatballs. $ *Average main: €15* ⊠ *Calle Capitán 13, Fuengirola* ☎ *952/467708* ⊕ *www.restaurantelasolera.es* ☉ *Closed Tues.*

### ★ Sollo

$$$$ | SPANISH | Perched high in the hills above Fuengirola, this is one of the best fish restaurants on the Costa del Sol. Michelin-starred chef Diego Gallegos champions sustainable and healthy cuisine, and his on-site aquaponics facility raises most of the fish and vegetables used here. **Known for:** coastal views; Latin American touches in dishes; sustainable and innovative cuisine. $ *Average main: €150* ⊠ *Higuerón Hotel, Avda. del Higuerón 48, Reserva del Higuerón, Fuengirola* ☎ *951/385622* ⊕ *www.sollo. es* ☉ *Closed Sun. and Mon. No lunch.*

### ★ Vegetalia

$ | VEGETARIAN | This long-established vegetarian restaurant has a large, pleasant dining space decorated with vibrant

A horseback rider in Fuengirola's El Real de la Feria

artwork. It's best known for its excellent, vast, and bargain-priced lunchtime buffet, which includes salads and hot dishes like red-lentil croquettes, vegetable paella, and soy "meatballs." Leave room for the house-made desserts, all delicious. **Known for:** soy meatballs; lunch buffet; vegetable dishes. ⑤ *Average main: €10* ✉ *Calle Santa Isabel 8, Fuengirola* ☎ *952/586031* ⊕ *www.restaurantevege-talia.com* ⊘ *No dinner. Closed July, Aug., and Sun.*

##  Hotels

### Hostal Italia

$ | **B&B/INN** | Right off the main plaza and near the beach, this deservedly popular family-run hotel has bright and comfortable but small rooms; guests return year after year, particularly during the October *feria* (fair). **Pros:** friendly owners; surrounded by restaurants and bars; most rooms have balconies. **Cons:** rooms are small; some street noise; could be a little basic for some. ⑤ *Rooms from:* €85 ✉ *Calle de la Cruz 1, Fuengirola* ☎ *952/474193* ⊕ *www.hostalitalia.com* ⇥ *40 rooms* ⟊ *No Meals.*

### Leonardo Hotel

$$$ | **HOTEL** | This glossy spa hotel has a sophisticated edge on its high-rise neighbors, with light and airy rooms and private terraces overlooking the port and surrounding beach. **Pros:** great location; views of mountains and coast; in-house spa. **Cons:** adults only; very small pool; can be an overload of tour groups. ⑤ *Rooms from: €150* ✉ *Calle Dr. Galvez Ginachero, Fuengirola* ☎ *952/922700* ⊕ *www.hotel-florida.es* ⇥ *184 rooms* ⟊ *No Meals.*

# Mijas

*8 km (5 miles) north of Fuengirola, 18 km (11 miles) west of Torremolinos.*

Mijas is in the foothills of the sierra just north of the coast. Long ago foreign retirees discovered the pretty, whitewashed town, and though the large, touristy square may look like an extension of the Costa, beyond it are hilly residential streets with timeworn homes. Try to visit late in the afternoon, after the tour buses have left.

Mijas extends down to the coast, and the coastal strip between Fuengirola and Marbella is officially called **Mijas-Costa**. This area has several hotels, restaurants, and golf courses.

## GETTING HERE AND AROUND
Buses leave Fuengirola every half hour for the 25-minute drive through hills peppered with large houses. If you have a car and don't mind a mildly hair-raising drive, take the more dramatic approach from Benalmádena-Pueblo, a winding mountain road with splendid views. You can park in the underground parking garage (€1, flat rate) signposted on the approach to the village.

## VISITOR INFORMATION
**CONTACTS Mijas Tourist Office.** ⊠ *Av. Virgen de la Peña, Mijas* ☎ *952/589034* ⊕ *turismo.mijas.es.*

# Sights

### Centro de Arte Contemporáneo
**ART MUSEUM** | This modern art center contains more than 400 works from the Remedios Medina Collection, including the second largest collection of Picasso ceramics in the world. A total of 130 works by Picasso are on display alongside paintings, etchings, and other pieces by artists such as Dalí, Braque, and Foujita. ⊠ *Calle Málaga 28, Mijas* ☎ *952/590442* ⊕ *www.cacmijas.info* ⊠ *€3.*

### Iglesia Parroquial de la Inmaculada Concepción (*Immaculate Conception*)
**CHURCH** | This delightful village church, up the hill from the bullring, is worth a visit. It's impeccably decorated, especially at Easter, and the terrace and spacious

gardens have a splendid panoramic view. ⊠ *Pl. de la Constitución, Mijas* ☜ *Free.*

### Museo Mijas
**ART MUSEUM** | This charming museum occupies the former ayuntamiento. Its themed rooms, including an old-fashioned bakery and bodega, surround a patio, and regular art exhibitions are mounted in the upstairs gallery. ⊠ *Pl. de la Libertad, Mijas* ☎ *952/590380* ⊠ *€1.*

# 🍴 Restaurants

### Restaurante El Mirlo Blanco
**$$$$ | SPANISH** | In an old house on the pleasant Plaza de la Constitución, this restaurant is run by a Basque family that's been in the Costa del Sol restaurant business since 1968. The cozy indoor dining room, with a log fire for cooler days, is welcoming and intimate, with original and noteworthy artwork interspersed among the arches, hanging plants, and traditional white paintwork. **Known for:** Grand Marnier soufflé; reputation as a local institution; Basque specialties. ⑤ *Average main: €23* ⊠ *Calle Cuesta de la Villa 13, Mijas* ☎ *952/485700* ⊕ *www.mirlo-blanco.es* ⊘ *Closed Tues. and Jan., no dinner Sun.*

### Tomillo Limón
**$ | INTERNATIONAL** | A bright and airy tapas bar offering traditional Spanish staples—croquettes and patatas bravas—as well more modern takes on quick bites. Try the pulled-pork bao with peanuts and honey or the *torta de boquerones y anchoas* (anchovy toast). **Known for:** quick bites; delicious desserts; patatas bravas. ⑤ *Average main: €6* ⊠ *Av. Virgen de la Peña 11, Mijas* ☎ *951/437298* ⊘ *Closed Mon., no dinner Sun.*

# Marbella

*27 km (17 miles) west of Fuengirola, 28 km (17 miles) east of Estepona, 50 km (31 miles) southeast of Ronda.*

Thanks to its year-round mild climate and a spectacular natural backdrop, Marbella has been a playground for the rich and famous since the 1950s, when wealthy Europeans first put it on the map as a high-end tourist destination. Grand hotels, luxury restaurants, and multimillion-euro mansions line the waterfront. The town is a mixture of a charming *casco antiguo* (old quarter), where visitors can get a taste of the real Andalusia; an ordinary, tree-lined main thoroughfare (Avenida Ricardo Soriano) flanked by high-rises; and a buzzing Paseo Marítimo (Seafront Promenade), which now stretches some 10 km (6 miles) to San Pedro in the west. The best beaches are to the east of the town between El Rosario and the Don Carlos Hotel. Puerto Banús, the place to see and be seen during the summer, is Spain's most luxurious marina, home to some of the most expensive yachts you will see anywhere. A bevy of restaurants, bars, and designer boutiques is nearby.

## GETTING HERE AND AROUND

There are regular buses to and from the surrounding resorts and towns, including Fuengirola, Estepona (both every 30 minutes), and Málaga (hourly).

**BUS CONTACT Bus Station.** ⊠ *Av. Trapiche, Marbella.*

## VISITOR INFORMATION

**CONTACTS Marbella Tourist Office.** ⊠ *Pl. de los Naranjos 1, Marbella* 🕾 *952/768707.*

##  Sights

### Museo del Grabado Español Contemporáneo

**ART MUSEUM** | In a restored 16th-century palace in the casco antiguo, this museum shows some of the best in contemporary Spanish prints. Some of Spain's most famous 20th-century artists, including Picasso, Miró, and Tàpies, are on display. Temporary exhibitions are also mounted here. ⊠ *Calle Hospital Bazán, Marbella* 🕾 *952/938840* 💷 *€3, free weekends.* ⊘ *Closed Sun.*

### Plaza de los Naranjos

**PLAZA/SQUARE** | Marbella's appeal lies in the heart of its casco antiguo, which remains surprisingly intact. Here, a block or two back from the main highway, narrow alleys of whitewashed houses cluster around the central Plaza de los Naranjos, where colorful, albeit pricey, restaurants vie for space under the orange trees. Climb onto what remains of the old fortifications and stroll along the Calle Virgen de los Dolores to the Plaza de Santo Cristo. ⊠ *Marbella.*

### Puerto Banús

**MARINA/PIER** | Marbella's wealth glitters most brightly along the Golden Mile, a tiara of star-studded clubs, restaurants, and hotels west of town and stretching from Marbella to Puerto Banús. A mosque and the former residence of Saudi Arabia's late King Fahd reveal the influence of Middle Eastern oil money in this wealthy enclave. About 7 km (4½ miles) west of central Marbella (between Km 175 and Km 174), a sign indicates the turnoff leading down to Puerto Banús. Though now hemmed in by a belt of high-rises, Marbella's plush marina, with 915 berths, is a Spanish answer to St. Tropez. Huge yachts and countless expensive stores and restaurants make for a glittering parade of beautiful people that continues long into the night. The backdrop is an Andalusian pueblo—built in the 1960s to resemble the fishing villages that once lined this coast. ⊠ *Marbella.*

## 🏖 Beaches

### Marbella East Side Beaches

BEACH | FAMILY | Marbella's best beaches are to the east of town, between the Monteros and Don Carlos hotels, and include Costa Bella and El Alicate. The 6-km (4-mile) stretch of yellow sand is lined with residential complexes and sand dunes (some of the last remaining on the Costa del Sol). The sea remains shallow for some distance, so bathing is safe. Beach bars catering to all tastes and budgets dot the sands, as do several exclusive beach clubs (look for Nikki Beach, for instance, where luxury yachts are anchored offshore). Tourists and locals flock to these beaches in the summer, but take a short walk away from the beach bars and parking lots, and you'll find a less crowded spot for your towel. **Amenities:** food and drink; lifeguards (mid-June–mid-September); parking (fee in summer); showers; toilets; water sports. **Best for:** swimming; walking. ⊠ *A7, Km 187–193, Marbella.*

### Playas de Puerto Banús

BEACH | These small sandy coves are packed almost to bursting in the summer, when they're crowded with young, bronzed, perfect bodies: topless sunbathing is almost de rigueur. The sea is shallow along the entire stretch, which is practically wave-free and seems warmer than other beaches nearby. In the area are excellent Caribbean-style beach bars with good seafood and fish, as well as lots of options for sundown drinks. This is also home to the famous Ocean and Sala Beach clubs with their oversize sun beds, Champagne, and nightlong parties. **Amenities:** food and drink; lifeguards (mid-June–mid-September); showers; toilets; water sports. **Best for:** partiers; sunset; swimming. ⊠ *Puerto Banús, Marbella.*

## 🍴 Restaurants

### Altamirano

$$ | SEAFOOD | The modest, old-fashioned exterior of this local favorite is a bit deceiving: inside you'll be greeted not with stodgy decor but with spacious dining rooms with soccer memorabilia, photos of famous patrons, and tanks of fish. Seafood choices include fried or grilled squid, spider crab, lobster, sole, red snapper, and sea bass. **Known for:** outdoor dining; homemade rice pudding; seafood. ⑤ *Average main: €15* ⊠ *Pl. Altamirano, Marbella* ☎ *952/824932* ⊕ *www.altamirano.es* ⊘ *Closed Wed.*

### ★ Cappuccino

$$$ | INTERNATIONAL | Just under the Don Pepe Hotel and right on the promenade, this is the perfect spot for some refreshment before or after a long stroll along the seafront. Done in navy and white with wicker chairs, this outdoor café-restaurant has a fitting nautical theme, and if the temperature drops, blankets and gas heaters are at the ready. **Known for:** stylish terrace; brunch; ocean views. ⑤ *Average main: €20* ⊠ *Calle de José Meliá, Marbella* ☎ *952/868790.*

### La Niña del Pisto

$$ | SPANISH | Tucked away in the casco antiguo, this small venue with upstairs and downstairs dining offers a taste of Córdoba tapas and Montilla wine in Marbella. There is a good choice of tapas (from €2.50) and sharing plates, including homemade croquettes, cold cuts, fried fish (the squid is particularly good), and the house *pisto* (ratatouille) served with a fried egg or pork. **Known for:** Montilla wine; pisto; tapas. ⑤ *Average main: €12* ⊠ *Calle Lázaro 2, Marbella* ☎ *633/320022* ⊘ *Closed Sun. and Mon.*

### Messina

$$$$ | MEDITERRANEAN | Between the casco antiguo and the seafront, this innovative restaurant has an unpromising plain exterior, but forge ahead: the interior's chocolate browns and deep

reds make for cozy surroundings for a quiet dinner from chef Mauricio Giovanni, who renewed his Michelin star in 2022. The menu has an international slant, with more than a sprinkling of Spanish cuisine in its unusual fusion dishes. **Known for:** cozy atmosphere; good-value tasting menus; innovative dining. $ *Average main: €35* ⊠ *Av. Severo Ochoa 12, Marbella* ☎ *952/864895* ⊕ *www.restaurante-messina.com* ⊗ *Closed Sun.*

### Paellas y Más

$$$ | SPANISH | Located on the west side of town, about a 10-minute walk from the center, this modern restaurant specializes in rice dishes; there are 14 on the menu, including the signature baked rice with pork and the squid rice with prawns and chickpeas. *Fideuá* (similar to paella but made with noodles instead of rice) also features on the menu. **Known for:** baked rice with pork; fideuá (a noodle version of paella); rice dishes. $ *Average main: €22* ⊠ *Calle Hermanos Salom 3, Marbella* ☎ *952/822511* ⊕ *www.restaurantepaellasymas.com.*

### Taberna Gaspar

$$ | SPANISH | A firm favorite with locals who flock here for the value cuisine, Taberna Gaspar offers a long list of traditional seasonal dishes on a handwritten menu. Portions come hearty, so go for sharing plates, or ask for the dish of the day (weekdays only) if you're less hungry. **Known for:** hearty, delicious dishes; eclectic interior; value for money. $ *Average main: €12* ⊠ *Calle Notario Luis Oliver 19, Marbella* ☎ *952/779098.*

##  Hotels

### Boho Club

$$$$ | HOTEL | At the far western end of the Golden Mile (and a few minutes' walk from the beach and Puerto Banús), Boho Club offers a chilled vibe in Scandinavian-style surroundings. **Pros:** stunning interiors; excellent restaurant on-site; pool and gardens with mountain views.

**Cons:** expensive; some distance from Marbella center; traffic noise in some rooms. $ *Rooms from: €500* ⊠ *Urb. Lomas de Río Verde, 144, Marbella* ☎ *952/157221* ⊕ *bohoclub.com* ⇆ *39 rooms* ⦿ *No Meals.*

### Hotel Claude

$$$$ | HOTEL | Enjoying a quiet location at the north end of the casco antiguo, this 17th-century mansion is one of the resort's longest-established boutique hotels, fully refurbished in 2020. **Pros:** exquisite decoration; good breakfast; historic atmosphere. **Cons:** could be too formal for some; street noise in some rooms; car park a short distance away. $ *Rooms from: €350* ⊠ *Calle San Francisco 5, Marbella* ☎ *952/900840* ⊕ *hotelclaudemarbella.com* ⇆ *7 rooms* ⦿ *Free Breakfast.*

### Hotel Lima

$$$$ | HOTEL | Two blocks from the beach and a short walk from the casco antiguo stands one of Marbella's oldest hotels, which had a total overhaul in 2019 to elevate it to a four-star property. **Pros:** downtown location is good for town and beach; open all year; newly refurbished. **Cons:** lacks character of other properties; street noise in some rooms; room size varies considerably. $ *Rooms from: €200* ⊠ *Av. Antonio Belón 2, Marbella* ☎ *952/770500* ⊕ *hotellimamarbella.com* ⇆ *61 rooms* ⦿ *No Meals.*

### La Morada Mas Hermosa

$$$ | HOTEL | On one of Marbella's prettiest plant-filled pedestrian streets, this small hotel has a warm, homey feel, and the rooms are lovely. **Pros:** real character; short walk from the beach; quiet street, yet near the action. **Cons:** no late-night check-in; no parking; some rooms accessed by steep stairs. $ *Rooms from: €130* ⊠ *Calle Ancha 12, Marbella* ☎ *952/924467* ⊕ *www.lamoradamashermosa.com* ⊗ *Closed Jan.–mid-Feb.* ⇆ *8 rooms* ⦿ *No Meals.*

## La Villa Marbella

**$$ | HOTEL |** Just a short walk from the Plaza de los Naranjos, these private rooms and apartments, decorated in Asian style with Thai screens, offer a quiet hideaway. **Pros:** central but quiet location; good breakfast (but not always included); rooftop terrace and pool. **Cons:** two-night minimum stay in July and August; no on-site parking; multiple buildings. ⑤ *Rooms from: €120* ✉ *Calle Príncipe 10, Marbella* ☎ *952/766220* ⊕ *www.lavillamarbella. com* ➭ *12 rooms* ⦿ *No Meals.*

## ★ Marbella Club

**$$$$ | HOTEL |** The grande dame of Marbella hotels offers luxurious rooms, tropical grounds, and sky-high rates; the sense of seclusion is emphasized by its lofty palm trees, dazzling flower beds, and a beachside tropical pool area. **Pros:** luxurious, classic hotel; some bungalow rooms have private pools; superb facilities. **Cons:** three-night minimum stay in July and August; extremely expensive; a drive from Marbella's restaurants and nightlife. ⑤ *Rooms from: €900* ✉ *Blvd. Principe Alfonso von Hohenlohe at Ctra. de Cádiz, Marbella* ✛ *3 km (2 miles) west of Marbella* ☎ *952/822211* ⊕ *www.marbellaclub. com* ➭ *130 rooms* ⦿ *No Meals.*

## ⓨ Nightlife

### Casino Marbella

**GATHERING PLACES |** This chic gambling spot is in the Hotel Andalucía Plaza, just west of Puerto Banús. Shorts and sports shoes are not allowed, and passports are required. It's open daily 8 pm–4 am. ✉ *Hotel Andalucía Pl., N340, Marbella* ☎ *952/814000* ⊕ *www.casinomarbella. com.*

### La Sala Banús

**DANCE CLUBS |** This is one of Marbella's most popular nightspots for "older" clubbers (those out or nearly out of their twenties). Dine in before you dance to the live music. ✉ *Calle Juan Belmonte, near bullring, Puerto Banús* ☎ *952/814145* ⊕ *www.lasalabanus.com.*

### Olivia Valére

**DANCE CLUBS |** Marbella's most famous nightspot, with an impressive celebrity guest list, attracts a sophisticated crowd with its roster of big-name DJs and stylish surroundings that resemble a Moorish palace. To get here, head inland from the town's mosque (it's easy to spot). Doors open at midnight (daily in July and August; Thursday through Saturday only, September–June) and close at 6 am. ✉ *Ctra. de Istán, Km 0.8, Marbella* ☎ *952/828861.*

### Tablao Flamenco Ana María

**THEMED ENTERTAINMENT |** Ana María and her troupe provide foot-stomping and hand-clapping flamenco shows nightly from 11pm. Admission includes one drink. ✉ *Pl. de Santo Cristo 4, Marbella* ☎ *952/823107.*

# Ojén

*10 km (6 miles) north of Marbella.*

For a contrast to the glamour of the coast, drive up to Ojén, in the hills above Marbella. Take note of the beautiful pottery and, if you're here the first week in August, don't miss the **Festival de Flamenco,** which attracts some of Spain's most respected flamenco names, including Juan Peña Fernández (aka El Lebrijano), Miguel Póveda, and Marina Heredia. Four kilometers (2½ miles) from Ojén is the **Refugio del Juanar,** a former hunting lodge in the heart of the Sierra Blanca, at the southern edge of the Serranía de Ronda, a mountainous wilderness. A walking trail takes you a mile from the refugio to the *mirador* (lookout), with a sweeping view of the Costa del Sol and the coast of North Africa.

### GETTING HERE AND AROUND

Approximately five buses leave from the Marbella main bus station for Ojén, Monday to Saturday, and three on Sunday.

## 🛏 Hotels

### La Posada del Angel

**$$ | B&B/INN |** With friendly Dutch owners and rooms with lots of traditional Andalusian features and even a few Moroccan touches, this hotel makes a perfect rural retreat. **Pros:** chance to sample Andalusian village life; some rooms have terraces with a view; heated pool. **Cons:** minimum two-night stay mid-July–mid-September; slightly off the beaten track; could be too quiet for some. $ *Rooms from: €105* ☒ *Calle Mesones 21, Ojén* ☎ *952/881808* ⊕ *www.laposadadelangel.net* ⮡ *16 rooms* ❍ *Free Breakfast.*

# Estepona

*17 km (11 miles) west of San Pedro de Alcántara, 22 km (14 miles) west of Marbella.*

Estepona is a pleasant and relatively tranquil seaside resort, despite being surrounded by lots of urban developments. The beach, more than 1 km (½ mile) long, has better-quality sand than the Costa norm, and the promenade is lined with well-kept, aromatic flower gardens. The gleaming white **Puerto Deportivo** is packed with bars and restaurants, serving everything from fresh fish to Chinese food. Back from the main Avenida de España, the old quarter of cobbled narrow streets and squares is surprisingly unspoiled and decorated with flowerpots. Keep your eyes open for the many modern sculptures in the squares and 60-odd giant murals that cover entire facades throughout the town. The tourist office provides a guide to the artists and a mural map.

### GETTING HERE AND AROUND

Buses run every half hour 6:20 am–11:30 pm from Marbella to Estepona, and there are around four buses a day from Málaga Airport. The town is compact enough to make most places accessible via foot.

**BUS CONTACT Bus Station.** ☒ *Av. de España, Estepona.*

### VISITOR INFORMATION

**CONTACTS Estepona Tourist Office.** ☒ *Pl. de las Flores s/n, Estepona* ☎ *952/802002.*

## 👁 Sights

### Museo de Arte de la Diputación

**ART MUSEUM |** Housed in the historic 18th-century Casa de las Tejerinas palace, this art museum, which opened in 2018 and is known as MAD, showcases contemporary Andalusian and Spanish artists. Focusing on work produced this century, it has 50 pieces from artists including Málaga-born Dadi Dreucol and Chema Lumbreras, Santiago Idáñez from Seville, and Judas Arrieta from the Basque Country. Also worthy of note are the central patio and ornate facade. ☒ *Casa de las Tejerinas, Pl. de las Flores, Estepona* ☎ *952/069695* ⊕ *www.madantequera.com* ☒ *Free* ⊘ *Closed Sun. and Mon.*

### ★ Orchidarium

**GARDEN |** This lush green space in the middle of Estepona houses Europe's largest orchidarium. More than 1,600 species and over 4,000 plants, from South America and Asia, are exhibited under a futuristic 100-foot glass dome containing a giant cascade. Guided tours are available. ☒ *Calle Terraza 86, Estepona* ☎ *951/517074* ⊕ *www.orchidariumestepona.com* ☒ *€3* ⊘ *Closed Mon.*

##  Beaches

### El Saladillo

**BEACH** | Something of a Costa del Sol secret, this quiet 4-km (2½-mile) beach of gray sand has long, empty stretches with plenty of room for towels, even in high summer, making it a great place to relax, walk, or swim. The water's safe for swimming when waves are low, but watch out for the undertow when it's windy. Between San Pedro and Estepona, and flanked by residential developments, El Saladillo has the occasional beach bar. **Amenities:** food and drink; lifeguards (mid-June–mid-September); showers; toilets; water sports. **Best for:** solitude; sunset; walking. ⊠ A7, Km 166–172, Estepona.

## 🍴 Restaurants

### La Casa del Rey

€€€ | SPANISH | Just a block from Plaza de las Flores, a 200-year-old building hides this sleek, modern wine bar, serving some of the best tapas in town. Choose from a long list of hot and cold *pinchos* (small snacks)—the *rabo de toro en hojaldre* (oxtail in pastry) and *graten de bacalao* (cod gratin) are perennial favorites—tostas, and miniburgers, or from the à la carte menu, where meat dishes star. **Known for:** rabo de toro; wine list; tapas. ⑤ *Average main: €18* ⊠ *Calle Raphael 7, Estepona* ☎ *951/965414* 🕙 *Closed Sun.*

### La Escollera

$$ | SPANISH | Located at the heart of Estepona port, this is one of the best places on the western Costa del Sol to try simply cooked fresh fish, delivered daily off the restaurant's own boat. The very busy venue (on weekends it's packed to bursting) has excellent service and a quick turnaround so you never have to wait very long for a table. **Known for:** authentic atmosphere; liveliness on weekends; fresh fish. ⑤ *Average main: €16* ⊠ *Calle Puerto Pesquero s/n, Estepona* ⊹ *Near lighthouse at east end*

of port ☎ 952/806361 🕙 *No dinner Sun. Closed Mon.*

## 🛏 Hotels

### Hotel Boutique Casa Veracruz

$$ | HOTEL | Housed in a beautifully restored historic mansion, this family-run hotel offers cozy accommodations off a stunning central patio. **Pros:** steps to Estepona's old quarter and the beach; complimentary refreshments; historic building. **Cons:** reception not staffed all day; decor may be a little too flowery for some; interior rooms dark. ⑤ *Rooms from: €120* ⊠ *Calle Veracruz 22, Estepona* ☎ *951/466470* ✉ *hotelcasaveracruz@gmail.com* ⊕ *www.hotelboutiquecasaveracruz.com* 🛏 *10 rooms* ⑩ *No Meals.*

### Kempinski Hotel Bahía

$$$$ | RESORT | This luxury resort, between the coastal highway and the sea, looks like a cross between a Moroccan casbah and a take on the Hanging Gardens of Babylon, with tropical gardens and a succession of large swimming pools meandering down to the beach. **Pros:** great location; all rooms have balconies with sea views; excellent amenities. **Cons:** expensive; some distance from Estepona; so-so beach. ⑤ *Rooms from: €600* ⊠ *Playa El Padrón, Ctra. A7, Km 159, Estepona* ☎ *952/809500* ⊕ *www.kempinski.com* 🛏 *144 rooms* ⑩ *No Meals.*

# Casares

*20 km (12 miles) northwest of Estepona.*

The mountain village of Casares lies high above Estepona in the Sierra Bermeja, with streets of ancient white houses piled one on top of the other, perched on the slopes beneath a ruined but impressive Moorish castle. The heights afford stunning views over orchards, olive groves, and woods to the Mediterranean sparkling in the distance.

Windsurfing at Tarifa

## GETTING HERE AND AROUND
Buses are few and far between to Casares, and the best way to visit the village is by your own means. Be prepared for some steep slopes when you sightsee.

## 🍽 Restaurants

### Sarmiento
$$$ | SPANISH | FAMILY | This restaurant has a loyal following among locals and visitors with its stunning location—the terrace has far-reaching views over the village and to the Strait of Gibraltar (don't miss the eagles soaring the thermals above you)—and delicious food. Local produce takes center stage, and you can try Casares cheese, goat, and lamb as well as locally sourced tropical fruits and fresh fish from the coast. **Known for:** meat croquettes; Casares cheese, goat, and lamb; stunning views. $ *Average main: €20* ✉ *Ctra. de Casares, Km 12.5, Estepona* ☎ *952/895035* 🌐 *restaurante-sarmiento.com* 🕐 *No dinner Sun. and Wed. Closed Mon. and Tues.*

# Tarifa

*74 km (46 miles) southwest of San Roque.*

Tarifa's strong winds helped keep it off the tourist maps for years, but now it is Europe's biggest center for windsurfing and kiteboarding, and the wide, white-sand beaches stretching north of the town have become a huge attraction. Those winds have proven a source of wealth in more direct ways also, via the electricity created by vast wind farms on the surrounding hills. Downtown cafés, which not that long ago were filled with men playing dominoes and drinking *anís* (a Spanish liquor), now serve croissants with their café con leche and make fancy tapas for a cosmopolitan crowd. The lovely hilltop village of Vejer de la Frontera, 51 km (32 miles) west of Tarifa, is an easy side trip, and its coastline offers stunning beaches and the historic Cape Trafalgar, where the English Armada beat Napoléon in an epic naval battle in 1805.

Buses connect Tarifa and Vejer de la Frontera with Algeciras, but this is an area best visited by car, especially if you want to explore the coastline. There's no public transportation to Baelo Claudia or NMAC.

### VISITOR INFORMATION

**CONTACTS Tarifa Tourist Office.** ✉ *Paseo de la Alameda s/n, Tarifa* ☎ *956/680993* ⊕ *turismodetarifa.com.*

##  Sights

### ★ Baelo Claudia

**RUINS** | On the Atlantic coast, 24 km (15 miles) north of Tarifa, stand the impressive Roman ruins of Baelo Claudia, once a thriving production center of garum, a salty, pungent fish paste appreciated in Rome. The visitor center includes a museum. Concerts are regularly held at the restored amphitheater during the summer months. ✉ *Tarifa* ✛ *Take N340 toward Cádiz 16 km (10 miles), then turn left for Bolonia on CA8202* ☎ *956/106797* 🎟 *€2* ⏰ *Closed Mon.*

### Castle

**CASTLE/PALACE** | Tarifa's 10th-century castle is famous for the siege of 1292, when the defender Guzmán el Bueno refused to surrender even though the attacking Moors threatened to kill his captive son. In defiance, he flung his own dagger down to them, shouting, "Here, use this"; they did indeed kill his son. The Spanish military turned the castle over to the town in the mid-1990s, and it now has a museum about Guzmán and the sacrifice of his son. There are impressive views of the African coast from the battlements and towers. ✉ *Av. Fuerza Armadas, Tarifa* 🎟 *€4* ⏰ *Closed Mon. and Tues.*

### ★ Fundación NMAC (*Contemporary Art and Nature*)

**ART MUSEUM** | The rolling hills and forest between Tarifa and Vejer provide the perfect stage for this unique outdoor art museum. The sculptures and installations are placed along the guided route and in restored army barracks, and include works by international and Spanish artists such as Olafur Eliasson, Marina Abramovic, James Turrell, Pascale Marthine Tayou, and Fernando Sánchez Castillo. Visit first thing to avoid the crowds and get the best of the birdsong. ✉ *Dehesa de Montenmedio, Ctra. N340, Km 42.5, Vejer de la Frontera* ☎ *956/455134* ⊕ *www.fundacionnmac.org* 🎟 *€5 (free 1st Sun. of month)* ⏰ *Closed Mon.*

##  Beaches

### Playa Los Lances

**BEACH** | This part of the Atlantic coast consists of miles of white and mostly unspoiled beaches, and this, to the north of Tarifa and the town's main beach, is one of the longest. Backed by low-lying scrub and lagoons, the beach is also close to the odd campground, boho-chic hotel, and kitesurfing school. Its windswept sands make for perfect kitesurfing: together with Punta Paloma (just up the coast) it's where you'll see most sails surfing the waves and wind. Amenities are concentrated at the Tarifa end of the beach, where there are a few bars and cafés, usually open mid-June–mid-September, and this is naturally where the crowds congregate in the summer. Otherwise, most of the beach is deserted year-round. Swimming is safe here, except in high winds, when there's a strong undertow. **Amenities:** food and drink (mid-June–mid-September); lifeguards; showers; toilets. **Best for:** solitude; sunset; walking; windsurfing. ✉ *Tarifa.*

##  Hotels

### ★ Hotel V... Vejer

**$$$$** | **HOTEL** | The spacious rooms at this restored 16th-century mansion in the heart of the spectacular village of Vejer de la Frontera overlook the coast and the countryside with white villages speckling the horizon. **Pros:** stunning views; rooftop

# Gibraltar

## Sights ▼

1  Apes' Den.................**C3**
2  Cable Car ................**B3**
3  Gibraltar
   National Museum
   and Moorish Baths.....**B2**
4  Gibraltar
   Nature Reserve..........**C2**
5  Gibraltar Town ..........**B2**
6  Great Siege Tunnels.....**C1**
7  Moorish Castle...........**C2**
8  St. Michael's Cave.......**C4**

## Restaurants ▼

1  Aquaterra ...............**B1**
2  Charlie's Steak
   House and Grill .........**B1**
3  Sacarello's..............**B2**

## Hotels ▼

1  The Rock................**C3**
2  Sunborn................**B1**

### KEY

1 Sights
1 Restaurants
1 Hotels

terrace; exquisite decor. **Cons:** some rooms are dark; no on-site parking; no elevator. $ *Rooms from: €300* ⊠ *Calle Rosario 11–13, Vejer de la Frontera* ☎ *956/451757* ⊕ *www.hotelv-vejer.com* ⟿ *11 rooms* ⦿⫯ *Free Breakfast.*

### Hurricane Hotel

$$$$ | **HOTEL** | Surrounded by lush subtropical gardens and fronting the beach, the Hurricane is one of the best-loved hip hotels on this stretch of coastline, famous for its Club Mistral wind- and kitesurfing school and its horseback-riding center. **Pros:** fun and sophisticated; lovely gardens with beach access; excellent restaurant. **Cons:** some noise from the highway; rooms are plain; 6 km (3½ miles) from Tarifa proper. $ *Rooms from: €200* ⊠ *N340, Km 78, Tarifa* ☎ *956/684919* ⊕ *www.hotelhurricane. com* ⟿ *21 rooms* ⦿⫯ *Free Breakfast.*

# Gibraltar

*20 km (12 miles) east of Algeciras, 77 km (48 miles) southwest of Marbella.*

The Rock of today is a bizarre anomaly of Moorish, Spanish, and especially British influences. There are double-decker buses, "bobbies" in helmets, and red mailboxes. Millions of pounds have been spent in developing its tourist potential, and a steady flow of expat Brits comes here from Spain to shop at Morrisons supermarket and other stores. This tiny British colony, whose impressive silhouette dominates the strait between Spain and Morocco, was one of the two Pillars of Hercules in ancient times, marking the western limits of the known world and commanding the narrow pathway between the Mediterranean Sea and the Atlantic Ocean. The Moors, headed by Tariq ibn Ziyad, seized the peninsula in 711, preliminary to the conquest of Spain. The Spaniards recaptured Tariq's Rock in 1462. The English, heading an Anglo-Dutch fleet in the War of the Spanish Succession, gained control in 1704, and, after several years of local skirmishes, Gibraltar was finally ceded to Great Britain in 1713 by the Treaty of Utrecht. Spain has been trying to get it back ever since. In 1779 a combined French and Spanish force laid siege to the Rock for three years, to no avail. During the Napoleonic Wars, Gibraltar served as Admiral Horatio Nelson's base for the decisive naval Battle of Trafalgar, and during the two world wars, it served the Allies well as a naval and air base. In 1967 Franco closed the land border with Spain to strengthen his claims over the colony, and it remained closed until 1985.

There are likely few places in the world that you enter by walking or driving across an airport runway, but that's what happens in Gibraltar. First you show your passport; then you make your way out onto the narrow strip of land linking Spain's Línea with Britain's Rock. Unless you have a good reason to take your car—such as loading up on cheap gas or duty-free goods—you're best off leaving it in a guarded parking area in La Línea, the Spanish border town. Note that non-resident vehicles are not permitted in the Upper Rock area. Make sure your Schengen visa is valid for re-entry into Spain.

In 2021, tensions between Gibraltar and Spain lessened due mainly to the planned entry of Gibraltar into the Schengen Area sometime in 2022. However, there is occasional diplomatic tension between the two sides, which usually result in lines for leaving the colony, both via car and on foot. They can be long—it can take up to three hours to cross the border into Spain. This situation is unlikely to change, as there's little sign of any progress on any sort of joint Anglo-Spanish sovereignty, which the majority of Gibraltarians fiercely oppose. You can check the status of the line in real time via ⊕ frontierqueue.gi.

The Rock of Gibraltar

When you call Gibraltar from Spain or another country, prefix the seven-digit telephone number with 00–350. Gibraltar's currency is the Gibraltar pound (£), whose exchange rate is the same as the British pound. Euros are accepted everywhere, although you will get a better exchange rate if you use pounds.

## GETTING HERE AND AROUND

There are frequent day tours organized from the Costa del Sol resorts, either via your hotel or any reputable travel agency.

## VISITOR INFORMATION

**CONTACTS Gibraltar.** ⊠ *13 John Mackintosh St., Gibraltar* ☎ *200/45000* ⊕ *www. visitgibraltar.gi.*

## 👁 Sights

### Apes' Den

**NATURE SIGHT** | The famous Barbary Apes are a breed of cinnamon-color, tailless macaques (not apes, despite their name) native to Morocco's Atlas Mountains. Legend holds that as long as they remain in Gibraltar, the British will keep the Rock; Winston Churchill went so far as to issue an order for their preservation when their numbers began to dwindle during World War II. They are publicly fed twice daily, at 8am and 4pm, at Apes' Den, a rocky area down Old Queens Road near the Wall of Carlos V. Among the macaques' talents are their grabbing of food, purses, cell phones, and cameras, so be on guard. ⊠ *Old Queens Rd., Gibraltar* ☎ *200/71633* 🎫 *£16 for Upper Rock Nature Reserve and attractions.*

### ★ Cable Car

**VIEWPOINT** | You can reach St. Michael's Cave—or ride all the way to the top of Gibraltar—on a cable car. The car doesn't go high off the ground, but the views of Spain and Africa from the Rock's pinnacle are superb. It leaves from a station at the southern end of Main Street, which is known as the Grand Parade. ⊠ *Grand Parade* 🎫 *£18 round trip.*

### Gibraltar National Museum and Moorish Baths

**HISTORY MUSEUM** | Often overlooked by visitors heading to the Upper Rock

Reserve, this museum houses a beautiful 14th-century Moorish bathhouse and an 1865 model of the Rock; the displays evoke the Great Siege and the Battle of Trafalgar. There's also a reproduction of the "Gibraltar Woman," the Neanderthal skull discovered here in 1848 and the remains of some Moorish baths, from the 14th-century Marinid dynasty, which are considered to be among the best-preserved in Europe. The museum also serves as an interpretation hub for the prehistoric remains found in the limestone caves of Gorham's Cave Complex, which received UNESCO World Heritage status in 2016. ⊠ *Bomb House La.* ☎ *200/74289* ⊕ *www.gibmuseum.gi* 🎫 *£5* ⊙ *Closed Sat. afternoon and Sun.*

### Gibraltar Nature Reserve

NATURE PRESERVE | The reserve, accessible from Jews' Gate, includes St. Michael's Cave, the Apes' Den, the Great Siege Tunnels, the Moorish Castle, and the Military Heritage Center, which chronicles the British regiments that have served on the Rock. The Skywalk, a glass viewing platform opened (appropriately) by Mark Hamill, aka Luke Skywalker, in 2018, offers 360-degree views of the Rock and the ocean from 370 yards up. You can access the reserve via the cable car. ⚬ *From Rosia Bay, drive along Queensway and Europa Rd. as far as Casino, above Alameda Gardens. Make a sharp right here, up Engineer Rd. to Jews' Gate, a lookout over docks and Bay of Gibraltar toward Algeciras* ☎ *200/71633* 🎫 *£16 for all attractions.*

### Gibraltar Town

TOWN | The dignified Regency architecture of Great Britain blends well with the shutters, balconies, and patios of southern Spain in colorful, congested Gibraltar town, where shops, restaurants, and pubs beckon on Main Street. At the Governor's Residence, the ceremonial Changing of the Guard takes place six times a year, and the Ceremony of the Keys takes place twice a year. Make sure

you see the Anglican Cathedral of the Holy Trinity; the Catholic Cathedral of St. Mary; and the Crowned Law Courts, where the famous case of the sailing ship *Mary Celeste* was heard in 1872.

### Great Siege Tunnels

TUNNEL | Formerly known as the Upper Galleries, these tunnels were carved out during the Great Siege of 1779-82. At the northern end of Old Queen's Road, you can plainly see the openings from which the guns were pointed at the Spanish invaders. They form part of what is arguably the most impressive defense system anywhere in the world. The privately managed World War II tunnels nearby (prebooking essential via email) are also open to the public but are less dramatic. ⊠ *Old Queen's Rd.* ⊕ *www.visitgibraltar.gi/see-and-do/military-history/the-great-siege-tunnels-50* 🎫 *£16 for Nature Reserve, Upper Rock, and attractions including tunnels.*

### Moorish Castle

CASTLE/PALACE | The castle was built by the descendants of the Moorish general Tariq ibn Ziyad (670–720), who conquered the Rock in 711. The present Tower of Homage dates to 1333, and its besieged walls bear the scars of stones from medieval catapults (and later, cannonballs). Adm. George Rooke hoisted the British flag from its summit when he captured the Rock in 1704, and it has flown here ever since. The castle may be viewed from the outside only. ⊠ *Willis's Rd.*

### St. Michael's Cave

CAVE | This is the largest of Gibraltar's 150 caves; a visit here is part of the tour of the Upper Rock Nature Preserve. This series of underground chambers full of stalactites and stalagmites is sometimes used for very atmospheric (albeit damp) concerts and other events. The skull of a Neanderthal woman (now in the British Museum) was found at the nearby Forbes Quarry eight years before the world-famous discovery in Germany's Neander Valley in 1856; nobody paid much attention to it at the time, which is why the prehistoric species is called Neanderthal rather than *Homo calpensis* (literally, "Gibraltar Man," after the Romans' name for the Rock: Calpe).

■ **TIP→ A Lower St. Michael's Tour with guide has a separate fee and can be arranged in advance by email.** ⊠ *Queen's Rd.* ⊕ *gibraltarinfo.gi/top-10-attractions/#st-michaels-cave* ⊠ *Included in Nature Reserve ticket (£16); £25 for tour of Lower Cave.*

##  Restaurants

### Aquaterra
**$$ | MEDITERRANEAN |** The menu at this local favorite includes a big nod to Andalusia across the border with its Iberian ham and cheese boards, croquettes, and garlicky clams. But there are also Mediterranean and fusion dishes such as duck magret with Cumberland sauce and several varieties of bao. **Known for:** ham and cheese boards; cocktail menu; generous portions. $ *Average main: £16* ⊠ *2 Main Street* ✛ *On Casemates Square, next to the pharmacy* ☎ *200/42875* ⊕ *aquaterragourmet.com.*

### Charlie's Steak House and Grill
**$$ | STEAKHOUSE |** Don't let the brash neon exterior put you off: inside is one of the best steak houses in the region. Hugely popular among locals for its long list of juicy steaks, this diner-style venue also serves lamb, fried fish, and Indian curries. **Known for:** English desserts; Indian curries; steak. $ *Average main: £16* ⊠ *Marina Bay, 4/5 Britannia House, Gibraltar* ☎ *200/69993* ⊕ *www.charliessteakandgrill.com.*

### Sacarello's
**$$ | BRITISH |** Right off Main Street, this busy restaurant is as well known for its excellent coffee and cakes as it is for the rest of its food. There's a varied salad and quiche buffet, as well as stuffed baked potatoes and daily specials, which could include beef curry, or baked lamb with honey mustard. **Known for:** cozy,

old-fashioned English setting; lunch menu; coffee and cakes. $ *Average main: £12* ⊠ *57 Irish Town* ☎ *200/70625* ⊕ *www.sacarellosgibraltar.com* ⊘ *Closed Sun. No dinner.*

## 🛏 Hotels

### The Rock
**$$$$ | HOTEL |** This hotel overlooking the straits first opened in 1932, and although furnishings in the rooms and restaurants are elegant and colorful, they still preserve something of the English colonial style, with bamboo, ceiling fans, and a terrace bar covered with wisteria. **Pros:** old-world atmosphere; good breakfast; magnificent bay views. **Cons:** some bathrooms are very small; up a steep hill; pool not on-site, but across a busy road. $ *Rooms from: £210* ⊠ *3 Europa Rd.* ☎ *200/73000* ⊕ *www.rockhotelgibraltar.com* ⇌ *84 rooms* ⦿ *No Meals.*

### Sunborn
**$$$$ | HOTEL |** This giant yacht hotel (it's seven floors high and 155 yards long) has a permanent home in Gibraltar's marina and offers luxury accommodations complete with ocean views, a casino, a spa, and a restaurant on the top deck, plus lots of luxury extras. **Pros:** unusual place to stay; central, waterfront location; luxury extras. **Cons:** noise from airport and nearby bars; not all cabins have views; some may find it claustrophobic. $ *Rooms from: £250* ⊠ *35 Ocean Village Promenade, Gibraltar* ☎ *200/16000* ⊕ *www.sunborngibraltar.com* ⇌ *189 rooms* ⦿ *No Meals.*

## 🍸 Nightlife

### Lord Nelson
**BARS |** A restaurant during the day and a lively bar at night, the Lord Nelson has karaoke on Saturday night and jam sessions and live music on Thursday and Friday nights. Many ales are on tap. ⊠ *Grand Casemates Sq.* ☎ *200/50009* ⊕ *www.lordnelson.gi.*

Chapter 14

# THE CANARY ISLANDS

Updated by
Benjamin Kemper

| 👁 Sights | 🍴 Restaurants | 🛏 Hotels | 🛍 Shopping | 🍸 Nightlife |
|---|---|---|---|---|
| ★★★★☆ | ★★★☆☆ | ★★★★☆ | ★★★☆☆ | ★★★★☆ |

# WELCOME TO THE CANARY ISLANDS

## TOP REASONS TO GO

★ **Carnaval:** Judge for yourself if Carnaval festivities in Santa Cruz de Tenerife and Las Palmas rival those of Rio.

★ **El Teide:** Be blown away by the views of Spain's highest peak, visible from most of the island of Tenerife and from the shores of neighboring islands.

★ **Relaxation:** Seek out solitude and tranquility in national parks, protected biospheres, rolling sand dunes, and secret beaches.

★ **Volcanoes:** Marvel at the stark beauty of Lanzarote's volcanoes and lava flows.

★ **Wine:** Go vineyard-hopping and taste award-winning wines made from distinctive Canarian grapes.

★ **Beaches:** Sunbathe on pure white sands lapped by pristine turquoise sea on Fuerteventura.

**1 Tenerife.** Ride a cable car up the slopes of El Teide, swim in a huge artificial lake, wander botanical gardens, or dance at beachside discos.

**2 Gran Canaria.** Maspalomas is one of the islands' most arresting beach resorts, and the magnificent sand dunes behind it are a must-visit nature reserve. The seaside capital, Las Palmas, is the Canaries' most cosmopolitan city.

**3 Lanzarote.** Lanzarote has golden beaches, white villages, caves, and a volcanic national park where heat from an eruption in 1730 is still rising through vents in the earth.

**4 Fuerteventura.** Fuerteventura is remote and beachy, perfect for those who come to windsurf and kitesurf and enjoy the endless white beaches, reminiscent of the Caribbean.

**5 La Palma.** In the news because of a massive volcanic eruption in late 2021, the island has since cooled off and is perfectly safe to visit. Take advantage of its dizzyingly varied terrain—a hiker's dream—with misty laurel forests in the north, rocky trails in the center, and steep vineyards and volcanic landscapes in the south.

ATLANTIC OCEAN

La Graciosa
Parque Natural Archipiélago Chinijo
Tahiche
Lanzarote
Parque Nacional
de Timanfaya
Yaiza
LZ-1
3
LZ-2
Playa Blanca
Puerto del
Carmen
Arrecife
Corralejo
Isla de
Lobos
Costa
Tequise
El Cotillo
Parque Natural
de Corralejo
Parque Rural
de Betancuria
4
FV-1
Puerto del
Betancuria
Rosario
Fuerteventura
FV-2
Cuchillos
de Vigán
Parque Natural
Jandía
Costa Calma
Moro
Jable

Gran Canaria
Las Palmas
de Gran Canaria
GC-2
rque Natural
Tamadaba
CENTRAL HIGHLANDS
Telde
gua
Pico de
las Nieves
2
GC-1
Maspalomas

La Palma
Lanzarote
Tenerife
Fuerteventura
La Gomera
El Hierro
Gran Canaria
The Canary Islands

A historical way station between Europe and the Americas, the Canary Islands have been influenced over the centuries by African, mainland European, and South American waves of immigration. Perhaps that constant cultural influx is what makes Canarians so welcoming and outgoing. Every day on the Canaries brings a new landscape: black-sand beaches, banana plantations, dormant volcanoes, and colonial cities, to name a few.

There are eight Canary Islands, a volcanic archipelago 1,280 km (800 miles) southwest of mainland Spain and 112 km (70 miles) off the coast of southern Morocco that lie at about the same latitude as Florida. La Gomera and El Hierro, as well as parts of La Palma and Gran Canaria, are fertile and overgrown with exotic tropical vegetation, while Lanzarote, Fuerteventura, La Graciosa, and stretches of Tenerife are as dry as a bone, with lava caves and desert sand dunes. Even so, Spain's highest peak, Mt. Teide, on Tenerife, is sometimes capped with snow. Geographically the Canaries are African, but culturally they're European; spiritually, some say they're Latin American (many islanders have close blood ties to Cuba and Venezuela). After all, the Spanish spoken here sounds more Latin American than Iberian. Salsa and reggaeton, less popular in mainland Spain, are basically all you'll hear at the Canaries' wild Carnaval fiestas.

Before the Spanish arrived, the Canaries were populated by a cave-dwelling people called the Guanches who were genetically similar to the Berber tribes of northern Africa. In the late 15th century, the islands fell one by one to Spanish conquistadores. Columbus resupplied his ships here in 1492 before heading west to the New World and helped establish the archipelago as an important trading center. The Guanches were decimated by slave traders by the end of the 16th century, and to this day, their customs and culture remain largely a mystery. The most significant Guanche remains are the Cenobio de Valerón ruins on Gran Canaria and the mummies on display at the Museo de la Naturaleza y el Hombre in Santa Cruz de Tenerife.

Each of the eight islands is a world unto itself with unique charms, landscapes, and patrimony. Our coverage focuses on five islands: Tenerife, Gran Canaria, Lanzarote, Fuerteventura, and La Palma. The smallor islands of El Hierro, La Gomera, and La Graciosa are no less attractive though a bit harder to get to. If you have a few days to spare, visit them from the larger islands via plane or boat.

# Planning

## When to Go

The Canaries enjoy warmth in the winter and cool breezes in summer. Regardless of the time of year you visit, expect highs of about 75°F and lows of about 60°F. Winter, especially Christmas, and Easter are peak tourism periods for northern Europeans, while Spaniards and Italians tend to come in the summer, particularly August, to escape the sweltering heat. October, when the summer heat and the winds drop, and spring, when wildflowers blanket the islands, are the most beautiful times to be here. Since the Canaries are a year-round destination, prices tend to be roughly the same no matter when you come, barring the holiday season. You may have some luck negotiating discounts during the slowest months, May and November.

## Getting Here and Around

### AIR

There are no nonstop flights to the Canary Islands from the United States. Americans usually transfer in Madrid or elsewhere in Europe. Iberia, its budget carrier Vueling, and Air Europa have direct flights to Tenerife, Gran Canaria, Lanzarote, Fuerteventura, and La Palma from mainland Spain (three hours from Madrid). Budget airlines like Ryanair and Easyjet often have good deals as well.

Inter-island flights are handled by carriers Binter Canarias and Canaryfly using small

join mid-turboprop planes with stunning low-altitude views of the islands.

**FLIGHT INFORMATION Air Europa.** ☎ 911/401501 ⊕ www.aireuropa. com. **Binter Canarias.** ☎ 902/875787 ⊕ www.bintercanarias.com. **Canaryfly.** ☎ 902/808065 ⊕ www.canaryfly.es. **Iberia.** ☎ 901/111500 ⊕ www.iberia.com. **Vueling.** ☎ 902/808005 ⊕ www.vueling. com.

**AIRPORTS Fuerteventura.** ☎ 913/211000 ⊕ www.aena.es. **Gran Canaria.** ☎ 928/579130 ⊕ www.aena.es. **Lanzarote.** ☎ 902/404704 ⊕ www.aena.es. **Tenerife North.** ☎ 902/404704 ⊕ www.aena.es. **Tenerife South.** ☎ 902/404704 ⊕ www. aena.es. **La Palma.** ☎ 91/321–1000 ⊕ www.aena.es.

### TRANSFERS ON TENERIFE
Tenerife has two airports: Tenerife South (TFS), near Playa de las Américas, and Tenerife North (TFN), near the capital city of Santa Cruz. Choose the airport closest to the area of the island that you'll be spending the most time in. The TITSA bus (Route 343, roughly €10) connects the airports directly; travel takes about 50 minutes. Driving time from one airport to the other is also about 50 minutes; you can hire a taxi for about €90 or rent a car for around €35.

### BOAT AND FERRY
Fred Olsen, Naviera Armas, Líneas Romero, and Trasmediterránea operate inexpensive ferries between all eight islands, although if you're traveling to or from El Hierro, La Gomera, or La Palma to the eastern islands, you usually need to get a connecting ferry in Tenerife. Most interisland trips take one to four hours; the few boats departing near midnight are equipped with sleeping cabins. Note that schedules change, particularly in high winds or storms, so keep an eye on your email for last-minute delays and cancellations. Fred Olsen's fleet has several ultrasleek trimarans,

which accommodate vehicles and are the quickest way to go between islands. Trasmediterránea runs a slow, comfortable ferry service weekly between Andalusia and the Canary Islands with trajectories ranging from 34 to 49 hours. Note that this is not a luxury cruise and clearly rather impractical, both money- and time-wise, for most travelers.

**CONTACTS Fred Olsen.** ☎ 902/100107 general information ⊕ www.fredolsen. es. **Líneas Romero.** ☎ 928/596107 ⊕ www. lineasromero.com. **Naviera Armas.** ☎ 902/456500 general information ⊕ www.navieraarmas.com. **Trasmediterránea.** ☎ 902/454645 general information ⊕ www.trasmediterranea.es.

## BUS

On the Canaries, buses are known as guaguas (pronounced wa-was), likely a hispanicization of the English word "wagon." A bus terminal is usually called an intercambiador rather than an estación de autobuses. Expect to see these terms on signs and brochures.

Bus travel is generally good between the main resorts, airports, and capitals. In Tenerife, TITSA runs a wide-reaching network of routes connecting the airports with Santa Cruz and the south, and Los Rodeos airport with Santa Cruz and Puerto de la Cruz. Global on Gran Canaria connects the capital and the south with the airport. Buses also transport ferry passengers to and from bus terminals and ports.

Each island has its own bus service geared toward residents. Buses generally leave each village early in the morning for the capital, then depart from the main plaza in early afternoon. Tourist offices have details, and Google Maps is generally reliable.

**CONTACTS Fuerteventura Buses.** ☎ 928/855726 ⊕ www.tiadhe.com. **Gran Canaria Buses.** ☎ 928/939407 ⊕ www.globalsu.net. **Lanzarote Buses.** ☎ 928/811522

⊕ www.intercitybuslanzarote.es. **Tenerife Buses.** ☎ 922/531300 ⊕ www.titsa.com. **La Palma Buses.**

## CAR

Most travelers rent a car for at least part of their stay on the Canaries, as this is by far the best way to explore the countryside. Mountain roads are sometimes narrow, which can be hair-raising if you meet a bus head on, so be alert. Expect traffic around urban centers. Rental hubs are found in all ferry terminals and airports.

### CAR RENTAL

Car-rental companies abound on every island. Reservations are usually necessary in high season. Cicar and Europcar, with branches in all the airports and major towns on all seven islands, tend to have the best rates.

**CONTACTS Cicar Fuerteventura.** ✉ Aeropuerto de Fuerteventura, Puerto del Rosario ☎ 928/822900 ⊕ www.cicar.com. **Cicar Gran Canaria.** ✉ Aeropuerto de Las Palmas, Gando ☎ 928/822900 ⊕ www. cicar.com. **Cicar Lanzarote.** ✉ Aeropuerto de Lanzarote, Arrecife ☎ 928/822900 ⊕ www.cicar.com. **Cicar Tenerife South.** ✉ Tenerife South Airport, Granadilla de Abona ☎ 928/822900 ⊕ www.cicar.com. **Europcar Fuerteventura.** ✉ Aeropuerto de

## Travel Tip

View all the options for interisland transportation (by land and sea) in one place on the Canary Island tourist board's Get Around the Archipelago travel tool (⊕ www.hellocanaryislands.com/travelling-between-the-islands), free and easy to use on the official government website. It comes in handy if, say, you want to know how to get from La Palma to El Hierro or from Tenerife to Gran Canaria and don't know where to start.

Fuerteventura ☎ 902/105055 ⊕ www.
europcar.es. **Europcar Gran Canaria.** ⊠ Aeropuerto de Las Palmas ☎ 902/105055 ⊕ www.europcar.es. **Europcar Lanzarote.** ⊠ Aeropuerto de Lanzarote ☎ 902/105055 ⊕ www.europcar.es. **Europcar Tenerife North.** ⊠ Tenerife North Airport, La Laguna ☎ 902/105055 ⊕ www.europcar.es. **Europcar Tenerife South.** ⊠ Tenerife South Airport, Granadilla de Abona ☎ 902/105055 ⊕ www.europcar.es. **Europcar La Palma Aeropuerto.** ⊠ Calle La Bajita, LP-5 ☎ 92/242–6192 ⊕ www.europcar.com. **Cicar Puerto de La Palma.** ⊠ Estación Marítima de Santa Cruz de La Palma, Santa Cruz de la Palma ☎ 92/242–0159 ⊕ www.cicar.com.

## CRUISE

Cruises to and among the Canaries are popular, but itineraries remained limited as of 2022 due to the pandemic. Las Palmas de Gran Canaria and Santa Cruz de Tenerife are Spain's most visited cruise ports after Barcelona and Palma de Mallorca. The islands are frequent stops on cruises that also visit Madeira, the Azores, and the west coast of Africa.

## TAXI

In major towns, taxis can be hailed on the street. Alternately, ask for the nearest taxi stand (parada de taxi). Taxis use meters to calculate the fare, though (shh) a cheaper flat rate can sometimes be negotiated in advance and paid in cash; passengers may be charged extra fees for luggage and holiday, weekend, and late-night trips. There are currently no third-party ride-hailing apps such as Uber or Cabify in service.

**CONTACTS Lanzarote Taxi.** (Asociación Cooperativa de Taxistas Ajey–Tamia) ☎ 630/207305 ⊕ www.lanzarotetaxi.com. **Radio-Taxi San Marcos Tenerife.** ☎ 922/641112, 922/641459, 682/391930 mobile/WhatsApp ⊕ www.taxisanmarcos.es. **Taxis Fuerteventura.** ☎ 928/850216 ⊕ www.taxisfuerteventura.es. **Taxi Radio Gran Canaria.** (Taragranca Sociedad Cooperativa de Taxistas) ☎ 928/160000 ⊕ www.taragranca.org. **Taxi La Palma.** ☎ 686/553868 ⊕ www.taxilapalma.com.

# Restaurants

Canarian cuisine revolves around local seafood, tropical fruits, potatoes, bread, and goat cheese. Meals often begin with a plato de cuchara, something hearty eaten with a spoon such as potaje canario (containing garden vegetables, pork, potatoes, chickpeas, and sometimes pears), rancho canario (with beef, noodles, and legumes), and potaje de berros (watercress soup). Gofio, a thick, savory porridge made with corn or wheat flour and enriched with milk or stock, adds ballast to otherwise light meals. The main culinary event is often fresh native fish, the best of which are white-fleshed vieja (parrotfish), cherne (wreckfish), sama (red-banded seabream), and the wonderfully rich patudo (bigeye) tuna, most of which is exported to Japan and other luxury markets. The most inescapable Canarian delicacy is papas arrugadas, "wrinkled" baby potatoes cooked in an abundance of salt water. The best examples use papas bonitas ("pretty" potatoes), the moniker for locally grown heirloom varieties.

Other specialties include cabrito (roast baby goat) and conejo (rabbit), both often served in salmorejo, a slightly spicy paprika sauce. No Canarian meal is complete without a dab of mojo: the spicy "rojo" (red) version is made with pimientas palmeras (mild local red chilies), garlic, and vinegar, plus any number of secret ingredients, while the "verde" (green) is milder and features parsley and/or cilantro. Most restaurants serve both sauces virtually by default, and Canarians heap it liberally on everything. Another island specialty is goat cheese, whose most prized specimens ripen in the seaside caves of La Palma.

Canarian wines are good and varied. The most popular red grape is Listán Negro, which makes a fruity, highly drinkable wine with a faint smokiness—probably that volcanic soil talking. Common whites include Malvasía and Listán Blanco, often blended to create floral, fruity expressions. Confusingly, off-dry wines are frequently labeled as *afrutado* ("fruity"), so if you like your whites on the dry side, ask for a *vino seco* ("dry") . Wine production on the Canaries dates back centuries—the Malmsey (fortified sweet) wines from Lanzarote were a favorite with Shakespeare's Falstaff. On the stronger side, the Canaries are also famous for dark rum and liqueurs flavored with everything from coffee to cocoa to hazelnut.

■**TIP**➜ **Although the tap water in the Canary Islands is technically safe to drink according to the Ministry of Health, most of it comes from desalination plants and is of inferior quality (and taste). Bottled water is the norm in both hotels and restaurants, and hotels generally do not charge restocking fees. To cut down on plastic waste, purchase large-format bottles, and ask your hotel to recycle empties. If you have a choice, go with Fuente Alta, the only bottled water brand in the Canaries that uses recycled materials in its production.**

*Restaurant reviews have been shortened. For full information, visit Fodors. com.*

### What It Costs in Euros

| $ | $$ | $$$ | $$$$ |
|---|---|---|---|
| **AT DINNER** | | | |
| Under €12 | €12–€17 | €18–€22 | over €22 |

# Hotels

It's important to read reviews closely and not jump at the first seemingly good deal when selecting accommodations. With a few exceptions, noted in the individual reviews, it's best to stay in newer facilities, ones that weren't built shoddily during the Canaries' tourism boom many decades ago. Many hotels include either a full buffet breakfast or a meal plan of breakfast and lunch or dinner in the price of a room. Hotels with spas and pools generally include the use of these in their rates, but be sure to check the fine print when comparing prices.

Apartment, villa, and cabin rentals at every budget have become wildly popular in recent years. Airbnb is the most common booking resource. Most accommodations are simply furnished with a kitchenette and small living space, though there are certainly diamond-in-the-rough design properties to be discovered for those willing to pony up the extra euros.

Package tours are generally best suited to groups as opposed to independent travelers. Especially in the post-pandemic economy, check for offers on hotel websites, and inquire about discounts for long stays or during low season. ■**TIP**➜ **Always call properties directly before booking via a third party to see if they'll offer you a lower rate.**

High season varies depending on the island and locale. In Tenerife, La Palma, and Gran Canaria, high season is from November to April with a second spike in July and August. Lanzarote and Fuerteventura's high seasons are during December and January plus July and August. Airfare to Tenerife and Gran Canaria increases during those islands' respective Carnaval celebrations in late February, so if you're keen to attend, make reservations a few months out if possible.

Note that many four- and five-star hotels have fusty dress codes that require you to change out of beachwear, shorts, and flip-flops at mealtimes.

*Hotel reviews have been shortened. For full information, visit Fodors.com.*

## What It Costs in Euros

| | $ | $$ | $$$ | $$$$ |
|---|---|---|---|---|
| **FOR TWO PEOPLE** | | | | |
| | under €90 | €90– €125 | €126– €180 | over €180 |

# Tenerife

Tenerife is the largest of the Canary Islands. Its standout feature is the volcanic peak of El Teide, which, at 12,198 feet, is Spain's highest mountain. Its slopes are blanketed with pines in the north and barren lava fields in the south. Tenerife's capital, Santa Cruz de Tenerife, is a spread-out urban center—forget whitewashed villas and sleepy streets, and imagine the traffic, activity, and crowds of an important shipping port. In the wetter north, mixed among the tourist attractions are banana plantations and vineyards, while in the dry south, resorts lining the coast spring up at the edge of what's essentially a desert.

## VILLA AND APARTMENT RENTAL

Villas and apartments abound in the Canary Islands. Self-catering apartments are competitively priced, and you can often find excellent deals, particularly if you stay for a week or more and do price comparisons on Airbnb and similar sites. For detailed listings and photos of apartments, villas and hotels throughout the islands, check out ⊕ *www.booking. com, www.vrbo.com, www.airbnb.com, www.nice2stay.com/en,* and ⊕ *www. spain-holiday.com.*

**LOCAL AGENTS Atlantic Horizons.** ⊠ *Av. Amsterdam 3, Los Cristianos* ☎ *922/790299* ⊕ *www.atlantichorizons. com.* **Tenerife Royal Gardens.** ⊠ *Apartamentos Royal Gardens 4, Playa de las Américas* ☎ *922/790211* ⊕ *www.tenerife-holiday-apartments.com.*

## VISITOR INFORMATION

**CONTACTS Santa Cruz de Tenerife Tourist Office.** ⊠ *Pl. de España, Santa Cruz de Tenerife* ☎ *922/892903* ⊕ *www.webtenerife.co.uk.*

# Santa Cruz de Tenerife

*10 km (6 miles) southeast of Los Rodeos Airport, 75 km (45 miles) northeast of Playa de las Américas.*

Although Tenerife's busy capital is smaller, quieter, and less attractive than Las Palmas in Gran Canaria, it has worthwhile attractions and monuments. Until 1833, the island's capital was La Laguna, not Santa Cruz, making the latter "new," at least by Spanish standards, with the city's oldest buildings (the fishermen's houses on Calle de la Noria) dating to the 18th century. From the busy Plaza de España, there are several pedestrian streets leading north and to the area west of the port, where you'll find a stunning auditorium and maritime park. Be sure to go for a stroll down the *ramblas,* the long, tree-lined boulevards that fall steeply from the north end of the city to the sea.

Santa Cruz is an ideal home base for adventures into the Parque Rural de Anaga (Anaga Nature Park), one of Tenerife's most scenic and untouched corners. Brave the switchbacks, and you'll be rewarded with subtropical forests, volcanic formations, and charming white villages.

Playa de las Teresitas is one of Tenerife's most popular beaches, thanks to its golden sand, many facilities, and beachfront restaurants.

### GETTING HERE AND AROUND

If you're arriving by sea, it can be a long and fairly uninteresting walk from your cruise ship into town, so take a shuttle bus if one is provided (most cruise companies do) to the Estación Marítima cruise station. From here, you can walk 10 minutes to Plaza de España, where there's a branch of the tourist office, and on to any of the main sights. If you're heading south to Los Cristianos or north to Puerto de la Cruz, go to the bus terminal (about a 15-minute walk from Plaza de España), where there are frequent connections. La Laguna can be reached by tram: There are stops at the bus station and near the Puente General Serrador.

From Tenerife you can catch a ferry to any of the other seven islands. From Santa Cruz, sail to Gran Canaria's two main ports: Agaete in the west (Fred Olsen is the quickest, at about an hour) or Las Palmas in the north. Ferries to La Palma (Santa Cruz de la Palma), La Gomera (San Sebastián), and El Hierro (Puerto de la Estaca) leave from Los Cristianos, in southern Tenerife. La Gomera can also be reached by ferry from Los Cristianos (55 minutes; 35 minutes by Fred Olsen's trimaran).

## ◉ Sights

### Auditorio de Tenerife Adán Martín

**PERFORMANCE VENUE** | A magnificent avant-garde auditorium designed by Santiago Calatrava dominates the west end of the city. To keep its pearly white *trencadís* (broken tile mosaics) exterior clear of pooping pigeons, a falconer visits regularly with his raptors. The auditorium has a year-round program of concerts and opera, though you can sometimes catch impromptu music acts rehearsing or performing in the adjacent square overlooking the sea. Guided tours are given in English and Spanish; book ahead by phone or email (*visitas@auditoriode-tenerife.com*). ✉ *Av. de la Constitución*

*1, Santa Cruz de Tenerife* ☎ *922/568625* ⊕ *www.auditoriodetenerife.com* ✉ *Tours* €8 ⊗ No tours Sun.

## Iglesia de Nuestra Señora de la Concepción
(*Church of Our Lady of the Conception*)
CHURCH | A six-story Moorish bell tower tops this church, which was renovated as part of an urban-renewal project that razed blocks of slums in this area. Opening times vary, but you can generally visit before and after Mass. ⊠ *Pl. de la Iglesia, Santa Cruz de Tenerife* ☎ *922/242387* ✉ *Free.*

## Mercado de Nuestra Señora de África (*La Recova Market*)
MARKET | FAMILY | This colorful city market is part bazaar and part food emporium. Stalls outside sell household goods; inside, stands displaying everything from flowers to canaries are arranged around a patio. Downstairs, a stroll through the seafood section will acquaint you with the local fish. A flea market with antiques and secondhand goods is held here on Sunday morning. Check the website for a monthly schedule of nighttime activities. ⊠ *Av. de San Sebastián, Santa Cruz de Tenerife* ⊕ *www.la-recova.com.*

## Museo de la Naturaleza y Arqueología
(*Museum of Nature and Archaeology*)
SCIENCE MUSEUM | FAMILY | Primitive ceramics and mummies are this museum's highlights. The ancient Guanches mummified their dead by rubbing the bodies with pine resin and salt and leaving them in the sun to dry for two weeks. Placards are in Spanish, but there's a downloadable app with English descriptions. ⊠ *Calle Fuente Morales, Santa Cruz de Tenerife* ☎ *922/535816* ⊕ *www.museosdetenerife.org* ✉ *€5 (free Fri. and Sat. 4–8)* ⊗ Closed Mon.

## Museo Municipal de Bellas Artes (*Museum of Fine Arts*)
ART MUSEUM | This 14-room, two-story gallery is lined with canvases by Breughel, Coecke, and Ribera as well as other famed works created between the 16th and 20th centuries. Many depict local events. The museum is on the Plaza Príncipe de Asturias. ⊠ *Calle José Murphy 12, Santa Cruz de Tenerife* ☎ *922/274786* ✉ *Free* ⊗ Closed Mon.

## Palmetum
GARDEN | FAMILY | Up on the hill just behind Parque Marítimo is Europe's largest collection of palms with some 600 species. The 29½-acre site, built over the former city dump and opened in 2014, houses palm trees from all over the world set around waterfalls and lagoons, all with panoramic views of the ocean and city. Guided tours in English cost €3 extra and last approximately one hour. ⊠ *Av. Constitución 5, Santa Cruz de Tenerife* ☎ *697/651127* ⊕ *palmetumtenerife.es* ✉ *€6* ⊗ Closed Mon.

## Parque Marítimo César Manrique
WATER PARK | FAMILY | West of the auditorium, this public water park with its three saltwater pools and tropical gardens is a favorite with locals. Designed by the Lanzarote-born architect César Manrique, it combines volcanic rock with palms and local flora. ⊠ *Av. de la Constitución 5, Santa Cruz de Tenerife* ☎ *922/229368* ⊕ *www.parquemaritimosantacruz.es* ✉ *€3.*

## ★ Parque Rural de Anaga (*Anaga Nature Park*)
NATURE PRESERVE | FAMILY | Thanks to its ornery terrain, Anaga Nature Park has managed to keep the tour-bus crowd (mostly) at bay—their loss. This magical oasis takes in misty laurel forests (aka laurisilva) with numerous endemic species, bizarre rock formations that jut above the trees, and hidden mountain villages like Taganana, founded in 1501. Explore the area by car, stopping to take a dip at Playa de Benijo, where you can catch a hiking trail into the surrounding countryside, and to snap a few postcard-worthy pics at the Pico de Inglés

## Tenerife

ATLANTIC OCEAN

Punta de Hidalgo
Benijo
Tagananao
Parque Rural de Anaga
Iguesta
San Cristóbal de La Laguna
Tenerife Norte Airport
Playa de las Teresitas
Santa Cruz de Tenerife
Playa del Bollullo
Playa Jardín
TF-5
Las Lagunetas
Puerto de la Cruz
Icod de los Vinos
La Orotava
Candelaria
Buenavista del Norte
Garachico
Malpaís de Güímar
Masca
Santiago del Tiede
Parque Nacional del Teide
El Teide
TF-1
Playa de los Gigantes
Fasnia
ATLANTIC OCEAN
Acantilados de Los Gigantes
TF-21
Parque Natural Corona Forestal
Playa San Juan
TF-1
Villaflor
Poris de Abona
Montaña Colorada
La Caleta
Arona
San Migual de Tajao
Montaña de Ifara y Los Riscos
Costa Adeje
Playa de las Américas
Los Christianos
El Médano
Aeropuerto Reina Sofia
Los Galletas

0          20 mi
0          20 km

---

viewpoint. ⊠ *Santa Cruz de Tenerife* ☎ *922/633576 for Anaga Visitor Center.*

### Plaza de España

**PLAZA/SQUARE** | The cross at the southern end of Santa Cruz's main square is a memorial to those who died in the Spanish Civil War, which—it bears remembering—was launched from Tenerife by General Franco during his exile here. The controversial monument's architect is Juan de Ávalos, who also designed the Francoist memorial and basilica at Valle de los Caídos. A 2006 refresh by Swiss firm Herzog & de Meuron added a shallow oblong pond, new pavilions, and modern lighting. It also uncovered the ruins of Castillo de San Cristóbal, today a small museum (free) housing the 18th-century "Tigre Cannon" that

reputedly cost Britain's Admiral Nelson his right arm in an attack he led in 1797. The entrance to the museum is via a stairway opposite the lake. ⊠ *Santa Cruz de Tenerife.*

### ★ Tenerife Espacio de las Artes (*TEA*)

**ART MUSEUM** | This museum is the leader in contemporary art on the islands due to its sleek low-rise design and avant-garde exhibitions. Designed by the Swiss architects Herzog & de Meuron, it's next to the Museo de la Naturaleza. Expect 20th- and 21st-century art with a political or sociological bent. TEA's crown jewel is the hall dedicated to *Tinerfeño* surrealist artist Óscar Domínguez. ⊠ *Av. San Sebastián 8, Santa Cruz de Tenerife* ☎ *922/849057* ⊕ *www.teatenerife.es* ☑ *Free* ☉ *Closed Mon.*

#  Beaches

### Playa de las Teresitas
**BEACH** | **FAMILY** | Santa Cruz's beach, Las Teresitas, is about 7 km (4½ miles) northeast of the city, near the town of San Andrés. The 1½ km (1 mile) of beach was created using white sand imported from the Sahara in 1973 and adorned with palms. Beachgoers in the 1970s were purportedly bitten by the occasional scorpion that had hitched a ride from Africa (they've since been eradicated). A man-made barrier runs parallel to the sands and ensures rip-tide-free bathing. Busy in the summer and on weekends, this beach is especially popular with local families. The 910 TITSA bus route connects the beach with Santa Cruz. There's a good choice of bars and restaurants, and plenty of lounge chairs for rent. **Amenities:** food and drink; lifeguards; parking (no fee); showers; toilets. **Good for:** sunrise; swimming; walking. ⊠ *San Andrés.*

# 🍴 Restaurants

### Bar Delicatessen La Garriga
**$** | **SPANISH** | **FAMILY** | Some of the best sandwiches in town are made here, and the *tortilla* (potato omelet) may be the tastiest on the island. Eat in or take your purchases to the quiet gardens in the Plaza de Príncipe, just down the road, for an impromptu picnic. **Known for:** fine cheeses and charcuterie; terrific tortilla; greasy-spoon sandwiches. ⑤ *Average main: €7* ⊠ *Calle Pérez Galdós 24, Santa Cruz de Tenerife* ☎ *922/285501* ⊕ *www. facebook.com/lagarrigatf* ⊙ *Closed Sun. No dinner Sat.*

### El Coto de Antonio
**$$** | **SPANISH** | **FAMILY** | The buzz around this down home Santa Cruz standby is well deserved, as you'll see when you sample chef Carlos's steak tartare, the best in town, or his rustic snail stew

enriched with trotters (don't knock it till you try it). The star dessert is *huevo mole,* egg yolk and sugar whipped into a creamy mousse. **Known for:** knockout steak tartare; Canarian comfort food; homey atmosphere. ⑤ *Average main: €17* ⊠ *Calle de General Goded 13, Santa Cruz de Tenerife* ☎ *922/272105* ⊙ *No dinner Sun.*

### El Lateral 27
**$$** | **SPANISH** | **FAMILY** | Situated on the main shopping street, this restaurant is a convenient place to stop for a meal after sightseeing, especially since the kitchen is open from 11 am to midnight. Try to snag a table on the terrace that overflows onto the leafy pedestrian street (the interior dining room is comparatively drab). **Known for:** good value for the city center; fresh fish; wide selection of salads. ⑤ *Average main: €15* ⊠ *Calle Bethencourt Alfonso 27, Santa Cruz de Tenerife* ☎ *922/287774* ⊙ *Closed Sun.*

### Los Pinchitos
**$$** | **SEAFOOD** | **FAMILY** | Los Pinchitos is one of those dying-breed restaurants where you can eat your fill of pristine seafood without maxing out your credit card. Settle in for a leisurely no-frills feast of octopus, scallops, squid, and whatever other sea creatures were hauled up onto the pier that morning, and wash it all down with a carafe of good house wine. **Known for:** mojo-topped limpets; homey atmosphere; heaping seafood platters. ⑤ *Average main: €14* ⊠ *Calle Guillén 14, Santa Cruz de Tenerife* ☎ *643/176630.*

### ★ San Sebastián 57
**$$$$** | **FUSION** | To fully grasp the potential of Canarian cuisine, book a table at this white-tablecloth standby that coaxes market ingredients—such as *patudo* (bigeye) tuna, black potatoes, and local heirloom tomatoes—into flawless, modern preparations like *tataki* (lightly seared), *ensaladilla rusa* (salade Olivier), and vinaigrette, respectively. Staff aren't

on island time and happily attend to your every need. **Known for:** subdued, minimalist decor; rave-worthy tasting menus; Canarian fusion cuisine. ⑤ *Average main: €26* ⊠ *Av. de San Sebastián 57, Santa Cruz de Tenerife* ☎ *822/104325* ⊘ *Closed Sun.*

### Tasca Tagoror

$ | SPANISH | FAMILY | Opposite the Iberostar Grand Mencey, this tiny no-frills bar serves simple Canarian cuisine—think grilled sardines and tomato-avocado salads—in abundant portions at reasonable prices. The dining room has a beamed ceiling, low wooden stools, and barrels for tables—perfect for a quick bite but perhaps not ideal for lingering. **Known for:** solid seafood and Spanish omelet; budget-friendly tapas; casual local crowd. ⑤ *Average main: €10* ⊠ *Calle Dr. José Naveiras 9, Santa Cruz de Tenerife* ☎ *922/274163* ⊕ *www.facebook.com/TascaTagoror* ⊘ *Closed Sun.*

 **Hotels**

### Hotel Colón Rambla

$ | HOTEL | FAMILY | This cheery budget hotel is situated in a residential area north of the city center, just off the Rambla Santa Cruz. **Pros:** quiet oasis in the city center; large bathrooms; well-maintained pool. **Cons:** could use an update; some rooms get noise from street traffic; breakfasts don't vary. ⑤ *Rooms from: €82* ⊠ *Calle Viera y Clavijo 49, Santa Cruz de Tenerife* ☎ *922/272550* ⊕ *www.hotelcolonrambla.com* ⇆ *40 rooms* ¡⊙¡ *No Meals.*

### ★ Iberostar Heritage Grand Mencey

$$ | HOTEL | The ancient Guanches' name for their kings was *mencey*, and you'll feel like one at this grand, white stucco-and-marble hotel north of the city center. **Pros:** quiet, leafy neighborhood; fairy-tale garden; well-oiled-machine staff. **Cons:** no kid-centric areas or programming; high fees for parking and spa

access; far from the action. ⑤ *Rooms from: €115* ⊠ *Calle Dr. José Naveiras 38, Santa Cruz de Tenerife* ☎ *922/609900* ⊕ *www.iberostar.com* ⇆ *286 rooms* ¡⊙¡ *No Meals.*

## 🍸 Nightlife

Santa Cruz nightlife revolves around Calle Antonio Domínguez Alfonso, known locally as Calle de la Noria, west of the Iglesia de la Concepción. Here you'll find plenty of good cocktail bars and pubs. If you're looking for tapas, try Callejón del Combate, west of Plaza del Príncipe. For upscale disco bars and dance clubs, head to **Avenida Anaga,** facing the port.

### Bambú Lounge

DANCE CLUBS | Shimmy—and twerk, if you want—at this tiki-inspired rooftop *discoteca* that attracts a young local crowd. Sunday nights are reserved for Latin (salsa, bachata, and more) dance parties. ⊠ *Calle Fernando Arozena Quintero 5, Santa Cruz de Tenerife* ☎ *922/202296* ⊕ *www.bambulounge.es.*

### La Guiri Bar

PUBS | Craft beer and well-made drinks lure *guiris* (foreigners) and locals alike to this wallpapered barroom three blocks from Plaza de España. ⊠ *Calle Clavel 9, Santa Cruz de Tenerife* ☎ *600/606558* ⊘ *Closed Mon. and Tues.*

## 🛍 Shopping

Santa Cruz de Tenerife is a major shopping center. Calle Castillo, the main pedestrian street through the center of town, is lined with souvenir shops, trendy boutiques, and big-brand apparel stores (e.g., Massimo Dutti, Bimba y Lola, Foot Locker). Calle del Pilar has higher-end fashions and the department stores Marks & Spencer and El Corte Inglés (another branch is next to the bus terminal).

### Artenerife

**CRAFTS** | Traditional crafts sold at this kiosk near the tourist office are made by local artisans and guaranteed by the island's government as *productos artesanos*. The selection includes *calado*—exquisitely embroidered linen tablecloths and place mats—and clay pottery made using the same methods as those used by the island's aboriginal settlers. (The Guanches didn't use potter's wheels; rather, they rolled the clay into *churros*, or cylindrical strips, and hand-kneaded these into bowls. Pebbles, branches, and shells were used to buff the results.) ⊠ *Pl. de España, Santa Cruz de Tenerife* ☎ *922/291523* ⊕ *www.artenerife.com* ⊘ *Closed Sat. afternoon and Sun.*

## San Cristóbal de La Laguna

*5 km (3 miles) northwest of Santa Cruz.*

Known colloquially as "La Laguna," this university town was the first capital of Tenerife. It was planned and built in a Renaissance style in 1500, a design that was later adopted in New World cities like La Habana (modern-day Havana) and Cartagena de Indias (in Colombia), and many original, UNESCO-protected buildings remain. The old town has kept its colonial feel through the centuries with its tree-lined promenades, pastel-colored facades, and elegant palaces. Pick up a map at the tourist office, on Calle Obispo Rey Redondo, and snake your way through the pedestrianized streets to be transported to Spain's Golden Age.

**GETTING HERE AND AROUND**
**CONTACTS Tranvía de Tenerife.** ⊠ *La Laguna* ⊕ *www.metrotenerife.com.*

**VISITOR INFORMATION**
**CONTACTS La Laguna Tourist Office.**
⊠ *Calle Obispo Rey Redondo 7, La Laguna* ☎ *922/631194* ⊕ *www.turismodelalaguna.com.*

## 🅞 Sights

**Museo de Historia y Antropología** (*Museum of History and Anthropology of Tenerife*)
**HISTORY MUSEUM** | **FAMILY** | Occupying the splendid 17th-century palace of an Italian merchant, this museum chronicles Tenerife's sociocultural history from the 15th to the 20th century with documents, artifacts, and religious relics. Signage is in Spanish, but English descriptions are available via app (ask personnel for details). The elegant courtyard blends Italian Renaissance architecture, like white marble columns, with local materials such as hardy Canary Island pine. ⊠ *Calle San Agustín 22, La Laguna* ☎ *922/825949* ⊕ *www.museosdetenerife.org* 💰 *€5 (free Fri. and Sat. 4–8).*

**Parroquia Matriz de Nuestra Señora de la Concepción**
**VIEWPOINT** | **FAMILY** | The arcaded bell tower of this 16th-century church is an architectural icon of La Laguna, visible from almost everywhere in the city. Climb to the top for 360-degree views of the rooftops and surrounding countryside. ⊠ *Pl. de la Concepción 10, La Laguna* 💰 *€1.*

## 🅡 Restaurants

### ★ Tasca El Obispado
**$$** | **SPANISH** | **FAMILY** | Figurines of the Virgin Mary and other religious paraphernalia line the walls of this eclectic tavern with low ceilings and a cozy, countrified feel. Hand-cut *jamón* (ham) and runny-in-the-center tortillas make wonderful appetizers; save room for the *conejo en salmorejo* (roast rabbit in a paprika-garlic sauce) and homemade desserts. **Known for:** one of the best tortillas on the island; rustic decor; cheery service. 💲 *Average main: €15* ⊠ *Calle Herradores 88, La Laguna* ☎ *922/251450* ⊘ *Closed Sun.*

La Laguna was the first unwalled colonial city and still preserves its original 15th century layout almost intact.

### Zumería Tamarindo

$ | SPANISH | FAMILY | Students and penny-pinching travelers flock to this no-frills juice bar, as famous for its colorful smoothies (made with local fruit) as it is for its club sandwiches and filling *platos combinados* (lunch and dinner combos), served with fries and salad. **Known for:** collegiate atmosphere; full lunches for under €5; tropical fruit juices and smoothies. ⑤ *Average main: €5* ⊠ *Calle Consistorio 22, La Laguna* ☎ *922/314353* ⊕ *www.facebook.com/ZumeriaTamarindo* ⊘ *Closed Sun.*

 **Hotels**

### Hotel Aguere

$$ | HOTEL | Get a taste of historic life in La Laguna at this 18th-century palace that became a hotel in 1885. **Pros:** historic building; welcoming staff; good value. **Cons:** steep stairs no and elevator; antique doors and walls mean poor soundproofing; small rooms with basic furnishings and space heaters. ⑤ *Rooms from: €95* ⊠ *Calle Obispo Rey Redondo 55, La Laguna* ☎ *922/314036* ⊕ *www.hotelaguere.es* ⊃ *23 rooms* ⑩ *Free Breakfast.*

### ★ La Laguna Gran Hotel

$$ | HOTEL | This chic four-star housed in an 18th-century palace opened in 2017. **Pros:** rooftop pool, gym, and bar; Michelin-starred restaurant on-site; varied breakfasts with local items. **Cons:** inconsistent service; strong-smelling cleaning products; poor soundproofing. ⑤ *Rooms from: €107* ⊠ *Calle Nava y Grimon 18, La Laguna* ☎ *922/108080* ⊕ *www.lalagunagranhotel.com* ⊃ *123 rooms* ⑩ *No Meals.*

## Puerto de la Cruz

*36 km (22 miles) west of Santa Cruz.*

This is the oldest resort in the Canaries, and sadly, cheap mass tourism and urban sprawl have all but drained it of local charm and island character. There are a few diamonds in the rough. Through and several sights on the outskirts of town make the area worth a visit. Don't stay at any of the bland, overpriced resorts by the beach, and when exploring, stick to the old sections of town, which have colonial plazas and paseos for evening strolls.

### GETTING HERE AND AROUND

An excellent bus service connects Puerto de la Cruz with the airport and Santa Cruz's bus terminal. Buses leave every 30 minutes weekdays and every 45–60 minutes on weekends; the journey takes around 50 minutes. You can also rent a car (from about €30 a day) or take a taxi (about €42).

The town is very hilly and getting anywhere outside the port involves a steep climb. To visit the Jardín Botánico or Parque Taoro without a car, your best bet is to take a cab or rent a motorcycle.

### VISITOR INFORMATION

**CONTACTS Más Que Motos Tenerife.** ⊠ Av. Marques Villanueva del Prado 15, Local 8, Puerto de la Cruz ☎ 922/371131 ⊕ www. masquemotostenerife.com. **Tourist Office.** ⊠ Casa de la Aduana, Calle Las Lonjas, Puerto de la Cruz ☎ 922/386000 ⊕ www. webtenerife.com.

## ◉ Sights

### ★ Casa del Vino de Tenerife

**WINERY** | Wine and food lovers shouldn't miss this wine museum and tasting room, opened by the Canary Islands' government to promote local vintners. The surprisingly well-appointed museum, which describes local grapes, viticultural methods, and history, has English-language placards; reasonably priced tastings in various formats are held in the abutting bar area, and you can buy your favorite bottle in the shop. The complex also has a tapas bar and a restaurant with creative Canarian fare and a curious little honey museum with exhibits and

tastings. Casa del Vino lies about halfway between Puerto de la Cruz and Tenerife North Airport, at the El Sauzal exit on the main highway. ⊠ Calle San Simon 49, at Autopista General del Norte, Km 21, Sauzal ☎ 922/572535 ⊕ www.casadelvinotenerife.com ⊠ Free ۝ Closed Mon.

### Jardín Botánico (Botanical Garden)

**GARDEN | FAMILY** | Filled with more than 4,000 varieties of tropical trees and plants, and sonorous birds, the Jardín Botánico was founded in 1788, on the orders of King Carlos III, to propagate warm-climate species brought back to Spain from the Americas. The gardens are closed during stormy weather or when the wind speed exceeds 40 kph (25 mph). ⊠ Calle Retama 2, Puerto de la Cruz ☎ 922/383572 ⊠ €3.

### Lago Martiánez (Lago Martiánez)

**POOL | FAMILY** | Because Puerto de la Cruz has uninviting black-sand beaches, the town commissioned Lanzarote artist César Manrique in 1965 to build Costa Martiánez, a forerunner of today's water parks. It's an immense, and immensely fun, public pool on the waterfront, with landscaped islands, bridges, and a volcanolike fountain that sprays sky high. The complex also includes several smaller pools and a restaurant-nightclub. ⊠ Av. de Colón, Puerto de la Cruz ☎ 922/385955 ⊕ www.lagomartianez.es ⊠ From €6.

### Loro Parque

**ZOO | FAMILY** | This huge subtropical garden and zoo holds 1,300 parrots, many of which are trained to ride bicycles and perform other tricks. The garden also has the world's largest penguin zoo. The dapper Antarctic birds receive round-the-clock care from marine biologists and other veterinary specialists in a climate-controlled environment. Also here is one of Europe's largest aquariums, with an underwater tunnel, a dolphin and killer-whale (orca) show, and some gorillas. Free trains leave for the park from

Jardín Beach in Puerto de la Cruz is a famous beach filled with dark-colored volcanic sand, palm trees, and hotels.

the Plaza Reyes Católicos. ✉ *Av. Loro Parque, Puerto de la Cruz* ☎ *922/373841* ⊕ *www.loroparque.com* ✉ *€38.*

### Plaza de la Iglesia

**PLAZA/SQUARE** | Stroll from Lago Martiánez along the coastal walkway to reach this square that's beautifully landscaped with flowering plants. Presiding over it is Nuestra Señora de la Peña Church (open before and after Mass), notable for its baroque altarpiece and elaborate pulpit. ✉ *Pl. de la Iglesia, Puerto de la Cruz.*

### Plaza del Charco

**PLAZA/SQUARE** | It's a two-minute walk from the Plaza de la Iglesia to this square, one of the prettiest and liveliest in town, with plenty of cafés and tapas bars. ✉ *Pl. del Charco, Puerto de la Cruz.*

## 🍽 Restaurants

### ★ Bodegas Monje

**$$** | **SPANISH** | A five-minute drive from the Casa del Vino, in the township of El Sauzal, you'll find this award-winning

winery and restaurant perched on a bluff overlooking the ocean. After a lunch of crackly pulled (local heritage-breed *cochino negro*) pork and roasted potatoes, waddle over to the bodega for a tour and tasting, and if you're looking for a gluggable souvenir, snap up a bottle of the tintilla, a smoky, complex red aged in French oak barrels that's nearly impossible to find in shops. **Known for:** production of some of the finest wines on the island; mojo-making demonstrations (call ahead to book); heritage-breed pulled pork. ⑤ *Average main: €14* ✉ *Calle Cruz de Leandro 36, Sauzal* ☎ *922/585027* ⊕ *www.bodegasmonje.com* ⊗ *No dinner.*

### Casa Paché

**$** | **SPANISH** | **FAMILY** | Down a plant-lined alley off the Plaza del Charco, this family-run restaurant is in a typical local house, with a labyrinth of small rooms leading off the main hall; you might find yourself sitting next to a collection of old photos, a pile of hats, or some rustic artifacts. Standouts on the traditional Canarian menu include *puchero canario* (chickpea stew with vegetables, pork, and chicken), *piñas con costillas y papas* (corn on the cob with spareribs and potatoes), and rabbit with *salmorejo* sauce. **Known for:** staff who treat you like family; Canarian comfort food and Tenerife wines; romantic ambience. $ *Average main: €10* ⊠ *Calle La Verdad 6, Puerto de la Cruz* ☎ *922/372524* ⊕ *www.facebook. com/casapache.rest* ⊗ *Closed Wed.*

### Tropical

$ | SPANISH | FAMILY | Those in the know come here for typical Canarian food, especially the local dayboat fish. The best tables are outside on the pedestrian street, a couple of blocks behind the port, but the interior's cheap and cheerful wooden tables and fishing nets are nearly as charming. **Known for:** local wines; unbeatable set lunch deal; ocean-fresh seafood. $ *Average main: €9* ⊠ *Calle El Lomo 7, Puerto de la Cruz* ☎ *922/385312* ⊗ *Closed Sat. and July.*

## 🛏 Hotels

### ★ Hacienda Cuatro Ventanas

$$$ | HOUSE | Until recently, if you wanted luxury on Tenerife, you had to settle for one of the big-brand resorts in the south—no longer; Cuatro Ventanas, hidden among rolling banana plantations that tumble into the sea, is the kind of place a celebrity might rent to disappear to for a few weeks. **Pros:** highly Instagrammable infinity pool; high-design interiors; a world away from the tourist hubbub. **Cons:** slow Wi-Fi; no full-time staff or daily cleaning service; minimum three-night stay. $ *Rooms from: €170* ⊠ *Calle Playa del Socorro 1–2, Puerto de la Cruz* ☎ *660/866678* ⊕ *www.haciendacuatroventanas.com* ⊃ *4 rooms* ⊙ *No Meals.*

### Hotel Tigaiga

$$$ | HOTEL | Take in sweeping views of the city, ocean, La Palma island, and Monte Teide from the lush tropical gardens at this family-owned hotel above

Taoro Park. **Pros:** intimate, noncorporate feel; well-appointed breakfast buffet; magnificent views. **Cons:** older clientele means it's quiet; 230-stair climb to the hotel from the city; slightly dated rooms. $ *Rooms from: €138* ⊠ *Parque Taoro 28, Puerto de la Cruz* ☎ *922/383500* ⊕ *www.tigaiga.com* ⊃ *76 rooms* ⊙ *Free Breakfast*

### Monopol

$ | HOTEL | Built as a private home in 1742, opened as a hotel in 1888, and run by the same family for several decades, this old-fashioned three-star has neatly furnished rooms with wooden balconies set around a verdant courtyard. **Pros:** central location; serene pool area; incredible rates. **Cons:** proximity to loud church bells; dowdy decor; communal areas could use refurbishment. $ *Rooms from: €35* ⊠ *Calle Quintana 15, Puerto de la Cruz* ☎ *922/384611* ⊕ *www.monopoltf. com* ⊃ *92 rooms* ⊙ *No Meals.*

## 🍸 Nightlife

Hotels often have live music or other entertainment at night, mostly geared toward a 50s-and-up crowd.

The side streets of Avenida Colón are packed with bars and clubs catering to a wide range of ages and musical tastes. For the pop and DJ beats, head to Blanco Bar and the venues on neighboring Calle Blanco.

**Azúcar**

DANCE CLUBS | You can dance to Cuban rhythms and live Latin jams at this busy nightclub that opens at 11 nightly. ⊠ *Calle Obispo Pérez Cáceres 12, Puerto de la Cruz* ☎ *682/286705.*

## 🎭 Performing Arts

**Sala Timanfaya**

ARTS CENTERS | The town's theater, a five-minute walk south of Plaza del Charco, has a year-round calendar of cultural events including a classical music concert every Sunday at noon (approximately €10). Purchase tickets at the tourist office or online. ⊠ *Calle Las Damas 1, Puerto de la Cruz* ☎ *922/376106* ⊕ *entradas. tickety.es/es/organizers/sala-timanfaya.*

# Icod de los Vinos

*26 km (16 miles) west of Puerto de la Cruz.*

Attractive plazas rimmed by unspoiled colonial architecture and pine balconies form the heart of Tenerife's most historic wine district. A 1,000-year-old dragon tree, the natural symbol of Tenerife, towers 57 feet above the coastal highway, C820. It's arguably the oldest living specimen of this species on earth, and special measures (like installing an electrical fan inside its trunk to prevent mold) have been undertaken to preserve it. The Guanches worshiped these trees as symbols of fertility and knowledge; the sap, which turns red upon contact with air, was used in healing rituals.

### GETTING HERE AND AROUND

Buses run every hour between here and Santa Cruz, and there's also reasonably frequent service from Puerto de la Cruz; however, it's best to drive so you can explore farther afield.

# Garachico

*5 km (3 miles) west of Icod de los Vinos.*

Garachico is one of the most idyllic and historic towns in the Canaries. It was the main port of Tenerife until May 5, 1706, when El Teide blew its top, sending twin rivers of lava downhill—one filled Garachico's harbor, and the other wiped out about 90% of the town (hence Garachico's nickname: "Pompeii of the Canaries"). Though most of the buildings are faithful reconstructions from the 18th century, a handful of original structures survived including the Castillo de San Miguel, a tiny 16th-century fortress on the waterfront. Save for the odd art exhibition or cultural event, it's closed to the public. The restored Convento de San Francisco (open Monday–Saturday), was also unscathed, as was the 18th-century parish church of Santa Ana with its elaborate baroque altarpiece.

## 👁 Sights

**Piscinas Naturales El Caletón**

HOT SPRING | FAMILY | Lava flows formed these seaside natural pools, to which stairs, paths, and railings have been added for easy access. There's a pleasant café selling drinks and snacks and a conventional swimming pool that comes in handy when the surf is rough. Far from luxurious or exclusive, the pools are owned by the town and popular with born-and-bred *tinerfeños* of all ages. ⊠ *Av. Tome Cano 5, Garachico.*

## 🛏 Hotels

 ★ **Boutique Hotel San Roque**

$$$$ | HOTEL | Museum-quality art by well-known painters lines the walls of this Bauhaus-inspired design property occupying a colonial palace in the old town. **Pros:** art by renowned artists; 17th-century building with great bones;

The last eruption of the mountain El Teide was in 1909, on the northwestern flank of the volcano.

paradisiacal pool and spa. **Cons:** cold when the weather is uncooperative; rooms and bathrooms a bit gloomy; kids not allowed. ⑤ *Rooms from. €217* ✉ *Calle Esteban de Ponte 31, Garachico* ☎ *922/133435* ⊕ *www.hotelsanroque. com* ⥵ *20 rooms* ⦿ *No Meals.*

## 👜 Shopping

### Tabacos Arturo

TOBACCO | Snap up local cigars at this tiny mom-and-pop shop that rolls its own smokes on-site. ✉ *Av. Tome Cano 8, Garachico* ☎ *689/359158* ⊗ *Closed Sun.*

# El Teide

*60 km (36 miles) southwest of Puerto de la Cruz, 63 km (39 miles) north of Playa de las Américas.*

The dormant volcano of El Teide, Spain's highest peak, looms on the horizon no matter where you are on the island, and its (often snowcapped) peak is visible from the neighboring islands of Gran Canaria and La Palma on clear days. You need a special permit (approximate processing time: two months; apply at ⊕ *www.reservasparquesnacionales. es*) to reach the highest point, but most hikers and tourists will be content with hitching a ride up most of the way on the cable car.

### GETTING HERE AND AROUND

Four roads lead to El Teide from different parts of Tenerife, each getting you to the park in about an hour, but the most beautiful approach is the road from Orotava, which is a mile uphill from Puerto de la Cruz. Orotava has a row of stately mansions on Calle San Francisco, north of the baroque church Nuestra Señora de la Concepción. Roads into the park are occasionally closed due to icy conditions; try to visit early on in your trip so you have an opportunity to return if this is the case.

## Sights

### Cable Car
VIEWPOINT | On its way to the top of El Teide, the cable car soars over sulfur steam vents. You can get a good view of southern Tenerife and Gran Canaria from the top, although you'll be confined to the tiny terrace of a bar. The station also has a basic restaurant. Online booking is a must, though it's important to note that there are no ticket refunds should the cable car be closed due to wind. ⊠ *La Orotava* ☎ *922/010440* ⊕ *www.volcano-teide.com* ✉ *From €37.*

### ★ Parque Nacional del Teide (*Teide National Park*)
MOUNTAIN | FAMILY | This park includes the volcano itself and the **Cañadas del Teide,** a violent jumble of volcanic leftovers from El Teide and the neighboring Pico Viejo. The last eruption here was in 1798. Within the park you can find blue-tinged hills (the result of a process called hydrothermal alteration); spiky, knobby rock protrusions; and lava in varied colors and textures. The bizarre, photogenic rock formations known as **Los Roques de García** are especially memorable; a two-hour trail around these rocks—one of 30 well-marked hikes inside the park—is a highlight. Visit in late May or early June to see the crimson, horn-shaped *tajinaste* flowers in bloom, a dramatic sight.

You enter the Parque Nacional del Teide at El Portillo. Exhibits at the visitor center explain the region's natural history; a garden outside labels the flora found within the park. The center also offers trail maps, video presentations, guided hikes, and bus tours. A second park information center is located near Los Roques de García beside the Parador Nacional Cañadas del Teide. ⊠ *La Orotava* ☎ *922/922371.*

## Shopping

### Casa de los Balcones
CRAFTS | Regional arts and crafts are available here. ⊠ *La Orotava* ✛ *Next to cable car* ☎ *922/694060* ⊕ *www.casa-balcones.com.*

## Activities

### Climbing the Teide Crater
HIKING & WALKING | If you're planning on hiking in the park, plan ahead. Take warm clothing even in summer, suitable footwear, sun protection, snacks, and plenty of drinking water. The trail to the top (No. 10) of the volcano is closed when it's snowy, usually three or four months of the year. The difficult final 656 feet to the volcano crater itself take about 40 minutes to climb, and you need a special (free) pass to do so—apply online (at least two months in advance in high season). If you stay at the refuge and access the crater before 9 am, you don't need a pass. ⊠ *Teide National Park, La Orotava* ⊕ *www.reservasparquesnacionales.es.*

# Los Cristianos, Playa de las Américas, and Costa Adeje

*74 km (44 miles) southwest of Santa Cruz, 10 km (6 miles) west of Reina Sofía Airport.*

The sunniest—and most touristy—area on Tenerife is the southwestern coast, where high-rise hotels are built chockablock above the beaches without a lick of feng-shui sensibility. Costa Adeje, to the west of Playa de las Américas, is the newest addition with lower-rise apartments and hotels packed into the hillside. Sun, beaches, and nightlife—no cultural or nature activities—constitute the attractions here for millions of northern Europeans desperate for sunshine in the winter months. Playa de las

Mïnï'ïl.ïïï, pïïïïlïïïly ïïï lïïï ïïïï ïïïïïïïl Las Verónicas, is a loud and brash resort, while Los Cristianos and Costa Adeje are quieter and more sedate, attracting a more mature crowd of holidaymakers. However, if you're looking for pin-drop-quiet solitude, you'll probably want to give this area a wide berth.

### GETTING HERE AND AROUND

Hourly buses connect the south of the island with the capital, stopping at Tenerife South Airport. If you rent a car from Santa Cruz (from about €30 a day), expect to get to the southern resorts in just over an hour. Once there, a good bus service connects the different locales, and hotels that are not within easy walking distance of the beach provide a shuttle service to the seafront.

## ◎ Beaches

### El Médano

BEACH | Stretching for more than 2 km (1 mile), this is the longest beach on the island and also one of the most distinctive—the conical top of Montaña Roja (Red Mountain) lies at its southern tip. The golden sands and exemplary facilities earn it the country's "Blue Flag" rating, and the gentle waves make for safe swimming. Strong winds make it a good beach for those who want to try their hand at windsurfing. To get here, drive along the TF1 past the Reina Sofía Airport and take the TF64 south shortly afterward. **Amenities:** food and drink; lifeguards; showers; toilets; water sports. **Best for:** sunset; swimming; walking; windsurfing. ⊠ *Arona*.

### Las Vistas

BEACH | Part of the eight beaches making up the sands in Playa de las Américas and Los Cristianos, Las Vistas has clean yellow sand and perfect bathing conditions thanks to a series of breakwalls that protect the beaches from high waves. Lounge chairs and parasols are available

# Masca  ◉

Sixteen km (10 miles) north of Guía de Isora, tucked deep in the Macizo de Teno mountains, lies Masca, colloquially known as the Macchu Picchu of the Canaries. If you squint, you can see the resemblance—a huddle of houses cling to a misty ridge beneath a massive, pyramid-shaped rock. Descend the cobblestone steps into the town center, grab a quick coffee or sandwich, and, if you're feeling adventurous, embark on the three-hour (each way) hike down to the beach.

for rent. After sunbathing on this Blue Flag beach, take a stroll along the seafront promenade, one of the longest of its kind in Europe. **Amenities:** food and drink; lifeguards; showers; toilets; water sports. **Best for:** sunset; swimming; walking. ⊠ *Los Cristianos*.

### Los Cristianos

BEACH | This was the first beach on the island to receive international tourists en masse, from the 1960s on; today its golden sands are flanked by apartment blocks and hotels. The nearby port protects the beach from high winds and waves, so bathing is safe. Lounge chairs and parasols are available for rent. This is a lively beach, with frequent concerts and sporting events, and finding a space for your towel can be a challenge in the summer. **Amenities:** food and drink; lifeguards; showers; toilets; water sports. **Best for:** partiers; sunset; swimming. ⊠ *Los Cristianos*.

### ★ Playa de los Guíos

BEACH | This small, placid cove situated 12 km (7 miles) from Playa de las Américas is dwarfed by Los Gigantes, the towering cliffs nearby. Its natural black sand, striking in appearance, can be hot on the toes, so be sure to strap on some sandals. A nearby marina provides boat trips along the coast to take in the full beauty of the cliffs. **Amenities:** food and drink; lifeguards; showers; toilets; water sports. **Best for:** sunset; swimming. ⊠ *Los Gigantes, Santiago del Teide.*

# 🍽 Restaurants

### Bar Baku

$ | RUSSIAN | Try wrapping your head around the fact that there's an Azerbaijani restaurant in Tenerife, where you can find Georgian specialties served by Russian waiters. Improbably, the food here—lamb kebabs, lemony stuffed grape leaves, plump *pelmeni*, juicy *khinkali* (Georgian soup dumplings), and other Russian and Caucasian delicacies—is fresh, well spiced, and wildly affordable. **Known for:** Russian crowd; grilled kebabs and boiled dumplings; Caucasian cuisine like it's made in the Old Country. ⑤ *Average main: €9* ⊠ *Centro Comercial Terra Nova, Av. de España 25, Costa Adeje* ✤ *Follow "Bar Baku" signs from shopping center's main entrance* ☎ *662/028096.*

### La Vieja

$$$ | SPANISH | A few minutes' drive from Costa Adeje lies this oceanfront restaurant overlooking the quaint harbor of La Caleta. Watch the sun set over La Gomera island while you savor fresh local fish and shellfish and Tenerife wines. **Known for:** local wines; fresh fish; ocean views. ⑤ *Average main: €20* ⊠ *Edificio Las Terrazas 1, La Caleta* ☎ *922/711548* ⊕ *www.restaurantelavieja.com.*

# 🛏 Hotels

### Arona Gran Hotel

$$$ | HOTEL | Prime views of the marina at Los Cristianos and La Gomera island are what you get from the balconies at this hotel, which is especially popular among retirees. **Pros:** adults-only policy means plenty of peace and quiet; good choice for those with mobility difficulties; professional, amicable service. **Cons:** access to spa and infinity pool costs extra; poolside real estate fills up fast; younger guests may feel out of place. ⑤ *Rooms from: €154* ⊠ *Av. Juan Carlos I 38, Los Cristianos* ☎ *922/750678* ⊕ *springhoteles.com/en/arona-gran-hotel-tenerife* ⟿ *392 rooms* ⑩ *No Meals.*

### ★ Bahía del Duque

$$$$ | RESORT | FAMILY | Built to resemble a 19th-century Canarian village—complete with a bell tower, Italianate villas, and leafy courtyards—this sprawling luxury resort takes in eight restaurants, five swimming pools, a 24-hour gym, and two tennis courts. **Pros:** warm, helpful staff; bountiful poolside real estate; good breakfast buffet with made-to-order eggs. **Cons:** overpriced spa; leaks in public areas when it rains; most pools aren't climatized. ⑤ *Rooms from: €326* ⊠ *Av. de Bruselas, Adeje* ☎ *922/746932* ⊕ *www.thetaishotels.com* ⟿ *351 rooms* ⑩ *No Meals.*

### Jardines de Nivaria

$$$$ | HOTEL | Step inside from views of El Teide to a world of Tiffany glass, palms, and orchids crowned by the largest privately owned stained-glass window in the world. **Pros:** fantastic spa; seafront location; tranquil atmosphere. **Cons:** dinner always in the same dated restaurant; evening entertainment sometimes a snooze; some may prefer a more modern style. ⑤ *Rooms from: €225* ⊠ *Calle Bruselas, Playa de Fanabé* ☎ *922/713333* ⊕ *www.hoteljardinesnivaria.com* ⟿ *271 rooms* ⑩ *Free Breakfast.*

### The Ritz-Carlton, Abama

$$$$ | RESORT | FAMILY | Rising like a Moorish citadel from the banana fields, the Ritz-Carlton Abama is an architectural stunner with a coral-red exterior, a semiprivate beach, seven pools, and

a two-Micholin-star restaurant and award-winning golf course. **Pros:** top-notch gym, spa, and restaurants; kids' club with original activities; gorgeous ocean views. **Cons:** below-average breakfasts and overpriced dining; stampedes of screaming children; small beach with ugly views. ⑤ *Rooms from: €320* ✉ *TF47, Km 9, Guía de Isora* ☎ *922/126000* ⊕ *www.ritzcarlton.com* ⤴ *461 rooms* ⊙ *No Meals.*

### Vincci Selección La Plantación del Sur

$$$$ | HOTEL | Centering around an original banana plantation house, this modern hotel retains its colonial essence with spacious communal areas, teak furniture, and potted palms. **Pros:** tranquil ambience; views of the mountains and Costa Adeje; excellent service. **Cons:** some noise from other rooms; 10- to 15-minute walk to nightlife; some distance from beach. ⑤ *Rooms from: €240* ✉ *Calle Roque Nublo 1, Costa Adeje* ☎ *902/454585* ⊕ *www.vinccihoteles.com* ⤴ *165 rooms* ⊙ *Free Breakfast.*

 Nightlife

Most of the area nightlife is centered in Playa de las Américas, in three main areas: Veronica's (or Veronica's Strip), Starco, and the Patch. Dozens of bars, pubs, and nightclubs compete here for the young, rowdy, mostly foreign crowds drawn to clubs.

## 🏃 Activities

### DIVING

#### Aquanautic Club Tenerife

DIVING & SNORKELING | FAMILY | This PADI-licensed diving center in the small resort of Playa Paraíso is one of the most well established on the island. ✉ *Lago Playa Paraíso, Playa Paraíso, Adeje* ☎ *922/741881* ⊕ *www.diving-tenerife. com.*

## GOLF

Southern Tenerife has five of the island's eight golf courses, and these six lie within 20 km (12 miles) of each other.

### Amarilla Golf Club

GOLF | In San Miguel, not far from Campo Golf, this 18-hole course has greens that front the ocean. ✉ *Urbanizacion Amarilla Golf, San Miguel* ☎ *922/730319* ⊕ *www. amarillagolf.com* ✒ *€81* 🏌 *18 holes, 6684 yards, par 72.*

### Campo Golf del Sur

GOLF | Near Reina Sofía Airport, this course has 27 holes and spectacular greens that are surrounded by cacti and palms. ✉ *Urbanización Golf del Sur, Av. Galván Bello, San Miguel* ☎ *922/738170* ⊕ *www.golfdelsur.es* ✒ *From €58* 🏌 *27 holes, 6458 yards, par 72.*

### Centro de Golf Los Palos

GOLF | In Arona, near Los Cristianos, Centro de Golf Los Palos has 9 holes (par 27) and is a good practice course. ✉ *Ctra. Guaza, Las Galletas, Km 7, Los Cristianos* ☎ *922/169080* ⊕ *www.golflospalos.com* ✒ *€26* 🏌 *9 holes, 1040 yards, par 27.*

### Golf Abama

GOLF | This exclusive course surrounded by banana plantations boasts more than 22 lakes and 90,000 palms along its 18 holes. It's part of the Ritz-Carlton Abama resort complex. Check the website for deals. ✉ *Playa de San Juan, Ctra. Gral TF47, Km 9, Guía de Isora* ☎ *922/126000* ⊕ *www.abamagolf.com* ✒ *€270* 🏌 *18 holes, 6858 yards, par 72.*

### Golf Costa Adeje

GOLF | There's a 27-hole course that runs alongside the ocean and has a small number of palm trees dotted throughout, black volcanic sand bunkers, and views of the sea. ✉ *Fince de los Olivos, Adeje* ☎ *922/710000* ⊕ *www.golfcostaadeje. com* ✒ *€105* 🏌 *27 holes, 6440 yards, par 72.*

### Golf Las Américas

GOLF | Adjacent to Playa de las Américas, Golf Las Américas has an 18-hole course with views of the ocean and La Gomera island. ✉ *Playa de las Américas, Arona* 🕾 *922/752005* ⊕ *https://www.golflasamericas.com* ✆ *€115* 🏌. *18 holes, 6409 yards, par 72.*

## KITESURFING

### Azul Kiteboarding

WINDSURFING | FAMILY | Kiteboard, surfboard, and windboard rentals and classes are available at this club on the seafront in Playa del Médano, which happens to be one of the best places on the island for beginners. If you're experienced and enjoy big waves, try Playa El Cabezo. ✉ *Edificio El Toscón, Paseo Nuestra Señora de Roja 26, El Médano* 🕾 *922/178314* ⊕ *www.azulkiteboarding.com.*

# Gran Canaria

Gran Canaria has three distinct identities. Its capital, Las Palmas (pop. 381,000), is a thriving business center and important shipping and cruise port; the white-sand beaches of the south coast are tourist magnets; and the rural interior has a forgotten-in-time allure and spectacular landscapes.

Las Palmas, the largest city in the Canary Islands, is awash with tourists, traffic, and hordes of locals—in other words, it's a *city,* the likes of which most first-time travelers don't readily associate with the archipelago. Even so, it's pretty and pleasant and consistently ranks as number one in air quality among Spanish metropolises. There are a number of worthwhile cultural attractions here including the 7-km (4½-mile) Canteras beach and well-preserved old town.

The south coast, a boxy '60s development along wide avenues, is a family resort, popular with millions of northern Europeans. At the southern tip of the island, the Playa del Inglés (a popular LGBT+ retreat) gives way to the vast, empty dunes of Maspalomas. The isle's interior is a steep highland that reaches 6,435 feet at Pozo de las Nieves. Although it's green in winter, Gran Canaria does not have the luxurious tropical foliage of the archipelago's western islands, and the landscape is often stark the rest of the year.

Since 2021, Gran Canaria (and to a lesser extent, Tenerife) has faced a migration crisis. Nearly 20,000 North Africans fleeing violence and poverty come ashore annually in the Canaries, but the clunky gears of bureaucracy are not moving fast enough, creating a bottleneck and leaving most migrants stranded, stateless, and in unsafe living conditions. There is tension within the native population: Some Canarians are helping the migrants (several hotels have graciously transformed into makeshift shelters to house them), most others simply look on, and a vocal minority is actively antagonizing them—throwing rocks at shelters and organizing vigilante groups—and seeking their extradition. The desperation—of both the migrants and the Canarians, who suffered greatly due to the pandemic—has understandably led to an uptick in petty crime, so it's best to keep your wits about you, particularly at night, in large resort towns and cities like La Palma and Santa Cruz de Tenerife.

■ TIP→ Traveling in the Canaries? Consider making a donation to the National Commission for Refugee Aid via www.cear.es. Both the migrants and the local population need all the assistance they can get.

# Gran Canaria

**ATLANTIC OCEAN**

Playa de las Canteras
Isleta
Gáldar
GC-2
Las Palmas
GC-2
Arucas
Agaete
Teror
Tafira Alta
GC-3
Playa de la Laja
Parque Natural Tamadaba
Artenara
GC-4
San Nicolás de Tolentino
Tejeda
San Mateo
Telde
Playa de Güigüi
Pico de las Nieves
Aueropuerto de Gran Canaria
Inagua
Ingenio
San Bartolomé de Tirajana
Los Rosas
Mogán
Fataga
Arinaga
Vecindario
Taurito
Puerto Rico
GC-1
GC-1
Maspalomas
Playa de las Mujeres
**ATLANTIC OCEAN**

0    20 mi

0    20 km

# Las Palmas

*35 km (21 miles) north of Gran Canaria Airport, 60 km (36 miles) north of Maspalomas.*

Las Palmas is a long, sprawling city, strung out for 10 km (6 miles) along two waterfronts of a peninsula. Though most of the action centers on the peninsula's northern end along the lovely Las Canteras beach, the historical sights are clustered around the city's southern edge. Begin in the old quarter, La Vegueta, at the **Plaza Santa Ana** (don't miss the bronze dog statues), for a tour through attractive colonial architecture. Then make your way to the neighboring quarter of Triana, a treasure trove of small shops and cafés and restaurants.

Both neighborhoods are protected by UNESCO. It's quite a walk from one end of town to the other, so at any point you may want to hop on one of the many canary-yellow buses. Buses 1, 2, and 12 run the length of the city.

## GETTING HERE AND AROUND

It's a short stroll from the cruise terminal into the northern part of Las Palmas. Here you can explore the beach and check out the market and the stores in El Muelle shopping mall and Calle Mesa y López, or take a bus (1, 2, or 12) into the older part of the city.

If you're planning to go north to Agaete or Teror, or south to Maspalomas or Puerto Mogán, good bus services run frequently from the Santa Catalina terminal just outside the port. You can also get an airport

The irregularities of house shapes in the colorful barrios of San Nicolas and San Juan in Las Palmas are an iconic image of the city.

bus from here. Alternatively, you can rent a car (from €30 a day) or take a taxi.

For those planning to island-hop, Las Palmas and Agaete have good connections with Santa Cruz de Tenerife. Fred Olsen provides the quickest travel between Santa Cruz de Tenerife and Gran Canaria (Agaete)—the trimaran takes an hour. Free bus service is provided between Agaete and Las Palmas in both directions. You can also ferry to Lanzarote (Arrecife) and Fuerteventura (Puerto del Rosario and Morro Jable). Fred Olsen runs several ferries a week between Las Palmas, Lanzarote (Arrecife), and Fuerteventura (Puerto del Rosario).

Note that Las Palmas and the highway south are always busy with traffic, so allow plenty of time for your journey, particularly on the return. Even a bus trip from one end of Las Palmas to the other can take up to an hour during rush hour.

## TOURS

Several companies offer sightseeing and themed tours. The hop-on, hop-off service is also good for just getting around.

### City Sightseeing Bus

**BUS TOURS** | **FAMILY** | Visiting the main sights of Las Palmas, this hop-on, hop-off bus has a Monumental City Tour (nine stops) and an Atlantic City Tour, with two additional stops. The buses leave from Parque Santa Catalina and Parque San Telmo. Tickets (cheaper if bought online) include a free walking tour in Vegueta. ⊠ *Las Palmas* ⊕ *www.city-sightseeing. com* ✉ *From €22.*

### Trip Gran Canaria

**SPECIAL-INTEREST TOURS** | **FAMILY** | This company's tours in Las Palmas cover Vegueta and Triana and take two to three hours. There are culinary tours available. Book ahead. ⊠ *Calle Colón 2, Vegueta* ☎ *674/128849* ⊕ *www.tripgrancanaria. com* ✉ *From €35 (for groups up to 4 people).*

# Sights

## ★ Casa Museo Colón (Columbus Museum)

HISTORY MUSEUM | FAMILY | In a palace where Christopher Columbus may have stayed when he stopped to repair the *Pinta*'s rudder, nautical instruments, copies of early navigational maps, and models of Columbus's three ships are on display in addition to interactive exhibits. The palace, which retains many original features, has two rooms holding pre-Columbian artifacts and one floor dedicated to paintings from the 16th to the 19th century. There's a glaring absence of criticism of Columbus's complicated legacy. ✉ *Calle Colón 1, Vegueta* ☎ *928/312373* ⊕ *www.casadecolon.com* ⛋ *€4 (free Sun.)*.

## Catedral Santa Ana

CHURCH | It took four centuries to complete St. Anne's Cathedral, so the neoclassical Roman columns of the 19th-century exterior contrast sharply with the Gothic ceiling vaulting of the interior. Baroque statues are displayed in the cathedral's **Museo de Arte Sacro** (Museum of Religious Art), arranged around a peaceful cloister. Ask the curator to open the *sala capitular* (chapter house) to see the 16th-century Valencian tile floor. Be sure to check out the black-bronze dog sculptures outside the cathedral's main entrance—these are four examples of the Gran Canaria hounds that gave the island its name. ✉ *Pl. Santa Ana 13, Vegueta* ☎ *928/314430* ⛋ *Cathedral free, museum €3* ⊘ *Closed Sun.*

## Centro Atlántico de Arte Moderno (Atlantic Center for Modern Art)

ART GALLERY | This art gallery has earned a name for curating some of the best avant-garde shows in Spain, with a year-round calendar of exhibitions. The excellent permanent collection includes Canarian art from the 1930s and 1940s and works by the well-known Lanzarote artist César Manrique. The center also has a fine collection of contemporary African art. ✉ *Calle los Balcones 11, Vegueta* ☎ *928/311800* ⊕ *www.caam.net* ⛋ *Free* ⊘ *Closed Mon.*

## Ermita de San Telmo (Parroquia de San Bernardo)

CHURCH | Destroyed by Dutch attackers in 1599, this chapel was rebuilt in the 17th century. Inside is a fine baroque altarpiece with rich gold leaf and wooden details. The chapel is generally open only before and after Mass. ✉ *Pl. de San Telmo, Triana* ⛋ *Free.*

## Fundación de Arte y Pensamiento Martín Chirino

ART MUSEUM | Housed in the Castillo de la Luz—the Canary Islands' oldest defensive fortress that once protected the port from pirates and other invaders—the Fundación de Arte y Pensamiento Martín Chirino opened in 2016 to celebrate the Canaries' most famous modern sculptor. Chirino's swooping, abstract designs are more poignant than ever given his death in 2019. ✉ *Calle Juan Rejón, La Isleta* ☎ *928/403102* ⊕ *www.fundacion-martinchirino.org* ⛋ *€4* ⊘ *Closed Mon.*

## Parque de Santa Catalina

CITY PARK | FAMILY | Ride a guagua (city bus) to this park, where you can visit the **Museo Néstor,** home to neoclassical and modernist works by brothers Miguel (architect) and Néstor (artist) Martín Fernández. There's also a kids' play area and cultural center with temporary exhibitions. On the way there, stop off at the neighboring Parque Doramas (stops are listed on big yellow signs; buses 2, 3, and 12 generally cover the entire city) to peek at the elegant Santa Catalina Hotel. Next to the Parque Doramas is the **Pueblo Canario,** a model village with typical Canarian architecture. ✉ *Calle León y Castillo, Las Palmas.*

## Poema del Mar Aquarium

AQUARIUM | This ultramodern fresh- and saltwater aquarium opened in 2017. It's organized by altitude: you start your visit gazing at the aquatic life of mountain lakes and rivers and finish in a room dedicated to alienlike deep-sea critters. The coral-filled pool is a highlight. ⊠ *Muelle del Sanapú 22, Las Palmas* ☎ *928/010350* ⊕ *www.poema-del-mar.com* ☑ *€25.*

## 🏊 Beaches

Although it can't quite compete with the endless stretches of golden sand to the south of the island, the northern beach here, frequented by locals of all ages, is one of Las Palmas's major attractions.

### ★ Las Canteras

BEACH | FAMILY | One of the best urban beaches in Spain is found at the northwest end of the city. Its yellow sands are flanked by a pleasant promenade that stretches more than 3 km (nearly 2 miles) from the Alfredo Kraus Auditorium, in the south, where surfers congregate, to the Playa del Confital, in the north. The beach is protected by a natural volcanic reef, La Barra, which runs parallel to the shore and makes for safe swimming. Lounge chairs and sunshades can be rented year-round. **Amenities:** food and drink; lifeguards; showers; toilets; water sports. **Best for:** sunset; surfing; swimming; walking. ⊠ *Paseo Las Canteras, Las Palmas.*

## 🍴 Restaurants

### Bistro La Champiñonería

$$ | SPANISH | FAMILY | Halfway up a pleasant pedestrian street in Vegueta, this French café-restaurant with red walls and old photos of Las Palmas specializes in mushroom dishes. Choose from more than 15 preparations, or forego the fungi and try the meat dishes and giant *revueltos* (scrambled-eggs). **Known for:** cozy atmosphere; large portions for the money; mushroom everything. ⑤ *Average main: €14* ⊠ *Calle Mendizábal 30, Vegueta* ☎ *928/334516* ⊕ *lachampivegueta.es.tl* ⊙ *Closed Mon.*

### Deliciosa Marta

$$ | SPANISH | Tables are hard to come by at this busy restaurant in a typical Triana house: there's usually a line outside the door. The concise, contemporary menu includes truffled gnocchi, baked cod with seasonal vegetables, and steak tartare, the house specialty. **Known for:** well-heeled local crowd; consistently fantastic food quality; steak tartare. ⑤ *Average main: €15* ⊠ *Calle Pérez Galdos 23, Triana* ☎ *676/377032* ⊙ *Closed Sun.*

### ★ El Santo

$$$ | FUSION | Freshly dug baby potatoes with mole sauce, tempura octopus with aerated spirulina, Canarian blood sausage soufflé with beer ice cream—these are a few of the palate-bending dishes you'll find on the menu at El Santo, one of Gran Canaria's most exciting fusion spots. Rustic stone walls give the restaurant an intimate, relaxed feel, while the white tablecloths and professional waiters make it feel like a special occasion. **Known for:** foams, reductions, and fine-dining touches; subdued yet stylish dining room; experimental Canarian cuisine. ⑤ *Average main: €22* ⊠ *Calle Escritor Benito Pérez Galdós 23, Las Palmas* ☎ *928/283366* ⊕ *www.elsantorestaurante.com* ⊙ *Closed Sun. and Mon.*

### La Bikina Cantina

$ | INTERNATIONAL | FAMILY | Skip the middling tourist-packed cafés and sandwich shops on the Las Canteras boardwalk and instead grab a bite at this sunny, casual storefront that serves tropical fare ranging from tacos to Cubano melts to pad Thai. **Known for:** beachside patio; craveable tacos and quesadillas; "slow" fast food. ⑤ *Average main: €10* ⊠ *Paseo las Canteras 63, Las Palmas* ☎ *828/065357* ⊕ *www.facebook.com/labikinacantina* ⊙ *Closed Tues.*

**Te Le Dije Pérez**

$ | **INTERNATIONAL** | Just below the cathedral square is one of the island's best bars for having a beer—there's a huge selection—along with some tapas. The bar feels a bit like a French café, with high ceilings and black and red furnishings. **Known for:** good tapas; fun ambience; choice of beers. $ *Average main: €8* ⊠ *Calle Obispo Codina 6, Vegueta* ☎ *928/249087* ⊕ *www.telodijeperez.com* ⊘ *Closed Sun.*

## ☕ Coffee and Quick Bites

**Cafetería Casa Suecia** (*Swiss Tea House*)
$ | **CAFÉ** | Escape to the tranquil, air-conditioned quiet of the Casa Suecia Salon de Té on Tomás Miller 70—near Playa de las Canteras—for comfortable booths, foreign newspapers, picture windows, pastries, breakfast plates, sandwiches, and perhaps the only free coffee refills on the islands. $ *Average main: €6* ⊠ *Calle Tomás Miller 70, Las Palmas* ☎ *928/271626* ⊘ *Closed Mon.*

★ **Caracolillo Coffee**
$ | **CAFÉ** | One of the Canaries' few great specialty coffee shops (think single origin beans, seasoned baristas, and Chemex pour-overs), Caracolillo, opened in 2021, is a trendy hangout in the Centro district. $ *Average main: €6* ⊠ *Calle León y Castillo 110, Las Palmas* ⊕ *caracolillo.coffee.*

**Guirlache**
$ | **ICE CREAM** | **FAMILY** | For a sweet treat, try Guirlache. There are at least 20 ice-cream flavors, and many of the cakes are made with that trusty island staple, condensed milk. **Known for:** popular with locals; quality ingredients; delicious cakes, ice creams, and chocolates. $ *Average main: €5* ⊠ *Calle Triana 68, Triana* ☎ *928/366723* ⊕ *www.guirlachelaspalmas.com.*

##  Hotels

**Bull Reina Isabel and Spa**
$$$ | **HOTEL** | **FAMILY** | With a location right on Las Canteras, this is a good midrange option for visiting the city and taking in its beach. **Pros:** rooftop swimming pool; varied breakfasts and above-average dining overall; beachfront location. **Cons:** steep competition to get a sunbed by the pool; street-view rooms are dreary; some areas look a little tired. $ *Rooms from: €139* ⊠ *Calle Alfredo Jones 40, Las Canteras* ☎ *928/260100* ⊕ *www.bullhotels.com* ⊐ *225 rooms* ⵙ *Free Breakfast.*

**Hotel Verol**
$ | **HOTEL** | **FAMILY** | This no-frills budget hotel has an uninspiring facade, but its location, sandwiched between the Las Canteras seafront promenade and the main shopping street, makes a great base for exploring and beachgoing. **Pros:** excellent value; kid- and pet-friendly; beachside location. **Cons:** poor-quality bath amenities; some street noise; basic, with small bathrooms. $ *Rooms from: €50* ⊠ *Calle Sagasta 25, Las Canteras* ☎ *928/262104* ⊕ *www.hotelverol.com* ⊐ *25 rooms* ⵙ *No Meals.*

★ **Veintiuno**
$$$ | **HOTEL** | This boutique adults-only hotel is a social-media darling, thanks to its drool-worthy rooftop pool overlooking the cathedral. **Pros:** serene and stylish decor; local art and quirky library; rooftop splash pool. **Cons:** no tea- and coffee-making facilities in entry-level rooms; cramped breakfast area; noisy ground-floor room. $ *Rooms from: €130* ⊠ *Calle Espíritu Santo 21, Las Palmas* ☎ *683/369723* ⊕ *www.hotelveintiuno.com* ⊐ *11 rooms* ⵙ *No Meals.*

## ⓨ Nightlife

Lively and sometimes a little rough around the edges, the bars and discos in Las Palmas are clustered between Playa de las Canteras and Parque Santa Catalina. The seafront promenade and **Calle Tomás Miller** are lined with restaurants serving dishes from every corner of the globe. Live music and entertainment are common—check out the online La Brújula guide for a lowdown on cultural events (⊕ *www.labrujulaocioycultura.com*).

### Ginger

COCKTAIL LOUNGES | Sip a colorful tiki drink while watching the tide come in at this Las Canteras hot spot, whose fishbowl *gin-tónics* and zippy mojitos lure a mixed local and international crowd until 2 am. ⊠ *Paseo de las Canteras 2, Las Palmas* ☎ *696/728992*.

### ★ Tao Club & Garden

DANCE CLUBS | Open until 5 am on weekends and past 1 am every other night, this swanky tropical nightclub playing a mix of pop and DJ music draws a local crowd of revelers ages 25 and up. The palm-lined outdoor terrace, with music and its own bar, is one of the city's top see-and-be-seen spots in the summer. Be sure to dress to impress (no shorts, sandals, or tanks). ⊠ *Paseo Alonso Quesada, Las Palmas* ☎ *928/243730* ⊕ *www. taolaspalmas.com*.

## 🎭 Performing Arts

### Orquesta Filarmónica de Gran Canaria

CONCERTS | One of Spain's oldest orchestras, the Filarmónica has an ample calendar of concerts between September and July that take place at the emblematic Auditorio Alfonso Kraus at the southwestern end of the Las Canteras seafront promenade. ⊠ *Paseo Príncipe de Asturias, Las Palmas* ☎ *928/472570* ⊕ *www.ofgrancanaria.com*.

### Teatro Pérez Galdós

THEATER | A varied program of plays, concerts, and opera is performed throughout the year at this 19th-century theater at the end of the Vegueta district. ⊠ *Pl. Stagno 1, Vegueta* ☎ *928/433334, 928/491770 box office* ⊕ *www.auditorio-teatrolaspalmasgc.es*.

## 🛍 Shopping

Las Palmas has the best shopping on the islands. The main commercial areas are around Calle Mesa y López (south of the port) and Triana in the old quarter. You'll find all the major international and Spanish fashion stores, duty-free stores, and shops selling local crafts, hats and clothes, tackle for fishing and catching crabs, surf gear, and lots more.

### Fundación Para El Estudio y Desarrollo de la Artesanía Canaria (*FEDAC*)

CRAFTS | This government-funded shop carries a selection of Gran Canaria crafts and handiwork. ⊠ *Calle Domingo J. Navarro 7, Triana* ☎ *928/369661* ⊕ *www. fedac.org* ⊗ *Closed weekends*.

### José Juan Sosa

CRAFTS | Out of his studio in Gáldar, a town west of Las Palmas, this award-winning knife maker sells handmade blades with ornate handles made from ebony, gold, silver, steel, and nickel. Every piece is one of a kind. Visits are by email appointment only: *kneron77@ gmail.com*. ⊠ *Lomo San Antón 90B, Las Palmas* ⊕ *www.cuchilloscanarios. blogspot.com*.

### Trastornados Showroom

FURNITURE | Part furniture showroom, part fashion boutique, and part home decorating store, this ultracool shopping spot sells designer wares from Spanish and international brands. If you're looking for a fancy gift for someone special—a beautiful handmade vase, perhaps, or a scented candle—you've come to the right place. ⊠ *Calle Pérez Galdós 13, Las Palmas* ☎ *928/433053* ⊗ *Closed Sun*.

Activities

## GOLF

### El Cortijo Club de Campo

GOLF | Just outside Las Palmas on the freeway to the south, this 18-hole, par-72 course is one of the longest in Spain. Set among magnificent palm groves and six lakes, it has several holes with ocean views. ⊠ *Autopista del Sur, Km 6.4, Telde* 🕾 *928/711111* ⊕ *www.elcortijo.es* ⊠ *€100* 🏌 *18 holes, 6899 yards, par 72.*

### Real Club de Golf de Las Palmas

GOLF | Founded in 1891, the Real Club de Golf de Las Palmas is Spain's oldest course. Redesigned and relocated in 1956, it has 18 holes (par 71), two putting greens, two tennis courts, a restaurant, and a bar. Fifteen minutes outside Las Palmas, the course sits on the rim of the impressive Bandama Crater overlooking the extinct Bandama Volcano. The club also rents horses; it has 48 stables and five riding rings. ⊠ *Ctra. de Bandama, Santa Brígida* 🕾 *928/351050* ⊕ *www. realclubdegolfdelaspalmas.com* ⊠ *€70* 🏌 *18 holes, 6288 yards, par 71.*

## Maspalomas and the Southern Coast

*60 km (36 miles) southwest of Las Palmas, 25 km (15 miles) southwest of Gran Canaria Airport.*

One of the first places in Spain to welcome international tourists (starting in 1962), Maspalomas remains a beach resort with all the trappings. It's improbably backed by empty sand dunes that resemble the Sahara—despite beachfront overdevelopment in the town—and retains appealing stretches of isolated beach on the outskirts, as well as a bird sanctuary. Much of the area around the dunes is a protected nature reserve. This is also one of Spain's most popular leisure destinations for LGBT+ travelers.

### GETTING HERE AND AROUND

From Las Palmas, a short bus journey (45 minutes, longer at rush hour) runs to the southern resorts. Note that not all return buses go to the bus terminal near the port (Intercambiador de Parque Santa Catalina); some end at Intercambiador de San Telmo in central Las Palmas. You may therefore need to take a bus from here to the port if you're on a cruise (buses 1 and 12 are the best options). If you rent a car from the port, it's an easy drive to the south coast via the GC1 highway, and there's plenty of parking in and around Maspalomas.

## ◉ Sights

### Aqualand Maspalomas

WATER PARK | FAMILY | The largest water park in the Canary Islands has wave pools, slides, and just about everything else splash-related. ⊠ *Ctra. Palmitos Park, Km 3, Maspalomas* 🕾 *928/140525* ⊕ *www.aqualand.es* ⊠ *€35.*

### Palmitos Park

ZOO | FAMILY | One of the main attractions in this part of the island, inland from Maspalomas, this part botanical garden and part zoo has 1,500 tropical birds, a butterfly sanctuary, an orchid house, 160 species of tropical fish, many crocodiles, and parrot shows. ⊠ *Ctra. Palmitos, Km 6, Maspalomas* 🕾 *928/797070* ⊕ *www. palmitospark.es* ⊠ *€33.*

## ⊕ Beaches

The below beaches abut one another, and you can walk them in sequence (hindered only by a pair of rocky dividers) along the shore. A boardwalk links Playa de Tarajalillo to the rest of the beaches until the dunes separate the boardwalk from the Maspalomas beach and Playa de la Mujer.

### ★ Maspalomas

**BEACH** | The island's most emblematic beach and one of the most beautiful, Maspalomas has golden sand that stretches for 2¾ km (1¾ miles) along the southern tip of Gran Canaria. Behind this beach are the famous Maspalomas dunes as well as palm groves and a saltwater lagoon, which lend an air of isolation and refuge to the beach. Bathing is safe everywhere except at La Punta de Maspalomas, where currents converge. Topless bathing is acceptable, and there's a nudist area at La Cañada de la Penca. This beach is busy year-round. **Amenities:** food and drink; lifeguards; showers; toilets. **Best for:** nudists; sunrise; sunset; walking. ⊠ *Maspalomas.*

### Playa de las Burras

**BEACH** | Sandwiched between Playa del Inglés and Playa de San Agustín, this little sandy beach is protected by a breakwall, making it a favorite with families. Small fishing boats are moored in the bay, and the seafront promenade connects the neighboring resorts. Swimming is safe. There are plenty of lounge chairs and sunshades. **Amenities:** food and drink; lifeguards; showers; toilets. **Best for:** sunrise; swimming. ⊠ *San Agustín.*

### Playa de las Mujeres

**BEACH** | The co-ed "Women's Beach" is around the corner from the Maspalomas lighthouse in Meloneras. A natural beach with gray shingles and small rocks, this quiet enclave currently has no amenities, although the expansion of Meloneras, along with the construction of several high-end hotels, may change that in the future. Swimming is generally safe. **Amenities:** none. **Best for:** solitude; sunset; walking. ⊠ *Meloneras.*

### Playa de San Agustín

**BEACH** | To the east of Maspalomas, this smaller beach consists of brown-black sand and some rocks. The promenade has lush vegetation nearby, making it one of the most picturesque on the island.

This is a quieter beach than Maspalomas and Playa del Inglés. Bathing is safe in calm conditions, but watch out for strong currents when the waves get up. Lounge chairs and sunshades line the beach. **Amenities:** food and drink; lifeguards; showers; toilets; water sports. **Best for:** sunrise; walking. ⊠ *San Agustín.*

### Playa del Inglés

**BEACH** | Rivaling Maspalomas for popularity, Playa del Inglés has a lot going for it, including partying at the beach bars, sports, competitions, and concerts. There are nearly 3 km (2 miles) of golden sands, flanked by a pleasant seafront promenade that's great for early-morning and evening strolls. Swimming is generally safe, although windy conditions can create waves—it's a favorite spot with surfers. Lounge chairs and sunshades are available along the beach, and there's also a nudist area, which is signposted. **Amenities:** food and drink; lifeguards; showers; toilets; water sports. **Best for:** nudists; partiers; swimming; windsurfing. ⊠ *Playa del Inglés.*

## 🛏 Hotels

### ★ Bohemia Suites & Spa

**$$$$** | **RESORT** | When Swiss architect Pia Smith was tasked with refurbishing the Hotel Apolo, the first hotel on the Playa del Inglés, she reached for the sledgehammer. **Pros:** standout spa and brand-new wellness facilities; characterful modern decor; most avant-garde cocktail bar in the Canaries. **Cons:** certain areas undergoing renovation or repair; poolside waiter service is slow; garden-view rooms face noisy construction site. ⑤ *Rooms from: €250* ⊠ *Av. Estados Unidos 28, Maspalomas* ☎ *928/563400* ⊕ *www.bohemia-grancanaria.com* ⌁ *67 rooms* ⑪ *Free Breakfast.*

### Bull Costa Canaria & Spa

**$$$$** | **RESORT** | One of the few hotels in the south of the island with direct access to the beach, Costa Canaria sits just

The dunes of Maspalomas were formed by sand from the bottom of the ocean, during the last ice age.

behind the Blue Flag sands on Playa de San Agustín. **Pros:** unbeatable oceanfront location; ultramodern pool facilities; one of the area's few adults-only hotels. **Cons:** unremarkable food; young travelers may feel out of place given older clientele; some distance from attractions. ⑤ *Rooms from: €200* ✉ *Calle Las Retamas 1, San Agustín* ☎ *928/760200* ⊕ *www.bullhotels.com* ⇱ *229 rooms, 15 bungalows* ⦾ *All-Inclusive.*

### Bull Eugenia Victoria & Spa

$$$ | HOTEL | One of the first hotels to pop up in the Playa del Inglés area in 1975, this is a longtime favorite among older northern Europeans in search of sun. **Pros:** Dead Sea pool; huge spa and gym; rooms overlook the pool and garden area. **Cons:** young travelers may feel out of place among older crowd; one-night stays not possible; not beachfront. ⑤ *Rooms from: €140* ✉ *Av. Gran Canaria 26, Maspalomas* ☎ *928/762500* ⊕ *www.bullhotels.com* ⇱ *400 rooms* ⦾ *Free Breakfast.*

### ★ Seaside Palm Beach

$$$$ | HOTEL | Sophisticated and luxurious, this hotel is a stone's throw from the edge of Maspalomas beach. **Pros:** exceptional design and facilities; room cleaning twice a day; above-and-beyond service. **Cons:** almost everyone is German and over 60; small bathrooms; expensive in high season. ⑤ *Rooms from: €300* ✉ *Av. del Oasis, Maspalomas* ☎ *928/721032* ⊕ *www.hotel-palm-beach.es* ⇱ *328 rooms* ⦾ *Free Breakfast.*

## 🍸 Nightlife

The days may be long, but the nights are even longer in Maspalomas and Playa del Inglés, party central of the Canary Islands. Freshly tanned vacationers pack the pubs at sundown; later, the clubs fill with writhing masses dancing to disco. Gran Canaria is one of Europe's biggest gay destinations, and gay bars and clubs abound near the four-story Yumbo Centrum shopping center at Playa del Inglés.

Las Meloneras is another nightlife center, where Aqua Ocean Club is one of the big attractions.

### Eiffel Bar

Slurping down a strawberry daiquiri at the gay-friendly Eiffel Bar is a rite of passage on the Playa del Inglés nightlife circuit; every cocktail comes with a complimentary bowl of peanuts and marshmallows. ⊠ *Yumbo Centrum, Av. Estados Unidos, Planta Baja, Local 121, Playa del Inglés* ☎ *634/310227.*

##  Activities

### BICYCLING

#### Bike 10Mil

BIKING | FAMILY | The tours offered by this company cater to all ages and fitness levels, or you can rent a bike and go it alone. ⊠ *Centro Comercial Gran Chaparral, Av. de Gran Canaria 30, Playa del Inglés* ☎ *663/535038* ⊕ *www.bike10mil.com.*

### BOAT TOURS

#### CoolPlaySail

SAILING | FAMILY | Hop on a sunset cruise or full-day sailing adventure on this 15.5-meter yacht complete with refreshments, tunes, and paddleboards. ⊠ *Puerto Deportivo Pasito Blanco, Maspalomas* ☎ *629/505606* ⊕ *www.coolplaysail.com.*

#### Multiacuatic

WILDLIFE-WATCHING | FAMILY | Two-hour whale- and dolphin-watching trips leave from Playa de Puerto Rico, about 13 km (8 miles) west of Maspalomas. Avoid rough-sea days. ⊠ *Muelle Puerto Base, Puerto Rico* ☎ *626/982152* ⊕ *www.dolphinwhales.es* 🎫 *€35.*

### CAMEL RIDES

#### Camello Safari

LOCAL SPORTS | FAMILY | Join a quick camel trek across the Maspalomas dunes. The rides, which take about 30 minutes, leave every 15 minutes. The website (on which tickets may be bought in advance) is so outdated that it looks fake, but it is

## Side Trip 👁

Drive up to the Cruz Grande summit on GC520. To the left are several of the island's reservoirs, known as the lakes of Gran Canaria; they're stocked with trout and carp, and you can fish in them with a permit (obtained in advance; inquire at any local tourist office). Continue along GC520 in the direction of Tejeda, past rural mountain villages. On the right is the Roque Nublo, an eroded volcanic chimney worshiped by the Guanches that juts 80 meters (262 feet) into the air. Explore the Roque and its surrounding trails, pausing for a picnic in the shade.

indeed correct. ⊠ *Calle Oceania, Maspalomas* ☎ *928/760781* ⊕ *www.camellosafari.com* 🎫 *€15.*

### GOLF

#### Lopesan Meloneras Golf

GOLF | Half of the 18 holes at this par-71 course face the mountains, and the other half face the sea. Several are practically on the beach. ⊠ *Autopista GC 500, Meloneras* ☎ *928/145309* ⊕ *www.grancanariagolf.com* 🎫 *From €96* 🏌 *18 holes, 6350 yards, par 71.*

#### Maspalomas Golf

GOLF | Surrounded by the famous Maspalomas dunes, this 18-hole, par-73 course has ocean views from many of its long, wide greens. The course was designed by Mackenzie Ross. ⊠ *Av. T. O. Neckerman, Maspalomas* ☎ *928/762581* ⊕ *www.maspalomasgolf.net* 🎫 *From €45* 🏌 *18 holes, 6723 yards, par 73.*

### HORSEBACK RIDING

#### El Salobre Horse Riding

HORSEBACK RIDING | Horseback riding trips through the rugged volcanic landscapes surrounding Maspalomas are for one

(€30) or two (€40) hours, with longer rides available on request. The company can pick you up from your hotel and take you to the stables. ⊠ *Calle Islas Malvinas 3, El Salobre* ☎ *616/418363* ⊕ *www. elsalobrehr.es.*

### WINDSURFING

**Pro Surfing Company**

**SURFING | FAMILY |** Learn from scratch or improve your windsurfing, kitesurfing, and paddleboarding skills here; they also have gear to rent. ⊠ *Centro Comercial Eurocenter Loc. 80, Av. de Moya 6, Playa del Inglés* ☎ *928/769719* ⊕ *www. prsurfing.com.*

## San Bartolomé de Tirajana

*23 km (14 miles) north of Maspalomas, 20 km (12 miles) east of Cruz de San Antonio.*

The administrative center of the south coast, San Bartolomé de Tirajana is an attractive town planted with pink geraniums. At its popular Sunday morning market, held every two weeks in front of the church, you'll find tropical produce and island crafts. To the east, the village of **Santa Lucía** has crafts shops and a small museum devoted to Guanche artifacts.

## Tejeda

*About 7 km (4½ miles) southwest of Las Palmas.*

At the misty mountain village of Tejeda, the road begins to ascend through a pine forest dotted with picnic spots to the Parador Cruz de Tejeda. From the parador, continue uphill about 21 km (13 miles) to the Mirador Pico de las Nieves, the highest lookout on Gran Canaria. Here, too, is the Pozo de la Nieve, a well built by clergymen in 1699 to store snow. Tejeda is locally famous for its fragrant almonds, which bakers fold into delectable confections sold in the town center.

## ◉ Sights

### Artenara

**TOWN |** From the road leading to the Parador Cruz de Tejeda, follow signs west to the village of Artenara (about 13 km [8 miles]) for views of the rocky valley and its chimneylike formations. You can see both Roque Nublo and Roque Ventaiga, sitting like temples on a long ridge in the valley. ⊠ *Artenara* ⊕ *www.artenara.es.*

### Mirador de la Cilla

**RESTAURANT |** The entrance to the touristy restaurant Mirador de la Cilla takes you through a 164-foot tunnel. Don't eat here—the food is subpar—but it's worth making a stop to take in the spectacular mountain view with a beer or coffee. ⊠ *C. de la Silla 3, Artenara* ☎ *609/163944.*

##  Hotels

### Parador Cruz de Tejeda

**$$$ | HOTEL |** In the geographical center of the island, this is the perfect spot to get away from it all and to take in some of Gran Canaria's best views. **Pros:** large rooms; incredible sunsets from the rooms; fantastic spa. **Cons:** inconsistent service; difficult access up a mountain road; fee to use the spa (€25 for guests and €32 for nonguests). ⑤ *Rooms from: €150* ⊠ *Calle Cruz de Tejeda, Tejeda* ☎ *928/012500* ⊕ *www.parador.es* ⇗ *43 rooms* ⎮◉⎮ *No Meals.*

## San Mateo

*15 km (9 miles) northeast of Parador Cruz de Tejeda.*

From Tejeda, the road winds down to San Mateo, whose goat cheese is famous across Gran Canaria. You can find it at the weekend market and in shops the island over. Pass Santa Brigida and turn right toward the golf club on the rim of the Bandama Crater. Continue to the village of Atalaya, where there are cave houses and pottery workshops carrying on a millennia-old tradition.

# Tafira Alta

*7 km (4½ miles) west of Las Palmas.*

Along the main road leading into Las Palmas from San Mateo is Tafira Alta, an exclusive suburb with a colonial air where many of the city's wealthiest families live.

## ◉ Sights

### ★ Jardín Botánico Canario Viero y Clavijo

GARDEN | FAMILY | Welcome to one of Spain's largest botanical gardens, with plants from all the islands grouped by their natural habitat. The cactuses are particularly arresting. ⊠ *Ctra. de Centro, Km 7, Tafira Alta* ☎ *928/219580* ⊕ *www. jardincanario.org* ☜ *Free.*

# Lanzarote

With hardened lava fields, black and red dunes, and treeless mountainsides, Lanzarote's interior is right out of a science-fiction movie (literally—*Clash of the Titans, One Million Years B.C.,* and a number of other blockbusters were filmed here). The entire island is a UNESCO biosphere reserve. There are no springs or lakes, and it rarely rains, so all freshwater comes from desalination plants. Despite its surreal and sometimes intimidating volcanic landscape, Lanzarote—the fourth-largest Canary—has turned itself into an inviting resort through good planning (although not so good around Playa Blanca, where illegal construction is slightly out of hand), an emphasis on outdoor adventure, and conservation of its natural beauty. No buildings taller than two stories are allowed in most places, and billboards are forbidden, leaving views of the spectacular geology unobstructed.

Lanzarote was named for the Italian explorer Lancelotto Alocello, who arrived in the 14th century, but the name most synonymous with the island today is César Manrique, the internationally acclaimed artist and architect who helped shape modern-day Canarian culture and share it on the world stage. Manrique designed many of the island's tourist attractions and convinced authorities to require that all new buildings be painted white with green or brown trim (white with blue on the coast), to suggest coolness and fertility. He also joined local activists in the fight against overdevelopment, lying down in front of bulldozers and galvanizing islanders. All over this island, and especially in Arrecife, Lanzarote has a North African feel. Like Moroccans, many locals sip their hot drinks, in this case *café bombón* (coffee with condensed milk), from little glasses rather than mugs.

Vying with Fuerteventura for the title of warmest island, Lanzarote often bakes in the summer. It's also very windy, particularly during July and August, when the trade winds (*vientos alisios*) from the northeast batter the island.

Despite the heat and lack of precipitation, the island produces some surprisingly excellent wine. Vines are buried (sometimes up to several feet deep) in a mantle of black lava shingle known as *picón* that attracts and retains moisture from dew, the only source of water for vines on this arid island. There are two designated wine tours that take in the main vineyards on the west side of the island. Ask at a tourist office for a wine-tour map.

Lanzarote is known for its year-round warm weather, volcanic landscape, and conservation of its natural beauty.

# Arrecife

*6 km (4 miles) east of the airport.*

Although Arrecife houses one-third of Lanzarote's population (146,000), it exudes a leisurely island energy, unlike bustling Santa Cruz or Las Palmas. Real talk: It's not an especially pretty city, and some Canarians will even tell you to skip it altogether, but it does have some of the best shopping and nightlife on the island. It's also a practical place to crash before an early-morning departure or after a late-night landing. The coastline is strung with line after line of rocky reefs (in fact, "reef" is what arrecife means in Spanish). While you're here, don't miss its two castles or its inland saltwater lagoon, Charco de San Ginés, where there's a gorgeous fleet of small fishing craft. A stroll around the backstreets near the lagoon gives you an idea of the old Arrecife. The local Playa del Reducto is a good place to squeeze in some beach time if you're spending the day here.

From Arrecife, you can walk or bike to Puerto del Carmen along the 12-km (7½-mile) seafront promenade, which takes in lovely stretches of golden sand and views of the Ajaches mountains in the south. Stop for a bite to eat in Playa Honda, and take the bus back if you're not up for the return trip.

## GETTING HERE AND AROUND

Cruise ships dock at Puerto Mármoles, about 3 km (2 miles) east of the capital. A walkway traces the shore from the port into the town, but it's a long and unattractive walk. Consider hopping on a shuttle bus or hailing a taxi outside the terminal.

Once in Arrecife, there are buses to Costa Teguise, Puerto del Carmen, and Playa Blanca run by the ambitiously named Intercity Bus company. If you want to travel farther afield, it's best to rent a car.

Island-hopping is possible by ferry from Arrecife to Fuerteventura and on to Gran Canaria, although the quickest way

Lanzarote and
Fuerteventura

to get to Fuerteventura is from Playa Blanca. Southern Lanzarote and northern Fuerteventura are linked by two companies, Fred Olsen and Naviera Armas, both of which make six round trips a day from Lanzarote. Interisland planes link Lanzarote quickly and frequently with the other islands.

### VISITOR INFORMATION

**Tourist Office**

VISITOR CENTER | Housed in the original bandstand in the municipal park, this visitor center has detailed maps and information about local points of interest. ⊠ *Parque Municipal, Arrecife* ☎ *928/811762* ⊕ *www.turismolanzarote. com* ☉ *Closed Sun.*

**Cruise Terminal Tourist Office**
The tourist office right on the port opens for three hours after cruise arrivals. ⊠ *Muelle de los Mármoles, Arrecife* ☎ *928/844690.*

##  Sights

**Castillo San Gabriel**
CASTLE/PALACE | This double-wall fortress was once used to keep pirates at bay. You can walk out to the fortress over Puente de las Bolas, with lovely views of the port and city, and then explore the small (Spanish-only) museum inside. There's usually an English-speaking attendant on hand able to provide basic historical info. ⊠ *Arrecife* ☜ *€3.*

**Museo Internacional de Arte Contemporáneo Castillo de San José** (*MIAC*)
ART MUSEUM | The old waterfront fortress Castillo San José was turned into this stunning modern art museum (aka MIAC) by the architect César Manrique. One of his paintings is on display, along with works by Cardenas, Beaudin, Zóbel, Tàpies, and others. ⊠ *Ctra. de los Castillos, Arrecife* ☎ *901/200300* ☜ *€4.*

## Beaches

**Playa del Reducto**
BEACH | FAMILY | Playa del Reducto is an attractive urban beach, ideal for relaxing after you've looked around Arrecife. It's well maintained and protected by natural reefs, so swimming is usually like swimming in a warm lake (just watch out for rocky outcrops at low tide). The beach, overlooked at the eastern end by the high-rise Arrecife Gran Hotel, is backed by a pleasant promenade that goes all the way to Puerto del Carmen. **Amenities:** food and drink; showers; toilets. **Best for:** sunrise; walking. ⊠ *Arrecife.*

## Restaurants

**Charco Vivo**
$ | SPANISH | Strewn with nautical gewgaws and awash with color, Charco Vivo has indoor and outdoor seating, with tables overlooking the sea or the San Ginés lagoon. House specials include *matrimonio* (a "marriage" of squid rings and fish) and clams washed down with local wines. **Known for:** local crowd; waterfront views; fresh fish. ⑤ *Average main: €9* ⊠ *Calle Juan de Quesada 7, Arrecife* ☎ *922/804046* ☉ *Closed Sun.*

**Lilium**
$$$ | SPANISH | Creative cooking with Canarian roots is the philosophy behind the dishes at this popular restaurant east of the San Ginés lagoon. In the white-tablecloth, blue-walled dining room—or at one of the handful of tables outside—feast on creamy croquetas with a variety of fillings and local fish spooned with nontraditional sauces. **Known for:** attentive service; €65 tasting menu; elevated Canarian cuisine. ⑤ *Average main: €20* ⊠ *Centro Comercial Marina Lanzarote, Av. Olof Palme, Arrecife* ☎ *928/524978* ⊕ *restaurantelilium.com* ☉ *Closed Sun. and Mon.*

## Naia

**$$ | SPANISH |** From your patio table overlooking the harbor, feast on attractively plated modern Spanish fare such as heirloom tomato *salmorejo* (creamy gazpacho), griddled Iberian pork with sautéed vegetables, and slow-poached cod over black rice. The interior dining area is almost as charming with pendant lights and mismatched vintage chairs. **Known for:** creative Canarian cuisine; pleasant harborside patio; artfully plated dishes. ⑤ *Average main: €15* ⊠ *Av. César Manrique 33, Arrecife* ☎ *928/805797* ⊘ *Closed Sun. and Mon.*

## 🛏 Hotels

### Arrecife Gran Hotel & Spa

**$$ | HOTEL |** This 17-story glass tower is a bit of an eyesore on an island where low-rises are the norm, but once inside, it's hard to hate the bird's-eye views from the guest rooms and inviting, comfy communal areas. **Pros:** sky-high restaurant with incredible views; soothing, well-maintained spa; spacious rooms. **Cons:** slow and undependable service; average breakfast; no room service. ⑤ *Rooms from: €119* ⊠ *Av. Fred Olsen 1, Arrecife* ☎ *928/800000* ⊕ *www.aghotel-spa.com* ⥮ *160 rooms* ⦿ *No Meals.*

### Hotel Lancelot

**$ | HOTEL |** Facing the attractive Playa del Reducto, this is a good budget option for a quick overnight. **Pros:** beachside location; rooftop pool; good value. **Cons:** drab environs; mattresses can be a little uncomfortable; dull breakfast that stops at 10 am. ⑤ *Rooms from: €87* ⊠ *Av. de la Mancomunidad 9, Arrecife* ☎ *928/805099* ⊕ *www.hotellancelot.com* ⥮ *110 rooms* ⦿ *No Meals.*

## 📺 Nightlife

### ★ Camarote Nao

**BREWPUBS |** What was once a fishnet factory is now a trendy industrial brewpub. On a vintage barstool beneath dangling plants at the pinewood bar, choose from an ever-rotating selection of award-winning Nao beers and bar food. ⊠ *Calle Foque 5, Arrecife* ☎ *656/676397* ⊕ *www.naobeer.com/tap-room-camarote* ⊘ *Closed Sun. and Mon.*

## 🛍 Shopping

Shopping is low-key in Arrecife. The main shops are on and around the pedestrian-only Calle León y Castilla.

### ★ Queso Project

**FOOD |** Some of Lanzarote's top artisan cheeses (and a wide selection of mainland European ones) are sold at this charming city-center shop. ⊠ *Calle José Molina 7, Arrecife* ☎ *636/714348* ⊕ *www.quesoproject.com* ⊘ *Closed Sat. at 2 pm and Sun.*

## 🏃 Activities

### ★ Eco Insider

**HIKING & WALKING | FAMILY |** Uncover hidden corners of Lanzarote with this company's specialty trips including bird-watching, volcano walks, food and wine tours, and visits to the remote islets of La Graciosa and uninhabited La Alegranza. Tours are led by local experts. The company can pick you up by prior arrangement from your hotel or cruise ship; book well in advance. Prices include lunch and transportation. ⊠ *Arrecife* ☎ *650/819069* ⊕ *www.eco-insider.com* ⦿ *From €55.*

# Costa Teguise

*7 km (4½ miles) northeast of Arrecife.*

A green-and-white puzzle of apartments and several large hotels, Costa Teguise is a typical '80s resort that some would say is past its heyday, although it still draws thousands of visitors every year. King Juan Carlos used to own a villa here, near the Meliá Salinas hotel. Teguise proper (aka La Villa), on the other hand, is situated 15 km (9 miles) inland from the

The incredible Jardín de Cactus was designed by César Manrique, the island's most influential artist and architect.

coastal enclave and is another experience entirely: It is Lanzarote's historical capital and the oldest settlement in the archipelago, dating to 1402. Many of local visionary artist César Manrique's architectural masterpieces are situated within easy driving distance of Teguise.

### GETTING HERE AND AROUND

Lanzarote Intercity buses connect the resort and Arrecife. On weekdays, a bus leaves every 20 minutes, and every 30 minutes on weekends. The trip takes about 20 minutes.

### VISITOR INFORMATION

**CONTACTS Costa Teguise Tourist Office.** ⊠ *Av. Islas Canarias, Costa Teguise* ☎ *928/592542* ⊕ *www.turismoteguise. com.*

##  Sights

**Castillo de Santa Bárbara** (*Museo de la Piratería*)
**CASTLE/PALACE | FAMILY |** For sweeping aerial views of Lanzarote's craggy coast and parched volcanic landscape, climb to the top of this 16th-century fortress that, since 2011, houses the Canaries' Museo de la Piratería (Piracy Museum; closed for renovations at the time of writing). The *castillo* warded off pirates for centuries from its perch on the Guanapay volcano. ⊠ *Calle Herrera y Rojas 5, Teguise* ☎ *686/470376, 928/594802* ⊕ *www. museodelapirateria.com.*

### ★ César Manrique House Museum

**HISTORIC HOME |** On a hillock overlooking the sleepy town of Haría you'll find César Manrique's final home, preserved as if in amber. The artist lived in this architecturally stunning estate, which he built for himself, until his untimely death by auto accident in 1992. Plant-filled courtyards lead into Bohemian living areas brimming with sculptures, paintings, and iconic furniture; the bathroom, with a floor-to-ceiling window into a leafy garden, is a highlight, as is the outdoor pool area and art studio, kept precisely how it was left on the day he died. ⊠ *Calle Elvira Sánchez 30, Haria* ☎ *928/843138* ⊕ *www. fcmanrique.org* ⊠ *€10.*

**Cueva de los Verdes** (*Verdes's Cave*)

CAVE | FAMILY | Guided walks take you through this 1-km (½-mile) section of an underground lava tube, said to be the longest in the world. It's one of the most stunning natural sights on the island. The entrance is just north of Costa Teguise, beyond Punta Mujeres. ⊠ *LZ204, Costa Teguise* ☎ *901/200300* ⊕ *www.cactlan-zarote.com/es/cact/cueva-los-verdes* 🖙 *€10.*

**Jameos del Agua**

NATURE SIGHT | These water caverns, turned into an architectural destination by César Manrique, is situated 15 km (9 miles) north of the Costa Teguise. They were created when molten lava streamed through an underground tunnel and hissed into the sea. Look for the tiny albino lobsters on the rocks in the underground lake—this blind species (*Munidopsis polimorpha*) is found nowhere else in the world. There's a pleasant if basic restaurant by the lake, and the Casa de los Volcanes is a good museum of volcanic science. Night visits are possible on Saturday. ⊠ *Punta de Mujeres, Costa Teguise* ☎ *901/200300* ⊕ *www.cactlanzarote.com/es/cact/jam-eos-del-agua* 🖙 *€10.*

★ **Jardín de Cactus** (*Cactus Garden*)

CITY PARK | FAMILY | North of Costa Teguise between Guatiza and Mala, this cactus garden with 10,000 specimens of more than 1,500 varieties was César Manrique's last creation for Lanzarote. Look beyond the park and you'll see prickly pear fields: for centuries locals have cultivated these plants for their cochineal, an insect living on the cacti from which scarlet carmine dye is extracted. ⊠ *Ctra. General del Norte, Guatiza* ☎ *901/200300* ⊕ *www.cactlanzarote.com/es/cact/jar-din-de-cactus* 🖙 *€7.*

**Mirador del Río**

NOTABLE BUILDING | Designed by César Manrique, this lookout at the northerly tip of a hairpin bend in the LZ202 road lets you see the islet of La Graciosa from an altitude of 1,550 feet. From the lookout you can also see smaller protected isles—Montaña Clara, Alegranza (the Canary closest to Europe), and Roque del Este. Arrive early to beat the crowds. ⊠ *LZ202, Costa Teguise* ⊕ *www.cactlan-zarote.com/es/cact/mirador-del-rio* 🖙 *€5.*

**Órzola**

TOWN | The little fishing village of Órzola is 9 km (5½ miles) north of Jameos del Agua. Small-boat excursions leave here each day for the neighboring one-town islet of La Graciosa, where there are fewer than 500 residents and plenty of quiet beaches. ⊠ *Órzola.*

## 🏖 Beaches

★ **Playa de Famara**

BEACH | Directly opposite Costa Teguise on the north coast of Lanzarote is perhaps the island's most breathtaking beach. Set in a natural cove, its 6 km (4 miles) of sand are flanked by spectacularly high cliffs. The riptide here makes for excellent surfing and windsurfing, and Playa de Famara is regularly used for world championships for those sports. That said, the strong currents mean swimming can be dangerous. **Amenities:** food and drink; lifeguards; showers; toilets; water sports. **Best for:** sunset; surfing; walking; windsurfing. ⊠ *Av. el Marinero, Las Palmas.*

**Playa de la Garita**

BEACH | FAMILY | Not far from the Jardín de Cactus, Playa de la Garita is a wide bay of crystalline water favored by surfers in winter and snorkelers in summer. Almost a kilometer (½ mile) of golden sands is safe for swimming, making this a popular spot for families. The beach gets busy in the summer but is reasonably quiet the rest of the year. Lounge chairs and umbrellas are available for rent. **Amenities:** food and drink; lifeguards; showers; toilets; water sports. **Best for:** snorkeling; surfing; swimming. ⊠ *Arrieta.*

### Playa de las Cucharas

**BEACH** | This is the best of Costa Teguise's several small beaches. The sands are protected from high wind and waves by the natural bay formed in the coastline. A pleasant seafront promenade takes you around the beach and into the southern stretches of the resort. Getting a spot for your towel in the summer can be a challenge, especially on weekends. **Amenities:** food and drink; lifeguards; showers; toilets; water sports. **Best for:** sunrise; swimming. ⊠ *Av. Arenas Blancas, Costa Teguise.*

 Restaurants

### El Navarro

$$$ | **INTERNATIONAL** | Although it's on a busy access road and inside a drab building, this restaurant is well worth a stop. Menu highlights include playfully plated appetizers and decadent meats. **Known for:** killer cheesecake; pleasant terrace; excellent value for money. $ *Average main: €19 ⊠ Av. del Mar 13, Costa Teguise ☎ 928/592145 ⊗ Closed Tues. and July.*

### Restaurante Las Caletas Casa Tomás

$$ | **SPANISH** | Off the tourist track, this no-frills seafood restaurant with stunning sea views is a favorite with locals. The outdoor terrace seems to hover over the sea. **Known for:** affordable seafood dishes; pleasant terrace; ocean views. $ *Average main: €17 ⊠ Calle Bambilote 2, Costa Teguise ☎ 928/591046 ⊕ www.facebook. com/casatomaslascaletas ⊗ Closed Tues. No dinner Mon.*

🛏 Hotels

### Club Santa Rosa Apartamentos

$ | **RESORT** | Outstanding value in pristine surroundings is the hallmark of the Santa Rosa resort, a collection of one- and two-bedroom apartments and villas centered around a large swimming pool. **Pros:** indoor pool and bowling (fee); well-appointed gym; spotless. **Cons:** maintenance could be improved; single beds only; longish walk to the beach. $ *Rooms from: €87 ⊠ Av. del Mar 19, Costa Teguise ☎ 928/346038 ⊕ www. apartamentossantarosa.com ⤵ 128 rooms ⊙ Free Breakfast.*

### H10 Suites Lanzarote Gardens

$$$ | **RESORT** | **FAMILY** | For a good, all-inclusive deal in tropical surroundings, this is one of the best bets in the area for families. **Pros:** good value; entertainment for all ages; excellent service. **Cons:** noisy breakfasts; no elevators; can be crowded in high season. $ *Rooms from: €140 ⊠ Av. Islas Canarias 13, Costa Teguise ☎ 900/444666 ⊕ www.h10hotels.com ⤵ 242 rooms ⊙ Free Breakfast.*

 Shopping

For island crafts and produce, go to the open market (one of the largest on the islands) in the village of **Teguise** on Sunday between 9 and 2. Some vendors set up stalls in the plaza; others just lay out a blanket in the street and sell embroidered tablecloths, leather goods, costume jewelry, African masks, and other items.

### Aloe Plus Lanzarote

**COSMETICS** | A wide range of lotions, balms, and serums made from locally grown aloe vera are sold at this shop, which also has a small "museum" detailing the history and uses of the plant. There are other branches in Yaiza, Arrieta, Punta Mujeres, La Graciosa, and beyond. ⊠ *Pl. de la Constitución 4, Teguise ☎ 928/594894 ⊕ www.alopeluslanzarote. com ⊗ Closed Sun. afternoon.*

🏃 Activities

### BIKING
### Evolution Bikes

**BIKING** | **FAMILY** | Both novice and expert cyclists are well served at this shop that rents mountain bikes, road bikes, quadricycles, and more. Child seats and trailers are also available. Should any technical issues arise while riding, a store associate will drive out and fix it. Rates start at €12 per day. ⊠ *Complejo La Galea, Paseo Marítimo 2, Costa Teguise* ☎ *672/330251* ⊕ *www.evolution-bikes.com.*

### DIVING

One of the island's official diving centers is located very near Las Cucharas beach.

**Aquatis Diving Center**

SCUBA DIVING | Diving Lanzarote rents equipment, leads dives, and offers a certification course. Adrenaline lovers shouldn't miss the "Dive with Sharks" experience. ⊠ *Playa de las Cucharas, Local 6, Costa Teguise* ☎ *928/590407* ⊕ *en.divinginlanzarote.com.*

**Calipso Diving Lanzarote**

DIVING & SNORKELING | This well-established dive school has PADI Resort Center status and offers experiences for kids and adults. Hotel pickup can be arranged. ⊠ *Centro Comercial Calipso, Av. Islas Canarias, Local 3, Costa Teguise* ☎ *928/590879* ⊕ *www.calipso-diving.com.*

### GOLF

**Costa Teguise Golf**

GOLF | These 18 holes, which are outside the Costa Teguise development, have unusual sand traps filled with black-lava cinders. ⊠ *Av. del Golf, Costa Teguise* ☎ *928/590512* ⊕ *www.lanzarote-golf.com* 🖭 *€90* ⅄ *18 holes, 7082 yards, par 72.*

### SURFING

Some of the best surfing in the world is on Lanzarote's west coast, particularly at Famara beach, where regular surfing championships take place. The variety of beaches and winds on the island makes it an excellent location for surfers of all abilities.

**★ Surf School Lanzarote**

SURFING | Surfers of all experience levels can take classes and rent gear from this company. ⊠ *Av. el Marinero 13, Teguise* ☎ *928/528528* ⊕ *www.surfcanarias.com.*

### WINDSURFING

**Windsurfing Club Las Cucharas**

WINDSURFING | The most thrilling place on the island for windsurfing is at Playa de las Cucharas; this club provides lessons and equipment rental. ⊠ *Centro Comercial Las Maretas 2, Calle de Marajo, Costa Teguise* ☎ *928/590731* ⊕ *www.lanzarotewindsurf.com.*

# Puerto del Carmen

*11 km (7 miles) southwest of Arrecife.*

Most beach-bound travelers to Lanzarote wind up in the sands of the Puerto del Carmen area, the island's busiest resort. The small fishing port and historic marina (called El Varadero) are surrounded by cafés and restaurants, with the main commercial center behind them. The charming Puerto Carlero, 6 km (4 miles) west, is the newest addition to the resort and makes a quieter base.

### GETTING HERE AND AROUND

Take the bus from Arrecife or the airport. Services run every 20 minutes on weekdays and every 30 minutes on weekends. The trip takes 40 minutes. If you're feeling energetic, walk or bike on the seafront promenade all the way to Puerto del Carmen from the capital.

### VISITOR INFORMATION

CONTACTS **Puerto del Carmen Tourist Office.** ⊠ *Av. de las Playas 6, Puerto del Carmen* ☎ *928/510542* ⊕ *www.puertodelcarmen.com.*

 **Beaches**

**Playa de los Pocillos**

BEACH | Slightly north of Puerto del Carmen, this beach is near most of the area's development; hotels and apartments are restricted, however, to the other side of the highway, leaving the 2-km (1-mile) yellow-sand beach surprisingly pristine. Finding a spot to lay your towel can be difficult in summer. Lounge chairs and umbrellas are available. **Amenities:** food and drink; lifeguards; showers; toilets; water sports. **Best for:** sunrise; swimming; walking. ⊠ *Av. de las Playas, Tías.*

### Playa Grande

BEACH | Puerto del Carmen's main beach is a busy strip of yellow sand that's as close as you can get to an urban beach on Lanzarote outside Arrecife. Lounge chairs and umbrellas are available for rent. Backing the beach is a seafront promenade with plenty of souvenir shops and restaurants. You can take the promenade all the way to Arrecife. **Amenities:** food and drink; lifeguards; showers; toilets; water sports. **Best for:** swimming. ⊠ *Av. de las Playas, Puerto del Carmen.*

### Playa Matagorda

BEACH | On this northern extension of Playa de los Pocillos, there are alternating sections of gravel and gray sand. A perpetually windy spot, this busy beach has gentle waves that are perfect for those learning to surf. Lounge chairs and beach umbrellas are available. **Amenities:** food and drink; lifeguards; showers; toilets; water sports. **Best for:** surfing; swimming; walking. ⊠ *Av. de las Playas, Tías.*

## 🍴 Restaurants

### Everest Indian Restaurant

$ | INDIAN | FAMILY | When you can't look at another plate of fish and taters without moaning—*mira*, it happens to the best of us in the Canaries—spring for a palate-jolting curry at Everest, whose heady dishes ranging from vindaloo to korma and jalfrezi are probably better than your neighborhood Indian joint's renditions. **Known for:** cheery service; unapologetically spicy curries; blistered made-to-order naan. ⑤ *Average main: €12* ⊠ *Av. de las Playas 41, Puerto del Carmen* ☎ *928/511181.*

### La Carmencita del Puerto

$$ | SPANISH | FAMILY | A surprisingly varied menu—from bruschette to charcuterie boards to lovingly cooked stews—keeps things interesting at this beachy restaurant strewn with crawling plants and twinkly lights. Surrender to your sangría cravings here without worrying about running up a high tab; it's affordable, house-made, and packs a punch. **Known for:** indoor-outdoor dining areas that book up fast; crowd-pleasing menu with Spanish and international dishes; terrific drinks and dessert. ⑤ *Average main: €13* ⊠ *Centro Comercial Marítimo, Av. de las Playas, Puerto del Carmen* ☎ *928/512318* ⊙ *Closed Sat. and Sun.*

### ★ Mardeleva

$$ | SEAFOOD | On a hill overlooking the port, this small family-run restaurant is all about the catch of the day (try the barracuda if available), served either fried or grilled and always accompanied by papas arrugadas. *Arroz caldoso con bogavante* (soupy rice with lobster) is another highlight. **Known for:** intimate, family-run atmosphere; pristine seafood; pleasant marina views. ⑤ *Average main: €12* ⊠ *Calle los Infantes 10, Puerto del Carmen* ☎ *928/510686* ⊕ *www.facebook.com/mardelevarestaurant* ⊙ *Closed Mon. and Tues.*

## 🛏 Hotels

### Hotel Costa Calero Talaso & Spa

$$$ | HOTEL | Sprawling gardens and serene pools await guests at this modern hotel, just south of Puerto del Carmen in the Puerto Calero marina. **Pros:** quiet location with lovely gardens; spa with Roman baths; free shuttle bus to the beach. **Cons:** spotty internet; lackluster entertainment and little food variety; slightly off the beaten track. ⑤ *Rooms from: €170* ⊠ *Urbanización Puerto Calero, Puerto del Carmen* ☎ *928/849595* ⊕ *www.hotelcostacalero.es* ↪ *312 rooms, 12 suites* ⑩ *Free Breakfast.*

## Did You Know?

The grapes used to make wines in Lanzarote are cultivated in a singular manner. Here, rows of volcanic stone semi-circles replace patchwork green fields. Called Zocos, these have been built for each individual vine and provide much needed protection from the sometimes-fierce winds.

### Seaside Los Jameos

$$$$ | HOTEL | FAMILY | César Manrique disciples were behind this giant colonial resort, where the tropical gardens, wooden balconies, and cane furniture all evoke old-school Havana. **Pros:** stunning architecture; renowned tennis club; complimentary glass of cava at check-in. **Cons:** kids' activities can be disappointing; not much variety for vegetarians; communal areas need a refresh. $ *Rooms from: €194* ✉ *Calle Marte 2, Playa de los Pocillos* 🕾 *928/763308* ⊕ *www.los-jameos.com* ➲ *526 rooms, 4 suites* ⍥ *Free Breakfast.*

## ▼ Nightlife

This is the center of Lanzarote's nightlife. The main party strip is Avenida de las Playas. For a more relaxed night out, head to the old town, where most locals spend their time. There, the crowd is still mostly foreign, but the bars are more intimate and the drinks cheaper.

### The Dubliner Live Music Lounge

LIVE MUSIC | These cover musicians are pros at getting everyone into party mode (and they keep it bumping till 3:30)—so grab a pint of Guinness and jump on the dance floor. Nobody takes themselves too seriously at the Dubliner, and that's precisely its allure. ✉ *Centro Comercial Marítimo, Av. de las Playas, Puerto del Carmen* 🕾 *711/002540.*

### Ruta 66

BARS | At the American bar Ruta 66, you can sip a frothy mixed drink on a cushioned wicker chair while taking in catchy tunes and ocean views. This is also the town's liveliest spot to catch a sports game and root for your team among fellow fans. ✉ *Av. de las Playas 19, Puerto del Carmen* 🕾 *928/514027.*

### Scotch Corner Bar

BARS | Guitars hang from the ceiling, and old pictures of Scotland adorn the walls in the Scotch Corner Bar. There's live music nightly usually acoustic and sometimes Scottish. Regulars love the mojitos. ✉ *Calle Tenerife 14, Puerto del Carmen* 🕾 *603/104416.*

## 🏃 Activities

### Lanzarote Golf

GOLF | This 18-hole course, which is between Puerto del Carmen and Tías, comes with spectacular ocean views along its wide greens. ✉ *Ctra. del Puerto del Carmen–Tías, Puerto del Carmen* 🕾 *928/514050* ⊕ *www.lanzarotegolfresort.com* ⌑ *€85* 🏌 *18 holes, 6707 yards, par 72.*

# Tahíche

*5 km (3 miles) south of Teguise.*

Only one thing makes Tahíche a destination rather than a drive-through town between Arrecife and the north of the island: the former estate of César Manrique.

### GETTING HERE AND AROUND

By car, head north out of Arrecife on the main avenue, Avenida Campoamor. The Fundación César Manrique is off to the left before you enter the village (follow the signs). From Arrecife, buses 7 and 9 go this way several times a day; Bus 10 runs weekdays only; all stop at the César Manrique Crossing.

## ◉ Sights

### ★ Fundación César Manrique

HISTORIC HOME | César Manrique (1919–92) made this high-design bachelor pad called Taro de Tahíche for himself in 1968 upon returning from New York City, where he'd been living and working thanks to a grant from Nelson Rockefeller. The artist managed to turn a barren lava field into an inviting and architecturally stunning abode—the first of its kind in the Canaries—that would play host to international celebrities and become the islands' most emblematic residence.

The spectacular volcanic landscape of Timanfaya National Park was created over six years of near continuous volcanic eruptions that took place between 1730 and 1736.

The artist called Taro home for 20 years and created some of his most celebrated works while residing here; his studio now displays original paintings. The real attraction is the house itself with its cave dwellings outfitted with splashy furniture, crystalline pools tucked between boulders, and palms shooting up through holes between floors. ✉ Calle Jorge Luis Borges 16, Tahíche ☎ 928/843138 ⊕ www.fcmanrique.org 🎫 €8.

# Yaiza

*13 km (8 miles) west of Puerto del Carmen.*

Yaiza is a quiet whitewashed village with good restaurants. Largely destroyed by a river of lava in the 1700s, it's best known as the gateway to the volcanic national park. The hamlet of El Golfo, situated within the Yaiza municipality, is a whitewashed coastal town with seafood restaurants and views of the **Charco Verde,** or "Green Lake."

## GETTING HERE AND AROUND

Bus service is infrequent, so rent a car to get here. To get to the volcanoes, you have to take a tour bus. There's no access for private vehicles.

## ◉ Sights

**El Charco Verde** (*Charco de los Clicos*)
**NATURE SIGHT** | This bizarre green lagoon, which looks like something out of a sci-fi thriller, is situated at the outer limits of Timanfaya National Park just uphill from El Golfo. It gets its radioactive hue from its sulfuric content and *Ruppia maritima* seagrass. It's forbidden to walk to the lake as it's within the reserve, but there's a viewpoint that's clearly marked at the turnoff to El Golfo where you can snap some excellent photos, especially at sunset. ⚠ **Wear grippy shoes and watch your step, as there are no guardrails around the viewpoint.** ✉ *Yaiza* 🎫 *Free.*

★ **Parque Nacional de Timanfaya** (*Timanfaya National Park*)

**VOLCANO | FAMILY** | Popularly known as the "Fire Mountains," this national park of barren volcanic landscapes takes up much of southern Lanzarote. The terrain is a violent jumble of exploded craters, cinder cones, lava formations, and heat fissures. The park is protected, and you can't drive or hike through it yourself (leave your car in the lot beside the middling, overhyped volcano-top restaurant, El Diablo); the only way to see the central volcanic area is on a 14-km (9-mile) bus circuit called the Ruta de los Volcanes, designed to have minimal environmental impact. (Photographers will be bummed that the only pics you can take on tour are through smudged windows.)

A taped English commentary explains how the parish priest of Yaiza took notes during the 1730 eruption that buried two villages. He had plenty of time— the eruption lasted six years, making it the longest known eruption in volcanic history. By the time it was over, more than 75% of Lanzarote was covered in lava. Throughout the park, on signs and road markers, you'll see a little devil with a pitchfork; this *diablito* was designed by Manrique. ∎ **TIP→ As you enter, you'll see the staging area for camel rides, which we recommend skipping due to recent animal cruelty complaints.** ✉ *Centro de Visitantes Mancha Blancha, Ctra. de Yaiza a Tinajo, Km 11.5, Tinajo* ☎ *928/118042* 🎫 *€10.*

## 🍴 Restaurants

### ★ La Bodega de Santiago

**$$ | SPANISH** | Shaded by a splendid ficus that keeps the *terraza* cool in the midday heat, La Bodega de Santiago is worth going out of your way to visit. The traditional Canarian menu is exquisite, integrating meats and produce from the surrounding farms and complementing dishes with island wines. **Known for:** locavore cuisine; terrific goat and roast meats; romantic dining beneath a gorgeous tree. $ *Average main: €17* ✉ *Calle Montañas del Fuego 27, Yaiza* ☎ *928/836204* ⊕ *www.labodegadesantiago.es* ⊗ *Closed Mon.*

### ★ Restaurante Mar Azul

**$$ | SEAFOOD** | Of all the seafood restaurants in the tiny hamlet of El Golfo, this harborside standby stands out for its ultrafresh fish and homemade Canarian dishes. Order the *parrillada de marisco*, or grilled seafood platter, for a sampling of local fish (the barracuda is consistently exceptional), calamari, and fried shellfish, all of which soar to new heights when dunked in cilantro-packed *mojo verde*. **Known for:** romantic seaside terrace; not-your-average mojos; bountiful seafood platters. $ *Average main: €15* ✉ *Av. Marítima 42, Yaiza* ☎ *928/173132.*

## 🛍 Shopping

### Ahumadería de Uga

**FOOD** | The hamlet of Uga is the improbable home of what's arguably Spain's finest smoked salmon producer. The Guerrero family won't relinquish its secret recipe, but what we know is that the salmon is imported from Scotland and Norway, cured with salt culled from nearby Janubio beach, and smoked over La Geria grapevines. The smoked fish is so delectable that the tiny shop sells more than 200 pounds of it each day. ✉ *LZ2 3, Yaiza* ☎ *928/830132* ⊕ *www.facebook.com/ahumaderiadeuga.*

# Playa Blanca

## 🛏 Hotels

### ★ Hotel Casa del Embajador

**$$$$ | B&B/INN** | Tucked behind one of Lanzarote's typically green front doors is an oasis of calm where all you'll want to do is curl up in one of the loungers and take in the views of Fuerteventura and the Isla de Lobos, **Pros:** peace and quiet by the sea; fresh fruit in the rooms; good breakfast. **Cons:** a tad overpriced; rooms need a revamp; no a/c. ⑤ *Rooms from: €220* ✉ *Calle La Tegala 56, Playa Blanca* ☎ *928/519191* ⊕ *www.hotelcasadelembajador.com* ➷ *13 rooms* ❍◉ *Free Breakfast.*

### Iberostar Selection Lanzarote Park

$$$$ | **RESORT** | **FAMILY** | Travelers looking for accessible luxury and all-inclusive pampering should look no further than this Iberostar outpost, a chic yet unpretentious oceanfront resort that reopened in 2017 after major renovations. **Pros:** separate family and adults-only areas; newly renovated public areas; spacious rooms. **Cons:** bland interiors convey no sense of place; you can hear the evening entertainment from some rooms; underwhelming food across the board. ⑤ *Rooms from: €202* ✉ *Av. Archipiélago 7, Playa Blanca* ☎ *928/517048* ⊕ *www.iberostar.com* ➷ *388 rooms* ❍◉ *No Meals.*

### Princesa Yaiza Suite Hotel Resort

$$$$ | **HOTEL** | **FAMILY** | It might be big, but this sprawling white hotel still manages to feel luxurious. **Pros:** great service; fantastic buffet breakfast with eggs cooked to order; superb spa. **Cons:** communal areas need a refresh; overpriced food at pool bar; long walk to some rooms. ⑤ *Rooms from: €234* ✉ *Av. de Papagayo, Playa Blanca* ☎ *928/519300* ⊕ *www.princesayaiza.com* ➷ *385 rooms* ❍◉ *Free Breakfast.*

##  Activities

### Papagayo Bike

**BIKING** | Daily bike rental from this company that's been around since 1998 starts at €12. Guided bike tours are also available. ✉ *Calle La Tegala 13, Playa Blanca* ☎ *928/349861* ⊕ *www.papagayobike.com.*

# Fuerteventura

Some of Fuerteventura's towering sand dunes blew in from the Sahara Desert, 96 km (60 miles) away, and indeed it's not hard to imagine Fuerteventura as a detached piece of Africa. Despite being the second-largest Canary Island by area, Fuerteventura's population reaches only 123,000. Tourism arrived relatively late on the island, compared with Gran Canaria and Lanzarote, and it's still somewhat off the radar. Visitors come mainly to enjoy the stunning white beaches and to windsurf; there's little else to do. The two main resort areas are at the island's far north and south ends: Corralejo, across from Lanzarote, known for its miles of protected dunes, and the Jandía peninsula with dozens of long beaches, respectively. Fuerteventura didn't fully escape the Spanish construction boom of the early 2000s, but it remains relatively unspoiled and has been a UNESCO biosphere reserve since 2009.

Prior to being conquered in the early 15th century by French crusaders, the island was inhabited by a tribal people called the Maxos with roots in North Africa; at the time of the colonists' arrival, the Maxos were split between two kingdoms, Jandía, in the south, and Maxorata, in the north. A stone wall, remnants of which are visible today, divided the two areas. The Catholic Monarchs claimed sovereignty over Fuerteventura in 1476 but were met with dozens of pirate attacks in the following decades, which led them to decree the construction of several fortifications along the coast, some of which remain. The island was largely dismissed by Spaniards as a desert wasteland until famed novelist Miguel de Unamuno chronicled his exile there in the 1920s under Primo de Rivera's reign—contrary to the dictator's wishes, Unamuno found Fuerteventura rather paradisiacal and would come to appreciate its "eternal springtime" temperatures and "naked hills that look like camels' humps."

Like Lanzarote, Fuerteventura is often windy, especially during the summer, when the northeast trade winds blow relentlessly for days at a time. It's also one of the hottest islands in the summer, and its winters are warm and dry.

### VISITOR INFORMATION

**CONTACTS Airport Tourist Office.** ⊠ *Fuerteventura Airport, Puerto del Rosario* ☎ *928/860604* ⊕ *www.visitfuerteventura.es.* **Center Tourist Office.** ⊠ *Av. Reyes de España, Puerto del Rosario* ☎ *928/530844.*

# Puerto del Rosario

Fuerteventura's capital, Puerto del Rosario, has long suffered from an image problem. It used to be called Puerto de Cabra (Goat Port), but the "rebranding" as Rosary Port has not changed the fact that there's little of interest here to the average traveler. If you arrive by boat, your best bet is to rent a car (Cicar has an office by the cruise terminal), skip town, and explore the island's natural wonders.

If you find yourself in Puerto del Rosario with an hour or two to spare before your boat leaves, stroll around the Parque Escultórico (Park of Sculptures) in the center, where there are more than 50 works on display. The tourist office outside the port can provide a map and guide to the 15 most prominent sculptures.

### GETTING HERE AND AROUND

Cruise ships dock at a terminal that's within easy walking distance of the town center. From there you can take a bus to Caleta de Fuste or Corralejo (departures every 30 minutes) or Morro Jable (every hour). If you plan to visit the southern beaches, make sure you rent a vehicle that's suitable for the dirt roads—you may need a 4x4 (inquire at the rental agency).

Ferries leave from Puerto del Rosario for Arrecife in Lanzarote and Las Palmas (via Morro Jable). Southern Lanzarote (Playa Blanca) and northern Fuerteventura (Corralejo) are linked by two companies, Fred Olsen and Naviera Armas. They both make six daily round trips from Lanzarote.

**CONTACTS Tiadhe Fuerteventura Bus.** ⊠ *Av. de la Constitución, Puerto del Rosario* ☎ *928/855726* ⊕ *www.tiadhe.com.*

## 🏃 Activities

### BIKING AND HIKING

**Natoural Adventure**

**BIKING** | Bike rentals and guided tours and hikes around the island are all available from this company, which can tailor excursions to different fitness levels. Horseback riding and boat trips can also be arranged. ⊠ *Calle Marisco 7, Puerto del Rosario* ☎ *664/849411* ⊕ *www.natouraladventure.com.*

### GOLF

**Fuerteventura Golf Club**

**GOLF** | This course with ocean views is near Caleta de Fuste, just south of Puerto del Rosario. ⊠ *Ctra. de Jandía, Km 11, Antigua* ☎ *928/160034* ⊕ *www.fuerteventuragolfclub.com* 🖥 *€80* 🏌 *18 holes, 6637 yards, par 70.*

**Golf Club Salinas de Antigua**

**GOLF** | Just down the road from Fuerteventura Golf Club, this course is surrounded by sand dunes. ⊠ *Ctra. de Jandía, Km 12, Antigua* ☎ *928/877272* ⊕ *www.salinasgolf.com* 🖥 *€62* 🏌 *18 holes, 6105 yards, par 70.*

# Corralejo

*38 km (23 miles) north of Puerto del Rosario.*

Most people visit this part of Fuerteventura for its magnificent sand dunes. Corralejo, a small port town where ferries from Lanzarote dock, has one street of tourist restaurants and some pedestrian plazas with good seafood.

### GETTING HERE AND AROUND

A bus service that leaves every 30 minutes connects Corralejo with Puerto del Rosario. Ferries leave from the marina, next to the original fishing port, for Lanzarote and Isla de Lobos, an uninhabited island that sits off the northwest coast.

##  Sights

### El Cotillo

**TOWN** | On Fuerteventura's most northwesterly tip, this fishing village has quaint and colorful houses and a sleepy, lost-in-time feel. Go at sunset, when the surrounding sands take on a red-orange glow, and peek into the 17th-century Castillo de El Tostón (Tostón Tower), which often holds temporary art exhibits. ⊠ *Corralejo.*

##  Beaches

### Playa de Corralejo

**BEACH** | Also known as Grandes Playas, Playa de Corralejo runs about 3½ km (2 miles) south from the Tres Islas hotel to the Playa de la Barreta. Its white sands are fringed by high sand dunes on one side and the ocean and Isla de Lobos on the other, so views are magnificent. Like many Fuerteventura beaches, it's windy, so waves can be rough. Lounge chairs and umbrellas are available on some parts of the beach, and nude sunbathing is common at the more remote spots. **Amenities:** food and drink; lifeguards; showers; toilets; water sports. **Best for:** nudists; sunrise; walking; windsurfing. ⊠ *Corralejo.*

### Playa del Aljibe de la Cueva

**BEACH** | On the northwest side of the island, this beach has a castle that once repelled pirates. The small stretch of white sand is rather isolated and is popular with locals. The beach is backed by dramatic ocher cliffs, and the sea tends to be rough. **Amenities:** none. **Best for:** nudists; solitude; sunset; windsurfing. ⊠ *Corralejo.*

## 🍴 Restaurants

### La Taberna Juan & Ana

**$$** | **SPANISH** | Behind the Atlantic Sol shopping mall, this well-established favorite is one of the oldest restaurants in town and has been under the same management since 1989. As you might expect from the name, its interior resembles a typical Spanish tavern, with wooden furniture and beams and cozy lighting. **Known for:** traditional Spanish ambience; to-die-for paella; cheery staff. ⑤ *Average main: €14* ⊠ *Calle Hernán Cortés 10, Corralejo* ☎ *928/535027* ⊗ *Closed Sun. No lunch.*

### ★ Restaurante El Moral

**$$** | **SPANISH** | In the small town of Villaverde, halfway between Puerto del Rosario and Corralejo, is one of the island's best-kept culinary secrets. At this small restaurant, Canarian dishes are served family style in the center of the table. **Known for:** gluggable house wines; good value; homemade Canarian tapas. ⑤ *Average main: €13* ⊠ *Ctra. General 94, Villaverde* ☎ *928/868285* ⊗ *Closed Mon.*

## 🛏 Hotels

### ★ Avanti Lifestyle Hotel

**$$$** | **HOTEL** | Fresh, ultramodern, Insta-ready design defines the aesthetic at Avanti, a 15-room adults-only hotel with gleaming blue-and-white rooms and an elegant rooftop bar. **Pros:** destination-worthy restaurant; exclusive (but not stuffy) feel; trendy interiors including four-person spa. **Cons:** rooftop bar open only in high season; small Jacuzzis; first-floor rooms are noisy. ⑤ *Rooms from: €155* ⊠ *Calle Delfín 1, Corralejo* ☎ *928/867523* ⊕ *www.avantihotelboutique.com* ⊗ *Restaurant closed Wed.* ⇥ *15 rooms* ⅼ❍ᵢ *Free Breakfast.*

#### ★ Bahiazul Villas & Club

**$$$$** | **APARTMENT** | Villas sleeping up to six comprise this private, tranquil luxury hotel with a blue-and-white color palette. **Pros:** spotlessly clean; great for both families and couples; inviting public areas. **Cons:** the occasional cockroach (par for the course on this island but still jarring); four- or seven-night minimum depending on the time of year; iffy Wi-Fi. $ *Rooms from: €230* ✉ *Calle Pardelas 7, Corralejo* ☎ *928/854598* ⊕ *www.bahiazul.com* ❙⨀❙ *Free Breakfast.*

#### Hotel Riu Palace Tres Islas

**$$$$** | **RESORT** | You can step right onto Grandes Playas, one of the best beaches on the island, from this hotel, which resembles a cruise ship with its six stories and curved white facade. **Pros:** two large, well-maintained pools; beachfront location; excellent service. **Cons:** dull entertainment; older clientele may not make it the best fit for families; some distance from Corralejo. $ *Rooms from: €192* ✉ *Av. Grandes Playas, Corralejo* ☎ *928/535700* ⊕ *www.riu.es* ↪ *372 rooms* ❙⨀❙ *Free Breakfast.*

#### ★ Secrets Bahía Real Resort & Spa

**$$$$** | **RESORT** | Straight out of the *Arabian Nights*, this oceanfront resort renovated in 2021 is a romantic retreat. **Pros:** excellent service; first-class cuisine; newly renovated. **Cons:** overpriced dining and room service; beach rocky in places; no bars or shops in the vicinity. $ *Rooms from: €237* ✉ *Av. Grandes Playas, Corralejo* ☎ *928/537153* ⊕ *www.atlantis-bahiareal.com* ↪ *170 rooms, 72 suites* ❙⨀❙ *Free Breakfast.*

## 🛍 Shopping

#### ★ Lapa Studio

**CRAFTS** | Snap up jewelry, hats, paper goods, and home decor items at this gorgeous little boutique (est. 2018) in El Cotillo run by four women. Many of the wares are made by local artisans.

✉ *Av. 3 de Abril de 1979 13, Corralejo* ⟊ *in El Cotillo* ☎ *669/616144* ⊕ *www.lapastudio.es.*

## 🏃 Activities

### BICYCLING

#### Easy Riders

**BIKING** | In addition to bike rental, Easy Riders also runs guided tours around the north of the island that cover 20–80 km (12½–50 miles) and can be made to suit most fitness levels. Some include a visit to the Isla de Lobos, off the north coast of the island. ✉ *Suite Atlantis Fuerteventura Resort, Las Dunas, Local 2, Corralejo* ☎ *928/867005* ⊕ *www.easyriders-bike-center.com.*

### BOATING AND OTHER WATER SPORTS

The channel between Corralejo and the tiny Isla de Lobos is rich in undersea life and favored by divers as well as sport fishermen.

#### Abyss Fuerteventura

**DIVING & SNORKELING** | This company organizes dives as well as PADI courses. ✉ *Calle Gravina 10, Corralejo* ☎ *928/949004* ⊕ *www.abyssfuerteventura.com.*

#### Fuertecharter Boat Trips

**BOATING** | This company, located in the marina, offers boat and fishing trips. ✉ *Marina, Muelle Deportivo, Corralejo* ☎ *928/344734* ⊕ *www.fuertecharter.com.*

#### ★ Kailua Surf School Fuerteventura

**SURFING** | Even if you've never surfed before, let the enthusiastic staff at Kailua show you the ropes. Classes for more advanced surfers are also available in addition to 7- and 14-night surf camps. Rates start at approximately €45 per four-hour group lesson. ✉ *Av. Corralejo Grandes Playas 75, Corralejo* ☎ *630/345560* ⊕ *www.kailuasurfschool.com.*

# Betancuria

*25 km (15 miles) west of Puerto del Rosario.*

Betancuria (pop. 731), set in the fertile center of the island, was once Fuerteventura's capital and has several historical monuments. Its quiet streets display typical Fuerteventura architecture. Betancuria is famously the only municipality in Spain to weather six waves of COVID-19 without registering a single positive case, a fact scientists chalk up to the area's sparse population density and high vaccination rates.

## GETTING HERE AND AROUND
Betancuria and its surroundings are best explored by car (the closest rental agencies are in Puerto del Rosario).

## ◉ Sights

### Museo del Queso Majorero (*Antigua Windmill*)
**WINDMILL | FAMILY |** In Antigua, 8 km (5 miles) east of Betancuria, you can visit a restored white Don Quixote–style windmill that was once used for grinding *gofio* (toasted grain) flour and is now part of a museum devoted to Fuerteventura's cheese-making tradition. Next to the windmill are a craft shop and cactus garden. Incidentally, the modern metal windmills throughout the island were imported from the United States and are used for pumping water. ⊠ *Calle Virgen de Antigua, Antigua* ☎ *928/878041* ⊕ *www.museoquesomajorero.es* ✉ *From €4.*

### Santa María de Betancuria
**CHURCH |** The weatherworn colonial church of Santa María de Betancuria was built in the early 15th century as the island's main church when Betancuria was the capital. The church was almost completely destroyed by Berbers in 1593 and then rebuilt. Outside Mass times, the church has no official opening hours, though weekday mornings are often a safe bet. ⊠ *Pl. Santa María de Betancuria 1, Betancuria* ☎ *928/549616* ✉ *€2.*

# Costa Calma

*7 km (4½ miles) south of Matas Blancas.*

As you continue south along the coast from Matas Blancas, the beaches get longer, the sand gets whiter, and the water gets bluer.

## GETTING HERE AND AROUND
The bus connecting Puerto del Rosario and Morro Jable stops at Costa Calma. Buses leave roughly every 30 minutes weekdays and every hour on weekends.

## ☺ Beaches

### Playa Costa Calma
**BEACH |** Like so many of the Fuerteventura beaches, this is yet another stretch of perfect white sands. Playa Costa Calma is actually made up of three beaches, a large one flanked by two smaller ones. You can walk along all three at low tide, but don't be caught by the rising tide: the rocky outcrops between the beaches will prevent your return. Lounge chair and umbrella rental is available near the hotels. Windy conditions draw windsurfers here. **Amenities:** food and drink; lifeguards; showers; toilets; water sports. **Best for:** sunrise; swimming; walking; windsurfing. ⊠ *Costa Calma.*

### ★ Playa de Sotavento
**BEACH |** This famous stretch of pure white sand rivals Corralejo for the title of best Fuerteventura beach. It extends for 6½ glorious km (4 miles)—at low tide you can walk over to neighboring beaches for 9 km (5½ miles). A sandbank that runs parallel to the beach creates a shallow lagoon that's perfect for swimming and for getting down the basics of windsurfing. Nude sunning is favored here,

Surrounded by mountains, Betancuria is a charming colonial village with cobbled streets, whitewashed cottages, and friendly villagers.

except directly in front of hotels—these areas are also the only place where amenities are available. **Amenities:** food and drink; water sports. **Best for:** nudists; solitude; sunrise; windsurfing. ⊠ *Jandía*.

## 🛏 Hotels

### H10 Tindaya
$$$ | **HOTEL** | Tuscany meets the Canary Islands at this neoclassical hotel with soaring towers and ocher-colored columns. **Pros:** hotel has its own sheltered beach; good service; squeaky-clean. **Cons:** small beach; entertainment can be noisy at times; all dining is buffet style. ⑤ *Rooms from: €153* ⊠ *Punta del Roquito, Costa Calma* ☎ *900/444666* ⊕ *www.h10hotels.com* ↬ *354 rooms* ⦿ *All-Inclusive.*

### Risco del Gato Suites The Senses Collection
$$$ | **HOTEL** | A far cry from the big-box resorts that abound on Fuerteventura, this suites-only sanctuary has spectacular ocean views—it's 2 km (1 mile) to the west of Costa Calma resort and perched about 650 feet above the magnificent Playa de Sotavento. **Pros:** tranquil location and setting; quality service; intriguing architecture. **Cons:** evening meals are bland; some rooms could use a refresh; slightly out of town. ⑤ *Rooms from: €160* ⊠ *Calle Sicasumbre 2, Costa Calma* ☎ *902/160630* ⊕ *www.hotelriscodelgato. com* ↬ *51 suites* ⦿ *Free Breakfast.*

## 🍸 Nightlife

### Los Piratas de Costa Calma
**COCKTAIL LOUNGES** | Staff at this popular tiki joint will happily get you buzzed on flamboyantly garnished cocktails. ⊠ *Calle Punta de los Molinillos, Costa Calma* ☎ *663/357689* ⊗ *Closed Sun.*

##  Activities

### GOLF

#### Playitas Golf

GOLF | This challenging course designed by Scottish golf course architect John Chilver Stainer is between Caleta de Fuste and Costa Calma. ⊠ *Guanchinerfe 2, Las Playitas* ☎ *928/860400* ⊕ *www. playitas.net* ⊠ *€69* ✗ *18 holes, 5276 yards, par 67.*

# Morro Jable

*At the southernmost tip of the island.*

The old fishing port of Morro Jable has a long stretch of golden sand. Many more miles of virgin coast stretch beyond here, down a dirt road that eventually leads to the lighthouse. Beaches along the entire windward side of the peninsula remain untouched.

### GETTING HERE AND AROUND

You can get to Morro Jable by bus from Puerto del Rosario. Buses leave every 30 minutes on weekdays and every hour weekends, but if you want to explore the main attraction in this part of the island — the stunning beaches—a car is a must.

## 🏖 Beaches

Beyond the town of Morro Jable, a dirt road leads to the isolated hamlet of Puerto de la Cruz, where there's a lighthouse. If you follow the dirt path across the narrow strip of land (make sure ahead of time that your rental is up to it), you can enjoy the equally empty beaches here. For scuba diving and snorkeling, head for the rocky outcrops on the windward side of Jandía.

#### Playa de Barlovento de Jandía

BEACH | Barlovento is spectacularly unspoiled. The fact that it can be reached only by 4x4s or other heavy-duty vehicles means it receives few visitors; in low season you might well have this 6-km (4-mile) stretch practically to yourself. Take plenty of drinking water, and watch out for strong currents, especially when the wind is strong. **Amenities:** none. **Best for:** nudists; solitude; sunset; windsurfing. ⊠ *Morro del Jable.*

#### Playa de Cofete

BEACH | Along with Barlovento next door, Playa de Cofete is one of Spain's most pristine beaches. This 14-km (9-mile) strip of golden sand faces north, making it the perfect spot for sunbathing, walking, and just getting away from it all. Currents are strong here, particularly when it's gusty. Take plenty of drinking water. **Amenities:** none. **Best for:** nudists; solitude; sunset; walking; windsurfing. ⊠ *Morro del Jable.*

#### Playa de Morro Jable

BEACH | The long stretch of powdery white sand and safe swimming conditions make Morro Jable's beach one of the island's most emblematic. It gets busy on weekends and during the summer, and finding a space for your towel can be difficult unless you're prepared to walk a ways. Lounge chairs and umbrellas are both available. **Amenities:** food and drink; lifeguards; showers; toilets; water sports. **Best for:** sunset; swimming; walking; windsurfing. ⊠ *Morro del Jable.*

# La Palma

The Canaries' most northwestern island is known as "La Isla Bonita" (The Pretty Island) for a reason: Its landscapes are some of the most breathtaking in the archipelago.

La Palma made international news in late 2021 because of a devastating volcanic eruption that lasted 85 days and covered more than 1,000 homes with lava and ash. Some 6,000 residents—13 percent of La Palma's population—were displaced, though much of the island

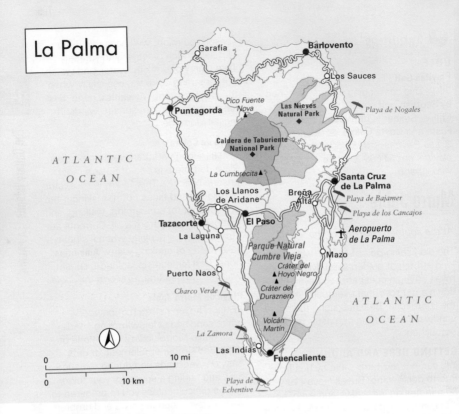

## La Palma

Garafía · Barlovento · Los Sauces · Pico Fuente Nova · Las Nieves Natural Park · Playa de Nogales · Puntagorda · Caldera de Taburiente National Park · La Cumbrecita · Santa Cruz de La Palma · Los Llanos de Aridane · Breña Alta · Playa de Bajamar · Playa de los Cancajos · Tazacorte · El Paso · Aeropuerto de La Palma · La Laguna · Parque Natural Cumbre Vieja · Mazo · Puerto Naos · Cráter del Hoyo Negro · Charco Verde · Cráter del Duraznero · Volcán Martín · La Zamora · Las Indias · Fuencaliente · Playa de Echentive

ATLANTIC OCEAN

ATLANTIC OCEAN

0 ——— 10 mi

0 ——— 10 km

---

emerged unscathed. Indeed, all of the listings in this section remained open through the eruption. At the time of writing, recovery was underway, La Palma was deemed seismologically sound, and hotels were eagerly welcoming visitors (just expect the occasional detour and unforeseen closure).

La Palma's main claim to fame prior to 2021 was hiking, and it remains virtually unspoiled by tourism. Some 1,000 km (621 miles) of waymarked trails spoke out from the center of the island, where the Caldera de Taburiente National Park, named for the pine-blanketed volcanic caldera, stretches 10 km (6 miles) across. The terrain is so varied on La Palma that you can take a morning hike in a misty subtropical rainforest and unwind in the evening with a glass of local wine overlooking barren lava fields and black-sand beaches.

The capital, Santa Cruz de La Palma, is a quaint colonial city of 16,000 with painted row houses and enough shops and restaurants to keep you busy for a few hours. Outside the urban centers, banana plantations stretch in virtually every direction, tumbling down to the coast, which is rocky and virtually beachless (relative to, say, Gran Canaria or Fuerteventura). Tropical fruits—most notably, delectable little pineapples—and flowers are the island's other main cultivars; some of the finest goat cheeses and wines in the Canaries are produced here as well.

The most famous cultural event is the Fiestas Lustrales de la Bajada de la Virgen de las Nieves, a religious march and

celebration that takes place every five
years; the next is scheduled for 2025.

## GETTING HERE AND AROUND
**AIR TRAVEL La Palma.** ☎ *91/321–1000*
⊕ *www.aena.es.*

**BUS TRAVEL La Palma Buses.**

**CAR TRAVEL Cicar Puerto de La Palma.**
⊠ *Estación Marítima de Santa Cruz de La
Palma, Santa Cruz de la Palma* ☎ *92/242–
0159* ⊕ *www.cicar.com.* **Europcar La
Palma Aeropuerto.** ⊠ *Calle La Bajita, LP-5*
☎ *92/242–6192* ⊕ *www.europcar.com.*

**TAXI TRAVEL Taxi La Palma.**
☎ *686/553868* ⊕ *www.taxilapalma.com.*

## VISITOR INFORMATION
**CONTACTS Airport Tourist Office.** ⊠ *La
Palma Airport* ☎ *922/967044* ⊕ *www.
visitlapalma.es.*

# Santa Cruz de La Palma

The island's capital and main port of entry
is Santa Cruz de La Palma, situated halfway down the east coast. Ferries depart
here for Lanzarote, Tenerife, and Gran
Canaria. Santa Cruz is far mellower than
other Canarian capitals and has a certain
Caribbean air, thanks to the colorful
colonial houses dating to the 16th and
17th centuries and cobblestone streets
shaded by palms and tropical plants.
It's a pleasant enough place to crash
after a long day of travel or ahead of an
early-morning departure, but you'll want
to head for more interesting environs for
longer stays.

## 🛏 Hotels

**Hotel San Telmo**
**$$ | B&B/INN | FAMILY |** In a centuries-old
building with painted wooden balconies
and a plant-filled courtyard, this tiny,
independently owned hotel offers charm
and tranquility at a good value. **Pros:** roof
deck with views; comfy, homey feel; on
a quiet side street. **Cons:** small TVs; no

a/c, pool, or gym; minimum four-night
stay depending on season. **⑤** *Rooms
from: €90* ⊠ *Calle San Telmo 5, Santa
Cruz de la Palma* ☎ *922/415385* ⊕ *www.
hotel-santelmo.com* ⇨ *8 rooms* ⍁ *Free
Breakfast.*

# El Paso

*27 km (17 miles) from Santa Cruz de La
Palma.*

El Paso is the only landlocked municipality in La Palma, and it's home to the
island's premier attraction, Caldera de
Taburiente National Park. The area is
sparsely populated with fewer than
10,000 inhabitants. Stone carvings show
that El Paso has ancient roots; it is
believed that the indigenous Benahoarite
people, a subset of Guanche culture
native to La Palma, tended to livestock
here before being colonized from the
15th century onward.

## ◉ Sights

### ★ Caldera de Taburiente National Park
**NATIONAL PARK** | What strikes you first
about Caldera de Taburiente National Park
is its sheer verticality, jutting over 3,000
feet (900 meters) above sea level, which
feels dramatic considering that the ocean
is only a couple of miles away as the
crow flies. Trails here take you through
dense Canarian pine forests, meadows
of wildflowers, dramatic gorges, and
burbling streams. All around you are even
higher, jagged cliff tops whose peaks are
often hidden above the cloud line. There
are essentially two routes: one uphill and
one downhill. The latter is far and away
more enjoyable, but you'll have to hire a
taxi (approximately €55; try to split the
fee with other hikers) at the Barranco de
las Angustias (aka Parking de la Villa) to
drop you at the trailhead at Mirador Los
Brecitos. You then walk the scenic route
from Los Brecitos back down to the taxi
stand, 4–7 hours depending on how

pokey you are. The hike is steep with lots of uneven surfaces and not suited to all travelers. Bring plenty of water and snacks. If you visit in spring or early summer, you'll be treated to jaw-dropping indigo tajinaste flowers in bloom. Islabonitatours (⊕ *www.islabonitatours.com*) is an outstanding English-speaking tour company that can make all transportation arrangements and provide knowledgeable mountain guides. ⊠ *Parque Nacional Caldera de Taburiente* ☎ *922/922280* ⊕ *www.reservasparquesnacionales.es.*

## 🍴 Restaurants

### El Duende del Fuego

$$ | SPANISH | FAMILY | This eccentric indoor-outdoor restaurant one municipality over from El Paso specializes in flavorful allergen-free food prepared for guests with any range of dietary requirements. All ingredients are organic; nearly every dish is gluten-, dairy-, and nut-free; and the best part is, you don't miss these common ingredients, thanks to the chef's creativity. **Known for:** characterful local wines; zero-kilometer menu; allergen-free food. ⑤ *Average main: €15* ⊠ *Pl. Elías Santos Abreu, Pl. Chica 2* ☎ *92/2401002* ⊕ *www.elduendedelfuego.com* ⏾ *Closed Sun. and Mon.*

## Fuencaliente

*22 km (14 miles) from El Paso.*

This municipality occupies the southernmost tip of La Palma. It stands out for its dramatic black-and-red volcanic landscape dotted with cacti and succulents. It's also a center of wine production.

## 👁 Sights

### Matías i Torres

WINERY | La Palma native Victoria Torres Pecis has been quietly making some of the finest Canarian wine on the market

since taking the reins at her late father's hilltop winery in 2010. A fifth-generation winemaker, she understands the island's soils and microclimates, and she adheres to a minimal-intervention philosophy in both vineyard and cellar. "A volcano constructs and at the same time destroys; my vines grow in volcanic ash, and this is part of who we are," she said, reflecting on the 2021 eruption. Snap up as many bottles as you can—Torres's wines (ranging from floral Malvasía to earthy Negramoll) sell out quickly and are hard to come by anywhere else. Visits are private and by email appointment only. ⊠ *in Los Canarios village* ☎ *617/967499* ✉ *victoriatorrespecis@gmail.com* ⊕ *www.facebook.com/matiasitorres* ⚠ *Reservations essential.*

### Salinas de Fuencaliente

NATURE SIGHT | FAMILY | Beside two picturesque lighthouses (one built in 1903 and the other in 1985) are salt flats set amid a starkly black lava landscape. Placards along a footpath explain how salt is extracted from ocean water according to an ancient method. There's a souvenir shop selling various types and textures of salt as well as local wines, T-shirts, postcards, and more, and a good oceanfront restaurant specializing in salt-baked fish that's filleted tableside. ⊠ *Ctra. la Costa el Faro 5* ☎ *922/696002* ⊕ *www.salinasdefuencaliente.es* 🎟 *Free.*

## Barlovento and the Northeast

*36 km (22 miles) from Santa Cruz de La Palma.*

The banana-tree-blanketed northeastern municipalities of Barlovento, San Andrés y Sauces, and Puntallana contain some of the most pristine nature on the island, with a highlight being the misty laurel forests of Las Nieves Natural Park.

#  Sights

## Las Nieves Natural Park

**NATURE PRESERVE | FAMILY |** Also known as Bosque de Los Tilos, this protected biosphere is home to one of the best-preserved laurisilva forests in the archipelago. Take a leisurely walk beneath mossy lianas and towering laurel trees up to the Espigón Atravesado viewpoint, about one hour each way, or take a three- to five-hour hike along the Marcos y Cordero route, skirting beneath waterfalls. There's also a quick out-and-back trail (30 minutes total, give or take) to the Los Tilos Waterfall; follow signs for "Sendero a la Cascada." There's a well-appointed visitor center at the end of the LP-105 road (follow signs for "Los Tilos") with maps and English placards on local history, flora, and fauna. ⚠ **Mudslides and inclement weather cause occasional closures; check with your hotel or the tourist office for updates.** ✉ *Parque Natural de Las Nieves, Calle Los Tilos* ☎ *922/451246.*

# 🛏 Hotels

## Faro de Punta Cumplida

**$$$$ | B&B/INN |** The Punta Cumplida lighthouse has been guiding ships to safety for 155 years, but since 2019, it has doubled as an end-of-the-earth luxury retreat for travelers looking for solitude amid the rolling banana plantations and crashing waves. **Pros:** breakfast basket dropped at your door each morning; steps from La Fajana natural pools; bucket-list experience. **Cons:** uncomfortably windy at times; sparse seating in living areas; unheated pool. ⑤ *Rooms from: €290* ✉ *Faro de Punta Cumplida* ☎ *91/4879017* ⊕ *www.floatel.de/en/hideaways/faro-cumplida* 🛏 *4 suites* ⑩ *Free Breakfast.*

# Tazacorte

*37 km (23 miles) from Santa Cruz de la Palma.*

The municipality of Tazacorte, midway down the western coast, is named for a small inland town and port (Puerto de Tazacorte). The former is home to the island's most emblematic hotel, while the latter is a popular beach destination. This is a good home base for hikes in the Caldera de Taburiente National Park, a 20-minute drive away. Tazacorte came dangerously close to being wiped off the map by the volcanic eruption in 2021, and 3,000 of its residents were temporarily evacuated. Thankfully, today it is perfectly safe to visit.

#  Beaches

## Playa de Tazacorte

**BEACH | FAMILY |** Powdery black sand is the main draw at this urban beach with a boardwalk. When the ocean is calm and the weather is slightly overcast (which makes the sand less likely to singe your toes!), it's an idyllic spot to relax and swim. There's a playground for kids. **Amenities:** food and drink; lifeguards; parking (free). **Best for:** sunset; swimming; walking. ✉ *Av. El Emigrante 15.*

# 🍴 Restaurants

## ★ Playa Mont

**$ | SEAFOOD | FAMILY |** Expertly grilled fish and fried seafood lure crowds night after night to this open-air restaurant steps from the beach. Let the chatty waitstaff talk you through the extensive, well-priced menu, which runs the gamut from *morena frita* (crisp-fried eel) to *alfonsino* (a delectable red-skinned fish) to *escaldón,* a hearty gofio porridge made with fish stock and topped with mojo. **Known for:** heavenly tres leches cake; perfectly cooked fish; beachy vibe.

⑤ *Average main: €11* ✉ *Av. Taburiente 2* ☎ *922/480443* ⊕ *www.playamont.com* ⊗ *Closed Wed.*

## 🛏 Hotels

### ★ Hacienda de Abajo

$$$$ | HOTEL | This sumptuous retreat tucked amid sloping banana plantations and set against the open Atlantic is a tropical oasis with colonial architecture and a distinctly old-world feel. **Pros:** a living museum dripping with priceless works of art; tranquil garden and pool; lovingly made breakfasts. **Cons:** bad lighting throughout the hotel doesn't do justice to the art; underwhelming restaurant; riches procured through multigenerational colonialism. ⑤ *Rooms from: €277* ✉ *Calle Miguel de Unamuno 11* ☎ *922/406000* ⊕ *www.hotelhaciendadeabajo.com* ⊷ *32 rooms* ⦿❘ *Free Breakfast.*

# Puntagorda and the Northwest

*28 km (17 miles) from Tazacorte.*

The dry northwest of the island is covered in cacti and low shrubs and succulents as well as Canarian pine forests in some areas. Many affluent northern Europeans have vacation homes here that they rent out as luxury villas for much of the year. Though rural tourism is on the upswing, the economy still relies heavily on agriculture: you'll spot orange, lemon, avocado, and almond trees. The sleepy town of Puntagorda is a pleasant place to stroll (and stock up on groceries, should you be staying in a vacation rental). There's a quaint farmers' market held on Saturday afternoon and Sunday morning a mile north of the town center (✉ *Mercadillo del Agricultor de Puntagorda, Camino el Pinar 56A, Puntagorda*).

## 🍴 Restaurants

### Jardín de los Naranjos

$$ | SPANISH | FAMILY | In a dining room oozing rustic charm (think green tablecloths, beamed ceilings, and squat wine glasses), feast on rich fall-off-the-bone goat stew made with local meat, or opt for the catch of the day, served with salad and papas arrugadas. **Known for:** warm service; local wines; slow-simmered goat stew. ⑤ *Average main: €14* ✉ *Camino el Pinar 33* ☎ *619/571125* ⊗ *Closed Mon.*

## 🛏 Hotels

### Villa Gran Atlántico

$$$$ | HOUSE | There's a smattering of villa rentals available in this tranquil corner of La Palma, but the most intriguing of the bunch—for both its magazine-cover-worthy Bauhaus-esque design and jaw-dropping views—is Villa Gran Atlántico, whose two ample suites comfortably sleep four guests each. **Pros:** architectural home with 180-degree ocean views; heated outdoor lap pool; high-end perks like Vitamix blender. **Cons:** booking through application; spotty Wi-Fi; far from main sights. ⑤ *Rooms from: €350* ✉ *Villa Gran Atlántico* ☎ *687/791163* ⊕ *www.villagranatlantico.com* ▭ *No credit cards* ⊷ *2 suites* ⦿❘ *No Meals.*

# Index

## A

A Coruña, *222, 253–257*
Abadía de Sacromonte, *669*
Abastos 2.0 ✕, *239*
Ábbatte (shop), *128*
Acinipo, *638*
Adego Eidos, *248*
Adrian Quetglas Restaurant ✕, *571*
Adventure tours, *374*
Agua Amarga, *684, 697*
Aínsa, *339, 375, 377*
Air travel, *41, 42, 53*
Barcelona, *393–395*
Basque Country, Navarra, and La Rioja, *286*
Canary Islands, *741*
Catalonia, Valencia, and the Costa Blanca, *496*
Central Spain, *154*
Costa del Sol and Costa de Almería, *692*
Galicia, Asturias, and Cantabria, *232*
Grenada, *655*
Ibiza and the Balearic Islands, *551*
Madrid, *73*
Pyrenees, *345*
Seville, *601*
Ajuntament (Palma de Mallorca), *566–567*
Ajuntament de Barcelona, *408–409*
Alameda del Tajo, *636*
Albaola boatbuilding factory, *323*
Albayzín, *650, 669–672*
Albores ✕, *643*
Albufera Nature Park, *535*
Alcazaba (Almería), *699*
Alcazaba (Málaga) *707*
Alcazaba (Mérida), *219*
Alcázar
Jerez de la Frontera, *641*
Segovia, *175*
Toledo, *159, 161*
Alcázar de los Reyes Cristianos, *624*
Alcúdia, *580–581*
Alderdi Eder, *309*
Alexandra Barcelona Hotel 🖫, *467*
Alfareria Aparicio (shop), *256*
Alhambra, *650, 657, 660–667*
Alicante (Alacant), *540–542*
Aljaferia, *367*
Alma Hotel Barcelona 🖫, *467*
Almagro, *33, 148, 168–169*
Almería, *684, 697, 699–700*
Almuñécar, *700–702*
Alpujarras, The, *650, 681–682*
Alquézar, *32, 339, 372–374*
Altamira Caves, *278*
Altea, *538–540*
Amphitheater (Tarragona), *523*
Andén Cero, *140–141*
Andrés Gallardo (shop), *111*
Annie b's Spanish Kitchen, *603*
Ansó Valley, *339, 381–383*
Antequera, *684, 713–715*
Antic Hospital de la Santa Creu i Sant Pau, *423, 425*
Antídoto Rooms 🖫, *167*
Antigua Casa Talavera (ceramics), *92*
Antiguo Convento de San Marcos, *197, 199*
Antonio Bar ✕, *312*
Apartment rentals, *745*
Apes' Den, *734*
Aqualand Maspolomas, *769*
Aquarium Donastia-San Sebastián, *310*
Aquarium Finisterrae, *253*
Aqueduct of Segovia, *175, 177*
Arc de Triomf, *446*
Archidona, *714*
Archivo General de Indias, *611–612*
Archivo Real y General de Navarra, *326–327*
Arco de Santa María, *193*
Arcos de la Frontera, *596, 639–640*
Arenales (wine bar), *316–317*
Arganzuela (Madrid), *69, 139–140*
Aribe, *383*
Arrecife, *775, 777–778*
Art Boutique Hotel Chamarel 🖫, *537*
Art Escudellers (ceramics), *421*
Art tours, *52, 396–397*
Artenara, *773*
Arties, *338, 364–365*
Artium Museum, *318*
Arzak ✕, *312*
As Catedrais Beach, *258*
Asador Bedua ✕, *307*
Asador Etxebarri ✕, *306*
Astorga, *148, 202–203*
Asturias, *20, 222–278*
Atrio Restaurante Hotel ✕, *211*
Auditorio de Tenerife Adán Martin, *746–747*
Auritz (Burguete), *339, 385*
Avanti Lifestyle Hotel 🖫, *791*
Ávila, *148, 181–184*
Axarquia, The, *684, 704–705*
Axpe Àtxondo, *280, 305–306*
Ayuntamiento (Alicante), *540–541*
Ayuntamiento (Baeza), *677*
Ayuntamiento (Laguardia), *321*
Ayuntamiento (Seville), *604*
Ayuntamiento Antiguo (Úbeda), *678–679*
Azkuna Zentroa, *289–290*
Azurmendi ✕, *295*

## B

Baelo Claudia, *731*
Baeza, *650, 677–678*
Baeza Cathedral, *677*
Bahía del Duque 🖫, *761*
Bahíazul Villas & Club 🖫, *792*
Baiona, *222, 251–252*
Baixada de Santa Eulàlia, *409*
Balcó del Mediterràni, *523*
Balcón de Europa, *703*
Balearic Islands, *22, 544–594*
Balius Bar, *453*
Ballooning, *574, 603, 657*
Bank of Sóller, *579*
Banker's Bar, *471*
Baños Árabes (Ronda), *636*
Banys Arabs (Girona), *501*
Banys Arabs (Palma de Mallorca), *567*
Baqueira-Beret, *364*
Bar Abaco, *573*
Bar Cañete ✕, *426*
Bar del Pla ✕, *437*
Bar Mut ✕, *464*
ΙΙΙΙ GΙΟΙΙΟ, *20, 390 400*
Barcelona EDITION, The 🖫, *440*
Barceloneta, *388, 443–453*
Barlovento and the Northeast, *798–799*
Barri Gòtic (Barcelona), *388, 408–423*
Barrio de la Macarena (Seville), *596, 619–620*
Barrio de las Letras (Madrid), *68, 103–110*
Barrio de Santa Cruz (Seville), *611–615*
Basílica de la Macarena, *619*
Basílica de Nuestra Señora del Pilar, *367*
Basílica de San Francisco el Grande, *130*
Basílica de San Isidoro, *198*
Basílica de San Vicente, *182–183*
Basílica de Sant Feliu, *501*
Basílica de Santa Eulàlia, *219*
Basílica de Santa María, *541*
Basílica de Santa María del Conceyu, *267*
Basque Country, Navarra, and La Rioja, *20, 280–336*
Basque culture, *303*
Bastió Promenade, *555*
Baztan Valley, *339, 385–386*
¡BE! Club, *317*
Beaches, *30–31, 41*
Barcelona, *448–449*
Basque Country, Navarra, and La Rioja, *302, 308, 311–312*
Canary Islands, *749, 759–760, 766, 769–770, 777, 780–781, 782–783, 791, 793–794, 795, 799*
Catalonia, Valencia, and the Costa Blanca, *499, 511–512, 515, 519, 531*
Costa del Sol and Costa de Almería, *688–689, 695–696, 703, 717, 719, 723, 729, 731*
Galicia, Asturias, and Cantabria, *244, 255, 258, 263, 265, 266, 267–268, 274*
Ibiza and the Balearic Islands, *548–549, 556–557, 563–564, 570–571, 578, 586, 591*
Bed and breakfasts, *50–51*
Beget, *33, 338, 349, 351*
Begoña Basilika, *290*
Begur, *514–516*
Bellver de Cerdanya, *338, 356, 358*
Belmond La Residencia 🖫, *578*
Bendito Vinos y Vinilos (wine bar), *138*
Benirràs, *549*
Benzina ✕, *464*
Bermeo, *280, 302*
Besalú, *508–509*
Best Western Premier Sofraga Palacio 🖫, *184*
Besta ✕, *464*
Betancuria, *793*
Betanzos, *223, 257–258*
Betlem ✕, *464*
Bibat Museum, *318*
Biblioteca de Bidebarrieta, *290*
Bicycling
Basque Country, Navarra, and La Rioja, *286*
Canary Islands, *772, 781–782, 789, 790, 792*
Costa del Sol and Costa de Almería, *692, 694, 695*
Galicia, Asturias, and Cantabria, *232*
Grenada, *657*

*Ibiza and the Balearic Islands, 551, 561, 574, 589*
Madrid, *73, 75*
Seville, *603*
tours, *75, 603, 657, 695*
Bihotz ✕ , *295*
Bilbao, *280, 288–302*
Bioparc Fuengirola, *718–719*
Bird-watching, *52, 574, 695*
Bistró Guggenheim Bilbao ✕ , *295*
Boat and ferry travel, *42–43, 53*
*Canary Islands, 741–742*
*Catalonia, Valencia, and the Costa Blanca, 496*
*Ibiza and the Balearic Islands, 551–552*
Boat tours, *289, 397, 554, 772*
Boating, *538, 559, 792*
Boca del Infierno, *381*
Bodega Antonio Nadal Rios, *567*
Bodega de la Ardosa ✕ , *102*
Bodega el Fabulista, *321–322*
Bodega La Puntual ✕ , *437*
Bodegas (Haro), *335*
Bodegas Baigorri, *322*
Bodegas Binifadet, *588–589*
Bodegas Campos ✕ , *631*
Bodegas del Palacio de Fefiñanes, *246*
Bodegas José Ferrer, *567*
Bodegas Lalanne, *373*
Bodegas Monje ✕ , *754*
Bodegas Muga, *335–336*
Bodegas Tradición, *641*
Bogatell, *30*
Bohemia Suites & Spa ▦ , *770*
Books and movies about, *34–35*
Boutique Hotel San Roque ▦ , *756–757*
Bretón de los Herreros, *331*
Broto, *377*
Bulls, running with, *326*
Burgos, *148, 192–197*
Burguete (Auritz), *339, 385*
Burgui, *383*
Bus travel, *43, 53*
*Barcelona, 395*
*Basque Country, Navarra, and La Rioja, 286*
*Canary Islands, 742*
*Catalonia, Valencia, and the Costa Blanca, 496–497*
*Central Spain, 154–155*
*Costa del Sol and Costa de Almería, 692–693*
*Galicia, Asturias, and Cantabria, 232*
Grenada, *655*
*Ibiza and the Balearic Islands, 552*
Madrid, *73–74*
Pyrenees, *345*
Seville, *601–602*
tours, *75, 397–398, 527, 566, 707–708, 742, 764*

**C**

Ca N'Alluny (La Casa de Robert Graves), *577*
Cabezuela del Valle, *204*
Cable cars, *271, 446, 734, 758*
Cabo de Gata Nature Reserve, *684, 689, 695–697*
Cáceres, *148, 208–213*
Cáceres Museum, *209–210*
Cadaqués, *32, 516–518*
Cadaqués ✕ , *124*
Cádiz, *596, 645–648*

Cádiz Cathedral, *646*
Caelis ✕ , *417*
Café Berlin (music club), *91*
Café Botanico ✕ , *673*
Café Central (jazz club), *111*
Café Iruña ✕ , *295, 298*
Caixa Forum (Palma de Mallorca), *567*
CaixaFòrum (Madrid), *103*
CaixaForum Barcelona, *483*
Cake Man Bakery, The ✕ , *452*
Cal Pep ✕ , *437–438*
Cal Serni ▦ , *359*
Cala Deia, *578*
Cala Galdana, *586*
Cala Macarella and Cala Macaralleta, *30, 549, 591*
Calatrava ▦ , *572*
Caldera de Taburiente National Park, *797–798*
Calella de Palafrugell, *514–515*
Calle Alfarería, *620*
Calle Castilla, *620*
Calle Cava Baja, *130, 131*
Calle Cuchilleria, *317*
Calle del Comercio, *161*
Calle Jacinto, *620*
Calle Ponzano, *141*
Calle Sierpes, *604*
Calleja de las Flores, *625*
Calpe (Calp), *537–538*
Calvari, *581, 583*
Camarote Nao (brewpub), *778*
Cambados, *222, 245–247*
Camel rides, *772*
Camí dels Enginyers, *352–353*
Caminito del Rey, *715*
Camino de Santiago, *197, 226–229*
Camp Nou: Futbol Club Barcelona, *482–483*
Camprodón, *338, 347–349*
Can Corbella, *567*
Can Forteza Rei, *567*
Can Gall ▦ , *561*
Can Po ✕ , *351*
Can Prunera, *579*
Can Ventura ✕ , *356*
Cañadas del Teide, *758*
Canary Islands, *22, 738–800*
Canfranc International Railway Station, *378*
Cangas de Onís, *223, 269–270*
Cantabria, *222–278*
Cap de Creus, *516*
Cap de Formentor, *583*
Cap Rocat ▦ , *572*
Cap Roig, *514*
Cap Roig ✕ , *587*
Capella de Sant Llàtzer, *425*
Capella d'en Marcús, *431*
Capilla de los Marineros, *620*
Capilla del Obispo, *131*
Capilla Real, *672*
Cappuccino ✕ , *723*
Car travel and rental, *44–45, 53*
*Basque Country, Navarra, and La Rioja, 286*
*Canary Islands, 742–743*
*Catalonia, Valencia, and the Costa Blanca, 497*
*Central Spain, 155*
*Costa del Sol and Costa de Almería, 693*
*Galicia, Asturias, and Cantabria, 232*
Grenada, *655–656*
*Ibiza and the Balearic Islands, 552*

Madrid, *74*
Pyrenees, *345*
Seville, *602*
Carmen de la Alcubilla del Caracol ▦ , *660*
Carmen de los Mártires, *660*
Caro Hotel ▦ , *533*
Carratraca, *715*
Carrer dels Escudellers, *399*
Carrer Flassaders, *431, 434*
Carrer Isabel II, *586*
Carrer Petritxol, *399, 401*
Cartoixa de Valldemossa, *576–577*
Cartuja de Miraflores, *193*
Carvajal, *689, 719*
Casa Amatller, *456*
Casa Anita ✕ , *517*
Casa Batlló, *456*
Casa Botines, *198–199*
Casa Bruno Cuadros, *401*
Casa Calvet, *456*
Casa Cámara ✕ , *324*
Casa Castellarnau, *523–524*
Casa Consistorial, *309*
Casa Dani ✕ , *125*
Casa de Campo, *92, 94*
Casa de Diego (fans), *86*
Casa de la Primica, *322*
Casa de l'Ardiaca, *409*
Casa de las Conchas, *187*
Casa de les Punxes, *456–457*
Casa de los Deanes, *183*
Casa de los Mensaque, *620*
Casa de los Pisa, *670*
Casa de los Tiros, *668*
Casa de Pilatos, *612*
Casa de Sefarad, *625*
Casa del Pópulo, *678*
Casa del Vino de Tenerife, *753*
Casa Gerardo ✕ , *132*
Casa Gispert (shop), *442*
Casa Golferichs, *457*
Casa González ✕ , *105*
Casa Irene ▦ , *365*
Casa Macareno ✕ , *102*
Casa Manteca ✕ , *647*
Casa Marcelo ✕ , *239*
Casa Milà, *457*
Casa Mira ✕ , *711*
Casa Morisca ▦ , *671*
Casa Museo Colón, *765*
Casa-Museo de Manuel de Falla, *660*
Casa-Museo Federico García Lorca, *674–675*
Casa Museo José Benlliure, *527*
Casa-Museu Gaudí, *473*
Casa Palacio Maria Luisa ▦ , *644*
Casa Revuelta ✕ , *132*
Casa Rufo ✕ , *298*
Casa Rufus ✕ , *365*
Casa Rural do Louteiro ▦ , *204*
Casa Salvador ✕ , *96–97*
Casa Salvador Dalí – Portlligat, *516*
Casa Sotero ✕ , *146*
Casa Urola ✕ , *312–313*
Casa Vicens, *473*
Casas Colgadas, *169–170*
Casares, *32, 685, 729–730*
Casco Antigua (Santiago de Compostela), *235*
Casinos, *274, 726*
Castell de Bellver, *567–568*

Castell de Montjuïc, *483*
Castell de Sant Ferran, *414–415*
Castell de Sant Nicolau, *590*
Castell Gala Dalí-Púbol, *508*
Castillo de Aínsa, *375*
Castillo de Arteaga ⌕, *300*
Castillo de Clavijo, *331*
Castillo de Coca, *180*
Castillo de Dénia, *536*
Castillo de Loarre, *372*
Castillo de San Antón (Museo Arqueológico e Histórico), *253*
Castillo de San Miguel (Almuñécar), *701*
Castillo de Santa Bárbara (Alicante), *541*
Castillo de Santa Bárbara (Costa Teguise), *779*
Castillo de Sigüenza, *172–173*
Castillo de Sohail, *719*
Castillo de Tossa de Mar, *511*
Castillo San Gabriel, *777*
Castle (Tarifa), *731*
Catalan culture, *40*
Catalonia, Valencia, and the Costa Blanca, *22, 490–542*
Catedral (Tarragona), *524*
Catedral-Bailica de Nuestra Señora del Pilar, *367–368*
Catedral de Ávila, *183*
Catedral de Burgos, *193, 195*
Catedral de Cuenca, *170*
Catedral de Girona, *501*
Catedral de Jerez, *641*
Catedral de la Almudena, *87*
Catedral de León, *199*
Catedral de Mallorca (La Seu), *568*
Catedral de Pamplona, *327*
Catedral de Santa Maria (La Seu D'Urgell), *358–359*
Catedral de Santa María (Vitoria-Gasteiz), *318*
Catedral de Santander, *272*
Catedral de Santiago de Bilbao, *290*
Catedral de Santiago de Compostela, *235*
Catedral de Segovia, *177*
Catedral de Sevilla, *604–605, 608*
Catedral de Sigüenza, *173*
Catedral de Valencia, *527–528*
Catedral del Buen Paster, *310*
Catedral del Salvador de Zaragoza (La Seo), *368*
Catedral Metropolitana de San Salvador de Oviedo, *261*
Catedral Santa Ana, *765*
Cathedral (Almería), *699*
Cathedral (Ciutadella), *590*
Cathedral (Elvissa), *555*
Cathedral (Granada), *672*
Cathedral (Toledo), *161*
Cava Baja, *130, 131*
Cemetery (Deià), *577*
Central Spain, *20, 148–220*
Centre de Cultura Contemporànea de Barcelona (CCCB), *425*
Centre del Carme Cultura Contempránia (CCCC), *528*
Centre d'Interpretació Madina Yasisa, *556*
Centre Pompidou Málaga, *707*
Centro (Granada), *650, 672–674*
Centro (Seville), *596, 604–611*

Centro Andaluz de Arte Contemporáneo, *601*
Centro Atlántico de Arte Moderno, *765*
Centro Botín, *274*
Centro de Arte Contemporáneo (Málaga), *707*
Centro de Arte Contemporáneo (Mijas), *721*
Centro de Arte Reina Sofía, *29, 114, 135*
Centro de Cerámica Triana, *620*
Centro de Creación Contemporánea de Andalucia, *625*
Centro de Interpretación del León Romano, *202*
Centro Galego de Arte Contemporánea, *236*
Centro José Guerrero, *672*
Ceramic mural (Mallorca), *565*
Cerámica de Sargadelos (shop), *258*
César Manrique House Museum, *779*
Chamartín (Madrid), *69, 144–146*
Chamberí (Madrid), *69, 140–144*
Charolés Restaurante ✕, *181*
Chillida Leku Museum, *310*
Chocolat Madrid ✕, *107*
Chueca (Madrid), *68, 96–101*
Church of San Bartolomé (Logroño), *331*
Church of San Bartomeu (Sóller), *579*
Churrería Santo Tomé ✕, *166*
Cidade da Cultura, *236*
Cimadevilla, *263*
Circ Romà, *524*
Ciudad Encantada, *170–171*
Ciudad Monumental, *210*
Ciudadela de Jaca, *378*
Ciutadella (Menorca), *590–593*
Ciutadella (Pamplona), *327*
Ciutadella Park (Barcelona), *446*
Ciutat de les Artes I las Ciències, *28, 528–529*
Ciutat Romana de Pol·lèntia, *581*
Clamores (club), *144*
Climate, *40–41, 48, 72, 153, 231, 285, 344, 393, 495, 551, 601, 655, 691, 741*
Climbing, *270, 758*
Cocó Madrid (dance club), *85*
Cocol (shop), *134*
Col·legi de los Teresianes, *477, 479*
Columbus, Christopher, *609*
Columnes del Temple d'August, *409*
Colección Visigoda, *219*
Colegiata de Santa Juliana, *278*
Colegiata de Santa María la Mayor, *373–374*
Colexiata de Santa Maria do Campo, *254*
Communications, *49*
Concatedral de San Nicolás de Bari, *541–542*
Concatedral de Santa Maria, *210*
Concatedral de Santa Maria de La Redonda, *332*
Consentido ✕, *190*
Convento de la Encarnación, *290*
Convento de Las Dueñas, *187*
Convento de San Clemente, *161*
Convento de San Estéban, *187*
Convento de San Francisco, *678*
Convento de Sant Agustí, *590*
Convento de Santa Paula, *619*

Convento de Santa Teresa, *163*
Convento de Santo Domingo el Antiguo, *161, 163*
Córdoba, *596, 623–635*
Corral de Comedias, *168*
Corral del Carbón, *672*
Corralejo, *790–792*
Costa Adeje, *758–762*
Costa Blanca, *22, 490–542*
Costa Brava, *499*
Costa Calma, *793–795*
Costa Daurada, *499*
Costa del Sol and Costa de Almeria, *22, 684–736*
Costa Teguise, *778–782*
Cova des Coloms, *594*
Covid-*19, 25, 158*
Cristine Bedfor ⌕, *587*
Cristo de los Faroles, *630*
Cristóbal Balenciaga Museum, *306–307*
Cruises, *694, 743*
Cruix ✕, *465*
Cudillero, *32–33, 260*
Cuenca, *148, 169–172*
Cuenllas ✕, *95*
Cuesta de la Alhacaba, *669*
Cuesta de Moyano, *111*
Cueva de la Pileta, *638*
Cueva de las Calaveras, *537*
Cueva de los Verdes, *780*
Cueva de Siete Palacios, *700–701*
Cuevas de Nerja, *703*
Cuevas del Drach, *570*
Cuisine, *41*
  Barcelona, *390–391, 418, 451*
  Basque Country, Navarra, and La Rioja, *282–283, 303*
  Catalonia, Valencia, and the Costa Blanca, *492–493, 522*
  Central Spain, *150–151, 207*
  Costa del Sol and Costa de Almería, *686–607*
  Galicia, Asturias, and Cantabria, *224–225*
  Grenada, *652–653*
  Ibiza and the Balearic Islands, *546–547*
  Madrid, *70–71*
  Pyrenees, *340–341*
Culinary and wine tours, *52, 397, 603, 657, 704, 707, 764*
City Walls (Lugo), *243*

**D**

Dalí, Salvador, *28, 506–507, 508, 516*
Dalt Vila, *555*
Damasqueros ✕, *668*
Dazz (club), *321*
Dear Hotel ⌕, *95*
Deià, *577–578*
DeLaCrem ✕, *467*
Delicatessen Ojeda, *197*
Dénia, *535–537*
DINS Sabti Taura ✕, *571*
Discounts and deals, *47, 393, 500*
Disfrutar ✕, *465*
DiverXO ✕, *145*
Doctor Cocktail, The (bar), *191*
Dolmens, *714*
Dolphin watching, *772*
Don Oligario, *246*
Doña Casilda Iturrizar Park, *290*
Donamariako Benta ✕, *386*

**E**

Echaurren ⊡ , 334–335
Eco Insider (tours), 778
Economy, 24
Eguren Ugarte, 322
Eivissa (Ibiza Town), 555–560
Eixample (Barcelona), 388, 453–472
El Arenal (Seville), 596, 615–618
El Bañuelo, 670
El Berbés, 249
El Bodegón ✕ , 271
El Cable ✕ , 520
El Call (Jewish Quarter; Barcelona), 415
El Call (Jewish Quarter; Girona), 501
El Camino de Santiago, 197, 226–229
El Castillo de Santa Catalina ⊡ , 712
El Celler de Can Roca ✕ , 503
El Charco Verde, 787
El Choco ✕ , 632
El Cid, statue of, 616
El Convento ⊡ , 640
El Cotillo, 791
El Cuarto Real, 668
El 58✕ , 451
El Fogón Sefardi ✕ , 178–179
El Greco, 159, 164
El Llorenç Parc de Mar ⊡ , 572
El Magnifico (shop), 443
El Médano, 759
El Mesón ✕ , 319–320
El Motel ✕ , 507
El Palmar, 535
El Paraguas ✕ , 125
El Paso, 797–798
El Playazo, 31, 695–696
El Prado, 29, 114, 115, 117–120
El Puchero de la Nieta ✕ , 220
El Rastro (Madrid), 134
El Raval (Barcelona), 388, 423–430
El Saladillo, 689, 729
El Salvador, 180
El Santo ✕ , 766
El Serrallo, 524
El 7 de Sillerias ✕ , 214
El Teide, 757–758
El Toro, 593–594
El Transbordador Aeri del Port, 446
El Trébol ✕ , 166
El Tributo de las Tres Vacas, 383
El Trillo ✕ , 670
El Tubo Neighborhood ✕ , 370
El Valle del Jerte, 204–205
El Vaso de Oro ✕ , 452
El Xampanyet (bar), 431
Eldiset (wine bar), 441
Elizondo, 385
Elkano ✕ , 307
Emergencies, 44, 53
EMOZ (Escuela Museo Origami Zaragoza), 368
Empúries, 515
Enoteca Paco Pérez ✕ , 451
Entre Vinos ✕ , 637
Equiberia (tours), 157
Era Coquèla ✕ , 363
Ermita de San Antonio de la Florida (Goya's tomb), 94
Ermita de San Frutos, 180
Ermita de San Telmo, 765
Es Cavellet Beach, 556–557
Es Trenc, 31, 549, 570–571
Es Moli de Foc ✕ , 587

Església de Betlem, 401
Església de Sant Pere, 508
Església de Sant Vicenç, 508
Espacio Eslava ✕ , 609
Estadi Olímpic Lluís Companys, 483, 485
Estany Pudent, 563
Estación de Atocha, 111, 114, 115
Estació de França, 446–447
Estepona, 685, 727, 729
Eth Galin Reiau (shop), 364
Eurostars Hotel de la Reconquista ⊡ , 262
Euskal Museoa Bilbao Museo Vasco, 290, 292
Ezcaray, 333–334

**F**

Faraday ✕ , 97
Farmhouse stays, 497
Faro de la Mola, 563
Farragut, David Glasgow, monument to, 590
Faustino Gran ⊡ , 592
Feria de Abril, 619
Festival de Flamenco, 726
Festivals, 64–66
Barcelona, 406
Catalonia, Valencia, and the Costa Blanca, 496, 522, 527
Costa del Sol and Costa de Almería, 726
Galicia, Asturias, and Cantabria, 258
Ibiza and the Balearic Islands, 583
Pyrenees, 348–349, 383
Seville, 619, 634
Figueres, 505–508
FIRMVM ✕ , 702
Fish Market (Calpe), 537–538
Fisterra, 222, 245
Flamenco, 598–599
Barcelona, 421, 488
Costa del Sol and Costa de Almería, 726
Grenada, 671–672
Madrid, 92, 135
Seville, 612, 615, 622, 634, 635
tours, 604
Flamenco La Quimera, 135
Flysch, 307
Fogón del Azogue ⊡ , 181
Fogony ✕ , 359–360
Fonda España ✕ , 427
Fonda Rigá ⊡ , 347
Fonseca family, 187
Font de Canaletes, 401
Formentera, 544, 563–564
Fornalutx, 32, 580
Fornells, 32, 594
Fragment (shop), 331
Frigiliana, 703
Fuencaliente, 798
Fuendetodos, 367
Fuengirola, 685, 718–720
Fuente de Cibeles, 115
Fuerteventura, 738, 789–795
Fundació Antoni Tàpies, 457
Fundació Joan Miró, 28, 485
Fundación César Manrique 786–787
Fundación de Arte y Pensamiento Martín Chirino, 765
Fundación-Museo Oteiza, 327
Fundación NMAC, 731
Fundación Rodríguez Acosta/Instituto Gómez Moreno, 668

Fundación Vela Zanetti, 199
Funicular de Artxanda, 292
Fus de Sa Geganta, 586
Fútbol, 145, 302, 303, 482–483

**G**

Galeria Juanjo San Pedro, 322
Galicia, Asturias, and Cantabria, 20, 222–278
Ganbara ✕ , 313
Garachico, 756–757
Garganta del Chorro, 715
Gaucho ✕ , 329
Gaudí, Antonio, 198–199, 202–203, 405, 406, 456–463, 473, 475, 477, 479, 480–481
Generalitat de Catalunya, 409, 412
Gernika, 304
Getaria, 280, 306–308
Gibralfaro, 707
Gibraltar, 685, 733–736
Gibraltar National Museum and Moorish Baths, 734–735
Gibraltar Nature Reserve, 735
Gibraltar Town, 735
Gijón, 223, 263–265
Girona, 498–504
Gocce di Latte ✕ , 440
Golf, 561, 575, 589, 694, 761–762, 769, 772, 782, 786, 790, 795
Golf Alcanada, 575
González Bypass, 641
Gràcia (Barcelona), 388, 473–477
Gran Canaria, 738, 762–714
Gran Casino del Sardinero, 274
Gran de Gràcia, 473
Gran Hotel La Perla ⊡ , 329–330
Gran Meliá Palacio de Los Duques ⊡ , 90
Gran Teatre del Liceu, 401
Gran Teatro Manuel de Falla, 646
Granada, 22, 650–682
Great Siege Tunnels, 735
Guadalhorce Valley, 684–685, 715
Guadalupe, 148, 215–218
Gure Toki ✕ , 298

**H**

Hacienda Cuatro Ventanas ⊡ , 755
Hacienda de Abajo ⊡ , 800
Haro, 280, 335–336
Hat, The ⊡ , 133
Hecho and Ansó Valleys, 339, 381–383
Herederos de Marqués de Riscal, 322
Hermandad de Pescadores ✕ , 325
Hiking and walking
Barcelona, 398
Canary Islands, 758, 778, 790
Costa del Sol and Costa de Almería, 694
Galicia, Asturias, and Cantabria, 235
Ibiza and the Balearic Islands, 575, 589
Madrid, 75, 131
Pyrenees, 345–346, 355, 362
Seville, 603–604
tours, 52, 75–76, 398, 603–604, 694
History, 36–38, 624
Hola Coffee ✕ , 137
Hondarribia, 33, 280, 325–326
Hontza, 322
Horseback riding, 251, 559, 593, 657, 772–773
Hospedería del Real Monasterio ⊡ , 217

Index

Hospes Palacio del Bailio ⌂, 633
Hospital de la Caridad, 616
Hospital de los Venerables, 612
Hospital de Santiago, 679
Hospital de Tavera, 163
Hostal de la Gavina ⌂, 513–514
Hostal dos Reis Católicos, 236–237
Hostal Loreto, 537
Hostal Restaurant Sa Rascassa ✕, 515
Hostal Rodri ⌂, 674
Hot springs, 242
Hotel Aigua Blava ⌂, 516
Hotel Alfonso XIII ⌂, 618
Hotel Amadeus Sevilla ⌂, 614
Hotel Arbaso ⌂, 315
Hotel Arts Barcelona ⌂, 452
Hotel Balcón de Córdoba ⌂, 634
Hotel Barosse ⌂, 379–380
Hotel Boutique Posada Dos Orillas ⌂, 215
Hotel Carabeo ⌂, 704
Hotel Casa de San Martín ⌂, 375
Hotel Casa del Embajador ⌂, 788–789
Hotel Casa 1800 ⌂, 614
Hotel Diana ⌂, 512
Hotel El Mirador de Ordiales ⌂, 265
Hotel Es Moli ⌂, 578
Hotel Maria Cristina ⌂, 315
Hotel Marqués de Riscal ⌂, 323
Hotel Neri ⌂, 419
Hotel NH Collection Madrid Euro-building ⌂, 146
Hotel Rec ⌂, 441
Hotel Rector ⌂, 191
Hotel Rural 3 Cabos ⌂, 260
Hotel Sauce ⌂, 371
Hotel Spa Relais & Châteaux A Quinta Da Auga ⌂, 240
Hotel V...Vejer ⌂, 731, 733
Hotels, 50–51, 53
Huerta de San Vicente, 650, 675
Huesca, 339, 371–372
Huesca Cathedral, 371

I
IAACC Pablo Serrano, 368
Ibañeta Pass, 384
Iberostar Heritage Grand Mencey ⌂, 750
Ibiza and the Balearic Islands, 22, 544–594
Ibiza Town, 555–560
Icod de los Vinos, 756
Iglesia de la Vera Cruz, 177
Iglesia de Nuestra Señora de la Concepción, 747
Iglesia de San Ildefonso, 163
Iglesia de San Luis de los Franceses, 608
Iglesia de San Mateo, 210
Iglesia de San Millán, 177
Iglesia de San Nicolás, 292
Iglesia de San Pablo, 368
Iglesia de San Román, 163
Iglesia de Santa Maria, 375
Iglesia de Santa Maria del Coro, 310–311
Iglesia de Santa Maria la Mayor, 213
Iglesia de Santiago, 254
Iglesia de Santo Tomé, 163

Iglesia del Salvador, 608
Igl... la Parroquial de la mauuuuuuu Concepción, 721
Igrexa de San Francisco de Betanzos, 257–258
Igrexa de Santa Maria do Azogue de Betanzos, 258
Igrexa de Santiago de Betanzos, 258
Illa de Cabrera, 569
Ilunion Mérida Palace ⌂, 220
Immunizations, 48
Institut Valencia d'Art Modern (IVAM), 529
Isaba, 383
Isla de la Cartuja, 620–621
Isla de Santa Clare, 311
Isla Mágica, 621
Islas Cíes, 31, 249–250
Itálica, 596, 622–623
Itineraries, 54–61
Itsasmuseum, 292
Iturrienea Ostatua ⌂, 301
Ivori (shop), 442

J
Jaca, 339, 378–380
Jaca Cathedral, 378–379
Jameos del Agua, 780
Jardi de Ses Bruixes Boutique Hotel ⌂, 588
Jardín Botánico (Canary Islands), 753
Jardín Botánico (Madrid), 114
Jardín Botánico Canario Viero y Clavijo, 774
Jardín de Cactus, 780
Jardines de Murillo, 612
Jardines de Sabatini, 87, 131
Jardines de la Victoria, 630
Javier, 327
Jerez de la Frontera, 596, 640–645
Jerte and El Valle del Jerte, 204–205
Jewish Quarter (Barcelona), 415
Jewish Quarter (Girona), 501
Jewish Quarter (Seville), 612
Jewish ritual baths, 508–509
Juan Peña El Lebrijano, 636
Juana la Loca ✕, 132
Judería (Jewish Quarter; Seville), 612

K
Kailua Surf School Fuerteventura, 792
Kaitxo, 292
Kayaking, 301–302
Kimpton Vividora Hotel ⌂, 419–420
Kitesurfing, 762
Kursaal, 311

L
La Alcoba Azul ✕, 417
La Alhambra, 650, 657, 660–667
La Bodega de Santiago ✕, 788
La Bodeguilla Lanciego ✕, 320
La Boqueria (food market), 403
La Brujidera ✕, 673
La Cabaña ✕, 673
La Campana ✕, 610
La Carboná ✕, 644
La Carihuela, 689, 717
La Casa de la Villa, 292
La Casa de los Arquillos ⌂, 320
La Casa del Flamenco, 615
La Casa Grande ⌂, 640

La Casa Marti–Els Quatre Gats, 412
La Catedral de Juana ✕, 275
La Catapa ✕, 122
La Catedral de Barcelona, 412–413
La Catedral de Santa Maria de Astorga, 202
La Catedral Vieja and La Catedral Nueva, 187–188
La Ciutadella (Barcelona), 388, 443–453
La Concepción, 707, 709
La Concha, 30, 308, 311
La Copita Asturiana ✕, 89
La Cova Fumada ✕, 452
La Encina de Ortega (shop), 168
La Fabrica de Hielo (bar), 534
La Galana ✕, 265
La Hoja 21 ✕, 190
La Huerta de San Vicente, 650, 675
La Laguna Gran Hotel ⌂, 752
La Latina (Madrid), 69, 128–135
La Llave de la Juderia ⌂, 634
La Llotja, 434
La Macarena, 596, 619–620
La Manual Alpargatera (shop), 423
La Mañueta ✕, 329
La Marina ✕, 211–212
La Moreneta, 518–519
La Noche Blanca del Flamenco, 634
La Palma, 738, 795–800
La Pepita ✕, 476
La Piedra, 249
La Platilleria ✕, 487
La Ponderosa ✕, 171
La Posada de los Sentidos ⌂, 208
La Rambla (Barcelona), 388, 398–408
La Ribera (Barcelona), 388, 431–443
La Ribera Sacra, 222
La Rioja, 20, 280–336
La Rioja Alta, 280, 333–335
La Soo cathodral, 367
La Seu d'Urgell, 338, 358–359
La Taberna de Baco ✕, 332
La Vera, 148, 207–208
La Villa, 213–214
La Viña ✕, 313
La Viña del Ensanche ✕, 298–299
Lago Martiánez, 753
Laguardia, 280, 321–323
Laguna de Fuente de Piedra, 714
Lambuzo ✕, 81, 84
Landa ⌂, 195–196
Language, 62–63, 303
Language programs, 52
Lanjarón, 681
Lanzarote, 738, 774–789
Lapa Studio (shop), 792
L'Arca (shop), 422
Las Alberquillas, 703
Las Canteras, 766
Las Fallas (festival), 496, 527
Las Médulas, 203–204
Las Nieves Natural Park, 799
Las Palmas, 763–769
Las Torres ✕, 372
Las Vistas, 759
Lasarte ✕, 466
L'Atelier ✕, 467
Lavapiés (Madrid), 69, 135–139
Le Bodeguilla Lanciego ✕, 320
Le Petit Train Jaune (little yellow train), 354
León, 148, 197–202

Lepanto ✕, 711
L'Estartit, 515
Ligne de Cerdagne, 354
Llafranc, 514
Llanes, 223, 267–269
Llívia, 338, 356
Lluc, 583–584
Logroño, 280, 331–333
Lonja (Zaragoza), 367
Lonja de la Seda, 529
Loro Parque, 753–754
Los Cristianos, 758–762
Los Jardines de Albia, 292–293
Los Millares, 699
Los Patios de Beatas ✕, 712
Los Roques de García, 758
Los Tarantos (flamenco), 421
Luarca, 223, 259–250
Lugo, 222, 243
Luis Méndez (shop), 192

**M**

M House ⬚, 572–573
Macera Taller Bar, 99
Madinat Al-Zahra, 625, 628
Madrid, 20, 68–146
Madrid Edition, The ⬚, 91
Madrid Río, 87
Mahón (Maó), 585–589
Majestic Hotel & Spa ⬚, 469
Málaga, 684, 705–713
Málaga Cathedral, 709
Malasaña (Madrid), 68, 101–103
Mallorca, 544, 564–584
Mandarin Oriental Barcelona ⬚, 469
Mandarin Oriental Ritz, Madrid ⬚, 122–123
Mar Menuda, 511
Marbella, 685, 722–726
Marbella Club ⬚, 726
Marbella East Side Beaches, 723
Mardeleva ✕, 783
Mare de Deu dels Àngels, 356
Martín Berasategui ✕, 313–314
Masca, 759
Maspalomas, 769–773
Matadero Madrid, 139–140
Mater Boat Museum, 324
Matias i Torres, 798
Mayor de Migueloa ⬚, 323
ME Barcelona ⬚, 470
ME Madrid Reina Victoria ⬚, 109
ME Sitges Terramar ⬚, 521
Medes Islands, 515
Melo's ✕, 137
Mendi Goikoa Bekoa ⬚, 306
Menorca, 544, 584–594
Mercado Central (Salamanca), 192
Mercado Central (Valencia), 529
Mercado Central de Almería, 699
Mercado de Abastos de Santiago, 237
Mercado de Antón Martín, 135
Mercado de Atarazanas, 709
Mercado de la Cebada, 130
Mercado de la Paz, 124
Mercado de la Ribera, 293
Mercado de Lanuza, 367
Mercado de Nuestra Señora de Africa, 747
Mercado de San Antón, 96

Mercado de San Miguel, 78
Mercado de Triana, 621
Mercado de Vallehermoso, 141
Mercat de la Llibertat, 473
Mercat Des Claustre, 586
Mercer ⬚, 610
Mérida, 148, 218–220
Metropol Parasol, 608
Mesa de los Tres Reyes, 381
Mesón de José María ✕, 179
Mezquita (Córdoba), 628–629
Mezquita del Cristo de la Luz, 163–164
Microtel Placetinos ⬚, 191
Mies van der Rohe Pavilion, 485
Mijas, 685, 720–721
Miluna ⬚, 167
Mirabó de Valldemossa ⬚, 577
Mirador de Colom, 403
Mirador de la Cilla, 773
Mirador de San Nicolás, 669–670
Mirador del Río, 780
Mirador d'es Port, 590
Mirador Panorámico La Boriza, 267
Misión Café ✕, 102
Moments ✕, 466
Monasterio de La Cartuja, 675
Monasterio de la Encarnación, 87, 131
Monasterio de las Descalzas Reales, 88
Monasterio de las Huelgas, 195
Monasterio de Piedra, 367
Monasterio de San Juan de la Peña, 339, 380–381
Monasterio de San Juan de los Reyes, 164
Monasterio de San Pedro de Siresa, 381–382
Monasterio de Santa María de las Cuevas, 621
Monasterio de Santa María de Poblet, 522
Monasterio de Suso, 334
Monasterio de Yuso, 334
Monasterio de Yuste, 148, 207–208
Monastery of Sant Joan de les Abadesses, 351
Monastery of Santa Maria de Ripoll, 352
Monastery of Santo Domingo de Silos, 196
Moncloa (Madrid), 68, 92, 94–95
Monestir de Miramar, 577–578
Monestir de Sant Pere de Galligants, 502
Monte Igueldo, 311
Monte Real, 251
Montjuïc, 388, 483–488
Moreria Archaeological Site, 219
Morro Fi (bar), 472
Morro Jable, 795
Montserrat, 518–519
Monument Hotel ⬚, 470
Monument to David Glasgow Farragut, 590
Monument to Jules Verne, 563
Moorish Castle (Gibraltar), 735
Mudejar churches, 367
Mulhacén, 680
Multisport, 301–302
Mundaka, 280, 302, 304–305

Muro Francisco de la Mata, 331
Muros, 222, 245
MUSAC (Museo de Arte Contemparánea de Castilla y León), 199
Museo Arqueológico (Córdoba), 629
Museo Arqueológico (Jerez de la Frontera), 641–642
Museo Arqueológico de Alicante, 542
Museo Arqueológico Nacional (Madrid), 29, 124
Museo Carmen Thyssen Málaga, 709
Museo Casa Natal de Picasso, 709
Museo Cerralbo, 94
Museo Cuevas del Sacromonte, 669
Museo de Armería de Álava, 318
Museo de Art Nouveau Art Déco-Casa Lis, 188
Museo de Arte Contempránes de Vigo (MARCO), 250
Museo de Arte de la Diputación, 727
Museo de Arte Sacro, 765
Museo de Artes y Costumbres Populares, 616
Museo de Baeza, 678
Museo de Bellas Artes (Bilbao), 293
Museo de Bellas Artes (Córdoba), 629
Museo de Bellas Artes (Seville), 616
Museo de Bellas Artes (Valencia), 529
Museo de Bellas Artes de Álava, 319
Museo de Cádiz, 646
Museo de Historia y Antropología, 751
Museo de Huesca, 371
Museo de la Ciudad de Antequera, 714
Museo de la Evolución Humana, 195
Museo de la Naturaleza y Arqueologia, 747
Museo de las Cortes, 646
Museo de León, 199
Museo de los Concilios y de la Cultura Visigoda, 163
Museo de los Patios, 630
Museo de Navarra, 327
Museo de Pontevedra, 248
Museo de Santa Cruz, 164
Museo de San Isidoro, 198
Museo de Zaragoza, 368
Museo del Baile Flamenco, 612
Museo del Foro de Caesaraugusta, 368
Museo del Grabado Español Contemporáneo, 722
Museo del Greco, 164
Museo del Pimentón, 208
Museo del Prado, 29, 114, 115, 117–120
Museo del Queso Majorero, 793
Museo del Romanticismo, 96
Museo del Teatro de Caesaraugusta, 368
Museo del Traje, 94
Museo del Vidrio y Cristal, 709, 711
Museo Diocesano, 278
Museo do Pobo Galego, 237
Museo Etnográfico Campo de Calatrava, 168
Museo Goya Colección Ibercaja, 369
Museo Guggenheim Bilbao, 29, 293–294
Museo Helga de Alvear, 210

Museo Internacional de Arte
Contemporáneo Contilla de San
Jose, *///*
Museo Mijas, *721*
Museo Municipal (Tossa de Mar), *511*
Museo Municipal de Bellas Artes,
*747*
Museo Nacional de Arte Romano,
*219–220*
Museo Nacional de Artes Decora-
tivas, *115*
Museo Nacional del Teatro, *168–169*
Museo Pablo Gargallo, *369*
Museo Picasso Málaga, *711*
Museo Provincial de Ávila, *183*
Museo Ruiz de Luna, *164*
Museo Sefardi, *166*
Museo Sorolla, *141*
Museo Taurino, *630*
Museo Thyssen-Bornemisza, *29, 103,
105, 114*
Museo Universidad de Navarra, *327*
Museo Vostell Malpartida, *210*
Museu Arqueològic, *502*
Museu d'Arqueologia de Catalunya,
*485–486*
Museu d'Art (Girona), *502*
Museu d'Art Contemporani (Eivissa),
*556*
Museu d'Art Contemporani de
Barcelona (MACBA), *425*
Meseu de la Farmacia, *356*
Museu de Maricel, *519*
Museu de la Xocolata, *434*
Museu del Cau Ferrat, *519–520*
Museu del Disseny de Barcelona,
*447*
Museu del Joguet de Catalunya, *506*
Museu del Modernisme de Barce-
lona, *457*
Museu del Pueblu d'Asturies, *263*
Museu d'Es Baluard, *565, 568–569*
Museu d'Història de Barcelona
(MUHBA), *413*
Museu d'Història de Catalunya, *447*
Museu d'Història de Girona, *502*
Museu d'Història de Sant Feliu
Guixols, *513*
Museu d'Història dels Jueus, *502–503*
Museu Fundació Pilar y Joan Miró,
*569*
Museu Fundación Juan March, *569*
Museu Marítim, *404*
Museu Municipal (Tossa de Mar), *511*
Museu Nacional d'Art de Catalunya,
*28, 486*
Meseu Paleocristià i Necrópolis, *524*
Museu Picasso, *29, 434–435*
Museum of Jewish History, *502–503*
Museum of Pilgrimage and Santiago,
*237*
Museum of the Asturian People, *263*
Museums, *28–29*
Muxía, *222, 243–244*

N

Nabucco Tiramisu ✕ , *477*
Nájera, *334*
Navarra, *20, 280–336*
Navarrete, *334*
Nerja, *684, 702–704*

NH Collection Cáceres Palacio de
Oquendo ⊞ , *711*
NH Collection León Plaza Mayor
⊞ , *201*
Nightlife and the arts, *25*
Barcelona, *408, 420–421, 428–430, 431,
441–442, 452, 471–472, 488*
Basque Country, Navarra, and La Rioja,
*316–317, 321, 330*
Canary Islands, *750, 755–756, 761, 768,
771–772, 778, 786, 794*
Catalonia, Valencia, and the Costa Blanca,
*504–505, 521, 525, 534–535, 542*
Central Spain, *191–192, 196, 201–202, 212*
Costa del Sol and Costa de Almería, *700,
713, 718, 726, 736*
Galicia, Asturias, and Cantabria, *240–241,
250–251, 256, 262, 277*
Grenada, *671–672, 674*
Ibiza and the Balearic Islands, *558–559,
573, 588*
Madrid, *76–77, 85–86, 91–92, 99–100,
102–103, 110–111, 123, 127, 133, 135,
138, 140, 146*
Pyrenees, *348–349, 363, 380*
Seville, *615, 618, 622, 634, 635*
Noor ✕ , *633*
Nuestra Señora del Carmen, *713*
Nuestra Senyora de Los Angeles, *581*

O

O Camino dos Faros, *243–244*
O Filendón (bar), *241*
Ochagavia (Otsagabia), *383*
Ojén, *685, 726–727*
Ojo Guareña, *196*
Olite, *327, 329*
Oliva ✕ , *703*
Olvera, *638*
One Shot Tabakalera House ⊞ , *316*
Only YOU Boutique Hotel ⊞ , *97*
Oratorio de la Santa Cueva, *848*
Oratorio de San Felipe Neri, *646–647*
Orchidarium, *727*
Ordesa and Monte Perdido National
Park, *339, 377–378*
Orreaga (Roncesvalles), *339, 384–385*
Orzán and Riazor Beaches, *255*
Órzola, *780*
Os Vinos, *241*
Oto, *377*
Ourense, *222, 241–243*
Oviedo, *223, 260–263*

P

Pa i Raïm ✕ , *514*
Packing, *41, 48*
Palacio (Madrid), *68, 87–92*
Palacio de Cibeles, *115, 121*
Palacio de Gaudí, *202–203*
Palacio de La Aljafería, *369*
Palacio de la Condesa de Lebrija,
*608*
Palacio de la Magdalena, *274*
Palacio de la Rambla ⊞ , *680*
Palacio de Liria, *101*
Palacio de las Dueñas, *608*
Palacio de los Golfines de Abajo,
*210–211*
Palacio de Mondragón, *636*
Palacio de Monterrey, *188*
Palacio de Orellana-Pizarro, *214*
Palacio de Viana, *630*
Palacio de Villapanés Hotel ⊞ , *610*

Palacio del Capitán Diego de
Luborra, *211*
Palacio del Marqués de Dos Aguas,
*529, 531*
Palacio Episcopal, *711*
Palacio Real (Madrid), *88, 131*
Palacio Real de La Granja, *177–178*
Palau Dalmases, *435*
Palau de la Generalitat, *531*
Palau de la Música Catalana, *435*
Palau del Lloctinet, *413*
Palau Güell, *404–405*
Palau Reial de l'Almudaina, *569*
Palau Salort, *591*
Palma de Mallorca, *565–574*
Palmetum, *747*
Palmitos Park, *769*
Palomeque ✕ , *370*
Pals, *515*
Pamplona, *280, 326–331*
Panteón de los Reyes, *198*
Parador de Almagro ⊞ , *169*
Parador de Baiona ⊞ , *251*
Parador de Cangas de Onis ⊞ , *269*
Parador de Cuenca ⊞ , *172*
Parador de Granada ⊞ , *660*
Parador de Hondarribia ⊞ , *325–326*
Parador de Málaga-Gibralfaro
⊞ , *713*
Parador de Santillana Gil Blas
⊞ , *278*
Parador de Santo Estevo ⊞ , *242*
Parador de Sigüenza ⊞ , *173*
Parador de Trujillo ⊞ , *215*
Parador de Úbeda ⊞ , *680*
Parador Hostel dos Reis Católicos
⊞ , *240*
Paradores, *51*
Parc de la Ciutadella, *446*
Parc Nacional d'Aigüestortes i
Estany de Sant Maurici, *338,
360–361*
Park Güell, *475*
Parlament de Catalunya, *448*
Parque Cultural del Río Vero, *374*
Parque de Ardales, *715*
Parque de las Ciencias, *675–676*
Parque de María Luisa, *615–616*
Parque de Santa Catalina, *765*
Parque del Buen Retiro, *114, 121*
Parque del Oeste, *94–95*
Parque Marítimo César Manrique,
*747*
Parque Monte del Castro, *250*
Parque Nacional de Ordesa y Monte
Perdido, *339, 377–378*
Parque Nacional de Timanfaya, *788*
Parque Nacional del Teide, *758*
Parque Natural de Monfragüe, *208*
Parque Natural del Torcal de Ante-
quera, *714*
Parque Natural Marítimo y Terrestre
Cabo de Gata-Níjar, *695*
Parque Rural de Anaga, *747–748*
Parroquia Matriz de Nuestra Señora
de la Concepción, *751*
Parte Vieja (San Sebastián), *309*
Pasaia, *280, 323–324*
Pasaje Chinitas, *711*
Pasarelas de Alquézar, *374*
Paseo del Espolón, *195*
Paseo del Prado, *114*

Paseo Maritimo, *254–255*
Paseo Padre Manjón, *670*
Passatge Permanyer, *458*
Passeig Arqueològic (Girona), *503*
Passeig Arqueològic (Tarragona), *524*
Passeig d'es Born (Barcelona), *435, 437*
Passeig des Born (Mallorca), *565, 569–570*
Passeig Maritim, *520*
Passports, *48*
Pasteleria Hofmann, *434, 443*
Pastisseria Confiteria Cosp, *355*
Pavellons de la Finca Güell-Càtedra Gaudí, *479*
Pavoneo (bar), *99–100*
Pazo Baión, *248*
Pazo de Rubianes, *246–247*
Pazo de Xelmírez, *237*
Pedralbes (Barcelona), *477–483*
Peña El Taranto, *700*
Peñón d'Ifach Natural Park, *538*
Pentxo ✕, *299*
Pepa Bar a Vins, *472*
Peratallada, *515*
Pez (shop), *100*
Picasso, Pablo, *29, 120, 304, 434–435, 709, 711*
Picnic ✕, *438, 440*
Pico de Veleta, *680–681*
Picos de Europa Visitor Center, *269*
Piscinas Naturales El Caletón, *756*
Pizarro House Museum, *214*
Plaça Cabrinetty, *354*
Plaça de Garriga I Bachs, *413–414*
Plaça de la Vila de Gràcia, *475*
Plaça de la Virreina, *475*
Plaça del Diamant, *475*
Plaça del Pedró, *425*
Plaça del Rei, *414*
Plaça d'Espanya, *486*
Plaça Major (Bellver de Cerdanya), *358*
Plaça Major (Palma de Mallorca), *570*
Plaça Reial, *405*
Plaça Rovira i Trias, *476*
Plaça Sant Felip Neri, *414*
Plaça Sant Jaume, *414*
Plaça Sant Just, *414–415*
Plaëa de s'Esplanada, *590*
Platja de la Barceloneta, *448–449*
Platja de la Mar Bella, *449*
Platja de la Nova Icária, *449*
Platja de Sant Sebastià, *449*
Platja Gran, *512*
Playa Ballota, *267*
Playa Blanca, *788–789*
Playa Costa Calma, *793*
Playa de Barlovento de Jandía, *795*
Playa de Cofete, *795*
Playa de Corralejo, *30, 791*
Playa de Famara, *780*
Playa de la Garita, *780*
Playa de la Ribera, *31*
Playa de la Victoria, *31*
Playa de las Américas, *758–762*
Playa de las Burras, *770*
Playa de las Cucharas, *781*
Playa de las Mujeres, *770*
Playa de las Teresitas, *749*
Playa de los Genoveses, *696*
Playa de los Guíos, *759–760*
Playa de los Pocillos, *782–783*
Playa de Morro Jable, *795*

Playa de Poniente, *265*
Playa de San Agustín, *770*
Playa de San Lorenzo, *265*
Playa de Santa Maria, *266*
Playa de Ses Illetes, *31, 549, 563–564*
Playa de Sotavento, *793–794*
Playa de Tazacorte, *799*
Playa de Torimbia, *267*
Playa de Toró, *267*
Playa del Aljibe de la Cueva, *791*
Playa del Inglés, *770*
Playa del Reducto, *777*
Playa del Sablón, *268*
Playa El Sardinero, *274*
Playa Grande, *783*
Playa las Arenas, *30, 531*
Playa Los Lances, *30, 689, 731*
Playa Mont ✕, *799–800*
Playa Matagorda, *783*
Playas de Puerto Banús, *723*
Plaza Cristo Rey, *267*
Plaza de España
  *El Arenal, 617*
  *Mérida, 220*
  *Santa Cruz de Tenerife, 748*
  *Vitoria-Gasteiz, 319*
Plaza de la Asunción, *642*
Plaza de la Iglesia, *754*
Plaza de la Paja, *130, 131, 132*
Plaza de la Villa, *88–89, 131*
Plaza de la Virgen Blanca, *319*
Plaza de los Dolores, *630*
Plaza de los Naranjos, *722*
Plaza de los Refinadores, *612*
Plaza de Oriente, *89, 131*
Plaza de San Martin, *199*
Plaza de San Miguel, *630*
Plaza de Santa Ana, *105*
Plaza de Santa Maria del Camino, *199*
Plaza de Toros, *636*
Plaza de Toros Real Maestranza, *617*
Plaza de Zocodover, *164–165*
Plaza del Altozano, *620*
Plaza del Castillo, *329*
Plaza del Charco, *754*
Plaza Mayor
  *Cáceres, 211*
  *Guadalupe, 217*
  *León, 201*
  *Madrid, 78, 81, 131*
  *Salamanca, 188*
  *Segovia, 178*
  *Sigüenza, 173*
  *Trujillo, 214*
Plaza Miguel de Unamuno, *294*
Plaza Nueva, *294*
Plaza Ochavada, *714*
Plaza San Francisco, *647*
Plaza Santa Ana, *763*
Plaza Santa Marína, *630*
Poble Espanyol, *486–487*
Poble Sec, *388, 483–488*
Poema del Mar Aquarium, *766*
Politics, *24*
Pollença, *581–583*
Pont Fortificat, *509*
Ponte Vella, *241*
Pontevedra, *222, 247–251*
Port (Ciutadella), *591*
Port de Barcelona, *405*
Port Olimpic, *448*
Port Vell, *448*

Portaferrissa Fountain, *405*
Posada de San José ☒, *172*
Posada Magoria ☒, *383*
Posada Naturista ☒, *380*
Potes, *223, 270–271*
Praetorium, *524*
Praia de Nemiña, *244*
Praza de Maria Pita, *255*
Praza do Obradoiro, *237*
Price categories
  dining, *76, 157, 233, 287, 346, 396, 498, 553, 603, 657, 694, 744*
  lodging, *76, 157, 233, 287, 346, 396, 498, 553, 603, 657, 694, 745*
Priego de Córdoba, *650, 676–677*
Proyecto Hemen (shop), *301*
Pueblo Canario, *765*
Puente de Alcántara, *165*
Puente de Isabel II, *620*
Puente de Piedra (Logroño), *332*
Puente de Piedra (Zaragoza), *367*
Puente de San Martin, *165*
Puente de San Pablo, *171*
Puente Romano (Salamanca), *188*
Puente Romano de Cangas de Onis, *269*
Puente Viesgo, *274*
Puerta de Alcalá, *121*
Puerta de Almadóvar, *630*
Puerta del Sol, *81, 131*
Puerto Banús, *689, 722*
Puerto de la Cruz, *752–758*
Puerto de Tornavacas, *204–205*
Puerto del Carmen, *782–783, 786*
Puerto del Rosario, *790*
Puerto Deportivo, *727*
Puigcerdà, *338, 354–355*
Puntagorda and the Northwest, *800*
Pyrenees, The, *20, 338–386*

**Q**
Queralbs, *353*
Queso Project (shop), *778*
Quinta de San Amaro ☒, *247*

**R**
Radisson Blu Hotel 1882 ☒, *470*
Rafting, *270*
Real Academia de Bellas Artes de San Fernando, *81*
Real Alcázar, *613*
Real Basilica de Santa Maria la Mayor, *248*
Real Colegiata de Santa Maria de Roncesvalles, *384*
Real Colegio Seminario del Corpus Christi, *531*
Real Escuela Andaluza del Arte Ecuestre, *642*
Real Fábrica de Tapices, *121*
Real Jardin Botánico, *121*
Real Monasterio de San Lorenzo de El Escorial, *181*
Real Monasterio de Santa María de Guadalupe, *217*
Real Monasterio de Santo Tomás, *183*
Real Monestir de Santa Maria de Pedralbes, *479*
Realejo (Granada), *640, 668–669*
Recinte Modernista de Sant Pau, *458*
Refugio del Juanar, *726*
Refugios de la Guerra Civil, *699*
Reial Cercle Artistic, *415*

Religion, 24–25
Restaurant Pont Vell ✕, 509
Restaurante El Molino de la Losa ✕, 184
Restaurante El Moral ✕, 791
Restaurante Filigrana ✕, 239–240
Restaurante Informal ✕, 418
Restaurante Iván Cerdeño ✕, 166–167
Restaurante Mar Azul ✕, 788
Restaurante Sorrento ✕, 201
Restaurants, 49–50
Retiro (Madrid), 68, 111–124
Riazor Beach, 255
Rías Baixas, 246
Ribadesella, 223, 266–267
Ribeira Sacra, 241–243
Ribes de Freser, 338, 352–353
Rideshare travel, 155, 287
Río Leza, 331
Ripoll, 338, 351–352
Riu Segre, 356
Rock Art Center of Tito Bustillo, 266
Roman aqueduct, 523
Roman bridge (Baiona), 251
Roman Bridge (Pollença), 581
Roman Bridge (Salamanca), 188
Roman Circus (Tarragona), 524
Roman ruins
Barcelona, 409
Catalonia, Valencia, and the Costa Blanca, 515, 523, 524
Central Spain, 175, 177, 188, 202, 219–220
Costa del Sol and Costa de Almería, 731
Galicia, Asturias, and Cantabria, 241, 243, 251, 263, 269
Ibiza and the Balearic Islands, 581
Pyrenees, 367, 368
Seville, 623, 638, 647
Roman Theater (Cádiz), 647
Roman walls (Zaragoza), 367
Romanesque bell tower, 354
Roncal Valley, 339, 383–384
Roncesvalles (Orreaga), 339, 384–385
Ronda and environs, 596, 635–638
Roostig ✕, 97
Rosewood Villa Magna ⛾, 127
Rúa Pescadería, 249
Ruta del Sol y del Vino and Ruta de la Pasa, 704

**S**

Sa Llotja, 570
Sa Penya, 555
Sacha ✕, 145–146
Sacra Capilla de El Salvador, 679
Sacromonte (Grenada), 650, 669
S'Agaró, 513–514
Sailing, 575–576, 594
St. George's Day, 406
St. Michael's Cave, 735–736
Sala Equis (cabaret), 133
Salamanca (Central Spain), 148, 184–192
Salamanca (Madrid), 68, 124–128
Salardú, 338, 365–367
Salinas de Fuencaliente, 798
Salmon Guru (bar), 110
Salobreña, 702
San Bartolomé de Tirajana, 773
San Cristóbal de La Laguna, 32, 751–752
San Julián de los Prados, 261
San Lorenzo de El Escorial, 148, 181

San Lorenzo y Jesús del Gran Poder, 619
San Mateo, 773–774
San Miguel, 642
San Miguel highlands, 381
San Millán de la Cogolla, 334
San Nicolás, 531
San Nicolás de los Servitas, 89
San Nicolás de Villa, 630
San Pedro el Viejo, 372
San Sebastián (church), 713
San Sebastián (town), 280, 308–317
San Sebastián 57 ✕, 749–750
Sanctuary of Loyola, 307
Sandeman, 642
Sant Cristófol, 349
Sant Domènec, 354
Sant Domingo, 556
Sant Feliu de Guixols, 512–513
Sant Francesc, 570
Sant Francesc Xavier, 563
Sant Jaume, 358
Sant Joan de les Abadesses, 338, 351
Sant Miquel del Port, 448
Sant Miqèu, 363
Sant Pau del Camp, 426
Sant Pere (Barcelona), 431–443
Sant Pere de Rodes, 516–517
Santa Cruz (Seville), 596
Santa Cruz de la Palma, 797
Santa Cruz de Tenerife, 745–751
Santa Eulàlia, 570
Santa Eulària des Riu, 560–561
Santa Gertrudis de Fruitera, 561–562
Santa Lucia, 773
Santa María (Mahón), 586
Santa María Bell Tower, 354–355
Santa María das Areas, 245
Santa María de Besalú, 509
Santa María de Betancuria, 793
Santa María de la Asunción, 639
Santa María de los Reyes, 322
Santa María de Montgarri, 364
Santa María de Palacio, 332
Santa María de Poblet, 522
Santa María del Mar, 437
Santa María del Naranco and San Miguel de Lillo, 261
Santa María la Mayor (Antequera), 713
Santa María la Mayor (Ronda), 636–637
Santander, 223, 271–277
Santes Creus, 521–522
Santiago de Compostela, 222, 233–241
Santiago el Real, 332
Santillana del Mar, 223, 277–278
Santo Domingo de la Calzada, 334
Santo Tomás, 336
Santuari de la Mare de Déu de Núria, 353
Santuari de Lluc, 584
Santuario de la Virgen de la Montaña, 211
Sarrià (Barcelona), 477, 479–480
Scuba diving, 559, 561, 576, 589, 761, 792
Seaside Palm Beach ⛾, 771
Secrets Bahía Real Resort & Spa ⛾, 792
Segore Etxe-Berri ✕, 308
Segovia, 148, 173, 175–180
Segway tours, 398
Selva de Irati, 384

Selva de Uza, 381
Semana Santa (Seville), 619
Semana Santa (Viveiro), 258
Seneca, statue of, 630
Sepúlveda, 148, 180–181
Ses Salines, 549, 557
Setenil de las Bodegas, 638
Seventy Barcelona ⛾, 477
Seville, 22, 596–648
Shopping
Barcelona, 421–423, 430, 434, 442–443, 477
Basque Country, Navarra, and La Rioja, 301, 308, 317, 321, 331
Canary Islands, 750–751, 757, 758, 768, 778, 781, 788, 792
Catalonia, Valencia, and the Costa Blanca, 505, 525, 535, 542
Central Spain, 167–168, 179–180, 192, 197, 202, 212–213, 215
Galicia, Asturias, and Cantabria, 247, 251, 256, 258, 262, 277
Grenada, 660, 674, 680
Ibiza and the Balearic Islands, 559, 562, 564, 573–574, 588–589, 592–593
Madrid, 77–78, 86, 100–101, 103, 111, 123–124, 128, 134–135, 139
Pyrenees, 349, 355, 364, 372, 380
Seville, 610–611, 615, 618, 622, 635
Sierra de Montánchez (shop), 213
Sierra Nevada, 650, 680–681
Sierra Rioja Alta, 280
Sigüenza, 148, 172–173
Sinagoga de Santa María La Blanca, 164
Sinagoga del Agua, 679
Sinagoga del Tránsito, 164–165
Sitges, 519–521
Skiing, 262–263, 347, 364, 380, 681
Slow & Low ✕, 466–467
Soccer, 145, 302, 303, 482–483
Sol (Madrid), 68, 78, 81–86
Sóller, 579–580
Sollo ✕, 719
Son Brull Hotel and Spa ⛾, 583
Son Marroig, 577, 578
Sort, 338, 359–360
Southern Coast (Canary Islands), 769–773
Sports and the outdoors, 25
Barcelona, 482–483
Basque Country, Navarra, and La Rioja, 301–302, 303
Canary Islands, 758, 761–762, 769, 772–773, 778, 781–782, 786, 789, 790, 792, 795
Catalonia, Valencia, and the Costa Blanca, 538
Costa del Sol and Costa de Almería, 694
Galicia, Asturias, and Cantabria, 251, 257, 262–263, 269–270
Grenada, 681
Ibiza and the Balearic Islands, 559–560, 561, 574–576, 580, 589, 593, 594
Madrid, 86, 145
Pyrenees, 345–346, 347, 355, 362, 364, 374, 377, 380
Station Building Galleries, 579
Street art, 319
Subways, 74, 395
Suculent ✕, 428
Surf School Lanzarote, 782
Surfing, 782, 792
Sylkar ✕, 143
Synagogues, 164–165, 630–631, 679

# T

Tabacelera (Madrid), *135–136*
Tabakalera (San Sebastián), *311*
Taberna La Elisa ✕ , *106–107*
Tafira Alta, *774*
Tahíche, *786–787*
Tao Club and Garden, *768*
Tapas 2.0 ✕ , *190–191*
Tarifa, *685, 730–731, 733*
Tarragna, *522–525*
Taüll, *338*
Tasca el Obispado ✕ , *751*
Taxes, *51*
Taxis, *74–75, 286, 395, 552, 602, 656, 693, 743*
Tazaorte, *799–800*
Teatre-Museu Dalí, *506–507*
Teatre Principal (Mallorca), *570*
Teatre Principal (Menorca), *586*
Teatro Kapital (club), *110*
Teatro Real (opera), *92*
Tejeda, *773*
Teleférico, *95*
Teleférico Fuente Dé, *271*
Telephones, *49*
Temple Expiatori de la Sagrada Família, *458–463*
Tenerife, *738, 745–762*
Tenerife Espacio de las Artes, *748*
Tennis, *560, 576*
Terete ✕ , *336*
Termas Romanas de Campo Valdés, *263*
Teteria Dar Al-Chai ✕ , *166*
Tetuán (Madrid), *69, 146*
Theatre-Museu Dalí Figueres, *28*
Thermal baths, *242*
Tibidabo, *480*
Timing the visit, *40–41, 48, 72–73, 153–154, 231–232, 285–286, 344–345, 393, 495–496, 551, 601, 655, 691–692, 741*
Tipping, *41, 52*
Toledo, *148, 158–168*
Toledo de la Mano (tours), *159*
Tondeluna ✕ , *332*
Torla, *377*
Torralba d'en Salort, *586*
Torre Bellesguard, *480–481*
Torre Calahorra, *631*
Torre de Doña Ochanda, *319*
Torre de Hércules, *255*
Torre de los Anda, *319*
Torre del Oro, *617*
Torre d'en Galmés, *586*
Torre Tavira, *647*
Torremolinos, *685, 716–718*
Tossa de Mar, *509–512*
Tours, *52*
Barcelona, *396–398*
Basque Country, Navarra, and La Rioja, *289*
Canary Island, *764, 772, 778, 790*
Catalonia, Valencia, and the Costa Blanca, *527*
Central Spain, *157, 159, 209*

Costa del Sol and Costa de Almería, *694–695, 704, 707–708*
Galicia, Asturias, and Cantabria, *235, 246*
Grenada, *657, 677*
Ibiza and the Balearic Islands, *554, 555, 566*
Madrid, *75–76*
Pyrenees, *346, 374*
Seville, *603–604, 642*
Town hall (Sóller), *579*
Train travel, *41, 45–47, 53*
Barcelona, *395–396*
Basque Country, Navarra, and La Rioja, *287*
Catalonia, Valencia, and the Costa Blanca, *497*
Central Spain, *155–156, 159*
Costa del Sol and Costa de Almería, *693*
Galicia, Asturias, and Cantabria, *232–233*
Grenada, *656*
Ibiza and the Balearic Islands, *552–553*
Pyrenees, *345, 353, 354*
Seville, *602*
Tram travel, *395*
Transportation, *41, 42–47, 53, 73–75, 154–156, 232–233, 286–287, 345, 393–396, 496–497, 551–553, 601–602, 655–656, 692–693, 741–743*
Triana (Seville), *596, 620–622*
Triumphal Arch of Berà, *523*
Trópico ✕ , *428*
Trucadors, *563*
Trujillo, *148, 213–215*
Trujillo Castle, *214*
Tui, *222, 252–253*
Tui Cathedral, *252*

# U

U.S. Embassy/Consulate, *48*
Úbeda, *650, 678–680*
Ullastret, *515*
Universidad de Salamanca, *188, 190*
University of Seville, *617*
Upper Barcelona, *388, 477–483*
Urdax, *385*
Urumea River, *309*

# V

Valencia, *22, 490–498, 525–535*
Vall de Núria, *338, 352–353*
Vall de Núria Rack Railway (Cremallera), *353*
Valldemossa, *576–577*
Valls, *522*
Vegetalia ✕ , *719–720*
Veintiuno 🖬 , *767*
Vélez-Málaga, *704–705*
Verne, Jules, monument to, *563*
Via Veneto ✕ , *482*
Victofer Conservas Artesanas, *321*
Victor Hugo House, *323*
Vielha, *338, 361, 363–364*
Vigo, *222, 249–251*
Viguera, *331*
Vila Vella, *511*
Vila Viniteca (shop), *443*
Villa and apartment rental, *745*
Villafranca del Bierzo, *148, 203–204*

Vineria San Telmo ✕ , *614*
Vinoteca Moratin ✕ , *107*
Visas, *48*
Visitor information, *53*
Barcelona, *398*
Costa del Sol and Costa de Almería, *695*
Grenada, *657*
Pyrenees, *355*
Vitoria-Gasteiz, *280, 317–321*
Viveiro, *223, 258*
Vizcaya Bridge, *294*
Volcanoes, *758, 772, 788*
Volunteer programs, *52*

# W

Walk and Eat Spain (tours), *76*
Water sports, *580, 792*
Weather, *40–41, 48, 72, 153, 231, 285, 344, 393, 495, 551, 601, 655, 691, 741*
Whale-watching, *772*
Windmill, *793*
Windsurfing, *773, 782*
Wine, *41, 52, 246*
Wineing (bar), *573*
Wineries
Basque Country, Navarra, and La Rioja, *321–322, 335–336*
Galicia, Asturias, and Cantabria, *246, 248*
Ibiza and the Balearic Islands, *567*
Pyrenees, *373*
Seville, *641, 642*
tours, *246, 642*

# X

Xerta ✕ , *467*

# Y

Yacimiento Arqueológico Gadir, *647*
Yaiza, *786–787*
Yeguada de la Cartuja, *643*
Yolanda Andrés (shop), *139*
Yurbban Passage Hotel & Spa 🖬 , *471*

# Z

Zahara de la Sierra, *638–639*
Zaragoza, *338, 367–371*
Zelaia Sagardotegia ✕ , *314*
Zentral (club), *330*
Zip lining, *377*
Zoos, *718, 753–754, 769*
Zubizuri Bridge, *295*
Zugarramurdi, *385*
Zumaia, *280, 306–308*
Zurriola, *312*

# Photo Credits

# Photo Credits

(543). Travelling-light/Dreamstime (546). Laurie Geffert Phelps / Fodor's.com member (547). Rafael Campillo / Alamy Stock Photo (547). Tagstiles (548). ArtesiaWells (549). Anibal Trejo/Shutterstock (549). Lara-sh/Shutterstock (558). Skowron/Shutterstock (568). Kovop58/Shutterstock (575). Bkrzyzanek/Shutterstock (581). Philippe Fritsch (582). LunaMarina (591). **Chapter 11: Seville and Around:** LucVi/Shutterstock (595). VicPhotoria/Shutterstock (598). KikoStock/Shutterstock (599). Pyroshot/Dreamstime (599). Sina Ettmer Photography/Shutterstock (605). Cezary Wojtkowski/Shutterstock (611). Sorincolac (629). RudiErnst/Shutterstock (632). Riverside / fodors.com member (637). Mamadela (639). Miquelito/Shutterstock (643). Fulcanelli/Shutterstock (645). **Chapter 12: Granada and Around:** Balate Dorin/Shutterstock (649). Pat_Hastings/Shutterstock (652). Carmen Martínez Banús/iStockphoto (653). AmpFotoStudio/Shutterstock (653). Botond Horvath/Shutterstock (661). Vladimir Korostyshevskiy/Shutterstock (661). Joserpizarro/ Shutterstock (662). Cezary Wojtkowski/Shutterstock (663). Ivan Soto Cobos/Shutterstock (664). Arenaphotouk/Dreamstime (664). Joserpizarro/Shutterstock (664). Reimar/Shutterstock (664). Guss.95/Shutterstock (664). Leon Rafael/Shutterstock (665). Kiev.Victor/Shutterstock (666). Julian Maldonado/Shutterstock (667). Fotografiecor. nl/Shutterstock (667). **Chapter 13: Costa del Sol and Costa de Almería:** Shutterstock / Artur Bogacki (683). Baghitsha/Dreamstime (686). Gildemax/wikipedia.org (687). Lia Sanz/Shutterstock (687). Valery Bareta/Shutterstock (688). Sunshinecity (689). Claus Mikosch/iStockphoto (689). Daniela Sachsenheimer/ Shutterstock (696). Westend61 GmbH/ Alamy Stock Photo (701). Anastasia Galkina/Shutterstock (710). Arsty/Dreamstime (716). Jupitersounds/ Shutterstock (720). Trabantos/Shutterstock (724). Sabine Klein/Shutterstock (728). Two meerkats/Shutterstock (730). Freefly/iStockphoto (734). **Chapter 14: The Canary Islands:** Turismo Lanzarote (737). Leoks/shutterstock (746). RossHelen/shutterstock (752). Elena19/shutterstock (754). Mikadun/shutterstock (757). Bellena/shutterstock (764). Valery Bareta/shutterstock (771). Alexilena/shutterstock (775). MisterStock/shutterstock (779). Turismo Lanzarote (784-785). Sergey Kelin/shutterstock (787). RossHelen/shutterstock (794). **About Our Writers:** All photos are courtesy of the writers.

*Every effort has been made to trace the copyright holders, and we apologize in advance for any accidental errors. We would be happy to apply the corrections in the following edition of this publication.

# Notes

# Notes

# Fodor's ESSENTIAL SPAIN 2023

**Publisher:** Stephen Horowitz, *General Manager*

**Editorial:** Douglas Stallings, *Editorial Director;* Jill Fergus, Amanda Sadlowski, *Senior Editors;* Kayla Becker, Brian Eschrich, Alexis Kelly, *Editors;* Angelique Kennedy-Chavannes, *Assistant Editor*

**Design:** Tina Malaney, *Director of Design and Production;* Jessica Gonzalez, *Senior Designer;* Erin Caceres, *Graphic Design Associate*

**Production:** Jennifer DePrima, *Editorial Production Manager;* Elyse Rozelle, *Senior Production Editor;* Monica White, *Production Editor*

**Maps:** Rebecca Baer, *Senior Map Editor;* Mark Stroud (Moon Street Cartography), *Cartographer*

**Photography:** Viviane Teles, *Senior Photo Editor;* Namrata Aggarwal, Neha Gupta, Payal Gupta, Ashok Kumar, *Photo Editors;* Eddie Aldrete, *Photo Production Intern;* Kadeem McPherson, *Photo Production Associate Intern*

**Business and Operations:** Chuck Hoover, *Chief Marketing Officer;* Robert Ames, *Group General Manager*

**Public Relations and Marketing:** Joe Ewaskiw, *Senior Director of Communications and Public Relations*

**Fodors.com:** Jeremy Tarr, *Editorial Director;* Rachael Levitt, *Managing Editor*

**Technology:** Jon Atkinson, *Director of Technology;* Rudresh Teotia, *Associate Director Of Technology;* Alison Lieu, *Project Manager*

**Writers:** Benjamin Kemper, Megan Francis Lloyd, Elizabeth Prosser, Joanna Styles

**Editor:** Angelique Kennedy-Chavannes

**Production Editor:** Jennifer DePrima

5th Edition

ISBN 978-1-64097-551-4

ISSN 2471-920X

All details in this book are based on information supplied to us at press time. Always confirm information when it matters, especially if you're making a detour to visit a specific place. Fodor's expressly disclaims any liability, loss, or risk, personal or otherwise, that is incurred as a consequence of the use of any of the contents of this book.

## SPECIAL SALES

This book is available at special discounts for bulk purchases for sales promotions or premiums. For more information, e-mail SpecialMarkets@fodors.com.

PRINTED IN THE UNITED STATES OF AMERICA

10 9 8 7 6 5 4 3 2

# About Our Writers

 **Benjamin Kemper** is a native New Englander based in Madrid, Spain, where he writes about the places that make him hungriest. The Caucasus and—*por supuesto*—Spain are his main beats. Beyond Benjamin's frequent contributions to Fodor's, his work appears regularly in *The Wall Street Journal, Bon Appétit, Condé Nast Traveler, AFAR,* and *Travel + Leisure,* among other publications. He is also a travel planner and culinary tour guide. Eavesdrop on his adventures on Instagram: @benjaminkemper.

 **Megan Frances Lloyd** is a food and travel writer writer based in Seville, Spain. Her work has appeared in *Condé Nast Traveler, Bon Appétit, Hemispheres Magazine, Serious Eats, Eater, PUNCH,* and *TASTE.* She also serves as the Spain correspondent for Migrants of the Mediterranean, a humanitarian storytelling organization.

 Originally from the north of England, **Elizabeth Prosser** has lived in Barcelona since 2007. When she is not indulging in her passion for travel, she works as a freelance writer and editor covering a range of topics including travel, lifestyle, property and technology for a range of print and online publications.

 **Joanna Styles** is a freelance writer based in Malaga, Andalusia, just about the perfect place to live. Since she first spotted orange trees in the sunshine and the snow-capped Sierra Nevada, she's been passionate about Andalusia, its people, places, and culture. Thirty years later she's still discovering hidden corners. Joanna is the author of www.guidetomalaga.com. Follow her and Malaga on social media @GuidetoMalaga.